C000320051

CONTENTS

Published by Collins
An imprint of HarperCollins*Publishers*
77-85 Fulham Palace Road, Hammersmith, London
W6 8JB

The HarperCollins website address is:
www.**fire**and**water**.com

Copyright © HarperCollins*Publishers* Ltd 2001
Mapping © Bartholomew Ltd 1998, 2000, 2001

Collins® is a registered trademark of
HarperCollins*Publishers* Limited

Mapping generated from Bartholomew digital databases

Bartholomew website address is:
www.bartholomewmaps.com

London Underground Map by permission of London
Regional Transport LRT Registered User No. 00/3264

Printed in Italy   OM10944   CDC

ISBN 0 00 448989 6 (spiral impression 004)
ISBN 0 00 448988 8 (paperback impression 004)
e-mail: roadcheck@harpercollins.co.uk

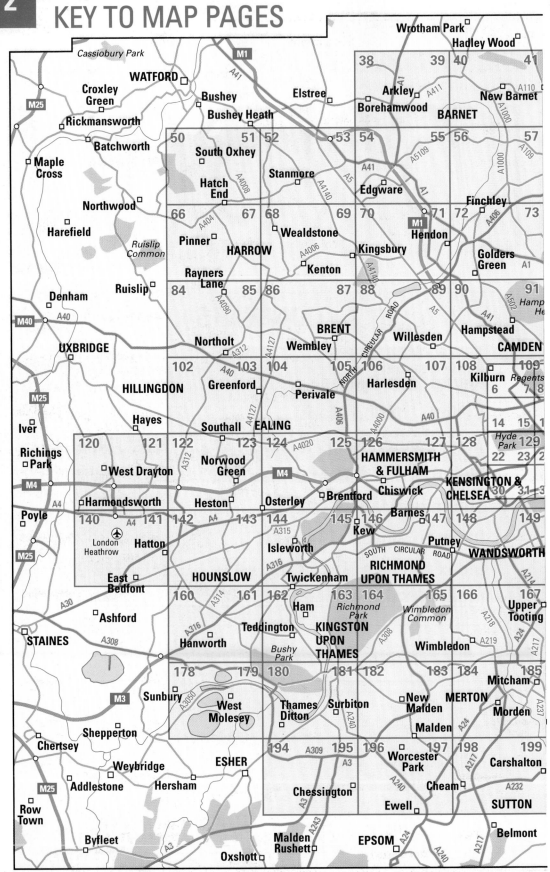

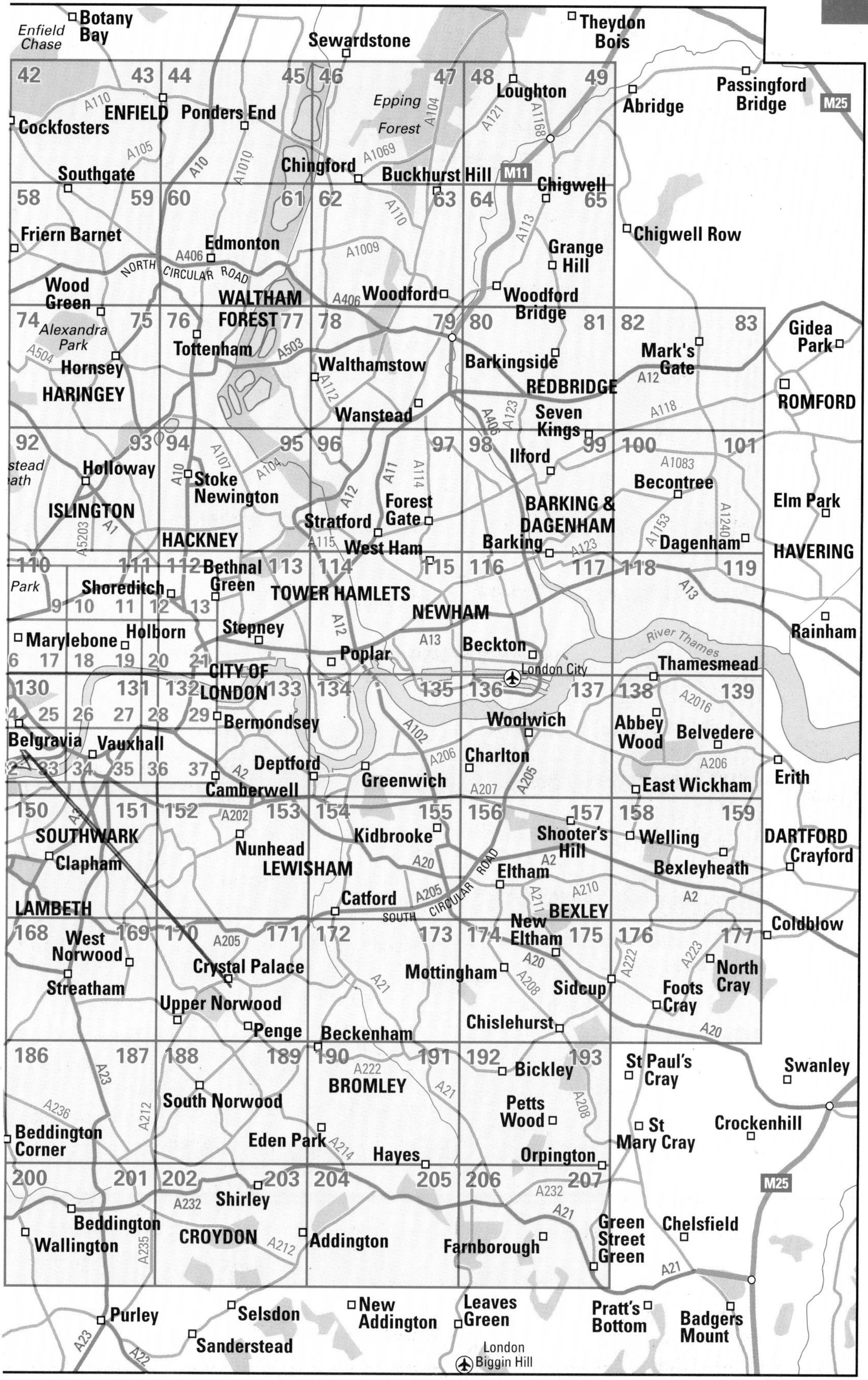

Botany Bay
Enfield Chase
Sewardstone
Theydon Bois

42 43 44 45 46 47 48 49
ENFIELD Ponders End Loughton Abridge Passingford Bridge
Cockfosters Epping Forest M25
A110 A105 A104 A121 A1168

Southgate Chingford Buckhurst Hill Chigwell
A10 A1010 A1069 M11

58 59 60 61 62 63 64 65
Friern Barnet Edmonton Grange Hill Chigwell Row
A406 A1009 A113
NORTH CIRCULAR ROAD
Wood Green WALTHAM Woodford Woodford Bridge
A406

74 75 76 77 78 79 80 81 82 83
Alexandra Park FOREST Walthamstow Barkingside Mark's Gate Gidea Park
A504 Hornsey A503 A112 REDBRIDGE A12
HARINGEY Tottenham Wanstead Seven Kings ROMFORD
A123 A118

92 93 94 95 96 97 98 99 100 101
Holloway Stoke Newington Forest Gate Ilford Becontree Elm Park
A10 A101 A104 A12 A11 A114 A406 A1083 A1153 A1240
ISLINGTON HACKNEY Stratford BARKING & Dagenham HAVERING
A5203 A1 A115 West Ham DAGENHAM Barking A123

110 111 112 113 114 115 116 117 118 119
Bethnal Green TOWER HAMLETS NEWHAM A13
Shoreditch Stepney Beckton Rainham
9 10 11 12 13 Poplar River Thames Thamesmead
Marylebone Holborn A12 A13
6 17 18 19 20 21 London City

130 131 132 133 134 135 136 137 138 139
CITY OF LONDON Woolwich Abbey Wood Belvedere
24 25 26 27 28 29 Bermondsey A102 A2016
Belgravia Vauxhall Deptford A206 Charlton East Wickham Erith
32 33 34 35 36 37 Camberwell Greenwich A206
A2 A207 A205

150 151 152 153 154 155 156 157 158 159
SOUTHWARK Nunhead Kidbrooke Shooter's Hill Welling DARTFORD
A202 CIRCULAR ROAD Crayford
Clapham LEWISHAM Eltham Bexleyheath
LAMBETH Catford A205 A2 A210 A2
SOUTH CIRCULAR ROAD BEXLEY A211

168 169 170 171 172 173 174 175 176 177
West Norwood Crystal Palace Mottingham New Eltham Foots Cray North Cray Coldblow
A205 A21 A20 A222 A223
Streatham Upper Norwood Sidcup A208
Penge Beckenham Chislehurst A20

186 187 188 189 190 191 192 193
BROMLEY Bickley St Paul's Cray Swanley
A23 A222 A21
A236 South Norwood A212 Petts Wood A208 St Mary Cray Crockenhill
Beddington Corner Eden Park Hayes Orpington

200 201 202 203 204 205 206 207
Shirley Addington Farnborough Green Street Green Chelsfield
A232 A232
Beddington Wallington CROYDON A212 A21 M25
A235 A21

Purley Selsdon New Addington Leaves Green Pratt's Bottom Badgers Mount
A23 Sanderstead London Biggin Hill
A22

4   KEY TO CENTRAL MAP SYMBOLS

M4	Motorway
Dual **A4**	Primary Route
Dual **A40**	'A' Road
B504	'B' Road
	Other Road
	Street Market
	Pedestrian Street
•————•	Access Restriction
===== -------	Track/Footpath
→	One Way Street
– – – – –	Riverbus
CITY	Borough Boundary
EC2	Postal District Boundary
≥	Main Railway Station
≥	Other Railway Station
⊖	London Underground Station
-DLR-	Docklands Light Railway Station
⬭	Bus/Coach Station
P	Car Park
WC	Public Toilet
i	Tourist Information Centre

■	Leisure & Tourism
■	Shopping
■	Administration
■	Health & Welfare
■	Education
■	Industry & Commerce
□	Public Open Space
■	Park/Garden/Sports Ground
✝ ✝ ✝	Cemetery
■ POL	Police Station
■ Fire Sta	Fire Station
■ PO	Post Office
🎥	Cinema
⊡	Theatre
⊠	Major Hotel
�	Embassy
+	Church
☾	Mosque
✡	Synagogue
Mormon ■	Other Place of Worship

The reference grid on this atlas coincides with the Ordnance Survey National Grid System. The grid interval is 250 metres.

A	Grid Reference	
8	Page Continuation Number	

Scale 1:8,100 (7.7 inches to 1 mile)

0	0.25	0.50	0.75	1 kilometre

0	¼	½ mile

KEY TO MAIN MAP SYMBOLS

M4	Motorway			Leisure & Tourism
Dual **A4**	Primary Route			Administration & Law
			USA	Embassy
Dual **A40**	'A' Road			Health & Welfare
B504	'B' Road			Education
	Other Road			Industry & Commerce
	Toll		↑ ↑	Cemetery
	Street Market			Golf Course
	Pedestrian Street			Public Open Space/ Allotments
	Cycle Path			Park/Garden/Sports Ground
- - - - - -	Track/Footpath			Wood/Forest
→	One Way Street		Pol	Police Station
- - P - -	Pedestrian Ferry		Fire Sta	Fire Station
- V -	Vehicle Ferry		PO	Post Office
	County/Borough Boundary		Lib	Library
	Postal District Boundary		▲	Youth Hostel
	Main Railway Station		□	Tower Block
	Other Railway Station		𝒊	Tourist Information Centre
	London Underground Station		Ⓗ	Heliport
DLR	Docklands Light Railway Station		WC	Public Toilet
	Tramway Station		+	Church
	Bus/Coach Station		☾	Mosque
P	Car Park		✡	Synagogue

The reference grid on this atlas coincides with the Ordnance Survey National Grid System. The grid interval is 500 metres.

A	Grid Reference	24	Page Continuation Number

Scale 1:16,300 (3.9 inches to 1 mile)

25	OS National Grid Kilometre Square	

```
0        0.25      0.50      0.75      1 kilometre
|----------|----------|----------|----------|
0               ¼               ½ mile
```

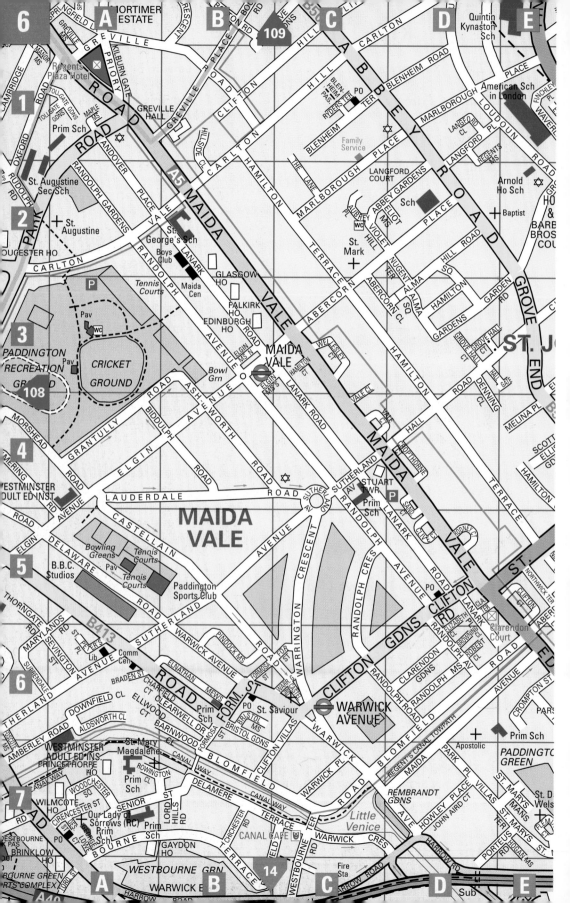

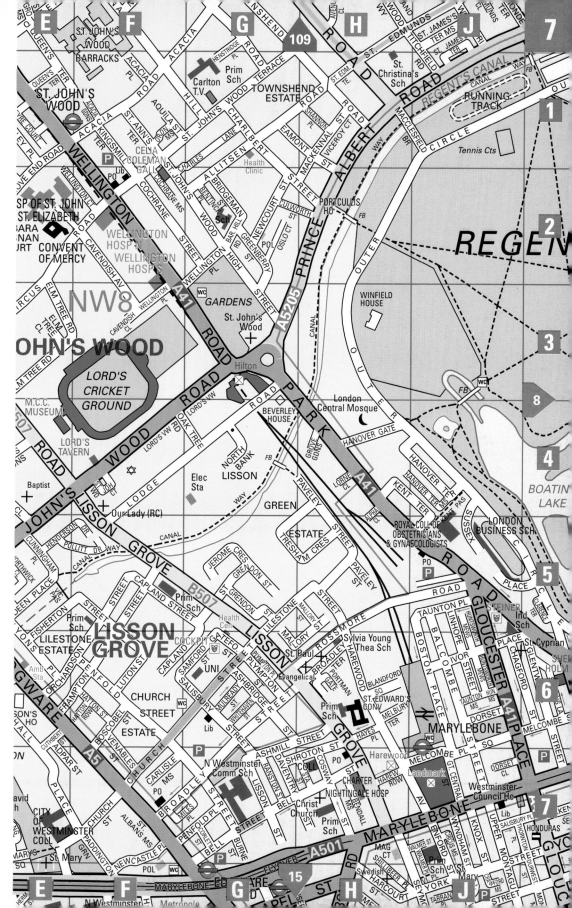

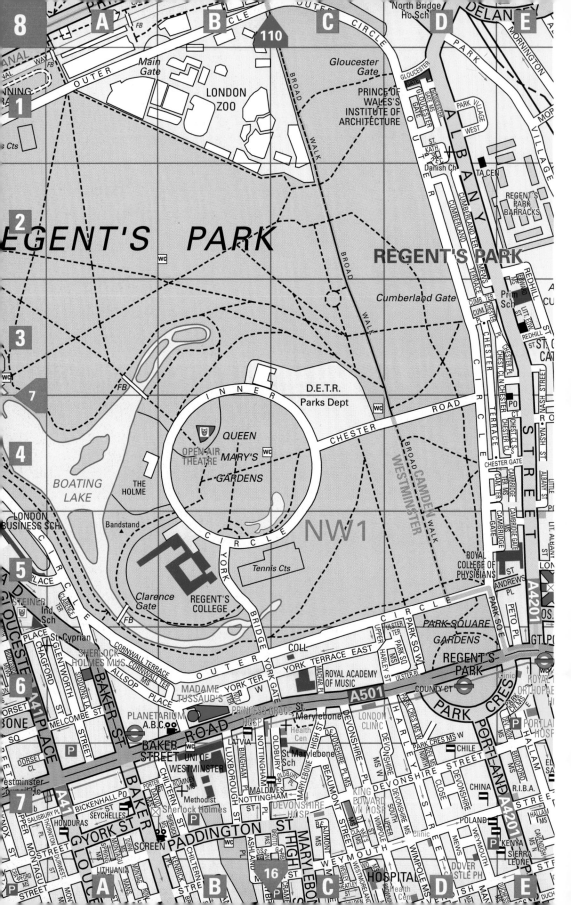

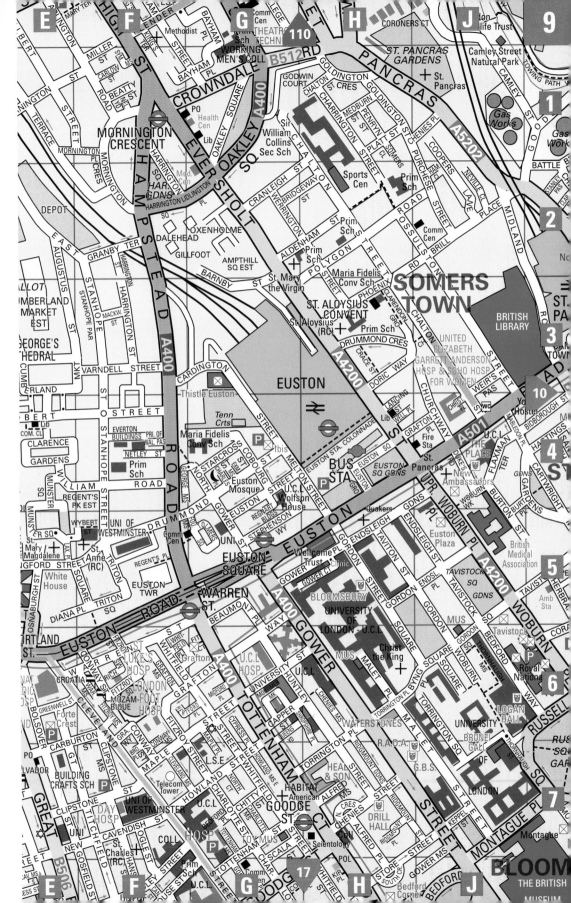

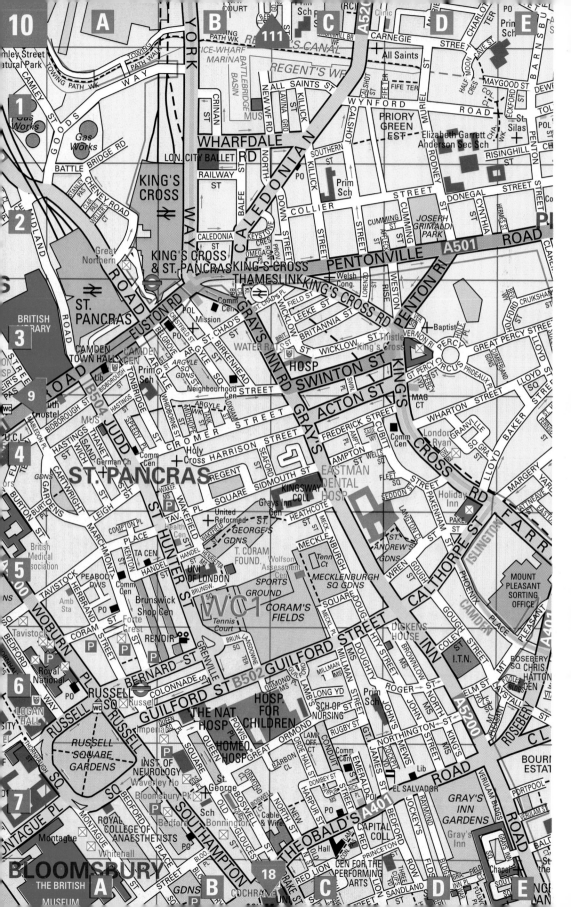

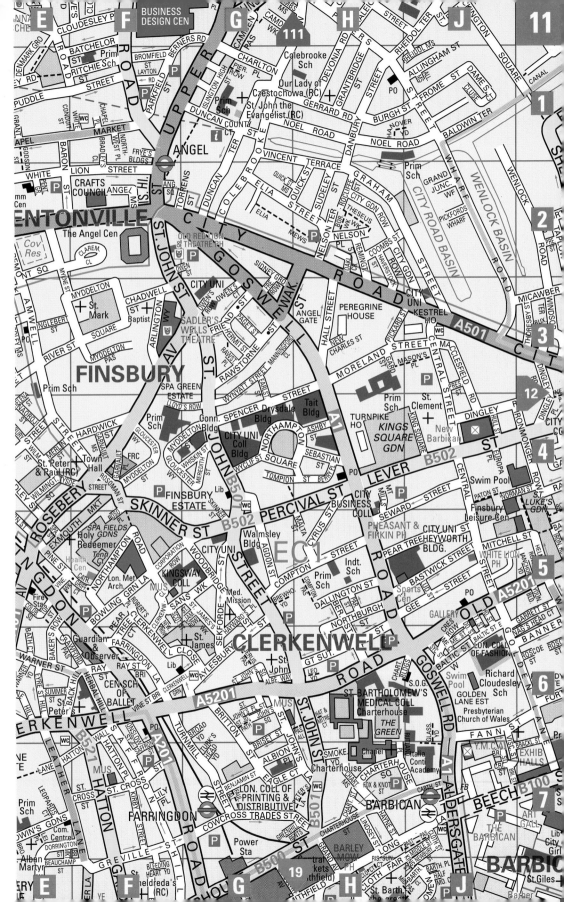

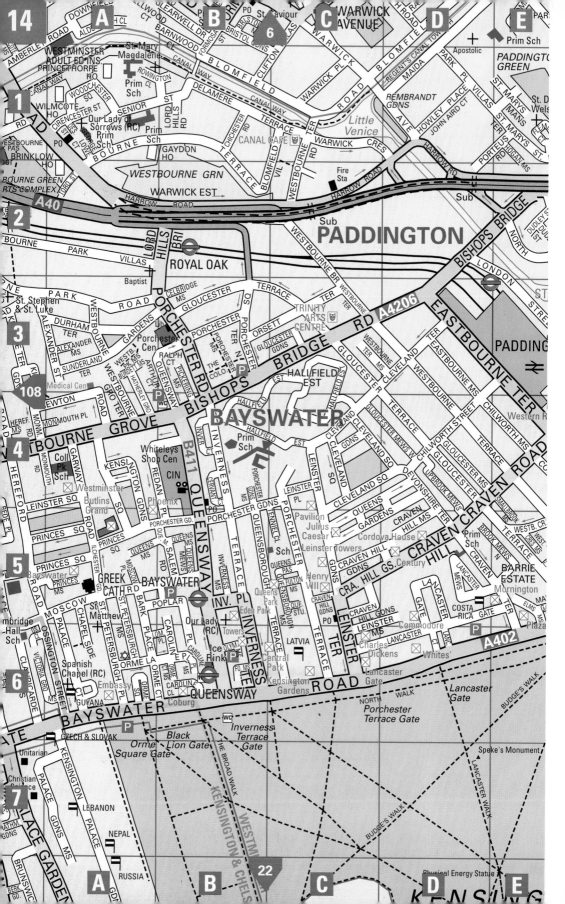

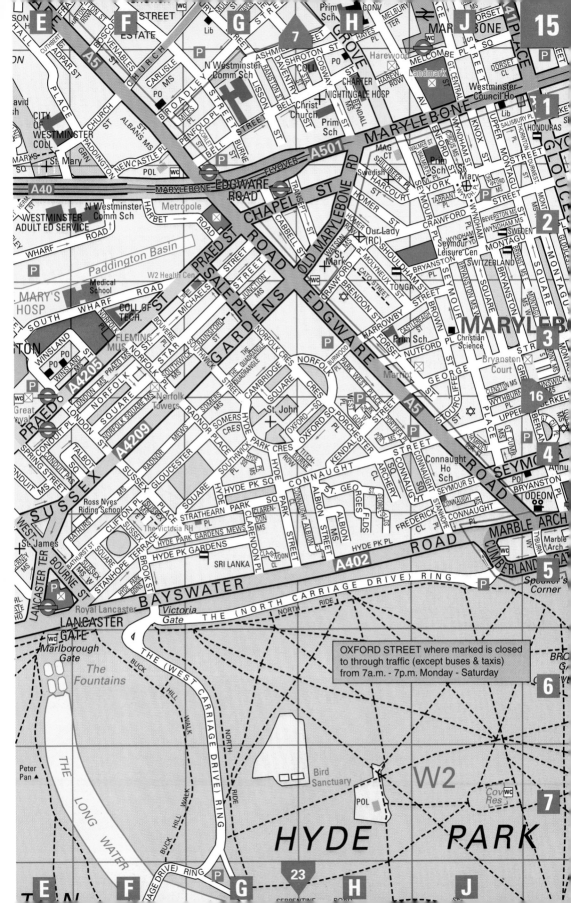

OXFORD STREET where marked is closed
to through traffic (except buses & taxis)
from 7a.m. - 7p.m. Monday - Saturday

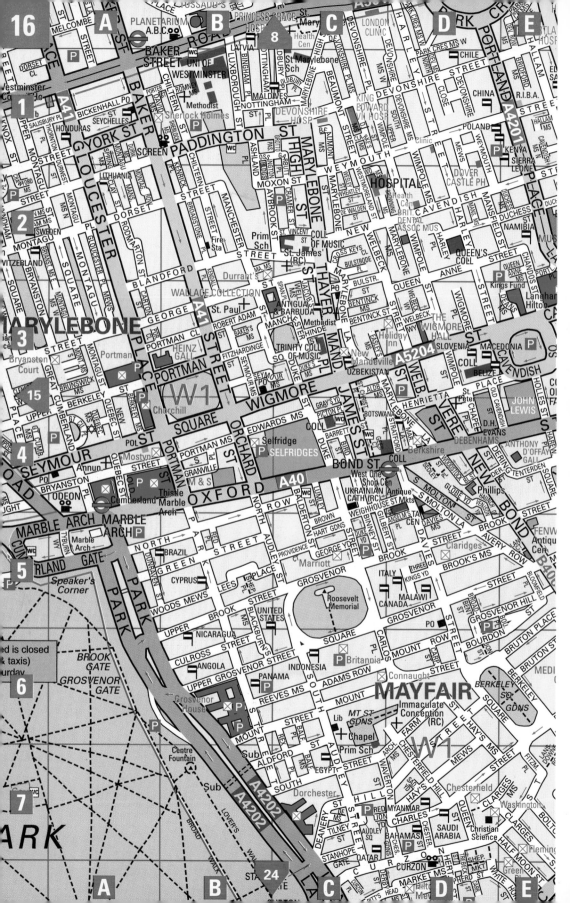

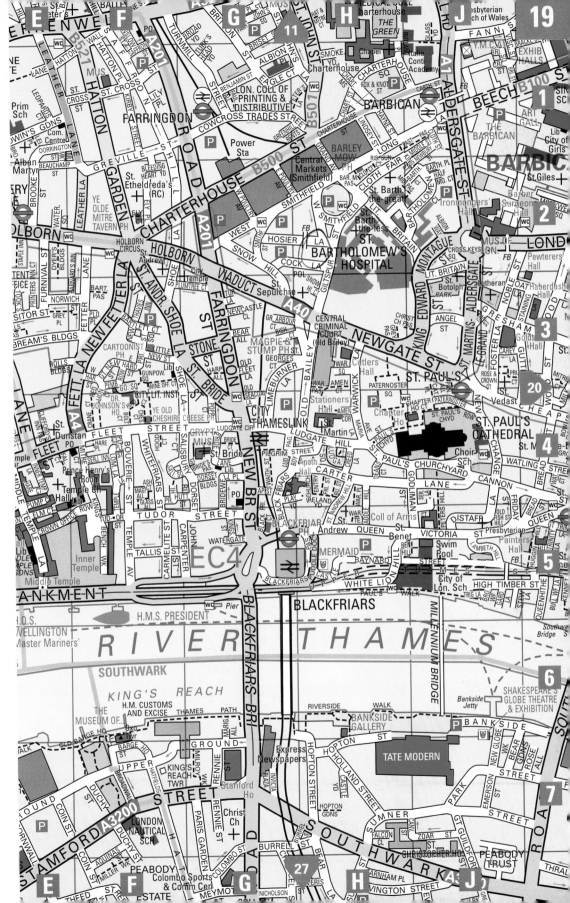

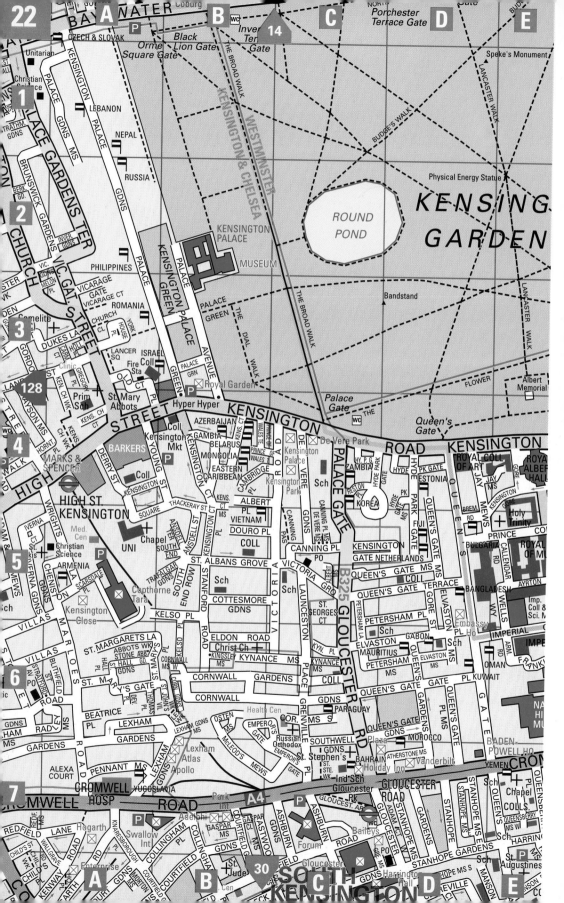

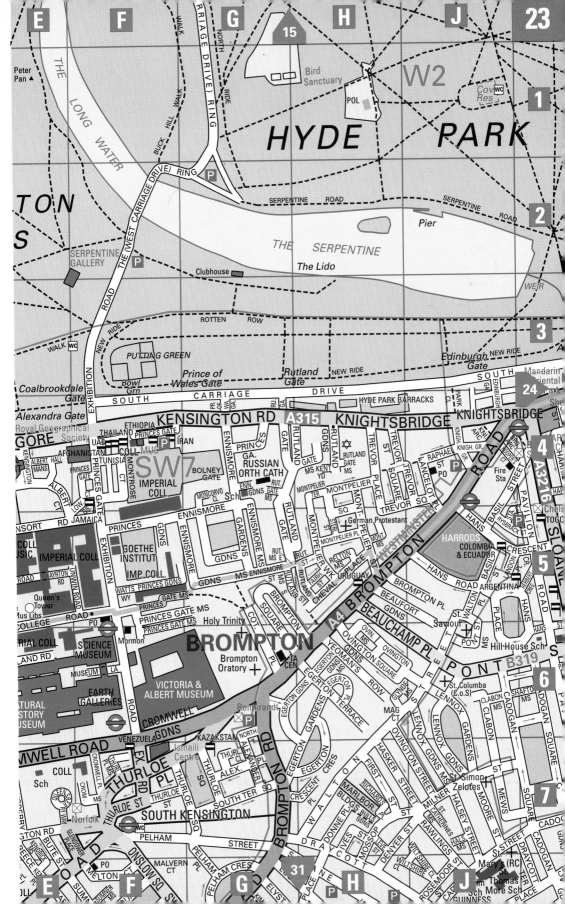

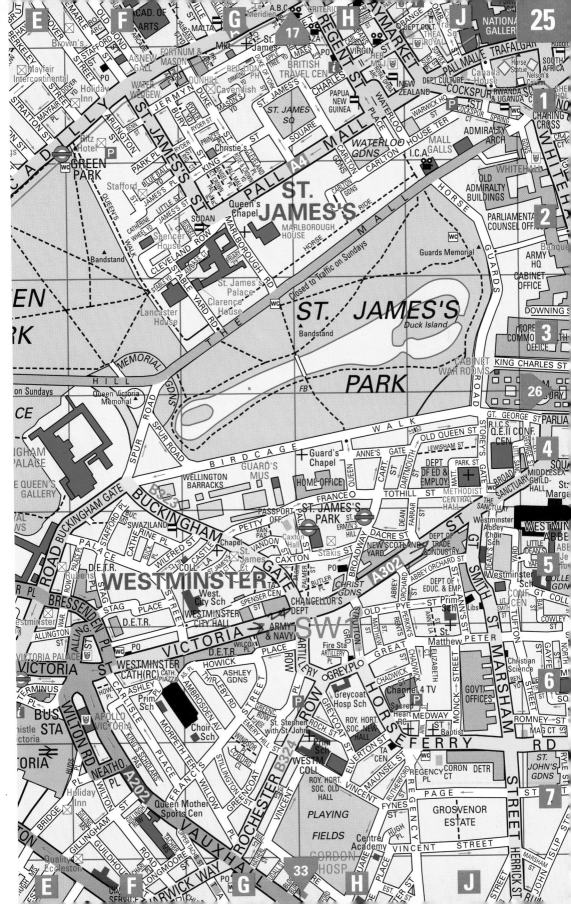

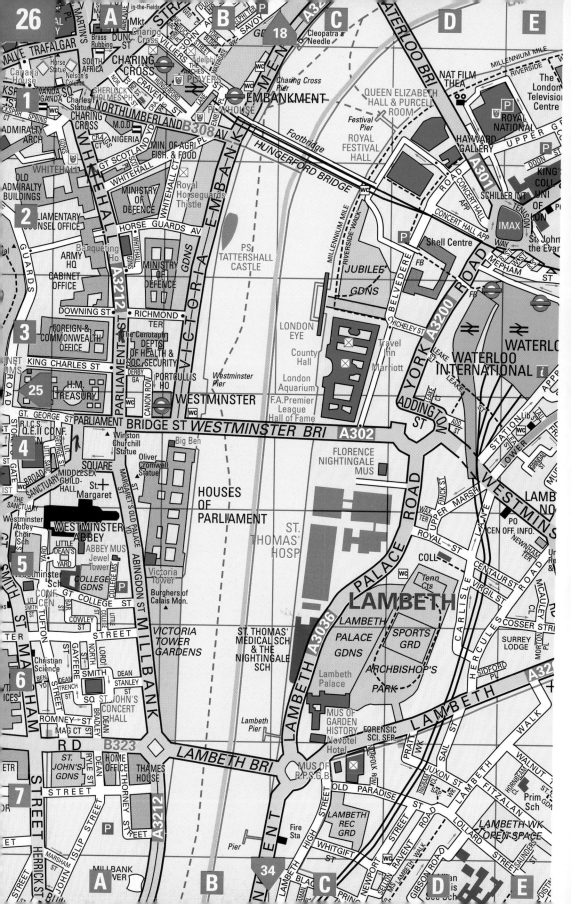

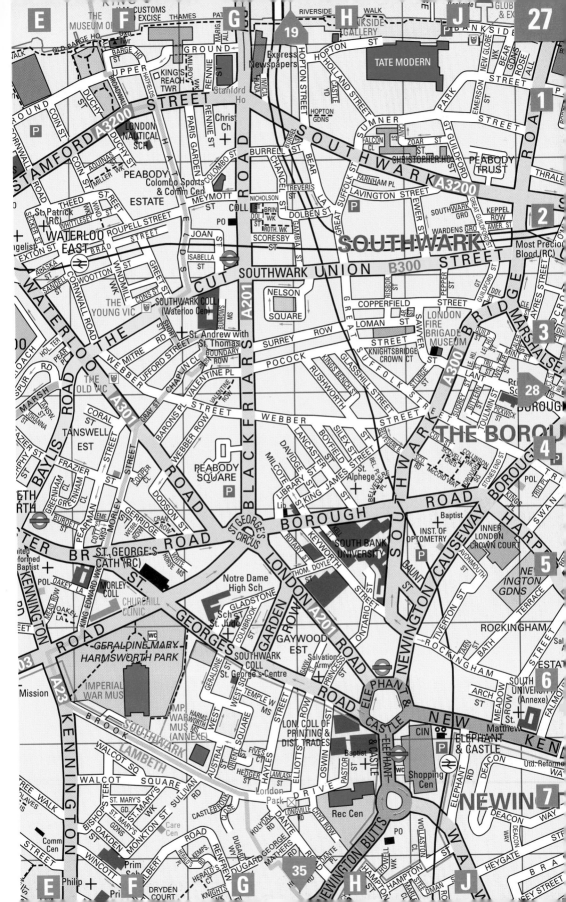

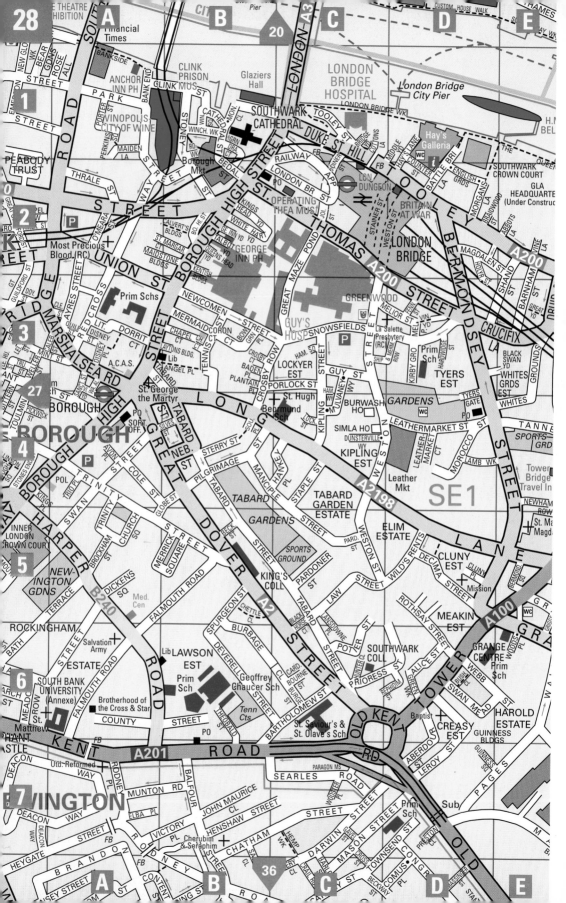

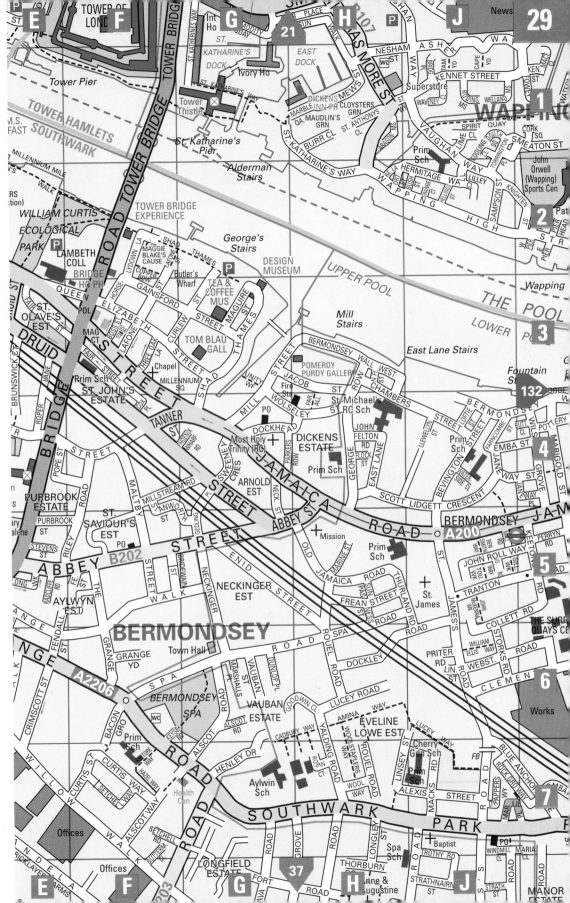

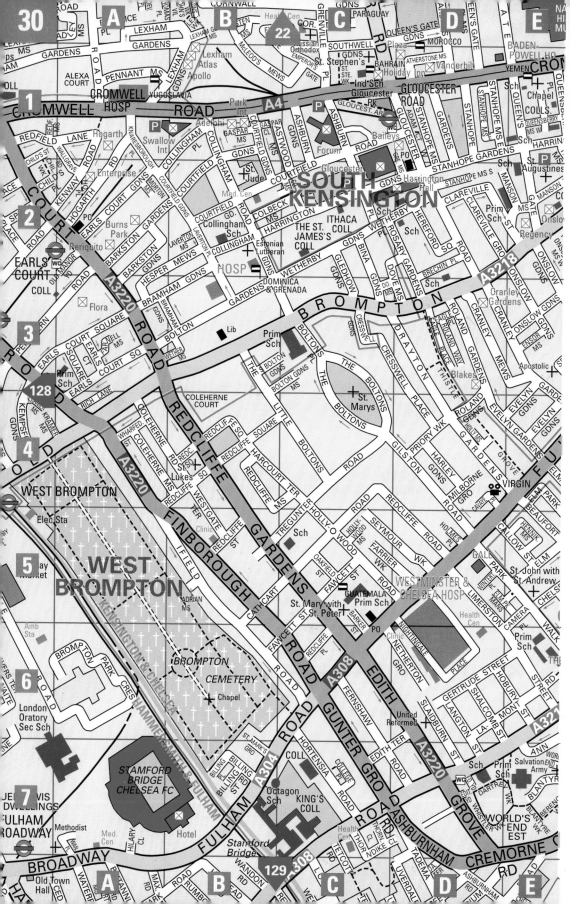

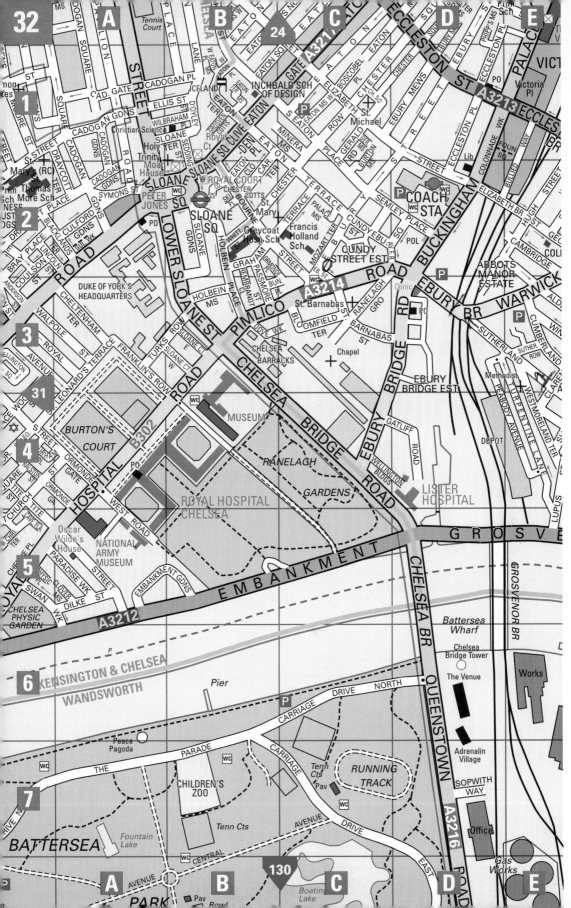

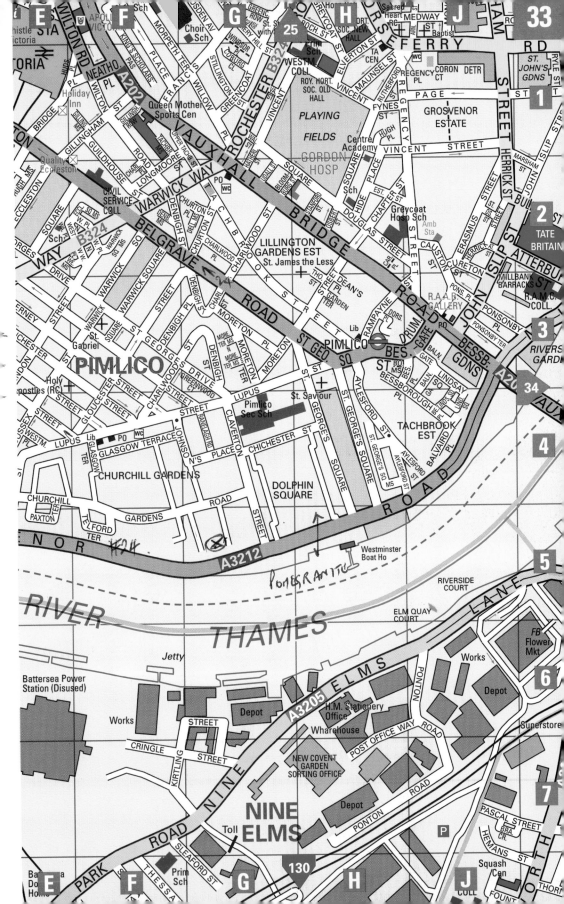

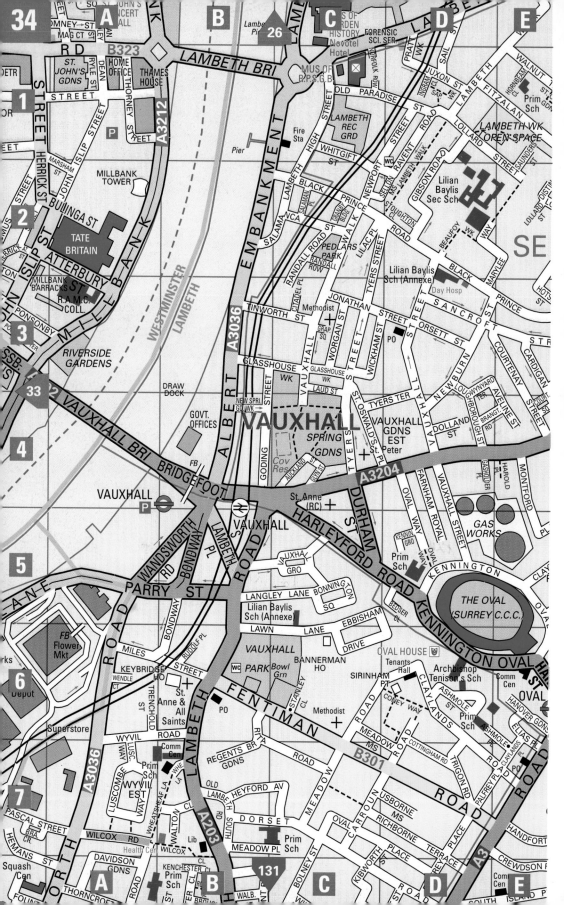

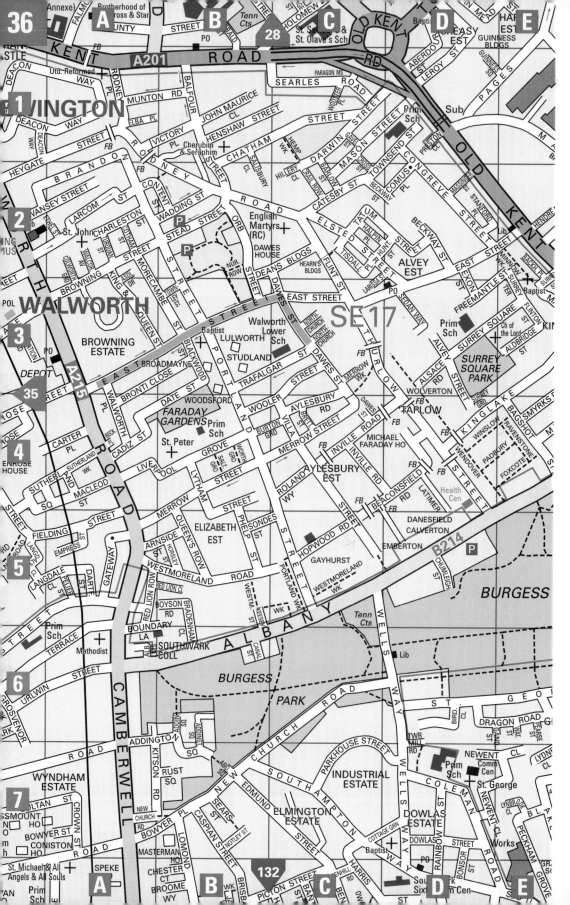

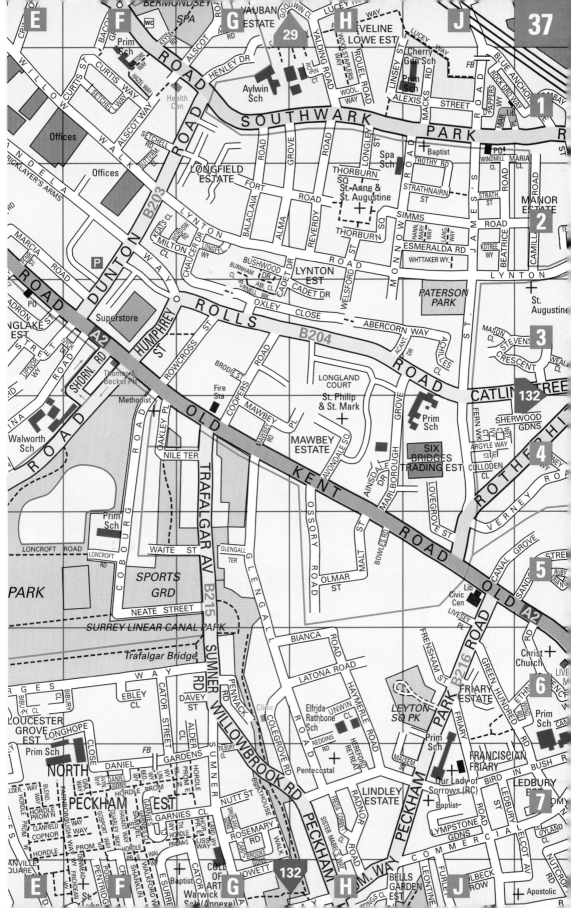

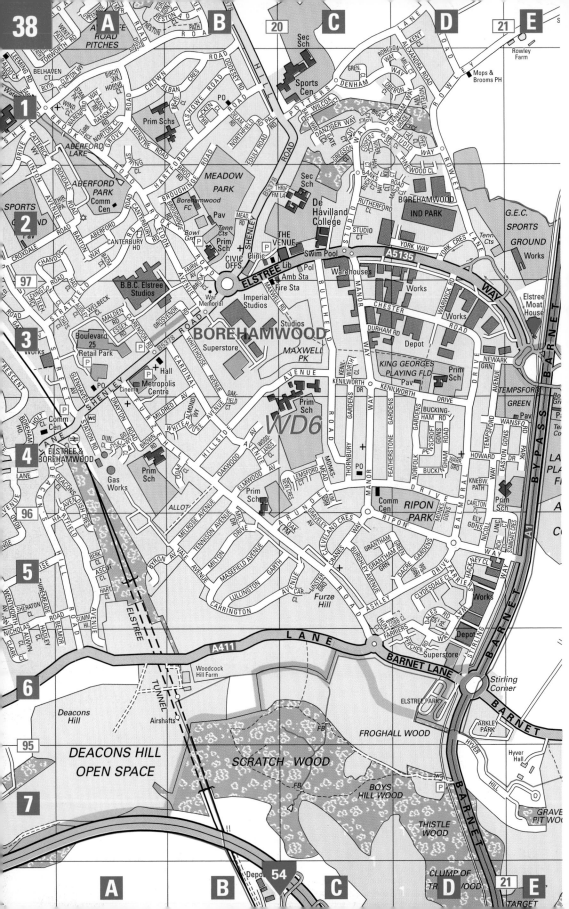

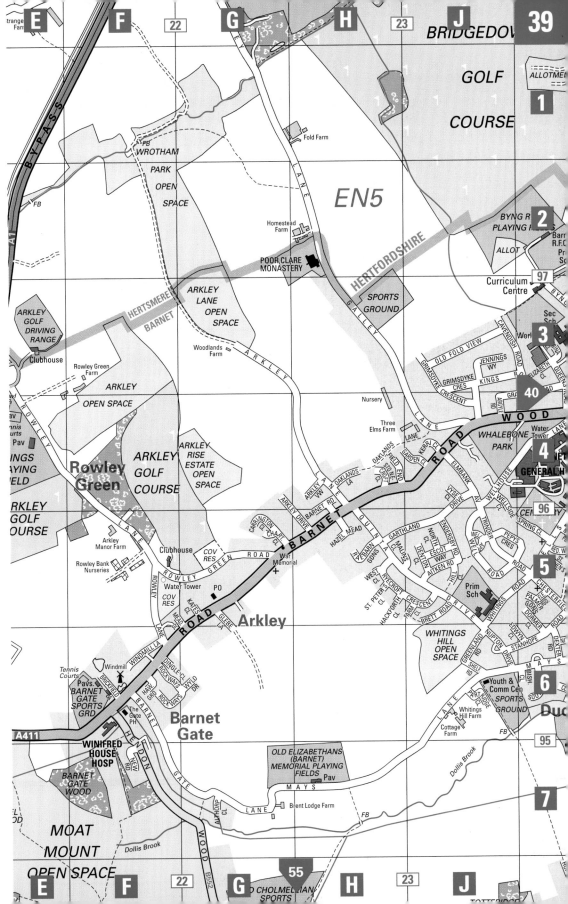

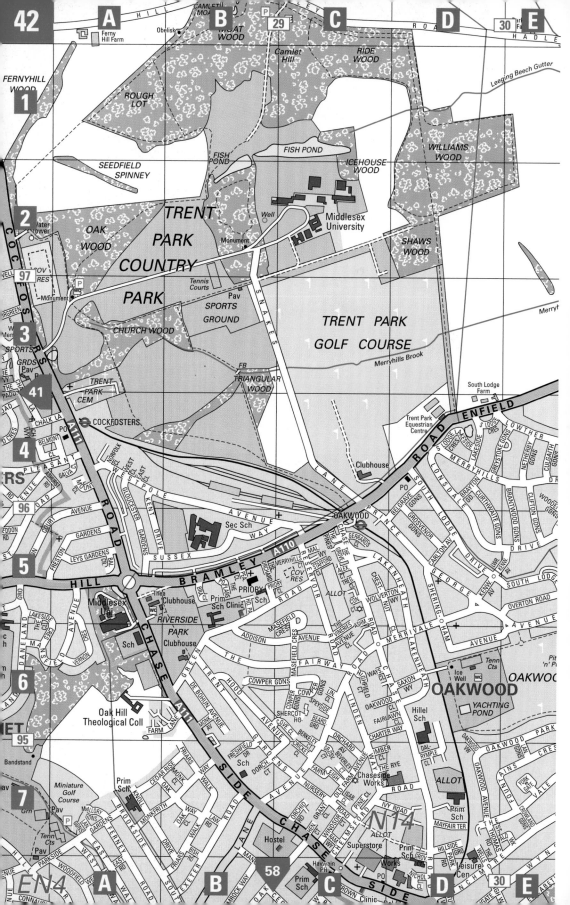

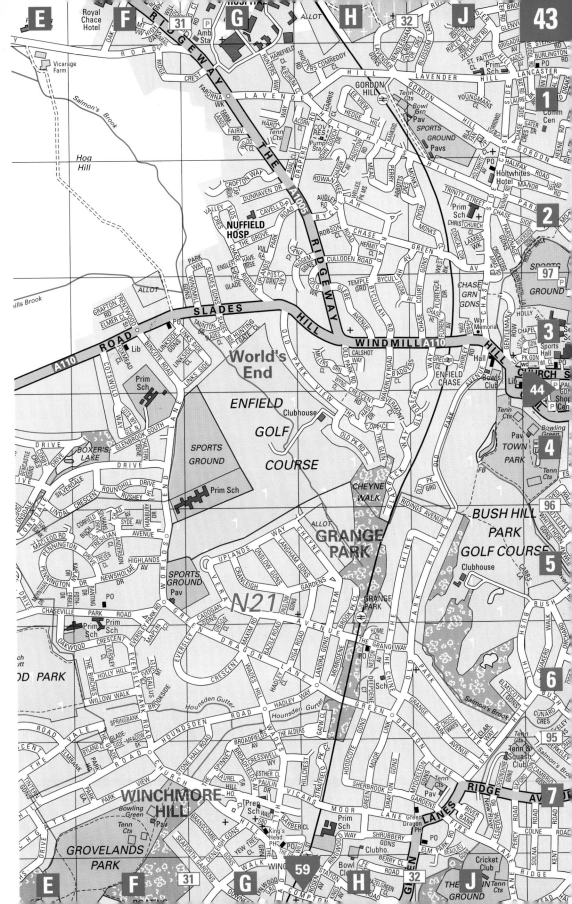

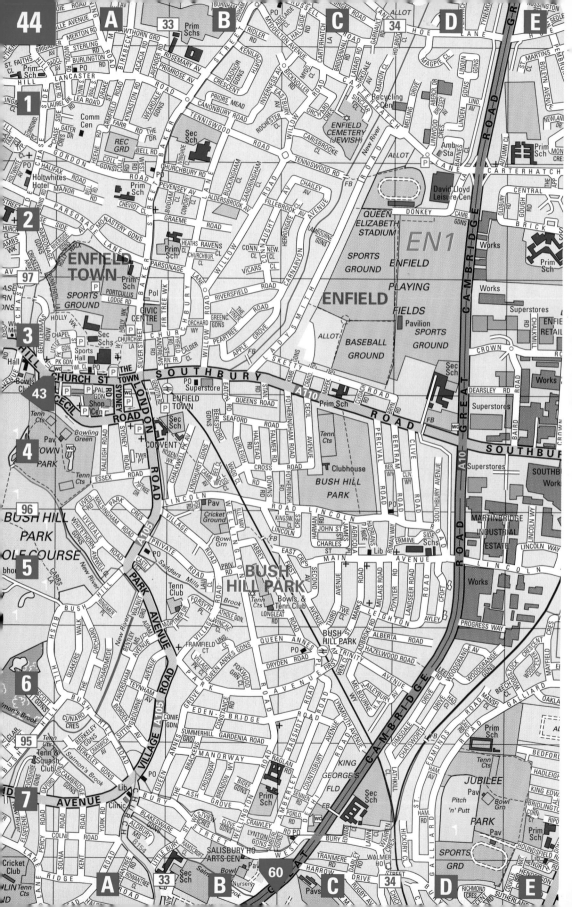

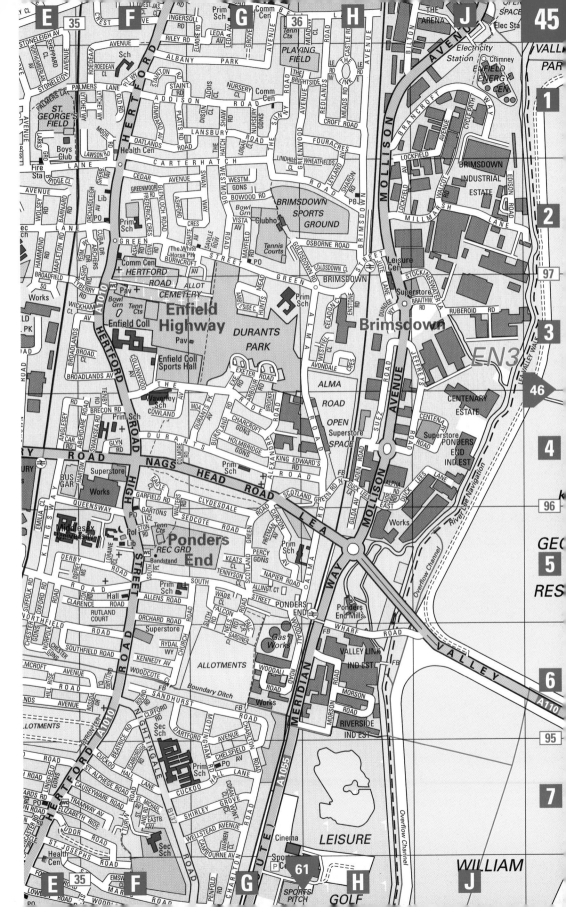

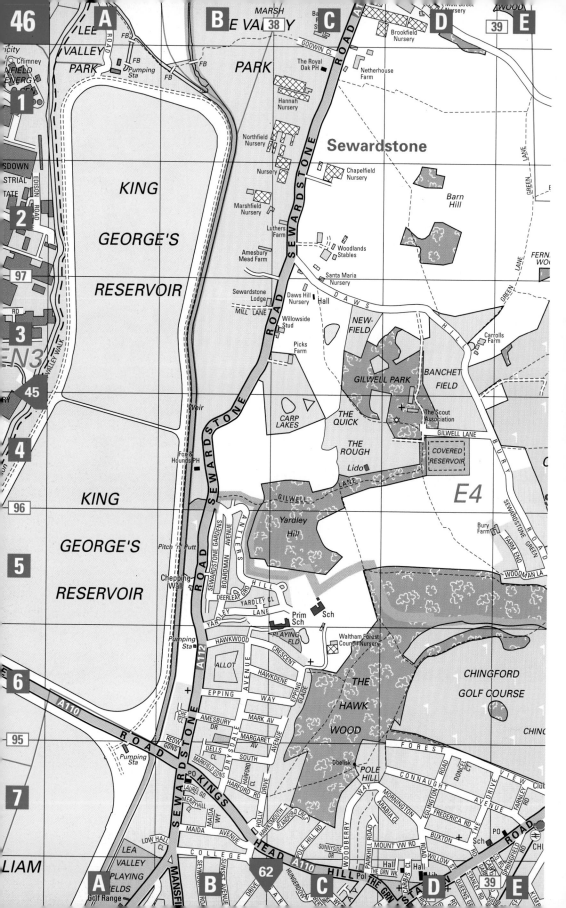

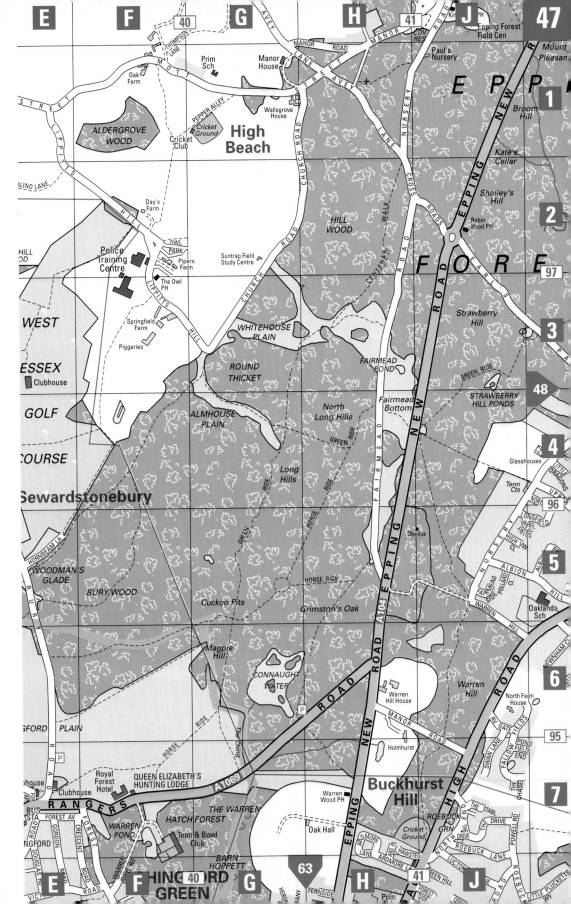

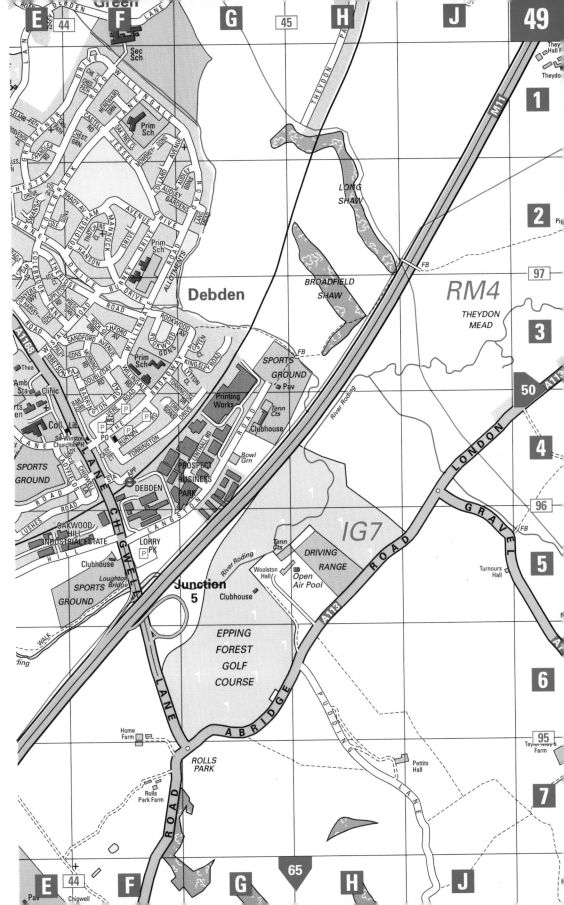

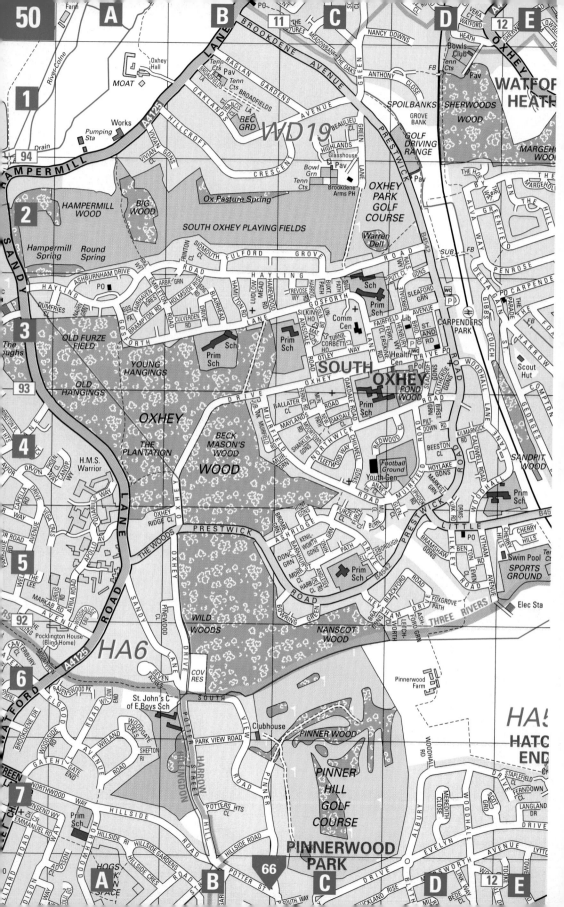

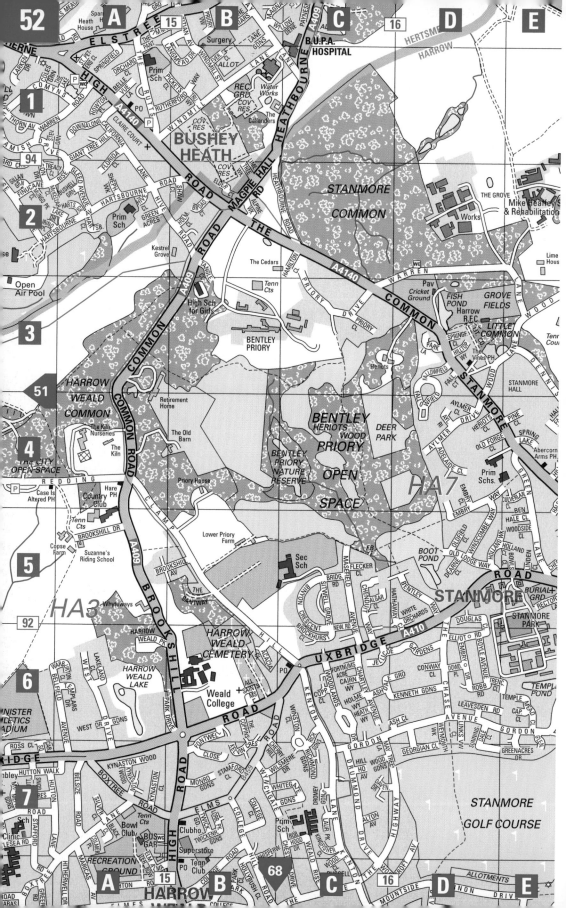

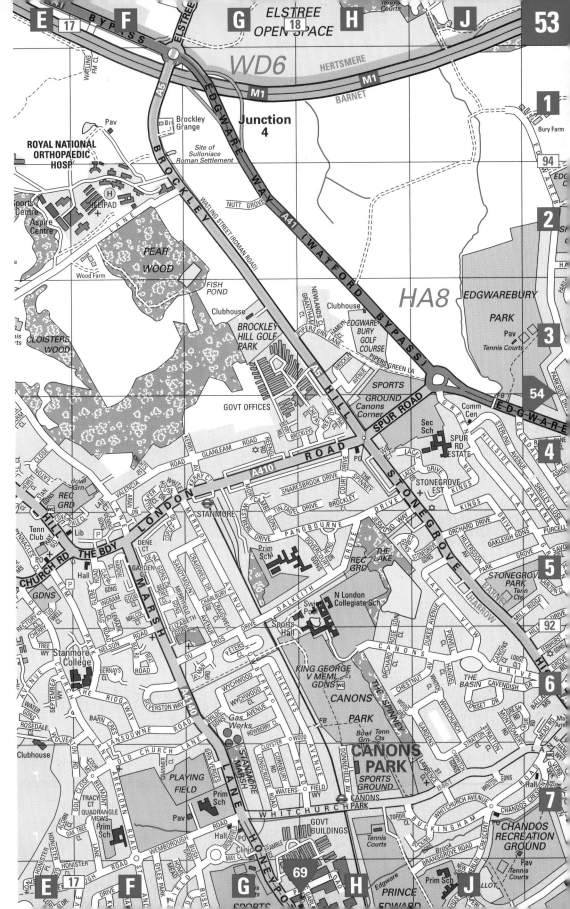

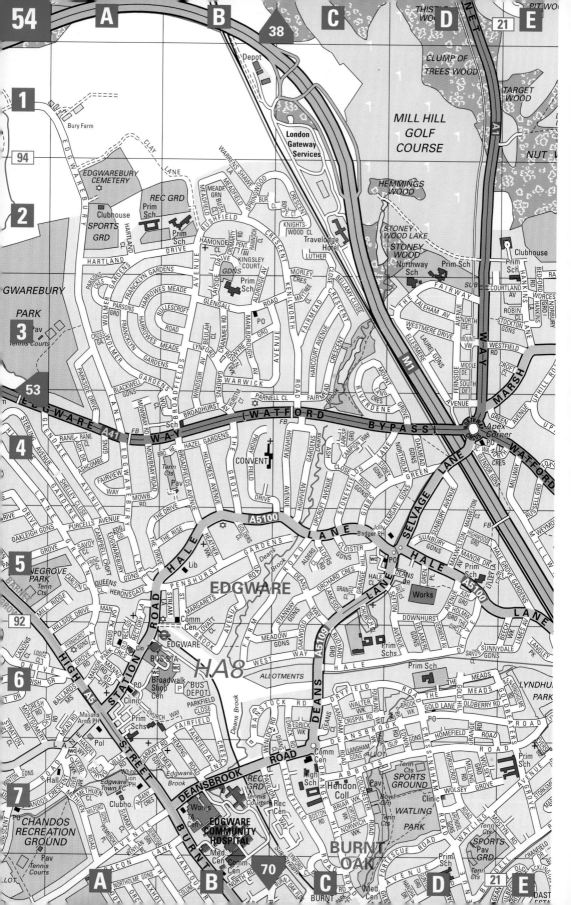

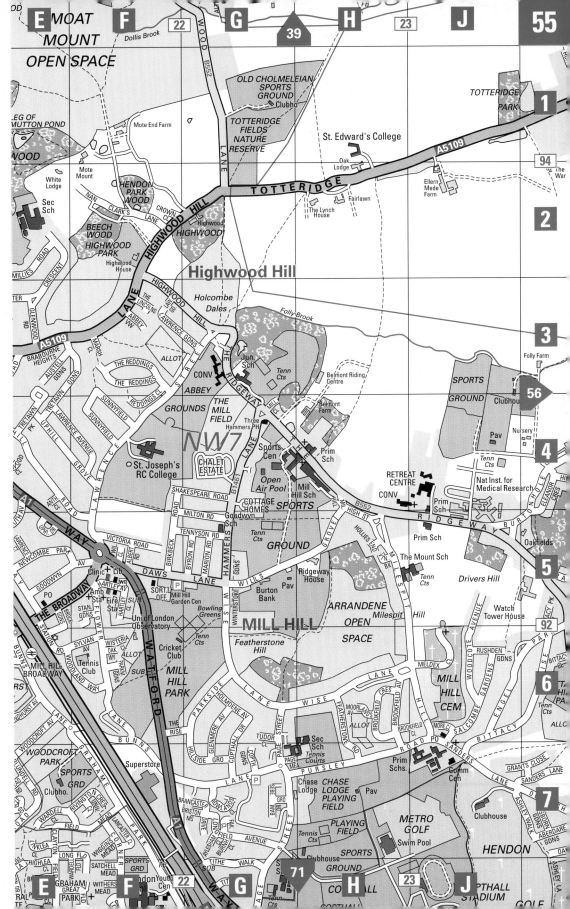

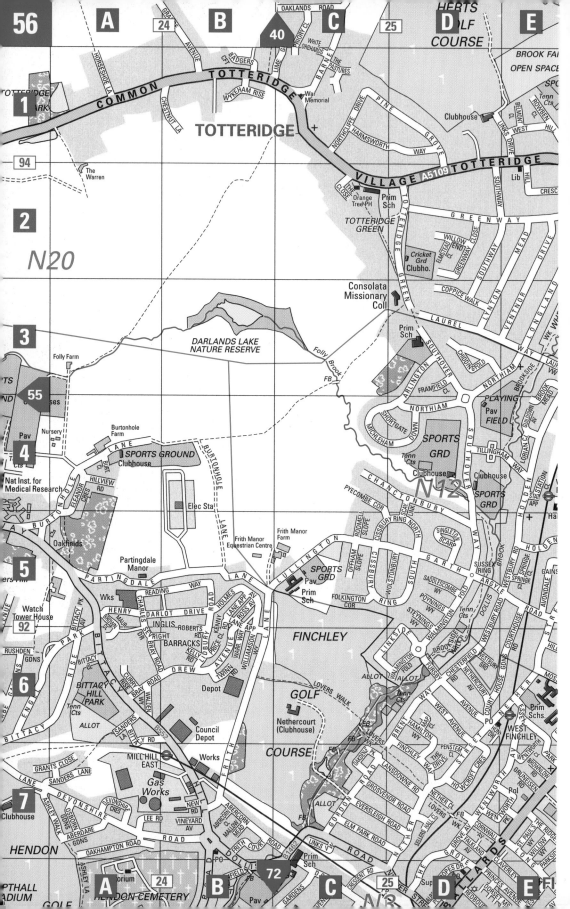

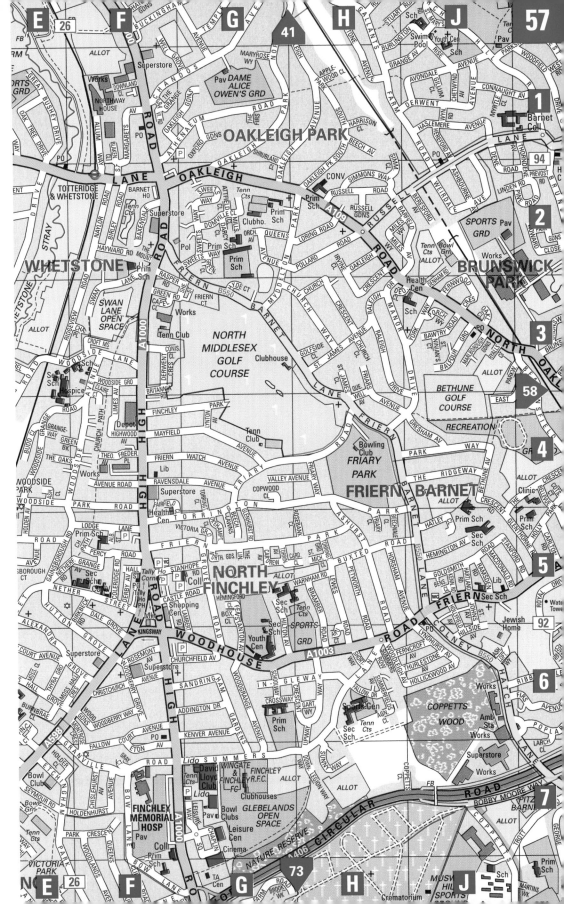

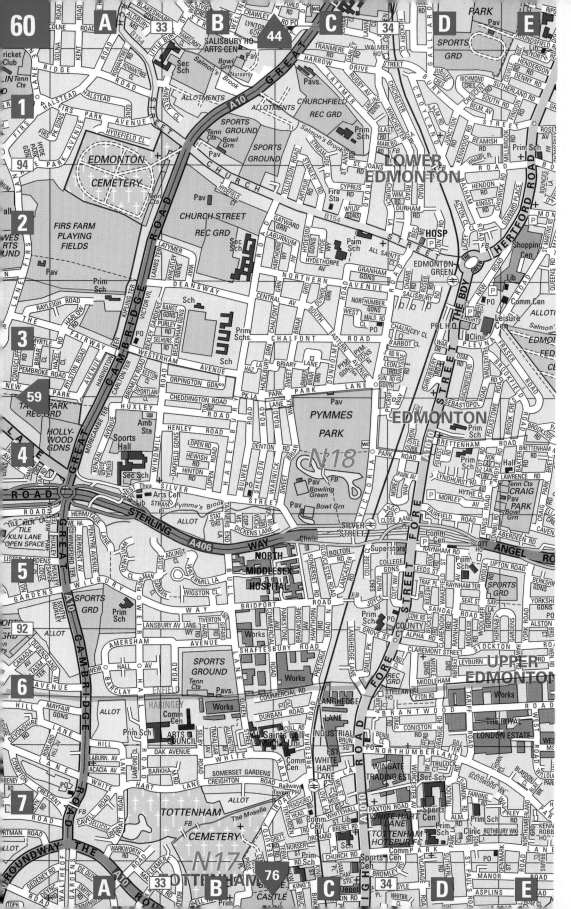

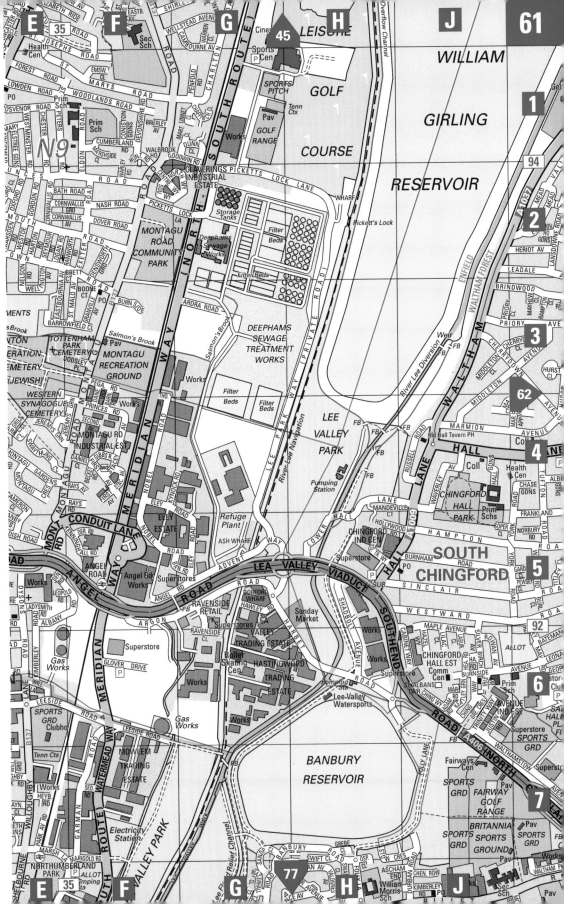

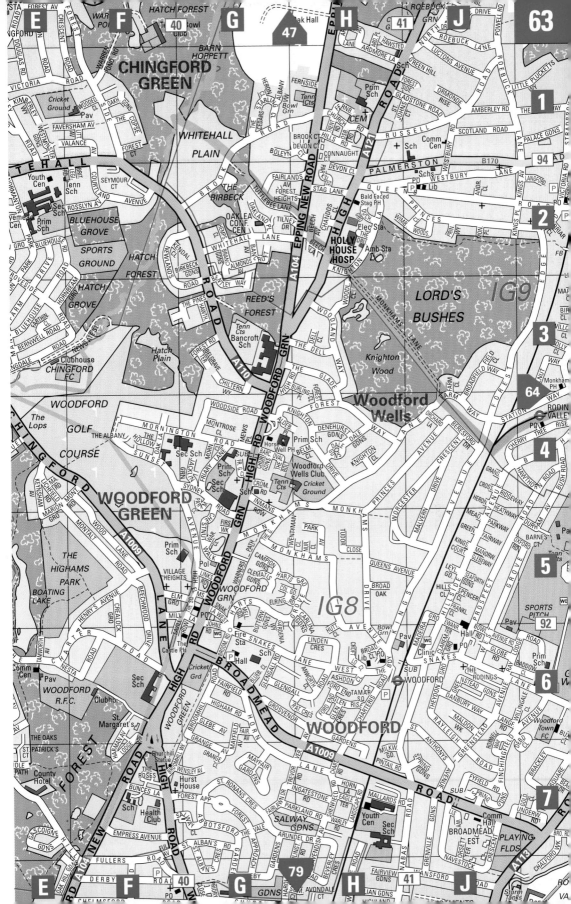

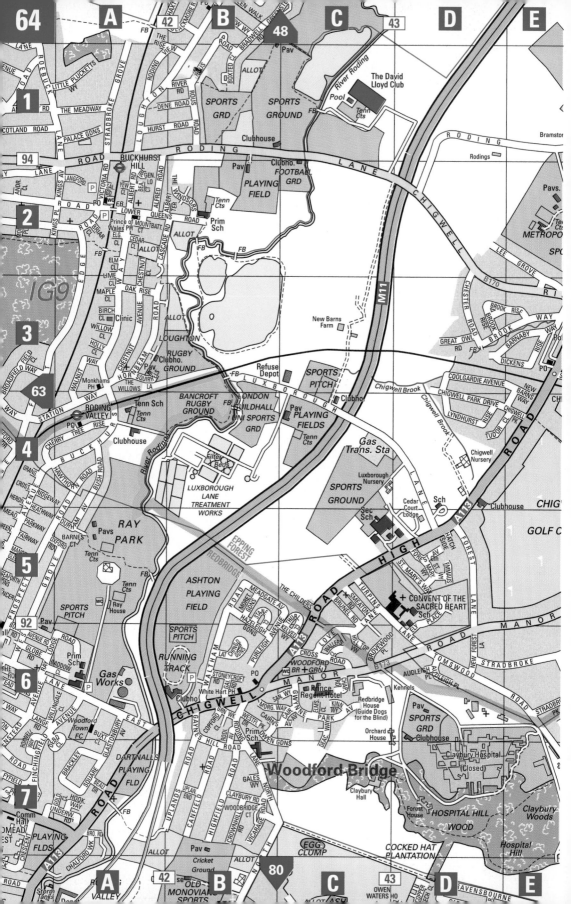

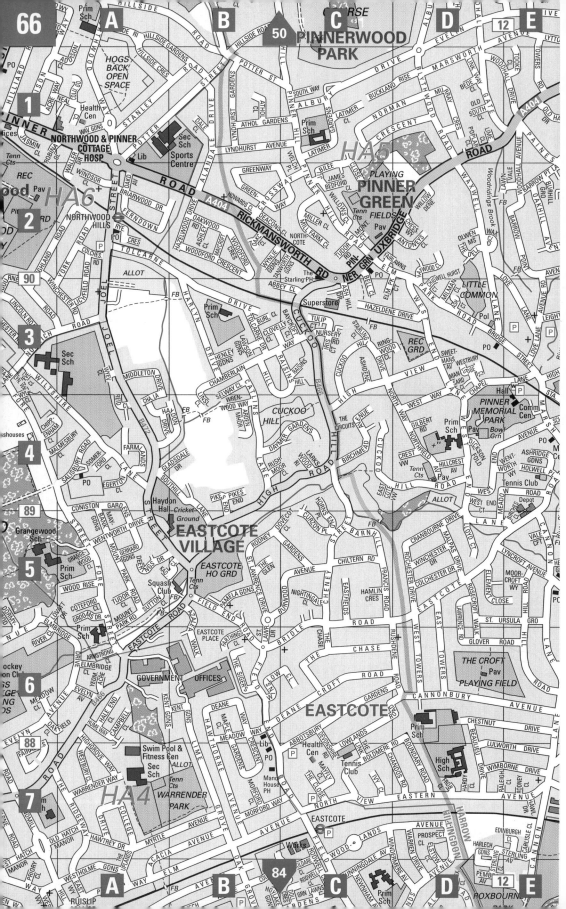

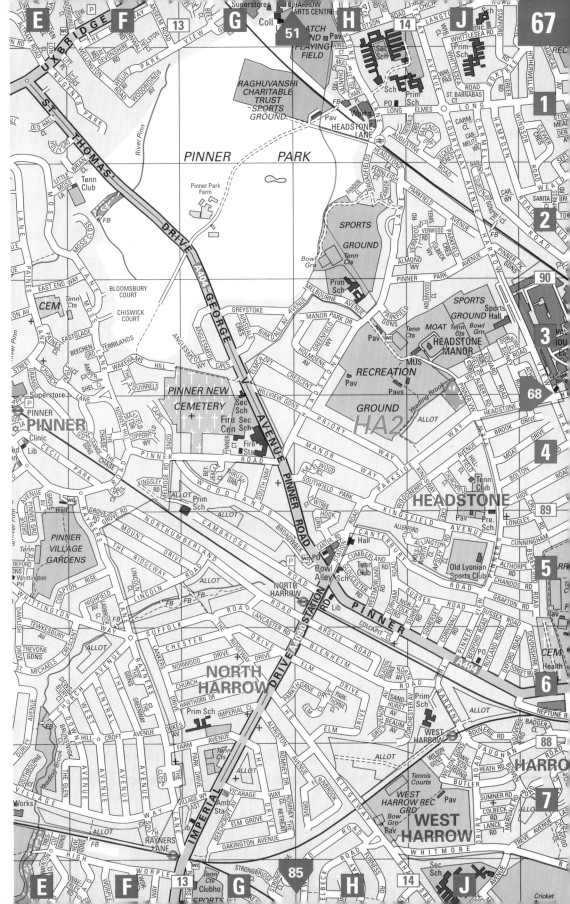

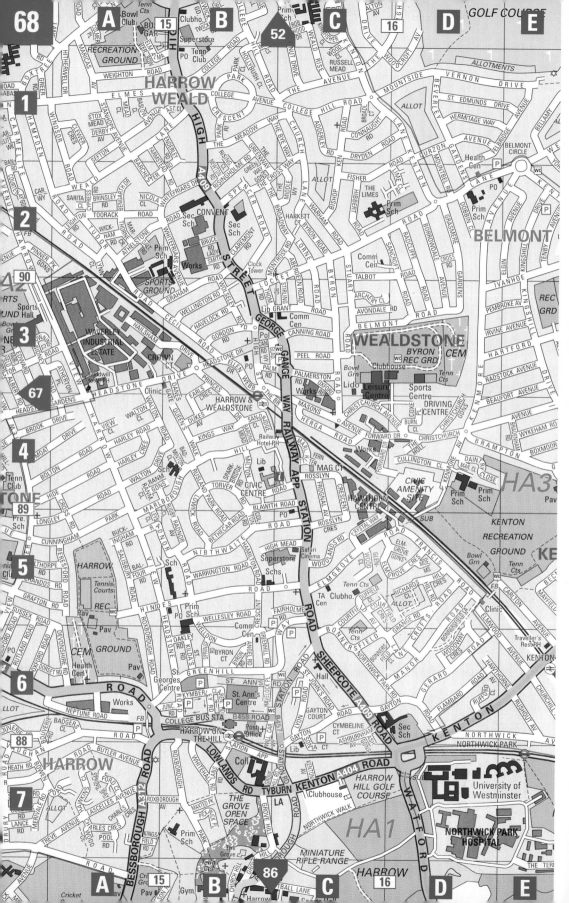

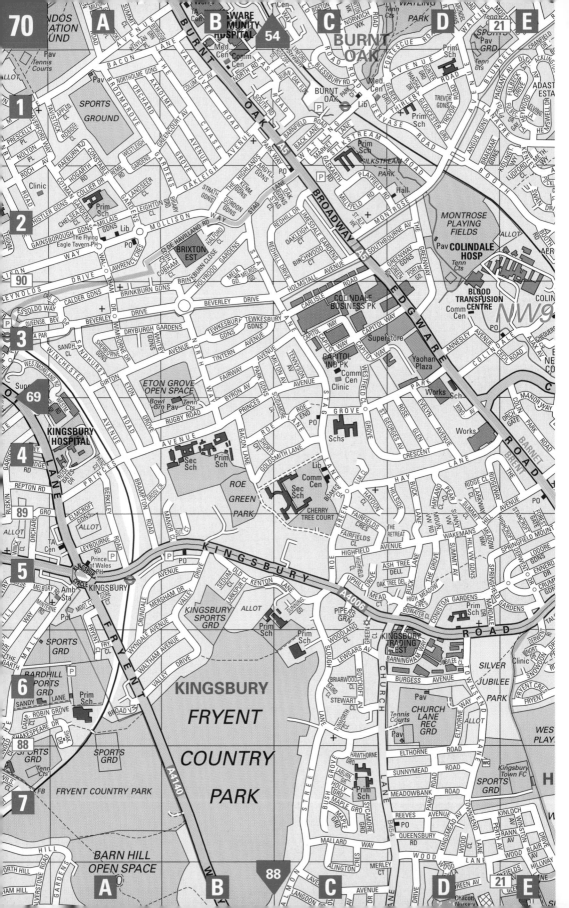

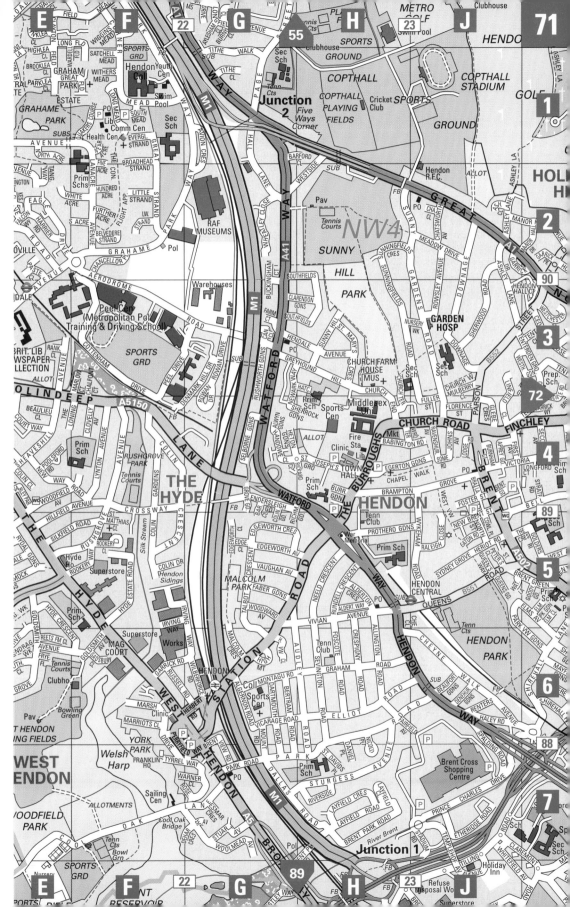

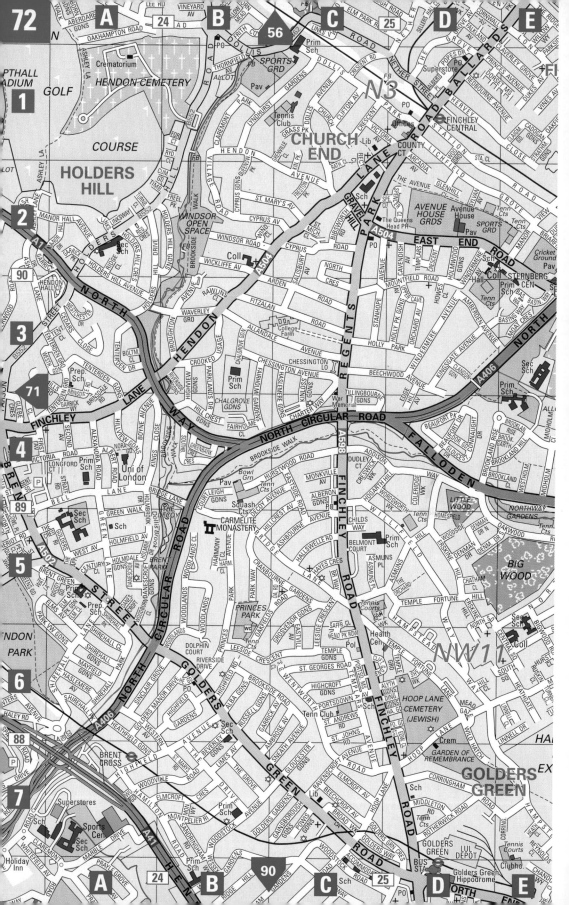

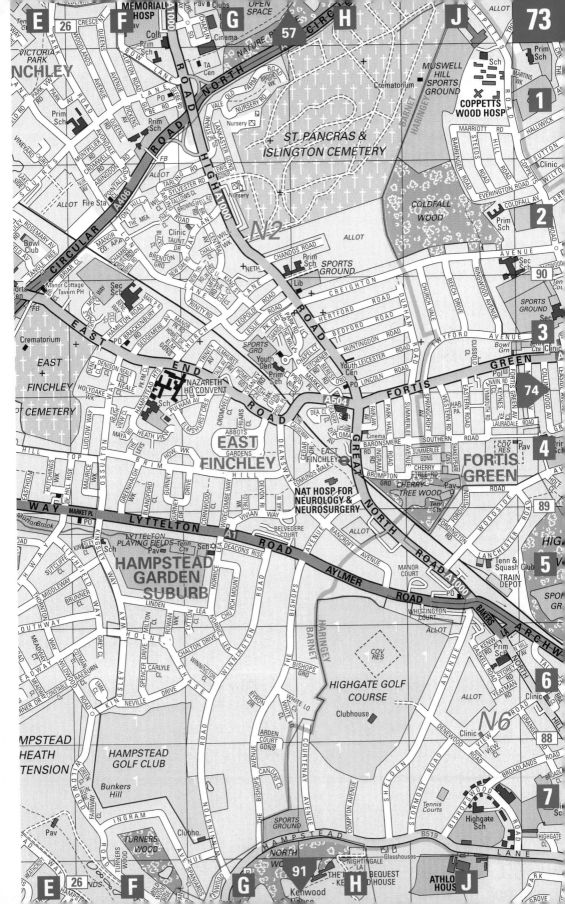

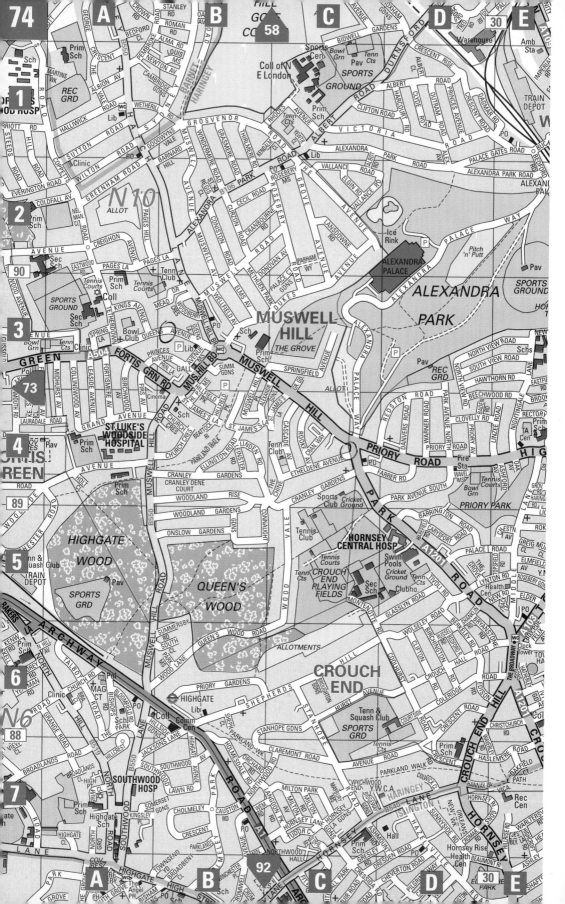

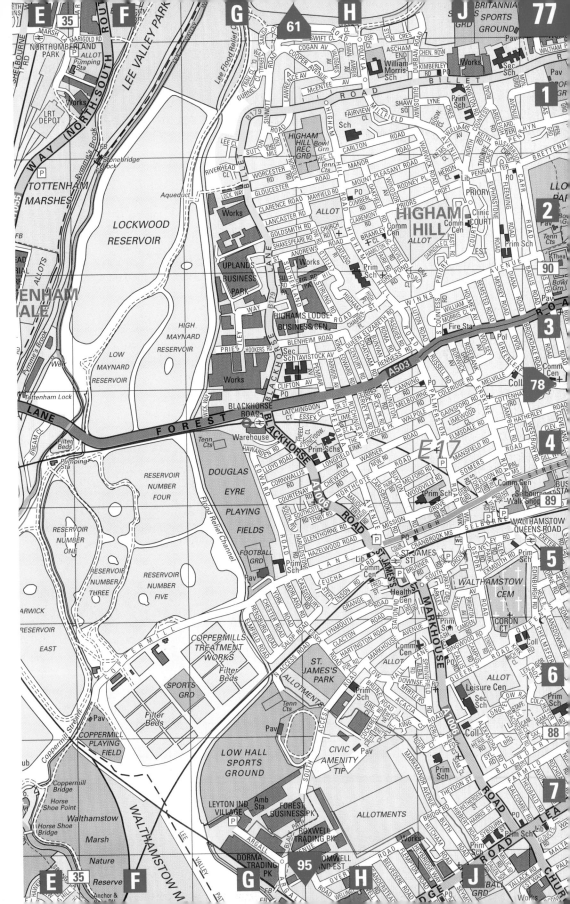

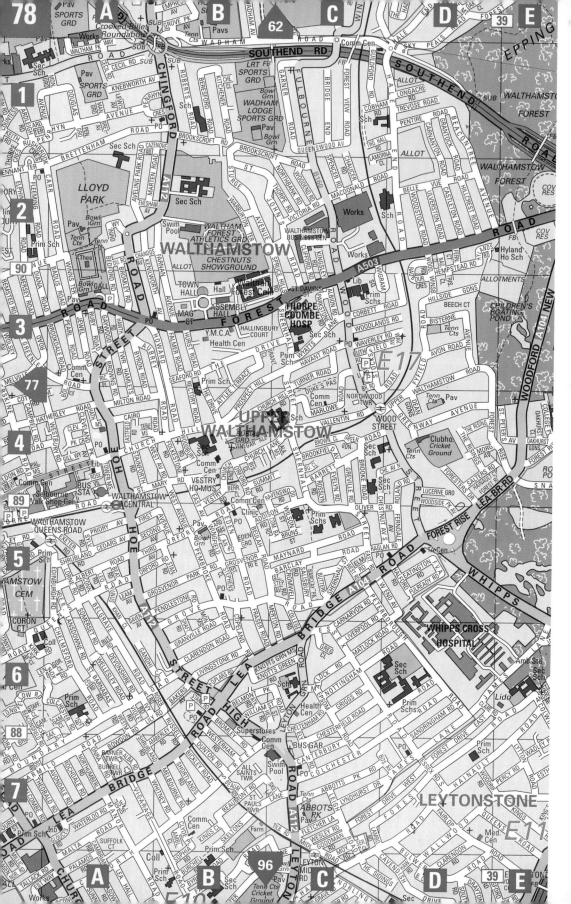

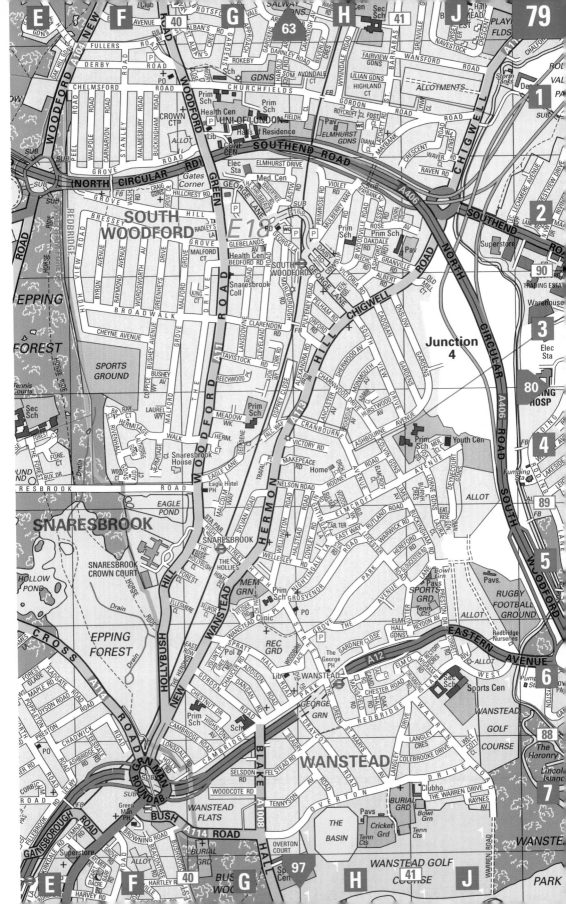

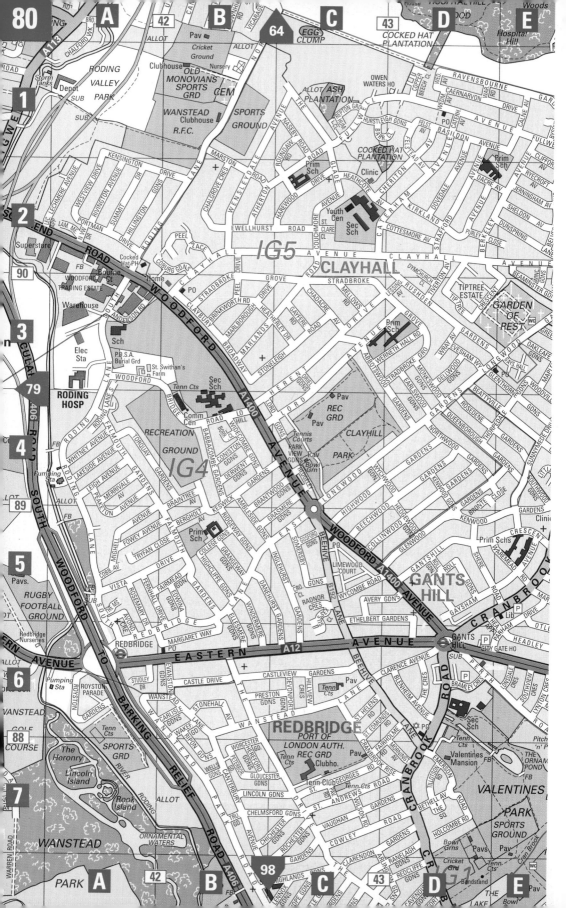

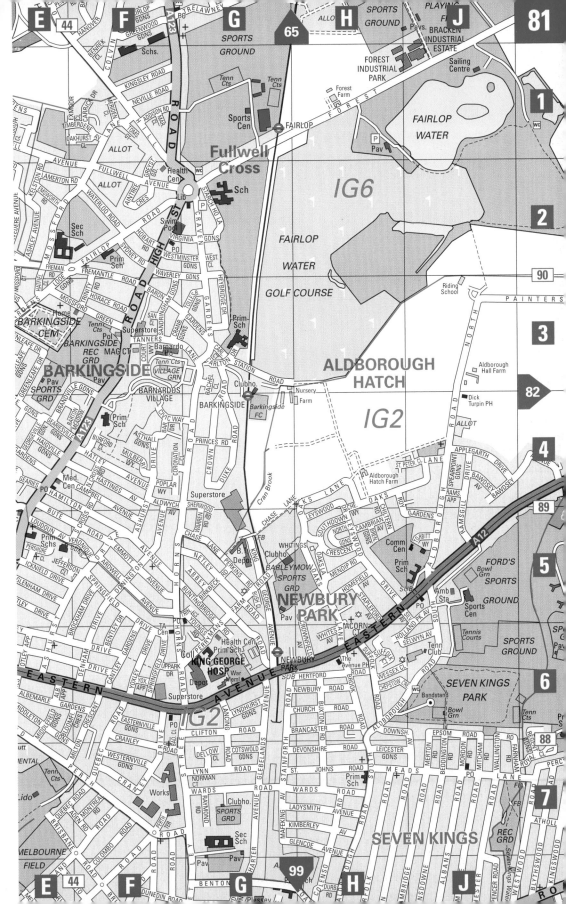

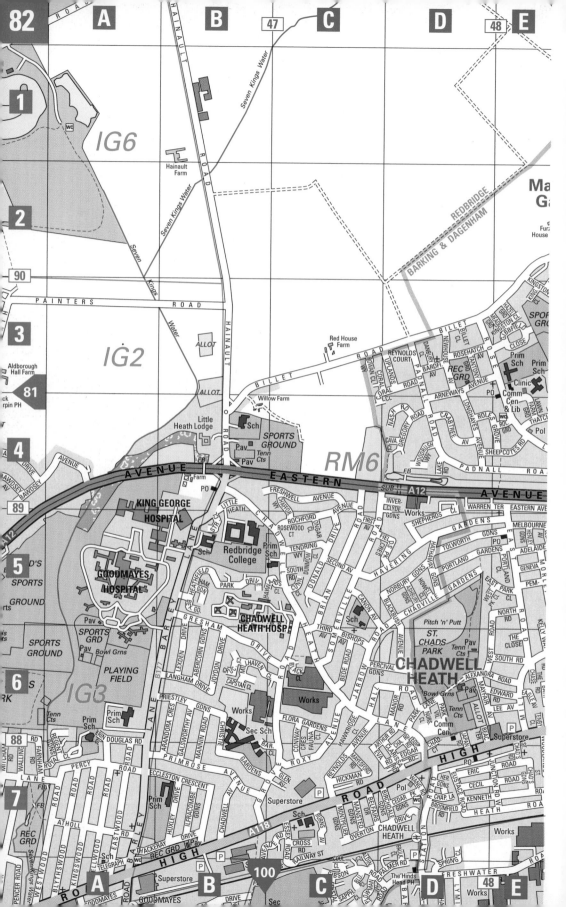

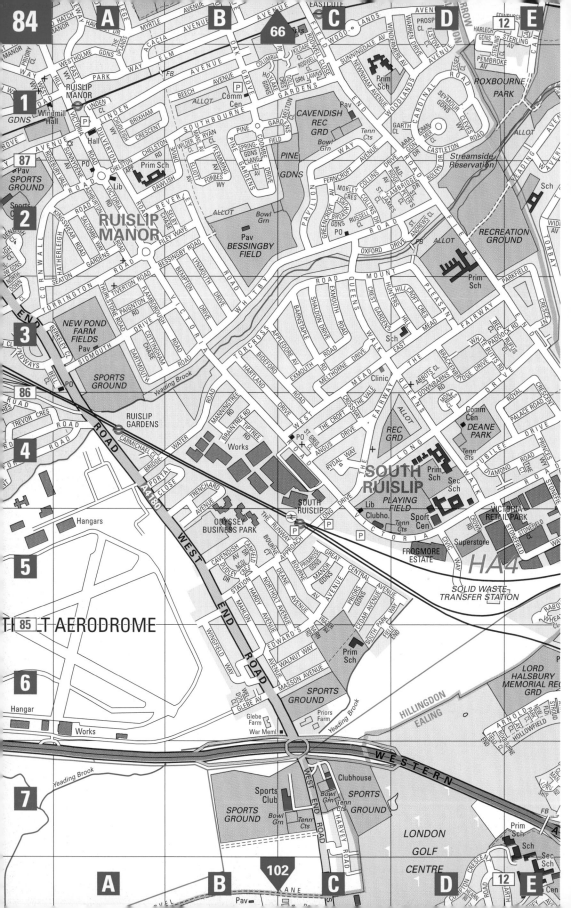

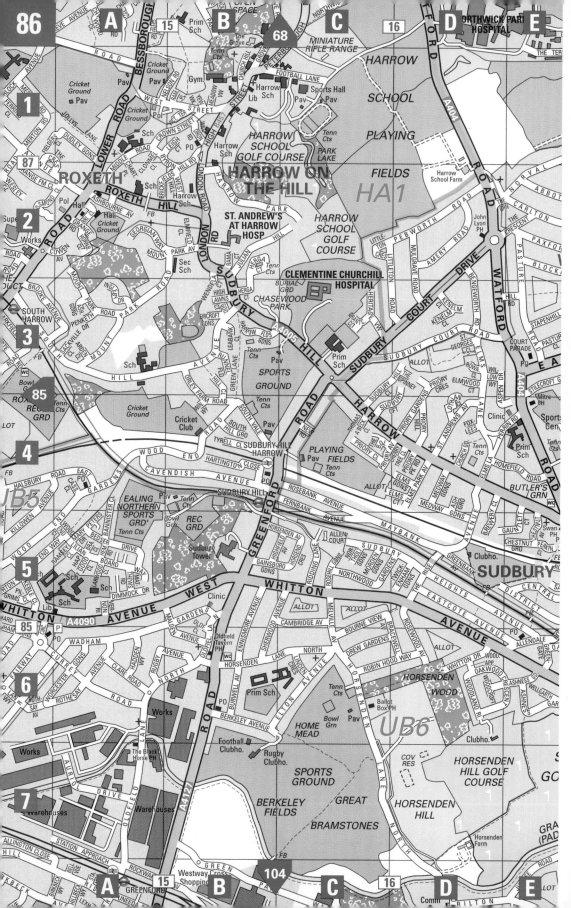

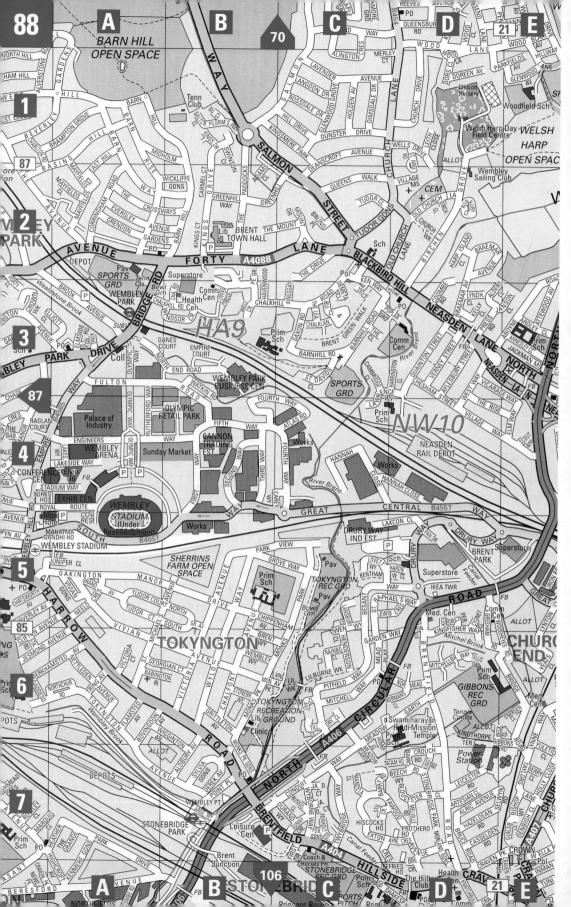

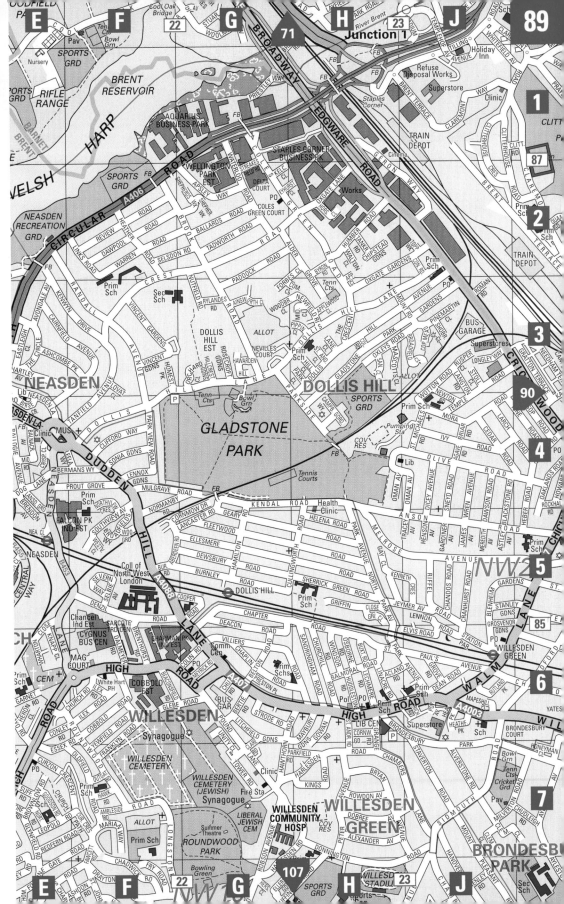

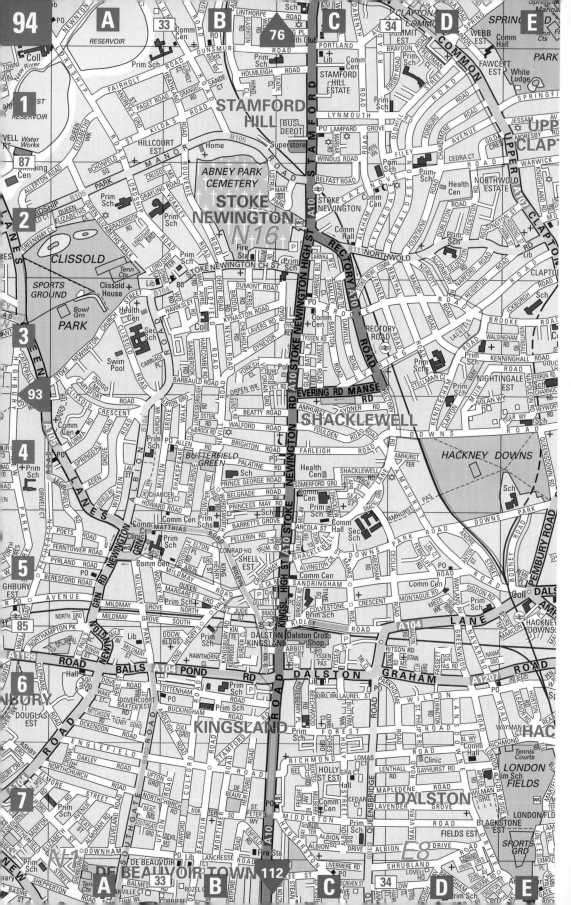

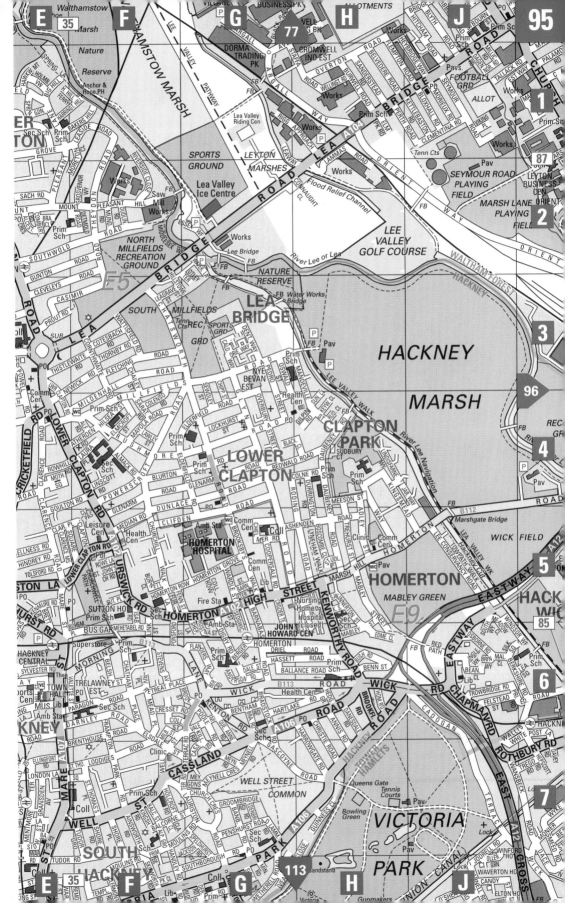

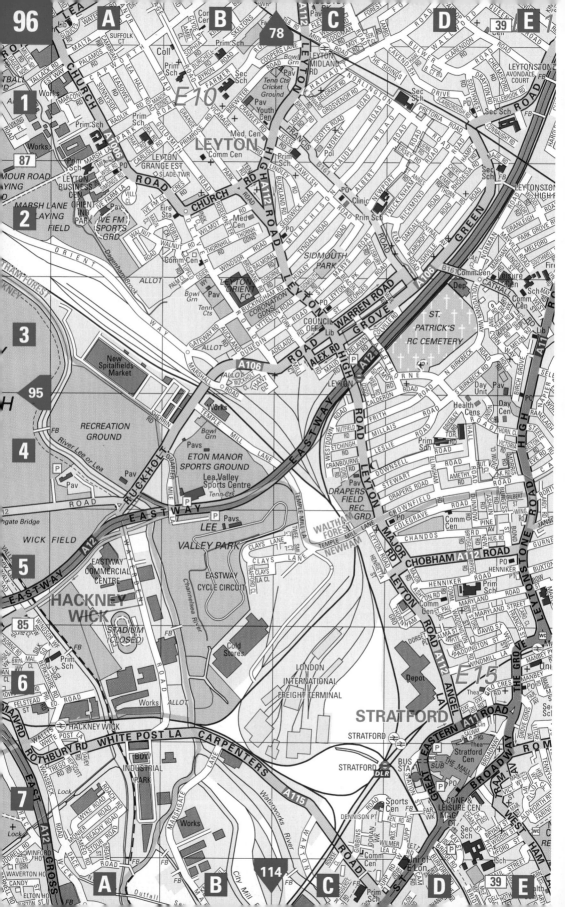

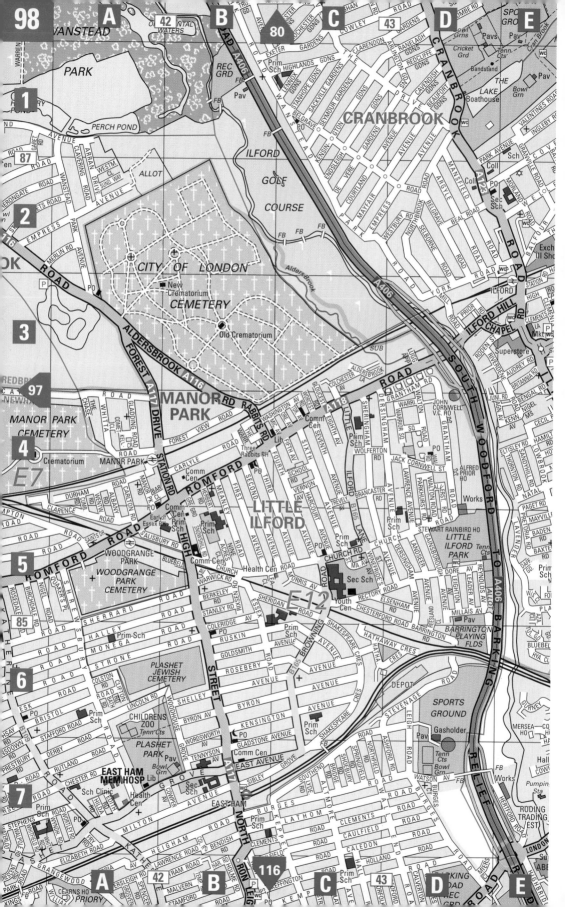

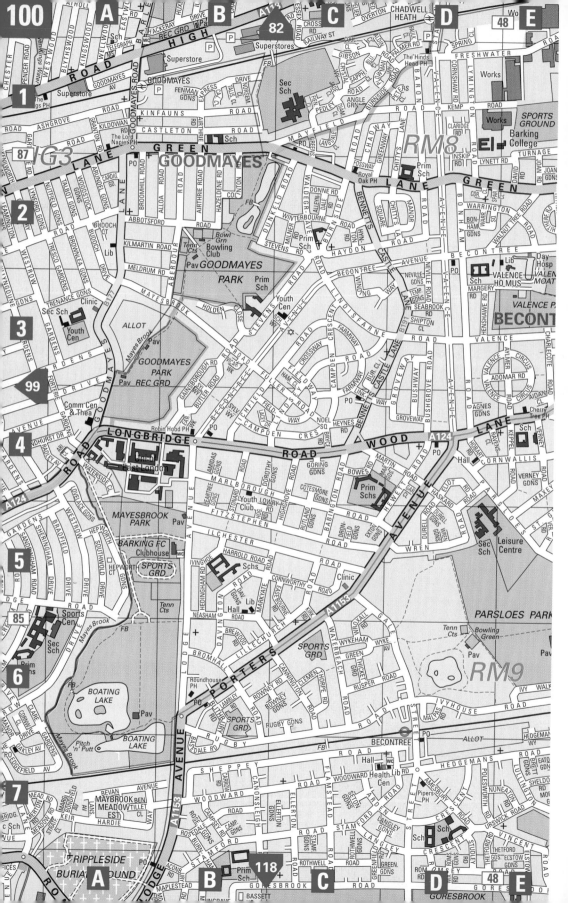

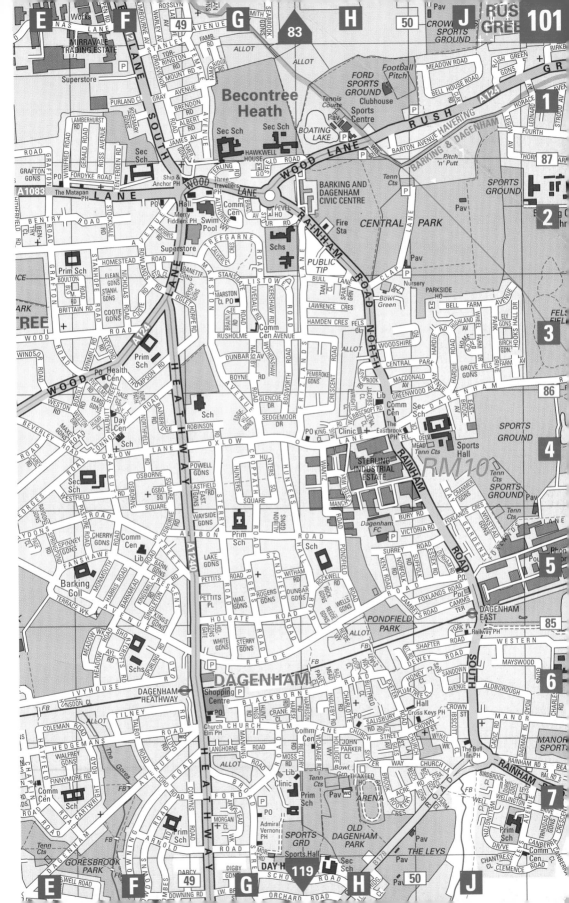

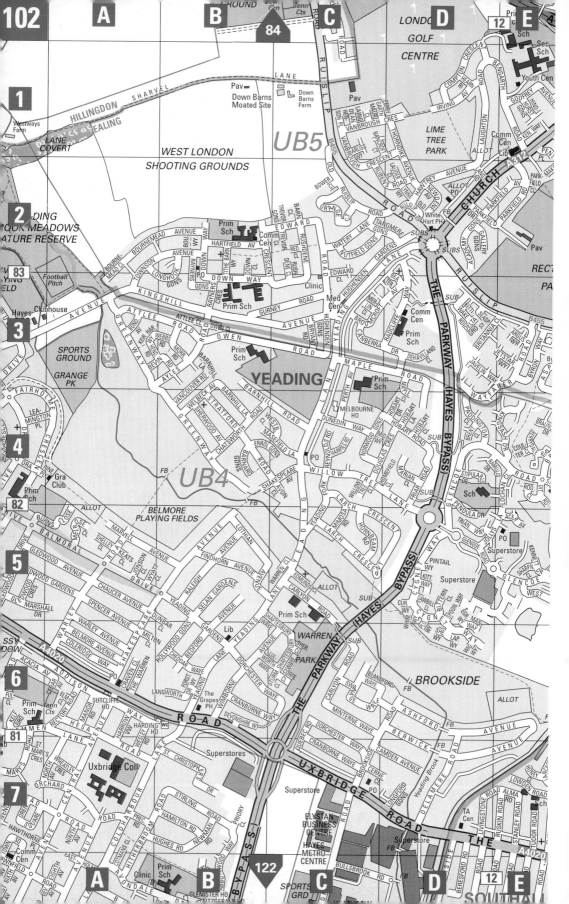

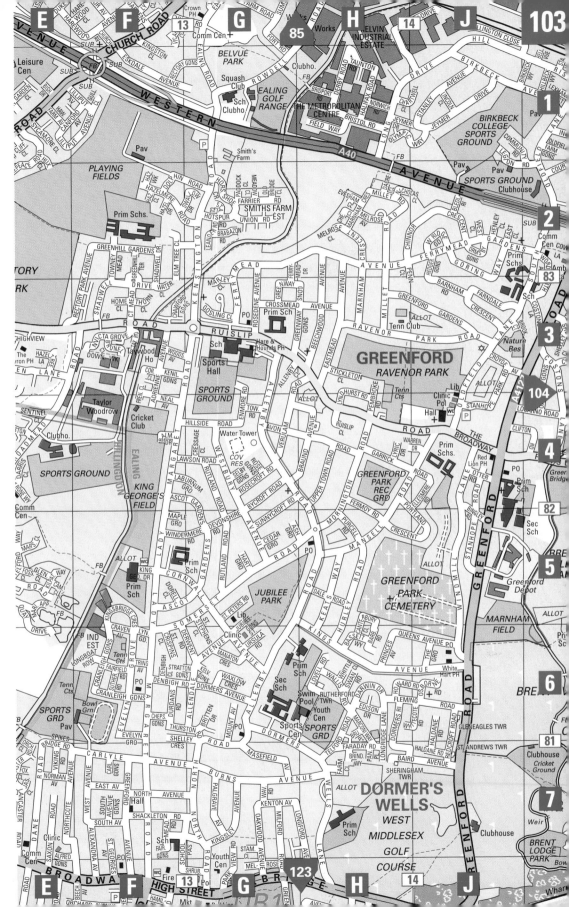

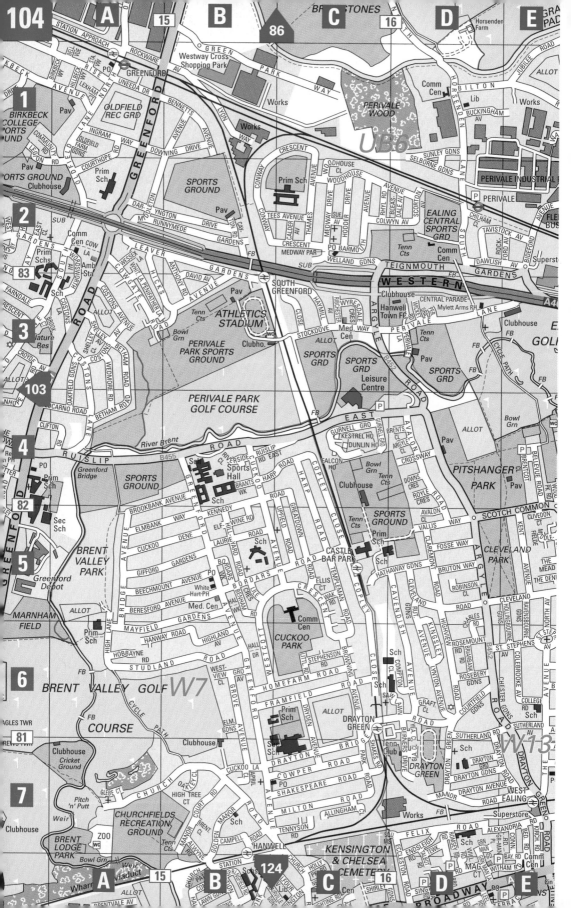

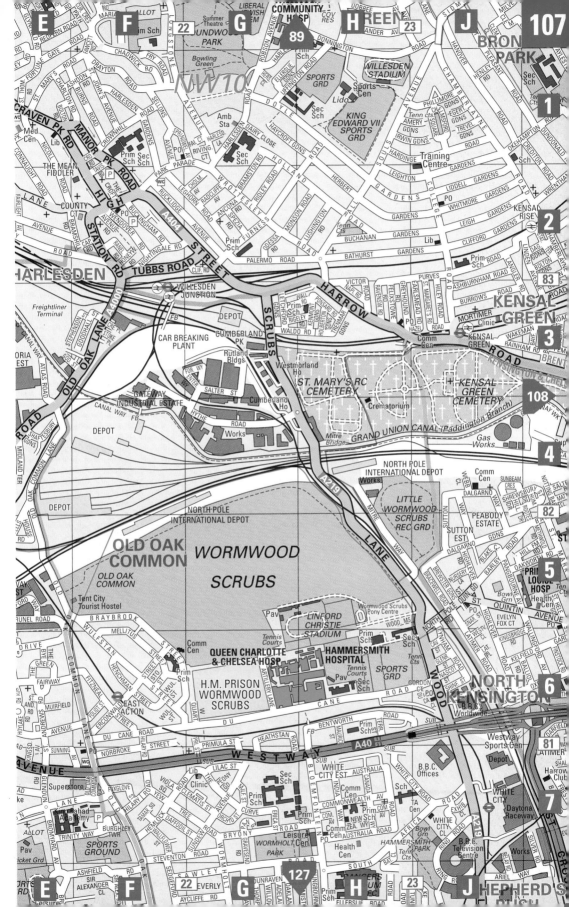

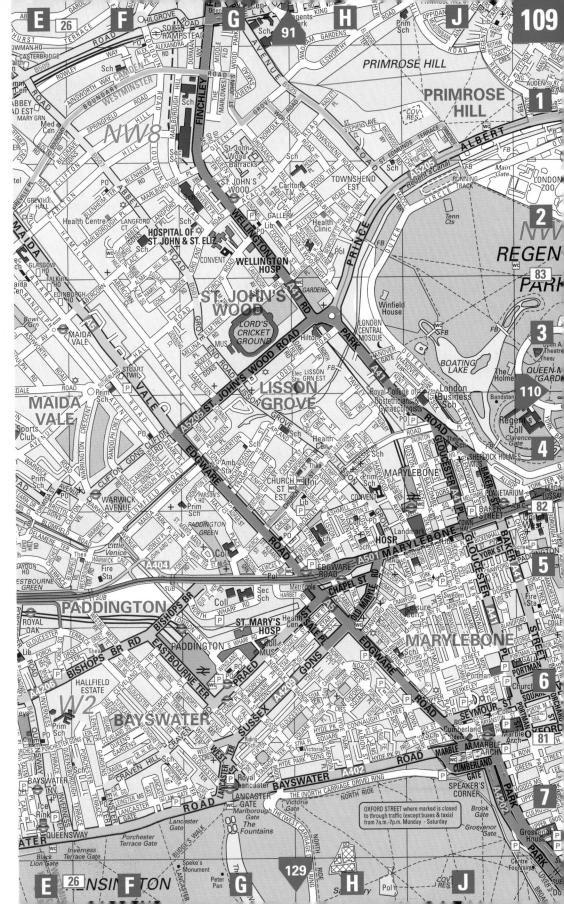

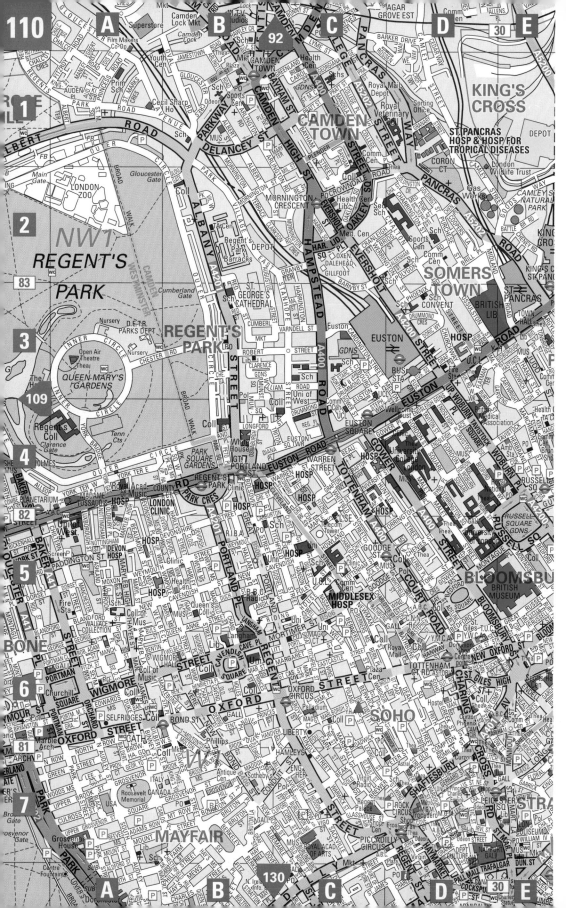

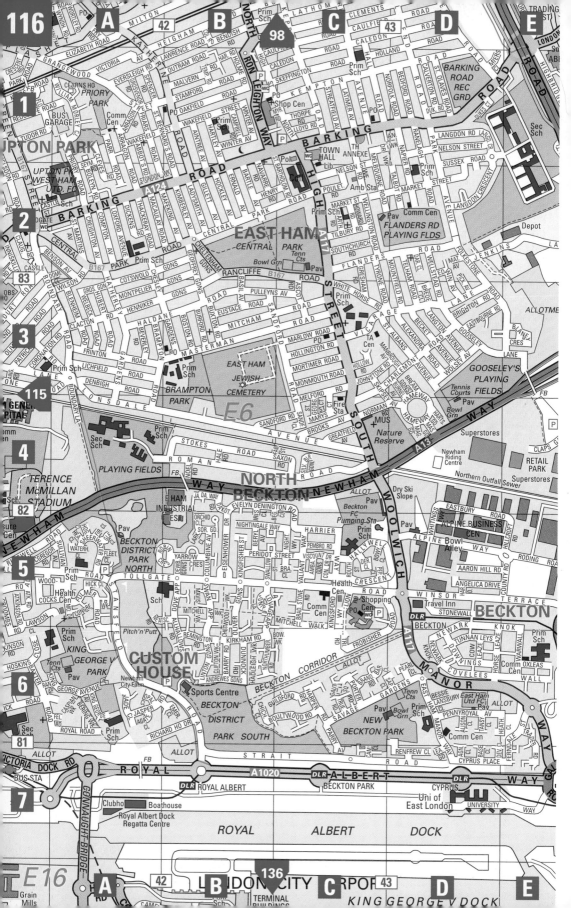

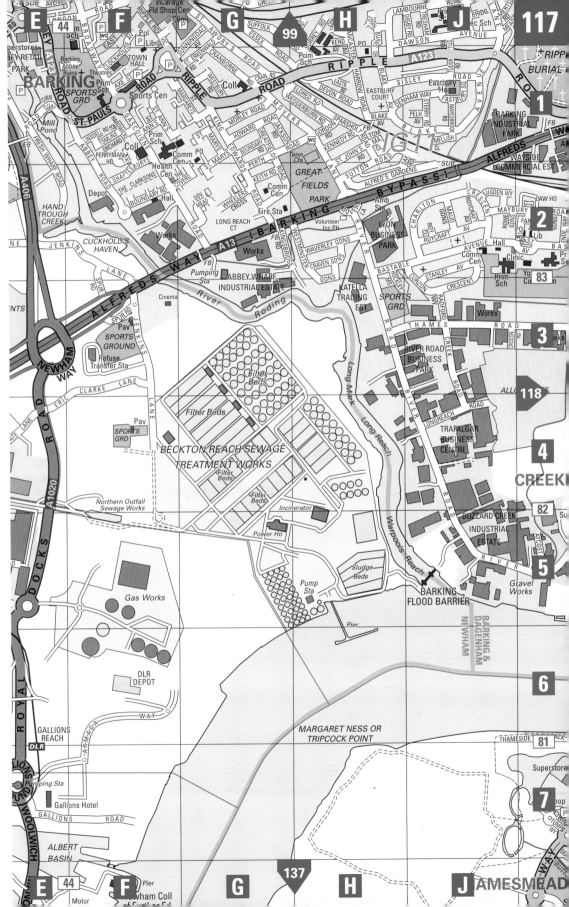

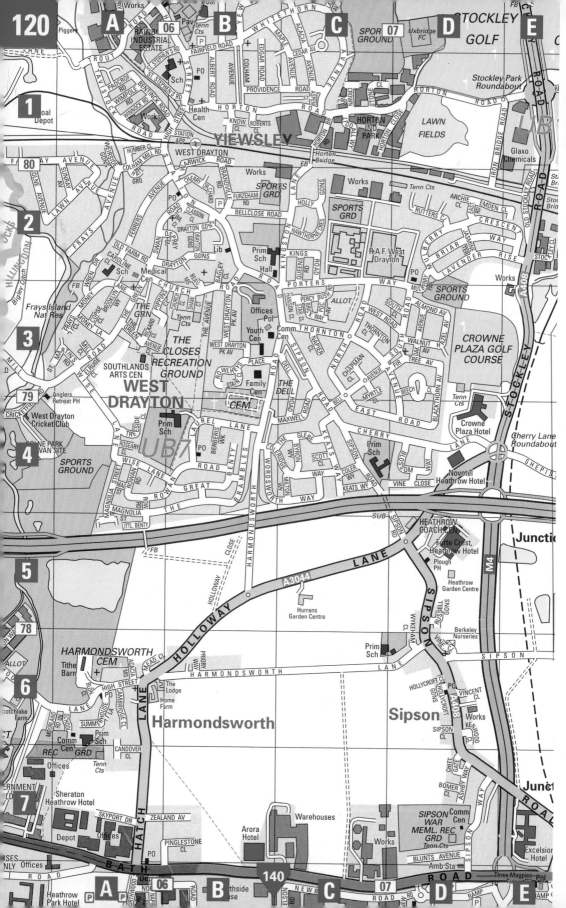

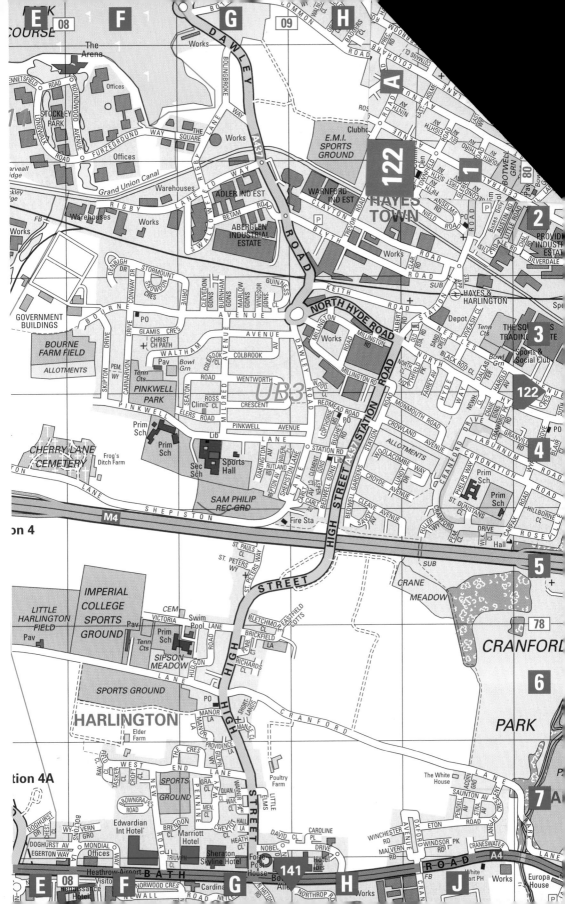

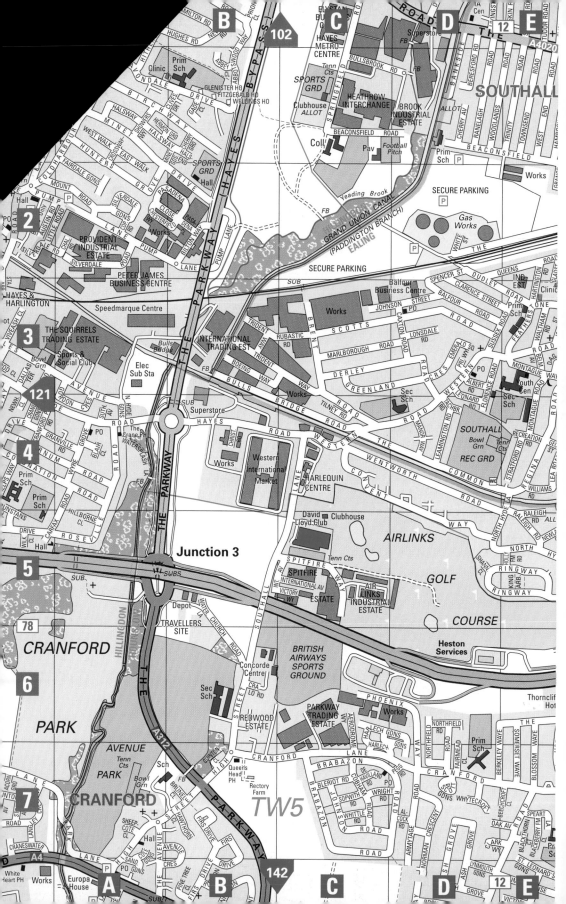

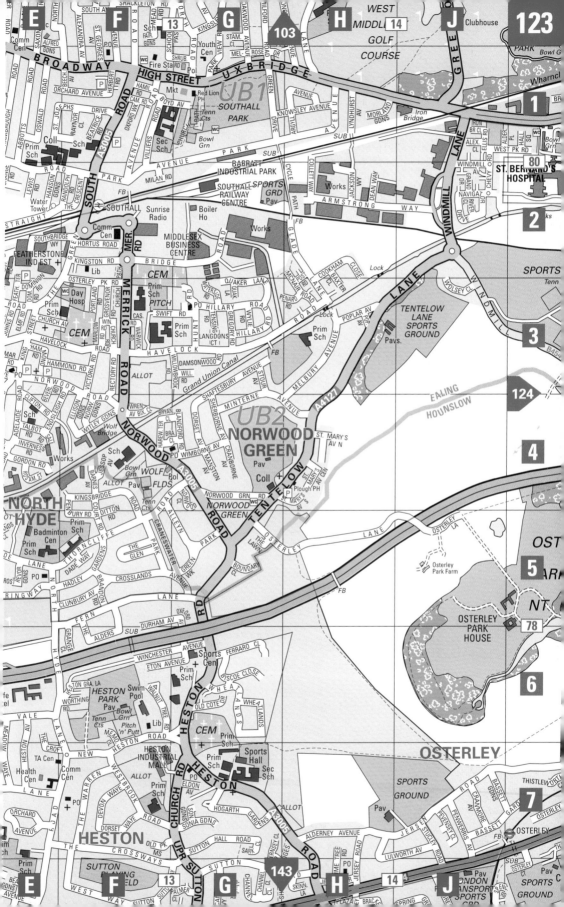

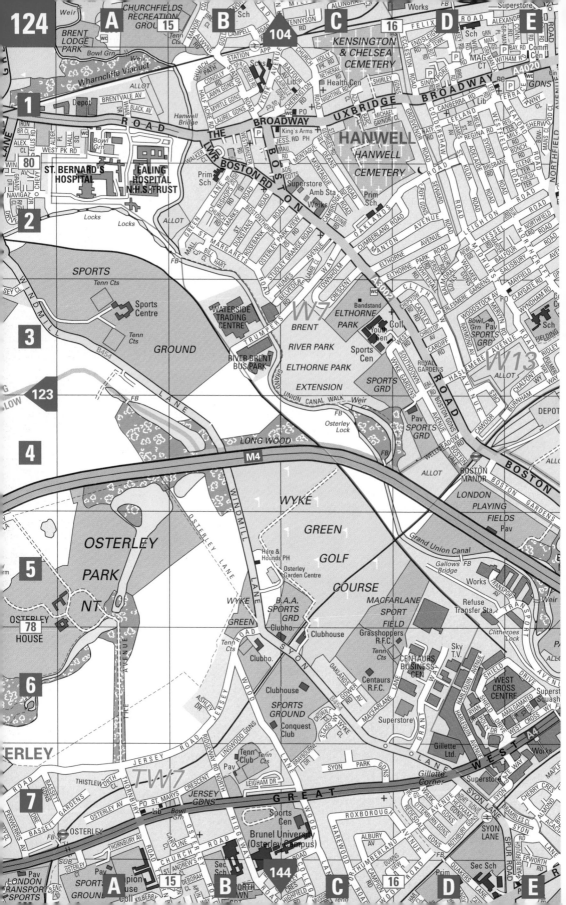

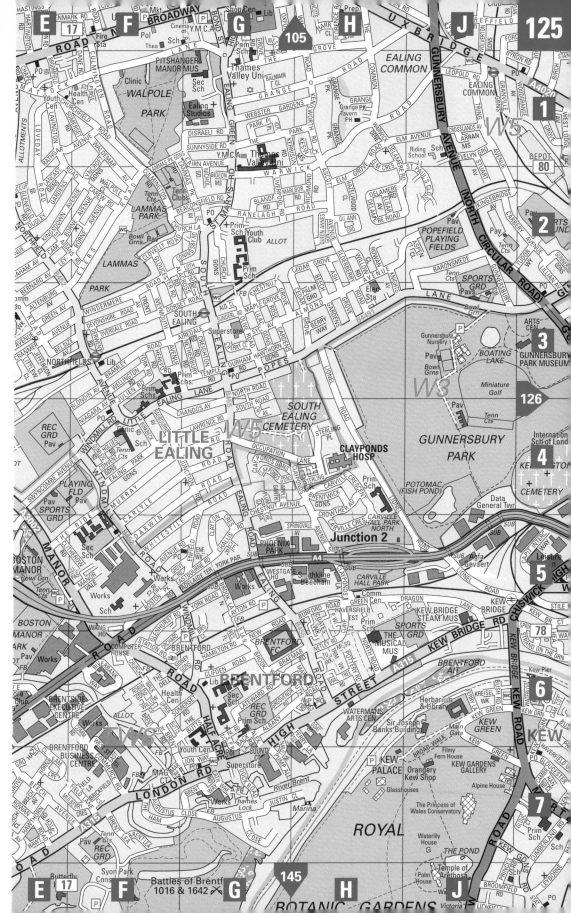

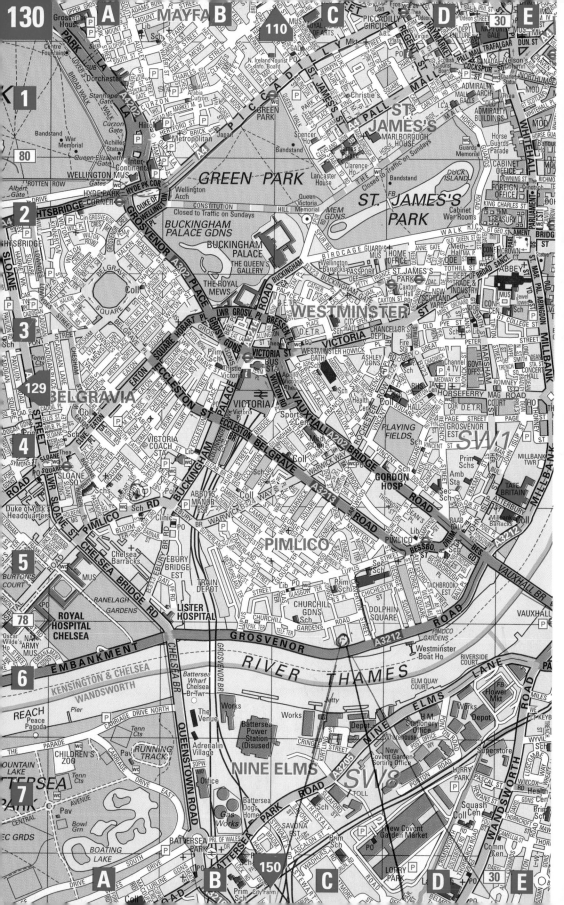

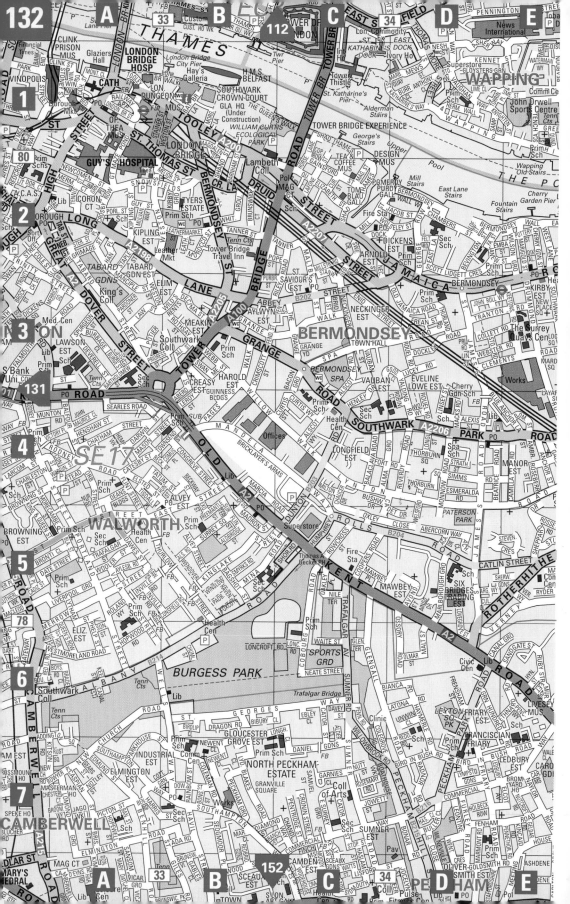

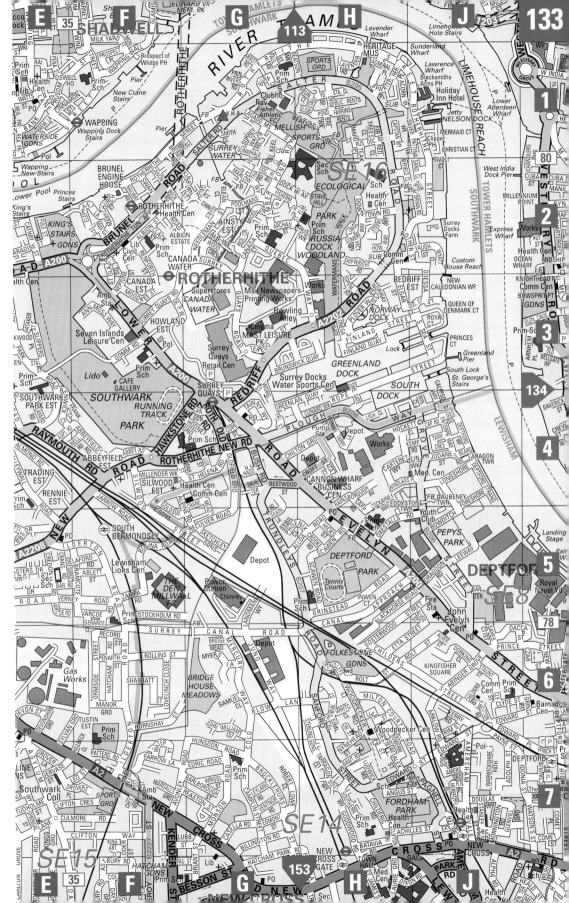

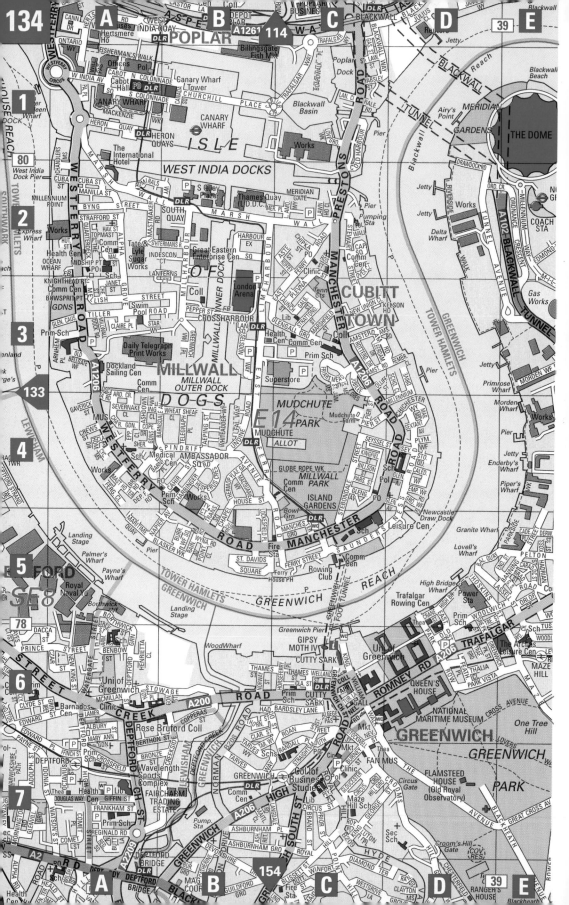

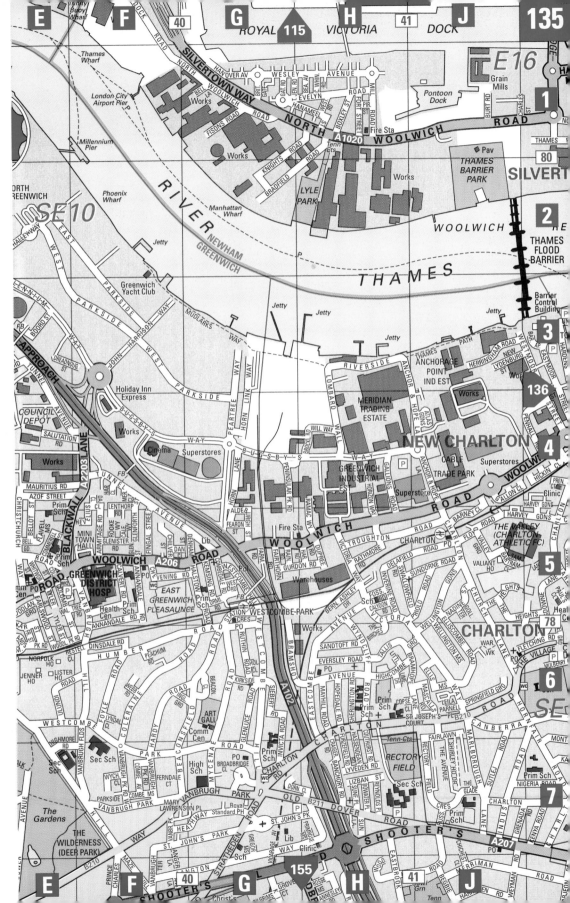

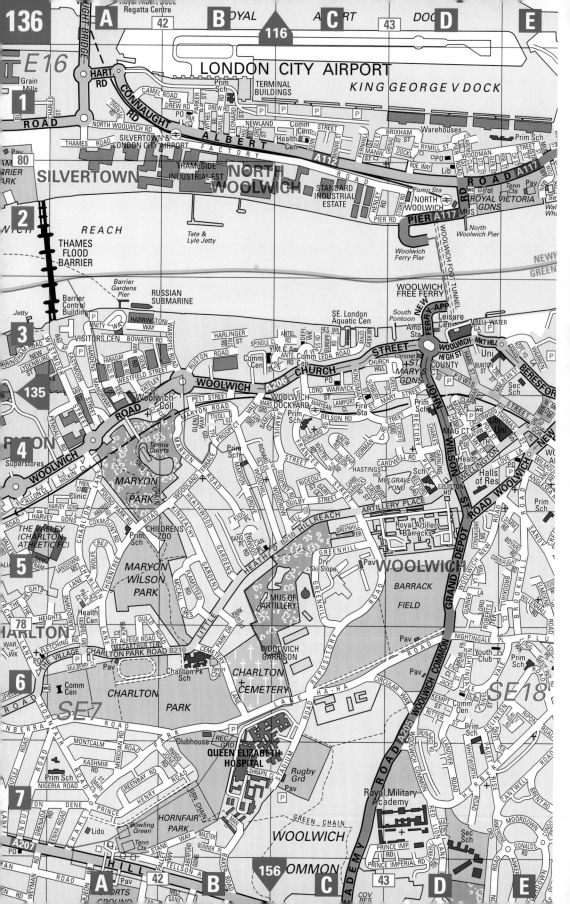

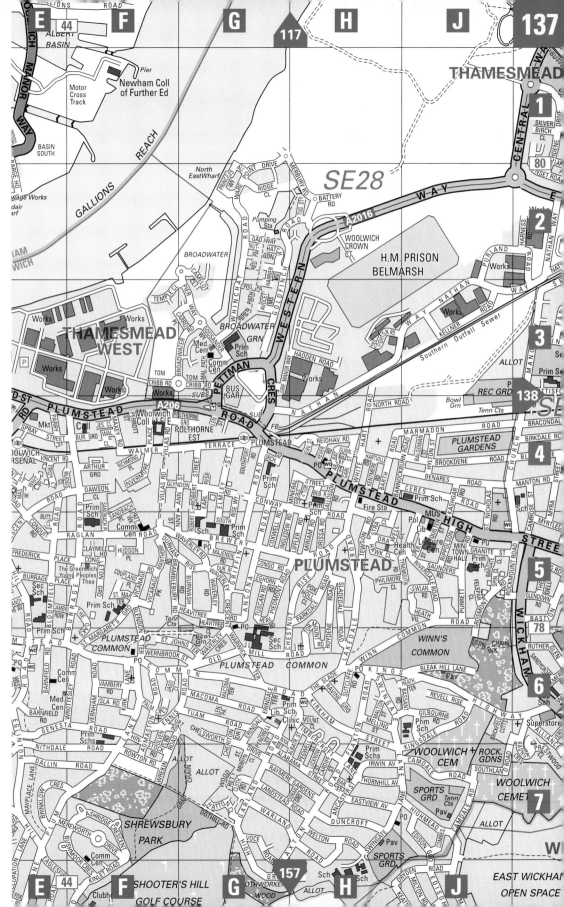

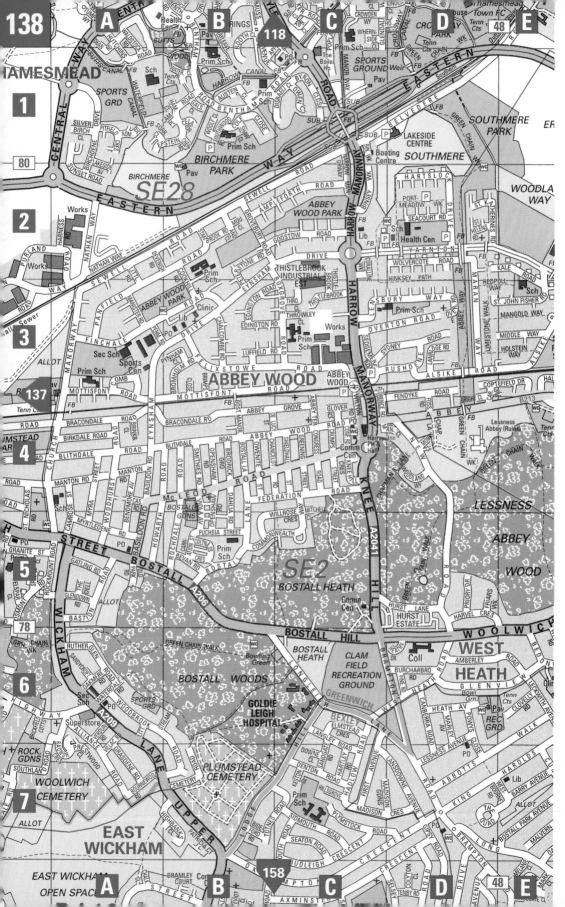

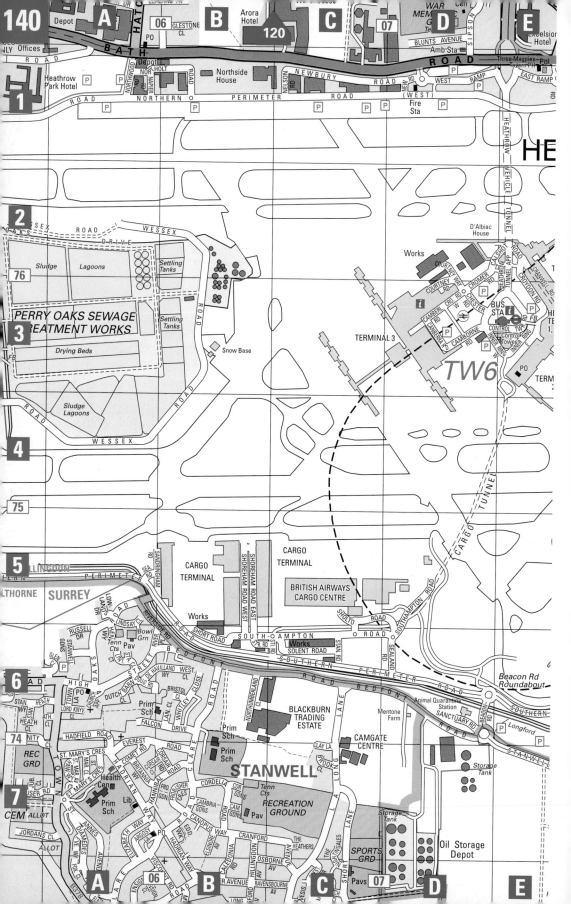

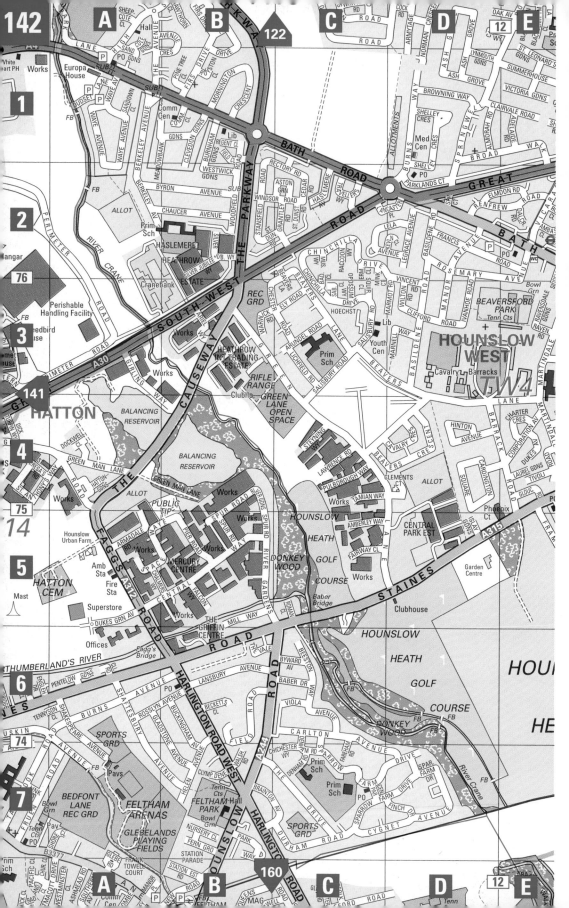

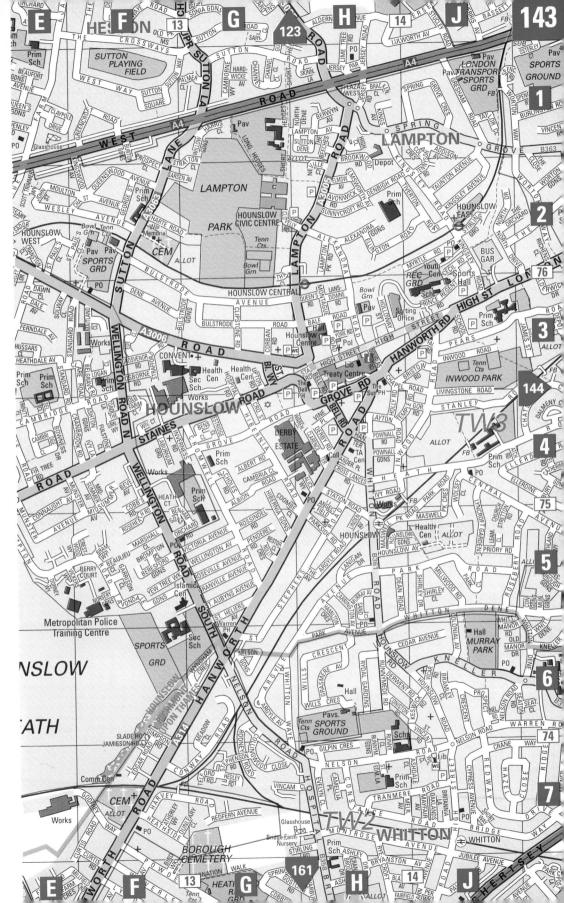

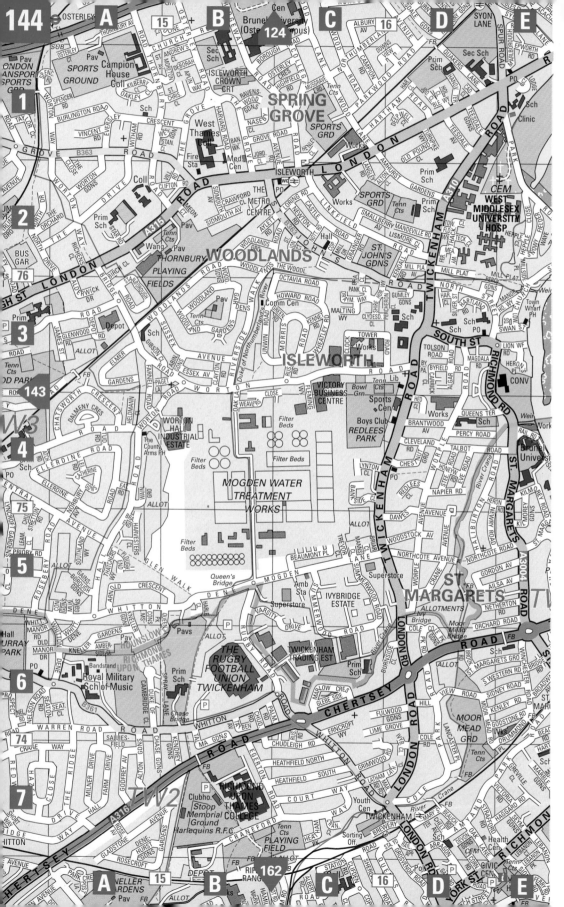

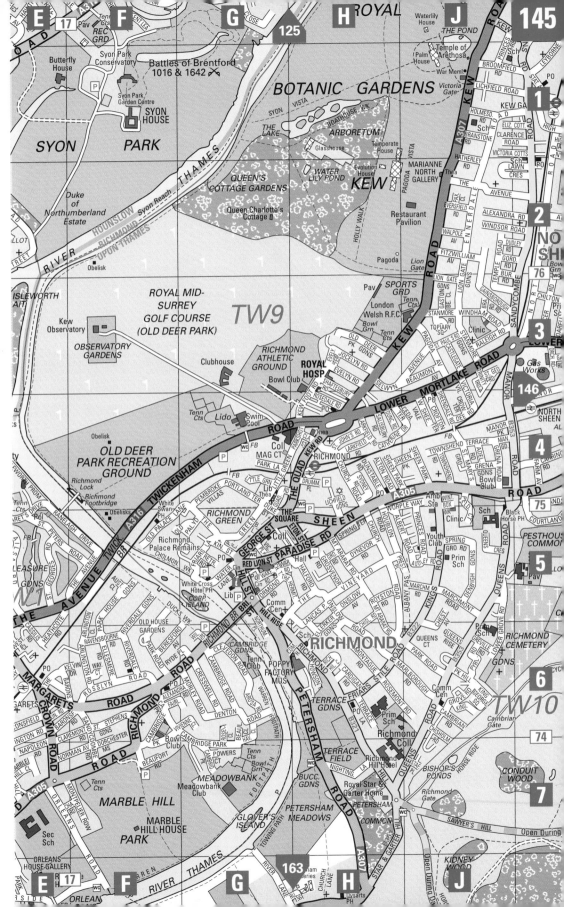

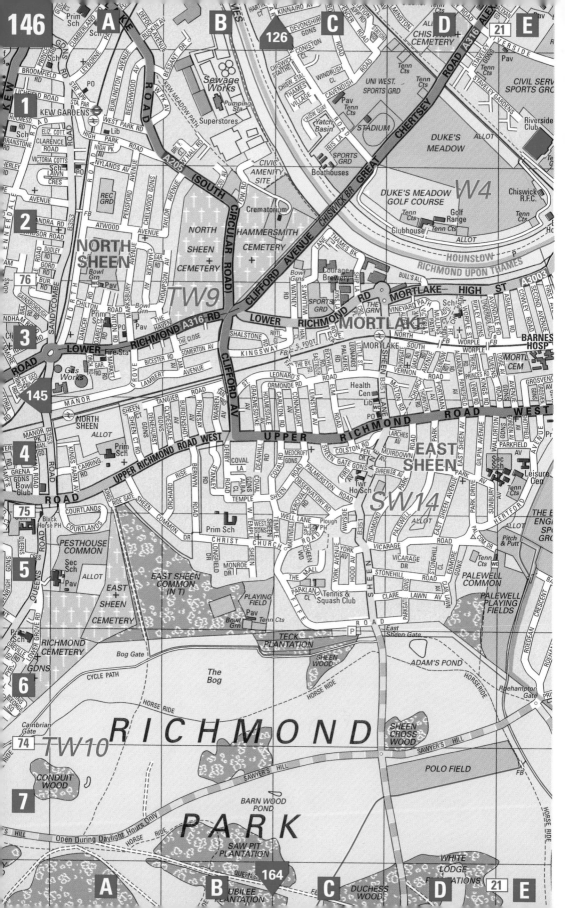

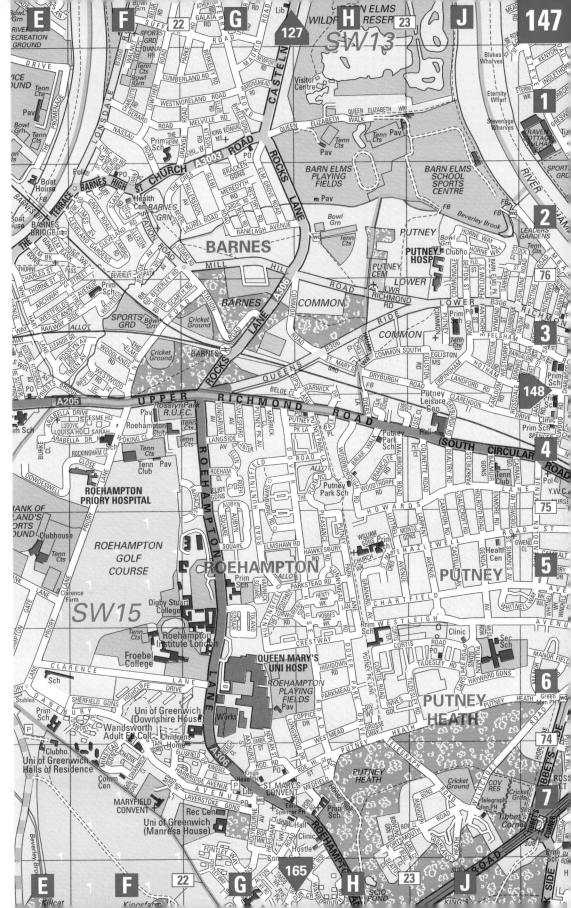

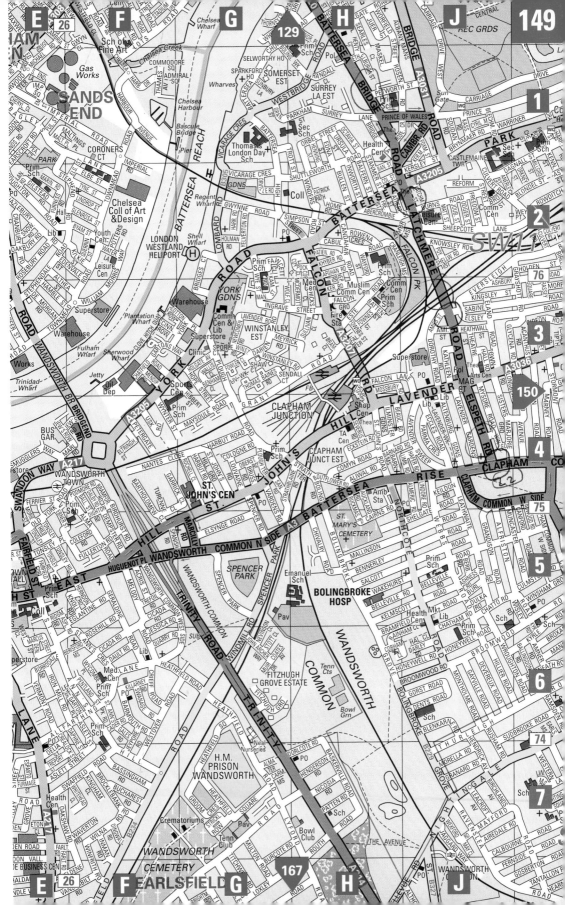

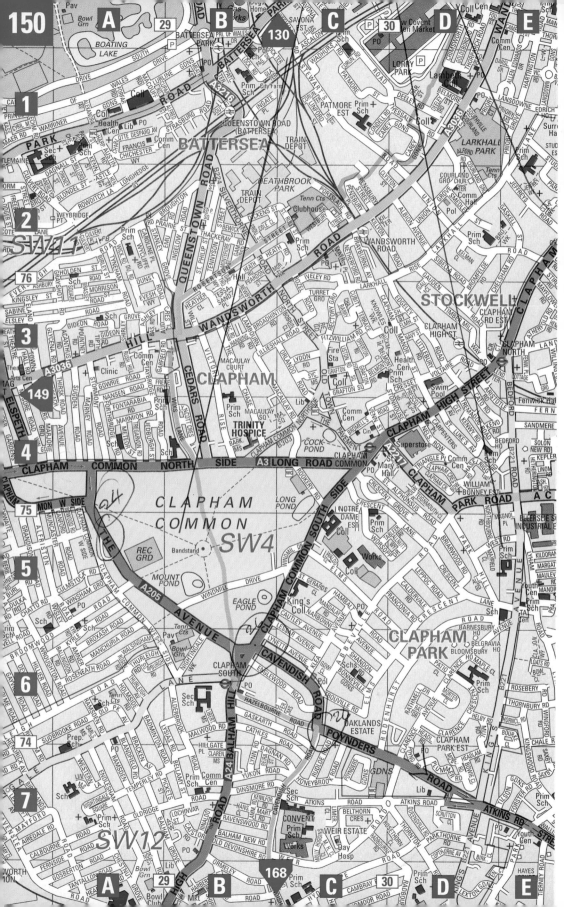

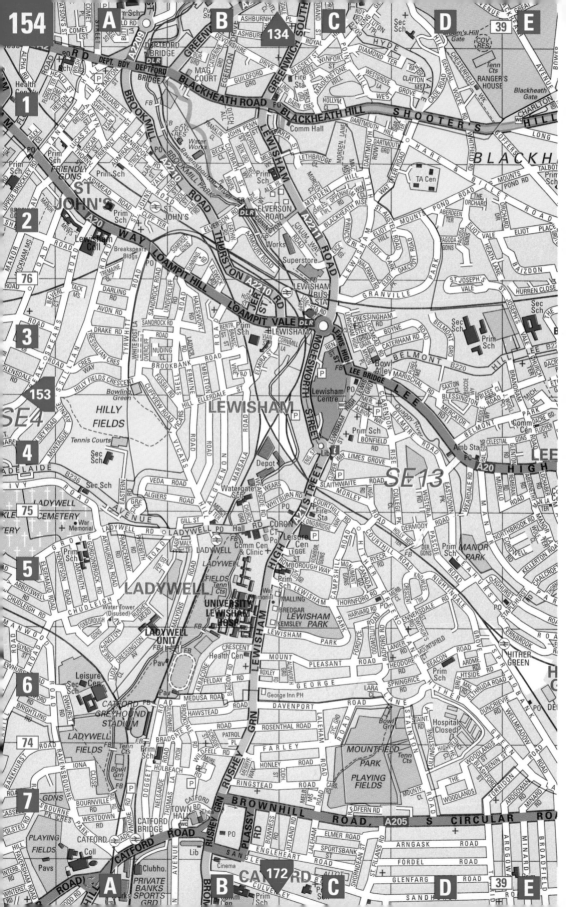

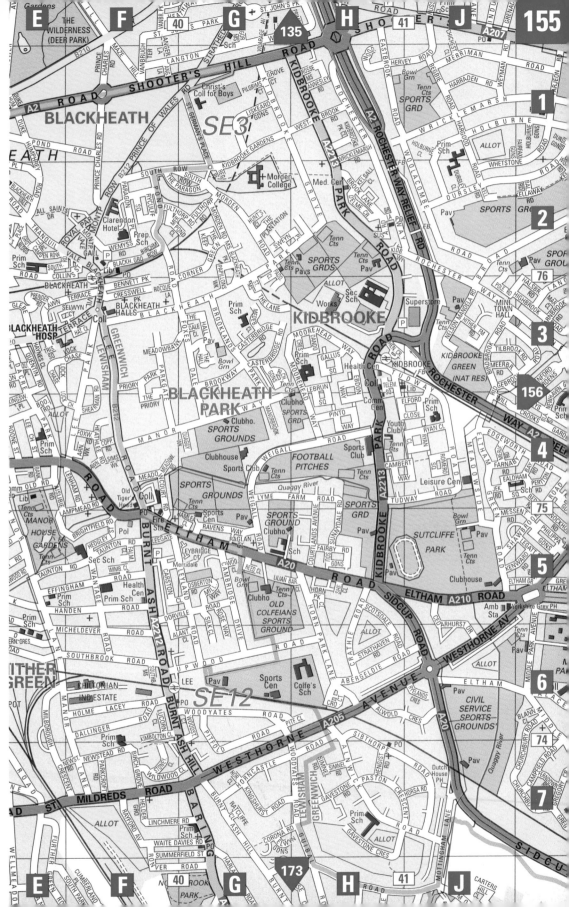

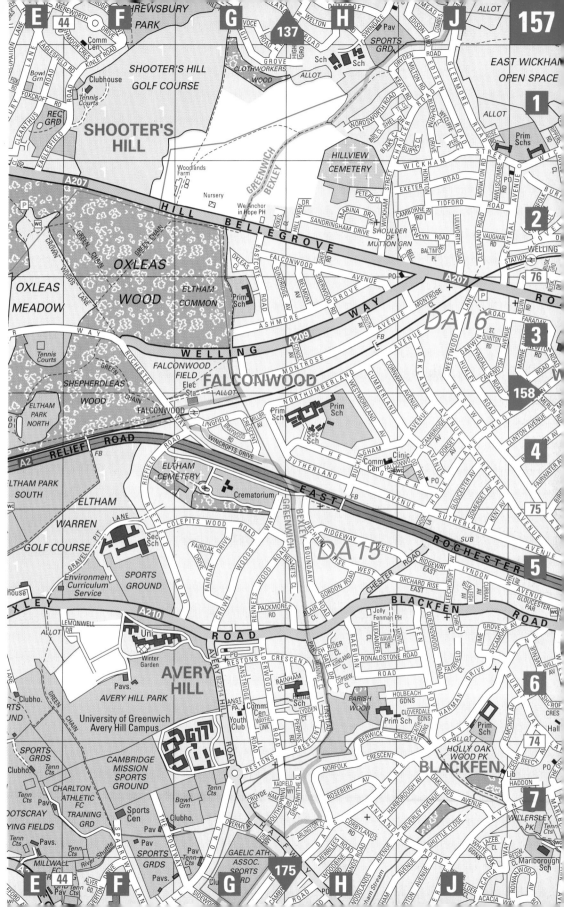

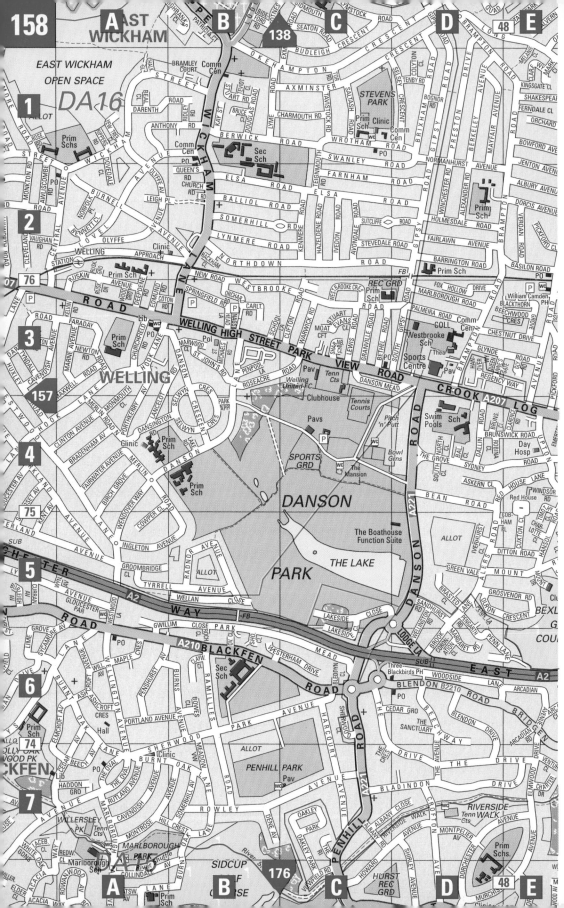

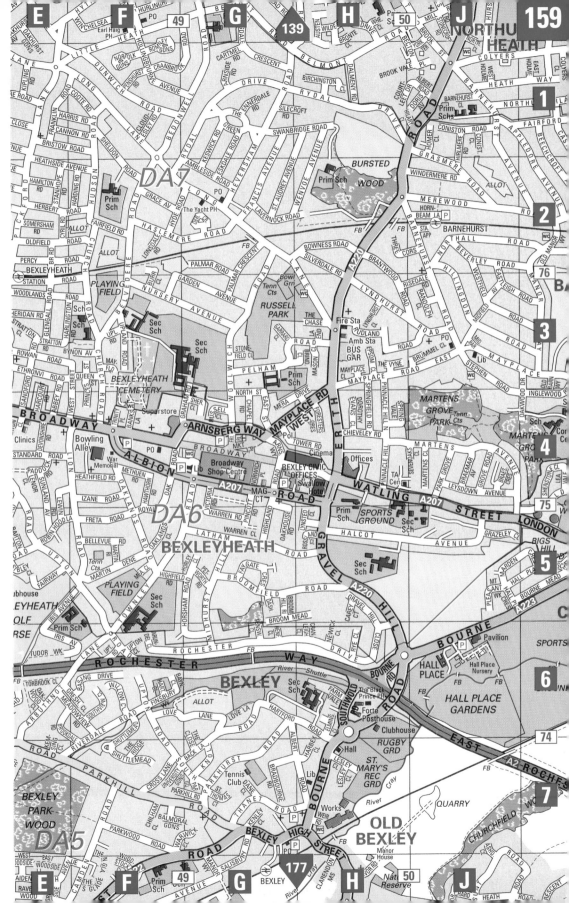

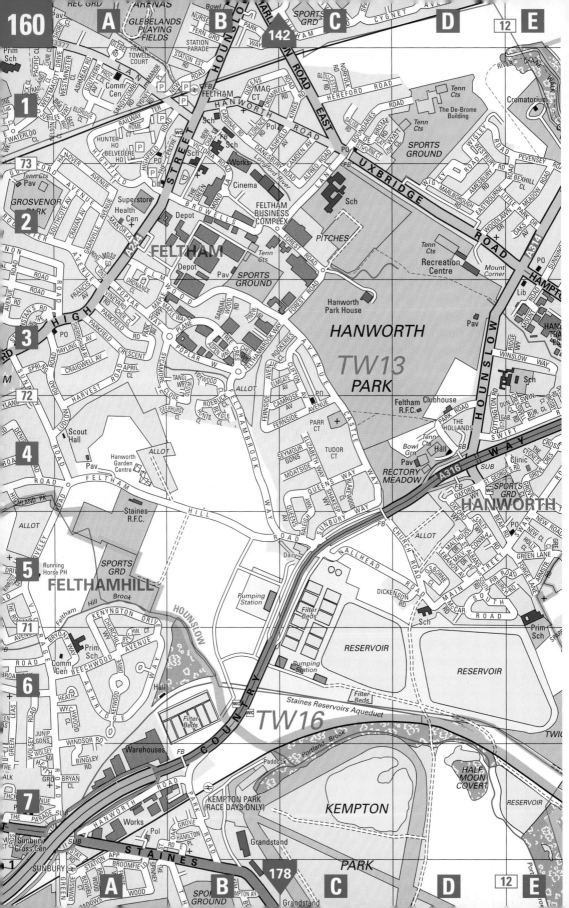

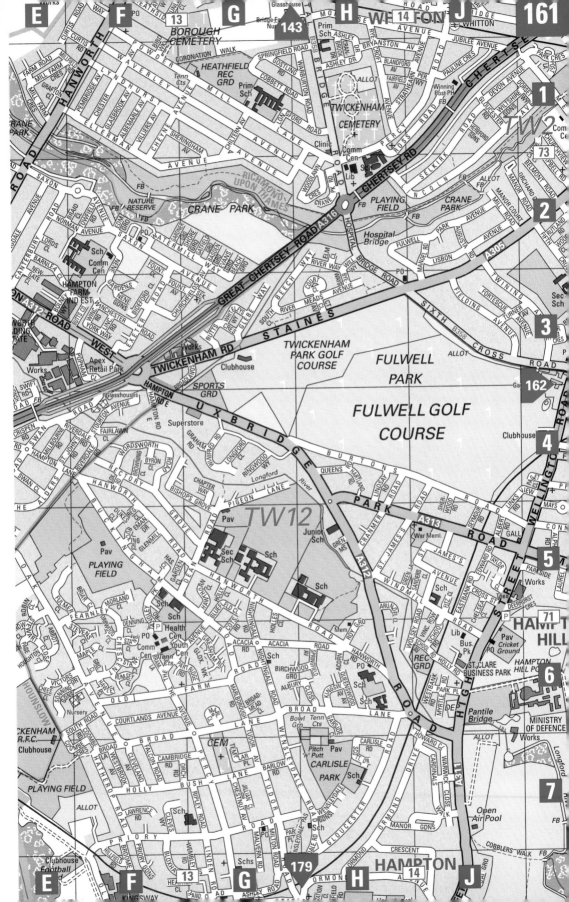

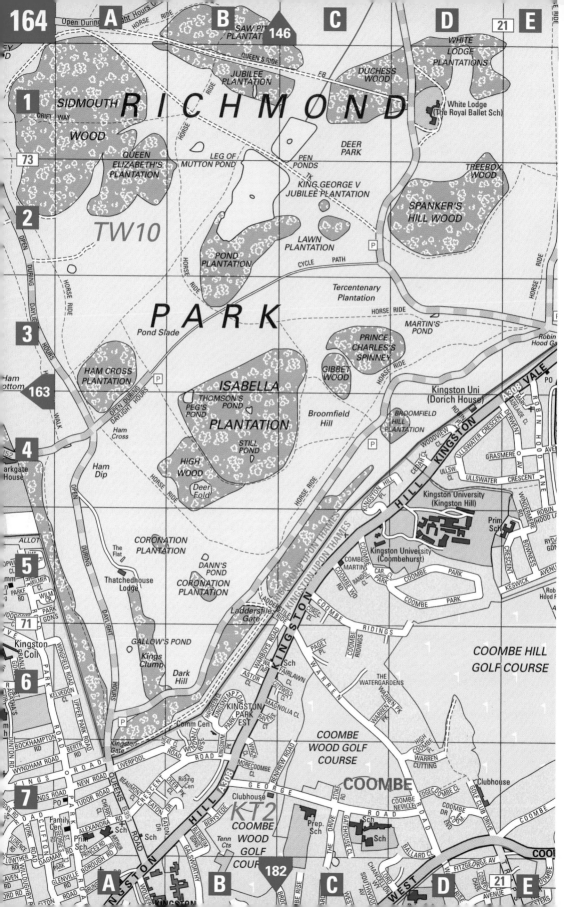

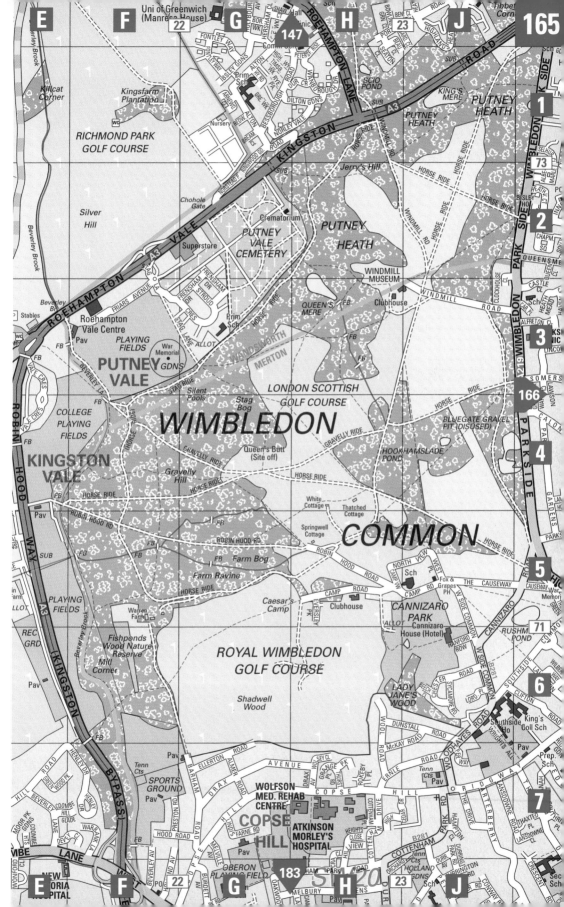

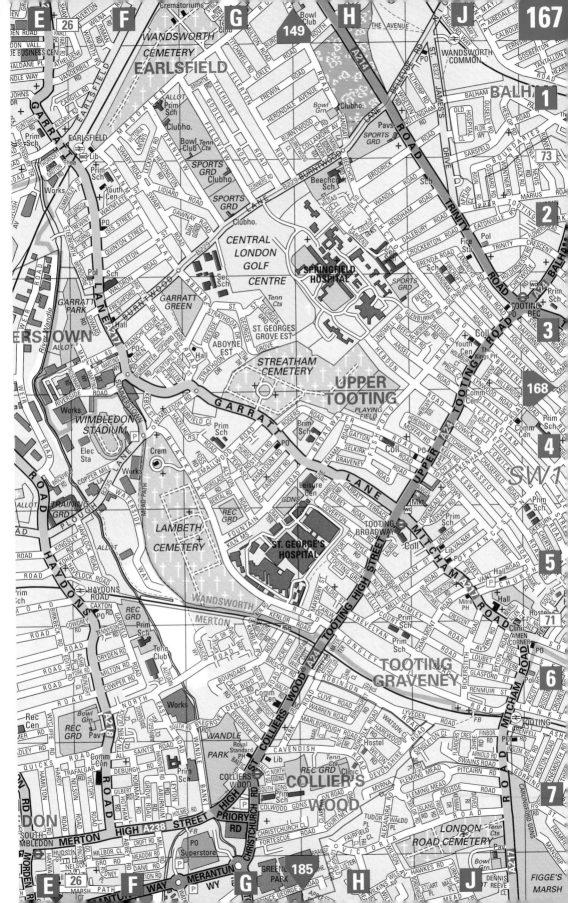

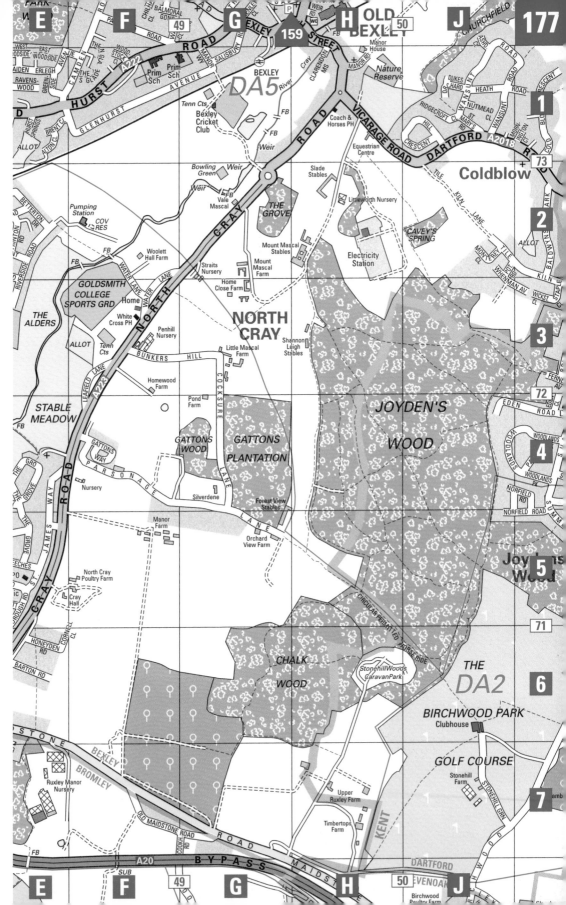

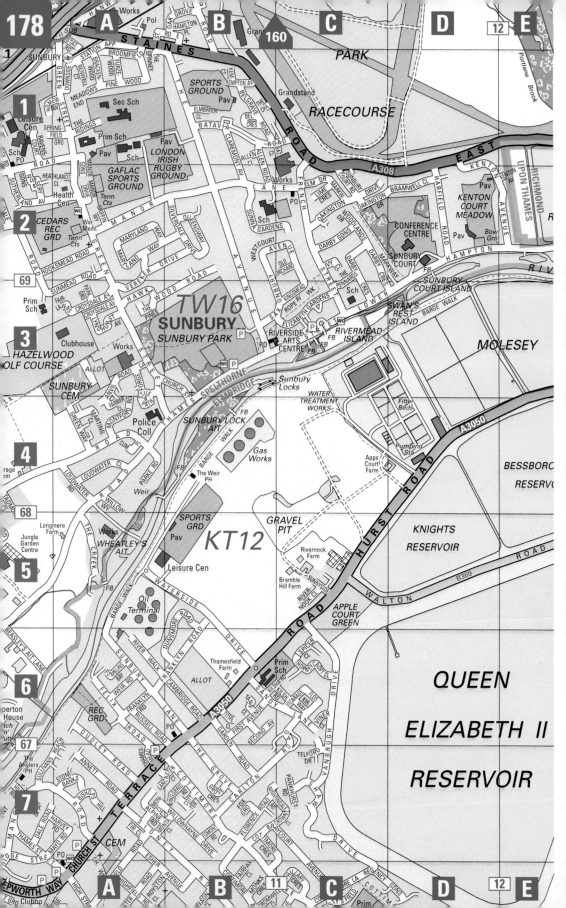

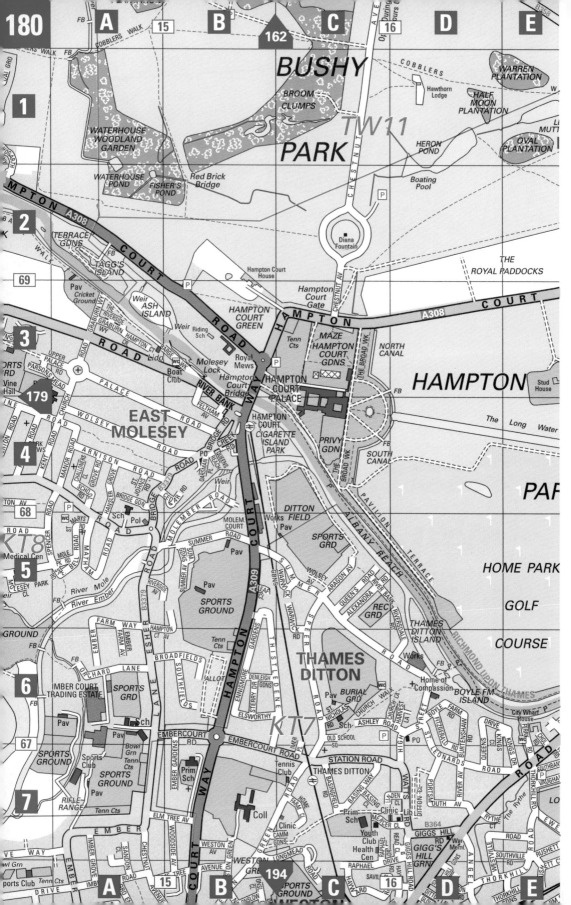

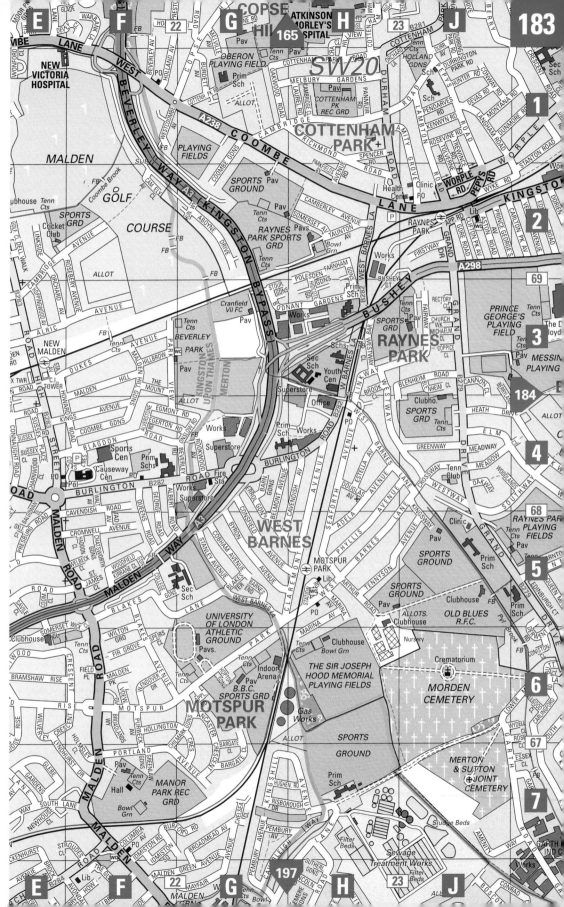

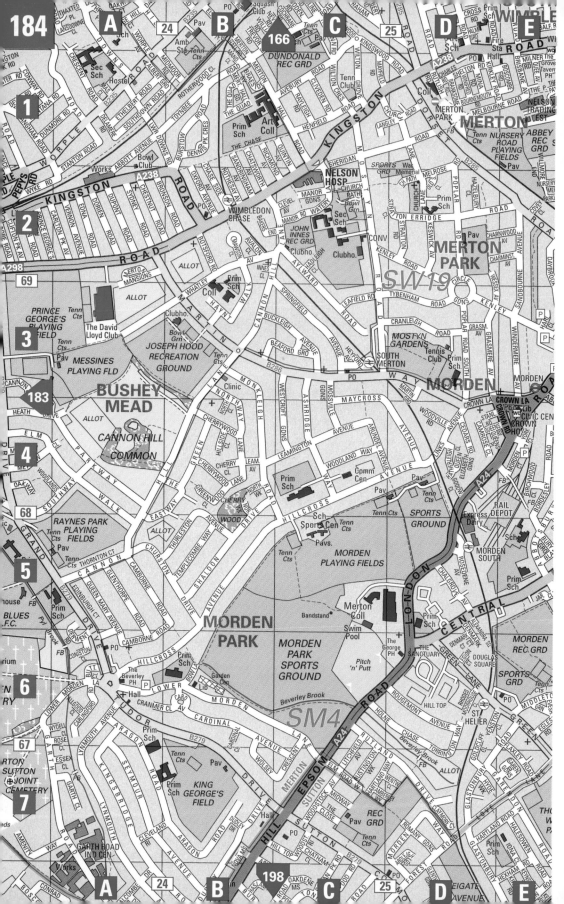

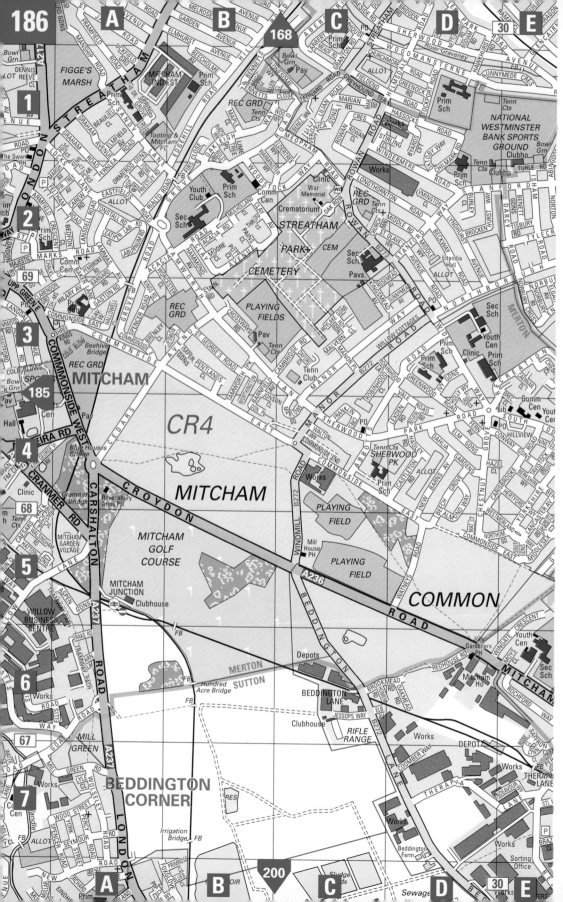

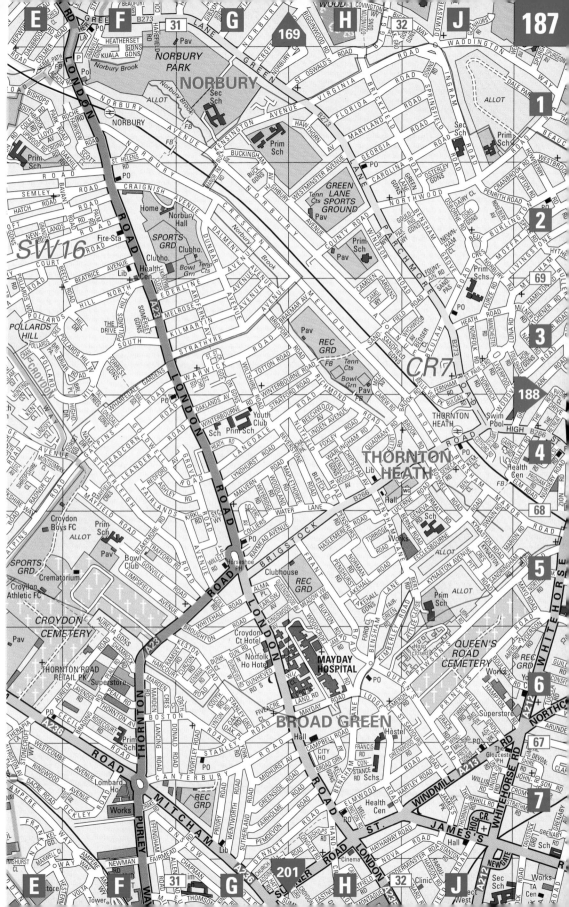

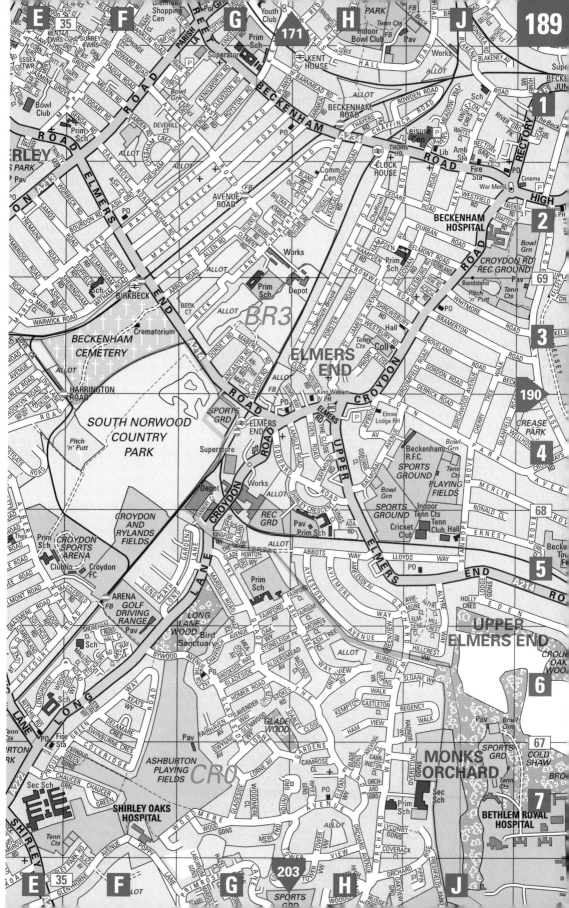

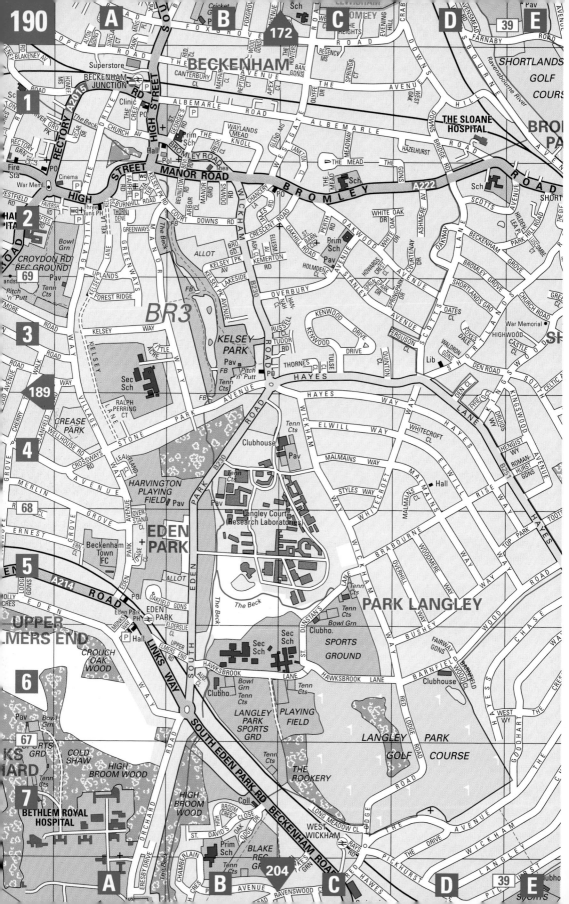

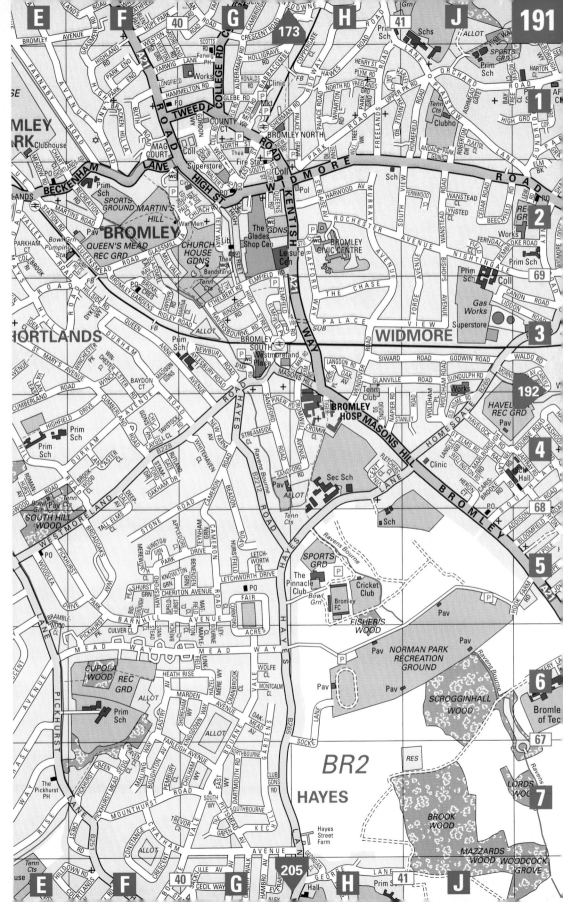

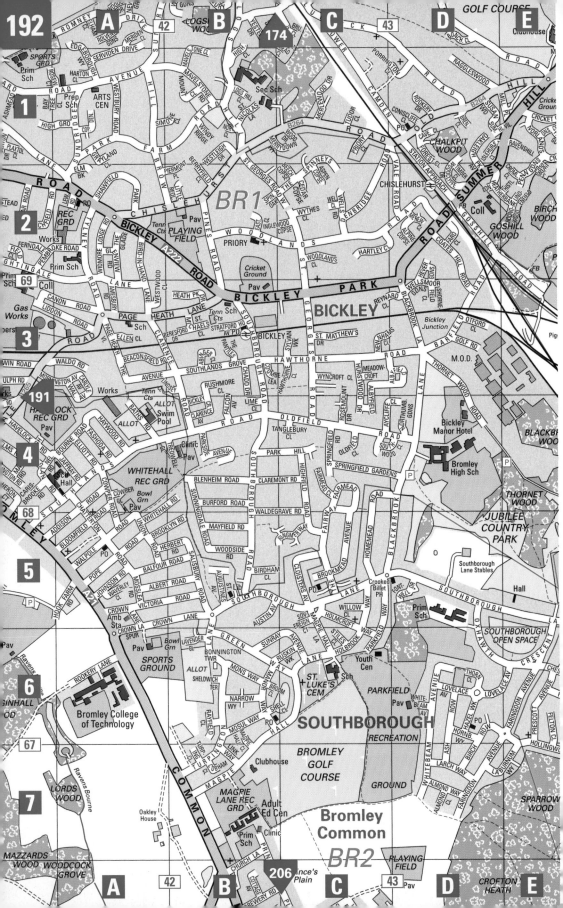

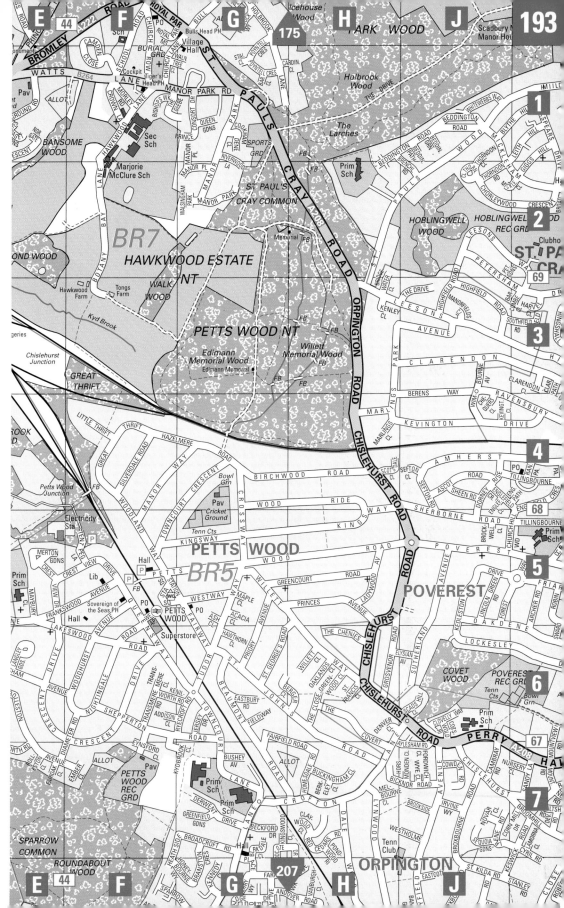

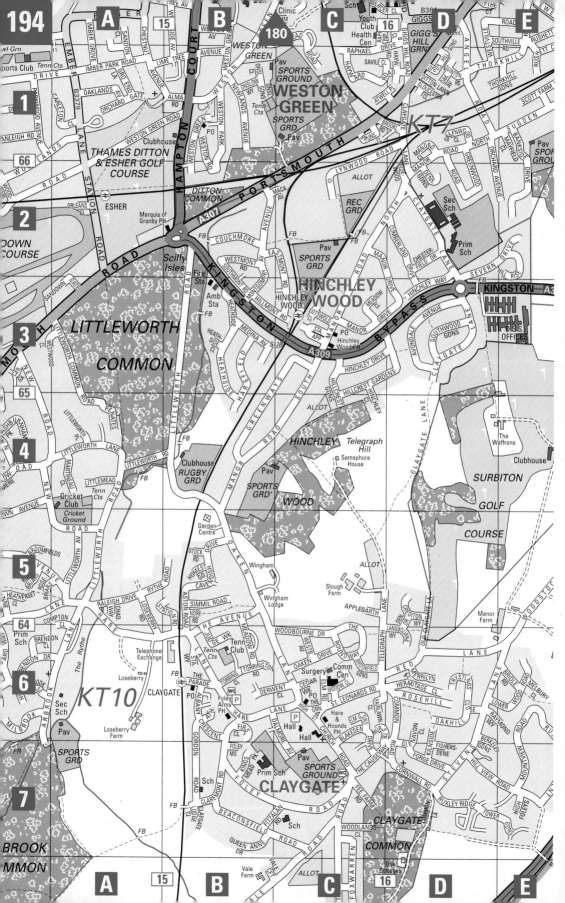

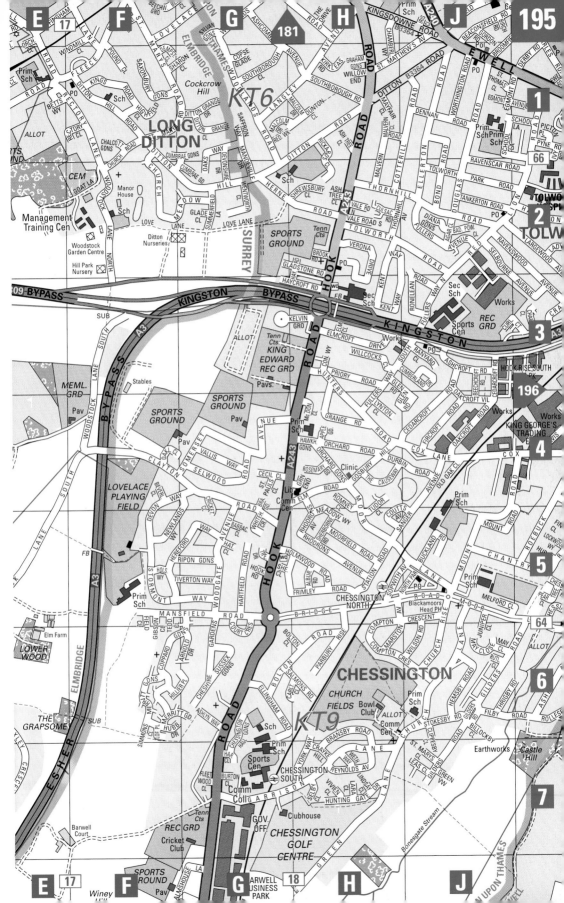

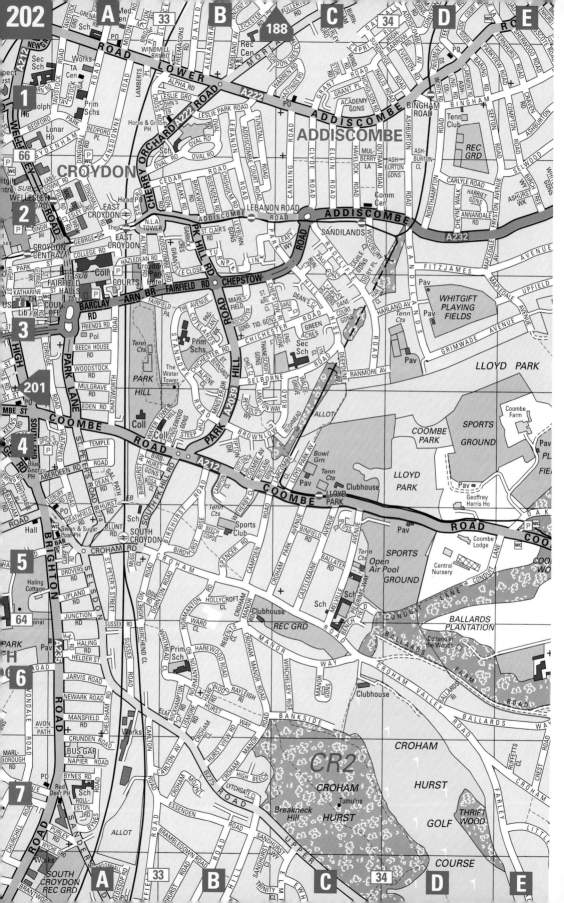

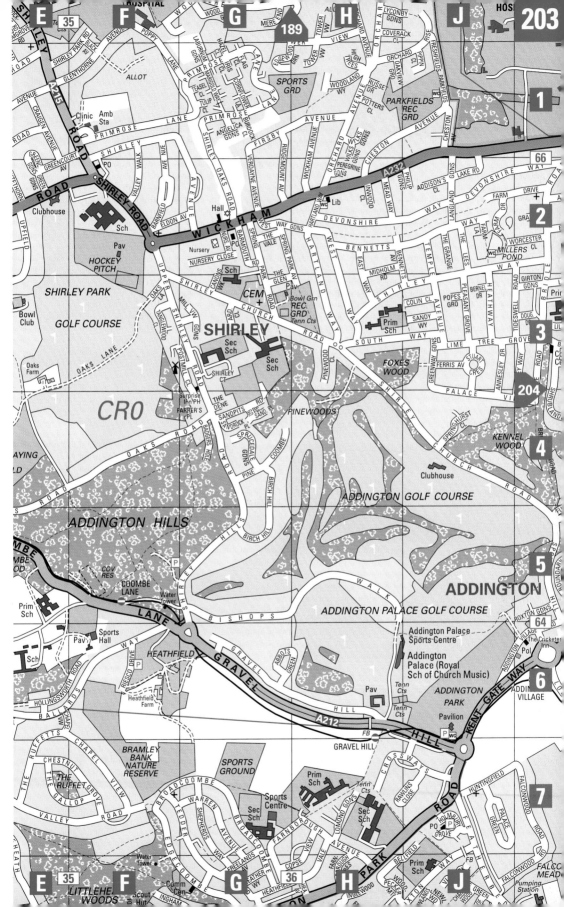

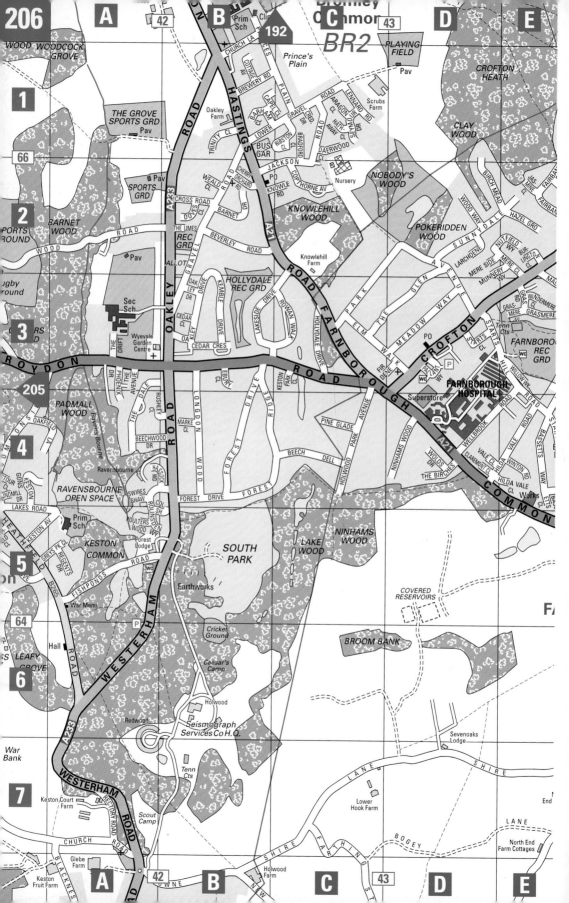

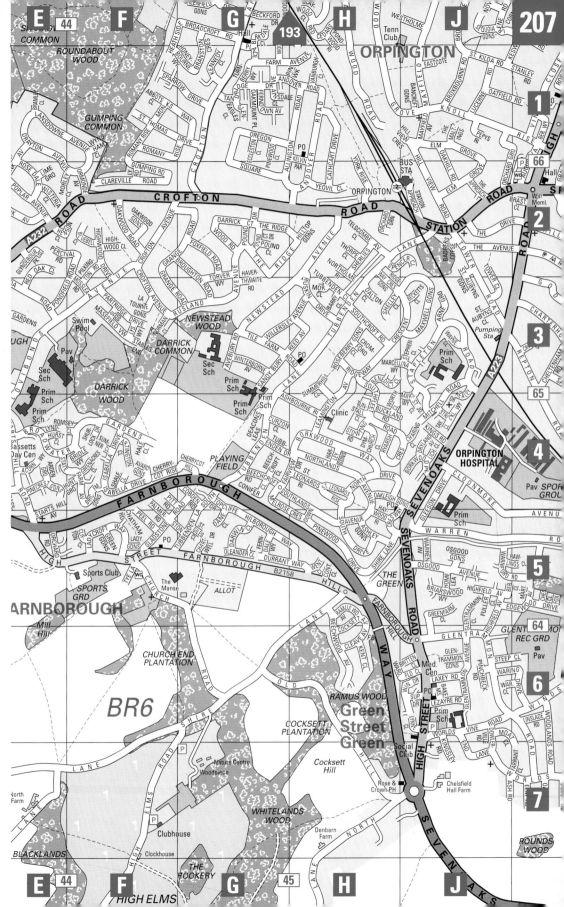

WEST END THEATRES & CINEMAS

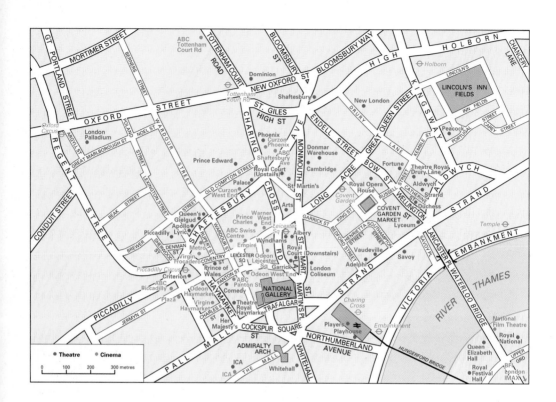

THEATRES

Adelphi *020 7344 0055*
Albery *020 7369 1730*
Aldwych *020 7416 6003*
Apollo *020 7416 6022*
Arts *020 7836 2132*
Cambridge *020 7494 5054*
Comedy *020 7369 1731*
Criterion *020 7369 1747*
Dominion *020 7656 1888*
Donmar Warehouse
 020 7369 1732
Duchess *020 7494 5075*
Fortune *020 7836 2238*
Garrick *020 7494 5085*
Gielgud *020 7494 5065*
Her Majesty's *020 7494 5400*
ICA *020 7930 3647*

London Coliseum *020 7632 8300*
London Palladium *020 7494 5020*
Lyceum *020 7420 8191*
Lyric *020 7494 5045*
New London *020 7405 0072*
Palace *020 7434 0909*
Peacock *020 7314 8800*
Phoenix *020 7369 1733*
Piccadilly *020 7369 1734*
Players *020 7839 1134*
Playhouse *020 7839 4401*
Prince Edward *020 7734 8951*
Prince of Wales *020 7839 5987*
Queen Elizabeth Hall
 020 7960 4242
Queen's *020 7494 5041*
Royal Court Theatre Downstairs
 020 7565 5000

Royal Court Theatre Upstairs
 020 7565 5000
Royal Festival Hall *020 7960 4242*
Royal National *020 7452 3000*
Royal Opera House
 020 7304 4000
St. Martin's *020 7836 1443*
Savoy *020 7836 8888*
Shaftesbury *020 7379 5399*
Strand *020 7930 8800*
Theatre Royal, Drury Lane
 020 7494 5550
Theatre Royal, Haymarket
 020 7930 8800
Vaudeville *020 7836 9987*
Whitehall *020 7369 1735*
Wyndhams *020 7369 1736*

CINEMAS

ABC Panton St *020 7930 0631*
ABC Piccadilly *020 7437 3561*
ABC ShaftesburyAvenue
 020 7836 6279
ABC Swiss Centre *020 7439 4470*
ABC Tottenham Court Rd
 020 7636 6148
BFI London IMAX *020 7902 1200*
Curzon Phoenix *020 7369 1721*
Curzon West End *020 7369 1722*

Empire *020 7437 1234*
ICA *020 7930 3647*
Metro *020 7437 0757*
National Film Theatre
 020 7928 3232
Odeon Haymarket *0426 915353*
Odeon Leicester Sq
 020 8315 4215
Odeon Mezzanine
(Odeon Leicester Sq)
 020 8315 4215

Odeon West End *020 8315 4221*
Plaza *020 7437 1234*
Prince Charles *020 7437 8181*
Virgin Haymarket *0870 907 0712*
Virgin Trocadero *0870 907 0716*
Warner West End *020 7437 4347*

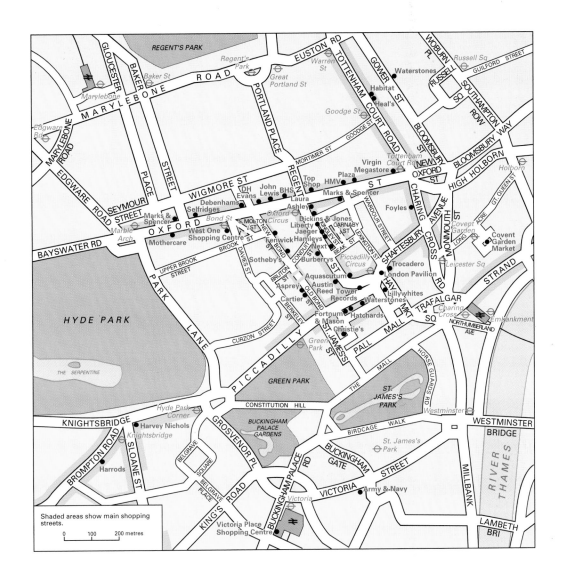

SHOPS

Aquascutum *020 7734 6090*
Army & Navy *020 7834 1234*
Asprey *020 7493 6767*
Austin Reed *020 7734 6789*
BHS (Oxford St) *020 7629 2011*
Cartier *020 7493 6962*
Christie's *020 7839 9060*
Covent Garden Market
  020 7836 9137
DH Evans *020 7629 8800*
Debenhams *020 7580 3000*
Dickins & Jones *020 7734 7070*
Fenwick *020 7629 9161*
Fortnum & Mason *020 7734 8040*
Foyles *020 7437 5660*
Habitat (Tottenham Court Rd)
  020 7631 3880
Hamleys *020 7734 3161*
Harrods *020 7730 1234*

Harvey Nichols *020 7235 5000*
Hatchards *020 7439 9921*
Heal's *020 7636 1666*
HMV *020 7631 3423*
Jaeger *020 7200 4000*
John Lewis *020 7629 7711*
Laura Ashley (Regent St)
  020 7355 1363
Liberty *020 7734 1234*
Lillywhites *020 7930 3181*
London Pavilion *020 7437 1838*
Marks & Spencer (Marble Arch)
  020 7935 7954
Marks & Spencer (Oxford St)
  020 7437 7722
Mothercare *020 7580 1688*
Next (Regent St) *020 7434 2515*
Plaza on Oxford St
  020 7637 8811

Selfridges *020 7629 1234*
Sotheby's *020 7493 8080*
Top Shop & Top Man
  020 7636 7700
Tower Records *020 7439 2500*
Trocadero *020 7439 1791*
Victoria Place Shopping Centre
  020 7931 8811
Virgin Megastore *020 7580 5822*
Waterstones (Gower St)
  020 7636 1577
Waterstones (Piccadilly)
  020 7851 2400

INDEX TO PLACES OF INTEREST

INDEX TO PLACE NAMES

INDEX TO STREET NAMES

General Abbreviations

All.	Alley	Embk.	Embankment	Pav.	Pavilion
Allot.	Allotments	Est.	Estate	Pk.	Park
Amb.	Ambulance	Ex.	Exchange	Pl.	Place
App.	Approach	Exhib.	Exhibition	Pol.	Police
Arc.	Arcade	F.B.	Footbridge	Prec.	Precinct
Av./Ave.	Avenue	F.C.	Football Club	Prim.	Primary
Bdy.	Broadway	Fld./Flds.	Field/Fields	Prom.	Promenade
Bk.	Bank	Fm.	Farm	Pt.	Point
Bldgs.	Buildings	Gall.	Gallery	Quad.	Quadrant
Boul.	Boulevard	Gar.	Garage	R.C.	Roman Catholic
Bowl.	Bowling	Gdn./Gdns.	Garden/Gardens	Rd./Rds	Road/Roads
Br./Bri.	Bridge	Govt.	Government	Rec.	Recreation
C. of E.	Church of England	Gra.	Grange	Res.	Reservoir
Cath.	Cathedral	Grd./Grds.	Ground/Grounds	Ri.	Rise
Cem.	Cemetery	Grn./Grns.	Green/Greens	S.	South
Cen.	Central, Centre	Gro./Gros.	Grove/Groves	Sch.	School
Cft./Cfts.	Croft/Crofts	Gt.	Great	Sec.	Secondary
Ch.	Church	Ho./Hos.	House/Houses	Shop.	Shopping
Chyd.	Churchyard	Hosp.	Hospital	Sq.	Square
Cin.	Cinema	Hts.	Heights	St.	Saint
Circ.	Circus	Ind.	Industrial	St./Sts.	Street/Streets
Cl./Clo.	Close	Int.	International	Sta.	Station
Co.	County	Junct.	Junction	Sub.	Subway
Coll.	College	La./Las.	Lane/Lanes	Swim.	Swimming
Comm.	Community	Lib.	Library	T.A.	Territorial Army
Conv.	Convent	Lo.	Lodge	T.H.	Town Hall
Cor./Cors.	Corner/Corners	Lwr.	Lower	Tenn.	Tennis
Coron.	Coroners	Mag.	Magistrates	Ter.	Terrace
Cotts.	Cottages	Mans.	Mansions	Thea.	Theatre
Cov.	Covered	Mem.	Memorial	Trd.	Trading
Crem.	Crematorium	Mkt./Mkts	Market/Markets	Twr./Twrs.	Tower/Towers
Cres.	Crescent	Ms.	Mews	Uni.	University
Ct./Cts.	Court/Courts	Mt.	Mount	Vil.	Villa, Villas
Ctyd.	Courtyard	Mus.	Museum	Vw.	View
Dep.	Depot	N.	North	W.	West
Dev.	Development	N.T.	National Trust	Wd.	Wood
Dr.	Drive	Nat.	National	Wds.	Woods
Dws.	Dwellings	P.H.	Public House	Wf.	Wharf
E.	East	P.O.	Post Office	Wk.	Walk
Ed.	Education	Par.	Parade	Wks.	Works
Elec.	Electricity	Pas.	Passage	Yd.	Yard

Post Town Abbreviations

Bark.	Barking	Har.	Harrow	Stai.	Staines
Barn.	Barnet	Hmptn.	Hampton	Stan.	Stanmore
Beck.	Beckenham	Houns.	Hounslow	Sthl.	Southall
Belv.	Belvedere	Ilf.	Ilford	Sun.	Sunbury-on-Thames
Bex.	Bexley	Islw.	Isleworth		
Bexh.	Bexleyheath	Kes.	Keston	Surb.	Surbiton
Borwd.	Borehamwood	Kings.T.	Kingston upon Thames	Sutt.	Sutton
Brent.	Brentford			T.Ditt.	Thames Ditton
Brom.	Bromley	Loug.	Loughton	Tedd.	Teddington
Buck.H.	Buckhurst Hill	Mitch.	Mitcham	Th.Hth.	Thornton Heath
Cars.	Carshalton	Mord.	Morden	Twick.	Twickenham
Chess.	Chessington	N.Mal.	New Malden	Uxb.	Uxbridge
Chig.	Chigwell	Nthlt.	Northolt	W.Mol.	West Molesey
Chis.	Chislehurst	Nthwd.	Northwood	W.Wick.	West Wickham
Cob.	Cobham	Orp.	Orpington	Wall.	Wallington
Croy.	Croydon	Pnr.	Pinner	Walt.	Walton-on-Thames
Dag.	Dagenham	Pot.B.	Potters Bar	Wat.	Watford
Dart.	Dartford	Pur.	Purley	Wdf.Grn.	Woodford Green
E.Mol.	East Molesey	Rain.	Rainham	Well.	Welling
Edg.	Edgware	Rich.	Richmond	Wem.	Wembley
Enf.	Enfield	Rom.	Romford	West Dr.	West Drayton
Epp.	Epping	Ruis.	Ruislip	Wor.Pk.	Worcester Park
Felt.	Feltham	S.Croy.	South Croydon		
Grnf.	Greenford	Sid.	Sidcup		

The street name and postal district or post town of an entry is followed by the page number and grid reference on which the name will be found, e.g. Abbey Road SW19 will be found on page 167 and in square F7.

All streets within the Central London enlarged scale section (pages 6-37) are shown in bold type when named in the index; **Abbey St. SE1** will be found on page 29 and in square E5.

This index contains some street names in standard text which are followed by another street named in italics. In these cases the street in standard text does not actually appear on the map due to insufficient space but can be located close to the street named in italics.

A

A.C. Ct., T.Ditt. 180 D6
Harvest La.
Aaron Hill Rd. E6 116 D5
Abberley Ms. SW4 150 B3
Cedars Rd.
Abbess Cl. E6 116 B5
Oliver Gdns.
Abbess Cl. SW2 169 H1
Abbeville Rd. N8 74 D4
Barrington Rd.
Abbeville Rd. SW4 150 C6
Abbey Av., Wem. 105 H2
Abbey Cl., Hayes 122 B1
Abbey Cl., Nthlt. 103 F3
Invicta Gro.
Abbey Cl., Pnr. 66 B3
Abbey Cres., Belv. 139 G4
Abbey Dr. SW17 168 A5
Church La.
Abbey Gdns. NW8 6 C2
Abbey Gdns. NW8 109 F2
Abbey Gdns. SE16 132 D4
Monnow Rd.
Abbey Gdns. W6 128 B6
Abbey Gro. SE2 138 B4
Abbey Ind. Est., Wem. 105 J1
Abbey La. E15 114 C2
Abbey La., Beck. 172 A7
Abbey Ms. E17 78 A5
Leamington Av.
Abbey Orchard St. SW1 25 J5
Abbey Orchard St. SW1 130 D3
Abbey Par. SW19 167 F7
Merton High St.
Abbey Par. W5 105 J3
Hanger La.
Abbey Pk., Beck. 172 A7
Abbey Retail Pk., Bark. 117 E1
Abbey Rd. E15 114 E2
Abbey Rd. NW6 6 C1
Abbey Rd. NW6 90 E7
Abbey Rd. NW8 109 F2
Abbey Rd. NW10 106 B2
Abbey Rd. SE2 138 D4
Abbey Rd. SW19 167 F7
Abbey Rd., Bark. 117 F1
Abbey Rd., Belv. 138 D4
Abbey Rd., Bexh. 159 E4
Abbey Rd., Croy. 201 H3
Abbey Rd., Enf. 44 B5
Abbey Rd., Ilf. 81 G5
Abbey Rd. Est. NW8 109 E1
Abbey St. E13 115 G4
Abbey St. SE1 29 E5
Abbey St. SE1 132 B3
Abbey Ter. SE2 138 C4
Abbey Vw. NW7 55 F3
Abbey Wk., W.Mol. 179 H3
Abbey Way SE2 138 D3
Abbey Wf. Ind. Est., Bark. 117 G2
Abbey Wd. Rd. SE2 138 B4
Abbeydale Rd., Wem. 106 A1
Abbeyfield Est. SE16 133 F4
Abbeyfield Rd. SE16 133 F4
Abbeyfields Cl. NW10 106 A2
Abbeyhill Rd., Sid. 176 C2
Abbot St. E8 94 C6
Abbots Cl. N1 93 J6
Alwyne Rd.
Abbots Cl., Orp. 207 F1
Abbots Cl., Ruis. 84 D3
Abbots Dr., Har. 85 G2
Abbots Gdns. N2 73 G4
Abbots Gdns. W8 22 A6
Abbots Grn., Croy. 203 G6
Abbots La. SE1 28 E2
Abbots Manor Est. SW1 32 D2
Abbots Manor Est. SW1 130 B4
Abbots Pk. SW2 169 G1
Abbot's Pl. NW6 108 E1
Abbot's Rd. E6 116 A1
Abbots Rd., Edg. 54 C7
Abbots Ter. N8 74 E6
Abbots Wk. W8 22 A6
Abbots Way, Beck. 189 H5
Abbotsbury Cl. E15 114 C2
Abbotsbury Cl. W14 128 C2
Abbotsbury Rd.
Abbotsbury Gdns., Pnr. 66 C6
Abbotsbury Ms. SE15 153 F3
Abbotsbury Rd. W14 128 B2
Abbotsbury Rd., Brom. 205 F2
Abbotsbury Rd., Mord. 184 E5
Abbotsford Av. N15 75 J4
Abbotsford Gdns., Wdf.Grn. 63 G7
Abbotsford Rd., Ilf. 100 A2
Abbotshade Rd. SE16 133 G1
Abbotshall Av. N14 58 C3
Abbotshall Rd. SE6 172 D1
Abbotsleigh Cl., Sutt. 198 E7
Abbotsleigh Rd. SW16 168 C4
Abbotsmede Cl., Twick. 162 C2
Abbotstone Rd. SW15 147 J3
Abbotswell Rd. SE4 153 J5
Abbotswood Cl., Belv. 138/139 E3
Coptefield Dr.
Abbotswood Gdns., Ilf. 80 C3
Abbotswood Rd. SE22 152 B4
Abbotswood Rd. SW16 168 D3
Abbotswood Way, Hayes 122 B1
Abbott Av. SW20 184 A2
Abbott Cl., Hmptn. 161 E6
Abbott Cl., Nthlt. 85 F6
Abbott Rd. E14 114 C5
Abbotts Cl. SE28 118 C7
Abbotts Cl., Rom. 83 H3
Abbotts Cres. E4 62 D4
Abbotts Cres., Enf. 43 H2
Abbotts Dr., Wem. 86 E2
Abbotts Pk. Rd. E10 78 C7
Abbotts Rd., Barn. 40 E4
Abbotts Rd., Mitch. 186 C4
Abbotts Rd., Sthl. 123 E1
Abbotts Rd., Sutt. 198 C3
Abbotts Wk., Bexh. 138 D7
Abchurch La. EC4 20 C5
Abchurch La. EC4 112 A7
Abchurch Yd. EC4 20 B5
Abdale Rd. W12 127 H1
Aberavon Rd. E3 113 H3
Abercairn Rd. SW16 168 C7
Aberconway Rd., Mord. 184 E3
Abercorn Cl. NW7 56 B7
Abercorn Cl. NW8 6 C3
Abercorn Cl. NW8 109 F3
Abercorn Cres., Har. 85 H1
Abercorn Gdns., Har. 69 G7
Abercorn Gdns., Rom. 82 B6
Abercorn Pl. NW8 6 C3
Abercorn Pl. NW8 109 F3
Abercorn Rd. NW7 56 B7
Abercorn Rd., Stan. 53 F7
Abercorn Way SE1 37 H3
Abercorn Way SE1 132 D5
Abercrombie Dr., Enf. 44 D1
Abercrombie St. SW11 149 H2
Aberdare Cl., W.Wick. 204 C2
Aberdare Gdns. NW6 91 E7
Aberdare Gdns. NW7 56 A7
Aberdare Rd., Enf. 45 F4
Aberdeen La. N5 93 H5
Aberdeen Par. N18 60/61 E5
Angel Rd.
Aberdeen Pk. N5 93 J5
Aberdeen Pk. Ms. N5 93 J4
Aberdeen Pl. NW8 6 E5
Aberdeen Pl. NW8 109 G4
Aberdeen Rd. N5 93 J4
Aberdeen Rd. N18 60 E5
Aberdeen Rd. NW10 89 F5
Aberdeen Rd., Croy. 201 J4
Aberdeen Rd., Har. 68 C2
Aberdeen Sq. E14 133 J1
Westferry Circ.
Aberdeen Ter. SE3 154 D2
Aberdour Rd., Ilf. 100 B3
Aberdour St. SE1 36 D1
Aberdour St. SE1 132 B4
Aberfeldy St. E14 114 C6
Aberford Gdns. SE18 156 B1
Aberford Rd., Borwd. 38 A2
Aberfoyle Rd. SW16 168 D6
Abergeldie Rd. SE12 155 H6
Aberglen Ind. Est., Hayes 121 G2
Abernethy Rd. SE13 154 E4
Abersham Rd. E8 94 C5
Abery St. SE18 137 H4
Abingdon Cl. NW1 92 D6
Camden Sq.
Abingdon Cl. SE1 37 G3
Abingdon Cl. SW19 167 F6
Abingdon Rd. N3 73 F2
Abingdon Rd. SW16 186 E2
Abingdon Rd. W8 128 D3
Abingdon St. SW1 26 A5
Abingdon St. SW1 130 E3
Abingdon Vil. W8 128 D3
Abinger Cl., Bark. 100 A4
Abinger Cl., Brom. 192 B3
Abinger Cl., Wall. 200/201 E5
Garden Cl.
Abinger Gdns., Islw. 144 B3
Abinger Gro. SE8 133 J6
Abinger Ms. W9 108 D4
Warlock Rd.
Abinger Rd. W4 127 E3
Ablett St. SE16 133 F5
Abney Gdns. N16 94 C2
Stoke Newington High St.
Aboyne Dr. SW20 183 G2
Aboyne Est. SW17 167 G3
Aboyne Rd. NW10 88 E3
Aboyne Rd. SW17 167 G3
Abridge Rd., Chig. 49 G6
Abridge Way, Bark. 118 B3
Abyssinia Cl. SW11 149 H4
Cairns Rd.
Acacia Av. N17 60 A7
Acacia Av., Brent. 124 E7
Acacia Av., Mitch. 186 B2
Acacia Rd.
Acacia Av., Ruis. 84 A1
Acacia Av., Wem. 87 H5
Acacia Cl. SE8 133 H4
Acacia Cl. SE20 188 D2
Selby Rd.
Acacia Cl., Orp. 193 G5
Acacia Cl., Stan. 52 B6
Acacia Dr., Sutt. 198 C1
Acacia Gdns. NW8 7 F1
Acacia Gdns., W.Wick. 204 C2
Acacia Gro. SE21 170 A2
Acacia Gro., N.Mal. 182 D3
Acacia Ms., West Dr. 120 A6
Acacia Pl. NW8 7 F1
Acacia Pl. NW8 109 G2
Acacia Rd. E11 97 E2
Acacia Rd. E17 77 H6
Acacia Rd. N22 75 G1
Acacia Rd. NW8 7 F1
Acacia Rd. NW8 109 G2
Acacia Rd. SW16 187 E1
Acacia Rd. W3 106 C7
Acacia Rd., Beck. 189 J3
Acacia Rd., Enf. 44 A1
Acacia Rd., Hmptn. 161 G6
Acacia Rd., Mitch. 186 B2
Acacia Way, Sid. 175 J1
Academy Gdns., Croy. 202 C1
Academy Gdns., Nthlt. 102 D2
Academy Pl. SE18 156 C1
Academy Rd. SE18 156 C1
Acanthus Dr. SE1 37 H3
Acanthus Dr. SE1 132 D5
Acanthus Rd. SW11 150 A3
Accommodation Rd. NW11 72 C7
Acer Av., Hayes 102 E5
Acfold Rd. SW6 148 E1
Achilles Cl. SE1 37 J3
Achilles Cl. SE1 132 D5
Achilles Rd. NW6 90 D5
Achilles St. SE14 133 H7
Achilles Way W1 24 C2
Acklam Rd. W10 108 C5
Acklington Dr. NW9 70 E1
Ackmar Rd. SW6 148 D1
Ackroyd Dr. E3 113 J5
Ackroyd Rd. SE23 153 G7
Ackworth Cl. N9 45 F7
Turin Rd.
Acland Cl. SE18 137 G7
Clothworkers Rd.
Acland Cres. SE5 152 A4
Acland Rd. NW2 89 H6
Acock Gro., Nthlt. 85 H5
Dorchester Rd.
Acol Cres., Ruis. 84 B5
Acol Rd. NW6 90 D7
Aconbury Rd., Dag. 118 B1
Acorn Cl. E4 62 B5
The Lawns
Acorn Cl., Chis. 175 F5
Acorn Cl., Enf. 43 H1
Acorn Cl., Hmptn. 161 H6
Acorn Cl., Stan. 53 E7
Acorn Ct., Ilf. 81 H6
Acorn Gdns. SE19 188 C1
Acorn Gdns. W3 106 D5
Acorn Gro., Hayes 121 J7
Acorn Par. SE15 132/133 E7
Carlton Gro.
Acorn Wk. SE16 133 H1
Acorn Way SE23 171 G3
Acorn Way, Orp. 207 E4
Acorns, The, Chig. 65 H4
Acre Dr. SE22 152 D4
Acre La. SW2 150 E4
Acre La., Cars. 200 A4
Acre La., Wall. 200 A4
Acre Path, Nthlt. 84/85 E6
Arnold Rd.
Acre Rd. SW19 167 G6
Acre Rd., Dag. 101 H7
Acre Rd., Kings.T. 181 H1
Acris St. SW18 149 F5
Acton Cl. N9 60 D2
Acton Hill Ms. W3 126 B1
Uxbridge Rd.
Acton La. NW10 106 E2
Acton La. W3 126 C2
Acton La. W4 126 D3
Acton Ms. E8 112 C1
Acton Pk. Ind. Est. W3 126 D2
Acton St. WC1 10 C4
Acton St. WC1 111 F3
Acuba Rd. SW18 166 E2
Acworth Cl. N9 45 F7
Turin Rd.
Ada Gdns. E14 114 D6
Ada Gdns. E15 115 F1
Ada Pl. E2 112 D1
Ada Rd. SE5 132 B7
Ada Rd., Wem. 87 G3
Ada St. E8 112 E1
Adair Cl. SE25 188 E3
Adair Rd. W10 108 B4
Adair Twr. W10 108 B4
Appleford Rd.
Adam & Eve Ct. W1 17 G3
Adam & Eve Ms. W8 128 D3
Adam Ct. SW7 30 D1
Adam Pl. N16 94 C2
Stoke Newington High St.
Adam Rd. E4 61 J6
Adam St. WC2 18 B6
Adam St. WC2 111 E7
Adam Wk. SW6 127 J7
Adams Cl. N3 56 D7
Falkland Av.
Adams Cl. NW9 88 B2
Adams Cl., Surb. 181 J6
Adams Ct. EC2 20 C3
Adams Gdns. Est. SE16 133 F2
St. Marychurch St.
Adams Pl. E14 134 B1
North Colonnade
Adams Pl. N7 93 F5
George's Rd.
Adams Rd. N17 76 B2
Adams Rd., Beck. 189 H5
Adams Row W1 16 C6
Adams Row W1 110 A7
Adams Sq., Bexh. 158/159 E3
Regency Way
Adams Wk., Kings.T. 181 H2
Adams Way, Croy. 188 C6
Adamson Rd. E16 115 G6
Adamson Rd. NW3 91 G7
Adamsrill Cl., Enf. 44 A6
Adamsrill Rd. SE26 171 H4
Adare Wk. SW16 169 F3
Adastral Est. NW9 70 E1
Adcock Wk., Orp. 207 J4
Borkwood Pk.
Adderley Gdns. SE9 174 D4
Adderley Gro. SW11 150 A5
Culmstock Rd.
Adderley Rd., Har. 68 C1
Adderley St. E14 114 C6
Addington Ct. SW14 146 D3
Addington Dr. N12 57 F6
Addington Gro. SE26 171 H4
Addington Rd. E3 114 A3
Addington Rd. E16 115 E4
Addington Rd. N4 75 G6
Addington Rd., Croy. 201 G1
Addington Rd., W.Wick. 205 E2
Addington Sq. SE5 36 A6
Addington Sq. SE5 131 J6
Addington St. SE1 26 D4
Addington Village Rd., Croy. 204 A5
Addis Cl., Enf. 45 G1
Addiscombe Av., Croy. 188 D7
Addiscombe Cl., Har. 69 F5
Addiscombe Ct. Rd., Croy. 202 B1
Addiscombe Gro., Croy. 202 A2
Addiscombe Rd., Croy. 202 B2
Addison Av. N14 42 B6
Addison Av. W11 128 B1
Addison Av., Houns. 143 J1
Addison Br. Pl. W14 128 C4

Addison Cl., Nthwd. 66 A1
Addison Cl., Orp. 193 F6
Addison Cres. W14 128 B3
Addison Dr. SE12 155 H5
Eltham Rd.
Addison Gdns. W14 128 A3
Addison Gdns., Surb. 181 J4
Addison Gro. W4 127 E3
Addison Pl. W11 128 B1
Addison Pl., Sthl. 103 G7
Longford Av.
Addison Rd. E11 79 G6
Addison Rd. E17 78 B5
Addison Rd. SE25 188 D4
Addison Rd. W14 128 C3
Addison Rd., Brom. 191 J5
Addison Rd., Enf. 45 F1
Addison Rd., Ilf. 81 F1
Addison Rd., Tedd. 162 E6
Addison Way NW11 72 C4
Addison Way, Hayes 102 A6
Addison's Cl., Croy. 203 J2
Addle Hill EC4 19 H5
Addle St. EC2 20 A2
Adecroft Way, W.Mol. 179 J3
Adela Av., N.Mal. 183 H5
Adela St. W10 108 B4
Kensal Rd.
Adelaide Av. SE4 153 J4
Adelaide Cl., Stan. 52 D4
Adelaide Cotts. W7 124 C2
Adelaide Gdns., Rom. 82 E5
Adelaide Gro. W12 127 G1
Adelaide Rd. E10 96 C3
Adelaide Rd. NW3 91 G7
Adelaide Rd. SW18 148 D5
Putney Br. Rd.
Adelaide Rd. W13 124 D1
Adelaide Rd., Chis. 175 E5
Adelaide Rd., Houns. 142 E1
Adelaide Rd., Ilf. 99 E2
Adelaide Rd., Rich. 145 J4
Adelaide Rd., Sthl. 123 E4
Adelaide Rd., Surb. 181 H5
Adelaide Rd., Tedd. 162 C6
Adelaide St. WC2 18 A6
Adelaide Ter., Brent. 125 G5
Adelaide Wk. SW9 151 G4
Sussex Wk.
Adelina Gro. E1 113 F5
Adelina Ms. SW12 168 D1
King's Av.
Adeline Pl. WC1 17 J2
Adeline Pl. WC1 110 D5
Adeliza Cl., Bark. 98/99 E7
North St.
Adelphi Ter. WC2 18 B6
Aden Gro. N16 94 A4
Aden Rd., Enf. 45 H4
Aden Rd., Ilf. 81 E7
Aden Ter. N16 94 A4
Adeney Cl. W6 128 A6
Adenmore Rd. SE6 154 A7
Adie Rd. W6 127 J3
Adine Rd. E13 115 H4
Adler Ind. Est., Hayes 121 G2
Adler St. E1 21 H3
Adler St. E1 112 D6
Adley St. E5 95 H5
Adlington Cl. N18 60 B5
Admaston Rd. SE18 137 F7
Admiral Ct. NW4 71 G5
Barton Cl.
Admiral Pl. SE16 133 H1
Admiral Seymour Rd. SE9 156 C4
Admiral Sq. SW10 149 G1
Admiral St. SE8 154 A1
Admiral Wk. W9 108 D5
Admirals Cl. E18 79 H4
Admirals Wk. NW3 91 F3
Admirals Way E14 134 A2
Admiralty Cl. SE8 134 A7
Reginald Sq.
Admiralty Rd., Tedd. 162 C6
Adolf St. SE6 172 B4
Adolphus Rd. N4 93 H2
Adolphus St. SE8 133 J7
Adomar Rd., Dag. 100 D3
Adpar St. W2 7 E6
Adpar St. W2 109 G4
Adrian Av. NW2 89 H1
North Circular Rd.
Adrian Ms. SW10 30 B5
Adrian Ms. SW10 129 E6
Adrienne Av., Sthl. 103 F4
Advance Rd. SE27 169 J4
Advent Ct., Wdf.Grn. 63 F4
Wood La.
Advent Way N18 61 G5
Adys Rd. SE15 152 C3
Aerodrome Rd. NW4 71 F3
Aerodrome Rd. NW9 71 F2
Aerodrome Way, Houns. 122 C6
Aeroville NW9 71 E2
Affleck St. N1 10 D2
Afghan Rd. SW11 149 H2
Agamemnon Rd. NW6 90 C5
Agar Cl., Surb. 195 J2
Agar Gro. NW1 92 C7
Agar Gro. Est. NW1 92 D7
Agar Pl. NW1 92 C7
Agar St. WC2 18 A6
Agar St. WC2 110 E7
Agate Cl. E16 116 A6
Agate Rd. W6 127 J3
Agatha Cl. E1 132/133 E1
Prusom St.
Agaton Rd. SE9 175 F2
Agave Rd. NW2 89 J4
Agdon St. EC1 11 G5
Agdon St. EC1 111 H4
Agincourt Rd. NW3 91 J4
Agnes Av., Ilf. 98 E4
Agnes Cl. E6 116 D7
Agnes Gdns., Dag. 100 D4
Agnes Rd. W3 127 F1
Agnes St. E14 113 J6
Agnesfield Cl. N12 57 H6
Agnew Rd. SE23 153 G7
Agricola Ct. E3 113 J1
Parnell Rd.
Agricola Pl., Enf. 44 C5
Aidan Cl., Dag. 100 E4
Aileen Wk. E15 97 F7
Ailsa Av., Twick. 144 D5
Ailsa Rd., Twick. 145 E5
Ailsa St. E14 114 C5
Ainger Ms. NW3 91 J7
Ainger Rd.
Ainger Rd. NW3 91 J7
Ainsdale Cl., Orp. 207 G1
Ainsdale Cres., Pnr. 67 G3
Ainsdale Dr. SE1 37 H4
Ainsdale Dr. SE1 132 D5
Ainsdale Rd. W5 105 G4
Ainsdale Rd., Wat. 50 C3
Ainsley Av., Rom. 83 H6
Ainsley Cl. N9 60 B1
Ainsley St. E2 113 E3
Ainslie Wk. SW12 150 B7
Ainslie Wd. Cres. E4 62 B5
Ainslie Wd. Gdns. E4 62 B4
Ainslie Wd. Rd. E4 62 A5
Ainsty Est. SE16 133 G2
Ainsworth Cl. NW2 89 G3
Ainsworth Cl. SE15 152 B2
Lyndhurst Gro.
Ainsworth Rd. E9 95 F7
Ainsworth Rd., Croy. 201 H2
Ainsworth Way NW8 109 F1
Aintree Av. E6 116 B1
Aintree Cres., Ilf. 81 F2
Aintree Est. SW6 128 B7
Dawes Rd.
Aintree Rd., Grnf. 105 E2
Aintree St. SW6 128 B7
Air Links Ind. Est., Houns. 122 C5
Air St. W1 17 G6
Air St. W1 110 C7
Aird Ct., Hmptn. 179 F1
Oldfield Rd.
Airdrie Cl. N1 93 F7
Airdrie Cl., Hayes 102/103 E5
Glencoe Rd.
Airedale Av. W4 127 F4
Airedale Av. S. W4 127 F5
Netheravon Rd. S.
Airedale Rd. SW12 149 J7
Airedale Rd. W5 125 F3
Airlie Gdns. W8 128 D1
Campden Hill Rd.
Airlie Gdns., Ilf. 99 E1
Airport Roundabout E16 136 A1
Connaught Br.
Airthrie Rd., Ilf. 100 B2
Aisgill Av. W14 128 C5
Aisher Rd. SE28 118 C7
Aislibie Rd. SE12 155 E4
Aitken Cl. E8 112 D1
Pownall Rd.
Aitken Cl., Mitch. 185 J7
Aitken Rd. SE6 172 B2
Aitken Rd., Barn. 39 J5
Ajax Av. NW9 70 E3
Ajax Rd. NW6 90 D5
Akabusi Cl., Croy. 188 D6
Akehurst St. SW15 147 G6
Akenside Rd. NW3 91 G5
Akerman Rd. SW9 151 H2
Akerman Rd., Surb. 181 F6
Alabama St. SE18 137 G7
Alacross Rd. W5 125 F2
Alan Dr., Barn. 40 B6
Alan Gdns., Rom. 83 G7
Alan Hocken Way E15 114 E2
Alan Rd. SW19 166 B5
Alandale Dr., Pnr. 66 B2
Alander Ms. E17 78 C4
Alanthus Cl. SE12 155 F6
Alaska St. SE1 27 E2
Alba Cl., Hayes 102 D4
Ramulis Dr.
Alba Gdns. NW11 72 B6
Alba Pl. W11 108 C6
Portobello Rd.
Albacore Cres. SE13 154 B6
Alban Cres., Borwd. 38 B1
Alban Highwalk EC2 111 J5
London Wall
Albany W1 17 F6
Albany, The, Wdf.Grn. 63 F4
Albany Cl. N15 75 H4
Albany Cl. SW14 146 B4
Albany Cl., Bex. 158 C7
Albany Ct. E4 46 B6
Chelwood Cl.
Albany Ctyd. W1 17 G6
Albany Cres., Edg. 54 A7
Albany Cres., Esher 194 B6
Albany Mans. SW11 129 H7
Albany Ms. N1 93 G7
Barnsbury Pk.
Albany Ms. SE5 36 A6
Albany Ms., Brom. 173 G6
Avondale Rd.
Albany Ms., Kings.T. 163 G6
Albany Pk. Rd.
Albany Ms., Sutt. 198/199 E5
Camden Rd.
Albany Pk. Av., Enf. 45 F1
Albany Pk. Rd., Kings.T. 163 H6
Albany Pas., Rich. 145 J5
Albany Pl. N7 93 G4
Benwell Rd.
Albany Pl., Brent. 125 H6
Albany Rd.
Albany Rd. E10 78 A7
Albany Rd. E12 98 A4
Albany Rd. E17 77 J6
Albany Rd. N4 75 F6
Albany Rd. N18 61 E5
Albany Rd. SE5 36 B6
Albany Rd. SE5 132 A6
Albany Rd. SW19 166 E5
Albany Rd. W13 104 E7
Albany Rd., Belv. 139 F6
Albany Rd., Bex. 158 C7
Albany Rd., Brent. 125 G6
Albany Rd., Chis. 175 E5
Albany Rd., N.Mal. 182 D4
Albany Rd., Rich. 145 J5
Albert Rd.
Albany Rd., Rom. 83 F6
Albany St. NW1 8 D1
Albany St. NW1 110 B2
Albany Ter. NW1 110 B4
Marylebone Rd.
Albany Vw., Buck.H. 63 G1
Albatross St. SE18 137 H7
Albatross Way SE16 133 G2
Albemarle SW19 166 A2
Albemarle App., Ilf. 81 E6
Albemarle Av., Twick. 161 F1
Albemarle Gdns., Ilf. 81 E6
Albemarle Gdns., N.Mal. 182 D4
Albemarle Pk., Stan. 53 F5
Marsh La.
Albemarle Rd., Barn. 41 H7
Albemarle Rd., Beck. 190 B1
Albemarle St. W1 17 E6
Albemarle St. W1 110 B7
Albemarle Way EC1 11 G6
Alberon Gdns. NW11 72 C4
Albert Av. E4 62 A4
Albert Av. SW8 131 F7
Albert Br. SW3 31 H6
Albert Br. SW3 129 H6
Albert Br. SW11 31 H6
Albert Br. SW11 129 H6
Albert Br. Rd. SW11 31 H7
Albert Br. Rd. SW11 129 H7
Albert Carr Gdns. SW16 168 E5
Albert Cl. E9 112/113 E1
Northiam St.
Albert Cl. N22 74 D1
Albert Ct. SW7 23 E4
Albert Ct. SW7 129 G2
Albert Cres. E4 62 A4
Albert Dr. SW19 166 B2
Albert Embk. SE1 34 B4
Albert Embk. SE1 131 E5
Albert Gdns. E1 113 G6
Albert Gate SW1 24 A3
Albert Gate SW1 129 J2
Albert Gro. SW20 184 A1
Albert Hall Mans. SW7 23 E4
Albert Mans. SW11 149 J1
Albert Br. Rd.
Albert Ms. E14 113 H7
Narrow St.
Albert Ms. W8 22 C5
Albert Pl. N3 72 D1
Albert Pl. N17 76 C3
High Rd.
Albert Pl. W8 22 B4
Albert Pl. W8 129 E2
Albert Rd. E10 96 C2
Albert Rd. E16 136 B1
Albert Rd. E17 78 A5
Albert Rd. E18 79 H3
Albert Rd. N4 93 F1
Albert Rd. N15 76 B6
Albert Rd. N22 74 C1
Albert Rd. NW4 72 A4
Albert Rd. NW6 108 C2
Albert Rd. NW7 55 F5
Albert Rd. SE9 174 B3
Albert Rd. SE20 171 G7
Albert Rd. SE25 188 D4
Albert Rd. W5 105 E4
Albert Rd., Barn. 41 F4
Albert Rd., Belv. 139 F5
Albert Rd., Bex. 159 G6
Albert Rd., Brom. 192 A5
Albert Rd., Buck.H. 64 A2
Albert Rd., Dag. 101 G1
Albert Rd., Hmptn. 161 J5
Albert Rd., Har. 67 J3
Albert Rd., Hayes 121 H3
Albert Rd., Houns. 143 G4
Albert Rd., Ilf. 99 E3
Albert Rd., Kings.T. 181 J2
Albert Rd., Mitch. 185 J3
Albert Rd., N.Mal. 183 F4
Albert Rd., Rich. 145 H5
Albert Rd., Sthl. 122 D3
Albert Rd., Sutt. 199 G5
Albert Rd., Tedd. 162 C6
Albert Rd., Twick. 162 C1
Albert Rd., West Dr. 120 B1
Albert Rd. Est., Belv. 139 F5
Albert Sq. E15 97 E5
Albert Sq. SW8 131 F7
Albert St. N12 57 F5
Albert St. NW1 110 B1
Albert Ter. NW1 110 A1
Albert Ter. NW10 106 D1
Albert Ter., Buck.H. 64 A2
Albert Ter. Ms. NW1 110 A1
Regents Pk. Rd.
Albert Way SE15 132 E7
Alberta Av., Sutt. 198 B4
Alberta Est. SE17 35 H3
Alberta Est. SE17 131 H5
Alberta Rd., Enf. 44 C6
Alberta Rd., Erith 159 J1
Alberta St. SE17 35 G3
Alberta St. SE17 131 H5
Albion Av. N10 74 A1
Albion Av. SW8 150 D2
Albion Bldgs. EC1 111 J5
Bartholomew Cl.
Albion Cl. W2 15 H5
Albion Dr. E8 94 C7
Albion Est. SE16 133 G2
Albion Gdns. W6 127 H4
Albion Gro. N16 94 B4
Albion Hill SE13 154 B2
Albion Hill, Loug. 47 J5
Albion Ms. N1 111 G1
Albion Ms. NW6 90 C7
Kilburn High Rd.
Albion Ms. W2 15 H4
Albion Ms. W2 109 H6
Albion Ms. W6 127 H4
Galena Rd.
Albion Par. N16 94 A4
Albion Rd.
Albion Pk., Loug. 48 A5
Albion Pl. EC1 19 G1
Albion Pl. EC1 111 H5
Albion Pl. SE25 188 D3
High St.
Albion Pl. W6 127 H4
Albion Rd. E17 78 C3
Albion Rd. N16 94 A4
Albion Rd. N17 76 C2
Albion Rd., Bexh. 159 F4
Albion Rd., Houns. 143 G4
Albion Rd., Kings.T. 182 C1
Albion Rd., Sutt. 199 G6
Albion Rd., Twick. 162 B1
Albion Sq. E8 94 C7
Albion St. SE16 133 F2

Albion St. W2 15 H4
Albion St. W2 109 H6
Albion St., Croy. 201 H1
Albion Ter. E8 94 C7
Albion Vil. Rd. SE26 171 F3
Albion Way EC1 19 J2
Albion Way SE13 154 C4
Albion Way, Wem. 88 B3 *North End Rd.*
Albion Yd. E1 113 E5
Albrighton Rd. SE22 152 B3
Albuhera Cl., Enf. 43 G1
Albury Av., Bexh. 158 E2
Albury Av., Islw. 124 C7
Albury Cl., Hmptn. 161 G6
Albury Dr., Pnr. 50 D7
Albury Ms. E12 97 J1
Albury Rd., Chess. 195 H5
Albury St. SE8 134 A6
Albyfield, Brom. 192 C3
Albyn Rd. SE8 154 A1
Alcester Cres. E5 95 E2
Alcester Rd., Wall. 200 B4
Alcock Cl., Wall. 200 D7
Alcock Rd., Houns. 122 D7
Alconbury Rd. E5 94 D2
Alcorn Cl., Sutt. 198 D2
Alcott Cl. W7 104 C5 *Westcott Cres.*
Alcuin Ct., Stan. 53 F7 *Old Ch. La.*
Aldborough Rd., Dag. 101 J6
Aldborough Rd. N., Ilf. 81 J5
Aldborough Rd. S., Ilf. 99 H1
Aldbourne Rd. W12 127 F1
Aldbridge St. SE17 36 E3
Aldbridge St. SE17 132 B5
Aldburgh Ms. W1 16 C3
Aldbury Av., Wem. 88 B7
Aldbury Ms. N9 44 A7
Aldebert Ter. SW8 131 E7
Aldeburgh Cl. E5 94/95 E2 *Southwold Rd.*
Aldeburgh Pl., Wdf.Grn. 63 G4
Aldeburgh St. SE10 135 G5
Alden Av. E15 115 F3
Aldenham St. NW1 9 G2
Aldenham St. NW1 110 D2
Aldensley Rd. W6 127 H3
Alder Cl. SE15 37 G6
Alder Cl. SE15 132 C6
Alder Gro. NW2 89 H2
Alder Ms. N19 92 C2 *Bredgar Rd.*
Alder Rd. SW14 146 D3
Alder Rd., Sid. 175 J3
Alder Wk., Ilf. 99 F5
Alderbrook Rd. SW12 150 B6
Alderbury Rd. SW13 127 G6
Aldergrove Gdns., Houns. 142/143 E2 *Bath Rd.*
Alderholt Way SE15 36 E7
Alderman Av., Bark. 118 A3
Alderman Judge Mall, Kings.T. 181 H2 *Eden St.*
Aldermanbury EC2 20 A3
Aldermanbury EC2 111 J6
Aldermanbury Sq. EC2 20 A2
Aldermans Hill N13 58 E4
Alderman's Wk. EC2 20 D2
Aldermary Rd., Brom. 191 G1
Aldermoor Rd. SE6 171 J3
Alderney Av., Houns. 123 H7
Alderney Gdns., Nthlt. 85 F7
Alderney Rd. E1 113 G4
Alderney St. SW1 32 E3
Alderney St. SW1 130 B4
Alders, The N21 43 G6
Alders, The, Felt. 161 E4
Alders, The, Houns. 123 F6
Alders, The, W.Wick. 204 B1
Alders Av., Wdf.Grn. 62 E6
Alders Cl. E11 97 H2 *Aldersbrook Rd.*
Alders Cl. W5 125 G3
Alders Cl., Edg. 54 C5
Alders Gro., E.Mol. 180 A5 *Esher Rd.*
Alders Rd., Edg. 54 C5
Aldersbrook Av., Enf. 44 B2
Aldersbrook Dr., Kings.T. 163 J6
Aldersbrook La. E12 98 C3
Aldersbrook Rd. E11 97 H2
Aldersbrook Rd. E12 98 A3
Aldersey Gdns., Bark. 99 G6
Aldersford Cl. SE4 153 G5
Aldersgate St. EC1 19 J3
Aldersgate St. EC1 111 J5
Aldersgrove Av. SE9 173 J3
Aldershot Rd. NW6 108 C1
Aldersmead Av., Croy. 189 G6
Aldersmead Rd., Beck. 171 H7
Alderson Pl., Sthl. 123 J1
Alderson St. W10 108 B4 *Kensal Rd.*
Alderton Cl. NW10 88 D3
Alderton Cl., Loug. 48 D4
Alderton Cres. NW4 71 H5
Alderton Hall La., Loug. 48 D4
Alderton Hill, Loug. 48 B5
Alderton Ms., Loug. 48 D4 *Alderton Hall La.*
Alderton Ri., Loug. 48 D4
Alderton Rd. SE24 151 J3
Alderton Rd., Croy. 188 C7
Alderton Way NW4 71 H5
Alderton Way, Loug. 48 C5
Alderville Rd. SW6 148 C2
Alderwick Dr., Houns. 144 A3
Alderwood Rd. SE9 157 G6
Aldford St. W1 24 B1
Aldford St. W1 130 A1
Aldgate EC3 21 F4
Aldgate EC3 112 C6
Aldgate Av. E1 21 F3
Aldgate High St. EC3 21 F4
Aldgate High St. EC3 112 C6
Aldine Ct. W12 127 J1 *Aldine St.*
Aldine Pl. W12 127 J1 *Uxbridge Rd.*
Aldine St. W12 127 J2
Aldington Cl., Dag. 82 C7
Aldington Rd. SE18 136 A3
Aldis Ms. SW17 167 H5 *Aldis St.*
Aldis St. SW17 167 H5
Aldred Rd. NW6 90 D5
Aldren Rd. SW17 167 F3
Aldrich Gdns., Sutt. 198 C3
Aldrich Ter. SW18 167 F2 *Lidiard Rd.*
Aldriche Way E4 62 C6
Aldridge Av., Edg. 54 B3
Aldridge Av., Ruis. 84 D2
Aldridge Av., Stan. 69 H1
Aldridge Ri., N.Mal. 182 E7
Aldridge Rd. Vil. W11 108 C5
Aldridge Wk. N14 42 E7
Aldrington Rd. SW16 168 C5
Aldsworth Cl. W9 6 A6
Aldsworth Cl. W9 108 E4
Aldwick Cl. SE9 175 G3
Aldwick Rd., Croy. 201 F3
Aldworth Gro. SE13 154 C6
Aldworth Rd. E15 96 E7
Aldwych WC2 18 C5
Aldwych WC2 111 F7
Aldwych Av., Ilf. 81 F4
Alers Rd., Bexh. 158 D5
Alesia Cl. N22 58/59 E7 *Nightingale Rd.*
Alestan Beck Rd. E16 116 A6 *Fulmer Rd.*
Alexa Ct. W8 30 A1
Alexander Av. NW10 89 H7
Alexander Cl., Barn. 41 G4
Alexander Cl., Brom. 205 G1
Alexander Cl., Sid. 157 H5
Alexander Cl., Sthl. 123 J1
Alexander Cl., Twick. 162 C2
Alexander Evans Ms. SE23 171 G1 *Sunderland Rd.*
Alexander Ms. W2 14 A3
Alexander Pl. SW7 31 G1
Alexander Pl. SW7 129 H4
Alexander Rd. N19 92 E3
Alexander Rd., Bexh. 158 D2
Alexander Rd., Chis. 175 E5
Alexander Sq. SW3 31 G1
Alexander Sq. SW3 129 H4
Alexander St. W2 108 D6
Alexandra Av. N22 74 D1
Alexandra Av. SW11 150 A1
Alexandra Av. W4 126 D7
Alexandra Av., Har. 85 F1
Alexandra Av., Sthl. 103 F7
Alexandra Av., Sutt. 198 D3
Alexandra Cl., Har. 85 G3 *Alexandra Av.*
Alexandra Cotts. SE14 153 J1
Alexandra Ct. N14 42 C5
Alexandra Ct., Wem. 87 J4
Alexandra Cres., Brom. 173 F6
Alexandra Dr. SE19 170 B5
Alexandra Dr., Surb. 182 A7
Alexandra Gdns. N10 74 B4
Alexandra Gdns. W4 126 D7
Alexandra Gdns., Houns. 143 H2
Alexandra Gro. N4 93 H1
Alexandra Gro. N12 57 E5
Alexandra Ms. N2 73 J3 *Fortis Grn.*
Alexandra Ms. SW19 166 D6 *Alexandra Rd.*
Alexandra Palace N22 74 D2
Alexandra Palace Way N22 74 C3
Alexandra Pk. Rd. N10 74 B2
Alexandra Pk. Rd. N22 74 D2
Alexandra Pl. NW8 109 F1
Alexandra Pl. SE25 188 A5
Alexandra Pl., Croy. 202 B1 *Alexandra Rd.*
Alexandra Rd. E6 116 D3
Alexandra Rd. E10 96 C3
Alexandra Rd. E17 77 J6
Alexandra Rd. E18 79 H3
Alexandra Rd. N8 75 G3
Alexandra Rd. N9 44 E7
Alexandra Rd. N10 58 B7
Alexandra Rd. N15 76 A5
Alexandra Rd. NW4 72 A4
Alexandra Rd. NW8 91 F7
Alexandra Rd. SE26 171 G6
Alexandra Rd. SW14 146 D3
Alexandra Rd. SW19 166 C6
Alexandra Rd. W4 126 D2
Alexandra Rd., Brent. 125 G6
Alexandra Rd., Croy. 202 B1
Alexandra Rd., Enf. 45 G4
Alexandra Rd., Houns. 143 H2
Alexandra Rd., Kings.T. 164 A7
Alexandra Rd., Mitch. 167 H7
Alexandra Rd., Rich. 145 J2
Alexandra Rd. (Chadwell Heath), Rom. 82 D6
Alexandra Rd., T.Ditt. 180 C5
Alexandra Rd., Twick. 145 F6
Alexandra Sq., Mord. 184 D5
Alexandra St. E16 115 G5
Alexandra St. SE14 133 H7
Alexandra Wk. SE19 170 B5
Alexandria Rd. W13 104 D7
Alexis St. SE16 37 H1
Alexis St. SE16 132 D4
Alfearn Rd. E5 95 F4
Alford Grn., Croy. 204 D6
Alford Pl. N1 12 A2
Alford Rd. SW8 150 D1
Alfoxton Av. N15 75 H4
Alfred Cl. W4 126 D4 *Belmont Rd.*
Alfred Gdns., Sthl. 103 E7
Alfred Ms. W1 17 H1
Alfred Ms. W1 110 D5
Alfred Pl. WC1 17 H1
Alfred Pl. WC1 110 D5
Alfred Prior Ho. E12 98 D4
Alfred Rd. E15 97 F5
Alfred Rd. SE25 188 D5
Alfred Rd. W2 108 D5
Alfred Rd. W3 126 C1
Alfred Rd., Belv. 139 F5
Alfred Rd., Buck.H. 64 A2
Alfred Rd., Felt. 160 C2
Alfred Rd., Kings.T. 181 H3
Alfred Rd., Sutt. 199 F5
Alfred St. E3 113 J3
Alfreda St. SW11 150 B1
Alfred's Gdns., Bark. 117 H2
Alfreds Way, Bark. 117 F3
Alfreds Way Ind. Est., Bark. 118 A1
Alfreton Cl. SW19 166 A3
Alfriston Av., Croy. 187 E7
Alfriston Av., Har. 67 G6
Alfriston Cl., Surb. 181 J5
Alfriston Rd. SW11 149 J5
Algar Cl., Islw. 144 D3 *Algar Rd.*
Algar Cl., Stan. 52 C5
Algar Rd., Islw. 144 D3
Algarve Rd. SW18 167 E1
Algernon Rd. NW4 71 G6
Algernon Rd. NW6 108 D1
Algernon Rd. SE13 154 B4
Algers Cl., Loug. 48 A5
Algers Mead, Loug. 48 A5
Algers Rd., Loug. 48 A5
Algiers Rd. SE13 154 A4
Alibon Gdns., Dag. 101 G5
Alibon Rd., Dag. 101 G5
Alice Ct. SW15 148 C4 *Deodar Rd.*
Alice Gilliatt Ct. W14 128 C6
Alice La. E3 113 J1
Alice Ms., Tedd. 162 C5 *Luther Rd.*
Alice St. SE1 28 D6
Alice St. SE1 132 B3
Alice Thompson Cl. SE12 173 J2
Alice Walker Cl. SE24 151 H4 *Shakespeare Rd.*
Alice Way, Houns. 143 H4
Alicia Av., Har. 69 E4
Alicia Cl., Har. 69 F4
Alicia Gdns., Har. 69 F4
Alie St. E1 21 G4
Alie St. E1 112 C6
Alington Cres. NW9 88 C1
Alison Cl. E6 116 D6
Alison Cl., Croy. 203 G1 *Shirley Oaks Rd.*
Aliwal Rd. SW11 149 H4
Alkerden Rd. W4 127 E5
Alkham Rd. N16 94 C2
All Hallows Rd. N17 76 B1
All Saints Cl. N9 60 C2
All Saints Dr. SE3 155 E2
All Saints Ms., Har. 52 B6
All Saints Pas. SW18 148/149 E5 *Wandsworth High St.*
All Saints Rd. SW19 167 F7
All Saints Rd. W3 126 C3
All Saints Rd. W11 108 C5
All Saints Rd., Sutt. 199 E3
All Saints St. N1 10 C1
All Saints St. N1 111 F2
All Saints Twr. E10 78 B7
All Souls Av. NW10 107 H2
All Souls Pl. W1 17 E2
Allan Barclay Cl. N15 76 C6 *High Rd.*
Allan Cl., N.Mal. 182 D5
Allan Way W3 106 C5
Allandale Av. N3 72 B3
Allard Cres., Bushey 51 J1
Allard Gdns. SW4 150 D5
Allardyce St. SW4 151 F4
Allbrook Cl., Tedd. 162 B5
Allcroft Rd. NW5 92 A5
Allen Cl., Mitch. 186 B1
Allen Cl., Sun. 178 B1
Allen Ct., Grnf. 86 C5
Allen Edwards Dr. SW8 150 E1
Allen Pl., Twick. 162 D1 *Church St.*
Allen Rd. E3 113 J2
Allen Rd. N16 94 B4
Allen Rd., Beck. 189 G2
Allen Rd., Croy. 187 F7
Allen Rd., Sun. 178 B1
Allen St. W8 128 D3
Allenby Cl., Grnf. 103 G3
Allenby Rd. SE23 171 H3
Allenby Rd., Sthl. 103 G6
Allendale Av., Sthl. 103 G6
Allendale Cl. SE5 152 A1 *Daneville Rd.*
Allendale Cl. SE26 171 G5
Allendale Rd., Grnf. 86 E6
Allens Rd., Enf. 45 F5
Allensbury Pl. NW1 92 D7
Allenswood Rd. SE9 156 B3
Allerford Ct., Har. 67 H5
Allerford Rd. SE6 172 B4
Allerton Ct. NW4 72 A2 *Holders Hill Rd.*
Allerton Rd. N16 93 J2
Allerton Wk. N7 93 F2 *Durham Rd.*
Allestree Rd. SW6 128 B7
Alleyn Cres. SE21 170 A2
Alleyn Pk. SE21 170 A2
Alleyn Pk., Sthl. 123 F4
Alleyn Rd. SE21 170 A3
Alleyndale Rd., Dag. 100 C2
Allfarthing La. SW18 149 E6
Allgood Cl., Mord. 184 A6
Allgood St. E2 13 G2
Allhallows La. EC4 20 B6
Allhallows Rd. E6 116 B5
Alliance Cl., Wem. 87 G4
Alliance Rd. E13 115 J4
Alliance Rd. SE18 138 A6
Alliance Rd. W3 106 B4

Allied Way W3 126/127 E2
Larden Rd.
Allingham Cl. W7 104 C7
Allingham Ms. N1 11 J1
Allingham St. N1 11 J1
Allingham St. N1 111 J2
Allington Av. N17 60 B6
Allington Cl. SW19 166 A5
High St. Wimbledon
Allington Cl., Grnf. 85 J7
Allington Ct. SW19 166 A5
High St. Wimbledon
Allington Ct., Enf. 45 G5
Allington Rd. NW4 71 H5
Allington Rd. W10 108 B2
Allington Rd., Har. 67 J5
Allington Rd., Orp. 207 G2
Allington St. SW1 25 F6
Allington St. SW1 130 B3
Allison Cl. SE10 154 C1
Dartmouth Hill
Allison Gro. SE21 170 B1
Allison Rd. N8 75 G5
Allison Rd. W3 106 C6
Allitsen Rd. NW8 7 G2
Allitsen Rd. NW8 109 H2
Allnutt Way SW4 150 D5
Alloa Rd. SE8 133 G5
Alloa Rd., Ilf. 100 A2
Allonby Gdns., Wem. 87 F1
Alloway Rd. E3 113 H3
Allsop Pl. NW1 8 A6
Allsop Pl. NW1 109 J4
Allum Way N20 57 F1
Allwood Cl. SE26 171 G4
Alma Av. E4 62 C7
Alma Cres., Sutt. 198 B5
Alma Gro. SE1 37 G2
Alma Gro. SE1 132 C4
Alma Pl. NW10 107 H3
Harrow Rd.
Alma Pl. SE19 170 C7
Alma Pl., Th.Hth. 187 G5
Alma Rd. N10 58 A7
Alma Rd. SW18 149 F5
Alma Rd., Cars. 199 H5
Alma Rd., Enf. 45 H5
Alma Rd., Esher 194 B1
Alma Rd., Sid. 176 A3
Alma Rd., Sthl. 102 E7
Alma Row, Har. 68 A1
Alma Sq. NW8 6 D3
Alma Sq. NW8 109 F3
Alma St. E15 96 D6
Alma St. NW5 92 B6
Alma Ter. SW18 149 G7
Alma Ter. W8 128 D3
Allen St.
Almack Rd. E5 95 F4
Almeida St. N1 93 H7
Almer Rd. SW20 165 G7
Almeric Rd. SW11 149 J4
Almington St. N4 93 F1
Almond Av. W5 125 H3
Almond Av., Cars. 199 J2
Almond Av., West Dr. 120 D3
Almond Cl. SE15 152 D2
Almond Cl., Brom. 192 D7
Almond Cl., Felt. 160 A1
Highfield Rd.
Almond Gro., Brent. 124 E7
Almond Rd. N17 60 D7
Almond Rd. SE16 133 E4
Almond Way, Borwd. 38 B4
Almond Way, Brom. 192 D7
Almond Way, Har. 67 H2
Almond Way, Mitch. 186 D5
Almonds Av., Buck.H. 63 G2
Almorah Rd. N1 94 A7
Almorah Rd., Houns. 142 D1
Alnwick Gro., Mord. 184/185 E4
Bordesley Rd.
Alnwick Rd. E16 115 J6
Alnwick Rd. SE12 155 H7
Alperton La., Grnf. 105 G3
Alperton La., Wem. 105 G3
Alperton St. W10 108 B4
Alpha Cl. NW1 7 H4
Alpha Gro. E14 134 A2
Alpha Pl. NW6 108 D2
Alpha Pl. SW3 31 H5
Alpha Pl. SW3 129 H6
Alpha Rd. E4 62 B3
Alpha Rd. N18 60 D6
Alpha Rd. SE14 153 J1
Alpha Rd., Croy. 202 B1
Alpha Rd., Enf. 45 H4
Alpha Rd., Surb. 181 J6
Alpha Rd., Tedd. 162 A5
Alpha St. SE15 152 D2
Alphabet Gdns., Cars. 185 G6
Alphabet Sq. E3 114 A5
Hawgood St.
Alphea Cl. SW19 167 H7
Courtney Rd.
Alpine Av., Surb. 196 C2
Alpine Cl., Croy. 202 B3
Alpine Copse, Brom. 192 D2
Alpine Gro. E9 95 F7
Alpine Rd. SE16 133 F4
Alpine Rd., Walt. 178 A7
Alpine Vw., Cars. 199 H5
Alpine Wk., Stan. 52 B2
Alpine Way E6 116 D5
Alric Av. NW10 88 D7
Alric Av., N.Mal. 183 E3
Alroy Rd. N4 75 G7
Alsace Rd. SE17 36 D3
Alsace Rd. SE17 132 B5
Alscot Rd. SE1 37 G1
Alscot Rd. SE1 132 C4
Alscot Way SE1 37 F1
Alscot Way SE1 132 C4
Alsike Rd. SE2 138 D3
Alsike Rd., Erith 138 E3
Alsom Av., Wor.Pk. 197 G4
Alston Cl., Surb. 181 E7
Alston Rd. N18 60 E5
Alston Rd. SW17 167 G4
Alston Rd., Barn. 40 B3
Alt Gro. SW19 166 C7
St. George's Rd.
Altair Cl. N17 60 C6
Altash Way SE9 174 C2
Altenburg Av. W13 125 E3
Altenburg Gdns. SW11 149 J4
Altham Rd., Pnr. 51 E7
Althea St. SW6 149 E3
Althorne Gdns. E18 79 F4
Althorne Way, Dag. 101 G2
Althorp Cl., Barn. 39 G7
Althorp Rd. SW17 167 J1
Althorpe Gro. SW11 149 G1
Westbridge Rd.
Althorpe Ms. SW11 149 G1
Westbridge Rd.
Althorpe Rd., Har. 67 J5
Altmore Av. E6 98 C7
Alton Av., Stan. 52 C7
Alton Cl., Bex. 177 E1
Alton Cl., Islw. 144 C2
Alton Gdns., Beck. 172 A7
Alton Gdns., Twick. 144 A7
Alton Rd. N17 76 A3
Alton Rd. SW15 165 G1
Alton Rd., Croy. 201 G3
Alton Rd., Rich. 145 H4
Alton St. E14 114 B5
Altyre Cl., Beck. 189 J5
Altyre Rd., Croy. 202 A2
Altyre Way, Beck. 189 J5
Alva Way, Wat. 50 D2
Alvanley Gdns. NW6 90 E5
Alverston Gdns. SE25 188 B5
Alverstone Av. SW19 166 D2
Alverstone Av., Barn. 41 H7
Alverstone Gdns. SE9 175 F1
Alverstone Rd. E12 98 D4
Alverstone Rd. NW2 89 J7
Alverstone Rd., N.Mal. 183 F4
Alverstone Rd., Wem. 87 J1
Alverton St. SE8 133 J5
Alveston Av., Har. 69 E3
Alvey Est. SE17 36 D2
Alvey Est. SE17 132 B4
Alvey St. SE17 36 D3
Alvey St. SE17 132 B5
Alvia Gdns., Sutt. 199 F4
Alvington Cres. E8 94 C5
Alway Av., Epsom 196 C5
Alwold Cres. SE12 155 H6
Alwyn Av. W4 126 D5
Alwyn Cl., Croy. 204 B7
Alwyn Gdns. NW4 71 G4
Alwyn Gdns. W3 106 B6
Alwyne La. N1 93 H7
Alwyne Vil.
Alwyne Pl. N1 93 J6
Alwyne Rd. N1 93 J7
Alwyne Rd. SW19 166 C6
Alwyne Rd. W7 104 B7
Alwyne Sq. N1 93 J6
Alwyne Vil. N1 93 H7
Alyth Gdns. NW11 72 D6
Alzette Ho. E2 113 G3
Amalgamated Dr., Brent. 124 D6
Amanda Cl., Chig. 65 G6
Amanda Ms., Rom. 83 J5
Amazon St. E1 112/113 E6
Hessel St.
Ambassador Cl., Houns. 142 E2
Ambassador Gdns. E6 116 C5
Ambassador Sq. E14 134 B4
Ambassador's Ct. SW1 25 G2
Amber Av. E17 77 H1
Amber Ct. SW17 168 A4
Brudenell Rd.
Amber Gro. NW2 90 A1
Prayle Gro.
Amber St. E15 96 D6
Salway Rd.
Amberden Av. N3 72 D3
Ambergate St. SE17 35 H3
Ambergate St. SE17 131 H5
Amberley Cl., Orp. 207 J5
Warnford Rd.
Amberley Cl., Pnr. 67 F3
Amberley Ct., Sid. 176 C5
Amberley Gdns., Enf. 44 B7
Amberley Gdns., Epsom 197 F4
Amberley Gro. SE26 170 E4
Amberley Gro., Croy. 188 C7
Amberley Rd. E10 78 B7
Amberley Rd. N13 59 F2
Amberley Rd. SE2 138 D6
Amberley Rd. W9 108 D5
Amberley Rd., Buck.H. 63 J1
Amberley Rd., Enf. 44 C7
Amberley Way, Houns. 142 C5
Amberley Way, Mord. 184 C7
Amberley Way, Rom. 83 H4
Amberside Cl., Islw. 144 A6
Amberwood Ri., N.Mal. 182 E6
Amblecote Cl. SE12 173 H3
Amblecote Meadows SE12 173 H3
Amblecote Rd. SE12 173 H3
Ambler Rd. N4 93 H3
Ambleside, Brom. 172 D6
Ambleside Av. SW16 168 D4
Ambleside Av., Beck. 189 H5
Ambleside Cl. E9 95 F5
Churchill Wk.
Ambleside Cl. E10 78 B7
Ambleside Cres., Enf. 45 G3
Ambleside Gdns. SW16 168 D5
Ambleside Gdns., Ilf. 80 B4
Ambleside Gdns., Sutt. 199 F6
Ambleside Gdns., Wem. 87 G1
Ambleside Rd. NW10 89 F7
Ambleside Rd., Bexh. 159 G2
Ambrooke Rd., Belv. 139 G3
Ambrosden Av. SW1 25 G6
Ambrosden Av. SW1 130 C3
Ambrose Av. NW11 72 B7
Ambrose Cl. E6 116 B5
Lovage App.
Ambrose Cl., Orp. 207 J3
Stapleton Rd.
Ambrose Ms. SW11 149 H2
Ambrose St. SE16 132 E4
Ambrose Wk. E3 114 A2
Malmesbury Rd.
Amelia St. SE17 35 H3
Amelia St. SE17 131 H5
Amen Cor. EC4 19 H4
Amen Cor. SW17 167 J6
Amen Ct. EC4 19 H3
Amenity Way, Mord. 183 J7
America Sq. EC3 21 F5
America St. SE1 27 J2
Amerland Rd. SW18 148 C6
Amersham Av. N18 60 A6
Amersham Gro. SE14 133 J7
Amersham Rd. SE14 153 J1
Amersham Rd., Croy. 187 J6
Amersham Vale SE14 133 J7
Amery Gdns. NW10 107 H1
Amery Rd., Har. 86 D2
Amesbury Av. SW2 169 E2
Amesbury Cl., Wor.Pk. 197 J1
Amesbury Dr. E4 46 B6
Amesbury Rd., Brom. 192 A3
Amesbury Rd., Dag. 100 D7
Amesbury Rd., Felt. 160 D2
Amethyst Rd. E15 96 D4
Amherst Av. W13 105 F6
Amherst Dr., Orp. 193 J4
Amherst Rd. W13 105 F6
Amhurst Gdns., Islw. 144 C1
Amhurst Par. N16 76 C7
Amhurst Pk.
Amhurst Pk. N16 76 A7
Amhurst Pas. E8 94 D5
Amhurst Rd. E8 94 E5
Amhurst Rd. N16 94 C4
Amhurst Ter. E8 94 D4
Amhurst Wk. SE28 138 A1
Pitfield Cres.
Amidas Gdns., Dag. 100 B4
Amiel St. E1 113 F4
Amies St. SW11 149 J3
Amina Way SE16 29 H6
Amis Av., Epsom 196 B6
Amity Gro. SW20 183 J1
Amity Rd. E15 115 F1
Ammanford Gdn. NW9 70/71 E6
Ruthin Cl.
Amner Rd. SW11 150 A6
Amor Rd. W6 127 J3
Amott Rd. SE15 152 D3
Amoy Pl. E14 114 A6
Ampere Way, Croy. 187 E7
Ampleforth Rd. SE2 138 B2
Ampthill Sq. Est. NW1 9 G2
Ampton Pl. WC1 10 C4
Ampton St. WC1 10 C4
Ampton St. WC1 111 F3
Amroth Cl. SE23 171 E1
Amsterdam Rd. E14 134 C3
Amundsen Ct. E14 134 A5
Napier Av.
Amwell Cl., Enf. 44 A5
Amwell Ct. Est. N4 93 J1
Amwell St. EC1 11 E3
Amwell St. EC1 111 G3
Amy Cl., Wall. 200/201 E7
Mollison Dr.
Amy Warne Cl. E6 116 B4
Evelyn Denington Rd.
Amyand Cotts., Twick. 144/145 E6
Amyand Pk. Rd.
Amyand La., Twick. 144/145 E7
Marble Hill Gdns.
Amyand Pk. Gdns., Twick. 144/145 E7
Amyand Pk. Rd.
Amyand Pk. Rd., Twick. 144 D7
Amyruth Rd. SE4 154 A5
Anatola Rd. N19 92 B2
Dartmouth Pk. Hill
Ancaster Cres., N.Mal. 183 G6
Ancaster Ms., Beck. 189 G3
Ancaster Rd., Beck. 189 G3
Ancaster St. SE18 137 H7
Anchor & Hope La. SE7 135 H3
Anchor Cl., Bark. 117 H3
Thames Rd.
Anchor Ms. SW12 150 B6
Hazelbourne Rd.
Anchor St. SE16 132 E4
Anchor Wf. E3 114 B5
Watts Gro.
Anchor Yd. EC1 12 A5
Anchorage Cl. SW19 166 D5
Anchorage Pt. Ind. Est. SE7 135 J3
Ancill Cl. W6 128 B6
Ancona Rd. NW10 107 G2
Ancona Rd. SE18 137 G5
Andace Pk. Gdns., Brom. 191 J1
Andalus Rd. SW9 151 E3
Ander Cl., Wem. 87 G4
Anderson Cl. N21 43 F5
Anderson Cl. W3 106 D6
Anderson Cl., Sutt. 198 D1
Anderson Ho., Bark. 117 G2
The Coverdales
Anderson Pl., Houns. 143 H4
Anderson Rd. E9 95 G6
Anderson Rd., Wdf.Grn. 80 A3
Anderson St. SW3 31 J3
Anderson St. SW3 129 J5
Anderson Way, Belv. 139 H2
Anderton Cl. SE5 152 A3
Andmark Ct., Sthl. 123 F1
Herbert Rd.
Andover Av. E16 116 A6
King George Av.
Andover Cl., Grnf. 103 H4
Ruislip Rd.
Andover Pl. NW6 6 A1
Andover Pl. NW6 108 E2
Andover Rd. N7 93 F2

Andover Rd., Orp. 207 G1
Andover Rd., Twick. 162 A1
Andre St. E8 94 D5
Andrew Borde St. WC2 17 J3
Andrew Cl., Ilf. 65 G6
Andrew Pl. SW8 150 D1
Cowthorpe Rd.
Andrew St. E14 114 C6
Andrewes Gdns. E6 116 B6
Andrews Cl. E6 116 B6
Linton Gdns.
Andrews Cl., Buck.H. 63 J2
Andrews Cl., Har. 68 A7
Bessborough Rd.
Andrews Cl., Wor.Pk. 198 A2
Andrews Crosse WC2 18 E4
Andrews Pl. SE9 156 E6
Andrew's Rd. E8 112 E1
Andrews Wk. SE17 35 H6
Andwell Cl. SE2 138 B2
Anerley Gro. SE19 170 C7
Anerley Hill SE19 170 C6
Anerley Pk. SE20 170 D7
Anerley Pk. Rd. SE20 170 E7
Anerley Rd. SE19 170 D7
Anerley Rd. SE20 170 D7
Anerley Sta. Rd. SE20 188 E1
Anerley St. SW11 149 J2
Anerley Vale SE19 170 C7
Anfield Cl. SW12 150 C7
Belthorn Cres.
Angel All. E1 21 G3
Angel Cl. N18 60 C4
Angel Cor. Par. N18 60 D5
Fore St.
Angel Ct. EC2 20 C3
Angel Ct. EC2 112 A6
Angel Ct. SW1 25 G2
Angel Ct. SW17 167 J4
Angel Gate EC1 11 H3
Angel Hill, Sutt. 198/199 E3
Sutton Common Rd.
Angel Hill Dr., Sutt. 199 E3
Angel La. E15 96 D6
Angel Ms. N1 11 F2
Angel Ms. N1 111 G2
Angel Ms. SW15 147 G7
Roehampton High St.
Angel Pas. EC4 20 B6
Angel Pl. N18 60 D5
Angel Pl. SE1 28 B3
Angel Rd. N18 60 E5
Angel Rd., Har. 68 B6
Angel Rd., T.Ditt. 180 D7
Angel Rd. Wks. N18 61 F5
Angel Sq. EC1 11 F2
Angel St. EC1 19 J3
Angel St. EC1 111 J6
Angel Wk. W6 127 J4
Angelfield, Houns. 143 H4
Angelica Dr. E6 116 D5
Angelica Gdns., Croy. 203 G1
Angell Pk. Gdns. SW9 151 G3
Angell Rd. SW9 151 G3
Angerstein La. SE3 135 F7
Angle Grn., Dag. 100 C1
Anglers Cl., Rich. 163 F4
Locksmeade Rd.
Angler's La. NW5 92 B6
Anglers Reach, Surb. 181 G5
Angles Rd. SW16 169 E4
Anglesea Av. SE18 136 E4
Anglesea Rd. SE18 136 E4
Anglesea Rd., Kings.T. 181 G4
Anglesea Ter. W6 127 H3
Wellesley Av.
Anglesey Ct. Rd., Cars. 200 A6
Anglesey Gdns., Cars. 200 A6
Anglesey Rd., Enf. 45 E4
Anglesey Rd., Wat. 50 C5
Anglesmede Cres., Pnr. 67 G3
Anglesmede Way, Pnr. 67 F3
Anglia Cl. N17 60/61 E7
Park La.
Anglia Ho. E14 113 H6
Anglia Wk. E6 116 C1
Anglian Rd. E11 96 D3
Anglo Rd. E3 113 J2
Angrave Ct. E8 112 C1
Angrave Pas. E8 112 C1
Haggerston Rd.
Angus Cl., Chess. 196 A5
Angus Dr., Ruis. 84 C4
Angus Gdns. NW9 70 D1
Angus Rd. E13 115 J3
Angus St. SE14 133 H7
Anhalt Rd. SW11 31 H7
Anhalt Rd. SW11 129 H7
Ankerdine Cres. SE18 136 D7
Anlaby Rd., Tedd. 162 B5
Anley Rd. W14 128 A2
Anmersh Gro., Stan. 69 G1
Ann La. SW10 30 E7
Ann La. SW10 129 G7
Ann Moss Way SE16 133 F3
Ann St. SE18 137 G4
Anna Cl. E8 112 C1
Anna Neagle Cl. E7 97 G4
Dames Rd.
Annabel Cl. E14 114 B6
Annandale Rd. SE10 135 F6
Annandale Rd. W4 126 E4
Annandale Rd., Croy. 202 D2
Annandale Rd., Sid. 157 H7
Anne Boleyn's Wk., Kings.T. 163 H5
Anne Boleyn's Wk., Sutt. 198 A7
Anne Case Ms., N.Mal. 182 D3
Sycamore Gro.
Anne St. E13 115 G4
Anne Way, Ilf. 65 F6
Anne Way, W.Mol. 179 H4
Annesley Av. NW9 70 D3
Annesley Cl. NW10 88 E3
Annesley Dr., Croy. 203 J3
Annesley Rd. SE3 155 H1
Annesley Wk. N19 92 C2
Annett Rd., Walt. 178 A7
Annette Cl., Har. 68 B2
Spencer Rd.
Annette Cres. N1 93 J7
Essex Rd.
Annette Rd. N7 93 F4
Annie Besant Cl. E3 113 J1
Anning St. EC2 13 E5
Annington Rd. N2 73 J3
Annis Rd. E9 95 H6
Ann's Cl. SW1 24 A4
Ann's Pl. E1 21 F2
Annsworthy Av., Th.Hth. 188 A3
Grange Pk. Rd.
Annsworthy Cres. SE25 188 A2
Grange Rd.
Ansdell Rd. SE15 153 F2
Ansdell St. W8 22 B5
Ansdell St. W8 129 E3
Ansdell Ter. W8 22 B5
Ansell Gro., Cars. 200 A1
Ansell Rd. SW17 167 H3
Anselm Cl., Croy. 202 C3
Park Hill Ri.
Anselm Rd. SW6 128 D6
Anselm Rd., Pnr. 51 F7
Ansford Rd., Brom. 172 C5
Ansleigh Pl. W11 108 A7
Anson Cl., Rom. 83 H2
Anson Rd. N7 92 D4
Anson Rd. NW2 90 A5
Anson Ter., Nthlt. 85 H6
Anstey Rd. SE15 152 D3
Anstey Wk. N15 75 H4
Anstice Cl. W4 127 E7
Anstridge Path SE9 157 G6
Anstridge Rd. SE9 157 G6
Antelope Rd. SE18 136 C3
Anthony Cl. NW7 55 E4
Anthony Cl., Wat. 50 C1
Anthony Rd. SE25 188 D6
Anthony Rd., Grnf. 104 B2
Anthony Rd., Well. 158 A1
Anthony St. E1 112/113 E6
Commercial Rd.
Antigua Cl. SE19 170 A5
Salters Hill
Antigua Wk. SE19 170 A5
Antill Rd. E3 113 H3
Antill Rd. N15 76 C4
Antill Ter. E1 113 G6
Antlers Hill E4 46 B5
Anton Cres., Sutt. 198 D3
Anton St. E8 94 D5
Antoneys Cl., Pnr. 66 D2
Antrim Gro. NW3 91 J6
Antrim Mans. NW3 91 H6
Antrim Rd. NW3 91 J6
Antrobus Cl., Sutt. 198 C5
Antrobus Rd. W4 126 C4
Anvil Cl. SW16 168 C7
Anvil Rd., Sun. 178 A3
Anworth Cl., Wdf.Grn. 63 H6
Apex Cl., Beck. 190 B1
Apex Cor. NW7 54 D4
Apex Retail Pk., Felt. 161 F3
Apex Twr., N.Mal. 182 E3
Aplin Way, Islw. 144 B1
Apollo Av., Brom. 191 H1
Rodway Rd.
Apollo Av., Nthwd. 50 A5
Apollo Pl. E11 96 E3
Apollo Pl. SW10 31 E7
Apollo Pl. SW10 129 G7
Apollo Way SE28 137 G3
Broadwater Rd.
Apostle Way, Th.Hth. 187 H2
Apothecary St. EC4 19 G4
Appach Rd. SW2 151 G6
Apple Garth, Brent. 125 G4
Apple Gro., Chess. 195 H4
Apple Gro., Enf. 44 B3
Apple Mkt., Kings.T. 181 G2
Eden St.
Apple Rd. E11 96 E3
Apple Tree Yd. SW1 25 G1
Appleby Cl. E4 62 C6
Appleby Cl. N15 76 A5
Appleby Cl., Twick. 162 A2
Appleby Rd. E8 94 D7
Appleby Rd. E16 115 F6
Appleby St. E2 13 F1
Appleby St. E2 112 C2
Appledore Av., Bexh. 159 J1
Appledore Av., Ruis. 84 B3
Appledore Cl. SW17 167 J2
Appledore Cl., Brom. 191 F5
Appledore Cl., Edg. 70 A1
Appledore Cres., Sid. 175 H3
Appleford Rd. W10 108 B4
Applegarth, Croy. 204 B7
Applegarth, Esher 194 C5
Applegarth Dr., Ilf. 81 J4
Applegarth Rd. SE28 138 B1
Applegarth Rd. W14 128 A3
Appleton Gdns., N.Mal. 183 G6
Appleton Rd. SE9 156 B3
Appleton Rd., Loug. 49 E3
Appleton Sq., Mitch. 185 H1
Appletree Cl. SE20 188/189 E1
Jasmine Gro.
Appletree Gdns., Barn. 41 H4
Applewood Cl. N20 57 H1
Applewood Cl. NW2 89 H3
Appold St. EC2 20 D1
Appold St. EC2 112 B5
Apprentice Way E5 94/95 E4
Clarence Rd.
Approach, The NW4 72 A5
Approach, The W3 106 D6
Approach, The, Enf. 44 E2
Approach, The, Orp. 207 J2
Approach Cl. N16 94 B5
Cowper Rd.
Approach Rd. E2 113 F2
Approach Rd. SW20 183 J2
Approach Rd., Barn. 41 G4
Approach Rd., W.Mol. 179 G5
Aprey Gdns. NW4 71 J4
April Cl. W7 104 B7
April Cl., Felt. 160 A3
April Cl., Orp. 207 J5
Briarswood Way
April Glen SE23 171 G3
April St. E8 94 C4
Apsley Cl., Har. 67 J5
Apsley Rd. SE25 188 E4
Apsley Rd., N.Mal. 182 C3
Apsley Way NW2 89 G2
Apsley Way W1 24 C3
Aquarius Business Pk. NW2 89 G1
Aquarius Way, Nthwd. 50 A5
Aquila St. NW8 7 F1
Aquila St. NW8 109 G2
Aquinas St. SE1 27 F2
Arabella Dr. SW15 147 E4
Arabia Cl. E4 46 D7
Arabin Rd. SE4 153 H4
Aragon Av., T.Ditt. 180 C5
Aragon Cl., Brom. 206 C1
Aragon Cl., Loug. 48 B6
Aragon Dr., Ilf. 65 F7
Aragon Dr., Ruis. 84 D1
Aragon Ms. E1 29 H1
Aragon Rd., Kings.T. 163 H5
Aragon Rd., Mord. 184 A6
Aran Dr., Stan. 53 F4
Arandora Cres., Rom. 82 B7
Arbery Rd. E3 113 H3
Arbor Cl., Beck. 190 B2
Arbor Ct. N16 94 A2
Lordship Rd.
Arbor Rd. E4 62 D3
Arborfield Cl. SW2 169 F1
Arbour Rd., Enf. 45 G4
Arbour Sq. E1 113 G6
Arbroath Grn., Wat. 50 A3
Arbroath Rd. SE9 156 B3
Arbury Ter. SE26 170/171 E3
Oaksford Av.
Arbuthnot La., Bex. 159 E6
Arbuthnot Rd. SE14 153 G2
Arbutus St. E8 112 B1
Arcade, The EC2 20 D2
Arcade, The, Croy. 201 J3
High St.
Arcadia Av. N3 72 D1
Arcadia Cl., Cars. 200 A4
Arcadia St. E14 114 A6
Arcadian Av., Bex. 158 E6
Arcadian Cl., Bex. 158 E6
Arcadian Gdns. N22 59 F7
Arcadian Rd., Bex. 158 E6
Arch St. SE1 27 J6
Arch St. SE1 131 J3
Archangel St. SE16 133 G2
Archbishops Pl. SW2 151 F6
Archdale Pl., N.Mal. 182 B3
Archdale Rd. SE22 152 C5
Archel Rd. W14 128 C6
Archer Cl., Kings.T. 163 H7
Archer Ho. SW11 149 G1
Vicarage Cres.
Archer Ms., Hmptn. 161 J6
Windmill Rd.
Archer Rd. SE25 188 E4
Archer St. W1 17 H5
Archers Dr., Enf. 45 F2
Archers Wk. SE15 152 C1
Wodehouse Av.
Archery Cl. W2 15 H4
Archery Cl. W2 109 H6
Archery Cl., Har. 68 C3
Archery Rd. SE9 156 C5
Arches, The SW6 148 C2
Munster Rd.
Arches, The WC2 26 B1
Arches, The, Har. 85 H2
Archibald Ms. W1 24 C1
Archibald Ms. W1 130 A1
Archibald Rd. N7 92 D4
Archibald St. E3 114 A3
Archie Cl., West Dr. 120 D2
Archway Cl. N19 92 C2
St. Johns Way
Archway Cl. SW19 166 E4
Archway Cl. W10 108 A5
Archway Cl., Wall. 200 D3
Archway Mall N19 92 C2
Magdala Av.
Archway Rd. N6 74 A6
Archway Rd. N19 92 C1
Archway St. SW13 147 E3
Arcola St. E8 94 C5
Arctic St. NW5 92 A5
Gillies St.
Arcus Rd., Brom. 173 E6
Ardbeg Rd. SE24 152 A6
Arden Cl., Har. 86 A3
Arden Ct. Gdns. N2 73 G6
Arden Cres. E14 134 A4
Arden Cres., Dag. 100 C7
Arden Est. N1 12 D2
Arden Est. N1 112 B2
Arden Gro., Orp. 207 E4
Arden Ms. E17 78 B5
Arden Mhor, Pnr. 66 B4
Arden Rd. N3 72 B3
Arden Rd. W13 105 F7
Ardent Cl. SE25 188 B3
Ardfern Av. SW16 187 G3
Ardfillan Rd. SE6 172 D1
Ardgowan Rd. SE6 154 E7
Ardilaun Rd. N5 93 J4
Ardingly Cl., Croy. 203 G3
Ardleigh Gdns., Sutt. 184 D7
Ardleigh Ho., Bark. 117 F1
St. Ann's
Ardleigh Ms., Ilf. 98/99 E3
Bengal Rd.
Ardleigh Rd. E17 77 J1
Ardleigh Rd. N1 94 A6
Ardleigh Ter. E17 77 J1
Ardley Cl. NW10 88 E3
Ardley Cl. SE6 171 H3
Ardlui Rd. SE27 169 J2
Ardmay Gdns., Surb. 181 H5
Ardmere Rd. SE13 154 D6
Ardmore La., Buck.H. 47 H7
Ardmore Pl., Buck.H. 47 H7
Ardoch Rd. SE6 172 D2
Ardra Rd. N9 61 G3
Ardrossan Gdns., Wor.Pk. 197 G3
Ardshiel Cl. SW15 148 A3
Bemish Rd.
Ardwell Av., Ilf. 81 F5

220 Ard-Ash

Ardwell Rd. SW2 169 E2
Ardwick Rd. NW2 90 D4
Arewater Grn., Loug. 48 C1
Argali Ho., Erith 138/139 E3
Kale Rd.
Argall Av. E10 77 G7
Argall Way E10 95 G1
Argent St. SE1 27 H3
Argenta Way NW10 88 B7
Argon Ms. SW6 128 D7
Argon Rd. N18 61 F5
Argosy La., Stai. 140 A7
Argus Cl., Rom. 83 H1
Argus Way W3 126 B3
Argus Way, Nthlt. 102 E3
Argyle Av., Houns. 143 G6
Argyle Cl. W13 104 D4
Argyle Pas. N17 76 C1
Argyle Pl. W6 127 H4
Argyle Rd. E1 113 G4
Argyle Rd. E15 96 E4
Argyle Rd. E16 115 J6
Argyle Rd. N12 56 D5
Argyle Rd. N17 76 D1
Argyle Rd. N18 60 D4
Argyle Rd. W13 104 D5
Argyle Rd., Barn. 39 J4
Argyle Rd., Grnf. 104 C3
Argyle Rd., Har. 67 H5
Argyle Rd., Houns. 143 H5
Argyle Rd., Ilf. 98 D2
Argyle Rd., Tedd. 162 B5
Argyle Sq. WC1 10 B3
Argyle Sq. WC1 111 E3
Argyle St. WC1 10 A3
Argyle St. WC1 110 E3
Argyle Wk. WC1 10 B4
Argyle Way SE16 37 J4
Argyle Way SE16 132 D5
Argyll Av., Sthl. 123 H1
Argyll Cl. SW9 151 F3
Dalyell Rd.
Argyll Gdns., Edg. 70 B2
Argyll Rd. W8 128 D2
Argyll St. W1 17 F4
Argyll St. W1 110 C6
Arica Rd. SE4 153 H4
Ariel Rd. NW6 90 D6
Ariel Way W12 127 J1
Ariel Way, Houns. 142 B3
Aristotle Rd. SW4 150 D3
Arkell Gro. SE19 169 H7
Arkindale Rd. SE6 172 C3
Arkley Cres. E17 77 J5
Arkley Dr., Barn. 39 G4
Arkley La., Barn. 39 G3
Arkley Pk., Barn. 38 D6
Arkley Rd. E17 77 J5
Arkley Vw., Barn. 39 H4
Arklow Ms., Surb. 195 H2
Vale Rd. S.
Arklow Rd. SE14 133 J6
Arkwright Rd. NW3 91 F5
Arlesey Cl. SW15 148 B6
Lytton Gro.
Arlesford Rd. SW9 151 E3
Arlingford Rd. SW2 151 G5
Arlington N12 56 D3
Arlington Av. N1 111 J2
Arlington Cl., Sid. 157 H7
Arlington Cl., Sutt. 198 D2
Arlington Cl., Twick. 145 F6
Arlington Ct., Hayes 121 G5
Shepiston La.
Arlington Dr., Cars. 199 J2
Arlington Gdns. W4 126 C5
Arlington Gdns., Ilf. 98 D1
Arlington Lo. SW2 151 F4
Arlington Ms., Twick. 144/145 E6
Arlington Rd.
Arlington Pl. SE10 134 C7
Greenwich S. St.
Arlington Rd. N14 58 B2
Arlington Rd. NW1 110 B1
Arlington Rd. W13 104 E6
Arlington Rd., Rich. 163 G2
Arlington Rd., Surb. 181 G6
Arlington Rd., Tedd. 162 C4
Arlington Rd., Twick. 145 F6
Arlington Rd., Wdf.Grn. 79 G1
Arlington Sq. N1 111 J1
Arlington St. SW1 25 F1
Arlington St. SW1 130 C1
Arlington Way EC1 11 F3
Arlington Way EC1 111 G3
Arliss Way, Nthlt. 102 C1
Arlow Rd. N21 59 G1
Armada Ct. SE8 134 A6
Watergate St.
Armada St. SE8 134 A6
Armada Way E6 117 F7
Armadale Cl. N17 76 E4
Armadale Rd. SW6 128 D7
Armadale Rd., Felt. 142 A5
Armagh Rd. E3 113 J1
Armfield Cl., W.Mol. 179 F5
Armfield Cres., Mitch. 185 J2
Armfield Rd., Enf. 44 A1
Arminger Rd. W12 127 H1
Armistice Gdns. SE25 188 D3
Penge Rd.
Armitage Rd. NW11 90 C1
Armitage Rd. SE10 135 F5
Armour Cl. N7 93 F6
Roman Way
Armoury Rd. SE8 154 B2
Armoury Way SW18 148 D5
Armstead Wk., Dag. 101 G7
Armstrong Av., Wdf.Grn. 62 E6
Armstrong Cl. E6 116 C6
Porter Rd.
Armstrong Cl., Dag. 100 D1
Palmer Rd.
Armstrong Cl., Pnr. 66 A6
Armstrong Cl., Walt. 178 A6
Sunbury La.
Armstrong Cres., Barn. 41 G3
Armstrong Rd. SW7 22 E6
Armstrong Rd. SW7 129 G3
Armstrong Rd. W3 127 F1
Armstrong Rd., Felt. 160 E5
Armstrong Way, Sthl. 123 H2
Armytage Rd., Houns. 122 D7
Arnal Cres. SW18 148 B7
Arncliffe Cl. N11 58 A6
Kettlewell Cl.
Arncroft Ct., Bark. 118 B3
Renwick Rd.
Arndale Cen. SW18 148 E6
Arndale Wk. SW18 148/149 E5
Garratt La.
Arne Gro., Orp. 207 J3
Arne St. WC2 18 B4
Arne St. WC2 111 E6
Arne Wk. SE3 155 F4
Arnett Sq. E4 61 J6
Silver Birch Av.
Arneway St. SW1 25 J6
Arneways Av., Rom. 82 D3
Arnewood Cl. SW15 165 G1
Arney's La., Mitch. 186 A6
Arngask Rd. SE6 154 D7
Arnhem Pl. E14 134 A3
Arnhem Way SE22 152 B5
East Dulwich Gro.
Arnhem Wf. E14 134 A3
Arnhem Pl.
Arnison Rd., E.Mol. 180 A4
Arnold Circ. E2 13 F4
Arnold Circ. E2 112 C3
Arnold Cl., Har. 69 J7
Arnold Cres., Islw. 144 A5
Arnold Dr., Chess. 195 G6
Arnold Est. SE1 29 G4
Arnold Est. SE1 132 C2
Arnold Gdns. N13 59 H5
Arnold Rd. E3 114 A3
Arnold Rd. N15 76 C3
Arnold Rd. SW17 167 J7
Arnold Rd., Dag. 101 F7
Arnold Rd., Nthlt. 84 D6
Arnos Gro. N14 58 D4
Arnos Rd. N11 58 C5
Arnott Cl. SE28 118 C7
Applegarth Rd.
Arnott Cl. W4 126 D4
Fishers La.
Arnould Av. SE5 152 A4
Arnsberg Way, Bexh. 159 G4
Arnside Gdns., Wem. 87 G1
Arnside Rd., Bexh. 159 G1
Arnside St. SE17 36 A5
Arnside St. SE17 131 J6
Arnulf St. SE6 172 B4
Arnulls Rd. SW16 169 G6
Arodene Rd. SW2 151 F6
Arosa Rd., Twick. 145 G6
Arragon Gdns. SW16 168 E7
Arragon Gdns., W.Wick. 204 B3
Arragon Rd. E6 116 A1
Arragon Rd. SW18 166 E1
Arragon Rd., Twick. 144 D7
Arran Cl., Wall. 200 B4
Arran Dr. E12 98 A1
Arran Grn., Wat. 50 C1
Prestwick Rd.
Arran Ms. W5 125 J1
Arran Rd. SE6 172 B2
Arran Wk. N1 93 J7
Arras Av., Mord. 185 F5
Arrol Rd., Beck. 189 F3
Arrow Rd. E3 114 B3
Arrowscout Wk., Nthlt. 102/103 E3
Argus Way
Arrowsmith Cl., Chig. 65 J5
Arrowsmith Path, Chig. 65 J5
Arrowsmith Rd., Chig. 65 H5
Arrowsmith Rd., Loug. 48 B3
Arsenal Rd. SE9 156 C2
Arterberry Rd. SW20 165 J7
Artesian Cl. NW10 88 D7
Artesian Gro., Barn. 41 F4
Artesian Rd. W2 108 D6
Artesian Wk. E11 96 E3
Arthingworth St. E15 114 E1
Arthur Ct. W2 14 A3
Arthur Gro. SE18 137 F4
Arthur Henderson Ho. SW6 148 C2
Arthur Horsley Wk. E7 97 F5
Magpie Cl.
Arthur Rd. E6 116 C2
Arthur Rd. N7 93 F4
Arthur Rd. N9 60 C2
Arthur Rd. SW19 166 D3
Arthur Rd., Kings.T. 164 A7
Arthur Rd., N.Mal. 183 H5
Arthur Rd., Rom. 82 C7
Arthur St. EC4 20 C6
Arthurdon Rd. SE4 154 A5
Artichoke Hill E1 112/113 E7
Pennington St.
Artichoke Pl. SE5 152 A1
Camberwell Ch. St.
Artillery Cl., Ilf. 81 F6
Horns Rd.
Artillery La. E1 21 E2
Artillery La. E1 112 B5
Artillery La. W12 107 G6
Artillery Pas. E1 21 E2
Artillery Pl. SE18 136 C4
Artillery Pl. SW1 25 H6
Artillery Pl., Har. 51 J7
Chicheley Rd.
Artillery Row SW1 25 H6
Artillery Row SW1 130 D3
Artington Cl., Orp. 207 F4
Artisan Cl. E6 116/117 E6
Ferndale St.
Artizan St. E1 21 E3
Arundel Av., Mord. 184 C4
Arundel Cl. E15 97 E4
Arundel Cl. SW11 149 H5
Chivalry Rd.
Arundel Cl., Bex. 159 F6
Arundel Cl., Croy. 201 H3
Arundel Cl., Hmptn. 161 H5
Arundel Ct. N12 57 H6
Arundel Ct., Har. 85 G4
Arundel Dr., Borwd. 38 C5
Arundel Dr., Har. 85 F4
Arundel Dr., Wdf.Grn. 63 G7
Arundel Gdns. N21 59 G1
Arundel Gdns. W11 108 C7
Arundel Gdns., Edg. 54 D7
Arundel Gdns., Ilf. 100 A2
Arundel Great Ct. WC2 18 D5
Arundel Gro. N16 94 B5
Arundel Pl. N1 93 G6
Arundel Rd., Barn. 41 H3
Arundel Rd., Croy. 188 A6
Arundel Rd., Houns. 142 C3
Arundel Rd., Kings.T. 182 B2
Arundel Rd., Sutt. 198 C7
Arundel Sq. N7 93 G6
Arundel St. WC2 18 D5
Arundel St. WC2 111 F7
Arundel Ter. SW13 127 H6
Arvon Rd. N5 93 G5
Asbaston Ter., Ilf. 99 F5
Buttsbury Rd.
Ascalon St. SW8 130 C7
Ascham Dr. E4 62 B7
Rushcroft Rd.
Ascham End E17 77 H1
Ascham St. NW5 92 C5
Aschurch Rd., Croy. 188 C7
Ascot Cl., Borwd. 38 A5
Ascot Cl., Ilf. 65 H6
Ascot Cl., Nthlt. 85 G5
Ascot Gdns., Sthl. 103 F5
Ascot Rd. E6 116 C3
Ascot Rd. N15 76 A5
Ascot Rd. N18 60 D4
Ascot Rd. SW17 168 A6
Ascot Rd., Orp. 193 J4
Ascott Av. W5 125 H2
Ash Cl. SE20 189 F2
Ash Cl., Cars. 199 J2
Ash Cl., Edg. 54 C4
Ash Cl., N.Mal. 182 D2
Ash Cl., Orp. 193 G5
Ash Cl., Sid. 176 B3
Ash Cl., Stan. 52 D6
Ash Ct., Epsom 196 C4
Ash Gro. E8 113 E1
Ash Gro. N13 59 J3
Ash Gro. NW2 90 A4
Ash Gro. SE20 189 F2
Ash Gro. W5 125 H2
Ash Gro., Enf. 44 B7
Ash Gro., Houns. 142 D1
Ash Gro., Sthl. 103 G5
Ash Gro., Wem. 86 D4
Ash Gro., W.Wick. 204 C2
Ash Hill Cl., Bushey 51 H1
Ash Hill Dr., Pnr. 66 C3
Ash Island, E.Mol. 180 A3
Ash Rd. E15 97 E5
Ash Rd., Croy. 204 A2
Ash Rd., Orp. 207 J7
Ash Rd., Sutt. 184 B7
Ash Row, Brom. 192 D7
Ash Tree Cl., Croy. 189 H6
Ash Tree Cl., Surb. 195 H1
Ash Tree Dell NW9 70 C5
Ash Tree Way, Croy. 189 H5
Ash Wk. SW2 169 F1
Ash Wk., Wem. 87 F4
Ashbourne Av. E18 79 H4
Ashbourne Av. N20 57 J2
Ashbourne Av. NW11 72 C5
Ashbourne Av., Bexh. 139 E7
Ashbourne Av., Har. 86 A2
Ashbourne Cl. N12 57 E4
Ashbourne Cl. W5 106 A5
Ashbourne Ct. E5 95 H4
Daubeney Rd.
Ashbourne Gro. NW7 54 D5
Ashbourne Gro. SE22 152 C5
Ashbourne Gro. W4 127 E5
Ashbourne Par. W5 105 J4
Ashbourne Rd.
Ashbourne Ri., Orp. 207 G4
Ashbourne Rd. W5 105 J5
Ashbourne Rd., Mitch. 168 A6
Ashbourne Ter. SW19 166 D7
Ashbourne Way NW11 72 C5
Ashbourne Av.
Ashbridge Rd. E11 79 F7
Ashbridge St. NW8 7 G6
Ashbridge St. NW8 109 H4
Ashbrook Rd. N19 92 D1
Ashbrook Rd., Dag. 101 H3
Ashburn Gdns. SW7 30 C1
Ashburn Gdns. SW7 129 F4
Ashburn Pl. SW7 30 C1
Ashburn Pl. SW7 129 F4
Ashburnham Av., Har. 68 C6
Ashburnham Cl. N2 73 G3
Ashburnham Cl., Wat. 50 A3
Ashburnham Dr.
Ashburnham Dr., Wat. 50 A3
Ashburnham Gdns., Har. 68 C6
Ashburnham Gro. SE10 134 B7
Ashburnham Pl. SE10 134 B7
Ashburnham Retreat SE10 134 B7
Ashburnham Rd. NW10 107 J3
Ashburnham Rd. SW10 129 F7
Ashburnham Rd., Belv. 139 J4
Ashburnham Rd., Rich. 163 E3
Ashburton Av., Croy. 202 E1
Ashburton Av., Ilf. 99 H4
Ashburton Cl., Croy. 202 D1
Ashburton Ct., Pnr. 66 D3
Ashburton Gdns., Croy. 202 D2
Ashburton Gro. N7 93 G4
Ashburton Rd. E16 115 G6
Ashburton Rd., Croy. 202 D1
Ashburton Rd., Ruis. 84 A2
Ashburton Ter. E13 115 G2
Grasmere Rd.
Ashbury Gdns., Rom. 82 D5
Ashbury Pl. SW19 167 F6
Ashbury Rd. SW11 149 J3
Ashby Av., Chess. 196 A6
Ashby Gro. N1 93 J7
Ashby Ms. SE4 153 J2

Ashby Rd. N15 76 D5
Ashby Rd. SE4 153 J2
Ashby St. EC1 11 H4
Ashby Wk., Croy. 187 J6
Ashby Way, West Dr. 120 D7
Ashchurch Gro. W12 127 G2
Ashchurch Pk. Vil. W12 127 G3
Ashchurch Ter. W12 127 G3
Ashcombe Av., Surb. 181 G7
Ashcombe Gdns., Edg. 54 A4
Ashcombe Pk. NW2 89 E3
Ashcombe Rd. SW19 166 D5
Ashcombe Rd., Cars. 200 A6
Ashcombe Sq., N.Mal. 182 C3
Ashcombe St. SW6 148 E2
Ashcroft, Pnr. 51 G6
Ashcroft Av., Sid. 158 A6
Ashcroft Cres., Sid. 158 A6
Ashcroft Rd. E3 113 H3
Ashcroft Rd., Chess. 195 J3
Ashcroft Sq. W6 127 J4
King St.
Ashdale Cl., Twick. 143 J7
Ashdale Gro., Stan. 52 C6
Ashdale Rd. SE12 173 H1
Ashdale Way, Twick. 143 J7
Ashdale Cl.
Ashdene SE15 152 E1
Ashdene, Pnr. 66 C3
Ashdon Cl., Wdf.Grn. 63 H6
Ashdon Rd. NW10 107 E1
Ashdown Cl., Beck. 190 B2
Ashdown Cl., Bex. 159 J7
Ashdown Cres. NW5 92 A5
Queens Cres.
Ashdown Est. E11 96/97 E4
High Rd. Leytonstone
Ashdown Rd., Enf. 45 F3
Ashdown Rd., Kings.T. 181 H2
Ashdown Wk. E14 134 A4
Ashdown Wk., Rom. 83 H2
Ashdown Way SW17 168 A2
Ashen E6 116 D6
Downings
Ashen Gro. SW19 166 D3
Ashenden Rd. E5 95 G5
Ashentree Ct. EC4 19 F4
Asher Loftus Way N11 57 J6
Asher Way E1 29 J1
Asher Way E1 112 D7
Ashfield Av., Felt. 160 B1
Ashfield Cl., Beck. 172 A7
Ashfield Cl., Rich. 163 H1
Ashfield La., Chis. 175 F6
Ashfield Par. N14 58 D1
Ashfield Rd. N4 75 J6
Ashfield Rd. N14 58 C3
Ashfield Rd. W3 127 F1
Ashfield St. E1 112 E5
Ashfield Yd. E1 112/113 E5
Ashfield St.
Ashfields, Loug. 48 C2
Ashford Av. N8 74 E4
Ashford Av., Hayes 102 D6
Ashford Cl. E17 77 J6
Ashford Cres., Enf. 45 F2
Ashford Grn., Wat. 50 D5
Ashford Rd. E6 98 D6
Ashford Rd. E18 79 H2
Ashford Rd. NW2 90 A4
Ashford St. N1 12 D3
Ashgrove Rd., Brom. 172 D6
Ashgrove Rd., Ilf. 99 J1
Ashingdon Cl. E4 62 C3
Ashington Rd. SW6 148 C2
Ashlake Rd. SW16 168 E4
Ashland Pl. W1 16 B1
Ashland Pl. W1 110 A5
Ashlar Pl. SE18 136/137 E4
Masons Hill
Ashleigh Gdns., Sutt. 198 E2
Ashleigh Rd. SE20 189 E3
Ashleigh Rd. SW14 146 E3
Ashley Av., Ilf. 81 E2
Ashley Av., Mord. 184 D5
Chalgrove Av.
Ashley Cl. NW4 71 J2
Ashley Cl., Pnr. 66 B2
Ashley Cres. N22 75 G2
Ashley Cres. SW11 150 A3
Ashley Dr., Borwd. 38 C5
Ashley Dr., Islw. 124 B6
Ashley Dr., Twick. 143 H7
Ashley Gdns. N13 59 J4
Ashley Gdns. SW1 25 G6
Ashley Gdns. SW1 130 C3
Ashley Gdns., Orp. 207 H5
Ashley Gdns., Rich. 163 G3
Ashley Gdns., Wem. 87 H2
Ashley Gro., Loug. 48 B3
Staples Rd.
Ashley La. NW4 71 J2
Ashley La., Croy. 201 H4
Ashley Pl. SW1 25 F6
Ashley Pl. SW1 130 C3
Ashley Rd. E4 62 A5
Ashley Rd. E7 97 J7
Ashley Rd. N17 76 D3
Ashley Rd. N19 92 E1
Ashley Rd. SW19 166 E6
Ashley Rd., Enf. 45 F2
Ashley Rd., Hmptn. 179 G1
Ashley Rd., Rich. 145 H3
Jocelyn Rd.
Ashley Rd., T.Ditt. 180 C6
Ashley Rd., Th.Hth. 187 F4
Ashley Wk. NW7 55 J7
Ashlin Rd. E15 96 D4
Ashling Rd., Croy. 202 D1
Ashlone Rd. SW15 147 J3
Ashlyns Way, Chess. 195 G6
Ashmead N14 42 C6
Ashmead Gate, Brom. 191 J1
Ashmead Rd. SE8 154 A2
Ashmead Rd., Felt. 160 A1
Ashmere Av., Beck. 190 D2
Ashmere Cl., Sutt. 197 J5
Ashmere Gro. SW2 150 E4
Ashmill St. NW1 15 G1
Ashmill St. NW1 109 H5
Ashmole Pl. SW8 34 E6
Ashmole Pl. SW8 131 F6
Ashmole St. SW8 34 D6
Ashmole St. SW8 131 F6
Ashmore Ct., Houns. 123 G6
Wheatlands
Ashmore Gro., Well. 157 G3
Ashmore Rd. W9 108 C4
Ashmount Est. N19 74 D7
Ashmount Rd.
Ashmount Rd. N15 76 C5
Ashmount Rd. N19 74 C7
Ashmount Ter. W5 125 G4
Murray Rd.
Ashneal Gdns., Har. 86 A3
Ashness Gdns., Grnf. 86 E6
Ashness Rd. SW11 149 J5
Ashridge Cl., Har. 69 F6
Ashridge Cres. SE18 137 F7
Ashridge Dr., Wat. 50 C5
Ashridge Gdns. N13 58 D5
Ashridge Gdns., Pnr. 66 E4
Ashridge Way, Mord. 184 C3
Ashridge Way, Sun. 160 A6
Ashtead Rd. E5 76 D7
Ashton Cl., Sutt. 198 D4
Ashton Gdns., Houns. 143 F4
Ashton Gdns., Rom. 83 E6
Ashton Rd. E15 96 D5
Ashton St. E14 114 C7
Ashtree Av., Mitch. 185 H2
Ashtree Cl., Orp. 206/207 E4
Broadwater Gdns.
Ashurst Cl. SE20 189 E1
Ashurst Dr., Ilf. 81 E6
Ashurst Rd. N12 57 H5
Ashurst Rd., Barn. 41 J5
Ashurst Wk., Croy. 202 E2
Ashvale Rd. SW17 167 J5
Ashville Rd. E11 96 D2
Ashwater Rd. SE12 173 G1
Ashwell Cl. E6 116 B6
Northumberland Rd.
Ashwin St. E8 94 C6
Ashwood Gdns., Croy. 204 B6
Ashwood Gdns., Hayes 121 J4
Cranford Dr.
Ashwood Rd. E4 62 D3
Ashworth Cl. SE5 152 A2
Hascombe Ter.
Ashworth Rd. W9 6 B3
Ashworth Rd. W9 109 E3
Aske St. N1 12 D3
Askern Cl., Bexh. 158 D4
Askew Cres. W12 127 F2
Askew Rd. W12 127 F1
Askham Ct. W12 127 G1
Askham Rd. W12 127 G1
Askill Dr. SW15 148 B5
Keswick Rd.
Asland Rd. E15 114 E1
Aslett St. SW18 149 E7
Asmara Rd. NW2 90 B5
Asmuns Hill NW11 72 D5
Asmuns Pl. NW11 72 C5
Asolando Dr. SE17 36 A2
Aspen Cl. N19 92 C2
Hargrave Pk.
Aspen Cl. W5 125 J2
Aspen Cl., West Dr. 120 C1
Aspen Copse, Brom. 192 C2
Aspen Ct., Hayes 121 H4
Aspen Dr., Wem. 86 D4
Aspen Gdns. W6 127 H5
Aspen Gdns., Mitch. 186 A5
Aspen Grn., Erith 139 F3
Aspen La., Nthlt. 102 E3
Aspen Way E14 114 B7
Aspen Way, Felt. 160 B3
Aspenlea Rd. W6 128 A6
Aspern Gro. NW3 91 H5
Aspinall Rd. SE4 153 G3
Aspinden Rd. SE16 133 E4
Aspley Rd. SW18 149 E5
Asplins Rd. N17 76 D1
Asquith Cl., Dag. 100 C1
Crystal Way
Ass Ho. La., Har. 51 H4
Assam St. E1 21 H3
Assata Ms. N1 93 H6
St. Paul's Rd.
Assembly Pas. E1 113 F5
Assembly Wk., Cars. 185 H7
Assurance Cotts., Belv. 139 F5
Heron Hill
Astall Cl., Har. 68 B1
Astbury Rd. SE15 153 F1
Aste St. E14 134 C2
Astell St. SW3 31 H3
Astell St. SW3 129 H5
Asteys Row N1 93 H7
River Pl.
Asthall Gdns., Ilf. 81 F4
Astle St. SW11 150 A2
Astley Av. NW2 89 J5
Aston Av., Har. 69 F7
Aston Cl., Sid. 176 A3
Aston Grn., Houns. 142 C2
Aston Ms., Rom. 82 C7
Reynolds Av.
Aston Rd. SW20 183 J2
Aston Rd. W5 105 G6
Aston Rd., Esher 194 B5
Aston St. E14 113 H6
Aston Ter. SW12 150 B6
Cathles Rd.
Astonville St. SW18 166 D1
Astor Av., Rom. 83 J6
Astor Cl., Kings.T. 164 B6
Astoria Wk. SW9 151 G3
Astrop Ms. W6 127 J3
Astrop Ter. W6 127 J3
Astwood Ms. SW7 30 C1
Astwood Ms. SW7 129 E4
Asylum Rd. SE15 133 E7
Atalanta St. SW6 148 A1
Atbara Ct., Tedd. 163 E6
Atbara Rd., Tedd. 163 E6
Atcham Rd., Houns. 143 J4
Atcost Rd., Bark. 118 A5
Atheldene Rd. SW18 167 E1
Athelney St. SE6 172 A3
Athelstan Rd., Kings.T. 181 J4
Athelstane Gro. E3 113 J2
Athelstane Ms. N4 93 G1
Stroud Grn. Rd.
Athelstone Rd., Har. 68 A2
Athena Cl., Har. 86 B2
Byron Hill Rd.
Athena Cl., Kings.T. 181 J3
Athenaeum Pl. N10 74 B3
Fortis Grn. Rd.
Athenaeum Rd. N20 57 F1
Athenlay Rd. SE15 153 G5
Athens Gdns. W9 108 D4
Elgin Av.
Atherden Rd. E5 95 F4
Atherfold Rd. SW9 150 E3
Atherley Way, Houns. 143 F7
Atherstone Ms. SW7 30 D1
Atherstone Ms. SW7 129 F4
Atherton Cl., Stai. 140 A6
Atherton Dr. SW19 166 A4
Atherton Hts., Wem. 87 F6
Atherton Ms. E7 97 F6
Atherton Pl., Har. 68 A3
Atherton Pl., Sthl. 103 H7
Longford Av.
Atherton Rd. E7 97 F5
Atherton Rd. SW13 127 G7
Atherton Rd., Ilf. 80 B2
Atherton St. SW11 149 H2
Athlon Rd., Wem. 105 G2
Athlone, Esher 194 B6
Athlone Cl. E5 94/95 E4
Goulton Rd.
Athlone Rd. SW2 151 F7
Athlone St. NW5 92 A6
Athol Cl., Pnr. 66 B1
Athol Gdns., Pnr. 66 B1
Athol Rd., Erith 139 J5
Athol Sq. E14 114 C6
Athole Gdns., Enf. 44 B5
Atholl Rd., Ilf. 82 A7
Atkins Dr., W.Wick. 204 D2
Atkins Rd. E10 78 B6
Atkins Rd. SW12 150 D7
Atkinson Rd. E16 115 J5
Atlantic Rd. SW9 151 G4
Atlantis Cl., Bark. 117 H3
Thames Rd.
Atlas Gdns. SE7 135 J4
Atlas Ms. E8 94 C6
Tyssen St.
Atlas Ms. N7 93 F6
Atlas Rd. E13 115 G2
Atlas Rd. N11 58 B6
Atlas Rd. NW10 107 E3
Atlas Rd., Wem. 88 C4
Atley Rd. E3 114 A1
Atlip Rd., Wem. 105 H1
Atney Rd. SW15 148 B4
Atria Rd., Nthwd. 50 A5
Attenborough Cl., Wat. 50/51 E3
Harrow Way
Atterbury Rd. N4 75 G6
Atterbury St. SW1 33 J2
Atterbury St. SW1 130 E4
Attewood Av. NW10 88 E3
Attewood Rd., Nthlt. 85 E6
Attfield Cl. N20 57 G2
Attlee Cl., Hayes 102 B3
Attlee Cl., Th.Hth. 187 J6
Attlee Rd. SE28 118 B7
Attlee Rd., Hayes 102 A3
Attlee Ter. E17 78 B4
Attneave St. WC1 10 E4
Atwater Cl. SW2 169 G1
Atwell Cl. E10 78 B6
Belmont Pk. Rd.
Atwell Pl., T.Ditt. 194 C1
Atwell Rd. SE15 152 D2
Rye La.
Atwood Av., Rich. 146 A2
Atwood Rd. W6 127 H4
Atwoods All., Rich. 146 A1
Leyborne Pk.
Aubert Pk. N5 93 H4
Aubert Rd. N5 93 H4
Aubrey Pl. NW8 6 C2
Aubrey Rd. E17 78 A3
Aubrey Rd. N8 75 E5
Aubrey Rd. W8 128 C1
Aubrey Wk. W8 128 C1
Aubyn Hill SE27 169 J4
Aubyn Sq. SW15 147 G4
Auckland Cl. SE19 188 C1
Auckland Gdns. SE19 188 B1
Auckland Hill SE27 169 J4
Auckland Ri. SE19 188 B1
Auckland Rd. E10 96 B3
Auckland Rd. SE19 188 C1
Auckland Rd. SW11 149 H4
Auckland Rd., Ilf. 99 E1
Auckland Rd., Kings.T. 181 J4
Auckland St. SE11 34 C4
Auden Pl. NW1 110 A1
Audleigh Pl., Chig. 64 D6
Audley Cl. N10 58 B7
Audley Cl. SW11 150 A3
Audley Cl., Borwd. 38 A3
Audley Ct. E18 79 F4
Audley Ct., Pnr. 66 C2
Rickmansworth Rd.
Audley Dr. E16 135 H1
Wesley Av.
Audley Gdns., Ilf. 99 J2
Audley Gdns., Loug. 49 F2
Audley Pl., Sutt. 198 D7
Audley Rd. NW4 71 H6
Audley Rd. W5 105 J5
Audley Rd., Enf. 43 H2
Audley Rd., Rich. 145 J5
Audley Sq. W1 24 C1
Audrey Cl., Beck. 190 B6
Audrey Gdns., Wem. 87 E2
Audrey Rd., Ilf. 98 E3
Audrey St. E2 13 H1
Audrey St. E2 112 D2
Audric Cl., Kings.T. 182 A1
Augurs La. E13 115 H3
Augusta Cl., W.Mol. 179 F3
Freeman Dr.
Augusta Rd., Twick. 161 J2
Augusta St. E14 114 B6
Augustine Rd. W14 128 A3
Augustine Rd., Har. 67 H1

Augustus Cl., Brent. 125 F7
Augustus Rd. SW19 166 B1
Augustus St. NW1 9 E2
Augustus St. NW1 110 B2
Aulton Pl. SE11 35 F4
Aulton Pl. SE11 131 G5
Aultone Way, Cars. 199 J3
Aultone Way, Sutt. 199 E2
Aurelia Gdns., Croy. 187 F5
Aurelia Rd., Croy. 187 E6
Auriga Ms. N16 94 A5
Auriol Cl., Wor.Pk. 196/197 E3
Auriol Pk. Rd.
Auriol Dr., Grnf. 86 A7
Auriol Pk. Rd., Wor.Pk. 197 E3
Auriol Rd. W14 128 B4
Austell Gdns. NW7 55 E3
Austen Cl. SE28 138 B1
Austen Cl., Loug. 49 G3
Austen Ho. NW6 108 D3
Austen Rd., Erith 139 H7
Austen Rd., Har. 85 H2
Austin Av., Brom. 192 B5
Austin Cl. SE23 153 J7
Austin Cl., Twick. 145 F5
Austin Ct. E6 115 J1
Kings Rd.
Austin Friars EC2 20 C3
Austin Friars EC2 112 A6
Austin Friars Pas. EC2 20 C3
Austin Friars Sq. EC2 20 C3
Austin Rd. SW11 150 A1
Austin Rd., Hayes 121 J2
Austin St. E2 13 F4
Austin St. E2 112 C3
Austral Cl., Sid. 175 J3
Austral St. SE11 35 G1
Austral St. SE11 131 H4
Australia Rd. W12 107 H7
Austyn Gdns., Surb. 196 B1
Autumn Cl. SW19 167 F6
Autumn Cl., Enf. 44 D1
Autumn St. E3 114 A1
Avalon Cl. SW20 184 B2
Avalon Cl. W13 104 D5
Avalon Cl., Enf. 43 G2
Avalon Rd. SW6 148 E1
Avalon Rd. W13 104 D4
Avard Gdns., Orp. 207 F4
Avarn Rd. SW17 167 J6
Ave Maria La. EC4 19 H4
Ave Maria La. EC4 111 H6
Avebury Ct. N1 112 A1
Poole St.
Avebury Pk., Surb. 181 G7
Avebury Rd. E11 96 D1
Southwest Rd.
Avebury Rd. SW19 184 C1
Avebury Rd., Orp. 207 G3
Avebury St. N1 112 A1
Poole St.
Aveline St. SE11 34 E3
Aveline St. SE11 131 G5
Aveling Pk. Rd. E17 78 A2
Avenell Rd. N5 93 H3
Avening Rd. SW18 148 D7
Brathway Rd.
Avening Ter. SW18 148 D6
Avenons Rd. E13 115 G4
Avenue, The E4 62 D6
Avenue, The (Leytonstone) E11 97 F2
Avenue, The (Wanstead) E11 97 F2
Avenue, The N3 72 D2
Avenue, The N8 75 G3
Avenue, The N10 74 C2
Avenue, The N11 58 B4
Avenue, The N17 76 B2
Avenue, The NW6 108 A1
Avenue, The SE7 135 J7
Avenue, The SE10 134 D7
Avenue, The SW4 150 A5
Avenue, The SW11 149 J7
Bellevue Rd.
Avenue, The SW18 149 H7
Avenue, The W4 126 E3
Avenue, The W13 104 E7
Avenue, The, Barn. 40 B3
Avenue, The, Beck. 190 B1
Avenue, The, Bex. 158 D7
Avenue, The, Brom. 192 A3
Avenue, The, Cars. 200 A7
Avenue, The, Croy. 202 B3
Avenue, The, Epsom 197 H7
Avenue, The, Esher 194 B6
Avenue, The, Hmptn. 161 F6
Avenue, The, Har. 68 C1
Avenue, The, Houns. 143 H5
Avenue, The (Cranford), Houns. 142 A1
Avenue, The, Islw. 124 A6
Avenue, The, Kes. 206 A3
Avenue, The, Loug. 48 A6
Avenue, The, Orp. 207 J2
Avenue, The (St. Paul's Cray), Orp. 176 B7
Avenue, The, Pnr. 67 F6
Avenue, The (Hatch End), Pnr. 51 G7
Avenue, The, Rich. 145 J2
Avenue, The, Sun. 178 B1
Avenue, The, Surb. 181 J6
Avenue, The (Cheam), Sutt. 197 J7
Avenue, The, Twick. 145 F5
Avenue, The, Wem. 87 J2
Avenue, The, West Dr. 120 B3
Avenue, The, W.Wick. 190 D7
Avenue, The, Wor.Pk. 197 F2
Avenue Cl. N14 42 C6
Avenue Cl. NW8 109 H1
Avenue Cl., Houns. 142 A1
The Av.
Avenue Cl., West Dr. 120 A3
Avenue Cres. W3 126 B2
Avenue Cres., Houns. 122 B7
Avenue Elmers, Surb. 181 H5
Avenue Gdns. SE25 188 D3
Avenue Gdns. SW14 146 E3
Avenue Gdns. W3 126 B2
Avenue Gdns., Houns. 122 A7
The Av.
Avenue Gdns., Tedd. 162 C7
Avenue Gate, Loug. 47 J6
Avenue Ind. Est. E4 61 J6
Avenue Ms. N10 74 B3
Avenue Pk. Rd. SE27 169 H2
Avenue Rd. E7 97 H5
Avenue Rd. N6 74 C7
Avenue Rd. N12 57 F4
Avenue Rd. N14 42 C7
Avenue Rd. N15 76 A5
Avenue Rd. NW3 91 G7
Avenue Rd. NW8 109 G1
Avenue Rd. NW10 107 F2
Avenue Rd. SE20 189 F1
Avenue Rd. SE25 188 D2
Avenue Rd. SW16 186 D2
Avenue Rd. SW20 183 H2
Avenue Rd. W3 126 B2
Avenue Rd., Beck. 189 F1
Avenue Rd., Belv. 139 J4
Avenue Rd., Bexh. 158 E3
Avenue Rd., Brent. 125 F5
Avenue Rd., Erith 139 J7
Avenue Rd., Hmptn. 179 H1
Avenue Rd., Islw. 144 C1
Avenue Rd., Kings.T. 181 H3
Avenue Rd., N.Mal. 182 E4
Avenue Rd., Pnr. 66 E3
Avenue Rd. (Chadwell Heath), Rom. 82 B7
Avenue Rd., Sthl. 123 F2
Avenue Rd., Tedd. 162 D7
Avenue Rd., Wall. 200 C7
Avenue Rd., Wdf.Grn. 63 J6
Avenue S., Surb. 181 J7
Avenue Ter., N.Mal. 182 C3
Kingston Rd.
Averil Gro. SW16 169 H6
Averill St. W6 128 A6
Avern Gdns., W.Mol. 179 H4
Avern Rd., W.Mol. 179 H5
Avery Fm. Row SW1 32 C2
Avery Gdns., Ilf. 80 C5
Avery Hill Rd. SE9 157 G6
Avery Row W1 16 D5
Avery Row W1 110 B7
Avey La., Loug. 47 H1
Aviary Cl. E16 115 F5
Aviemore Cl., Beck. 189 J5
Aviemore Way, Beck. 189 H5
Avignon Rd. SE4 153 G3
Avington Ct. SE1 132 B4
Old Kent Rd.
Avington Gro. SE20 171 F7
Avington Way SE15 37 F7
Avion Cres. NW9 71 G1
Avis Sq. E1 113 G6
Avoca Rd. SW17 168 A4
Avocet Ms. SE28 137 G3
Avon Cl., Hayes 102 C4
Avon Cl., Sutt. 199 F4
Avon Cl., Wor.Pk. 197 G2
Avon Ct., Grnf. 103 H4
Braund Av.
Avon Ms., Pnr. 67 F1
Avon Path, S.Croy. 201 J6
Avon Pl. SE1 28 A4
Avon Rd. E17 78 D3
Avon Rd. SE4 154 A3
Avon Rd., Grnf. 103 G4
Avon Way E18 79 G3
Avondale Av. N12 56 E5
Avondale Av. NW2 89 E3
Avondale Av., Barn. 57 J1
Avondale Av., Esher 194 D3
Avondale Av., Wor.Pk. 197 F1
Avondale Cl., Loug. 48 C7
Avondale Ct. E11 96 E1
Avondale Ct. E16 114/115 E5
Avondale Rd.
Avondale Ct. E18 79 H1
Avondale Cres., Enf. 45 H3
Avondale Cres., Ilf. 80 A5
Avondale Dr., Hayes 122 A1
Avondale Dr., Loug. 48 C7
Avondale Gdns., Houns. 143 F5
Avondale Ms., Brom. 173 G6
Avondale Rd.
Avondale Pk. Gdns. W11 108 B7
Avondale Pk. Rd. W11 108 B7
Avondale Pavement SE1 132 D5
Avondale Sq.
Avondale Ri. SE15 152 C3
Avondale Rd. E16 115 E5
Avondale Rd. E17 78 A7
Avondale Rd. N3 73 F1
Avondale Rd. N13 59 G2
Avondale Rd. N15 75 H5
Avondale Rd. SE9 174 B2
Avondale Rd. SW14 146 D3
Avondale Rd. SW19 166 E5
Avondale Rd., Brom. 173 E6
Avondale Rd., Har. 68 C3
Avondale Rd., S.Croy. 201 J6
Avondale Rd., Well. 158 C2
Avondale Sq. SE1 37 H4
Avondale Sq. SE1 132 D5
Avonley Rd. SE14 133 F7
Avonmore Gdns. W14 128 B4
Avonmore Rd.
Avonmore Pl. W14 128 B4
Avonmore Rd.
Avonmore Rd. W14 128 C4
Avonmouth St. SE1 27 J5
Avonmouth St. SE1 131 J3
Avonwick Rd., Houns. 143 H2
Avril Way E4 62 C5
Avro Way, Wall. 201 E7
Awlfield Av. N17 76 A1
Awliscombe Rd., Well. 157 J2
Axe St., Bark. 117 F1
Axholme Av., Edg. 70 A1
Axminster Cres., Well. 158 C1
Axminster Rd. N7 93 E3
Aybrook St. W1 16 B2
Aybrook St. W1 110 A5
Aycliffe Cl., Brom. 192 C4
Aycliffe Rd. W12 127 F1
Aylands Cl., Wem. 87 H2
Preston Rd.
Ayles Rd., Hayes 102 B3
Aylesbury Cl. E7 97 F6
Atherton Rd.
Aylesbury Est. SE17 36 C4
Aylesbury Rd. SE17 36 C4
Aylesbury Rd. SE17 132 A5
Aylesbury Rd., Brom. 191 G3
Aylesbury St. EC1 11 G6
Aylesbury St. EC1 111 H4
Aylesbury St. NW10 88 D3
Aylesford Av., Beck. 189 H5
Aylesford St. SW1 33 H3
Aylesford St. SW1 130 D5
Aylesham Cl. NW7 55 G7
Aylesham Rd., Orp. 193 J7
Aylestone Av. NW6 108 A1
Aylett Rd. SE25 188 E4
Aylett Rd., Islw. 144 B2
Ayley Cft., Enf. 44 D5
Ayliffe Cl., Kings.T. 182 A2
Cambridge Gdns.
Aylmer Cl., Stan. 52 D4
Aylmer Dr., Stan. 52 D4
Aylmer Par. N2 73 J5
Aylmer Rd.
Aylmer Rd. E11 97 F1
Aylmer Rd. N2 73 H5
Aylmer Rd. W12 127 F2
Aylmer Rd., Dag. 100 E3
Ayloffe Rd., Dag. 101 F6
Aylton Est. SE16 133 F2
Renforth St.
Aylward Rd. SE23 171 G2
Aylward Rd. SW20 184 C2
Aylward St. E1 113 F6
Aylwards Ri., Stan. 52 D4
Aylwyn Est. SE1 29 F5
Aylwyn Est. SE1 132 B3
Aynhoe Rd. W14 128 A4
Aynscombe La. SW14 146 C3
Aynscombe Path SW14 146 C2
Thames Bank
Ayr Ct. W3 106 A5
Monks Dr.
Ayres Cl. E13 115 G3
Ayres Cres. NW10 88 D7
Ayres St. SE1 28 A3
Ayres St. SE1 131 J2
Ayrsome Rd. N16 94 B3
Ayrton Rd. SW7 23 E5
Aysgarth Rd. SE21 152 B6
Aytoun Pl. SW9 151 F2
Aytoun Rd. SW9 151 F2
Azalea Cl. W7 124 C1
Azalea Cl., Ilf. 98 E5
Azalea Ct., Wdf.Grn. 62/63 E7
The Bridle Path
Azalea Wk., Pnr. 66 B5
Azalea Wk., Sthl. 123 J2
Navigator Dr.
Azenby Rd. SE15 152 C2
Azile Everitt Ho. SE18 137 F5
Vicarage Pk.
Azof St. SE10 135 E4

B

Baalbec Rd. N5 93 H5
Babbacombe Cl., Chess. 195 G5
Babbacombe Gdns., Ilf. 80 B4
Babbacombe Rd., Brom. 191 G1
Baber Dr., Felt. 142 C6
Babington Ri., Wem. 88 A6
Babington Rd. NW4 71 H4
Babington Rd. SW16 168 D5
Babington Rd., Dag. 100 C5
Babmaes St. SW1 17 G6
Bacchus Wk. N1 12 D2
Baches St. N1 12 C4
Baches St. N1 112 A3
Back Ch. La. E1 21 H5
Back Ch. La. E1 112 D7
Back Hill EC1 11 E6
Back Hill EC1 111 G4
Back La. N8 74 E5
Back La. NW3 91 F4
Heath St.
Back La., Bex. 159 G7
Back La., Brent. 125 G6
Back La., Edg. 70 C1
Back La., Rich. 163 F3
Back La., Rom. 82/83 E7
St. Chad's Rd.
Back Rd., Sid. 176 A4
Backhouse Pl. SE17 36 E2
Backley Gdns. SE25 188 D6
Bacon Gro. SE1 29 F6
Bacon Gro. SE1 132 C3
Bacon La. NW9 70 B4
Bacon La., Edg. 70 A1
Bacon St. E1 13 G5
Bacon St. E1 112 C4
Bacon St. E2 13 G5
Bacon St. E2 112 C4
Bacon Ter., Dag. 100 B5
Fitzstephen Rd.
Bacons La. N6 92 A1
Bacton NW5 92 A5
Bacton St. E2 113 F3
Roman Rd.
Baddow Cl., Dag. 119 G1
Baddow Cl., Wdf.Grn. 64 A6
Baddow Wk. N1 111 J1
Baden Pl. SE1 28 B3
Baden Powell Cl., Dag. 119 E1
Baden Powell Cl., Surb. 195 J2
Baden Rd. N8 74 D4
Baden Rd., Ilf. 98 E5
Badger Cl., Felt. 160 A3
Sycamore Cl.
Badger Cl., Houns. 142 C3
Badger Cl., Ilf. 81 F7
Badgers Cl., Enf. 43 H3
Badgers Cl., Har. 68 A6
Badgers Copse, Orp. 207 J2
Badgers Copse, Wor.Pk. 197 F2

Badgers Cft. N20 56 B1
Badgers Cft. SE9 174 D3
Badgers Hole, Croy. 203 G4
Badgers Wk., N.Mal. 182 E2
Badlis Rd. E17 78 A3
Badminton Cl., Borwd. 38 A2
Badminton Cl., Har. 68 B4
Badminton Cl., Nthlt. 85 G6
Badminton Ms. E16 135 G1
Hanameel St.
Badminton Rd. SW12 150 A6
Badsworth Rd. SE5 131 J7
Baffin Way E14 114 C7
Prestons Rd.
Bagley Cl., West Dr. 120 B2
Bagley's La. SW6 149 E1
Bagleys Spring, Rom. 83 E4
Bagshot Ct. SE18 156 D1
Prince Imperial Rd.
Bagshot Rd., Enf. 44 C7
Bagshot St. SE17 36 E4
Bagshot St. SE17 132 B5
Baildon St. SE8 134 A7
Watson's St.
Bailey Cl. E4 62 C4
Bailey Cl., Chess. 195 G6
Ashlyns Way
Bailey Pl. SE26 171 G6
Baillies Wk. W5 125 G2
Liverpool Rd.
Bainbridge Rd., Dag. 101 F4
Bainbridge St. WC1 17 J3
Bainbridge St. WC1 110 D6
Baines Cl., S.Croy. 201 J5
Brighton Rd.
Baird Av., Sthl. 103 H7
Baird Cl. E10 96 A1
Church Rd.
Baird Cl. NW9 70 C6
Baird Gdns. SE19 170 B4
Baird Rd., Enf. 44 E4
Baird St. EC1 12 A5
Baizdon Rd. SE3 154 E2
Baker La., Mitch. 186 A2
Baker Pas. NW10 106/107 E1
Acton La.
Baker Rd. NW10 106 E1
Baker Rd. SE18 136 B7
Baker St. NW1 8 A6
Baker St. NW1 109 J4
Baker St. W1 16 A1
Baker St. W1 109 J5
Baker St., Enf. 44 A3
Bakers Av. E17 78 B6
Bakers Ct. SE25 188 B3
Bakers End SW20 184 B2
Bakers Fld. N7 92 D4
Crayford Rd.
Bakers Gdns., Cars. 199 H2
Bakers Hill E5 95 F1
Bakers Hill, Barn. 41 E2
Bakers La. N6 73 J5
Baker's Ms. W1 16 B3
Bakers Ms., Orp. 207 J6
Bakers Pas. NW3 91 F4
Heath St.
Baker's Rents E2 13 F4
Bakers Row E15 114 E2
Baker's Row EC1 11 E6
Baker's Row EC1 111 G4
Baker's Yd. EC1 111 G4
Baker's Row
Bakery Cl. SW9 151 F1
Bakery Path, Edg. 54 B6
Station Rd.
Bakery Pl. SW11 149 J4
Altenburg Gdns.
Bakewell Way, N.Mal. 182 E2
Bala Gdn. NW9 70/71 E6
Snowdon Dr.
Balaam St. E13 115 G3
Balaams La. N14 58 D2
Balaclava Rd. SE1 37 G2
Balaclava Rd. SE1 132 C4
Balaclava Rd., Surb. 181 F7
Balcaskie Rd. SE9 156 C5
Balchen Rd. SE3 156 A2
Balchier Rd. SE22 152 E6
Balcombe Cl., Bexh. 158 D4
Balcombe St. NW1 7 J6
Balcombe St. NW1 109 J4
Balcon Way, Borwd. 38 C1
Balcorne St. E9 95 F7
Balder Ri. SE12 173 H2
Balderton St. W1 16 C4
Balderton St. W1 110 A6
Baldock St. E3 114 B2
Baldry Gdns. SW16 169 E6
Baldwin Cres. SE5 151 J1
Baldwin Gdns., Houns. 143 J1
Gresham Rd.
Baldwin St. EC1 12 B4
Baldwin Ter. N1 11 J1
Baldwin Ter. N1 111 J2
Baldwin's Gdns. EC1 18 E1
Baldwin's Gdns. EC1 111 G5
Baldwins Hill, Loug. 48 C2
Baldwyn Gdns. W3 106 D7
Balfe St. N1 10 B2
Balfe St. N1 111 E2
Balfern Gro. W4 127 E5
Balfern St. SW11 149 H1
Balfour Av. W7 124 C1
Balfour Gro. N20 57 J3
Balfour Ho. W10 108 A5
St. Charles Sq.
Balfour Ms. N9 60 D3
The Bdy.
Balfour Ms. W1 24 C1
Balfour Pl. SW15 147 H4
Balfour Pl. W1 16 C6
Balfour Rd. N5 93 J4
Balfour Rd. SE25 188 D4
Balfour Rd. SW19 166 E7
Balfour Rd. W3 106 C5
Balfour Rd. W13 124 D2
Balfour Rd., Brom. 192 A5
Balfour Rd., Cars. 199 J7
Balfour Rd., Har. 68 A5
Balfour Rd., Houns. 143 H3
Balfour Rd., Ilf. 98 E2
Balfour Rd., Sthl. 122 D3
Balfour St. SE17 36 B1
Balfour St. SE17 132 A4
Balgonie Rd. E4 62 D1
Balgowan Cl., N.Mal. 183 E5
Balgowan Rd., Beck. 189 H3
Balgowan St. SE18 137 J4
Balham Continental Mkt. SW12 168 B1
Balham Gro. SW12 150 A7
Balham High Rd. SW12 168 A1
Balham High Rd. SW17 168 A2
Balham Hill SW12 150 B7
Balham New Rd. SW12 150 B7
Balham Pk. Rd. SW12 167 J1
Balham Rd. N9 60 D2
Balham Sta. Rd. SW12 168 B1
Balkan Wk. E1 112/113 E7
Pennington St.
Balladier Wk. E14 114 B5
Ballamore Rd., Brom. 173 G3
Ballance Rd. E9 95 G6
Ballantine St. SW18 149 F4
Ballard Cl., Kings.T. 164 D7
Ballards Cl., Dag. 119 H1
Ballards Fm. Rd., Croy. 202 D6
Ballards Fm. Rd., S.Croy. 202 D6
Ballards La. N3 72 D1
Ballards La. N12 72 D1
Ballards Ms., Edg. 54 A6
Ballards Ri., S.Croy. 202 D6
Ballards Rd. NW2 89 G2
Ballards Rd., Dag. 119 H1
Ballards Way, Croy. 203 E6
Ballards Way, S.Croy. 202 D6
Ballast Quay SE10 134 D5
Ballater Cl., Wat. 50 C4
Ballater Rd. SW2 151 E4
Ballater Rd., S.Croy. 202 C5
Ballina St. SE23 153 G6
Ballingdon Rd. SW11 150 A6
Ballinger Pt. E3 114 B3
Bromley High St.
Balliol Av. E4 62 D4
Balliol Rd. N17 76 B1
Balliol Rd. W10 107 J6
Balliol Rd., Well. 158 B2
Balloch Rd. SE6 172 D1
Ballogie Av. NW10 89 E4
Ballow Cl. SE5 132 B7
Harris St.
Balls Pond Pl. N1 94 A6
Balls Pond Rd.
Balls Pond Rd. N1 94 A6
Balmain Cl. W5 125 G1
Balmer Rd. E3 113 J2
Balmes Rd. N1 112 A1
Balmoral Av. N11 58 A5
Balmoral Av., Beck. 189 H4
Balmoral Cl. SW15 148 A6
Westleigh Av.
Balmoral Cres., W.Mol. 179 G3
Balmoral Dr., Borwd. 38 D5
Balmoral Dr., Hayes 102 A5
Balmoral Dr., Sthl. 103 F4
Balmoral Gdns. W13 124 D3
Balmoral Gdns., Bex. 159 F7
Balmoral Gdns., Ilf. 99 J1
Balmoral Gro. N7 93 F6
Balmoral Ms. W12 127 F2
Balmoral Rd. E7 97 J4
Balmoral Rd. E10 96 B2
Balmoral Rd. NW2 89 H6
Balmoral Rd., Har. 85 G4
Balmoral Rd., Kings.T. 181 J4
Balmoral Rd., Wor.Pk. 197 H3
Balmore Cres., Barn. 42 A5
Balmore St. N19 92 B2
Balmuir Gdns. SW15 147 J4
Balnacraig Av. NW10 89 E4
Balniel Gate SW1 33 J3
Balniel Gate SW1 130 D5
Baltic Cl. SW19 167 G7
Baltic Ct. SE16 133 G2
Timber Pond Rd.
Baltic Pl. N1 112 B1
Kingsland Rd.
Baltic St. E. EC1 11 J6
Baltic St. E. EC1 111 J4
Baltic St. W. EC1 11 J6
Baltic St. W. EC1 111 J4
Baltimore Pl., Well. 157 J2
Balvaird Pl. SW1 33 J4
Balvaird Pl. SW1 130 D5
Balvernie Gro. SW18 148 C7
Bamber Ho., Bark. 117 F1
St. Margarets
Bamborough Gdns. W12 127 J2
Bamford Av., Wem. 105 J1
Bamford Ct. E15 96 B5
Clays La.
Bamford Rd., Bark. 99 F6
Bamford Rd., Brom. 172 C5
Bampfylde Cl., Wall. 200 C3
Bampton Dr. NW7 55 G7
Bampton Rd. SE23 171 G3
Banavie Gdns., Beck. 190 C1
Banbury Cl., Enf. 43 H1
Holtwhites Hill
Banbury Ct. WC2 18 A5
Banbury Ct., Sutt. 198 D7
Banbury Enterprise Cen., Croy. 201 H2
Factory La.
Banbury Rd. E9 95 G7
Banbury Rd. E17 61 G7
Banbury St. SW11 149 H2
Banbury Wk., Nthlt. 103 G2
Brabazon Rd.
Banchory Rd. SE3 135 H7
Bancroft Av. N2 73 H5
Bancroft Av., Buck.H. 63 G2
Bancroft Ct., Nthlt. 102 C1
Bancroft Gdns., Har. 67 J1
Bancroft Gdns., Orp. 207 J1
Bancroft Rd. E1 113 F3
Bancroft Rd., Har. 67 J2
Bandon Ri., Wall. 200 D5
Bangalore St. SW15 147 J3
Bangor Cl., Nthlt. 85 H5
Banim St. W6 127 H3
Banister Rd. W10 108 A3
Bank, The N6 92 B1
Cholmeley Pk.
Bank Av., Mitch. 185 G2
Bank End SE1 28 A1
Bank End SE1 131 J1
Bank La. SW15 146 E5
Bank La., Kings.T. 163 H7
Bankfoot Rd., Brom. 173 E4
Bankhurst Rd. SE6 153 J7
Banks La., Bexh. 159 F4
Banks Rd., Borwd. 38 C2
Banks Way E12 98 D4
Grantham Rd.
Banksia Rd. N18 61 F5
Banksian Wk., Islw. 144 B1
Bankside SE1 19 J6
Bankside SE1 111 J7
Bankside, Enf. 43 H1
Bankside, S.Croy. 202 C6
Bankside, Sthl. 122 D1
Bankside Av., Nthlt. 102 A2
Townson Av.
Bankside Cl., Cars. 199 H6
Bankside Cl., Islw. 144 C4
Bankside Dr., T.Ditt. 194 E1
Bankside Rd., Ilf. 99 F5
Bankside Way SE19 170 B6
Lunham Rd.
Bankton Rd. SW2 151 G4
Bankwell Rd. SE13 155 E4
Banner St. EC1 12 A6
Banner St. EC1 111 J4
Bannerman Ho. SW8 34 C6
Bannerman Ho. SW8 131 F6
Banning St. SE10 134 E5
Bannister Cl. SW2 169 G1
Ewen Cres.
Bannister Cl., Grnf. 86 A5
Bannister Ho. E9 95 G5
Homerton High St.
Bannockburn Rd. SE18 137 H4
Banstead Gdns. N9 60 B3
Banstead Rd., Cars. 199 H6
Banstead St. SE15 153 F3
Banstead Way, Wall. 201 E5
Banstock Rd., Edg. 54 B6
Banting Dr. N21 43 F5
Banton Cl., Enf. 44/45 E2
Central Av.
Bantry St. SE5 132 A7
Banwell Rd., Bex. 158 D6
Woodside La.
Banyard Rd. SE16 132/133 E3
Southwark Pk. Rd.
Baptist Gdns. NW5 92 A6
Queens Cres.
Barandon Wk. W11 108 A7
Barb Ms. W6 127 J3
Barbara Brosnan Ct. NW8 6 E2
Barbara Hucklesby Cl. N22 75 H2
The Sandlings
Barbauld Rd. N16 94 B3
Barber Cl. N21 43 G7
Barber's All. E13 115 H3
Barbers Rd. E15 114 B2
Barbican, The EC2 19 J1
Barbican, The EC2 111 J5
Barbican Rd., Grnf. 103 H6
Barbon Cl. WC1 18 C1
Barbot Cl. N9 60 D3
Barchard St. SW18 148 E5
Barchester Cl. W7 124 C1
Barchester Rd., Har. 68 A2
Barchester St. E14 114 B5
Barclay Cl. SW6 128 D7
Barclay Oval, Wdf.Grn. 63 G4
Barclay Path E17 78 C5
Barclay Rd. E11 97 E1
Barclay Rd. E13 115 J4
Barclay Rd. E17 78 C5
Barclay Rd. N18 60 A6
Barclay Rd. SW6 128 D7
Barclay Rd., Croy. 202 A3
Barclay Way SE22 152 D7
Lordship La.
Barcombe Av. SW2 169 E2
Barcombe Cl., Orp. 193 J3
Bard Rd. W10 108 A7
Barden St. SE18 137 H7
Bardfield Av., Rom. 82 D3
Bardney Rd., Mord. 185 E4
Bardolph Rd. N7 92 E4
Bardolph Rd., Rich. 145 J3
St. Georges Rd.
Bardsey Pl. E1 113 F5
Mile End Rd.
Bardsey Wk. N1 93 J6
Clephane Rd.
Bardsley Cl., Croy. 202 C3
Bardsley La. SE10 134 C6
Barfett St. W10 108 C4
Barfield Av. N20 57 H2
Barfield Rd. E11 97 F1
Barfield Rd., Brom. 192 D3
Barfields, Loug. 48 D4
Barfields Gdns., Loug. 48 D4
Barfields
Barfields Path, Loug. 48 D4
Barford Cl. NW4 71 G1
Barford St. N1 111 G1
Barforth Rd. SE15 153 E3
Barfreston Way SE20 189 E1
Bargate Cl. SE18 137 J5
Bargate Cl., N.Mal. 183 G6
Barge Ho. Rd. E16 137 E1
Barge Ho. St. SE1 27 F1
Barge Wk., E.Mol. 181 G2
Barge Wk., Kings.T. 181 G1
Barge Wk., Walt. 179 J2
Bargery Rd. SE6 172 B1
Bargrove Cl. SE20 170 D7
Bargrove Cres. SE6 171 J2
Elm La.
Barham Cl., Brom. 206 B1
Barham Cl., Chis. 174 E5
Barham Cl., Rom. 83 H2
Barham Cl., Wem. 87 E6
Barham Rd. SW20 165 G7
Barham Rd., Chis. 174 E5

Barham Rd., S.Croy. 201 J5
Baring Cl. SE12 173 G2
Baring Rd. SE12 155 G7
Baring Rd., Barn. 41 G3
Baring Rd., Croy. 202 D1
Baring St. N1 112 A1
Bark Pl. W2 14 A5
Bark Pl. W2 108 E7
Barkantine Shop. Par., The E14 134 A2
The Quarterdeck
Barker Cl., N.Mal. 182 C3
California Rd.
Barker Dr. NW1 92 C7
Barker Ms. SW4 150 B4
Barker St. SW10 30 C5
Barker St. SW10 129 F6
Barker Wk. SW16 168 D3
Barker Way SE22 170 D1
Dulwich Common
Barkham Rd. N17 60 A7
Barking Ind. Pk., Bark. 117 J1
Barking Rd. E6 116 A2
Barking Rd. E13 115 H4
Barking Rd. E16 115 F5
Barkston Gdns. SW5 30 A3
Barkston Gdns. SW5 128 E4
Barkway Ct. N4 93 J3
Queens Dr.
Barkwood Cl., Rom. 83 J5
Barkworth Rd. SE16 133 E5
Barlborough St. SE14 133 F7
Barlby Gdns. W10 108 A4
Barlby Rd. W10 108 A5
Barley La., Ilf. 82 A7
Barley La., Rom. 82 B6
Barley Mow Pas. EC1 19 H2
Barley Mow Pas. W4 126 D5
Barley Shotts Business Pk. W10 108 C5
St. Ervans Rd.
Barleycorn Way E14 113 J7
Barleyfields Cl., Rom. 82 B7
Barlow Cl., Wall. 200/201 E6
Cobham Cl.
Barlow Pl. W1 17 E6
Barlow Rd. NW6 90 C6
Barlow Rd. W3 126 B1
Barlow Rd., Hmptn. 161 G7
Barlow St. SE17 36 C2
Barmeston Rd. SE6 172 B2
Barmor Cl., Har. 67 H2
Barmouth Av., Grnf. 104 C2
Barmouth Rd. SW18 149 F6
Barmouth Rd., Croy. 203 G2
Barn Cl., Nthlt. 102 C2
Barn Cres., Stan. 53 F6
Barn Elms Pk. SW15 147 J2
Barn Hill, Wem. 88 B2
Barn Ms., Har. 85 G3
Barn Ri., Wem. 88 A1
Barn St. N16 94 B3
Stoke Newington Ch. St.
Barn Way, Wem. 88 A1
Barnabas Ct. N21 43 G5
Cheyne Wk.
Barnabas Rd. E9 95 G5
Barnaby Cl., Har. 85 J2
Barnaby Pl. SW7 31 E2
Barnaby Pl. SW7 129 G4
Barnaby Way, Chig. 64 E3
Barnard Cl. SE18 136 D4
Barnard Cl., Chis. 193 G1
Barnard Cl., Sun. 160 B7
Oak Gro.
Barnard Cl., Wall. 200 D7
Barnard Gdns., Hayes 102 B4
Barnard Gdns., N.Mal. 183 G4
Barnard Gro. E15 97 F7
Vicarage La.
Barnard Hill N10 74 A2
Barnard Ms. SW11 149 H4
Barnard Rd. SW11 149 H4
Barnard Rd., Enf. 45 E2
Barnard Rd., Mitch. 186 A3
Barnardo Dr., Ilf. 81 F4
Barnardo St. E1 113 G6
Devonport St.
Barnardos Village, Ilf. 81 F3
Barnard's Inn EC1 19 F3
Barnby Sq. E15 114/115 E1
Barnby St.
Barnby St. E15 114 E1
Barnby St. NW1 9 G2
Barnby St. NW1 110 C2
Barncroft Cl., Loug. 48 D5
Barncroft Grn., Loug. 48 D5
Barncroft Rd., Loug. 48 D5
Barnehurst Av., Bexh. 159 J1
Barnehurst Av., Erith 159 J1
Barnehurst Cl., Erith 159 J1
Barnehurst Rd., Bexh. 159 J2
Barnes All., Hmptn. 179 J2
Hampton Ct. Rd.
Barnes Av. SW13 127 G7
Barnes Av., Sthl. 123 F4
Barnes Br. SW13 147 E2
Barnes Br. W4 147 E2
Barnes Cl. E12 98 A4
Barnes Ct. E16 115 J5
Ridgwell Rd.
Barnes Ct., Wdf.Grn. 64 A5
Barnes End, N.Mal. 183 G5
Barnes High St. SW13 147 F2
Barnes Ho., Bark. 117 G1
St. Marys
Barnes Pikle W5 105 F7
Barnes Rd. N18 61 F4
Barnes Rd., Ilf. 99 F5
Barnes St. E14 113 H6
Barnes Ter. SE8 133 J5
Barnesbury Ho. SW4 150 D5
Barnet Bypass, Barn. 38 E3
Barnet Dr., Brom. 206 B2
Barnet Gate La., Barn. 39 F6
Barnet Gro. E2 13 H3
Barnet Gro. E2 112 D3
Barnet Hill, Barn. 40 D4
Barnet Ho. N20 57 F2
Barnet La. N20 56 C1
Barnet La., Barn. 40 C6
Barnet Rd. (Arkley), Barn. 39 H5
Barnet Trd. Est., Barn. 40 C3
Barnet Way NW7 38 D7
Barnet Wd. Rd., Brom. 205 J2
Barnett St. E1 112/113 E6
Cannon St. Rd.
Barney Cl. SE7 135 J5
Barnfield, N.Mal. 182 E6
Barnfield Av., Croy. 203 F2
Barnfield Av., Kings.T. 163 H5
Barnfield Av., Mitch. 186 B4
Barnfield Cl. N4 74/75 E7
Crouch Hill
Barnfield Cl. SW17 167 F3
Barnfield Gdns. SE18 136/137 E6
Plumstead Common Rd.
Barnfield Gdns., Kings.T. 163 H4
Barnfield Pl. E14 134 A4
Barnfield Rd. SE18 137 E6
Barnfield Rd. W5 105 F4
Barnfield Rd., Belv. 139 F6
Barnfield Rd., Edg. 70 C1
Barnfield Wd. Cl., Beck. 190 D6
Barnfield Wd. Rd., Beck. 190 D6
Barnham Rd., Grnf. 103 J3
Barnham St. SE1 28 E3
Barnham St. SE1 132 B2
Barnhill, Pnr. 66 C5
Barnhill Av., Brom. 191 F5
Barnhill La., Hayes 102 B3
Barnhill Rd., Hayes 102 B3
Barnhill Rd., Wem. 88 C3
Barnhurst Path, Wat. 50 C5
Barningham Way NW9 70 D6
Barnlea Cl., Felt. 161 E2
Barnmead Gdns., Dag. 101 F5
Barnmead Rd., Beck. 189 H1
Barnmead Rd., Dag. 101 F5
Barnsbury Cl., N.Mal. 182 C4
Barnsbury Cres., Surb. 196 C1
Barnsbury Est. N1 111 G1
Barnsbury Rd.
Barnsbury Gro. N7 93 F7
Barnsbury La., Surb. 196 B2
Barnsbury Pk. N1 93 G7
Barnsbury Rd. N1 10 E1
Barnsbury Rd. N1 111 G2
Barnsbury Sq. N1 93 G7
Barnsbury St. N1 93 G7
Barnsbury Ter. N1 93 F7
Barnscroft SW20 183 H3
Barnsdale Av. E14 134 A4
Barnsdale Rd. W9 108 C4
Barnsley St. E1 113 E4
Barnstaple Rd., Ruis. 84 C3
Barnston Wk. N1 111 J1
Popham St.
Barnwell Rd. SW2 151 G5
Barnwood Cl. W9 6 A6
Barnwood Cl. W9 108 E4
Baron Cl. N11 58 A5
Balmoral Av.
Baron Gdns., Ilf. 81 F3
Baron Gro., Mitch. 185 H4
Baron Rd., Dag. 100 D1
Baron St. N1 11 E1
Baron St. N1 111 G2
Baron Wk. E16 115 F5
Baron Wk., Mitch. 185 H4
Baroness Rd. E2 13 G3
Baronet Gro. N17 76 D1
St. Paul's Rd.
Baronet Rd. N17 76 D1
Barons, The, Twick. 145 E6
Barons Ct., Wall. 200 D3
Whelan Way
Barons Ct. Rd. W14 128 B5
Barons Gate, Barn. 41 H6
Barons Keep W14 128 B5
Barons Mead, Har. 68 B4
Barons Pl. SE1 27 F4
Barons Pl. SE1 131 G2
Barons Wk., Croy. 189 H6
Baronsfield Rd., Twick. 145 E6
Baronsmead Rd. SW13 147 G1
Baronsmede W5 125 J2
Baronsmere Rd. N2 73 H4
Barque Ms. SE8 134 A6
Watergate St.
Barrack Rd., Houns. 142 D4
Barracks La., Barn. 40 B3
High St.
Barratt Av. N22 75 F2
Barratt Ind. Pk., Sthl. 123 G2
Barratt Way, Har. 68 A3
Tudor Rd.
Barrenger Rd. N10 73 J1
Barrett Rd. E17 78 C4
Barrett St. W1 16 C4
Barrett St. W1 110 A6
Barretts Grn. Rd. NW10 106 C2
Barretts Gro. N16 94 B5
Barrhill Rd. SW2 169 E2
Barrie Est. W2 14 E5
Barrie Ho. W3 126 B2
Barriedale SE14 153 H2
Barrier App. SE7 136 A3
Barrier Pt. Rd. E16 135 G1
North Woolwich Rd.
Barringer Sq. SW17 168 A4
Barrington Cl. NW5 92 A5
Barrington Cl., Ilf. 80 C1
Barrington Cl., Loug. 49 F4
Barrington Rd.
Barrington Grn., Loug. 49 F4
Barrington Rd. E12 98 D6
Barrington Rd. N8 74 D5
Barrington Rd. SW9 151 H3
Barrington Rd., Bexh. 158 D2
Barrington Rd., Loug. 49 F3
Barrington Rd., Sutt. 198 D1
Barrington Vil. SE18 156 D1
Barrow Av., Cars. 199 J7
Barrow Cl. N21 59 H3
Barrow Hedges Cl., Cars. 199 H7
Barrow Hedges Way, Cars. 199 H7
Barrow Hill, Wor.Pk. 196 E2
Barrow Hill Cl., Wor.Pk. 196/197 E2
Barrow Hill
Barrow Hill Rd. NW8 7 G2
Barrow Hill Rd. NW8 109 H2
Barrow Pt. Av., Pnr. 66 E2
Barrow Pt. La., Pnr. 66 E2
Barrow Rd. SW16 168 D6
Barrow Rd., Croy. 201 G5
Barrow Wk., Brent. 125 F5
Glenhurst Rd.
Barrowdene Cl., Pnr. 66/67 E2
Paines La.
Barrowell Grn. N21 59 H2
Barrowfield Cl. N9 61 E3
Barrowgate Rd. W4 126 C5
Barrs Rd. NW10 88 D7
Barry Av. N15 76 C6
Craven Pk. Rd.
Barry Av., Bexh. 138 E7
Barry Cl., Orp. 207 H3
Barry Rd. E6 116 B6
Barry Rd. NW10 88 C7
Barry Rd. SE22 152 D6
Barset Rd. SE15 153 F3
Barson Cl. SE20 171 F7
Barston Rd. SE27 169 J3
Barstow Cres. SW2 169 F1
Barter St. WC1 18 B2
Barter St. WC1 111 E5
Barters Wk., Pnr. 66/67 E3
High St.
Barth Rd. SE18 137 H4
Bartholomew Cl. EC1 19 J2
Bartholomew Cl. EC1 111 J5
Bartholomew Cl. SW18 149 F4
Bartholomew La. EC2 20 C4
Bartholomew Pl. EC1 19 J2
Bartholomew Rd. NW5 92 C6
Bartholomew Sq. E1 112/113 E4
Coventry Rd.
Bartholomew Sq. EC1 12 A5
Bartholomew Sq. EC1 111 J4
Bartholomew St. SE1 28 B6
Bartholomew St. SE1 132 A3
Bartholomew Vil. NW5 92 C6
Bartle Av. E6 116 B2
Bartle Rd. W11 108 B6
Bartlett Cl. E14 114 A6
Bartlett Ct. EC4 19 F3
Bartlett St., S.Croy. 202 A5
Bartletts Pas. EC4 19 F3
Barton Av., Rom. 101 H1
Barton Cl. E6 116 C6
Barton Cl. E9 95 F5
Churchill Wk.
Barton Cl. NW4 71 G4
Barton Cl. SE15 152/153 E3
Kirkwood Rd.
Barton Cl., Bexh. 158 E5
Barton Cl., Chig. 65 F2
Barton Grn., N.Mal. 182 D2
Barton Meadows, Ilf. 81 F4
Barton Rd. W14 128 B5
Barton Rd., Sid. 177 E6
Barton St. SW1 26 A5
Barton Way, Borwd. 38 A2
Bartonway NW8 109 G2
Queen's Ter.
Bartram Rd. SE4 153 H5
Barville Cl. SE4 153 H4
St. Norbert Rd.
Barwick Rd. E7 97 H4
Barwood Av., W.Wick. 204 B1
Basden Gro., Felt. 161 G2
Basedale Rd., Dag. 100 B7
Baseing Cl. E6 116 D7
Bashley Rd. NW10 106 D4
Basil Av. E6 116 B2
Basil Gdns. SE27 169 J5
Basil Gdns., Croy. 203 G1
Primrose La.
Basil St. SW3 23 J5
Basil St. SW3 129 J3
Basildene Rd., Houns. 142 D2
Basildon Av., Ilf. 80 D1
Basildon Rd. SE2 138 A5
Basilon Rd., Bexh. 158 E2
Basin S. E16 137 E1
Basing Cl., T.Ditt. 180 C7
Basing Ct. SE15 152 C1
Basing Dr., Bex. 159 F6
Basing Hill NW11 90 C1
Basing Hill, Wem. 87 J2
Basing Ho., Bark. 117 G1
St. Margarets
Basing Ho. Yd. E2 13 E3
Basing Pl. E2 12 E3
Basing St. W11 108 C6
Basing Way N3 72 E3
Basing Way, T.Ditt. 180 C7
Basingdon Way SE5 152 A4
Basingfield Rd., T.Ditt. 180 C7
Basinghall Av. EC2 20 B2
Basinghall Av. EC2 112 A5
Basinghall St. EC2 20 B3
Basinghall St. EC2 111 J5
Basire St. N1 111 J1
Baskerville Rd. SW18 149 H7
Basket Gdns. SE9 156 B5
Baslow Cl., Har. 68 A1
Baslow Wk. E5 95 G4
Overbury St.
Basnett Rd. SW11 150 A3
Basque Ct. SE16 133 G2
Poolmans St.

Bassano St. SE22 152 C5
Bassant Rd. SE18 137 J6
Bassein Pk. Rd. W12 127 F2
Bassett Gdns., Islw. 123 J7
Bassett Ho., Dag. 118 B1
Bassett Rd. W10 108 A6
Bassett St. NW5 92 A6
Bassett Way, Grnf. 103 H6
Bassetts Cl., Orp. 206 E4
Bassetts Way, Orp. 206 E4
Bassingham Rd. SW18 149 F7
Bassingham Rd., Wem. 87 G6
Bassishaw Highwalk EC2 111 J5
London Wall
Basswood Cl. SE15 152/153 E3
Linden Gro.
Bastable Av., Bark. 117 H2
Bastion Highwalk EC2 111 J5
London Wall
Bastion Rd. SE2 138 A5
Baston Manor Rd., Brom. 205 H3
Baston Rd., Brom. 205 H1
Bastwick St. EC1 11 J5
Bastwick St. EC1 111 J4
Basuto Rd. SW6 148 D1
Batavia Cl., Sun. 178 C1
Batavia Ms. SE14 133 H7
Goodwood Rd.
Batavia Rd. SE14 133 H7
Batavia Rd., Sun. 178 B1
Batchelor St. N1 11 E1
Batchelor St. N1 111 G2
Bate St. E14 113 J7
Three Colt St.
Bateman Cl., Bark. 99 F6
Glenny Rd.
Bateman Ho. SE17 35 G6
Bateman Rd. E4 62 A6
Bateman St. W1 17 H4
Bateman's Bldgs. W1 17 H4
Bateman's Row EC2 12 E5
Bateman's Row EC2 112 B4
Bates Cres. SW16 168 C7
Bates Cres., Croy. 201 G5
Bateson St. SE18 137 H4
Bath Cl. SE15 132/133 E7
Asylum Rd.
Bath Ct. EC1 11 E6
Bath Ho. Rd., Croy. 200 E1
Bath Pas., Kings.T. 181 G2
St. James Rd.
Bath Pl. EC2 12 D4
Bath Pl., Barn. 40 C3
Bath Rd. E7 98 A6
Bath Rd. N9 61 E2
Bath Rd. W4 127 E4
Bath Rd., Hayes 141 F1
Bath Rd., Houns. 142 C1
Bath Rd., Mitch. 185 G3
Bath Rd., Rom. 82 E6
Bath Rd., West Dr. 140 A1
Bath St. EC1 12 A4
Bath St. EC1 112 A3
Bath Ter. SE1 27 J6
Bath Ter. SE1 131 J3
Bathgate Rd. SW19 166 A3
Baths Rd., Brom. 192 A4
Bathurst Av. SW19 184/185 E1
Brisbane Av.
Bathurst Gdns. NW10 107 H2
Bathurst Ms. W2 15 E5
Bathurst Rd., Ilf. 98 E1
Bathurst St. W2 15 E5
Bathurst St. W2 109 G7
Bathway SE18 136 D4
Batley Cl., Mitch. 185 J7
Batley Pl. N16 94 C3
Batley Rd. N16 94 C3
Stoke Newington High St.
Batley Rd., Enf. 43 J1
Batman Cl. W12 127 H1
Batoum Gdns. W6 127 J3
Batson St. W12 127 G2
Batsworth Rd., Mitch. 185 G3
Batten Cl. E6 116 C6
Savage Gdns.
Batten St. SW11 149 H3
Battenburg Wk. SE19 170 B5
Brabourne Cl.
Battersby Rd. SE6 172 D2
Battersea Br. SW3 31 F7
Battersea Br. SW3 129 G7
Battersea Br. SW11 31 F7
Battersea Br. SW11 129 G7
Battersea Br. Rd. SW11 129 H7
Battersea Ch. Rd. SW11 149 G1
Battersea High St. SW11 149 G1
Battersea Pk. SW11 31 J7
Battersea Pk. SW11 129 J7
Battersea Pk. Rd. SW8 150 B1
Battersea Pk. Rd. SW11 149 H2
Battersea Ri. SW11 149 H5
Battersea Sq. SW11 149 G1
Battersea High St.
Battery Rd. SE28 137 H2
Battishill Gdns. N1 93 H7
Waterloo Ter.
Battishill St. N1 93 H7
Waterloo Ter.
Battle Br. La. SE1 28 D2
Battle Br. La. SE1 132 B1
Battle Br. Rd. NW1 10 A2
Battle Br. Rd. NW1 110 E2
Battle Cl. SW19 167 F6
North Rd.
Battle Rd., Belv. 139 J4
Battle Rd., Erith 139 J4
Battledean Rd. N5 93 H5
Batty St. E1 21 J3
Batty St. E1 112 D6
Baudwin Rd. SE6 172 E2
Baugh Rd., Sid. 176 C5
Baulk, The SW18 148 D7
Bavant Rd. SW16 187 E2
Bavaria Rd. N19 92 E2
Bavdene Ms. NW4 71 H4
The Burroughs
Bavent Rd. SE5 151 J2
Bawdale Rd. SE22 152 C5
Bawdsey Av., Ilf. 81 J4
Bawtree Rd. SE14 133 H7
Bawtry Rd. N20 57 J3
Baxendale N20 57 F2
Baxendale St. E2 13 H3
Baxendale St. E2 112 D3
Baxter Cl., Sthl. 123 H2
Baxter Rd. E16 115 J6
Baxter Rd. N1 94 A6
Baxter Rd. N18 60 E4
Baxter Rd. NW10 106 E4
Baxter Rd., Ilf. 98 E5
Bay Ct. W5 125 H3
Popes La.
Bay Tree Cl., Brom. 191 J1
Baycroft Cl., Pnr. 66 C3
Baydon Ct., Brom. 191 F3
Bayes Cl. SE26 171 F5
Bayfield Rd. SE9 156 A4
Bayford Ms. E8 94/95 E7
Bayford St.
Bayford Rd. NW10 108 A3
Bayford St. E8 95 E7
Bayham Pl. NW1 9 F1
Bayham Pl. NW1 110 C1
Bayham Rd. W4 126 D3
Bayham Rd. W13 104 E7
Bayham Rd., Mord. 185 E4
Bayham St. NW1 110 C1
Bayley St. WC1 17 H2
Bayley St. WC1 110 D5
Bayley Wk. SE2 138/139 E5
Woolwich Rd.
Baylin Rd. SW18 148/149 E6
Garratt La.
Baylis Rd. SE1 27 E4
Baylis Rd. SE1 131 G2
Bayliss Av. SE28 118 D7
Bayliss Cl. N21 42/43 E5
Macleod Rd.
Bayne Cl. E6 116 C6
Savage Gdns.
Baynes Cl., Enf. 44 D2
Baynes Ms. NW3 91 G6
Belsize La.
Baynes St. NW1 92 C7
Baynham Cl., Bex. 159 F6
Bayonne Rd. W6 128 B6
Bayshill Ri., Nthlt. 85 H6
Bayston Rd. N16 94 C3
Bayswater Rd. W2 15 F5
Bayswater Rd. W2 108 E7
Baythorne St. E3 113 J5
Baytree Cl., Sid. 175 J1
Baytree Rd. SW2 151 F4
Bazalgette Cl., N.Mal. 182 D5
Bazalgette Gdns., N.Mal. 182 D5
Bazely St. E14 114 C7
Bazile Rd. N21 43 G6
Beach Gro., Felt. 161 G2
Beacham Cl. SE7 136 A5
Beachborough Rd., Brom. 172 C4
Beachcroft Rd. E11 97 E3
Beachcroft Way N19 92 D1
Beachy Rd. E3 96 A7
Beacon Gate SE14 153 G3
Beacon Gro., Cars. 200 A4
Beacon Hill N7 92 E5
Beacon Rd. SE13 154 D6
Beacon Rd., Houns. 140 D6
Beacon Rd. Roundabout, Houns. 140 E6
Beacons Cl. E6 116 B5
Oliver Gdns.
Beaconsfield Cl. N11 58 A4
Beaconsfield Cl. SE3 135 G6
Beaconsfield Cl. W4 126 C5
Beaconsfield Par. SE9 174 B4
Beaconsfield Rd.
Beaconsfield Rd. E10 96 C2
Beaconsfield Rd. E16 115 F4
Beaconsfield Rd. E17 77 J6
Beaconsfield Rd. N9 60 D4
Beaconsfield Rd. N11 58 A3
Beaconsfield Rd. N15 76 B4
Beaconsfield Rd. NW10 89 F6
Beaconsfield Rd. SE3 135 F7
Beaconsfield Rd. SE9 174 B2
Beaconsfield Rd. SE17 36 C4
Beaconsfield Rd. SE17 132 A5
Beaconsfield Rd. W4 126 D3
Beaconsfield Rd. W5 125 F2
Beaconsfield Rd., Brom. 192 A3
Beaconsfield Rd., Croy. 188 A6
Beaconsfield Rd., Esher 194 B7
Beaconsfield Rd., Hayes 122 C1
Beaconsfield Rd., N.Mal. 182 D2
Beaconsfield Rd., Sthl. 122 D1
Beaconsfield Rd., Surb. 181 J7
Beaconsfield Rd., Twick. 144 E6
Beaconsfield Ter., Rom. 82 D6
Beaconsfield Ter. Rd. W14 128 B3
Beaconsfield Wk. E6 116 D6
East Ham Manor Way
Beaconsfield Wk. SW6 148 C1
Beacontree Av. E17 78 D1
Beacontree Rd. E11 79 F7
Beadlow Cl., Cars. 185 G6
Olveston Wk.
Beadman Pl. SE27 169 H4
Norwood High St.
Beadman St. SE27 169 H4
Beadnell Rd. SE23 171 G1
Beadon Rd. W6 127 J4
Beadon Rd., Brom. 191 G4
Beaford Gro. SW20 184 B3
Beagle Cl., Felt. 160 B4
Beak St. W1 17 G5
Beak St. W1 110 C7
Beal Cl., Well. 158 A1
Beal Rd., Ilf. 98 D2
Beale Cl. N13 59 H5
Beale Pl. E3 113 J2
Beale Rd. E3 113 J1
Beam Av., Dag. 119 H1
Beaminster Gdns., Ilf. 80 E2
Beamish Dr., Bushey 51 J1
Beamish Rd. N9 60 D1
Bean Rd., Bexh. 158 D4
Beanacre Cl. E9 95 J6
Beanshaw SE9 174 D4
Beansland Gro., Rom. 83 E2
Bear All. EC4 19 G3
Bear Cl., Rom. 83 H6
Bear Gdns. SE1 27 J1
Bear Gdns. SE1 131 J1
Bear La. SE1 27 H1
Bear La. SE1 131 H1
Bear Rd., Felt. 160 D5
Bear St. WC2 17 J5
Beard Rd., Kings.T. 163 J5
Beardell St. SE19 170 C6
Beardow Gro. N14 42 C6
Beard's Hill, Hmptn. 179 G1
Beard's Hill Cl., Hmptn. 179 G1
Beard's Hill
Beardsfield E13 115 G1
Valetta Gro.
Beardsley Ter., Dag. 100 B5
Fitzstephen Rd.
Beardsley Way W3 126 D2
Bearfield Rd., Kings.T. 163 H7
Bearstead Ri. SE4 153 J5
Bearstead Ter., Beck. 190 A1
Copers Cope Rd.
Beatrice Av. SW16 187 F3
Beatrice Av., Wem. 87 H5
Beatrice Cl. E13 115 G4
Chargeable La.
Beatrice Cl., Pnr. 66 A4
Reid Cl.
Beatrice Ct., Buck.H. 64 A2
Beatrice Pl. W8 22 A6
Beatrice Pl. W8 128 E3
Beatrice Rd. E17 78 A5
Beatrice Rd. N4 75 G7
Beatrice Rd. N9 45 F7
Beatrice Rd. SE1 37 J2
Beatrice Rd. SE1 132 D4
Beatrice Rd., Rich. 145 J5
Albert Rd.
Beatrice Rd., Sthl. 123 F1
Beatson Wk. SE16 133 H1
Beattock Ri. N10 74 B4
Beatty Rd. N16 94 B4
Beatty Rd., Stan. 53 F6
Beatty St. NW1 9 F1
Beatty St. NW1 110 C2
Beattyville Gdns., Ilf. 80 D3
Beauchamp Cl. W4 126 C3
Church Path
Beauchamp Ct., Stan. 53 F5
Hardwick Cl.
Beauchamp Pl. SW3 23 H5
Beauchamp Pl. SW3 129 H3
Beauchamp Rd. E7 97 H7
Beauchamp Rd. SE19 188 A1
Beauchamp Rd. SW11 149 H4
Beauchamp Rd., E.Mol. 179 H5
Beauchamp Rd., Sutt. 198 D5
Beauchamp Rd., Twick. 144 D7
Beauchamp Rd., W.Mol. 179 H5
Beauchamp St. EC1 19 E2
Beauchamp Ter. SW15 147 H3
Dryburgh Rd.
Beauclerc Rd. W6 127 H3
Beauclerk Cl., Felt. 160 B1
Florence Rd.
Beaudesert Ms., West Dr. 120 B2
Beaufort E6 116 D5
Newark Knok
Beaufort Av., Har. 68 D4
Beaufort Cl. E4 62 B6
Higham Sta. Av.
Beaufort Cl. SW15 147 H7
Beaufort Cl. W5 105 J5
Beaufort Cl., Rom. 83 J4
Beaufort Ct., Rich. 163 F4
Beaufort Rd.
Beaufort Dr. NW11 72 D4
Beaufort Gdns. NW4 71 J6
Beaufort Gdns. SW3 23 H5
Beaufort Gdns. SW3 129 H3
Beaufort Gdns. SW16 169 F7
Beaufort Gdns., Houns. 143 E1
Beaufort Gdns., Ilf. 98 D1
Beaufort Ms. SW6 128 C6
Lillie Rd.
Beaufort Pk. NW11 72 D4
Beaufort Rd. W5 105 J5
Beaufort Rd., Kings.T. 181 H4
Beaufort Rd., Rich. 163 F4
Beaufort Rd., Twick. 145 F7
Beaufort St. SW3 31 F6
Beaufort St. SW3 129 G6
Beaufort Way, Epsom 197 G7
Beaufoy Rd. N17 60 B7
Beaufoy Wk. SE11 34 D2
Beaufoy Wk. SE11 131 F4
Beaulieu Av. E16 135 H1
Beaulieu Av. SE26 170 E4
Beaulieu Cl. NW9 71 E4
Beaulieu Cl. SE5 152 A3
Beaulieu Cl., Houns. 143 F5
Beaulieu Cl., Mitch. 186 A1
Beaulieu Cl., Twick. 145 G7
Beaulieu Cl., Wat. 50 C1
Beaulieu Dr., Pnr. 66 D6
Beaulieu Gdns. N21 43 J7
Beaulieu Pl. W4 126 C3
Rothschild Rd.
Beaumanor Gdns. SE9 174 D4
Beaumaris Dr., Wdf.Grn. 64 A7
Beaumont Av. W14 128 C5

Beaumont Av., Har. 67 H6
Beaumont Av., Rich. 145 J3
Beaumont Av., Wem. 87 F5
Beaumont Cl., 164 A7
  Kings.T.
Beaumont Cres. W14 128 C5
Beaumont Gdns. 90 D3
  NW3
Beaumont Ms. W1 **16 C1**
Beaumont Pl. W1 **9 G5**
Beaumont Pl. W1 110 C4
Beaumont Pl., Barn. 40 C1
Beaumont Pl., Islw. 144 C5
Beaumont Ri. N19 92 D1
Beaumont Rd. E10 78 B7
Beaumont Rd. E13 115 H3
Beaumont Rd. SE19 169 J6
Beaumont Rd. SW19 148 B7
Beaumont Rd. W4 126 C3
Beaumont Rd., Orp. 193 G6
Beaumont Sq. E1 113 G4
Beaumont St. W1 **16 C1**
Beaumont St. W1 110 A4
Beaumont Wk. NW3 91 J7
Beauvais Ter., Nthlt. 102 D3
Beauval Rd. SE22 152 C6
Beaver Cl. SE20 170 D7
  Lullington Rd.
Beaver Cl., Hmptn. 179 H1
Beaver Gro., 102/103 E3
  Nthlt.
  Jetstar Way
Beaverbank Rd. SE9 175 G1
Beavers Cres. 142 C4
  Houns.
Beavers La., Houns. 142 C3
Beavers La. Camp, 142 C3
  Houns.
  Beavers La.
Beaverwood Rd., 175 H6
  Chis.
Beavor Gro. W6 127 G4
  Beavor La.
Beavor La. W6 127 G4
Bebbington Rd. SE18 137 H4
Bebletts Cl., Orp. 207 J5
Bec Cl., Ruis. 84 D3
Beccles Dr., Bark. 99 H6
Beccles St. E14 113 J7
Beck Cl. SE13 154 B1
Beck Ct., Beck. 189 G3
Beck La., Beck. 189 G3
Beck River Pk., Beck. 190 A1
  Rectory Rd.
Beck Rd. E8 112 E1
Beck Way, Beck. 189 J3
Beckenham Business 171 H6
  Cen., Beck.
Beckenham Gdns. 60 B3
  N9
Beckenham Gro., 190 D2
  Brom.
Beckenham Hill Rd. 172 B5
  SE6
Beckenham Hill Rd., 172 B5
  Beck.
Beckenham La., 191 E2
  Brom.
Beckenham Pl. Pk., 172 B7
  Beck.
Beckenham Rd., 189 G1
  Beck.
Beckenham Rd., 190 B7
  W.Wick.
Beckers, The N16 94 D3
  Rectory Rd.
Becket Av. E6 116 D3
Becket Cl. SE25 188 D6
Becket Fold, Har. 68 C5
  Courtfield Cres.
Becket Rd. N18 61 F4
Becket St. SE1 **28 B5**
Beckett Cl. NW10 88 D6
Beckett Cl. SW16 168 D2
Beckett Cl., Belv. 138/139 E3
  Tunstock Way
Beckett Wk., Beck. 171 H6
Becketts Cl., Felt. 142 B6
Becketts Cl., Orp. 207 J3
Becketts Pl., Kings.T. 181 G1
Beckford Dr., Orp. 193 G3
Beckford Pl. SE17 **36 A4**
Beckford Rd., Croy. 188 C6
Becklow Gdns. W12 127 G2
  Becklow Rd.
Becklow Ms. W12 127 F2
  Becklow Rd.
Becklow Rd. W12 127 G2
Becks Rd., Sid. 176 A3
Beckton Pk. 116 C7
  Roundabout E16
  Royal Albert Way
Beckton Rd. E16 115 F5

Beckway Rd. SW16 186 D2
Beckway St. SE17 **36 C2**
Beckway St. SE17 132 A4
Beckwith Rd. SE24 152 A6
Beclands Rd. SW17 168 A6
Becmead Av. SW16 168 D4
Becmead Av., Har. 68 E5
Becondale Rd. SE19 170 B5
Bective Pl. SW15 148 C4
  Bective Rd.
Bective Rd. E7 97 G4
Bective Rd. SW15 148 C4
Becton Pl., Erith 139 H7
Bedale St. SE1 **28 B2**
Bedale St. SE1 132 A1
Beddington 186/187 E7
  Cross, Croy.
  Beddington Fm. Rd.
Beddington Fm. Rd., 200 E1
  Croy.
Beddington Gdns., 200 A6
  Cars.
Beddington Gdns., 200 B6
  Wall.
Beddington Grn. 193 J1
  Orp.
Beddington Gro., 200 D5
  Wall.
Beddington La., Croy. 186 C5
Beddington Path, 193 J1
  Orp.
Beddington Rd., Ilf. 81 J7
Beddington Rd., Orp. 193 H2
Beddington Trd. Pk. 200 E1
  W., Croy.
Bede Cl., Pnr. 66 D1
Bede Rd., Rom. 82 C6
Bedenham Way **37 F7**
  SE15
Bedens Rd., Sid. 176 E6
Bedfont Cl., Mitch. 186 A2
Bedfont Cl., Felt. 141 F6
Bedfont La., Felt. 141 J7
Bedfont Rd., Stai. 140 B6
Bedford Av. WC1 **17 J2**
Bedford Av. WC1 110 D5
Bedford Av., Barn. 40 C5
Bedford Av., Hayes 102 B6
Bedford Cl. N10 58 A7
Bedford Cl. W4 127 E6
Bedford Cor. W4 126/127 E4
  The Av.
Bedford Ct. WC2 **18 A6**
Bedford Gdns. W8 128 D1
Bedford Hill SW12 168 B1
Bedford Hill SW16 168 B1
Bedford Ho. SW4 150 D4
  Bedford Ms. N2 73 H3
Bedford Pk.
Bedford Pk., Croy. 201 J1
Bedford Pk. Cor. 126/127 E4
  W4
  Bath Rd.
Bedford Pas. SW6 128 B7
  Dawes Rd.
Bedford Pl. W1 **17 G1**
Bedford Pl. WC1 **18 A1**
Bedford Pl. WC1 110 E5
Bedford Pl., Croy. 202 A1
Bedford Rd. E6 116 D1
Bedford Rd. E17 78 A2
Bedford Rd. E18 79 G2
Bedford Rd. N2 73 H3
Bedford Rd. N8 74 D6
Bedford Rd. N9 44 E7
Bedford Rd. N15 76 B4
Bedford Rd. N22 74 E1
Bedford Rd. NW7 54 E3
Bedford Rd. SW4 150 E3
Bedford Rd. W4 126 D3
Bedford Rd. W13 104 E7
Bedford Rd., Har. 67 J6
Bedford Rd., Ilf. 99 E3
Bedford Rd., Sid. 175 H3
Bedford Rd., Twick. 162 A3
Bedford Rd., Wor.Pk. 197 J2
Bedford Row WC1 **18 D1**
Bedford Row WC1 111 F5
Bedford Sq. WC1 **17 J2**
Bedford Sq. WC1 110 D5
Bedford St. WC2 **18 A5**
Bedford St. WC2 111 E7
  Lyham Rd.
Bedford Way WC1 **9 J6**
Bedford Way WC1 110 D4
Bedfordbury WC2 **18 A5**
Bedgebury Gdns. 166 B2
  SW19
Bedgebury Rd. SE9 156 A4
Bedivere Rd., Brom. 173 G3
Bedlow Way, Croy. 201 F4
Bedonwell Rd. SE2 138 E6

Bedonwell Rd., Belv. 139 G6
Bedonwell Rd., Bexh. 139 G6
Bedser Cl. SE11 **34 D5**
Bedser Cl., Th.Hth. 187 J3
Bedser Dr., Grnf. 86 A5
Bedster Gdns., 179 H2
  W.Mol.
Bedwardine Rd. 170 B7
  SE19
Bedwell Gdns., 121 H5
  Hayes
Bedwell Rd. N17 76 B1
Bedwell Rd., Belv. 139 G5
Beeby Rd. E16 115 H6
Beech Av. N20 57 H1
Beech Av. W3 126 E1
Beech Av., Brent. 125 E7
Beech Av., Buck.H. 63 H2
Beech Av., Ruis. 84 B1
Beech Av., Sid. 158 A7
Beech Cl. N9 44 D6
Beech Cl. SE8 133 J6
  Clyde St.
Beech Cl. SW15 147 G7
Beech Cl. SW19 165 J6
Beech Cl., Cars. 199 J2
Beech Cl., Loug. 48/49 E2
  Cedar Dr.
Beech Cl., Stai. 140 A7
  St. Mary's Cres.
Beech Cl., Sun. 178 D2
  Harfield Rd.
Beech Cl., West Dr. 120 D3
Beech Copse, Brom. 192 C2
Beech Copse, S.Croy. 202 B5
Beech Ct. E17 78 D3
Beech Ct. SE9 156 B6
Beech Ct., Ilf. 98 D3
  Riverdene Rd.
Beech Ct., Surb. 181 H7
Beech Dell, Kes. 206 C4
Beech Dr. N2 73 J3
Beech Gdns. EC2 111 J5
  Aldersgate St.
Beech Gdns. W5 125 H2
Beech Gdns., Dag. 101 H7
Beech Gro., Ilf. 65 H6
Beech Gro., Mitch. 186 D4
Beech Gro., N.Mal. 182 D3
Beech Hall Cres. E4 62 D7
Beech Hall Rd. E4 62 C7
Beech Hill Av., Barn. 41 F1
Beech Ho., Croy. 204 B6
Beech Ho. Rd., Croy. 202 A3
Beech La., Buck.H. 63 H2
Beech Lawns N12 57 G5
Beech Rd. N11 59 E6
Beech Rd. SW16 187 E2
Beech Rd., Felt. 141 H7
Beech Row, Rich. 163 H4
Beech St. EC2 **19 J1**
Beech St. EC2 111 J5
Beech St., Rom. 83 J4
Beech Tree Cl., 53 F5
  Stan.
Beech Tree Glade E4 63 F1
  Forest Side
Beech Tree Pl., 198/199 E5
  Sutt.
  St. Nicholas Way
Beech Wk. NW7 54 E6
Beech Way NW10 88 D7
Beech Way, Twick. 161 G3
Beechcroft, Chis. 174 D7
Beechcroft Av. NW11 72 C7
Beechcroft Av., Har. 67 G7
Beechcroft Av., 182 C1
  N.Mal.
Beechcroft Av., Sthl. 123 H1
Beechcroft Cl., Orp. 207 H1
Beechcroft Cl., 122 E7
  Houns.
Beechcroft Cl., Orp. 207 G4
Beechcroft Gdns., 87 J3
  Wem.
Beechcroft Rd. E18 79 H2
Beechcroft Rd. SW14 146 C3
  Elm Rd.
Beechcroft Rd. 167 H2
  SW17
Beechcroft Rd., 195 J3
  Chess.
Beechcroft Rd., Orp. 207 G4
Beechdale N21 59 F2
Beechdale Rd. SW2 151 F6
Beechen Cliff Way, 144 C1
  Islw.
  Henley Cl.
Beechen Gro., Pnr. 67 F3
Beeches, The, Houns. 143 H1
Beeches Av., Cars. 199 H7
Beeches Cl. SE20 189 F1
  Genoa Rd.
Beeches Ct., Brom. 173 G6
  Avondale Rd.

Beeches Rd. SW17 167 H3
Beeches Rd., Sutt. 198 B1
Beechfield Cotts., 191 J2
  Brom.
  Widmore Rd.
Beechfield Gdns., 83 J7
  Rom.
Beechfield Rd. N4 75 J6
Beechfield Rd. SE6 171 J1
Beechfield Rd., 191 J2
  Brom.
Beechhill Rd. SE9 156 D5
Beechmont Cl., 172 E5
  Brom.
Beechmore Gdns., 198 A2
  Sutt.
Beechmore Rd. 149 J1
  SW11
Beechmount Av. W7 104 A5
Beecholme Av., 186 B1
  Mitch.
Beecholme Est. E5 94/95 E3
  Prout Rd.
Beechvale Cl. N12 57 H5
Beechway, Bex. 158 D6
Beechwood Av. N3 72 C3
Beechwood Av., 103 H3
  Grnf.
Beechwood Av., Har. 85 H3
Beechwood Av., Orp. 207 H5
Beechwood Av., 146 A1
  Rich.
Beechwood Av., Sun. 160 A6
Beechwood Av., 187 H4
  Th.Hth.
Beechwood Circle, 85 H3
  Har.
  Beechwood Gdns.
Beechwood Cl. NW7 54 D5
Beechwood Cl., 181 F7
  Surb.
Beechwood Ct., Cars. 199 J4
Beechwood Ct., Sun. 160 A6
Beechwood Cres. 158 D3
  Bexh.
Beechwood Dr., Kes. 206 A4
Beechwood Dr., 63 F5
  Wdf.Grn.
Beechwood Gdns. 105 J3
  NW10
  St. Annes Gdns.
Beechwood Gdns., 85 H3
  Har.
Beechwood Gdns., Ilf. 80 C5
Beechwood Gro. 106/107 E7
  W3
  East Acton La.
Beechwood Gro., 181 F7
  Surb.
Beechwood Ms. N9 60 D2
Beechwood Pk. E18 79 G3
Beechwood Ri., Chis. 175 E4
Beechwood Rd. E8 94 C6
Beechwood Rd. N8 74 D4
Beechwoods Ct. 170 C5
  SE19
  Crystal Palace Par.
Beechworth Cl. NW3 90 D2
Beecroft Rd. SE4 153 H5
Beehive Cl. E8 94 C7
Beehive La., Ilf. 80 C6
Beehive Pas. EC3 **20 D4**
Beehive Pl. SW9 151 G3
Beeken Dene, Orp. 207 F4
  Isabella Dr.
Beeleigh Rd., Mord. 185 E4
Beeston Cl. E8 94 D5
  Ferncliff Rd.
Beeston Cl., Wat. 50 D4
Beeston Pl. SW1 **24 E6**
Beeston Pl. SW1 130 B3
Beeston Rd., Barn. 41 G6
Beeston Way, Felt. 142 C6
Beethoven St. W10 108 B3
Beeton Cl., Pnr. 51 G7
Begbie Rd. SE3 155 J1
Beggars Hill, Epsom 197 F7
Beggars Roost La., 198 D6
  Sutt.
Begonia Cl. E6 116 B5
Begonia Pl., Hmptn. 161 G6
  Gresham Rd.
Begonia Wk. W12 107 F6
  Du Cane Rd.
Beira St. SW12 150 B7
Bekesbourne St. E14 113 H6
  Ratcliffe La.
Belcroft Cl., Brom. 173 F7
  Hope Pk.
Beldham Gdns., 179 H3
  W.Mol.
Belfairs Dr., Rom. 82 C7
Belfairs Grn., Wat. 50 D5
  Heysham Dr.

Belfast Rd. N16 94 C2
Belfast Rd. SE25 188 E4
Belfont Wk. N7 93 E4
Belfort Rd. SE15 153 F2
Belfry Cl. SE16 132/133 E5
  Masters Dr.
Belgrade Rd. N16 94 B4
Belgrade Rd., Hmptn. 179 H1
Belgrave Cl. N14 42 C5
  Prince George Av.
Belgrave Cl. NW7 54 D5
Belgrave Cl. W3 126 C2
  Avenue Rd.
Belgrave Cres., Sun. 178 B1
Belgrave Gdns. N14 42 D5
Belgrave Gdns. NW8 109 E1
Belgrave Gdns., Stan. 53 F5
  Copley Rd.
Belgrave Ms. N. SW1 24 B4
Belgrave Ms. N. SW1 130 A3
Belgrave Ms. S. SW1 24 C5
Belgrave Ms. S. SW1 130 A3
Belgrave Ms. W. SW1 24 B5
Belgrave Ms. W. SW1 130 A3
Belgrave Pl. SW1 24 C5
Belgrave Pl. SW1 130 A3
Belgrave Rd. E10 96 C1
Belgrave Rd. E11 97 G2
Belgrave Rd. E13 115 J4
Belgrave Rd. E17 78 A5
Belgrave Rd. SE25 188 C4
Belgrave Rd. SW1 33 F2
Belgrave Rd. SW1 130 B4
Belgrave Rd. SW13 127 F7
Belgrave Rd., Houns. 143 F3
Belgrave Rd., Ilf. 98 C1
Belgrave Rd., Mitch. 185 G3
Belgrave Rd., Sun. 178 B1
Belgrave Sq. SW1 24 B5
Belgrave Sq. SW1 130 A3
Belgrave St. E1 113 G6
Belgrave Ter., Wdf.Grn. 63 G3
Belgrave Wk., Mitch. 185 G3
Belgrave Yd. SW1 24 D6
Belgravia Cl., Barn. 40 C3
Belgravia Gdns., Brom. 172 E6
Belgravia Ho. SW4 150 E6
Belgravia Ms., Kings.T. 181 G4
Belgrove St. WC1 10 A3
Belgrove St. WC1 111 E3
Belham Wk. SE5 152 A1
  D'Eynsford Rd.
Belinda Rd. SW9 151 H3
Belitha Vil. N1 93 F7
Bell Av., West Dr. 120 C4
Bell Cl., Pnr. 66 C3
Bell Ct., Surb. 196 B2
  Barnsbury La.
Bell Dr. SW18 148 B7
Bell Fm. Av., Dag. 101 J3
Bell Gdns. E10 96 A1
  Church Rd.
Bell Gdns. E17 77 J5
  Markhouse Rd.
Bell Grn. SE26 171 J3
Bell Grn. La. SE26 171 H5
Bell Hill, Croy. 201 J3
  Surrey St.
Bell Ho. Rd., Rom. 101 J1
Bell Inn Yd. EC3 20 C4
Bell La. E1 21 F2
Bell La. E1 112 C5
Bell La. E16 135 G1
Bell La. NW4 72 A4
Bell La., Twick. 162 D1
  The Embk.
Bell La., Wem. 87 G2
  Magnet Rd.
Bell Meadow SE19 170 B4
  Dulwich Wd. Av.
Bell Rd., E.Mol. 180 A5
Bell Rd., Enf. 44 A1
Bell Rd., Houns. 143 H4
Bell St. NW1 15 G1
Bell St. NW1 109 H5
Bell Water Gate SE18 136 D3
Bell Wf. La. EC4 20 A5
Bell Wf. La. EC4 111 J7
Bell Yd. WC2 18 E3
Bell Yd. WC2 111 G6
Bellamy Cl. E14 134 A2
  Byng St.
Bellamy Cl. W14 128 C5
  Aisgill Av.
Bellamy Cl., Edg. 54 C3
Bellamy Dr., Stan. 68 E1
Bellamy Rd. E4 62 B6

Bellamy Rd., Enf. 44 A2
Bellamy St. SW12 150 B7
Bellasis Av. SW2 168 E2
Bellclose Rd., West Dr. 120 B2
Belle Vue, Grnf. 104 A1
Belle Vue Est. NW4 71 J4
  Bell La.
Belle Vue La., Bushey 52 A1
Belle Vue Pk., Th.Hth. 187 J3
Belle Vue Rd. E17 78 D2
Belle Vue Rd. NW4 71 J4
  Bell La.
Bellefields Rd. SW9 151 F3
Bellegrove Cl., Well. 157 J2
Bellegrove Par., Well. 157 J3
  Bellegrove Rd.
Bellegrove Rd., Well. 157 G2
Bellenden Rd. SE15 152 C2
Bellestaines Pleasaunce E4 62 A2
Belleville Rd. SW11 149 J5
Bellevue Ms. N11 58 A5
  Bellevue Rd.
Bellevue Par. SW17 167 H1
  Bellevue Rd.
Bellevue Pl. E1 113 F4
Bellevue Rd. N11 58 A4
Bellevue Rd. SW13 147 G2
Bellevue Rd. SW17 167 H1
Bellevue Rd. W13 104 E4
Bellevue Rd., Bexh. 159 F5
Bellevue Rd., Kings.T. 181 H3
Bellew St. SW17 167 F3
Bellfield Av., Har. 52 A6
Bellflower Cl. E6 116 B5
  Sorrel Gdns.
Bellgate Ms. NW5 92 B3
  York Ri.
Bellingham Cl., Bark. 118 B3
  Renwick Rd.
Bellingham Grn. SE6 172 A3
Bellingham Rd. SE6 172 B3
Bello Cl. SE24 151 H7
Bellot Gdns. SE10 135 E5
Bellot St. SE10 135 E5
Bellring Cl., Belv. 139 G6
Bells All. SW6 148 D2
Bells Gdn. Est. SE15 132 D7
  Buller Cl.
Bells Hill, Barn. 40 A5
Belltrees Gro. SW16 169 F5
Bellwood Rd. SE15 153 G4
Belmarsh Rd. SE28 137 H2
  Western Way
Belmont Av. N9 60 D1
Belmont Av. N13 59 E5
Belmont Av. N17 75 J3
Belmont Av., Barn. 41 J5
Belmont Av., N.Mal. 183 G5
Belmont Av., Sthl. 122 E3
Belmont Av., Well. 157 H3
Belmont Av., Wem. 105 J1
Belmont Circle, Har. 68 E1
Belmont Cl. E4 62 D5
Belmont Cl. N20 56 E1
Belmont Cl. SW4 150 C3
Belmont Cl., Barn. 41 J4
Belmont Cl., Wdf.Grn. 63 H4
Belmont Ct. NW11 72 C5
Belmont Gro. SE13 154 D3
Belmont Gro. W4 126 D4
  Belmont Rd.
Belmont Hall Ct. SE13 154 D3
  Belmont Gro.
Belmont Hill SE13 154 D3
Belmont La., Chis. 175 F5
Belmont La., Stan. 53 F7
Belmont Ms. SW19 166 A2
  Chapman Sq.
Belmont Pk. SE13 154 D4
Belmont Pk. Cl. SE13 154 D4
  Belmont Pk.
Belmont Pk. Rd. E10 78 B6
Belmont Rd. N15 75 J4
Belmont Rd. N17 75 J4
Belmont Rd. SE25 188 E5
Belmont Rd. SW4 150 C3
Belmont Rd. W4 126 D4
Belmont Rd., Beck. 189 J2
Belmont Rd., Chis. 175 E5
Belmont Rd., Erith 139 G7
Belmont Rd., Har. 68 C3
Belmont Rd., Ilf. 99 F3
Belmont Rd., Twick. 162 A2
Belmont Rd., Wall. 200 B5
Belmont St. NW1 92 A7
Belmont Ter. W4 126 D4
  Belmont Rd.
Belmor, Borwd. 38 A5
Belmore Av., Hayes 102 A6

Belmore La. N7 92 D5
Belmore St. SW8 150 D1
Beloe Cl. SW15 147 G3
Belper Ct. E5 95 G4
  Pedro St.
Belsham St. E9 95 F6
Belsize Av. N13 59 F6
Belsize Av. NW3 91 H6
Belsize Av. W13 125 E3
Belsize Cl. NW3 91 H5
  Belsize La.
Belsize Cres. NW3 91 G5
Belsize Gdns., Sutt. 199 E4
Belsize Gro. NW3 91 H6
Belsize La. NW3 91 G6
Belsize Ms. NW3 91 G6
  Belsize La.
Belsize Pk. NW3 91 G6
Belsize Pk. Gdns. NW3 91 H6
Belsize Pk. Ms. NW3 91 G6
  Belsize La.
Belsize Pl. NW3 91 G6
  Belsize La.
Belsize Rd. NW6 91 F7
Belsize Rd., Har. 52 A7
Belsize Sq. NW3 91 G6
Belsize Ter. NW3 91 G6
Belson Rd. SE18 136 C4
Beltane Dr. SW19 166 A3
Belthorn Cres. SW12 150 C7
Belton Rd. E7 97 H7
Belton Rd. E11 96 E4
Belton Rd. N17 76 B3
Belton Rd. NW2 89 G6
Belton Rd., Sid. 176 A4
Belton Way E3 114 A5
Beltran Rd. SW6 148 E2
Beltwood Rd., Belv. 139 J4
Belvedere Av. SW19 166 B5
Belvedere Av., Ilf. 80 E2
Belvedere Bldgs. SE1 27 H4
Belvedere Cl., Tedd. 162 B5
Belvedere Ct. N2 73 G5
Belvedere Dr. SW19 166 B5
Belvedere Gdns., W.Mol. 179 F5
Belvedere Gro. SW19 166 B5
Belvedere Ho., Felt. 160 A1
Belvedere Ind. Est., Belv. 139 J3
Belvedere Ms. SE15 153 E3
Belvedere Pl. SE1 27 H4
Belvedere Pl. SE1 131 H2
Belvedere Rd. E10 95 H1
Belvedere Rd. SE1 26 D3
Belvedere Rd. SE1 131 F1
Belvedere Rd. SE2 138 D1
Belvedere Rd. SE19 170 C7
Belvedere Rd. W7 124 C3
Belvedere Rd., Bexh. 159 F3
Belvedere Sq. SW19 166 B5
Belvedere Strand NW9 71 F2
Belvedere Way, Har. 69 H6
Belvoir Cl. SE9 174 B3
Belvoir Rd. SE22 152 D7
Belvue Cl., Nthlt. 85 G7
Belvue Rd., Nthlt. 85 G7
Bembridge Cl. NW6 90 B7
Bemerton Est. N1 93 F7
Bemerton St. N1 111 F1
Bemish Rd. SW15 148 A3
Bempton Dr., Ruis. 84 B2
Bemsted Rd. E17 77 J3
Ben Hale Cl., Stan. 52 E4
Ben Jonson Rd. E1 113 H5
Ben Smith Way SE16 29 J5
Ben Tillet Cl., Bark. 100 A7
Ben Tillett Cl. E16 136 C1
  Newland St.
Benares Rd. SE18 137 J4
Benbow Rd. W6 127 H3
Benbow St. SE8 134 A6
Benbury Cl., Brom. 172 C5
Bench Fld., S.Croy. 202 C6
Bencroft Rd. SW16 168 C7
Bencurtis Pk., W.Wick. 204 D3
Bendall Ms. NW1 15 H1
Bendemeer Rd. SW15 148 A3
Bendish Rd. E6 98 B7
Bendmore Av. SE2 138 A5
Bendon Valley SW18 148 E7
Benedict Cl., Belv. 138/139 E3
  Tunstock Way
Benedict Cl., Orp. 207 H3
Benedict Dr., Felt. 141 G7
Benedict Rd. SW9 151 F3
Benedict Rd., Mitch. 185 G3

Benedict Way N2 73 F3
Benenden Grn., Brom. 191 G5
Benett Gdns. SW16 186 E2
Benfleet Cl., Sutt. 199 F3
Bengal Ct. EC3 112 A6
  Birchin La.
Bengal Rd., Ilf. 98 E4
Bengarth Dr., Har. 68 A2
Bengarth Rd., Nthlt. 102 D1
Bengeworth Rd. SE5 151 J3
Bengeworth Rd., Har. 86 D2
Benham Cl. SW11 149 G3
Benham Cl., Chess. 195 F6
  Merritt Gdns.
Benham Gdns., Houns. 143 F4
Benham Rd. W7 104 B5
Benhams Pl. NW3 91 F4
  Holly Wk.
Benhill Av., Sutt. 199 E4
Benhill Rd. SE5 132 A7
Benhill Rd., Sutt. 199 F3
Benhill Wd. Rd., Sutt. 199 F3
Benhilton Gdns., Sutt. 199 E3
Benhurst Ct. SW16 169 G5
Benhurst La. SW16 169 G5
Benin St. SE13 154 D7
Benjafield Cl. N18 60/61 E4
  Brettenham Rd.
Benjamin Cl. E8 112 D1
Benjamin St. EC1 19 G1
Benjamin St. EC1 111 H5
Benledi St. E14 114 D6
Benn St. E9 95 H6
Bennerley Rd. SW11 149 H5
Bennet's Hill EC4 19 H5
Bennetsfield Rd., Uxb. 120 E1
Bennett Cl., Kings.T. 181 F1
Bennett Cl., Well. 158 A2
Bennett Gro. SE13 154 B1
Bennett Pk. SE3 155 F3
Bennett Rd. E13 115 J4
Bennett Rd. N16 94 B4
Bennett Rd., Rom. 83 E6
Bennett St. SW1 25 F1
Bennett St. W4 127 E6
Bennetts Av., Croy. 203 H2
Bennetts Av., Grnf. 104 B2
Bennetts Castle La., Dag. 100 C4
Bennetts Cl. N17 60 C6
Bennetts Cl., Mitch. 186 B1
Bennetts Copse, Chis. 174 B6
Bennetts Way, Croy. 203 H2
Bennetts Yd. SW1 25 J6
Benningholme Rd., Edg. 54 E6
Bennington Rd. N17 76 B1
Bennington Rd., Wdf.Grn. 62 E7
Benn's Wk., Rich. 145 H4
  Rosedale Rd.
Benrek Cl., Ilf. 81 F1
Bensbury Cl. SW15 147 H7
Bensham Cl., Th.Hth. 187 J4
Bensham Gro., Th.Hth. 187 J2
Bensham La., Croy. 187 H7
Bensham La., Th.Hth. 187 H4
Bensham Manor Rd., Th.Hth. 187 J4
Bensington Ct., Felt. 141 G6
Bensley Cl. N11 57 J5
Benson Av. E6 115 J2
Benson Cl., Houns. 143 G4
Benson Quay E1 113 F7
  Garnet St.
Benson Rd. SE23 171 F1
Benson Rd., Croy. 201 G3
Bentfield Gdns. SE9 173 J3
  Aldersgrove Av.
Benthal Rd. N16 94 D2
Bentham Ct. N1 93 J7
  Rotherfield St.
Bentham Rd. E9 95 G6
Bentham Rd. SE28 118 B7
Bentham Wk. NW10 88 C5
Bentinck Ms. W1 16 C3
Bentinck Pl. NW8 7 G2
Bentinck St. W1 16 C3
Bentinck St. W1 110 A6
Bentley Dr. NW2 90 C3
Bentley Dr., Ilf. 81 F6
Bentley Ms., Enf. 44 A6
Bentley Rd. N1 94 B6
  Tottenham Rd.
Bentley Way, Stan. 52 D5

Bentley Way, Wdf.Grn. 63 G2
Benton Rd., Ilf. 99 G1
Benton Rd., Wat. 50 D5
Bentons La. SE27 169 J4
Bentons Ri. SE27 170 A5
Bentry Cl., Dag. 101 E2
Bentry Rd., Dag. 101 E2
Bentworth Rd. W12 107 H6
Benwell Ct., Sun. 178 A1
Benwell Rd. N7 93 G4
Benwick Cl. SE16 133 E3
Benworth St. E3 113 J3
Benyon Rd. N1 112 A1
Southgate Rd.
Berber Rd. SW11 149 J5
Berberis Wk., West Dr. 120 B4
Berberry Cl., Edg. 54 C4
Larkspur Gro.
Bercta Rd. SE9 175 F2
Bere St. E1 113 G7
Cranford St.
Berenger Wk. SW10 30 E7
Berens Rd. NW10 108 A3
Berens Way, Chis. 193 J4
Beresford Av. N20 57 J2
Beresford Av. W7 104 A5
Beresford Av., Surb. 196 B1
Beresford Av., Twick. 145 F6
Beresford Av., Wem. 105 J1
Beresford Dr., Brom. 192 A3
Beresford Dr., Wdf.Grn. 63 J4
Beresford Gdns., Enf. 44 B4
Beresford Gdns., Houns. 143 F5
Beresford Gdns., Rom. 83 E5
Beresford Rd. E4 62 E1
Beresford Rd. E17 78 B1
Beresford Rd. N2 73 H3
Beresford Rd. N5 93 J5
Beresford Rd. N8 75 G5
Beresford Rd., Har. 68 A5
Beresford Rd., Kings.T. 181 J1
Beresford Rd., N.Mal. 182 C4
Beresford Rd., Sthl. 122 D1
Beresford Rd., Sutt. 198 C7
Beresford Sq. SE18 136 E4
Beresford St. SE18 136 E3
Beresford Ter. N5 93 J5
Berestede Rd. W6 127 F5
Bergen Sq. SE16 133 H3
Norway Gate
Berger Cl., Orp. 193 G6
Berger Rd. E9 95 G6
Berghem Ms. W14 128 A3
Blythe Rd.
Bergholt Av., Ilf. 80 B5
Bergholt Cres. N16 76 B7
Bergholt Ms. NW1 92 C7
Rossendale Way
Bering Sq. E14 134 A5
Napier Av.
Bering Wk. E16 116 A6
Berisford Ms. SW18 149 F6
Berkeley Av., Bexh. 158 D1
Berkeley Av., Grnf. 86 B6
Berkeley Av., Houns. 142 A2
Berkeley Av., Ilf. 80 D2
Berkeley Cl., Borwd. 38 A5
Berkeley Cl., Kings.T. 163 H7
Berkeley Cl., Orp. 193 H7
Berkeley Cl., Ruis. 84 A3
Berkeley Ct. N14 42 C6
Berkeley Ct., Wall. 200 C3
Berkeley Cres., Barn. 41 G5
Berkeley Dr., W.Mol. 179 F3
Berkeley Gdns. N21 44 A7
Berkeley Gdns. W8 128 D1
Brunswick Gdns.
Berkeley Gdns., Esher 194 D6
Berkeley Ho. E3 114 A4
Berkeley Ms. W1 16 A3
Berkeley Pl. SW19 166 A6
Berkeley Rd. E12 98 B5
Berkeley Rd. N8 74 D5
Berkeley Rd. N15 76 A6
Berkeley Rd. NW9 70 A4
Berkeley Rd. SW13 147 G1
Berkeley Sq. W1 16 E6
Berkeley Sq. W1 110 B7
Berkeley St. W1 17 E6
Berkeley St. W1 110 B7
Berkeley Wk. N7 93 F2
Durham Rd.
Berkeley Waye, Houns. 122 D7
Berkhampstead Rd., Belv. 139 G5
Berkhamsted Av., Wem. 87 J6
Berkley Gro. NW1 91 J7
Berkley Rd.
Berkley Rd. NW1 91 J7
Berkshire Gdns. N13 59 G6
Berkshire Gdns. N18 60 E5
Berkshire Rd. E9 95 J6
Berkshire Sq., Mitch. 186/187 E4
Berkshire Way
Berkshire Way, Mitch. 186 E4
Bermans Way NW10 89 E4
Bermondsey Sq. SE1 28 E5
Bermondsey St. SE1 28 D2
Bermondsey St. SE1 132 B2
Bermondsey Wall E. SE16 29 J4
Bermondsey Wall E. SE16 132 D2
Bermondsey Wall W. SE16 29 H3
Bermondsey Wall W. SE16 132 D2
Bernal Cl. SE28 118 D7
Haldane Rd.
Bernard Ashley Dr. SE7 135 H5
Bernard Av. W13 125 E3
Bernard Cassidy St. E16 115 F5
Bernard Gdns. SW19 166 C5
Bernard Rd. N15 76 C5
Bernard Rd., Rom. 83 J7
Bernard Rd., Wall. 200 B4
Bernard St. WC1 10 A6
Bernard St. WC1 110 E4
Bernards Cl., Ilf. 65 F6
Bernays Cl., Stan. 53 F6
Bernays Gro. SW9 151 F4
Berne Rd., Th.Hth. 187 J5
Bernel Dr., Croy. 203 J3
Berners Dr. W13 104 D6
Berners Ms. W1 17 G2
Berners Ms. W1 110 C5
Berners Pl. W1 17 G3
Berners Pl. W1 110 C6
Berners Rd. N1 11 F1
Berners Rd. N1 111 G1
Berners Rd. N22 75 G1
Berners St. W1 17 G2
Berners St. W1 110 C5
Bernersmede SE3 155 G3
Blackheath Pk.
Berney Rd., Croy. 188 A7
Bernhart Cl., Edg. 54 C7
Orange Hill Rd.
Bernville Way, Har. 69 J5
Kenton Rd.
Bernwell Rd. E4 63 E3
Berridge Grn., Edg. 54 A7
Berridge Ms. NW6 90 D5
Hillfield Rd.
Berridge Rd. SE19 170 A5
Berriman Rd. N7 93 F3
Berriton Rd., Har. 85 F1
Berry Cl. N21 59 H1
Berry Cl. NW10 88 E7
Berry Ct., Houns. 143 F5
Berry Hill, Stan. 53 G4
Berry La. SE21 170 A4
Berry Pl. EC1 11 H4
Berry St. EC1 11 H5
Berry St. EC1 111 H4
Berry Way W5 125 H3
Berrybank Cl. E4 62 C2
Greenbank Cl.
Berrydale Rd., Hayes 102 E4
Berryfield Cl. E17 78 B4
Berryfield Cl., Brom. 192 B1
Berryfield Rd. SE17 35 H3
Berryfield Rd. SE17 131 H5
Berryhill SE9 156 E4
Berryhill Gdns. SE9 156 E4
Berrylands SW20 183 J3
Berrylands, Surb. 182 A5
Berrylands Rd., Surb. 181 J6
Berryman Cl., Dag. 100 C3
Bennetts Castle La.
Berrymans La. SE26 171 G4
Berrymead Gdns. W3 126 C1
Berrymede Rd. W4 126 D3
Bert Rd., Th.Hth. 187 J5
Bertal Rd. SW17 167 G4
Berthon St. SE8 134 A7
Bertie Rd. NW10 89 G6
Bertie Rd. SE26 171 G6
Bertram Cotts. SW19 166 D7
Hartfield Rd.
Bertram Rd. NW4 71 G6
Bertram Rd., Enf. 44 D4
Bertram Rd., Kings.T. 164 A7
Bertram St. N19 92 B2
Bertram Way, Enf. 44 C4
Bertrand St. SE13 154 B3
Bertrand Way SE28 118 B7
Berwick Av., Hayes 102 D6
Berwick Cl., Stan. 52 C7
Gordon Av.
Berwick Cres., Sid. 157 H6
Berwick Rd. E16 115 H6
Berwick Rd. N22 75 H1
Berwick Rd., Well. 158 B1
Berwick St. W1 17 H4
Berwick St. W1 110 D6
Berwyn Av., Houns. 143 H1
Berwyn Rd. SE24 169 H1
Berwyn Rd., Rich. 146 B4
Beryl Av. E6 116 B5
Beryl Ho. SE18 137 J5
Spinel Cl.
Beryl Rd. W6 128 A5
Berystede, Kings.T. 164 B7
Besant Ct. N1 94 A5
Newington Grn. Rd.
Besant Rd. NW2 90 B4
Besant Wk. N7 93 F2
Newington Barrow Way
Besant Way NW10 88 C5
Besley St. SW16 168 C6
Bessant Dr., Rich. 146 B1
Bessborough Gdns. SW1 33 J3
Bessborough Gdns. SW1 130 D5
Bessborough Pl. SW1 33 J3
Bessborough Pl. SW1 130 D5
Bessborough Rd. SW15 165 G1
Bessborough Rd., Har. 86 A1
Bessborough St. SW1 33 H3
Bessborough St. SW1 130 D5
Bessemer Rd. SE5 151 J2
Bessie Lansbury Cl. E6 116 D6
Bessingby Rd., Ruis. 84 A2
Bessingham Wk. SE4 153 G4
Frendsbury Rd.
Besson St. SE14 153 F1
Bessy St. E2 113 F3
Roman Rd.
Bestwood St. SE8 133 G4
Beswick Ms. NW6 90/91 E6
Lymington Rd.
Betam Rd., Hayes 121 G2
Betchworth Cl., Sutt. 199 G5
Turnpike La.
Betchworth Rd., Ilf. 99 H2
Betham Rd., Grnf. 104 A3
Bethany Waye, Felt. 141 H7
Bethecar Rd., Har. 68 B5
Bethel Rd., Well. 158 C3
Bethell Av. E16 115 F4
Bethell Av., Ilf. 80 D7
Bethersden Cl., Beck. 171 J7
Bethnal Grn. Rd. E1 13 F5
Bethnal Grn. Rd. E1 112 C4
Bethnal Grn. Rd. E2 13 F5
Bethnal Grn. Rd. E2 112 C4
Bethune Av. N11 57 J4
Bethune Rd. N16 76 A7
Bethune Rd. NW10 106 D4
Bethwin Rd. SE5 35 H7
Bethwin Rd. SE5 131 H7
Betjeman Cl., Pnr. 67 G4
Betony Cl., Croy. 203 G1
Primrose La.
Betoyne Av. E4 62 E4
Betstyle Rd. N11 58 B4
Betterton Dr., Sid. 177 E2
Betterton St. WC2 18 A4
Betterton St. WC2 111 E6
Bettons Pk. E15 115 E1
Bettridge Rd. SW6 148 C2
Betts Cl., Beck. 189 H2
Kendall Rd.
Betts Ms. E17 77 J6
Queen's Rd.
Betts Rd. E16 115 H7
Victoria Dock Rd.
Betts St. E1 112/113 E7
The Highway
Betts Way SE20 189 E1
Betts Way, Surb. 195 E1
Beulah Av., Th.Hth. 187 F4
Beulah Rd.
Beulah Cl., Edg. 54 B3
Beulah Cres., Th.Hth. 187 J2
Beulah Gro., Croy. 187 J6
Beulah Hill SE19 169 H6
Beulah Path E17 78 B5
Addison Rd.
Beulah Rd. E17 78 B5
Beulah Rd. SW19 166 C7
Beulah Rd., Sutt. 198 D4
Beulah Rd., Th.Hth. 187 J3
Bev Callender Cl. SW8 150 B3
Daley Thompson Way
Bevan Av., Bark. 100 A7
Bevan Ct., Croy. 201 G5
Bevan Rd. SE2 138 B5
Bevan Rd., Barn. 41 J4
Bevan St. N1 111 J1
Bevenden St. N1 12 C3
Bevenden St. N1 112 A3
Bevercote Wk., Belv. 139 F6
Osborne Rd.
Beveridge Rd. NW10 88/89 E7
Curzon Cres.
Beverley Av. SW20 183 F1
Beverley Av., Houns. 143 F4
Beverley Av., Sid. 157 J7
Beverley Cl. N21 59 J1
Beverley Cl. SW11 149 G4
Maysoule Rd.
Beverley Cl. SW13 147 F2
Beverley Cl., Chess. 195 F4
Beverley Cl., Enf. 44 B4
Beverley Cotts. SW15 164 D4
Kingston Vale
Beverley Ct. N14 42 C7
Beverley Ct. SE4 153 J3
Beverley Cres., Wdf.Grn. 79 H1
Beverley Dr., Edg. 70 B3
Beverley Gdns. NW11 72 B7
Beverley Gdns. SW13 147 F3
Beverley Gdns., Stan. 68 D1
Beverley Gdns., Wem. 87 J1
Beverley Gdns., Wor.Pk. 197 G1
Green La.
Beverley Ho. NW8 7 G4
Beverley La. SW15 165 F3
Beverley La., Kings.T. 165 E7
Beverley Ms. E4 62 D6
Beverley Rd.
Beverley Path SW13 147 F2
Beverley Rd. E4 62 D6
Beverley Rd. E6 116 A3
Beverley Rd. SE20 188/189 E2
Wadhurst Cl.
Beverley Rd. SW13 147 F3
Beverley Rd. W4 127 F5
Beverley Rd., Bexh. 159 J2
Beverley Rd., Brom. 206 B2
Beverley Rd., Dag. 101 E4
Beverley Rd., Kings.T. 181 F1
Beverley Rd., Mitch. 186 D4
Beverley Rd., N.Mal. 183 G4
Beverley Rd., Ruis. 84 A2
Beverley Rd., Sthl. 123 E3
Beverley Rd., Wor.Pk. 197 J2
Beverley Way SW20 183 F1
Beverley Way, N.Mal. 183 F1
Beversbrook Rd. N19 92 D3
Beverston Ms. W1 15 J2
Beverstone Rd. SW2 151 F5
Beverstone Rd., Th.Hth. 187 G4
Bevill Allen Cl. SW17 167 J5
Bevill Cl. SE25 188 D3
Bevin Cl. SE16 133 H1
Stave Yd. Rd.
Bevin Ct. WC1 111 G3
Holford St.
Bevin Rd., Hayes 102 A3
Bevin Sq. SW17 167 J3
Bevin Way WC1 10 E3
Bevington Rd. W10 108 B5
Bevington Rd., Beck. 190 B2
Bevington St. SE16 29 J4
Bevington St. SE16 132 D2
Bevis Marks EC3 20 E3
Bevis Marks EC3 112 B6
Bewcastle Gdns., Enf. 43 E4
Bewdley St. N1 93 G7
Bewick St. SW8 150 B2
Bewley St. E1 112/113 E7
Dellow St.
Bewlys Rd. SE27 169 H5
Bexhill Cl., Felt. 160 E2
Bexhill Rd. N11 58 D5
Bexhill Rd. SE4 153 J6
Bexhill Rd. SW14 146 C3
Bexhill Wk. E15 114/115 E2
Mitre Rd.
Bexley Gdns. N9 60 A3

Bexley Gdns., Rom. 82 B5
Bexley High St., Bex. 159 G7
Bexley La., Sid. 176 C3
Bexley Rd. SE9 156 E5
Bexley Rd., Erith 139 J7
Beynon Rd., Cars. 199 J5
Bianca Ho. N1 112 B2
Crondall St.
Bianca Rd. SE15 37 H6
Bianca Rd. SE15 132 C6
Bibsworth Rd. N3 72 C2
Bibury Cl. SE15 37 E6
Bibury Cl. SE15 132 B6
Bicester Rd., Rich. 146 A3
Bickenhall St. W1 16 A1
Bickenhall St. W1 109 J5
Bickersteth Rd. SW17 167 J6
Bickerton Rd. N19 92 C2
Bickley Cres., Brom. 192 B4
Bickley Pk. Rd., Brom. 192 B3
Bickley Rd. E10 78 B7
Bickley Rd., Brom. 192 A2
Bickley St. SW17 167 H5
Bicknell Rd. SE5 151 J3
Bicknoller Rd., Enf. 44 C1
Bicknor Rd., Orp. 193 H7
Bidborough Cl., Brom. 191 F5
Bidborough St. WC1 10 A4
Bidborough St. WC1 110 D3
Biddenden Way SE9 174 D4
Bidder St. E16 114 E5
Biddestone Rd. N7 93 F4
Biddulph Rd. W9 6 A4
Biddulph Rd. W9 108 E3
Bideford Av., Grnf. 104 E2
Bideford Cl., Edg. 70 A1
Bideford Cl., Felt. 161 F3
Bideford Gdns., Enf. 44 B7
Bideford Rd., Brom. 173 F3
Bideford Rd., Ruis. 84 B3
Bideford Rd., Well. 138 B7
Bidwell Gdns. N11 58 C7
Bidwell St. SE15 153 E1
Big Hill E5 95 E1
Bigbury Cl. N17 60 A7
Weir Hall Rd.
Bigbury Rd. N17 60 B7
Barkham Rd.
Biggerstaff Rd. E15 114 C1
Biggerstaff St. N4 93 G2
Biggin Av., Mitch. 185 J1
Biggin Hill SE19 169 H7
Biggin Hill Cl., Kings.T. 163 F5
Biggin Way SE19 169 H7
Bigginwood Rd. SW16 169 H7
Biggs Row SW15 148 A3
Felsham Rd.
Bigland St. E1 112 E6
Bignell Rd. SE18 136 E5
Bignold Rd. E7 97 G4
Bigwood Rd. NW11 72 E5
Bill Hamling Cl. SE9 174 C2
Bill Nicholson Way N17 76 C3
High Rd.
Billet Cl., Rom. 82 D3
Billet Rd. E17 77 G2
Billet Rd., Rom. 82 B3
Billets Hart Cl. W7 124 B2
Billing Pl. SW10 30 B7
Billing Pl. SW10 129 E7
Billing Rd. SW10 30 B7
Billing Rd. SW10 129 E7
Billing St. SW10 30 B7
Billing St. SW10 129 E7
Billingford Cl. SE4 153 G4
Billings Cl., Dag. 100 C7
Ellerton Rd.
Billington Rd. SE14 133 G7
Billiter Sq. EC3 20 E5
Billiter St. EC3 20 E4
Billiter St. EC3 112 B6
Billockby Cl., Chess. 195 J6
Billson St. E14 134 C4
Bilsby Gro. SE9 174 A4
Bilton Rd., Grnf. 105 F1
Bilton Way, Enf. 45 H1
Bilton Way, Hayes 122 B2
Bina Gdns. SW5 30 C2
Bina Gdns. SW5 129 F4
Bincote Rd., Enf. 43 F3
Binden Rd. W12 127 F3
Bindon Grn., Mord. 185 E4
Binfield Rd. SW4 151 E1
Binfield Rd., S.Croy. 202 C5
Bingfield St. N1 111 E1
Bingham Ct. N1 93 H7
Halton Rd.
Bingham Pl. W1 16 B1
Bingham Rd., Croy. 202 D1
Bingham St. N1 94 A6
Bingley Rd. E16 115 J6
Bingley Rd., Grnf. 103 J5
Bingley Rd., Sun. 160 A7
Binney St. W1 16 C5
Binney St. W1 110 A6
Binns Rd. W4 126 E5
Binns Ter. W4 126/127 E5
Binns Rd.
Binsey Wk. SE2 138 C1
Binyon Cres., Stan. 52 C5
Birbetts Rd. SE9 174 C2
Birch Av. N13 59 J3
Birch Cl. E16 115 E5
Birch Cl. N19 92 C2
Hargrave Pk.
Birch Cl. SE15 152 D2
Bournemouth Rd.
Birch Cl., Brent. 124 E7
Birch Cl., Buck.H. 64 A3
Birch Cl., Houns. 144 A3
Birch Cl., Rom. 83 H3
Birch Cl., Tedd. 162 D5
Birch Gdns., Dag. 101 J3
Birch Grn. NW9 54/55 E7
Clayton Fld.
Birch Gro. E11 96 E3
Birch Gro. SE12 155 F7
Birch Gro. W3 126 A1
Birch Gro., Well. 158 A4
Birch Hill, Croy. 203 G5
Birch Mead, Orp. 206 D2
Birch Pk., Har. 51 J7
Birch Rd., Felt. 160 D5
Birch Rd., Rom. 83 H3
Birch Row, Brom. 192 D7
Birch Tree Av., W.Wick. 205 F5
Birch Tree Way, Croy. 202 E2
Birch Wk., Borwd. 38 A1
Birch Wk., Erith 139 J6
Birch Wk., Mitch. 186 B1
Bircham Path SE4 153 G4
St. Norbert Rd.
Birchanger Rd. SE25 188 D5
Birchdale Gdns., Rom. 82 D7
Birchdale Rd. E7 97 J5
Birchdene Dr. SE28 138 A2
Birchen Cl. NW9 88 D2
Birchen Gro. NW9 88 D2
Birchend Cl., S.Croy. 202 A6
Birches, The N21 43 F6
Birches, The SE7 135 H6
Birches, The, Orp. 206 D4
Birches Cl., Mitch. 185 J3
Birches Cl., Pnr. 66 E5
Birchfield St. E14 114 A7
Birchin La. EC3 20 C4
Birchin La. EC3 112 A6
Birchington Cl., Bexh. 159 H1
Birchington Rd. N8 74 D6
Birchington Rd. NW6 108 D1
Birchington Rd., Surb. 181 J7
Birchlands Av. SW12 149 J7
Birchmead Av., Pnr. 66 C4
Birchmere Row SE3 155 F2
Birchmore Wk. N5 93 J3
Birchville Ct., Bushey 52 B1
Heathbourne Rd.
Birchway, Hayes 122 A1
Birchwood Av. N10 74 A3
Birchwood Av., Beck. 189 J4
Birchwood Av., Sid. 176 B2
Birchwood Av., Wall. 200 A3
Birchwood Cl., Mord. 184 E4
Birchwood Ct. N13 59 H5
Birchwood Ct., Edg. 70 C2
Birchwood Dr. NW3 91 E3
Birchwood Gro., Hmptn. 161 G6
Birchwood Rd. SW17 168 B5
Birchwood Rd., Orp. 193 G4
Bird in Bush Rd. SE15 132 D7
Bird St. W1 16 C4
Bird Wk., Twick. 161 F1
Bird-in-Hand La., Brom. 192 A2
Bird-in-Hand Pas. SE23 171 F2
Dartmouth Rd.
Birdbrook Cl., Dag. 101 J7
Birdbrook Rd. SE3 155 J3
Birdcage Wk. SW1 25 G4
Birdcage Wk. SW1 130 C2
Birdham Cl., Brom. 192 B5
Birdhurst Av., S.Croy. 202 A4
Birdhurst Gdns., S.Croy. 202 A4
Birdhurst Ri., S.Croy. 202 B5
Birdhurst Rd. SW18 149 F4
Birdhurst Rd. SW19 167 H6
Birdhurst Rd., S.Croy 202 B5
Birdlip Cl. SE15 36 D6
Birdlip Cl. SE15 132 B6
Birds Fm. Av., Rom. 83 H1
Birdsfield La. E3 113 J1
Birdwood Cl., Tedd. 162 B4
Birkbeck Av. W3 106 C7
Birkbeck Av., Grnf. 103 J1
Birkbeck Gdns., Wdf.Grn. 63 F2
Birkbeck Gro. W3 126 D2
Birkbeck Hill SE21 169 H2
Birkbeck Ms. E8 94 C5
Sandringham Rd.
Birkbeck Pl. SE21 169 J1
Birkbeck Rd. E8 94 C5
Birkbeck Rd. N8 75 E4
Birkbeck Rd. N12 57 F5
Birkbeck Rd. N17 76 C1
Birkbeck Rd. NW7 55 F5
Birkbeck Rd. SW19 167 E5
Birkbeck Rd. W3 126 D1
Birkbeck Rd. W5 125 F4
Birkbeck Rd., Beck. 189 F2
Birkbeck Rd., Enf. 44 A1
Birkbeck Rd., Ilf. 81 G5
Birkbeck Rd., Sid. 176 A3
Birkbeck St. E2 113 E3
Birkbeck Way, Grnf. 103 J1
Birkdale Av., Pnr. 67 G3
Birkdale Cl. SE16 132/133 E5
Masters Dr.
Birkdale Cl., Orp. 193 G7
Birkdale Gdns., Croy. 203 G4
Birkdale Gdns., Wat. 50 D3
Birkdale Rd. SE2 138 A4
Birkdale Rd. W5 105 H5
Birkenhead Av., Kings.T. 181 J2
Birkenhead St. WC1 10 B3
Birkenhead St. WC1 111 E3
Birkhall Rd. SE6 172 D1
Birkwood Cl. SW12 150 D7
Birley Rd. N20 57 F2
Birley St. SW11 150 A2
Birnam Rd. N4 93 F2
Birse Cres. NW10 89 E4
Birstall Grn., Wat. 50 D4
Birstall Rd. N15 76 B5
Biscay Rd. W6 128 A5
Biscoe Cl., Houns. 123 G6
Biscoe Way SE13 154 D3
Bisenden Rd., Croy. 202 B2
Bisham Cl., Cars. 199 J1
Bisham Gdns. N6 92 A1
Bishop Butt Cl., Orp. 207 J3
Stapleton Rd.
Bishop Cl. W4 126 C5
Bishop Fox Way, W.Mol. 179 F4
Bishop Ken Rd., Har. 68 C2
Bishop Kings Rd. W14 128 B4
Bishop Rd. N14 42 B7
Bishop St. N1 111 J1
Bishop Way NW10 88 E7
Bishop Wilfred Wd. Cl. SE15 152 D2
Moncrieff St.
Bishop's Av. E13 115 H1
Bishop's Av. SW6 148 A2
Bishops Av., Brom. 191 J2
Bishops Av., Rom. 82 C6
Bishops Av., The N2 73 G7
Bishops Br. W2 14 D2
Bishops Br. W2 109 F5
Bishops Br. Rd. W2 14 B4
Bishops Br. Rd. W2 109 F6
Bishops Cl. E17 78 B4
Bishops Cl. N19 92 C3
Wyndham Cres.
Bishops Cl. SE9 175 F2
Bishops Cl., Barn. 40 A6
Bishops Cl., Enf. 44/45 E2
Central Av.
Bishops Cl., Rich. 163 G3
Bishop's Cl., Sutt. 198 D3
Bishop's Ct. EC4 19 G3
Bishop's Ct. WC2 18 E3
Bishops Dr., Felt. 141 G6
Bishops Dr., Nthlt. 103 E1
Bishops Gro. N2 73 G6
Bishops Gro., Hmptn. 161 F4
Bishop's Hall, Kings.T. 181 G2
Bishops Hill, Walt. 178 A7
Bishop's Pk. SW6 148 A2
Bishop's Pk. Rd. SW6 148 A2
Bishops Pk. Rd. SW16 187 E1
Bishops Pl., Sutt. 199 F5
Lind Rd.
Bishops Rd. N6 74 A6
Bishops Rd. SW6 148 C1
Bishops Rd. W7 124 B2
Bishops Rd., Croy. 187 H7
Bishops Ter. SE11 35 F1
Bishops Ter. SE11 131 G4
Bishops Wk., Chis. 193 F1
Bishops Wk., Croy. 203 G5
Bishop's Wk., Pnr. 66/67 E3
High St.
Bishops Way E2 113 E2
Bishopsford Rd., Mord. 185 F7
Bishopsgate EC2 20 E2
Bishopsgate EC2 112 B6
Bishopsgate Arc. EC2 20 E2
Bishopsgate Chyd. EC2 20 D3
Bishopsthorpe Rd. SE26 171 G4
Bishopswood Rd. N6 73 J7
Bisley Cl., Wor.Pk. 197 J1
Bispham Rd. NW10 105 J3
Bisson Rd. E15 114 C2
Bisterne Av. E17 78 D3
Bittacy Cl. NW7 56 A6
Bittacy Hill NW7 56 A6
Bittacy Pk. Av. NW7 56 A6
Bittacy Ri. NW7 55 J6
Bittacy Rd. NW7 56 A6
Bittern Cl., Hayes 102 D5
Bittern St. SE1 27 J4
Bittoms, The, Kings.T. 181 G3
Bixley Cl., Sthl. 123 F4
Black Boy La. N15 75 J5
Black Fan Cl., Enf. 43 J1
Black Friars Ct. EC4 19 G5
Black Friars La. EC4 19 G5
Black Friars La. EC4 111 H7
Black Gates, Pnr. 67 F3
Church La.
Black Horse Ct. SE1 28 C5
Black Lion La. W6 127 G4
Black Lion Ms. W6 127 G4
Black Lion La.
Black Path E10 77 G7
Black Prince Rd. SE1 34 C2
Black Prince Rd. SE1 131 F4
Black Prince Rd. SE11 34 D2
Black Prince Rd. SE11 131 F4
Black Rod Cl., Hayes 121 J3
Black Swan Yd. SE1 28 E3
Blackall St. EC2 12 D5
Blackberry Fm. Cl., Houns. 122 E7
Blackbird Hill NW9 88 C2
Blackbird Yd. E2 13 G3
Blackborne Rd., Dag. 101 G6
Blackbrook La., Brom. 192 D3
Blackburn Rd. NW6 90 E6
Blackburn Trd. Est., Stai. 140 C6
Blackburne's Ms. W1 16 B5
Blackburne's Ms. W1 110 A7
Blackbush Av., Rom. 82 D5
Blackbush Cl., Sutt. 199 E7
Blackdown Cl. N2 73 F2
Blackdown Ter. SE18 136 D7
Prince Imperial Rd.
Blackett St. SW15 148 A3
Blackfen Rd., Sid. 157 H5
Blackford Rd., Wat. 50 D5
Blackford's Path SW15 147 G7
Roehampton High St.
Blackfriars Br. EC4 19 G5
Blackfriars Br. EC4 111 H7
Blackfriars Br. SE1 19 G5
Blackfriars Br. SE1 111 H7
Blackfriars Pas. EC4 19 G5
Blackfriars Rd. SE1 27 G4
Blackfriars Rd. SE1 131 H1
Blackheath Av. SE10 134 D7
Blackheath Gro. SE3 155 F2
Blackheath Hill SE10 154 C1
Blackheath Pk. SE3 155 F3
Blackheath Ri. SE13 154 C2
Blackheath Rd. SE10 154 B1
Blackheath Vale SE3 155 E2
Blackheath Village SE3 155 F2
Blackhorse La. E17 77 G4
Blackhorse La., Croy. 188 D7
Blackhorse Ms. E17 77 G3
Blackhorse La.
Blackhorse Rd. E17 77 G4
Blackhorse Rd. SE8 133 H5

Blackhorse Rd., Sid. 176 A4
Blacklands Rd. SE6 172 C4
Blacklands Ter. SW3 31 J2
Blacklands Ter. SW3 129 J4
Blackmore Av., Sthl. 124 A1
Blackmore Rd., Buck.H. 48 B7
Blackmores Gro., Tedd. 162 D6
Blackpool Rd. SE15 152 E2
Blacks Rd. W6 127 J4
Queen Caroline St.
Blackshaw Pl. N1 94 B7
Hertford Rd.
Blackshaw Rd. SW17 167 F4
Blacksmiths Cl., Rom. 82 C6
Blackstock Ms. N4 93 H2
Blackstock Rd.
Blackstock Rd. N4 93 H2
Blackstock Rd. N5 93 H2
Blackstone Est. E8 94 E7
Blackstone Rd. NW2 89 J5
Blackthorn Av., West Dr. 120 D4
Blackthorn Ct., Houns. 122 E7
Blackthorn Gro., Bexh. 158 E3
Blackthorn St. E3 114 A4
Blackthorne Av., Croy. 189 F7
Blackthorne Dr. E4 62 D4
Blacktree Ms. SW9 151 G3
Blackwall La. SE10 135 E5
Blackwall Pier E14 114 E7
Blackwall Tunnel E14 134 D1
Blackwall Tunnel App. SE10 134 E2
Blackwall Tunnel Northern App. E3 114 A2
Blackwall Tunnel Northern App. E14 114 A2
Blackwall Way E14 114 C7
Blackwater Cl. E7 97 F4
Blackwater Rd., Sutt. 198/199 E4
High St.
Blackwater St. SE22 152 C5
Blackwell Cl. E5 95 G4
Blackwell Cl., Har. 52 A7
Blackwell Gdns., Edg. 54 A3
Blackwood St. SE17 36 B3
Blackwood St. SE17 132 A5
Blade Ms. SW15 148 C4
Deodar Rd.
Blades Ct. SW15 148 C4
Deodar Rd.
Bladindon Dr., Bex. 158 C7
Bladon Gdns., Har. 67 H6
Blagdens Cl. N14 58 C2
Blagdens La. N14 58 D2
Blagdon Rd. SE13 154 B6
Blagdon Rd., N.Mal. 183 F4
Blagdon Wk., Tedd. 163 F6
Blagrove Rd. W10 108 B5
Blair Av. NW9 70 E7
Blair Cl. N1 93 J6
Blair Cl., Hayes 122 A4
Blair Cl., Sid. 157 H5
Blair St. E14 114 C6
Blairderry Rd. SW2 169 E2
Blairhead Dr., Wat. 50 B3
Blake Av., Bark. 117 H1
Blake Cl. W10 107 J5
Blake Cl., Cars. 185 H7
Blake Cl., Well. 157 H1
Blake Gdns. SW6 148 E1
Blake Hall Cres. E11 97 G1
Blake Hall Rd. E11 79 G7
Blake Ho., Beck. 172 A6
Blake Rd. E16 115 F4
Blake Rd. N11 58 C7
Blake Rd., Croy. 202 B2
Blake Rd., Mitch. 185 H3
Blake St. SE8 134 A6
Watergate St.
Blakeden Dr., Esher 194 C6
Blakehall Rd., Cars. 199 J6
Blakeley Cotts. SE10 134 D2
Tunnel Av.
Blakemore Rd. SW16 168 E3
Blakemore Rd., Th.Hth. 187 F5
Blakemore Way, Belv. 139 E3
Blakeney Av., Beck. 189 J1
Blakeney Cl. E8 94 D5
Ferncliff Rd.
Blakeney Cl. N20 57 F1
Blakeney Cl. NW1 92 D7
Rossendale Way
Blakeney Rd., Beck. 171 J7
Blakenham Rd. SW17 167 J4
Blaker Ct. SE7 135 J7
Fairlawn
Blaker Rd. E15 114 C1
Blakes Av., N.Mal. 183 F5
Blake's Grn., W.Wick. 204 C1
Blakes La., N.Mal. 183 F5
Blakes Rd. SE15 36 E7
Blakes Rd. SE15 132 B7
Blakes Ter., N.Mal. 183 G5
Blakesley Av. W5 105 F6
Blakesley Wk. SW20 184 C2
Kingston Rd.
Blakesware Gdns. N9 44 A7
Blakewood Cl., Felt. 160 C4
Blanch Cl. SE15 133 F7
Culmore Rd.
Blanchard Cl. SE9 174 B3
Blanchard Way E8 94 D6
Blanche St. E16 115 F4
Blanchedowne SE5 152 A4
Blanchland Rd., Mord. 184 E5
Bland St. SE9 156 A4
Blandfield Rd. SW12 150 A6
Blandford Av., Beck. 189 H2
Blandford Av., Twick. 161 H1
Blandford Cl. N2 73 F4
Blandford Cl., Croy. 201 E3
Blandford Cl., Rom. 83 H4
Blandford Cres. E4 46 C7
Blandford Rd. W4 126 E3
Blandford Rd. W5 125 G2
Blandford Rd., Beck. 189 F2
Blandford Rd., Sthl. 123 G4
Blandford Rd., Tedd. 162 A5
Blandford Sq. NW1 7 H6
Blandford Sq. NW1 109 H4
Blandford St. W1 16 A3
Blandford St. W1 110 A5
Blandford Waye, Hayes 102 C6
Blaney Cres. E6 116 E3
Blanmerle Rd. SE9 174 E1
Blann Cl. SE9 156 A6
Blantyre St. SW10 30 E7
Blantyre St. SW10 129 G7
Blantyre Wk. SW10 30 E7
Blashford NW3 91 J7
Blashford St. SE13 154 D7
Blasker Wk. E14 134 A5
Blawith Rd., Har. 68 B4
Blaydon Cl. N17 60 E7
Blaydon Wk. N17 60 E7
Bleak Hill La. SE18 137 J6
Blean Gro. SE20 171 F7
Bleasdale Av., Grnf. 104 D2
Blechynden St. W10 108 A7
Bramley Rd.
Bleddyn Cl., Sid. 158 C6
Bledlow Cl. SE28 118 C7
Bledlow Ri., Grnf. 103 J2
Bleeding Heart Yd. EC1 19 F2
Blegborough Rd. SW16 168 C6
Blendon Dr., Bex. 158 D6
Blendon Path, Brom. 173 F7
Blendon Rd., Bex. 158 D6
Blendon Ter. SE18 137 F5
Blendworth Way SE15 37 E7
Blenheim Av., Ilf. 80 D6
Blenheim Cl. N21 59 J1
Elm Pk. Rd.
Blenheim Cl. SW20 183 J3
Blenheim Cl., Grnf. 104 A2
Leaver Gdns.
Blenheim Cl., Rom. 83 J4
Blenheim Cl., Wall. 200 C7
Blenheim Ct. N19 92/93 E2
Marlborough Rd.
Blenheim Ct., Sid. 175 G3
Blenheim Cres. W11 108 B6
Blenheim Cres., S.Croy. 201 J7
Blenheim Dr., Well. 157 J1
Blenheim Gdns. NW2 89 J5
Blenheim Gdns. SW2 151 F6
Blenheim Gdns., Kings.T. 164 B7
Blenheim Gdns., Wall. 200 C6
Blenheim Gdns., Wem. 87 H3
Blenheim Gro. SE15 152 D2
Blenheim Pas. NW8 6 C1
Blenheim Ri. N15 76 C4
Talbot Rd.
Blenheim Rd. E6 116 A3
Blenheim Rd. E15 97 E4
Blenheim Rd. E17 77 G3
Blenheim Rd. NW8 6 C1
Blenheim Rd. NW8 109 F2
Blenheim Rd. SE20 171 F7
Maple Rd.
Blenheim Rd. SW20 183 J3
Blenheim Rd. W4 126 E3
Blenheim Rd., Barn. 40 A3
Blenheim Rd., Brom. 192 B4
Blenheim Rd., Har. 67 H6
Blenheim Rd., Nthlt. 85 H6
Blenheim Rd., Sid. 176 C1
Blenheim Rd., Sutt. 198 D3
Blenheim St. W1 16 D4
Blenheim Ter. NW8 6 C1
Blenheim Ter. NW8 109 F2
Blenheim Way, Islw. 144 D1
Blenkarne Rd. SW11 149 J6
Bleriot Rd., Houns. 122 C7
Blessbury Rd., Edg. 70 C1
Blessing Way, Bark. 118 C3
Blessington Cl. SE13 154 D3
Blessington Rd. SE13 154 D3
Bletchingley Cl., Th.Hth. 187 H4
Bletchley Ct. N1 12 B2
Bletchley Ct. N1 112 A2
Bletchley St. N1 12 A2
Bletchley St. N1 111 J2
Bletchmore Cl., Hayes 121 G5
Bletsoe Wk. N1 12 A1
Blewbury Ho. SE2 138 D2
Yarnton Way
Blincoe Cl. SW19 166 A2
Blind La., Loug. 47 E2
Bliss Cres. SE13 154 B2
Coldbath St.
Blissett St. SE10 154 C1
Blisworth Cl., Hayes 102/103 E4
Braunston Dr.
Blithbury Rd., Dag. 100 B6
Blithdale Rd. SE2 138 A4
Blithfield St. W8 22 A6
Blithfield St. W8 128 E3
Blockley Rd., Wem. 86 E2
Bloemfontein Av. W12 127 H1
Bloemfontein Rd. W12 107 H7
Blomfield Rd. W9 14 D1
Blomfield Rd. W9 109 F5
Blomfield St. EC2 20 C2
Blomfield St. EC2 112 A5
Blomfield Vil. W2 14 B2
Blomfield Vil. W2 109 E5
Blomville Rd., Dag. 101 E3
Blondel St. SW11 150 A2
Blondell Cl., West Dr. 120 A6
Blondin Av. W5 125 F4
Blondin St. E3 114 A2
Bloom Gro. SE27 169 H3
Bloom Pk. Rd. SW6 128 C7
Bloomburg St. SW1 33 G2
Bloomfield Cres., Ilf. 81 E6
Bloomfield Pl. W1 16 E5
Bloomfield Pl. W1 110 B7
Bloomfield Rd. N6 74 A6
Bloomfield Rd. SE18 137 E5
Bloomfield Rd., Brom. 192 A5
Bloomfield Rd., Kings.T. 181 H4
Bloomfield Ter. SW1 32 C3
Bloomfield Ter. SW1 130 A5
Bloomhall Rd. SE19 170 A5
Bloomsbury Cl. W5 105 J7
Bloomsbury Ct. WC1 18 B2
Bloomsbury Ct., Pnr. 67 F3
Bloomsbury Ho. SW4 150 D6
Bloomsbury Pl. SW18 149 F5
Fullerton Rd.
Bloomsbury Pl. WC1 18 B1
Bloomsbury Pl. WC1 111 E5
Bloomsbury Sq. WC1 18 B2
Bloomsbury Sq. WC1 111 E5
Bloomsbury St. WC1 17 J2
Bloomsbury St. WC1 110 D5
Bloomsbury Way WC1 18 A3
Bloomsbury Way WC1 110 E6
Blore Cl. SW8 150 D1
Thessaly Rd.
Blore Ct. W1 17 H4
Blossom Cl. W5 125 H2
Almond Av.
Blossom Cl., Dag. 119 F1
Blossom Cl., S.Croy. 202 C5
Blossom La., Enf. 43 J1
Blossom Pl. E1 13 E6
Blossom St. E1 21 E1
Blossom St. E1 112 B4
Blossom Way, West Dr. 120 D4
Blossom Waye, Houns. 122 E7
Blount St. E14 113 H5
Bloxam Gdns. SE9 156 B5
Bloxhall Rd. E10 95 J1
Bloxham Cres., Hmptn. 179 F1
Bloxworth Cl., Wall. 200 C3
Blucher Rd. SE5 131 J7
Blue Anchor All., Rich. 145 H4
Kew Rd.
Blue Anchor La. SE16 37 J1
Blue Anchor La. SE16 132 D4
Blue Anchor Yd. E1 21 H5
Blue Anchor Yd. E1 112 D7
Blue Ball Yd. SW1 25 F2
Bluebell Av. E12 98 B5
Bluebell Cl. E9 113 F1
Moulins Rd.
Bluebell Cl. SE26 170 C4
Bluebell Cl., Orp. 207 F2
Bluebell Cl., Wall. 200 B1
Bluebell Way, Ilf. 98 E6
Blueberry Cl., Wdf.Grn. 63 G6
Bluefield Cl., Hmptn. 161 G5
Bluegates, Epsom 197 G7
Bluehouse Rd. E4 63 E3
Blundell Rd., Edg. 70 D1
Blundell St. N7 93 E7
Blunden Cl., Dag. 100 C1
Blunt Rd., S.Croy. 202 A5
Blunts Av., West Dr. 120 D7
Blunts Rd. SE9 156 D5
Blurton Rd. E5 95 F4
Blyth Cl. E14 134 D4
Manchester Rd.
Blyth Cl., Twick. 144 C6
Grimwood Rd.
Blyth Rd. E17 77 J7
Blyth Rd. SE28 118 C7
Blyth Rd., Brom. 191 F1
Blyth Rd., Hayes 121 H2
Blythe Cl. SE6 153 J7
Blythe Hill SE6 153 J7
Blythe Hill, Orp. 193 J1
Blythe Hill La. SE6 153 J7
Blythe Rd. W14 128 A3
Blythe St. E2 112 E3
Blythe Vale SE6 171 J1
Blythswood Rd., Ilf. 100 A1
Blythwood Rd. N4 75 E7
Blythwood Rd., Pnr. 66 D1
Boades Ms. NW3 91 G4
New End
Boadicea St. N1 111 F1
Copenhagen St.
Boakes Cl. NW9 70 C4
Boardman Av. E4 46 B5
Boardman Cl., Barn. 40 B5
Boardwalk Pl. E14 134 C1
Boar's Head Yd., Brent. 125 G7
Brent Way
Boat Lifter Way SE16 133 H4
Sweden Gate
Boathouse Wk. SE15 37 G7
Boathouse Wk. SE15 132 C7
Boathouse Wk., Rich. 145 H1
Bob Anker Cl. E13 115 G3
Chesterton Rd.
Bob Marley Way SE24 151 G4
Mayall Rd.
Bobbin Cl. SW4 150 C3
Bobby Moore Way N10 57 J7
Bockhampton Rd., Kings.T. 163 J7
Bocking St. E8 112 E1
Boddicott Cl. SW19 166 B2
Bodiam Cl., Enf. 44 A2
Bodiam Rd. SW16 168 D7
Bodley Cl., N.Mal. 182 E5
Bodley Manor Way SW2 151 G7
Papworth Way
Bodley Rd., N.Mal. 182 D6
Bodmin Cl., Har. 85 F3
Bodmin Gro., Mord. 185 E5
Bodmin St. SW18 166 D1
Bodnant Gdns. SW20 183 G3

Bodney Rd. E8 94 E5
Boeing Way, Sthl. 122 B3
Boevey Path, Belv. 139 F6
Bogey La., Orp. 206 D7
Bognor Gdns., Wat. 50 C5
Bowring Grn.
Bognor Rd., Well. 158 D1
Bohemia Pl. E8 95 E6
Bohun Gro., Barn. 41 H6
Boileau Par. W5 105 J6
Boileau Rd.
Boileau Rd. SW13 127 G7
Boileau Rd. W5 105 J6
Bolden St. SE8 154 B2
Bolderwood Way, W.Wick. 204 B2
Boldmere Rd., Pnr. 66 C7
Boleyn Av., Enf. 44 E1
Boleyn Cl. E17 78 A4
Boleyn Cl., Loug. 48 B6
Roding Gdns.
Boleyn Ct., Buck.H. 63 G1
Boleyn Dr., Ruis. 84 D2
Boleyn Dr., W.Mol. 179 F3
Boleyn Gdns., Dag. 101 J7
Boleyn Gdns., W.Wick. 204 B2
Boleyn Gro., W.Wick. 204 C2
Boleyn Rd. E6 116 A2
Boleyn Rd. E7 97 G7
Boleyn Rd. N16 94 B5
Boleyn Way, Barn. 41 F3
Boleyn Way, Ilf. 65 F6
Bolina Rd. SE16 133 F5
Bolingbroke Gro. SW11 149 H4
Bolingbroke Rd. W14 128 A3
Bolingbroke Wk. SW11 129 G7
Bolingbroke Way, Hayes 121 G1
Bolliger Ct. NW10 106 C4
Park Royal Rd.
Bollo Br. Rd. W3 126 B3
Bollo La. W3 126 B2
Bollo La. W4 126 C4
Bolney Gate SW7 23 G4
Bolney St. SW8 131 F7
Bolney Way, Felt. 161 E3
Bolsover St. W1 9 E6
Bolsover St. W1 110 B4
Bolstead Rd., Mitch. 186 B1
Bolt Ct. EC4 19 F4
Boltmore Cl. NW4 72 A3
Bolton Cl. SE20 188 D2
Selby Rd.
Bolton Cl., Chess. 195 G6
Bolton Cres. SE5 35 F6
Bolton Cres. SE5 131 H6
Bolton Gdns. NW10 108 A2
Bolton Gdns. SW5 30 B3
Bolton Gdns. SW5 129 E5
Bolton Gdns., Brom. 173 F6
Bolton Gdns., Tedd. 162 D6
Bolton Gdns. Ms. SW10 30 C3
Bolton Gdns. Ms. SW10 129 E5
Bolton Rd. E15 97 F6
Bolton Rd. N18 60 C5
Bolton Rd. NW8 109 E1
Bolton Rd. NW10 107 E1
Bolton Rd. W4 126 C7
Bolton Rd., Chess. 195 G6
Bolton Rd., Har. 67 J4
Bolton St. W1 24 E1
Bolton St. W1 130 B1
Bolton Wk. N7 93 F2
Durham Rd.
Boltons, The SW10 30 C3
Boltons, The SW10 129 F5
Boltons, The, Wem. 86 C4
Boltons, The, Wdf.Grn. 63 G4
Boltons La., Hayes 121 F7
Boltons Pl. SW5 30 C3
Boltons Pl. SW5 129 F5
Bombay St. SE16 132 E4
Bomer Cl., West Dr. 120 D7
Bomore Rd. W11 108 A7
Bon Marche Ter. Ms. SE27 170 B4
Gipsy Rd.
Bonar Pl., Chis. 174 B7
Bonar Rd. SE15 132 D7
Bonchester Cl., Chis. 174 D7
Bonchurch Cl., Sutt. 199 E7
Bonchurch Rd. W10 108 B5
Bonchurch Rd. W13 124 E1
Bond Ct. EC4 20 B4
Bond Ct. EC4 112 A6
Bond Gdns., Wall. 200 C4
Bond Rd., Mitch. 185 H2
Bond Rd., Surb. 195 J2
Bond St. E15 96 E5
Bond St. W4 126 E4
Bond St. W5 105 G7
Bondfield Av., Hayes 102 A3
Bondfield Rd. E6 116 B5
Lovage App.
Bonding Yd. Wk. SE16 133 H3
Finland St.
Bondway SW8 34 B5
Bondway SW8 131 E6
Boneta Rd. SE18 136 C3
Bonfield Rd. SE13 154 C4
Bonham Gdns., Dag. 100 D2
Bonham Rd. SW2 151 F5
Bonham Rd., Dag. 100 D2
Bonheur Rd. W4 126 D2
Bonhill St. EC2 12 C6
Bonhill St. EC2 112 A4
Boniface Gdns., Har. 51 H7
Boniface Wk., Har. 51 H7
Bonner Hill Rd., Kings.T. 181 J3
Bonner Rd. E2 113 F2
Bonner St. E2 113 F2
Bonnersfield Cl., Har. 68 C6
Bonnersfield La., Har. 68 D6
Bonneville Gdns. SW4 150 C6
Bonnington Sq. SW8 34 C5
Bonnington Sq. SW8 131 F6
Bonnington Twr., Brom. 192 B6
Bonny St. NW1 92 C7
Bonser Rd., Twick. 162 C2
Bonsor St. SE5 132 B7
Bonville Gdns. NW4 71 G4
Handowe Cl.
Bonville Rd., Brom. 173 F5
Book Ms. WC2 17 J4
Bookbinders' Cotts. N20 57 J3
Manor Dr.
Booker Cl. E14 113 J5
Wallwood St.
Booker Rd. N18 60 D5
Boone Ct. N9 61 F3
Boone St. SE13 155 E4
Boones Rd. SE13 155 E4
Boord St. SE10 135 E3
Boot St. N1 12 D4
Boot St. N1 112 B3
Booth Cl. E9 112/113 E1
Victoria Pk. Rd.
Booth Cl. SE28 118 B7
Booth Rd. NW9 70 E2
Booth Rd., Croy. 201 H2
Waddon New Rd.
Boothby Rd. N19 92 D2
Booth's Pl. W1 17 G2
Bordars Rd. W7 104 B5
Bordars Wk. W7 104 B5
Borden Av., Enf. 44 A6
Border Cres. SE26 170 E5
Border Gdns., Croy. 204 B4
Border Rd. SE26 171 E5
Bordergate, Mitch. 185 H1
Borders La., Loug. 48 D4
Bordesley Rd., Mord. 185 E4
Bordon Wk. SW15 147 G7
Boreas Wk. N1 11 H2
Boreham Av. E16 115 G6
Boreham Cl. E11 96 C1
Hainault Rd.
Boreham Rd. N22 75 J2
Borehamwood Ind. Pk., Borwd. 38 D2
Borgard Rd. SE18 136 C4
Borkwood Pk., Orp. 207 J4
Borkwood Way, Orp. 207 H4
Borland Rd. SE15 153 F4
Borland Rd., Tedd. 163 E6
Borneo St. SW15 147 J3
Borough High St. SE1 27 J4
Borough High St. SE1 131 J2
Borough Hill, Croy. 201 H3
Borough Rd. SE1 27 G5
Borough Rd. SE1 131 H3
Borough Rd., Islw. 144 B1
Borough Rd., Kings.T. 182 A1
Borough Rd., Mitch. 185 H2
Borough Sq. SE1 27 J4
Borrett Cl. SE17 35 J4
Borrodaile Rd. SW18 149 E6
Borrowdale Av., Har. 68 D2
Borrowdale Cl., Ilf. 80 B4
Borrowdale Ct., Enf. 43 J1
Borthwick Ms. E15 96/97 E4
Borthwick Rd.
Borthwick Rd. E15 96 E4
Borthwick Rd. NW9 71 F6
West Hendon Bdy.
Borthwick St. SE8 134 A5
Borwick Av. E17 77 J3
Bosbury Rd. SE6 172 C3
Boscastle Rd. NW5 92 B3
Bosco Cl., Orp. 207 J4
Strickland Way
Boscobel Pl. SW1 32 C1
Boscobel Pl. SW1 130 A4
Boscobel St. NW8 7 F6
Boscobel St. NW8 109 G4
Boscombe Av. E10 78 D7
Boscombe Cl. E5 95 H5
Boscombe Gdns. SW16 169 E6
Boscombe Rd. SW17 168 A6
Boscombe Rd. SW19 184 E1
Boscombe Rd. W12 127 G1
Boscombe Rd., Wor.Pk. 197 J1
Bosgrove E4 62 C1
Boss St. SE1 29 F3
Bostal Row, Bexh. 159 F3
Harlington Rd.
Bostall Heath SE2 138 C5
Bostall Hill SE2 138 A5
Bostall La. SE2 138 B5
Bostall Manorway SE2 138 B4
Bostall Pk. Av., Bexh. 138 E7
Bostall Rd., Orp. 176 B7
Boston Gdns. W4 127 E6
Boston Gdns. W7 124 D4
Boston Gdns., Brent. 124 D4
Boston Manor Rd., Brent. 124 E4
Boston Pk. Rd., Brent. 125 F5
Boston Pl. NW1 7 J6
Boston Pl. NW1 109 J4
Boston Rd. E6 116 B3
Boston Rd. E17 78 A6
Boston Rd. W7 124 B1
Boston Rd., Croy. 187 F6
Boston Rd., Edg. 54 C7
Boston St. E2 13 H1
Boston Vale W7 124 D4
Bostonthorpe Rd. W7 124 B2
Bosun Cl. E14 134 A2
Byng St.
Boswell Ct. WC1 18 B1
Boswell Path, Hayes 121 J4
Croyde Av.
Boswell Rd., Th.Hth. 187 J4
Boswell St. WC1 18 B1
Boswell St. WC1 111 E5
Bosworth Cl. E17 77 J1
Bosworth Rd. N11 58 D6
Bosworth Rd. W10 108 B4
Bosworth Rd., Barn. 40 D3
Bosworth Rd., Dag. 101 G4
Botany Bay La., Chis. 193 F2
Botany Cl., Barn. 41 H4
Boteley Cl. E4 62 D2
Botha Rd. E13 115 H5
Botham Cl., Edg. 54 C7
Pavilion Way
Bothwell Cl. E16 115 F5
Bothwell St. W6 128 A6
Delorme St.
Botolph All. EC3 20 D5
Botolph La. EC3 20 D5
Botsford Rd. SW20 184 B2
Botts Ms. W2 108 D6
Chepstow Rd.
Botts Pas. W2 108 D6
Chepstow Rd.
Botwell La., Hayes 121 H1
Boucher Cl., Tedd. 162 C5
Boughton Av., Brom. 191 F7
Boughton Rd. SE28 137 H3
Boulcott St. E1 113 G6
Boulevard, The SW17 168 A2
Balham High Rd.
Boulevard, The, Pnr. 67 G4
Pinner Rd.
Boulevard 25 Retail Pk., Borwd. 38 A3
Boulogne Rd., Croy. 187 J6
Boulton Ho., Brent. 125 H5
Green Dragon La.
Boulton Rd., Dag. 101 E3
Boultwood Rd. E6 116 B6
Bounces La. N9 60 E2
Bounces Rd. N9 60 E1
Boundaries Rd. SW12 167 J2
Boundaries Rd., Felt. 160 C1
Boundary Av. E17 77 J7
Boundary Cl. SE20 188 D2
Haysleigh Gdns.
Boundary Cl., Barn. 40 C1
Boundary Cl., Ilf. 99 H4
Loxford La.
Boundary Cl., Kings.T. 182 B3
Boundary Cl., Sthl. 123 G5
Boundary La. E13 116 A3
Boundary La. SE17 36 A6
Boundary La. SE17 131 J6
Boundary Pas. E2 13 F5
Boundary Rd. E13 115 J3
Boundary Rd. E17 77 J7
Boundary Rd. N9 45 F6
Boundary Rd. N22 75 H3
Boundary Rd. NW8 109 E1
Boundary Rd. SW19 167 G6
Boundary Rd., Bark. 117 F2
Boundary Rd., Cars. 200 B6
Boundary Rd., Pnr. 66 D6
Boundary Rd., Sid. 157 H5
Boundary Rd., Wall. 200 B6
Boundary Rd., Wem. 87 H3
Boundary Row SE1 27 G3
Boundary St. E2 13 F4
Boundary St. E2 112 C4
Boundary Way, Croy. 204 A5
Boundfield Rd. SE6 172 E3
Bounds Grn. Rd. N11 58 C6
Bounds Grn. Rd. N22 58 C6
Bourchier St. W1 17 H5
Bourdon Pl. W1 16 E5
Bourdon Rd. SE20 189 F2
Bourdon St. W1 16 D6
Bourdon St. W1 110 B7
Bourke Cl. NW10 88/89 E6
Mayo Rd.
Bourke Cl. SW4 150 E6
Bourlet Cl. W1 17 F2
Bourn Av. N15 76 A4
Bourn Av., Barn. 41 G5
Bournbrook Rd. SE3 156 A3
Bourne, The N14 58 D1
Bourne Av. N14 58 E2
Bourne Av., Hayes 121 F3
Bourne Av., Ruis. 84 C5
Bourne Ct., Ruis. 84 B5
Bourne Dr., Mitch. 185 G2
Bourne Est. EC1 18 E1
Bourne Est. EC1 111 G5
Bourne Gdns. E4 62 B4
Bourne Hill N13 58 E1
Bourne Pl. W4 126 D5
Dukes Av.
Bourne Rd. E7 97 F3
Bourne Rd. N8 75 E6
Bourne Rd., Bex. 159 H6
Bourne Rd., Brom. 192 A4
Bourne Rd., Dart. 159 J6
Bourne St. SW1 32 B2
Bourne St. SW1 130 A4
Bourne St., Croy. 201 H2
Waddon New Rd.
Bourne Ter. W2 14 A1
Bourne Ter. W2 108 E5
Bourne Vale, Brom. 191 G7
Bourne Vw., Grnf. 86 C6
Bourne Way, Brom. 205 F2
Bourne Way, Epsom 196 C4
Bourne Way, Sutt. 198 C5
Bournemead Av., Nthlt. 102 A2
Bournemead Cl., Nthlt. 102 A2
Bournemead Way, Nthlt. 102 B2
Bournemouth Cl. SE15 152 D2
Bournemouth Rd. SE15 152 D2
Bournemouth Rd. SW19 184 D1
Bourneside Cres. N14 58 D1
Bourneside Gdns. SE6 172 C5
Bournevale Rd. SW16 168 E4
Bournewood Rd. SE18 138 A7
Bournville Rd. SE6 154 A7
Bournwell Cl., Barn. 41 J3
Bourton Cl., Hayes 122 A1
Avondale Dr.
Bousfield Rd. SE14 153 G2
Boutflower Rd. SW11 149 H4
Bouverie Gdns., Har. 69 G6
Bouverie Ms. N16 94 B2
Bouverie Rd.
Bouverie Pl. W2 15 F3

Bouverie Pl. W2	109	G6
Bouverie Rd. N16	94	B2
Bouverie Rd., Har.	67	J6
Bouverie St. EC4	**19**	**F4**
Bouverie St. EC4	111	G6
Boveney Rd. SE23	153	G7
Bovill Rd. SE23	153	G7
Bovingdon Av., Wem.	88	A6
Bovingdon Cl. N19	92	C2
Junction Rd.		
Bovingdon La. NW9	71	E1
Bovingdon Rd. SW6	148	E1
Bovingdon Sq., Mitch.	186/187	E4
Leicester Av.		
Bow Br. Est. E3	114	B3
Bow Chyd. EC4	**20**	**A4**
Bow Common La. E3	113	H4
Bow Ind. Pk. E15	96	A7
Bow La. EC4	**20**	**A4**
Bow La. EC4	111	J6
Bow La. N12	73	F1
Bow La., Mord.	184	B6
Bow Rd. E3	113	J3
Bow St. E15	96	E5
Bow St. WC2	**18**	**B4**
Bow St. WC2	111	E6
Bowater Cl. NW9	70	D5
Bowater Cl. SW2	150	E6
Bowater Pl. SE3	135	H7
Bowater Rd. SE18	136	A3
Bowden St. SE11	**35**	**F4**
Bowden St. SE11	131	G5
Bowditch SE8	133	J5
Bowdon Rd. E17	78	A7
Bowen Dr. SE21	170	B3
Bowen Rd., Har.	67	J7
Bowen St. E14	114	B6
Bower Av. SE10	154	E1
Bower Cl., Nthlt.	102	C2
Bower St. E1	113	G6
Bowerdean St. SW6	148	E1
Bowerman Av. SE14	133	H6
Bowers Wk. E6	116	C6
Bowes Cl., Sid.	158	B6
Bowes Rd. N11	58	B5
Bowes Rd. N13	58	E5
Bowes Rd. W3	106	E7
Bowes Rd., Dag.	100	C4
Bowfell Rd. W6	127	J6
Bowford Av., Bexh.	158	E1
Bowhill Cl. SW9	131	G7
Bowie Cl. SW4	150	D7
Bowl Ct. EC2	**13**	**E6**
Bowl Ct. EC2	112	B4
Bowland Rd. SW4	150	D4
Bowland Rd., Wdf.Grn.	63	J6
Bowland Yd. SW1	**24**	**A4**
Bowles Rd. SE1	**37**	**H5**
Bowley Cl. SE19	170	C6
Bowley La. SE19	170	C5
Bowling Grn. Cl. SW15	147	H7
Bowling Grn. La. EC1	**11**	**F5**
Bowling Grn. La. EC1	111	G4
Bowling Grn. Pl. SE1	**28**	**B3**
Bowling Grn. Pl. SE1	132	A2
Bowling Grn. Row SE18	136	C3
Samuel St.		
Bowling Grn. St. SE11	**35**	**E5**
Bowling Grn. St. SE11	131	G6
Bowling Grn. Wk. N1	**12**	**D3**
Bowls, The, Chig.	65	H4
Bowls Cl., Stan.	52	E5
Bowman Av. E16	115	F7
Bowman Ms. SW18	166	C1
Bowmans Cl. W13	124	E1
Bowmans Lea SE23	153	F7
Bowmans Meadow, Wall.	200	B3
Bowmans Ms. E1	**21**	**H5**
Bowmans Ms. N7	92/93	E3
Seven Sisters Rd.		
Bowmans Pl. N7	92/93	E3
Holloway Rd.		
Bowman's Trd. Est. NW9	69	J3
Westmoreland Rd.		
Bowmead SE9	174	C2
Bowmore Wk. NW1	92	D7
St. Paul's Cres.		
Bowness Cl. E8	94	C6
Beechwood Rd.		
Bowness Cres. SW15	164	E5
Bowness Dr., Houns.	143	E4
Bowness Rd. SE6	154	B7
Bowness Rd., Bexh.	159	H2
Bowood Rd. SW11	150	A4
Bowood Rd., Enf.	45	G2
Bowring Grn., Wat.	50	C5
Bowrons Av., Wem.	87	G7
Bowsley Ct., Felt.	160	A1
Highfield Rd.		
Bowyer Cl. E6	116	C5
Bowyer Pl. SE5	**36**	**A7**
Bowyer Pl. SE5	132	A7
Bowyer St. SE5	**35**	**J7**
Bowyer St. SE5	131	J7
Box La., Bark.	118	B2
Boxall Rd. SE21	152	B6
Boxgrove Rd. SE2	138	C3
Boxley Rd., Mord.	185	F4
Boxley St. E16	135	H1
Boxmoor Rd., Har.	68	E4
Boxoll Rd., Dag.	101	F4
Boxted Cl., Buck.H.	64	B1
Boxtree La., Har.	67	J1
Boxtree Rd., Har.	52	A7
Boxwood Cl., West Dr.	120	C2
Hawthorne Cres.		
Boxworth Cl. N12	57	G5
Boxworth Gro. N1	111	F1
Richmond Av.		
Boyard Rd. SE18	136	E5
Boyce St. SE1	**26**	**D2**
Boyce Way E13	115	G4
Boycroft Av. NW9	70	C6
Boyd Av., Sthl.	123	F1
Boyd Cl., Kings.T.	164	A7
Crescent Rd.		
Boyd Rd. SW19	167	G6
Boyd St. E1	**21**	**H4**
Boyd St. E1	112	D6
Boydell Ct. NW8	91	G7
St. John's Wd. Pk.		
Boyfield St. SE1	**27**	**H4**
Boyfield St. SE1	131	H2
Boyland Rd., Brom.	173	F5
Boyle Av., Stan.	52	D6
Boyle Fm. Island, T.Ditt.	180	D6
Boyle Fm. Rd., T.Ditt.	180	D6
Boyle St. W1	**17**	**F5**
Boyne Av. NW4	72	A4
Boyne Rd. SE13	154	C3
Boyne Rd., Dag.	101	G3
Boyne Ter. Ms. W11	128	C1
Boyseland Ct., Edg.	54	C2
Boyson Rd. SE17	**36**	**B5**
Boyson Rd. SE17	132	A6
Boyton Cl. E1	113	G4
Stayner's Rd.		
Boyton Cl. N8	75	E3
Boyton Rd. N8	75	E3
Brabant Ct. EC3	**20**	**D5**
Brabant Rd. N22	75	F2
Brabazon Av., Wall.	200	E7
Brabazon Rd., Houns.	122	C7
Brabazon Rd., Nthlt.	103	G2
Brabazon St. E14	114	B6
Brabourn Gro. SE15	153	F2
Brabourne Cl. SE19	170	B5
Brabourne Cres., Bexh.	139	F6
Brabourne Hts. NW7	55	E3
Brabourne Ri., Beck.	190	C5
Bracewell Av., Grnf.	86	C5
Bracewell Rd. W10	107	J5
Bracewood Gdns., Croy.	202	C3
Bracey Ms. N4	92/93	E2
Bracey St.		
Bracey St. N4	93	E2
Bracken, The E4	62	C2
Hortus Rd.		
Bracken Av. SW12	150	A6
Bracken Av., Croy.	204	B3
Bracken Cl. E6	116	C5
Bracken Cl., Borwd.	38	B1
Bracken Cl., Twick.	143	G7
Hedley Rd.		
Bracken Dr., Chig.	65	E6
Bracken End, Islw.	144	A5
Bracken Gdns. SW13	147	G2
Bracken Hill Cl., Brom.	191	F1
Bracken Hill La.		
Bracken Hill La., Brom.	191	F1
Bracken Ind. Est., Ilf.	65	J7
Bracken Ms. E4	62	C2
Hortus Rd.		
Bracken Ms., Rom.	83	G6
Brackenbridge Dr., Ruis.	84	D3
Brackenbury Gdns. W6	127	H3
Brackenbury Rd. N2	73	F3
Brackenbury Rd. W6	127	H3
Brackendale N21	59	F2
Brackendale Cl., Houns.	143	H1
Brackenfield Cl. E5	94/95	E4
Tiger Way		
Brackens, The, Enf.	44	B7
Brackenwood, Sun.	178	A1
Brackley Cl., Wall.	201	E7
Brackley Rd. W4	127	E5
Brackley Rd., Beck.	171	J7
Brackley Sq., Wdf.Grn.	64	A7
Brackley St. EC1	**19**	**J1**
Brackley Ter. W4	127	E5
Bracklyn Cl. N1	**12**	**B1**
Bracklyn Ct. N1	**12**	**B1**
Bracklyn St. N1	**12**	**B1**
Bracklyn St. N1	112	A2
Bracknell Cl. N22	75	G1
Bracknell Gdns. NW3	90	E4
Bracknell Gate NW3	90	E5
Bracknell Way NW3	90	E4
Bracondale Rd. SE2	138	A4
Brad St. SE1	**27**	**F2**
Bradbourne Rd., Bex.	159	G7
Bradbourne St. SW6	148	D2
Bradbury Cl., Borwd.	38	B1
Bradbury Cl., Sthl.	123	F4
Bradbury Ms. N16	94	B5
Bradbury St.		
Bradbury St. N16	94	B5
Braddock Cl., Islw.	144	C3
Braddon Rd., Rich.	145	J3
Braddyll St. SE10	134	E5
Braden St. W9	**6**	**A6**
Bradenham Av., Well.	158	A4
Bradenham Cl. SE17	**36**	**B5**
Bradenham Cl. SE17	132	A6
Bradenham Rd., Har.	68	E4
Bradfield Dr., Bark.	100	A5
Bradfield Rd. E16	135	G2
Bradfield Rd., Ruis.	85	E5
Bradford Cl. N17	60	B6
Commercial Rd.		
Bradford Cl. SE26	170/171	E4
Coombe Rd.		
Bradford Cl., Brom.	206	C1
Bradford Dr., Epsom	197	F6
Bradford Rd. W3	126/127	E2
Warple Way		
Bradford Rd., Ilf.	99	G1
Bradgate Rd. SE6	154	A6
Brading Cres. E11	97	H2
Brading Rd. SW2	151	F7
Brading Rd., Croy.	187	F6
Bradiston Rd. W9	108	C3
Bradley Cl. N7	93	F6
Sutterton St.		
Bradley Gdns. W13	104	E6
Bradley Ms. SW17	167	J1
Bellevue Rd.		
Bradley Rd. N22	75	F2
Bradley Rd. SE19	169	J6
Bradley Stone Rd. E6	116	C5
Bradley's Cl. N1	**11**	**F1**
Bradman Row, Edg.	54	C7
Pavilion Way		
Bradmead SW8	130	B7
Bradmore Ho. E1	113	F5
Bradmore Pk. Rd. W6	127	H3
Bradshaw Cl. SW19	166	D6
Bradshaws Cl. SE25	188	D3
Bradstock Rd. E9	95	G6
Bradstock Rd., Epsom	197	G5
Bradwell Av., Dag.	101	G2
Bradwell Cl. E18	79	F4
Bradwell Ms. N18	60	D4
Lyndhurst Rd.		
Bradwell Rd., Buck.H.	64	B1
Bradwell St. E1	113	G3
Brady Av., Loug.	49	F2
Brady St. E1	112	E4
Bradymead E6	116/117	E6
Warwall		
Braemar Av. N22	75	E1
Braemar Av. NW10	88	D3
Braemar Av. SW19	166	D2
Braemar Av., Bexh.	159	J4
Braemar Av., Th.Hth.	187	G3
Braemar Av., Wem.	87	G7
Braemar Gdns. NW9	70	D1
Braemar Gdns., Sid.	175	G3
Braemar Gdns., W.Wick.	204	C1
Braemar Rd. E13	115	F4
Braemar Rd. N15	76	B5
Braemar Rd., Brent.	125	H6
Braemar Rd., Wor.Pk.	197	H3
Braes St. N1	93	H7
Braeside, Beck.	172	A5
Braeside Av. SW19	184	B1
Braeside Cl., Pnr.	51	G7
The Av.		
Braeside Cres., Bexh.	159	J4
Braeside Rd. SW16	168	C7
Braesyde Cl., Belv.	139	F4
Brafferton Rd., Croy.	201	J4
Braganza St. SE17	**35**	**G3**
Braganza St. SE17	131	H5
Bragg Cl., Dag.	100	B6
Porters Av.		
Braham St. E1	**21**	**G3**
Braham St. E1	112	C6
Braid Av. W3	106	E6
Braid Cl., Felt.	161	F2
Braidwood Rd. SE6	172	D1
Braidwood St. SE1	**28**	**D2**
Brailsford Cl., Mitch.	167	H7
Brailsford Rd. SW2	151	G5
Brainton Av., Felt.	142	B7
Braintree Av., Ilf.	80	B4
Braintree Rd., Dag.	101	G3
Braintree Rd., Ruis.	84	B4
Braintree St. E2	113	F3
Braithwaite Av., Rom.	83	G7
Braithwaite Gdns., Stan.	69	F1
Braithwaite Rd., Enf.	45	J3
Bramah Grn. SW9	151	G1
Bramalea Cl. N6	74	A6
Bramall Cl. E15	97	F5
Idmiston Rd.		
Bramber Ct., Brent.	125	H4
Sterling Pl.		
Bramber Rd. N12	57	H5
Bramber Rd. W14	128	C6
Bramble Cl., Croy.	204	A4
Bramble Cl., Stan.	53	G7
Bramble Cft., Erith	139	J4
Bramble Gdns. W12	107	F7
Wallflower St.		
Bramble La., Hmptn.	161	F6
Brambleacres Cl., Sutt.	198	D7
Bramblebury Rd. SE18	137	F5
Brambledown Cl., W.Wick.	191	E5
Brambledown Rd., Cars.	200	A7
Brambledown Rd., S.Croy.	202	B7
Brambledown Rd., Wall.	200	B7
Brambles, The, Chig.	65	F5
Clayside		
Brambles, The, West Dr.	120	B4
Brambles Cl., Islw.	124	E7
Bramblewood Cl., Cars.	199	H1
Bramblings, The E4	62	D4
Bramcote Av., Mitch.	185	J4
Bramcote Ct., Mitch.	185	J4
Bramcote Av.		
Bramcote Gro. SE16	133	F5
Bramcote Rd. SW15	147	H4
Bramdean Cres. SE12	173	G1
Bramdean Gdns. SE12	173	G1
Bramerton Rd., Beck.	189	J3
Bramerton St. SW3	**31**	**G5**
Bramerton St. SW3	129	H6
Bramfield Ct. N4	93	J2
Queens Dr.		
Bramfield Rd. SW11	149	H6
Bramford Ct. N14	58	D2
Bramford Rd. SW18	149	F4
Bramham Gdns. SW5	**30**	**A3**
Bramham Gdns. SW5	129	E5
Bramham Gdns., Chess.	195	G4
Bramhope La. SE7	135	H6
Bramlands Cl. SW11	149	H3
Bramley Cl. E17	77	H2
Bramley Cl. N14	42	B5
Bramley Cl., Hayes	102	A7
Orchard Rd.		
Bramley Cl., Orp.	207	E1
Bramley Cl., S.Croy.	201	H5
Bramley Cl., Twick.	143	J6

Name	Page	Grid
Bramley Ct., Well.	158	B1
Bramley Cres. SW8	**33**	**J7**
Bramley Cres., Ilf.	80	D6
Bramley Gdns., Wat.	50	C5
Bramley Hill, S.Croy.	201	H5
Bramley Rd. N14	42	B5
Bramley Rd. W5	125	F3
Bramley Rd. W10	108	A7
Bramley Rd., Sutt.	199	G5
Bramley Way, Houns.	143	F5
Bramley Way, W.Wick.	204	B2
Brampton Cl. E5	95	E2
Brampton Gdns. N15	75	J5
Brampton Rd.		
Brampton Gro. NW4	71	H4
Brampton Gro., Har.	68	D4
Brampton Gro., Wem.	88	A1
Brampton La. NW4	71	J4
Brampton Pk. Rd. N22	75	G3
Brampton Rd. E6	116	A3
Brampton Rd. N15	75	J5
Brampton Rd. NW9	70	A4
Brampton Rd. SE2	138	C6
Brampton Rd., Bexh.	138	D7
Brampton Rd., Croy.	188	C7
Brampton Rd., Wat.	50	A3
Bramshaw Gdns., Wat.	50	D5
Bramshaw Ri., N.Mal.	183	E6
Bramshaw Rd. E9	95	G6
Bramshill Cl., Chig.	65	H5
Tine Rd.		
Bramshill Gdns. NW5	92	B3
Bramshill Rd. NW10	107	F2
Bramshot Av. SE7	135	G6
Bramshot Way, Wat.	50	A2
Bramston Cl., Ilf.	65	J6
Bramston Rd. NW10	107	G2
Bramston Rd. SW17	167	F3
Bramwell Cl., Sun.	178	D2
Bramwell Ms. N1	111	F1
Brancaster Dr. NW7	55	F7
Brancaster Pl., Loug.	48	C3
Brancaster Rd. E12	98	C4
Brancaster Rd. SW16	168	E3
Brancaster Rd., Ilf.	81	G6
Brancepeth Gdns., Buck.H.	63	G2
Branch Hill NW3	91	F3
Branch Pl. N1	112	A1
Branch Rd. E14	113	H7
Branch St. SE15	132	B7
Brancker Cl., Wall.	200/201	E7
Brown Cl.		
Brancker Rd., Har.	69	G3
Brancroft Way, Enf.	45	H1
Brand St. SE10	134	C7
Brandlehow Rd. SW15	148	C4
Brandon Est. SE17	**35**	**H6**
Brandon Est. SE17	131	H6
Brandon Rd. E17	78	C3
Brandon Rd. N7	92	E7
Brandon Rd., Sthl.	123	F5
Brandon Rd., Sutt.	198	E4
Brandon St. SE17	**36**	**A2**
Brandon St. SE17	131	J4
Brandram Rd. SE13	154	E3
Brandreth Rd. E6	116	C6
Brandreth Rd. SW17	168	B2
Brandries, The, Wall.	200	D3
Brandville Gdns., Ilf.	81	E4
Brandville Rd., West Dr.	120	B2
Brandy Way, Sutt.	198	D7
Brangbourne Rd., Brom.	172	C5
Brangton Rd. SE11	**34**	**D4**
Brangton Rd. SE11	131	F5
Brangwyn Cres. SW19	185	G1
Branksea St. SW6	128	B7
Branksome Av. N18	60	C5
Branksome Rd. SW2	151	E5
Branksome Rd. SW19	184	D1
Branksome Way, Har.	69	H6
Branksome Way, N.Mal.	182	C1
Bransby Rd., Chess.	195	H6
Branscombe Gdns. N21	43	G7
Branscombe St. SE13	154	B3
Bransdale Cl. NW6	108/109	E1
West End La.		
Bransgrove Rd., Edg.	69	J1
Branston Cres., Orp.	207	G1
Branstone Rd., Rich.	145	J1
Brants Wk. W7	104	B4
Brantwood Av., Erith	139	J7
Brantwood Av., Islw.	144	D4
Brantwood Cl. E17	78	B3
Brantwood Gdns., Enf.	42	E4
Brantwood Gdns., Ilf.	80	B4
Brantwood Rd. N17	60	D6
Brantwood Rd. SE24	151	J5
Brantwood Rd., Bexh.	159	H2
Brasenose Dr. SW13	127	J6
Brasher Cl., Grnf.	86	A5
Brass Tally All. SE16	133	G2
Middleton Dr.		
Brassey Cl., Felt.	160	A1
Brassey Rd. NW6	90	C6
Brassey Sq. SW11	150	A3
Brassie Av. W3	106	E6
Brasted Cl. SE26	171	F4
Brasted Cl., Bexh.	158	D5
Brathway Rd. SW18	148	D7
Bratley St. E1	**13**	**H6**
Braund Av., Grnf.	103	H4
Braundton Av., Sid.	175	J1
Braunston Dr., Hayes	102	E4
Bravington Pl. W9	108	C4
Bravington Rd.		
Bravington Rd. W9	108	C2
Brawne Ho. SE17	**35**	**G6**
Braxfield Rd. SE4	153	H4
Braxted Pk. SW16	169	F6
Bray NW3	91	H7
Bray Cl., Borwd.	38	C1
Bray Cres. SE16	133	G2
Marlow Way		
Bray Dr. E16	115	F7
Bray Pas. E16	115	G7
Bray Pl. SW3	**31**	**J2**
Bray Pl. SW3	129	J4
Bray Rd. NW7	56	A6
Brayards Rd. SE15	152	E2
Brayards Rd. Est. SE15	153	E2
Braybourne Dr., Islw.	124	C7
Braybrook St. W12	107	F5
Braybrooke Gdns. SE19	170	C7
Fox Hill		
Brayburne Av. SW4	150	C2
Braycourt Av., Walt.	178	B7
Braydon Rd. N16	94	D1
Brayfield Ter. N1	93	G7
Lofting Rd.		
Brayford Sq. E1	113	F6
Summercourt Rd.		
Brayton Gdns., Enf.	42	D4
Braywood Rd. SE9	157	G4
Brazil Cl., Croy.	186	E7
Breach La., Dag.	119	G3
Bread St. EC4	**20**	**A4**
Bread St. EC4	111	J7
Breakspears Ms. SE4	154	A2
Breakspears Rd.		
Breakspears Rd. SE4	153	J4
Bream Cl. N17	77	E4
Bream Gdns. E6	116	D3
Bream St. E3	96	A7
Breamore Cl. SW15	165	G1
Breamore Rd., Ilf.	99	J2
Bream's Bldgs. EC4	**19**	**E3**
Bream's Bldgs. EC4	111	G6
Breamwater Gdns., Rich.	163	E3
Brearley Cl., Edg.	54	C7
Pavilion Way		
Breasley Cl. SW15	147	H4
Brechin Pl. SW7	**30**	**D2**
Brecknock Rd. N7	92	C4
Brecknock Rd. N19	92	C4
Brecknock Rd. Est. N7	92	C4
Breckonmead, Brom.	191	J2
Wanstead Rd.		
Brecon Cl., Mitch.	186	E3
Brecon Cl., Wor.Pk.	197	J2
Brecon Rd. W6	128	B6
Brecon Rd., Enf.	45	F4
Brede Cl. E6	116	D3
Bredgar Rd. N19	92	C2
Bredhurst Cl. SE20	171	F6
Bredon Rd. SE5	151	J3
Bredon Rd., Croy.	188	C7
Breer St. SW6	148	E3
Breezers Hill E1	**21**	**J6**
Brember Rd., Har.	85	J2
Bremer Ms. E17	78	B4
Church La.		
Bremner Rd. SW7	**22**	**D4**
Bremner Rd. SW7	129	F2
Brenchley Cl., Brom.	191	F6
Brenchley Cl., Chis.	192	D1
Brenchley Gdns. SE23	153	F6
Brenchley Rd., Orp.	193	J1
Brenda Rd. SW17	167	J2
Brende Gdns., W.Mol.	179	H4
Brendon Av. NW10	89	E4
Brendon Cl., Hayes	121	F7
Brendon Gdns., Har.	85	H4
Brendon Gdns., Ilf.	81	H5
Brendon Gro. N2	73	F2
Brendon Rd. SE9	175	G2
Brendon Rd., Dag.	101	F1
Brendon St. W1	**15**	**H3**
Brendon St. W1	109	H6
Brendon Way, Enf.	44	B7
Brenley Cl., Mitch.	186	A3
Brenley Gdns. SE9	156	A4
Brent Cl., Bex.	177	E1
Brent Cres. NW10	105	J2
Brent Cross Gdns. NW4	72	A6
Haley Rd.		
Brent Cross Shop. Cen. NW4	71	J7
Brent Grn. NW4	71	J5
Brent Grn. Wk., Wem.	88	C3
Brent Lea, Brent.	125	F7
Brent Pk. NW10	88	D5
Brent Pk. Rd. NW4	71	H7
Brent Pk. Rd. NW9	89	G1
Brent Pl., Barn.	40	D5
Brent Rd. E16	115	G5
Brent Rd. SE18	136	E7
Brent Rd., Brent.	125	F6
Brent Rd., Sthl.	122	C3
Brent Side, Brent.	125	F6
Brent St. NW4	71	J4
Brent Ter. NW2	89	J2
Brent Vw. Rd. NW9	71	G7
Brent Way N3	56	D6
Brent Way, Brent.	125	G7
Brent Way, Wem.	88	B6
Brentcot Cl. W13	104	E4
Brentfield NW10	88	B7
Brentfield Cl. NW10	88	D6
Normans Mead		
Brentfield Gdns. NW2	72	A7
Hendon Way		
Brentfield Rd. NW10	88	D6
Brentford Business Cen., Brent.	125	F7
Brentford Cl., Hayes	102	D4
Brentham Way W5	105	G4
Brenthouse Rd. E9	95	F7
Brenthurst Rd. NW10	89	F6
Brentmead Cl. W7	104	B7
Brentmead Gdns. NW10	105	J2
Brentmead Pl. NW11	72	A6
North Circular Rd.		
Brenton St. E14	113	H6
Brentside Cl. W13	104	D4
Brentside Executive Cen., Brent.	125	E6
Brentvale Av., Sthl.	124	A1
Brentvale Av., Wem.	105	J1
Brentwick Gdns., Brent.	125	H4
Brentwood Cl. SE9	175	F1
Brentwood Ho. SE18	136	A7
Shooter's Hill Rd.		
Brereton Rd. N17	60	C7
Bressenden Pl. SW1	**25**	**E5**
Bressenden Pl. SW1	130	B3
Bressey Av., Enf.	44	D1
Bressey Gro. E18	79	F2
Brett Cl. N16	94	B2
Yoakley Rd.		
Brett Cl., Nthlt.	102	D3
Broomcroft Av.		
Brett Ct. N9	61	F2
Brett Cres. NW10	88	D7
Brett Gdns., Dag.	100	E7
Brett Ho. Cl. SW15	148	A6
Putney Heath La.		
Brett Pas. E8	94/95	E5
Kenmure Rd.		
Brett Rd. E8	95	E5
Brett Rd., Barn.	39	J5
Brettell St. SE17	**36**	**C4**
Brettenham Av. E17	78	A1
Brettenham Rd. E17	78	A2
Brettenham Rd. N18	60	E4
Brewer St. W1	**17**	**G5**
Brewer St. W1	110	C7
Brewer's Grn. SW1	**25**	**H5**
Brewers Hall Gdns. EC2	**20**	**A2**
Brewers La., Rich.	145	G5
Brewery Cl., Wem.	86	D5
Brewery La., Twick.	144	C7
Brewery Rd. N7	92	E7
Brewery Rd. SE18	137	G5
Brewery Rd., Brom.	206	B1
Brewery Sq. SE1	132	C1
Horselydown La.		
Brewhouse La. E1	133	E1
Brewhouse Rd. SE18	136	C4
Brewhouse St. SW15	148	B3
Brewhouse Wk. SE16	133	H1
Brewhouse Yd. EC1	**11**	**G5**
Brewood Rd., Dag.	100	B6
Brewster Gdns. W10	107	J5
Brewster Ho. E14	113	J7
Brewster Rd. E10	96	B1
Brian Rd., Rom.	82	C5
Briant St. SE14	153	G1
Briants Cl., Pnr.	67	F2
Briar Av. SW16	169	F7
Briar Cl. N2	73	E3
Briar Cl. N13	59	J3
Briar Cl., Buck.H.	64	A2
Briar Cl., Hmptn.	161	F5
Briar Cl., Islw.	144	C5
Briar Ct., Sutt.	197	J4
Briar Cres., Nthlt.	85	H6
Briar Gdns., Brom.	205	F1
Briar La., Croy.	204	B4
Briar Pas. SW16	187	E3
Briar Pl. SW16	187	F3
Briar Rd. NW2	89	J4
Briar Rd. SW16	187	E3
Briar Rd., Har.	69	F5
Briar Rd., Twick.	162	B1
Briar Wk. SW15	147	H4
Briar Wk. W10	108	B4
Droop St.		
Briar Wk., Edg.	54	C7
Briar Way, West Dr.	120	D2
Briarbank Rd. W13	104	D6
Briardale Gdns. NW3	90	D3
Briarfield Av. N3	72	E2
Briaris Cl. N17	60	E7
Briarswood Way, Orp.	207	J5
Briarwood Cl. NW9	70	C6
Briarwood Dr., Nthwd.	66	A2
Briarwood Rd. SW4	150	D5
Briarwood Rd., Epsom	197	G6
Briary Cl. NW3	91	H7
Fellows Rd.		
Briary Ct., Sid.	176	B5
Briary Gdns., Brom.	173	H5
Briary Gro., Edg.	70	B2
Briary La. N9	60	C3
Brick Ct. EC4	**18**	**E4**
Brick Fm. Cl., Rich.	146	B1
Brick La. E1	**13**	**G6**
Brick La. E1	112	C5
Brick La. E2	**13**	**G4**
Brick La. E2	112	C3
Brick La., Enf.	44	E2
Brick La., Stan.	53	G7
Honeypot La.		
Brick St. W1	**24**	**D2**
Brick St. W1	130	B1
Brickfield Cl., Brent.	125	F6
Brickfield Cotts. SE18	137	J6
Brickfield Fm. Gdns., Orp.	207	F4
Brickfield La., Barn.	39	F6
Brickfield La., Hayes	121	G6
Brickfield Rd. SW19	167	E4
Brickfield Rd., Th.Hth.	187	H1
Brickfields, Har.	86	A2
Brickfields Way, West Dr.	120	C3
Bricklayer's Arms SE1	**36**	**E1**
Bricklayer's Arms SE1	132	B4
Brickwood Cl. SE26	171	E3
Brickwood Rd., Croy.	202	B2
Bride Ct. EC4	**19**	**G4**

Bride La. EC4 19 G4
Bride St. N7 93 F6
Brideale Cl. SE15 132 C7
Colegrove Rd.
Bridewain St. SE1 29 G5
Bridewain St. SE1 132 C3
Bridewell Pl. E1 132/133 E1
Brewhouse La.
Bridewell Pl. EC4 19 G4
Bridford Ms. W1 16 E1
Bridge, The, Har. 68 B3
Bridge App. NW1 92 A7
Bridge Av. W6 127 J5
Bridge Av. W7 104 A5
Bridge Cl. W10 108 A6
Kingsdown Cl.
Bridge Cl., Enf. 45 E2
Bridge Cl., Tedd. 162 C4
Shacklegate La.
Bridge Dr. N13 59 F4
Bridge End E17 78 C1
Bridge Gdns., E.Mol. 180 A4
Bridge Gate N21 43 J7
Ridge Av.
Bridge Ho. Quay E14 134 C1
Prestons Rd.
Bridge La. NW11 72 B5
Bridge La. SW11 149 H1
Bridge Meadows SE14 133 G6
Bridge Pk. SW18 148 D5
Bridge Pl. SW1 33 E1
Bridge Pl. SW1 130 B4
Bridge Pl., Croy. 188 A7
Bridge Rd. E6 98 C7
Bridge Rd. E15 96 D7
Bridge Rd. E17 77 J7
Bridge Rd. N9 60 D3
The Bdy.
Bridge Rd. N22 75 E1
Bridge Rd. NW10 88 E6
Bridge Rd., Beck. 171 J7
Bridge Rd., Bexh. 159 E2
Bridge Rd., Chess. 195 H5
Bridge Rd., Croy. 201 J3
Duppas Hill Rd.
Bridge Rd., E.Mol. 180 B4
Bridge Rd., Houns. 144 A3
Bridge Rd., Islw. 144 A3
Bridge Rd., Sthl. 123 F2
Bridge Rd., Sutt. 199 E6
Bridge Rd., Twick. 144 E6
Bridge Rd., Wall. 200 C5
Bridge Rd., Wem. 88 A3
Bridge Row, Croy. 202 A1
Cross Rd.
Bridge St. SW1 26 A4
Bridge St. SW1 130 E2
Bridge St. W4 126 D4
Bridge St., Pnr. 66 D3
Bridge St., Rich. 145 G5
Bridge Ter. E15 96 D7
Bridge Vw. W6 127 J5
Bridge Way N11 58 C3
Pymmes Grn. Rd.
Bridge Way NW11 72 C5
Bridge Way, Twick. 143 J7
Bridge Wf. Rd., Islw. 144/145 E3
Church St.
Bridge Yd. SE1 28 C1
Bridgefield Rd., Sutt. 198 D6
Bridgefoot SE1 34 A4
Bridgefoot SE1 131 E5
Bridgeland Rd. E16 115 G7
Bridgeman Rd. N1 93 F7
Bridgeman Rd., Tedd. 162 D6
Bridgeman St. NW8 7 G2
Bridgeman St. NW8 109 H2
Bridgen Rd., Bex. 158 E6
Bridgend Rd. SW18 149 F4
Bridgenhall Rd., Enf. 44 C1
Bridgeport Pl. E1 29 J1
Bridges Ct. SW11 149 G3
Bridges La., Croy. 200 E4
Bridges Ms. SW19 166/167 E6
Bridges Rd.
Bridges Pl. SW6 148 C1
Bridges Rd. SW19 166 E6
Bridges Rd., Stan. 52 C5
Bridges Rd. Ms. SW19 166/167 E6
Bridges Rd.
Bridgetown Cl. SE19 170 B5
St. Kitts Ter.
Bridgeview Ct., Ilf. 65 G6
Bridgewater Cl., Chis. 193 H3
Bridgewater Gdns., Edg. 69 J2
Bridgewater Rd., Ruis. 84 A4
Bridgewater Rd., Wem. 87 F7
Bridgewater Sq. EC2 19 J1
Bridgewater St. EC2 19 J1
Bridgeway, Bark. 99 J7
Bridgeway, Wem. 87 H7
Bridgeway St. NW1 9 H2
Bridgeway St. NW1 110 C2
Bridgewood Cl. SE20 170 E7
Bridgewood Rd. SW16 168 D7
Bridgewood Rd., Wor.Pk. 197 G4
Bridgford St. SW18 167 F3
Bridgman Rd. W4 126 C3
Bridgwater Rd. E15 114 C1
Bridle Cl., Epsom 196 D5
Bridle Cl., Kings.T. 181 G4
Bridle Cl., Sun. 178 A3
Forge La.
Bridle La. W1 17 G5
Bridle La., Twick. 144/145 E6
Crown Rd.
Bridle Path, Croy. 201 F3
Bridle Path, The, Wdf.Grn. 62 E7
Bridle Rd., Croy. 204 A3
Bridle Rd., Esher 194 E6
Bridle Rd., Pnr. 66 C6
Bridle Way, Croy. 204 A5
Bridle Way, Orp. 207 F4
Bridleway, The, Wall. 200 C4
Bridlington Rd. N9 44 E7
Bridlington Rd., Wat. 50 D3
Bridport Av., Rom. 83 H6
Bridport Pl. N1 12 C1
Bridport Pl. N1 112 A2
Bridport Rd. N18 60 B5
Bridport Rd., Grnf. 103 H1
Bridport Rd., Th.Hth. 187 G3
Bridport Ter. SW8 150 D1
Wandsworth Rd.
Bridstow Pl. W2 108 D6
Talbot Rd.
Brief St. SE5 151 H1
Brierley, Croy. 204 B6
Brierley Av. N9 61 F1
Brierley Cl. SE25 188 D4
Brierley Rd. E11 96 D4
Brierley Rd. SW12 168 C2
Brierly Gdns. E2 113 F2
Royston St.
Brig Ms. SE8 134 A6
Watergate St.
Brigade Cl., Har. 86 A2
Brigade St. SE3 155 F2
Royal Par.
Brigadier Av., Enf. 43 J1
Briggeford Cl. E5 94 D2
Geldeston Rd.
Briggs Cl., Mitch. 186 B1
Bright Cl., Belv. 138 D4
Bright St. E14 114 B6
Brightfield Rd. SE12 155 F5
Brightling Rd. SE4 153 J6
Brightlingsea Pl. E14 113 J7
Brightman Rd. SW18 167 G1
Brighton Av. E17 77 J5
Brighton Dr., Nthlt. 85 G6
Brighton Gro. SE14 153 H1
New Cross Rd.
Brighton Rd. E6 116 D3
Brighton Rd. N2 73 F2
Brighton Rd. N16 94 B4
Brighton Rd., S.Croy. 201 J5
Brighton Rd., Surb. 181 F6
Brighton Ter. SW9 151 F4
Brightside, The, Enf. 45 G1
Brightside Rd. SE13 154 D6
Brightwell Cl., Croy. 201 G1
Sumner Rd.
Brightwell Cres. SW17 167 J5
Brigstock Rd., Belv. 139 H4
Brigstock Rd., Th.Hth. 187 G5
Brill Pl. NW1 9 J2
Brill Pl. NW1 110 D2
Brim Hill N2 73 F4
Brimpsfield Cl. SE2 138 B3
Brimsdown Av., Enf. 45 H2
Brimsdown Ind. Est., Enf. 45 J2
Brindle Gate, Sid. 175 H1
Brindley Cl., Bexh. 159 H3
Brindley Cl., Wem. 105 G1
Brindley St. SE14 153 J1
Brindley Way, Brom. 173 G5
Brindley Way, Sthl. 103 H7
Brindwood Rd. E4 61 J3
Brinkburn Cl. SE2 138 A4
Brinkburn Cl., Edg. 70 B2
Brinkburn Gdns., Edg. 70 A3
Brinkley Rd., Wor.Pk. 197 H2
Brinklow Cres. SE18 137 E7
Brinklow Ho. W2 14 A1
Brinklow Ho. W2 108 E5
Brinkworth Rd., Ilf. 80 B3
Brinkworth Way E9 95 J6
Brinsdale Rd. NW4 72 A4
Brinsley Rd., Har. 68 A2
Brinsley St. E1 112/113 E6
Watney St.
Brinsworth Cl., Twick. 162 A2
Brinton Wk. SE1 27 G2
Brion Pl. E14 114 C5
Brisbane Av. SW19 184 E1
Brisbane Ct. N10 58 B7
Sydney Rd.
Brisbane Rd. E10 96 B2
Brisbane Rd. W13 124 D2
Brisbane Rd., Ilf. 81 E7
Brisbane St. SE5 132 A7
Briscoe Cl. E11 97 F2
Briscoe Rd. SW19 167 G6
Briset Rd. SE9 156 A3
Briset St. EC1 19 G1
Briset Way N7 93 F2
Bristol Cl., Stai. 140 B6
Bristol Gdns. SW15 147 J7
Portsmouth Rd.
Bristol Gdns. W9 6 B6
Bristol Gdns. W9 109 E4
Bristol Ms. W9 6 B6
Bristol Pk. Rd. E17 77 H4
Bristol Rd. E7 97 J6
Bristol Rd., Grnf. 103 H1
Bristol Rd., Mord. 185 F5
Briston Gro. N8 75 E6
Briston Ms. NW7 55 G7
Bristow Rd. SE19 170 B5
Bristow Rd., Bexh. 159 E1
Bristow Rd., Croy. 200 E4
Bristow Rd., Houns. 143 J3
Britannia Cl. SW4 150 D4
Bowland Rd.
Britannia Cl., Nthlt. 102 D3
Britannia Gate E16 135 G1
Britannia La., Twick. 143 J7
Britannia Rd. E14 134 A4
Britannia Rd. N12 57 F3
Britannia Rd. SW6 128 E7
Britannia Rd., Ilf. 98 E3
Britannia Rd., Surb. 181 J7
Britannia Row N1 111 H1
Britannia St. WC1 10 C3
Britannia St. WC1 111 F3
Britannia Wk. N1 12 B3
Britannia Wk. N1 112 A2
Britannia Way NW10 106 B4
Britannia Way SW6 148/149 E1
Britannia Rd.
Britannia Way, Stai. 140 A7
British Gro. W4 127 F5
British Gro. Pas. W4 127 F5
British Gro. S. W4 127 F5
British Gro. Pas.
British Legion Rd. E4 63 F2
British St. E3 113 J3
Brittain Rd., Dag. 101 E3
Britten Cl. NW11 90 E1
Britten Dr., Sthl. 103 G6
Britten St. SW3 31 G4
Britten St. SW3 129 H5
Brittenden Cl., Orp. 207 H6
Britten's Ct. E1 112 E7
Britton Cl. SE6 154 D7
Brownhill Rd.
Britton St. EC1 11 G6
Britton St. EC1 111 H4
Brixham Cres., Ruis. 84 A1
Brixham Gdns., Ilf. 99 H5
Brixham Rd., Well. 158 D1
Brixham St. E16 136 D1
Brixton Est., Edg. 70 B2
Brixton Hill SW2 151 E7
Brixton Hill Pl. SW2 150/151 E7
Brixton Hill
Brixton Oval SW2 151 G4
Brixton Rd. SW9 151 G2
Brixton Sta. Rd. SW9 151 G4
Brixton Water La. SW2 151 F5
Broad Ct. WC2 18 B4
Broad Grn. Av., Croy. 187 H7
Broad La. EC2 20 D1
Broad La. EC2 112 B5
Broad La. N8 75 F5
Tottenham La.
Broad La. N15 76 C4
Broad La., Hmptn. 161 G6
Broad Lawn SE9 174 D2
Broad Oak, Wdf.Grn. 63 H5
Broad Oak Cl. E4 62 A5
Royston Av.
Broad Sanctuary SW1 25 J4
Broad Sanctuary SW1 130 D2
Broad St., Dag. 101 G7
Broad St., Tedd. 162 C6
Broad St. Av. EC2 20 D2
Broad St. Pl. EC2 20 C2
Broad Vw. NW9 70 A6
Broad Wk. N21 59 F2
Broad Wk. NW1 8 D4
Broad Wk. NW1 110 B3
Broad Wk. SE3 155 J2
Broad Wk. W1 24 B1
Broad Wk. W1 130 A1
Broad Wk., Houns. 142 D1
Broad Wk., Rich. 125 J7
Broad Wk., The W8 22 B1
Broad Wk., The W8 129 E1
Broad Wk., The, E.Mol. 180 C3
Broad Wk. La. NW11 72 C7
Broad Yd. EC1 11 G6
Broadbent Cl. N6 92 B1
Broadbent St. W1 16 D5
Broadberry Ct. N18 60 E5
Broadbridge Cl. SE3 135 G7
Broadcoombe, S.Croy. 203 F7
Broadcroft Av., Stan. 69 G2
Broadcroft Rd., Orp. 193 G7
Broadfield Cl. NW2 89 J3
Broadfield Cl., Croy. 201 F2
Progress Way
Broadfield Ct., Bushey 52 B2
Broadfield La. NW1 92 E7
Broadfield Rd. SE6 154 E7
Broadfield Sq., Enf. 45 E2
Broadfield Way, Buck.H. 63 J3
Broadfields, E.Mol. 180 A6
Broadfields, Har. 67 H2
Broadfields Av. N21 43 G7
Broadfields Av., Edg. 54 B4
Broadfields Hts., Edg. 54 B4
Broadfields La., Wat. 50 B1
Broadfields Way NW10 89 F5
Broadgate E13 115 J2
Broadgate EC2 112 B5
Liverpool St.
Broadgate Circle EC2 20 D1
Broadgate Rd. E16 116 A6
Fulmer Rd.
Broadgates Av., Barn. 41 E1
Broadgates Rd. SW18 167 G1
Ellerton Rd.
Broadhead Strand NW9 71 F1
Broadheath Dr., Chis. 174 C5
Broadhinton Rd. SW4 150 B3
Broadhurst Av., Edg. 54 B4
Broadhurst Av., Ilf. 99 J4
Broadhurst Cl. NW6 91 F6
Broadhurst Gdns.
Broadhurst Cl., Rich. 145 J5
Lower Gro. Rd.
Broadhurst Gdns. NW6 90 E6
Broadhurst Gdns., Chig. 65 F4
Broadhurst Gdns., Ruis. 84 C2
Broadlands, Felt. 161 F3
Broadlands Av. SW16 168 E2
Broadlands Av., Enf. 45 E3
Broadlands Cl. N6 74 A7
Broadlands Cl. SW16 168 E2
Broadlands Cl., Enf. 45 E3
Broadlands Rd. N6 73 J7
Broadlands Rd., Brom. 173 H4
Broadlands Way, N.Mal. 183 F6
Broadlawns Ct., Har. 68 C1
Broadley St. NW8 15 F1
Broadley St. NW8 109 H5
Broadley Ter. NW1 7 H6
Broadley Ter. NW1 109 H4
Broadmayne SE17 36 B3
Broadmead SE6 172 A3
Broadmead Av., Wor.Pk. 183 G7

Name	Page	Grid
Broadmead Cl., Hmptn.	161	G6
Broadmead Cl., Pnr.	51	E7
Broadmead Est., Wdf.Grn.	63	J7
Broadmead Rd., Hayes	102	E4
Broadmead Rd., Nthlt.	102	E4
Broadmead Rd., Wdf.Grn.	63	G6
Broadoaks, Surb.	196	B1
Broadoaks Way, Brom.	191	F5
Broadstone Pl. W1	**16**	**B2**
Broadview Rd. SW16	168	D7
Broadwalk E18	79	F3
Broadwalk, Har.	67	G5
Broadwall SE1	**27**	**F1**
Broadwall SE1	131	G1
Broadwater Gdns., Orp.	207	E4
Broadwater Rd. N17	76	B1
Broadwater Rd. SE28	137	G3
Broadwater Rd. SW17	167	H4
Broadway E15	96	D7
Broadway SW1	**25**	**H5**
Broadway SW1	130	D3
Broadway W13	124	D1
Broadway, Bark.	99	F7
Broadway, Bexh.	159	E4
Broadway, Surb.	196	B1
Broadway, The E4	62	D6
Broadway, The E13	115	H2
Broadway, The N8	74	E6
Broadway, The N9	60	D3
Broadway, The N14	58	D1
Winchmore Hill Rd.		
Broadway, The N22	75	G2
Broadway, The NW7	55	E5
Broadway, The SW13	146/147	E2
The Ter.		
Broadway, The SW19	166	C6
Broadway, The W5	105	G7
Broadway, The W7	124	B1
Broadway, The, Croy.	200/201	E4
Croydon Rd.		
Broadway, The, Dag.	101	F2
Whalebone La. S.		
Broadway, The, Grnf.	103	J4
Broadway, The, Har.	68	B2
Broadway, The, Loug.	51	F7
Broadway, The, Pnr.	51	F7
Broadway, The, Sthl.	102	D7
Broadway, The, Stan.	53	F5
Broadway, The, Sutt.	198	B6
Broadway, The, T.Ditt.	194	B1
Hampton Ct. Way		
Broadway, The, Wem.	87	H3
East La.		
Broadway, The, Wdf.Grn.	63	H6
Broadway Av., Croy.	188	A5
Broadway Av., Twick.	144	E6
Broadway Cl., Wdf.Grn.	63	H6
Broadway Ct. SW19	166	D6
The Bdy.		
Broadway Gdns., Mitch.	185	H4
Broadway Mkt. E8	112	E1
Broadway Mkt. Ms. E8	112	D1
Brougham Rd.		
Broadway Ms. E5	76	C7
Broadway Ms. N13	59	F5
Elmdale Rd.		
Broadway Ms. N21	59	H1
Compton Rd.		
Broadway Par. N8	74	E6
Broadway Pl. SW19	166	C6
Hartfield Rd.		
Broadwick St. W1	**17**	**G5**
Broadwick St. W1	110	C6
Broadwood Ter. W8	128	C4
Pembroke Rd.		
Brocas Cl. NW3	91	H7
Fellows Rd.		
Brock Pl. E3	114	B4
Brock Rd. E13	115	H5
Brock St. SE15	153	F3
Evelina Rd.		
Brockdish Av., Bark.	99	J5
Brockenhurst, W.Mol.	179	F6
Brockenhurst Av., Wor.Pk.	197	E1
Brockenhurst Gdns. NW7	55	E5
Brockenhurst Gdns., Ilf.	99	F5
Brockenhurst Ms. N18	60	D4
Lyndhurst Rd.		
Brockenhurst Rd., Croy.	188	E7
Brockenhurst Way SW16	186	D2
Brocket Cl., Chig.	65	J5
Burrow Rd.		
Brocket Way, Chig.	65	H5
Brockham Cl. SW19	166	C5
Brockham Cres., Croy.	204	D7
Brockham Dr. SW2	151	F7
Fairview Pl.		
Brockham Dr., Ilf.	81	E6
Brockham St. SE1	**28**	**A5**
Brockham St. SE1	131	J3
Brockhurst Cl., Stan.	52	C6
Brockill Cres. SE4	153	H4
Brocklebank Rd. SE7	135	H4
Brocklebank Rd. SW18	149	F7
Brocklehurst St. SE14	133	G7
Brocklesby Rd. SE25	188	E4
Brockley Av., Stan.	53	H3
Brockley Cl., Stan.	53	H4
Brockley Cross SE4	153	H3
Endwell Rd.		
Brockley Footpath SE15	153	F4
Brockley Gdns. SE4	153	J2
Brockley Gro. SE4	153	J5
Brockley Hall Rd. SE4	153	H6
Brockley Hill, Stan.	53	F1
Brockley Ms. SE4	153	H5
Brockley Pk. SE23	153	H7
Brockley Ri. SE23	153	H6
Brockley Rd. SE4	153	J3
Brockley Vw. SE23	153	H7
Brockley Way SE4	153	G5
Brockleyside, Stan.	53	G4
Brockman Ri., Brom.	172	D4
Brocks Dr., Sutt.	198	B3
Brockshot Cl., Brent.	125	G5
Brockway Cl. E11	97	E1
Brockwell Cl., Orp.	193	J5
Brockwell Pk. Gdns. SE24	151	G7
Brodewater Rd., Borwd.	38	B2
Brodia Rd. N16	94	B3
Brodie Rd. E4	62	C1
Brodie St. SE1	**37**	**G3**
Brodlove La. E1	113	G7
Brodrick Gro. SE2	138	B4
Brodrick Rd. SW17	167	H2
Brograve Gdns., Beck.	190	B2
Broke Wk. E8	112	D1
Broken Wf. EC4	**19**	**J5**
Brokesley St. E3	113	J4
Bromar Rd. SE5	152	B3
Bromborough Grn., Wat.	50	C5
Brome Rd. SE9	156	C3
Bromefield, Stan.	69	F1
Bromehead Rd. E1	113	F6
Bromell's Rd. SW4	150	C4
Bromfelde Rd. SW4	150	D2
Bromfelde Wk. SW4	150	D2
Bromfield St. N1	**11**	**F1**
Bromfield St. N1	111	G2
Bromhall Rd., Dag.	100	B6
Bromhedge SE9	174	C3
Bromholm Rd. SE2	138	B3
Bromleigh Ct. SE23	170/171	E2
Lapse Wd. Wk.		
Bromley Av., Brom.	173	E7
Bromley Common, Brom.	191	J4
Bromley Cres., Brom.	191	F3
Bromley Gdns., Brom.	191	F3
Bromley Gro., Brom.	190	D2
Bromley Hall Rd. E14	114	C5
Bromley High St. E3	114	B3
Bromley Hill, Brom.	172	E6
Bromley La., Chis.	175	F7
Bromley Pk., Brom.	191	F1
London Rd.		
Bromley Pl. W1	**17**	**F1**
Bromley Rd. E10	78	B6
Bromley Rd. E17	78	A3
Bromley Rd. N17	60	A3
Bromley Rd. N18	76	C1
Bromley Rd. SE6	172	B1
Bromley Rd., Beck.	190	B1
Bromley Rd., Brom.	190	C2
Bromley Rd. (Downham), Brom.	172	C4
Bromley Rd., Chis.	193	E1
Bromley St. E1	113	G5
Brompton Arc. SW3	23	J4
Brompton Cl. SE20	188	D2
Selby Rd.		
Brompton Cl., Houns.	143	F5
Brompton Gro. N2	73	H4
Brompton Pk. Cres. SW6	**30**	**A6**
Brompton Pk. Cres. SW6	128	E6
Brompton Pl. SW3	**23**	**H5**
Brompton Pl. SW3	129	H3
Brompton Rd. SW1	**23**	**H5**
Brompton Rd. SW1	129	H3
Brompton Rd. SW3	**23**	**H5**
Brompton Rd. SW3	129	H3
Brompton Rd. SW7	**23**	**H5**
Brompton Rd. SW7	129	H3
Brompton Sq. SW3	**23**	**G5**
Brompton Sq. SW3	129	H3
Brompton Ter. SE18	156	D1
Prince Imperial Rd.		
Bromwich Av. N6	92	A2
Bromyard Av. W3	127	E1
Bromyard Ho. SE15	**37**	**J7**
Bromyard Ho. SE15	132	E7
Brondesbury Ct. NW2	89	J6
Brondesbury Ms. NW6	90	D7
Willesden La.		
Brondesbury Pk. NW2	89	H6
Brondesbury Pk. NW6	90	A7
Brondesbury Rd. NW6	108	C2
Brondesbury Vil. NW6	108	C2
Bronsart Rd. SW6	128	B7
Bronson Rd. SW20	184	A2
Bronte Cl. E7	97	G4
Bective Rd.		
Bronte Cl., Erith	139	H7
Bronte Cl., Ilf.	80	D5
Bronte Ho. NW6	108	D3
Bronti Cl. SE17	**36**	**A4**
Bronti Cl. SE17	131	J5
Bronze Age Way, Belv.	139	J3
Bronze Age Way, Erith	139	J3
Bronze St. SE8	134	A7
Brook Av., Dag.	101	H7
Brook Av., Edg.	54	B6
Brook Av., Wem.	88	A3
Brook Cl. NW7	56	B7
Frith Ct.		
Brook Cl. SW17	168	A2
Balham High Rd.		
Brook Cl. SW20	183	H3
Brook Cl. W3	126	A1
West Lo. Av.		
Brook Cl., Borwd.	38	B3
Brook Cl., Stai.	140	C7
Brook Cres. E4	62	A4
Brook Cres. N9	60	E4
Brook Dr. SE11	**27**	**F6**
Brook Dr. SE11	131	G4
Brook Dr., Har.	67	J4
Brook Gdns. E4	62	B4
Brook Gdns. SW13	147	F3
Brook Gdns., Kings.T.	182	C1
Brook Gate W1	**16**	**A6**
Brook Gate W1	109	J7
Brook Grn. W6	128	A4
Brook Ind. Est., Hayes	122	D1
Brook La. SE3	155	H2
Brook La., Bex.	158	D6
Brook La., Brom.	173	G6
Brook La. N., Brent.	125	G5
Brook Mead, Epsom	197	E6
Brook Meadow N12	56	E4
Brook Meadow Cl., Wdf.Grn.	62	E6
Brook Ms. N. W2	**14**	**D5**
Brook Par., Chig.	64/65	E3
High Rd.		
Brook Path, Loug.	48	B4
Brook Pl., Barn.	40	D5
Brook Ri., Chig.	64	D3
Brook Rd. N8	74	E4
Brook Rd. N22	75	F3
Brook Rd. NW2	89	G2
Brook Rd., Borwd.	38	A2
Brook Rd., Buck.H.	63	G2
Brook Rd., Ilf.	81	H6
Brook Rd., Loug.	48	B5
Brook Rd., Surb.	195	H2
Brook Rd., Th.Hth.	187	J4
Brook Rd., Twick.	144	D6
Brook Rd. S., Brent.	125	G6
Brook St. N17	76	C2
High Rd.		
Brook St. W1	**16**	**C5**
Brook St. W1	110	B6
Brook St. W2	**15**	**F5**
Brook St. W2	109	G7
Brook St., Belv.	139	H5
Brook St., Erith	139	H6
Brook St., Kings.T.	181	H2
Brook Vale, Erith	159	H1
Brook Wk. N2	73	G1
Brook Wk., Edg.	54	D6
Brook Way, Chig.	64	D3
Brookbank Av. W7	104	A5
Brookbank Rd. SE13	154	A3
Brookdale N11	58	C4
Brookdale Rd. E17	78	A3
Brookdale Rd. SE6	154	B6
Brookdale Rd., Bex.	159	E6
Brookdene Rd. SE18	137	J4
Brooke Av., Har.	85	J3
Brooke Rd. E5	94	D3
Brooke Rd. E17	78	C4
Brooke Rd. N16	94	C3
Brooke St. EC1	**19**	**E2**
Brooke St. EC1	111	G5
Brookehowse Rd. SE6	172	B3
Brookend Rd., Sid.	175	H1
Brooke's Ct. EC1	**19**	**E1**
Brookes Mkt. EC1	**19**	**F1**
Brookfield N6	92	A3
Brookfield Av. E17	78	C4
Brookfield Av. NW7	55	H6
Brookfield Av. W5	105	G4
Brookfield Av., Sutt.	199	G4
Brookfield Cl. NW7	55	H6
Brookfield Ct., Grnf.	103	J3
Brookfield Ct., Har.	69	G5
Brookfield Cres. NW7	55	H6
Brookfield Cres., Har.	69	H5
Brookfield Gdns., Esher	194	C6
Brookfield Pk. NW5	92	B3
Brookfield Path, Wdf.Grn.	62	E6
Brookfield Rd. E9	95	H6
Brookfield Rd. N9	60	D3
Brookfield Rd. W4	126	D2
Brookfields, Enf.	45	G4
Brookfields Av., Mitch.	185	H5
Brookhill Cl. SE18	136	E5
Brookhill Cl., Barn.	41	H5
Brookhill Rd. SE18	136	E5
Brookhill Rd., Barn.	41	H5
Brookhouse Gdns. E4	62	E4
Brooking Rd. E7	97	G5
Brookland Cl. NW11	72	D4
Brookland Garth NW11	72	E4
Brookland Hill NW11	72	D4
Brookland Ri. NW11	72	D4
Brooklands Av. SW19	166	E2
Brooklands Av., Sid.	175	G2
Brooklands Dr., Grnf.	105	G1
Brooklands Pk. SE3	155	G3
Brooklands Rd., T.Ditt.	194	C1
Brooklea Cl. NW9	71	E1
Brooklyn Av. SE25	189	E4
Brooklyn Av., Loug.	48	B4
Brooklyn Cl., Cars.	199	H2
Brooklyn Gro. SE25	189	E4
Brooklyn Rd. SE25	188	E4
Brooklyn Rd., Brom.	192	A5
Brooklyn Way, West Dr.	120	A3
Brookmarsh Trd. Est. SE10	134	B7
Norman Rd.		
Brookmead Av., Brom.	192	C5
Brookmead Rd., Croy.	186	C6
Brookmeads Est., Mitch.	185	H5
Brookmill Rd. SE8	154	A1
Brooks Av. E6	116	C4
Brooks Cl. SE9	174	D2
Brooks Ct. E15	96	B5
Clays La.		
Brooks La. W4	126	A6
Brook's Ms. W1	**16**	**D5**

Brook's Ms. W1 110 B7
Brooks Rd. E13 115 G1
Brooks Rd. W4 126 A5
Brooksbank St. E9 95 G6
Brooksby Ms. N1 93 G7
Brooksby St.
Brooksby St. N1 93 G7
Brooksby's Wk. E9 95 G5
Brookscroft Rd. E17 78 B1
Brookshill, Har. 52 A5
Brookshill Av., Har. 52 A5
Brookshill Dr., Har. 52 A5
Brookside N21 43 F6
Brookside, Barn. 41 H6
Brookside, Cars. 200 A5
Brookside, Ilf. 65 F6
Brookside, Orp. 193 J7
Brookside Cl., Barn. 40 B6
Brookside Cl., Felt. 160 A3
Sycamore Cl.
Brookside Cl., Har. 69 G5
Brookside Cl. (Kenton), Har. 85 E4
Brookside Cres., Wor.Pk. 197 G1
Green La.
Brookside Rd. N9 60 E4
Brookside Rd. N19 92 C2
Junction Rd.
Brookside Rd. NW11 72 B6
Brookside Rd., Hayes 102 C7
Brookside S., Barn. 42 A7
Brookside Wk. N3 72 B2
Brookside Wk. N12 56 D6
Brookside Wk. NW4 72 B4
Brookside Wk. NW11 72 B4
Brookside Way, Croy. 189 G6
Brooksville Av. NW6 108 B1
Brookview Rd. SW16 168 C5
Brookville Rd. SW6 128 C7
Brookway SE3 155 G3
Brookwood Av. SW13 147 F2
Brookwood Cl., Brom. 191 F4
Brookwood Rd. SW18 166 C1
Brookwood Rd., Houns. 143 H1
Broom Cl., Brom. 192 B6
Broom Cl., Tedd. 163 G7
Broom Gdns., Croy. 204 A3
Broom Lock, Tedd. 163 F6
Broom Mead, Bexh. 159 G5
Broom Pk., Tedd. 163 G7
Broom Rd., Croy. 204 A3
Broom Rd., Tedd. 163 F6
Broom Water, Tedd. 163 F6
Broom Water W., Tedd. 163 F5
Broomcroft Av., Nthlt. 102 C3
Broome Rd., Hmptn. 161 F7
Broome Way SE5 131 J7
Broomfield E17 77 J7
Broomfield, Sun. 178 A1
Broomfield Av. N13 59 F5
Broomfield Av., Loug. 48 C6
Broomfield La. N13 59 F4
Broomfield Pl. W13 124/125 E1
Broomfield Rd.
Broomfield Rd. N13 59 E5
Broomfield Rd. W13 125 E1
Broomfield Rd., Beck. 189 H3
Broomfield Rd., Bexh. 159 G5
Broomfield Rd., Rich. 145 J1
Broomfield Rd., Rom. 82 D7
Broomfield Rd., Surb. 195 J1
Broomfield Rd., Tedd. 163 F6
Melbourne Rd.
Broomfield St. E14 114 A5
Broomgrove Gdns., Edg. 70 A1
Broomgrove Rd. SW9 151 F2
Broomhill Ri., Bexh. 159 G5
Broomhill Rd. SW18 148 D5
Broomhill Rd., Ilf. 100 A2
Broomhill Rd., Wdf.Grn. 63 G6
Broomhill Wk., Wdf.Grn. 63 F7
Broomhouse La. SW6 148 D2
Broomhouse Rd. SW6 148 D2
Broomloan La., Sutt. 198 D2
Broomsleigh St. NW6 90 C5
Broomwood Cl., Croy. 189 G5
Broomwood Rd. SW11 149 J6
Broseley Gro. SE26 171 H5
Broster Gdns. SE25 188 C3
Brough Cl. SW8 130/131 E7
Kenchester Cl.
Brough Cl., Kings.T. 163 G5
Brougham Rd. E8 112 D1
Brougham Rd. W3 106 C6
Brougham St. SW11 149 J2
Broughinge Rd., Borwd. 38 B2
Broughton Av. N3 72 B3
Broughton Av., Rich. 163 E3
Broughton Dr. SW9 151 G4
Broughton Gdns. N6 74 C6
Broughton Rd. SW6 148 E2
Broughton Rd. W13 105 E7
Broughton Rd., Orp. 207 G2
Broughton Rd., Th.Hth. 187 G6
Broughton Rd. App. SW6 148/149 E2
Wandsworth Br. Rd.
Broughton St. SW8 150 A2
Brouncker Rd. W3 126 C2
Browells La., Felt. 160 B2
Brown Cl., Wall. 200 E7
Brown Hart Gdns. W1 16 C5
Brown Hart Gdns. W1 110 A7
Brown St. W1 15 J3
Brown St. W1 109 J6
Brownfield St. E14 114 B6
Browngraves Rd., Hayes 121 F7
Brownhill Rd. SE6 154 B7
Browning Av. W7 104 C6
Browning Av., Sutt. 199 H4
Browning Av., Wor.Pk. 197 H1
Browning Cl. E17 78 C4
Browning Cl. W9 6 D6
Browning Cl., Hmptn. 161 F4
Browning Cl., Well. 157 H1
Browning Est. SE17 36 A3
Browning Est. SE17 131 J5
Browning Ho. W12 107 J6
Wood La.
Browning Ms. W1 16 D2
Browning Rd. E11 79 F7
Browning Rd. E12 98 C6
Browning St. SE17 36 A3
Browning St. SE17 131 J5
Browning Way, Houns. 142 D1
Brownlea Gdns., Ilf. 100 A2
Brownlow Ms. WC1 10 D6
Brownlow Ms. WC1 111 F4
Brownlow Rd. E7 97 H4
Woodford Rd.
Brownlow Rd. E8 112 C1
Brownlow Rd. N3 56 E7
Brownlow Rd. N11 58 E6
Brownlow Rd. NW10 89 E7
Brownlow Rd. W13 124 D1
Brownlow Rd., Borwd. 38 A4
Brownlow Rd., Croy. 202 B4
Brownlow St. WC1 18 D2
Brown's Bldgs. EC3 20 E4
Brown's Bldgs. EC3 112 B6
Browns La. NW5 92 B5
Browns Rd. E17 78 A3
Browns Rd., Surb. 181 J7
Brownspring Dr. SE9 175 E4
Brownswell Rd. N2 73 G2
Brownswood Rd. N4 93 H3
Broxash Rd. SW11 150 A6
Broxbourne Av. E18 79 H4
Broxbourne Rd. E7 97 G3
Broxbourne Rd., Orp. 193 J7
Broxholm Rd. SE27 169 G3
Broxted Rd. SE6 171 J2
Broxwood Way NW8 109 H1
Bruce Castle Rd. N17 76 C1
Bruce Cl. W10 108 B5
Ladbroke Gro.
Bruce Cl., Well. 158 B1
Bruce Gdns. N20 57 J3
Balfour Gro.
Bruce Gro. N17 76 B1
Bruce Hall Ms. SW17 168 A4
Brudenell Rd.
Bruce Rd. E3 114 B3
Bruce Rd. NW10 88 D7
Bruce Rd. SE25 188 A4
Bruce Rd., Barn. 40 B3
St. Albans Rd.
Bruce Rd., Har. 68 B2
Bruce Rd., Mitch. 168 A7
Bruckner St. W10 108 C3
Brudenell Rd. SW17 167 J3
Bruffs Meadow, Nthlt. 85 E6
Bruges Pl. NW1 92 C7
Randolph St.
Brumfield Rd., Epsom 196 C5
Brummel Cl., Bexh. 159 J3
Brune St. E1 21 F2
Brune St. E1 112 C5
Brunel Cl. SE19 170 C6
Brunel Cl., Houns. 122 B7
Brunel Cl., Nthlt. 103 F3
Brunel Est. W2 108 D5
Brunel Pl., Sthl. 103 H6
Brunel Rd. E17 77 H6
Brunel Rd. SE16 133 F2
Brunel Rd. W3 106 E5
Brunel Rd., Wdf.Grn. 64 C5
Brunel St. E16 115 F6
Victoria Dock Rd.
Brunel Wk. N15 76 B4
Brunel Wk., Twick. 143 G7
Stephenson Rd.
Brunner Cl. NW11 73 F5
Brunner Rd. E17 77 J5
Brunner Rd. W5 105 G4
Bruno Pl. NW9 88 C2
Brunswick Av. N11 58 A3
Brunswick Cen. WC1 10 A5
Brunswick Cl., Bexh. 158 D4
Brunswick Cl., Pnr. 67 E6
Brunswick Cl., T.Ditt. 194 C1
Brunswick Cl., Twick. 162 A3
Brunswick Ct. EC1 111 H3
Northampton Sq.
Brunswick Ct. SE1 29 E4
Brunswick Ct. SE1 132 B2
Brunswick Ct., Barn. 41 G5
Brunswick Cres. N11 58 A3
Brunswick Gdns. W5 105 H3
Brunswick Gdns. W8 128 D1
Brunswick Gdns., Ilf. 65 F7
Brunswick Gro. N11 58 A3
Brunswick Ind. Pk. N11 58 B4
Brunswick Ms. SW16 168 D6
Potters La.
Brunswick Ms. W1 16 A3
Brunswick Pk. SE5 152 A1
Brunswick Pk. Gdns. N11 58 A2
Brunswick Pk. Rd. N11 58 A2
Brunswick Pl. N1 12 C4
Brunswick Pl. N1 112 A3
Brunswick Pl. SE19 170 D7
Brunswick Quay SE16 133 G3
Brunswick Rd. E10 96 C1
Brunswick Rd. E14 114 C6
Blackwall Tunnel Northern App.
Brunswick Rd. N15 76 B5
Brunswick Rd. W5 105 G4
Brunswick Rd., Bexh. 158 D4
Brunswick Rd., Kings.T. 182 A1
Brunswick Rd., Sutt. 199 E4
Brunswick Sq. N17 60 C6
Brunswick Sq. WC1 10 B6
Brunswick Sq. WC1 111 E4
Brunswick St. E17 78 C5
Brunswick Vil. SE5 152 B1
Brunswick Way N11 58 B4
Brunton Pl. E14 113 H6
Brushfield St. E1 21 E2
Brushfield St. E1 112 B5
Brussels Rd. SW11 149 G4
Bruton Cl., Chis. 174 C7
Bruton La. W1 17 E6
Bruton La. W1 110 B7
Bruton Pl. W1 16 E6
Bruton Pl. W1 110 B7
Bruton Rd., Mord. 185 F5
Bruton St. W1 16 E6
Bruton St. W1 110 B7
Bruton Way W13 104 D5
Bryan Av. NW10 89 H7
Bryan Cl., Sun. 160 A7
Bryan Rd. SE16 133 J2
Bryan's All. SW6 148/149 E2
Wandsworth Br. Rd.
Bryanston Av., Twick. 161 H1
Bryanston Cl., Sthl. 123 F4
Bryanston Ms. E. W1 15 J2
Bryanston Ms. W. W1 15 J2
Bryanston Pl. W1 15 J2
Bryanston Pl. W1 109 J5
Bryanston Sq. W1 15 J2
Bryanston Sq. W1 109 J5
Bryanston St. W1 15 J4
Bryanston St. W1 109 J6
Bryanstone Rd. N8 74 D5
Bryant Cl., Barn. 40 C5
Bryant Ct. E2 13 F1
Bryant Ct. E2 112 C2
Bryant Rd., Nthlt. 102 C3
Bryant St. E15 96 D7
Bryantwood Rd. N7 93 G5
Bryce Rd., Dag. 100 C4
Brycedale Cres. N14 58 D4
Bryden Cl. SE26 171 H5
Brydges Pl. WC2 18 A6
Brydges Rd. E15 96 D5
Brydon Wk. N1 110/111 E1
Outram Pl.
Bryer Ct. EC2 111 J5
Aldersgate St.
Bryett Rd. N7 93 E3
Brymay Cl. E3 114 A2
Bryn-y-Mawr Rd., Enf. 44 C4
Brynmaer Rd. SW11 149 J1
Bryony Cl., Loug. 48 E4
Bryony Rd. W12 107 G7
Buchan Rd. SE15 153 F3
Buchanan Cl. N21 43 F5
Buchanan Ct., Borwd. 38 C2
Buchanan Gdns. NW10 107 H2
Bucharest Rd. SW18 149 F7
Buck Hill Wk. W2 15 F6
Buck La. NW9 70 D5
Buck St. NW1 92 B7
Buck Wk. E17 78 D4
Foresters Dr.
Buckden Cl. N2 73 J4
Southern Rd.
Buckden Cl. SE12 155 F6
Upwood Rd.
Buckfast Rd., Mord. 185 E4
Buckfast St. E2 13 J4
Buckfast St. E2 112 D3
Buckhold Rd. SW18 148 D6
Buckhurst Av., Cars. 199 H1
Buckhurst St. E1 113 E4
Buckhurst Way, Buck.H. 64 A4
Buckingham Arc. WC2 18 B6
Buckingham Av. N20 41 F7
Buckingham Av., Felt. 142 B6
Buckingham Av., Grnf. 104 D1
Buckingham Av., Th.Hth. 187 G1
Buckingham Av., Well. 157 H4
Buckingham Av., W.Mol. 179 H3
Buckingham Cl. W5 105 F5
Buckingham Cl., Enf. 44 B2
Buckingham Cl., Hmptn. 161 F5
Buckingham Cl., Orp. 193 H7
Buckingham Ct. NW4 71 G3
Buckingham Dr., Chis. 175 E5
Buckingham Gdns., Edg. 53 J7
Buckingham Gdns., Th.Hth. 187 G2
Buckingham Gdns., W.Mol. 179 H2
Buckingham Av.
Buckingham Gate SW1 25 F4
Buckingham Gate SW1 130 C3
Buckingham La. SE23 153 H7
Buckingham Ms. N1 94 B6
Buckingham Rd.
Buckingham Ms. NW10 107 F2
Buckingham Rd.
Buckingham Ms. SW1 25 F5
Buckingham Palace Rd. SW1 32 D2
Buckingham Palace Rd. SW1 130 B4
Buckingham Pl. SW1 25 F5
Buckingham Rd. E10 96 B3
Buckingham Rd. E11 79 J5
Buckingham Rd. E15 97 F5
Buckingham Rd. E18 79 F1
Buckingham Rd. N1 94 B6
Buckingham Rd. N22 74 E1
Buckingham Rd. NW10 107 F2

Buckingham Rd., Borwd. 38 D4
Buckingham Rd., Edg. 53 J7
Buckingham Rd., Hmptn. 161 F5
Buckingham Rd., Har. 68 A5
Buckingham Rd., Ilf. 99 G2
Buckingham Rd., Kings.T. 181 J4
Buckingham Rd., Mitch. 186 E5
Buckingham Rd., Rich. 163 G2
Buckingham St. WC2 18 B6
Buckland Cres. NW3 91 G7
Buckland Ri., Pnr. 66 C1
Buckland Rd. E10 96 C2
Buckland Rd., Chess. 195 J5
Buckland Rd., Orp. 207 H4
Buckland St. N1 12 C2
Buckland St. N1 112 A2
Buckland Wk. W3 126 C2
Church Rd.
Buckland Wk., Mord. 185 F4
Buckland Way, Wor.Pk. 197 J1
Bucklands Rd., Tedd. 163 F6
Buckle St. E1 21 G3
Buckleigh Av. SW20 184 B3
Buckleigh Rd. SW16 168 D6
Buckleigh Way SE19 188 C1
Buckler Gdns. SE9 174 C3
Southold Ri.
Bucklers All. SW6 128 C6
Bucklers Way, Cars. 199 J3
Bucklersbury EC4 20 B4
Bucklersbury EC4 112 A6
Bucklersbury Pas. EC4 20 B4
Buckles Ct., Belv. 138 D3
Fendyke Rd.
Buckley Rd. NW6 90 C7
Buckley St. SE1 26 E2
Buckmaster Cl. SW9 151 F3
Stockwell Pk. Rd.
Buckmaster Rd. SW11 149 H4
Bucknall St. WC2 17 J3
Bucknall St. WC2 110 D6
Bucknell Cl. SW2 151 F4
Buckner Rd. SW2 151 F4
Buckrell Rd. E4 62 D2
Buckstone Cl. SE23 153 F6
Buckstone Rd. N18 60 D5
Buckters Rents SE16 133 H1
Buckthorne Rd. SE4 153 H6
Budd Cl. N12 57 E4
Buddings Circle, Wem. 88 C3
Budd's All., Twick. 145 F5
Arlington Cl.
Budge La., Mitch. 185 J7
Budge Row EC4 20 B5
Budge's Wk. W2 22 C1
Budge's Wk. W2 109 F7
Budleigh Cres., Well. 158 C1
Budoch Ct., Ilf. 100 A2
Budoch Dr., Ilf. 100 A2
Buer Rd. SW6 148 B2
Bugsby's Way SE7 135 H4
Bugsby's Way SE10 135 F4
Bulganak Rd., Th.Hth. 187 J4
Bulinga St. SW1 34 A2
Bulinga St. SW1 130 D4
Bull All., Well. 158 B3
Welling High St.
Bull Inn Ct. WC2 18 B6
Bull La. N18 60 B5
Bull La., Chis. 175 G7
Bull La., Dag. 101 H3
Bull Rd. E15 115 F2
Bull Wf. La. EC4 20 A5
Bullace Row SE5 151 J1
Camberwell Rd.
Bullards Pl. E2 113 G3
Bullbanks Rd., Belv. 139 J4
Bullen St. SW11 149 H2
Buller Cl. SE15 132 D7
Buller Rd. N17 76 D2
Buller Rd. N22 75 G2
Buller Rd. NW10 108 A3
Chamberlayne Rd.
Buller Rd., Bark. 99 H7
Buller Rd., Th.Hth. 188 A2
Bullers Cl., Sid. 176 E5
Bullers Wd. Dr., Chis. 174 B7
Bullescroft Rd., Edg. 54 A3
Bullhead Rd., Borwd. 38 C3
Bullied Way SW1 32 E2
Bullivant St. E14 114 C7
Bullrush Cl., Croy. 188 B6
Bull's All. SW14 146 D2
Bulls Br. Ind. Est., Sthl. 122 B3
Hayes Rd.
Bulls Br. Rd., Sthl. 122 B3
Bulls Gdns. SW3 31 H1
Bull's Head Pas. EC3 20 D4
Bullsbrook Rd., Hayes 122 C1
Bulmer Gdns., Har. 69 G7
Bulmer Ms. W11 108 D7
Ladbroke Rd.
Bulmer Pl. W11 128 D1
Bulow Est. SW6 148/149 E2
Broughton Rd.
Bulstrode Av., Houns. 143 F2
Bulstrode Gdns., Houns. 143 F3
Bulstrode Pl. W1 16 C2
Bulstrode Rd., Houns. 143 G3
Bulstrode St. W1 16 C3
Bulstrode St. W1 110 A6
Bulwer Ct. Rd. E11 96 D1
Bulwer Gdns., Barn. 41 F4
Bulwer Rd.
Bulwer Rd. E11 78 D7
Bulwer Rd. N18 60 B4
Bulwer Rd., Barn. 41 E4
Bulwer St. W12 127 J1
Bunces La., Wdf.Grn. 63 F7
Bungalow Rd. SE25 188 B4
Bungalows, The SW16 168 B7
Bungalows, The, Wall. 200 B5
Bunhill Row EC1 12 B5
Bunhill Row EC1 112 A4
Bunhouse Pl. SW1 32 B3
Bunhouse Pl. SW1 130 A5
Bunkers Hill NW11 73 F7
Bunkers Hill, Belv. 139 G4
Bunkers Hill, Sid. 177 F3
Bunning Way N7 93 E7
Bunns La. NW7 55 F6
Bunsen St. E3 113 H2
Kenilworth Rd.
Bunting Cl. N9 61 G1
Dunnock Cl.
Bunting Cl., Mitch. 185 J5
Buntingbridge Rd., Ilf. 81 G5
Bunton St. SE18 136 D3
Bunyan Rd. E17 77 H3
Buonaparte Ms. SW1 33 H3
Burbage Cl. SE1 28 B6
Burbage Cl. SE1 132 A3
Burbage Rd. SE21 152 A6
Burbage Rd. SE24 151 J6
Burberry Cl., N.Mal. 182 E2
Burbridge Way N17 76 C2
Burcham St. E14 114 B6
Burcharbro Rd. SE2 138 D6
Burchell Rd. E10 96 B1
Burchell Rd. SE15 153 E1
Burchett Way, Rom. 83 F6
Burcote Rd. SW18 167 G1
Burden Cl., Brent. 125 F5
Burden Way E11 97 H2
Brading Cres.
Burdenshott Av., Rich. 146 B4
Burder Cl. N1 94 B6
Burder Rd. N1 94 B6
Balls Pond Rd.
Burdett Av. SW20 183 G1
Burdett Cl. W7 124 C2
Cherington Rd.
Burdett Cl., Sid. 176 E5
Burdett Ms. NW3 91 G6
Belsize Cres.
Burdett Ms. W2 14 A3
Burdett Rd. E3 113 J4
Burdett Rd. E14 113 J4
Burdett Rd., Croy. 188 A6
Burdett Rd., Rich. 145 J3
Burdett St. SE1 27 E5
Burdetts Rd., Dag. 119 F1
Burdock Cl., Croy. 203 G1
Burdock Rd. N17 76 D3
Burdon La., Sutt. 198 B7
Burfield Cl. SW17 167 G4
Burford Cl., Dag. 100 C3
Burford Cl., Ilf. 81 F4
Burford Gdns. N13 59 F3
Burford Rd. E6 116 B3
Burford Rd. E15 96 D7
Burford Rd. SE6 171 J2
Burford Rd., Brent. 125 H5
Burford Rd., Brom. 192 B4
Burford Rd., Sutt. 198 D2
Burford Rd., Wor.Pk. 183 F7
Burford Wk. SW6 128/129 E7
Cambria St.
Burford Way, Croy. 204 C6
Burge St. SE1 28 C6
Burge St. SE1 132 A3
Burges Ct. E6 98 D7
Burges Gro. SW13 127 H7
Burges Rd. E6 98 B7
Burgess Av. NW9 70 D6
Burgess Cl., Felt. 160 E4
Burgess Hill NW2 90 D4
Burgess Rd. E15 96 E4
Burgess Rd., Sutt. 198 E4
Burgess St. E14 114 A5
Burgh St. N1 11 H1
Burgh St. N1 111 H2
Burghill Rd. SE26 171 H4
Burghley Av., Borwd. 38 C5
Burghley Av., N.Mal. 182 D1
Burghley Hall Cl. SW19 166 B1
Princes Way
Burghley Pl., Mitch. 186 A5
Burghley Rd. E11 97 E1
Burghley Rd. N8 75 G3
Burghley Rd. NW5 92 B5
Burghley Rd. SW19 166 A4
Burghley Twr. W3 107 F7
Burgon St. EC4 19 H4
Burgos Cl., Croy. 201 G6
Burgos Gro. SE10 154 B1
Burgoyne Rd. N4 75 H6
Burgoyne Rd. SE25 188 C4
Burgoyne Rd. SW9 151 F3
Burham Cl. SE20 171 F7
Maple Rd.
Burhill Gro., Pnr. 66 E2
Burke Cl. SW15 147 E4
Burke St. E16 115 F6
Burket Cl., Sthl. 123 F4
Kingsbridge Rd.
Burland Rd. SW11 149 J5
Burleigh Av., Sid. 157 J5
Burleigh Av., Wall. 200 A3
Burleigh Gdns. N14 58 C1
Burleigh Ho. W10 108 A5
St. Charles Sq.
Burleigh Pl. SW15 148 A5
Burleigh Rd., Enf. 44 B4
Burleigh Rd., Sutt. 198 B1
Burleigh St. WC2 18 C5
Burleigh Wk. SE6 172 C1
Muirkirk Rd.
Burleigh Way, Enf. 44 A3
Church St.
Burley Cl. E4 62 A5
Burley Cl. SW16 186 D2
Burley Rd. E16 115 J6
Burlington Arc. W1 17 F6
Burlington Arc. W1 110 C7
Burlington Av., Rich. 146 A1
Burlington Av., Rom. 83 H6
Burlington Cl. E6 116 B6
Northumberland Rd.
Burlington Cl. W9 108 C4
Burlington Cl., Felt. 141 G7
Burlington Cl., Orp. 206 E2
Burlington Cl., Pnr. 66 B3
Burlington Gdns. W1 17 F6
Burlington Gdns. W1 110 C7
Burlington Gdns. W3 126 C1
Burlington Gdns. W4 126 C5
Burlington Gdns., Rom. 83 E7
Burlington La. W4 126 E7
Burlington Ms. SW15 148 C5
Upper Richmond Rd.
Burlington Ms. W3 126 C1
Burlington Pl. SW6 148 B2
Burlington Rd.
Burlington Pl., Wdf.Grn. 63 G3
Burlington Ri., Barn. 57 H1
Burlington Rd. N10 74 A2
Tetherdown
Burlington Rd. N17 76 D1
Burlington Rd. SW6 148 B2
Burlington Rd. W4 126 C5
Burlington Rd., Enf. 44 A1
Burlington Rd., Islw. 144 A1
Burlington Rd., N.Mal. 183 G4
Burlington Rd., Th.Hth. 187 J2
Burma Rd. N16 94 A4
Burmester Rd. SW17 167 F3
Burn Side N9 61 F3
Burnaby Cres. W4 126 B6
Burnaby Gdns. W4 126 C6
Burnaby St. SW10 129 F7
Burnbrae Cl. N12 57 E6
Burnbury Rd. SW12 168 C1
Burncroft Av., Enf. 45 F2
Burne Jones Ho. W14 128 C4
Burne St. NW1 15 G1
Burne St. NW1 109 H5
Burnell Av., Rich. 163 F5
Burnell Av., Well. 158 A2
Burnell Gdns., Stan. 69 G1
Burnell Rd., Sutt. 199 E4
Burnell Wk. SE1 37 G3
Burnels Av. E6 116 D3
Burness Cl. N7 93 F6
Roman Way
Burnett Cl. E9 95 F5
Burney Av., Surb. 181 J5
Burney Dr., Loug. 49 E2
Burney St. SE10 134 C7
Burnfoot Av. SW6 148 B1
Burnfoot Ct. SE22 170 E1
Burnham NW3 91 H7
Burnham Cl. NW7 55 G7
Burnham Cl. SE1 37 G2
Burnham Cl., Har. 68 D4
Burnham Ct. NW4 71 J4
Burnham Cres. E11 79 J4
Burnham Dr., Wor.Pk. 198 A2
Burnham Gdns., Croy. 188 C7
Burnham Gdns., Hayes 121 G3
Burnham Gdns., Houns. 142 B1
Burnham Rd. E4 61 J5
Burnham Rd., Dag. 100 B7
Burnham Rd., Mord. 185 E5
Burnham Rd., Sid. 176 E2
Burnham St. E2 113 F3
Burnham St., Kings.T. 182 A1
Burnham Way SE26 171 J5
Burnham Way W13 124 E4
Burnhill Rd., Beck. 190 A2
Burnley Cl., Wat. 50 C5
Burnley Rd. NW10 89 G5
Burnley Rd. SW9 151 F2
Burns Av., Felt. 142 A6
Burns Av., Rom. 82 C7
Burns Av., Sid. 158 B6
Burns Av., Sthl. 103 G7
Burns Cl. E17 78 C4
Burns Cl. SW19 167 G6
North Rd.
Burns Cl., Well. 157 J1
Burns Rd. NW10 107 F1
Burns Rd. SW11 149 J2
Burns Rd. W13 124 E2
Burns Rd., Wem. 105 G2
Burns Way, Houns. 142 D2
Burnsall St. SW3 31 H3
Burnsall St. SW3 129 H5
Burnside Av. E4 61 J6
Burnside Cl. SE16 133 G1
Burnside Cl., Barn. 40 D3
Burnside Cl., Twick. 144 D6
Burnside Cres., Wem. 105 G1
Burnside Rd., Dag. 100 C2
Burnt Ash Hill SE12 155 F6
Burnt Ash La., Brom. 173 G6
Burnt Ash Rd. SE12 155 F5
Burnt Oak Bdy., Edg. 54 B7
Burnt Oak Flds., Edg. 70 C1
Burnt Oak La., Sid. 158 A6
Burnthwaite Rd. SW6 128 D7
Burntwood Cl. SW18 167 G1
Burntwood Gra. Rd. SW18 167 G1
Burntwood La. SW17 167 H2
Burntwood Vw. SE19 170 C5
Bowley La.
Buross St. E1 112/113 E6
Commercial Rd.
Burr Cl. E1 29 H1
Burr Cl. E1 132 D1
Burr Cl., Bexh. 159 F3
Burr Rd. SW18 148 D7
Burrage Gro. SE18 137 F4
Burrage Pl. SE18 137 E5
Burrage Rd. SE18 137 F5
Burrard Rd. E16 115 H6
Burrard Rd. NW6 90 D4
Burrell Cl., Croy. 189 H6
Burrell Cl., Edg. 54 B2
Burrell Row, Beck. 190 A2
High St.
Burrell St. SE1 27 G1
Burrell St. SE1 131 H1
Burrell Twr. E10 78 A7
Burrells Wf. Sq. E14 134 B5
Burritt Rd., Kings.T. 182 A2
Burroughs, The NW4 71 H5
Burroughs Gdns. NW4 71 H4

Street	Page	Grid
Caistor Ms. SW12	150	B7
Caistor Rd.		
Caistor Pk. Rd. E15	115	F1
Caistor Rd. SW12	150	B7
Caithness Gdns., Sid.	157	J6
Caithness Rd. W14	128	A4
Caithness Rd., Mitch.	168	B7
Calabria Rd. N5	93	H6
Calais Gate SE5	151	H1
Calais St.		
Calais St. SE5	151	H1
Calbourne Rd. SW12	149	J7
Calcott Wk. SE9	174	A4
Caldbeck Av., Wor.Pk.	197	G2
Caldecot Rd. SE5	151	J2
Caldecott Way E5	95	G3
Calder Av., Grnf.	104	C2
Calder Cl., Enf.	44	B3
Calder Gdns., Edg.	70	A3
Calder Rd., Mord.	185	F5
Calderon Pl. W10	107	J5
St. Quintin Gdns.		
Calderon Rd. E11	96	C4
Caldervale Rd. SW4	150	D5
Calderwood St. SE18	136	D4
Caldicot Grn. NW9	70/71	E6
Snowdon Dr.		
Caldwell Rd., Wat.	50	D4
Caldwell St. SW9	131	F7
Caldwell Yd. EC4	111	J7
Upper Thames St.		
Caldy Rd., Belv.	139	H3
Caldy Wk. N1	93	J6
Clephane Rd.		
Cale St. SW3	31	G3
Cale St. SW3	129	H5
Caleb St. SE1	27	J3
Caledon Rd. E6	116	C1
Caledon Rd., Wall.	200	A4
Caledonia St. N1	10	B2
Caledonia St. N1	111	F2
Caledonian Cl., Ilf.	100	B1
Caledonian Rd. N1	10	B2
Caledonian Rd. N1	111	F2
Caledonian Rd. N7	93	F5
Caledonian Wf. E14	134	D4
Caletock Way SE10	135	F5
Calico Row SW11	149	F3
York Pl.		
Calidore Cl. SW2	151	F6
Endymion Rd.		
California La., Bushey	52	A1
California Rd., N.Mal.	182	C4
Callaby Ter. N1	94	A6
Wakeham St.		
Callaghan Cl. SE13	154/155	E4
Glenton Rd.		
Callander Rd. SE6	172	B2
Callard Av. N13	59	H5
Callcott Rd. NW6	90	C7
Callcott St. W8	128	D1
Hillgate Pl.		
Callendar Rd. SW7	22	E5
Callendar Rd. SW7	129	G3
Callingham Cl. E14	113	J5
Wallwood St.		
Callis Fm. Cl., Stai.	140	B6
Bedfont Rd.		
Callis Rd. E17	77	J6
Callow St. SW3	30	D5
Callow St. SW3	129	G6
Calmont Rd., Brom.	172	D6
Calne Av., Ilf.	80	E1
Calonne Rd. SW19	166	A4
Calshot Rd., Houns.	140	D2
Calshot St. N1	10	C1
Calshot St. N1	111	F2
Calshot Way, Enf.	43	H3
Calshot Way, Houns.	140/141	E2
Calshot Rd.		
Calthorpe Gdns., Edg.	53	H5
Jesmond Way		
Calthorpe Gdns., Sutt.	199	F3
Calthorpe St. WC1	10	D5
Calthorpe St. WC1	111	F4
Calton Av. SE21	152	B5
Calton Rd., Barn.	41	F6
Calverley Cl., Beck.	172	B6
Calverley Cres., Dag.	101	G2
Calverley Gro., Har.	69	G7
Calverley Gro. N19	92	D1
Calverley Rd., Epsom	197	G6
Calvert Av. E2	13	E4
Calvert Av. E2	112	B3
Calvert Cl., Belv.	139	G4
Calvert Cl., Sid.	176	E6
Calvert Rd. SE10	135	F5
Calvert Rd., Barn.	40	A2
Calvert St. NW1	110	A1
Chalcot Rd.		
Calverton SE5	36	D5
Calverton Rd. E6	116	D1
Calvert's Bldgs. SE1	28	B2
Calvin St. E1	13	F6
Calvin St. E1	112	C4
Calydon Rd. SE7	135	H5
Calypso Way SE16	133	J3
Cam Rd. E15	114	D1
Camac Rd., Twick.	162	A1
Cambalt Rd. SW15	148	A5
Camberley Av. SW20	183	H2
Camberley Av., Enf.	44	B4
Camberley Cl., Sutt.	198	A3
Camberley Rd., Houns.	140	D3
Cambert Way SE3	155	H4
Camberwell Ch. St. SE5	152	A1
Camberwell Glebe SE5	152	A1
Camberwell Grn. SE5	152	A1
Camberwell Gro. SE5	152	A1
Camberwell New Rd. SE5	35	E6
Camberwell New Rd. SE5	131	G7
Camberwell Pas. SE5	151	J1
Camberwell Grn.		
Camberwell Rd. SE5	36	A6
Camberwell Rd. SE5	131	J6
Camberwell Sta. Rd. SE5	151	J1
Cambeys Rd., Dag.	101	H5
Camborne Av. W13	125	E2
Camborne Ms. W11	108	B6
St. Marks Rd.		
Camborne Rd. SW18	148	D7
Camborne Rd., Croy.	188	D7
Camborne Rd., Houns.	140	D3
Camborne Rd., Mord.	184	A5
Camborne Rd., Sid.	176	C3
Camborne Rd., Sutt.	198	D7
Camborne Rd., Well.	157	J2
Camborne Way, Houns.	143	G1
Cambourne Av. N9	45	G7
Cambray Rd. SW12	168	C3
Cambray Rd., Orp.	193	J7
Cambria Cl., Houns.	143	G4
Cambria Cl., Sid.	175	G1
Cambria Cl., Felt.	142	B7
Hounslow Rd.		
Cambria Gdns., Stai.	140	B7
Cambria Rd. SE5	151	J3
Cambria St. SW6	129	E7
Cambrian Av., Ilf.	81	H5
Cambrian Cl. SE27	169	H3
Cambrian Rd. E10	78	A7
Cambrian Rd., Rich.	145	J6
Cambridge Av. NW6	108	D2
Cambridge Av., Grnf.	86	C5
Cambridge Av., N.Mal.	183	F2
Cambridge Av., Well.	157	J4
Cambridge Barracks Rd. SE18	136	C4
Cambridge Circ. WC2	17	J4
Cambridge Circ. WC2	110	D6
Cambridge Cl. E17	77	J6
Cambridge Cl. N22	75	G1
Pellatt Gro.		
Cambridge Cl. NW10	88	C3
Cambridge Cl. SW20	183	H1
Cambridge Cl., Houns.	143	E4
Cambridge Cl., West Dr.	120	A6
Cambridge Cotts., Rich.	126	A6
Cambridge Cres. E2	112	E2
Cambridge Cres., Tedd.	162	D5
Cambridge Dr. SE12	155	G5
Cambridge Dr., Ruis.	84	C2
Cambridge Gdns. N10	74	B1
Cambridge Gdns. N13	59	G5
Cambridge Gdns. N17	60	A7
Great Cambridge Rd.		
Cambridge Gdns. N21	44	A7
Cambridge Gdns. NW6	108	D2
Cambridge Gdns. W10	108	B6
Cambridge Gdns. Enf.	44	D2
Cambridge Gdns., Kings.T.	182	A2
Cambridge Gate NW1	8	E4
Cambridge Gate Ms. NW1	8	E4
Cambridge Grn. SE9	174	E1
Cambridge Gro. SE20	170	E7
Cambridge Gro. W6	127	H4
Cambridge Gro. Rd., Kings.T.	182	A2
Cambridge Heath Rd. E1	113	E2
Cambridge Heath Rd. E2	113	E2
Cambridge Mans. SW11	149	J1
Cambridge Rd.		
Cambridge Par., Enf.	44	D1
Great Cambridge Rd.		
Cambridge Pk. E11	79	G7
Cambridge Pk. Twick.	145	G7
Cambridge Pk. Rd. E11	79	F7
Cambridge Pk.		
Cambridge Pl. W8	22	B4
Cambridge Pl. W8	129	E2
Cambridge Rd. E4	62	D1
Cambridge Rd. E11	79	F6
Cambridge Rd. NW6	108	D3
Cambridge Rd. SE20	188	E3
Cambridge Rd. SW11	149	J1
Cambridge Rd. SW13	147	F2
Cambridge Rd. SW20	183	G1
Cambridge Rd. W7	124	C2
Cambridge Rd., Bark.	99	F7
Cambridge Rd., Brom.	173	G7
Cambridge Rd., Cars.	199	H6
Cambridge Rd., Hmptn.	161	F7
Cambridge Rd., Har.	67	G5
Cambridge Rd., Houns.	143	E4
Cambridge Rd., Ilf.	99	H1
Cambridge Rd., Kings.T.	181	J2
Cambridge Rd., Mitch.	186	C3
Cambridge Rd., N.Mal.	182	E4
Cambridge Rd., Rich.	126	A7
Cambridge Rd., Sid.	175	H4
Cambridge Rd., Sthl.	123	F1
Cambridge Rd., Tedd.	162	C4
Cambridge Rd., Twick.	145	G6
Cambridge Rd., Walt.	178	B6
Cambridge Rd., W.Mol.	179	F4
Cambridge Rd. N. W4	126	B5
Cambridge Rd. S. W4	126	B5
Oxford Rd. S.		
Cambridge Row SE18	137	E5
Cambridge Sq. W2	15	G3
Cambridge Sq. W2	109	H6
Cambridge St. SW1	32	E2
Cambridge St. SW1	130	B5
Cambridge Ter. N13	59	G5
Cambridge Ter. NW1	8	E4
Cambridge Ter. Ms. NW1	8	E4
Cambstone Cl. N11	58	A2
Cambus Cl., Hayes	103	E5
Cambus Rd. E16	115	G5
Camdale Rd. SE18	137	J7
Camden Av., Felt.	160	C2
Camden Av., Hayes	102	C7
Camden Cl., Chis.	175	F7
Camden Est. SE15	152	C1
Camden Gdns. NW1	92	B7
Kentish Town Rd.		
Camden Gdns., Sutt.	198	E5
Camden Gdns., Th.Hth.	187	H3
Camden Gro., Chis.	175	E6
Camden High St. NW1	110	B1
Camden Hill Rd. SE19	170	B6
Camden La. N7	92	D6
Rowscroft Gdns.		
Camden Lock Pl. NW1	92	B7
Chalk Fm. Rd.		
Camden Ms. NW1	92	D6
Camden Pk. Rd. NW1	92	D6
Camden Pk. Rd., Chis.	174	C7
Camden Pas. N1	111	H1
Camden Rd. E11	79	H6
Camden Rd. E17	77	J6
Camden Rd. N7	92	D5
Camden Rd. NW1	92	C7
Camden Rd., Bex.	177	F1
Camden Rd., Cars.	199	J4
Camden Rd., Sutt.	198	D5
Camden Row SE3	155	E2
Camden Sq. NW1	92	D6
Camden Sq. SE15	152	C1
Watts St.		
Camden St. NW1	92	C7
Camden Ter. NW1	92	D6
North Vil.		
Camden Wk. N1	111	H1
Camden Way, Chis.	174	C7
Camden Way, Th.Hth.	187	H3
Camdenhurst St. E14	113	H6
Camel Gro., Kings.T.	163	G5
Camel Rd. E16	136	A1
Camelford Wk. W11	108	B6
Lancaster Rd.		
Camellia Ct., Wdf.Grn.	62/63	E7
The Bridle Path		
Camellia Pl., Twick.	143	H7
Camellia St. SW8	130	E7
Camelot Cl. SE28	137	G2
Camelot Cl. SW19	166	D4
Camelot St. SE15	132/133	E7
Bird in Bush Rd.		
Camera Pl. SW10	30	E5
Camera Pl. SW10	129	G6
Cameron Cl. N18	61	E4
Cameron Cl. N20	57	H2
Myddelton Pk.		
Cameron Pl. E1	112/113	E6
Varden St.		
Cameron Rd. SE6	171	J2
Cameron Rd., Brom.	191	G4
Cameron Rd., Croy.	187	H6
Cameron Rd., Ilf.	99	H1
Cameron Sq., Mitch.	185	H1
Camerton Cl. E8	94	C6
Buttermere Wk.		
Camgate Cen., Stai.	140	C6
Camilla Rd. SE16	132	E4
Camille Cl. SE25	188	D3
Camlan Rd., Brom.	173	F4
Camlet St. E2	13	F5
Camlet St. E2	112	C4
Camlet Way, Barn.	40	D2
Camley St. NW1	9	J1
Camley St. NW1	92	D7
Camm Gdns., Kings.T.	181	J2
Church Rd.		
Camm Gdns., T.Ditt.	180	B7
Camms Ter., Dag.	101	J5
Camomile Av., Mitch.	185	J1
Camomile St. EC3	20	D3
Camomile St. EC3	112	B6
Camp Rd. SW19	165	J5
Camp Vw. SW19	165	H5
Campana Rd. SW6	148	D1
Campbell Av., Ilf.	81	F4
Campbell Cl. SE18	156	D1
Moordown		
Campbell Cl. SW16	168	D4
Campbell Cl., Ruis.	66	A6
Campbell Cl., Twick.	162	A2
Campbell Ct. N17	76	C1
Campbell Cft., Edg.	54	A5
Campbell Gordon Way NW2	89	H4
Campbell Rd. E3	114	A3
Campbell Rd. E6	116	B1
Campbell Rd. E15	97	F4
Trevelyan Rd.		
Campbell Rd. E17	77	J4
Campbell Rd. N17	76	D1
Campbell Rd. W7	104	B7
Campbell Rd., Croy.	187	H7
Campbell Rd., E.Mol.	180	C3
Hampton Ct. Rd.		
Campbell Rd., Twick.	162	A2
Campbell Wk. N1	110/111	E1
Outram Pl.		
Campdale Rd. N7	92	D3
Campden Cres., Dag.	100	D3
Campden Cres., Wem.	87	E2
Campden Gro. W8	128	D2
Campden Hill W8	128	D2
Campden Hill Gdns. W8	128	D1
Campden Hill Gate W8	128	D2
Duchess of Bedford's Wk.		
Campden Hill Pl. W11	128	C1
Holland Pk. Av.		
Campden Hill Rd. W8	128	D1
Campden Hill Sq. W8	128	C1
Campden Ho. Cl. W8	128	D2
Hornton St.		

Carlos Pl. W1	**16**	**C6**
Carlos Pl. W1	110	A7
Carlow St. NW1	**9**	**F1**
Carlton Av. N14	42	D5
Carlton Av., Felt.	142	C6
Carlton Av., Har.	68	E5
Carlton Av., Hayes	121	H4
Carlton Av., S.Croy.	202	B7
Carlton Av. E., Wem.	87	H1
Carlton Av. W., Wem.	86	E2
Carlton Cl. NW3	90	D2
Carlton Cl., Borwd.	38	D4
Carlton Cl., Chess.	195	G6
Carlton Cl., Edg.	54	A5
Carlton Cl., Nthlt.	85	J5
Whitton Av. W.		
Carlton Ct. SW9	151	H1
Carlton Ct., Ilf.	81	G3
Carlton Cres., Sutt.	198	B4
Carlton Dr. SW15	148	B5
Carlton Dr., Ilf.	81	G3
Carlton Gdns. SW1	**25**	**H2**
Carlton Gdns. SW1	130	D1
Carlton Gdns. W5	105	F6
Carlton Gro. SE15	152	E1
Carlton Hill NW8	**6**	**B2**
Carlton Hill NW8	109	E2
Carlton Ho., Felt.	141	J7
Carlton Ho. Ter. SW1	**25**	**H2**
Carlton Ho. Ter. SW1	130	D1
Carlton Pk. Av. SW20	183	J2
Carlton Rd. E11	97	F1
Carlton Rd. E12	98	A4
Carlton Rd. E17	77	H1
Carlton Rd. N4	75	G7
Carlton Rd. N11	58	A5
Carlton Rd. SW14	146	C3
Carlton Rd. W4	126	D2
Carlton Rd. W5	105	F7
Carlton Rd., Erith	139	H6
Carlton Rd., N.Mal.	182	E2
Carlton Rd., Sid.	175	J5
Carlton Rd., S.Croy.	202	A6
Carlton Rd., Walt.	178	B7
Carlton Rd., Well.	158	B3
Carlton Sq. E1	113	G4
Argyle Rd.		
Carlton St. SW1	**17**	**H6**
Carlton Ter. E11	79	H5
Carlton Ter. N18	60	A3
Carlton Ter. SE26	171	F3
Carlton Twr. Pl. SW1	**24**	**A5**
Carlton Twr. Pl. SW1	129	J3
Carlton Vale NW6	108	E2
Carlton Vil. SW15	147	J5
St. John's Av.		
Carlwell St. SW17	167	H5
Carlyle Av., Brom.	192	A3
Carlyle Av., Sthl.	103	F7
Carlyle Cl. N2	73	F6
Carlyle Cl. NW10	106	D1
Carlyle Cl., W.Mol.	179	H2
Carlyle Gdns., Sthl.	103	F7
Carlyle Ms. E1	113	G4
Alderney Rd.		
Carlyle Pl. SW15	148	A4
Carlyle Rd. E12	98	B4
Carlyle Rd. SE28	118	B7
Carlyle Rd. W5	125	F5
Carlyle Rd., Croy.	202	D2
Carlyle Sq. SW3	**31**	**F4**
Carlyle Sq. SW3	129	G5
Carlyon Av., Har.	85	F4
Carlyon Cl., Wem.	105	H1
Carlyon Rd., Hayes	102	C6
Carlyon Rd., Wem.	105	H2
Carmalt Gdns. SW15	147	J4
Carmarthen Gdn. NW9	70/71	E6
Snowdon Dr.		
Carmel Ct. W8	**22**	**A3**
Carmel Ct., Wem.	88	B2
Carmelite Cl., Har.	67	J1
Carmelite Rd., Har.	67	J1
Carmelite St. EC4	**19**	**F5**
Carmelite St. EC4	111	G7
Carmelite Wk., Har.	67	J1
Carmelite Way, Har.	67	J2
Carmen St. E14	114	B6
Carmichael Cl. SW11	149	G3
Darien Rd.		
Carmichael Cl., Ruis.	84	A4
Carmichael Ms. SW18	149	G7
Carmichael Rd. SE25	188	D5
Carminia Rd. SW17	168	B2
Carnaby St. W1	**17**	**F4**
Carnaby St. W1	110	C6
Carnac St. SE27	170	A4
Carnanton Rd. E17	78	D1
Carnarvon Av., Enf.	44	C3
Carnarvon Dr., Hayes	121	F3
Carnarvon Rd. E10	78	C6
Carnarvon Rd. E15	97	F6
Carnarvon Rd. E18	79	F1
Carnarvon Rd., Barn.	40	B3
Carnation St. SE2	138	B5
Carnbrook Rd. SE3	156	A3
Carnecke Gdns. SE9	156	B5
Carnegie Cl., Surb.	195	J2
Fullers Av.		
Carnegie Pl. SW19	166	A3
Carnegie St. N1	111	F1
Carnforth Cl., Epsom	196	B6
Carnforth Rd. SW16	168	D7
Carnie Lo. SW17	168	B3
Manville Rd.		
Carnoustie Dr. N1	93	F7
Carnwath Rd. SW6	148	D3
Carol St. NW1	110	C1
Carolina Cl. E15	96	E5
Carolina Rd., Th.Hth.	187	H2
Caroline Cl. N10	74	B2
Alexandra Pk. Rd.		
Caroline Cl. SW16	169	F4
Caroline Cl. W2	**14**	**B6**
Caroline Cl., Croy.	202	B4
Brownlow Rd.		
Caroline Cl., Islw.	124	A7
Caroline Cl., West Dr.	120	A2
Caroline Ct., Stan.	52	D6
The Chase		
Caroline Gdns. SE15	132	E7
Caroline Pl. SW11	150	A2
Caroline Pl. W2	**14**	**B5**
Caroline Pl. W2	109	E7
Caroline Pl., Hayes	121	H7
Caroline Pl. Ms. W2	**14**	**B6**
Caroline Rd. SW19	166	C7
Caroline St. E1	113	G6
Caroline Ter. SW1	**32**	**B2**
Caroline Ter. SW1	130	A4
Caroline Wk. W6	128	B6
Carpenders Av., Wat.	50	E3
Carpenders Pk., Wat.	51	E2
Carpenter Gdns. N21	59	H2
Carpenter St. W1	**16**	**D6**
Carpenters Ct., Twick.	162	B2
Carpenters Pl. SW4	150	D4
Carpenters Rd. E15	96	B6
Carr Gro. SE18	136	B4
Carr Rd. E17	77	J2
Carr Rd., Nthlt.	85	H6
Carr St. E14	113	H5
Carrara Wk. SW9	151	G4
Somerleyton Rd.		
Carriage Dr. E. SW11	**32**	**B7**
Carriage Dr. E. SW11	130	A7
Carriage Dr. N. SW11	**32**	**C6**
Carriage Dr. N. SW11	130	A6
Carriage Dr. S. SW11	149	J1
Carriage Dr. W. SW11	129	J7
Carriage Ms., Ilf.	99	F2
Carriage Pl. N16	94	A3
Carrick Cl., Islw.	144	D3
Carrick Dr., Ilf.	81	F1
Carrick Gdns. N17	60	B7
Flexmere Rd.		
Carrick Ms. SE8	134	A6
Watergate St.		
Carrill Way, Belv.	138	D4
Carrington Av., Borwd.	38	B5
Carrington Av., Houns.	143	H5
Carrington Cl., Barn.	39	G5
Carrington Cl., Borwd.	38	C5
Carrington Cl., Croy.	189	H7
Carrington Cl., Kings.T.	164	C5
Carrington Gdns. E7	97	H4
Woodford Rd.		
Carrington Rd., Rich.	146	A4
Carrington Sq., Har.	51	J7
Carrington St. W1	**24**	**D2**
Carrol Cl. NW5	92	B4
Carroll Cl. E15	97	F5
Carroll Hill, Loug.	48	C3
Carron Cl. E14	114	B6
Carronade Pl. SE28	137	F3
Carroun Rd. SW8	**34**	**C7**
Carroun Rd. SW8	131	F7
Carrow Rd., Dag.	100	B7
Carroway La., Grnf.	104	A3
Cowgate Rd.		
Carrs La. N21	43	J5
Carshalton Gro., Sutt.	199	G4
Carshalton Pk. Rd., Cars.	199	J5
Carshalton Pl., Cars.	200	A4
Carshalton Rd., Cars.	199	F5
Carshalton Rd., Mitch.	186	A4
Carshalton Rd., Sutt.	199	F5
Carslake Rd. SW15	147	J6
Carson Rd. E16	115	G4
Carson Rd. SE21	170	A2
Carson Rd., Barn.	41	J4
Carstairs Rd. SE6	172	C3
Carston Cl. SE12	155	G5
Carswell Cl., Ilf.	80	A4
Roding La. S.		
Carswell Rd. SE6	154	C7
Cart La. E4	46	D7
Carter Cl., Wall.	200	D7
Carter Ct. EC4	111	H6
Carter La.		
Carter La. EC4	**19**	**H4**
Carter La. EC4	111	H6
Carter Pl. SE17	**36**	**A4**
Carter Pl. SE17	131	J5
Carter Rd. E13	115	H1
Carter Rd. SW19	167	G6
Carter St. SE17	**35**	**J5**
Carter St. SE17	131	J6
Carteret St. SW1	**25**	**H4**
Carteret St. SW1	130	D2
Carteret Way SE8	133	H4
Carterhatch La., Enf.	44	D2
Carterhatch Rd., Enf.	45	F2
Carters Cl., Wor.Pk.	198	A2
Carters Hill Cl. SE9	173	J1
Carters La. SE23	171	H2
Carters Yd. SW18	148	D5
Wandsworth High St.		
Carthew Rd. W6	127	H3
Carthew Vil. W6	127	H3
Carthusian St. EC1	**19**	**J1**
Carthusian St. EC1	111	J5
Cartier Circle E14	134	B1
Carting La. WC2	**18**	**B6**
Carting La. WC2	111	E7
Cartmel Cl. N17	60/61	E7
Heybourne Rd.		
Cartmel Gdns., Mord.	185	F5
Cartmel Rd., Bexh.	159	G1
Carton St. W1	**16**	**A3**
Cartwright Gdns. WC1	**10**	**A4**
Cartwright Gdns. WC1	110	E3
Cartwright Rd., Dag.	101	F7
Cartwright St. E1	**21**	**G5**
Cartwright St. E1	112	C7
Cartwright Way SW13	127	H7
Carver Cl. W4	126	C3
Carver Rd. SE24	151	J6
Carville Cres., Brent.	125	H5
Cary Rd. E11	97	E4
Carysfort Rd. N8	74	D5
Carysfort Rd. N16	94	A3
Cascade Av. N10	74	C4
Cascade Cl., Buck.H.	64	A2
Cascade Rd.		
Cascade Rd., Buck.H.	64	A2
Casella Rd. SE14	133	G7
Casewick Rd. SE27	169	H4
Casimir Rd. E5	95	E3
Casino Av. SE24	151	J5
Caspian St. SE5	**36**	**B7**
Caspian St. SE5	132	A7
Caspian Wk. E16	116	A6
Caspian Wf. E3	114	B5
Violet Rd.		
Cassandra Cl., Nthlt.	86	A4
Casselden Rd. NW10	88	D7
Cassidy Rd. SW6	128	D7
Cassilda Rd. SE2	138	A4
Cassilis Rd., Twick.	145	E5
Cassiobury Av., Felt.	141	J6
Cassiobury Rd. E17	77	G5
Cassis Ct., Loug.	49	F4
Cassland Rd. E9	95	F7
Cassland Rd., Th.Hth.	188	A4
Casslee Rd. SE6	153	J7
Casson St. E1	**21**	**H2**
Casson St. E1	112	D5
Castalia Sq. E14	134	C2
Roserton St.		
Castalia St. E14	134	C2
Plevna St.		
Castell Rd., Loug.	49	F1
Castellain Rd. W9	**6**	**C6**
Castellain Rd. W9	108	E4
Castellane Cl., Stan.	52	C7
Daventer Dr.		
Castello Av. SW15	147	J5
Castelnau SW13	127	H6
Castelnau Gdns. SW13	127	H6
Arundel Ter.		
Castelnau Pl. SW13	127	H6
Castelnau		
Castelnau Row SW13	127	H6
Lonsdale Rd.		
Casterbridge NW6	109	E1
Casterbridge Rd. SE3	155	G3
Casterton St. E8	94/95	E6
Wilton Way		
Castile Rd. SE18	136	D4
Castillon Rd. SE6	172	E2
Castlands Rd. SE6	171	J2
Castle Av. E4	62	D5
Castle Baynard St. EC4	**19**	**H5**
Castle Cl. E9	95	H5
Swinnerton St.		
Castle Cl. SW19	166	A3
Castle Cl. W3	126	B2
Park Rd. E.		
Castle Cl., Brom.	190	E3
Castle Ct. EC3	**20**	**C4**
Castle Ct. SE26	171	H4
Champion Rd.		
Castle Dr., Ilf.	80	B6
Castle La. SW1	**25**	**G5**
Castle La. SW1	130	C3
Castle Ms. N12	57	F5
Castle Rd.		
Castle Ms. NW1	92	B6
Castle Rd.		
Castle Par., Epsom	197	G7
Ewell Bypass		
Castle Pl. NW1	92	B6
Castle Pl. W4	126/127	E4
Windmill Rd.		
Castle Pt. E13	115	J2
Castle Rd. N12	57	F5
Castle Rd. NW1	92	B6
Castle Rd., Dag.	118	B1
Castle Rd., Enf.	45	H1
Castle Rd., Islw.	144	C2
Castle Rd., Nthlt.	85	H6
Castle Rd., Sthl.	123	F3
Castle St. E6	115	J2
Castle St., Kings.T.	181	H2
Castle Wk., Sun.	178	C3
Elizabeth Gdns.		
Castle Way SW19	166	A3
Castle Way, Felt.	160	C4
Castle Yd. N6	74	A7
North Rd.		
Castle Yd. SE1	**27**	**H1**
Castle Yd., Rich.	145	G5
Hill St.		
Castlebar Hill W5	105	E5
Castlebar Ms. W5	105	F5
Castlebar Pk. W5	105	E5
Castlebar Rd. W5	105	F5
Castlebrook Cl. SE11	**35**	**G1**
Castlebrook Cl. SE11	131	H4
Castlecombe Dr. SW19	148	A7
Castlecombe Rd. SE9	174	B4
Castledine Rd. SE20	170	E7
Castleford Av. SE9	174	E1
Castleford Cl. N17	60	C6
Castlegate, Rich.	145	J3
Castlehaven Rd. NW1	92	B7
Castleleigh Ct., Enf.	44	A5
Castlemaine Av., S.Croy.	202	C5
Castlemaine Twr. SW11	149	J1
Castlereagh St. W1	**15**	**J3**
Castleton Av., Wem.	87	H4
Castleton Cl., Croy.	189	H6
Castleton Gdns., Wem.	87	H3
Castleton Rd. E17	78	D2
Castleton Rd. SE9	174	A4
Castleton Rd., Ilf.	100	A1
Castleton Rd., Mitch.	186	D4
Castleton Rd., Ruis.	84	D1
Castletown Rd. W14	128	B5
Castleview Cl. N4	93	J1
Castleview Gdns., Ilf.	80	B6
Castlewood Dr. SE9	156	C2
Castlewood Rd. N15	76	D6
Castlewood Rd. N16	76	D7
Castlewood Rd., Barn.	41	G3
Castor La. E14	114	B7
Cat Hill, Barn.	41	H6
Caterham Av., Ilf.	80	C2
Caterham Rd. SE13	154	C3
Catesby St. SE17	**36**	**C2**
Catesby St. SE17	132	A4
Catford Bdy. SE6	154	B7
Catford Hill SE6	171	J2
Catford Ms. SE6	154	B7
Holbeach Rd.		
Catford Rd. SE6	154	A7
Cathall Rd. E11	96	D3
Cathay St. SE16	133	E2
Cathay Wk., Nthlt.	103	G2
Brabazon Rd.		

Chadville Gdns., Rom. 82 D5
Chadway, Dag. 100 C1
Chadwell Av., Rom. 82 B7
Chadwell Heath La., Rom. 82 B5
Chadwell St. EC1 11 F3
Chadwell St. EC1 111 G3
Chadwick Av. E4 62 D4
Chadwick Av. N21 43 F5
Chadwick Av. SW19 166 D6
Chadwick Cl. SW15 147 F7
Chadwick Cl. W7 104 C5
Westcott Cres.
Chadwick Cl., Tedd. 162 D6
Chadwick Pl., Surb. 181 F7
Chadwick Rd. E11 79 E7
Chadwick Rd. NW10 107 F1
Chadwick Rd. SE15 152 C2
Chadwick Rd., Ilf. 99 E3
Chadwick St. SW1 25 J6
Chadwick St. SW1 130 D3
Chadwick Way SE28 118 D7
Chadwin Rd. E13 115 H5
Chadworth Way, Esher 194 A5
Chaffinch Av., Croy. 189 G6
Chaffinch Cl. N9 61 G1
Chaffinch Cl., Croy. 189 G6
Chaffinch Cl., Surb. 196 A3
Chaffinch Rd., Beck. 189 H1
Chafford Way, Rom. 82 C4
Chagford St. NW1 7 J6
Chagford St. NW1 109 J4
Chailey Av., Enf. 44 C2
Chailey Cl., Houns. 142 D1
Springwell Rd.
Chailey St. E5 95 F3
Chalbury Wk. N1 111 F2
Chalcombe Rd. SE2 138 B3
Chalcot Cl., Sutt. 198 D7
Chalcot Cres. NW1 109 J1
Chalcot Gdns. NW3 91 J6
Chalcot Ms. SW16 168 E3
Chalcot Rd. NW1 92 A7
Chalcot Sq. NW1 92 A7
Chalcott Gdns., Surb. 195 F1
Chalcroft Rd. SE13 154 E5
Chaldon Path, Th.Hth. 187 H4
Chaldon Rd. SW6 128 B7
Chale Rd. SW2 150 E6
Chalet Est. NW7 55 G4
Chalfont Av., Wem. 88 B6
Chalfont Ct. NW9 71 F3
Chalfont Grn. N9 60 B3
Chalfont Rd. N9 60 C3
Chalfont Rd. SE25 188 C3
Chalfont Rd., Hayes 122 A4
Chalfont Wk., Pnr. 66 C2
Willows Cl.
Chalfont Way W13 124 E3
Chalford Cl., W.Mol. 179 G4
Chalford Rd. SE21 170 A4
Chalford Wk., Wdf.Grn. 80 A1
Chalgrove Av., Mord. 184 D5
Chalgrove Cres., Ilf. 80 B2
Chalgrove Gdns. N3 72 B3
Chalgrove Rd. N17 76 E1
Chalgrove Rd., Sutt. 199 G7
Chalice Cl., Wall. 200 D6
Lavender Vale
Chalk Fm. Rd. NW1 92 A7
Chalk Hill Rd. W6 128 A4
Shortlands
Chalk La., Barn. 41 J4
Chalk Pit Way, Sutt. 199 F5
Chalk Rd. E13 115 J5
Chalkenden Cl. SE20 170 E7
Chalkhill Rd., Wem. 88 B3
Chalklands, Wem. 88 C3
Chalkley Cl., Mitch. 185 J2
Chalkmill Rd., Enf. 44 E3
Chalkstone Cl., Well. 158 A1
Chalkwell Pk. Av., Enf. 44 B4
Challice Way SW2 169 F1
Challin St. SE20 189 F1
Challis Rd., Brent. 125 G5
Challoner Cl. N2 73 G2
Challoner Cres. W14 128 C5
Challoner St.
Challoner St. W14 128 C5
Challoners Cl., E.Mol. 180 A4
Chalmers Wk. SE17 35 H6
Chalmers Way, Felt. 142 A5
Chaloner Ct. SE1 28 B3
Chalsey Rd. SE4 153 J4
Chalton Dr. N2 73 F6
Chalton St. NW1 9 J3
Chalton St. NW1 110 D2

Chamber St. E1 21 G5
Chamber St. E1 112 C7
Chamberlain Cl. SE28 137 G3
Broadwater Rd.
Chamberlain Cotts. 152 A1
SE5
Camberwell Gro.
Chamberlain Cres., 204 B1
W.Wick.
Gresham Rd.
Chamberlain Gdns., 143 J1
Houns.
Chamberlain La., Pnr. 66 A4
Chamberlain Pl. E17 77 H3
Chamberlain Rd. N2 73 F2
Chamberlain Rd. N9 60 D3
Chamberlain Rd. W13 124 D2
Midhurst Rd.
Chamberlain St. NW1 91 J7
Regents Pk. Rd.
Chamberlain Wk., 160/161 E4
Felt.
Burgess Cl.
Chamberlain Way, 66 B3
Pnr.
Chamberlain Way, 181 H7
Surb.
Chamberlayne Rd. 108 A3
NW10
Chambers Gdns. N2 73 G1
Chambers La. NW10 89 H7
Chambers Pl., 202 A7
S.Croy.
Rolleston Rd.
Chambers Rd. N7 92 E4
Chambers St. SE16 29 H3
Chambers St. SE16 132 D2
Chambord St. E2 13 G4
Chambord St. E2 112 C3
Champion Cres. 171 H4
SE26
Champion Gro. SE5 152 A3
Champion Hill SE5 152 A3
Champion Hill Est. 152 B3
SE5
Champion Pk. SE5 152 A2
Champion Pk. SE5 152 A3
SE5
Denmark Hill
Champion Rd. SE26 171 H4
Champness Cl. SE27 170 A4
Rommany Rd.
Champneys Cl., 198 C7
Sutt.
Chance St. E1 13 F5
Chance St. E1 112 C4
Chance St. E2 13 F5
Chance St. E2 112 C4
Chancel St. SE1 27 G1
Chancel St. SE1 131 H1
Chancellor Gro. SE21 169 J2
Chancellor Pas. E14 134 A1
South Colonnade
Chancellor Pl. NW9 71 F2
Chancellors Rd. W6 127 J5
Chancellors St. W6 127 J5
Chancelot Rd. SE2 138 B4
Chancery La. WC2 18 E3
Chancery La. WC2 111 G5
Chancery La., Beck. 190 B2
Chancery Ms. SW17 167 H2
Beechcroft Rd.
Chanctonbury Cl. 175 E3
SE9
Chanctonbury Gdns., 198 E7
Sutt.
Chanctonbury Way 56 C4
N12
Chandler Av. E16 115 G5
Chandler Cl., 179 G1
Hmptn.
Chandler Rd., Loug. 49 E1
Chandler St. E1 132/133 E1
Wapping La.
Chandler Way SE15 132 C7
Chandlers Cl., Felt. 141 J7
Chandlers Ms. E14 134 A2
Chandlers Way SW2 151 G7
Chandos Av. E17 78 A2
Chandos Av. N14 58 C3
Chandos Av. N20 57 F1
Chandos Av. W5 125 F4
Chandos Cl., 63 H2
Buck.H.
Chandos Cres., Edg. 53 J7
Chandos Par., Edg. 53 J7
Chandos Cres.
Chandos Pl. WC2 18 A6
Chandos Pl. WC2 110 E7
Chandos Rd. E15 96 D5
Chandos Rd. N2 73 G2
Chandos Rd. N17 76 B2
Chandos Rd. NW2 89 J5
Chandos Rd. NW10 106 E4

Chandos Rd., Har. 67 J5
Chandos Rd., Pnr. 66 C7
Chandos St. W1 16 E2
Chandos St. W1 110 B5
Chandos Way NW11 90 E1
Change All. EC3 20 C4
Channel Cl., Houns. 143 G1
Channel Gate Rd. 107 F3
NW10
Old Oak La.
Channelsea Rd. E15 114 D1
Chant Sq. E15 96 D7
Chant St. E15 96 D7
Chantrey Rd. SW9 151 F3
Chantry Cl. NW7 39 F6
Hendon Wd. La.
Chantry Cl., Har. 69 J5
Chantry Cl., Sid. 176/177 E5
Ellenborough Rd.
Chantry La., Brom. 192 A5
Bromley Common
Chantry Pl., Har. 67 H1
Chantry Pt. W9 108 C4
Chantry Rd., Chess. 195 J5
Chantry Rd., Har. 67 H1
Chantry St. N1 111 H1
Chantry Way, Mitch. 185 G3
Chapel Ct. SE1 28 B3
Chapel Ct. N2 73 H3
Chapel Fm. Rd. SE9 174 C3
Chapel Ho. St. E14 134 B5
Chapel La., Chig. 65 J3
Chapel La., Pnr. 66 D3
Chapel La., Rom. 82 D7
Chapel Mkt. N1 10 E1
Chapel Mkt. N1 111 G2
Chapel Pl. EC2 12 D4
Chapel Pl. N1 11 F1
Chapel Pl. N17 60 C7
White Hart La.
Chapel Pl. W1 16 D4
Chapel Pl. W1 110 B6
Chapel Rd. SE27 169 H4
Chapel Rd. W13 125 E1
Chapel Rd., Bexh. 159 G4
Chapel Rd., Houns. 143 H3
Chapel Rd., Ilf. 98 D3
Chapel Rd., Twick. 145 E7
Chapel Side W2 14 A5
Chapel Side W2 108 E7
Chapel Stones N17 76 C1
Chapel St. NW1 15 G2
Chapel St. NW1 109 H5
Chapel St. SW1 24 C5
Chapel St. SW1 130 A3
Chapel St., Enf. 43 J3
Chapel Ter., Loug. 48 B4
Forest Rd.
Chapel Vw., S.Croy. 203 E6
Chapel Wk. NW4 71 H4
Chapel Wk., Croy. 201 J2
Wellesley Rd.
Chapel Way N7 93 F3
Sussex Way
Chapel Yd. SW18 148 D5
Wandsworth High St.
Chapelmount Rd., 64 C6
Wdf.Grn.
Chaplin Cl. SE1 27 F3
Chaplin Cl. SE1 131 G2
Chaplin Rd. E15 115 E2
Chaplin Rd. N17 76 C3
Chaplin Rd. NW2 89 G6
Chaplin Rd., Dag. 101 E7
Chaplin Rd., Wem. 87 F6
Chaplin Sq. N12 57 G7
Chapman Cl., West Dr. 120 C3
Chapman Cres., Har. 69 H5
Chapman Pk. Ind. 89 F6
Est. NW10
Chapman Rd. E9 95 J6
Chapman Rd., Belv. 139 G5
Chapman Rd., Croy. 201 G1
Chapman Sq. SW19 166 A2
Chapman St. E1 112 E7
Chapman's La. SE2 138 C4
Chapman's La., Belv. 138 D4
Chapone Pl. W1 17 H4
Chapter Cl. W4 126 C3
Beaumont Rd.
Chapter Ho. Ct. EC4 19 J4
Chapter Rd. NW2 89 G5
Chapter Rd. SE17 35 H4
Chapter Rd. SE17 131 H5
Chapter St. SW1 33 H2
Chapter St. SW1 130 D4
Chapter Way, 161 G4
Hmptn.
Chara Pl. W4 126 D6
Charcroft Gdns., Enf. 45 G4
Chardin Rd. W4 126/127 A4
Elliott Rd.

Chardmore Rd. N16 94 D1
Chardwell Cl. E6 116 B6
Northumberland Rd.
Charecroft Way W12 128 A2
Charfield Ct. W9 6 A6
Charford Rd. E16 115 G5
Chargeable La. E13 115 F4
Chargeable St. E16 115 F4
Chargrove Cl. SE16 133 G2
Marlow Way
Charing Cl., Orp. 207 J4
Charing Cross SW1 26 A1
Charing Cross Rd. 17 J3
WC2
Charing Cross Rd. 110 D6
WC2
Charlbert St. NW8 7 G1
Charlbert St. NW8 109 H2
Charlbury Av., Stan. 53 G5
Charlbury Gdns., Ilf. 99 J2
Charlbury Gro. W5 105 F6
Charldane Rd. SE9 174 E3
Charlecote Gro. SE26 171 E3
Charlecote Rd., Dag. 100 E3
Charlemont Rd. E6 116 C3
Charles Babbage Cl. 195 G6
Chess.
Ashlyns Way
Charles Barry Cl. 150 C3
SW4
Charles Burton Ct. E5 95 H5
Ashenden Rd.
Charles Cl., Sid. 176 B4
Charles Cobb Gdns., 201 G5
Croy.
Charles Coveney Rd. 152 C1
SE15
Charles Cres., Har. 68 A7
Charles Dickens Ho. 112 E3
E2
Charles Flemwell 135 G1
Ms. E16
Hanameel St.
Charles Grinling Wk. 136 D4
SE18
Love La.
Charles Ho. N17 60 C7
Love La.
Charles La. NW8 7 F2
Charles Pl. NW1 9 G4
Charles Rd. E7 97 J7
Lens Rd.
Charles Rd. SW19 184 D1
Charles Rd. W13 104 D5
Charles Rd., Rom. 82 D7
Charles II St. SW1 25 H1
Charles II St. SW1 130 D1
Charles Sevright Dr. 56 A5
NW7
Charles Sq. N1 12 C4
Charles Sq. N1 112 A3
Charles Sq. Est. N1 112 A3
Pitfield St.
Charles St. E16 136 A1
Charles St. SW13 147 E2
Charles St. W1 24 D1
Charles St. W1 130 B1
Charles St., Croy. 201 J3
Charles St., Enf. 44 C6
Charles St., Houns. 143 F2
Charles Whincup Rd. 135 H1
E16
Charlesfield SE9 173 J3
Charleston Cl., Felt. 160 A3
Vineyard Rd.
Charleston St. SE17 36 A2
Charleston St. SE17 131 J4
Charleville Circ. SE26 170 D5
Charleville Rd. W14 128 B5
Charleville Rd., Erith 139 J7
Northumberland Pk.
Charlmont Rd. SW17 167 J6
Charlotte Cl., Bexh. 158 E5
Charlotte Cl., Ilf. 80 C1
Fullwell Av.
Charlotte Despard 150 A1
Av. SW11
Charlotte Ms. W1 17 G1
Charlotte Ms. W10 108 A6
Charlotte Ms. W14 128 B4
Munden St.
Charlotte Pl. NW9 70 C5
Uphill Dr.
Charlotte Pl. SW1 33 F2
Charlotte Pl. W1 17 G2
Charlotte Rd. EC2 12 D5
Charlotte Rd. EC2 112 B4
Charlotte Rd. SW13 147 F1
Charlotte Rd., Dag. 101 H6
Charlotte Rd., Wall. 200 C6
Charlotte Row SW4 150 C3
North St.
Charlotte Sq., Rich. 145 J6
Greville Rd.
Charlotte St. W1 17 G2

Charlotte St. W1 110 C5
Charlotte Ter. N1 111 F1
Charlow Cl. SW6 149 F2
Townmead Rd.
Charlton Ch. La. SE7 135 J5
Charlton Cres., Bark. 117 J2
Charlton Dene SE7 135 J7
Charlton Kings Rd. NW5 92 D5
Charlton La. SE7 136 A5
Charlton Pk. La. SE7 136 A7
Charlton Pk. Rd. SE7 136 A6
Charlton Pl. N1 11 G1
Charlton Pl. N1 111 H2
Charlton Rd. N9 61 G1
Charlton Rd. NW10 107 E1
Charlton Rd. SE3 135 G7
Charlton Rd. SE7 135 H6
Charlton Rd., Har. 69 G4
Charlton Rd., Wem. 87 J1
Charlton Way SE3 154 E1
Charlwood Cl., Har. 52 B7
Kelvin Cres.
Charlwood Pl. SW1 33 G2
Charlwood Pl. SW1 130 C4
Charlwood Rd. SW15 148 A3
Charlwood Sq., Mitch. 185 G3
Charlwood St. SW1 33 G2
Charlwood St. SW1 130 C5
Charlwood Ter. SW15 148 A4
Cardinal Pl.
Charmian Av., Stan. 69 G3
Charminster Av. SW19 184 E2
Charminster Ct., Surb. 181 G7
Charminster Rd. SE9 174 A4
Charminster Rd., Wor.Pk. 198 A1
Charmouth Rd., Well. 158 C1
Charnock Rd. E5 94 E3
Charnwood Av. SW19 184 D2
Charnwood Cl., N.Mal. 183 E4
Charnwood Dr. E18 79 H3
Charnwood Gdns. E14 134 A4
Charnwood Pl. N20 57 F3
Charnwood Rd. SE25 188 A5
Charnwood St. E5 94 D2
Charrington Rd., Croy. 201 H2
Drayton Rd.
Charrington St. NW1 9 H1
Charrington St. NW1 110 D2
Charsley Rd. SE6 172 B2
Chart Cl., Brom. 191 E1
Chart Cl., Croy. 189 F6
Stockbury Rd.
Chart St. N1 12 C3
Chart St. N1 112 A3
Charter Av., Ilf. 99 G1
Charter Ct., N.Mal. 182 E3
Charter Cres., Houns. 142 E4
Charter Dr., Bex. 158 E7
Charter Rd., Kings.T. 182 B3
Charter Rd., The, Wdf.Grn. 62 E6
Charter Sq., Kings.T. 182 B2
Charter Way N3 72 C4
Charter Way N14 42 C6
Charterhouse Av., Wem. 87 F4
Charterhouse Bldgs. EC1 11 H6
Charterhouse Ms. EC1 19 H1
Charterhouse Sq. EC1 19 H1
Charterhouse Sq. EC1 111 H5
Charterhouse St. EC1 19 F2
Charterhouse St. EC1 111 H5
Charteris Rd. N4 93 G1
Charteris Rd. NW6 108 C1
Charteris Rd., Wdf.Grn. 63 H7
Charters Cl. SE19 170 B5
Chartfield Av. SW15 147 H5
Chartfield Sq. SW15 148 A5
Chartham Gro. SE27 169 G3
Royal Circ.
Chartham Rd. SE25 188 E3
Chartley Av. NW2 88 E3
Chartley Av., Stan. 52 C6
Charton Cl., Belv. 139 F6
Nuxley Rd.
Chartridge Cl., Barn. 39 G5
Chartwell Cl. SE9 175 F2
Chartwell Cl., Croy. 202 A1
Tavistock Rd.
Chartwell Cl., Grnf. 103 H1
Chartwell Dr., Orp. 207 G5
Chartwell Gdns., Sutt. 198 B4
Chartwell Pl., Har. 86 A2
Chartwell Pl., Sutt. 198 C4
Chartwell Way SE20 188 E1
Charwood SW16 169 G4
Chase, The E12 98 A4
Chase, The SW4 150 B3
Chase, The SW16 169 F7
Chase, The SW20 184 B1
Chase, The, Bexh. 159 H3
Chase, The, Brom. 191 H3
Chase, The, Chig. 65 F4
Chase, The, Edg. 70 B1
Chase, The, Loug. 47 J7
Chase, The, Pnr. 67 F4
Chase, The (Eastcote), Pnr. 66 C6
Chase, The (Chadwell Heath), Rom. 82 E6
Chase, The, Stan. 52 D5
Chase, The, Sun. 178 B1
Chase, The, Wall. 200 E5
Chase Ct. Gdns., Enf. 43 J3
Chase Gdns. E4 62 A4
Chase Gdns., Twick. 144 A6
Chase Grn., Enf. 43 J3
Chase Grn. Av., Enf. 43 H2
Chase Hill, Enf. 43 J3
Chase La., Ilf. 81 G5
Chase Ridings, Enf. 43 G2
Chase Rd. N14 42 D6
Chase Rd. NW10 106 D4
Chase Rd. W3 106 D4
Chase Side N14 42 A6
Chase Side, Enf. 43 J3
Chase Side Av. SW20 184 B1
Chase Side Av., Enf. 43 J2
Chase Side Cres., Enf. 43 J1
Chase Side Pl., Enf. 43 J2
Chase Side
Chase Way N14 58 B2
Chasefield Rd. SW17 167 J4
Chaseley Dr. W4 146 B1
Wellesley Rd.
Chaseley St. E14 113 H6
Chasemore Cl., Mitch. 185 J7
Chasemore Gdns., Croy. 201 H5
Thorneloe Gdns.
Chaseville Pk. Rd. N21 43 E5
Chasewood Av., Enf. 43 H2
Chasewood Pk., Har. 86 C3
Chatfield Rd. SW11 149 F3
Chatfield Rd., Croy. 201 H1
Chatham Av., Brom. 191 F7
Chatham Cl. NW11 72 D5
Chatham Cl., Sutt. 184 C7
Chatham Pl. E9 95 F6
Chatham Rd. E17 77 H3
Chatham Rd. E18 79 F2
Grove Hill
Chatham Rd. SW11 149 J6
Chatham Rd., Kings.T. 182 A2
Chatham Rd., Orp. 207 F5
Chatham St. SE17 36 B1
Chatham St. SE17 132 A4
Chatsfield Pl. W5 105 H6
Chatsworth Av. NW4 71 J2
Chatsworth Av. SW20 184 B1
Chatsworth Av., Brom. 173 H4
Chatsworth Av., Sid. 176 A1
Chatsworth Av., Wem. 87 J5
Chatsworth Cl. NW4 71 J2
Chatsworth Cl., Borwd. 38 A3
Chatsworth Cl., W.Wick. 205 F2
Chatsworth Ct. W8 128 D4
Chatsworth Ct., Stan. 53 F5
Marsh La.
Chatsworth Cres., Houns. 144 A4
Chatsworth Dr., Enf. 44 D7
Chatsworth Est. E5 95 G4
Elderfield Rd.
Chatsworth Gdns. W3 106 B7
Chatsworth Gdns., Har. 85 H1
Chatsworth Gdns., N.Mal. 183 F5
Chatsworth Par., Orp. 193 F5
Queensway
Chatsworth Pl., Mitch. 185 J3
Chatsworth Pl., Tedd. 162 D4
Chatsworth Ri. W5 105 J4
Chatsworth Rd. E5 95 F3
Chatsworth Rd. E15 97 F5
Chatsworth Rd. NW2 90 A6
Chatsworth Rd. W4 126 C6
Chatsworth Rd. W5 105 J4
Chatsworth Rd., Croy. 202 A4
Chatsworth Rd., Hayes 102 B4
Chatsworth Rd., Sutt. 198 A5
Chatsworth Way SE27 169 H3
Chatterton Rd. N4 93 H3
Chatterton Rd., Brom. 192 A4
Chatto Rd. SW11 149 J5
Chaucer Av., Hayes 102 A5
Chaucer Av., Houns. 142 B2
Chaucer Av., Rich. 146 A2
Chaucer Cl. N11 58 C5
Chaucer Ct. N16 94 B4
Chaucer Dr. SE1 37 G2
Chaucer Dr. SE1 132 C4
Chaucer Gdns., Sutt. 198 D3
Chaucer Grn., Croy. 189 E7
Chaucer Ho., Sutt. 198 D3
Chaucer Rd. E7 97 G6
Chaucer Rd. E11 79 G6
Chaucer Rd. E17 78 C2
Chaucer Rd. SE24 151 G5
Chaucer Rd. W3 126 C1
Chaucer Rd., Sid. 176 C1
Chaucer Rd., Sutt. 198 D4
Chaucer Rd., Well. 157 H1
Chaucer Way SW19 167 G6
Chauncey Cl. N9 60 D3
Chaundrye Cl. SE9 156 B6
Chauntler Cl. E16 115 H6
Cheam Common Rd., Wor.Pk. 197 H2
Cheam Mans., Sutt. 198 B7
Cheam Pk. Way, Sutt. 198 B6
Cheam Rd., Sutt. 198 C6
Cheam St. SE15 152/153 E3
Evelina Rd.
Cheapside EC2 20 A4
Cheapside EC2 111 J6
Cheapside N13 59 J4
Taplow Rd.
Cheddar Rd., Houns. 140 D2
Cromer Rd.
Cheddar Waye, Hayes 102 B6
Cheddington Rd. N18 60 B3
Chedworth Cl. E16 115 F6
Hallsville Rd.
Cheeseman Cl., Hmptn. 161 E6
Cheesemans Ter. W14 128 C5
Chelford Rd., Brom. 172 D5
Chelmer Cres., Bark. 118 B2
Chelmer Rd. E9 95 G5
Chelmsford Cl. E6 116 C6
Guildford Rd.
Chelmsford Cl. W6 128 A6
Chelmsford Gdns., Ilf. 80 B7
Chelmsford Rd. E11 96 D1
Chelmsford Rd. E17 78 A6
Chelmsford Rd. E18 79 F1
Chelmsford Rd. N14 42 C7
Chelmsford Sq. NW10 107 J1
Chelsea Br. SW1 32 D5
Chelsea Br. SW1 130 B6
Chelsea Br. SW8 32 D5
Chelsea Br. SW8 130 B6
Chelsea Br. Rd. SW1 32 B3
Chelsea Br. Rd. SW1 130 A5
Chelsea Cloisters SW3 129 H4
Lucan Pl.
Chelsea Cl. NW10 106 D1
Winchelsea Rd.
Chelsea Cl., Edg. 70 A2
Chelsea Cl., Hmptn. 161 J5
Chelsea Cl., Wor.Pk. 183 G7
Chelsea Embk. SW3 31 H6
Chelsea Embk. SW3 129 H6
Chelsea Gdns., Sutt. 198 B4
Chelsea Harbour SW10 149 G1
Chelsea Harbour Dr. SW10 149 F1
Chelsea Manor Gdns. SW3 31 G5
Chelsea Manor Gdns. SW3 129 H6
Chelsea Manor St. SW3 31 G4
Chelsea Manor St. SW3 129 H5
Chelsea Pk. Gdns. SW3 31 E5
Chelsea Pk. Gdns. SW3 129 G6
Chelsea Sq. SW3 31 F3
Chelsea Sq. SW3 129 G5
Chelsea Wf. SW10 129 G7
Chelsfield Av. N9 45 G7
Chelsfield Gdns. SE26 171 F3
Chelsfield Grn. N9 45 G7
Chelsfield Av.
Chelsham Rd. SW4 150 D3
Chelsham Rd., S.Croy. 202 A6
Chelston App., Ruis. 84 A2
Chelston Rd., Ruis. 84 A1
Chelsworth Dr. SE18 137 G6
Cheltenham Av., Twick. 144 D7
Cheltenham Cl., N.Mal. 182 C3
Northcote Rd.
Cheltenham Cl., Nthlt. 85 H6
Cheltenham Gdns. E6 116 B2
Cheltenham Gdns., Loug. 48 B6
Cheltenham Pl. W3 126 B1
Cheltenham Pl., Har. 69 H4
Cheltenham Rd. E10 78 C6
Cheltenham Rd. SE15 153 F4
Cheltenham Ter. SW3 32 A3
Cheltenham Ter. SW3 129 J5
Chelverton Rd. SW15 148 A4
Chelwood Cl. E4 46 B6
Chelwood Gdns., Rich. 146 A2
Chelwood Gdns. Pas., Rich. 146 A2
Chelwood Gdns.
Chelwood Wk. SE4 153 H4
Chenappa Cl. E13 115 G3
Chenduit Way, Stan. 52 C5
Cheney Rd. NW1 10 A2
Cheney Rd. NW1 110 E2
Cheney Row E17 77 J1
Cheney St., Pnr. 66 C5
Cheneys Rd. E11 97 E3
Chenies, The, Orp. 193 H6
Chenies Ms. WC1 9 H6
Chenies Pl. NW1 9 J1
Chenies Pl. NW1 110 D2
Chenies St. WC1 17 H1
Chenies St. WC1 110 D5
Cheniston Gdns. W8 22 A5
Cheniston Gdns. W8 128 E3
Chepstow Cl. SW15 148 B6
Lytton Gro.
Chepstow Cres. W11 108 D7
Chepstow Cres., Ilf. 81 H6
Chepstow Gdns., Sthl. 103 F6
Chepstow Pl. W2 108 D6
Chepstow Ri., Croy. 202 B3
Chepstow Rd. W2 108 D6
Chepstow Rd. W7 124 D3
Chepstow Rd., Croy. 202 B3
Chepstow Vil. W11 108 C7
Chepstow Way SE15 152 C1
Chequer St. EC1 12 A6
Chequers Cl. NW9 70 E3
Chequers Cl., Orp. 193 J4
Chequers Gdns. N13 59 H5
Chequers La., Dag. 119 F4
Chequers Par. SE9 156 C6
Eltham High St.
Chequers Rd., Loug. 48 D5
Chequers Way N13 59 J5
Cherbury Cl. SE28 118 D6
Cherbury Ct. N1 112 A2
Cherbury St.
Cherbury St. N1 12 C2
Cherbury St. N1 112 A2
Cherchefelle Ms., Stan. 52 E5
Cherimoya Gdns., W.Mol. 179 H3
Kelvinbrook
Cherington Rd. W7 124 C1
Cheriton Av., Brom. 191 F5
Cheriton Av., Ilf. 80 C2
Cheriton Cl. W5 105 F5
Cheriton Cl., Barn. 41 J3
Cheriton Dr. SE18 137 G7
Cheriton Sq. SW17 168 A2
Cherry Av., Sthl. 122 D1
Cherry Blossom Cl. N13 59 H5
Cherry Cl. E17 78 B5
Eden Rd.
Cherry Cl. SW2 151 G7
Tulse Hill
Cherry Cl. W5 125 G3
Cherry Cl., Cars. 199 J2
Cherry Cl., Mord. 184 B4
Cherry Cres., Brent. 124 E7
Cherry Gdn. St. SE16 132 E2
Cherry Gdns., Dag. 101 F5
Cherry Gdns., Nthlt. 85 H7
Cherry Garth, Brent. 125 G4

Cherry Gro., Hayes	122	B1
Cherry Hill, Barn.	41	E6
Cherry Hill, Har.	52	B6
Cherry Hill Gdns., Croy.	201	F4
Cherry Hills, Wat.	50	E5
Cherry La., West Dr.	120	C4
Cherry La. Roundabout, West Dr.	120	E4
Cherry Laurel Wk. SW2	151	F6
Beechdale Rd.		
Cherry Orchard, West Dr.	120	B2
Cherry Orchard Gdns., Croy.	202	A2
Oval Rd.		
Cherry Orchard Gdns., W.Mol.	179	F3
Cherry Orchard Rd., Brom.	206	B2
Cherry Orchard Rd., Croy.	202	A2
Cherry Orchard Rd., W.Mol.	179	G3
Cherry Tree Cl. E9	113	F1
Moulins Rd.		
Cherry Tree Cl., Wem.	86	C4
Cherry Tree Ct. NW9	70	C4
Cherry Tree Dr. SW16	169	E3
Cherry Tree Ri., Buck.H.	63	J4
Cherry Tree Rd. E15	96/97	E4
Wingfield Rd.		
Cherry Tree Rd. N2	73	J4
Cherry Tree Wk. EC1	12	A6
Cherry Tree Wk., Beck.	189	J4
Cherry Tree Wk., W.Wick.	205	F4
Cherry Tree Way, Stan.	53	E6
Cherry Wk., Brom.	205	G1
Cherry Way, Epsom	196	D6
Cherry Wd. Way W5	106	A5
Hanger Vale La.		
Cherrycot Hill, Orp.	207	G4
Cherrycot Ri., Orp.	207	F4
Cherrycroft Gdns., Pnr.	51	F7
Westfield Pk.		
Cherrydown Av. E4	61	J3
Cherrydown Cl. E4	61	J3
Cherrydown Rd., Sid.	176	D2
Cherrydown Wk., Rom.	83	H2
Cherrywood Cl. E3	113	H3
Cherrywood Cl., Kings.T.	164	A7
Cherrywood Dr. SW15	148	A5
Cherrywood La., Mord.	184	B4
Cherston Gdns., Loug.	48	D4
Cherston Rd.		
Cherston Rd., Loug.	48	D4
Chertsey Dr., Sutt.	198	B2
Chertsey Rd. E11	96	D2
Chertsey Rd., Ilf.	99	G4
Chertsey Rd., Twick.	144	C6
Chertsey St. SW17	168	A5
Chervil Cl., Felt.	160	A3
Chervil Ms. SE28	138	B1
Cherwell Cl., Epsom	196	C4
Cheryls Cl. SW6	149	E1
Cheseman St. SE26	171	E3
Chesfield Rd., Kings.T.	163	H7
Chesham Av., Orp.	192	G6
Chesham Cl. SW1	24	B6
Chesham Cres. SE20	189	F2
Chesham Ms. SW1	24	B5
Chesham Ms. SW1	130	A3
Chesham Pl. SW1	24	B6
Chesham Pl. SW1	130	A3
Chesham Rd. SE20	189	F2
Chesham Rd. SW19	167	G5
Chesham Rd., Kings.T.	182	A1
Chesham St. NW10	88	D3
Chesham St. SW1	24	B6
Chesham St. SW1	130	A3
Chesham Ter. W13	124	E2
Cheshire Cl. E17	78	B1
Cheshire Cl. SE4	153	J2
Cheshire Cl., Mitch.	186	E3
Cheshire Ct. EC4	19	F4
Cheshire Gdns., Chess.	195	G6
Cheshire Rd. N22	59	F7
Cheshire St. E2	13	G5
Cheshire St. E2	112	C4

Chesholm Rd. N16	94	B3
Cheshunt Rd. E7	97	H6
Cheshunt Rd., Belv.	139	G5
Chesil Ct. E2	113	E2
Chesilton Rd. SW6	148	C1
Chesley Gdns. E6	116	A2
Chesney Cres., Croy.	204	C7
Chesney St. SW11	150	A1
Chesnut Est. N17	76	C3
Chesnut Gro. N17	76	C3
Chesnut Rd.		
Chesnut Rd. N17	76	C3
Chessington Av. N3	72	B3
Chessington Av., Bexh.	139	E7
Chessington Cl., Epsom	196	C6
Chessington Ct., Pnr.	67	F4
Chessington Hall Gdns., Chess.	195	G7
Chessington Hill Pk., Chess.	196	A5
Chessington Lo. N3	72	C3
Chessington Way, W.Wick.	204	B2
Chesson Rd. W14	128	C6
Chesswood Way, Pnr.	66	D2
Chester Av., Rich.	145	J5
Chester Av., Twick.	161	F1
Chester Cl. SW1	24	C4
Chester Cl. SW1	130	A2
Chester Cl. SW13	147	H3
Chester Cl., Loug.	49	F1
Chester Cl., Sutt.	198	D2
Chester Cl. N. NW1	8	E3
Chester Cl. S. NW1	8	E4
Chester Cotts. SW1	32	B2
Chester Ct. NW1	8	E3
Chester Ct. SE5	132	A7
Chester Cres. E8	94	C6
Ridley Rd.		
Chester Dr., Har.	67	F6
Chester Gdns. W13	104	D6
Chester Gdns., Enf.	45	E6
Chester Gdns., Mord.	185	F6
Chester Gate NW1	8	D4
Chester Gate NW1	110	B3
Chester Grn., Loug.	49	F1
Chester Ms. SW1	24	D5
Chester Ms. SW1	130	B3
Chester Path, Loug.	49	F1
Chester Pl. NW1	8	E3
Chester Rd. E7	98	A7
Chester Rd. E11	79	H6
Chester Rd. E16	115	E4
Chester Rd. E17	77	G5
Chester Rd. N9	61	E1
Chester Rd. N17	76	A3
Chester Rd. N19	92	B2
Chester Rd. NW1	8	C4
Chester Rd. NW1	110	A3
Chester Rd. SW19	165	J6
Chester Rd., Borwd.	38	C3
Chester Rd., Chig.	64	D3
Chester Rd., Houns.	142	B3
Chester Rd. (Heathrow Airport), Houns.	140	B3
Chester Rd., Ilf.	99	J1
Chester Rd., Loug.	49	E2
Chester Rd., Sid.	157	H5
Chester Row SW1	32	B2
Chester Row SW1	130	A4
Chester Sq. SW1	32	D1
Chester Sq. SW1	130	B3
Chester Sq. Ms. SW1	24	D6
Chester St. E2	13	J5
Chester St. E2	112	D4
Chester St. SW1	24	C5
Chester St. SW1	130	A3
Chester Ter. NW1	8	D3
Chester Way SE11	35	F2
Chester Way SE11	131	G4
Chesterfield Dr., Esher	194	D2
Chesterfield Gdns. N4	75	H5
Chesterfield Gdns. SE10	134	D7
Crooms Hill		
Chesterfield Gdns. W1	24	D1
Chesterfield Gdns. W1	130	B1
Chesterfield Gro. SE22	152	C5
Chesterfield Hill W1	16	D6
Chesterfield Hill W1	110	B7
Chesterfield Ms. N4	75	H5
Chesterfield Gdns.		
Chesterfield Rd. E10	78	C6
Chesterfield Rd. N3	56	D6
Chesterfield Rd. W4	126	C6
Chesterfield Rd., Barn.	40	A5

Chesterfield Rd., Epsom	196	D7
Chesterfield St. W1	24	D1
Chesterfield St. W1	130	B1
Chesterfield Wk. SE10	154	D1
Chesterfield Way SE15	133	F7
Chesterfield Way, Hayes	122	A2
Chesterford Gdns. NW3	91	E4
Chesterford Ho. SE18	136	A7
Shooter's Hill Rd.		
Chesterford Rd. E12	98	C5
Chesters, The, N.Mal.	182	E1
Chesterton Cl. SW18	148	D5
Ericcson Cl.		
Chesterton Cl., Grnf.	103	H2
Chesterton Rd. E13	115	G3
Chesterton Rd. W10	108	A5
Chesterton Sq. W8	128	C4
Pembroke Rd.		
Chesterton Ter. E13	115	G3
Chesterton Ter., Kings.T.	182	A2
Chesthunte Rd. N17	75	J1
Chestnut All. SW6	128	C6
Lillie Rd.		
Chestnut Av. E7	97	H4
Chestnut Av. N8	74	E5
Chestnut Av. SW14	146	D3
Thornton Rd.		
Chestnut Av., Brent.	125	G4
Chestnut Av., Buck.H.	64	A3
Chestnut Av., E.Mol.	180	C3
Chestnut Av., Edg.	53	H6
Chestnut Av., Epsom	196	E4
Chestnut Av., Esher	180	A7
Chestnut Av., Hmptn.	161	G7
Chestnut Av., Tedd.	180	C2
Chestnut Av., Wem.	86	E5
Chestnut Av., W.Wick.	205	E5
Chestnut Av. N. E17	78	C4
Chestnut Av. S. E17	78	C4
Chestnut Cl. N14	42	C5
Chestnut Cl. N16	94	A2
Lordship Gro.		
Chestnut Cl. SE6	172	C5
Chestnut Cl. SE14	153	J3
Shardeloes Rd.		
Chestnut Cl. SW16	169	G4
Chestnut Cl., Buck.H.	64	A3
Chestnut Cl., Cars.	199	J1
Chestnut Cl., Sid.	176	A1
Chestnut Cl., WestDr.	121	E7
Chestnut Ct. SW6	128	C6
North End Rd.		
Chestnut Ct., Surb.	181	H7
Penners Gdns.		
Chestnut Dr. E11	79	G6
Chestnut Dr., Bexh.	158	D3
Chestnut Dr., Har.	52	C7
Chestnut Dr., Pnr.	66	D6
Chestnut Gro. SE20	171	F7
Chestnut Gro. SW12	150	A7
Chestnut Gro. W5	125	G3
Chestnut Gro., Barn.	41	J5
Chestnut Gro., Ilf.	65	H6
Chestnut Gro., Islw.	144	D4
Chestnut Gro., Mitch.	186	D4
Chestnut Gro., N.Mal.	182	D3
Chestnut Gro., S.Croy.	203	E7
Chestnut Gro., Wem.	86	E5
Chestnut La. N20	56	B1
Chestnut Ri. SE18	137	G6
Chestnut Rd. SE27	169	H3
Chestnut Rd. SW20	184	A2
Chestnut Rd., Kings.T.	163	H7
Chestnut Rd., Twick.	162	B2
Chestnut Wk., Wdf.Grn.	63	G5
Chestnut Way, Felt.	160	B3
Chestnuts, The SE14	153	J1
Cheston Av., Croy.	203	H2
Chettle Cl. SE1	28	B5
Chettle Ct. N8	75	G6
Chetwode Rd. SW17	167	J3
Chetwood Wk. E6	116	B6
Chetwynd Av., Barn.	57	J1
Chetwynd Rd. NW5	92	B4
Cheval Pl. SW7	23	H5
Cheval Pl. SW7	129	H3
Cheval St. E14	134	A3
Chevalier Cl., Stan.	53	H4
Cheveney Wk., Brom.	191	G3
Marina Cl.		

Chevening Rd. NW6	108	A2
Chevening Rd. SE10	135	F5
Chevening Rd. SE19	170	A6
Chevenings, The, Sid.	176	C3
Cheverton Rd. N19	92	D1
Chevet St. E9	95	H5
Kenworthy Rd.		
Cheviot Cl., Enf.	44	A2
Cheviot Cl., Hayes	121	G7
Cheviot Gdns. NW2	90	A2
Cheviot Gdns. SE27	169	H4
Cheviot Gate NW2	90	B2
Cheviot Rd. SE27	169	G5
Cheviot Way, Ilf.	81	H4
Chevron Cl. E16	115	G6
Chevy Rd., Sthl.	123	J2
Chewton Rd. E17	77	H4
Cheyne Av. E18	79	F1
Cheyne Av., Twick.	161	F1
Cheyne Cl. NW4	71	J5
Cheyne Cl., Brom.	206	B3
Cedar Cres.		
Cheyne Ct. SW3	31	J5
Cheyne Gdns. SW3	31	H5
Cheyne Gdns. SW3	129	H6
Cheyne Hill, Surb.	181	J4
Cheyne Ms. SW3	31	H5
Cheyne Ms. SW3	129	H6
Cheyne Path W7	104	C6
Copley Cl.		
Cheyne Pl. SW3	31	J5
Cheyne Pl. SW3	129	J6
Cheyne Row SW3	31	G6
Cheyne Row SW3	129	H6
Cheyne Wk. N21	43	H5
Cheyne Wk. NW4	71	J6
Cheyne Wk. SW3	31	H6
Cheyne Wk. SW3	129	H6
Cheyne Wk. SW10	31	E7
Cheyne Wk. SW10	129	G7
Cheyne Wk., Croy.	202	D2
Cheyneys Av., Edg.	53	G6
Chichele Gdns., Croy.	202	C4
Brownlow Rd.		
Chichele Rd. NW2	90	A5
Chicheley Gdns., Har.	51	J7
Chicheley Rd., Har.	51	J7
Chicheley St. SE1	26	D3
Chicheley St. SE1	131	F2
Chichester Cl. E6	116	B6
Chichester Cl. SE3	155	J1
Chichester Cl., Hmptn.	161	F6
Maple Cl.		
Chichester Ct., Stan.	69	H3
Chichester Gdns., Ilf.	80	B7
Chichester Ms. SE27	169	G4
Chichester Rents WC2	18	E3
Chichester Rd. E11	97	E3
Chichester Rd. N9	60	D1
Chichester Rd. NW6	108	D2
Chichester Rd. W2	14	B1
Chichester Rd. W2	109	E5
Chichester Rd., Croy.	202	B3
Chichester St. SW1	33	G4
Chichester St. SW1	130	C5
Chichester Way E14	134	D4
Chichester Way, Felt.	142	B7
Chicksand St. E1	21	G2
Chicksand St. E1	112	C5
Chiddingfold N12	56	D3
Chiddingstone Av., Bexh.	139	F7
Chiddingstone St. SW6	148	D2
Chieveley Rd., Bexh.	159	H4
Chignell Pl. W13	124	D1
Broadway		
Chigwell Hill E1	112/113	E7
Pennington St.		
Chigwell Hurst Ct., Pnr.	66	D3
Chigwell La., Loug.	49	F5
Chigwell Pk., Chig.	64	E4
Chigwell Pk. Dr., Chig.	64	D3
Chigwell Ri., Chig.	64	D2
Chigwell Rd. E18	79	H3
Chigwell Rd., Wdf.Grn.	79	J3
Chilcot Cl. E14	114	B6
Grundy St.		
Childebert Rd. SW17	168	B2
Childeric Rd. SE14	133	H7
Childerley St. SW6	148	A1
Fulham Palace Rd.		
Childers, The, Wdf.Grn.	64	C5
Childers St. SE8	133	H6
Childs Hill Wk. NW2	90	C3
Childs La. SE19	170	B6
Westow St.		

Church Rd., Felt. 160 D5
Church Rd., Hayes 121 J1
Church Rd. (Cranford), Houns. 122 B5
Church Rd. (Heston), Houns. 123 G7
Church Rd., Ilf. 81 H6
Church Rd., Islw. 144 A1
Church Rd., Kes. 206 A7
Church Rd., Kings.T. 181 J2
Church Rd., Loug. 47 H2
Church Rd., Mitch. 185 G2
Church Rd., Nthlt. 85 F7
Church Rd. (Farnborough), Orp. 207 F5
Church Rd., Rich. 145 H5
Church Rd. (Ham), Rich. 163 J5
Church Rd., Sid. 176 A4
Church Rd., Sthl. 123 F3
Church Rd., Stan. 53 E5
Church Rd., Surb. 195 F2
Church Rd., Sutt. 198 B6
Church Rd., Tedd. 162 B4
Church Rd., Wall. 200 C3
Church Rd., Well. 158 B2
Church Rd., West Dr. 120 A3
Church Rd., Wor.Pk. 196 E1
Church Rd. Merton SW19 185 G1
Church Row NW3 91 F4
Church Row, Chis. 175 F7
Church St. E15 115 E1
Church St. E16 136 E1
Church St. N9 60 B2
Church St. NW8 15 F1
Church St. NW8 109 G4
Church St. W2 15 F1
Church St. W2 109 G5
Church St. W4 127 E6
Church St., Croy. 201 J2
Church St., Dag. 101 H6
Church St., Enf. 44 A3
Church St., Hmptn. 179 J1
Church St., Islw. 144 E3
Church St., Kings.T. 181 G2
Church St., Sun. 178 B3
Church St., Sutt. 198/199 E5
High St.
Church St., Twick. 162 D1
Church St. Est. NW8 7 F6
Church St. Est. NW8 109 G4
Church St. N. E15 115 E1
Church St. Pas. E15 114/115 E1
Church St.
Church Stretton Rd., Houns. 143 J5
Church Ter. NW4 71 H3
Church Ter. SE13 154 E3
Church Ter. SW8 150 D2
Church Ter., Rich. 145 G5
Church Vale N2 73 J3
Church Vale SE23 171 F2
Church Wk. N6 92 A3
Swains La.
Church Wk. N16 94 A4
Church Wk. NW2 90 C3
Church Wk. NW4 71 J3
Church Wk. NW9 88 D2
Church Wk. SW13 147 G1
Church Wk. SW15 147 H5
Church Wk. SW16 186 C2
Church Wk. SW20 183 J3
Church Wk., Brent. 125 F6
Church Wk., Enf. 44 A3
Church La.
Church Wk., Rich. 145 G5
Red Lion St.
Church Wk., T.Ditt. 180 C6
Church Way N20 57 H3
Church Way, Barn. 41 J4
Church Way, Edg. 54 A6
Churchbury Cl., Enf. 44 B2
Churchbury La., Enf. 44 A3
Churchbury Rd. SE9 156 A7
Churchbury Rd., Enf. 44 A2
Churchcroft Cl. SW12 150 A7
Endlesham Rd.
Churchdown, Brom. 173 E4
Churchfield Av. N12 57 F6
Churchfield Cl., Har. 67 J4
Churchfield Rd. W3 126 C1
Churchfield Rd. W7 124 B2
Churchfield Rd. W13 125 E1
Churchfield Rd., Well. 158 A3
Churchfields E18 79 G1
Churchfields SE10 134 C6
Roan St.
Churchfields, Loug. 48 B4
Churchfields, W.Mol. 179 G3
Churchfields Av., Felt. 161 F3
Churchfields Rd., Beck. 189 G2
Churchill Av., Har. 68 E6
Churchill Ct. W5 105 J4
Churchill Ct., Nthlt. 85 G5
Churchill Gdns. SW1 33 F4
Churchill Gdns. SW1 130 C5
Churchill Gdns. W3 106 A6
Churchill Gdns. Rd. SW1 33 E4
Churchill Gdns. Rd. SW1 130 B5
Churchill Ms., Wdf.Grn. 63 F6
High Rd. Woodford Grn.
Churchill Pl. E14 134 B1
Churchill Pl., Har. 68 B4
Sandridge Cl.
Churchill Rd. E16 115 J6
Churchill Rd. NW2 89 H6
Churchill Rd. NW5 92 B4
Churchill Rd., Edg. 53 J6
Churchill Rd., S.Croy. 201 J7
Churchill Ter. E4 62 A4
Churchill Wk. E9 95 F5
Churchill Way, Brom. 191 G3
Ethelbert Rd.
Churchill Way, Sun. 160 A5
Churchley Rd. SE26 171 E4
Churchmead Cl., Barn. 41 H6
Churchmead Rd. NW10 89 G6
Churchmore Rd. SW16 186 C1
Churchview Rd., Twick. 162 A1
Churchway NW1 9 J3
Churchway NW1 110 D3
Churchwell Path E9 95 F5
Churchwood Gdns., Wdf.Grn. 63 G4
Churchyard Row SE11 35 H1
Churston Av. E13 115 H1
Churston Cl. SW2 169 H1
Tulse Hill
Churston Dr., Mord. 184 A5
Churston Gdns. N11 58 C6
Churton Pl. SW1 33 G2
Churton Pl. SW1 130 C4
Churton St. SW1 33 G2
Churton St. SW1 130 C4
Chusan Pl. E14 113 J6
Commercial Rd.
Chyngton Cl., Sid. 175 J3
Cibber Rd. SE23 171 G2
Cicada Rd. SW18 149 F5
Cicely Rd. SE15 152 D1
Cinderford Way, Brom. 173 E4
Cinema Par. W5 105 J4
Ashbourne Rd.
Cinnamon Cl., Croy. 186 E7
Cinnamon Row SW11 149 F3
Cinnamon St. E1 133 E1
Cintra Pk. SE19 170 C7
Circle, The NW2 89 E3
Circle, The NW7 54 D5
Circle Gdns. SW19 184 D2
Circuits, The, Pnr. 66 C4
Circular Rd. N17 76 C3
Circular Way SE18 136 C6
Circus Ms. W1 15 J1
Circus Pl. EC2 20 C2
Circus Rd. NW8 6 E3
Circus Rd. NW8 109 G3
Circus St. SE10 134 C7
Cirencester St. W2 14 A1
Cirencester St. W2 108 E5
Cissbury Ring N. N12 56 C5
Cissbury Ring S. N12 56 C5
Cissbury Rd. N15 76 A5
Citadel Pl. SE11 34 C3
Citizen Rd. N7 93 G4
Citron Ter. SE15 152/153 E3
Nunhead La.
City Gdn. Row N1 11 H2
City Gdn. Row N1 111 H2
City Rd. EC1 11 G2
City Rd. EC1 111 H2
Civic Way, Ilf. 81 F4
Civic Way, Ruis. 84 D5
Clabon Ms. SW1 23 J6
Clabon Ms. SW1 129 J3
Clack St. SE16 133 F2
Clacton Rd. E6 116 A3
Clacton Rd. E17 77 H6
Clacton Rd. N17 76 C2
Sperling Rd.
Claigmar Gdns. N3 72 E1
Claire Ct. N12 57 F3
Claire Ct., Bushey 52 A1
Claire Ct., Pnr. 51 F7
Westfield Pk.
Claire Gdns., Stan. 53 F5
Claire Pl. E14 134 A3
Clairvale Rd., Houns. 142 D1
Clairview Rd. SW16 168 B5
Clairville Gdns. W7 124 C1
Clairville Pt. SE23 171 G3
Clamp Hill, Stan. 52 A4
Clancarty Rd. SW6 148 D2
Clandon Cl. W3 126 B2
Avenue Rd.
Clandon Cl., Epsom 197 F6
Clandon Gdns. N3 72 D3
Clandon Rd., Ilf. 99 H2
Clandon St. SE8 154 A2
Clanfield Way SE15 37 E7
Clanricarde Gdns. W2 108 D7
Clap La., Dag. 101 H3
Clapham Common N. Side SW4 150 B4
Clapham Common S. Side SW4 150 B5
Clapham Common W. Side SW4 150 A4
Clapham Cres. SW4 150 D4
Clapham High St. SW4 150 D4
Clapham Junct. Est. SW11 149 H4
Clapham Manor St. SW4 150 C3
Clapham Pk. Est. SW4 150 D6
Clapham Pk. Rd. SW4 150 D4
Clapham Rd. SW9 150 E3
Clapham Rd. Est. SW4 150 D3
Claps Gate La. E6 116 E4
Clapton Common E5 76 C7
Clapton Pk. Est. E5 95 H4
Blackwell Cl.
Clapton Pas. E5 95 F5
Clapton Sq. E5 95 E5
Clapton Ter. N16 94 D1
Oldhill St.
Clapton Way E5 94 D4
Clara Pl. SE18 136 D4
Clare Cl. N2 73 F3
Thomas More Way
Clare Cor. SE9 156 E7
Clare Gdns. E7 97 G4
Clare Gdns. W11 108 B6
Westbourne Pk. Rd.
Clare Gdns., Bark. 99 J6
Clare La. N1 93 J7
Clare Lawn Av. SW14 146 D5
Clare Mkt. WC2 18 C4
Clare Ms. SW6 128/129 E7
Waterford Rd.
Clare Pl. SW15 147 F7
Minstead Gdns.
Clare Rd. E11 78 D6
Clare Rd. NW10 89 G7
Clare Rd. SE14 153 J1
Clare Rd., Grnf. 86 A6
Clare Rd., Houns. 143 F3
Clare Rd., Stai. 140 B7
Clare St. E2 113 E2
Clare Way, Bexh. 158 E1
Claredale St. E2 13 J2
Claredale St. E2 112 D2
Claremont Av., Har. 69 H5
Claremont Av., N.Mal. 183 G5
Claremont Av., Sun. 178 B1
Claremont Cl. E16 136 D1
Claremont Cl. N1 11 F2
Claremont Cl. N1 111 G2
Claremont Cl. SW2 168/169 E1
Streatham Hill
Claremont Cl., Orp. 206 D4
Claremont Ct., Surb. 181 G6
St. James Rd.
Claremont Gdns., Ilf. 99 H2
Claremont Gdns., Surb. 181 H5
Claremont Gro. W4 126/127 E7
Edensor Gdns.
Claremont Gro., Wdf.Grn. 63 J6
Claremont Pk. N3 72 B1
Claremont Rd. E7 97 H5
Claremont Rd. E17 77 H2
Claremont Rd. N6 74 C7
Claremont Rd. NW2 90 A3
Claremont Rd. W9 108 B2
Claremont Rd. W13 104 D5
Claremont Rd., Brom. 192 B4
Claremont Rd., Croy. 202 D1
Claremont Rd., Esher 194 B7
Claremont Rd., Har. 68 B2
Claremont Rd., Surb. 181 H6
Claremont Rd., Tedd. 162 C5
Claremont Rd., Twick. 145 F6
Claremont Sq. N1 10 E2
Claremont Sq. N1 111 G2
Claremont St. E16 136 D1
Claremont St. N18 60 D6
Claremont St. SE10 134 B6
Claremont Way NW2 89 J1
Clarence Av. SW4 150 D6
Clarence Av., Brom. 192 B4
Clarence Av., Ilf. 80 D6
Clarence Av., N.Mal. 182 C2
Clarence Cres. SW4 150 D6
Clarence Cres., Sid. 176 B3
Clarence Gdns. NW1 9 E4
Clarence Gdns. NW1 110 B3
Clarence La. SW15 147 E6
Clarence Ms. E5 95 E5
Clarence Ms. SE16 133 G1
Clarence Ms. SW12 150 B7
Clarence Pas. NW1 10 A2
Clarence Pl. E5 95 E5
Clarence Rd. E5 95 E4
Clarence Rd. E12 98 A5
Clarence Rd. E16 115 E4
Clarence Rd. E17 77 G2
Clarence Rd. N15 75 J5
Clarence Rd. N22 59 E7
Clarence Rd. NW6 90 C7
Clarence Rd. SE9 174 B2
Clarence Rd. SW19 166 E6
Clarence Rd. W4 126 A5
Clarence Rd., Bexh. 158 E4
Clarence Rd., Brom. 192 A3
Clarence Rd., Croy. 188 A7
Clarence Rd., Enf. 45 E5
Clarence Rd., Rich. 145 J1
Clarence Rd., Sid. 176 B3
Clarence Rd., Sutt. 198 E4
Clarence Rd., Tedd. 162 C6
Clarence Rd., Wall. 200 B5
Clarence St., Kings.T. 181 H2
Clarence St., Rich. 145 H4
Clarence St., Sthl. 122 D3
Clarence Ter. NW1 8 A5
Clarence Ter., Houns. 143 H4
Clarence Wk. SW4 150 E2
Clarence Way NW1 92 B7
Clarence Way Est. NW1 92 B7
Clarendon Cl. E9 95 F7
Clarendon Cl. W2 15 G5
Clarendon Cres., Twick. 162 A3
Clarendon Cross W11 108 B7
Portland Rd.
Clarendon Dr. SW15 147 J4
Clarendon Gdns. NW4 71 H3
Clarendon Gdns. W9 6 D6
Clarendon Gdns. W9 109 F4
Clarendon Gdns., Ilf. 98 C1
Clarendon Gdns., Wem. 87 G3
Clarendon Gro. NW1 9 H3
Clarendon Gro., Mitch. 185 J3
Clarendon Ms. W2 15 G4
Clarendon Ms., Bex. 177 H1
Clarendon Ms., Borwd. 38 A3
Clarendon Rd.
Clarendon Pl. W2 15 G5
Clarendon Pl. W2 109 H7
Clarendon Ri. SE13 154 C3
Clarendon Rd. E11 96 D1
Clarendon Rd. E17 78 B6
Clarendon Rd. E18 79 G3
Clarendon Rd. N8 75 F3
Clarendon Rd. N15 75 H4
Clarendon Rd. N18 60 D6
Clarendon Rd. N22 75 F2
Clarendon Rd. SW19 167 H7
Clarendon Rd. W5 105 H4
Clarendon Rd. W11 108 B7
Clarendon Rd., Borwd. 38 A3
Clarendon Rd., Croy. 201 H2
Clarendon Rd., Har. 68 B6
Clarendon Rd., Hayes 121 J2
Clarendon Rd., Wall. 200 C6
Clarendon St. SW1 32 E4
Clarendon St. SW1 130 B5
Clarendon Ter. W9 6 D5
Clarendon Wk. W11 108 B6
Clarendon Way N21 43 J6
Clarendon Way, Chis. 193 J3
Clarendon Way, Orp. 193 J3
Clarens St. SE6 171 J2
Claret Gdns. SE25 188 B4

248 Cla-Cli

Clareville Gro. SW7 30 D2
Clareville Gro. SW7 129 F4
Clareville Rd., Orp. 207 F2
Clareville St. SW7 30 D2
Clareville St. SW7 129 F4
Clarewood Wk. SW9 151 G4
Somerleyton Rd.
Clarges Ms. W1 24 D1
Clarges Ms. W1 130 B1
Clarges St. W1 24 E1
Clarges St. W1 130 B1
Claribel Rd. SW9 151 H2
Claridge Rd., Dag. 100 D1
Clarina Rd. SE20 171 G7
Evelina Rd.
Clarissa Rd., Rom. 82 D7
Clarissa St. E8 112 C1
Clark St. E1 113 E5
Clark Way, Houns. 122 D7
Clarke Path N16 94 D1
Braydon Rd.
Clarkes Av., Wor.Pk. 198 A1
Clarke's Ms. W1 16 C1
Clarks Pl. EC2 20 D3
Clarks Rd., Ilf. 99 G2
Clarkson Rd. E16 115 F6
Clarkson Row NW1 110 B2
Clarkson St. E2 112 E3
Clarksons, The, Bark. 117 F2
Classon Cl., West Dr. 120 B2
Claude Rd. E10 96 C2
Claude Rd. E13 115 H1
Claude Rd. SE15 152 E2
Claude St. E14 134 A4
Claudia Jones Way SW2 150 E6
Claudia Pl. SW19 166 B1
Claughton Rd. E13 115 J2
Clauson Av., Nthlt. 85 H5
Clave St. E1 132/133 E1
Cinnamon St.
Clavell St. SE10 134 C6
Claverdale Rd. SW2 151 F7
Clavering Av. SW13 127 H6
Clavering Cl., Twick. 162 D4
Clavering Rd. E12 98 A1
Claverings Ind. Est. N9 61 G2
Claverley Gro. N3 56 D7
Claverley Vil. N3 56/57 E7
Claverley Gro.
Claverton St. SW1 33 G4
Claverton St. SW1 130 C5
Claxton Gro. W6 128 A5
Clay Av., Mitch. 186 B2
Clay La., Edg. 54 A1
Clay La., Stai. 140 C7
Clay Rd., The, Loug. 48 B1
Clay St. W1 16 A2
Claybank Gro. SE13 154 B3
Algernon Rd.
Claybourne Ms. SE19 170 B7
Church Rd.
Claybridge Rd. SE12 173 J4
Claybrook Cl. N2 73 G3
Claybrook Rd. W6 128 A6
Claybury Bdy., Ilf. 80 B3
Claybury Rd., Wdf.Grn. 64 B7
Claydon Dr., Croy. 201 E4
Claydown Ms. SE18 136 D5
Woolwich New Rd.
Clayfarm Rd. SE9 175 F2
Claygate Cres., Croy. 204 C6
Claygate La., Esher 194 D2
Claygate La., T.Ditt. 194 D1
Claygate Lo. Cl., Esher 194 B7
Claygate Rd. W13 124 E3
Clayhall Av., Ilf. 80 B3
Clayhill, Surb. 182 A5
Clayhill Cres. SE9 174 A4
Claylands Pl. SW8 34 E7
Claylands Pl. SW8 131 G7
Claylands Rd. SW8 34 D6
Claylands Rd. SW8 131 F6
Claymill Ho. SE18 137 F5
Claymore Cl., Mord. 184 D7
Claymore Ct. E17 77 G1
Billet Rd.
Claypole Dr., Houns. 143 E1
Claypole Rd. E15 114 C2
Clayponds Av., Brent. 125 H4
Clayponds Gdns. W5 125 G4
Clayponds La., Brent. 125 H5
Clays La. E15 96 B5
Clay's La., Loug. 48 D1
Clays La. Cl. E15 96 B5
Clayside, Chig. 65 F6
Clayton Av., Wem. 87 H7
Clayton Cl. E6 116 C6
Brandreth Rd.
Clayton Cres., Brent. 125 G5
Clayton Fld. NW9 55 E7
Clayton Ms. SE10 154 D1
Clayton Rd. SE15 152 D1
Clayton Rd., Chess. 195 F4
Clayton Rd., Hayes 121 H2
Clayton Rd., Islw. 144 B3
Clayton Rd., Rom. 101 J1
Clayton St. SE11 34 E5
Clayton St. SE11 131 G6
Clayton Ter., Hayes 102 D5
Jollys La.
Claywood Cl., Orp. 193 H7
Clayworth Cl., Sid. 158 B6
Cleanthus Cl. SE18 156/157 E1
Cleanthus Rd.
Cleanthus Rd. SE18 157 E1
Clearbrook Way E1 113 G6
West Arbour St.
Clearwater Ter. W11 128 A2
Lorne Gdns.
Clearwell Dr. W9 6 A6
Clearwell Dr. W9 108 E4
Cleave Av., Hayes 121 H4
Cleave Av., Orp. 207 H6
Cleaveland Rd., Surb. 181 G5
Cleaver Sq. SE11 35 F3
Cleaver Sq. SE11 131 G5
Cleaver St. SE11 35 F3
Cleaver St. SE11 131 G5
Cleaverholme Cl. SE25 188 E6
Cleeve Hill SE23 171 E1
Cleeve Pk. Gdns., Sid. 176 B2
Cleeve Way SW15 147 F7
Danebury Av.
Clegg St. E1 132/133 E1
Prusom St.
Clegg St. E13 115 G2
Cleland Path, Loug. 49 E1
Clem Attlee Ct. SW6 128 C6
Clem Attlee Est. SW6 128 C6
Lillie Rd.
Clem Attlee Par. SW6 128 C6
Clem Attlee Ct.
Clematis Gdns., Wdf.Grn. 63 G5
Clematis St. W12 107 F7
Clemence Rd., Dag. 119 J1
Clemence St. E14 113 J5
Clement Av. SW4 150 D4
Clement Cl. NW6 89 J7
Clement Cl. W4 126 D4
Acton La.
Clement Gdns., Hayes 121 H4
Clement Rd. SW19 166 B5
Clement Rd., Beck. 189 G2
Clementhorpe Rd., Dag. 100 C6
Clementina Rd. E10 95 J1
Clementine Cl. W13 124/125 E2
Balfour Rd.
Clements Av. E16 115 G7
Clements Ct., Houns. 142 D4
Clements Ct., Ilf. 98/99 E3
Clements La.
Clement's Inn WC2 18 D4
Clement's Inn WC2 111 F6
Clement's Inn Pas. WC2 18 D4
Clements La. EC4 20 C5
Clements La. EC4 112 A7
Clements La., Ilf. 98 E3
Clements Pl., Brent. 125 G5
Clements Rd. E6 98 C7
Clements Rd. SE16 29 J6
Clements Rd. SE16 132 D3
Clements Rd., Ilf. 98 E3
Clendon Way SE18 137 G4
Polthorne Gro.
Clennam St. SE1 28 A3
Clensham La., Sutt. 198 D2
Clenston Ms. W1 15 J3
Clephane Rd. N1 94 A6
Clere St. EC2 12 C5
Clerkenwell Cl. EC1 11 F5
Clerkenwell Cl. EC1 111 G4
Clerkenwell Grn. EC1 11 F6
Clerkenwell Grn. EC1 111 H4
Clerkenwell Rd. EC1 10 E6
Clerkenwell Rd. EC1 111 G4
Clerks Piece, Loug. 48 C3
Clermont Rd. E9 113 F1
Cleve Rd. NW6 90 D7
Cleve Rd., Sid. 176 D3
Clevedon Cl. N16 94 C3
Smalley Cl.
Clevedon Gdns., Hayes 121 G3
Clevedon Gdns., Houns. 142 B1
Clevedon Rd. SE20 189 G1
Clevedon Rd., Kings.T. 182 A2
Clevedon Rd., Twick. 145 G6
Cleveland Av. SW20 184 C2
Cleveland Av. W4 127 F4
Cleveland Av., Hmptn. 161 F7
Cleveland Cres., Borwd. 38 C5
Cleveland Gdns. N4 75 J5
Cleveland Gdns. NW2 90 A2
Cleveland Gdns. SW13 147 F2
Cleveland Gdns. W2 14 C4
Cleveland Gdns. W2 109 F6
Cleveland Gdns., Wor.Pk. 197 E2
Cleveland Gro. E1 113 F4
Cleveland Way
Cleveland Ms. W1 17 F1
Cleveland Pk., Stai. 140 B6
Northumberland Cl.
Cleveland Pk. Av. E17 78 A4
Cleveland Pk. Cres. E17 78 A4
Cleveland Pl. SW1 25 G1
Cleveland Ri., Mord. 184 A7
Cleveland Rd. E18 79 G3
Cleveland Rd. N1 94 A7
Cleveland Rd. N9 45 E7
Cleveland Rd. SW13 147 F2
Cleveland Rd. W4 126 C3
Antrobus Rd.
Cleveland Rd. W13 104 E5
Cleveland Rd., Ilf. 99 E3
Cleveland Rd., Islw. 144 D4
Cleveland Rd., N.Mal. 182 E4
Cleveland Rd., Well. 157 J2
Cleveland Rd., Wor.Pk. 197 E2
Cleveland Row SW1 25 F2
Cleveland Row SW1 130 C1
Cleveland Sq. W2 14 C4
Cleveland Sq. W2 109 F6
Cleveland St. W1 9 F6
Cleveland St. W1 110 B4
Cleveland Ter. W2 14 D3
Cleveland Ter. W2 109 F6
Cleveland Way E1 113 F4
Cleveley Cl. SE7 136 A4
Cleveley Cres. W5 105 H2
Cleveleys Rd. E5 95 E3
Cleverly Est. W12 127 G1
Cleves Cl., Loug. 48 B6
Cleves Rd. E6 116 A1
Cleves Rd., Rich. 163 F3
Cleves Wk., Ilf. 65 F7
Cleves Way, Hmptn. 161 F7
Cleves Way, Ruis. 84 D1
Clewer Cres., Har. 68 A1
Clewer Ho. SE2 138 D2
Wolvercote Rd.
Clichy Est. E1 113 F5
Clifden Rd. E5 95 F5
Clifden Rd., Brent. 125 G6
Clifden Rd., Twick. 162 C1
Cliff Rd. NW1 92 D6
Cliff Ter. SE8 154 A2
Cliff Vil. NW1 92 D6
Cliff Wk. E16 115 F5
Cliffe Rd., S.Croy. 202 A5
Cliffe Wk., Sutt. 199 F5
Turnpike La.
Clifford Av. SW14 146 B3
Clifford Av., Chis. 174 C6
Clifford Av., Ilf. 80 E1
Clifford Av., Wall. 200 C4
Clifford Cl., Nthlt. 103 E1
Clifford Dr. SW9 151 H4
Clifford Gdns. NW10 107 J2
Clifford Rd. E16 115 F4
Clifford Rd. E17 78 C2
Clifford Rd. N9 45 F6
Clifford Rd. SE25 188 D4
Clifford Rd., Barn. 41 E3
Clifford Rd., Houns. 142 D3
Clifford Rd., Rich. 163 G2
Clifford Rd., Wem. 105 G1
Clifford St. W1 17 F6
Clifford St. W1 110 C7
Clifford Way NW10 89 F4
Clifford's Inn Pas. EC4 19 E4
Cliffview Rd. SE13 154 A3
Clifton Av. E17 77 G3
Clifton Av. N3 72 C1
Clifton Av. W12 127 F1
Clifton Av., Felt. 160 C3
Clifton Av., Stan. 69 E2
Clifton Av., Wem. 87 J6
Clifton Cl., Orp. 207 F5
Clifton Ct. N4 93 G2
Playford Rd.
Clifton Ct. NW8 6 E5
Clifton Cres. SE15 133 E7
Clifton Est. SE15 152/153 E1
Consort Rd.
Clifton Gdns. N15 76 C6
Clifton Gdns. NW11 72 C6
Clifton Gdns. W4 126 D4
Dolman Rd.
Clifton Gdns. W9 6 C6
Clifton Gdns. W9 109 F4
Clifton Gdns., Enf. 42 E4
Clifton Gro. E8 94 D6
Clifton Hill NW8 6 B1
Clifton Hill NW8 109 E2
Clifton Pk. Av. SW20 183 J2
Clifton Pl. SE16 133 F2
Canon Beck Rd.
Clifton Pl. W2 15 F5
Clifton Pl. W2 109 G7
Clifton Ri. SE14 133 H7
Clifton Rd. E7 98 A6
Clifton Rd. E16 115 E5
Clifton Rd. N3 73 F1
Clifton Rd. N8 74 D6
Clifton Rd. N22 74 C1
Clifton Rd. NW10 107 G2
Clifton Rd. SE25 188 B4
Clifton Rd. SW19 166 A6
Clifton Rd. W9 6 D5
Clifton Rd. W9 109 F4
Clifton Rd., Grnf. 103 J4
Clifton Rd., Har. 69 J5
Clifton Rd., Ilf. 81 G6
Clifton Rd., Islw. 144 B2
Clifton Rd., Kings.T. 163 J7
Clifton Rd., Loug. 48 B4
Clifton Rd., Sid. 175 H4
Clifton Rd., Sthl. 123 E4
Clifton Rd., Tedd. 162 B4
Clifton Rd., Wall. 200 B5
Clifton Rd., Well. 158 C3
Clifton St. EC2 12 D6
Clifton St. EC2 112 B4
Clifton Ter. N4 93 G2
Clifton Vil. W9 14 B1
Clifton Vil. W9 109 E5
Clifton Wk. E6 116 B6
Clifton Wk. W6 127 H4
King St.
Clifton Way SE15 133 F7
Clifton Way, Borwd. 38 A1
Clifton Way, Wem. 105 H1
Clinch Ct. E16 115 G5
Cline Rd. N11 58 C6
Clinger Ct. N1 112 B1
Pitfield St.
Clink St. SE1 28 A1
Clink St. SE1 132 A1
Clinton Av., E.Mol. 179 J4
Clinton Av., Well. 157 J4
Clinton Cres., Ilf. 65 H6
Clinton Rd. E3 113 H3
Clinton Rd. E7 97 G4
Clinton Rd. N15 76 A4
Clipper Cl. SE16 133 G2
Kinburn St.
Clipper Way SE13 154 C4
Clippesby Cl., Chess. 195 J6
Clipstone Ms. W1 9 F6
Clipstone Ms. W1 110 C4
Clipstone Rd., Houns. 143 G3
Clipstone St. W1 17 E1
Clipstone St. W1 110 C5
Clissold Cl. N2 73 J3
Clissold Ct. N4 93 J2
Clissold Cres. N16 94 A3
Clissold Rd. N16 94 A3
Clitheroe Av., Har. 85 G1
Clitheroe Gdns., Wat. 50 D3
Clitheroe Rd. SW9 151 E2
Clitherow Av. W7 124 D3
Clitherow Pas., Brent. 125 F5
Clitherow Rd., Brent. 125 F5
Clitterhouse Cres. NW2 89 J1
Clitterhouse Rd. NW2 89 J1
Clive Av. N18 60 D6
Claremont St.
Clive Ct. W9 6 D5
Clive Pas. SE21 170 A3
Clive Rd.
Clive Rd. SE21 170 A3
Clive Rd. SW19 167 H6
Clive Rd., Belv. 139 G4
Clive Rd., Enf. 44 D4
Clive Rd., Felt. 142 A6
Clive Rd., Twick. 162 C4
Clive Way, Enf. 44 D4
Cliveden Cl. N12 57 F4
Woodside Av.
Cliveden Pl. SW1 32 B1
Cliveden Pl. SW1 130 A4
Cliveden Rd. SW19 184 C1

Clivedon Ct. W13 104 E5
Clivedon Rd. E4 62 E5
Clivesdale Dr., Hayes 122 B1
Cloak La. EC4 20 A5
Cloak La. EC4 111 J7
Clock Ho. Rd., Beck. 189 H3
Clock Twr. Ms. N1 111 J1
Arlington Av.
Clock Twr. Ms. SE28 118 B7
Clock Twr. Pl. N7 92 E6
Clock Twr. Rd., Islw. 144 C3
Clockhouse Av., Bark. 117 F1
Clockhouse Cl. SW19 165 J3
Clockhouse Pl. SW15 148 B5
Cloister Cl., Tedd. 162 E5
Cloister Gdns. SE25 188 E6
Cloister Gdns., Edg. 54 C5
Cloister Rd. NW2 90 C3
Cloister Rd. W3 106 C5
Cloisters Av., Brom. 192 C5
Cloisters Mall, Kings.T. 181 G2
Union St.
Clonard Way, Pnr. 51 G6
Clonbrock Rd. N16 94 B4
Cloncurry St. SW6 148 A2
Clonmel Cl., Har. 86 A1
Clonmel Rd. SW6 128 C7
Clonmel Rd., Tedd. 162 A4
Clonmell Rd. N17 76 A3
Clonmore St. SW18 166 C1
Cloonmore Av., Orp. 207 J4
Clorane Gdns. NW3 90 D3
Close, The E4 62 C7
Beech Hall Rd.
Close, The N14 58 D2
Close, The N20 56 C2
Close, The SE3 154 D2
Heath La.
Close, The, Barn. 41 J6
Close, The, Beck. 189 H4
Close, The, Bex. 159 G6
Close, The, Har. 67 J2
Close, The, Islw. 144 A2
Close, The, Mitch. 185 J4
Close, The, N.Mal. 182 C2
Close, The, Orp. 193 H6
Close, The (Eastcote), Pnr. 66 C7
Close, The (Rayners La.), Pnr. 67 F7
Close, The, Rich. 146 B3
Close, The, Rom. 82 E6
Close, The, Sid. 176 B5
Close, The, Sutt. 184 C7
Close, The (Barnhill Rd.), Wem. 88 C3
Close, The (Lyon Pk. Av.), Wem. 87 H6
Cloth Ct. EC1 19 H2
Cloth Fair EC1 19 H2
Cloth Fair EC1 111 H5
Cloth St. EC1 19 J1
Clothier St. E1 21 E3
Clothworkers Rd. SE18 137 G7
Cloudesdale Rd. SW17 168 B2
Cloudesley Pl. N1 111 G1
Cloudesley Rd. N1 111 G1
Cloudesley Rd., Bexh. 159 F1
Cloudesley Sq. N1 111 G1
Cloudesley St. N1 111 G1
Clouston Cl., Wall. 200 E5
Clova Rd. E7 97 F6
Clove Cres. E14 114 D7
Clove Hitch Quay SW11 149 F3
Clove St. E13 115 G4
Barking Rd.
Clovelly Av. NW9 71 F4
Clovelly Cl., Pnr. 66 B3
Clovelly Gdns. SE19 188 C1
Clovelly Gdns., Enf. 44 B7
Clovelly Gdns., Rom. 83 H1
Clovelly Rd. N8 74 D4
Clovelly Rd. W4 126 C2
Clovelly Rd. W5 125 F2
Clovelly Rd., Bexh. 138 E6
Clovelly Rd., Houns. 143 G2
Clovelly Way E1 113 F6
Jamaica St.
Clovelly Way, Har. 85 F2
Clovelly Way, Orp. 193 J6
Clover Cl. E11 96 D2
Norman Rd.
Clover Ms. SW3 31 J5
Clover Way, Wall. 200 A1
Cloverdale Gdns., Sid. 157 J6
Cloverleys, Loug. 48 A5
Clowders Rd. SE6 171 J3
Clowser Cl., Sutt. 199 F5
Turnpike La.
Cloyster Wd., Edg. 53 G7
Cloysters Grn. E1 29 H1
Cloysters Grn. E1 132 D1
Club Gdns. Rd., Brom. 191 G7
Club Row E1 13 F5
Club Row E1 112 C4
Club Row E2 13 F5
Club Row E2 112 C4
Clunbury Av., Sthl. 123 F5
Clunbury St. N1 12 C2
Cluny Est. SE1 28 D5
Cluny Ms. SW5 128 D4
Cluny Pl. SE1 28 D5
Cluse Ct. N1 11 J1
Clutton St. E14 114 B5
Clydach Rd., Enf. 44 C4
Clyde Circ. N15 76 B4
Clyde Pl. E10 78 B7
Clyde Rd. N15 76 B4
Clyde Rd. N22 74 D1
Clyde Rd., Croy. 202 C1
Clyde Rd., Sutt. 198 D5
Clyde Rd., Wall. 200 C5
Clyde St. SE8 133 J6
Clyde Ter. SE23 171 F2
Clyde Vale SE23 171 F2
Clydesdale, Enf. 45 G4
Clydesdale Av., Stan. 69 G3
Clydesdale Cl., Borwd. 38 D5
Clydesdale Cl., Islw. 144 C3
Clydesdale Gdns., Rich. 146 B4
Clydesdale Ho., Erith 138/139 E2
Kale Rd.
Clydesdale Rd. W11 108 C6
Clymping Dene, Felt. 142 B7
Clyston St. SW8 150 C2
Coach & Horses Yd. W1 17 E5
Coach Ho. La. N5 93 H4
Highbury Hill
Coach Ho. La. SW19 166 A4
Coach Ho. Ms. SE23 153 G6
Coach Ho. Yd. SW18 148/149 E4
Ebner St.
Coach Yd. Ms. N19 92/93 E1
Trinder Rd.
Coachhouse Ms. SE20 170 E7
Coal Wf. Rd. W12 128 A2
Shepherds Bush Pl.
Coaldale Wk. SE21 151 J7
Lairdale Cl.
Coalecroft Rd. SW15 147 J4
Coate St. E2 13 J2
Coate St. E2 112 D2
Coates Av. SW18 149 G6
Coates Hill Rd., Brom. 192 D2
Coates Wk., Brent. 125 H5
Cobb Cl., Borwd. 38 C5
Cobb St. E1 21 F2
Cobb St. E1 112 C5
Cobbett Rd. SE9 156 B3
Cobbett Rd., Twick. 161 G1
Cobbett St. SW8 131 F7
Cobbetts Av., Ilf. 80 A5
Cobblers Wk., E.Mol. 180 D1
Cobblers Wk., Hmptn. 161 J7
Cobblers Wk., Kings.T. 180 D1
Cobblers Wk., Tedd. 162 A7
Cobblestone Pl., Croy. 201 J1
Oakfield Rd.
Cobbold Est. NW10 89 F6
Cobbold Ms. W12 127 F2
Cobbold Rd.
Cobbold Rd. E11 97 F3
Cobbold Rd. NW10 89 F6
Cobbold Rd. W12 127 F2
Cobb's Ct. EC4 111 H6
Carter La.
Cobb's Rd., Houns. 143 F4
Cobden Rd. E11 97 E3
Cobden Rd. SE25 188 D5
Cobden Rd., Orp. 207 G4
Cobham Av., N.Mal. 183 G5
Cobham Cl. SW11 149 H6
Cobham Cl., Brom. 192 B7
Cobham Cl., Edg. 70 B2
Cobham Cl., Sid. 158 B6
Park Mead
Cobham Cl., Wall. 200 E6
Cobham Ho., Bark. 117 F1
St. Margarets
Cobham Ms. NW1 92 D7
Agar Gro.
Cobham Pl., Bexh. 158 D5
Cobham Rd. E17 78 C1
Cobham Rd. N22 75 H3
Cobham Rd., Houns. 122 C7
Cobham Rd., Ilf. 99 H2
Cobham Rd., Kings.T. 182 A1
Cobland Rd. SE12 173 J4
Coborn Rd. E3 113 J3
Coborn St. E3 113 J3
Cobourg Rd. SE5 37 F5
Cobourg Rd. SE5 132 C6
Cobourg St. NW1 9 G4
Cobourg St. NW1 110 C3
Coburg Cl. SW1 33 G1
Coburg Cres. SW2 169 F1
Coburg Gdns., Ilf. 80 A2
Coburg Rd. N22 75 F3
Cochrane Ms. NW8 7 F2
Cochrane Rd. SW19 166 C7
Cochrane St. NW8 7 F2
Cochrane St. NW8 109 G2
Cock Hill E1 21 E2
Cock La. EC1 19 G2
Cock La. EC1 111 H5
Cockayne Way SE8 133 H5
Cockerell Rd. E17 77 H6
Cockfosters Rd., Barn. 41 J2
Cockpit Steps SW1 25 J4
Cockpit Yd. WC1 18 D1
Cocks Cres., N.Mal. 183 F4
Cocksett Av., Orp. 207 H6
Cockspur Ct. SW1 25 J1
Cockspur St. SW1 25 J1
Cockspur St. SW1 130 D1
Cocksure La., Sid. 177 G3
Code St. E1 13 G6
Code St. E1 112 C4
Codicote Ter. N4 93 J2
Green Las.
Codling Cl. E1 29 J2
Codling Way, Wem. 87 G4
Codrington Hill SE23 153 H7
Codrington Ms. W11 108 B6
Blenheim Cres.
Cody Cl., Har. 69 G3
Cody Cl., Wall. 200 D7
Alcock Cl.
Cody Rd. E16 114 D4
Cody Rd. Business Cen. E16 114 D4
Coe Av. SE25 188 D6
Coe's All., Barn. 40 B4
Wood St.
Coffers Circle, Wem. 88 B3
Cogan Av. E17 77 H1
Coin St. SE1 27 E1
Coin St. SE1 131 G1
Coity Rd. NW5 92 A6
Coke St. E1 21 H3
Coke St. E1 112 D6
Cokers La. SE21 170 A1
Perifield
Colas Ms. NW6 108 D1
Birchington Rd.
Colbeck Ms. SW7 30 B2
Colbeck Ms. SW7 129 E4
Colbeck Rd., Har. 67 J7
Colberg Pl. N16 76 B7
Colborne Way, Wor.Pk. 197 J3
Colbrook Av., Hayes 121 G3
Colbrook Cl., Hayes 121 G3
Colburn Av., Pnr. 51 E6
Colburn Way, Sutt. 199 G3
Colby Ms. SE19 170 B5
Gipsy Hill
Colby Rd. SE19 170 B5
Colchester Av. E12 98 C3
Colchester Dr., Pnr. 66 D5
Colchester Rd. E10 78 C7
Colchester Rd. E17 78 A6
Colchester Rd., Edg. 54 C7
Colchester Rd., Nthwd. 66 A2
Colchester St. E1 21 G3
Cold Blow La. SE14 133 G7
Cold Blows, Mitch. 186 A3
Cold Harbour E14 134 C2
Coldbath Sq. EC1 11 E5
Coldbath St. SE13 154 B1
Coldershaw Rd. W13 124 D1
Coldfall Av. N10 73 J2
Coldharbour La. SE5 151 G4
Coldharbour La. SW9 151 G4
Coldharbour La., Hayes 102 A7
Coldharbour Pl. SE5 151 J2
Denmark Hill
Coldharbour Rd., Croy. 201 G5
Coldharbour Way, Croy. 201 G5
Coldstream Gdns. SW18 148 C6
Cole Cl. SE28 138 B1
Cole Gdns., Houns. 122 A7
Cole Pk. Gdns., Twick. 144 D6
Cole Pk. Rd., Twick. 144 D6
Cole Pk. Vw., Twick. 144 D6
Hill Vw. Rd.
Cole Rd., Twick. 144 D6
Cole St. SE1 28 A4
Cole St. SE1 131 J2
Colebeck Ms. N1 93 H6
Colebert Av. E1 113 F4
Colebrook Cl. SW15 148 A7
West Hill
Colebrook Gdns., Loug. 49 E2
Colebrook Ho. E14 114 B6
Brabazon St.
Colebrook La., Loug. 49 E2
Colebrook Path, Loug. 49 E2
Colebrook Rd. SW16 187 E1
Colebrook Way N11 58 B5
Colebrooke Av. W13 104 E6
Colebrooke Dr. E11 79 H7
Colebrooke Pl. N1 111 H1
St. Peters St.
Colebrooke Ri., Brom. 191 E2
Colebrooke Row N1 11 G2
Colebrooke Row N1 111 H2
Coleby Path SE5 132 A7
Harris St.
Coledale Dr., Stan. 69 F1
Coleford Rd. SW18 149 F5
Colegrave Rd. E15 96 D5
Colegrove Rd. SE15 37 G6
Colegrove Rd. SE15 132 C7
Coleherne Ct. SW5 30 B4
Coleherne Ct. SW5 129 E5
Coleherne Ms. SW10 30 A4
Coleherne Ms. SW10 128 E5
Coleherne Rd. SW10 30 A4
Coleherne Rd. SW10 128 E5
Colehill Gdns. SW6 148 B2
Fulham Palace Rd.
Colehill La. SW6 148 B1
Coleman Cl. SE25 188 D2
Warminster Rd.
Coleman Flds. N1 111 J1
Coleman Rd. SE5 36 D7
Coleman Rd. SE5 132 B7
Coleman Rd., Belv. 139 G4
Coleman Rd., Dag. 101 E6
Coleman St. EC2 20 B3
Coleman St. EC2 112 A6
Colemans Heath SE9 174 E3
Colenso Dr. NW7 55 G7
Bunns La.
Colenso Rd. E5 95 F4
Colenso Rd., Ilf. 99 H1
Colepits Wd. Rd. SE9 157 F5
Coleraine Rd. N8 75 G3
Coleraine Rd. SE3 135 F6
Coleridge Av. E12 98 B6
Coleridge Av., Sutt. 199 H4
Coleridge Cl. SW8 150 B2
Coleridge Gdns. NW6 91 F7
Fairhazel Gdns.
Coleridge La. N8 74/75 E6
Coleridge Rd.
Coleridge Rd. E17 77 J4
Coleridge Rd. N4 93 G2
Coleridge Rd. N8 74 D6
Coleridge Rd. N12 57 F5
Coleridge Rd., Croy. 189 F7
Coleridge Sq. W13 104 D6
Berners Dr.
Coleridge Wk. NW11 72 D4
Coleridge Way, Hayes 102 A6
Coleridge Way, West Dr. 120 C4
Coles Cres., Har. 85 H2
Coles Grn., Bushey 51 J1
Coles Grn., Loug. 48 D1
Coles Grn. Ct. NW2 89 G2
Coles Grn. Rd. NW2 89 G1
Colesburg Rd., Beck. 189 J3
Coleshill Rd., Tedd. 162 B6
Colestown St. SW11 149 H2
Colet Cl. N13 59 H6
Colet Gdns. W14 128 A4
Coley St. WC1 10 D6
Coley St. WC1 111 F4
Colfe Rd. SE23 171 H1
Colham Av., West Dr. 120 B1
Colham Mill Rd., West Dr. 120 A2
Colin Cl. NW9 71 E4

Colin Cl., Croy. 203 J3
Colin Cl., W.Wick. 205 F3
Colin Cres. NW9 71 F4
Colin Dr. NW9 71 F5
Colin Gdns. NW9 71 F5
Colin Par. NW9 70/71 E4
Edgware Rd.
Colin Pk. Rd. NW9 70 E4
Colin Rd. NW10 89 G6
Colina Ms. N15 75 H5
Harringay Rd.
Colina Rd. N15 75 H5
Colindale Av. NW9 70 D3
Colindale Business Pk. NW9 70 C3
Colindeep Gdns. NW4 71 G5
Colindeep La. NW4 70 E3
Colindeep La. NW9 70 E3
Colinette Rd. SW15 147 J4
Colinton Rd., Ilf. 100 B2
Coliston Pas. SW18 148 D7
Coliston Rd.
Coliston Rd. SW18 148 D7
Collamore Av. SW18 167 H1
Collapit Cl., Har. 67 H5
Collard Av., Loug. 49 F2
Collard Grn., Loug. 49 F2
Collard Av.
College App. SE10 134 C6
College Av., Har. 68 B1
College Cl. E9 95 F5
Median Rd.
College Cl. N18 60 C5
College Cl., Har. 52 B7
College Cl., Twick. 162 A1
Meadway
College Cres. NW3 91 G6
College Cross N1 93 G7
College Dr., Ruis. 66 A7
College Gdns. E4 46 B7
College Gdns. N18 60 C5
College Gdns. SE21 170 B1
College Gdns. SW17 167 H2
College Gdns., Enf. 44 A1
College Gdns., Ilf. 80 B5
College Gdns., N.Mal. 183 F5
College Grn. SE19 170 B7
College Gro. NW1 110 D1
St. Pancras Way
College Hill EC4 20 A5
College Hill Rd., Har. 68 C1
College La. NW5 92 B4
College Ms. SW1 26 A5
College Ms. SW18 148/149 E5
St. Ann's Hill
College Pk. Cl. SE13 154 D4
College Pk. Rd. N17 60 C6
College Rd.
College Pl. E17 78 E4
College Pl. NW1 110 C1
College Pl. SW10 30 C7
College Pt. E15 97 F6
College Rd. E17 78 C5
College Rd. N17 60 C6
College Rd. N21 59 G2
College Rd. NW10 107 J2
College Rd. SE19 170 C5
College Rd. SE21 152 B7
College Rd. SW19 167 G6
College Rd. W13 104 E6
College Rd., Brom. 173 G7
College Rd., Croy. 202 A2
College Rd., Enf. 44 A2
College Rd. (Harrow on the Hill), Har. 68 B6
College Rd. (Harrow Weald), Har. 68 B1
College Rd., Islw. 144 C1
College Rd., Wem. 87 G1
College Row E9 95 G5
College Slip, Brom. 191 G1
College St. EC4 20 B5
College Ter. E3 113 J3
College Ter. N3 72 C2
Hendon La.
College Vw. SE9 174 A1
College Wk., Kings.T. 181 H2
Grange Rd.
College Yd. NW5 92 B4
College La.
Collent St. E9 95 F6
Colless Rd. N15 76 C5
Collett Rd. SE16 29 J6
Collett Rd. SE16 132 D3
Collett Way, Sthl. 123 H1
Collier Cl. E6 116/117 E6
Trader Rd.
Collier Cl., Epsom 196 A6
Collier Dr., Edg. 70 A2
Collier Row Rd., Rom. 83 F1
Collier St. N1 10 C2
Collier St. N1 111 F2
Colliers Shaw, Kes. 206 A4
Colliers Water La., Th.Hth. 187 G5
Collindale Av., Erith 139 H6
Collindale Av., Sid. 176 A1
Collingbourne Rd. W12 127 H1
Collingham Gdns. SW5 30 B2
Collingham Gdns. SW5 129 E4
Collingham Pl. SW5 30 A2
Collingham Pl. SW5 128 E4
Collingham Rd. SW5 30 B1
Collingham Rd. SW5 129 E4
Collings Cl. N22 59 F6
Whittington Rd.
Collingtree Rd. SE26 171 F4
Collingwood Av. N10 74 A3
Collingwood Av., Surb. 196 C1
Collingwood Cl. SE20 189 E1
Collingwood Cl., Twick. 143 G6
Collingwood Rd. E17 78 A6
Collingwood Rd. N15 76 B4
Collingwood Rd., Mitch. 185 H2
Collingwood Rd., Sutt. 198 D3
Collingwood St. E1 113 E4
Collins Av., Stan. 69 H2
Collins Dr., Ruis. 84 C2
Collins Rd. N5 93 J4
Collins Sq. SE3 155 F2
Tranquil Vale
Collins St. SE3 155 E2
Collin's Yd. N1 111 H1
Islington Grn.
Collinson St. SE1 27 J4
Collinson Wk. SE1 27 J4
Collinwood Av., Enf. 45 F3
Collinwood Gdns., Ilf. 80 C5
Collis All., Twick. 162 B1
The Grn.
Colls Rd. SE15 153 F1
Collyer Av., Croy. 200 E4
Collyer Pl. SE15 152 D1
Peckham High St.
Collyer Rd., Croy. 201 E4
Colman Rd. E16 115 J5
Colmar Cl. E1 113 G4
Alderney Rd.
Colmer Pl., Har. 52 A7
Colmer Rd. SW16 187 E1
Colmore Ms. SE15 153 E1
Colmore Rd., Enf. 45 F4
Colnbrook St. SE1 27 G6
Colnbrook St. SE1 131 H3
Colne Ct., Epsom 196 C4
Colne Ho., Bark. 99 E6
Colne Rd. E5 95 H4
Colne Rd. N21 44 A7
Colne Rd., Twick. 162 B1
Colne St. E13 115 G3
Grange Rd.
Colney Hatch La. N10 74 B2
Colney Hatch La. N11 57 J6
Cologne Rd. SW11 149 G4
Colomb St. SE10 135 E5
Colombo Rd., Ilf. 99 F1
Colombo St. SE1 27 G2
Colombo St. SE1 131 H1
Colonels Wk., Enf. 43 H3
Colonial Av., Twick. 143 J5
Colonial Rd., Felt. 141 H7
Colonnade WC1 10 A6
Colonnade WC1 110 E4
Colonnade Wk. SW1 32 D2
Colonnades, The W2 14 B3
Colonnades, The W2 109 E6
Colson Gdns., Loug. 48/49 E4
Colson Rd.
Colson Grn., Loug. 48/49 E4
Colson Rd.
Colson Path, Loug. 48 D4
Colson Rd., Croy. 202 B2
Colson Rd., Loug. 48 E4
Colson Way SW16 168 C4
Colsterworth Rd. N15 76 C4
Colston Av., Cars. 199 H4
Colston Cl., Cars. 199 J4
West St.
Colston Rd. E7 98 A6
Colston Rd. SW14 146 C4
Colthurst Cres. N4 93 J2
Coltness Cres. SE2 138 B5
Colton Gdns. N17 75 J3
Colton Rd., Har. 68 B5
Columbia Av., Edg. 70 B1
Columbia Av., Ruis. 84 B1
Columbia Av., Wor.Pk. 183 F7
Columbia Ctyd. E14 134 A1
West India Av.
Columbia Rd. E2 13 F3
Columbia Rd. E2 112 C3
Columbia Rd. E13 115 F4
Columbia Sq. SW14 146 C4
Upper Richmond Rd. W.
Columbine Av. E6 116 B5
Columbine Av., S.Croy. 201 H7
Columbine Way SE13 154 C2
Columbus Ct. SE16 133 F1
Rotherhithe St.
Columbus Ctyd. E14 134 A1
West India Av.
Columbus Gdns., Nthwd. 66 A1
Colva Wk. N19 92 B2
Chester Rd.
Colvestone Cres. E8 94 C5
Colview Ct. SE9 174 A1
Mottingham La.
Colville Est. N1 112 B1
Colville Gdns. W11 108 C6
Colville Hos. W11 108 C6
Colville Ms. W11 108 C6
Lonsdale Rd.
Colville Pl. W1 17 G2
Colville Rd. E11 96 C3
Colville Rd. E17 77 H2
Colville Rd. N9 60 E1
Colville Rd. W3 126 B3
Colville Rd. W11 108 C6
Colville Sq. W11 108 C6
Colville Sq. Ms. W11 108 C6
Portobello Rd.
Colville Ter. W11 108 C6
Colvin Cl. SE26 171 F5
Colvin Gdns. E4 62 C3
Colvin Gdns. E11 79 H4
Colvin Gdns., Ilf. 81 F1
Colvin Rd. E6 98 B7
Colvin Rd., Th.Hth. 187 G5
Colwall Gdns., Wdf.Grn. 63 G5
Colwell Rd. SE22 152 C5
Colwick Cl. N6 74 D7
Colwith Rd. W6 127 J6
Colwood Gdns. SW19 167 G7
Colworth Gro. SE17 36 A2
Colworth Rd. E11 78 E6
Colworth Rd., Croy. 202 D1
Colwyn Av., Grnf. 104 C2
Colwyn Cl. SW16 168 C5
Colwyn Cres., Houns. 143 J1
Colwyn Grn. NW9 70/71 E6
Snowdon Dr.
Colwyn Rd. NW2 89 H3
Colyer Cl. N1 10 D1
Colyer Cl. N1 111 F2
Colyer Cl. SE9 175 E2
Colyers La., Erith 159 J1
Colyton Cl., Well. 158 D1
Colyton Cl., Wem. 87 F6
Bridgewater Rd.
Colyton Rd. SE22 153 E5
Colyton Way N18 60 D5
Combe Av. SE3 135 F7
Combe Lo. SE7 135 J6
Elliscombe Rd.
Combe Martin, Kings.T. 164 C5
Combe Ms. SE3 135 F7
Combedale Rd. SE10 135 G5
Combemartin Rd. SW18 148 B7
Comber Cl. NW2 89 H3
Comber Gro. SE5 151 J1
Combermere Rd. SW9 151 F3
Combermere Rd., Mord. 185 E6
Comberton Rd. E5 95 E2
Combeside SE18 137 J7
Combwell Cres. SE2 138 A3
Comely Bank Rd. E17 78 C5
Comer Cres., Sthl. 123 J2
Windmill Av.
Comeragh Ms. W14 128 B5
Comeragh Rd. W14 128 B5
Comerford Rd. SE4 153 H4
Comet Cl. E12 98 A4
Comet Pl. SE8 134 A7
Comet Rd., Stai. 140 A7
Comet St. SE8 134 A7
Commerce Rd. N22 75 F1
Commerce Rd., Brent. 125 F7
Commerce Way, Croy. 201 F2
Commercial Rd. E1 21 H3
Commercial Rd. E1 112 D6
Commercial Rd. E14 113 F6
Commercial Rd. N17 60 B6
Commercial Rd. N18 60 B5
Commercial St. E1 13 F6
Commercial St. E1 112 C4
Commercial Way NW10 106 B2
Commercial Way SE15 132 C7
Commerell St. SE10 135 E5
Commodity Quay E1 21 G6
Commodore Sq. SW10 149 G1
Commodore St. E1 113 H4
Common, The W5 105 H7
Common, The, Rich. 163 G3
Common, The, Sthl. 122 C4
Common, The, Stan. 52 B2
Common La., Esher 194 D7
Common Rd. SW13 147 G3
Common Rd., Esher 194 D6
Common Rd., Stan. 52 A4
Commondale SW15 147 J3
Commonfield La. SW17 167 H5
Tooting Gro.
Commonside, Kes. 205 J4
Commonside E., Mitch. 185 J3
Commonside W., Mitch. 185 J3
Commonwealth Av. W12 107 H7
Commonwealth Rd. N17 60 D7
Commonwealth Way SE2 138 B5
Community Cl., Houns. 142 B1
Community La. N7 92 D5
Community Rd. E15 96 D5
Community Rd., Grnf. 103 J1
Como Rd. SE23 171 H2
Compass Hill, Rich. 145 G6
Compayne Gdns. NW6 90 E7
Compton Av. E6 116 A2
Compton Av. N1 93 H6
Compton Av. N6 73 H7
Compton Cl. E3 114 A5
Compton Cl. NW1 9 E4
Compton Cl. NW11 90 A3
The Vale
Compton Cl. W13 104 D6
Compton Cl., Edg. 54 C7
Pavilion Way
Compton Ct. SE19 170 B5
Victoria Cres.
Compton Cres. N17 59 J7
Compton Cres. W4 126 C6
Compton Cres., Chess. 195 H6
Compton Cres., Nthlt. 102 D1
Compton Pas. EC1 11 H5
Compton Pl. WC1 10 A5
Compton Pl., Wat. 50 E3
Compton Ri., Pnr. 67 E5
Compton Rd. N1 93 H6
Compton Rd. N21 59 G1
Compton Rd. NW10 108 A3
Compton Rd. SW19 166 C6
Compton Rd., Croy. 202 E1
Compton St. EC1 11 G5
Compton St. EC1 111 H4
Compton Ter. N1 93 H6
Comreddy Cl., Enf. 43 H1
Comus Pl. SE17 36 D2
Comus Pl. SE17 132 B4
Comyn Rd. SW11 149 H4
Comyns, The, Bushey 51 J1
Comyns Cl. E16 115 F5
Comyns Rd., Dag. 101 G7
Conant Ms. E1 21 H5
Concanon Rd. SW2 151 F4
Concert Hall App. SE1 26 D2
Concert Hall App. SE1 131 F1
Concord Cl., Nthlt. 102 D3
Britannia Cl.
Concord Rd. W3 106 B4
Concord Rd., Enf. 45 F5
Concorde Cl., Houns. 143 H2
Lampton Rd.
Concorde Dr. E6 116 C5
Concourse, The N9 60 D2
New Rd.
Concourse, The NW9 71 F1
Condell Rd. SW8 150 C1
Conder St. E14 113 H6
Salmon La.

Name	Page	Grid
Conderton Rd. SE5	151	J3
Condor Path, Nthlt.	103	G2
Brabazon Rd.		
Condover Cres. SE18	136	E7
Condray Pl. SW11	129	H7
Crooms Hill		
Conduit Ct. WC2	**18**	**A5**
Conduit La. N18	61	F5
Conduit La., Croy.	202	D5
Conduit La., Enf.	45	H6
Morson Rd.		
Conduit La., S.Croy.	202	D5
Conduit Ms. W2	**14**	**E4**
Conduit Ms. W2	109	G6
Conduit Pas. W2	**15**	**E4**
Conduit Pl. W2	**15**	**E4**
Conduit Pl. W2	109	G6
Conduit Rd. SE18	137	E5
Conduit St. W1	**17**	**E5**
Conduit St. W1	110	B7
Conduit Way NW10	88	C7
Conewood St. N5	93	H3
Coney Acre SE21	169	J1
Coney Burrows E4	62/63	E2
Wyemead Cres.		
Coney Hill Rd., W.Wick.	205	G2
Coney Way SW8	**34**	**D6**
Coney Way SW8	131	F6
Coneygrove Path, Nthlt.	84/85	E6
Arnold Rd.		
Conference Cl. E4	62	C2
Greenbank Cl.		
Conference Rd. SE2	138	C4
Congleton Gro. SE18	137	F5
Congo Rd. SE18	137	G5
Congress Rd. SE2	138	C4
Congreve Rd. SE9	156	C3
Congreve St. SE17	**36**	**D1**
Congreve St. SE17	132	B4
Congreve Wk. E16	116	A5
Conical Cor., Enf.	43	J2
Conifer Cl., Orp.	207	G4
Conifer Gdns. SW16	169	E3
Conifer Gdns., Enf.	44	B6
Conifer Gdns., Sutt.	198	E2
Conifer Way, Hayes	102	A7
Longmead Rd.		
Conifer Way, Wem.	87	F3
Conifers Cl., Tedd.	163	E7
Coniger Rd. SW6	148	D2
Coningham Ms. W12	127	G1
Percy Rd.		
Coningham Rd. W12	127	H1
Coningsby Cotts. W5	125	G2
Coningsby Rd.		
Coningsby Gdns. E4	62	B6
Coningsby Rd. N4	75	H7
Coningsby Rd. W5	125	F2
Conington Rd. SE13	154	B2
Conisbee Ct. N14	42	C5
Conisborough Cres. SE6	172	C3
Coniscliffe Cl., Chis.	192	D1
Coniscliffe Rd. N13	59	J3
Coniston Av., Bark.	99	H7
Coniston Av., Grnf.	105	E3
Coniston Av., Well.	157	H3
Coniston Cl. N20	57	F3
Coniston Cl. SW13	127	F7
Lonsdale Rd.		
Coniston Cl. SW20	184	A6
Coniston Cl. W4	146	C1
Coniston Cl., Bark.	99	H7
Coniston Av.		
Coniston Cl., Bexh.	159	J1
Coniston Gdns. N9	61	F1
Coniston Gdns. NW9	70	D5
Coniston Gdns., Ilf.	80	B4
Coniston Gdns., Pnr.	66	A4
Coniston Gdns., Sutt.	199	G6
Coniston Gdns., Wem.	87	F1
Coniston Ho. SE5	**35**	**J7**
Coniston Ho. SE5	131	J7
Coniston Rd. N10	74	B2
Coniston Rd. N17	60	D6
Coniston Rd., Bexh.	159	J1
Coniston Rd., Brom.	172	E6
Coniston Rd., Croy.	188	D7
Coniston Rd., Twick.	143	H6
Coniston Wk. E9	95	F5
Clifden Rd.		
Coniston Way, Chess.	195	H3
Conistone Way N7	93	E7
Conlan St. W10	108	B4
Conley Rd. NW10	88	E6
Conley St. SE10	134/135	E5
Pelton Rd.		
Connaught Av. E4	46	D7
Connaught Av. SW14	146	C3
Connaught Av., Barn.	57	J1
Connaught Av., Enf.	44	B2
Connaught Av., Houns.	143	E5
Connaught Av., Loug.	48	A4
Connaught Br. E16	116	A7
Connaught Cl. E10	95	H2
Connaught Cl. W2	**15**	**G4**
Connaught Cl., Enf.	44	B2
Connaught Cl., Sutt.	199	G2
Connaught Dr. NW11	72	D4
Connaught Gdns. N10	74	B5
Connaught Gdns. N13	59	H4
Connaught Gdns., Mord.	185	F4
Connaught Hill, Loug.	48	A4
Connaught La., Ilf.	99	G2
Connaught Rd.		
Connaught Ms. W2	**15**	**G4**
Connaught Ms. SE18	136	D5
Connaught Ms., Ilf.	99	G2
Connaught Rd.		
Connaught Pl. W2	**15**	**J5**
Connaught Pl. W2	109	J7
Connaught Rd. E4	46	E7
Connaught Rd. E11	96	D1
Connaught Rd. E16	136	A1
Connaught Rd. E17	78	A5
Connaught Rd. N4	75	G7
Connaught Rd. NW10	107	E1
Connaught Rd. SE18	136	D5
Connaught Rd. W13	104	E7
Connaught Rd., Barn.	40	A6
Connaught Rd., Har.	68	C1
Connaught Rd., Ilf.	99	G2
Connaught Rd., N.Mal.	183	E4
Connaught Rd., Rich.	145	J5
Albert Rd.		
Connaught Rd., Sutt.	199	G2
Connaught Rd., Tedd.	162	A5
Connaught Roundabout E16	116	A7
Connaught Br.		
Connaught Sq. W2	**15**	**J4**
Connaught Sq. W2	109	J6
Connaught St. W2	**15**	**G4**
Connaught St. W2	109	H6
Connaught Way N13	59	H4
Connell Cres. W5	105	J4
Connemara Cl., Borwd.	38	D6
Percheron Rd.		
Connington Cres. E4	62	D3
Connor Cl., Ilf.	80	C1
Fullwell Av.		
Connor Rd., Dag.	101	F4
Connor St. E9	113	G1
Lauriston Rd.		
Conolly Rd. W7	124	B1
Conrad Dr., Wor.Pk.	197	J1
Conrad Ho. N16	94	B5
Cons St. SE1	**27**	**F3**
Consfield Av., N.Mal.	183	G4
Consort Ms., Islw.	144	A5
Consort Rd. SE15	152	E1
Constable Av. E16	135	H1
Wesley Av.		
Constable Cl. NW11	73	E6
Constable Cres. N15	76	D5
Constable Gdns., Edg.	70	A1
Constable Gdns., Islw.	144	A5
Constable Ms., Dag.	100	B4
Stonard Rd.		
Constable Wk. SE21	170	C3
Constance Cres., Brom.	191	F7
Constance Rd., Croy.	187	H7
Constance Rd., Enf.	44	B6
Constance Rd., Sutt.	199	F4
Constance Rd., Twick.	143	H7
Constance St. E16	136	B1
Albert Rd.		
Constitution Hill SW1	**24**	**D3**
Constitution Hill SW1	130	B2
Constitution Ri. SE18	156	D1
Consul Av., Dag.	119	J3
Content St. SE17	**36**	**A2**
Content St. SE17	132	A4
Contessa Cl., Orp.	207	H5
Control Twr. Rd., Houns.	140	D3
Convair Wk., Nthlt.	102	D3
Kittiwake Rd.		
Convent Cl., Beck.	172	C7
Convent Gdns. W5	125	F4
Convent Gdns. W11	108	C6
Kensington Pk. Rd.		
Convent Hill SE19	169	J6
Convent Way, Sthl.	122	C4
Conway Cres., Grnf.	104	B2
Conway Cres., Rom.	82	C7
Conway Dr., Hayes	121	F3
Conway Dr., Sutt.	198	E6
Conway Gdns., Mitch.	186	D4
Conway Gdns., Wem.	69	F7
Conway Gro. W3	106	D5
Conway Ms. W1	**9**	**F6**
Conway Rd. N14	59	E3
Conway Rd. N15	75	H5
Conway Rd. N9	89	J2
Conway Rd. SE18	137	G4
Conway Rd. SW20	183	J1
Conway Rd., Felt.	160	D5
Conway Rd., Houns.	143	F7
Conway Rd. (Heathrow Airport), Houns.	140/141	E3
Inner Ring E.		
Conway St. E13	115	G4
Conway St. W1	**9**	**F6**
Conway St. W1	110	C5
Conway Wk., Hmptn.	161	F6
Fearnley Cres.		
Conybeare NW3	91	H7
King Henry's Rd.		
Conyer St. E3	113	H2
Conyers Cl., Wdf.Grn.	62	E6
Conyers Rd. SW16	168	D5
Conyers Way, Loug.	49	E3
Cooden Cl., Brom.	173	H7
Plaistow La.		
Cooderidge Cl. N17	60	C6
Brantwood Rd.		
Cook Ct. SE16	133	F1
Rotherhithe St.		
Cook Rd., Dag.	118	E1
Cooke Cl. E14	134	A1
Cabot Sq.		
Cookes Cl. E11	97	F2
Cookes La., Sutt.	198	B6
Cookham Cl., Sthl.	123	H2
Cookham Cres. SE16	133	G2
Marlow Way		
Cookham Dene Cl., Chis.	193	G1
Cookham Rd., Sid.	177	G7
Cookhill Rd. SE2	138	B2
Cooks Cl., Rom.	83	J1
Cook's Rd. E15	114	B2
Cooks Rd. SE17	**35**	**G5**
Cooks Rd. SE17	131	H6
Cookson Gro., Erith	139	H7
Cool Oak La. NW9	71	E7
Coolfin Rd. E16	115	G6
Coolgardie Av. E4	62	C5
Coolgardie Av., Chig.	64	D3
Coolhurst Rd. N8	74	D6
Coomassie Rd. W9	108	C4
Bravington Rd.		
Coombe Av., Croy.	202	B4
Coombe Bank, Kings.T.	182	E1
Coombe Cl., Edg.	69	J2
Coombe Cl., Houns.	143	G4
Coombe Cor. N21	59	H1
Coombe Cres., Hmptn.	161	E7
Coombe Dr., Kings.T.	164	D7
Coombe Dr., Ruis.	84	B1
Coombe End, Kings.T.	164	D7
Coombe Gdns. SW20	183	G2
Coombe Gdns., N.Mal.	183	F4
Coombe Hts., Kings.T.	165	E7
Coombe Hill Glade, Kings.T.	165	E7
Coombe Hill Rd., Kings.T.	164	E7
Coombe Ho. Chase, N.Mal.	182	D1
Coombe La. SW20	183	H2
Coombe La., Croy.	202	E5
Coombe La. W., Kings.T.	183	G1
Coombe Lea, Brom.	192	B3
Coombe Neville, Kings.T.	164	D7
Coombe Pk., Kings.T.	164	D5
Coombe Ridings, Kings.T.	164	C5
Coombe Ri., Kings.T.	182	C1
Coombe Rd. N22	75	G1
Coombe Rd. NW10	88	D3
Coombe Rd. SE26	170	E4
Coombe Rd. W4	127	E5
Coombe Rd. W13	124/125	E3
Northcroft Rd.		
Coombe Rd., Croy.	202	A4
Coombe Rd., Hmptn.	161	F6
Coombe Rd., Kings.T.	182	A1
Coombe Rd., N.Mal.	182	E2
Coombe Rd., Sutt.	198	E3
Coombe Wd. Rd., Kings.T.	164	C5
Coombefield Cl., N.Mal.	183	E5
Coombehurst Cl., Barn.	41	J2
Coomber Way, Croy.	186	D7
Coombes Rd., Dag.	119	F4
Coombewood Dr., Rom.	83	F6
Coombs St. N1	**11**	**H2**
Coombs St. N1	111	H2
Coomer Ms. SW6	128	C6
Coomer Pl.		
Coomer Pl. SW6	128	C6
Coomer Rd. SW6	128	C6
Coomer Pl.		
Cooms Wk., Edg.	70	C1
East Rd.		
Cooper Av. E17	77	G1
Cooper Cl. SE1	**27**	**F4**
Cooper Ct. E15	96	B5
Clays La.		
Cooper Cres., Cars.	199	J3
Cooper Rd. NW4	72	A6
Cooper Rd. NW10	89	G5
Cooper Rd., Croy.	201	G4
Cooper St. E16	115	F5
Lawrence St.		
Cooperage Cl. N17	60	C6
Brantwood Rd.		
Coopers Cl. E1	113	F4
Coopers Cl., Dag.	101	H6
Coopers Cres., Borwd.	38	C1
Coopers La. E10	96	B1
Coopers La. NW1	**9**	**J1**
Coopers La. NW1	110	D2
Coopers La. SE12	173	H2
Coopers Rd. SE1	**37**	**G4**
Coopers Rd. SE1	132	C5
Cooper's Row EC3	**21**	**F5**
Coopers Wk. E15	96	D5
Maryland St.		
Cooper's Yd. SE19	170	B6
Westow Hill		
Coopersale Cl., Wdf.Grn.	63	J7
Navestock Cres.		
Coopersale Rd. E9	95	G5
Coote Gdns., Dag.	101	F3
Coote Rd., Bexh.	159	F1
Coote Rd., Dag.	101	F3
Cope Pl. W8	128	D3
Cope St. SE16	133	G4
Copeland Dr. E14	134	A4
Copeland Rd. E17	78	B5
Copeland Rd. SE15	152	D2
Copeman Cl. SE26	171	F5
Copenhagen Gdns. W4	126	C2
Copenhagen Pl. E14	113	J6
Copenhagen St. N1	111	E1
Copers Cope Rd., Beck.	171	J6
Copford Cl., Wdf.Grn.	64	B6
Copford Wk. N1	111	J1
Popham St.		
Copgate Path SW16	169	F6
Copinger Wk., Edg.	70	B1
North Rd.		
Copland Av., Wem.	87	G5
Copland Cl., Wem.	87	F5
Copland Ms., Wem.	87	H6
Copland Rd.		
Copland Rd., Wem.	87	H6
Copleston Ms. SE15	152	C2
Copleston Rd.		
Copleston Pas. SE15	152	C3
Copleston Rd. SE15	152	C3
Copley Cl. SE17	**35**	**H6**
Copley Cl. W7	104	C5
Copley Dene, Brom.	192	A1
Copley Pk. SW16	169	F6
Copley Rd., Stan.	53	F5
Copley St. E1	113	G5
Stepney Grn.		
Copnor Way SE15	**37**	**E7**
Coppard Gdns., Chess.	195	F6
Copped Hall SE21	170	A2
Glazebrook Cl.		

Coppelia Rd. SE3 155 F4
Coppen Rd., Dag. 83 F7
Copper Beech Cl. NW3 91 G6
Daleham Ms.
Copper Beech Cl., Ilf. 80 D1
Copper Beech Ct., Loug. 48 D1
Copper Beeches, Islw. 144 A1
Eversley Cres.
Copper Cl. SE19 170 C7
Auckland Rd.
Copper Mead Cl. NW2 89 J3
Copper Mill Dr., Islw. 144 C2
Copper Mill La. SW17 167 F4
Copper Row SE1 29 F2
Copper Row SE1 132 C1
Copperas St. SE8 134 B6
Copperbeech Cl. NW3 91 G5
Akenside Rd.
Copperdale Rd., Hayes 122 A2
Copperfield, Chig. 65 G6
Copperfield App., Chig. 65 G6
Copperfield Ct., Pnr. 67 F4
Copperfield Way
Copperfield Dr. N15 76 C4
Copperfield Ms. N18 60 B5
Copperfield Rd. E3 113 H4
Copperfield Rd. SE28 118 C6
Copperfield St. SE1 27 H3
Copperfield St. SE1 131 H2
Copperfield Way, Chis. 175 F6
Copperfield Way, Pnr. 67 F4
Coppergate Cl., Brom. 191 H1
Coppermill La. E17 77 F6
Coppetts Cl. N12 57 H7
Coppetts Rd. N10 74 A2
Coppice, The, Enf. 43 H4
Coppice Cl. SW20 183 J3
Coppice Cl., Stan. 52 C6
Coppice Dr. SW15 147 H6
Coppice Wk. N20 56 D3
Coppice Way E18 79 F4
Coppies Gro. N11 58 A4
Copping Cl., Croy. 202 B4
Tipton Dr.
Coppins, The, Croy. 204 B6
Coppins, The, Har. 52 B6
Coppock Cl. SW11 149 H2
Coppsfield, W.Mol. 179 G3
Hurst Rd.
Copse, The E4 63 F1
Copse Av., W.Wick. 204 B3
Copse Cl. SE7 135 H6
Copse Cl., West Dr. 120 A3
Copse Glade, Surb. 195 G1
Copse Hill SW20 165 H7
Copse Hill, Sutt. 199 E7
Copsewood Cl., Sid. 157 H6
Coptefield Dr., Belv. 138 D3
Copthall Av. EC2 20 C3
Copthall Av. EC2 112 A6
Copthall Bldgs. EC2 20 B3
Copthall Cl. EC2 20 B3
Copthall Ct. EC2 112 A6
Copthall Dr. NW7 55 G7
Copthall Gdns. NW7 55 G7
Copthall Gdns., Twick. 162 C1
Copthorne Av. SW12 150 D7
Copthorne Av., Brom. 206 C2
Copthorne Av., Ilf. 65 E6
Copthorne Ms., Hayes 121 H4
Coptic St. WC1 18 A2
Coptic St. WC1 110 E5
Copwood Cl. N12 57 G4
Coral Cl., Rom. 82 C3
Coral Row SW11 149 F3
Gartons Way
Coral St. SE1 27 F4
Coral St. SE1 131 G2
Coraline Cl., Sthl. 103 F3
Coralline Wk. SE2 138 C2
Coram St. WC1 10 A6
Coram St. WC1 110 E4
Coran Cl. N9 45 G7
Corban Rd., Houns. 143 G3
Corbet Cl., Wall. 200 A1
Corbet Ct. EC3 20 C4
Corbet Pl. E1 21 F1
Corbett Gro. N22 58 E7
Corbett Ho., Wat. 50 C3
Corbett Rd. E11 79 J6
Corbett Rd. E17 78 C3
Corbetts La. SE16 133 F4
Rotherhithe New Rd.
Corbetts Pas. SE16 133 F4
Rotherhithe New Rd.
Corbicum E11 79 E7
Corbiere Ct. SW19 166 A6
Thornton Rd.
Corbiere Ho. N1 112 B1
Corbins La., Har. 85 H3
Corbridge Cres. E2 112 E2
Corby Cres., Enf. 43 E4
Corby Rd. NW10 106 D2
Corby Way E3 114 A4
Knapp Rd.
Corbylands Rd., Sid. 157 H7
Corbyn St. N4 93 E1
Cord Way E14 134 A3
Mellish St.
Cordelia Cl. SE24 151 H4
Cordelia Gdns., Stai. 140 B7
Cordelia Rd., Stai. 140 B7
Cordelia St. E14 114 B6
Cording St. E14 114 B5
Chrisp St.
Cordova Rd. E3 113 H3
Cordwainers Wk. E13 115 G2
Clegg St.
Cordwell Rd. SE13 154 E5
Corelli Rd. SE3 156 B2
Corfe Av., Har. 85 G4
Corfe Cl., Hayes 102 C6
Corfe Twr. W3 126 B2
Corfield Rd. N21 43 F5
Corfield St. E2 113 E3
Corfton Rd. W5 105 H6
Coriander Av. E14 114 D6
Cories Cl., Dag. 100 D2
Corinium Cl., Wem. 87 J4
Corinne Rd. N19 92 C4
Corinthian Way, Stai. 140 A7
Clare Rd.
Cork Sq. E1 132/133 E1
Smeaton St.
Cork St. W1 17 F6
Cork St. W1 110 C7
Cork St. Ms. W1 17 F6
Cork Tree Way E4 61 H5
Corker Wk. N7 93 F2
Corkran Rd., Surb. 181 G7
Corkscrew Hill, W.Wick. 204 D2
Corlett St. NW1 15 G1
Corlett St. NW1 109 H5
Cormont Rd. SE5 151 H1
Cormorant Cl. E17 77 G7
Banbury Rd.
Cormorant Pl., Sutt. 198 B2
Gander Grn. La.
Cormorant Rd. E7 97 F5
Corn Mill Dr., Orp. 193 J7
Corn Way E11 96 D3
Cornbury Rd., Edg. 53 G7
Cornelia St. N7 93 F6
Cornell Cl., Sid. 177 E6
Corner Grn. SE3 155 G2
Corner Ho. St. WC2 26 A1
Corner Mead NW9 55 F7
Corney Reach Way W4 127 E7
Corney Rd. W4 127 E6
Cornflower La., Croy. 203 G1
Cornflower Ter. SE22 152 E6
Cornford Cl., Brom. 191 G5
Cornford Gro. SW12 168 B2
Cornhill EC3 20 C4
Cornhill EC3 112 A6
Cornish Ct. N9 44 E7
Cornish Gro. SE20 171 E7
Cornish Ho. SE17 35 G6
Cornish Ho., Brent. 125 J5
Green Dragon La.
Cornmill La. SE13 154 B3
Cornmow Dr. NW10 89 F5
Cornshaw Rd., Dag. 100 D1
Cornthwaite Rd. E5 95 F3
Cornwall Av. E2 113 F3
Cornwall Av. N3 56 D7
Cornwall Av. N22 75 E1
Cornwall Av., Esher 194 C7
The Causeway
Cornwall Av., Sthl. 103 F5
Cornwall Av., Well. 157 H3
Cornwall Cl., Bark. 99 J6
Cornwall Cres. W11 108 B7
Cornwall Dr., Orp. 176 C7
Cornwall Gdns. NW10 89 H6
Cornwall Gdns. SW7 22 B6
Cornwall Gdns. SW7 129 F3
Cornwall Gdns. Wk. SW7 22 B6
Cornwall Gro. W4 127 E5
Cornwall Ms. S. SW7 22 C6
Cornwall Ms. S. SW7 129 F3
Cornwall Ms. W. SW7 22 B6
Cornwall Rd. N4 75 G7
Cornwall Rd. N15 76 A5
Cornwall Rd. N18 60 D5
Fairfield Rd.
Cornwall Rd. SE1 26 E1
Cornwall Rd. SE1 131 G1
Cornwall Rd., Croy. 201 H2
Cornwall Rd., Esher 194 D7
Cornwall Rd., Har. 67 J6
Cornwall Rd., Pnr. 51 F7
Cornwall Rd., Sutt. 198 C7
Cornwall Rd., Twick. 162 D1
Cornwall St. E1 112/113 E7
Watney St.
Cornwall Ter. NW1 8 A6
Cornwall Ter. Ms. NW1 8 A6
Cornwallis Av. N9 61 E2
Cornwallis Av. SE9 175 G2
Cornwallis Gro. N9 61 E2
Cornwallis Rd. E17 77 G4
Cornwallis Rd. N9 61 E2
Cornwallis Rd. N19 92 E2
Cornwallis Rd., Dag. 100 D4
Cornwallis Sq. N19 92 E2
Cornwallis Wk. SE9 156 C3
Cornwood Cl. N2 73 G5
Cornwood Dr. E1 113 F6
Cornworthy Rd., Dag. 100 C5
Corona Rd. SE12 155 G7
Coronation Av. N16 94 C3
Victorian Rd.
Coronation Cl., Bex. 158 D6
Coronation Cl., Ilf. 81 F4
Coronation Rd. E13 115 J3
Coronation Rd. NW10 105 J3
Coronation Rd., Hayes 121 J4
Coronation Wk., Twick. 161 F1
Coronet St. N1 12 D4
Coronet St. N1 112 B3
Corporation Av., Houns. 142 E4
Corporation Row EC1 11 F5
Corporation Row EC1 111 G4
Corporation St. E15 115 E2
Corporation St. N7 92 E5
Corrance Rd. SW2 151 E4
Corri Av. N14 58 D4
Corrib Dr., Sutt. 199 H5
Corringham Ct. NW11 72/73 E7
Corringham Rd.
Corringham Rd. NW11 72 D7
Corringham Rd., Wem. 88 A2
Corringway NW11 72 E7
Corringway W5 106 A4
Corsair Cl., Stai. 140 A7
Corsair Rd., Stai. 140 B7
Corscombe Cl., Kings.T. 164 C5
Corsehill St. SW16 168 C6
Corsham St. N1 12 C4
Corsham St. N1 112 A3
Corsica St. N5 93 H6
Corsley Way E9 95 J6
Osborne Rd.
Cortayne Rd. SW6 148 C2
Cortis Rd. SW15 147 H6
Cortis Ter. SW15 147 H6
Corunna Rd. SW8 150 C1
Corunna Ter. SW8 150 C1
Corvette Sq. SE10 134 D6
Feathers Pl.
Coryton Path W9 108 C4
Ashmore Rd.
Cosbycote Av. SE24 151 J5
Cosdach Av., Wall. 200 D7
Cosedge Cres., Croy. 201 G5
Cosgrove Cl. N21 59 J2
Cosgrove Cl., Hayes 102/103 E4
Kingsash Dr.
Cosmo Pl. WC1 18 B1
Cosmur Cl. W12 127 F3
Cossall Wk. SE15 153 E1
Cosser St. SE1 26 E5
Cosser St. SE1 131 G3
Costa St. SE15 152 D2
Coston Wk. SE4 153 G4
Frendsbury Rd.
Costons Av., Grnf. 104 A3
Costons La., Grnf. 104 A3
Cosway St. NW1 15 H1
Cosway St. NW1 109 H5
Cotall St. E14 114 A6
Coteford Cl., Loug. 48 E2
Coteford Cl., Pnr. 66 A5
Coteford St. SW17 167 J4
Cotelands, Croy. 202 B3
Cotesbach Rd. E5 95 F3
Cotesmore Gdns., Dag. 100 C4
Cotford Rd., Th.Hth. 187 J4
Cotham St. SE17 36 A2
Cotherstone Rd. SW2 169 F1
Cotleigh Av., Bex. 176 D2
Cotleigh Rd. NW6 90 D7
Cotman Cl. NW11 73 F6
Cotman Cl. SW15 148 A6
Westleigh Av.
Cotman Gdns., Edg. 70 A2
Cotman Ms., Dag. 100 C5
Highgrove Rd.
Cotmans Cl., Hayes 122 A1
Coton Rd., Well. 158 A3
Cotsford Av., N.Mal. 182 C5
Cotswold Cl., Esher 194 C3
Cotswold Cl., Kings.T. 164 B6
Cotswold Ct. N11 58 A4
Cotswold Gdns. E6 116 A3
Cotswold Gdns. NW2 90 A2
Cotswold Gdns., Ilf. 81 G7
Cotswold Gate NW2 90 B1
Cotswold Gdns.
Cotswold Grn., Enf. 43 F4
Cotswold Way
Cotswold Ms. SW11 149 G1
Battersea High St.
Cotswold Ri., Orp. 193 J6
Cotswold Rd., Hmptn. 161 G6
Cotswold St. SE27 169 H4
Norwood High St.
Cotswold Way, Enf. 43 F4
Cotswold Way, Wor.Pk. 197 J2
Cottage Av., Brom. 206 B1
Cottage Fld. Cl., Sid. 176 C1
Cottage Grn. SE5 36 C7
Cottage Grn. SE5 132 A7
Cottage Gro. SW9 150 E3
Cottage Gro., Surb. 181 G6
Cottage Homes NW7 55 G4
Cottage Pl. SW3 23 G5
Cottage Pl. SW3 129 H3
Cottage Rd., Epsom 196 D7
Cottage St. E14 114 B7
Cottage Wk. N16 94 C3
Smalley Cl.
Cottage Wk. SE15 132 C7
Sumner Est.
Cottenham Dr. NW9 71 F3
Cottenham Dr. SW20 165 H7
Cottenham Par. SW20 183 H2
Durham Rd.
Cottenham Pk. Rd. SW20 165 H7
Cottenham Pl. SW20 165 H7
Cottenham Rd. E17 77 J4
Cotterill Rd., Surb. 195 H2
Cottesbrook St. SE14 133 H7
Nynehead St.
Cottesloe Ms. SE1 27 F5
Cottesmore Av., Ilf. 80 D2
Cottesmore Gdns. W8 22 B5
Cottesmore Gdns. W8 129 E3
Cottimore Cres., Walt. 178 B7
Cottimore Ter., Walt. 178 B7
Cottingham Chase, Ruis. 84 A3
Cottingham Rd. SE20 171 G7
Cottingham Rd. SW8 34 D6
Cottingham Rd. SW8 131 F7
Cottington Rd., Felt. 160 D4
Cottington St. SE11 35 F3
Cottle St. SE16 133 F2
St. Marychurch St.
Cotton Av. W3 106 D6
Cotton Cl., Dag. 100 C7
Ellerton Rd.
Cotton Hill, Brom. 172 D4
Cotton Row SW11 149 F3
Cotton St. E14 114 C7
Cottongrass Cl., Croy. 203 G1
Cornflower La.
Cottons Gdns. E2 13 E3
Cottons La. SE1 28 C1
Cotts Cl. W7 104 C5
Westcott Cres.
Couchmore Av., Esher 194 B2
Couchmore Av., Ilf. 80 C2
Coulgate St. SE4 153 H3
Coulson Cl., Dag. 82 C7
Coulson St. SW3 31 J3
Coulson St. SW3 129 J4
Coulter Cl., Hayes 102 E4

Coulter Rd. W6	127	H3
Councillor St. SE5	131	J7
Counter Ct. SE1	132	A1
Southwark St.		
Counter St. SE1	**28**	**D2**
Countess Rd. NW5	92	C5
Countisbury Av.,	44	C7
Enf.		
Country Way, Felt.	160	B6
Country Way, Sun.	160	B6
County Gdns., Bark.	117	H2
River Rd.		
County Gate SE9	175	F3
County Gate, Barn.	41	E6
County Gro. SE5	151	J1
County Rd. E6	116	E5
County Rd., Th.Hth.	187	H2
County St. SE1	**28**	**A6**
County St. SE1	132	A3
Coupland Pl. SE18	137	F5
Courcy Rd. N8	75	G3
Courier Rd., Dag.	119	J4
Courland Gro. SW8	150	D1
Courland St. SW8	150	D1
Course, The SE9	174	D3
Court, The, Ruis.	84	E4
Court Av., Belv.	139	F5
Court Cl., Har.	69	H3
Court Cl., Twick.	161	H3
Court Cl., Wall.	200	D7
Court Cl. Av.,	161	H3
Twick.		
Court Cres., Chess.	195	G5
Court Downs Rd.,	190	B2
Beck.		
Court Dr., Croy.	201	F4
Court Dr., Stan.	53	H4
Court Dr., Sutt.	199	H4
Court Fm. Av., Epsom	196	D5
Court Fm. Rd. SE9	174	A2
Court Fm. Rd., Nthlt.	85	G7
Court Gdns. N7	93	G6
Court Ho. Gdns. N3	56	D6
Court La. SE21	152	B6
Court La. Gdns. SE21	152	B7
Court Mead, Nthlt.	103	F3
Court Par., Wem.	86	E3
Court Rd. SE9	174	B2
Court Rd. SE25	188	C2
Court Rd., Sthl.	123	F4
Court St. E1	112/113	E5
Durward St.		
Court St., Brom.	191	G2
Court Way NW9	71	E4
Court Way W3	106	C5
Court Way, Ilf.	81	F3
Court Way, Twick.	144	C7
Court Yd. SE9	156	B6
Courtauld Cl. SE28	138	A1
Pitfield Cres.		
Courtauld Rd. N19	92	D1
Courtenay Av. N6	73	H7
Courtenay Av., Har.	67	J1
Courtenay Dr., Beck.	190	D2
Courtenay Gdns.,	67	J2
Har.		
Courtenay Ms. E17	77	H5
Cranbrook Ms.		
Courtenay Pl. E17	77	H5
Courtenay Rd. E11	97	F3
Courtenay Rd. E17	77	G4
Courtenay Rd. SE20	171	G7
Courtenay Rd., Wem.	87	G3
Courtenay Rd.,	197	J3
Wor.Pk.		
Courtenay Sq. SE11	**34**	**E4**
Courtenay St. SE11	**34**	**E3**
Courtenay St. SE11	131	G5
Courtens Ms., Stan.	53	F7
Courtfield W5	105	F5
Castlebar Hill		
Courtfield Av., Har.	68	C5
Courtfield Cres., Har.	68	C5
Courtfield Gdns.	**30**	**B1**
SW5		
Courtfield Gdns. SW5	129	E4
Courtfield Gdns. W13	104	D6
Courtfield Ms. SW5	**30**	**C2**
Courtfield Ri.,	204	D3
W.Wick.		
Courtfield Rd. SW7	**30**	**B2**
Courtfield Rd. SW7	129	E4
Courthill Rd. SE13	154	C4
Courthope Rd. NW3	91	J4
Courthope Rd. SW19	166	B5
Courthope Rd., Grnf.	104	A2
Courthope Vil. SW19	166	B7
Courthouse Rd. N12	56	E6
Courtland Av. E4	63	F2
Courtland Av. NW7	54	D3
Courtland Av. SW16	169	F7
Courtland Av., Ilf.	98	C2
Courtland Dr., Chig.	65	E3
Courtland Gro. SE28	118	D7
Courtland Rd. E6	116	B1
Harrow Rd.		
Courtlands, Rich.	146	A4
Courtlands Av. SE12	155	H5
Courtlands Av.,	205	F1
Brom.		
Courtlands Av.,	161	F6
Hmptn.		
Courtlands Av.,	146	B2
Rich.		
Courtlands Dr.,	197	E6
Epsom		
Courtlands Rd., Surb.	182	A7
Courtleet Dr., Erith	159	H1
Courtleigh Gdns.	72	B4
NW11		
Courtman Rd. N17	59	J7
Courtmead Cl. SE24	151	J6
Courtnell St. W2	108	D6
Courtney Cl. SE19	170	B6
Courtney Cres., Cars.	199	J7
Courtney Pl., Croy.	201	G3
Courtney Rd. N7	93	G5
Bryantwood Rd.		
Courtney Rd. SW19	167	H7
Courtney Rd., Croy.	201	G3
Courtney Rd., Houns.	140	D3
Courtney Way,	140	D2
Houns.		
Courtrai Rd. SE23	153	H6
Courtside N8	74	D6
Courtway, Wdf.Grn.	63	J5
Courtway, The, Wat.	51	E2
Cousin La. EC4	**20**	**B6**
Couthurst Rd. SE3	135	H6
Coutts Av., Chess.	195	H5
Coutts Cres. NW5	92	A3
Coval Gdns. SW14	146	B4
Coval La. SW14	146	B4
Coval Rd. SW14	146	B4
Covelees Wall E6	116	D6
Covell Ct. SE8	134	A7
Reginald Sq.		
Covent Gdn. WC2	**18**	**B5**
Covent Gdn. WC2	111	E7
Coventry Cl. E6	116	C6
Harper Rd.		
Coventry Cl. NW6	108	D1
Kilburn High Rd.		
Coventry Cross E3	114	C4
Gillender St.		
Coventry Rd. E1	113	E4
Coventry Rd. E2	113	E4
Coventry Rd. SE25	188	D4
Coventry Rd., Ilf.	98	E1
Coventry St. W1	**17**	**H6**
Coventry St. W1	110	D7
Coverack Cl. N14	42	C6
Coverack Cl., Croy.	189	H7
Coverdale Cl., Stan.	53	E5
Coverdale Gdns.,	202	C3
Croy.		
Park Hill Ri.		
Coverdale Rd. N11	58	A6
Coverdale Rd. NW2	90	A7
Coverdale Rd. W12	127	H1
Coverdales, The,	117	G2
Bark.		
Coverley Cl. E1	**21**	**J1**
Coverley Cl. E1	112	D5
Covert, The, Orp.	193	H6
Covert Rd., Ilf.	65	J6
Covert Way, Barn.	41	F2
Coverton Rd. SW17	167	H5
Covet Wd. Cl., Orp.	193	J6
Lockesley Dr.		
Covey Cl. SW19	184	E2
Covington Gdns.	169	H7
SW16		
Covington Way SW16	169	F6
Cow La., Grnf.	104	A2
Cow Leaze E6	116	D6
Cowan Cl. E6	116	B5
Oliver Gdns.		
Cowbridge La., Bark.	98	E7
Cowbridge Rd., Har.	69	J4
Cowcross St. EC1	**19**	**G1**
Cowcross St. EC1	111	H5
Cowden Rd., Orp.	193	J7
Cowden St. SE6	172	A4
Cowdenbeath Path	111	F1
N1		
Cowdrey Cl., Enf.	44	B2
Cowdrey Rd. SW19	167	E5
Cowdry Rd. E9	95	H6
Wick Rd.		
Cowen Av., Har.	85	J2
Cowgate Rd., Grnf.	104	A2
Cowick Rd. SW17	167	J4
Cowings Mead, Nthlt.	85	E7
Cowland Av., Enf.	45	F4
Cowleaze Rd.,	181	H1
Kings.T.		
Cowley La. E11	96/97	E3
Cathall Rd.		
Cowley Pl. NW4	71	J5
Cowley Rd. E11	79	H5
Cowley Rd. SW9	151	G1
Cowley Rd. SW14	146	E3
Cowley Rd. W3	127	F1
Cowley Rd., Ilf.	80	C7
Cowley St. SW1	**26**	**A5**
Cowling Cl. W11	128	B1
Wilsham St.		
Cowper Av. E6	98	B7
Cowper Av., Sutt.	199	G4
Cowper Cl., Brom.	192	A4
Cowper Cl., Well.	158	A5
Cowper Gdns. N14	42	C6
Cowper Gdns., Wall.	200	C6
Cowper Rd. N14	58	B1
Cowper Rd. N16	94	B5
Cowper Rd. N18	60	D5
Cowper Rd. SW19	167	F6
Cowper Rd. W3	126	D1
Cowper Rd. W7	104	C7
Cowper Rd., Belv.	139	G4
Cowper Rd., Brom.	192	A4
Cowper Rd., Kings.T.	163	J5
Cowper St. EC2	**12**	**C5**
Cowper St. EC2	112	A4
Cowper Ter. W10	108	A5
St. Marks Rd.		
Cowslip Rd. E18	79	H2
Cowthorpe Rd. SW8	150	D1
Cox La., Chess.	195	J4
Cox La., Epsom	196	B5
Coxe Pl., Har.	68	D4
Coxmount Rd. SE7	136	A5
Cox's Wk. SE21	170	D1
Coxson Pl. SE1	**29**	**F4**
Coxwell Rd. SE18	137	G5
Coxwell Rd. SE19	170	B7
Coxwold Path, Chess.	195	H7
Garrison La.		
Crab Hill, Beck.	172	D7
Crabbs Cft. Cl., Orp.	207	F5
Ladycroft Way		
Crabtree Av., Rom.	82	D4
Crabtree Av., Wem.	105	H2
Crabtree Cl. E2	**13**	**F2**
Crabtree Cl. E2	112	C2
Crabtree Ct. E15	96	B5
Clays La.		
Crabtree La. SW6	128	A7
Crabtree Manorway	139	J2
N., Belv.		
Crabtree Manorway	139	J3
S., Belv.		
Crabtree Wk. SE15	152	C1
Lisford St.		
Crace St. NW1	**9**	**H3**
Craddock Rd., Enf.	44	C3
Craddock St. NW5	92	A6
Prince of Wales Rd.		
Cradley Rd. SE9	175	G1
Craig Gdns. E18	79	F2
Craig Pk. Rd. N18	60	E5
Craig Rd., Rich.	163	F4
Craigen Av., Croy.	203	E1
Craigerne Rd. SE3	135	H7
Craigholm SE18	156	D2
Craigmuir Pk., Wem.	105	J1
Craignair Rd. SW2	151	G7
Craignish Av. SW16	187	F2
Craigs Ct. SW1	**26**	**A1**
Craigton Rd. SE9	156	C4
Craigweil Cl., Stan.	53	G5
Craigweil Dr., Stan.	53	G5
Craigwell Av., Felt.	160	A3
Craik Ct. NW6	108	C2
Carlton Vale		
Crail Row SE17	**36**	**C2**
Cramer St. W1	**16**	**C2**
Cramond Cl. W6	128	B6
Crampton Rd. SE20	171	F6
Crampton St. SE17	**35**	**J2**
Crampton St. SE17	131	J4
Cranberry Cl., Nthlt.	102	D2
Parkfield Av.		
Cranberry La. E16	114	E4
Cranborne Av., Sthl.	123	G4
Cranborne Av.,	196	A3
Surb.		
Cranborne Rd., Bark.	117	G1
Cranborne Waye,	102	C7
Hayes		
Cranbourn All. WC2	**17**	**J5**
Cranbourn Pas.	132/133	E2
SE16		
Marigold St.		
Cranbourn St. WC2	**17**	**J5**
Cranbourn St. WC2	110	D7
Cranbourne Av. E11	79	H4
Cranbourne Cl.	187	E3
SW16		
Cranbourne Dr., Pnr.	66	D5
Cranbourne Gdns.	72	B5
NW11		
Cranbourne Gdns., Ilf.	81	F3
Cranbourne Rd. E12	98	B5
High St. N.		
Cranbourne Rd. E15	96	C4
Cranbourne Rd. N10	74	B2
Cranbrook Cl.,	191	G6
Brom.		
Cranbrook Dr., Twick.	161	H1
Cranbrook Ms. E17	77	J5
Cranbrook Pk. N22	75	F1
Cranbrook Ri., Ilf.	80	C7
Cranbrook Rd. SE8	154	A1
Cranbrook Rd. SW19	166	B7
Cranbrook Rd. W4	127	E5
Cranbrook Rd., Barn.	41	G6
Cranbrook Rd., Bexh.	159	F1
Cranbrook Rd.,	143	F4
Houns.		
Cranbrook Rd., Ilf.	98	D1
Cranbrook Rd.,	187	J2
Th.Hth.		
Cranbrook St. E2	113	G2
Mace La.		
Cranbury Rd. SW6	149	E2
Crane Av. W3	106	C7
Crane Av., Islw.	144	D5
Crane Cl., Dag.	101	G6
Crane Cl., Har.	85	J3
Crane Ct. EC4	**19**	**F4**
Crane Ct., Epsom	196	C4
Crane Gdns., Hayes	121	J4
Crane Gro. N7	93	G6
Crane Lo. Rd.,	122	B6
Houns.		
Crane Mead SE16	133	G4
Crane Pk. Rd., Twick.	161	H2
Crane Rd., Twick.	162	B1
Crane St. SE10	134	D5
Crane St. SE15	152	C1
Crane Way, Twick.	143	J7
Cranebrook, Twick.	161	J2
Manor Rd.		
Craneford Cl.,	144	C7
Twick.		
Craneford Way,	144	B7
Twick.		
Cranes Dr., Surb.	181	H4
Cranes Pk., Surb.	181	H4
Cranes Pk. Av.,	181	H4
Surb.		
Cranes Pk. Cres.,	181	J4
Surb.		
Cranes Way, Borwd.	38	C5
Cranesbill Cl. NW9	70	D3
Colindale Av.		
Craneswater, Hayes	121	J7
Craneswater Pk.,	123	F5
Sthl.		
Cranfield Cl. SE27	169	J3
Dunelm Gro.		
Cranfield Dr. NW9	54	E7
Cranfield Rd. SE4	153	J3
Cranfield Row SE1	**27**	**F5**
Cranford Av. N13	59	E5
Cranford Av., Stai.	140	B7
Cranford Cl. SW20	183	H1
Cranford Cl., Stai.	140	B7
Canopus Way		
Cranford Cotts. E1	113	G7
Cranford St.		
Cranford Dr., Hayes	121	J4
Cranford La., Hayes	121	G6
Cranford La.	141	J1
(Cranford), Houns.		
Cranford La.	141	J3
(Hatton Cross), Houns.		
Cranford La.	122	D7
(Heston), Houns.		
Cranford Pk. Rd.,	121	J4
Hayes		
Cranford St. E1	113	G7
Cranford Way N8	75	F5
Cranhurst Rd. NW2	89	J5
Cranleigh Cl. SE20	188	E2
Cranleigh Cl., Bex.	159	J6
Cranleigh Gdns. N21	43	G5
Cranleigh Gdns.	188	B3
SE25		
Cranleigh Gdns.,	99	G7
Bark.		
Cranleigh Gdns., Har.	69	H5
Cranleigh Gdns.,	163	J6
Kings.T.		
Cranleigh Gdns.,	48	C6
Loug.		
Cranleigh Gdns., Sthl.	103	F6
Cranleigh Gdns., Sutt.	198	E2
Cranleigh Gdns. Ind.	103	F6
Est., Sthl.		
Cranleigh Ms. SW11	149	H2
Cranleigh Rd. N15	75	J5
Cranleigh Rd. SW19	184	D3

Cranleigh St. NW1	**9**	**G2**
Cranleigh St. NW1	110	C2
Cranley Dene Ct. N10	74	B4
Cranley Dr., Ilf.	81	F7
Cranley Gdns. N10	74	C4
Cranley Gdns. N13	59	F3
Cranley Gdns. SW7	**30**	**D3**
Cranley Gdns. SW7	129	F5
Cranley Gdns., Wall.	200	C7
Cranley Ms. SW7	**30**	**D3**
Cranley Ms. SW7	129	F5
Cranley Par. SE9 *Beaconsfield Rd.*	174	B4
Cranley Pl. SW7	**31**	**E2**
Cranley Pl. SW7	129	G4
Cranley Rd. E13	115	H5
Cranley Rd., Ilf.	81	F6
Cranmer Av. W13	125	E3
Cranmer Cl., Mord.	184	A6
Cranmer Cl., Ruis.	84	D1
Cranmer Cl., Stan.	53	F7
Cranmer Ct. SW3	**31**	**H2**
Cranmer Ct. SW4	150	D3
Cranmer Ct., Hmptn. *Cranmer Rd.*	161	H5
Cranmer Fm. Cl., Mitch.	185	J4
Cranmer Gdns., Dag.	101	J4
Cranmer Rd. E7	97	H4
Cranmer Rd. SW9	**35**	**F7**
Cranmer Rd. SW9	131	G7
Cranmer Rd., Croy.	201	H3
Cranmer Rd., Edg.	54	B3
Cranmer Rd., Hmptn.	161	H5
Cranmer Rd., Kings.T.	163	H5
Cranmer Rd., Mitch.	185	J4
Cranmer Ter. SW17	167	G5
Cranmore Av., Islw.	123	J7
Cranmore Rd., Brom.	173	E3
Cranmore Rd., Chis.	174	C5
Cranmore Way N10	74	C4
Cranston Cl., Houns.	143	E2
Cranston Est. N1	**12**	**C2**
Cranston Est. N1	112	A2
Cranston Gdns. E4	62	B5
Cranston Rd. SE23	171	H1
Cranswick Rd. SE16	133	E5
Crantock Rd. SE6	172	B2
Cranwell Cl. E3	114	B4
Cranwell Rd., Houns.	140	E2
Cranwich Av. N21	44	A7
Cranwich Rd. N16	76	A7
Cranwood St. EC1	**12**	**B4**
Cranwood St. EC1	112	A3
Cranworth Cres. E4	62	D1
Cranworth Gdns. SW9	151	G1
Craster Rd. SW2	151	F7
Crathie Rd. SE12	155	H6
Cravan Av., Felt.	160	A2
Craven Av. W5	105	F7
Craven Av., Sthl.	103	F5
Craven Cl., Hayes	102	A6
Craven Gdns. SW19	166	D5
Craven Gdns., Bark.	117	H2
Craven Gdns., Ilf.	81	G2
Craven Hill W2	**14**	**D5**
Craven Hill W2	109	F7
Craven Hill Gdns. W2	**14**	**C5**
Craven Hill Gdns. W2	109	F7
Craven Hill Ms. W2	**14**	**D5**
Craven Hill Ms. W2	109	F7
Craven Ms. SW11 *Taybridge Rd.*	150	A3
Craven Pk. NW10	106	E1
Craven Pk. Ms. NW10	106	E1
Craven Pk. Rd. N15	76	C6
Craven Pk. Rd. NW10	107	E1
Craven Pas. WC2	**26**	**A1**
Craven Pas. WC2	130	E1
Craven Rd. NW10	106	D1
Craven Rd. W2	**14**	**D5**
Craven Rd. W2	109	F7
Craven Rd. W5	105	F7
Craven Rd., Croy.	202	E1
Craven Rd., Kings.T.	181	J1
Craven St. WC2	**26**	**A1**
Craven St. WC2	130	E1
Craven Ter. W2	**14**	**D5**
Craven Ter. W2	109	F7
Craven Wk. N16	76	D7
Crawford Av., Wem.	87	G5
Crawford Cl., Islw.	144	B2
Crawford Est. SE5	151	J2
Crawford Gdns. N13	59	H3
Crawford Gdns., Nthlt.	103	F3
Crawford Ms. W1	**15**	**J2**
Crawford Pas. EC1	**11**	**E6**
Crawford Pl. W1	**15**	**H3**
Crawford Pl. W1	109	H6
Crawford Rd. SE5	151	J1
Crawford St. W1	**15**	**J2**
Crawford St. W1	109	J5
Crawley Rd. E10	96	B1
Crawley Rd. N22	75	J2
Crawley Rd., Enf.	44	B7
Crawshay Ct. SW9 *Eythorne Rd.*	151	G1
Crawthew Gro. SE22	152	C4
Cray Rd., Belv.	139	G6
Cray Rd., Sid.	176	C7
Craybrooke Rd., Sid.	176	B4
Craybury End SE9	175	F2
Crayford Cl. E6 *Neatscourt Rd.*	116	B5
Crayford Rd. N7	92	D4
Crayke Hill, Chess.	195	H7
Crealock Gro., Wdf.Grn.	63	F5
Crealock St. SW18	149	E6
Creasy Est. SE1	**28**	**D6**
Creasy Est. SE1	132	B3
Crebor St. SE22	152	D6
Credenhall Dr., Brom.	206	C1
Credenhill St. SW16	168	C6
Crediton Hill NW6	90	E5
Crediton Rd. E16 *Pacific Rd.*	115	G6
Crediton Rd. NW10	108	A1
Crediton Way, Esher	194	D5
Credon Rd. E13	115	J2
Credon Rd. SE16	133	E5
Creechurch La. EC3	**21**	**E4**
Creechurch La. EC3	112	B6
Creechurch Pl. EC3	**21**	**E4**
Creed Ct. EC4 *Ludgate Hill*	111	H6
Creed La. EC4	**19**	**H4**
Creek, The, Sun.	178	A5
Creek Rd. SE8	134	A6
Creek Rd. SE10	134	A6
Creek Rd., Bark.	117	J3
Creek Rd., E.Mol.	180	B4
Creekside SE8	134	B7
Creeland Gro. SE6 *Catford Hill*	171	J1
Crefeld Cl. W6	128	A6
Creffield Rd. W3	105	J7
Creffield Rd. W5	105	J7
Creighton Av. E6	116	A2
Creighton Av. N2	73	H3
Creighton Av. N10	73	H3
Creighton Cl. W12 *Bloemfontein Rd.*	107	H7
Creighton Rd. N17	60	B7
Creighton Rd. NW6	108	A2
Creighton Rd. W5	125	G3
Cremer St. E2	**13**	**F2**
Cremer St. E2	112	C2
Cremorne Est. SW10	**31**	**E7**
Cremorne Rd. SW10	129	F7
Crescent EC3	**21**	**F5**
Crescent, The E17	77	H5
Crescent, The N11	57	J4
Crescent, The NW2	89	H3
Crescent, The SW13	147	F2
Crescent, The SW19	166	D3
Crescent, The W3	106	E6
Crescent, The, Barn.	40	E3
Crescent, The, Beck.	190	A1
Crescent, The, Bex.	158	C7
Crescent, The, Croy.	188	A5
Crescent, The, Har.	86	A1
Crescent, The, Hayes	121	F7
Crescent, The, Ilf.	80	D6
Crescent, The, Loug.	48	A5
Crescent, The, N.Mal.	182	C2
Crescent, The, Sid.	175	J4
Crescent, The, Sthl.	123	F2
Crescent, The, Surb.	181	H5
Crescent, The, Sutt.	199	G4
Crescent, The, Wem.	86	E2
Crescent, The, W.Mol.	179	G4
Crescent, The, W.Wick.	190	E6
Crescent Ct., Surb.	181	G5
Crescent Dr., Orp.	193	E6
Crescent Gdns. SW19	166	D3
Crescent Gdns., Ruis.	66	B6
Crescent Gro. SW4	150	C4
Crescent Gro., Mitch.	185	H4
Crescent La. SW4	150	D5
Crescent Ms. N22 *Palace Gates Rd.*	74/75	E1
Crescent Pl. SW3	**31**	**G1**
Crescent Pl. SW3	129	H4
Crescent Ri. N22	74	D1
Crescent Ri., Barn.	41	H5
Crescent Rd. E4	47	E7
Crescent Rd. E6	115	J1
Crescent Rd. E10	96	B2
Crescent Rd. E13	115	G1
Crescent Rd. E18	79	J2
Crescent Rd. N3	72	C1
Crescent Rd. N8	74	D7
Crescent Rd. N9	60	D1
Crescent Rd. N11	57	J4
Crescent Rd. N15 *Carlingford Rd.*	75	H3
Crescent Rd. N22	74	D1
Crescent Rd. SE18	136	E5
Crescent Rd. SW20	184	A1
Crescent Rd., Barn.	41	H5
Crescent Rd., Beck.	190	B2
Crescent Rd., Brom.	173	G7
Crescent Rd., Dag.	101	H4
Crescent Rd., Enf.	43	H3
Crescent Rd., Kings.T.	164	A7
Crescent Rd., Sid.	175	J3
Crescent Row EC1	**11**	**J6**
Crescent Stables SW15 *Upper Richmond Rd.*	148	B4
Crescent St. N1	93	F7
Crescent Vw., Loug.	48	A6
Crescent Way N12	57	H6
Crescent Way SE4	154	A3
Crescent Way SW16	169	F7
Crescent Way, Orp.	207	H5
Crescent Wd. Rd. SE26	170	D3
Cresford Rd. SW6	148	E1
Crespigny Rd. NW4	71	H6
Cressage Cl., Sthl.	103	G4
Cresset Rd. E9	95	F6
Cresset St. SW4	150	D3
Cressfield Cl. NW5	92	A5
Cressida Rd. N19	92	C1
Cressingham Gro., Sutt.	199	F4
Cressingham Rd. SE13	154	C3
Cressingham Rd., Edg.	54	D6
Cressington Cl. N16 *Wordsworth Rd.*	94	B5
Cresswell Gdns. SW5	**30**	**C3**
Cresswell Gdns. SW5	129	F5
Cresswell Pk. SE3	155	F3
Cresswell Pl. SW10	**30**	**C3**
Cresswell Pl. SW10	129	F5
Cresswell Rd. SE25	188	D4
Cresswell Rd., Felt.	160	E4
Cresswell Rd., Twick.	145	G6
Cresswell Way N21	43	G7
Cressy Ct. E1 *Cressy Pl.*	113	F5
Cressy Ct. W6	127	H3
Cressy Pl. E1	113	F5
Cressy Rd. NW3	91	J4
Crest, The N13	59	G4
Crest, The NW4	71	J5
Crest, The, Surb.	182	A5
Crest Gdns., Ruis.	84	C3
Crest Rd. NW2	89	F3
Crest Rd., Brom.	191	F7
Crest Rd., S.Croy.	202	E7
Crest Vw., Pnr.	66	D4
Crest Vw. Dr., Orp.	193	E5
Crestbrook Av. N13	59	H3
Crestbrook Pl. N13	59	H3
Crestfield St. WC1	**10**	**B3**
Crestfield St. WC1	111	E3
Creston Way, Wor.Pk.	198	A1
Crestway SW15	147	H6
Crestwood Way, Houns.	143	F5
Creswick Rd. W3	106	B7
Creswick Wk. E3 *Malmesbury Rd.*	114	A3
Creswick Wk. NW11	72	C4
Creton St. SE18	136	D3
Crewdson Rd. SW9	131	G7
Crewe Pl. NW10	107	F3
Crews St. E14	134	A4
Crewys Rd. NW2	90	C2
Crewys Rd. SE15	153	E2
Crichton Av., Wall.	200	D5
Crichton Rd., Cars.	199	J6
Cricket Grn., Mitch.	185	J3
Cricket Grd. Rd., Chis.	192	E1
Cricket La., Beck.	171	H6
Cricketers Arms Rd., Enf.	43	J2
Cricketers Cl. N14	42	C7
Cricketers Cl., Chess.	195	G4
Cricketers Ct. SE11	**35**	**G2**
Cricketers Ct. SE11	131	H4
Cricketers Ms. SW18 *East Hill*	148/149	E5
Cricketers Ter., Cars. *Wrythe La.*	199	H3
Cricketfield Rd. E5	95	E4
Cricklade Av. SW2	169	E2
Cricklewood Bdy. NW2	90	A3
Cricklewood La. NW2	90	A4
Cricklewood Trd. Est. NW2	90	B3
Cridland St. E15 *Church St.*	115	F1
Crieff Ct., Tedd.	163	F7
Crieff Rd. SW18	149	F6
Criffel Av. SW2	168	D2
Crimscott St. SE1	**29**	**E6**
Crimscott St. SE1	132	B3
Crimsworth Rd. SW8	150	D1
Crinan St. N1	**10**	**B1**
Crinan St. N1	111	E2
Cringle St. SW8	**33**	**F7**
Cringle St. SW8	130	C7
Cripplegate St. EC2	**19**	**J1**
Cripps Grn., Hayes *Stratford Rd.*	102	B4
Crisp Rd. W6	127	J5
Crispe Ho., Bark. *Dovehouse Mead*	117	G2
Crispen Rd., Felt.	160	E4
Crispian Cl. NW10	89	E4
Crispin Cl., Croy. *Harrington Cl.*	200/201	E2
Crispin Cres., Croy.	200	D3
Crispin Rd., Edg.	54	C6
Crispin St. E1	**21**	**F2**
Crispin St. E1	112	C5
Cristowe Rd. SW6	148	C2
Criterion Ms. N19	92	D2
Crockerton Rd. SW17	167	J2
Crockham Way SE9	174	D4
Crocus Cl., Croy. *Cornflower La.*	203	G1
Crocus Fld., Barn.	40	C6
Croft, The E4	62	E2
Croft, The NW10	107	F2
Croft, The W5	105	H5
Croft, The, Barn.	40	A4
Croft, The, Houns.	123	E6
Croft, The, Loug.	48	D2
Croft, The, Pnr. *Rayners La.*	67	F7
Croft, The, Ruis.	84	C4
Croft, The, Wem.	87	F5
Croft Av., W.Wick.	204	C1
Croft Cl. NW7	54	E3
Croft Cl., Belv.	139	F5
Croft Cl., Chis.	174	C4
Croft Cl., Hayes	121	F7
Croft End Cl., Chess. *Ashcroft Rd.*	195	J3
Croft Gdns. W7	124	D2
Croft Lo. Cl., Wdf.Grn.	63	H6
Croft Ms. N12	57	F3
Croft Rd. SW16	187	G1
Croft Rd. SW19	167	F7
Croft Rd., Brom.	173	G6
Croft Rd., Enf.	45	H1
Croft Rd., Sutt.	199	H5
Croft St. SE8	133	H4
Croft Way NW3 *Ferncroft Av.*	90	D4
Croft Way, Sid.	175	H3
Croftdown Rd. NW5	92	A3
Crofters Cl., Islw. *Ploughmans End*	144	A5
Crofters Ct. SE8 *Croft St.*	133	H4
Crofters Way NW1	110	D1
Crofton Av. W4	126	D7
Crofton Av., Bex.	158	D7
Crofton Av., Orp.	207	F2
Crofton Gro. E4	62	D4
Crofton La., Orp.	193	H7
Crofton Pk. Rd. SE4	153	J6
Crofton Rd. E13	115	H4
Crofton Rd. SE5	152	B1
Crofton Rd., Orp.	206	D3
Crofton Ter. E5 *Studley Cl.*	95	H5
Crofton Ter., Rich.	145	J4
Crofton Way, Barn. *Wycherley Cres.*	40/41	E6
Crofton Way, Enf.	43	G2
Croftongate Way SE4	153	H5
Crofts La. N22 *Glendale Av.*	59	G7
Crofts Rd., Har.	68	D6
Crofts St. E1	**21**	**H6**
Crofts St. E1	112	D7
Croftside SE25 *Sunny Bank*	188	D3
Croftway NW3	90	D4
Croftway, Rich.	163	E3
Crogsland Rd. NW1	92	A7
Croham Cl., S.Croy.	202	B6
Croham Manor Rd., S.Croy.	202	B7

Name	Page	Grid
Cubitts Yd. WC2	18	B5
Cuckoo Av. W7	104	B4
Cuckoo Dene W7	104	A5
Cuckoo Hall La. N9	45	F7
Cuckoo Hill, Pnr.	66	C3
Cuckoo Hill Dr., Pnr.	66	C3
Cuckoo Hill Rd., Pnr.	66	C4
Cuckoo La. W7	104	B7
Cudas Cl., Epsom	197	F4
Cuddington Av., Wor.Pk.	197	F3
Cudham St. SE6	154	C7
Cudworth St. E1	113	E4
Cuff Cres. SE9	156	A6
Cuff Pt. E2	**13**	**F3**
Cuff Pt. E2	112	C3
Culford Gdns. SW3	**32**	**A2**
Culford Gdns. SW3	129	J4
Culford Gro. N1	94	B6
Culford Ms. N1	94	B6
Culford Rd.		
Culford Rd. N1	94	B7
Culgaith Gdns., Enf.	42	E4
Cullen Way NW10	106	C4
Culling Rd. SE16	133	F3
Lower Rd.		
Cullington Cl., Har.	68	D4
Cullingworth Rd. NW10	89	G5
Culloden Cl. SE16	**37**	**J4**
Culloden Cl. SE16	132	D5
Culloden Rd., Enf.	43	H2
Culloden St. E14	114	C6
Cullum St. EC3	**20**	**D5**
Culmington Rd. W13	125	F2
Culmore Cross SW12	168	B3
Culmore Rd. SE15	133	E7
Culmstock Rd. SW11	150	A5
Culpeper Cl., Ilf.	65	E6
Culross Cl. N15	75	J4
Culross St. W1	**16**	**B6**
Culross St. W1	110	A7
Culsac Rd., Surb.	195	H2
Culver Gro., Stan.	69	F2
Culverden Rd. SW12	168	C2
Culverden Rd., Wat.	50	B3
Culverhouse Gdns. SW16	169	F3
Culverlands Cl., Stan.	52	E4
Culverley Rd. SE6	172	B1
Culvers Av., Cars.	199	J2
Culvers Retreat, Cars.	199	J1
Culvers Way, Cars.	199	J2
Culverstone Cl., Brom.	191	F6
Culvert Pl. SW11	150	A2
Culvert Rd. N15	76	B5
Culvert Rd. SW11	149	J2
Culworth St. NW8	**7**	**G2**
Cumberland Av. NW10	106	B3
Cumberland Av., Well.	157	H3
Cumberland Cl. E8	94	C6
Cumberland Cl. SW20	166	A7
Lansdowne Rd.		
Cumberland Cl., Ilf.	81	F1
Carrick Dr.		
Cumberland Cl., Twick.	144/145	E6
Westmorland Cl.		
Cumberland Cres. W14	128	B4
Cumberland Dr., Bexh.	138	E7
Cumberland Dr., Chess.	195	J3
Cumberland Dr., Esher	194	D2
Cumberland Gdns. NW4	72	B2
Cumberland Gdns. WC1	**10**	**D3**
Cumberland Gate W1	**15**	**J5**
Cumberland Gate W1	109	J7
Cumberland Mkt. NW1	**9**	**E3**
Cumberland Mkt. NW1	110	B3
Cumberland Mkt. Est. NW1	**9**	**E3**
Cumberland Mills Sq. E14	134	D5
Saunders Ness Rd.		
Cumberland Pk. W3	107	G3
Cumberland Pl. NW1	**8**	**D3**
Cumberland Pl. SE6	173	F1
Cumberland Pl., Sun.	178	A4
Cumberland Rd. E12	98	A4
Cumberland Rd. E13	115	H5
Cumberland Rd. E17	77	H2
Cumberland Rd. N9	61	F1
Cumberland Rd. N22	75	F2
Cumberland Rd. SE25	189	E6
Cumberland Rd. SW13	147	F1
Cumberland Rd. W3	106	C7
Cumberland Rd. W7	124	C2
Cumberland Rd., Brom.	191	E4
Cumberland Rd., Har.	67	H5
Cumberland Rd., Rich.	126	A7
Cumberland Rd., Stan.	69	J3
Cumberland St. SW1	**32**	**E3**
Cumberland St. SW1	130	B5
Cumberland Ter. NW1	**8**	**D3**
Cumberland Ter. Ms. NW1	**8**	**D2**
Cumberland Vil. W3	106	C7
Cumberland Rd.		
Cumberlow Av. SE25	188	C3
Cumberton Rd. N17	76	A1
Cumbrae Gdns., Surb.	195	F1
Cumbrian Gdns. NW2	90	A2
Cumming St. N1	**10**	**C2**
Cumming St. N1	111	F2
Cumnor Gdns., Epsom	197	G6
Cumnor Rd., Sutt.	199	F6
Cunard Cres. N21	44	A6
Cunard Pl. EC3	**20**	**E4**
Cunard Rd. NW10	106	D3
Cunard St. SE5	132	B6
Albany Rd.		
Cunard Wk. SE16	133	H4
Cundy Rd. E16	115	J6
Cundy St. SW1	**32**	**C2**
Cundy St. SW1	130	A4
Cundy St. Est. SW1	**32**	**C2**
Cunliffe Rd., Epsom	197	F4
Cunliffe St. SW16	168	C6
Cunningham Cl., Rom.	82	C5
Cunningham Cl., W.Wick.	204	B2
Cunningham Pk., Har.	67	J5
Cunningham Pl. NW8	**7**	**E5**
Cunningham Rd. N15	76	D4
Cunnington St. W4	126	C3
Cupar Rd. SW11	150	A1
Cupola Cl., Brom.	173	H5
Cureton St. SW1	**33**	**J2**
Cureton St. SW1	130	D4
Curfew Ho., Bark.	117	F1
St. Ann's		
Curlew Cl. SE28	118	D7
Curlew Ct., Surb.	195	J3
Curlew St. SE1	**29**	**F3**
Curlew St. SE1	132	C2
Curlew Way, Hayes	102	D5
Curnick's La. SE27	169	J4
Chapel Rd.		
Curnock Est. NW1	110	C1
Plender St.		
Curran Av., Sid.	157	J5
Curran Av., Wall.	200	A3
Currey Rd., Grnf.	86	A6
Curricle St. W3	126	E1
Currie Hill Cl. SW19	166	C4
Curry Ri. NW7	56	A6
Cursitor St. EC4	**18**	**E3**
Cursitor St. EC4	111	G6
Curtain Pl. EC2	112	B3
Curtain Rd.		
Curtain Rd. EC2	**12**	**D6**
Curtain Rd. EC2	112	B4
Curthwaite Gdns., Enf.	42	D4
Curtis Dr. W3	106	D6
Curtis Fld. Rd. SW16	169	F4
Curtis La., Wem.	87	H6
Montrose Cres.		
Curtis Rd., Epsom	196	C4
Curtis Rd., Houns.	143	F7
Curtis St. SE1	**37**	**F1**
Curtis St. SE1	132	C4
Curtis Way SE1	**37**	**F1**
Curtis Way SE1	132	C4
Curtis Way SE28	118	B7
Tawney Rd.		
Curve, The W12	107	G7
Curwen Av. E7	97	H4
Woodford Rd.		
Curwen Rd. W12	127	G2
Curzon Av., Enf.	45	G5
Curzon Av., Stan.	68	C7
Curzon Cl., Orp.	207	G4
Curzon Cres. NW10	89	F7
Curzon Cres., Bark.	117	J2
Curzon Gate W1	**24**	**C2**
Curzon Gate W1	130	A1
Curzon Pl. W1	**24**	**C2**
Curzon Pl., Pnr.	66	C5
Curzon Rd. N10	74	B2
Curzon Rd. W5	105	E4
Curzon Rd., Th.Hth.	187	G6
Curzon St. W1	**24**	**C2**
Curzon St. W1	130	A1
Cusack Cl., Twick.	162	C4
Waldegrave Rd.		
Custom Ho. Reach SE16	133	J2
Custom Ho. Wk. EC3	**20**	**D6**
Custom Ho. Wk. EC3	112	B7
Cut, The SE1	**27**	**F3**
Cut, The SE1	131	G2
Cutcombe Rd. SE5	151	J2
Cuthberga Cl., Bark.	99	F7
George St.		
Cuthbert Gdns. SE25	188	B3
Cuthbert Rd. E17	78	C3
Cuthbert Rd. N18	60	D5
Fairfield Rd.		
Cuthbert Rd., Croy.	201	H2
Cuthbert St. W2	**15**	**E1**
Cuthbert St. W2	109	G4
Cuthill Wk. SE5	152	A1
Cutler St. E1	**21**	**E3**
Cutler St. E1	112	B6
Cutlers Gdns. E1	**21**	**E3**
Cutlers Gdns. Arc. EC2	112	B6
Cutler St.		
Cutlers Sq. E14	134	A4
Britannia Rd.		
Cutthroat All., Rich.	163	F2
Ham St.		
Cutty Sark Gdns. SE10	134	C6
King William Wk.		
Cuxton Cl., Bexh.	158	E5
Cyclamen Cl., Hmptn.	161	G6
Cyclamen Way, Epsom	196	B5
Cyclops Ms. E14	134	A4
Cygnet Av., Felt.	142	C7
Cygnet Cl. NW10	88	D5
Cygnet Cl., Borwd.	38	C1
Cygnet St. E1	**13**	**G5**
Cygnet Way, Hayes	102	D5
Cygnets, The, Felt.	160	E4
Cygnus Business Cen. NW10	89	F6
Cymbeline Ct., Har.	68	C6
Cynthia St. N1	**10**	**D2**
Cynthia St. N1	111	F2
Cyntra Pl. E8	94/95	E7
Mare St.		
Cypress Av., Twick.	143	J7
Cypress Gro., Ilf.	65	H6
Cypress Pl. W1	**9**	**G6**
Cypress Rd. SE25	188	B2
Cypress Rd., Har.	68	A2
Cypress Tree Cl., Sid.	157	J7
White Oak Gdns.		
Cyprus Av. N3	72	B2
Cyprus Cl. N4	75	H6
Atterbury Rd.		
Cyprus Gdns. N3	72	B2
Cyprus Pl. E2	113	F2
Cyprus Pl. E6	116	D7
Cyprus Rd. N3	72	C2
Cyprus Rd. N9	60	C2
Cyprus Roundabout E16	116	D7
Royal Albert Way		
Cyprus St. E2	113	F2
Cyrena Rd. SE22	152	C6
Cyril Mans. SW11	149	J1
Cyril Rd., Bexh.	159	E2
Cyrus St. EC1	**11**	**H5**
Cyrus St. EC1	111	H4
Czar St. SE8	134	A6

D

Name	Page	Grid
Da Gama Pl. E14	134	A5
Napier Av.		
Dabbs Hill La., Nthlt.	85	H5
Dabin Cres. SE10	154	C1
Dacca St. SE8	133	J6
Dace Rd. E3	96	A7
Dacre Av., Ilf.	80	D2
Dacre Cl., Chig.	65	F4
Dacre Cl., Grnf.	103	H2
Dacre Gdns. SE13	154	E4
Dacre Gdns., Borwd.	38	D5
Dacre Gdns., Chig.	65	F4
Dacre Pk. SE13	155	E3
Dacre Pl. SE13	154	E3
Dacre Rd. E11	97	F1
Dacre Rd. E13	115	H1
Dacre Rd., Croy.	187	E7
Dacre St. SW1	**25**	**H5**
Dacre St. SW1	130	D3
Dacres Rd. SE23	171	G3
Dade Way, Sthl.	123	F5
Daerwood Cl., Brom.	206	C1
Daffodil Cl., Croy.	203	G1
Primrose La.		
Daffodil Gdns., Ilf.	98	E5
Daffodil Pl., Hmptn.	161	G6
Gresham Rd.		
Daffodil St. W12	107	F7
Dafforne Rd. SW17	168	A3
Dagenham Av., Dag.	118	E1
Dagenham Rd. E10	95	J1
Dagenham Rd., Dag.	101	J4
Dagmar Av., Wem.	87	J4
Dagmar Gdns. NW10	108	A2
Dagmar Ms., Sthl.	122/123	E3
Dagmar Rd.		
Dagmar Pas. N1	111	H1
Cross St.		
Dagmar Rd. N4	75	G7
Dagmar Rd. N15	76	A4
Cornwall Rd.		
Dagmar Rd. N22	74	D1
Dagmar Rd. SE5	152	B1
Dagmar Rd. SE25	188	B5
Dagmar Rd., Dag.	101	J7
Dagmar Rd., Kings.T.	181	J1
Dagmar Rd., Sthl.	122	E3
Dagmar Ter. N1	111	H1
Dagnall Pk. SE25	188	B6
Dagnall Rd. SE25	188	B5
Dagnall St. SW11	149	J2
Dagnan Rd. SW12	150	B7
Dagonet Gdns., Brom.	173	G3
Shroffold Rd.		
Dagonet Rd., Brom.	173	G3
Dahlia Gdns., Ilf.	99	E6
Dahlia Gdns., Mitch.	186	D4
Dahlia Rd. SE2	138	B4
Dahomey Rd. SW16	168	C6
Daimler Way, Wall.	200	E7
Daines Cl. E12	98	C3
Colchester Av.		
Dainford Cl., Brom.	172	D5
Dainton Cl., Brom.	191	H1
Daintry Cl., Har.	68	D4
Daintry Way E9	95	J6
Eastway		
Dairsie Rd. SE9	156	D3
Dairy Cl. NW10	107	G1
Dairy Cl., Th.Hth.	187	J2
Dairy La. SE18	136	C4
Dairy Ms. SW9	151	E3
Dairy Wk. SW19	166	B4
Dairyman Cl. NW2	90	B3
Claremont Rd.		
Daisy Cl., Croy.	203	G1
Primrose La.		
Daisy Dobbins Wk. N19	74/75	E7
Hillrise Rd.		
Daisy La. SW6	148	D3
Daisy Rd. E16	114/115	E4
Cranberry La.		
Daisy Rd. E18	79	H2
Dakota Gdns. E6	116	B4
Dakota Gdns., Nthlt.	102/103	E3
Argus Way		
Dalberg Rd. SW2	151	G5
Dalberg Way SE2	138	D3
Lanridge Rd.		
Dalby Rd. SW18	149	F4
Dalby St. NW5	92	B6
Dalcross Rd., Houns.	142	E2
Dale, The, Kes.	206	A4
Dale Av., Edg.	69	J1
Dale Av., Houns.	143	E3
Dale Cl. SE3	155	G3
Dale Cl., Barn.	41	E6
Dale Cl., Pnr.	66	B1
Dale Gdns., Wdf.Grn.	63	H4
Dale Grn. Rd. N11	58	B3
Dale Gro. N12	57	F5
Dale Pk. Av., Cars.	199	J2
Dale Pk. Rd. SE19	187	J1
Dale Rd. NW5	92	A5
Grafton Rd.		
Dale Rd. SE17	**35**	**H6**
Dale Rd. SE17	131	H6
Dale Rd., Grnf.	103	H5
Dale Rd., Sutt.	198	C4
Dale Row W11	108	B6
St. Marks Rd.		
Dale St. W4	126	E5
Dale Vw. E4	62	C2
Dale Vw. Cres. E4	62	C2
Dale Vw. Gdns. E4	62	D3

Dale Wd. Rd., Orp. 193 H7
Dalebury Rd. SW17 167 H2
Daleham Gdns. NW3 91 G5
Daleham Ms. NW3 91 G6
Dalehead NW1 9 F2
Dalehead NW1 110 C2
Dalemain Ms. E16 135 G1
Hanover Av.
Dales Path, Borwd. 38 D5
Farriers Way
Dales Rd., Borwd. 38 D5
Daleside Gdns., Chig. 65 F3
Daleside Rd. SW16 168 B5
Daleside Rd., Epsom 196 D6
Daleview Rd. N15 76 B6
Dalewood Gdns., Wor.Pk. 197 H2
Daley St. E9 95 G6
Daley Thompson Way SW8 150 B2
Dalgarno Gdns. W10 107 J5
Dalgarno Way W10 107 J4
Dalgleish St. E14 113 H6
Daling Way E3 113 H1
Dalkeith Gro., Stan. 53 G5
Dalkeith Rd. SE21 169 J1
Dalkeith Rd., Ilf. 99 F3
Dallas Rd. NW4 71 G7
Dallas Rd. SE26 170 E4
Dallas Rd. W5 105 J5
Dallas Rd., Sutt. 198 B6
Dallas Ter., Hayes 121 J3
Dallin Rd. SE18 137 E7
Dallin Rd., Bexh. 158 D4
Dalling Rd. W6 127 H3
Dallinger Rd. SE12 155 F6
Dallington St. EC1 11 H5
Dallington St. EC1 111 H4
Dalmain Rd. SE23 171 G1
Dalmally Rd., Croy. 188 C7
Dalmeny Av. N7 92 D4
Dalmeny Av. SW16 187 G2
Dalmeny Cl., Wem. 87 F6
Dalmeny Cres., Houns. 144 A4
Dalmeny Rd. N7 92 D3
Dalmeny Rd., Barn. 41 F6
Dalmeny Rd., Cars. 200 A7
Dalmeny Rd., Erith 159 H1
Dalmeny Rd., Wor.Pk. 197 H3
Dalmeyer Rd. NW10 89 F6
Dalmore Av., Esher 194 C6
Dalmore Rd. SE21 169 J2
Dalrymple Cl. N14 42 D7
Dalrymple Rd. SE4 153 H4
Dalston Cross Shop. Cen. E8 94 C6
Dalston Gdns., Stan. 69 H1
Dalston La. E8 94 C6
Dalton Av., Mitch. 185 H2
Dalton Cl., Orp. 207 H3
Dalton Rd., Har. 68 A2
Dalton St. SE27 169 H2
Dalwood St. SE5 152 B1
Daly Ct. E15 96 C5
Clays La.
Dalyell Rd. SW9 151 F3
Damascene Wk. SE21 169 J1
Lovelace Rd.
Damask Cres. E16 114/115 E4
Cranberry La.
Dame St. N1 11 J1
Dame St. N1 111 J2
Damer Ter. SW10 129 F7
Tadema Rd.
Dames Rd. E7 97 G3
Damien St. E1 113 E6
Damon Cl., Sid. 176 B3
Damsonwood Rd., Sthl. 123 G3
Dan Leno Wk. SW6 128/129 E7
Britannia Rd.
Danbrook Rd. SW16 187 E1
Danbury Cl., Rom. 82 D3
Danbury Ms., Wall. 200 B4
Danbury Rd., Loug. 48 B7
Danbury St. N1 11 H1
Danbury St. N1 111 H2
Danbury Way, Wdf.Grn. 63 J6
Danby St. SE15 152 C3
Dancer Rd. SW6 148 C1
Dancer Rd., Rich. 146 A3
Dando Cres. SE3 155 H3
Dandridge Cl. SE10 135 F5
Dane Cl., Bex. 159 G7
Dane Cl., Orp. 207 G5
Dane Pl. E3 113 H2
Roman Rd.
Dane Rd. N18 61 F3
Dane Rd. SW19 185 F1
Dane Rd. W13 125 F1
Dane Rd., Ilf. 99 F5
Dane Rd., Sthl. 103 E7
Dane St. WC1 18 C2
Danebury, Croy. 204 B6
Danebury Av. SW15 147 E6
Daneby Rd. SE6 172 B3
Danecourt Gdns., Croy. 202 C3
Danecroft Rd. SE24 151 J5
Danehill Wk., Sid. 176 A3
Hatherley Rd.
Danehurst Gdns., Ilf. 80 B5
Danehurst St. SW6 148 B1
Daneland, Barn. 41 J6
Danemead Gro., Nthlt. 85 H5
Danemere St. SW15 147 J3
Danes Ct., Wem. 88 B3
Danes Gate, Har. 68 B3
Danes Rd., Rom. 83 J7
Danesbury Rd., Felt. 160 B1
Danescombe SE12 173 G1
Winn Rd.
Danescourt Cres., Sutt. 199 F2
Danescroft NW4 72 A5
Danescroft Av. NW4 72 A5
Danescroft Gdns. NW4 72 A5
Danesdale Rd. E9 95 H6
Danesfield SE5 36 D5
Daneswood Av. SE6 172 C3
Danethorpe Rd., Wem. 87 G6
Danetree Cl., Epsom 196 C7
Danetree Rd., Epsom 196 C7
Danette Gdns., Dag. 101 F2
Daneville Rd. SE5 152 A1
Dangan Rd. E11 79 G6
Daniel Bolt Cl. E14 114 B5
Uamvar St.
Daniel Cl. N18 61 F4
Daniel Cl. SW17 167 H6
Daniel Gdns. SE15 37 F7
Daniel Gdns. SE15 132 C7
Daniel Pl. NW4 71 H7
Daniel Rd. W5 105 J7
Daniell Way, Croy. 201 E1
Daniels Ms. SE4 153 J4
Daniels Rd. SE15 153 F3
Dansey Pl. W1 17 H5
Dansington Rd., Well. 158 A4
Danson Cres., Well. 158 B3
Danson La., Well. 158 B4
Danson Mead, Well. 158 C3
Danson Pk., Bexh. 158 C4
Danson Rd., Bex. 158 D5
Danson Rd., Bexh. 158 D5
Danson Underpass, Sid. 158 C6
Danson Rd.
Dante Pl. SE11 35 H1
Dante Rd. SE11 35 G1
Dante Rd. SE11 131 H4
Danube St. SW3 31 H3
Danvers Rd. N8 74 D4
Danvers St. SW3 31 F6
Danvers St. SW3 129 G6
Danziger Way, Borwd. 38 C1
Daphne Gdns. E4 62 C3
Gunners Gro.
Daphne St. SW18 149 F6
Daplyn St. E1 21 H1
D'Arblay St. W1 17 G4
D'Arblay St. W1 110 C6
Darby Cres., Sun. 178 C2
Darby Gdns., Sun. 178 C2
Darcy Av., Wall. 200 C4
Darcy Cl. N20 57 G2
D'Arcy Dr., Har. 69 G4
Darcy Gdns., Dag. 119 F1
D'Arcy Gdns., Har. 69 H4
Darcy Rd. SW16 186 E2
Darcy Rd., Islw. 144 D1
London Rd.
D'Arcy Rd., Sutt. 198 A4
Dare Gdns., Dag. 100/101 E3
Grafton Rd.
Darell Rd., Rich. 146 A3
Darenth Rd. N16 76 C7
Darenth Rd., Well. 158 A1
Darfield Rd. SE4 153 J5
Darfield Way W10 108 A6
Darfur St. SW15 148 A3
Dargate Cl. SE19 170 C7
Chipstead Cl.
Darien Rd. SW11 149 G3
Darlan Rd. SW6 128 C7
Darlaston Rd. SW19 166 A7
Darley Cl., Croy. 189 H6
Darley Dr., N.Mal. 182 D2
Darley Gdns., Mord. 185 E6
Darley Rd. N9 60 C1
Darley Rd. SW11 149 J6
Darling Rd. SE4 154 A3
Darling Row E1 113 E4
Darlington Rd. SE27 169 H5
Darmaine Cl., S.Croy. 201 J7
Churchill Rd.
Darndale Cl. E17 77 J2
Darnley Ho. E14 113 H6
Darnley Rd. E9 95 E6
Darnley Rd., Wdf.Grn. 79 G1
Darnley Ter. W11 128 B1
St. James's Gdns.
Darrell Rd. SE22 152 D5
Darren Cl. N4 75 F7
Darrick Wd. Rd., Orp. 207 G2
Darris Cl., Hayes 103 E4
Darsley Dr. SW8 150 E1
Dart St. W10 108 B3
Dartford Av. N9 45 F6
Dartford Gdns., Rom. 82 B6
Heathfield Pk. Dr.
Dartford Rd., Bex. 177 J1
Dartford St. SE17 36 A5
Dartford St. SE17 131 J6
Dartmoor Wk. E14 134 A4
Charnwood Gdns.
Dartmouth Cl. W11 108 C6
Dartmouth Gro. SE10 154 C1
Dartmouth Hill SE10 154 C1
Dartmouth Pk. Av. NW5 92 B3
Dartmouth Pk. Hill N19 92 B1
Dartmouth Pk. Hill NW5 92 B4
Dartmouth Pk. Rd. NW5 92 B4
Dartmouth Pl. SE23 171 F2
Dartmouth Rd.
Dartmouth Pl. W4 127 E6
Dartmouth Rd. E16 115 G6
Fords Pk. Rd.
Dartmouth Rd. NW2 90 A6
Dartmouth Rd. NW4 71 G6
Dartmouth Rd. SE23 171 F3
Dartmouth Rd. SE26 171 F3
Dartmouth Rd., Brom. 191 G7
Dartmouth Rd., Ruis. 84 A3
Dartmouth Row SE10 154 C1
Dartmouth St. SW1 25 H4
Dartmouth St. SW1 130 D2
Dartmouth Ter. SE10 154 D1
Dartnell Rd., Croy. 188 C7
Dartrey Wk. SW10 30 D7
Darville Rd. N16 94 C3
Darwell Cl. E6 116 D2
Darwin Cl. N11 58 B3
Darwin Cl., Orp. 207 G5
Darwin Dr., Sthl. 103 H6
Darwin Gdns., Wat. 50 C5
Barnhurst Path
Darwin Rd. N22 75 H1
Darwin Rd. W5 125 F5
Darwin Rd., Well. 157 J3
Darwin St. SE17 36 C1
Darwin St. SE17 132 A4
Daryngton Dr., Grnf. 104 A2
Dashwood Cl., Bexh. 159 G5
Dashwood Rd. N8 75 F6
Dassett Rd. SE27 169 H5
Datchelor Pl. SE5 152 A1
Datchet Rd. SE6 171 J3
Datchworth Ct. N4 93 J3
Queens Dr.
Date St. SE17 36 B4
Date St. SE17 131 J5
Daubeney Gdns. N17 59 J7
Daubeney Rd. E5 95 H4
Daubeney Rd. N17 59 J7
Daubeney Twr. SE8 133 J4
Dault Rd. SW18 149 F6
Davema Cl., Chis. 192 D1
Brenchley Cl.
Davenant Rd. N19 92 D2
Davenant Rd., Croy. 201 H4
Duppas Hill Rd.
Davenant St. E1 21 J2
Davenant St. E1 112 D5
Davenport Cl., Tedd. 162 D6
Davenport Rd. SE6 154 B6
Davenport Rd., Sid. 176 D2
Daventer Dr., Stan. 52 C7
Daventry Av. E17 78 A5
Daventry St. NW1 15 G1
Daventry St. NW1 109 H5
Davern Cl. SE10 135 F4
Davey Cl. N7 93 F6
Davey Rd. E9 96 A7
Davey St. SE15 37 G6
Davey St. SE15 132 C6
David Av., Grnf. 104 B3
David Cl., Hayes 121 G7
David Ms. W1 16 A1
David Rd., Dag. 100 E2
David St. E15 96 D6
Davidge St. SE1 27 G4
Davidge St. SE1 131 H2
Davids Rd. SE23 171 F1
David's Way, Ilf. 65 H7
Davidson Gdns. SW8 130 E7
Davidson La., Har. 68 C7
Grove Hill
Davidson Rd., Croy. 188 C6
Davies Cl., Croy. 188 D6
Davies La. E11 97 E2
Davies Ms. W1 16 D5
Davies St. W1 16 D5
Davies St. W1 110 B7
Davington Gdns., Dag. 100 B5
Davington Rd., Dag. 100 B6
Davinia Cl., Wdf.Grn. 64 C6
Deacon Way
Davis Rd. W3 127 F1
Davis Rd., Chess. 196 A4
Davis St. E13 115 H2
Davisville Rd. W12 127 G2
Dawes Av., Islw. 144 D5
Dawes Ho. SE17 36 C2
Dawes Rd. SW6 128 B7
Dawes St. SE17 36 C3
Dawes St. SE17 132 A5
Dawley Rd., Hayes 121 H3
Dawlish Av. N13 58 E4
Dawlish Av. SW18 166 E2
Dawlish Av., Grnf. 104 D2
Dawlish Dr., Ilf. 99 H4
Dawlish Dr., Pnr. 67 E5
Dawlish Dr., Ruis. 84 A2
Dawlish Rd. E10 96 C2
Dawlish Rd. N17 76 D3
Dawlish Rd. NW2 90 A6
Dawn Cl., Houns. 143 E3
Dawn Cres. E15 114 D1
Bridge Rd.
Dawnay Gdns. SW18 167 G2
Dawnay Rd. SW18 167 F2
Dawpool Rd. NW2 89 F2
Daws Hill E4 46 C3
Daws La. NW7 55 F5
Dawson Av., Bark. 99 J7
Dawson Cl. SE18 137 F4
Dawson Gdns., Bark. 99 J7
Dawson Av.
Dawson Hts. Est. SE22 152 D7
Dawson Pl. W2 108 D7
Dawson Rd. NW2 89 J5
Dawson Rd., Kings.T. 181 J3
Dawson St. E2 13 G2
Dawson St. E2 112 C2
Dax Ct., Sun. 178 C3
Thames St.
Daybrook Rd. SW19 184 E2
Daylesford Av. SW15 147 G4
Daymer Gdns., Pnr. 66 B4
Days La., Sid. 157 H7
Daysbrook Rd. SW2 169 F1
Dayton Gro. SE15 153 F1
De Barowe Ms. N5 93 H4
Leigh Rd.
De Beauvoir Cres. N1 112 B1
De Beauvoir Est. N1 112 A1
De Beauvoir Rd. N1 112 B1
De Beauvoir Sq. N1 94 B7
De Bohun Av. N14 42 B6
De Brome Rd., Felt. 160 C1
De Crespigny Pk. SE5 152 A2
De Frene Rd. SE26 171 G4
De Havilland Rd., Edg. 70 B2
De Havilland Rd., Houns. 122 C7
De Havilland Rd., Wall. 201 E7
De Havilland Way, Stai. 140 A6
De Laune St. SE17 35 G4
De Laune St. SE17 131 H5
De Luci Rd., Erith 139 J5
De Lucy St. SE2 138 B4
De Mandeville Gate, Enf. 44 D4
Southbury Rd.
De Montfort Par. SW16 168/169 E3
Streatham High Rd.
De Montfort Rd. SW16 168 E3
De Morgan Rd. SW6 149 E3
De Quincey Ms. E16 135 G1
Wesley Av.
De Quincey Rd. N17 76 A1
De Vere Gdns. W8 22 C4

De Vere Gdns. W8 129 F2
De Vere Gdns., Ilf. 98 C2
De Vere Ms. W8 22 C5
De Walden St. W1 16 C2
Deacon Ms. N1 94 A7
Deacon Rd. NW2 89 G5
Deacon Rd., Kings.T. 181 J1
Deacon Way SE17 35 J1
Deacon Way SE17 131 J4
Deacon Way, Wdf.Grn. 64 C7
Deacons Cl., Borwd. 38 A4
Deacons Cl., Pnr. 66 B2
Deacons Leas, Orp. 207 G4
Deacons Ri. N2 73 G5
Deacons Wk., Hmptn. 161 F4
Bishops Gro.
Deal Ms. W5 125 G4
Darwin Rd.
Deal Porters Way SE16 133 F3
Deal Rd. SW17 168 A6
Deal St. E1 21 H1
Deal St. E1 112 D5
Deal Wk. SW9 131 G7
Mandela St.
Deal's Gateway SE10 154 B1
Blackheath Rd.
Dealtry Rd. SW15 147 J4
Dean Bradley St. SW1 26 A6
Dean Bradley St. SW1 130 E3
Dean Cl. E9 95 F5
Churchill Wk.
Dean Cl. SE16 133 G1
Surrey Water Rd.
Dean Ct., Wem. 87 E3
Dean Dr., Stan. 69 H2
Dean Farrar St. SW1 25 H5
Dean Farrar St. SW1 130 D3
Dean Gdns. E17 78 D4
Dean Gdns. W13 124/125 E1
Northfield Av.
Dean Rd. NW2 89 J6
Dean Rd. SE28 118 A7
Dean Rd., Croy. 202 A4
Dean Rd., Hmptn. 161 G5
Dean Rd., Houns. 143 H5
Dean Ryle St. SW1 34 A1
Dean Ryle St. SW1 130 E4
Dean Stanley St. SW1 26 A6
Dean Stanley St. SW1 130 E3
Dean St. E7 97 G5
Dean St. W1 17 H3
Dean St. W1 110 D6
Dean Trench St. SW1 26 A6
Dean Trench St. SW1 130 E3
Dean Wk., Edg. 54 C6
Deansbrook Rd.
Dean Way, Sthl. 123 H2
Deancross St. E1 113 F6
Deane Av., Ruis. 84 C5
Deane Cft. Rd., Pnr. 66 C6
Deane Way, Ruis. 66 B6
Deanery Cl. N2 73 H4
Deanery Ms. W1 24 C1
Deanery Rd. E15 97 E6
Deanery St. W1 24 C1
Deanery St. W1 130 A1
Deanhill Rd. SW14 146 B4
Deans Bldgs. SE17 36 B2
Deans Bldgs. SE17 132 A4
Deans Cl. W4 126 B6
Dean's Cl., Croy. 202 C3
Deans Cl., Edg. 54 C6
Deans Ct. EC4 19 H4
Deans Dr. N13 59 H6
Deans Dr., Edg. 54 D5
Dean's Gate Cl. SE23 171 G3
Deans La. W4 126 B6
Deans La., Edg. 54 C6
Deans Ms. W1 16 E3
Dean's Pl. SW1 33 H3
Dean's Pl. SW1 130 D5
Deans Rd. W7 124 C1
Deans Rd., Sutt. 198 E3
Deans Way, Edg. 54 C5
Dean's Yd. SW1 25 J5
Deansbrook Cl., Edg. 54 C7
Deansbrook Rd., Edg. 54 C6
Deanscroft Av. NW9 88 C2
Deansway N2 73 G4
Deansway N9 60 B3
De'Arn Gdns., Mitch. 185 H3
Dearne Cl., Stan. 52 D5
Dearsley Rd., Enf. 44 D3
Deason St. E15 114 C1
High St.
Debden Cl., Kings.T. 163 G5
Debden Cl., Wdf.Grn. 63 J7
Debnams Rd. SE16 133 F4
Rotherhithe New Rd.
Deborah Cl., Islw. 144 B1
Deburgh Rd. SW19 167 F7
Decima St. SE1 28 D5
Decima St. SE1 132 B3
Deck Cl. SE16 133 G2
Thame Rd.
Decoy Av. NW11 72 B5
Dee Rd., Rich. 145 J4
Dee St. E14 114 C6
Deeley Rd. SW8 150 D1
Deena Cl. W3 105 J6
Deepdale SW19 166 A4
Deepdale Av., Brom. 191 F4
Deepdale Cl. N11 58 A6
Ribblesdale Av.
Deepdene W5 105 J4
Deepdene Av., Croy. 202 C3
Deepdene Cl. E11 79 G4
Deepdene Ct. N21 43 H6
Deepdene Gdns. SW2 151 F7
Deepdene Path, Loug. 48 D4
Deepdene Rd. SE5 152 A4
Deepdene Rd., Loug. 48 D4
Deepdene Rd., Well. 158 A3
Deepwell Cl., Islw. 144 D1
Deepwood La., Grnf. 104 A3
Cowgate Rd.
Deer Pk. Cl., Kings.T. 164 B7
Deer Pk. Gdns., Mitch. 185 G3
Deer Pk. Rd. SW19 185 E2
Deer Pk. Way, W.Wick. 205 F2
Deerbrook Rd. SE24 169 H1
Deerdale Rd. SE24 151 J4
Deerhurst Cl., Felt. 160 A4
Deerhurst Cres., Hmptn. 161 J5
Deerhurst Rd. NW2 90 A6
Deerhurst Rd. SW16 169 F5
Deerings Dr., Pnr. 66 A5
Deerleap Gro. E4 46 B5
Deeside Rd. SW17 167 G3
Defiance Wk. SE18 136 C3
Defiant Way, Wall. 200 E7
Defoe Av., Rich. 126 A7
Defoe Cl. SE16 133 J2
Vaughan St.
Defoe Cl. SW17 167 H6
Defoe Rd. N16 94 B2
Degema Rd., Chis. 174 E5
Dehar Cres. NW9 71 F7
Dehavilland Cl., Nthlt. 102 D3
Dekker Rd. SE21 152 B6
Delacourt Rd. SE3 135 H7
Old Dover Rd.
Delafield Rd. SE7 135 H5
Delaford Rd. SE16 133 E5
Delaford St. SW6 128 B7
Delamare Cres., Croy. 189 F6
Delamere Gdns. NW7 54 D6
Delamere Rd. SW20 184 A1
Delamere Rd. W5 125 H1
Delamere Rd., Borwd. 38 B1
Delamere Rd., Hayes 102 D7
Delamere Ter. W2 14 B1
Delamere Ter. W2 109 E5
Delancey Pas. NW1 110 B1
Delancey St.
Delancey St. NW1 110 B1
Delaware Rd. W9 6 A5
Delaware Rd. W9 108 E4
Delawyk Cres. SE24 151 J6
Delcombe Av., Wor.Pk. 197 J1
Delft Way SE22 152 B5
East Dulwich Gro.
Delhi Rd., Enf. 44 C7
Delhi St. N1 111 E1
Delia St. SW18 149 E7
Delisle Rd. SE28 137 H1
Merbury Rd.
Delius Gro. E15 114 D2
Dell, The SE2 138 A5
Dell, The SE19 188 C1
Dell, The, Brent. 125 F6
Dell, The, Felt. 142 B7
Harlington Rd. W.
Dell, The, Pnr. 66 D2
Dell, The, Wem. 87 E5
Dell, The, Wdf.Grn. 63 H3
Dell Cl. E15 114 D1
Dell Cl., Wall. 200 D4
Dell Cl., Wdf.Grn. 63 H3
Dell La., Epsom 197 G5
Dell Rd., Epsom 197 G6
Dell Rd., West Dr. 120 C3
Dell Wk., N.Mal. 183 E2
Dell Way W13 105 F6
Della Path E5 94/95 E3
Napoleon Rd.
Dellbow Rd., Felt. 142 B5
Central Way
Dellfield Cl., Beck. 172 C7
Foxgrove Rd.
Dellors Cl., Barn. 40 A5
Dellow Cl., Ilf. 81 G7
Dellow St. E1 113 E7
Dells Cl. E4 46 B7
Dell's Ms. SW1 33 G2
Dellwood Gdns., Ilf. 80 D3
Delmare Cl. SW9 151 F4
Brighton Ter.
Delme Cres. SE3 155 H2
Delmey Cl., Croy. 202 C3
Radcliffe Rd.
Deloraine St. SE8 154 A1
Delorme St. W6 128 A6
Delta Cl., Wor.Pk. 197 F3
Delta Ct. NW2 89 G2
Delta Gain, Wat. 50 D2
Delta Gro., Nthlt. 102 D3
Delta Rd., Wor.Pk. 197 E3
Delta St. E2 13 H3
Delvan Cl. SE18 136 D7
Ordnance Rd.
Delvers Mead, Dag. 101 J4
Delverton Rd. SE17 35 H4
Delverton Rd. SE17 131 H5
Delvino Rd. SW6 148 D1
Demesne Rd., Wall. 200 D5
Demeta Cl., Wem. 88 C3
Dempster Cl., Surb. 195 F1
Dempster Rd. SW18 149 F5
Den Cl., Beck. 190 D3
Den Rd., Brom. 190 D3
Denbar Par., Rom. 83 J4
Mawney Rd.
Denberry Dr., Sid. 176 B3
Denbigh Cl. NW10 88 E7
Denbigh Cl. W11 108 C7
Denbigh Cl., Chis. 174 C6
Denbigh Cl., Sthl. 103 F6
Denbigh Cl., Sutt. 198 C5
Denbigh Dr., Hayes 121 F2
Denbigh Gdns., Rich. 145 J5
Denbigh Ms. SW1 33 F2
Denbigh Pl. SW1 33 F3
Denbigh Pl. SW1 130 C5
Denbigh Rd. E6 116 A3
Denbigh Rd. W11 108 C7
Denbigh Rd. W13 105 E7
Denbigh Rd., Houns. 143 H2
Denbigh Rd., Sthl. 103 F6
Denbigh St. SW1 33 F2
Denbigh St. SW1 130 C4
Denbigh Ter. W11 108 C7
Denbridge Rd., Brom. 192 C2
Dene, The W13 104 E5
Dene, The, Croy. 203 G4
Dene, The, Wem. 87 H4
Dene, The, W.Mol. 179 F5
Dene Av., Houns. 143 F3
Dene Av., Sid. 158 B7
Dene Cl. SE4 153 H3
Dene Cl., Brom. 205 F1
Dene Cl., Wor.Pk. 197 F2
Dene Ct., Stan. 53 F5
Marsh La.
Dene Gdns., Stan. 53 F5
Dene Gdns., T.Ditt. 194 D2
Dene Rd. N11 57 J1
Dene Rd., Buck.H. 64 A1
Denehurst Gdns. NW4 71 J6
Denehurst Gdns. W3 126 B1
Denehurst Gdns., Rich. 146 A4
Denehurst Gdns., Twick. 144 A7
Denehurst Gdns., Wdf.Grn. 63 H4
Denewood, Barn. 41 F5
Denewood Rd. N6 73 J6
Dengie Wk. N1 111 J1
Basire St.
Denham Cl., Well. 158 C3
Park Vw. Rd.
Denham Cres., Mitch. 185 J4
Denham Dr., Ilf. 81 F6
Denham Rd. N20 57 J3
Denham Rd., Felt. 142 C6
Denham St. SE10 135 G5
Denham Way, Bark. 117 H1
Denham Way, Borwd. 38 D1
Denholme Rd. W9 108 C3
Denison Cl. N2 73 F3
Denison Rd. SW19 167 G6
Denison Rd. W5 105 F4
Deniston Av., Bex. 176 E1
Denleigh Gdns. N21 59 G1
Denleigh Gdns., T.Ditt. 180 B6
Denman Dr. NW11 72 D5
Denman Dr., Esher 194 D5
Denman Dr. N. NW11 72 D5
Denman Dr. S. NW11 72 D5
Denman Rd. SE15 152 C1
Denman St. W1 17 H6
Denmark Av. SW19 166 B7
Denmark Ct., Mord. 184 D5
Denmark Gdns., Cars. 200 A3
Denmark Gro. N1 11 E1
Denmark Gro. N1 111 G2
Denmark Hill SE5 152 A1
Denmark Hill Dr. NW9 71 F4
Denmark Hill Est. SE5 152 A4
Denmark Pl. WC2 17 J3
Denmark Rd. N8 75 F4
Denmark Rd. NW6 108 C2
Denmark Rd. SE5 151 J1
Denmark Rd. SE25 188 D5
Denmark Rd. SW19 166 A6
Denmark Rd. W13 105 E7
Denmark Rd., Brom. 191 H1
Denmark Rd., Cars. 199 J3
Denmark Rd., Kings.T. 181 H3
Denmark Rd., Twick. 162 A3
Denmark St. E11 96/97 E3
High Rd. Leytonstone
Denmark St. E13 115 H5
Denmark St. N17 76 E1
Denmark St. WC2 17 J4
Denmark St. WC2 110 D6
Denmark Wk. SE27 169 J4
Denmead Ho. SW15 147 F6
Highcliffe Dr.
Denmead Rd., Croy. 201 H1
Denmead Way SE15 37 F7
Dennan Rd., Surb. 195 J1
Denne Ter. E8 112 C1
Denner Rd. E4 62 A2
Dennett Rd., Croy. 187 G7
Dennetts Gro. SE14 153 G2
Dennetts Rd.
Dennetts Rd. SE14 153 F1
Denning Av., Croy. 201 G4
Denning Cl. NW8 6 D3
Denning Cl. NW8 109 F3
Denning Cl., Hmptn. 161 F6
Denning Rd. NW3 91 G4
Dennington Cl. E5 94/95 E2
Detmold Rd.
Dennington Pk. Rd. NW6 90 D6
Denningtons, The, Wor.Pk. 197 E2
Dennis Av., Wem. 87 J5
Dennis Gdns., Stan. 53 F5
Dennis La., Stan. 52 E3
Dennis Pk. Cres. SW20 184 B1
Dennis Reeve Cl., Mitch. 185 J1
Dennis Rd., E.Mol. 179 J4
Dennis Way SW4 150 D3
Gauden Rd.
Dennison Pt. E15 96 C7
Denny Cl. E6 116 B5
Linton Gdns.
Denny Cres. SE11 35 F2
Denny Gdns., Dag. 100 B7
Canonsleigh Rd.
Denny Rd. N9 60 E1
Denny St. SE11 35 F3
Denny St. SE11 131 G5
Densham Rd. E15 115 E1
Densole Cl., Beck. 189 H1
Kings Hall Rd.
Densworth Gro. N9 61 F2
Denton Cl., Barn. 39 J5
Denton Rd. N8 75 F5
Denton Rd. N18 60 B4
Denton Rd., Twick. 145 G6
Denton Rd., Well. 138 C7
Denton St. SW18 149 E6
Denton Way E5 95 G3
Dents Rd. SW11 149 J6
Denver Cl., Orp. 193 H6
Denver Rd. N16 76 B7
Denyer St. SW3 31 H2
Denyer St. SW3 129 H4
Denzil Rd. NW10 89 F5
Deodar Rd. SW15 148 B4
Deodara Cl. N20 57 H3
Depot Rd., Houns. 144 A3
Deptford Br. SE8 154 A1
Deptford Bdy. SE8 154 A1
Deptford Ch. St. SE8 134 A6

Deptford Ferry Rd. E14 134 A4
Deptford Grn. SE8 134 A6
Deptford High St. SE8 134 A6
Deptford Strand SE8 133 J4
Deptford Wf. SE8 133 J4
Derby Av. N12 57 F5
Derby Av., Har. 68 A1
Derby Av., Rom. 83 J6
Derby Ct. E5 95 G4
Overbury St.
Derby Est., Houns. 143 G4
Derby Gate SW1 26 A3
Derby Hill SE23 171 F2
Derby Hill Cres. SE23 171 F2
Derby Rd. E7 97 J7
Derby Rd. E9 113 G1
Derby Rd. E18 79 F1
Derby Rd. N18 61 F5
Derby Rd. SW14 146 B4
Derby Rd. SW19 166 D7
Russell Rd.
Derby Rd., Croy. 201 H2
Derby Rd., Enf. 45 E5
Derby Rd., Grnf. 103 H1
Derby Rd., Houns. 143 H4
Derby Rd., Surb. 196 A1
Derby Rd., Sutt. 198 C6
Derby St. W1 24 C2
Derbyshire St. E2 13 J4
Derbyshire St. E2 112 D3
Dereham Pl. EC2 12 E4
Dereham Rd., Bark. 99 J6
Derek Av., Epsom 196 A5
Derek Av., Wall. 200 B4
Derek Av., Wem. 88 B7
Derek Cl., Epsom 196 B5
Derek Walcott Cl. SE24 151 H5
Shakespeare Rd.
Dericote St. E8 112 D1
Deridene Cl., Stai. 140 B6
Bedfont Rd.
Derifall Cl. E6 116 C5
Dering Pl., Croy. 201 J4
Dering Rd., Croy. 201 J4
Dering St. W1 16 D4
Dering St. W1 110 B6
Derinton Rd. SW17 167 J4
Derley Rd., Sthl. 122 C3
Dermody Gdns. SE13 154 D5
Dermody Rd. SE13 154 D5
Deronda Rd. SE24 169 H1
Deroy Cl., Cars. 199 J6
Derrick Gdns. SE7 135 J4
Anchor & Hope La.
Derrick Rd., Beck. 189 J3
Derry Rd., Croy. 200 E3
Derry St. W8 22 A4
Derry St. W8 128 E2
Dersingham Av. E12 98 D5
Dersingham Rd. NW2 90 B3
Derwent Av. N18 60 A5
Derwent Av. NW7 54 D5
Derwent Av. SW15 164 E4
Derwent Av., Barn. 57 J1
Derwent Av., Pnr. 51 E6
Derwent Cl., Esher 194 B6
Derwent Cres. N20 57 F3
Derwent Cres., Bexh. 159 G2
Derwent Cres., Stan. 69 F2
Derwent Dr. NW9 70 E5
Derwent Dr., Orp. 193 G7
Derwent Gdns., Ilf. 80 B4
Derwent Gdns., Wem. 69 F7
Derwent Gro. SE22 152 C4
Derwent Ri. NW9 70 E6
Derwent Rd. N13 59 F4
Derwent Rd. SE20 188 D2
Derwent Rd. SW20 184 A6
Derwent Rd. W5 125 F3
Derwent Rd., Sthl. 103 G6
Derwent Rd., Twick. 143 H6
Derwent St. SE10 134 E5
Derwent Wk., Wall. 200 B7
Derwent Yd. W5 125 F3
Northfield Av.
Derwentwater Rd. W3 126 C1
Desborough St. W2 14 A1
Desenfans Rd. SE21 152 B6
Desford Ms. E16 114/115 E4
Desford Rd.
Desford Rd. E16 115 E4
Desmond St. SE14 133 H6
Despard Rd. N19 92 C1
Detling Rd., Brom. 173 G5
Detmold Rd. E5 95 F2
Devalls Cl. E6 116 D7
Devana End, Cars. 199 J3
Devas Rd. SW20 183 J1
Devas St. E3 114 B4
Devenay Rd. E15 97 F7
Devenish Rd. SE2 138 A2
Deventer Cres. SE22 152 B5
Deverell St. SE1 28 B6
Deverell St. SE1 132 A3
Devereux Ct. WC2 18 E4
Devereux La. SW13 127 H7
Devereux Rd. SW11 149 J6
Deverill Ct. SE20 189 F1
Devey Cl., Kings.T. 165 E7
Devizes St. N1 112 A1
Poole St.
Devon Av., Twick. 161 J1
Devon Cl. N17 76 C3
Devon Cl., Buck.H. 63 H2
Devon Cl., Grnf. 105 F1
Devon Gdns. N4 75 H6
Devon Ri. N2 73 G4
Devon Rd., Bark. 117 H1
Devon St. SE15 133 E6
Devon Way, Chess. 195 F5
Devon Way, Epsom 196 B5
Devon Waye, Houns. 123 F7
Devoncroft Gdns., Twick. 144 D7
Devonhurst Pl. W4 126 D5
Heathfield Ter.
Devonia Gdns. N18 59 J6
Devonia Rd. N1 11 H1
Devonia Rd. N1 111 H2
Devonport Gdns., Ilf. 80 C6
Devonport Ms. W12 127 H1
Devonport Rd.
Devonport Rd. W12 127 H2
Devonport St. E1 113 F6
Devons Est. E3 114 B3
Devons Rd. E3 114 A5
Devonshire Av., Sutt. 199 F7
Devonshire Cl. E15 97 E4
Devonshire Cl. N13 59 G4
Devonshire Cl. W1 16 D1
Devonshire Cl. W1 110 B5
Devonshire Cres. NW7 56 A7
Devonshire Dr. SE10 134 B7
Devonshire Dr., Surb. 195 G1
Devonshire Gdns. N17 59 J6
Devonshire Gdns. N21 43 J7
Devonshire Gdns. W4 126 C7
Devonshire Gro. SE15 133 E6
Devonshire Hill La. N17 59 J6
Devonshire Ms. W4 126/127 E5
Glebe St.
Devonshire Ms. N. W1 16 D1
Devonshire Ms. S. W1 16 D1
Devonshire Ms. S. W1 110 B5
Devonshire Ms. W. W1 8 D6
Devonshire Ms. W. W1 110 B5
Devonshire Pas. W4 126 E5
Devonshire Pl. NW2 90 D3
Devonshire Pl. W1 8 C6
Devonshire Pl. W1 110 A4
Devonshire Pl. W4 126 E5
Devonshire Pl. W8 22 A6
Devonshire Pl. Ms. W1 8 C6
Devonshire Rd. E15 96/97 E4
Janson Rd.
Devonshire Rd. E16 115 H6
Devonshire Rd. E17 78 A6
Devonshire Rd. N9 61 F1
Devonshire Rd. N13 59 F4
Devonshire Rd. N17 59 J6
Devonshire Rd. NW7 56 A7
Devonshire Rd. SE9 174 B2
Devonshire Rd. SE23 171 F1
Devonshire Rd. SW19 167 H7
Devonshire Rd. W4 126 E5
Devonshire Rd. W5 125 F3
Devonshire Rd., Bexh. 159 E4
Devonshire Rd., Cars. 200 A4
Devonshire Rd., Croy. 188 A7
Devonshire Rd., Felt. 160 E3
Devonshire Rd., Har. 68 A6
Devonshire Rd., Ilf. 81 H7
Devonshire Rd. (Eastcote), Pnr. 66 C6
Devonshire Rd. (Hatch End), Pnr. 67 F1
Devonshire Rd., Sthl. 103 G5
Devonshire Rd., Sutt. 199 F7
Devonshire Row EC2 20 E2
Devonshire Row Ms. W1 8 E6
Devonshire Sq. EC2 20 E3
Devonshire Sq., Brom. 191 H4
Devonshire St. W1 16 C1
Devonshire St. W1 110 B5
Devonshire St. W4 126 E5
Devonshire Ter. W2 14 D4
Devonshire Ter. W2 109 F6
Devonshire Way, Croy. 203 H2
Devonshire Way, Hayes 102 B6
Dewar St. SE15 152 D3
Dewberry Gdns. E6 116 B5
Dewberry St. E14 114 C5
Dewey Rd. N1 10 E1
Dewey Rd. N1 111 G2
Dewey Rd., Dag. 101 H6
Dewey St. SW17 167 J5
Dewhurst Rd. W14 128 A3
Dewlands Ct. NW4 72 A2
Holders Hill Rd.
Dewsbury Cl., Pnr. 67 F6
Dewsbury Ct. W4 126 C4
Chiswick Rd.
Dewsbury Gdns., Wor.Pk. 197 G3
Dewsbury Rd. NW10 89 G5
Dewsbury Ter. NW1 110 B1
Camden High St.
Dexter Ho., Erith 138/139 E3
Kale Rd.
Dexter Rd., Barn. 40 A6
Deyncourt Rd. N17 75 J1
Deynecourt Gdns. E11 79 J4
D'Eynsford Rd. SE5 152 A1
Diadem Ct. W1 17 H4
Dial Wk., The W8 22 B3
Dial Wk., The W8 129 E2
Diamedes Av., Stai. 140 A7
Diameter Rd., Orp. 193 E7
Diamond Cl., Dag. 100 C1
Diamond Rd., Ruis. 84 D4
Diamond St. SE15 132 B7
Diamond Ter. SE10 154 C1
Diamond Way SE8 134 A7
Deptford High St.
Diana Cl. E18 79 H1
Diana Gdns., Surb. 195 J2
Diana Ho. SW13 147 F1
Diana Pl. NW1 9 E5
Diana Pl. NW1 110 B4
Diana Rd. E17 77 J3
Dianne Way, Barn. 41 H5
Dianthus Cl. SE2 138 B5
Carnation St.
Dibden Row SE1 131 G3
Gerridge St.
Dibden St. N1 111 J1
Dibdin Cl., Sutt. 198 D3
Dibdin Rd., Sutt. 198 D3
Dicey Av. NW2 89 J5
Dick Turpin Way, Felt. 141 J4
Dickens Av. N3 73 F1
Dickens Cl., Erith 139 H7
Dickens Cl., Hayes 121 H4
Croyde Av.
Dickens Cl., Rich. 163 H2
Dickens Dr., Chis. 175 F6
Dickens Est. SE1 29 H4
Dickens Est. SE1 132 D2
Dickens Est. SE16 29 H4
Dickens Est. SE16 132 D2
Dickens La. N18 60 B5
Dickens Ri., Chig. 64 D3
Dickens Rd. E6 116 A2
Dickens Sq. SE1 28 A5
Dickens Sq. SE1 131 J3
Dickens St. SW8 150 B2
Dickenson Cl. N9 60 D1
Croyland Rd.
Dickenson Rd. N8 75 E7
Dickenson Rd., Felt. 160 C5
Dickenson St. NW5 92 B6
Dalby St.
Dickensons La. SE25 188 D5
Dickensons Pl. SE25 188 D6
Dickenswood Cl. SE19 169 H7
Dickerage La., N.Mal. 182 C3
Dickerage Rd., Kings.T. 182 C1
Dickerage Rd., N.Mal. 182 C1
Dickson Fold, Pnr. 66 D4
Dickson Rd. SE9 156 B3
Didsbury Cl. E6 116 C1
Barking Rd.
Digby Cres. N4 93 J2
Digby Gdns., Dag. 119 G1
Digby Pl., Croy. 202 C3
Digby Rd. E9 95 G5
Digby Rd., Bark. 99 J7
Digby St. E2 113 F3
Dighton Ct. SE5 35 J6
Dighton Ct. SE5 131 J6
Dighton Rd. SW18 149 F5
Digswell St. N7 93 G6
Holloway Rd.
Dilhorne Cl. SE12 173 H3
Dilke St. SW3 32 A5
Dilke St. SW3 129 J6
Dillwyn Cl. SE26 171 H4
Dilston Cl., Nthlt. 102 C3
Yeading La.
Dilston Gro. SE16 133 F4
Abbeyfield Rd.
Dilton Gdns. SW15 165 G1
Dimes Pl. W6 127 H4
King St.
Dimmock Dr., Grnf. 86 A5
Dimond Cl. E7 97 G4
Dimsdale Dr. NW9 88 C1
Dimsdale Dr., Enf. 44 D6
Dimsdale Wk. E13 115 G1
Stratford Rd.
Dimson Cres. E3 114 A4
Dingle Cl., Barn. 39 F6
Dingle Gdns. E14 114 A7
Dingley La. SW16 168 D2
Dingley Pl. EC1 12 A4
Dingley Pl. EC1 111 J3
Dingley Rd. EC1 11 J4
Dingley Rd. EC1 111 J3
Dingwall Av., Croy. 201 J2
Dingwall Gdns. NW11 72 D6
Dingwall Pl., Croy. 202 A2
Dingwall Rd.
Dingwall Rd. SW18 149 F7
Dingwall Rd., Croy. 202 A2
Dinmont St. E2 112/113 E2
Coate St.
Dinsdale Gdns. SE25 188 B5
Dinsdale Gdns., Barn. 41 E5
Dinsdale Rd. SE3 135 F6
Dinsmore Rd. SW12 150 B7
Dinton Rd. SW19 167 G6
Dinton Rd., Kings.T. 163 J7
Diploma Av. N2 73 H4
Dirleton Rd. E15 115 F1
Disbrowe Rd. W6 128 B6
Discovery Wk. E1 132 E1
Dishforth La. NW9 70 E1
Disney Ms. N4 75 H5
Chesterfield Gdns.
Disney Pl. SE1 28 A3
Disney St. SE1 28 A3
Dison Cl., Enf. 45 G1
Disraeli Cl. SE28 138 C1
Disraeli Cl. W4 126 D4
Acton La.
Disraeli Gdns. SW15 148 C4
Fawe Pk. Rd.
Disraeli Rd. E7 97 G6
Disraeli Rd. NW10 106 C2
Disraeli Rd. SW15 148 B4
Disraeli Rd. W5 125 G1
Diss St. E2 13 F3
Diss St. E2 112 C3
Distaff La. EC4 19 J5
Distaff La. EC4 111 J7
Distillery La. W6 127 J5
Fulham Palace Rd.
Distillery Rd. W6 127 J5
Distillery Wk., Brent. 125 H6
Pottery Rd.
Distin St. SE11 34 E2
Distin St. SE11 131 G4
District Rd., Wem. 86 E5
Ditch All. SE10 154 B1
Ditchburn St. E14 114 C7
Ditchfield Rd., Hayes 102 E4
Dittisham Rd. SE9 174 B4
Ditton Cl., T.Ditt. 180 D7
Ditton Gra. Cl., Surb. 195 G1
Ditton Gra. Dr., Surb. 195 G1
Ditton Hill, Surb. 195 F1
Ditton Hill Rd., Surb. 195 F1
Ditton Lawn, T.Ditt. 194 D1
Ditton Pl. SE20 189 E1
Ditton Reach, T.Ditt. 181 E6
Ditton Rd., Bexh. 158 D5
Ditton Rd., Sthl. 123 F4
Ditton Rd., Surb. 195 H1
Dittoncroft Cl., Croy. 202 B4
Divis Way SW15 147 H6
Dixon Clark Ct. N1 93 H6
Canonbury Rd.
Dixon Cl. E6 116 C6
Brandreth Rd.
Dixon Pl., W.Wick. 204 B1
Dixon Rd. SE14 153 H1
Dixon Rd. SE25 188 B3
Dixon's All. SE16 132 E2
Dobbin Cl., Har. 68 D2
Dobell Rd. SE9 156 C5

Dobree Av. NW10 89 H7
Dobson Cl. NW6 91 G7
Dock Hill Av. SE16 133 G2
Dock Rd. E16 115 F7
Dock Rd., Brent. 125 G7
Dock St. E1 21 H5
Dock St. E1 112 D7
Dockers Tanner Rd. E14 134 A3
Dockhead SE1 29 G4
Dockhead SE1 132 C2
Dockland St. E16 136 D1
Dockley Rd. SE16 29 H6
Dockley Rd. SE16 132 D3
Dockwell Cl., Felt. 142 A4
Dockyard Ind. Est. SE18 136 B3
Woolwich Ch. St.
Doctor Johnson Av. SW17 168 B3
Doctors Cl. SE26 171 F5
Docwra's Bldgs. N1 94 B6
Dod St. E14 114 A6
Dodbrooke Rd. SE27 169 G3
Doddington Gro. SE17 35 G5
Doddington Gro. SE17 131 H6
Doddington Pl. SE17 35 G5
Doddington Pl. SE17 131 H6
Dodsley Pl. N9 61 E3
Dodson St. SE1 27 F4
Dodson St. SE1 131 G2
Doebury Wk. SE18 138 A6
Prestwood Cl.
Doel Cl. SW19 167 F7
Dog Kennel Hill SE22 152 B3
Dog Kennel Hill Est. SE22 152 B3
Dog La. NW10 89 E4
Doggets Ct., Barn. 41 H5
Doggett Rd. SE6 154 A7
Doghurst Av., Hayes 121 E7
Doghurst Dr., West Dr. 121 E7
Doherty Rd. E13 115 G4
Dokal Ind. Est., Sthl. 122 E2
Dolben St. SE1 27 G2
Dolben St. SE1 131 H1
Dolby Ct. EC4 20 A5
Dolby Rd. SW6 148 C2
Dolland St. SE11 34 D4
Dolland St. SE11 131 F5
Dollis Av. N3 72 C1
Dollis Brook Wk., Barn. 40 B6
Dollis Cres., Ruis. 84 C1
Dollis Hill Av. NW2 89 H3
Dollis Hill Est. NW2 89 G3
Dollis Hill La. NW2 89 H3
Dollis Ms. N3 72 C1
Dollis Pk.
Dollis Pk. N3 72 C1
Dollis Rd. N3 56 B7
Dollis Rd. NW7 56 B7
Dollis Valley Grn. Wk. N20 57 F2
Totteridge La.
Dollis Valley Grn. Wk., Barn. 40 B6
Dollis Valley Way, Barn. 40 C6
Dolman Cl. N3 73 F2
Avondale Rd.
Dolman Rd. W4 126 D4
Dolman St. SW4 151 F4
Dolphin Cl. SE16 133 G2
Kinburn St.
Dolphin Cl. SE28 118 D6
Dolphin Cl., Surb. 181 G6
Dolphin Ct. NW11 72 B6
Dolphin La. E14 114 B7
Dolphin Rd., Nthlt. 103 F2
Dolphin Sq. SW1 33 G4
Dolphin Sq. SW1 130 C5
Dolphin Sq. W4 126 E7
Dolphin St., Kings.T. 181 H1
Dombey St. WC1 18 C1
Dombey St. WC1 111 F5
Dome Hill Pk. SE26 170 C4
Domett Cl. SE5 152 A4
Domfe Pl. E5 95 F4
Rushmore Rd.
Domingo St. EC1 11 J5
Dominica Cl. E13 115 J2
Dominion Rd., Croy. 188 C7
Dominion Rd., Sthl. 123 E3
Dominion St. EC2 20 C1
Domonic Dr. SE9 174 E4
Domville Cl. N20 57 G2
Don Phelan Cl. SE5 152 A1
Donald Dr., Rom. 82 C5
Donald Rd. E13 115 H1
Donald Rd., Croy. 187 F6
Donald Wds. Gdns., Surb. 196 B2
Donaldson Rd. NW6 108 C1
Donaldson Rd. SE18 156 D1
Doncaster Dr., Nthlt. 85 F5
Doncaster Gdns. N4 75 J6
Stanhope Gdns.
Doncaster Gdns., Nthlt. 85 F5
Doncaster Grn., Wat. 50 C5
Doncaster Rd. N9 44 E7
Doncel Ct. E4 46 D7
Donegal St. N1 10 D2
Donegal St. N1 111 F2
Doneraile St. SW6 148 A2
Dongola Rd. E13 115 H3
Dongola Rd. N17 76 B3
Dongola Rd. W. E13 115 H3
Balaam St.
Donington Av., Ilf. 81 F5
Donkey All. SE22 152 D7
Donkey La., Enf. 44 D2
Donne Ct. SE24 151 J6
Donne Pl. SW3 31 H1
Donne Pl. SW3 129 H4
Donne Pl., Mitch. 186 B4
Donne Rd., Dag. 100 C2
Donnefield Av., Edg. 53 H7
Donnington Rd. NW10 89 H7
Donnington Rd., Har. 69 G5
Donnington Rd., Wor.Pk. 197 G2
Donnybrook Rd. SW16 168 C7
Donovan Av. N10 74 B2
Doon St. SE1 26 E2
Doone Cl., Tedd. 162 D6
Dora Rd. SW19 166 D5
Dora St. E14 113 J6
Doral Way, Cars. 199 J5
Doran Gro. SE18 137 H7
Doran Mans. N2 73 J5
Great N. Rd.
Doran Wk. E15 96 C7
Dorchester Av. N13 59 J4
Dorchester Av., Bex. 176 D1
Dorchester Av., Har. 67 J6
Dorchester Cl., Nthlt. 85 H5
Dorchester Cl., Orp. 176 A7
Grovelands Rd.
Dorchester Ct. N14 42 B7
Dorchester Ct. SE24 151 J5
Dorchester Dr. SE24 151 J5
Dorchester Dr., Felt. 141 H6
Dorchester Gdns. E4 62 A4
Dorchester Gdns. NW11 72 D4
Dorchester Gro. W4 127 E5
Dorchester Ms., N.Mal. 182 D4
Elm Rd.
Dorchester Ms., Twick. 145 F7
Dorchester Rd., Mord. 185 E7
Dorchester Rd., Nthlt. 85 H5
Dorchester Rd., Wor.Pk. 197 J1
Dorchester Way, Har. 69 J6
Dorchester Waye, Hayes 102 C6
Dorcis Av., Bexh. 158 E2
Dordrecht Rd. W3 127 E1
Dore Av. E12 98 D5
Dore Gdns., Mord. 185 E7
Doreen Av. NW9 88 D1
Dorell Cl., Sthl. 103 F5
Doria Rd. SW6 148 C2
Doric Way NW1 9 H3
Doric Way NW1 110 D3
Dorien Rd. SW20 184 A2
Doris Av., Erith 159 J1
Doris Rd. E7 97 G7
Dorking Cl. SE8 133 J6
Dorking Cl., Wor.Pk. 198 A2
Dorlcote Rd. SW18 149 H7
Dorma Trd. Pk. E10 95 G1
Dorman Pl. N9 60 D2
Balham Rd.
Dorman Wk. NW10 88 D5
Garden Way
Dorman Way NW8 109 G1
Dormay St. SW18 148 E5
Dormer Cl. E15 97 F6
Dormer Cl., Barn. 40 A5
Dormers Av., Sthl. 103 G6
Dormers Ri., Sthl. 103 H6
Dormers Wells La., Sthl. 103 G6
Dornberg Cl. SE3 135 G7
Dornberg Rd. SE3 135 H7
Banchory Rd.
Dorncliffe Rd. SW6 148 B2
Dorney NW3 91 H7
Dorney Ri., Orp. 193 J4
Dorney Way, Houns. 143 E5
Dornfell St. NW6 90 C5
Dornton Rd. SW12 168 B2
Dornton Rd., S.Croy. 202 A5
Dorothy Av., Wem. 87 H7
Dorothy Evans Cl., Bexh. 159 H4
Dorothy Gdns., Dag. 100 B4
Dorothy Rd. SW11 149 J3
Dorrell Pl. SW9 151 G4
Brixton Rd.
Dorrien Wk. SW16 168 D2
Dorrington Ct. SE25 188 B2
Dorrington Pt. E3 114 B3
Bromley High St.
Dorrington St. EC1 19 E1
Dorrington St. EC1 111 G5
Dorrit Ms. N18 60 B4
Dorrit Way, Chis. 175 F6
Dors Cl. NW9 88 D1
Dorset Av., Sthl. 123 G4
Dorset Av., Well. 157 J4
Dorset Bldgs. EC4 19 G4
Dorset Cl. NW1 15 J1
Dorset Dr., Edg. 53 J6
Dorset Est. E2 13 G3
Dorset Est. E2 112 C3
Dorset Gdns., Mitch. 187 F4
Dorset Ms. N3 72 D1
Dorset Ms. SW1 24 D5
Dorset Pl. E15 96 D6
Dorset Pl. SW1 33 H3
Dorset Ri. EC4 19 G4
Dorset Ri. EC4 111 H6
Dorset Rd. E7 97 J7
Dorset Rd. N15 76 A4
Dorset Rd. N22 75 E1
Dorset Rd. SE9 174 B2
Dorset Rd. SW8 34 B7
Dorset Rd. SW8 131 F7
Dorset Rd. SW19 184 D1
Dorset Rd. W5 125 F3
Dorset Rd., Beck. 189 G3
Dorset Rd., Har. 67 J6
Dorset Rd., Mitch. 185 H2
Dorset Sq. NW1 7 J6
Dorset Sq. NW1 109 J4
Dorset St. W1 16 A2
Dorset St. W1 110 A5
Dorset Way, Twick. 162 A1
Dorset Waye, Houns. 123 F7
Dorville Cres. W6 127 H3
Dorville Rd. SE12 155 F5
Dothill Rd. SE18 137 G7
Douai Gro., Hmptn. 179 J1
Doubleday Rd., Loug. 49 F3
Doughty Ms. WC1 10 C6
Doughty Ms. WC1 111 F4
Doughty St. WC1 10 C5
Doughty St. WC1 111 F4
Douglas Av. E17 78 A1
Douglas Av., N.Mal. 183 H4
Douglas Av., Wem. 87 H7
Douglas Cl., Stan. 52 D5
Douglas Cl., Wall. 201 E7
Douglas Cres., Hayes 102 C4
Douglas Dr., Croy. 204 A3
Douglas Est. N1 93 J6
Douglas Ms. NW2 90 B3
Douglas Rd. E4 47 E7
Douglas Rd. E16 115 G5
Douglas Rd. N1 93 J7
Douglas Rd. N22 75 G1
Douglas Rd. NW6 108 C1
Douglas Rd., Houns. 143 H3
Douglas Rd., Ilf. 82 A6
Douglas Rd., Kings.T. 182 B2
Douglas Rd., Stai. 140 A6
Douglas Rd., Surb. 195 J2
Douglas Rd., Well. 158 B1
Douglas Sq., Mord. 184 D6
Douglas St. SW1 33 H2
Douglas St. SW1 130 D4
Douglas Ter. E17 78 A1
Douglas Av.
Douglas Way SE8 133 J7
Doulton Ms. NW6 90/91 E6
Lymington Rd.
Dounesforth Gdns. SW18 166 E1
Douro Pl. W8 22 B5
Douro Pl. W8 129 E3
Douro St. E3 114 A2
Douthwaite Sq. E1 29 J1
Dove App. E6 116 B5
Dove Cl. NW7 55 F7
Bunns La.
Dove Cl., Nthlt. 102 D4
Wayfarer Rd.
Dove Ct. EC2 20 B4
Dove Ho. Gdns. E4 62 A2
Dove Ms. SW5 30 C2
Dove Ms. SW5 129 F4
Dove Pk., Pnr. 51 G7
Dove Rd. N1 94 A6
Dove Row E2 112 D1
Dove Wk. SW1 32 B3
Dovecot Cl., Pnr. 66 B5
Dovecote Av. N22 75 G3
Dovecote Gdns. SW14 146 D3
Avondale Rd.
Dovecott Gdns. SW14 146 D3
North Worple Way
Dovedale Av., Har. 69 F6
Dovedale Av., Ilf. 80 D2
Dovedale Cl., Well. 158 A2
Dovedale Ri., Mitch. 167 J7
Dovedale Rd. SE22 153 E5
Dovedon Cl. N14 58 E2
Dovehouse Mead, Bark. 117 G2
Dovehouse St. SW3 31 G3
Dovehouse St. SW3 129 G5
Dover Cl. NW2 90 A2
Brent Ter.
Dover Cl., Rom. 83 J2
Dover Flats SE1 132 B4
Old Kent Rd.
Dover Gdns., Cars. 199 J3
Dover Ho. Rd. SW15 147 G4
Dover Pk. Dr. SW15 147 H6
Dover Patrol SE3 155 H2
Kidbrooke Way
Dover Rd. E12 97 J2
Dover Rd. N9 61 F2
Dover Rd. SE19 170 A6
Dover Rd., Rom. 82 E6
Dover St. W1 17 E6
Dover St. W1 110 B7
Dover Yd. W1 25 F1
Dovercourt Av., Th.Hth. 187 G4
Dovercourt Est. N1 94 A6
Dovercourt Gdns., Stan. 53 H5
Dovercourt La., Sutt. 199 F3
Dovercourt Rd. SE22 152 B6
Doverfield Rd. SW2 151 E6
Doveridge Gdns. N13 59 H4
Doves Cl., Brom. 206 B2
Dove's Yd. N1 111 G1
Doveton Rd., S.Croy. 202 A5
Doveton St. E1 113 F4
Malcolm Rd.
Dowanhill Rd. SE6 172 D1
Dowdeswell Cl. SW15 147 E4
Dowding Pl., Stan. 52 D6
Dowgate Hill EC4 20 B5
Dowgate Hill EC4 112 A7
Dowland St. W10 108 B2
Dowlas Est. SE5 36 D7
Dowlas St. SE5 36 D7
Dowlas St. SE5 132 B7
Dowlerville Rd., Orp. 207 J6
Dowman Cl. SW19 184/185 E1
Nelson Gro. Rd.
Down Cl., Nthlt. 102 B2
Down Hall Rd., Kings.T. 181 G1
Down Pl. W6 127 H4
Down Rd., Tedd. 163 E6
Down St. W1 24 D2
Down St. W1 130 B1
Down St., W.Mol. 179 G5
Down St. Ms. W1 24 D2
Down Way, Nthlt. 102 B3
Downage NW4 71 J3
Downalong, Bushey 52 A1
Downbarns Rd., Ruis. 84 D3
Downbury Ms. SW18 148 D6
Merton Rd.
Downderry Rd., Brom. 172 D3
Downe Cl., Well. 138 C7
Downe Rd., Mitch. 185 J2
Downend SE18 136/137 E7
Moordown
Downers Cotts. SW4 150 C4
The Pavement
Downes Cl., Twick. 144/145 E6
St. Margarets Rd.
Downes Ct. N21 59 G1
Downfield, Wor.Pk. 197 F1
Downfield Cl. W9 6 A6
Downfield Cl. W9 108 E4
Downham La., Brom. 172 D5
Downham Way
Downham Rd. N1 94 A7
Downham Way, Brom. 172 D5
Downhills Av. N17 76 A3
Downhills Pk. Rd. N17 75 J3

Downhills Way N17 75 J3
Downhurst Av. NW7 54 D5
Downing Cl., Har. 67 J3
Downing Dr., Grnf. 104 A1
Downing Rd., Dag. 119 F1
Downing St. SW1 26 A3
Downing St. SW1 130 E2
Downings E6 116 D6
Downland Cl. N20 57 F1
Downleys Cl. SE9 174 B2
Downman Rd. SE9 156 B3
Downs, The SW20 166 A7
Downs Av., Chis. 174 C5
Downs Av., Pnr. 67 F6
Downs Br. Rd., Beck. 190 D1
Downs Hill, Beck. 190 D1
Downs La. E5 94/95 E4
Downs Rd.
Downs Pk. Rd. E5 94 D5
Downs Pk. Rd. E8 94 C5
Downs Rd. E5 94 D4
Downs Rd., Beck. 190 B2
Downs Rd., Enf. 44 B4
Downs Rd., Th.Hth. 187 J1
Downs Vw., Islw. 124 C7
Downsbury Ms. SW18 148 D5
Merton Rd.
Downsell Rd. E15 96 C4
Downsfield Rd. E17 77 H6
Downshall Av., Ilf. 81 H6
Downshire Hill NW3 91 G4
Downside, Sun. 178 A1
Downside, Twick. 162 C3
Downside Cl. SW19 167 F6
Downside Cres. NW3 91 H5
Downside Cres. W13 104 D4
Downside Rd., Sutt. 199 G6
Downside Wk., Nthlt. 103 F3
Downsview Gdns. SE19 169 H7
Downsview Rd. SE19 169 J7
Downsway, Orp. 207 H5
Downton Av. SW2 169 E2
Downtown Rd. SE16 133 H2
Downway N12 57 H7
Dowrey St. N1 111 G1
Richmond Av.
Dowsett Rd. N17 76 C2
Dowson Cl. SE5 152 A4
Doyce St. SE1 27 J3
Doyle Gdns. NW10 107 G1
Doyle Rd. SE25 188 D4
D'Oyley St. SW1 32 B1
D'Oyley St. SW1 130 A4
Doynton St. N19 92 B2
Draco St. SE17 35 J5
Draco St. SE17 131 J6
Dragmire La., Mitch. 185 G4
Dragon Rd. SE15 36 D6
Dragon Rd. SE15 132 B6
Dragonfly Cl. E13 115 H3
Hollybush St.
Dragoon Rd. SE8 133 J5
Dragor Rd. NW10 106 C4
Drake Cl. SE16 133 G2
Middleton Dr.
Drake Ct. SE19 170 C5
Drake Ct., Har. 85 F1
Drake Cres. SE28 118 C6
Drake Rd. SE4 154 A3
Drake Rd., Chess. 196 A5
Drake Rd., Croy. 187 F7
Drake Rd., Har. 85 F2
Drake Rd., Mitch. 186 A6
Drake St. WC1 18 C2
Drake St., Enf. 44 A1
Drakefell Rd. SE4 153 G2
Drakefell Rd. SE14 153 G2
Drakefield Rd. SW17 168 A3
Drakeley Ct. N5 93 H4
Highbury Hill
Drakes Ctyd. NW6 90 C7
Drakes Wk. E6 116 C1
Drakewood Rd. SW16 168 D7
Draper Cl., Belv. 139 F4
Draper Cl., Islw. 124 A7
Thornbury Rd.
Draper Pl. N1 111 H1
Essex Rd.
Drapers Gdns. EC2 112 A6
Copthall Av.
Drapers Rd. E15 96 D4
Drapers Rd. N17 76 C3
Drapers Rd., Enf. 43 H2
Drappers Way SE16 37 J1
Draven Cl., Brom. 191 F7
Drawdock Rd. SE10 134 D1
Drawell Cl. SE18 137 H5
Drax Av. SW20 165 G7
Draxmont SW19 166 B6
Dray Gdns. SW2 151 F5
Draycot Rd. E11 79 H6
Draycot Rd., Surb. 196 A1
Draycott Av. SW3 31 H1
Draycott Av. SW3 129 H4
Draycott Av., Har. 69 E6
Draycott Cl., Har. 69 E6
Draycott Ms. SW6 148 C2
New Kings Rd.
Draycott Pl. SW3 31 J2
Draycott Pl. SW3 129 J4
Draycott Ter. SW3 32 A1
Draycott Ter. SW3 129 J4
Drayford Cl. W9 108 C4
Draymans Way, Islw. 144 C3
Drayside Ms., Sthl. 123 F2
Kingston Rd.
Drayson Ms. W8 128 D2
Drayton Av. W13 104 D7
Drayton Av., Loug. 48 C6
Drayton Av., Orp. 207 E1
Drayton Br. Rd. W7 104 C7
Drayton Br. Rd. W13 104 C7
Drayton Cl., Houns. 143 F5
Bramley Way
Drayton Cl., Ilf. 99 G1
Drayton Gdns. N21 43 H7
Drayton Gdns. SW10 30 D3
Drayton Gdns. SW10 129 F5
Drayton Gdns. W13 104 D7
Drayton Gdns., West Dr. 120 B2
Drayton Grn. W13 104 D7
Drayton Grn. Rd. W13 104 E7
Drayton Gro. W13 104 D7
Drayton Pk. N5 93 G5
Drayton Pk. Ms. N5 93 G5
Drayton Pk.
Drayton Rd. E11 96 D1
Drayton Rd. N17 76 B2
Drayton Rd. NW10 107 F1
Drayton Rd. W13 104 D7
Drayton Rd., Borwd. 38 A4
Drayton Rd., Croy. 201 H2
Drayton Waye, Har. 69 E6
Dreadnought St. SE10 135 E3
Dresden Cl. NW6 91 E6
Dresden Rd. N19 92 D1
Dressington Av. SE4 154 A6
Drew Av. NW7 56 B6
Drew Gdns., Grnf. 86 C6
Drew Rd. E16 136 B1
Drewstead Rd. SW16 168 D2
Driffield Rd. E3 113 H2
Drift, The, Brom. 206 A3
Drift Way, Rich. 163 J1
Driftway, The, Mitch. 186 A1
Drinkwater Rd., Har. 85 H2
Drive, The E4 46 D7
Drive, The E17 78 B4
Drive, The E18 79 G4
Drive, The N3 56 D7
Drive, The N6 73 J5
Fordington Rd.
Drive, The N11 58 C6
Drive, The NW10 107 F1
Longstone Av.
Drive, The NW11 72 B7
Drive, The SW6 148 B2
Fulham Rd.
Drive, The SW16 187 F3
Drive, The SW20 165 J7
Drive, The W3 106 C6
Drive, The, Bark. 99 J7
Drive, The, Barn. 40 B3
Drive, The (New Barnet), Barn. 41 F6
Drive, The, Beck. 190 A2
Drive, The, Bex. 158 C6
Drive, The, Buck.H. 47 J7
Drive, The, Chis. 193 J3
Drive, The (Scadbury Pk.), Chis. 193 H1
Drive, The, Edg. 54 A5
Drive, The, Enf. 44 A1
Drive, The, Epsom 197 F6
Drive, The, Erith 139 H7
Drive, The, Felt. 142 C7
Drive, The, Har. 67 G7
Drive, The, Houns. 144 A2
Drive, The, Ilf. 98 C1
Drive, The, Islw. 144 A2
Drive, The, Kings.T. 164 C7
Drive, The, Loug. 48 B3
Drive, The, Mord. 185 G5
Drive, The, Orp. 207 J2
Drive, The, Rom. 83 J1
Drive, The, Sid. 176 B3
Drive, The, Surb. 181 H7
Drive, The, Th.Hth. 188 A4
Drive, The, Wem. 88 C2
Drive, The, W.Wick. 190 D7
Driveway, The E17 78 B6
Hoe St.
Droitwich Cl. SE26 170 D3
Dromey Gdns., Har. 52 C7
Dromore Rd. SW15 148 B6
Dronfield Gdns., Dag. 100 C5
Droop St. W10 108 B4
Drover La. SE15 133 E7
Drovers Pl. SE15 133 E7
Drovers Rd., S.Croy. 202 A5
Droveway, Loug. 49 E2
Druce Rd. SE21 152 B6
Druid St. SE1 28 E3
Druid St. SE1 132 B2
Druids Way, Brom. 190 D4
Drum St. E1 21 G3
Drumaline Ridge, Wor.Pk. 197 E2
Drummond Cres. NW1 9 H3
Drummond Cres. NW1 110 D3
Drummond Dr., Stan. 52 C7
Drummond Gate SW1 33 J3
Drummond Gate SW1 130 D5
Drummond Pl., Rich. 145 H4
Drummond Pl., Twick. 144 E6
Drummond Rd. E11 79 J6
Drummond Rd. SE16 132 E3
Drummond Rd., Croy. 201 J2
Drummond St. NW1 9 F5
Drummond St. NW1 110 C4
Drummonds, The, Buck.H. 63 H2
Drury Cres., Croy. 201 G2
Drury La. WC2 18 B4
Drury La. WC2 111 E6
Drury Rd., Har. 67 J7
Drury Way NW10 88 D5
Drury Way Ind. Est. NW10 88 C5
Dryad St. SW15 148 A3
Dryburgh Gdns. NW9 70 A3
Dryburgh Rd. SW15 147 H3
Dryden Av. W7 104 C6
Dryden Cl., Ilf. 65 J6
Dryden Ct. SE11 35 F2
Dryden Ct. SE11 131 G4
Dryden Rd. SW19 167 F6
Dryden Rd., Enf. 44 B6
Dryden Rd., Har. 68 C1
Dryden Rd., Well. 157 H1
Dryden St. WC2 18 B4
Dryfield Cl. NW10 88 C6
Dryfield Rd., Edg. 54 C6
Dryfield Wk. SE8 134 A6
New King St.
Dryhill Rd., Belv. 139 F6
Dryland Av., Orp. 207 J4
Drylands Rd. N8 75 E6
Drysdale Av. E4 46 B7
Drysdale Pl. N1 12 E3
Drysdale St. N1 12 E3
Drysdale St. N1 112 B3
Du Burstow Ter. W7 124 B2
Du Cane Cl. W12 107 J6
Du Cane Ct. SW17 168 A1
Du Cane Rd. W12 107 F6
Du Cros Dr., Stan. 53 F6
Du Cros Rd. W3 126/127 E1
The Vale
Dublin Av. E8 112 D1
Ducal St. E2 13 G4
Duchess Cl. N11 58 B5
Duchess Cl., Sutt. 199 F4
Duchess Gro., Buck.H. 63 H2
Duchess Ms. W1 16 E2
Duchess of Bedford's Wk. W8 128 D2
Duchess St. W1 16 E2
Duchess St. W1 110 B5
Duchy St. SE1 27 F1
Duchy St. SE1 131 G1
Ducie St. SW4 151 F4
Duck La. W1 17 H4
Duck Lees La., Enf. 45 H4
Duckett Ms. N4 75 H6
Duckett Rd.
Duckett Rd. N4 75 H6
Duckett St. E1 113 G5
Ducks Wk., Twick. 145 F5
Dudden Hill La. NW10 89 F4
Duddington Cl. SE9 174 A4
Dudley Av., Har. 69 F3
Dudley Ct. NW11 72 C4
Dudley Dr., Mord. 184 B7
Dudley Dr., Ruis. 84 B5
Dudley Gdns. W13 125 E2
Dudley Gdns., Har. 86 A1
Dudley Rd. E17 78 A2
Dudley Rd. N3 72 E2
Dudley Rd. NW6 108 B2
Dudley Rd. SW19 166 D6
Dudley Rd., Har. 85 J2
Dudley Rd., Ilf. 99 E4
Dudley Rd., Kings.T. 181 J3
Dudley Rd., Rich. 145 J2
Dudley Rd., Sthl. 122 D2
Dudley Rd., Walt. 178 A6
Dudley St. W2 14 E2
Dudley St. W2 109 G5
Dudlington Rd. E5 95 F2
Dudmaston Ms. SW3 31 F3
Dudsbury Rd., Sid. 176 B6
Dudset La., Houns. 142 A1
Duff St. E14 114 B6
Dufferin Av. EC1 12 B6
Dufferin St. EC1 12 A6
Dufferin St. EC1 111 J4
Duffield Cl., Har. 68 C5
Duffield Dr. N15 76 C4
Copperfield Dr.
Dufour's Pl. W1 17 G4
Dugard Way SE11 35 G1
Dugard Way SE11 131 H4
Duke Gdns., Ilf. 81 G4
Duke Rd.
Duke Humphrey Rd. SE3 155 E1
Duke of Cambridge Cl., Twick. 144 A6
Duke of Edinburgh Rd., Sutt. 199 G2
Duke of Wellington Pl. SW1 24 C3
Duke of Wellington Pl. SW1 130 A2
Duke of York St. SW1 25 G1
Duke of York St. SW1 130 C1
Duke Rd. W4 126 D5
Duke Rd., Ilf. 81 G4
Duke Shore Pl. E14 113 J7
Narrow St.
Duke Shore Wf. E14 113 J7
Narrow St.
Duke St. SW1 25 G1
Duke St. SW1 130 C1
Duke St. W1 16 C3
Duke St. W1 110 A6
Duke St., Rich. 145 G4
Duke St., Sutt. 199 G4
Duke St. Hill SE1 28 C1
Dukes Av. N3 72 E1
Dukes Av. N10 74 C3
Dukes Av. W4 126 D5
Dukes Av., Edg. 53 J6
Dukes Av., Har. 67 F6
Dukes Av. (Wealdstone), Har. 68 B4
Dukes Av., Houns. 142 E4
Dukes Av., Kings.T. 163 F4
Dukes Av., N.Mal. 183 F3
Dukes Av., Nthlt. 85 E7
Dukes Av., Rich. 163 F4
Dukes Cl., Hmptn. 161 F5
Dukes Ct. E6 116 D1
Dukes Grn. Av., Felt. 142 A5
Dukes Head Yd. N6 92 B1
Highgate High St.
Dukes La. W8 128 D2
Duke's Meadows W4 146 C2
Great Chertsey Rd.
Dukes Ms. N10 74 B3
Dukes Av.
Duke's Ms. W1 16 C3
Dukes Orchard, Bex. 177 J1
Duke's Pas. E17 78 C4
Dukes Pl. EC3 21 E4
Dukes Pl. EC3 112 B6
Dukes Rd. E6 116 D1
Dukes Rd. W3 106 A5
Duke's Rd. WC1 9 J4
Duke's Rd. WC1 110 D3
Dukes Way, W.Wick. 205 E3
Duke's Yd. W1 16 C5
Dukesthorpe Rd. SE26 171 G4
Dulas St. N4 93 F1
Everleigh St.
Dulford St. W11 108 B7
Dulka Rd. SW11 149 J5
Dulverton Rd. SE9 175 F2
Dulverton Rd., Ruis. 84 A1
Dulwich Common SE21 170 B1
Dulwich Common SE22 170 B1
Dulwich Lawn Cl. SE22 152 C5
Colwell Rd.
Dulwich Oaks, The SE21 170 B3
Dulwich Rd. SE24 151 G5
Dulwich Village SE21 152 B6
Dulwich Wd. Av. SE19 170 B4
Dulwich Wd. Pk. SE19 170 B4

Dumbarton Rd. SW2 151 E6
Dumbleton Cl., Kings.T. 182 B1
Gloucester Rd.
Dumbreck Rd. SE9 156 D4
Dumont Rd. N16 94 B3
Dumpton Pl. NW1 92 A7
Gloucester Av.
Dunbar Av. SW16 187 G2
Dunbar Av., Beck. 189 H4
Dunbar Av., Dag. 101 G3
Dunbar Cl., Hayes 102 A5
Dunbar Ct., Sutt. 199 G5
Dunbar Gdns., Dag. 101 G5
Dunbar Rd. E7 97 G6
Dunbar Rd. N22 75 G1
Dunbar Rd., N.Mal. 182 C4
Dunbar St. SE27 169 J3
Dunblane Cl., Edg. 54 B2
Tayside Dr.
Dunblane Rd. SE9 156 B3
Dunboyne Rd. NW3 91 J5
Dunbridge St. E2 13 J5
Dunbridge St. E2 112 D4
Duncan Cl., Barn. 41 F4
Duncan Gro. W3 106 E6
Duncan Rd. E8 112 E1
Duncan Rd., Rich. 145 H4
Duncan St. N1 11 G1
Duncan St. N1 111 H2
Duncan Ter. N1 11 G2
Duncan Ter. N1 111 H2
Duncannon St. WC2 18 A6
Duncannon St. WC2 110 E7
Dunch St. E1 112/113 E6
Watney St.
Duncombe Hill SE23 153 H7
Duncombe Rd. N19 92 D1
Duncrievie Rd. SE13 154 D6
Duncroft SE18 137 H7
Dundalk Rd. SE4 153 H3
Dundas Gdns., W.Mol. 179 H3
Dundas Rd. SE15 153 F2
Dundee Rd. E13 115 H2
Dundee Rd. SE25 188 E5
Dundee St. E1 132 E1
Dundee Way, Enf. 45 H3
Dundela Gdns., Wor.Pk. 197 H4
Dundonald Cl. E6 116 B6
Northumberland Rd.
Dundonald Rd. NW10 108 A1
Dundonald Rd. SW19 166 B7
Dunedin Rd. E10 96 B3
Dunedin Rd., Ilf. 99 F1
Dunedin Way, Hayes 102 C4
Dunelm Gro. SE27 169 J4
Dunelm St. E1 113 G6
Dunfield Gdns. SE6 172 B4
Dunfield Rd. SE6 172 B5
Dunford Rd. N7 93 F4
Dungarvan Av. SW15 147 G4
Dunheved Cl., Th.Hth. 187 G6
Dunheved Rd. N., Th.Hth. 187 G6
Dunheved Rd. S., Th.Hth. 187 G6
Dunheved Rd. W., Th.Hth. 187 G6
Dunholme Grn. N9 60 C3
Dunholme La. N9 60 C3
Dunholme Rd.
Dunholme Rd. N9 60 C3
Dunkeld Rd. SE25 188 A4
Dunkeld Rd., Dag. 100 B2
Dunkery Rd. SE9 174 A4
Dunkirk St. SE27 169 J4
Waring St.
Dunlace Rd. E5 95 F4
Dunleary Cl., Houns. 143 F7
Dunley Dr., Croy. 204 B7
Dunlin Ho. W13 104 C4
Dunloe Av. N17 76 A3
Dunloe St. E2 13 F2
Dunloe St. E2 112 C2
Dunlop Pl. SE16 29 G6
Dunmore Pt. E2 13 F4
Dunmore Rd. NW6 108 B1
Dunmore Rd. SW20 183 J1
Dunmow Cl., Felt. 160 E4
Dunmow Cl., Loug. 48 B6
Dunmow Cl., Rom. 82 C5
Dunmow Ho., Dag. 118 B1
Dunmow Rd. E15 96 D4
Dunmow Wk. N1 111 J1
Popham St.
Dunn Mead NW9 55 F7
Field Mead
Dunn St. E8 94 C5
Dunnage Cres. SE16 133 H4
Plough Way
Dunnock Cl. N9 61 G1
Dunnock Cl., Borwd. 38 A4
Dunnock Rd. E6 116 B6
Dunns Pas. WC1 18 B3
Dunollie Pl. NW5 92 C5
Dunollie Rd.
Dunollie Rd. NW5 92 C5
Dunoon Rd. SE23 153 F7
Dunraven Dr., Enf. 43 G2
Dunraven Rd. W12 127 G1
Dunraven St. W1 16 A5
Dunsany Rd. W14 128 A3
Dunsfold Way, Croy. 204 B7
Dunsford Way SW15 147 H6
Dover Pk. Dr.
Dunsmore Cl., Hayes 102/103 E4
Kingsash Dr.
Dunsmore Rd., Walt. 178 B6
Dunsmure Rd. N16 94 B1
Dunspring La., Ilf. 80 E2
Dunstable Ms. W1 16 C1
Dunstable Rd., Rich. 145 H4
Dunstable Rd., W.Mol. 179 F4
Dunstall Rd. SW20 165 H6
Dunstall Way, W.Mol. 179 H3
Dunstan Cl. N2 73 F3
Thomas More Way
Dunstan Rd. NW11 90 C1
Dunstans Gro. SE22 152 E6
Dunstans Rd. SE22 152 D7
Dunster Av., Mord. 198 A1
Dunster Cl., Barn. 40 A4
Dunster Cl., Rom. 83 J2
Dunster Ct. EC3 20 E5
Dunster Dr. NW9 88 C1
Dunster Gdns. NW6 90 C7
Dunster Way, Har. 85 E3
Dunsterville Way SE1 28 C4
Dunston Rd. E8 112 C1
Dunston Rd. SW11 150 A2
Dunston St. E8 112 C1
Dunton Cl., Surb. 195 H1
Dunton Rd. E10 78 B7
Dunton Rd. SE1 37 F3
Dunton Rd. SE1 132 C5
Duntshill Rd. SW18 167 E1
Dunvegan Cl., W.Mol. 179 H4
Dunvegan Rd. SE9 156 C4
Dunwich Rd., Bexh. 159 F1
Dunworth Ms. W11 108 C6
Portobello Rd.
Duplex Ride SW1 24 A4
Dupont Rd. SW20 184 A2
Dupont St. E14 113 H5
Maroon St.
Duppas Av., Croy. 201 H4
Violet La.
Duppas Hill La., Croy. 201 H4
Duppas Hill Rd.
Duppas Hill Rd., Croy. 201 H4
Duppas Hill Ter., Croy. 201 H3
Duppas Rd., Croy. 201 G3
Dupree Rd. SE7 135 H5
Dura Den Cl., Beck. 172 B7
Durand Cl., Cars. 199 J1
Durand Gdns. SW9 151 F1
Durand Way NW10 88 C7
Durands Wk. SE16 133 J2
Durant St. E2 13 H3
Durant St. E2 112 D3
Durants Pk. Av., Enf. 45 G4
Durants Rd., Enf. 45 F4
Durban Gdns., Dag. 101 J7
Durban Rd. E15 114 E3
Durban Rd. E17 77 J1
Durban Rd. N17 60 B6
Durban Rd. SE27 169 J4
Durban Rd., Beck. 189 J2
Durban Rd., Ilf. 99 H1
Durbin Rd., Chess. 195 H4
Durdans Rd., Sthl. 103 F6
Durell Gdns., Dag. 100 D5
Durell Rd., Dag. 100 D5
Durford Cres. SW15 165 H1
Durham Av., Brom. 191 F4
Durham Av., Houns. 123 F5
Durham Av., Wdf.Grn. 64 A5
Durham Cl. SW20 183 H2
Durham Rd.
Durham Hill, Brom. 173 F4
Durham Ho. St. WC2 18 B6
Durham Pl. SW3 31 J4
Durham Pl., Ilf. 99 F4
Eton Rd.
Durham Ri. SE18 137 F5
Durham Rd. E12 98 A4
Durham Rd. E16 115 E4
Durham Rd. N2 73 H3
Durham Rd. N7 93 F2
Durham Rd. N9 60 D2
Durham Rd. SW20 183 H1
Durham Rd. W5 125 G3
Durham Rd., Borwd. 38 C3
Durham Rd., Brom. 191 F3
Durham Rd., Dag. 101 J5
Durham Rd., Felt. 142 C7
Durham Rd., Har. 67 H5
Durham Rd., Sid. 176 B5
Durham Row E1 113 H5
Durham St. SE11 34 C4
Durham St. SE11 131 F5
Durham Ter. W2 14 A3
Durham Ter. W2 108 E6
Durham Wf., Brent. 125 F7
London Rd.
Durham Yd. E2 112/113 E3
Teesdale St.
Durley Av., Pnr. 67 E7
Durley Rd. N16 76 B7
Durlston Rd. E5 94 D2
Durlston Rd., Kings.T. 163 H6
Durnell Way, Loug. 48 D3
Durnford St. N15 76 B5
Durnford St. SE10 134 C6
Greenwich Ch. St.
Durning Rd. SE19 170 A5
Durnsford Av. SW19 166 D2
Durnsford Rd. N11 74 D1
Durnsford Rd. SW19 166 D2
Durrant Way, Orp. 207 G5
Durrell Rd. SW6 148 C1
Durrington Av. SW20 183 J1
Durrington Pk. Rd. SW20 165 J7
Durrington Rd. E5 95 H4
Dursley Cl. SE3 155 J2
Dursley Gdns. SE3 156 A1
Dursley Rd. SE3 155 J2
Durward St. E1 112 E5
Durweston Ms. W1 16 A1
Durweston St. W1 16 A1
Durweston St. W1 109 J5
Dury Rd., Barn. 40 C1
Dutch Barn Cl., Stai. 140 A6
Dutch Gdns., Kings.T. 164 B6
Windmill Ri.
Dutch Yd. SW18 148 D5
Wandsworth High St.
Duthie St. E14 114 C7
Prestons Rd.
Dutton St. SE10 154 C1
Duxberry Cl., Brom. 192 B5
Southborough La.
Duxford Ho. SE2 138 D2
Wolvercote Rd.
Dwight Ct. SW6 148 B2
Burlington Rd.
Dye Ho. La. E3 114 A1
Dyer's Bldgs. EC1 19 E2
Dyers Hall Rd. E11 96 E1
Dyers La. SW15 147 H4
Dykes Way, Brom. 191 F3
Dylan Rd. SE24 151 H4
Dylan Rd., Belv. 139 G3
Dylan Thomas Ho. N8 75 F4
Dylways SE5 152 A4
Dymchurch Cl., Ilf. 80 D2
Dymchurch Cl., Orp. 207 H4
Dymes Path SW19 166 A2
Queensmere Rd.
Dymock St. SW6 148 E3
Dymond Est. SW17 167 H3
Glenburnie Rd.
Dyne Rd. NW6 90 C7
Dyneley Rd. SE12 173 J4
Dynevor Rd. N16 94 B3
Dynevor Rd., Rich. 145 H5
Dynham Rd. NW6 90 D7
Dyott St. WC1 18 A3
Dyott St. WC1 110 D6
Dysart Av., Kings.T. 163 F5
Dysart St. EC2 12 D6
Dyson Rd. E11 79 E6
Dyson Rd. E15 97 F6
Dysons Rd. N18 61 E5

E

Eade Rd. N4 75 J7
Eagans Cl. N2 73 H3
Market Pl.
Eagle Av., Rom. 82 E6
Eagle Cl. SE16 133 F5
Varcoe Rd.
Eagle Cl., Enf. 45 F4
Eagle Cl., Wall. 201 E6
Eagle Ct. EC1 19 G1
Eagle Ct. EC1 111 H5
Eagle Dr. NW9 71 E2
Eagle Hill SE19 170 A6
Eagle La. E11 79 G4
Eagle Ms. N1 94 B6
Tottenham Rd.
Eagle Pl. SW1 17 G6
Eagle Pl. SW7 30 D3
Eagle Rd., Wem. 87 G7
Eagle St. WC1 18 C2
Eagle St. WC1 111 F5
Eagle Ter., Wdf.Grn. 63 H7
Eagle Wf. E14 114 B5
Broomfield St.
Eagle Wf. Rd. N1 12 A1
Eagle Wf. Rd. N1 111 J2
Eaglesfield Rd. SE18 137 E7
Ealdham Sq. SE9 155 J4
Ealing Cl., Borwd. 38 D1
Ealing Downs Ct., Grnf. 104 D3
Perivale La.
Ealing Grn. W5 125 G1
Ealing Pk. Gdns. W5 125 F4
Ealing Rd., Brent. 125 G5
Ealing Rd., Nthlt. 85 G7
Ealing Rd., Wem. 105 H1
Ealing Village W5 105 H6
Eamont St. NW8 7 G1
Eamont St. NW8 109 H2
Eardley Cres. SW5 128 D5
Eardley Pt. SE18 136/137 E4
Wilmount St.
Eardley Rd. SW16 168 C5
Eardley Rd., Belv. 139 G5
Earl Cl. N11 58 B5
Earl Ri. SE18 137 G4
Earl Rd. SW14 146 C4
Elm Rd.
Earl St. EC2 20 D1
Earl St. EC2 112 A5
Earldom Rd. SW15 147 J4
Earle Gdns., Kings.T. 163 H6
Earlham Gro. E7 97 F5
Earlham Gro. N22 59 F7
Earlham St. WC2 17 J4
Earlham St. WC2 110 D6
Earls Ct. Gdns. SW5 30 A2
Earls Ct. Gdns. SW5 128 E4
Earls Ct. Rd. SW5 128 D4
Earls Ct. Rd. W8 128 D3
Earls Ct. Sq. SW5 30 A3
Earls Ct. Sq. SW5 128 E5
Earls Cres., Har. 68 B4
Earl's Path, Loug. 47 J2
Earls Ter. W8 128 C3
Earls Wk. W8 128 D3
Earls Wk., Dag. 100 B4
Earls Way, Orp. 207 J2
Station Rd.
Earlsdown Ho., Bark. 117 G2
Wheelers Cross
Earlsferry Way N1 111 F1
Earlsfield Rd. SW18 167 F1
Earlshall Rd. SE9 156 C4
Earlsmead, Har. 85 F4
Earlsmead Rd. N15 76 C5
Earlsmead Rd. NW10 107 J2
Earlsthorpe Ms. SW12 150 A6
Earlsthorpe Rd. SE26 171 G4
Earlstoke St. EC1 11 G3
Earlston Gro. E9 113 E1
Earlswood Av., Th.Hth. 187 G5
Earlswood Cl. SE10 134/135 E5
Earlswood St.
Earlswood Gdns., Ilf. 80 D3
Earlswood St. SE10 135 E5
Early Ms. NW1 110 B1
Arlington Rd.
Earnshaw St. WC2 17 J3
Earnshaw St. WC2 110 D6
Earsby St. W14 128 B4
Easby Cres., Mord. 185 E6
Easebourne Rd., Dag. 100 C5
Easedale Ho., Islw. 144 C5
Summerwood Rd.
Easley's Ms. W1 16 C3
East Acton La. W3 126 E1
East Arbour St. E1 113 G6
East Av. E12 98 B7
East Av. E17 78 B4
East Av., Hayes 121 J2
East Av., Sthl. 103 F7
East Av., Wall. 201 F5
East Bank N16 76 B7
East Barnet Rd., Barn. 41 H6
East Churchfield Rd. W3 126 D1
East Cl. W5 106 A4
East Cl., Barn. 42 A4
East Cl., Grnf. 103 J2
East Ct., Wem. 87 F2
East Cres. N11 57 J4
East Cres., Enf. 44 C5

East Cross Route E3 114 A1
East Duck Lees La., Enf. 45 H4
East Dulwich Gro. SE22 152 B6
East Dulwich Rd. SE15 152 C4
East Dulwich Rd. SE22 152 C4
East End Rd. N2 73 F3
East End Rd. N3 72 D2
East End Way, Pnr. 67 E3
East Entrance, Dag. 119 H2
East Ferry Rd. E14 134 B3
East Gdns. SW17 167 H6
East Ham Ind. Est. E6 116 B4
East Ham Manor Way E6 116 D6
East Harding St. EC4 19 F3
East Heath Rd. NW3 91 G3
East Hill SW18 149 E5
East Hill, Wem. 88 A2
East India Dock Rd. E14 114 D6
East La. SE16 29 H4
East La. SE16 132 D2
East La., Kings.T. 181 G3
High St.
East La., Wem. 87 G3
East Mascalls SE7 135 J6
Mascalls Rd.
East Mead, Ruis. 84 D3
East Mt. St. E1 113 E5
East Pk. Cl., Rom. 82 D5
East Parkside SE10 135 E2
East Pas. EC1 19 H1
East Pier E1 132/133 E1
Wapping High St.
East Pl. SE27 169 J4
Pilgrim Hill
East Poultry Av. EC1 19 G2
East Ramp, Houns. 140 E1
East Rd. E15 115 G1
East Rd. N1 12 B4
East Rd. N1 112 A3
East Rd. SW19 167 F6
East Rd., Barn. 58 A1
East Rd., Edg. 70 B1
East Rd., Felt. 141 G7
East Rd., Kings.T. 181 H1
East Rd. (Chadwell Heath), Rom. 82 E5
East Rd., Well. 158 B2
East Rd., West Dr. 120 C4
East Rochester Way SE9 157 H4
East Rochester Way, Bex. 159 J7
East Rochester Way, Sid. 157 H4
East Row E11 79 G6
East Row W10 108 B4
East Sheen Av. SW14 146 D4
East Smithfield E1 21 G6
East Smithfield E1 112 C7
East St. SE17 36 A3
East St. SE17 131 J5
East St., Bark. 99 F7
East St., Bexh. 159 G4
East St., Brent. 125 F7
East St., Brom. 191 G2
East Surrey Gro. SE15 132 C7
East Tenter St. E1 21 G4
East Tenter St. E1 112 C6
East Twrs., Pnr. 66 D5
East Vw. E4 62 C5
East Vw., Barn. 40 C3
East Wk., Barn. 42 A7
East Wk., Hayes 122 A1
East Way E11 79 H5
East Way, Brom. 191 G7
East Way, Croy. 203 H2
East Way, Hayes 122 A1
East Way, Ruis. 84 A1
East Woodside, Bex. 177 E1
Eastbank Rd., Hmptn. 161 J5
Eastbourne Av. W3 106 D6
Eastbourne Gdns. SW14 146 C3
Eastbourne Ms. W2 14 D3
Eastbourne Ms. W2 109 F6
Eastbourne Rd. E6 116 D3
Eastbourne Rd. E15 115 E1
Eastbourne Rd. N15 76 B6
Eastbourne Rd. SW17 168 A6
Eastbourne Rd. W4 126 C6
Eastbourne Rd., Brent. 125 F5
Eastbourne Rd., Felt. 160 D2
Eastbourne Ter. W2 14 D3
Eastbourne Ter. W2 109 F6
Eastbournia Av. N9 61 E3
Eastbrook Av. N9 45 F7
Eastbrook Av., Dag. 101 J4
Eastbrook Rd. SE3 135 H7
Eastbury Av., Bark. 117 H1
Eastbury Av., Enf. 44 B1
Eastbury Ct., Bark. 117 H1
Eastbury Gro. W4 127 E5
Eastbury Ho., Bark. 117 J1
Eastbury Rd. E6 116 D4
Eastbury Rd., Kings.T. 163 H7
Eastbury Rd., Orp. 193 G6
Eastbury Sq., Bark. 117 J1
Eastbury Ter. E1 113 G4
Eastcastle St. W1 17 F3
Eastcastle St. W1 110 C6
Eastcheap EC3 20 C5
Eastcheap EC3 112 A7
Eastchurch Rd., Houns. 141 H2
Eastcombe Av. SE7 135 H6
Eastcote, Orp. 207 J1
Eastcote Av., Grnf. 86 D5
Eastcote Av., Har. 85 H2
Eastcote Av., W.Mol. 179 F5
Eastcote La., Har. 85 G3
Eastcote La., Nthlt. 85 G7
Eastcote La. N., Nthlt. 85 F6
Eastcote Pl., Pnr. 66 B6
Eastcote Rd., Har. 85 J3
Eastcote Rd., Pnr. 66 D5
Eastcote Rd. (Eastcote Village), Pnr. 66 A6
Eastcote Rd., Well. 157 G2
Eastcote St. SW9 151 F2
Eastcote Vw., Pnr. 66 C4
Eastcroft Rd., Epsom 197 E7
Eastdown Pk. SE13 154 D4
Eastern Av. E11 79 J6
Eastern Av., Ilf. 80 B6
Eastern Av., Pnr. 66 D7
Eastern Av., Rom. 82 C4
Eastern Av. W., Rom. 82 E4
Eastern Ind. Est., Erith 139 G2
Eastern Perimeter Rd., Houns. 141 J3
Eastern Rd. E13 115 H2
Eastern Rd. E17 78 C5
Eastern Rd. N2 73 J3
Eastern Rd. N22 75 E1
Eastern Rd. SE4 154 A4
Eastern Way SE2 138 D1
Eastern Way SE28 138 A2
Eastern Way, Belv. 139 H2
Eastern Way, Erith 138 D1
Easternville Gdns., Ilf. 81 F6
Eastfield Cotts., Hayes 121 H5
Eastfield Gdns., Dag. 101 G4
Eastfield Rd. E17 78 A4
Eastfield Rd. N8 74 E3
Eastfield Rd., Dag. 101 G4
Eastfields, Pnr. 66 C5
Eastfields Rd. W3 106 C5
Eastfields Rd., Mitch. 186 A2
Eastgate Cl. SE28 118 D6
Eastglade, Pnr. 67 E3
Eastham Cl., Barn. 40 B5
Eastholm NW11 73 E4
Eastholme, Hayes 122 A1
Eastlake Rd. SE5 151 H2
Eastlands Cres. SE21 152 C6
Eastlea Ms. E16 114/115 E4
Desford Rd.
Eastleigh Av., Har. 85 H2
Eastleigh Cl. NW2 89 E3
Eastleigh Cl., Sutt. 199 E7
Eastleigh Rd. E17 77 J2
Eastleigh Rd., Bexh. 159 J2
Eastleigh Rd., Houns. 141 J3
Cranford La.
Eastleigh Wk. SW15 147 G7
Eastleigh Way, Felt. 160 A1
Eastman Rd. W3 126 D1
Eastmead Av., Grnf. 103 H3
Eastmead Cl., Brom. 192 B2
Eastmearn Rd. SE21 169 J2
Eastmont Rd., Esher 194 B2
Eastmoor Pl. SE7 136 A3
Eastmoor St.
Eastmoor St. SE7 136 A3
Eastney Rd., Croy. 201 H1
Eastney St. SE10 134 D5
Eastnor Rd. SE9 175 F1
Easton Gdns., Borwd. 38 D4
Easton St. WC1 10 E4
Eastry Av., Brom. 191 F6
Eastry Rd., Erith 139 G7
Eastside Rd. NW11 72 C4
Eastview Av. SE18 137 H7
Eastville Av. NW11 72 C6
Eastway E9 95 J6
Eastway E10 96 C4
Eastway E15 96 A5
Eastway, Mord. 184 A5
Eastway, Wall. 200 C4
Eastway Commercial Cen. E9 96 A5
Eastwell Cl., Beck. 189 H1
Eastwood Cl. E18 79 G2
George La.
Eastwood Cl. N17 60/61 E7
Northumberland Gro.
Eastwood Rd. E18 79 G2
Eastwood Rd. N10 74 A2
Eastwood Rd., Ilf. 82 A7
Eastwood Rd., West Dr. 120 D2
Eastwood St. SW16 168 C6
Eatington Rd. E10 78 D5
Eaton Cl. SW1 32 B2
Eaton Cl. SW1 130 A4
Eaton Cl., Stan. 53 E4
Eaton Dr. SW9 151 H4
Eaton Dr., Kings.T. 164 A7
Eaton Gdns., Dag. 100 E7
Eaton Gate SW1 32 B1
Eaton Gate SW1 130 A4
Eaton La. SW1 24 E6
Eaton La. SW1 130 B3
Eaton Ms. N. SW1 32 B1
Eaton Ms. N. SW1 130 A3
Eaton Ms. S. SW1 32 C1
Eaton Ms. S. SW1 130 B3
Eaton Ms. W. SW1 32 C1
Eaton Ms. W. SW1 130 A4
Eaton Pk. Rd. N13 59 G2
Eaton Pl. SW1 24 B6
Eaton Pl. SW1 130 A3
Eaton Ri. E11 79 J5
Eaton Ri. W5 105 G6
Eaton Rd. NW4 71 J5
Eaton Rd., Enf. 44 B3
Eaton Rd., Houns. 144 A4
Eaton Rd., Sid. 176 D2
Eaton Rd., Sutt. 199 G6
Eaton Row SW1 24 D6
Eaton Row SW1 130 B3
Eaton Sq. SW1 24 D5
Eaton Sq. SW1 130 A4
Eaton Ter. SW1 32 B1
Eaton Ter. SW1 130 A4
Eaton Ter. Ms. SW1 32 B1
Eaton Wk. SE15 132 C7
Sumner Est.
Eatons Mead E4 62 A2
Eatonville Rd. SW17 167 J2
Eatonville Vil. SW17 167 J2
Eatonville Rd.
Ebbisham Dr. SW8 34 C5
Ebbisham Dr. SW8 131 F6
Ebbisham Rd., Wor.Pk. 197 J2
Ebbsfleet Rd. NW2 90 B4
Ebdon Way SE3 155 H3
Ebenezer St. N1 12 B3
Ebenezer St. N1 112 A3
Ebenezer Wk. SW16 186 C1
Ebley Cl. SE15 37 F6
Ebley Cl. SE15 132 C6
Ebner St. SW18 149 E5
Ebor St. E1 13 F5
Ebor St. E1 112 C4
Ebrington Rd., Har. 69 G6
Ebsworth St. SE23 153 G7
Eburne Rd. N7 93 E3
Ebury Br. SW1 32 D3
Ebury Br. SW1 130 B5
Ebury Br. Est. SW1 32 D3
Ebury Br. Est. SW1 130 B5
Ebury Br. Rd. SW1 32 C4
Ebury Br. Rd. SW1 130 A5
Ebury Cl., Kes. 206 B3
Ebury Ms. SE27 169 H3
Ebury Ms. SW1 32 D1
Ebury Ms. SW1 130 B4
Ebury Ms. E. SW1 32 D1
Ebury Sq. SW1 32 C2
Ebury Sq. SW1 130 A4
Ebury St. SW1 32 D1
Ebury St. SW1 130 A4
Eccles Rd. SW11 149 J4
Ecclesbourne Cl. N13 59 G5
Ecclesbourne Gdns. N13 59 G5
Ecclesbourne Rd. N1 93 J7
Ecclesbourne Rd., Th.Hth. 187 J5
Eccleston Br. SW1 32 E1
Eccleston Br. SW1 130 B4
Eccleston Cl., Barn. 41 J4
Eccleston Cl., Orp. 207 G1
Eccleston Cres., Rom. 82 A7
Eccleston Ms. SW1 24 C6
Eccleston Ms. SW1 130 A3
Eccleston Pl. SW1 32 D1
Eccleston Pl. SW1 130 B4
Eccleston Rd. W13 104 D7
Eccleston Sq. SW1 33 E2
Eccleston Sq. SW1 130 B4
Eccleston Sq. Ms. SW1 33 F2
Eccleston St. SW1 24 D6
Eccleston St. SW1 130 A3
Ecclestone Ct., Wem. 87 H5
St. John's Rd.
Ecclestone Pl., Wem. 87 J5
Echo Hts. E4 62 B1
Mount Echo Dr.
Eckersley St. E1 112 D4
Buxton St.
Eckford St. N1 10 E1
Eckford St. N1 111 G2
Eckstein Rd. SW11 149 H4
Eclipse Rd. E13 115 H5
Ector Rd. SE6 172 E2
Edbrooke Rd. W9 108 D4
Eddiscombe Rd. SW6 148 C2
Eddy Cl., Rom. 83 H6
Eddystone Rd. SE4 153 H5
Eddystone Wk., Stai. 140 B7
Ede Cl., Houns. 143 F3
Eden Cl. NW3 90 D2
Eden Cl. W8 128 D3
Adam & Eve Ms.
Eden Cl., Wem. 105 G1
Eden Gro. E17 78 B5
Eden Gro. N7 93 F5
Eden Ms. SW17 167 F3
Huntspill St.
Eden Pk. Av., Beck. 189 H4
Eden Rd. E17 78 B5
Eden Rd. SE27 169 H5
Eden Rd., Beck. 189 H4
Eden Rd., Bex. 177 J4
Eden Rd., Croy. 202 A4
Eden St., Kings.T. 181 G2
Eden Wk., Kings.T. 181 H2
Eden St.
Eden Way, Beck. 189 J5
Edenbridge Cl. SE16 132/133 E5
Masters Dr.
Edenbridge Rd. E9 95 G7
Edenbridge Rd., Enf. 44 B6
Edencourt Rd. SW16 168 B6
Edenfield Gdns., Wor.Pk. 197 F3
Edenham Way W10 108 C5
Elkstone Rd.
Edenhurst Av. SW6 148 C3
Edensor Gdns. W4 127 E7
Edensor Rd. W4 126 E7
Edenvale Cl., Mitch. 168 A7
Edenvale Rd.
Edenvale Rd., Mitch. 168 A7
Edenvale St. SW6 149 E2
Ederline Av. SW16 187 F3
Edgar Kail Way SE22 152 B4
Edgar Rd. E3 114 B3
Edgar Rd., Houns. 143 F7
Edgar Rd., Rom. 82 D7
Edgarley Ter. SW6 148 B1
Edgbaston Rd., Wat. 50 B3
Edge Hill SE18 136 E6
Edge Hill SW19 166 A7
Edge Hill Av. N3 72 D3
Edge Hill Ct. SW19 166 A7
Edge St. W8 128 D1
Kensington Ch. St.
Edgeborough Way, Brom. 174 A7
Edgebury, Chis. 175 E4
Edgebury Wk., Chis. 175 F4
Edgecombe Ho. SW19 166 B1
Edgecoombe, S.Croy. 203 F7
Edgecoombe Cl., Kings.T. 164 D7
Edgecot Gro. N15 76 A5
Oulton Rd.
Edgecote Cl. W3 126 C1
Cheltenham Pl.
Edgefield Av., Bark. 99 J7
Edgehill Gdns., Dag. 101 G4
Edgehill Rd. W13 105 F5
Edgehill Rd., Chis. 175 F3
Edgehill Rd., Mitch. 186 B1
Edgel St. SW18 148/149 E4
Ferrier St.
Edgeley La. SW4 150 D3
Edgeley Rd.
Edgeley Rd. SW4 150 D3
Edgepoint Cl. SE27 169 H5
Knights Hill
Edgewood Dr., Orp. 207 J5
Edgewood Grn., Croy. 203 G1
Edgeworth Av. NW4 71 G5
Edgeworth Cl. NW4 71 G5
Edgeworth Cres. NW4 71 G5

264 Edg-Elk

Edgeworth Rd. SE9 155 J4
Edgeworth Rd., Barn. 41 H4
Edgington Rd. SW16 168 D6
Edgington Way, Sid. 176 C7
Edgware Ct., Edg. 54 A6
Cavendish Dr.
Edgware Rd. NW2 89 H1
Edgware Rd. NW9 70 D3
Edgware Rd. W2 15 H3
Edgware Rd. W2 109 H6
Edgware Way, Edg. 53 J4
Edgwarebury Gdns., Edg. 54 A5
Edgwarebury La., Edg. 54 A4
Edinburgh Cl. E2 113 F2
Russia La.
Edinburgh Cl., Pnr. 66 D7
Edinburgh Ct. SW20 184 A5
Edinburgh Dr., Rom. 83 J4
Eastern Av. W.
Edinburgh Gate SW1 23 J3
Edinburgh Gate SW1 129 J2
Edinburgh Ho. W9 6 B3
Edinburgh Ho. W9 109 F3
Edinburgh Rd. E13 115 H2
Edinburgh Rd. E17 78 A5
Edinburgh Rd. N18 60 D5
Edinburgh Rd. W7 124 C2
Edinburgh Rd., Sutt. 199 F2
Edington Rd. SE2 138 B3
Edington Rd., Enf. 45 F2
Edis St. NW1 110 A1
Edison Cl. E17 78 A5
Exeter Rd.
Edison Dr., Sthl. 103 H6
Edison Gro. SE18 137 J7
Edison Rd. N8 74 D6
Edison Rd., Brom. 191 G2
Edison Rd., Enf. 45 J2
Edison Rd., Well. 157 J1
Edith Cavell Cl. N19 74 D7
Hornsey Ri. Gdns.
Edith Gdns., Surb. 182 B7
Edith Gro. SW10 30 C6
Edith Gro. SW10 129 F6
Edith Rd. E6 98 A7
Edith Rd. E15 96 D5
Chandos Rd.
Edith Rd. N11 58 D7
Edith Rd. SE25 188 A5
Edith Rd. SW19 167 E6
Edith Rd. W14 128 B4
Edith Rd., Rom. 82 D6
Edith Row SW6 149 E1
Edith St. E2 13 H1
Edith St. E2 112 D2
Edith Ter. SW10 30 C7
Edith Ter. SW10 129 F7
Edith Turbeville Ct. N19 74/75 E7
Hillrise Rd.
Edith Vil. W14 128 C4
Edith Yd. SW10 30 D7
Edithna St. SW9 151 E3
Edmansons Cl. N17 76 B1
Bruce Gro.
Edmeston Cl. E9 95 H6
Edmond Halley Way SE10 134 E2
Edmonds Ct., W.Mol. 179 H4
Avern Rd.
Edmonton Grn. N9 60/61 E2
Hertford Rd.
Edmund Gro., Felt. 161 F2
Edmund Hurst Cl. E6 116 D5
Winsor Ter.
Edmund Rd., Mitch. 185 H3
Edmund Rd., Well. 158 A3
Edmund St. SE5 36 B7
Edmund St. SE5 132 A7
Edmunds Cl., Hayes 102 C5
Edmunds Wk. N2 73 G4
Edna Rd. SW20 184 A2
Edna St. SW11 149 H1
Edric Rd. SE14 133 G7
Edrich Ho. SW4 150 E1
Edrick Rd., Edg. 54 C6
Edrick Wk., Edg. 54 C6
Edridge Rd., Croy. 201 J3
Edulf Rd., Borwd. 38 B1
Edward Av. E4 62 B6
Edward Av., Mord. 185 G5
Edward Cl. N9 44 C7
Edward Cl., Hmptn. 161 J5
Edward Rd.
Edward Cl., Nthlt. 102 C2
Edward Ct. E16 115 G5
Alexandra St.
Edward Gro., Barn. 41 G5
Edward Ms. NW1 8 E2
Edward Pl. SE8 133 J6
Edward Rd. E17 77 G4
Edward Rd. SE20 171 G7
Edward Rd., Barn. 41 G5
Edward Rd., Brom. 173 H7
Edward Rd., Chis. 175 E5
Edward Rd., Croy. 188 B7
Edward Rd., Felt. 141 G5
Edward Rd., Hmptn. 161 J5
Edward Rd., Har. 67 J3
Edward Rd., Nthlt. 102 C2
Edward Rd., Rom. 82 E6
Edward Sq. N1 111 F1
Caledonian Rd.
Edward Sq. SE16 133 H1
Rotherhithe St.
Edward St. E16 115 G4
Edward St. SE8 133 J6
Edward St. SE14 133 H7
Edward Temme Av. E15 97 F7
Edward Tyler Rd. SE12 173 H2
Edwardes Pl. W8 128 C3
Edwardes Sq.
Edwardes Sq. W8 128 D3
Edward's Av., Ruis. 84 B6
Edwards Cl., Wor.Pk. 198 A2
Edwards Cotts. N1 93 H6
Compton Av.
Edwards Dr. N11 58 D7
Gordon Rd.
Edwards La. N16 94 A2
Edwards Ms. N1 93 G7
Edwards Ms. W1 16 B4
Edwards Ms. W1 110 A6
Edwards Rd., Belv. 139 G4
Edwards Yd., Wem. 105 H1
Mount Pleasant
Edwin Av. E6 116 D2
Edwin Cl., Bexh. 139 F6
Edwin Pl., Croy. 202 A1
Cross Rd.
Edwin Rd., Edg. 54 D6
Edwin Rd., Twick. 162 C1
Edwin St. E1 113 F4
Edwin St. E16 115 G5
Edwina Gdns., Ilf. 80 B5
Edwin's Mead E9 95 H4
Lindisfarne Way
Edwyn Cl., Barn. 39 J6
Eel Brook Studios SW6 128 D7
Moore Pk. Rd.
Eel Pie Island, Twick. 162 E1
Effie Pl. SW6 128 D7
Effie Rd. SW6 128 D7
Effingham Cl., Sutt. 199 E7
Effingham Rd. N8 75 G5
Effingham Rd. SE12 155 E5
Effingham Rd., Croy. 187 F7
Effingham Rd., Surb. 181 E7
Effort St. SW17 167 H5
Effra Par. SW2 151 G5
Effra Rd. SW2 151 G4
Effra Rd. SW19 166 E6
Egbert St. NW1 110 A1
Egerton Cl., Pnr. 66 A4
Egerton Cres. SW3 31 H1
Egerton Cres. SW3 129 H4
Egerton Dr. SE10 154 B1
Egerton Gdns. NW4 71 H4
Egerton Gdns. NW10 107 J1
Egerton Gdns. SW3 23 G6
Egerton Gdns. SW3 129 H3
Egerton Gdns. W13 105 E6
Egerton Gdns., Ilf. 99 J3
Egerton Gdns. Ms. SW3 23 H6
Egerton Gdns. Ms. SW3 129 H3
Egerton Pl. SW3 23 H6
Egerton Pl. SW3 129 H3
Egerton Rd. N16 76 C7
Egerton Rd. SE25 188 B3
Egerton Rd., N.Mal. 183 F4
Egerton Rd., Twick. 144 B7
Egerton Rd., Wem. 87 J7
Egerton Ter. SW3 23 H6
Egerton Ter. SW3 129 H3
Egerton Way, Hayes 121 E7
Egham Cl. SW19 166 B2
Winterfold Cl.
Egham Cl., Sutt. 198 B2
Egham Cres., Sutt. 198 A3
Egham Rd. E13 115 H5
Eglantine Rd. SW18 149 F5
Egleston Rd., Mord. 184 E6
Eglington Ct. SE17 35 J5
Eglington Rd. E4 46 D7
Eglinton Hill SE18 137 E6
Eglinton Rd. SE18 136 D6
Egliston Ms. SW15 147 J3
Egliston Rd. SW15 147 J3
Eglon Ms. NW1 91 J7
Berkley Rd.
Egmont Av., Surb. 195 J1
Egmont Rd., N.Mal. 183 F4
Egmont Rd., Surb. 195 J1
Egmont Rd., Sutt. 199 F7
Egmont Rd., Walt. 178 B7
Egmont St. SE14 133 G7
Egremont Rd. SE27 169 G3
Egret Way, Hayes 102 D5
Eider Cl. E7 97 F5
Eider Cl., Hayes 102 D5
Cygnet Way
Eighteenth Rd., Mitch. 186 E4
Eighth Av. E12 98 C4
Eighth Av., Hayes 122 A1
Eileen Rd. SE25 188 A5
Eindhoven Cl., Cars. 200 A1
Eisenhower Dr. E6 116 B5
Elaine Gro. NW5 92 A5
Elam Cl. SE5 151 H2
Elam St. SE5 151 H2
Eland Pl., Croy. 201 H3
Eland Rd.
Eland Rd. SW11 149 J3
Eland Rd., Croy. 201 H3
Elba Pl. SE17 36 A1
Elbe St. SW6 149 F2
Elberon Av., Croy. 186 C6
Elborough Rd. SE25 188 D5
Elborough St. SW18 166 D1
Elbury Dr. E16 115 G6
Elcho St. SW11 129 H7
Elcot Av. SE15 132 E7
Elder Av. N8 74 E5
Elder Cl., Sid. 175 J1
Elder Ct., Bushey 52 B2
Elder Gdns. SE27 169 J4
Gladstone Ter.
Elder Oak Cl. SE20 188 E1
Elder Rd. SE27 169 J5
Elder St. E1 13 F6
Elder St. E1 112 C5
Elder Wk. N1 111 H1
Essex Rd.
Elderberry Gro. SE27 169 J5
Linton Gro.
Elderberry Rd. W5 125 H2
Elderfield Pl. SW17 168 B4
Elderfield Rd. E5 95 F4
Elderfield Wk. E11 79 H5
Elderflower Way E15 96 E7
Elderslie Cl., Beck. 190 B5
Elderslie Rd. SE9 156 D5
Elderton Rd. SE26 171 H4
Eldertree Pl., Mitch. 186 C1
Eldertree Way
Eldertree Way, Mitch. 186 B1
Elderwood Pl. SE27 169 J5
Elder Rd.
Eldon Av., Borwd. 38 A2
Eldon Av., Croy. 203 F2
Eldon Av., Houns. 123 G7
Eldon Gro. NW3 91 G5
Eldon Pk. SE25 188 E4
Eldon Rd. E17 77 J4
Eldon Rd. N9 61 F2
Eldon Rd. N22 75 H1
Eldon Rd. W8 22 B6
Eldon Rd. W8 129 E3
Eldon St. EC2 20 C2
Eldon St. EC2 112 A5
Eldon Way NW10 106 B2
Eldred Rd., Bark. 117 H1
Eldridge Cl., Felt. 160 A1
Eleanor Cl. N15 76 C3
Arnold Rd.
Eleanor Cl. SE16 133 G2
Eleanor Cres. NW7 56 A4
Eleanor Gdns., Barn. 40 A5
Eleanor Gdns., Dag. 101 F3
Eleanor Gro. SW13 147 E3
Eleanor Rd. E8 94 E7
Eleanor Rd. E15 97 F6
Eleanor Rd. N11 58 E6
Eleanor St. E3 114 A3
Eleanor Wk. SE18 136 C4
Samuel St.
Electric Av. SW9 151 G4
Electric La. SW9 151 G4
Electric Par., Surb. 181 G6
Elephant & Castle SE1 27 H6
Elephant & Castle SE1 131 H4
Elephant La. SE16 133 F2
Elephant Rd. SE17 35 J1
Elephant Rd. SE17 131 J4
Elers Rd. W13 125 F2
Elers Rd., Hayes 121 G4
Eleven Acre Ri., Loug. 48 C3
Eley Est. N18 61 F5
Eley Rd. N18 61 G5
Elf Row E1 113 F7
Elfin Gro., Tedd. 162 C5
Broad St.
Elfindale Rd. SE24 151 J5
Elford Cl. SE3 155 H4
Elfort Rd. N5 93 G4
Elfrida Cres. SE6 172 A4
Elfwine Rd. W7 104 B5
Elgal Cl., Orp. 206/207 E5
Orchard Rd.
Elgar Av. NW10 88 D6
Mitchellbrook Way
Elgar Av. SW16 186 E3
Elgar Av. W5 125 H2
Elgar Av., Surb. 182 B7
Elgar Cl. E13 115 J2
Bushey Rd.
Elgar Cl. SE8 134 A7
Comet St.
Elgar Cl., Buck.H. 64 A2
Elgar St. SE16 133 H3
Elgin Av. W9 6 A4
Elgin Av. W9 108 E3
Elgin Av., Har. 68 E2
Elgin Cres. W11 108 C6
Elgin Cres., Houns. 141 H2
Eastern Perimeter Rd.
Elgin Ms. W11 108 B6
Ladbroke Gro.
Elgin Ms. N. W9 6 B3
Elgin Ms. S. W9 6 B3
Elgin Rd. N22 74 C2
Elgin Rd., Croy. 202 C1
Elgin Rd., Ilf. 99 H1
Elgin Rd., Sutt. 199 F3
Elgin Rd., Wall. 200 C6
Elgood Av., Nthwd. 50 A6
Elgood Cl. W11 108 B7
Avondale Pk. Rd.
Elham Cl., Brom. 174 A7
Elia Ms. N1 11 G2
Elia Ms. N1 111 H2
Elia St. N1 11 G2
Elia St. N1 111 H2
Elias Pl. SW8 34 E6
Elias Pl. SW8 131 G6
Elibank Rd. SE9 156 D4
Elim Est. SE1 28 D5
Elim Est. SE1 132 B3
Elim Way E13 115 F3
Eliot Bank SE23 170 E2
Eliot Cotts. SE3 154/155 E2
Eliot Pl.
Eliot Dr., Har. 85 H2
Eliot Gdns. SW15 147 G4
Eliot Hill SE13 154 C2
Eliot Ms. NW8 6 D2
Eliot Ms. NW8 109 F2
Eliot Pk. SE13 154 C3
Eliot Pl. SE3 154 E2
Eliot Rd., Dag. 100 D4
Eliot Vale SE3 154 D2
Elizabeth Av. N1 93 J7
Elizabeth Av., Enf. 43 H3
Elizabeth Av., Ilf. 99 G2
Elizabeth Blackwell Ho. N22 75 G1
Progress Way
Elizabeth Br. SW1 32 D2
Elizabeth Br. SW1 130 B4
Elizabeth Cl. E14 114 B6
Grundy St.
Elizabeth Cl. W9 6 D6
Elizabeth Cl., Barn. 40 A3
Elizabeth Cl., Rom. 83 H1
Elizabeth Cl., Sutt. 198 C4
Elizabeth Clyde Cl. N15 76 B4
Elizabeth Cotts., Rich. 145 J1
Elizabeth Ct. SW1 25 J6
Elizabeth Est. SE17 36 B5
Elizabeth Est. SE17 132 A6
Elizabeth Fry Rd. E8 94/95 E7
Lamb La.
Elizabeth Gdns. W3 127 F1
Elizabeth Gdns., Stan. 53 F6
Elizabeth Gdns., Sun. 178 C3
Elizabeth Ms. NW3 91 H6
Elizabeth Pl. N15 76 A4
Elizabeth Ride N9 45 E7
Elizabeth Rd. E6 116 A1
Elizabeth Rd. N15 76 B5
Elizabeth Sq. SE16 113 H7
Rotherhithe St.
Elizabeth St. SW1 32 C1
Elizabeth St. SW1 130 A4
Elizabeth Ter. SE9 156 C6
Elizabeth Way SE19 170 A7
Elizabeth Way, Felt. 160 C4
Elizabethan Cl., Stai. 140 A7
Elizabethan Way
Elizabethan Way, Stai. 140 A7
Elkanette Ms. N20 57 F2
Ridgeview Rd.

Elkington Rd. E13 115 H4
Elkstone Rd. W10 108 C5
Ella Rd. N8 75 E7
Ellaline Rd. W6 128 A6
Ellanby Cres. N18 60 E5
Elland Rd. SE15 153 F4
Ellement Cl., Pnr. 66 D5
Ellen Cl., Brom. 192 A3
Ellen Ct. N9 61 F2
Densworth Gro.
Ellen St. E1 21 J4
Ellen St. E1 112 D6
Ellen Webb Dr., Har. 68 B3
Ellenborough Pl. SW15 147 G4
Ellenborough Rd. N22 75 J1
Ellenborough Rd., Sid. 176 D5
Elleray Rd., Tedd. 162 C6
Ellerby St. SW6 148 A1
Ellerdale Cl. NW3 91 F4
Ellerdale Rd.
Ellerdale Rd. NW3 91 F5
Ellerdale St. SE13 154 B4
Ellerdine Rd., Houns. 143 J4
Ellerker Gdns., Rich. 145 H6
Ellerman Av., Twick. 161 F1
Ellerslie Gdns. NW10 107 G1
Ellerslie Rd. W12 127 H1
Ellerslie Sq. Ind. Est. SW2 150 E5
Ellerton Gdns., Dag. 100 C7
Ellerton Rd. SW13 147 G1
Ellerton Rd. SW18 167 G1
Ellerton Rd. SW20 165 G7
Ellerton Rd., Dag. 100 C7
Ellerton Rd., Surb. 195 J2
Ellery Rd. SE19 170 A7
Ellery St. SE15 153 E2
Ellesborough Cl., Wat. 50 C5
Ellesmere Av. NW7 54 D3
Ellesmere Av., Beck. 190 B2
Ellesmere Cl. E11 79 F5
Ellesmere Gdns., Ilf. 80 B5
Ellesmere Gro., Barn. 40 C5
Ellesmere Rd. E3 113 H2
Ellesmere Rd. NW10 89 G5
Ellesmere Rd. W4 126 D6
Ellesmere Rd., Grnf. 103 J4
Ellesmere Rd., Twick. 145 F6
Ellesmere St. E14 114 B6
Ellingfort Rd. E8 95 E7
Ellingham Rd. E15 96 D4
Ellingham Rd. W12 127 G2
Ellingham Rd., Chess. 195 G6
Ellington Rd. N10 74 B4
Ellington Rd., Houns. 143 H2
Ellington St. N7 93 G6
Elliot Cl. E15 96 E7
Elliot Rd. NW4 71 H6
Elliot Rd., Stan. 52 D6
Elliott Av., Ruis. 84 B2
Elliott Cl., Wem. 87 J3
Elliott Rd. SW9 131 H7
Elliott Rd. W4 126 E4
Elliott Rd., Brom. 192 A4
Elliott Rd., Th.Hth. 187 H4
Elliott Sq. NW3 91 H7
Elliott's Pl. N1 111 H1
St. Peters St.
Elliotts Row SE11 35 G1
Elliotts Row SE11 131 H4
Ellis Cl. NW10 89 H6
High Rd.
Ellis Cl. SE9 175 F2
Ellis Ct. W7 104 C5
Ellis Ms. SE7 135 J6
Ellis Rd., Mitch. 185 J6
Ellis Rd., Sthl. 123 J1
Ellis St. SW1 32 A1
Ellis St. SW1 129 J4
Elliscombe Rd. SE7 135 J5
Ellisfield Dr. SW15 147 F7
Ellison Gdns., Sthl. 123 F4
Ellison Rd. SW13 147 F2
Ellison Rd. SW16 168 D7
Ellison Rd., Sid. 175 G1
Elliston Ho. SE18 136 D4
Ellora Rd. SW16 168 D5
Ellsworth St. E2 113 E3
Ellwood Ct. W9 6 A6
Elm Av. W5 125 H1
Elm Av., Ruis. 84 A1
Elm Bank, Brom. 192 A2
Elm Bank Gdns. SW13 147 E2
Elm Cl. E11 79 H6
Elm Cl. N19 92 C2
Hargrave Pk.
Elm Cl. NW4 72 A5
Elm Cl. SW20 183 J4
Grand Dr.
Elm Cl., Buck.H. 64 A2
Elm Cl., Cars. 199 J1
Elm Cl., Har. 67 H6
Elm Cl., Hayes 102 A6
Elm Cl., Rom. 83 H2
Elm Cl., S.Croy. 202 B6
Elm Cl., Surb. 182 C7
Elm Cl., Twick. 161 H2
Elm Ct. EC4 19 E5
Elm Ct., Mitch. 185 J2
Armfield Cres.
Elm Cres. W5 125 H1
Elm Cres., Kings.T. 181 H1
Elm Dr., Har. 67 H6
Elm Dr., Sun. 178 C2
Elm Friars Wk. NW1 92 D7
Elm Gdns. N2 73 F3
Elm Gdns., Esher 194 C6
Elm Gdns., Mitch. 186 D4
Elm Grn. W3 106 E6
Elm Gro. N8 75 E6
Elm Gro. NW2 90 A4
Elm Gro. SE15 152 C2
Elm Gro. SW19 166 B7
Elm Gro., Har. 67 G7
Elm Gro., Kings.T. 181 H1
Elm Gro., Orp. 207 J1
Elm Gro., Sutt. 199 E4
Elm Gro., Wdf.Grn. 63 F5
Elm Gro. Par., Wall. 200 A3
Butter Hill
Elm Gro. Rd. SW13 147 G2
Elm Gro. Rd. W5 125 H2
Elm Hall Gdns. E11 79 H5
Elm La. SE6 171 J2
Elm Ms., Rich. 145 J6
Grove Rd.
Elm Pk. SW2 151 F6
Elm Pk., Stan. 53 E5
Elm Pk. Av. N15 76 C5
Elm Pk. Ct., Pnr. 66 C3
Elm Pk. Gdns. NW4 72 A5
Elm Pk. Gdns. SW10 31 E4
Elm Pk. Gdns. SW10 129 G5
Elm Pk. La. SW3 30 E4
Elm Pk. La. SW3 129 G5
Elm Pk. Mans. SW10 30 D5
Elm Pk. Rd. E10 95 H1
Elm Pk. Rd. N3 56 C7
Elm Pk. Rd. N21 43 J7
Elm Pk. Rd. SE25 188 C3
Elm Pk. Rd. SW3 30 E5
Elm Pk. Rd. SW3 129 G6
Elm Pk. Rd., Pnr. 66 C2
Elm Pl. SW7 31 E3
Elm Pl. SW7 129 G5
Elm Quay Ct. SW8 33 H5
Elm Quay Ct. SW8 130 D6
Elm Rd. E7 97 F6
Elm Rd. E11 96 D2
Elm Rd. E17 78 C5
Elm Rd. N22 75 H1
Granville Rd.
Elm Rd. SW14 146 C3
Elm Rd., Barn. 40 C4
Elm Rd., Beck. 189 J2
Elm Rd., Chess. 195 H4
Elm Rd., Epsom 197 F6
Elm Rd., Esher 194 C6
Elm Rd., Kings.T. 181 J1
Elm Rd., N.Mal. 182 D4
Elm Rd., Rom. 83 H2
Elm Rd., Sid. 176 A4
Elm Rd., Th.Hth. 188 A4
Elm Rd., Wall. 200 A1
Elm Rd., Wem. 87 H5
Elm Rd. W., Sutt. 184 C7
Elm Row NW3 91 F3
Elm St. WC1 10 D6
Elm St. WC1 111 F4
Elm Ter. NW2 90 D3
Elm Ter. NW3 91 H4
Constantine Rd.
Elm Ter. SE9 156 D6
Elm Ter., Har. 52 A7
Elm Tree Av., Esher 180 A7
Elm Tree Cl. NW8 7 E3
Elm Tree Cl. NW8 109 G3
Elm Tree Cl., Nthlt. 103 F2
Elm Tree Rd. NW8 6 E3
Elm Tree Rd. NW8 109 G3
Elm Wk. NW3 90 D2
Elm Wk. SW20 183 J4
Elm Wk., Orp. 206 C3
Elm Way N11 58 A6
Elm Way NW10 88 E4
Elm Way, Epsom 196 D5
Elm Way, Wor.Pk. 197 J3
Elmar Rd. N15 76 A4
Elmbank N14 43 E7
Elmbank Av., Barn. 39 J4
Elmbank Way W7 104 A5
Elmbourne Dr., Belv. 139 H4
Elmbourne Rd. SW17 168 A3
Elmbridge Av., Surb. 182 B5
Elmbridge Cl., Ruis. 66 A6
Elmbridge Wk. E8 94 D7
Wilman Gro.
Elmbrook Cl., Sun. 178 B1
Elmbrook Gdns. SE9 156 B4
Elmbrook Rd., Sutt. 198 C4
Elmcourt Rd. SE27 169 H2
Elmcroft N8 75 F5
Elmcroft Av. E11 79 H5
Elmcroft Av. N9 44 E6
Elmcroft Av. NW11 72 C7
Elmcroft Av., Sid. 157 J6
Elmcroft Cl. E11 79 H4
Elmcroft Cl. W5 105 G6
Elmcroft Cl., Chess. 195 H3
Elmcroft Cl., Felt. 141 J6
Elmcroft Cres. NW11 72 B7
Elmcroft Cres., Har. 67 G3
Elmcroft Dr., Chess. 195 H3
Elmcroft Gdns. NW9 70 A5
Elmcroft St. E5 95 F4
Elmdale Rd. N13 59 F5
Elmdene, Surb. 196 C1
Elmdene Cl., Beck. 189 J5
Elmdene Rd. SE18 136 E5
Elmdon Rd., Houns. 142 D2
Elmdon Rd. (Hatton Cross), Houns. 141 J3
Elmer Cl., Enf. 43 F3
Elmer Gdns., Edg. 54 B7
Elmer Gdns., Islw. 144 A3
Elmer Rd. SE6 154 C7
Elmers Dr., Tedd. 162/163 E6
Kingston Rd.
Elmers End Rd. SE20 189 F2
Elmers End Rd., Beck. 189 F2
Elmers Rd. SE25 188 D7
Elmerside Rd., Beck. 189 H4
Elmfield Av. N8 74 E5
Elmfield Av., Mitch. 186 A1
Elmfield Av., Tedd. 162 C5
Elmfield Cl., Har. 86 B2
Elmfield Pk., Brom. 191 G3
Elmfield Rd. E4 62 C2
Elmfield Rd. E17 77 G6
Elmfield Rd. N2 73 G3
Elmfield Rd. SW17 168 A2
Elmfield Rd., Brom. 191 G3
Elmfield Rd., Sthl. 123 E3
Elmfield Way W9 108 D5
Elmgate Av., Felt. 160 B3
Elmgate Gdns., Edg. 54 D5
Elmgreen Cl. E15 114/115 E1
Church St. N.
Elmgrove Cres., Har. 68 C5
Elmgrove Gdns., Har. 68 D5
Elmgrove Rd., Croy. 188 E7
Elmgrove Rd., Har. 68 C5
Elmhurst, Belv. 139 E6
Elmhurst Av. N2 73 G3
Elmhurst Av., Mitch. 168 B7
Elmhurst Dr. E18 79 G2
Elmhurst Gdns. E18 79 H1
Elmhurst Dr.
Elmhurst Rd. E7 97 H7
Elmhurst Rd. N17 76 C2
Elmhurst Rd. SE9 174 B2
Elmhurst St. SW4 150 D3
Elmhurst Vil. SE15 153 F4
Cheltenham Rd.
Elmhurst Way, Loug. 48 C7
Elmington Cl., Bex. 159 H6
Elmington Est. SE5 36 C7
Elmington Est. SE5 132 A7
Elmington Rd. SE5 152 A1
Elmira St. SE13 154 B3
Elmlee Cl., Chis. 174 C6
Elmley Cl. E6 116 B5
Northumberland Rd.
Elmley St. SE18 137 G4
Elmore Cl., Wem. 105 H2
Elmore Rd. E11 96 C3
Elmore Rd., Enf. 45 G1
Elmore St. N1 93 J7
Elmores, Loug. 48 D3
Elms, The SW13 147 F3
Elms Av. N10 74 B3
Elms Av. NW4 72 A5
Elms Ct., Wem. 86 C4
Elms Cres. SW4 150 C6
Elms Gdns., Dag. 101 F4
Elms Gdns., Wem. 86 D4
Elms La., Wem. 86 D4
Elms Ms. W2 14 E5
Elms Ms. W2 109 G7
Elms Pk. Av., Wem. 86 D4
Elms Rd. SW4 150 C5
Elms Rd., Har. 52 B7
Elmscott Gdns. N21 43 J6
Elmscott Rd., Brom. 173 F5
Elmsdale Rd. E17 77 J4
Elmshaw Rd. SW15 147 G5
Elmshurst Cres. N2 73 G4
Elmside, Croy. 204 B6
Elmside Rd., Wem. 88 A3
Elmsleigh Av., Har. 69 E4
Elmsleigh Ct., Sutt. 198 E3
Elmsleigh Rd., Twick. 162 A2
Elmslie Cl., Wdf.Grn. 64 C6
Elmslie Pt. E3 113 J5
Elmstead Av., Chis. 174 C5
Elmstead Av., Wem. 87 H1
Elmstead Cl. N20 56 D2
Elmstead Cl., Epsom 197 E5
Elmstead Cres., Well. 138 C6
Elmstead Gdns., Wor.Pk. 197 G3
Elmstead Glade, Chis. 174 C6
Elmstead La., Chis. 174 C5
Elmstead Rd., Ilf. 99 H2
Elmstone Rd. SW6 148 D1
Elmsworth Av., Houns. 143 H2
Elmton Way E5 94 D3
Rendlesham Rd.
Elmtree Rd., Tedd. 162 B4
Elmwood Av. N13 59 E5
Elmwood Av., Borwd. 38 B4
Elmwood Av., Felt. 160 A2
Elmwood Av., Har. 68 D5
Elmwood Cl., Epsom 197 G7
Elmwood Cl., Wall. 200 A2
Elmwood Ct., Wem. 86 D3
Elmwood Cres. NW9 70 C4
Elmwood Dr., Bex. 158 E7
Elmwood Dr., Epsom 197 G6
Elmwood Gdns. W7 104 B6
Elmwood Rd. SE24 152 A5
Elmwood Rd. W4 126 C6
Elmwood Rd., Croy. 187 H7
Elmwood Rd., Mitch. 185 J3
Elmworth Gro. SE21 170 A2
Elnathan Ms. W9 6 B6
Elphinstone Rd. E17 77 J2
Elphinstone St. N5 93 H4
Avenell Rd.
Elrington Rd. E8 94 D6
Elrington Rd., Wdf.Grn. 63 G5
Elruge Cl., West Dr. 120 A3
Elsa Rd., Well. 158 B2
Elsa St. E1 113 H5
Elsdale St. E9 95 F6
Elsden Ms. E2 113 F2
Old Ford Rd.
Elsden Rd. N17 76 C1
Elsenham Rd. E12 98 D5
Elsenham St. SW18 166 C1
Elsham Rd. E11 96 E3
Elsham Rd. W14 128 B2
Elsham Ter. W14 128 B2
Elsie Rd. SE22 152 C4
Elsiedene Rd. N21 43 J7
Elsiemaud Rd. SE4 153 J5
Elsinore Av., Stai. 140 B7
Elsinore Gdns. NW2 90 B3
Elsinore Rd. SE23 171 H1
Elsinore Way, Rich. 146 B3
Lower Richmond Rd.
Elsley Rd. SW11 149 J3
Elspeth Rd. SW11 149 J4
Elspeth Rd., Wem. 87 H5
Elsrick Av., Mord. 184 D5
Chalgrove Av.
Elstan Way, Croy. 189 H7
Elsted St. SE17 36 C2
Elsted St. SE17 132 A4
Elstow Cl. SE9 156 D5
Elstow Cl., Ruis. 66 D7
Elstow Gdns., Dag. 118 E1
Elstow Rd., Dag. 100 E7
Elstree Gdns. N9 61 E1
Elstree Gdns., Belv. 139 E4
Elstree Gdns., Ilf. 99 F5
Elstree Hill, Brom. 173 E7
Elstree Pk., Borwd. 38 D6
Elstree Way, Borwd. 38 B3
Elswick Rd. SE13 154 B2
Elswick St. SW6 149 F2
Elsworthy, T.Ditt. 180 B6
Elsworthy Ri. NW3 91 H7
Elsworthy Rd. NW3 109 H1
Elsworthy Ter. NW3 91 H7
Elsynge Rd. SW18 149 G5
Eltham Grn. SE9 155 J5
Eltham Grn. Rd. SE9 155 J4
Eltham High St. SE9 156 C6
Eltham Hill SE9 156 A5
Eltham Palace Rd. SE9 155 J6
Eltham Pk. Gdns. SE9 156 D4
Eltham Rd. SE9 155 J5
Eltham Rd. SE12 155 F5

Elthiron Rd. SW6 148 D1
Elthorne Av. W7 124 C2
Elthorne Ct., Felt. 160 C1
Elthorne Pk. Rd. W7 124 C2
Elthorne Rd. N19 92 D2
Elthorne Rd. NW9 70 D7
Elthorne Way NW9 70 D6
Elthruda Rd. SE13 154 D6
Eltisley Rd., Ilf. 98 E4
Elton Av., Barn. 40 C5
Elton Av., Grnf. 86 C6
Elton Av., Wem. 87 E5
Elton Cl., Kings.T. 163 F7
Elton Ho. E3 113 J1
Elton Pl. N16 94 B5
Elton Rd., Kings.T. 181 J1
Eltringham St. SW18 149 F4
Elvaston Ms. SW7 22 D5
Elvaston Ms. SW7 129 F3
Elvaston Pl. SW7 22 C6
Elvaston Pl. SW7 129 F3
Elveden Pl. NW10 106 A2
Elveden Rd. NW10 106 A2
Elvendon Rd. N13 58 E6
Elver Gdns. E2 13 J3
Elverson Rd. SE8 154 B2
Elverton St. SW1 33 H1
Elverton St. SW1 130 D4
Elvington Grn., Brom. 191 F5
Elvington La. NW9 70 E1
Elvino Rd. SE26 171 H5
Elvis Rd. NW2 89 J6
Elwill Way, Beck. 190 C4
Elwin St. E2 13 H3
Elwin St. E2 112 D3
Elwood St. N5 93 H3
Elwyn Gdns. SE12 155 G7
Ely Cl., N.Mal. 183 F2
Ely Ct. EC1 19 F2
Ely Gdns., Borwd. 38 D5
Ely Gdns., Dag. 101 J3
Ely Gdns., Ilf. 80 B7
Canterbury Av.
Ely Pl. EC1 19 F2
Ely Pl., Wdf.Grn. 64 D6
Ely Rd. E10 78 C6
Ely Rd., Croy. 188 A5
Ely Rd. (Heathrow Airport), Houns. 141 J2
Eastern Perimeter Rd.
Ely Rd. (Hounslow W.), Houns. 142 C3
Elyne Rd. N4 75 G6
Elysian Av., Orp. 193 J6
Elysium Pl. SW6 148 C2
Fulham Pk. Gdns.
Elysium St. SW6 148 C2
Fulham Pk. Gdns.
Elystan Business Cen., Hayes 102 C7
Elystan Pl. SW3 31 H3
Elystan Pl. SW3 129 H5
Elystan St. SW3 31 G2
Elystan St. SW3 129 H4
Elystan Wk. N1 111 G1
Cloudesley Rd.
Emanuel Av. W3 106 C6
Emanuel Dr., Hmptn. 161 F5
Emba St. SE16 29 J4
Emba St. SE16 132 D2
Embankment SW15 148 A2
Embankment, The, Twick. 162 D1
Embankment Gdns. SW3 32 A5
Embankment Gdns. SW3 129 J6
Embankment Pl. WC2 26 B1
Embankment Pl. WC2 131 E1
Embassy Ct., Sid. 176 B3
Embassy Ct., Well. 158 B3
Welling High St.
Embassy Gdns., Beck. 189 J1
Blakeney Rd.
Ember Cl., Orp. 193 F7
Ember Fm. Av., E.Mol. 180 A6
Ember Fm. Way, E.Mol. 180 A6
Ember Gdns., T.Ditt. 180 B7
Ember La., E.Mol. 194 A1
Ember La., Esher 180 A7
Embercourt Rd., T.Ditt. 180 B6
Emberton SE5 36 C5
Embleton Rd. SE13 154 B3
Embleton Rd., Wat. 50 A3
Embleton Wk., Hmptn. 161 F6
Fearnley Cres.
Embley Pt. E5 94/95 E4
Tiger Way
Embry Cl., Stan. 52 D4
Embry Dr., Stan. 52 D6
Embry Way, Stan. 52 D5
Emden Cl., West Dr. 120 D2
Emden St. SW6 149 E1
Emerald Cl. E16 116 B6
Emerald Gdns., Dag. 101 G1
Emerald Sq., Sthl. 122 D3
Emerald St. WC1 18 C1
Emerald St. WC1 111 F5
Emerson Gdns., Har. 69 J6
Emerson Rd., Ilf. 80 D7
Emerson St. SE1 27 J1
Emerson St. SE1 131 J1
Emerton Cl., Bexh. 159 E4
Emery Hill St. SW1 25 G6
Emery Hill St. SW1 130 C3
Emery St. SE1 27 F5
Emes Rd., Erith 139 J7
Emilia Cl., Enf. 45 E5
Emily Pl. N7 93 G4
Emlyn Gdns. W12 127 E2
Emlyn Rd. W12 127 E3
Emma Rd. E13 115 F2
Emma St. E2 112 E2
Emmanuel Rd. SW12 168 C1
Emmaus Way, Chig. 64 D5
Emmott Av., Ilf. 81 F5
Emmott Cl. E1 113 H4
Emmott Cl. NW11 73 F6
Emms Pas., Kings.T. 181 G2
High St.
Emperor's Gate SW7 22 B6
Emperor's Gate SW7 129 E3
Empire Av. N18 59 J5
Empire Ct., Wem. 88 B3
Empire Rd., Grnf. 105 F1
Empire Sq. N7 92/93 E3
Holloway Rd.
Empire Way, Wem. 87 J4
Empire Wf. Rd. E14 134 D4
Empire Yd. N7 92/93 E3
Holloway Rd.
Empress Av. E4 62 A7
Empress Av. E12 97 J2
Empress Av., Ilf. 98 C2
Empress Av., Wdf.Grn. 63 F7
Empress Dr., Chis. 174 E6
Empress Pl. SW6 128 D5
Empress St. SE17 36 A5
Empress St. SE17 131 J6
Empson St. E3 114 B4
Emsworth Cl. N9 61 F1
Emsworth Rd., Ilf. 81 E2
Emsworth St. SW2 169 F2
Emu Rd. SW8 150 B2
Ena Rd. SW16 186 E3
Enbrook St. W10 108 B3
Endale Cl., Cars. 199 J2
Endeavour Way SW19 166 E4
Endeavour Way, Bark. 118 A2
Endeavour Way, Croy. 186 D7
Endell St. WC2 18 A3
Endell St. WC2 110 E6
Enderby St. SE10 134 E5
Enderley Cl., Har. 68 B1
Enderley Rd.
Enderley Rd., Har. 68 B1
Endersby Rd., Barn. 39 J5
Endersleigh Gdns. NW4 71 G4
Endlebury Rd. E4 62 C2
Endlesham Rd. SW12 150 A7
Endsleigh Gdns. WC1 9 H5
Endsleigh Gdns. WC1 110 D4
Endsleigh Gdns., Ilf. 98 C2
Endsleigh Gdns., Surb. 181 F6
Endsleigh Pl. WC1 9 J5
Endsleigh Pl. WC1 110 D4
Endsleigh Rd. W13 104 D7
Endsleigh Rd., Sthl. 123 E4
Endsleigh St. WC1 9 H5
Endsleigh St. WC1 110 D4
Endway, Surb. 182 A7
Endwell Rd. SE4 153 H2
Endymion Rd. N4 75 G7
Endymion Rd. SW2 151 F6
Energen Cl. NW10 88 E6
Enfield Retail Pk., Enf. 44 E3
Enfield Rd. N1 94 B7
Enfield Rd. W3 126 B2
Enfield Rd., Brent. 125 G5
Enfield Rd., Enf. 42 D4
Enfield Rd., Houns. 141 H2
Eastern Perimeter Rd.
Enfield Wk., Brent. 125 G5
Enford St. W1 15 J1
Enford St. W1 109 J5
Engadine Cl., Croy. 202 C3
Engadine St. SW18 166 C1
Engate St. SE13 154 C4
Engel Pk. NW7 55 J6
Engineer Cl. SE18 136 D6
Engineers Way, Wem. 88 A4
England Way, N.Mal. 182 C3
California Rd.
Englands La. NW3 91 J6
Englands La., Loug. 48 D2
Englefield Cl., Croy. 187 J6
Queen's Rd.
Englefield Cl., Enf. 43 G2
Englefield Cl., Orp. 193 J4
Englefield Cres., Orp. 193 J4
Englefield Path, Orp. 193 J4
Englefield Rd. N1 94 A6
Engleheart Dr., Felt. 141 J6
Engleheart Rd. SE6 154 B7
Englewood Rd. SW12 150 B6
English Grds. SE1 28 D2
English St. E3 113 J4
Enid St. SE16 29 G5
Enid St. SE16 132 C3
Enmore Av. SE25 188 D5
Enmore Gdns. SW14 146 D5
Enmore Rd. SE25 188 D5
Enmore Rd. SW15 147 J4
Enmore Rd., Sthl. 103 G4
Ennerdale Av., Stan. 69 F3
Ennerdale Cl. (Cheam), Sutt. 198 C4
Ennerdale Dr. NW9 70 E5
Ennerdale Gdns., Wem. 87 G1
Ennerdale Ho. E3 113 J4
Ennerdale Rd., Bexh. 159 G1
Ennerdale Rd., Rich. 145 J2
Ennersdale Rd. SE13 154 D5
Ennis Rd. N4 93 G1
Ennis Rd. SE18 137 F6
Ennismore Av. W4 127 F4
Ennismore Av., Grnf. 86 B6
Ennismore Gdns. SW7 23 G4
Ennismore Gdns. SW7 129 H2
Ennismore Gdns., T.Ditt. 180 B6
Ennismore Gdns. Ms. SW7 23 G5
Ennismore Gdns. Ms. SW7 129 H3
Ennismore Ms. SW7 23 G4
Ennismore Ms. SW7 129 H2
Ennismore St. SW7 23 G5
Ennismore St. SW7 129 H3
Ensign Dr. N13 59 J3
Ensign St. E1 21 H5
Ensign St. E1 112 D7
Enslin Rd. SE9 156 D6
Ensor Ms. SW7 30 E3
Enstone Rd., Enf. 45 H3
Enterprise Cl., Croy. 201 G1
Enterprise Way NW10 107 G3
Enterprise Way SW18 148 D4
Enterprise Way, Tedd. 162 C5
Enterprize Way SE8 133 J4
Epirus Ms. SW6 128 D7
Epirus Rd. SW6 128 C7
Epping Cl. E14 134 A4
Epping Cl., Rom. 83 H3
Epping Glade E4 46 C6
Epping New Rd., Buck.H. 63 H2
Epping New Rd., Loug. 47 H5
Epping Pl. N1 93 G6
Liverpool Rd.
Epping Way E4 46 B6
Epple Rd. SW6 148 C1
Epsom Cl., Bexh. 159 H3
Epsom Cl., Nthlt. 85 F5
Epsom Rd. E10 78 C6
Epsom Rd., Croy. 201 G4
Epsom Rd., Ilf. 81 J6
Epsom Rd., Mord. 184 C6
Epsom Rd., Sutt. 184 C7
Epsom Sq., Houns. 141 J2
Eastern Perimeter Rd.
Epstein Rd. SE28 138 A1
Epworth Rd., Islw. 124 E7
Epworth St. EC2 12 C6
Epworth St. EC2 112 A4
Equity Sq. E2 112 C3
Shacklewell St.
Erasmus St. SW1 33 J2
Erasmus St. SW1 130 D4
Erconwald St. W12 107 F6
Eresby Dr., Beck. 204 A1
Eresby Pl. NW6 90 D7
Eric Clarke La., Bark. 117 E4
Eric Cl. E7 97 G4
Eric Rd. E7 97 G4
Eric Rd. NW10 89 F6
Church Rd.
Eric Rd., Rom. 82 D7
Eric St. E3 113 J4
Erica Gdns., Croy. 204 B4
Erica St. W12 107 G7
Ericcson Cl. SW18 148 D5
Eridge Rd. W4 126 D3
Erin Cl., Brom. 172 E7
Erin Cl., Ilf. 82 A6
Erindale SE18 137 G6
Erindale Ter. SE18 137 G6
Erith Cres., Rom. 83 J1
Erith Rd., Belv. 139 G5
Erith Rd., Bexh. 159 H4
Erith Rd., Erith 159 H4
Erlanger Rd. SE14 153 G1
Erlesmere Gdns. W13 124 D3
Ermine Cl., Houns. 142 C2
Ermine Ho. N17 60 C7
Moselle St.
Ermine Rd. N15 76 C6
Ermine Rd. SE13 154 B3
Ermine Side, Enf. 44 D5
Ermington Rd. SE9 175 F2
Ernald Av. E6 116 B2
Erncroft Way, Twick. 144 C6
Ernest Av. SE27 169 H4
Ernest Cl., Beck. 190 A5
Ernest Gdns. W4 126 B6
Ernest Gro., Beck. 189 J5
Ernest Rd., Kings.T. 182 B2
Ernest Sq., Kings.T. 182 B2
Ernest St. E1 113 G4
Ernle Rd. SW20 165 H7
Ernshaw Pl. SW15 148 B5
Carlton Dr.
Erpingham Rd. SW15 147 J3
Erridge Rd. SW19 184 D2
Errington Rd. W9 108 C4
Errol Gdns., Hayes 102 B4
Errol Gdns., N.Mal. 183 G4
Errol St. EC1 12 A6
Errol St. EC1 111 J4
Erskine Cl., Sutt. 199 H3
Erskine Cres. N17 76 E4
Erskine Hill NW11 72 D5
Erskine Ms. NW3 91 J7
Erskine Rd.
Erskine Rd. E17 77 J4
Erskine Rd. NW3 91 J7
Erskine Rd., Sutt. 199 G4
Erskine Rd., Wat. 50 C3
Erwood Rd. SE7 136 B5
Esam Way SW16 169 G5
Escot Way, Barn. 39 J5
Escott Gdns. SE9 174 B4
Escreet Gro. SE18 136 D4
Esher Av., Rom. 83 J6
Esher Av., Sutt. 198 A3
Esher Av., Walt. 178 A7
Esher Bypass, Chess. 195 F4
Esher Bypass, Cob. 195 E7
Esher Cl., Bex. 176 E1
Esher Cres., Houns. 141 H2
Eastern Perimeter Rd.
Esher Gdns. SW19 166 A2
Esher Ms., Mitch. 185 J3
Esher Rd., E.Mol. 180 A6
Esher Rd., Ilf. 99 H3
Esk Rd. E13 115 G4
Eskdale Av., Nthlt. 103 F1
Eskdale Cl., Wem. 87 G2
Eskdale Rd., Bexh. 159 G2
Eskmont Ridge SE19 170 B7
Esmar Cres. NW9 71 G7
Esme Ho. SW15 147 F4
Esmeralda Rd. SE1 37 J2
Esmeralda Rd. SE1 132 D4
Esmond Rd. NW6 108 C1
Esmond Rd. W4 126 D4
Esmond St. SW15 148 B4
Esparto St. SW18 149 E7
Essenden Rd., Belv. 139 G5
Essenden Rd., S.Croy. 202 B7
Essendine Rd. W9 108 D4
Essex Av., Islw. 144 B3
Essex Cl. E17 77 H4
Essex Cl., Mord. 184 A7
Essex Cl., Rom. 83 H4
Essex Cl., Ruis. 84 D1
Essex Ct. EC4 18 E4
Essex Ct. SW13 147 F2
Essex Gdns. N4 75 H6
Essex Gro. SE19 170 A6
Essex Ho. E14 114 B6
Giraud St.
Essex Pk. N3 56 E6
Essex Pk. Ms. W3 126 E1
Essex Pl. W4 126 C4
Essex Pl. Sq. W4 126 D4
Essex Pl.

Street	Page	Grid
Essex Rd. E4	62	E1
Essex Rd. E10	78	C6
Essex Rd. E12	98	B5
Essex Rd. E17	77	H6
Essex Rd. E18	79	H2
Essex Rd. N1	111	H1
Essex Rd. NW10	89	E7
Essex Rd. W3	106	C7
Essex Rd. W4	126	D4
Belmont Rd.		
Essex Rd., Bark.	99	G7
Essex Rd., Borwd.	38	A3
Essex Rd., Dag.	101	J5
Essex Rd., Enf.	44	A4
Essex Rd., Rom.	83	H4
Essex Rd. (Chadwell Heath), Rom.	82	C7
Essex Rd. S. E11	78	D7
Essex St. E7	97	G5
Essex St. WC2	**18**	**E5**
Essex Twr. SE20	189	E1
Essex Vil. W8	128	D2
Essex Wf. E5	95	G2
Essian St. E1	113	H5
Essoldo Way, Edg.	69	J3
Estate Way E10	95	J1
Estcourt Rd. SE25	189	E6
Estcourt Rd. SW6	128	C7
Este Rd. SW11	149	H3
Estella Av., N.Mal.	183	H4
Estelle Rd. NW3	91	J4
Esterbrooke St. SW1	**33**	**H2**
Esterbrooke St. SW1	130	D4
Esther Cl. N21	43	G7
Esther Rd. E11	78	E7
Estoria Cl. SW2	151	G7
Estreham Rd. SW16	168	D6
Estridge Cl., Houns.	143	G4
Estuary Cl., Bark.	118	B3
Eswyn Rd. SW17	167	J4
Etchingham Pk. Rd. N3	57	E7
Etchingham Rd. E15	96	C4
Eternit Wk. SW6	147	J1
Etfield Gro., Sid.	176	B5
Ethel Rd. E16	115	H6
Ethel St. SE17	**35**	**J2**
Ethelbert Cl., Brom.	191	G3
Ethelbert Gdns., Ilf.	80	C5
Ethelbert Rd. SW20	184	A1
Ethelbert Rd., Brom.	191	G3
Ethelbert Rd., Erith	139	J7
Ethelbert St. SW12	168	B1
Fernlea Rd.		
Ethelburga St. SW11	149	H1
Ethelden Rd. W12	127	H1
Etheldene Av. N10	74	C4
Etheridge Grn., Loug.	49	F3
Etheridge Rd.		
Etheridge Rd. NW2	71	J7
Etheridge Rd., Loug.	49	E2
Etherley Rd. N15	75	J5
Etherow St. SE22	152	D6
Etherstone Grn. SW16	169	G4
Etherstone Rd.		
Etherstone Rd. SW16	169	G4
Ethnard Rd. SE15	132	E6
Ethronvi Rd., Bexh.	159	E3
Etloe Rd. E10	96	A2
Eton Av. N12	57	F7
Eton Av. NW3	91	G7
Eton Av., Barn.	41	H6
Eton Av., Houns.	123	F6
Eton Av., N.Mal.	182	D5
Eton Av., Wem.	87	E4
Eton Cl. SW18	149	E7
Eton College Rd. NW3	91	J6
Eton Ct. NW3	91	G7
Eton Av.		
Eton Ct., Wem.	87	F4
Eton Av.		
Eton Garages NW3	91	H6
Lambolle Pl.		
Eton Gro. NW9	70	A3
Eton Gro. SE13	154	E3
Eton Hall NW3	91	J6
Eton College Rd.		
Eton Pl. NW3	92	A7
Haverstock Hill		
Eton Ri. NW3	91	J6
Eton College Rd.		
Eton Rd. NW3	91	J7
Eton Rd., Hayes	121	J7
Eton Rd., Ilf.	99	F5
Eton St., Rich.	145	H5
Eton Vil. NW3	91	J6
Etta St. SE8	133	H6
Ettrick St. E14	114	C6
Etwell Pl., Surb.	181	J6
Eugenia Rd. SE16	133	F4
Eureka Rd., Kings.T.	182	A2
Washington Rd.		
Europa Pl. EC1	**11**	**J4**
Europe Rd. SE18	136	C3
Eustace Rd. E6	116	B3
Eustace Rd. SW6	128	D7
Eustace Rd., Rom.	82	D7
Euston Cen. NW1	110	C4
Triton Sq.		
Euston Gro. NW1	**9**	**H4**
Euston Gro. NW1	110	D3
Euston Rd. N1	**10**	**A3**
Euston Rd. N1	110	D4
Euston Rd. NW1	**9**	**E6**
Euston Rd. NW1	110	B4
Euston Rd., Croy.	201	G1
Euston Sq. NW1	**9**	**H4**
Euston Sq. NW1	110	D3
Euston Sta. Colonnade NW1	**9**	**H4**
Euston St. NW1	**9**	**G5**
Euston St. NW1	110	C3
Eva Rd., Rom.	82	C7
Evandale Rd. SW9	151	G2
Evangelist Rd. NW5	92	B4
Evans Cl. E8	94	C6
Buttermere Wk.		
Evans Gro., Felt.	161	G2
Evans Rd. SE6	173	E2
Evanston Av. E4	62	C7
Evanston Gdns., Ilf.	80	B6
Eve Rd. E11	96	E4
Eve Rd. E15	115	E2
Eve Rd. N17	76	B3
Eve Rd., Islw.	144	D4
Evelina Rd. SE15	153	F3
Evelina Rd. SE20	171	G7
Eveline Lowe Est. SE16	**29**	**H6**
Eveline Lowe Est. SE16	132	D3
Eveline Rd., Mitch.	185	J1
Evelyn Av. NW9	70	D4
Evelyn Cl., Twick.	143	H7
Evelyn Ct. N1	**12**	**B2**
Evelyn Denington Rd. E6	116	B4
Evelyn Dr., Pnr.	50	D7
Evelyn Fox Ct. W10	107	J5
Evelyn Gdns. SW7	**30**	**E4**
Evelyn Gdns. SW7	129	G5
Evelyn Gdns., Rich.	145	H4
Kew Rd.		
Evelyn Gro. W5	125	J1
Evelyn Gro., Sthl.	103	F6
Evelyn Rd. E16	135	H1
Evelyn Rd. E17	78	C4
Evelyn Rd. SW19	166	E5
Evelyn Rd. W4	126	D3
Evelyn Rd., Barn.	41	J4
Evelyn Rd., Rich.	145	H3
Evelyn Rd. (Ham), Rich.	163	F3
Evelyn St. SE8	133	H5
Evelyn Ter., Rich.	145	H3
Evelyn Wk. N1	**12**	**B2**
Evelyn Wk. N1	112	A2
Evelyn Way, Wall.	200	D4
Evelyn Yd. W1	**17**	**H3**
Evening Hill, Beck.	172	C7
Evenwood Cl. SW15	148	B5
Everard Av., Brom.	205	G1
Everard Way, Wem.	87	H3
Everatt Cl. SW18	148	C6
Amerland Rd.		
Everdon Rd. SW13	127	G6
Everest Pl. E14	114	C5
Everest Rd. SE9	156	C5
Everest Rd., Stai.	140	A7
Everett Cl., Bushey	52	B1
Everett Wk., Belv.	139	F5
Osborne Rd.		
Everglade Strand NW9	71	F1
Evergreen Ct., Stai.	140	A7
Evergreen Way		
Evergreen Way, Stai.	140	A7
Everilda St. N1	111	F1
Evering Rd. E5	94	C3
Evering Rd. N16	94	C3
Everington Rd. N10	73	J2
Everington St. W6	128	A6
Everitt Rd. NW10	106	D3
Everleigh St. N4	93	F1
Eversfield Gdns. NW7	54	E7
Eversfield Rd., Rich.	145	J2
Evershed Wk. W4	126	D4
Eversholt St. NW1	**9**	**G1**
Eversholt St. NW1	110	C2
Evershot Rd. N4	93	F1
Eversleigh Rd. E6	116	A1
Eversleigh Rd. N3	56	C7
Eversleigh Rd. SW11	150	A2
Eversleigh Rd., Barn.	41	F5
Eversley Av., Wem.	88	A2
Eversley Cl. N21	43	F6
Eversley Cres. N21	43	F6
Eversley Cres., Islw.	144	A1
Eversley Mt. N21	43	F6
Eversley Pk. SW19	165	H5
Eversley Pk. Rd. N21	43	F6
Eversley Rd. SE7	135	H6
Eversley Rd. SE19	170	A7
Eversley Rd., Surb.	181	J4
Eversley Way, Croy.	204	A4
Everthorpe Rd. SE15	152	C3
Everton Bldgs. NW1	**9**	**F4**
Everton Dr., Stan.	69	J3
Everton Rd., Croy.	202	D1
Evesham Av. E17	78	A2
Evesham Cl., Grnf.	103	H2
Evesham Cl., Sutt.	198	D7
Evesham Grn., Mord.	184	E6
Evesham Rd. E15	115	F1
Evesham Rd. N11	58	C5
Evesham Rd., Felt.	142	C7
Sparrow Fm. Dr.		
Evesham Rd., Mord.	185	E6
Evesham St. W11	108	A7
Evesham Wk. SE5	152	A2
Love Wk.		
Evesham Wk. SW9	151	G2
Evesham Way SW11	150	A3
Evesham Way, Ilf.	80	D3
Evry Rd., Sid.	176	C6
Ewald Rd. SW6	148	C2
Ewanrigg Ter., Wdf.Grn.	63	J5
Ewart Gro. N22	75	G1
Ewart Pl. E3	113	J2
Ewart Rd. SE23	153	G7
Ewe Cl. N7	93	E6
Ewell Bypass, Epsom	197	G7
Ewell Ct. Av., Epsom	197	E5
Ewell Pk. Gdns., Epsom	197	G7
Ewell Pk. Way, Epsom	197	G6
Ewell Rd., Surb.	181	H6
Ewell Rd. (Long Ditton), Surb.	180	E7
Ewell Rd., Sutt.	198	B6
Ewellhurst Rd., Ilf.	80	B2
Ewelme Rd. SE23	171	F1
Ewen Cres. SW2	169	G1
Ewer St. SE1	**27**	**J2**
Ewer St. SE1	131	J1
Ewhurst Ho. E1	113	F5
Ewhurst Rd. SE4	153	J6
Exbury Rd. SE6	172	A2
Excel Ct. WC2	**17**	**J6**
Excelsior Cl., Kings.T.	182	A2
Washington Rd.		
Excelsior Gdns. SE13	154	C2
Exchange Arc. EC2	**20**	**E1**
Exchange Bldgs. E1	112	B6
Cutler St.		
Exchange Ct. WC2	**18**	**B6**
Exchange Pl. EC2	**20**	**D1**
Exchange Sq. EC2	**20**	**D1**
Exchange Sq. EC2	112	B5
Exeter Cl. E6	116	C6
Harper Rd.		
Exeter Gdns., Ilf.	98	B1
Exeter Ho. SW15	147	J6
Putney Heath		
Exeter Ms. NW6	90/91	E6
West Hampstead Ms.		
Exeter Rd. E16	115	G5
Exeter Rd. E17	78	A5
Exeter Rd. N9	61	F2
Exeter Rd. N14	58	B1
Exeter Rd. NW2	90	B5
Exeter Rd., Croy.	188	B7
Exeter Rd., Dag.	101	H6
Exeter Rd., Enf.	45	G3
Exeter Rd., Felt.	161	F3
Exeter Rd., Har.	85	E2
Exeter Rd., Houns.	141	H2
Exeter Rd., Well.	157	J2
Exeter St. WC2	**18**	**B5**
Exeter St. WC2	111	E7
Exeter Way SE14	133	J7
Exeter Way, Houns.	141	H3
Exford Gdns. SE12	173	H1
Exford Rd. SE12	173	H2
Exhibition Cl. W12	107	J7
Exhibition Rd. SW7	**23**	**F4**
Exhibition Rd. SW7	129	G2
Exmoor Cl., Ilf.	81	F1
Exmoor St. W10	108	A4
Exmouth Mkt. EC1	**11**	**E5**
Exmouth Mkt. EC1	111	G4
Exmouth Ms. NW1	**9**	**G4**
Exmouth Pl. E8	94	E7
Exmouth Rd. E17	77	J5
Exmouth Rd., Brom.	191	H3
Exmouth Rd., Ruis.	84	C3
Exmouth Rd., Well.	158	C1
Exmouth St. E1	113	F6
Commercial Rd.		
Exning Rd. E16	115	F4
Exon St. SE17	**36**	**D3**
Exon St. SE17	132	B5
Express Dr., Ilf.	100	B1
Exton Cres. NW10	88	C7
Exton Gdns., Dag.	100	C5
Exton St. SE1	**27**	**E2**
Exton St. SE1	131	G1
Eyebright Cl., Croy.	203	G1
Primrose La.		
Eyhurst Cl. NW2	89	G2
Eylewood Rd. SE27	169	J5
Eynella Rd. SE22	152	C7
Eynham Rd. W12	107	J6
Eynsford Cl., Orp.	193	F7
Eynsford Cres., Bex.	176	C1
Eynsford Rd., Ilf.	99	H2
Eynsham Dr. SE2	138	A4
Eynswood Dr., Sid.	176	B5
Eyot Gdns. W6	127	F5
Eyot Grn. W4	127	F6
Chiswick Mall		
Eyre Ct. NW8	**7**	**E1**
Eyre St. Hill EC1	**11**	**E6**
Eythorne Rd. SW9	151	G1
Ezra St. E2	**13**	**G3**
Ezra St. E2	112	C3

F

Street	Page	Grid
Faber Gdns. NW4	71	G5
Fabian Rd. SW6	128	C7
Fabian St. E6	116	C4
Factory La. N17	76	C2
Factory La., Croy.	201	G1
Factory Rd. E16	136	B1
Factory Sq. SW16	168	E6
Factory Yd. W7	124	B1
Uxbridge Rd.		
Faggs Rd., Felt.	142	A5
Fair Acres, Brom.	191	G5
Fair St. SE1	**29**	**E3**
Fair St., Houns.	143	J3
High St.		
Fairacre, N.Mal.	182	E3
Fairacres SW15	147	G4
Fairbairn Grn. SW9	151	G1
Fairbank Av., Orp.	206	E2
Fairbanks Rd. N17	76	C3
Fairbourne Rd. N17	76	B3
Fairbridge Rd. N19	92	D2
Fairbrook Cl. N13	59	G5
Fairbrook Rd. N13	59	G6
Fairburn Cl., Borwd.	38	A1
Fairburn Ct. SW15	148	B5
Mercier Rd.		
Fairby Rd. SE12	155	H5
Faircharm Trd. Est. SE8	134	B7
Fairchild Cl. SW11	149	G2
Wye St.		
Fairchild Pl. EC2	**12**	**E6**
Fairchild St. EC2	**13**	**E6**
Fairclough St. E1	**21**	**J4**
Fairclough St. E1	112	D6
Faircross Av., Bark.	99	F6
Fairdale Gdns. SW15	147	H4
Fairdale Gdns., Hayes	122	A1
Fairey Av., Hayes	121	J4
Fairfax Gdns. SE3	156	A1
Fairfax Ms. E16	135	H1
Wesley Av.		
Fairfax Ms. SW15	147	J4
Upper Richmond Rd.		
Fairfax Pl. NW6	91	F7
Fairfax Rd. N8	75	G4
Fairfax Rd. NW6	91	F7
Fairfax Rd. W4	127	E3
Fairfax Rd., Tedd.	162	D6
Fairfax Way N10	58	A7
Cromwell Rd.		
Fairfield Av. NW4	71	H6
Fairfield Av., Edg.	54	B6
Fairfield Av., Twick.	161	H1
Fairfield Av., Wat.	50	C3
Fairfield Cl. N12	57	F4
Fairfield Cl., Enf.	45	H4
Scotland Grn. Rd. N.		
Fairfield Cl., Epsom	196	E5
Fairfield Cl., Mitch.	167	H7
Fairfield Cl., Sid.	157	J6
Fairfield Ct. NW10	107	G1
Fairfield Cres., Edg.	54	B6
Fairfield Dr. SW18	149	E5
Fairfield Dr., Grnf.	105	F1
Fairfield Dr., Har.	67	J3
Fairfield E., Kings.T.	181	H2
Fairfield Gdns. N8	74/75	E5
Elder Av.		
Fairfield Gro. SE7	136	A5

Fairfield Ind. Est., Kings.T. 181 J3
Fairfield N., Kings.T. 181 H2
Fairfield Path, Croy. 202 A3
Fairfield Pl., Kings.T. 181 H3
Fairfield Rd. E3 114 A2
Fairfield Rd. E17 77 H2
Fairfield Rd. N8 75 E5
Fairfield Rd. N18 60 D4
Fairfield Rd. W7 124 D3
Fairfield Rd., Beck. 190 A2
Fairfield Rd., Bexh. 159 F2
Fairfield Rd., Brom. 173 G7
Fairfield Rd., Croy. 202 B3
Fairfield Rd., Ilf. 99 E6
Fairfield Rd., Kings.T. 181 H2
Fairfield Rd., Orp. 193 G6
Fairfield Rd., Sthl. 103 F6
Fairfield Rd., West Dr. 120 B1
Fairfield Rd., Wdf.Grn. 63 G6
Fairfield S., Kings.T. 181 H2
Fairfield St. SW18 149 E5
Fairfield Way, Barn. 40 D5
Fairfield Way, Epsom 196 E5
Fairfield W., Kings.T. 181 H2
Fairfields Cl. NW9 70 C5
Fairfields Cres. NW9 70 C4
Fairfields Rd., Houns. 143 J3
Fairfoot Rd. E3 114 A4
Fairford Av., Croy. 189 G5
Fairford Cl., Croy. 189 H5
Fairford Gdns., Wor.Pk. 197 F2
Fairgreen, Barn. 41 J3
Fairgreen E., Barn. 41 J3
Fairgreen Rd., Th.Hth. 187 H5
Fairhaven Av., Croy. 189 G6
Fairhaven Cres., Wat. 50 A3
Fairhazel Gdns. NW6 91 E6
Fairholme, Felt. 141 G7
Fairholme Cl. N3 72 B4
Fairholme Gdns. N3 72 B3
Fairholme Rd. W14 128 B5
Fairholme Rd., Croy. 187 G7
Fairholme Rd., Har. 68 C5
Fairholme Rd., Ilf. 80 C7
Fairholme Rd., Sutt. 198 C6
Fairholt Cl. N16 94 B1
Fairholt Rd. N16 94 A1
Fairholt St. SW7 23 H5
Fairland Rd. E15 97 F6
Fairlands Av., Buck.H. 63 G2
Fairlands Av., Sutt. 198 D2
Fairlands Av., Th.Hth. 187 F4
Fairlands Ct. SE9 156 D6
North Pk.
Fairlawn SE7 135 J6
Fairlawn Av. N2 73 H4
Fairlawn Av. W4 126 C4
Fairlawn Av., Bexh. 158 D2
Fairlawn Cl. N14 42 C6
Fairlawn Cl., Esher 194 C6
Fairlawn Cl., Felt. 161 F4
Fairlawn Cl., Kings.T. 164 C6
Fairlawn Dr., Wdf.Grn. 63 G7
Fairlawn Gdns., Sthl. 103 F7
Fairlawn Gro. W4 126 C4
Fairlawn Pk. SE26 171 H5
Fairlawn Rd. SW19 166 C7
Fairlawns, Pnr. 66 C2
Fairlawns, Sun. 178 A3
Fairlawns, Twick. 145 F6
Fairlea Pl. W5 105 G4
Fairlie Gdns. SE23 153 F7
Fairlight Av. E4 62 D2
Fairlight Av. NW10 107 E2
Fairlight Av., Wdf.Grn. 63 G6
Fairlight Cl. E4 62 D2
Fairlight Cl., Wor.Pk. 197 J4
Fairlight Rd. SW17 167 G4
Fairlop Gdns., Ilf. 65 F7
Fairlop Rd. E11 78 D7
Fairlop Rd., Ilf. 81 F2
Fairmead, Brom. 192 C4
Fairmead, Surb. 196 B1
Fairmead Cl., Brom. 192 C4
Fairmead Cl., Houns. 122 D7
Fairmead Cl., N.Mal. 182 D3
Fairmead Cres., Edg. 54 C3
Fairmead Gdns., Ilf. 80 B5
Fairmead Rd. N19 92 D3
Fairmead Rd., Croy. 201 F1
Fairmead Rd., Loug. 47 H4
Fairmead Side, Loug. 47 J5
Fairmeads, Loug. 48 E2
Fairmile Av. SW16 168 D5
Fairmont Cl., Belv. 139 F5
Lullingstone Rd.
Fairmount Rd. SW2 151 F6
Fairoak Cl., Orp. 193 E7
Fairoak Dr. SE9 157 G5
Fairseat Cl., Bushey 52 B2
Hive Rd.
Fairstead Wk. N1 111 J1
Popham Rd.
Fairthorn Rd. SE7 135 G5
Fairview Av., Wem. 87 G6
Fairview Cl. E17 77 H1
Fairview Cl., Chig. 65 H4
Fairview Cres., Har. 85 G1
Fairview Dr., Chig. 65 H4
Fairview Dr., Orp. 207 G4
Fairview Gdns., Wdf.Grn. 79 H1
Fairview Pl. SW2 151 F7
Fairview Rd. N15 76 C5
Fairview Rd. SW16 187 F1
Fairview Rd., Chig. 65 H4
Fairview Rd., Enf. 43 G1
Fairview Rd., Sutt. 199 G5
Fairview Way, Edg. 54 A4
Fairwater Av., Well. 158 A4
Fairway SW20 183 J3
Fairway, Bexh. 159 E5
Fairway, Orp. 193 G5
Fairway, Wdf.Grn. 63 J5
Fairway, The N13 59 J3
Fairway, The N14 42 B6
Fairway, The NW7 54 D3
Fairway, The W3 106 E6
Fairway, The, Barn. 41 E6
Fairway, The, Brom. 192 C5
Fairway, The, N.Mal. 182 D1
Fairway, The, Nthlt. 85 J6
Fairway, The, Ruis. 84 D3
Fairway, The, Wem. 87 E3
Fairway, The, W.Mol. 179 H3
Fairway Av. NW9 70 B3
Fairway Av., Borwd. 38 B2
Fairway Cl. NW11 73 F7
Fairway Cl., Croy. 189 H5
Fairway Cl., Epsom 196 C4
Fairway Cl., Houns. 142 C5
Fairway Ct. NW7 54 D3
The Fairway
Fairway Dr. SE28 118 D6
Fairway Dr., Grnf. 85 H7
Fairway Gdns., Beck. 190 D6
Fairway Gdns., Ilf. 99 F5
Fairways, Stan. 69 H2
Fairways, Tedd. 163 G7
Fairweather Cl. N15 76 B4
Fairweather Rd. N16 76 D6
Fairwyn Rd. SE26 171 H4
Fakenham Cl. NW7 55 G7
Fakenham Cl., Nthlt. 85 G6
Goodwood Dr.
Fakruddin St. E1 13 J6
Fakruddin St. E1 112 D4
Falcon Av., Brom. 192 B4
Falcon Cl. SE1 27 H1
Falcon Cl. W4 126 C6
Sutton La. S.
Falcon Ct. EC4 19 E4
Falcon Ct. EC4 111 G6
Falcon Cres., Enf. 45 G5
Falcon Dr., Stai. 140 A6
Falcon Gro. SW11 149 H3
Falcon Ho. W13 104 C4
Falcon La. SW11 149 H3
Falcon Pk. Ind. Est. NW10 89 F5
Falcon Rd. SW11 149 H2
Falcon Rd., Enf. 45 G5
Falcon Rd., Hmptn. 161 F7
Falcon St. E13 115 G4
Falcon Ter. SW11 149 H3
Falcon Way E11 79 G4
Falcon Way E14 134 B4
Falcon Way NW9 71 E2
Falcon Way, Felt. 142 B5
Falcon Way, Har. 69 H5
Falconberg Ct. W1 17 J3
Falconberg Ms. W1 17 H3
Falconer Wk. N7 93 F2
Newington Barrow Way
Falconwood Av., Well. 157 G2
Falconwood Par., Well. 157 H4
Falconwood Rd., Croy. 204 A7
Falcourt Cl., Sutt. 198 E5
Falkirk Gdns., Wat. 50 D5
Blackford Rd.
Falkirk Ho. W9 6 B3
Falkirk Ho. W9 109 E3
Falkirk St. N1 12 E2
Falkirk St. N1 112 B2
Falkland Av. N3 56 D7
Falkland Av. N11 58 A4
Falkland Pk. Av. SE25 188 B3
Falkland Pl. NW5 92 C5
Falkland Rd.
Falkland Rd. N8 75 G4
Falkland Rd. NW5 92 C5
Falkland Rd., Barn. 40 B2
Fallaize Av., Ilf. 98/99 E4
Riverdene Rd.
Falloden Way NW11 72 D4
Fallow Cl., Chig. 65 J5
Fallow Ct. SE16 37 J4
Fallow Ct. Av. N12 57 F7
Fallow Flds., Loug. 47 J7
Fallowfield, Stan. 52 D3
Fallowfield Ct., Stan. 52 D3
Fallowfields Dr. N12 57 H6
Fallows Cl. N2 73 F2
Fallsbrook Rd. SW16 168 C7
Falman Cl. N9 60 D1
Croyland Rd.
Falmer Rd. E17 78 B3
Falmer Rd. N15 75 J5
Falmer Rd., Enf. 44 B4
Falmouth Av. E4 62 D5
Falmouth Cl. N22 59 F7
Truro Rd.
Falmouth Cl. SE12 155 F5
Falmouth Gdns., Ilf. 80 B5
Falmouth Rd. SE1 28 A5
Falmouth Rd. SE1 131 J3
Falmouth St. E15 96 D5
Falstaff Ms., Hmptn. 162 A5
Hampton Rd.
Fambridge Cl. SE26 171 J4
Fambridge Rd., Dag. 101 G1
Fane St. W14 128 C6
North End Rd.
Fann St. EC1 11 J6
Fann St. EC1 111 J4
Fann St. EC2 11 J6
Fann St. EC2 111 J4
Fanshaw St. N1 12 D3
Fanshaw St. N1 112 B3
Fanshawe Av., Bark. 99 F6
Fanshawe Cres., Dag. 101 E5
Fanshawe Rd., Rich. 163 F4
Fanthorpe St. SW15 147 J3
Faraday Av., Sid. 176 A2
Faraday Cl. N7 93 F6
Bride St.
Faraday Rd. E15 97 F6
Faraday Rd. SW19 166 D6
Faraday Rd. W3 106 C7
Faraday Rd. W10 108 B5
Faraday Rd., Sthl. 103 H7
Faraday Rd., Well. 158 A3
Faraday Rd., W.Mol. 179 G4
Faraday Way SE18 136 A3
Faraday Way, Croy. 201 F1
Ampere Way
Fareham Rd., Felt. 142 C7
Fareham St. W1 17 H3
Farewell Pl., Mitch. 185 H1
Faringdon Av., Brom. 192 E6
Faringford Rd. E15 96 E7
Farjeon Rd. SE3 156 A1
Farleigh Av., Brom. 191 F6
Farleigh Pl. N16 94 C4
Farleigh Rd.
Farleigh Rd. N16 94 C4
Farley Dr., Ilf. 99 H1
Farley Pl. SE25 188 D4
Farley Rd. SE6 154 B7
Farley Rd., S.Croy. 202 E7
Farlington Pl. SW15 147 H7
Roehampton La.
Farlow Rd. SW15 148 A3
Farlton Rd. SW18 149 E7
Farm Av. NW2 90 B3
Farm Av. SW16 169 E4
Farm Av., Har. 67 F7
Farm Av., Wem. 87 F6
Farm Cl., Barn. 39 J5
Farm Cl., Buck.H. 63 J3
Farm Cl., Dag. 101 J7
Farm Cl., Sthl. 103 H7
Farm Cl., Sutt. 199 G7
Farm Cl., W.Wick. 205 E3
Farm Ct. NW4 71 G3
Farm Dr., Croy. 203 J2
Farm End E4 46 E5
Farm La. N14 42 A6
Farm La. SW6 128 D6
Farm La., Croy. 203 J2
Farm Pl. W8 128 D1
Uxbridge St.
Farm Rd. N21 59 J1
Farm Rd., Edg. 54 B6
Farm Rd., Houns. 161 E1
Farm Rd., Mord. 185 E5
Farm Rd., Sutt. 199 G7
Farm St. W1 16 D6
Farm St. W1 110 B7
Farm Vale, Bex. 159 H6
Farm Wk. NW11 72 C5
Farm Way, Buck.H. 63 J4
Farm Way, Wor.Pk. 197 J3
Farman Gro., Nthlt. 102 D3
Wayfarer Rd.
Farmborough Cl., Har. 68 A7
Pool Rd.
Farmcote Rd. SE12 173 G1
Farmdale Rd. SE10 135 G5
Farmdale Rd., Cars. 199 H7
Farmer Rd. E10 96 B1
Farmer St. W8 128 D1
Uxbridge St.
Farmers Rd. SE5 35 H7
Farmers Rd. SE5 131 H7
Farmfield Rd., Brom. 172 E5
Farmhouse Rd. SW16 168 C7
Farmilo Rd. E17 77 J7
Farmington Av., Sutt. 199 G3
Farmland Wk., Chis. 174 E5
Farmlands, Enf. 43 G1
Farmlands, Pnr. 66 A4
Farmlands, The, Nthlt. 85 F6
Farmleigh N14 42 C7
Farmstead Rd. SE6 172 B4
Farmstead Rd., Har. 68 A1
Farmway, Dag. 100 C4
Farnaby Rd. SE9 155 J4
Farnaby Rd., Brom. 172 D7
Farnan Av. E17 78 A2
Farnan Rd. SW16 169 E5
Farnborough Av. E17 77 H3
Farnborough Av., S.Croy. 203 G7
Farnborough Cl., Wem. 88 B2
Chalkhill Rd.
Farnborough Common, Orp. 206 C3
Farnborough Cres., Brom. 205 F1
Saville Row
Farnborough Hill, Orp. 207 G5
Farnborough Way SE15 37 E7
Farnborough Way, Orp. 207 F4
Farncombe St. SE16 29 J4
Farncombe St. SE16 132 D2
Farndale Av. N13 59 H3
Farndale Cres., Grnf. 103 J3
Farnell Ms. SW5 30 A3
Farnell Rd., Islw. 144 A3
Farnham Cl. N20 41 F7
Farnham Gdns. SW20 183 H2
Farnham Pl. SE1 27 H2
Farnham Rd., Ilf. 81 J7
Farnham Rd., Well. 158 C2
Farnham Royal SE11 34 D4
Farnham Royal SE11 131 F5
Farningham Rd. N17 60 D7
Farnley Rd. E4 46 E7
Farnley Rd. SE25 188 A4
Faro Cl., Brom. 192 D2
Faroe Rd. W14 128 A3
Farorna Wk., Enf. 43 G1
Farquhar Rd. SE19 170 C5
Farquhar Rd. SW19 166 D3
Farquharson Rd., Croy. 201 J1
Farr Av., Bark. 118 A2
Farr Rd., Enf. 44 A1
Farrance Rd., Rom. 83 E6
Farrance St. E14 113 J6
Farrans Ct., Har. 69 E7
Farrant Av. N22 75 G2
Farrell Ho. E1 113 F6
Farren Rd. SE23 171 H2
Farrer Ms. N8 74 C4
Farrer Rd.
Farrer Rd. N8 74 C4
Farrer Rd., Har. 69 H5
Farrer's Pl., Croy. 203 G4
Farrier Cl., Sun. 178 A4
Farrier Rd., Nthlt. 103 G2
Farrier St. NW1 92 B7
Farrier Wk. SW10 30 C5
Farrier Wk. SW10 129 F6
Farriers Way, Borwd. 38 C6
Farringdon La. EC1 11 F6
Farringdon La. EC1 111 G4
Farringdon Rd. EC1 10 E5
Farringdon Rd. EC1 111 G4
Farringdon St. EC4 19 G3
Farringdon St. EC4 111 H5
Farrington Pl., Chis. 175 G7

Farrins Rents SE16 133 H1
Farrow La. SE14 133 F7
Farrow Pl. SE16 133 H3
Ropemaker Rd.
Farthing All. SE1 29 H4
Farthing Flds. E1 132/133 E1
Raine St.
Farthing St., Orp. 206 C7
Farthingale Wk. E15 96 D7
Farthings, The, Kings.T. 182 A1
Brunswick Rd.
Farthings Cl. E4 63 E3
Farthings Cl., Pnr. 66 B6
Farwell Rd., Sid. 176 B3
Farwig La., Brom. 191 F1
Fashion St. E1 21 F2
Fashion St. E1 112 C5
Fashoda Rd., Brom. 192 A4
Fassett Rd. E8 94 D6
Fassett Rd., Kings.T. 181 H4
Fassett Sq. E8 94 D6
Fauconberg Rd. W4 126 C6
Faulkner Cl., Dag. 82 D7
Faulkner St. SE14 153 F1
Faulkner's All. EC1 19 G1
Fauna Cl., Rom. 82 C7
Faunce St. SE17 35 G5
Favart Rd. SW6 148 D1
Faversham Av. E4 63 E1
Faversham Av., Enf. 44 A6
Faversham Rd. SE6 153 J7
Faversham Rd., Beck. 189 J2
Faversham Rd., Mord. 185 E6
Fawcett Cl. SW11 149 G2
Fawcett Cl. SW16 169 G4
Fawcett Est. E5 94 D1
Fawcett Rd. NW10 107 F1
Fawcett Rd., Croy. 201 H3
Fawcett St. SW10 30 C5
Fawcett St. SW10 129 F6
Fawcus Cl., Esher 194 C6
Dalmore Av.
Fawe Pk. Rd. SW15 148 C4
Fawe St. E14 114 B5
Fawley Rd. NW6 90 E5
Fawn Rd. E13 115 J2
Fawn Rd., Chig. 65 J5
Fawnbrake Av. SE24 151 H5
Fawood Av. NW10 88 D7
Faygate Cres., Bexh. 159 G5
Faygate Rd. SW2 169 F2
Fayland Av. SW16 168 C5
Fearnley Cres., Hmptn. 161 F5
Fearon St. SE10 135 G5
Featherbed La., Croy. 203 J7
Feathers Pl. SE10 134 D6
Featherstone Av. SE23 171 E2
Featherstone Gdns., Borwd. 38 C4
Featherstone Ind. Est., Sthl. 123 E2
Featherstone Rd. NW7 55 H6
Featherstone Rd., Sthl. 122 E3
Featherstone St. EC1 12 B5
Featherstone St. EC1 112 A4
Featherstone Ter., Sthl. 123 E3
Featley Rd. SW9 151 H3
Federal Rd., Grnf. 105 F2
Federation Rd. SE2 138 B4
Fee Fm. Rd., Esher 194 C7
Felbridge Av., Stan. 68 D1
Felbridge Cl. SW16 169 G4
Felbrigge Rd., Ilf. 99 J2
Felday Rd. SE13 154 B6
Felden Cl., Pnr. 51 E7
Felden St. SW6 148 C1
Feldman Cl. N16 94 D1
Felgate Ms. W6 127 H4
Felhampton Rd. SE9 174 E2
Felhurst Cres., Dag. 101 H4
Felix Av. N8 74 E6
Felix Rd. W13 104 D7
Felix Rd., Walt. 178 A6
Felix St. E2 112/113 E2
Hackney Rd.
Felixstowe Ct. E16 136/137 E2
Barge Ho. Rd.
Felixstowe Rd. N9 60 D4
Felixstowe Rd. N17 76 C3
Felixstowe Rd. NW10 107 H3
Felixstowe Rd. SE2 138 B3
Fell Rd., Croy. 201 J3
Fell Wk., Edg. 70 B1
East Rd.
Fellbrigg Rd. SE22 152 C5
Fellbrigg St. E1 112/113 E4
Headlam St.
Fellbrook, Rich. 163 E3
Fellmongers Yd., Croy. 201 J2
Surrey St.
Fellowes Cl., Hayes 102 D4
Paddington Cl.
Fellowes Rd., Cars. 199 H3
Fellows Ct. E2 13 F2
Fellows Ct. E2 112 C2
Fellows Rd. NW3 91 G7
Felltram Way SE7 135 G5
Woolwich Rd.
Felmersham Cl. SW4 150 D4
Haselrigge Rd.
Felmingham Rd. SE20 189 F2
Felnex Trd. Est., Wall. 200 A2
Fels Cl., Dag. 101 H3
Fels Fm. Av., Dag. 101 J3
Felsberg Rd. SW2 151 E6
Felsham Rd. SW15 148 A3
Felspar Cl. SE18 137 J5
Felstead Av., Ilf. 80 D1
Felstead Gdns. E14 134 C5
Ferry St.
Felstead Rd. E11 79 G7
Felstead Rd., Loug. 48 B7
Felstead St. E9 95 J6
Felsted Rd. E16 116 A6
Feltham Av., E.Mol. 180 B4
Feltham Business Complex, Felt. 160 B2
Feltham Hill Rd., Felt. 160 A4
Feltham Rd., Mitch. 185 J2
Felthambrook Way, Felt. 160 B3
Felton Cl., Orp. 192 E6
Felton Gdns., Bark. 117 H1
Sutton Rd.
Felton Lea, Sid. 175 J5
Felton Rd. W13 125 F2
Camborne Av.
Felton Rd., Bark. 117 H2
Sutton Rd.
Felton St. N1 112 A1
Fen Ct. EC3 20 D5
Fen Gro., Sid. 157 J6
Fen St. E16 115 F7
Victoria Dock Rd.
Fencepiece Rd., Chig. 65 F5
Fencepiece Rd., Ilf. 65 F5
Fenchurch Av. EC3 20 D4
Fenchurch Av. EC3 112 B6
Fenchurch Bldgs. EC3 20 E4
Fenchurch Pl. EC3 20 E5
Fenchurch St. EC3 20 D5
Fenchurch St. EC3 112 B7
Fendall Rd., Epsom 196 C5
Fendall St. SE1 29 E6
Fendall St. SE1 132 B3
Fendt Cl. E16 115 F7
Bowman Av.
Fendyke Rd., Belv. 138 D3
Fenelon Pl. W14 128 C4
Fenham Rd. SE15 132 D7
Fenman Ct. N17 76/77 E1
Shelbourne Rd.
Fenman Gdns., Ilf. 100 B1
Fenn Cl., Brom. 173 G6
Fenn St. E9 95 F5
Fennel Cl. E16 114/115 E4
Cranberry La.
Fennel Cl., Croy. 203 G1
Primrose La.
Fennel St. SE18 136 D6
Fenner Cl. SE16 132/133 E4
Layard Rd.
Fenner Sq. SW11 149 G3
Thomas Baines Rd.
Fenning St. SE1 28 D3
Fenstanton Av. N12 57 G5
Fenswood Cl., Bex. 159 G5
Fentiman Rd. SW8 34 B6
Fentiman Rd. SW8 131 E6
Fenton Cl. E8 94 C6
Laurel St.
Fenton Cl. SW9 151 F2
Fenton Cl., Chis. 174 C5
Fenton Rd. N17 59 J7
Fentons Av. E13 115 H2
Fenwick Cl. SE18 136 D6
Ritter St.
Fenwick Gro. SE15 152 D3
Fenwick Pl. SW9 150 E3
Fenwick Rd. SE15 152 D3
Ferdinand Pl. NW1 92 A7
Ferdinand St.
Ferdinand St. NW1 92 A6
Fergus Rd. N5 93 H5
Calabria Rd.
Ferguson Av., Surb. 181 J5
Ferguson Cl. E14 134 A4
Ferguson Cl., Brom. 190 C3
Ferguson Dr. W3 106 D6
Ferme Pk. Rd. N4 75 E5
Ferme Pk. Rd. N8 75 E5
Fermor Rd. SE23 171 H1
Fermoy Rd. W9 108 C4
Fermoy Rd., Grnf. 103 H4
Fern Av., Mitch. 186 D4
Fern Dene W13 104/105 E5
Templewood
Fern Gro., Felt. 142 B7
Fern La., Houns. 123 F5
Fern St. E3 114 A4
Fern Wk. SE16 37 J4
Fernbank, Buck.H. 63 H1
Fernbank Av., Walt. 179 E7
Fernbank Av., Wem. 86 C4
Fernbank Ms. SW12 150 C6
Fernbrook Av., Sid. 157 H5
Blackfen Rd.
Fernbrook Cres. SE13 154 E6
Fernbrook Dr., Har. 67 H7
Fernbrook Rd. SE13 154 E6
Ferncliff Rd. E8 94 D5
Ferncroft Av. N12 57 H6
Ferncroft Av. NW3 90 D3
Ferncroft Av., Ruis. 84 C2
Ferndale, Brom. 191 J2
Ferndale Av. E17 78 D5
Ferndale Av., Houns. 143 E3
Ferndale Cl., Bexh. 158 E1
Ferndale Ct. SE3 135 F7
Ferndale Rd. E7 97 H7
Ferndale Rd. E11 97 E2
Ferndale Rd. N15 76 C6
Ferndale Rd. SE25 188 E5
Ferndale Rd. SW4 150 E4
Ferndale Rd. SW9 151 F3
Ferndale Rd., Rom. 83 J2
Ferndale St. E6 116 E7
Ferndale Ter., Har. 68 C4
Ferndale Way, Orp. 207 G5
Fernden Way, Rom. 83 H6
Ferndene Rd. SE24 151 J4
Ferndown, Nthwd. 66 A2
Ferndown Av., Orp. 207 G1
Ferndown Cl., Pnr. 50 E7
Ferndown Cl., Sutt. 199 G6
Ferndown Rd. SE9 156 A7
Ferndown Rd., Wat. 50 C3
Ferney Meade Way, Islw. 144 D2
Ferney Rd., Barn. 42 A7
Fernhall Dr., Ilf. 80 A5
Fernham Rd., Th.Hth. 187 J3
Fernhead Rd. W9 108 C4
Fernhill Ct. E17 78 D2
Fernhill Gdns., Kings.T. 163 G5
Fernhill St. E16 136 C1
Fernholme Rd. SE15 153 G5
Fernhurst Gdns., Edg. 54 A6
Fernhurst Rd. SW6 148 B1
Fernhurst Rd., Croy. 188 D7
Fernlea Rd. SW12 168 B1
Fernlea Rd., Mitch. 186 A2
Fernleigh Cl., Croy. 201 G4
Stafford Rd.
Fernleigh Ct., Har. 67 H2
Fernleigh Ct., Wem. 87 H2
Fernleigh Rd. N21 59 G2
Ferns Rd. E15 97 F6
Fernsbury St. WC1 10 E4
Fernshaw Rd. SW10 30 C6
Fernshaw Rd. SW10 129 F6
Fernside NW11 90 D2
Finchley Rd.
Fernside, Buck.H. 63 H1
Fernside Av. NW7 54 D3
Fernside Av., Felt. 160 B4
Fernside Rd. SW12 167 J1
Fernthorpe Rd. SW16 168 C6
Ferntower Rd. N5 94 A5
Fernways, Ilf. 98/99 E4
Cecil Rd.
Fernwood Av. SW16 168 D4
Fernwood Av., Wem. 87 F5
Bridgewater Rd.
Fernwood Cl., Brom. 191 J2
Fernwood Cres. N20 57 J3
Ferranti Cl. SE18 136 A3
Ferraro Cl., Houns. 123 G6
Ferrers Av., Wall. 200 D4
Ferrers Av., West Dr. 120 A2
Ferrers Rd. SW16 168 D5
Ferrestone Rd. N8 75 F4
Ferriby Cl. N1 93 G7
Bewdley St.
Ferrier Pt. E16 115 H5
Forty Acre La.
Ferrier St. SW18 149 E4
Ferring Cl., Har. 85 J1
Ferrings SE21 170 B2
Ferris Av., Croy. 203 J3
Ferris Rd. SE22 152 D4
Ferron Rd. E5 94 E3
Ferrour Ct. N2 73 G3
Ferry La. N17 76 E4
Ferry La. SW13 127 F6
Ferry La., Brent. 125 H6
Ferry La., Rich. 125 J6
Ferry Pl. SE18 136 D3
Woolwich High St.
Ferry Rd. SW13 127 G7
Ferry Rd., Tedd. 162 E5
Ferry Rd., T.Ditt. 180 E6
Ferry Rd., Twick. 162 E1
Ferry Rd., W.Mol. 179 G3
Ferry Sq., Brent. 125 G6
Ferry St. E14 134 C5
Ferryhills Cl., Wat. 50 C3
Ferrymead Av., Grnf. 103 G3
Ferrymead Dr., Grnf. 103 G2
Ferrymead Gdns., Grnf. 103 J2
Ferrymoor, Rich. 163 E3
Festing Rd. SW15 148 A3
Festival Cl., Bex. 176 D1
Festival Wk., Cars. 199 J5
Fetter La. EC4 19 F4
Fetter La. EC4 111 G6
Ffinch St. SE8 134 A7
Field Cl. E4 62 B6
Field Cl., Brom. 191 J2
Field Cl., Buck.H. 63 J3
Field Cl., Chess. 195 F5
Field Cl., Hayes 121 F7
Field Cl., Houns. 142 B1
Field Cl., W.Mol. 179 H5
Field Ct. WC1 18 D2
Field End, Barn. 39 H4
Field End, Nthlt. 84 D6
Field End, Ruis. 84 C6
Field End, Twick. 162 C4
Field End Rd., Pnr. 66 B6
Field End Rd., Ruis. 85 E4
Field La., Brent. 125 F7
Field La., Tedd. 162 D5
Field Mead NW7 55 E7
Field Mead NW9 55 E7
Field Pl., N.Mal. 183 F6
Field Rd. E7 97 G4
Field Rd. N17 76 A3
Field Rd. W6 128 B5
Field Rd., Felt. 142 B6
Field St. WC1 10 C3
Field St. WC1 111 F3
Field Way NW10 88 C7
Twybridge Way
Field Way, Croy. 204 B6
Field Way, Grnf. 103 H1
Fieldcommon La., Walt. 179 F7
Fieldend Rd. SW16 186 C1
Fielders Cl., Enf. 44 B4
Woodfield Cl.
Fielders Cl., Har. 85 J1
Fieldfare Rd. SE28 118 C7
Fieldgate La., Mitch. 185 H3
Fieldgate St. E1 21 J2
Fieldgate St. E1 112 D5
Fieldhouse Cl. E18 79 G1
Fieldhouse Rd. SW12 168 C1
Fielding Av., Twick. 161 J3
Fielding Ho. NW6 108 D3
Fielding Ms. SW13 127 H6
Castelnau
Fielding Rd. W4 126 D3
Fielding Rd. W14 128 A3
Fielding St. SE17 35 J5
Fielding St. SE17 131 J6
Fielding Wk. W13 124 E3
Fieldings, The SE23 171 F1
Fields Est. E8 94 D7
Fields Pk. Cres., Rom. 82 D5
Fieldsend Rd., Sutt. 198 B5
Fieldside Cl., Orp. 207 F4
State Fm. Av.
Fieldside Rd., Brom. 172 D5
Fieldview SW18 167 G1
Fieldway, Dag. 100 B4
Fieldway, Orp. 193 G6
Fieldway Cres. N5 93 G5
Fiennes Cl., Dag. 100 C1
Fiesta Dr., Dag. 119 J4
Fife Rd. E16 115 G5
Fife Rd. N22 59 H7
Fife Rd. SW14 146 C5
Fife Rd., Kings.T. 181 H2
Fife Ter. N1 10 D1
Fife Ter. N1 111 F2
Fifield Path SE23 171 G3
Bampton Rd.
Fifth Av. E12 98 C4
Fifth Av. W10 108 B3
Fifth Av., Hayes 121 J1
Fifth Cross Rd., Twick. 162 A2

Fifth Way, Wem. 88 B4
Fig Tree Cl. NW10 106/107 E1
Craven Pk.
Figges Rd., Mitch. 168 A7
Filby Rd., Chess. 195 J6
Filey Av. N16 94 D1
Filey Cl., Sutt. 199 F7
Filey Waye, Ruis. 84 A2
Filigree Ct. SE16 133 J1
Silver Wk.
Fillebrook Av., Enf. 44 B2
Fillebrook Rd. E11 96 D1
Filmer Rd. SW6 148 B1
Filston Rd., Erith 139 H5
Riverdale Rd.
Finborough Rd. SW10 30 B5
Finborough Rd. SW10 128 E5
Finborough Rd. SW17 167 J6
Finch Av. SE27 170 A4
Finch Cl. NW10 88 D5
Finch Cl., Barn. 40 D5
Finch Dr., Felt. 142 D7
Finch La. EC3 20 C4
Finch Ms. SE15 132 C7
Finchale Rd. SE2 138 A3
Finchdean Way SE15 132 C7
Daniel Gdns.
Finchingfield Av., Wdf.Grn. 63 J7
Finchley Ct. N3 57 E6
Finchley La. NW4 71 J4
Finchley Pk. N12 57 F4
Finchley Pl. NW8 6 E1
Finchley Pl. NW8 109 G2
Finchley Rd. NW2 90 D3
Finchley Rd. NW3 91 F6
Finchley Rd. NW8 109 G1
Finchley Rd. NW11 72 C6
Finchley Way N3 56 D7
Finck St. SE1 26 D4
Finden Rd. E7 97 H5
Findhorn Av., Hayes 102 B5
Findhorn St. E14 114 C6
Findon Cl. SW18 148 D6
Wimbledon Pk. Rd.
Findon Cl., Har. 85 H3
Findon Rd. N9 60 E1
Findon Rd. W12 127 G2
Fingal St. SE10 135 F5
Finland Quay SE16 133 H3
Finland Rd. SE4 153 H3
Finland St. SE16 133 H3
Finlay St. SW6 148 A1
Finlays Cl., Chess. 196 A5
Finnis St. E2 113 E3
Finnymore Rd., Dag. 101 E7
Finsbury Av. EC2 20 C2
Finsbury Circ. EC2 20 C2
Finsbury Circ. EC2 112 A5
Finsbury Cotts. N22 58/59 E7
Clarence Rd.
Finsbury Est. EC1 11 G4
Finsbury Est. EC1 111 G3
Finsbury Ho. N22 75 E1
Finsbury Mkt. EC2 12 D6
Finsbury Mkt. EC2 112 B4
Finsbury Pk. Av. N4 75 J6
Finsbury Pk. Rd. N4 93 H3
Finsbury Pavement EC2 20 C1
Finsbury Pavement EC2 112 A5
Finsbury Rd. N22 75 F1
Finsbury Sq. EC2 20 C1
Finsbury Sq. EC2 112 A5
Finsbury St. EC2 20 B1
Finsbury St. EC2 112 A5
Finsbury Way, Bex. 159 F6
Finsen Rd. SE5 151 J3
Finstock Rd. W10 108 A6
Finucane Ri., Bushey 51 J2
Fir Cl., Walt. 178 A7
Fir Dene, Orp. 206 C3
Fir Gro., N.Mal. 183 F6
Fir Rd., Felt. 160 D5
Fir Rd., Sutt. 198 C1
Fir Tree Av., Mitch. 186 A2
Fir Tree Av., West Dr. 120 D3
Fir Tree Cl. SW16 168 C5
Fir Tree Cl. W5 105 H6
Fir Tree Cl., Epsom 197 F4
Fir Tree Cl., Orp. 207 J5
Highfield Av.
Fir Tree Gdns., Croy. 204 A4
Fir Tree Gro., Cars. 199 J7
Fir Tree Rd., Houns. 143 E4
Fir Tree Wk., Dag. 101 J3
Wheel Fm. Dr.
Fir Tree Wk., Enf. 44 A3
Fir Trees Cl. SE16 133 H1
Firbank Cl. E16 116 A5
Firbank Cl., Enf. 43 J4
Gladbeck Way
Firbank Rd. SE15 153 E2
Fircroft Gdns., Har. 86 B3
Fircroft Rd. SW17 167 J2
Fircroft Rd., Chess. 195 J4
Firdene, Surb. 196 C1
Fire Bell All., Surb. 181 H6
Fire Sta. All., Barn. 40 C2
Christchurch La.
Firecrest Dr. NW3 91 E3
Firefly Cl., Wall. 200 E7
Firefly Gdns. E6 116 B4
Jack Dash Way
Firethorn Cl., Edg. 54 C4
Larkspur Gro.
Firhill Rd. SE6 172 A4
Firs, The E17 77 H5
Leucha Rd.
Firs, The N20 57 G1
Firs, The W5 105 G5
Firs Av. N10 74 A3
Firs Av. N11 58 A6
Firs Av. SW14 146 C4
Firs Cl. N10 74 A3
Firs Av.
Firs Cl. SE23 153 G7
Firs Cl., Esher 194 B6
Firs Cl., Mitch. 186 B2
Firs Dr., Houns. 122 B7
Firs Dr., Loug. 48 D1
Firs La. N13 59 J3
Firs La. N21 59 J2
Firs Pk. Av. N21 60 A1
Firs Pk. Gdns. N21 59 J1
Firs Wk., Wdf.Grn. 63 G5
Firsby Av., Croy. 203 G1
Firsby Rd. N16 94 C1
Firscroft N13 59 J3
Firside Gro., Sid. 175 J1
First Av. E12 98 B4
First Av. E13 115 G3
First Av. E17 78 A5
First Av. N18 61 F4
First Av. NW4 71 J4
First Av. SW14 146 E3
First Av. W3 127 F1
First Av. W10 108 C4
First Av., Bexh. 138 C7
First Av., Dag. 119 H2
First Av., Enf. 44 C6
First Av., Hayes 121 J1
First Av., Rom. 82 C5
First Av., Walt. 178 B6
First Av., Wem. 87 G2
First Av., W.Mol. 179 F4
First Cl., W.Mol. 179 J3
First Cross Rd., Twick. 162 B2
First Dr. NW10 88 C7
First St. SW3 31 H1
First St. SW3 129 H4
First Way, Wem. 88 B4
Firstway SW20 183 J2
Firswood Av., Epsom 197 F5
Firth Gdns. SW6 148 B1
Fish St. Hill EC3 20 C5
Fish St. Hill EC3 112 A7
Fisher Cl., Croy. 202 C1
Grant Rd.
Fisher Cl., Grnf. 103 G3
Gosling Cl.
Fisher Rd., Har. 68 C2
Fisher St. E16 115 G5
Fisher St. WC1 18 C2
Fisher St. WC1 111 F5
Fisherman Cl., Rich. 163 F4
Locksmeade Rd.
Fishermans Dr. SE16 133 G2
Fisherman's Wk. E14 134 A1
Fishermans Wk. SE28 137 H2
Tugboat St.
Fishers Ct. SE14 153 G1
Besson St.
Fishers La. W4 126 D4
Fishers Way, Belv. 139 J1
Fishersdene, Esher 194 D7
Fisherton St. NW8 7 E6
Fisherton St. NW8 109 G4
Fishguard Way E16 136/137 E2
Barge Ho. Rd.
Fishponds Rd. SW17 167 H4
Fishponds Rd., Kes. 206 A5
Fisons Rd. E16 135 G1
Fitzalan Rd. N3 72 B3
Fitzalan Rd., Esher 194 B7
Fitzalan St. SE11 34 D1
Fitzalan St. SE11 131 F4
Fitzgeorge Av. W14 128 B4
Fitzgeorge Av., N.Mal. 182 D1
Fitzgerald Av. SW14 147 E3
Fitzgerald Cl. E11 79 G5
Fitzgerald Rd.
Fitzgerald Ho. E14 114 B6
Fitzgerald Ho., Hayes 122 B1
Fitzgerald Rd. E11 79 G5
Fitzgerald Rd. SW14 146 D3
Fitzgerald Rd., T.Ditt. 180 D6
Fitzhardinge St. W1 16 B3
Fitzhardinge St. W1 110 A6
Fitzhugh Gro. SW18 149 G6
Fitzhugh Gro. Est. SW18 149 G6
Fitzjames Av. W14 128 B4
Fitzjames Av., Croy. 202 D2
Fitzjohn Av., Barn. 40 B5
Fitzjohn's Av. NW3 91 G5
Fitzmaurice Pl. W1 24 E1
Fitzmaurice Pl. W1 110 B7
Fitzneal St. W12 107 F6
Fitzroy Cl. N6 91 J1
Fitzroy Ct. W1 9 G6
Fitzroy Cres. W4 126 D7
Fitzroy Gdns. SE19 170 B7
Fitzroy Ms. W1 9 F6
Fitzroy Pk. N6 91 J1
Fitzroy Rd. NW1 110 A1
Fitzroy Sq. W1 9 F6
Fitzroy Sq. W1 110 C4
Fitzroy St. W1 9 F6
Fitzroy St. W1 110 C4
Fitzroy Yd. NW1 110 A1
Fitzroy Rd.
Fitzstephen Rd., Dag. 100 B5
Fitzwarren Gdns. N19 92 C1
Fitzwilliam Av., Rich. 145 J2
Fitzwilliam Ms. E16 135 G1
Hanover Av.
Fitzwilliam Rd. SW4 150 C3
Fitzwygram Cl., Hmptn. 161 J5
Five Acre NW9 71 F1
Five Bell All. E14 113 J7
Three Colt St.
Five Elms Rd., Brom. 205 H3
Five Elms Rd., Dag. 101 F3
Five Flds. Cl., Wat. 51 F3
Fiveacre Cl., Th.Hth. 187 G6
Fives Ct. SE11 35 G1
Fiveways Rd. SW9 151 H2
Fladbury Rd. N15 76 A6
Fladgate Rd. E11 79 E6
Flag Cl., Croy. 203 G1
Flag Wk., Pnr. 66 A6
Eastcote Rd.
Flambard Rd., Har. 68 D6
Flamborough Rd., Ruis. 84 A3
Flamborough St. E14 113 H6
Flamingo Gdns., Nthlt. 102/103 E3
Jetstar Way
Flamstead Gdns., Dag. 100 C7
Flamstead Rd.
Flamstead Rd., Dag. 100 C7
Flamsted Av., Wem. 88 A6
Flamsteed Rd. SE7 136 B5
Flanchford Rd. W12 127 F3
Flanders Cres. SW17 167 J7
Flanders Rd. E6 116 C2
Flanders Rd. W4 127 E4
Flanders Way E9 95 G6
Flank St. E1 21 H5
Flask Cotts. NW3 91 G4
New End Sq.
Flask Wk. NW3 91 G4
Flavell Ms. SE10 135 E5
Flaxen Cl. E4 62 B3
Flaxen Rd.
Flaxen Rd. E4 62 B3
Flaxley Rd., Mord. 184 E6
Flaxman Ct. W1 17 H4
Flaxman Rd. SE5 151 H2
Flaxman Ter. WC1 9 J4
Flaxman Ter. WC1 110 D3
Flaxton Rd. SE18 157 G1
Flecker Cl., Stan. 52 C5
Fleece Dr. N9 60 D4
Fleece Rd., Surb. 195 F1
Fleece Wk. N7 92/93 E6
Manger Rd.
Fleeming Cl. E17 77 J2
Pennant Ter.
Fleeming Rd. E17 77 J2
Fleet Cl., W.Mol. 179 F5
Fleet La., W.Mol. 179 F6
Fleet Pl. EC4 111 G6
Farringdon St.
Fleet Rd. NW3 91 H5
Fleet Sq. WC1 10 C4
Fleet St. EC4 19 E4
Fleet St. EC4 111 G6
Fleet St. Hill E1 13 H6
Fleetside, W.Mol. 179 F6
Fleetway Business Pk., Grnf. 105 E2
Fleetwood Cl. E16 116 A5
Fleetwood Cl., Chess. 195 G7
Fleetwood Cl., Croy. 202 B3
Chepstow Ri.
Fleetwood Ct. E6 116 C5
Evelyn Denington Rd.
Fleetwood Gro. W3 106/107 E7
East Acton La.
Fleetwood Rd. NW10 89 G5
Fleetwood Rd., Kings.T. 182 B3
Fleetwood Sq., Kings.T. 182 B3
Fleetwood St. N16 94 B2
Stoke Newington Ch. St.
Fleetwood Way, Wat. 50 C4
Fleming Ct. W2 14 E1
Fleming Ct., Croy. 201 G5
Fleming Dr. N21 43 F5
Sydenham Av.
Fleming Mead, Mitch. 167 H7
Fleming Rd. SE17 35 H5
Fleming Rd. SE17 131 H6
Fleming Rd., Sthl. 103 H6
Fleming Way SE28 118 D7
Fleming Way, Islw. 144 C3
Flemming Av., Ruis. 84 B1
Flempton Rd. E10 95 H1
Fletcher Cl. E6 116/117 E6
Trader Rd.
Fletcher La. E10 78 C7
Fletcher Path SE8 134 A7
New Butt La.
Fletcher Rd. W4 126 C3
Fletcher Rd., Chig. 65 J5
Fletcher St. E1 21 J5
Fletcher St. E1 112 D7
Fletchers Cl., Brom. 191 H4
Fletching Rd. E5 95 F3
Fletching Rd. SE7 135 J6
Fletton Rd. N11 58 E7
Fleur de Lis St. E1 13 E6
Fleur de Lis St. E1 112 B4
Fleur Gates SW19 148 A7
Princes Way
Flexmere Gdns. N17 76 A1
Flexmere Rd.
Flexmere Rd. N17 76 A1
Flight App. NW9 71 F2
Flimwell Cl., Brom. 172 E5
Flint St. SE17 36 C2
Flint St. SE17 132 A4
Flintmill Cres. SE3 156 B2
Flinton St. SE17 36 E3
Flinton St. SE17 132 B5
Flitcroft St. WC2 17 J3
Flock Mill Pl. SW18 166 E1
Flockton St. SE16 29 H4
Flodden Rd. SE5 151 J1
Flood La., Twick. 162 D1
Church La.
Flood Pas. SE18 136 C4
Samuel St.
Flood St. SW3 31 H4
Flood St. SW3 129 H5
Flood Wk. SW3 31 H5
Flood Wk. SW3 129 H6
Flora Cl. E14 114 B6
Flora Gdns. W6 127 H4
Ravenscourt Rd.
Flora Gdns., Rom. 82 C6
Flora St., Belv. 139 F5
Victoria St.
Floral St. WC2 18 A5
Floral St. WC2 110 E7
Florence Av., Enf. 43 J3
Florence Av., Mord. 185 F5
Florence Cantwell Wk. N19 74/75 E7
Hillrise Rd.
Florence Cl., Walt. 178 B7
Florence Rd.
Florence Dr., Enf. 43 J3
Florence Elson Cl. E12 98 D4
Grantham Rd.
Florence Gdns. W4 126 C6
Florence Gdns., Rom. 82 C7
Roxy Av.
Florence Nightingale Ho. N1 94 A6
Clephane Rd.
Florence Rd. E6 115 J1
Florence Rd. E13 115 F2
Florence Rd. N4 93 G1
Florence Rd. SE2 138 C3
Florence Rd. SE14 153 J1
Florence Rd. SW19 166 E6
Florence Rd. W4 126 D3
Florence Rd. W5 105 H7

Florence Rd., Beck. 189 G2
Florence Rd., Brom. 191 G1
Florence Rd., Felt. 160 B1
Florence Rd., 163 J7
  Kings.T.
Florence Rd., Sthl. 122 D4
Florence Rd., Walt. 178 B7
Florence St. E16 115 F4
Florence St. N1 93 H7
Florence St. NW4 71 J4
Florence Ter. SE14 153 J1
Florence Way SW12 167 J1
Florfield Pas. E8 94/95 E6
  Reading La.
Florfield Rd. E8 94/95 E6
  Reading La.
Florian Av., Sutt. 199 G4
Florian Rd. SW15 148 B4
Florida Cl., Bushey 52 A2
Florida Rd., Th.Hth. 187 H1
Florida St. E2 13 H4
Florida St. E2 112 D3
Floriston Cl., Stan. 69 E1
Floriston Gdns., Stan. 69 E1
Floss St. SW15 147 J2
Flower & Dean Wk. 21 G2
E1
Flower La. NW7 55 F5
Flower Pot Cl. N15 76 C6
  St. Ann's Rd.
Flower Wk., The SW7 22 C4
Flower Wk., The SW7 129 F2
Flowers Ms. N19 92 C2
  Tollhouse Way
Flowersmead SW17 168 A2
Floyd Rd. SE7 135 J5
Fludyer St. SE13 154 E4
Foley Ms., Esher 194 B7
Foley Rd., Esher 194 B7
Foley St. W1 17 F2
Foley St. W1 110 C5
Folgate St. E1 21 E1
Folgate St. E1 112 B5
Foliot St. W12 107 F6
Folkestone Rd. E6 116 D2
Folkestone Rd. E17 78 B4
Folkestone Rd. N18 60 D4
Folkingham La. NW9 70 D1
Folkington Cor. N12 56 C5
Follett St. E14 114 C6
Folly La. E4 61 J7
Folly La. E17 77 H1
Folly Ms. W11 108 C6
  Portobello Rd.
Folly Wall E14 134 C2
Font Hills N2 73 F2
Fontaine Rd. SW16 169 F7
Fontarabia Rd. SW11 150 A4
Fontayne Av., Chig. 65 F4
Fontenoy Rd. SW12 168 B2
Fonteyne Gdns., 80 A2
  Wdf.Grn.
  Lechmere Av.
Fonthill Cl. SE20 188 D2
  Selby Rd.
Fonthill Ms. N4 93 G2
  Lennox Rd.
Fonthill Rd. N4 93 F1
Fontley Way SW15 147 G7
Fontwell Cl., Har. 52 B7
Fontwell Cl., Nthlt. 85 G6
Fontwell Dr., Brom. 192 D5
Football La., Har. 86 B1
Footpath, The SW15 147 G5
Foots Cray High St., 176 C6
  Sid.
Foots Cray La., Sid. 176 C1
Footway, The SE9 157 F7
Forbes Cl. NW2 89 G3
Forbes Cl. SE19 170 B5
Forbes St. E1 21 J4
Forbes Way, Ruis. 84 B2
Forburg Rd. N16 94 D1
Ford Cl. E3 113 H2
  Roman Rd.
Ford Cl., Har. 68 A7
Ford Cl., Th.Hth. 187 H6
Ford End, Wdf.Grn. 63 H6
Ford Rd. E3 113 H1
Ford Rd., Dag. 101 F7
Ford Sq. E1 113 E5
Ford St. E3 113 H1
Ford St. E16 115 F6
Forde Av., Brom. 191 J3
Fordel Rd. SE6 172 D1
Fordham Cl., Barn. 41 H3
Fordham Rd., Barn. 41 G3
Fordham St. E1 21 J3
Fordham St. E1 112 D6
Fordhook Av. W5 105 J7
Fordingley Rd. W9 108 C3
Fordington Rd. N6 73 J5
Fordmill Rd. SE6 172 A2

Fords Gro. N21 59 J1
Fords Pk. Rd. E16 115 G6
Fordwich Cl., Orp. 193 J7
Fordwych Rd. NW2 90 B5
Fordyce Rd. SE13 154 C6
Fordyke Rd., Dag. 101 F2
Fore St. EC2 20 A2
Fore St. EC2 111 J5
Fore St. N9 60 D5
Fore St. N18 60 C6
Fore St., Pnr. 66 A5
Fore St. Av. EC2 20 B2
Foreland Cl. NW4 72 B1
Foreland St. SE18 137 G4
  Plumstead Rd.
Foreman Ct. W6 127 J4
  Hammersmith Bdy.
Foremark Cl., Ilf. 65 J5
Foreshore SE8 133 J4
Forest, The E11 79 E4
Forest App. E4 47 E1
Forest App., Wdf.Grn. 63 F7
Forest Av. E4 47 E1
Forest Av., Chig. 64 D5
Forest Business Pk. 77 G7
  E17
Forest Cl. E11 79 F5
Forest Cl., Chis. 192 D1
Forest Cl., Wdf.Grn. 63 H3
Forest Ct. E4 63 F1
Forest Ct. E11 79 E4
Forest Cft. SE23 171 E2
Forest Dr. E12 98 A3
Forest Dr., Kes. 206 B4
Forest Dr. E. E11 78 D7
Forest Dr. W. E11 78 C7
Forest Edge, Buck.H. 63 J4
Forest Gdns. N17 76 C2
Forest Gate NW9 70 E5
Forest Glade E4 62 E4
Forest Glade E11 79 E6
Forest Gro. E8 94 C7
Forest Hts., Buck.H. 63 G2
Forest Hill Business 171 F2
  Cen. SE23
Forest Hill Ind. Est. 171 F2
  SE23
  Perry Vale
Forest Hill Rd. SE22 153 E5
Forest Hill Rd. SE23 153 E5
Forest Ind. Pk., Ilf. 81 H1
Forest La. E7 97 E5
Forest La. E15 97 E5
Forest La., Chig. 64 D5
Forest Mt. Rd., 62 D7
  Wdf.Grn.
Forest Ridge, Beck. 190 A3
Forest Ridge, Kes. 206 B4
Forest Ri. E17 78 D5
Forest Rd. E7 97 G4
Forest Rd. E8 94 C6
Forest Rd. E11 78 D7
Forest Rd. E17 77 F4
Forest Rd. N9 61 E1
Forest Rd. N17 77 F4
Forest Rd., Felt. 160 C2
Forest Rd., Ilf. 81 H1
Forest Rd., Loug. 48 A3
Forest Rd., Rich. 126 A7
Forest Rd., Rom. 83 H3
Forest Rd., Sutt. 198 D1
Forest Rd., Wdf.Grn. 78 B3
Forest Side E4 47 F7
Forest Side E7 97 H4
  Capel Rd.
Forest Side, Buck.H. 63 J1
Forest Side, Wor.Pk. 197 F1
Forest Side E7 97 G5
  High Rd. Leytonstone
Forest Vw. Av. E10 78 D5
Forest Vw. Rd. E12 98 B4
Forest Vw. Rd. E17 78 C1
Forest Vw. Rd., Loug. 48 A4
Forest Way N19 92 C2
  Hargrave Pk.
Forest Way, Orp. 193 J5
Forest Way, Sid. 157 G7
Forest Way, Wdf.Grn. 63 H4
Forestdale N14 58 D4
Forester Rd. SE15 153 E4
Foresters Cl., Bexh. 159 H4
Foresters Cres., Bexh. 159 H4
Foresters Dr. E17 78 D4
Foresters Dr., Wall. 200 E7
Forestholme Cl. 171 F2
  SE23
Forfar Rd. N22 75 H1
Forfar Rd. SW11 150 A1
Forge Cl., Brom. 205 G1
Forge Cl., Hayes 121 G6
  High St.

Forge Cotts. W5 125 G1
  Ealing Grn.
Forge Dr., Esher 194 D7
Forge La., Felt. 160 E6
Forge La., Sun. 178 A3
Forge La., Sutt. 198 B7
Forge Ms., Sun. 178 A3
  Forge La.
Forge Pl. NW1 92 A6
  Malden Cres.
Forlong Path, Nthlt. 84/85 E6
  Arnold Rd.
Forman Pl. N16 94 C4
  Farleigh Rd.
Formby Av., Stan. 69 F3
Formosa St. W9 6 C6
Formosa St. W9 109 E4
Formunt Cl. E16 115 F5
  Vincent St.
Forres Gdns. NW11 72 D6
Forrest Gdns. SW16 187 F3
Forrester Path SE26 171 G4
Forris Av., Hayes 121 J1
Forset St. W1 15 H3
Forset St. W1 109 H6
Forstal Cl., Brom. 191 G3
  Ridley Rd.
Forster Rd. E17 77 H6
Forster Rd. N17 76 C3
Forster Rd. SW2 150 E7
Forster Rd., Beck. 189 H3
Forster Rd., Croy. 187 J7
  Windmill Rd.
Forsters Cl., Rom. 83 F6
Forster's Way SW18 166 E1
Forsters Way, Hayes 102 B6
Forston St. N1 12 B1
Forsyte Cres. SE19 188 B1
Forsyth Gdns. SE17 131 H6
Forsyth Gdns. SE17 35 H5
Forsyth Pl., Enf. 44 B5
Forsythia Cl., Ilf. 98 E5
Fort Rd. SE1 37 G2
Fort Rd. SE1 132 C4
Fort Rd., Nthlt. 85 G7
Fort St. E1 21 E2
Fort St. E16 135 H1
Forterie Gdns., Ilf. 100 A3
Fortescue Av. E8 94/95 E7
  Mentmore Ter.
Fortescue Av., 161 J3
  Twick.
Fortescue Rd. SW19 167 G7
Fortescue Rd., Edg. 70 D1
Fortess Gro. NW5 92 B5
  Fortess Rd.
Fortess Rd. NW5 92 B5
Fortess Wk. NW5 92 B5
  Fortess Rd.
Forthbridge Rd. 150 A4
  SW11
Fortis Cl. E16 115 J6
Fortis Grn. N2 73 H4
Fortis Grn. N10 73 H4
Fortis Grn. Av. N2 73 J3
Fortis Grn. Rd. N10 74 A3
Fortismere Av. N10 74 A3
Fortnam Rd. N19 92 D2
Fortnums Acre, Stan. 52 C6
Fortrose Gdns. SW2 168 D1
  New Pk. Rd.
Fortuna Cl. N7 93 F6
  Vulcan Way
Fortune Gate Rd. 107 E1
  NW10
Fortune Grn. Rd. NW6 90 D4
Fortune St. EC1 12 A6
Fortune St. EC1 111 J4
Fortune Wk. SE28 137 G3
  Broadwater Rd.
Fortune Way NW10 107 G3
Fortunes Mead, Nthlt. 85 E6
Forty Acre La. E16 115 G5
Forty Av., Wem. 87 J3
Forty Cl., Wem. 87 J2
Forty Footpath SW14 146 C3
Forty La., Wem. 88 B2
Forum, The, W.Mol. 179 H4
Forum Way, Edg. 54 A6
  High St.
Forumside, Edg. 54 A6
  High St.
Forval Cl., Mitch. 185 J5
Forward Dr., Har. 68 C4
Fosbury Ms. W2 14 B6
Foscote Ms. W9 108 D5
  Amberley Rd.
Foscote Rd. NW4 71 H6
Foskett Rd. SW6 148 C2
Foss Av., Croy. 201 G5
Foss Rd. SW17 167 G4
Fossdene Rd. SE7 135 H5
Fossdyke Cl., Hayes 103 E5
Fosse Way W13 104 D5

Fossil Rd. SE13 154 A3
Fossington Rd., Belv. 138 D4
Fossway, Dag. 100 C2
Foster La. EC2 19 J3
Foster La. EC2 111 J6
Foster Rd. E13 115 G4
Foster Rd. W3 106 E7
Foster Rd. W4 126 D5
Foster St. NW4 71 J4
Foster Wk. NW4 71 J4
  New Brent St.
Fosters Cl. E18 79 H1
Fosters Cl., Chis. 174 C5
Fothergill Cl. E13 115 G2
Fothergill Dr. N21 43 F5
Fotheringham Rd., 44 C4
  Enf.
Foubert's Pl. W1 17 F4
Foubert's Pl. W1 110 C6
Foulden Rd. N16 94 C4
Foulden Ter. N16 94 C4
  Foulden Rd.
Foulis Ter. SW7 31 F3
Foulis Ter. SW7 129 G5
Foulser Rd. SW17 167 J3
Foulsham Rd., 187 J3
  Th.Hth.
Founder Cl. E6 116/117 E6
  Trader Rd.
Founders Ct. EC2 20 B3
Founders Gdns. SE19 169 J7
Foundry Cl. SE16 133 H1
Foundry Ms. NW1 9 G5
Fount St. SW8 130 D7
Fountain Ct. EC4 19 E5
Fountain Dr. SE19 170 C4
Fountain Dr., Cars. 199 J1
Fountain Grn. Sq. 132 D2
  SE16
  Bermondsey Wall E.
Fountain Ms. N5 93 J4
  Kelross Rd.
Fountain Pl. SW9 151 G1
Fountain Rd. SW17 167 G5
Fountain Rd., Th.Hth. 187 J2
Fountain Sq. SW1 32 D1
Fountain Sq. SW1 130 B4
Fountain St. E2 112 C3
  Columbia Rd.
Fountains, The, Loug. 47 J7
  Fallow Flds.
Fountains Av., Felt. 161 F3
Fountains Cl., Felt. 161 F2
Fountains Cres. N14 42 E7
Fountayne Rd. N15 76 D4
Fountayne Rd. N16 94 D2
Four Seasons Cl. E3 114 A2
Four Seasons Cres., 198 C2
  Sutt.
  Kimpton Rd.
Four Wents, The E4 62 D2
  Kings Rd.
Fouracres SW12 168 B2
  Little Dimocks
Fouracres, Enf. 45 H1
Fourland Wk., Edg. 54 C6
Fournier St. E1 21 F1
Fournier St. E1 112 C5
Fourth Av. E12 98 C4
Fourth Av. W10 108 B4
Fourth Av., Hayes 121 J1
Fourth Cross Rd., 162 A2
  Twick.
Fourth Way, Wem. 88 C4
Fowey Av., Ilf. 80 A5
Fowey Cl. E1 132/133 E1
  Kennet St.
Fowler Cl. SW11 149 G3
Fowler Rd. E7 97 G4
Fowler Rd. N1 93 H7
  Halton Rd.
Fowler Rd., Mitch. 186 A2
Fowlers Cl., Sid. 176/177 E5
  Thursland Rd.
Fowlers Wk. W5 105 G4
Fownes St. SW11 149 H3
Fox & Knot St. EC1 19 H1
Fox Cl. E1 113 F4
Fox Cl. E16 115 G5
Fox Gro., Walt. 178 B7
Fox Hill SE19 170 C7
Fox Hill, Kes. 205 J5
Fox Hill Gdns. SE19 170 C7
Fox Hollow Cl. SE18 137 H5
Fox Hollow Dr., Bexh. 158 D3
Fox Ho. Rd., Belv. 139 H4
Fox La. N13 59 F3
Fox La. W5 105 H4
Fox La., Kes. 205 H5
Fox Rd. E16 115 F5
Foxberry Rd. SE4 153 H3
Foxborough Gdns. 154 A5
  SE4
Foxbourne Rd. SW17 168 A2

Foxbury Av., Chis. 175 G6
Foxbury Cl., Brom. 173 H6
Foxbury Rd., Brom. 173 G6
Foxcombe, Croy. 204 B6
Foxcombe Cl. E6 116 A2
Boleyn Rd.
Foxcombe Rd. SW15 165 G1
Alton Rd.
Foxcote SE5 36 E4
Foxcote SE5 132 B5
Foxcroft Rd. SE18 157 E1
Foxes Dale SE3 155 G3
Foxes Dale, Brom. 190 D3
Foxfield Rd., Orp. 207 G2
Foxglove Cl., Sthl. 103 E7
Foxglove Gdns. E11 79 J4
Foxglove La., Chess. 196 A4
Foxglove St. W12 107 F7
Foxglove Way, Wall. 200 B1
Foxgrove N14 58 E3
Foxgrove Av., Beck. 172 B7
Foxgrove Path, Wat. 50 D5
Foxgrove Rd., Beck. 172 B7
Foxham Rd. N19 92 D3
Foxhole Rd. SE9 156 B5
Foxholt Gdns. NW10 88 C7
Foxhome Cl., Chis. 174 D6
Foxlands Cres., Dag. 101 J5
Foxlands La., Dag. 101 J5
Foxlands Rd., Dag. 101 J5
Foxlees, Wem. 86 D4
Foxley Cl. E8 94 D5
Ferncliff Rd.
Foxley Cl., Loug. 49 E2
Foxley Rd. SW9 35 F7
Foxley Rd. SW9 131 G7
Foxley Rd., Th.Hth. 187 H4
Foxley Sq. SW9 131 H7
Cancell Rd.
Foxleys, Wat. 51 E3
Foxmead Cl., Enf. 43 F3
Foxmore St. SW11 149 J1
Fox's Path, Mitch. 185 H2
Foxton Gro., Mitch. 185 G2
Foxwell Ms. SE4 153 H3
Foxwell St.
Foxwell St. SE4 153 H3
Foxwood Cl. NW7 54 E4
Foxwood Cl., Felt. 160 B3
Foxwood Grn. Cl., Enf. 44 B6
Foxwood Rd. SE3 155 F4
Foyle Rd. N17 76 D1
Foyle Rd. SE3 135 F6
Framfield Cl. N12 56 D3
Framfield Ct., Enf. 44 B6
Framfield Rd. N5 93 H5
Framfield Rd. W7 104 B6
Framfield Rd., Mitch. 168 A7
Framlingham Cl. E5 95 F2
Detmold Rd.
Framlingham Cres. SE9 174 B4
Frampton Cl., Sutt. 198 D7
Frampton Pk. Rd. E9 95 F6
Frampton Rd., Houns. 142 E5
Frampton St. NW8 7 E6
Frampton St. NW8 109 G4
Francemary Rd. SE4 154 A5
Frances Rd. E4 62 A6
Frances St. SE18 136 C4
Franche Ct. Rd. SW17 167 F3
Francis Av., Bexh. 159 G2
Francis Av., Felt. 160 A3
Francis Av., Ilf. 99 G2
Francis Barber Cl. SW16 169 F4
Well Cl.
Francis Chichester Way SW11 150 A1
Francis Cl. E14 134 D4
Saunders Ness Rd.
Francis Cl., Epsom 196 D4
Francis Gro. SW19 166 C6
Francis Rd. E10 96 C1
Francis Rd. N2 73 J4
Lynmouth Rd.
Francis Rd., Croy. 187 H7
Francis Rd., Grnf. 105 F1
Francis Rd., Har. 68 D5
Francis Rd., Houns. 142 D2
Francis Rd., Ilf. 99 G2
Francis Rd., Pnr. 66 C5
Francis Rd., Wall. 200 C6
Francis St. E15 96 E5
Francis St. SW1 33 F1
Francis St. SW1 130 C4
Francis St., Ilf. 99 G2
Francis Ter. N19 92 C3
Junction Rd.
Francis Wk. N1 111 F1
Bingfield St.
Franciscan Rd. SW17 167 J5
Francklyn Gdns., Edg. 54 A3
Franconia Rd. SW4 150 C5
Frank Bailey Wk. E12 98 D5
Gainsborough Av.
Frank Burton Cl. SE7 135 H5
Victoria Way
Frank Dixon Cl. SE21 170 B1
Frank Dixon Way SE21 170 B1
Frank St. E13 115 G4
Frank Towell Ct., Felt. 160 A1
Frankfurt Rd. SE24 151 J5
Frankham St. SE8 134 A7
Frankland Cl. SE16 133 F4
Frankland Cl., Wdf.Grn. 63 J5
Frankland Rd. E4 62 A5
Frankland Rd. SW7 22 E6
Frankland Rd. SW7 129 G3
Franklin Cl. N20 41 F7
Franklin Cl. SE13 154 B1
Franklin Cl. SE27 169 H3
Franklin Cl., Kings.T. 182 A3
Franklin Cres., Mitch. 186 C4
Franklin Ho. NW9 71 F7
Franklin Pas. SE9 156 B3
Franklin Rd. SE20 171 F7
Franklin Rd., Bexh. 159 E1
Franklin Sq. W14 128 C5
Marchbank Rd.
Franklin St. E3 114 B3
St. Leonards St.
Franklin St. N15 76 B6
Franklin Way, Croy. 187 E7
Franklins Ms., Har. 85 J2
Franklin's Row SW3 32 A3
Franklin's Row SW3 129 J5
Franklyn Gdns., Ilf. 65 G6
Franklyn Rd. NW10 89 F7
Franklyn Rd., Walt. 178 A6
Franks Av., N.Mal. 182 C4
Frankswood Av., Orp. 193 E5
Franlaw Cres. N13 59 J4
Fransfield Gro. SE26 171 E3
Frant Cl. SE20 171 F7
Frant Rd., Th.Hth. 187 H5
Franthorne Way SE6 172 B2
Fraser Cl. E6 116 B6
Linton Gdns.
Fraser Cl., Bex. 177 J1
Dartford Rd.
Fraser Ho., Brent. 125 J5
Green Dragon La.
Fraser Rd. E17 78 B5
Fraser Rd. N9 60 E3
Fraser Rd., Erith 139 J5
Fraser Rd., Grnf. 105 E1
Fraser St. W4 126 E5
Frating Cres., Wdf.Grn. 63 G6
Frays Av., West Dr. 120 A2
Frays Cl., West Dr. 120 A3
Frazer Av., Ruis. 84 C5
Frazier St. SE1 26 E4
Frazier St. SE1 131 G2
Frean St. SE16 29 H5
Frean St. SE16 132 D3
Fred Wigg Twr. E11 97 F2
Freda Corbett Cl. SE15 37 H7
Frederic Ms. SW1 24 A4
Frederic St. E17 77 H5
Frederica Rd. E4 46 D7
Frederica St. N7 93 F7
Caledonian Rd.
Frederick Cl. W2 15 J5
Frederick Cl. W2 109 H7
Frederick Cl., Sutt. 198 C4
Frederick Ct. NW2 90 B3
Douglas Ms.
Frederick Cres. SW9 131 H7
Frederick Cres., Enf. 45 F2
Frederick Gdns., Sutt. 198 C5
Frederick Pl. SE18 137 E5
Frederick Rd. SE17 35 H5
Frederick Rd., Sutt. 198 C5
Frederick Sq. SE16 113 H7
Rotherhithe St.
Frederick St. WC1 10 C4
Frederick St. WC1 111 F3
Frederick Ter. E8 112 C1
Haggerston Rd.
Frederick Vil. W7 124 B1
Lower Boston Rd.
Frederick's Pl. EC2 20 B4
Fredericks Pl. N12 57 F4
Frederick's Row EC1 11 G3
Freedom Cl. E17 77 H4
Freedom Rd. N17 76 A2
Freedom St. SW11 149 J2
Freegrove Rd. N7 93 E5
Freeland Pk. NW4 72 B2
Freeland Rd. W5 105 J7
Freelands Gro., Brom. 191 H1
Freelands Rd., Brom. 191 H1
Freeling St. N1 93 F7
Caledonian Rd.
Freeman Cl., Nthlt. 85 E7
Freeman Ct. N7 92/93 E3
Tollington Way
Freeman Dr., W.Mol. 179 F3
Freeman Rd., Mord. 185 G5
Freemantle Av., Enf. 45 G5
Freemantle St. SE17 36 D3
Freemantle St. SE17 132 B5
Freemasons Rd. E16 115 H5
Freemasons Rd., Croy. 202 B1
Freesia Cl., Orp. 207 J5
Briarswood Way
Freethorpe Cl. SE19 188 A1
Freke Rd. SW11 150 A3
Fremantle Rd., Belv. 139 G4
Fremantle Rd., Ilf. 81 F2
Fremont St. E9 113 F1
French Ordinary Ct. EC3 21 E5
French Pl. E1 13 E4
French St., Sun. 178 C2
Frendsbury Rd. SE4 153 H4
Frensham Cl., Sthl. 103 F4
Frensham Ct., Mitch. 185 G3
Phipps Br. Rd.
Frensham Dr. SW15 165 G2
Frensham Dr., Croy. 204 C7
Frensham Rd. SE9 175 G2
Frensham St. SE15 37 J6
Frensham St. SE15 132 D6
Frere St. SW11 149 H2
Fresh Wf. Rd., Bark. 117 E1
Freshfield Av. E8 94 C7
Freshfield Cl. SE13 154 D4
Marischal Rd.
Freshfield Dr. N14 42 B7
Freshfields, Croy. 189 J7
Freshford St. SW18 167 F3
Freshwater Cl. SW17 168 A6
Freshwater Rd. SW17 168 A6
Freshwater Rd., Dag. 100 D1
Freshwell Av., Rom. 82 C4
Freshwood Cl., Beck. 190 B1
Freston Gdns., Barn. 42 A5
Freston Pk. N3 72 C2
Freston Rd. W10 108 A7
Freston Rd. W11 108 A7
Freta Rd., Bexh. 159 F5
Frewin Rd. SW18 167 G1
Friar Ms. SE27 169 H3
Prioress Rd.
Friar Rd., Hayes 102 D4
Friar St. EC4 19 H4
Friars, The, Chig. 65 H4
Friars Av. N20 57 H3
Friars Av. SW15 165 F3
Friars Cl. E4 62 C3
Friars Cl. N2 73 G4
Friars Cl., Nthlt. 102 D3
Broomcroft Av.
Friars Gdns. W3 106 D6
St. Dunstans Av.
Friars Gate Cl., Wdf.Grn. 63 G4
Friars La., Rich. 145 G5
Friars Mead E14 134 C3
Friars Ms. SE9 156 D5
Friars Pl. La. W3 106 D7
Friars Rd. E6 116 A1
Friars Stile Pl., Rich. 145 H6
Friars Stile Rd.
Friars Stile Rd., Rich. 145 H6
Friars Wk. N14 58 B1
Friars Wk. SE2 138 D5
Friars Way W3 106 D6
Friary Cl. N12 57 H5
Friary Ct. SW1 25 G2
Friary Est. SE15 37 J6
Friary Est. SE15 132 D6
Friary La., Wdf.Grn. 63 G4
Friary Rd. N12 57 G4
Friary Rd. SE15 37 J6
Friary Rd. SE15 132 D7
Friary Rd. W3 106 C6
Friary Way N12 57 H4
Friday Hill E4 62 E2
Friday Hill E. E4 62 E3
Friday Hill W. E4 62 E2
Friday Rd., Mitch. 167 J7
Friday St. EC4 19 J4
Friday St. EC4 111 J6
Frideswide Pl. NW5 92 C5
Islip St.
Friend St. EC1 11 G3
Friend St. EC1 111 H3
Friendly Pl. SE13 154 B1
Lewisham Rd.
Friendly St. SE8 154 A1
Friendly St. Ms. SE8 154 A2
Friendly St.
Friends Rd., Croy. 202 A3
Friendship Wk., Nthlt. 102 D3
Wayfarer Rd.
Friern Barnet La. N11 57 H4
Friern Barnet La. N20 57 H4
Friern Barnet Rd. N11 57 J5
Friern Br. Retail Pk. N11 58 B6
Friern Ct. N20 57 G3
Friern Mt. Dr. N20 41 F7
Friern Pk. N12 57 F5
Friern Rd. SE22 152 D6
Friern Watch Av. N12 57 F4
Frigate Ms. SE8 134 A6
Watergate St.
Frimley Av., Wall. 201 E5
Frimley Cl. SW19 166 B2
Frimley Cl., Croy. 204 C7
Frimley Ct., Sid. 176 B5
Frimley Cres., Croy. 204 C7
Frimley Gdns., Mitch. 185 H3
Frimley Rd., Chess. 195 H5
Frimley Rd., Ilf. 99 H3
Frimley Way E1 113 G4
Frinton Cl., Wat. 50 B2
Frinton Dr., Wdf.Grn. 62 D7
Frinton Ms., Ilf. 80 D6
Bramley Cres.
Frinton Rd. E6 116 A3
Frinton Rd. N15 76 B6
Frinton Rd. SW17 168 A6
Frinton Rd., Sid. 177 E2
Friston Path, Chig. 65 H5
Friston St. SW6 148 E2
Friswell Pl., Bexh. 159 G4
Frith Ct. NW7 56 B7
Frith La. NW7 56 B7
Frith Rd. E11 96 C4
Frith Rd., Croy. 201 J2
Frith St. W1 17 H4
Frith St. W1 110 D6
Fritham Cl., N.Mal. 182 E6
Frithville Gdns. W12 127 J1
Frizlands La., Dag. 101 H4
Frobisher Cl., Pnr. 66 D7
Frobisher Cres., Stai. 140 B7
Frobisher Gdns., Stai. 140 B7
Frobisher Pas. E14 134 A1
North Colonnade
Frobisher Rd. E6 116 C6
Frobisher Rd. N8 75 G4
Frobisher St. SE10 135 E6
Froghall La., Chig. 65 G4
Frogley Rd. SE22 152 C4
Frogmore SW18 148 D5
Frogmore Cl., Sutt. 198 A3
Frogmore Est., Ruis. 84 D5
Frogmore Gdns., Sutt. 198 B4
Frogmore Ind. Est. NW10 106 C3
Frognal NW3 91 F5
Frognal Av., Har. 68 C4
Frognal Av., Sid. 176 A6
Frognal Cl. NW3 91 F5
Frognal Ct. NW3 91 F6
Frognal Gdns. NW3 91 F4
Frognal La. NW3 91 E5
Frognal Par. NW3 91 F6
Frognal Ct.
Frognal Pl., Sid. 176 A6
Frognal Ri. NW3 91 F4
Frognal Way NW3 91 F4
Froissart Rd. SE9 156 A5
Frome Rd. N22 75 H3
Westbury Av.
Frome St. N1 11 J1
Frome St. N1 111 J2
Fromondes Rd., Sutt. 198 B5
Frostic Wk. E1 21 G2
Frostic Wk. E1 112 C5
Froude St. SW8 150 B2
Fruen Rd., Felt. 141 J7
Fry Rd. E6 98 A7
Fry Rd. NW10 107 F1
Fryatt Rd. N17 60 A7
Fryatt St. E14 114/115 E6
Orchard Pl.
Fryent Cl. NW9 70 A6
Fryent Cres. NW9 70 E6
Fryent Flds. NW9 71 E6
Fryent Gro. NW9 70 E6
Fryent Way NW9 70 A6
Frye's Bldgs. N1 11 F1
Frying Pan All. E1 21 F2
Fryston Av., Croy. 202 D2
Fuchsia St. SE2 138 B5
Fulbeck Dr. NW9 70 E1
Fulbeck Wk., Edg. 54 B2
Bushfield Cres.
Fulbeck Way, Har. 67 J2

Name	Page	Grid
Fulbourne Rd. E17	78	C1
Fulbourne St. E1	112/113	E5
Durward St.		
Fulbrook Ms. N19	92	C4
Junction Rd.		
Fulbrook Rd. N19	92	C4
Junction Rd.		
Fulford Gro., Wat.	50	B2
Fulford Rd., Epsom	196	D7
Fulford St. SE16	133	E2
Fulham Bdy. SW6	128	D7
Fulham Cl. SW6	128	D7
Fulham Rd.		
Fulham High St. SW6	148	B2
Fulham Palace Rd. SW6	128	A7
Fulham Palace Rd. W6	127	J5
Fulham Pk. Gdns. SW6	148	C2
Fulham Pk. Rd. SW6	148	C2
Fulham Rd. SW3	**30**	**E4**
Fulham Rd. SW3	129	F6
Fulham Rd. SW6	**30**	**B7**
Fulham Rd. SW6	148	B2
Fulham Rd. SW10	**30**	**E4**
Fulham Rd. SW10	129	E7
Fullbrooks Av., Wor.Pk.	197	F1
Fuller Cl. E2	**13**	**H5**
Fuller Cl., Orp.	207	J5
Fuller Rd., Dag.	100	B3
Fuller St. NW4	71	J4
Fuller Ter., Ilf.	99	F5
Oaktree Gro.		
Fuller Way, Hayes	121	J5
Fullers Av., Surb.	195	J2
Fullers Av., Wdf.Grn.	63	F7
Fullers Rd. E18	79	F1
Fullers Way N., Surb.	195	J3
Fullers Way S., Chess.	195	H4
Fullers Wd., Croy.	204	A5
Fullerton Rd. SW18	149	F5
Fullerton Rd., Croy.	188	C7
Fullwell Av., Ilf.	80	C1
Fullwell Cross Roundabout, Ilf.	81	G2
Fencepiece Rd.		
Fullwoods Ms. N1	**12**	**C3**
Fulmar Ct., Surb.	181	J6
Fulmead St. SW6	149	E1
Fulmer Cl., Hmptn.	161	E5
Fulmer Rd. E16	116	A5
Fulmer Way W13	124	E3
Fulready Rd. E10	78	D5
Fulstone Cl., Houns.	143	F4
Fulthorp Rd. SE3	155	F2
Fulton Ms. W2	**14**	**C5**
Fulton Rd., Wem.	88	A3
Fulwell Pk. Av., Twick.	161	H2
Fulwell Rd., Tedd.	162	A4
Fulwood Av., Wem.	105	J1
Fulwood Gdns., Twick.	144	C6
Fulwood Pl. WC1	**18**	**D2**
Fulwood Pl. WC1	111	F5
Fulwood Wk. SW19	166	B1
Furber St. W6	127	H3
Furham Feild, Pnr.	51	G7
Furley Rd. SE15	132	D7
Furlong Cl., Wall.	200	A1
Furlong Rd. N7	93	G6
Furmage St. SW18	149	E7
Furneaux Av. SE27	169	H5
Furness Rd. NW10	107	G2
Furness Rd. SW6	149	E2
Furness Rd., Har.	67	H7
Furness Rd., Mord.	185	E7
Furnival St. EC4	**19**	**E3**
Furnival St. EC4	111	G6
Furrow La. E9	95	F5
Fursby Av. N3	56	D6
Further Acre NW9	71	F2
Further Grn. Rd. SE6	155	E7
Furtherfield Cl., Croy.	187	G6
Furze Cl., Wat.	50	C5
Furze Fm. Cl., Rom.	83	E2
Furze Rd., Th.Hth.	187	J3
Furze St. E3	114	A4
Furzedown Dr. SW17	168	B5
Furzedown Rd. SW17	168	B5
Furzefield Cl., Chis.	174	E6
Furzefield Rd. SE3	135	H6
Furzeground Way, Uxb.	121	F1
Furzeham Rd., West Dr.	120	B2
Furzehill Rd., Borwd.	38	A4
Furzewood, Sun.	178	A1
Fuschia Ct., Wdf.Grn.	62/63	E7
The Bridle Path		
Fyfe Way, Brom.	191	G2
Widmore Rd.		
Fyfield Cl., Brom.	190	D4
Fyfield Ct. E7	97	G6
Fyfield Rd. E17	78	D3
Fyfield Rd. SW9	151	G3
Fyfield Rd., Enf.	44	B3
Fyfield Rd., Wdf.Grn.	63	J7
Fynes St. SW1	**33**	**H1**
Fynes St. SW1	130	D4

G

Name	Page	Grid
G.E.C. Est., Wem.	87	G3
Gable Cl., Pnr.	51	G7
Gable Ct. SE26	170/171	E5
Lawrie Pk. Av.		
Gables, The, Wem.	87	J4
Gables Cl. SE5	152	B1
Gables Cl. SE12	173	G1
Gabriel Cl., Felt.	160	D4
Gabriel St. SE23	153	G7
Gabrielle Cl., Wem.	87	J3
Gabrielle Ct. NW3	91	G6
Gad Cl. E13	115	H3
Gaddesden Av., Wem.	87	J6
Gade Cl., Hayes	122	B1
Gadesden Rd., Epsom	196	C6
Gadsbury Cl. NW9	71	F6
Gadwall Cl. E16	115	H6
Freemasons Rd.		
Gadwall Way SE28	137	G2
Gage Rd. E16	114/115	E5
Malmesbury Rd.		
Gage St. WC1	**18**	**B1**
Gainford St. N1	111	G1
Richmond Av.		
Gainsboro Gdns., Grnf.	86	B5
Gainsborough Av. E12	98	D5
Gainsborough Cl., Beck.	172	A7
Gainsborough Cl., Esher	194	B1
Lime Tree Av.		
Gainsborough Ct. N12	57	E5
Gainsborough Ct. W12	127	J2
Lime Gro.		
Gainsborough Gdns. NW3	91	G3
Gainsborough Gdns. NW11	72	C7
Gainsborough Gdns., Edg.	69	J2
Gainsborough Gdns., Islw.	144	A5
Gainsborough Ms. SE26	170/171	E3
Panmure Rd.		
Gainsborough Pl., Chig.	65	J3
Gainsborough Rd. E11	79	E7
Gainsborough Rd. E15	114	E3
Gainsborough Rd. N12	57	E5
Gainsborough Rd. W4	127	F4
Gainsborough Rd., Dag.	100	B4
Gainsborough Rd., N.Mal.	182	D7
Gainsborough Rd., Rich.	145	J3
Gainsborough Rd., Wdf.Grn.	64	B6
Gainsborough Sq., Bexh.	158	D3
Regency Way		
Gainsford Rd. E17	77	J4
Gainsford St. SE1	**29**	**F3**
Gainsford St. SE1	132	C2
Gairloch Rd. SE5	152	B2
Gaisford St. NW5	92	C6
Gaitskell Rd. SE9	175	F1
Galahad Rd., Brom.	173	G3
Galata Rd. SW13	127	G7
Galatea Sq. SE15	152/153	E3
Scylla Rd.		
Galbraith St. E14	134	C3
Galdana Av., Barn.	41	F3
Gale Cl., Hmptn.	160/161	E6
Stewart Cl.		
Gale Cl., Mitch.	185	G3
Gale St. E3	114	A5
Gale St., Dag.	118	D1
Galeborough Av., Wdf.Grn.	62	D7
Galen Pl. WC1	**18**	**B2**
Galena Ho. SE18	137	J5
Grosmont Rd.		
Galena Rd. W6	127	H4
Gales Gdns. E2	113	E3
Gales Way, Wdf.Grn.	64	B7
Galesbury Rd. SW18	149	F6
Galgate Cl. SW19	166	B1
Gallants Fm. Rd., Barn.	41	H7
Galleon Cl. SE16	133	G2
Kinburn St.		
Galleons Dr., Bark.	117	H3
Thames Rd.		
Gallery Gdns., Nthlt.	102	D2
Gallery Rd. SE21	170	A1
Galley La., Barn.	39	H3
Galleywall Rd. SE16	132	E4
Gallia Rd. N5	93	H5
Galliard Cl. N9	45	F6
Galliard Rd. N9	60	D1
Gallions Cl., Bark.	118	A3
Gallions Rd. E16	117	E7
Gallions Rd. SE7	135	H4
Gallions Roundabout E16	116	E7
Gallions Vw. Rd. SE28	137	G2
Goldfinch Rd.		
Gallon Cl. SE7	135	J4
Gallop, The, S.Croy.	203	E7
Gallop, The, Sutt.	199	F7
Gallosson Rd. SE18	137	H4
Galloway Path, Croy.	202	A4
Galloway Rd. W12	127	G1
Gallus Cl. N21	43	F6
Gallus Sq. SE3	155	H3
Galpins Rd., Th.Hth.	187	F4
Galsworthy Av., Rom.	82	B7
Galsworthy Cl. SE28	138	B1
Galsworthy Cres. SE3	155	J1
Merriman Rd.		
Galsworthy Rd. NW2	90	B4
Galsworthy Rd., Kings.T.	164	B7
Galsworthy Ter. N16	94	B3
Hawksley Rd.		
Galton St. W10	108	B4
Galva Cl., Barn.	42	A4
Galvani Way, Croy.	201	F1
Ampere Way		
Galveston Rd. SW15	148	C5
Galway Cl. SE16	132/133	E5
Masters Dr.		
Galway St. EC1	**12**	**A4**
Galway St. EC1	111	J3
Gambetta St. SW8	150	B2
Gambia St. SE1	**27**	**H2**
Gamble St. SW17	167	H4
Gamlen Rd. SW15	148	A4
Gamuel Cl. E17	78	A6
Gander Grn. Cres., Hmptn.	179	G1
Gander Grn. La., Sutt.	198	B2
Gandhi Cl. E17	78	A6
Gandolfi St. SE15	36	E6
Gane Cl., Wall.	200/201	E7
Kingsford Av.		
Ganton St. W1	**17**	**F5**
Ganton Wk., Wat.	50/51	E4
Woodhall La.		
Gantshill Cres., Ilf.	80	D5
Gantshill Cross, Ilf.	80	D6
Eastern Av.		
Gap Rd. SW19	166	D5
Garage Rd. W3	106	A6
Garbutt Pl. W1	**16**	**C1**
Gard St. EC1	11	H3
Garden Av., Bexh.	159	G3
Garden Av., Mitch.	168	B7
Garden City, Edg.	54	A6
Garden Cl. E4	62	A5
Garden Cl. SE12	173	H3
Garden Cl. SW15	147	H7
Garden Cl., Barn.	39	J4
Garden Cl., Hmptn.	161	F5
Garden Cl., Nthlt.	103	E1
Garden Cl., Wall.	200	E5
Garden Ct. EC4	**18**	**E5**
Garden Ct. SE15	152	C1
Sumner Est.		
Garden Ct., Rich.	145	J1
Lichfield Rd.		
Garden Ct., Stan.	53	F5
Marsh La.		
Garden Ct., W.Mol.	179	H4
Avern Rd.		
Garden La. SW2	169	F1
Christchurch Rd.		
Garden La., Brom.	173	H6
Garden Ms. W2	108	D7
Linden Gdns.		
Garden Rd. NW8	**6**	**D3**
Garden Rd. NW8	109	F3
Garden Rd. SE20	189	F1
Garden Rd., Brom.	173	H7
Garden Rd., Rich.	146	A3
Garden Rd., Walt.	178	B6
Garden Row SE1	**27**	**G6**
Garden Row SE1	131	H3
Garden St. E1	113	G5
Garden Ter. SW1	**33**	**H3**
Garden Wk. EC2	**12**	**D4**
Garden Wk., Beck.	189	J1
Hayne Rd.		
Garden Way NW10	88	C4
Gardeners Cl. N11	58	A2
Gardeners Rd., Croy.	201	H1
Gardenia Rd., Enf.	44	B6
Gardenia Way, Wdf.Grn.	63	G5
Gardens, The SE22	152	D4
Gardens, The, Beck.	190	C2
Gardens, The, Felt.	141	G5
Gardens, The, Har.	67	J6
Gardens, The, Pnr.	67	F6
Gardiner Av. NW2	89	J5
Gardiner Cl., Dag.	100	D4
Gardiner Cl., Enf.	45	G6
Gardner Cl. E11	79	H6
Gardner Gro., Felt.	161	F4
Gardner Rd. E13	115	H4
Gardners La. EC4	**19**	**J5**
Gardnor Rd. NW3	91	G4
Flask Wk.		
Garendon Gdns., Mord.	184	E7
Garendon Rd., Mord.	184	E7
Gareth Cl., Wor.Pk.	198	A2
Burnham Dr.		
Gareth Gro., Brom.	173	G4
Garfield Ms. SW11	150	A3
Garfield Rd.		
Garfield Rd. E4	62	D1
Garfield Rd. E13	115	F4
Garfield Rd. SW11	150	A3
Garfield Rd. SW19	167	F5
Garfield Rd., Enf.	45	F4
Garfield Rd., Twick.	162	D1
Garford St. E14	114	A7
Garganey Wk. SE28	118	D7
Garibaldi St. SE18	137	H4
Garland Rd. SE18	137	G7
Garland Rd., Stan.	69	H1
Garlands Rd., Croy.	202	A4
Chatsworth Rd.		
Garlick Hill EC4	**20**	**A5**
Garlick Hill EC4	111	J7
Garlies Rd. SE23	171	H3
Garlinge Rd. NW2	90	C6
Garman Cl. N18	60	A5
Garman Rd. N17	61	F7
Garnault Ms. EC1	**11**	**F4**
Garnault Pl. EC1	**11**	**F4**
Garner Rd. E17	78	C1
Garner St. E2	**13**	**J2**
Garnet Rd. NW10	89	F6
Garnet Rd., Th.Hth.	188	A4
Garnet St. E1	113	F7
Garnet Wk. E6	116	B5
Kingfisher St.		
Garnett Cl. SE9	156	C3
Garnett Rd. NW3	91	J5
Garnett Way E17	77	H1
McEntee Av.		
Garnham Cl. N16	94	C2
Garnham St.		
Garnies Cl. SE15	**37**	**F7**
Garnies Cl. SE15	132	C7
Garrad's Rd. SW16	168	D3
Garrard Cl., Bexh.	159	F3
Garrard Cl., Chis.	175	E5
Garrard Wk. NW10	88/89	A7
Garnet Rd.		
Garratt La. SW17	167	G4
Garratt La. SW18	148	E5
Garratt Rd., Edg.	54	A7
Garratt Ter. SW17	167	H4
Garratt Wk. W3	106	D5
Jenner Av.		
Garrett St. EC1	**12**	**A5**
Garrick Av. NW11	72	B6
Garrick Cl. SW18	149	F4
Garrick Cl. W5	105	H4
Garrick Cl., Rich.	145	G5
The Grn.		
Garrick Cres., Croy.	202	B2
Garrick Dr. NW4	71	J2
Garrick Dr. SE28	137	G3
Broadwater Rd.		
Garrick Gdns., W.Mol.	179	G3
Garrick Pk. NW4	72	A2
Garrick Rd. NW9	71	F6
Garrick Rd., Grnf.	103	H4

Garrick Rd., Rich.	146	A2
Garrick St. WC2	**18**	**A5**
Garrick St. WC2	110	E7
Garrick Way NW4	72	A4
Garrison Cl. SE18	136	D7
Red Lion La.		
Garrison Cl., Houns.	143	F5
Garrison La., Chess.	195	G7
Garsdale Cl. N11	58	A6
Garside Cl. SE28	137	G3
Goosander Way		
Garside Cl., Hmptn.	161	H6
Garsington Ms. SE4	153	J3
Garter Way SE16	133	G2
Poolmans St.		
Garth, The, Hmptn.	161	H6
Uxbridge Rd.		
Garth, The, Har.	69	J6
Garth Cl. W4	126	D5
Garth Cl., Kings.T.	163	J5
Garth Cl., Mord.	184	A7
Garth Cl., Ruis.	84	D1
Garth Ct. W4	126	D5
Garth Rd.		
Garth Ms. W5	105	H4
Greystoke Gdns.		
Garth Rd. NW2	90	C2
Garth Rd. W4	126	D6
Garth Rd., Kings.T.	163	J5
Garth Rd., Mord.	183	J6
Garth Rd. Ind. Cen., Mord.	184	A7
Garthland Dr., Barn.	39	H5
Garthorne Rd. SE23	153	G7
Garthside, Rich.	163	H5
Garthway N12	57	H6
Gartmoor Gdns. SW19	166	C1
Gartmore Rd., Ilf.	99	J1
Garton Pl. SW18	149	F6
Gartons Cl., Enf.	45	F5
Gartons Way SW11	149	F3
Garvary Rd. E16	115	H6
Garway Rd. W2	**14**	**A4**
Garway Rd. W2	108	E6
Gascoigne Gdns., Wdf.Grn.	63	E7
Gascoigne Pl. E2	**13**	**F4**
Gascoigne Pl. E2	112	C3
Gascoigne Rd., Bark.	117	F1
Gascony Av. NW6	90	D7
Gascoyne Rd. E9	95	G7
Gaselee St. E14	114	C7
Gasholder Pl. SE11	**34**	**D4**
Gaskarth Rd. SW12	150	B6
Gaskarth Rd., Edg.	70	C1
Gaskell Rd. N6	73	J6
Gaskell St. SW4	150	E2
Gaskin St. N1	111	H1
Gaspar Cl. SW5	**30**	**B1**
Gaspar Ms. SW5	**30**	**B1**
Gassiot Rd. SW17	167	J4
Gassiot Way, Sutt.	199	G3
Gastein Rd. W6	128	A6
Gaston Bell Cl., Rich.	145	J3
Gaston Rd., Mitch.	186	A3
Gataker St. SE16	133	E3
Gatcombe Rd. E16	135	G1
Gatcombe Rd. N19	92	D3
Gatcombe Way, Barn.	41	J3
Gate Cl., Borwd.	38	C1
Gate End, Nthwd.	50	A7
Gate Ms. SW7	**23**	**H4**
Gate Ms. SW7	129	H2
Gate St. WC2	**18**	**C3**
Gateforth St. NW8	**7**	**G6**
Gateforth St. NW8	109	H4
Gatehouse Cl., Kings.T.	164	C7
Gatehouse Sq. SE1	131	J1
Southwark Br. Rd.		
Gateley Rd. SW9	151	F3
Gater Dr., Enf.	44	A1
Gates Grn. Rd., Kes.	205	G4
Gates Grn. Rd., W.Wick.	205	F3
Gatesborough St. EC2	**12**	**D5**
Gateside Rd. SW17	167	J3
Gatestone Rd. SE19	170	B6
Gateway SE17	**36**	**A5**
Gateway SE17	131	J6
Gateway Arc. N1	111	H2
SET		
Gateway Ind. Est. NW10	107	F3
Gateway Ms. E8	94	C5
Shacklewell La.		
Gateway Rd. E10	96	B3
Gateways, The SW3	**31**	**H2**
Gateways, The SW3	129	J4
Gatfield Gro., Felt.	161	G2
Gathorne Rd. N22	75	G2
Gathorne St. E2	113	G2
Mace St.		
Gatley Av., Epsom	196	B5
Gatliff Rd. SW1	**32**	**D4**
Gatliff Rd. SW1	130	B5
Gatling Rd. SE2	138	A5
Gatting Cl., Edg.	54	C7
Pavilion Way		
Gatton Rd. SW17	167	H4
Gattons Way, Sid.	177	F4
Gatward Cl. N21	43	H6
Gatward Grn. N9	60	B2
Gatwick Rd. SW18	148	C7
Gauden Cl. SW4	150	D3
Gauden Rd. SW4	150	D2
Gaumont Ter. W12	127	J2
Lime Gro.		
Gaunt St. SE1	**27**	**J5**
Gauntlet Cl., Nthlt.	84	E7
Gauntlett Ct., Wem.	86	E5
Gauntlett Rd., Sutt.	199	G5
Gautrey Rd. SE15	153	F2
Gautrey Sq. E6	116	C6
Gavel St. SE17	**36**	**C1**
Gaverick St. E14	134	A4
Gavestone Cres. SE12	155	H7
Gavestone Rd. SE12	155	H7
Gaviller Pl. E5	94/95	E4
Clarence Rd.		
Gavin St. SE18	137	H4
Gavina Cl., Mord.	185	H5
Gawber St. E2	113	F3
Gawsworth Cl. E15	96/97	E5
Ash Rd.		
Gawthorne Av. NW7	56	B5
Lane App.		
Gawthorne Ct. E3	114	A2
Mostyn Gro.		
Gay Cl. NW2	89	H5
Gay Gdns., Dag.	101	J4
Gay Rd. E15	114	D2
Gay St. SW15	148	A3
Gaydon Ho. W2	**14**	**B1**
Gaydon Ho. W2	109	E5
Gaydon La. NW9	70	E1
Gayfere Rd., Epsom	197	G5
Gayfere Rd., Ilf.	80	C3
Gayfere St. SW1	**26**	**A6**
Gayfere St. SW1	130	E3
Gayford Rd. W12	127	F2
Gayhurst SE17	**36**	**C5**
Gayhurst Rd. E8	94	D7
Gaylor Rd., Nthlt.	85	F5
Gaynes Hill Rd., Wdf.Grn.	64	B6
Gaynesford Rd. SE23	171	G2
Gaynesford Rd., Cars.	199	J7
Gaysham Av., Ilf.	80	D5
Gaysham Hall, Ilf.	80	E3
Gayton Ct., Har.	68	C6
Gayton Cres. NW3	91	G4
Gayton Rd. NW3	91	G4
Gayton Rd. SE2	138	C3
Florence Rd.		
Gayton Rd., Har.	68	C6
Gayville Rd. SW11	149	J6
Gaywood Cl. SW2	169	F1
Gaywood Est. SE1	**27**	**H6**
Gaywood Est. SE1	131	H3
Gaywood Rd. E17	78	A3
Gaywood St. SE1	**27**	**H6**
Gaza St. SE17	**35**	**G4**
Geariesville Gdns., Ilf.	81	E4
Geary Rd. NW10	89	G5
Geary St. N7	93	F5
Geddes Pl., Bexh.	159	G4
Market Pl.		
Gedeney Rd. N17	75	J1
Gedling Pl. SE1	**29**	**G5**
Gedling Pl. SE1	132	C2
Gee St. EC1	**11**	**J5**
Gee St. EC1	111	J4
Geere Rd. E15	115	F1
Gees Ct. W1	**16**	**C4**
Geffrye Ct. N1	**12**	**E2**
Geffrye Est. N1	112	B2
Stanway St.		
Geffrye St. E2	**13**	**F1**
Geffrye St. E2	112	C2
Geldart Rd. SE15	132	E7
Geldeston Rd. E5	94	D2
Gellatly Rd. SE14	153	F2
Gemini Gro., Nthlt.	102/103	E3
Javelin Way		
General Gordon Pl. SE18	136	E4
General Wolfe Rd. SE10	154	D1
Genesta Rd. SE18	137	E6
Geneva Dr. SW9	151	G4
Geneva Gdns., Rom.	82	E5
Geneva Rd., Kings.T.	181	H4
Geneva Rd., Th.Hth.	187	J5
Genever Cl. E4	62	A5
Genista Rd. N18	61	E5
Genoa Av. SW15	147	J5
Genoa Rd. SE20	189	F1
Genotin Rd., Enf.	44	A3
Genotin Ter., Enf.	44	A3
Genotin Rd.		
Gentian Row SE13	154	C1
Sparta St.		
Gentlemans Row, Enf.	43	J3
Gentry Gdns. E13	115	G4
Whitwell Rd.		
Geoffrey Cl. SE5	151	J2
Geoffrey Gdns. E6	116	B2
Geoffrey Rd. SE4	153	J3
George Beard Rd. SE8	133	J4
George Comberton Wk. E12	98	D5
Gainsborough Av.		
George Ct. WC2	**18**	**B6**
George Cres. N10	58	A7
George Downing Est. N16	94	C2
Cazenove Rd.		
George V Av., Pnr.	67	G3
George V Cl., Pnr.	67	G3
George V Av.		
George V Way, Grnf.	105	E1
George Gange Way, Har.	68	B3
George Gro. Rd. SE20	188	D1
George Inn Yd. SE1	**28**	**B2**
George La. E18	79	G2
George La. SE13	154	C6
George La., Brom.	205	H1
George Lansbury Ho. N22	75	G1
Progress Way		
George Loveless Ho. E2	**13**	**G3**
George Lowe Ct. W2	**14**	**A1**
George Mathers Rd. SE11	**35**	**G1**
George Mathers Rd. SE11	131	H4
George Ms. NW1	**9**	**F4**
George Ms., Enf.	44	A3
Sydney Rd.		
George Pl. N17	76	B3
Dongola Rd.		
George Rd. E4	62	A6
George Rd., Kings.T.	164	B7
George Rd., N.Mal.	183	F4
George Row SE16	**29**	**H4**
George Row SE16	132	D2
George Sq. SW19	184	C3
Mostyn Rd.		
George St. E16	115	F6
George St. W1	**16**	**A3**
George St. W1	110	A6
George St. W7	124	B1
The Bdy.		
George St., Bark.	99	F7
George St., Croy.	202	A2
George St., Houns.	143	F2
George St., Rich.	145	G5
George St., Sthl.	122	E4
George St., Sutt.	198	E5
George Wyver Cl. SW19	148	B7
Beaumont Rd.		
George Yd. EC3	**20**	**C4**
George Yd. W1	**16**	**C5**
George Yd. W1	110	A7
George's Rd. N7	93	F5
Georges Sq. SW6	128	C6
North End Rd.		
Georgetown Cl. SE19	170	A5
St. Kitts Ter.		
Georgette Pl. SE10	134	C7
King George St.		
Georgeville Gdns., Ilf.	81	E4
Georgia Rd., N.Mal.	182	C4
Georgia Rd., Th.Hth.	187	H1
Georgian Cl., Brom.	191	H7
Georgian Cl., Stan.	52	D7
Georgian Ct. SW16	168/169	E4
Gleneldon Rd.		
Georgian Ct., Wem.	88	A6
Georgian Way, Har.	86	A2
Georgiana St. NW1	110	C1
Georgina Gdns. E2	**13**	**G3**
Geraint Rd., Brom.	173	G4
Gerald Ms. SW1	**32**	**C1**
Gerald Rd. E16	115	F4
Gerald Rd. SW1	**32**	**C1**
Gerald Rd. SW1	130	A4
Gerald Rd., Dag.	101	F2
Geraldine Rd. SW18	149	F5
Geraldine Rd. W4	126	A6
Geraldine St. SE11	**27**	**G6**
Geraldine St. SE11	131	H3
Gerard Av., Houns.	143	G7
Redfern Av.		
Gerard Rd. SW13	147	F1
Gerard Rd., Har.	68	D6
Gerards Cl. SE16	133	F5
Gerda Rd. SE9	175	F2
Germander Way E15	115	E3
Gernon Rd. E3	113	H2
Geron Way NW2	89	H1
Gerrard Gdns., Pnr.	66	A5
Gerrard Pl. W1	**17**	**J5**
Gerrard Rd. N1	**11**	**H1**
Gerrard Rd. N1	111	H2
Gerrard St. W1	**17**	**H5**
Gerrard St. W1	110	D7
Gerrards Cl. N14	42	C5
Gerridge St. SE1	**27**	**F4**
Gerridge St. SE1	131	G3
Gerry Raffles Sq. E15	96	D6
Salway Rd.		
Gertrude Rd., Belv.	139	G4
Gertrude St. SW10	**30**	**D6**
Gertrude St. SW10	129	F6
Gervase Cl., Wem.	88	C3
Gervase Rd., Edg.	70	C1
Gervase St. SE15	133	E7
Ghent St. SE6	172	A2
Ghent Way E8	94	C6
Tyssen St.		
Giant Arches Rd. SE24	151	J7
Giant Tree Hill, Bushey	52	A1
Gibbard Ms. SW19	166	A5
Gibbfield Cl., Rom.	82	E3
Gibbins Rd. E15	96	C7
Gibbon Rd. SE15	153	F2
Gibbon Rd. W3	106	E7
Gibbon Rd., Kings.T.	181	H1
Gibbon Wk. SW15	147	G4
Swinburne Rd.		
Gibbons Rd. NW10	88	D6
Gibbs Av. SE19	170	A5
Gibbs Cl. SE19	170	A5
Gibbs Couch, Wat.	50	D3
Gibbs Grn. W14	128	C5
Gibbs Grn., Edg.	54	C5
Gibbs Rd. N18	61	F4
Gibbs Sq. SE19	170	A5
Gibraltar Wk. E2	**13**	**G4**
Gibraltar Wk. E2	112	C3
Gibson Cl. E1	113	F4
Colebert Av.		
Gibson Cl. N21	43	G6
Gibson Cl., Chess.	195	F6
Gibson Cl., Islw.	144	A3
Gibson Gdns. N16	94	C2
Northwold Rd.		
Gibson Rd. SE11	**34**	**D2**
Gibson Rd. SE11	131	F4
Gibson Rd., Dag.	100	C1
Gibson Rd., Sutt.	198	E5
Gibson Sq. N1	111	G1
Gibson St. SE10	134	E5
Gibson's Hill SW16	169	G6
Gideon Cl., Belv.	139	H4
Gideon Ms. W5	125	G2
Gideon Rd. SW11	150	A3
Giesbach Rd. N19	92	C2
Giffard Rd. N18	60	B5
Giffin St. SE8	134	A7
Gifford Gdns. W7	104	A5
Gifford St. N1	93	E7
Gift La. E15	115	E1
Giggs Hill Gdns., T.Ditt.	194	D1
Giggs Hill Rd., T.Ditt.	180	D7
Gilbert Cl. SE18	156	C1
Gilbert Gro., Edg.	70	D1
Gilbert Ho. SE8	134	A6
McMillan St.		
Gilbert Pl. WC1	**18**	**A2**
Gilbert Rd. SE11	**35**	**F2**
Gilbert Rd. SE11	131	G4
Gilbert Rd. SW19	167	F7
Gilbert Rd., Belv.	139	G3
Gilbert Rd., Brom.	173	G7
Gilbert Rd., Pnr.	66	D4
Gilbert St. E15	96	E4
Gilbert St. W1	**16**	**C5**
Gilbert St. W1	110	A6
Gilbert St., Houns.	143	J3
High St.		
Gilbert Way, Croy.	200/201	E1
Beddington Fm. Rd.		
Gilbey Rd. SW17	167	H4
Gilbeys Yd. NW1	110	B1
Oval Rd.		
Gilbourne Rd. SE18	137	J6

Gilda Av., Enf. 45 H5
Gilda Cres. N16 94 D1
Gildea Cl., Pnr. 51 G7
Gildea St. W1 17 E2
Gilden Cres. NW5 92 A5
Gilders Rd., Chess. 195 J6
Gildersome St. SE18 136 D6
Nightingale Vale
Giles Coppice SE19 170 C4
Gilkes Cres. SE21 152 B6
Gilkes Pl. SE21 152 B6
Gill Av. E16 115 G6
Gill St. E14 113 J6
Gillan Grn., Bushey 51 J2
Gillards Ms. E17 78 A4
Gillards Way
Gillards Way E17 78 A4
Gillender St. E3 114 C4
Gillender St. E14 114 C4
Gillespie Rd. N5 93 G3
Gillett Av. E6 116 B2
Gillett Pl. N16 94 B5
Gillett St.
Gillett Rd., Th.Hth. 188 A4
Gillett St. N16 94 B5
Gillette Cor., Islw. 124 D7
Gillfoot NW1 9 G2
Gillfoot NW1 110 C2
Gillham Ter. N17 60 D6
Gillian Pk. Rd., Sutt. 198 C1
Gillian St. SE13 154 B5
Gillies St. NW5 92 A5
Gilling Ct. NW3 91 H6
Gillingham Ms. SW1 33 F1
Gillingham Rd. NW2 90 B3
Gillingham Row SW1 33 F1
Gillingham St. SW1 33 F1
Gillingham St. SW1 130 B4
Gillison Wk. SE16 29 J5
Gillman Dr. E15 115 F1
Gillum Cl., Barn. 57 J1
Gilmore Rd. SE13 154 D4
Gilpin Av. SW14 146 D4
Gilpin Cl., Mitch. 185 H2
Gilpin Cres. N18 60 C5
Gilpin Cres., Twick. 143 H7
Gilpin Rd. E5 95 H4
Gilpin Way, Hayes 121 G7
Gilsland Rd., Th.Hth. 188 A4
Gilstead Ho., Bark. 118 B2
Gilstead Rd. SW6 149 E2
Gilston Rd. SW10 30 D4
Gilston Rd. SW10 129 F5
Gilton Rd. SE6 173 E3
Giltspur St. EC1 19 H3
Giltspur St. EC1 111 H6
Gilwell Cl. E4 46 B4
Antlers Hill
Gilwell La. E4 46 C4
Gilwell Pk. E4 46 C3
Gippeswyck Cl., Pnr. 66 D1
Uxbridge Rd.
Gipsy Hill SE19 170 B5
Gipsy La. SW15 147 G3
Gipsy Rd. SE27 169 J4
Gipsy Rd., Well. 158 D1
Gipsy Rd. Gdns. SE27 169 J4
Giralda Cl. E16 116 A5
Fulmer Rd.
Giraud St. E14 114 B6
Girdlers Rd. W14 128 A4
Girdlestone Wk. N19 92 C2
Girdwood Rd. SW18 148 B7
Girling Way, Felt. 142 A3
Gironde Rd. SW6 128 C7
Girton Av. NW9 70 A3
Girton Cl., Nthlt. 85 J6
Girton Gdns., Croy. 204 A3
Girton Rd. SE26 171 G5
Girton Rd., Nthlt. 85 J6
Girton Vil. W10 108 A6
Gisbourne Cl., Wall. 200 D3
Gisburn Rd. N8 75 F4
Gissing Wk. N1 93 G7
Lofting Rd.
Gittens Cl., Brom. 173 F4
Given Wilson Wk. E13 115 F2
Glacier Way, Wem. 105 G2
Gladbeck Way, Enf. 43 H4
Gladding Rd. E12 98 A4
Glade, The N21 43 F6
Glade, The SE7 135 J7
Glade, The, Brom. 192 A2
Glade, The, Croy. 189 G5
Glade, The, Enf. 43 G3
Glade, The, Epsom 197 G5
Glade, The, Ilf. 80 C1
Glade, The, W.Wick. 204 B3
Glade, The, Wdf.Grn. 63 H3
Glade Cl., Surb. 195 G2
Glade Ct., Ilf. 80 C1
The Glade
Glade Gdns., Croy. 189 H7
Glade La., Sthl. 123 H2
Glades Pl., Brom. 191 G2
Widmore Rd.
Glades Shop. Cen., The, Brom. 191 G2
Gladeside N21 43 F6
Gladeside, Croy. 189 G6
Gladeside Cl., Chess. 195 G7
Leatherhead Rd.
Gladesmore Rd. N15 76 C6
Gladeswood Rd., Belv. 139 H4
Gladiator St. SE23 153 H6
Glading Ter. N16 94 C3
Gladioli Cl., Hmptn. 161 G6
Gresham Rd.
Gladsdale Dr., Pnr. 66 A4
Gladsmuir Rd. N19 92 C1
Gladsmuir Rd., Barn. 40 B2
Gladstone Av. E12 98 B7
Gladstone Av. N22 75 G2
Gladstone Av., Felt. 142 A6
Gladstone Av., Twick. 144 A7
Gladstone Gdns., Houns. 143 J1
Gresham Rd.
Gladstone Ms. NW6 90 C7
Cavendish Rd.
Gladstone Ms. SE20 171 F7
Gladstone Par. NW2 89 H1
Edgware Rd.
Gladstone Pk. Gdns. NW2 89 H3
Gladstone Pl. E3 113 J2
Roman Rd.
Gladstone Pl., Barn. 40 A4
Gladstone Rd. SW19 166 D7
Gladstone Rd. W4 126 D3
Acton La.
Gladstone Rd., Buck.H. 63 H1
Gladstone Rd., Croy. 188 A7
Gladstone Rd., Kings.T. 182 A3
Gladstone Rd., Orp. 207 F5
Gladstone Rd., Sthl. 122 E3
Gladstone Rd., Surb. 195 G2
Gladstone St. SE1 27 G5
Gladstone St. SE1 131 H3
Gladstone Ter. SE27 169 J4
Gladstone Ter. SW8 150 B1
Gladstone Way, Har. 68 B3
Gladwell Rd. N8 75 F6
Gladwell Rd., Brom. 173 G6
Gladwyn Rd. SW15 148 A3
Gladys Rd. NW6 90 D7
Glamis Cres., Hayes 121 F3
Glamis Pl. E1 113 F7
Glamis Rd. E1 113 F7
Glamis Way, Nthlt. 85 J6
Glamorgan Cl., Mitch. 187 E3
Glamorgan Rd., Kings.T. 163 F7
Glanfield Rd., Beck. 189 J4
Glanleam Rd., Stan. 53 G4
Glanville Rd. SW2 151 E5
Glanville Rd., Brom. 191 H3
Glasbrook Av., Twick. 161 F1
Glasbrook Rd. SE9 156 A7
Glaserton Rd. N16 76 B7
Glasford St. SW17 167 J6
Glasgow Ho. W9 6 B3
Glasgow Ho. W9 109 E2
Glasgow Rd. E13 115 H2
Glasgow Rd. N18 60/61 E5
Aberdeen Rd.
Glasgow Ter. SW1 33 F4
Glasgow Ter. SW1 130 C5
Glass St. E2 112/113 E4
Coventry Rd.
Glass Yd. SE18 136 D3
Woolwich High St.
Glasse Cl. W13 104 D7
Glasshill St. SE1 27 H3
Glasshill St. SE1 131 H2
Glasshouse All. EC4 19 F4
Glasshouse Flds. E1 113 G7
Glasshouse St. W1 17 G6
Glasshouse St. W1 110 C7
Glasshouse Wk. SE11 34 B3
Glasshouse Wk. SE11 131 E5
Glasshouse Yd. EC1 19 J1
Glasslyn Rd. N8 74 D5
Glassmill La., Brom. 191 F2
Glastonbury Av., Wdf.Grn. 64 A7
Glastonbury Rd. N9 60 C1
Glastonbury Rd., Mord. 184 D7
Glastonbury St. NW6 90 C5
Glaucus St. E3 114 B5
Glazbury Rd. W14 128 B4
Glazebrook Cl. SE21 170 A2
Glazebrook Rd., Tedd. 162 C7
Glebe, The SE3 154 E3
Glebe, The SW16 168 D4
Glebe, The, Chis. 193 F1
Glebe, The, West Dr. 120 C4
Glebe, The, Wor.Pk. 197 F1
Glebe Av., Enf. 43 H3
Glebe Av., Har. 69 H3
Glebe Av., Mitch. 185 H2
Glebe Av., Ruis. 84 B6
Glebe Av., Wdf.Grn. 63 G6
Glebe Cl. W4 126/127 E5
Glebe St.
Glebe Cotts., Sutt. 198/199 E4
Vale Rd.
Glebe Ct. W7 104 A7
Glebe Ct., Mitch. 185 J3
Glebe Ct., Stan. 53 F5
Glebe Rd.
Glebe Cres. NW4 71 J4
Glebe Cres., Har. 69 H3
Glebe Gdns., N.Mal. 183 E7
Glebe Ho. Dr., Brom. 205 H1
Glebe Hyrst SE19 170 C4
Giles Coppice
Glebe La., Barn. 39 G5
Glebe La., Har. 69 H4
Glebe Path, Mitch. 185 H3
Glebe Pl. SW3 31 G5
Glebe Pl. SW3 129 H6
Glebe Rd. E8 94 C7
Middleton Rd.
Glebe Rd. N3 73 F1
Glebe Rd. N8 75 F4
Glebe Rd. NW10 89 F6
Glebe Rd. SW13 147 G2
Glebe Rd., Brom. 191 G1
Glebe Rd., Cars. 199 J6
Glebe Rd., Dag. 101 H6
Glebe Rd., Hayes 121 J1
Glebe Rd., Stan. 53 F5
Glebe Side, Twick. 144 C6
Glebe St. W4 126 E5
Glebe Ter. E3 114 A3
Bow Rd.
Glebe Way, Felt. 161 G3
Glebe Way, W.Wick. 204 C2
Glebelands, W.Mol. 179 H5
Glebelands Av. E18 79 G2
Glebelands Av., Ilf. 81 G7
Glebelands Cl. SE5 152 B3
Grove Hill Rd.
Glebelands Rd., Felt. 142 A7
Glebeway, Wdf.Grn. 63 J5
Gledhow Gdns. SW5 30 C2
Gledhow Gdns. SW5 129 F4
Gledstanes Rd. W14 128 B5
Gleed Av., Bushey 52 A2
Gleeson Dr., Orp. 207 J5
Glegg Pl. SW15 148 A4
Glen, The, Brom. 190 E2
Glen, The, Croy. 203 G2
Glen, The, Enf. 43 H4
Glen, The, Orp. 206 C3
Glen, The, Pnr. 67 E7
Glen, The (Eastcote), Pnr. 66 B5
Glen, The, Sthl. 123 F5
Glen, The, Wem. 87 G4
Glen Albyn Rd. SW19 166 A2
Glen Cres., Wdf.Grn. 63 H6
Glen Gdns., Croy. 201 G3
Glen Ri., Wdf.Grn. 63 H6
Glen Rd. E13 115 J4
Glen Rd. E17 77 J5
Glen Rd., Chess. 195 H3
Glen Ter. E14 134 C2
Manchester Rd.
Glen Wk., Islw. 144 A5
Glena Mt., Sutt. 199 F4
Glenaffric Av. E14 134 D4
Glenalmond Rd., Har. 69 H4
Glenalvon Way SE18 136 B4
Glenarm Rd. E5 95 F5
Glenavon Cl., Esher 194 D7
Glenavon Rd. E15 97 E7
Glenbarr Cl. SE9 156/157 E3
Dumbreck Rd.
Glenbow Rd., Brom. 172 E6
Glenbrook N., Enf. 43 F4
Glenbrook Rd. NW6 90 D5
Glenbrook S., Enf. 43 F4
Glenbuck Ct., Surb. 181 G6
Glenbuck Rd.
Glenbuck Rd., Surb. 181 G6
Glenburnie Rd. SW17 167 J3
Glencairn Dr. W5 105 F4
Glencairn Rd. SW16 168 E7
Glencairne Cl. E16 116 A5
Glencoe Av., Ilf. 81 G7
Glencoe Dr., Dag. 101 G4
Glencoe Rd., Hayes 102 D5
Glencorse Grn., Wat. 50 D4
Caldwell Rd.
Glendale Av. N22 59 G7
Glendale Av., Edg. 53 J4
Glendale Av., Rom. 82 C7
Glendale Cl. SE9 156 D3
Dumbreck Rd.
Glendale Dr. SW19 166 C5
Glendale Gdns., Wem. 87 G1
Glendale Ms., Beck. 190 B1
Glendale Rd., Erith 139 J4
Glendale Way SE28 118 C7
Glendall St. SW9 151 F4
Glendarvon St. SW15 148 A3
Glendevon Cl., Edg. 54 B3
Tayside Dr.
Glendish Rd. N17 76 E1
Glendor Gdns. NW7 54 D4
Glendower Gdns. SW14 146 D3
Glendower Rd.
Glendower Pl. SW7 31 E1
Glendower Pl. SW7 129 G4
Glendower Rd. E4 62 D1
Glendower Rd. SW14 146 D3
Glendown Rd. SE2 138 A5
Glendun Rd. W3 107 E7
Gleneagle Ms. SW16 168 D5
Ambleside Av.
Gleneagle Rd. SW16 168 D5
Gleneagles, Stan. 52 E6
Gleneagles Cl. SE16 132/133 E5
Ryder Dr.
Gleneagles Cl., Orp. 207 G1
Gleneagles Cl., Stai. 140 A6
Gleneagles Cl., Wat. 50 D4
Gleneagles Grn., Orp. 207 G1
Tandridge Dr.
Gleneagles Twr., Sthl. 103 J6
Gleneldon Ms. SW16 168 E4
Gleneldon Rd. SW16 168 E4
Glenelg Rd. SW2 151 E5
Glenesk Rd. SE9 156 D3
Glenfarg Rd. SE6 172 D1
Glenfield Rd. SW12 168 C1
Glenfield Rd. W13 125 E2
Glenfield Ter. W13 124 E2
Glenfinlas Way SE5 35 H7
Glenfinlas Way SE5 131 H7
Glenforth St. SE10 135 F5
Glengall Causeway E14 134 A3
Glengall Gro. E14 134 C3
Glengall Rd. NW6 108 C1
Glengall Rd. SE15 37 G5
Glengall Rd. SE15 132 C6
Glengall Rd., Bexh. 159 E3
Glengall Rd., Edg. 54 B3
Glengall Rd., Wdf.Grn. 63 G6
Glengall Ter. SE15 37 G5
Glengall Ter. SE15 132 C6
Glengarnock Av. E14 134 C4
Glengarry Rd. SE22 152 B5
Glenham Dr., Ilf. 80 E5
Glenhaven Av., Borwd. 38 A3
Glenhead Cl. SE9 156/157 E3
Dumbreck Rd.
Glenhill Cl. N3 72 D2
Glenhouse Rd. SE9 156 D5
Glenhurst Av. NW5 92 A4
Glenhurst Av., Bex. 177 F1
Glenhurst Ct. SE19 170 C5
Glenhurst Ri. SE19 169 J7
Glenhurst Rd. N12 57 G5
Glenhurst Rd., Brent. 125 F6
Glenilla Rd. NW3 91 H6
Glenister Ho., Hayes 122 B1
Glenister Pk. Rd. SW16 168 D7
Glenister Rd. SE10 135 F5
Glenister St. E16 136 D1
Glenlea Rd. SE9 156 C5
Glenloch Rd. NW3 91 H6
Glenloch Rd., Enf. 45 F2
Glenluce Rd. SE3 135 G6
Glenlyon Rd. SE9 156 D5
Glenmere Av. NW7 55 G7
Glenmill, Hmptn. 161 F5
Glenmore Rd. NW3 91 H6
Glenmore Rd., Well. 157 J1
Glenmore Way, Bark. 118 A2
Glenmount Path SE18 137 F5
Raglan Rd.
Glennie Rd. SE27 169 G3
Glenny Rd., Bark. 99 F6
Glenorchy Cl., Hayes 103 E5

Glenparke Rd. E7 97 H6
Glenrosa St. SW6 149 F2
Glenrose Ct., Sid. 176 B5
Glenroy St. W12 107 J6
Glensdale Rd. SE4 153 J3
Glenshiel Rd. SE9 156 D5
Glenside, Chig. 65 E6
Glentanner Way SW17 167 G3
  Aboyne Rd.
Glentham Gdns. 127 H6
  SW13
  Glentham Rd.
Glentham Rd. SW13 127 G6
Glenthorne Av., 203 E1
  Croy.
Glenthorne Cl., Sutt. 198 D1
Glenthorne Gdns., Ilf. 80 D3
Glenthorne Gdns., 198 D1
  Sutt.
Glenthorne Ms. W6 127 H4
  Glenthorne Rd.
Glenthorne Rd. E17 77 H5
Glenthorne Rd. N11 57 J5
Glenthorne Rd. W6 127 J4
Glenthorne Rd., 181 J4
  Kings.T.
Glenthorpe Rd., 184 A5
  Mord.
Glenton Rd. SE13 154 E4
Glentrammon Av., 207 J6
  Orp.
Glentrammon Cl., 207 J6
  Orp.
Glentrammon Gdns., 207 J6
  Orp.
Glentrammon Rd., 207 J6
  Orp.
Glentworth St. NW1 8 A6
Glentworth St. NW1 109 J4
Glenure Rd. SE9 156 D5
Glenview SE2 138 D6
Glenview Rd., Brom. 192 A2
Glenville Gro. SE8 133 J7
Glenville Ms. SW18 148 E7
Glenville Rd., 182 A1
  Kings.T.
Glenwood Av. NW9 88 E1
Glenwood Cl., Har. 68 C5
Glenwood Gdns., Ilf. 80 D5
Glenwood Gro. NW9 88 C1
Glenwood Rd. N15 75 H5
Glenwood Rd. NW7 55 E3
Glenwood Rd. SE6 171 J1
Glenwood Rd., 197 G6
  Epsom
Glenwood Rd., 144 A3
  Houns.
Glenwood Way, Croy. 189 G6
Glenworth Av. E14 134 D4
Gliddon Rd. W14 128 B4
Glimpsing Grn., Erith 139 E3
Global App. E3 114 B2
  Hancock Rd.
Globe Pond Rd. SE16 133 H1
Globe Rd. E1 113 F3
Globe Rd. E2 113 F3
Globe Rd. E15 97 F5
Globe Rd., Wdf.Grn. 63 J6
Globe Rope Wk. E14 134 C4
Globe St. SE1 28 A5
Globe St. SE1 132 A3
Globe Ter. E2 113 F3
  Globe Rd.
Globe Yd. W1 16 D4
Gloster Rd., N.Mal. 182 E4
Gloucester Arc. SW7 30 C1
Gloucester Av. NW1 92 A7
Gloucester Av., Sid. 175 H2
Gloucester Av., 157 J4
  Well.
Gloucester Circ. SE10 134 C7
Gloucester Cl. NW10 88 D7
Gloucester Cl., 194 D1
  T.Ditt.
Gloucester Ct. EC3 21 E6
Gloucester Ct., Rich. 126 A7
Gloucester Cres. NW1 110 B1
Gloucester Dr. N4 93 H2
Gloucester Dr. NW11 72 D4
Gloucester Gdns. 72 C7
  NW11
Gloucester Gdns. W2 14 B3
Gloucester Gdns., 42 A4
  Barn.
Gloucester Gdns., Ilf. 80 B7
Gloucester Gdns., 199 E2
  Sutt.
Gloucester Gate NW1 8 D1
Gloucester Gate NW1 110 B2
Gloucester Gate Ms. 8 D1
  NW1
Gloucester Gro., Edg. 70 D1
Gloucester Gro. Est. 37 E6
  SE15

Gloucester Gro. Est. 132 B6
  SE15
Gloucester Ho. N7 93 E3
Gloucester Ho. NW6 108 D2
Gloucester Ms. E10 78 A7
  Gloucester Rd.
Gloucester Ms. W2 14 D4
Gloucester Ms. W2 109 F6
Gloucester Ms. W. W2 14 C4
Gloucester Par., Sid. 158 A5
Gloucester Pl. NW1 7 J5
Gloucester Pl. NW1 109 J4
Gloucester Pl. W1 16 A1
Gloucester Pl. W1 109 J5
Gloucester Pl., Enf. 43 J2
  Chase Side
Gloucester Pl. Ms. W1 16 A2
Gloucester Rd. E10 78 A7
Gloucester Rd. E11 79 H5
Gloucester Rd. E12 98 C3
Gloucester Rd. E17 77 G2
Gloucester Rd. N17 76 A2
Gloucester Rd. N18 60 C5
Gloucester Rd. SW7 22 C5
Gloucester Rd. SW7 129 F4
Gloucester Rd. W3 126 C2
Gloucester Rd. W5 125 F2
Gloucester Rd., Barn. 41 F5
Gloucester Rd., Belv. 139 F5
Gloucester Rd., Croy. 188 A6
Gloucester Rd., Felt. 160 C1
Gloucester Rd., 161 H7
  Hmptn.
Gloucester Rd., Har. 67 H5
Gloucester Rd., Houns. 142 E4
Gloucester Rd., 182 B2
  Kings.T.
Gloucester Rd., Rich. 126 A7
Gloucester Rd., Tedd. 162 B5
Gloucester Rd., 161 J1
  Twick.
Gloucester Sq. E2 112 D1
  Whiston Rd.
Gloucester Sq. W2 15 F4
Gloucester Sq. W2 109 G6
Gloucester St. SW1 33 F4
Gloucester St. SW1 130 C5
Gloucester Ter. W2 14 C3
Gloucester Ter. W2 109 G7
Gloucester Wk. W8 128 D2
Gloucester Way EC1 11 F4
Gloucester Way EC1 111 G3
Glover Cl. SE2 138 C4
Glover Dr. N18 61 F6
Glover Rd., Pnr. 66 D6
Gloxinia Wk., Hmptn. 161 G6
Glycena Rd. SW11 149 J3
Glyn Av., Barn. 41 G4
Glyn Cl. SE25 188 B2
Glyn Ct. SW16 169 G3
Glyn Dr., Sid. 176 B4
Glyn Rd. E5 95 G4
Glyn Rd., Enf. 45 F4
Glyn Rd., Wor.Pk. 198 A2
Glyn St. SE11 34 C4
Glynde Ms. SW3 23 H6
Glynde Rd., Bexh. 158 D3
Glynde St. SE4 153 J6
Glyndebourne Pk., 207 E2
  Orp.
Glyndon Rd. SE18 137 F4
Glynfield Rd. NW10 89 E7
Glynne Rd. N22 75 G2
Glynwood Ct. SE23 171 F2
Goat La., Surb. 195 F2
Goat Rd., Mitch. 186 A7
Goat St. SE1 29 F3
Goat Wf., Brent. 125 H6
Goaters All. SW6 128 C7
Godalming Av., 201 E5
  Wall.
Godalming Rd. E14 114 B5
Godbold Rd. E15 114 E3
Goddard Rd., Beck. 189 G4
Goddards Way, Ilf. 99 G1
Godfrey Av., Nthlt. 102 E1
Godfrey Av., Twick. 144 A7
Godfrey Hill SE18 136 B4
Godfrey Rd. SE18 136 C4
Godfrey St. E15 114 C2
Godfrey St. SW3 31 H3
Godfrey Way, Houns. 143 F7
Goding St. SE11 34 B4
Goding St. SE11 131 E5
Godley Rd. SW18 167 G1
Godliman St. EC4 19 J4
Godliman St. EC4 111 J6
Godman Rd. SE15 152 E2
Godolphin Cl. N13 59 H6
Godolphin Pl. W3 106 D7
  Vyner St.
Godolphin Rd. W12 127 H2

Godson Rd., Croy. 201 G3
Godson St. N1 11 E1
Godson St. N1 111 G2
Godstone Rd., Sutt. 199 F4
Godstone Rd., Twick. 144 E6
Godstow Rd. SE2 138 C2
Godwin Cl. N1 12 A1
Godwin Cl., Epsom 196 C6
Godwin Cl. NW1 9 G1
Godwin Rd. E7 97 H4
Godwin Rd., Brom. 191 J3
Goffers Rd. SE3 154 D1
Goidel Cl., Wall. 200 D4
Golborne Gdns. W10 108 C4
  Golborne Rd.
Golborne Ms. W10 108 B5
  Portobello Rd.
Golborne Rd. W10 108 B5
Gold Hill, Edg. 54 D6
Gold La., Edg. 54 D6
Golda Cl., Barn. 40 A6
Goldbeaters Gro., 54 E6
  Edg.
Goldcliff Cl., Mord. 184 D6
Goldcrest Cl. E16 116 A5
  Sheerwater Rd.
Goldcrest Cl. SE28 118 C7
Goldcrest Ms. W5 105 G5
  Montpelier Av.
Goldcrest Way, 51 J1
  Bushey
Golden Ct., Rich. 145 G5
  George St.
Golden Cres., Hayes 121 J1
Golden Cross Ms. 108 C6
  W11
  Basing St.
Golden La. EC1 11 J6
Golden La. EC1 111 J4
Golden La. Est. EC1 11 J6
Golden Manor W7 104 B7
Golden Plover Cl. 115 H6
  E16
  Maplin Rd.
Golden Sq. W1 17 G5
Golden Sq. W1 110 C7
Golden Yd. NW3 91 F4
  Heath St.
Golders Cl., Edg. 54 B5
Golders Gdns. NW11 72 B7
Golders Grn. Cres. 72 C7
  NW11
Golders Grn. Rd. 72 B6
  NW11
Golders Manor Dr. 72 A6
  NW11
Golders Pk. Cl. NW11 90 E1
Golders Ri. NW4 72 A5
Golders Way NW11 72 C7
Goldfinch Rd. SE28 137 G3
Goldfinch Way, 38 A4
  Borwd.
Goldhawk Ms. W12 127 H2
  Devonport Rd.
Goldhawk Rd. W6 127 F4
Goldhawk Rd. W12 127 G3
Goldhaze Cl., 64 A7
  Wdf.Grn.
Goldhurst Ter. NW6 90 E7
Golding Cl., Chess. 195 F6
  Coppard Gdns.
Golding St. E1 21 J4
Golding St. E1 112 D6
Golding Ter. SW11 150 A2
  Longhedge St.
Goldingham Av., 49 F2
  Loug.
Goldings Hill, Loug. 48 D1
Goldings Ri., Loug. 48 D1
Goldings Rd., Loug. 48 D1
Goldington Cres. NW1 9 H1
Goldington Cres. 110 D2
  NW1
Goldington St. NW1 9 H1
Goldington St. NW1 110 D2
Goldman Cl. E2 13 H5
Goldman Cl. E2 112 D4
Goldney Rd. W9 108 D4
Goldrill Dr. N11 58 A2
Goldsboro Rd. SW8 150 D1
Goldsborough Cres. 62 B2
  E4
Goldsdown Cl., Enf. 45 H2
Goldsdown Rd., Enf. 45 G2
Goldsmid St. SE18 137 H5
  Sladedale Rd.
Goldsmith Av. E12 98 B6
Goldsmith Av. NW9 71 F6
Goldsmith Av. W3 106 D7
Goldsmith Av., Rom. 83 G7
Goldsmith Cl. W3 126/127 E1
  East Acton La.
Goldsmith Cl., Har. 85 H1
Goldsmith La. NW9 70 B4

Goldsmith Rd. E10 96 A1
Goldsmith Rd. E17 77 G2
Goldsmith Rd. N11 57 J5
Goldsmith Rd. SE15 152 D1
Goldsmith Rd. W3 126 D1
Goldsmith St. EC2 20 A3
Goldsmith's Row E2 13 J2
Goldsmith's Row E2 112 D2
Goldsmith's Sq. E2 13 J1
Goldsmith's Sq. E2 112 D2
Goldsworthy Gdns. 133 F4
  SE16
Goldwell Rd., Th.Hth. 187 F4
Goldwin Cl. SE14 153 F1
Goldwing Cl. E16 115 G6
Golf Cl., Stan. 53 F7
Golf Cl., Th.Hth. 187 G1
  Kensington Av.
Golf Club Dr., 164 D7
  Kings.T.
Golf Rd. W5 105 J6
  Boileau Rd.
Golf Rd., Brom. 192 D3
Golf Side, Twick. 162 A3
Golfe Rd., Ilf. 99 G3
Golfside Cl. N20 57 H3
Golfside Cl., N.Mal. 183 E2
Goliath Cl., Wall. 200 E7
Gollogly Ter. SE7 135 J5
Gomer Gdns., Tedd. 162 D6
Gomer Pl., Tedd. 162 D6
Gomm Rd. SE16 133 F3
Gomshall Av., Wall. 200 E5
Gondar Gdns. NW6 90 C5
Gonson Pl. SE8 134 A6
Gonson St. SE8 134 B6
Gonston Cl. SW19 166 B2
  Boddicott Cl.
Gonville Cres., Nthlt. 85 H6
Gonville Rd., Th.Hth. 187 F5
Gonville St. SW6 148 B3
  Putney Br. App.
Goodall Rd. E11 96 C3
Gooden Ct., Har. 86 B3
Goodenough Rd. 166 C7
  SW19
Goodge Pl. W1 17 G2
Goodge St. W1 17 G2
Goodge St. W1 110 C5
Goodhall St. NW10 107 E3
Goodhart Pl. E14 113 H7
Goodhart Way, 190 E7
  W.Wick.
Goodhew Rd., Croy. 188 D6
Gooding Cl., N.Mal. 182 C4
Goodinge Cl. N7 92 E6
Goodman Cres. SW2 168 D2
Goodman Rd. E10 78 C7
Goodmans Ct., Wem. 87 G4
Goodman's Stile E1 21 H4
Goodman's Stile E1 112 D6
Goodmans Yd. E1 21 F5
Goodmans Yd. E1 112 C7
Goodmayes Av., Ilf. 100 A1
Goodmayes La., Ilf. 100 A4
Goodmayes Rd., Ilf. 100 A1
Goodrich Rd. SE22 152 C6
Goods Way NW1 10 A1
Goods Way NW1 110 E2
Goodson Rd. NW10 89 E7
Goodway Gdns. E14 114 D6
Goodwin Cl. SE16 29 G6
Goodwin Cl. SE16 132 D3
Goodwin Cl., Mitch. 185 G3
Goodwin Dr., Sid. 176 D3
Goodwin Gdns., 201 H6
  Croy.
Goodwin Rd. N9 61 F1
Goodwin Rd. W12 127 G2
Goodwin Rd., Croy. 201 H5
Goodwin St. N4 93 G2
  Fonthill Rd.
Goodwins Ct. WC2 18 A5
Goodwood Cl., 184 D4
  Mord.
Goodwood Cl., Stan. 53 F5
Goodwood Dr., Nthlt. 85 G6
Goodwood Path, 38 A3
  Borwd.
  Stratfield Rd.
Goodwood Rd. SE14 133 H7
Goodwyn Av. NW7 55 E5
Goodwyns Vale N10 74 A1
Goodyers Gdns. NW4 72 A5
Goosander Way SE28 137 G3
Goose Sq. E6 116 C6
  Harper Rd.
Gooseacre La., Har. 69 G5
Gooseley La. E6 116 D3
Goosens Cl., Sutt. 199 F5
  Turnpike La.
Gophir La. EC4 20 B5
Gopsall St. N1 112 A1
Gordon Av. E4 62 E6

Gordon Av. SW14 146 E4
Gordon Av., Stan. 52 E6
Gordon Av., Twick. 144 D5
Gordon Cl. E17 78 A6
Gordon Cl. N19 92 C1
Highgate Hill
Gordon Ct. W12 107 J6
Gordon Cres., Croy. 202 B1
Gordon Cres., Hayes 122 A3
Gordon Gdns., Edg. 70 B2
Gordon Gro. SE5 151 H2
Gordon Hill, Enf. 43 J1
Gordon Ho. Rd. NW5 92 A4
Gordon Pl. W8 128 D2
Gordon Rd. E4 47 E7
Gordon Rd. E11 79 G6
Gordon Rd. E15 96 C4
Gordon Rd. E18 79 H1
Gordon Rd. N3 56 C7
Gordon Rd. N9 61 E2
Gordon Rd. N11 58 D7
Gordon Rd. SE15 152 E2
Gordon Rd. W4 126 B6
Gordon Rd. W5 105 F7
Gordon Rd. W13 105 E7
Gordon Rd., Bark. 117 H1
Gordon Rd., Beck. 189 J3
Gordon Rd., Belv. 139 J4
Gordon Rd., Cars. 199 J6
Gordon Rd., Enf. 43 J1
Gordon Rd., Esher 194 B6
Gordon Rd., Har. 68 B3
Gordon Rd., Houns. 143 J4
Gordon Rd., Ilf. 99 G3
Gordon Rd., Kings.T. 181 J1
Gordon Rd., Rich. 145 J2
Gordon Rd., Rom. 83 F6
Gordon Rd., Sid. 157 H5
Gordon Rd., Sthl. 123 E4
Gordon Rd., Surb. 181 J7
Gordon Sq. WC1 9 J6
Gordon Sq. WC1 110 D4
Gordon St. E13 115 G3
Grange Rd.
Gordon St. WC1 9 H5
Gordon St. WC1 110 D4
Gordon Way, Barn. 40 C4
Gordon Way, Brom. 191 G1
Gordonbrock Rd. SE4 154 A5
Gordondale Rd. SW19 166 D2
Gore Ct. NW9 70 A5
Gore Rd. E9 113 F1
Gore Rd. SW20 183 J2
Gore St. SW7 22 D5
Gore St. SW7 129 F3
Gorefield Pl. NW6 108 D2
Goresbrook Rd., Dag. 118 B1
Goresbrook Village, Dag. 118 B1
Goresbrook Rd.
Gorham Pl. W11 108 B7
Mary Pl.
Goring Cl., Rom. 83 J1
Goring Gdns., Dag. 100 C4
Goring Rd. N11 58 E6
Goring St. EC3 21 E3
Goring St. EC3 112 B6
Goring Way, Grnf. 103 J2
Gorleston Rd. N15 76 A5
Gorleston St. W14 128 B4
Gorman Rd. SE18 136 C4
Gorringe Pk. Av., Mitch. 167 J7
Gorse Cl. E16 115 G6
Gorse Ri. SW17 168 A5
Gorse Rd., Croy. 204 A4
Gorst Rd. NW10 106 C4
Gorst Rd. SW11 149 J6
Gorsuch Pl. E2 13 F3
Gorsuch St. E2 13 F3
Gorsuch St. E2 112 C3
Gosberton Rd. SW12 168 A1
Gosbury Hill, Chess. 195 H4
Gosfield Rd., Dag. 101 G2
Gosfield St. W1 17 F1
Gosfield St. W1 110 C5
Gosford Gdns., Ilf. 80 C5
Gosforth La., Wat. 50 C3
Gosforth Path, Wat. 50 A3
Goslett Yd. WC2 17 J4
Gosling Cl., Grnf. 103 G3
Gosling Way SW9 151 G1
Gospatrick Rd. N17 75 J1
Gospel Oak Est. NW5 91 J5
Gosport Rd. E17 77 J5
Gosport Wk. N17 76/77 E5
Yarmouth Cres.
Gosport Way SE15 37 F7
Gossage Rd. SE18 137 G5
Ancona Rd.
Gosset St. E2 13 G3
Gosset St. E2 112 C3
Gosshill Rd., Chis. 192 D2
Gossington Cl., Chis. 174/175 E4
Beechwood Ri.
Gosterwood St. SE8 133 H6
Gostling Rd., Twick. 161 G1
Goston Gdns., Th.Hth. 187 G3
Goswell Rd. EC1 11 J6
Goswell Rd. EC1 111 H3
Gothic Ct., Hayes 121 G6
Sipson La.
Gothic Rd., Twick. 162 A2
Gottfried Ms. NW5 92 C4
Fortess Rd.
Goudhurst Rd., Brom. 173 E5
Gough Rd. E15 97 F4
Gough Rd., Enf. 44 E2
Gough Sq. EC4 19 F3
Gough Sq. EC4 111 G6
Gough St. WC1 10 D5
Gough St. WC1 111 F4
Gough Wk. E14 114 A6
Saracen St.
Gould Ct. SE19 170 C5
Gould Rd., Felt. 141 H7
Gould Rd., Twick. 162 B1
Gould Ter. E8 94/95 E5
Kenmure Rd.
Goulding Gdns., Th.Hth. 187 H2
Goulston St. E1 21 F3
Goulston St. E1 112 C6
Goulton Rd. E5 95 E4
Gourley Pl. N15 76 B5
Gourley St.
Gourley St. N15 76 B5
Gourock Rd. SE9 156 D5
Govan St. E2 112 D1
Whiston Rd.
Govier Cl. E15 97 E7
Gowan Av. SW6 148 B1
Gowan Rd. NW10 89 H6
Gower Cl. SW4 150 C6
Gower Ct. WC1 9 H5
Gower Ms. WC1 17 H2
Gower Ms. WC1 110 D5
Gower Pl. WC1 9 G5
Gower Pl. WC1 110 C4
Gower Rd. E7 97 G6
Gower Rd., Islw. 124 C6
Gower St. WC1 9 H6
Gower St. WC1 110 C4
Gower's Wk. E1 21 H3
Gower's Wk. E1 112 D6
Gowland Pl., Beck. 189 J2
Gowlett Rd. SE15 152 D3
Gowrie Rd. SW11 150 A3
Graburn Way, E.Mol. 180 A3
Grace Av., Bexh. 159 F2
Grace Cl. SE9 174 A3
Grace Cl., Borwd. 38 D1
Grace Cl., Edg. 54 C7
Pavilion Way
Grace Cl., Ilf. 65 J6
Grace Jones Cl. E8 94 D6
Parkholme Rd.
Grace Path SE26 171 F4
Silverdale
Grace Pl. E3 114 B3
St. Leonards St.
Grace Rd., Croy. 187 J6
Grace St. E3 114 B3
Gracechurch St. EC3 20 C5
Gracechurch St. EC3 112 A7
Gracedale Rd. SW16 168 B5
Gracefield Gdns. SW16 169 E3
Grace's All. E1 21 H5
Grace's All. E1 112 D7
Graces Ms. SE5 152 B2
Graces Rd. SE5 152 B2
Gradient, The SE26 170 D4
Graeme Rd., Enf. 44 A2
Graemesdyke Av. SW14 146 B4
Grafton Cl. W13 104 D6
Grafton Cl., Houns. 161 E1
Grafton Cl., Wor.Pk. 197 E3
Grafton Cres. NW1 92 B6
Grafton Gdns. N4 75 J6
Grafton Gdns., Dag. 101 E2
Grafton Ho. E3 114 A3
Grafton Ms. W1 9 F6
Grafton Pk. Rd., Wor.Pk. 196 E2
Grafton Pl. NW1 9 H4
Grafton Pl. NW1 110 D3
Grafton Rd. NW5 92 A5
Grafton Rd. W3 106 C7
Grafton Rd., Croy. 201 G1
Grafton Rd., Dag. 101 E2
Grafton Rd., Enf. 43 F3
Grafton Rd., Har. 67 J5
Grafton Rd., N.Mal. 182 E3
Grafton Rd., Wor.Pk. 196 D3
Grafton Sq. SW4 150 C3
Grafton St. W1 17 E6
Grafton St. W1 110 B7
Grafton Ter. NW5 91 J5
Grafton Way W1 9 F6
Grafton Way W1 110 C4
Grafton Way WC1 9 F6
Grafton Way WC1 110 C4
Grafton Way, W.Mol. 179 F4
Grafton Yd. NW5 92 B6
Prince of Wales Rd.
Graftons, The NW2 90 D3
Hermitage La.
Graham Av. W13 124 E2
Graham Av., Mitch. 186 A1
Graham Cl., Croy. 204 A2
Graham Gdns., Surb. 195 H1
Graham Rd. E8 94 D6
Graham Rd. E13 115 G4
Graham Rd. N15 75 H3
Graham Rd. NW4 71 H6
Graham Rd. SW19 166 C7
Graham Rd. W4 126 D3
Graham Rd., Bexh. 159 G4
Graham Rd., Hmptn. 161 G4
Graham Rd., Har. 68 B3
Graham Rd., Mitch. 186 A1
Graham St. N1 11 H2
Graham St. N1 111 H2
Graham Ter. SW1 32 B2
Graham Ter. SW1 130 A4
Grahame Pk. Est. NW9 71 F1
Grahame Pk. Way NW7 55 F7
Grahame Pk. Way NW9 71 F2
Grainger Cl., Nthlt. 85 J5
Lancaster Rd.
Grainger Rd. N22 75 J1
Grainger Rd., Islw. 144 C2
Gramer Cl. E11 96 D2
Norman Rd.
Grampian Cl., Hayes 121 G7
Grampian Cl., Orp. 193 J6
Cotswold Ri.
Grampian Gdns. NW2 90 B1
Granard Av. SW15 147 H5
Granard Rd. SW12 149 J7
Granary Cl. N9 45 F7
Turin Rd.
Granary Rd. E1 112 E4
Granary St. NW1 110 D1
Granby Bldgs. SE11 34 C2
Granby Rd. SE9 156 C2
Granby St. E2 13 G5
Granby St. E2 112 C4
Granby Ter. NW1 9 F2
Granby Ter. NW1 110 C2
Grand Arc. N12 57 F5
Ballards La.
Grand Av. EC1 19 H1
Grand Av. N10 74 A4
Grand Av., Surb. 182 B5
Grand Av., Wem. 88 A5
Grand Av. E., Wem. 88 B5
Grand Depot Rd. SE18 136 D5
Grand Dr. SW20 183 J2
Grand Dr., Sthl. 123 J2
Grand Junct. Wf. N1 11 J2
Grand Junct. Wf. N1 111 J2
Grand Par. Ms. SW15 148 B5
Upper Richmond Rd.
Grand Union Canal Wk. W7 124 B3
Grand Union Cl. W9 108 C5
Woodfield Rd.
Grand Union Cres. E8 94 D7
Grand Union Ind. Est. NW10 106 B2
Grand Union Wk. NW1 92 B7
Grand Wk. E1 113 H4
Solebay St.
Granden Rd. SW16 187 E2
Grandison Rd. SW11 149 J5
Grandison Rd., Wor.Pk. 197 J2
Granfield St. SW11 149 G1
Grange, The N2 73 G2
Central Av.
Grange, The N20 57 F1
Grange, The SE1 29 F5
Grange, The SE1 132 C3
Grange, The SW19 166 A6
Grange, The, Croy. 203 J2
Grange, The, Wem. 88 A7
Grange, The, Wor.Pk. 196 D3
Grange Av. N12 57 F5
Grange Av. N20 40 B7
Grange Av. SE25 188 B2
Grange Av., Barn. 57 H1
Grange Av., Stan. 69 E2
Grange Av., Twick. 162 B2
Grange Av., Wdf.Grn. 63 G6
Grange Cl., Edg. 54 C5
Grange Cl., Houns. 123 F6
Grange Cl., Sid. 176 A3
Grange Cl., W.Mol. 179 H4
Grange Cl., Wdf.Grn. 63 G7
Grange Ct. E8 94 C7
Grange Ct. WC2 18 D4
Grange Ct., Chig. 65 F2
Grange Ct., Loug. 48 A5
Grange Ct., Nthlt. 102 C2
Grange Cres. SE28 118 C6
Grange Cres., Chig. 65 G5
Grange Dr., Chis. 174 B6
Grange Fm. Cl., Har. 85 J2
Grange Gdns. N14 58 D1
Grange Gdns. NW3 91 E3
Grange Gdns. SE25 188 B2
Grange Gdns., Pnr. 67 F4
Grange Gro. N1 93 J6
Grange Hill SE25 188 B2
Grange Hill, Edg. 54 C5
Grange Ho., Bark. 117 G1
St. Margarets
Grange La. SE21 170 C2
Grange Mans., Epsom 197 F7
Grange Ms. SE10 134 D7
Crooms Hill
Grange Pk. W5 125 H1
Grange Pk. Av. N21 43 H6
Grange Pk. Pl. SW20 165 H7
Grange Pk. Rd. E10 96 B1
Grange Pk. Rd., Th.Hth. 188 A4
Grange Pl. NW6 90 D7
Grange Rd. E10 96 A1
Grange Rd. E13 115 F3
Grange Rd. E17 77 H5
Grange Rd. N6 74 A6
Grange Rd. N17 60 D6
Grange Rd. N18 60 D6
Grange Rd. NW10 89 H6
Grange Rd. SE1 28 E6
Grange Rd. SE1 132 B3
Grange Rd. SE19 188 A4
Grange Rd. SE25 188 A4
Grange Rd. SW13 147 G1
Grange Rd. W4 126 B5
Grange Rd. W5 125 G1
Grange Rd., Chess. 195 H4
Grange Rd., Edg. 54 D6
Grange Rd., Har. 68 D6
Grange Rd. (South Harrow), Har. 86 A2
Grange Rd., Ilf. 99 E4
Grange Rd., Kings.T. 181 H3
Grange Rd., Orp. 207 F2
Grange Rd., Sthl. 122 E2
Grange Rd., Sutt. 198 D7
Grange Rd., Th.Hth. 188 A4
Grange Rd., W.Mol. 179 H4
Grange St. N1 112 A1
Grange Vale, Sutt. 199 E7
Grange Vw. Rd. N20 57 F1
Grange Wk. SE1 28 E5
Grange Wk. SE1 132 B3
Grange Yd. SE1 29 F6
Grange Yd. SE1 132 C3
Grangecliffe Gdns. SE25 188 B2
Grangecourt Rd. N16 94 B1
Grangehill Pl. SE9 156 C3
Westmount Rd.
Grangehill Rd. SE9 156 C3
Grangemill Rd. SE6 172 A3
Grangemill Way SE6 172 A2
Grangeway N12 57 E4
Grangeway NW6 90 D7
Messina Av.
Grangeway, Wdf.Grn. 63 J4
Grangeway, The N21 43 H6
Grangeway Gdns., Ilf. 80 B5
Grangewood, Bex. 177 F1
Hurst Rd.
Grangewood Cl., Pnr. 66 A5
Grangewood La., Beck. 171 J6
Grangewood St. E6 115 J1
Grangewood Ter. SE25 188 A3
Grange Rd.
Granham Gdns. N9 60 C2
Granite St. SE18 137 J5
Granleigh Rd. E11 96 E2
Gransden Av. E8 95 E7
Gransden Rd. W12 127 F2
Wendell Rd.
Grant Cl. N14 42 C7
Grant Pl., Croy. 202 C1
Grant Rd. SW11 149 G4
Grant Rd., Croy. 202 C1
Grant Rd., Har. 68 C3

Grant St. E13 115 G3
Grant St. N1 11 E1
Grant Way, Islw. 124 D6
Grantbridge St. N1 11 H1
Grantbridge St. N1 111 H2
Grantchester Cl., Har. 86 C3
Grantham Cl., Edg. 53 H3
Grantham Gdns., Rom. 83 F6
Grantham Grn., Borwd. 38 C5
Grantham Pl. W1 24 D2
Grantham Rd. E12 98 D4
Grantham Rd. SW9 151 E2
Grantham Rd. W4 126 E7
Grantley Rd., Houns. 142 C2
Grantley St. E1 113 G3
Grantock Rd. E17 78 D1
Granton Rd. SW16 186 C1
Granton Rd., Ilf. 100 A1
Granton Rd., Sid. 176 C6
Grants Cl. NW7 55 J7
Grantully Rd. W9 6 A4
Grantully Rd. W9 108 E3
Granville Av. N9 61 F3
Granville Av., Felt. 160 A2
Granville Av., Houns. 143 G5
Granville Cl., Croy. 202 B2
Granville Ct. N1 112 A1
Granville Gdns. SW16 187 F1
Granville Gdns. W5 125 J1
Granville Gro. SE13 154 C3
Granville Ms., Sid. 176 A4
Granville Pk. SE13 154 C3
Granville Pl. (North Finchley) N12 57 F7
High Rd.
Granville Pl. W1 16 B4
Granville Pl. W1 110 A6
Granville Pl., Pnr. 66 D2
Elm Pk. Rd.
Granville Rd. E17 78 B6
Granville Rd. E18 79 H2
Granville Rd. N4 75 F6
Granville Rd. N12 57 E7
Granville Rd. N13 59 F6
Russell Rd.
Granville Rd. N22 75 H1
Granville Rd. NW2 90 C2
Granville Rd. NW6 108 D2
Granville Rd. SW18 148 D7
Granville Rd. SW19 166 D7
Russell Rd.
Granville Rd., Barn. 39 J4
Granville Rd., Hayes 121 J4
Granville Rd., Ilf. 98 E1
Granville Rd., Sid. 176 A4
Granville Rd., Well. 158 C3
Granville Sq. SE15 132 B7
Granville Sq. WC1 10 D4
Granville Sq. WC1 111 F3
Granville St. WC1 10 D4
Grape St. WC2 18 A3
Graphite Sq. SE11 34 C3
Grapsome Cl., Chess. 195 G6
Ashlyns Way
Grasdene Rd. SE18 138 A7
Grasmere Av. SW15 164 D4
Grasmere Av. SW19 184 D3
Grasmere Av. W3 106 C7
Grasmere Av., Houns. 143 H6
Grasmere Av., Orp. 206 E3
Grasmere Av., Wem. 69 G7
Grasmere Cl., Loug. 48 C2
Grasmere Ct. N22 59 F6
Palmerston Rd.
Grasmere Gdns., Har. 68 D2
Grasmere Gdns., Ilf. 80 C5
Grasmere Gdns., Orp. 206 E3
Grasmere Rd. E13 115 G2
Grasmere Rd. N10 74 B1
Grasmere Rd. N17 60 D6
Grasmere Rd. SE25 189 E6
Grasmere Rd. SW16 169 F5
Grasmere Rd., Bexh. 159 J1
Grasmere Rd., Brom. 191 F1
Grasmere Rd., Orp. 206 E3
Grass Pk. N3 72 C1
Grassington Cl. N11 58 A6
Ribblesdale Av.
Grassington Rd., Sid. 176 A4
Grassmount SE23 171 E2
Grassway, Wall. 200 C4
Grasvenor Av., Barn. 40 D6
Grately Way SE15 37 F7
Gratton Rd. W14 128 B3
Gratton Ter. NW2 90 A3
Gravel Hill N3 72 C2
Gravel Hill, Bexh. 159 H5
Gravel Hill, Croy. 203 G6
Gravel Hill Cl., Bexh. 159 H5
Gravel La. E1 21 F3
Gravel Pit La. SE9 157 F5
Gravel Rd., Brom. 206 B2
Gravel Rd., Twick. 162 B1
Graveley Av., Borwd. 38 C4
Gravelly Ride SW19 165 H4
Gravelwood Cl., Chis. 175 F3
Graveney Gro. SE20 171 F7
Graveney Rd. SW17 167 H4
Gravesend Rd. W12 107 G7
Gray Av., Dag. 101 F1
Gray St. SE1 27 F4
Grayham Cres., N.Mal. 182 D4
Grayham Rd., N.Mal. 182 D4
Grayland Cl., Brom. 192 A1
Grayling Cl. E16 114/115 E4
Cranberry La.
Grayling Rd. N16 94 A2
Grayling Sq. E2 13 J3
Grayling Sq. E2 112 D3
Gray's Inn WC1 18 D1
Gray's Inn WC1 111 G5
Gray's Inn Pl. WC1 18 D2
Gray's Inn Rd. WC1 10 C4
Gray's Inn Rd. WC1 111 F4
Gray's Inn Sq. WC1 18 D1
Gray's Yd. W1 16 C4
Grayscroft Rd. SW16 168 D7
Grayshott Rd. SW11 150 A2
Grayswood Gdns. SW20 183 H2
Farnham Gdns.
Graywood Ct. N12 57 F7
Grazebrook Rd. N16 94 A2
Grazeley Cl., Bexh. 159 J5
Grazeley Ct. SE19 170 B4
Gipsy Hill
Great Acre Ct. SW4 150 D4
St. Alphonsus Rd.
Great Bell All. EC2 20 B3
Great Benty, West Dr. 120 B4
Great Brownings SE21 170 C4
Great Bushey Dr. N20 57 E1
Great Cambridge Rd. N9 60 C1
Great Cambridge Rd. N17 60 A5
Great Cambridge Rd. N18 60 A5
Great Cambridge Rd., Enf. 44 D4
Great Castle St. W1 17 E3
Great Castle St. W1 110 C6
Great Cen. Av., Ruis. 84 C5
Great Cen. St. NW1 15 J1
Great Cen. St. NW1 109 J5
Great Cen. Way NW10 88 E5
Great Cen. Way, Wem. 88 C4
Great Chapel St. W1 17 H3
Great Chapel St. W1 110 D6
Great Chertsey Rd. W4 146 C2
Great Chertsey Rd., Felt. 161 G3
Great Ch. La. W6 128 A5
Great College St. SW1 26 A5
Great College St. SW1 130 E3
Great Cross Av. SE10 134 E7
Great Cumberland Ms. W1 15 J4
Great Cumberland Pl. W1 15 J3
Great Cumberland Pl. W1 109 J6
Great Dover St. SE1 28 A4
Great Dover St. SE1 132 A2
Great Eastern Rd. E15 96 D7
Great Eastern St. EC2 12 D4
Great Eastern St. EC2 112 B3
Great Eastern Wk. EC2 20 E2
Great Elms Rd., Brom. 191 J4
Great Fld. NW9 71 E1
Great Fleete Way, Bark. 118 C2
Great Galley Cl., Bark. 118 B3
Great George St. SW1 25 J4
Great George St. SW1 130 D2
Great Guildford St. SE1 27 J1
Great Guildford St. SE1 131 J1
Great Harry Dr. SE9 174 D3
Great James St. WC1 10 C6
Great James St. WC1 111 F5
Great Marlborough St. W1 17 F4
Great Marlborough St. W1 110 C6
Great Maze Pond SE1 28 C3
Great Maze Pond SE1 132 A2
Great New St. EC4 19 F3
Great Newport St. WC2 110 D7
Cranbourn St.
Great N. Rd. N2 73 H4
Great N. Rd. N6 73 H4
Great N. Rd. (New Barnet), Barn. 40 D5
Great N. Way NW4 71 J2
Great Oaks, Chig. 65 F4
Great Ormond St. WC1 18 B1
Great Ormond St. WC1 111 E5
Great Owl Rd., Chig. 64 D3
Great Percy St. WC1 10 D3
Great Percy St. WC1 111 F3
Great Peter St. SW1 25 H6
Great Peter St. SW1 130 D3
Great Portland St. W1 17 E1
Great Portland St. W1 110 B5
Great Pulteney St. W1 17 G5
Great Pulteney St. W1 110 C7
Great Queen St. WC2 18 B4
Great Queen St. WC2 111 E6
Great Russell St. WC1 17 J3
Great Russell St. WC1 110 E5
Great St. Helens EC3 20 D3
Great St. Helens EC3 112 B6
Great St. Thomas Apostle EC4 20 A5
Great Scotland Yd. SW1 26 A2
Great Scotland Yd. SW1 130 E1
Great Smith St. SW1 25 J5
Great Smith St. SW1 130 D3
Great South-West Rd., Felt. 141 F7
Great South-West Rd., Houns. 141 J4
Great Spilmans SE22 152 B5
Great Strand NW9 71 F1
Great Suffolk St. SE1 27 H2
Great Suffolk St. SE1 131 H2
Great Sutton St. EC1 11 H6
Great Sutton St. EC1 111 H4
Great Swan All. EC2 20 B3
Great Thrift, Orp. 193 F4
Great Titchfield St. W1 17 F3
Great Titchfield St. W1 110 C6
Great Twr. St. EC3 20 D5
Great Twr. St. EC3 112 B7
Great Trinity La. EC4 20 A5
Great Turnstile WC1 18 D2
Great W. Rd. W4 126 B5
Great W. Rd. W6 127 F5
Great W. Rd., Brent. 126 B5
Great W. Rd., Houns. 142 D2
Great W. Rd., Islw. 124 C7
Great Western Rd. W2 108 C5
Great Western Rd. W9 108 C5
Great Western Rd. W11 108 C5
Great Wf. Rd. E14 134 B1
Churchill Pl.
Great Winchester St. EC2 20 C3
Great Winchester St. EC2 112 A6
Great Windmill St. W1 17 H5
Great Windmill St. W1 110 D7
Great Yd. SE1 28 E3
Greatdown Rd. W7 104 C4
Greatfield Av. E6 116 C4
Greatfield Cl. N19 92 C4
Warrender Rd.
Greatfield Cl. SE4 154 A4
Greatfields Rd., Bark. 117 G1
Greatham Wk. SW15 165 G1
Greatorex St. E1 21 H1
Greatorex St. E1 112 D5
Greatwood, Chis. 174 D7
Greaves Cl., Bark. 99 H7
Norfolk Rd.
Greaves Pl. SW17 167 H4
Grebe Av., Hayes 102 D6
Cygnet Way
Grebe Cl. E7 97 F5
Cormorant Rd.
Grebe Cl. E17 61 H7
Grebe Cl., Bark. 117 H3
Thames Rd.
Grebe Ct., Sutt. 198 B2
Gander Grn. La.
Grecian Cres. SE19 169 H6
Gredo Ho., Bark. 118 B3
Greek Ct. W1 17 J4
Greek St. W1 17 J4
Greek St. W1 110 D6
Greek Yd. WC2 18 A5
Green, The E4 62 C1
Green, The E11 79 H6
Green, The E15 97 E6
Green, The N9 60 D2
Green, The N14 58 D3
Green, The N21 43 G7
Green, The SW14 146 C3
Green, The SW19 166 A5
Green, The W3 107 E6
Green, The W5 125 G1
High St.
Green, The, Bexh. 159 G1
Green, The, Brom. 191 G7
Green, The, Cars. 200 A4
Green, The, Esher 194 C6
Green, The, Felt. 160 B2
Green, The, Houns. 123 G6
Heston Rd.
Green, The, Mord. 184 B4
Green, The, N.Mal. 182 C3
Green, The (St. Paul's Cray), Orp. 176 B7
The Av.
Green, The, Rich. 145 G5
Green, The, Sid. 176 A4
Green, The, Sthl. 123 E3
Green, The, Sutt. 198 E3
Green, The, Twick. 162 B1
Green, The, Well. 157 H4
Green, The, Wem. 86 D2
Green, The, West Dr. 120 A3
Green, The, Wdf.Grn. 63 G5
Green Acres, Croy. 202 C3
Green Arbour Ct. EC1 19 G3
Green Av. NW7 54 D4
Green Av. W13 125 E3
Green Bank E1 132 E1
Green Bank N12 57 E4
Green Cl. NW9 70 C6
Green Cl. NW11 73 F7
Green Cl., Brom. 190 E3
Green Cl., Cars. 199 J2
Green Cl., Felt. 160 E5
Green Cft., Edg. 54 C5
Deans La.
Green Dale SE5 152 A4
Green Dale SE22 152 B5
Green Dale Cl. SE22 152 B5
Green Dale
Green Dragon Ct. SE1 28 B1
Green Dragon La. N21 43 H6
Green Dragon La., Brent. 125 H5
Green Dragon Yd. E1 21 H2
Green Dr., Sthl. 123 G1
Green End N21 59 H2
Green End, Chess. 195 H4
Green Gdns., Orp. 207 F5
Green Hill, Buck.H. 63 J1
Green Hundred Rd. SE15 132 D6
Green La. E4 46 E3
Green La. NW4 72 A5
Green La. SE9 174 D2
Green La. SE20 171 G7
Green La. SW16 169 F7
Green La. W7 124 B2
Green La., Chig. 65 G2
Green La., Chis. 174 E4
Green La., Dag. 100 D2
Green La., Edg. 54 A5
Green La., Felt. 160 E5
Green La., Har. 86 B3
Green La., Houns. 142 B3
Green La., Ilf. 99 F2
Green La., Mord. 184 E6
Green La., N.Mal. 182 C5
Green La., Stan. 52 E4
Green La., Th.Hth. 187 G1
Green La., Wat. 50 C1
Green La., W.Mol. 179 H5
Green La., Wor.Pk. 197 G1
Green La. Gdns., Th.Hth. 187 J2
Green Las. N4 93 J1
Green Las. N8 75 H3
Green Las. N13 59 F6
Green Las. N15 75 H3
Green Las. N16 93 J3
Green Las. N21 59 H1
Green Lawns, Ruis. 84 C1
Green Leaf Av., Wall. 200 D4
Green Man Gdns. W13 104 D7
Green Man La. W13 124 D1
Green Man La., Felt. 142 A4
Green Man Pas. W13 104 D7
Green Man Roundabout E11 79 F7

Green Moor Link N21 43 H7
Green Pk. Way, Grnf. 104 B1
Green Pt. E15 97 E6
Green Pond Cl. E17 77 J3
Green Pond Rd. E17 77 H3
Green Ride, Loug. 47 G5
Green Rd. N14 42 B6
Green Rd. N20 57 F3
Green Shield Ind. Est. E16 135 G1
Bradfield Rd.
Green St. E7 97 H6
Green St. E13 115 J1
Green St. W1 16 B5
Green St. W1 110 A7
Green St., Enf. 45 F2
Green St., Sun. 178 A1
Green Vale W5 105 J6
Green Vale, Bexh. 158 D5
Green Verges, Stan. 53 G7
Green Vw., Chess. 195 J7
Green Wk. NW4 72 A5
Green Wk. SE1 28 D6
Green Wk., Buck.H. 48 B7
Green Wk., Hmptn. 161 F6
Orpwood Cl.
Green Wk., Sthl. 123 G5
Green Wk., Wdf.Grn. 64 B6
Green Wk., The E4 62 C1
Green Way SE9 156 A5
Green Way, Brom. 192 B6
Green Way, Sun. 178 A4
Green Wrythe Cres., Cars. 199 H1
Green Wrythe La., Cars. 185 G6
Greenacre Cl., Nthlt. 85 F5
Eastcote La.
Greenacre Gdns. E17 78 C4
Greenacre Pl., Wall. 200 B2
Park Rd.
Greenacre Sq. SE16 133 G2
Fishermans Dr.
Greenacre Wk. N14 58 E3
Greenacres SE9 156 D6
Greenacres, Bushey 52 A2
Greenacres Cl., Orp. 207 F4
Greenacres Dr., Stan. 52 E7
Greenaway Gdns. NW3 90 E4
Greenbank Av., Wem. 86 D5
Greenbank Cl. E4 62 C2
Greenbank Cres. NW4 72 B4
Greenbay Rd. SE7 136 A7
Greenberry St. NW8 7 G2
Greenberry St. NW8 109 H2
Greenbrook Av., Barn. 41 F1
Greencoat Pl. SW1 33 G1
Greencoat Pl. SW1 130 C4
Greencoat Row SW1 25 G6
Greencourt Av., Croy. 203 E2
Greencourt Av., Edg. 70 B1
Greencourt Gdns., Croy. 203 E1
Greencourt Rd., Orp. 193 G5
Greencrest Pl. NW2 89 H3
Dollis Hill La.
Greencroft Av., Ruis. 84 C2
Greencroft Cl. E6 116 B5
Neatscourt Rd.
Greencroft Gdns. NW6 91 E7
Greencroft Gdns., Enf. 44 B3
Greencroft Rd., Houns. 143 F1
Greenend Rd. W4 126 E2
Greenfarm Cl., Orp. 207 J5
Greenfield Av., Surb. 182 B7
Greenfield Av., Wat. 50 D2
Greenfield Gdns. NW2 90 B2
Greenfield Gdns., Dag. 118 D1
Greenfield Gdns., Orp. 193 G7
Greenfield Rd. E1 21 J2
Greenfield Rd. E1 112 D5
Greenfield Rd. N15 76 B5
Greenfield Rd., Dag. 118 C1
Greenfield Way, Har. 67 H3
Greenfields, Loug. 48 D4
Greenfields Cl., Loug. 48 D4
Greenford Av. W7 104 B4
Greenford Av., Sthl. 103 F7
Greenford Gdns., Grnf. 103 H3
Greenford Rd., Grnf. 103 J5
Greenford Rd., Har. 104 A2
Greenford Rd., Sthl. 123 J1
Greenford Rd., Sutt. 198 E4
Greengate, Grnf. 86 E6
Greengate St. E13 115 H2
Greenhalgh Wk. N2 73 F4
Greenham Cl. SE1 27 E4
Greenham Cl. SE1 131 G2
Greenham Cres. E4 61 J6
Greenham Rd. N10 74 A2
Greenheys Dr. E18 79 F3
Greenhill NW3 91 G4
Hampstead High St.
Greenhill SE18 136 C5
Greenhill, Sutt. 199 F2
Greenhill, Wem. 88 B2
Greenhill Gdns., Nthlt. 103 F2
Greenhill Gro. E12 98 B4
Greenhill Pk. NW10 106 E1
Greenhill Pk., Barn. 40 E5
Greenhill Rd. NW10 106 E1
Greenhill Rd., Har. 68 B6
Greenhill Ter. SE18 136 C5
Greenhill Ter., Nthlt. 103 F2
Greenhill Way, Har. 68 B6
Greenhill Way, Wem. 88 B2
Greenhill's Rents EC1 19 H1
Greenhills Ter. N1 94 A6
Baxter Rd.
Greenhithe Cl., Sid. 157 H7
Greenholm Rd. SE9 156 E5
Greenhurst Rd. SE27 169 G5
Greening St. SE2 138 C4
Greenland Cres., Sthl. 122 C3
Greenland Ms. SE8 133 G5
Trundleys Rd.
Greenland Pl. NW1 110 B1
Greenland Rd.
Greenland Quay SE16 133 G4
Greenland Rd. NW1 110 C1
Greenland Rd., Barn. 39 J6
Greenland St. NW1 110 B1
Camden High St.
Greenlaw Gdns., N.Mal. 183 F7
Greenlaw St. SE18 136 D3
Greenlea Pk. SW19 185 G1
Greenleaf Cl. SW2 151 G7
Tulse Hill
Greenleaf Rd. E6 115 J1
Redclyffe Rd.
Greenleaf Rd. E17 77 J3
Greenleafe Dr., Ilf. 81 E4
Greenman St. N1 93 J7
Greenmead Cl. SE25 188 D5
Greenmoor Rd., Enf. 45 F2
Greenoak Pl., Barn. 41 J3
Cockfosters Rd.
Greenoak Way SW19 166 A4
Greenock Rd. SW16 186 D1
Greenock Rd. W3 126 B3
Greenpark Ct., Wem. 87 F7
Greens Cl., The, Loug. 48 D2
Green's Ct. W1 17 H5
Green's End SE18 136 E4
Greenshank Cl. E17 61 H7
Banbury Rd.
Greenside, Bex. 177 E1
Greenside, Dag. 100 C1
Greenside Cl. N20 57 G2
Greenside Cl. SE6 172 D2
Greenside Rd. W12 127 G3
Greenside Rd., Croy. 187 G7
Greenslade Rd., Bark. 99 G7
Greenstead Av., Wdf.Grn. 63 J7
Greenstead Cl., Wdf.Grn. 63 J6
Greenstead Gdns.
Greenstead Gdns. SW15 147 G5
Greenstead Gdns., Wdf.Grn. 63 J6
Greensted Rd., Loug. 48 B7
Greenstone Ms. E11 79 G6
Greenvale Rd. SE9 156 C4
Greenview Av., Beck. 189 H6
Greenview Av., Croy. 189 H6
Greenway N14 58 E2
Greenway N20 56 D2
Greenway SW20 183 J4
Greenway, Chis. 174 D5
Greenway, Dag. 100 C2
Greenway, Har. 69 H5
Greenway, Hayes 102 B4
Greenway, Pnr. 66 B2
Greenway, Wall. 200 C4
Greenway, Wdf.Grn. 63 J5
Greenway, The NW9 70 D2
Greenway, The, Har. 68 B1
Greenway, The, Houns. 143 F4
Greenway, The, Pnr. 67 F6
Greenway Av. E17 78 D4
Greenway Cl. N4 93 J2
Greenway Cl. N11 58 A6
Greenway Cl. N15 76 C4
Copperfield Dr.
Greenway Cl. N20 56 D2
Greenway Cl. NW9 70 D2
Greenway Gdns. NW9 70 D2
Greenway Gdns., Croy. 203 J3
Greenway Gdns., Grnf. 103 G3
Greenway Gdns., Har. 68 B1
Greenways, Beck. 190 A2
Greenways, Esher 194 B4
Greenways, The, Twick. 144 D6
South Western Rd.
Greenwell St. W1 9 E6
Greenwell St. W1 110 B4
Greenwich Ch. St. SE10 134 C6
Greenwich Cres. E6 116 B5
Swan App.
Greenwich Foot Tunnel E14 134 C5
Greenwich Foot Tunnel SE10 134 C5
Greenwich High Rd. SE10 154 B1
Greenwich Ind. Est. SE7 135 H4
Greenwich Mkt. SE10 134 C6
Greenwich Pk. SE10 134 D7
Greenwich Pk. St. SE10 134 D5
Greenwich S. St. SE10 154 B1
Greenwich Vw. Pl. E14 134 B3
Greenwood Av., Dag. 101 H4
Greenwood Av., Enf. 45 H2
Greenwood Cl., Mord. 184 B4
Greenwood Cl., Orp. 193 H6
Greenwood Cl., Sid. 176 A2
Hurst Rd.
Greenwood Cl., T.Ditt. 194 D1
Greenwood Ct. SW1 33 F3
Greenwood Ct. SW1 130 C5
Greenwood Dr. E4 62 C5
Avril Way
Greenwood Gdns. N13 59 H3
Greenwood Gdns., Ilf. 65 F7
Greenwood La., Hmptn. 161 H5
Greenwood Pk., Kings.T. 165 E7
Greenwood Pl. NW5 92 B5
Highgate Rd.
Greenwood Rd. E8 94 D6
Greenwood Rd. E13 115 F2
Maud Rd.
Greenwood Rd., Croy. 187 H7
Greenwood Rd., Islw. 144 B3
Greenwood Rd., Mitch. 186 D3
Greenwood Rd., T.Ditt. 194 D1
Greenwood Ter. NW10 106 D1
Greenwoods, The, Har. 85 J2
Sherwood Rd.
Greer Rd., Har. 67 J1
Greet St. SE1 27 F2
Greet St. SE1 131 G1
Greg Cl. E10 78 C6
Gregor Ms. SE3 135 G7
Gregory Cres. SE9 156 A7
Gregory Pl. W8 22 A3
Gregory Pl. W8 128 E2
Gregory Rd., Rom. 82 D4
Gregory Rd., Sthl. 123 G3
Gregson Cl., Borwd. 38 C1
Greig Cl. N8 74 E5
Greig Ter. SE17 35 H5
Grena Gdns., Rich. 145 J4
Grena Rd., Rich. 145 J4
Grenaby Av., Croy. 188 A7
Grenaby Rd., Croy. 188 A7
Grenada Rd. SE7 135 J7
Grenade St. E14 113 J7
Grenadier St. E16 136 D1
Grendon Gdns., Wem. 88 A2
Grendon St. NW8 7 G5
Grendon St. NW8 109 H4
Grenfell Cl., Borwd. 38 C1
Grenfell Gdns., Har. 69 H7
Grenfell Rd. W11 108 A7
Grenfell Rd., Mitch. 167 J6
Grenfell Twr. W11 108 A7
Grenfell Wk. W11 108 A7
Grennell Cl., Sutt. 199 G2
Grennell Rd., Sutt. 199 F2
Grenoble Gdns. N13 59 G6
Grenville Cl. N3 72 C1
Grenville Cl., Surb. 196 C1
Grenville Gdns., Wdf.Grn. 79 J1
Grenville Ms. SW7 30 D1
Grenville Ms. SW7 129 F4
Grenville Ms., Hmptn. 161 H5
Grenville Pl. NW7 54 D5
Grenville Pl. SW7 22 C6
Grenville Pl. SW7 129 F3
Grenville Rd. N19 92 E1
Grenville St. WC1 10 B6
Grenville St. WC1 111 E4
Gresham Av. N20 57 J4
Gresham Cl., Bex. 159 E6
Gresham Cl., Enf. 43 J3
Gresham Dr., Rom. 82 B5
Gresham Gdns. NW11 90 B1
Gresham Rd. E6 116 C2
Gresham Rd. E16 115 H6
Gresham Rd. NW10 88 D5
Gresham Rd. SE25 188 D4
Gresham Rd. SW9 151 G3
Gresham Rd., Beck. 189 H2
Gresham Rd., Edg. 53 J6
Gresham Rd., Hmptn. 161 G6
Gresham Rd., Houns. 143 J1
Gresham St. EC2 19 J3
Gresham St. EC2 111 J6
Gresham Way SW19 166 D3
Gresley Cl. E17 77 H6
Gresley Cl. N15 76 A4
Clinton Rd.
Gresley Rd. N19 92 C1
Gresse St. W1 17 H2
Gresse St. W1 110 D5
Gressenhall Rd. SW18 148 C6
Gresswell Cl., Sid. 176 A3
Greswell St. SW6 148 A1
Gretton Rd. N17 60 B7
Greville Cl., Twick. 144 E7
Greville Hall NW6 6 A1
Greville Hall NW6 109 E2
Greville Pl. NW6 6 B1
Greville Pl. NW6 109 E2
Greville Rd. E17 78 C4
Greville Rd. NW6 108 E1
Greville Rd., Rich. 145 J6
Greville St. EC1 19 F2
Greville St. EC1 111 G5
Grey Cl. NW11 73 F6
Grey Eagle St. E1 21 F1
Grey Eagle St. E1 112 C5
Greycoat Pl. SW1 25 H6
Greycoat Pl. SW1 130 D3
Greycoat St. SW1 25 H6
Greycoat St. SW1 130 D3
Greycot Rd., Beck. 172 A5
Greyfell Cl., Stan. 52/53 E5
Coverdale Cl.
Greyfriars Pas. EC1 19 H3
Greyhound Hill NW4 71 G3
Greyhound La. SW16 168 D6
Greyhound Rd. N17 76 B3
Greyhound Rd. NW10 107 H3
Greyhound Rd. W6 128 A6
Greyhound Rd. W14 128 A6
Greyhound Rd., Sutt. 199 F5
Greyhound Ter. SW16 186 C1
Greys Pk. Cl., Kes. 205 J5
Greystead Rd. SE23 153 F7
Greystoke Av., Pnr. 67 G3
Greystoke Gdns. W5 105 H4
Greystoke Gdns., Enf. 42 D4
Greystoke Pk. Ter. W5 105 G3
Greystoke Pl. EC4 19 E3
Greystone Gdns., Har. 69 F6
Greystone Gdns., Ilf. 81 F2
Greystone Path E11 79 F7
Grove Rd.
Greyswood St. SW16 168 B6
Grierson Rd. SE23 153 G7
Griffin Cen., The, Felt. 142 B5
Griffin Cl. NW10 89 H5
Griffin Manor Way SE28 137 G3
Griffin Rd. N17 76 B2
Griffin Rd. SE18 137 G5
Griffin Way, Sun. 178 A2
Griffith Cl., Dag. 100 C1
Gibson Rd.
Griffiths Cl., Wor.Pk. 197 H2
Griffiths Rd. SW19 166 D7
Griggs App., Ilf. 99 F2
Griggs Pl. SE1 28 E6
Griggs Rd. E10 78 C6

Gurney Cl. E15 96/97 E5
Gurney Rd.
Gurney Cl. E17 77 G1
Gurney Cl., Bark. 98 E6
Gurney Cres., Croy. 201 F1
Gurney Dr. N2 73 F5
Gurney Rd. E15 96 E5
Gurney Rd., Cars. 200 A4
Gurney Rd., Nthlt. 102 B3
Guthrie St. SW3 31 G3
Gutter La. EC2 20 A3
Gutter La. EC2 111 J6
Guy Barnett Gro. SE3 155 G3
Casterbridge Rd.
Guy Rd., Wall. 200 D3
Guy St. SE1 28 C3
Guy St. SE1 132 A2
Guyatt Gdns., Mitch. 186 A2
Ormerod Gdns.
Guyscliff Rd. SE13 154 C5
Gwalior Rd. SW15 148 A3
Felsham Rd.
Gwendolen Av. SW15 148 A5
Gwendolen Cl. SW15 148 A5
Gwendoline Av. E13 115 H1
Gwendwr Rd. W14 128 B5
Gwillim Cl., Sid. 158 A5
Gwydor Rd., Beck. 189 G4
Gwydyr Rd., Brom. 191 F3
Gwyn Cl. SW6 129 F7
Gwynne Av., Croy. 189 G7
Gwynne Cl. W4 127 F6
Gwynne Pk. Av., Wdf.Grn. 64 C6
Gwynne Pl. WC1 10 D4
Gwynne Rd. SW11 149 G2
Gylcote Cl. SE5 152 A4
Gyles Pk., Stan. 69 F1
Gyllyngdune Gdns., Ilf. 99 J2

H

Ha-Ha Rd. SE18 136 C6
Haarlem Rd. W14 128 A3
Haberdasher Pl. N1 12 C3
Haberdasher St. N1 12 C3
Haberdasher St. N1 112 A3
Habgood Rd., Loug. 48 B3
Haccombe Rd. SW19 167 F6
Haydons Rd.
Hackbridge Grn., Wall. 200 A2
Hackbridge Pk. Gdns., Cars. 200 A2
Hackbridge Rd., Wall. 200 A2
Hackford Rd. SW9 151 F1
Hackforth Cl., Barn. 39 H5
Hackington Cres., Beck. 172 A6
Hackney Cl., Borwd. 38 D5
Hackney Gro. E8 94/95 E6
Reading La.
Hackney Rd. E2 13 F4
Hackney Rd. E2 112 C3
Hadden Rd. SE28 137 H3
Hadden Way, Grnf. 86 A6
Haddington Rd., Brom. 172 D3
Haddo St. SE10 134 B6
Haddon Cl., Borwd. 38 A3
Haddon Cl., Enf. 44 D6
Haddon Cl., N.Mal. 183 F5
Haddon Gro., Sid. 158 A7
Haddon Rd., Sutt. 198 E4
Haddonfield SE8 133 G4
Hadfield Cl., Sthl. 103 F3
Adrienne Av.
Hadfield Rd., Stai. 140 A6
Hadleigh Cl. E1 113 F4
Mantus Rd.
Hadleigh Cl. SW20 184 C2
Hadleigh Rd. N9 44 E7
Hadleigh St. E2 113 F4
Hadleigh Wk. E6 116 B6
Hadley Cl. N21 43 G6
Hadley Common, Barn. 40 D2
Hadley Gdns. W4 126 D5
Hadley Gdns., Sthl. 123 F5
Hadley Grn., Barn. 40 C2
Hadley Grn. Rd., Barn. 40 C2
Hadley Grn. W., Barn. 40 C2
Hadley Gro., Barn. 40 B2
Hadley Highstone, Barn. 40 C1
Hadley Ridge, Barn. 40 C3
Hadley Rd. (New Barnet), Barn. 41 E4
Hadley Rd., Belv. 139 F4
Hadley Rd., Mitch. 186 D4
Hadley St. NW1 92 B6
Hadley Way N21 43 G6
Hadlow Pl. SE19 170 D7
Hadlow Rd., Sid. 176 A4
Hadlow Rd., Well. 138 C7
Hadrian Cl., Wall. 201 E7
Hadrian Est. E2 13 J2
Hadrian Est. E2 112 D2
Hadrian St. SE10 134 E5
Hadrian Way, Stai. 140 B7
Hadrians Ride, Enf. 44 C5
Hadyn Pk. Rd. W12 127 G2
Hafer Rd. SW11 149 J4
Hafton Rd. SE6 173 E1
Haggard Rd., Twick. 144 E7
Haggerston Rd. E8 94 C7
Hague St. E2 13 J4
Haig Pl., Mord. 184 D6
Green La.
Haig Rd., Stan. 53 F5
Haig Rd. E. E13 115 J3
Haig Rd. W. E13 115 J3
Haigville Gdns., Ilf. 81 E4
Hailes Cl. SW19 167 F6
North Rd.
Hailey Rd., Erith 139 G2
Haileybury Av., Enf. 44 C6
Hailsham Av. SW2 169 F2
Hailsham Cl., Surb. 181 G7
Hailsham Dr., Har. 68 A3
Hailsham Rd. SW17 168 A6
Hailsham Ter. N18 59 J5
Haimo Rd. SE9 156 A5
Hainault Ct. E17 78 D4
Hainault Gore, Rom. 83 E5
Hainault Gro., Chig. 65 F4
Hainault Rd. E11 96 C1
Hainault Rd., Chig. 65 E3
Hainault Rd., Rom. 83 J2
Hainault Rd. (Chadwell Heath), Rom. 83 F6
Hainault Rd. (Hainault), Rom. 82 B3
Hainault St. SE9 175 E1
Hainault St., Ilf. 99 E2
Haines Wk., Mord. 184/185 E7
Dorchester Rd.
Hainford Cl. SE4 153 G4
Haining Cl. W4 126 A5
Wellesley Rd.
Hainthorpe Rd. SE27 169 H3
Hainton Cl. E1 113 E6
Halberd Ms. E5 94/95 E2
Knightland Rd.
Halbutt Gdns., Dag. 101 F3
Halbutt St., Dag. 101 F4
Halcomb St. N1 112 B1
Halcot Av., Bexh. 159 H5
Halcrow St. E1 112/113 E5
Newark St.
Halcyon Ct., Wem. 88 B3
Coffers Circle
Haldan Rd. E4 62 C6
Haldane Cl. N10 58 B7
Haldane Pl. SW18 166 E1
Haldane Rd. E6 116 A3
Haldane Rd. SE28 118 D7
Haldane Rd. SW6 128 C7
Haldane Rd., Sthl. 103 J6
Haldon Cl., Chig. 65 H5
Arrowsmith Rd.
Haldon Rd. SW18 148 C5
Hale, The E4 62 D7
Hale, The N17 76 D4
Hale Cl. E4 62 C3
Hale Cl., Edg. 54 C5
Hale Cl., Orp. 207 F4
Hale Dr. NW7 54 C6
Hale End Cl., Ruis. 66 A6
Hale End Rd. E4 62 D6
Hale End Rd. E17 78 D1
Hale End Rd., Wdf.Grn. 62 D7
Hale Gdns. N17 76 D3
Hale Gdns. W3 126 A1
Hale Gro. Gdns. NW7 54 D5
Hale La. NW7 54 D5
Hale La., Edg. 54 B5
Hale Path SE27 169 H4
Hale Rd. E6 116 B4
Hale Rd. N17 76 D3
Hale St. E14 114 B7
Hale Wk. W7 104 B5
Halefield Rd. N17 76 D1
Hales St. SE8 134 A7
Deptford High St.
Halesowen Rd., Mord. 184 E7
Halesworth Cl. E5 95 F2
Theydon Rd.
Halesworth Rd. SE13 154 B3
Haley Rd. NW4 71 J6
Half Acre, Brent. 125 G6
Half Acre Rd. W7 124 B1
Half Moon Ct. EC1 19 J2
Half Moon Cres. N1 10 D1
Half Moon Cres. N1 111 F2
Half Moon La. SE24 151 J6
Half Moon Pas. E1 21 G4
Half Moon St. W1 24 E1
Half Moon St. W1 130 B1
Halford Cl., Edg. 70 B2
Halford Rd. E10 78 D5
Halford Rd. SW6 128 D6
Halford Rd., Rich. 145 H5
Halfway St., Sid. 157 G7
Haliburton Rd., Twick. 144 D5
Haliday Wk. N1 94 A6
Balls Pond Rd.
Halidon Cl. E9 95 F5
Urswick Rd.
Halifax Rd., Enf. 43 J2
Halifax Rd., Grnf. 103 H1
Halifax St. SE26 171 E4
Halifield Dr., Belv. 138 E3
Haling Gro., S.Croy. 201 J7
Haling Pk., S.Croy. 201 J6
Haling Pk. Gdns., S.Croy. 201 H6
Haling Pk. Rd., S.Croy. 201 H5
Haling Rd., S.Croy. 202 A6
Halkin Arc. SW1 24 B5
Halkin Arc. SW1 130 A3
Halkin Ms. SW1 24 B5
Halkin Pl. SW1 24 B5
Halkin Pl. SW1 130 A3
Halkin St. SW1 24 C4
Halkin St. SW1 130 A2
Hall, The SE3 155 G3
Hall Av. N18 60 A6
Weir Hall Av.
Hall Cl. W5 105 H5
Hall Ct., Tedd. 162 C5
Teddington Pk.
Hall Dr. SE26 171 F5
Hall Dr. W7 104 B6
Hall Fm. Cl., Stan. 52 E4
Hall Fm. Dr., Twick. 144 A7
Hall Gdns. E4 61 J4
Hall Gate NW8 6 D3
Hall La. E4 61 H5
Hall La. NW4 71 G1
Hall La., Hayes 121 G7
Hall Oak Wk. NW6 90 C6
Maygrove Rd.
Hall Pl. W2 7 E6
Hall Pl. W2 109 G4
Hall Pl. Cres., Bex. 159 J5
Hall Rd. E6 116 C1
Hall Rd. E15 96 D4
Hall Rd. NW8 6 D4
Hall Rd. NW8 109 F3
Hall Rd., Islw. 144 A5
Hall Rd., Rom. 82 C6
Hall St. EC1 11 H3
Hall St. EC1 111 H3
Hall St. N12 57 F5
Hall Vw. SE9 174 A2
Hallam Cl., Chis. 174 C5
Hallam Gdns., Pnr. 51 E7
Hallam Ms. W1 16 E1
Hallam Rd. N15 75 H4
Hallam Rd. SW13 147 H3
Hallam St. W1 8 E6
Hallam St. W1 110 B5
Halley Gdns. SE13 154 D4
Halley Rd. E7 97 J6
Halley Rd. E12 98 A6
Halley St. E14 113 H5
Hallfield Est. W2 14 C4
Hallfield Est. W2 109 F6
Halliards, The, Walt. 178 A6
Felix Rd.
Halliday Sq., Sthl. 124 A1
Halliford St. N1 93 J7
Hallingbury Ct. E17 78 B3
Halliwell Rd. SW2 151 F6
Halliwick Rd. N10 74 A1
Hallmark Trd. Est. NW10 88 C4
Great Cen. Way
Hallmead Rd., Sutt. 198 E3
Hallowell Av., Croy. 200 E4
Hallowell Cl., Mitch. 186 A3
Hallowes Cres., Wat. 50 A3
Hayling Rd.
Hallowfield Way, Mitch. 185 H3
Hallsville Rd. E16 115 F6
Hallswelle Rd. NW11 72 C5
Hallywell Cres. E6 116 C5
Halons Rd. SE9 156 D7
Halpin Pl. SE17 36 C2
Halsbrook Rd. SE3 156 A3
Halsbury Cl., Stan. 52 E4
Halsbury Rd. W12 127 H1
Halsbury Rd. E., Nthlt. 85 J4
Halsbury Rd. W., Nthlt. 85 H5
Halsend, Hayes 122 B1
Halsey Ms. SW3 31 J1
Halsey St. SW3 31 J1
Halsey St. SW3 129 J4
Halsham Cres., Bark. 99 J6
Halsmere Rd. SE5 151 H1
Halstead Cl., Croy. 201 J3
Charles St.
Halstead Ct. N1 12 C2
Halstead Gdns. N21 60 A1
Halstead Rd. E11 79 G5
Halstead Rd. N21 59 J1
Halstead Rd., Enf. 44 B4
Halston Cl. SW11 149 J6
Halstow Rd. NW10 108 A3
Halstow Rd. SE10 135 G5
Halsway, Hayes 122 A1
Halt Robin La., Belv. 139 H4
Halt Robin Rd.
Halt Robin Rd., Belv. 139 G4
Halter Cl., Borwd. 38 D5
Clydesdale Cl.
Halton Cross St. N1 111 H1
Halton Pl. N1 111 J1
Dibden St.
Halton Rd. N1 93 H7
Ham, The, Brent. 125 F7
Ham Cl., Rich. 163 F3
Ham Common, Rich. 163 J4
Ham Fm. Rd., Rich. 163 G4
Ham Gate Av., Rich. 163 G3
Ham Pk. Rd. E7 97 F7
Ham Pk. Rd. E15 97 F7
Ham Ridings, Rich. 163 J5
Ham St., Rich. 163 F2
Ham Vw., Croy. 189 H6
Ham Yd. W1 17 H5
Hambalt Rd. SW4 150 C5
Hamble Ct., Kings.T. 163 G7
Hamble St. SW6 149 E3
Hamble Wk., Nthlt. 103 G2
Brabazon Rd.
Hambledon Gdns. SE25 188 C3
Hambledon Pl. SE21 170 B1
Hambledon Rd. SW18 148 C7
Hambledown Rd., Sid. 157 G7
Hambleton Cl., Wor.Pk. 197 J2
Cotswold Way
Hambridge Way SW2 151 G7
Hambro Av., Brom. 205 G1
Hambro Rd. SW16 168 D6
Hambrook Rd. SE25 188 E3
Hambrough Rd., Sthl. 122 E1
Hamden Cres., Dag. 101 H3
Hamel Cl., Har. 69 G3
Hamelin St. E14 114 C6
St. Leonards Rd.
Hameway E6 116 D4
Hamfrith Rd. E15 97 F6
Hamilton Av. N9 44 D7
Hamilton Av., Ilf. 81 E4
Hamilton Av., Surb. 196 B1
Hamilton Av., Sutt. 198 B2
Hamilton Cl. N17 76 C3
Hamilton Cl. NW8 6 E4
Hamilton Cl. NW8 109 G3
Hamilton Cl. SE16 133 H2
Somerford Way
Hamilton Cl., Barn. 41 H4
Hamilton Cl., Stan. 52 C2
Hamilton Ct. W5 105 J7
Hamilton Ct. W9 6 C3
Hamilton Cres. N13 59 G4
Hamilton Cres., Har. 85 F3
Hamilton Cres., Houns. 143 H5
Hamilton Gdns. NW8 6 D3
Hamilton Gdns. NW8 109 F3
Hamilton La. N5 93 H4
Hamilton Pk.
Hamilton Ms. W1 24 D3
Hamilton Pk. N5 93 H4
Hamilton Pk. W. N5 93 H4
Hamilton Pl. N19 92 D3
Wedmore St.
Hamilton Pl. W1 24 C2
Hamilton Pl. W1 130 A1
Hamilton Pl., Sun. 160 B7
Hamilton Rd. E15 115 E3
Hamilton Rd. E17 77 H2
Hamilton Rd. N2 73 F3
Hamilton Rd. N9 44 D7
Hamilton Rd. NW10 89 G5
Hamilton Rd. NW11 72 A7
Hamilton Rd. SE27 170 A4
Hamilton Rd. SW19 167 E7
Hamilton Rd. W4 126 E2
Hamilton Rd. W5 105 H7
Hamilton Rd., Barn. 41 H4
Hamilton Rd., Bexh. 159 E2
Hamilton Rd., Brent. 125 G6

Hamilton Rd., Har. 68 B5
Hamilton Rd., Hayes 102 B7
Hamilton Rd., Ilf. 98 E4
Hamilton Rd., Sid. 176 A4
Hamilton Rd., Sthl. 123 F1
Hamilton Rd., Th.Hth. 188 A3
Hamilton Rd., Twick. 162 B1
Hamilton Rd., Wat. 50 B3
Hamilton Sq. SE1 28 C3
Hamilton St. SE8 134 A6
Deptford High St.
Hamilton Ter. NW8 6 D3
Hamilton Ter. NW8 109 E2
Hamilton Way N3 56 D6
Hamilton Way N13 59 H4
Hamlea Cl. SE12 155 F5
Hamlet, The SE5 152 A3
Hamlet Cl. SE13 154/155 E4
Old Rd.
Hamlet Gdns. W6 127 G4
Hamlet Rd. SE19 170 C7
Hamlet Sq. NW2 90 B3
The Vale
Hamlet Way SE1 28 C3
Hamlets Way E3 113 J4
Hamlin Cres., Pnr. 66 C5
Hamlyn Cl., Edg. 53 H3
Hamlyn Gdns. SE19 170 B7
Hammelton Grn. SW9 151 H1
Cromwell Rd.
Hammelton Rd., Brom. 191 F1
Hammers La. NW7 55 G5
Hammersmith Br. SW13 127 H5
Hammersmith Br. W6 127 H5
Hammersmith Br. Rd. W6 127 J5
Hammersmith Bdy. W6 127 J4
Hammersmith Flyover W6 127 J5
Hammersmith Gro. W6 127 J3
Hammersmith Rd. W6 128 A4
Hammersmith Rd. W14 128 A4
Hammersmith Ter. W6 127 G5
Hammet Cl., Hayes 102 D5
Willow Tree La.
Hammett St. EC3 21 F5
Hammond Av., Mitch. 186 B2
Hammond Cl., Barn. 40 B5
Hammond Cl., Grnf. 86 A5
Lilian Board Way
Hammond Cl., Hmptn. 179 G1
Hammond Rd., Enf. 45 E2
Hammond Rd., Sthl. 123 E3
Hammond St. NW5 92 C6
Hammond Way SE28 118 B7
Oriole Way
Hammonds Cl., Dag. 100 C3
Hamonde Cl., Edg. 54 B2
Hampden Av., Beck. 189 H2
Hampden Cl. NW1 9 J2
Hampden Gurney St. W1 15 J4
Hampden La. N17 76 C1
Hampden Rd. N8 75 G4
Hampden Rd. N10 58 A7
Hampden Rd. N17 76 D1
Hampden Rd. N19 92 D2
Holloway Rd.
Hampden Rd., Beck. 189 H2
Hampden Rd., Har. 67 J1
Hampden Rd., Kings.T. 182 A3
Hampden Sq. N14 58 B1
Osidge La.
Hampden Way N14 58 B2
Hampshire Cl. N18 60/61 E5
Berkshire Gdns.
Hampshire Hog La. W6 127 H4
King St.
Hampshire Rd. N22 59 F7
Hampshire St. NW5 92 D6
Torriano Av.
Hampson Way SW8 151 F1
Hampstead Cl. SE28 138 B1
Hampstead Gdns. NW11 72 D6
Hampstead Gdns., Rom. 82 B5
Hampstead Grn. NW3 91 H5
Hampstead Gro. NW3 91 F3
Hampstead Hts. N2 73 F4
Hampstead High St. NW3 91 F4
Hampstead Hill Gdns. NW3 91 G4
Hampstead La. N6 73 G7
Hampstead La. NW3 73 G7
Hampstead Rd. NW1 9 F2
Hampstead Rd. NW1 110 C2
Hampstead Sq. NW3 91 F3
Hampstead Wk. E3 113 J1
Parnell Rd.
Hampstead Way NW11 91 F1
Hampton Cl. N11 58 B5
Balmoral Av.
Hampton Cl. NW6 108 D3
Hampton Cl. SW20 165 J7
Hampton Ct. N1 93 H6
Upper St.
Hampton Ct. Av., E.Mol. 180 A5
Hampton Ct. Cres., E.Mol. 180 A3
Hampton Ct. Palace, E.Mol. 180 C3
Hampton Ct. Par., E.Mol. 180 B4
Creek Rd.
Hampton Ct. Rd., E.Mol. 180 C3
Hampton Ct. Rd., Hmptn. 179 J2
Hampton Ct. Rd., Kings.T. 180 C3
Hampton Ct. Way, E.Mol. 180 B6
Hampton Ct. Way, T.Ditt. 194 B2
Hampton Fm. Ind. Est., Felt. 161 F3
Hampton La., Felt. 161 E4
Hampton Mead, Loug. 48 E3
Hampton Ms. NW10 106 D3
Minerva Rd.
Hampton Ri., Har. 69 H6
Hampton Rd. E4 61 J5
Hampton Rd. E7 97 H5
Hampton Rd. E11 96 D1
Hampton Rd., Croy. 187 J6
Hampton Rd., Hmptn. 162 A5
Hampton Rd., Ilf. 99 E4
Hampton Rd., Tedd. 162 A5
Hampton Rd., Twick. 162 A3
Hampton Rd., Wor.Pk. 197 G2
Hampton Rd. E., Felt. 161 F3
Hampton Rd. W., Felt. 160 E2
Hampton St. SE1 35 H2
Hampton St. SE1 131 H4
Hampton St. SE17 35 H2
Hampton St. SE17 131 H4
Hamshades Cl., Sid. 175 J3
Hanah Ct. SW19 166 A7
Hanameel St. E16 135 H1
Hanbury Cl. NW4 71 J3
Parson St.
Hanbury Dr. N21 43 F5
Hanbury Ms. N1 111 J1
Mary St.
Hanbury Rd. N17 76 E2
Hanbury Rd. W3 126 B2
Hanbury St. E1 21 F1
Hanbury St. E1 112 C5
Hancock Ct., Borwd. 38 C1
Hancock Rd. E3 114 C3
Hancock Rd. SE19 170 A6
Hand Ct. WC1 18 D2
Hand Ct. WC1 111 F5
Handa Wk. N1 94 A6
Clephane Rd.
Handcroft Rd., Croy. 187 H7
Handel Cl., Edg. 53 J6
Handel Pl. NW10 88 D6
Mitchellbrook Way
Handel St. WC1 10 A5
Handel St. WC1 110 E4
Handel Way, Edg. 54 A7
Handen Rd. SE12 155 E5
Handforth Rd. SW9 34 E7
Handforth Rd. SW9 131 G7
Handforth Rd., Ilf. 98/99 E3
Winston Way
Handley Rd. E9 95 F7
Handowe Cl. NW4 71 G4
Hands Wk. E16 115 G6
Handside Cl., Wor.Pk. 198 A1
Carters Cl.
Handsworth Av. E4 62 D6
Handsworth Rd. N17 76 A3
Handsworth Way, Wat. 50 A3
Hayling Rd.
Handtrough Way, Bark. 116/117 E2
Fresh Wf. Rd.
Hanford Cl. SW18 166 D1
Hanford Row SW19 165 J6
Hangar Ruding, Wat. 51 F3
Hanger Grn. W5 106 A4
Hanger La. W5 105 J4
Hanger Vale La. W5 105 J6
Hanger Vw. Way W3 106 A6
Hankey Pl. SE1 28 C4
Hankey Pl. SE1 132 A2
Hankins La. NW7 54 E3
Hanley Pl., Beck. 172 A7
Hanley Rd. N4 93 E1
Hanmer Wk. N7 93 F3
Newington Barrow Way
Hannah Cl. NW10 88 C4
Hannah Cl., Beck. 190 C3
Hannah Mary Way SE1 37 J2
Hannah Ms., Wall. 200 C7
Hannay La. N8 74 D7
Hannay Wk. SW16 168 D2
Hannell Rd. SW6 128 B7
Hannen Rd. SE27 169 H3
Norwood High St.
Hannibal Rd. E1 113 F5
Hannibal Rd., Stai. 140 A7
Hannibal Way, Croy. 201 F5
Hannington Rd. SW4 150 B3
Hanover Av. E16 135 G1
Hanover Av., Felt. 160 A1
Hanover Cl., Rich. 126 A7
Hanover Cl., Sutt. 198 C4
Hanover Ct. W12 127 G1
Uxbridge Rd.
Hanover Dr., Chis. 175 F4
Hanover Gdns. SE11 34 E6
Hanover Gdns. SE11 131 G6
Hanover Gdns., Ilf. 65 F7
Hanover Gate NW1 7 H4
Hanover Gate NW1 109 H3
Hanover Pk. SE15 152 D1
Hanover Pl. E3 113 J3
Brokesley St.
Hanover Pl. WC2 18 B4
Hanover Rd. N15 76 C4
Hanover Rd. NW10 89 J7
Hanover Rd. SW19 167 F7
Hanover Sq. W1 17 E4
Hanover Sq. W1 110 B6
Hanover St. W1 17 E4
Hanover St. W1 110 B6
Hanover St., Croy. 201 H3
Abbey Rd.
Hanover Ter. NW1 7 J4
Hanover Ter. NW1 109 H3
Hanover Ter., Islw. 144 D1
Hanover Ter. Ms. NW1 7 H4
Hanover Way, Bexh. 158 D3
Hanover W. Ind. Est. NW10 106 D2
Hanover Yd. N1 11 H1
Hans Cres. SW1 23 J5
Hans Cres. SW1 129 J3
Hans Pl. SW1 24 A5
Hans Pl. SW1 129 J3
Hans Rd. SW3 23 J5
Hans Rd. SW3 129 J3
Hans St. SW1 24 A6
Hansard Ms. W14 128 A2
Holland Rd.
Hansart Way, Enf. 43 G1
The Ridgeway
Hanselin Cl., Stan. 52 C5
Chenduit Way
Hansen Dr. N21 43 F5
Hansha Dr., Edg. 70 D1
Hansler Gro., E.Mol. 180 A4
Hansler Rd. SE22 152 C5
Hansol Rd., Bexh. 158 E5
Hanson Cl. SW12 150 B7
Hanson Cl. SW14 146 C3
Hanson Cl., Beck. 172 B6
Hanson Cl., Loug. 49 F2
Hanson Dr.
Hanson Cl., West Dr. 120 C3
Hanson Dr., Loug. 49 F2
Hanson Gdns., Sthl. 123 E2
Hanson Grn., Loug. 49 F2
Hanson Dr.
Hanson St. W1 17 F1
Hanson St. W1 110 C5
Hanway Pl. W1 17 H3
Hanway Rd. W7 104 A6
Hanway St. W1 17 H3
Hanway St. W1 110 D6
Hanworth Rd., Felt. 160 B1
Hanworth Rd., Hmptn. 161 H6
Hanworth Rd., Houns. 143 H3
Hanworth Rd., Sun. 160 A7
Hanworth Ter., Houns. 143 H4
Hanworth Trd. Est., Felt. 161 E3
Hapgood Cl., Grnf. 86 A5
Harads Pl. E1 21 H6
Harben Rd. NW6 91 F7
Harberson Rd. E15 115 F1
Harberson Rd. SW12 168 B1
Harberton Rd. N19 92 C1
Harbet Rd. E4 61 G5
Harbet Rd. N18 61 G5
Harbet Rd. W2 15 F2
Harbet Rd. W2 109 G5
Harbex Cl., Bex. 159 H7
Harbinger Rd. E14 134 B4
Harbledown Rd. SW6 148 D1
Harbord Cl. SE5 152 A2
De Crespigny Pk.
Harbord St. SW6 148 A1
Harborne Cl., Wat. 50 C5
Harborough Av., Sid. 157 H7
Harborough Rd. SW16 169 F4
Harbour Av. SW10 149 F1
Harbour Ex. Sq. E14 134 B2
Harbour Rd. SE5 151 J3
Harbridge Av. SW15 147 F7
Harbut Rd. SW11 149 G4
Harcombe Rd. N16 94 B3
Harcourt Av. E12 98 C4
Harcourt Av., Edg. 54 C3
Harcourt Av., Sid. 158 C6
Harcourt Av., Wall. 200 B4
Harcourt Cl., Islw. 144 D3
Harcourt Fld., Wall. 200 B4
Harcourt Rd. E15 115 F2
Harcourt Rd. N22 74 D1
Harcourt Rd. SE4 153 H4
Harcourt Rd. SW19 166 D7
Russell Rd.
Harcourt Rd., Bexh. 159 E4
Harcourt Rd., Th.Hth. 187 F6
Harcourt Rd., Wall. 200 B4
Harcourt St. W1 15 H2
Harcourt St. W1 109 H5
Harcourt Ter. SW10 30 B4
Harcourt Ter. SW10 129 E5
Hardcastle Cl., Croy. 188 D6
Hardcourts Cl., W.Wick. 204 B3
Hardel Ri. SW2 169 H2
Hardel Wk. SW2 151 G7
Papworth Way
Hardens Manorway SE7 136 A3
Harders Rd. SE15 152 E2
Hardess St. SE24 151 J3
Herne Hill Rd.
Hardie Cl. NW10 88 D5
Hardie Rd., Dag. 101 J3
Harding Cl. SE17 35 J5
Harding Cl., Croy. 202 C3
Harding Ho., Hayes 102 B6
Harding Rd., Bexh. 159 F2
Hardinge La. E1 113 F6
Hardinge St.
Hardinge Rd. N18 60 B5
Hardinge Rd. NW10 107 H1
Hardinge St. E1 113 F6
Harding's Cl., Kings.T. 181 J1
Hardings La. SE20 171 G6
Hardman Rd. SE7 135 H5
Hardman Rd., Kings.T. 181 H2
Hardwick Cl., Stan. 53 F5
Hardwick Grn. W13 105 E5
Hardwick St. EC1 11 F4
Hardwick St. EC1 111 G3
Hardwicke Av., Houns. 143 G1
Hardwicke Rd. N13 58 E6
Hardwicke Rd. W4 126 D4
Hardwicke Rd., Rich. 163 F4
Hardwicke St., Bark. 117 F1
Hardwicks Way SW18 148 D5
Buckhold Rd.
Hardwidge St. SE1 28 D3
Hardy Av. E16 135 G1
Wesley Av.
Hardy Av., Ruis. 84 B5
Hardy Cl. SE16 133 G2
Middleton Dr.
Hardy Cl., Barn. 40 B6
Hardy Cl., Pnr. 66 D7
Hardy Rd. E4 61 J6
Hardy Rd. SE3 135 F7
Hardy Rd. SW19 167 E7
Hardy Way, Enf. 43 G1
Hare & Billet Rd. SE3 154 D1
Hare Ct. EC4 19 E4
Hare La., Esher 194 B6
Hare Marsh E2 13 H5
Hare Pl. EC4 19 F4
Hare Row E2 113 E2
Hare St. SE18 136 D3
Hare Wk. N1 13 E2
Hare Wk. N1 112 B2
Harebell Dr. E6 116 D5

Harecastle Cl., 102/103 E4
Hayes
Braunston Dr.
Harecourt Rd. N1 93 J6
Haredale Rd. SE24 151 J4
Haredon Cl. SE23 153 F7
Harefield, Esher 194 B4
Harefield Cl., Enf. 43 G1
Harefield Ms. SE4 153 J3
Harefield Rd. N8 74 D5
Harefield Rd. SE4 153 J3
Harefield Rd. SW16 169 F7
Harefield Rd., Sid. 176 D2
Haresfield Rd., Dag. 101 G6
Harewood Av. NW1 7 H6
Harewood Av. NW1 109 H4
Harewood Av., Nthlt. 85 E7
Harewood Cl., Nthlt. 85 F7
Harewood Dr., Ilf. 80 C2
Harewood Pl. W1 16 E4
Harewood Rd. SW19 167 H6
Harewood Rd., Islw. 124 C7
Harewood Rd., 202 B6
S.Croy.
Harewood Rd., Wat. 50 B3
Harewood Row NW1 15 H1
Harewood Ter., Sthl. 123 F4
Harfield Gdns. SE5 152 B3
Harfield Rd., Sun. 178 D2
Harford Cl. E4 46 B7
Harford Rd. E4 46 B7
Harford St. E1 113 H4
Harford Wk. N2 73 G5
Hargood Cl., Har. 69 H6
Hargood Rd. SE3 155 J1
Hargrave Pk. N19 92 C2
Hargrave Pl. N7 92 D5
Brecknock Rd.
Hargrave Rd. N19 92 C2
Hargwyne St. SW9 151 F3
Haringey Pk. N8 75 E6
Haringey Pas. N4 75 H6
Haringey Pas. N8 75 G4
Haringey Rd. N8 74 E4
Harington Ter. N9 60 A3
Harington Ter. N18 60 A3
Harkett Cl., Har. 68 C2
Byron Rd.
Harkett Ct., Har. 68 C2
Harland Av., Croy. 202 C3
Harland Av., Sid. 175 G3
Harland Cl. SW19 184 E3
Harland Rd. SE12 173 G1
Harlands Gro., 206/207 E4
Orp.
Pinecrest Gdns.
Harlech Gdns., 122 C6
Houns.
Harlech Gdns., Pnr. 66 D7
Harlech Rd. N14 59 E3
Harlech Twr. W3 126 B2
Harlequin Av., Brent. 124 D6
Harlequin Cl., Hayes 102 D5
Cygnet Way
Harlequin Cl., Islw. 144 B5
Harlequin Ho., 138/139 E3
Erith
Kale Rd.
Harlequin Rd., Tedd. 162 E7
Harlescott Rd. SE15 153 G4
Harlesden Gdns. 107 F1
NW10
Harlesden La. NW10 107 G1
Harlesden Rd. NW10 107 G1
Harleston Cl. E5 95 F2
Theydon Rd.
Harley Cl., Wem. 87 G6
Harley Ct. E11 79 G7
Blake Hall Rd.
Harley Cres., Har. 68 A4
Harley Gdns. SW10 30 D4
Harley Gdns. SW10 129 F6
Harley Gdns., Orp. 207 H4
Harley Gro. E3 113 J3
Harley Pl. W1 16 D2
Harley Pl. W1 110 B5
Harley Rd. NW3 91 G7
Harley Rd. NW10 106 E2
Harley Rd., Har. 68 A4
Harley St. W1 16 D2
Harley St. W1 110 B4
Harleyford, Brom. 191 H1
Harleyford Rd. SE11 34 C5
Harleyford Rd. SE11 131 F6
Harleyford St. SE11 34 E6
Harleyford St. SE11 131 G6
Harlinger St. SE18 136 B3
Harlington Cl., Hayes 121 F7
New Rd.
Harlington Rd., Bexh. 159 E3
Harlington Rd., 141 J4
Houns.
Harlington Rd. E., 142 B7
Felt.

Harlington Rd. W., 142 B6
Felt.
Harlow Rd. N13 60 A3
Harlyn Dr., Pnr. 66 B3
Harman Av., 63 F7
Wdf.Grn.
Harman Cl. E4 62 D4
Harman Cl. NW2 90 B3
Harman Dr. NW2 90 B3
Harman Dr., Sid. 157 J6
Harman Rd., Enf. 44 C5
Harmondsworth La., 120 B6
West Dr.
Harmondsworth Rd., 120 B5
West Dr.
Harmony Cl. NW11 72 B5
Harmony Way NW4 71 J4
Victoria Rd.
Harmood Gro. NW1 92 B7
Clarence Way
Harmood Pl. NW1 92 B7
Harmood St.
Harmood St. NW1 92 B7
Harmsworth Ms. SE11 27 G6
Harmsworth St. SE17 35 G4
Harmsworth St. SE17 131 H5
Harmsworth Way N20 56 C1
Harness Rd. SE28 138 A2
Harold Av., Belv. 139 F5
Harold Av., Hayes 121 J3
Harold Est. SE1 28 E6
Harold Est. SE1 132 B3
Harold Gibbons Ct. 135 J6
SE7
Victoria Way
Harold Pl. SE11 34 E4
Harold Pl. SE11 131 G5
Harold Rd. E4 62 C4
Harold Rd. E11 96 E1
Harold Rd. E13 115 H1
Harold Rd. N8 75 F5
Harold Rd. N15 76 C5
Harold Rd. NW10 106 D3
Harold Rd. SE19 170 A7
Harold Rd., Sutt. 199 G4
Harold Rd., Wdf.Grn. 79 G1
Haroldstone Rd. E17 77 G5
Harp All. EC4 19 G3
Harp Island Cl. NW10 88 D2
Harp La. EC3 20 D6
Harp Rd. W7 104 C4
Harpenden Rd. E12 97 J2
Harpenden Rd. SE27 169 H3
Harper Cl. N14 42 C5
Alexandra Ct.
Harper Rd. E6 116 C6
Harper Rd. SE1 131 J3
Harpers Yd. N17 76 C1
Ruskin Rd.
Harpley Sq. E1 113 F3
Harpour Rd., Bark. 99 F6
Harpsden St. SW11 150 A1
Harpur Ms. WC1 18 C1
Harpur St. WC1 18 C1
Harpur St. WC1 111 F5
Harraden Rd. SE3 155 J1
Harrap St. E14 114 C7
Harrier Av. E11 79 H6
Eastern Av.
Harrier Ms. SE28 137 G3
Harrier Rd. NW9 71 E2
Harrier Way E6 116 C5
Harriers Cl. W5 105 H7
Harriers Rd., Hayes 102 C4
Harriet Cl. E8 112 D1
Harriet Gdns., Croy. 202 D2
Harriet St. SW1 24 A4
Harriet Tubman Cl. 151 G7
SW2
Harriet Wk. SW1 24 A4
Harriet Wk. SW1 129 J2
Harringay Gdns. N8 75 H4
Harringay Rd. N15 75 H5
Harrington Cl. NW10 88 D3
Harrington Cl., Croy. 200 E2
Harrington Ct. W10 108 C3
Dart St.
Harrington Gdns. SW7 30 B2
Harrington Gdns. 129 E4
SW7
Harrington Hill E5 95 E1
Harrington Rd. E11 97 E1
Harrington Rd. SE25 188 E4
Harrington Rd. SW7 30 E1
Harrington Rd. SW7 129 G4
Harrington Sq. NW1 9 F2
Harrington Sq. NW1 110 C2
Harrington St. NW1 9 F3
Harrington St. NW1 110 C3
Harrington Way SE18 136 A3
Harriott Cl. SE10 135 F4
Harris Cl., Enf. 43 H1
Harris Cl., Houns. 143 G1

Harris Rd., Bexh. 159 E1
Harris Rd., Dag. 101 F5
Harris St. E17 77 J7
Harris St. SE5 132 A7
Harrison Cl. N20 57 H1
Harrison Rd., Dag. 101 H6
Harrison St. WC1 10 B4
Harrison St. WC1 111 E3
Harrisons Ri., Croy. 201 H3
Harrogate Rd., Wat. 50 C3
Harrold Rd., Dag. 100 B5
Harrow Av., Enf. 44 C6
Harrow Cl., Chess. 195 G7
Harrow Dr. N9 60 C1
Harrow Flds. Gdns., 86 B3
Har.
Harrow Grn. E11 96/97 E3
Harrow Rd.
Harrow La. E14 114 C7
Harrow Manorway 138 C1
SE2
Harrow Pk., Har. 86 B2
Harrow Pas., Kings.T. 181 G2
Market Pl.
Harrow Pl. E1 21 E3
Harrow Pl. E1 112 B6
Harrow Rd. E6 116 B1
Harrow Rd. E11 97 E3
Harrow Rd. NW10 107 H3
Harrow Rd. W2 108 C4
Harrow Rd. W9 108 C4
Harrow Rd. W10 108 A4
Harrow Rd., Bark. 117 H1
Harrow Rd., Cars. 199 H5
Harrow Rd., Ilf. 99 F4
Harrow Rd., Wem. 87 F5
Harrow Rd. 88 B6
(Tokyngton), Wem.
Harrow Vw., Har. 68 A4
Harrow Vw., Hayes 102 A6
Harrow Vw. Rd. W5 105 E4
Harrow Way, Wat. 50 E3
Harrow Weald Pk., 52 A6
Har.
Harroway Rd. SW11 149 G2
Harrowby St. W1 15 H3
Harrowby St. W1 109 H6
Harrowdene Cl., Wem. 87 G4
Harrowdene Gdns., 162 D6
Tedd.
Harrowdene Rd., Wem. 87 G3
Harrowes Meade, 54 A3
Edg.
Harrowgate Rd. E9 95 H6
Hart Cres., Chig. 65 J5
Hart Gro. W5 126 A1
Hart Gro., Sthl. 103 G5
Hart St. EC3 20 E5
Harte Rd., Houns. 143 F2
Hartfield Av., Borwd. 38 A5
Hartfield Av., Nthlt. 102 B2
Hartfield Cl., Borwd. 38 A5
Hartfield Cres. SW19 166 C6
Hartfield Cres., 205 G3
W.Wick.
Hartfield Gro. SE20 189 E1
Hartfield Rd. SW19 166 C7
Hartfield Rd., Chess. 195 G5
Hartfield Rd., W.Wick. 205 G4
Hartfield Ter. E3 114 A2
Hartford Av., Har. 68 D3
Hartford Rd., Bex. 159 G6
Hartford Rd., Epsom 196 A6
Hartforde Rd., Borwd. 38 A2
Hartham Cl. N7 93 E5
Hartham Cl., Islw. 144 D1
Hartham Rd. N7 92 E5
Hartham Rd. N17 76 C2
Hartham Rd., Islw. 144 C1
Harting Rd. SE9 174 B4
Hartington Cl., Har. 86 B4
Hartington Ct. W4 126 B7
Hartington Rd. E16 115 H6
Hartington Rd. E17 77 H6
Hartington Rd. SW8 150 E1
Hartington Rd. W4 126 B7
Hartington Rd. W13 105 E7
Hartington Rd., Sthl. 122 E2
Hartington Rd., 124 E7
Twick.
Hartismere Rd. SW6 128 C7
Hartlake Rd. E9 95 G6
Hartland Cl. N21 43 J6
Elmscott Gdns.
Hartland Cl., Edg. 54 A2
Hartland Dr., Edg. 54 A2
Hartland Dr., Ruis. 84 B3
Hartland Rd. E15 97 F7
Hartland Rd. N11 57 J5
Hartland Rd. NW1 92 B7
Hartland Rd. NW6 108 C2
Hartland Rd., Hmptn. 161 H4
Hartland Rd., Islw. 144 D3

Hartland Rd., Mord. 184 D7
Hartland Way, Croy. 203 H2
Hartland Way, Mord. 184 C7
Hartlands Cl., Bex. 159 F6
Hartlepool Ct. E16 136/137 E2
Barge Ho. Rd.
Hartley Av. E6 116 B1
Hartley Av. NW7 55 F5
Hartley Cl. NW7 55 F5
Hartley Cl., Brom. 192 C2
Hartley Rd. E11 97 F1
Hartley Rd., Croy. 187 H7
Hartley Rd., Well. 138 C7
Hartley St. E2 113 F3
Hartmann Rd. E16 136 A1
Hartnoll St. N7 93 F5
Eden Gro.
Harton Cl., Brom. 192 A1
Harton Rd. N9 61 E2
Harton St. SE8 154 A1
Harts Gro., Wdf.Grn. 63 G5
Harts La. SE14 133 H7
Harts La., Bark. 98 E6
Hartsbourne Av., 51 J2
Bushey
Hartsbourne Cl., 52 A2
Bushey
Hartsbourne Rd., 52 A2
Bushey
Hartshorn All. EC3 21 E4
Hartshorn Gdns. E6 116 D4
Hartslock Dr. SE2 138 D2
Hartsmead Rd. SE9 174 C2
Hartsway, Enf. 45 F4
Hartswood Gdns. W12 127 F3
Hartswood Grn., 52 A2
Bushey
Hartswood Rd. W12 127 F2
Hartsworth Cl. E13 115 F2
Hartville Rd. SE18 137 H4
Hartwell Dr. E4 62 C6
Hartwell St. E8 94 C6
Dalston La.
Harvard La. W4 126 B6
Harvard La. W4 126 B5
Harvard Rd. SE13 154 C5
Harvard Rd. W4 126 B5
Harvard Rd., Islw. 144 B1
Harvel Cres. SE2 138 D5
Harvest Bank Rd., 205 F3
W.Wick.
Harvest La., Loug. 47 J7
Fallow Flds.
Harvest La., T.Ditt. 180 D6
Harvest Rd., Felt. 160 A4
Harvesters Cl., Islw. 144 A5
Harvey Dr., Hmptn. 179 H1
Harvey Gdns. E11 97 F1
Harvey Rd.
Harvey Gdns. SE7 136 A4
Harvey Gdns., Loug. 49 E3
Harvey Ho., Brent. 125 H5
Green Dragon La.
Harvey Pt. E16 115 H5
Fife Rd.
Harvey Rd. E11 97 F1
Harvey Rd. N8 75 F5
Harvey Rd. SE5 152 A1
Harvey Rd., Houns. 143 F7
Harvey Rd., Ilf. 99 E5
Harvey Rd., Nthlt. 84 C7
Harvey Rd., Walt. 178 A7
Harvey St. N1 112 A1
Harvill Rd., Sid. 176 D5
Harvington Wk. E8 94 D7
Wilman Gro.
Harvist Est. N7 93 G4
Harvist Rd. NW6 108 A2
Harwater Dr., Loug. 48 C2
Harwell Pas. N2 73 J4
Harwich La. EC2 20 E1
Harwich La. EC2 112 B5
Harwood Av., Brom. 191 G2
Harwood Av., Mitch. 185 H3
Harwood Cl. N12 57 H6
Summerfields Av.
Harwood Cl., Wem. 87 G4
Harrowdene Rd.
Harwood Rd. SW6 128 D7
Harwood Ter. SW6 148 E1
Harwoods Yd. N21 43 G7
Wades Hill
Hascombe Ter. SE5 152 A2
Haselbury Rd. N9 60 B4
Haselbury Rd. N18 60 B4
Haseley End SE23 153 F7
Tyson Rd.
Haselrigge Rd. SW4 150 D4
Haseltine Rd. SE26 171 J4
Haselwood Dr., Enf. 43 H4
Haskard Rd., Dag. 100 D4
Haskell Ho. NW10 106 D1
Hasker St. SW3 31 H1
Hasker St. SW3 129 H4

Hayfield Pas. E1 113 F4
Stepney Grn.
Hayfield Yd. E1 113 F4
Mile End Rd.
Haygarth Pl. SW19 166 A5
Haygreen Cl., Kings.T. 164 B6
Hayland Cl. NW9 70 D4
Hayles St. SE11 35 G1
Hayles St. SE11 131 H4
Haylett Gdns., Kings.T. 181 G4
Anglesea Rd.
Hayling Av., Felt. 160 A3
Hayling Cl. N16 94 B5
Pellerin Rd.
Hayling Rd., Wat. 50 B2
Hayman St. N1 93 H7
Cross St.
Haymarket SW1 17 H6
Haymarket SW1 110 D7
Haymarket Arc. SW1 17 H6
Haymer Gdns., Wor.Pk. 197 G3
Haymerle Rd. SE15 37 H6
Haymerle Rd. SE15 132 D6
Haymill Cl., Grnf. 104 C3
Hayne Rd., Beck. 189 J2
Hayne St. EC1 19 H1
Haynes Cl. N11 58 A3
Haynes Cl. N17 60 E7
Haynes Cl. SE3 155 E3
Haynes La. SE19 170 B6
Haynes Rd., Wem. 87 H7
Haynt Wk. SW20 184 B3
Hay's La. SE1 28 D2
Hay's Ms. W1 16 D6
Hay's Ms. W1 110 B7
Haysleigh Gdns. SE20 188 D2
Hayter Rd. SW2 151 E5
Hayton Cl. E8 94 C6
Buttermere Wk.
Hayward Cl. SW19 185 E1
Hayward Gdns. SW15 147 J6
Hayward Rd. N20 57 F2
Hayward Rd., T.Ditt. 194 D1
Haywards Cl., Rom. 82 B5
Hayward's Pl. EC1 11 G5
Haywood Cl., Pnr. 66 D2
Haywood Ri., Orp. 207 H4
Haywood Rd., Brom. 192 A4
Hayworth Cl., Enf. 45 H2
Green St.
Hazel Av., West Dr. 120 D3
Hazel Cl. N13 60 A3
Hazel Cl. N19 92 C2
Hargrave Pk.
Hazel Cl. SE15 152 D2
Hazel Cl., Brent. 125 E7
Hazel Cl., Croy. 189 G7
Hazel Cl., Mitch. 186 D4
Hazel Cl., Twick. 143 J7
Hazel Gdns., Edg. 54 B4
Hazel Gro. SE26 171 G4
Hazel Gro., Enf. 44 D6
Dimsdale Dr.
Hazel Gro., Orp. 206 E2
Hazel Gro., Rom. 82 E3
Hazel Gro., Wem. 105 H1
Carlyon Rd.
Hazel Gro. Est. SE26 171 G4
Hazel La., Rich. 163 H2
Hazel Mead, Barn. 39 H5
Hazel Rd. E15 96/97 E5
Wingfield Rd.
Hazel Rd. NW10 107 J3
Hazel Wk., Brom. 192 D6
Hazel Way E4 61 J6
Hazel Way SE1 37 F1
Hazelbank, Surb. 196 C1
Hazelbank Rd. SE6 172 D2
Hazelbourne Rd. SW12 150 B6
Hazelbrouck Gdns., Ilf. 65 G7
Hazelbury Cl. SW19 184 D2
Hazelbury Grn. N9 60 B3
Hazelbury La. N9 60 B3
Hazelcroft, Pnr. 51 G6
Hazeldean Rd. NW10 88 D7
Hazeldene Dr., Pnr. 66 C3
Hazeldene Rd., Ilf. 100 B2
Hazeldene Rd., Well. 158 C2
Hazeldon Rd. SE4 153 H5
Hazeleigh Gdns., Wdf.Grn. 64 B5
Hazelgreen Cl. N21 59 H1
Hazelhurst, Beck. 190 D1
Hazelhurst Rd. SW17 167 F4
Hazell Cres., Rom. 83 H1
Hazellville Rd. N19 74 D7
Hazelmere Cl., Felt. 141 G6
Hazelmere Cl., Nthlt. 103 F2
Hazelmere Dr., Nthlt. 103 F2
Hazelmere Rd. NW6 108 D1
Hazelmere Rd., Nthlt. 103 F2
Hazelmere Rd., Orp. 193 F4
Hazelmere Wk., Nthlt. 103 F2
Hazelmere Way, Brom. 191 G6
Hazeltree La., Nthlt. 103 E3
Hazelwood, Loug. 48 A5
Hazelwood Av., Mord. 185 E4
Hazelwood Cl. W5 125 H2
Hazelwood Cl., Har. 67 H4
Hazelwood Ct. NW10 88/89 E3
Neasden La. N.
Hazelwood Cres. N13 59 G4
Hazelwood Cft., Surb. 181 H6
Hazelwood Dr., Pnr. 66 B2
Hazelwood La. N13 59 G4
Hazelwood Pk. Cl., Chig. 65 H5
Hazelwood Rd. E17 77 H5
Hazelwood Rd., Enf. 44 C6
Hazlebury Rd. SW6 149 E2
Hazledean Rd., Croy. 202 A2
Hazledene Rd. W4 126 C6
Hazlemere Gdns., Wor.Pk. 197 H1
Hazlewell Rd. SW15 147 J5
Hazlewood Cl. E5 95 H3
Mandeville St.
Hazlewood Cres. W10 108 B4
Hazlitt Ms. W14 128 B3
Hazlitt Rd.
Hazlitt Rd. W14 128 B3
Head St. E1 113 G6
Headcorn Pl., Th.Hth. 187 F4
Headcorn Rd.
Headcorn Rd. N17 60 C7
Headcorn Rd., Brom. 173 F5
Headcorn Rd., Th.Hth. 187 F4
Headfort Pl. SW1 24 C4
Headfort Pl. SW1 130 A2
Headingley Cl., Ilf. 65 J6
Headington Rd. SW18 167 F2
Headlam Rd. SW4 150 D6
Headlam St. E1 113 E4
Headley App., Ilf. 80 D5
Headley Av., Wall. 201 F5
Headley Cl., Epsom 196 A6
Headley Ct. SE26 171 E5
Headley Dr., Croy. 204 B7
Headley Dr., Ilf. 80 E6
Head's Ms. W11 108 D6
Artesian Rd.
Headstone Dr., Har. 68 B3
Headstone Gdns., Har. 67 J4
Headstone La., Har. 67 H4
Headstone Rd., Har. 68 B5
Headway Cl., Rich. 163 F4
Locksmeade Rd.
Heald St. SE14 153 J1
Healey Dr., Orp. 207 J4
Healey St. NW1 92 B6
Heanor Ct. E5 95 G3
Pedro St.
Hearn Ri., Nthlt. 102 D1
Hearn St. EC2 12 E6
Hearn St. EC2 112 B4
Hearne Rd. W4 126 A6
Hearn's Bldgs. SE17 36 C2
Hearnville Rd. SW12 168 A1
Heath, The W7 124 B1
Lower Boston Rd.
Heath Av., Bexh. 138 D6
Heath Brow NW3 91 F3
North End Way
Heath Cl. NW11 72 E7
Heath Cl. W5 105 J4
Heath Cl., Hayes 121 G7
Heath Ct., Houns. 143 F4
Heath Dr. NW3 90 E4
Heath Dr. SW20 183 J4
Heath Gdns., Twick. 162 C1
Heath Gro. SE20 171 F7
Maple Rd.
Heath Hurst Rd. NW3 91 H4
Heath La. SE3 154 D2
Heath Mead SW19 166 A3
Heath Pk. Dr., Brom. 192 B3
Heath Pas. NW3 91 E2
Heath Ri. SW15 148 A6
Heath Ri., Brom. 191 F6
Heath Rd. SW8 150 B2
Heath Rd., Bex. 177 J1
Heath Rd., Har. 67 J7
Heath Rd., Houns. 143 H4
Heath Rd., Rom. 82 D7
Heath Rd., Th.Hth. 187 J3
Heath Rd., Twick. 162 C1
Heath Side NW3 91 G4
Heath Side, Orp. 207 F1
Heath St. NW3 91 F4
Heath Vw. N2 73 F4
Heath Vw. Cl. N2 73 F4
Heath Vil. SE18 137 J5
Heath Vil. SW18 167 F1
Cargill Rd.
Heath Way, Erith 159 J1
Heatham Pk., Twick. 144 C7
Heathbourne Rd., Bushey 52 B2
Heathbourne Rd., Stan. 52 B2
Heathcock Ct. WC2 110/111 E7
Strand
Heathcote Av., Ilf. 80 C2
Heathcote Gro. E4 62 C3
Heathcote Rd., Twick. 145 E6
Heathcote St. WC1 10 C5
Heathcote St. WC1 111 F4
Heathcote Way, West Dr. 120 A1
Tavistock Rd.
Heathcroft NW11 91 E1
Heathcroft W5 105 J4
Heathcroft Gdns. E17 78 D1
Hale End Rd.
Heathdale Av., Houns. 143 E3
Heathdene Dr., Belv. 139 H4
Heathdene Rd. SW16 169 F7
Heathdene Rd., Wall. 200 B7
Heathedge SE26 170 E2
Heather Cl. E6 116 E6
Heather Cl. SE13 154 D7
Heather Cl. SW8 150 B3
Heather Cl., Hmptn. 179 F1
Heather Cl., Islw. 144 A5
Harvesters Cl.
Heather Dr., Enf. 43 H2
Chasewood Av.
Heather Gdns. NW11 72 B6
Heather Gdns., Sutt. 198 D6
Heather Pk. Dr., Wem. 88 A7
Heather Rd. E4 61 J6
Heather Rd. NW2 89 F2
Heather Rd. SE12 173 G2
Heather Wk. W10 108 B4
Droop St.
Heather Wk., Edg. 54 B5
Heather Wk., Twick. 143 G7
Stephenson Rd.
Heather Way, Stan. 52 C6
Heatherbank SE9 156 C2
Heatherbank, Chis. 192 D2
Heatherdale Cl., Kings.T. 164 A6
Heatherdene Cl. N12 73 F1
Bow La.
Heatherdene Cl., Mitch. 185 H4
Heatherlands, Sun. 160 A6
Heatherley Dr., Ilf. 80 B3
Heathers, The, Stai. 140 C7
Heatherset Gdns. SW16 169 F7
Heatherside Rd., Epsom 196 D7
Heatherside Rd., Sid. 176 D3
Wren Rd.
Heatherwood Cl. E12 97 J2
Heathfield E4 62 C3
Heathfield, Chis. 175 F6
Heathfield Av. SW18 149 G7
Heathfield Rd.
Heathfield Cl. E16 116 A5
Heathfield Cl., Kes. 205 J5
Heathfield Dr., Mitch. 185 H1
Heathfield Gdns. NW11 72 A6
Heathfield Gdns. SW18 149 G6
Heathfield Rd.
Heathfield Gdns. W4 126 C5
Heathfield Gdns., Croy. 202 A4
Coombe Rd.
Heathfield La., Chis. 175 E6
Heathfield N., Twick. 144 C7
Heathfield Pk. NW2 89 J6
Heathfield Pk. Dr., Rom. 82 B5
Heathfield Rd. SW18 149 F6
Heathfield Rd. W3 126 B2
Heathfield Rd., Bexh. 159 F4
Heathfield Rd., Brom. 173 F7
Heathfield Rd., Croy. 202 A4
Heathfield Rd., Kes. 205 J5
Heathfield S., Twick. 144 C7
Heathfield Sq. SW18 149 G7
Heathfield St. W11 108 B7
Portland Rd.
Heathfield Ter. SE18 137 J6
Heathfield Ter. W4 126 C5
Heathfields Ct., Houns. 142/143 E5
Frampton Rd.
Heathgate NW11 72 E6
Heathgate Pl. NW3 91 J5
Agincourt Rd.
Heathland Rd. N16 94 B1
Heathlands Cl., Sun. 178 A2
Heathlands Cl., Twick. 162 C2
Heathlands Way, Houns. 142/143 E5
Frampton Rd.
Heathlee Rd. SE3 155 F4
Heathley End, Chis. 175 F6
Heathmans Rd. SW6 148 C1
Heathrow Interchange, Hayes 122 C1
Heathrow Int. Trd. Est., Houns. 142 B3
Heathrow Tunnel App., Houns. 140 E3
Heathrow Vehicle Tunnel, Houns. 140 E1
Heaths Cl., Enf. 44 B2
Heathside, Esher 194 B3
Heathside, Houns. 143 F7
Heathside Av., Bexh. 159 E1
Heathside Cl., Esher 194 B3
Heathstan Rd. W12 107 G6
Heathview Ct. SW19 166 A2
Heathview Dr. SE2 138 D6
Heathview Gdns. SW15 147 J7
Heathview Rd., Th.Hth. 187 G4
Heathville Rd. N19 74 E7
Heathwall St. SW11 149 J3
Heathway SE3 135 F7
Heathway, Croy. 203 J3
Heathway, Dag. 101 G7
Heathway, Wdf.Grn. 63 J4
Heathway Ind. Est., Dag. 101 H4
Manchester Way
Heathwood Gdns. SE7 136 B4
Heaton Cl. E4 62 C3
Friars Cl.
Heaton Rd. SE15 152 D3
Heaton Rd., Mitch. 168 A7
Heaver Rd. SW11 149 G3
Wye St.
Heavitree Cl. SE18 137 G5
Heavitree Rd. SE18 137 G5
Hebden Ct. E2 112 C1
Laburnum St.
Hebden Ter. N17 60 B6
Commercial Rd.
Hebdon Rd. SW17 167 H3
Heber Rd. NW2 90 A5
Heber Rd. SE22 152 C6
Hebron Rd. W6 127 H3
Hecham Cl. E17 77 H2
Heckfield Pl. SW6 128 D7
Fulham Rd.
Heckford St. E1 113 G7
The Highway
Hector St. SE18 137 H4
Heddington Gro. N7 93 F5
Heddon Cl., Islw. 144 D4
Heddon Ct. Av., Barn. 41 J5
Heddon Rd., Barn. 41 J5
Heddon St. W1 17 F5
Heddon St. W1 110 C7
Hedge Hill, Enf. 43 H1
Hedge La. N13 59 H3
Hedge Wk. SE6 172 B4
Hedgeley, Ilf. 80 C4
Hedgemans Rd., Dag. 100 D7
Hedgemans Way, Dag. 100 E6
Hedger St. SE11 35 G1
Hedgerley Gdns., Grnf. 103 J2
Hedgers Cl., Loug. 48 D4
Newmans La.
Hedgers Gro. E9 95 H6
Hedgewood Gdns., Ilf. 80 D5
Hedgley St. SE12 155 F5
Hedingham Cl. N1 93 J7
Popham Rd.
Hedingham Rd., Dag. 100 B5
Hedley Rd., Twick. 143 G7
Hedley Row N5 94 A5
Poets Rd.
Heenan Cl., Bark. 99 F6
Glenny Rd.
Heene Rd., Enf. 44 A1
Heidegger Cres. SW13 127 H6
Trinity Ch. Rd.
Heigham Rd. E6 98 A7
Heighton Gdns., Croy. 201 H5

Heights, The SE7	135	J5
Heights, The, Beck.	172	C7
Heights, The, Loug.	48	C2
Heights, The, Nthlt.	85	F5
Heights Cl. SW20	165	H7
Heiron St. SE17	**35**	**H6**
Heiron St. SE17	131	H6
Helby Rd. SW4	150	D6
Helder Gro. SE12	155	F7
Helder St., S.Croy.	202	A6
Heldmann Cl., Houns.	144	A4
Helen Av., Felt.	142	B7
Helen Cl. N2	73	F3
Thomas More Way		
Helen Cl., W.Mol.	179	H4
Helen St. SE18	136/137	E4
Wilmount St.		
Helena Cl., Wall.	201	E7
Helena Pl. E9	113	F1
Fremont St.		
Helena Rd. E13	115	F2
Helena Rd. E17	78	A5
Helena Rd. NW10	89	H5
Helena Rd. W5	105	G5
Helena Sq. SE16	113	H7
Rotherhithe St.		
Helen's Pl. E2	113	F3
Roman Rd.		
Helenslea Av. NW11	90	C1
Helix Gdns. SW2	151	F6
Helix Rd.		
Helix Rd. SW2	151	F6
Hellings St. E1	**29**	**J2**
Helme Cl. SW19	166	C5
Helmet Row EC1	**12**	**A5**
Helmet Row EC1	111	J4
Helmsdale Cl., Hayes	102/103	E4
Berrydale Rd.		
Helmsdale Rd. SW16	186	C1
Helmsley Pl. E8	94	E7
Helsinki Sq. SE16	133	H3
Finland St.		
Helston Cl., Pnr.	51	F7
Helvetia St. SE6	171	J2
Hemans St. SW8	**33**	**J7**
Hemans St. SW8	130	D7
Hemberton Rd. SW9	150	E3
Hemery Rd., Grnf.	86	A5
Heming Rd., Edg.	54	B7
Hemingford Cl. N12	57	G5
Hemingford Rd. N1	111	F1
Hemingford Rd., Sutt.	197	J4
Hemington Av. N11	57	J5
Hemlock Rd. W12	107	F7
Hemming Cl., Hmptn.	179	G1
Chandler Cl.		
Hemming St. E1	**13**	**J6**
Hemming St. E1	112	D4
Hemmings Cl., Sid.	176	B2
Hemp Wk. SE17	**36**	**C1**
Hemp Wk. SE17	132	A4
Hempstead Cl., Buck.H.	63	G2
Hempstead Rd. E17	78	D2
Hemsby Rd., Chess.	195	J6
Hemstal Rd. NW6	90	D7
Hemswell Dr. NW9	70	E1
Hemsworth St. N1	**12**	**D1**
Hemsworth St. N1	112	B2
Hemus Pl. SW3	**31**	**H4**
Hen & Chicken Ct. EC4	111	G6
Fleet St.		
Henbury Way, Wat.	50	D3
Henchman St. W12	107	F6
Hendale Av. NW4	71	G3
Henderson Cl. NW10	88	C6
Henderson Dr. NW8	**7**	**E5**
Henderson Rd. E7	97	J6
Henderson Rd. N9	60	E1
Henderson Rd. SW18	149	H7
Henderson Rd., Croy.	188	A6
Henderson Rd., Hayes	102	A3
Hendham Rd. SW17	167	H2
Hendon Av. N3	72	B1
Hendon Hall Ct. NW4	72	A3
Hendon La. N3	72	B3
Hendon Pk. Row NW11	72	C6
Hendon Rd. N9	60	D2
Hendon Way NW2	90	C3
Hendon Way NW4	71	H6
Hendon Way, Stai.	140	A6
Hendon Wd. La. NW7	39	F6
Hendre Rd. SE1	**36**	**E2**
Hendren Cl., Grnf.	86	A5
Dimmock Dr.		
Hendrick Av. SW12	149	J7
Heneage La. EC3	**21**	**E4**
Heneage St. E1	**21**	**G1**
Heneage St. E1	112	C5
Henfield Cl. N19	92	C1
Henfield Cl., Bex.	159	G6
Henfield Rd. SW19	184	C1
Hengelo Gdns., Mitch.	185	G4
Hengist Rd. SE12	155	H7
Hengist Rd., Erith	139	H7
Hengist Way, Brom.	190	E4
Hengrave Rd. SE23	153	G7
Hengrove Ct., Bex.	176/177	E1
Hurst Rd.		
Henley Av., Sutt.	198	B3
Henley Cl., Grnf.	103	J2
Henley Cl., Islw.	144	C1
Henley Ct. N14	42	C7
Henley Cross SE3	155	H3
Henley Dr. SE1	**37**	**G1**
Henley Dr. SE1	132	C4
Henley Dr., Kings.T.	165	F7
Henley Gdns., Pnr.	66	B3
Henley Gdns., Rom.	82	E5
Henley Rd. E16	136	C2
Henley Rd. N18	60	B4
Henley Rd. NW10	107	J1
Henley Rd., Ilf.	99	F4
Henley St. SW11	150	A2
Henley Way, Felt.	160	D5
Henlow Pl., Rich.	163	G2
Sandpits Rd.		
Hennel Cl. SE23	171	F3
Henniker Gdns. E6	116	A3
Henniker Ms. SW3	**30**	**E5**
Henniker Pt. E15	96	E5
Henniker Rd. E15	96	D5
Henning St. SW11	149	H1
Henningham Rd. N17	76	A1
Henrietta Cl. SE8	134	A6
Henrietta Ms. WC1	**10**	**B5**
Henrietta Pl. W1	**16**	**D4**
Henrietta Pl. W1	110	B6
Henrietta St. E15	96	C5
Henrietta St. WC2	**18**	**B5**
Henrietta St. WC2	111	E7
Henriques St. E1	**21**	**J3**
Henriques St. E1	112	D6
Henry Addlington Cl. E6	116	D5
Winsor Ter.		
Henry Cooper Way SE9	174	A3
Henry Darlot Dr. NW7	56	A5
Henry Dickens Ct. W11	128	A1
Henry Doulton Dr. SW17	168	B4
Henry Jackson Rd. SW15	148	A3
Henry Macaulay Av., Kings.T.	181	G1
Henry Rd. E6	116	B2
Henry Rd. N4	93	J1
Henry Rd., Barn.	41	G5
Henry St., Brom.	191	H1
Henry's Av., Wdf.Grn.	63	F5
Henry's Wk., Ilf.	65	G7
Henryson Rd. SE4	154	A5
Hensford Gdns. SE26	170/171	E4
Wells Pk. Rd.		
Henshall St. N1	94	A6
Henshaw St. SE17	**36**	**B1**
Henshaw St. SE17	132	A4
Henshawe Rd., Dag.	100	D3
Henshill Pt. E3	114	B3
Bromley High St.		
Henslowe Rd. SE22	152	D5
Henson Av. NW2	89	J5
Henson Cl., Orp.	207	E2
Henson Path, Har.	69	G3
Henson Pl., Nthlt.	102	C1
Henstridge Pl. NW8	**7**	**G1**
Henstridge Pl. NW8	109	H2
Henty Cl. SW11	129	H7
Henty Wk. SW15	147	H5
Henville Rd., Brom.	191	H1
Henwick Rd. SE9	156	A3
Henwood Side, Wdf.Grn.	64	C6
Love La.		
Hepburn Gdns., Brom.	205	E1
Hepburn Ms. SW11	149	J5
Webbs Rd.		
Hepple Cl., Islw.	144	E2
Hepplestone Cl. SW15	147	H6
Dover Pk. Dr.		
Hepscott Rd. E9	96	A7
Hepworth Ct., Bark.	100	A5
Hepworth Gdns., Bark.	100	A5
Hepworth Rd. SW16	169	E7
Hepworth Wk. NW3	91	H5
Haverstock Hill		
Heracles Cl., Wall.	200	E7
Herald Gdns., Wall.	200	B3
Herald St. E2	112/113	E4
Three Colts La.		
Herald's Ct. SE11	**35**	**G2**
Herald's Pl. SE11	**35**	**F1**
Herbal Hill EC1	**11**	**F6**
Herbal Hill EC1	111	G4
Herbert Cres. SW1	**24**	**A5**
Herbert Gdns. NW10	107	H2
Herbert Gdns. W4	126	B6
Magnolia Rd.		
Herbert Gdns., Rom.	82	D7
Herbert Pl. SE18	136/137	E6
Plumstead Common Rd.		
Herbert Rd. E12	98	B4
Herbert Rd. E17	77	J7
Herbert Rd. N11	58	E7
Herbert Rd. N15	76	C5
Herbert Rd. NW9	71	G6
Herbert Rd. SE18	136	D7
Herbert Rd. SW19	166	C7
Herbert Rd., Bexh.	159	E2
Herbert Rd., Brom.	192	A5
Herbert Rd., Ilf.	99	H2
Herbert Rd., Kings.T.	181	J3
Herbert Rd., Sthl.	123	F1
Herbert St. E13	115	G2
Herbert St. NW5	92	A6
Herbert Ter. SE18	136/137	E6
Herbert Rd.		
Herbrand St. WC1	**10**	**A5**
Herbrand St. WC1	110	E4
Hercules Pl. N7	92/93	E3
Hercules St.		
Hercules Rd. SE1	**26**	**D6**
Hercules Rd. SE1	131	F3
Hercules St. N7	93	E3
Hercules Twr. SE14	133	H6
Milton Ct. Rd.		
Hereford Av., Barn.	57	J1
Hereford Gdns. SE13	154/155	E5
Longhurst Rd.		
Hereford Gdns., Ilf.	80	B7
Hereford Gdns., Pnr.	66	E5
Hereford Gdns., Twick.	161	J1
Hereford Ho. NW6	108	D2
Hereford Ms. W2	108	D6
Hereford Rd.		
Hereford Pl. SE14	133	J7
Hereford Retreat SE15	**37**	**H6**
Hereford Rd. E11	79	H5
Hereford Rd. W2	108	D6
Hereford Rd. W3	106	B7
Hereford Rd. W5	125	F3
Hereford Rd., Felt.	160	C1
Hereford Sq. SW7	**30**	**D2**
Hereford Sq. SW7	129	F4
Hereford St. E2	**13**	**H5**
Hereford St. E2	112	D4
Hereford Way, Chess.	195	F5
Herent Dr., Ilf.	80	C3
Hereward Gdns. N13	59	G5
Hereward Grn., Loug.	49	F1
Hereward Rd. SW17	167	J4
Herga Ct., Har.	86	B3
Herga Rd., Har.	68	C4
Heriot Av. E4	62	A2
Heriot Rd. NW4	71	J5
Heriots Cl., Stan.	52	D4
Heritage Cl. SW9	151	H3
Heritage Hill, Kes.	205	J5
Heritage Vw., Har.	86	C3
Herlwyn Gdns. SW17	167	J4
Hermes Pt. W9	108	D4
Hermes St. N1	**10**	**E2**
Hermes Wk., Nthlt.	103	G2
Hotspur Rd.		
Hermes Way, Wall.	200	D7
Hermiston Av. N8	75	E5
Hermit Pl. NW6	108/109	E1
Belsize Rd.		
Hermit Rd. E16	115	F5
Hermit St. EC1	**11**	**G3**
Hermit St. EC1	111	H3
Hermitage, The SE23	171	F1
Hermitage, The SW13	147	F1
Hermitage, The, Rich.	145	G5
Hermitage Cl. E18	79	F4
Hermitage Cl., Enf.	43	H2
Hermitage Cl., Esher	194	D6
Hermitage Ct. E18	79	G4
Hermitage Ct. NW2	90	D3
Hermitage La.		
Hermitage Gdns. NW2	90	D3
Hermitage Gdns. SE19	169	J6
Hermitage La. N18	60	A5
Hermitage La. NW2	90	D3
Hermitage La. SE25	188	D6
Hermitage La. SW16	169	F7
Hermitage La., Croy.	188	D6
Hermitage Path SW16	187	E1
Hermitage Rd. N4	75	H7
Hermitage Rd. N15	75	H7
Hermitage Rd. SE19	169	J7
Hermitage Row E8	94	D5
Hermitage St. W2	**15**	**E2**
Hermitage St. W2	109	G5
Hermitage Wk. E18	79	F4
Hermitage Wall E1	**29**	**J2**
Hermitage Wall E1	132	D1
Hermitage Way, Stan.	68	D1
Hermon Gro., Hayes	122	A1
Hermon Hill E11	79	G5
Hermon Hill E18	79	G5
Herndon Rd. SW18	149	F5
Herne Cl. NW10	88	D5
North Circular Rd.		
Herne Hill SE24	151	J6
Herne Hill Rd. SE24	151	J3
Herne Ms. N18	60	D4
Lyndhurst Rd.		
Herne Pl. SE24	151	H5
Herne Rd., Surb.	195	G2
Heron Cl. E17	77	J2
Heron Cl. NW10	89	E6
Heron Cl., Buck.H.	63	G1
Heron Cl., Sutt.	198	B2
Gander Grn. La.		
Heron Ct., Brom.	191	J4
Heron Cres., Sid.	175	H3
Heron Dr. N4	93	J2
Heron Hill, Belv.	139	F4
Heron Ms., Ilf.	98/99	E2
Balfour Rd.		
Heron Pl. SE16	133	H1
Heron Quay E14	134	A1
Heron Rd. SE24	151	J4
Heron Rd., Croy.	202	B2
Tunstall Rd.		
Heron Rd., Twick.	144	D4
Heron Sq., Rich.	145	G5
Bridge St.		
Herondale Av. SW18	167	G1
Herongate Rd. E12	97	J2
Herons, The E11	79	F6
Heron's Pl., Islw.	144	E3
Herons Ri., Barn.	41	H4
Heronsforde W13	105	F6
Heronsgate, Edg.	54	A5
Heronslea Dr., Stan.	53	H5
Heronway, Wdf.Grn.	63	J4
Herrick Rd. N5	93	J3
Herrick St. SW1	**33**	**J1**
Herrick St. SW1	130	D4
Herries St. W10	108	B2
Herringham Rd. SE7	135	J3
Herrongate Cl., Enf.	44	C2
Hersant Cl. NW10	107	G1
Herschell Rd. SE23	153	H7
Hersham Cl. SW15	147	G7
Hertford Av. SW14	146	E5
Hertford Cl., Barn.	41	G3
Hertford Pl. W1	**9**	**F6**
Hertford Rd. N1	112	B1
Hertford Rd. N2	73	H3
Hertford Rd. N9	60	E2
Hertford Rd., Bark.	98	E7
Hertford Rd., Barn.	41	F3
Hertford Rd., Enf.	45	F3
Hertford Rd., Ilf.	81	H6
Hertford Sq., Mitch.	186/187	E4
Hertford Way		
Hertford St. W1	**24**	**D1**
Hertford St. W1	130	B1
Hertford Wk., Belv.	139	G5
Hoddesdon Rd.		
Hertford Way, Mitch.	186	E4
Hertslet Rd. N7	93	F3
Hertsmere Rd. E14	114	A7
Hervey Cl. N3	72	D1
Hervey Pk. Rd. E17	77	H4
Hervey Rd. SE3	155	H1
Hesa Rd., Hayes	102	A6
Hesewall Cl. SW4	150	C2
Brayburne Av.		
Hesketh Pl. W11	108	B7
Hesketh Rd. E7	97	G3
Heslop Rd. SW12	167	J1
Hesper Ms. SW5	**30**	**A3**
Hesper Ms. SW5	128	E5
Hesperus Cres. E14	134	B4
Hessel Rd. W13	124	D2
Hessel St. E1	112	E6
Hester Rd. N18	60	D5
Hester Rd. SW11	129	H7
Hester Ter., Rich.	146	A3
Chilton Rd.		
Hestercombe Av. SW6	148	B2
Hesterman Way, Croy.	201	F1
Heston Av., Houns.	123	E7
Heston Gra. La., Houns.	123	F6
Heston Ind. Mall, Houns.	123	F7

Street	Page	Grid
Hildenborough Gdns., Brom.	173	E6
Hildenlea Pl., Brom.	190	E2
Hildreth St. SW12	168	B1
Hildyard Rd. SW6	128	D6
Hiley Rd. NW10	107	J3
Hilgrove Rd. NW6	91	F7
Hiliary Gdns., Stan.	69	F2
Hill Brow, Brom.	192	A1
Hill Cl. NW2	89	H3
Hill Cl. NW11	72	D6
Hill Cl., Barn.	39	J5
Hill Cl., Chis.	174	E5
Hill Cl., Har.	86	B3
Hill Cl., Stan.	52	E4
Hill Ct., Nthlt.	85	G5
Hill Cres. N20	56	E2
Hill Cres., Bex.	177	J1
Hill Cres., Har.	68	D5
Hill Cres., Surb.	181	J5
Hill Cres., Wor.Pk.	197	J2
Hill Crest, Sid.	158	A7
Hill Dr. NW9	88	C1
Hill Dr. SW16	187	F3
Hill End, Orp. *The App.*	207	J2
Hill Fm. Rd. W10	107	J5
Hill Gro., Felt. *Watermill Way*	161	F2
Hill Ho. Av., Stan.	52	C7
Hill Ho. Cl. N21	43	G7
Hill Ho. Dr., Hmptn.	179	G1
Hill Ho. Rd. SW16	169	F5
Hill Path SW16 *Valley Rd.*	169	F5
Hill Ri. N9	45	E6
Hill Ri. NW11	73	E4
Hill Ri. SE23 *London Rd.*	170/171	E1
Hill Ri., Esher	194	E2
Hill Ri., Grnf.	85	J7
Hill Ri., Rich.	145	G5
Hill Rd. N10	73	J1
Hill Rd. NW8	**6**	**D2**
Hill Rd. NW8	109	F2
Hill Rd., Cars.	199	H6
Hill Rd., Har.	68	D5
Hill Rd., Mitch.	186	B1
Hill Rd., Pnr.	66	E5
Hill Rd., Sutt.	199	E5
Hill Rd., Wem.	86	E3
Hill St. W1	**24**	**C1**
Hill St. W1	130	B1
Hill St., Rich.	145	G5
Hill Top NW11	73	E4
Hill Top, Loug.	48	D2
Hill Top, Mord.	184	D6
Hill Top, Sutt.	184	C7
Hill Top Cl., Loug.	48	D3
Hill Top Pl., Loug.	48	D3
Hill Top Vw., Wdf.Grn.	64	C6
Hill Vw. Cres., Orp.	207	J1
Hill Vw. Dr., Well.	157	H2
Hill Vw. Gdns. NW9	70	D5
Hill Vw. Rd., Esher	194	D7
Hill Vw. Rd., Orp.	207	J1
Hill Vw. Rd., Twick.	144	D6
Hillary Ri., Barn.	40	D4
Hillary Rd., Sthl.	123	G3
Hillbeck Cl. SE15	133	F7
Hillbeck Way, Grnf.	104	A1
Hillborne Cl., Hayes	122	A5
Hillborough Cl. SW19	167	F7
Hillbrook Rd. SW17	167	J3
Hillbrow, N.Mal.	183	F3
Hillbrow Rd., Brom.	172	E7
Hillbury Av., Har.	69	E5
Hillbury Rd. SW17	168	B3
Hillcote Av. SW16	169	G7
Hillcourt Av. N12	56	E6
Hillcourt Est. N16	94	A1
Hillcourt Rd. SE22	152	E6
Hillcrest N6	74	A7
Hillcrest N21	43	H7
Hillcrest Av. NW11	72	B5
Hillcrest Av., Edg.	54	B4
Hillcrest Av., Pnr.	66	D4
Hillcrest Cl. SE26	170	D4
Hillcrest Cl., Beck.	189	J5
Hillcrest Gdns. N3	72	B4
Hillcrest Gdns. NW2	89	G3
Hillcrest Gdns., Esher	194	C3
Hillcrest Rd. E17	78	D2
Hillcrest Rd. E18	79	F2
Hillcrest Rd. W3	126	A1
Hillcrest Rd. W5	105	H5
Hillcrest Rd., Brom.	173	G5
Hillcrest Rd., Loug.	48	A6
Hillcrest Vw., Beck.	189	J6
Hillcroft, Loug.	48	D2
Hillcroft Av., Pnr.	67	F6
Hillcroft Cres. W5	105	H6
Hillcroft Cres., Ruis.	84	D3
Hillcroft Cres., Wat.	50	B1
Hillcroft Cres., Wem.	87	J4
Hillcroft Rd. E6	116	E5
Hillcroome Rd., Sutt.	199	G6
Hillcross Av., Mord.	184	C5
Hilldale Rd., Sutt.	198	C4
Hilldown Rd. SW16	169	E7
Hilldown Rd., Brom.	205	E1
Hilldrop Cres. N7	92	D5
Hilldrop Est. N7	92	D5
Hilldrop La. N7	92	D5
Hilldrop Rd. N7	92	D5
Hilldrop Rd., Brom.	173	G6
Hillend SE18	156	D1
Hillersdon Av. SW13	147	G2
Hillersdon Av., Edg.	53	J5
Hillery Cl. SE17	**36**	**C2**
Hillfield Av. N8	75	E5
Hillfield Av. NW9	71	E5
Hillfield Av., Wem.	87	H7
Hillfield Cl., Har.	67	J4
Hillfield Ct. NW3	91	H5
Hillfield Par., Mord.	185	H6
Hillfield Pk. N10	74	B4
Hillfield Pk. N21	59	G2
Hillfield Pk. Ms. N10	74	B4
Hillfield Rd. NW6	90	C5
Hillfield Rd., Hmptn.	161	F7
Hillfoot Av., Rom.	83	J1
Hillfoot Rd., Rom.	83	J1
Hillgate Pl. SW12	150	B7
Hillgate Pl. W8	128	D1
Hillgate St. W8	128	D1
Hilliards Ct. E1 *Wapping High St.*	132/133	E1
Hillier Cl., Barn.	40	E6
Hillier Gdns., Croy. *Crowley Cres.*	201	G5
Hillier Pl., Chess.	195	F6
Hillier Rd. SW11	149	J6
Hilliers La., Croy.	200	E3
Hillingdon Rd., Bexh.	159	J2
Hillingdon St. SE5	**35**	**H6**
Hillingdon St. SE5	131	H6
Hillingdon St. SE17	**35**	**H6**
Hillingdon St. SE17	131	H6
Hillington Gdns., Wdf.Grn.	80	A2
Hillman Dr. W10	107	J4
Hillman St. E8	95	E6
Hillmarton Rd. N7	93	E5
Hillmead Dr. SW9	151	H4
Hillmont Rd., Esher	194	B3
Hillmore Gro. SE26	171	G5
Hillreach SE18	136	C5
Hillrise Rd. N19	74	E7
Hills Ms. W5	105	H7
Hills Pl. W1	**17**	**F4**
Hills Rd., Buck.H.	63	H1
Hillsborough Grn., Wat. *Ashburnham Dr.*	50	A3
Hillsborough Rd. SE22	152	B5
Hillsgrove, Well.	138	C7
Hillside NW9	70	D4
Hillside NW10	106	C1
Hillside SW19	166	A6
Hillside, Barn.	41	F5
Hillside Av. N11	57	J6
Hillside Av., Borwd.	38	B4
Hillside Av., Wem.	87	J4
Hillside Av., Wdf.Grn.	63	J5
Hillside Cl. NW8	**6**	**B1**
Hillside Cl. NW8	109	E2
Hillside Cl., Mord.	184	B4
Hillside Cl., Wdf.Grn.	63	J5
Hillside Cres., Har.	85	J1
Hillside Cres., Nthwd.	66	A1
Hillside Dr., Edg.	54	A6
Hillside Est. N15	76	C6
Hillside Gdns. E17	78	D3
Hillside Gdns. N6	74	A6
Hillside Gdns. SW2	169	G2
Hillside Gdns., Barn.	40	B4
Hillside Gdns., Edg.	53	J4
Hillside Gdns., Har.	69	H7
Hillside Gdns., Nthwd.	50	A7
Hillside Gdns., Wall.	200	C7
Hillside Gro. N14	42	D7
Hillside Gro. NW7	55	G7
Hillside La., Brom.	205	G2
Hillside Pas. SW2	169	F2
Hillside Ri., Nthwd.	50	A7
Hillside Rd. N15	76	B7
Hillside Rd. SW2	169	G2
Hillside Rd. W5	105	H5
Hillside Rd., Brom.	191	F3
Hillside Rd., Croy.	201	H5
Hillside Rd., Nthwd.	50	A7
Hillside Rd., Pnr.	50	B7
Hillside Rd., Sthl.	103	G4
Hillside Rd., Surb.	181	J5
Hillside Rd., Sutt.	198	C7
Hillsleigh Rd. W8	128	C1
Hillstowe St. E5	95	F2
Hilltop Gdns. NW4 *Great N. Way*	71	H1
Hilltop Gdns., Orp.	207	H2
Hilltop Rd. NW6	90	D7
Hilltop Way, Stan.	52	D3
Hillview SW20	165	H7
Hillview, Mitch.	186	E4
Hillview Av., Har.	69	H5
Hillview Cl., Pnr.	51	F6
Hillview Cres., Ilf.	80	C6
Hillview Gdns. NW4	72	A4
Hillview Gdns., Har.	67	G3
Hillview Rd. NW7	56	A4
Hillview Rd., Chis.	174	D5
Hillview Rd., Pnr.	51	F7
Hillview Rd., Sutt.	199	F3
Hillway N6	92	A2
Hillway NW9	88	E1
Hillworth Rd. SW2	151	G7
Hilly Flds. Cres. SE4	154	A3
Hillyard Rd. W7	104	B5
Hillyard St. SW9	151	G1
Hillyfield E17	77	H3
Hillyfields, Loug.	48	D2
Hilsea St. E5	95	F4
Hilton Av. N12	57	G5
Hilversum Cres. SE22 *East Dulwich Gro.*	152	B5
Himley Rd. SW17	167	H5
Hinchcliffe Cl., Wall.	201	F7
Hinchley Cl., Esher	194	C3
Hinchley Dr., Esher	194	C3
Hinchley Way, Esher	194	D3
Hinckley Rd. SE15	152	D4
Hind Cl., Chig.	65	J5
Hind Ct. EC4	**19**	**F4**
Hind Gro. E14	114	A6
Hinde Ms. W1 *Marylebone La.*	110	A6
Hinde St. W1	**16**	**C3**
Hinde St. W1	110	A6
Hindes Rd., Har.	68	A5
Hindhead Cl. N16	94	B1
Hindhead Gdns., Nthlt.	102	E1
Hindhead Grn., Wat.	50	C5
Hindhead Way, Wall.	200	E5
Hindmans Rd. SE22	152	D5
Hindmans Way, Dag.	119	F4
Hindmarsh Cl. E1	**21**	**J5**
Hindrey Rd. E5	95	E5
Hindsley's Pl. SE23	171	F2
Hinkler Cl., Wall.	201	E7
Hinkler Rd., Har.	69	G3
Hinksey Path SE2	138	D3
Hinstock Rd. SE18	137	F6
Hinton Av., Houns.	142	D4
Hinton Cl. SE9	174	B1
Hinton Rd. N18	60	B4
Hinton Rd. SE24	151	H3
Hinton Rd., Wall.	200	C6
Hippodrome Ms. W11 *Portland Rd.*	108	B7
Hippodrome Pl. W11	108	B7
Hiscocks Ho. NW10	88	C7
Hitcham Rd. E17	77	J7
Hitchin Sq. E3	113	H2
Hither Fm. Rd. SE3	155	J3
Hither Grn. La. SE13	154	C5
Hitherbroom Rd., Hayes	122	A1
Hitherfield Rd. SW16	169	F2
Hitherfield Rd., Dag.	101	E2
Hitherlands SW12	168	B2
Hitherwell Dr., Har.	68	A1
Hitherwood Dr. SE19	170	C4
Hive Cl., Bushey	52	A2
Hive Rd., Bushey	52	A2
Hoadly Rd. SW16	168	D3
Hobart Cl. N20 *Oakleigh Rd. N.*	57	H2
Hobart Cl., Hayes	102	D4
Hobart Dr., Hayes	102	D4
Hobart Gdns., Th.Hth.	188	A3
Hobart La., Hayes	102	D4
Hobart Pl. SW1	**24**	**D5**
Hobart Pl. SW1	130	B3
Hobart Pl., Rich. *Chisholm Rd.*	145	J6
Hobart Rd., Dag.	100	D4
Hobart Rd., Hayes	102	D4
Hobart Rd., Ilf.	81	F2
Hobart Rd., Wor.Pk.	197	H3
Hobbayne Rd. W7	104	A6
Hobbes Wk. SW15	147	H5
Hobbs Grn. N2	73	F3
Hobbs Ms., Ilf. *Ripley Rd.*	99	J2
Hobbs Pl. Est. N1 *Pitfield St.*	112	B1
Hobbs Rd. SE27	169	J4
Hobday St. E14	114	B5
Hobill Wk., Surb.	181	J6
Hoblands End, Chis.	175	H6
Hobsons Pl. E1	**21**	**H1**
Hobury St. SW10	**30**	**D6**
Hobury St. SW10	129	F6
Hocker St. E2	**13**	**F4**
Hockett Cl. SE8	133	H4
Hockley Av. E6	116	B2
Hockley Ms., Bark.	117	H2
Hocroft Av. NW2	90	C3
Hocroft Rd. NW2	90	C4
Hocroft Wk. NW2	90	C3
Hodder Dr., Grnf.	104	C2
Hoddesdon Rd., Belv.	139	G5
Hodford Rd. NW11	90	C2
Hodgkin Cl. SE28 *Fleming Way*	118	D7
Hodister Cl. SE5 *Badsworth Rd.*	131	J7
Hodnet Gro. SE16	133	G4
Hodson Cl., Har.	85	F3
Hoe, The, Wat.	50	D2
Hoe St. E17	78	A4
Hofland Rd. W14	128	A3
Hogan Ms. W2	**14**	**E1**
Hogan Way E5 *Geldeston Rd.*	94	D2
Hogarth Cl. E16	116	A5
Hogarth Cl. W5	105	H5
Hogarth Ct. EC3	**20**	**E5**
Hogarth Ct. SE19 *Fountain Dr.*	170	C4
Hogarth Cres. SW19	185	G1
Hogarth Cres., Croy.	187	J7
Hogarth Gdns., Houns.	123	G7
Hogarth Hill NW11	72	C4
Hogarth La. W4	126	E6
Hogarth Pl. SW5	**30**	**A2**
Hogarth Reach, Loug.	48	C5
Hogarth Rd. SW5	**30**	**A2**
Hogarth Rd. SW5	128	E4
Hogarth Rd., Dag.	100	B5
Hogarth Rd., Edg.	70	A2
Hogarth Roundabout W4	127	E6
Hogarth Roundabout Flyover W4 *Burlington La.*	126/127	E6
Hogarth Way, Hmptn.	179	J1
Hogshead Pas. E1 *Pennington St.*	112/113	E7
Hogsmill Way, Epsom	196	C5
Holbeach Gdns., Sid.	157	H6
Holbeach Ms. SW12 *Harberson Rd.*	168	B1
Holbeach Rd. SE6	154	A7
Holbeck Row SE15	132	D7
Holbein Ms. SW1	**32**	**B3**
Holbein Ms. SW1	130	A5
Holbein Pl. SW1	**32**	**B2**
Holbein Pl. SW1	130	A4
Holbein Ter., Dag. *Marlborough Rd.*	100	B4
Holberton Gdns. NW10	107	H3
Holborn EC1	**18**	**E2**
Holborn EC1	111	G5
Holborn Circ. EC1	**19**	**F2**
Holborn Pl. WC1	**18**	**C2**
Holborn Rd. E13	115	H4
Holborn Viaduct EC1	**19**	**F2**
Holborn Viaduct EC1	111	G5
Holborn Way, Mitch.	185	J2
Holbrook Cl. N19 *Dartmouth Pk. Hill*	92	B1
Holbrook Cl., Enf.	44	C1
Holbrook La., Chis.	175	G7
Holbrook Rd. E15	115	F2
Holbrook Way, Brom.	192	C6
Holbrooke Ct. N7	93	E4
Holbrooke Pl., Rich. *Hill Ri.*	145	G5
Holburne Cl. SE3	155	J1
Holburne Gdns. SE3	156	A1
Holburne Rd. SE3	155	J1
Holcombe Hill NW7 *Highwood Hill*	55	G3
Holcombe Rd. N17	76	C3
Holcombe Rd., Ilf.	80	D7
Holcombe St. W6	127	H4
Holcote Cl., Belv. *Blakemore Way*	138/139	E3
Holcroft Rd. E9	95	F7
Holden Av. N12	57	E5
Holden Av. NW9	88	C1
Holden Cl., Dag.	100	B3
Holden Pt. E15 *Waddington Rd.*	96	D6
Holden Rd. N12	56	E5
Holden St. SW11	150	A2
Holdenby Rd. SE4	153	H5
Holdenhurst Av. N12	57	E7
Holder Cl. N3	57	E7
Holderness Way SE27	169	H5

Holdernesse Cl., Islw. 144 D1
Holdernesse Rd. SW17 167 J3
Holders Hill Av. NW4 72 A2
Holders Hill Circ. NW7 56 B7
Dollis Rd.
Holders Hill Cres. NW4 72 A2
Holders Hill Dr. NW4 72 A3
Holders Hill Gdns. NW4 72 B2
Holders Hill Rd. NW4 72 A2
Holders Hill Rd. NW7 72 B1
Holdgate St. SE7 136 A3
Westmoor St.
Holford Pl. WC1 10 D3
Holford Rd. NW3 91 F3
Holford St. WC1 10 E3
Holford St. WC1 111 G3
Holgate Av. SW11 149 G3
Holgate Gdns., Dag. 101 G5
Holgate Rd., Dag. 101 G5
Holland Av. SW20 183 F1
Holland Cl., Barn. 41 G7
Holland Cl., Brom. 205 F2
Holland Cl., Rom. 83 J5
Holland Cl., Stan. 52 E5
Holland Dr. SE23 171 H3
Holland Gdns. W14 128 B3
Holland Gro. SW9 131 G7
Holland Pk. W8 128 C2
Holland Pk. W11 128 C2
Holland Pk. Av. W11 128 B2
Holland Pk. Av., Ilf. 81 H6
Holland Pk. Gdns. W14 128 B1
Holland Pk. Ms. W11 128 B1
Holland Pk. Rd. W14 128 C3
Holland Pas. N1 111 J1
Basire St.
Holland Pl. W8 22 A3
Holland Rd. E6 116 C1
Holland Rd. E15 115 E3
Holland Rd. NW10 107 G1
Holland Rd. SE25 188 D5
Holland Rd. W14 128 A2
Holland Rd., Wem. 87 G6
Holland St. SE1 27 H1
Holland St. SE1 131 H1
Holland St. W8 128 D2
Holland Vil. Rd. W14 128 B2
Holland Wk. N19 92 D1
Duncombe Rd.
Holland Wk. W8 128 C2
Holland Wk., Stan. 52 D5
Holland Way, Brom. 205 F2
Hollands, The, Felt. 160 D4
Hollands, The, Wor.Pk. 197 F1
Hollar Rd. N16 94 C3
Stoke Newington High St.
Hollen St. W1 17 H3
Hollen St. W1 110 C6
Holles Cl., Hmptn. 161 G6
Holles St. W1 16 E3
Holles St. W1 110 B6
Holley Rd. W3 127 E2
Hollickwood Av. N12 57 J6
Holliday Sq. SW11 149 G3
Fowler Cl.
Hollidge Way, Dag. 101 H6
Hollies, The E11 79 G5
Hollies, The N20 57 G1
Oakleigh Pk. N.
Hollies, The, Har. 68 D4
Hollies Av., Sid. 175 J2
Hollies Cl. SW16 169 G6
Hollies Cl., Twick. 162 C2
Hollies End NW7 55 H5
Hollies Rd. W5 125 F4
Hollies Way SW12 150 A7
Bracken Av.
Holligrave Rd., Brom. 191 G1
Hollingbourne Av., Bexh. 139 F7
Hollingbourne Gdns. W13 104 E5
Hollingbourne Rd. SE24 151 J5
Hollingsworth Rd., Croy. 203 E6
Hollington Cres., N.Mal. 183 F6
Hollington Rd. E6 116 C3
Hollington Rd. N17 76 D2
Hollingworth Cl., W.Mol. 179 F4
Hollingworth Rd., Orp. 192 E6
Hollman Gdns. SW16 169 H6
Hollow, The, Wdf.Grn. 63 F4
Hollow Wk., Rich. 125 H7
Kew Rd.
Holloway Cl., West Dr. 120 B5
Holloway La., West Dr. 120 B6
Holloway Rd. E6 116 C3
Holloway Rd. E11 96 E3
Holloway Rd. N7 93 G6
Holloway Rd. N19 92 D2
Holloway St., Houns. 143 H3
Hollowfield Wk., Nthlt. 84 E6
Hollows, The, Brent. 125 J6
Kew Br. Rd.
Holly Av., Stan. 69 H2
Holly Bush Hill NW3 91 F4
Holly Bush La., Hmptn. 161 F7
Holly Bush Steps NW3 91 F4
Heath St.
Holly Bush Vale NW3 91 F4
Heath St.
Holly Cl. NW10 88 E7
Holly Cl., Buck.H. 64 A3
Holly Cl., Felt. 160 E5
Holly Cl., Wall. 200 B7
Holly Cres., Beck. 189 J5
Holly Cres., Wdf.Grn. 62 D7
Holly Dr. E4 46 B7
Holly Dr., Brent. 124 D6
Holly Fm. Rd., Sthl. 122 E5
Holly Gdns., West Dr. 120 C2
Holly Gro. NW9 70 C7
Holly Gro. SE15 152 C2
Holly Gro., Pnr. 67 E1
Holly Hedge Ter. SE13 154 D5
Holly Hill N21 43 F6
Holly Hill NW3 91 F4
Holly Hill Rd., Belv. 139 H5
Holly Hill Rd., Erith 139 H5
Holly Lo. Gdns. N6 92 A2
Holly Ms. SW10 30 D4
Holly Mt. NW3 91 F4
Holly Bush Hill
Holly Pk. N3 72 C3
Holly Pk. N4 75 F7
Holly Pk. Est. N4 75 F7
Blythwood Rd.
Holly Pk. Gdns. N3 72 D3
Holly Pk. Rd. N11 58 A5
Holly Pk. Rd. W7 124 C1
Holly Pl. NW3 91 F4
Holly Wk.
Holly Rd. E11 79 F7
Holly Rd. W4 126 D4
Dolman Rd.
Holly Rd., Hmptn. 161 J6
Holly Rd., Houns. 143 H4
Holly Rd., Twick. 162 D1
Holly St. E8 94 C6
Holly St. Est. E8 94 C7
Holly Ter. N6 92 A1
Highgate W. Hill
Holly Ter. N20 57 F2
Swan La.
Holly Vw. Cl. NW4 71 G6
Holly Village N6 92 B2
Swains La.
Holly Wk. NW3 91 F4
Holly Wk., Enf. 44 A3
Holly Wk., Rich. 145 H2
Holly Way, Mitch. 186 D4
Hollybank Cl., Hmptn. 161 G5
Hollyberry La. NW3 91 F4
Holly Wk.
Hollybrake Cl., Chis. 175 G7
Hollybush Cl. E11 79 G5
Hollybush Cl., Har. 68 B1
Hollybush Gdns. E2 113 E3
Hollybush Hill E11 79 F6
Hollybush Pl. E2 112/113 E3
Bethnal Grn. Rd.
Hollybush Rd., Kings.T. 163 H5
Hollybush St. E13 115 H3
Hollybush Wk. SW9 151 H4
Hollycroft Av. NW3 90 D3
Hollycroft Av., Wem. 87 J2
Hollycroft Cl., S.Croy. 202 B5
Hollycroft Cl., West Dr. 120 D6
Hollycroft Gdns., West Dr. 120 D6
Hollydale Cl., Nthlt. 85 H4
Dorchester Rd.
Hollydale Dr., Brom. 206 C3
Hollydale Rd. SE15 153 F1
Hollydene SE15 152 E1
Hollydown Way E11 96 D3
Hollyfield Av. N11 57 J5
Hollyfield Rd., Surb. 181 J7
Hollymead, Cars. 199 J3
Hollymount Cl. SE10 154 C1
Hollytree Cl. SW19 166 A1
Hollywood Gdns., Hayes 102 B6
Hollywood Ms. SW10 30 C5
Hollywood Rd. E4 61 H5
Hollywood Rd. SW10 30 C5
Hollywood Rd. SW10 129 F6
Hollywood Way, Wdf.Grn. 62 D7
Holm Oak Cl. SW15 148 C6
West Hill
Holm Oak Ms. SW4 150/151 E5
King's Av.
Holm Wk. SE3 155 G2
Blackheath Pk.
Holman Rd. SW11 149 G2
Holman Rd., Epsom 196 C5
Holmbridge Gdns., Enf. 45 G4
Holmbrook Dr. NW4 72 A5
Holmbury Ct. SW17 167 J3
Holmbury Ct. SW19 167 H7
Cavendish Rd.
Holmbury Gdns., Hayes 121 J1
Church Rd.
Holmbury Gro., Croy. 203 J7
Holmbury Pk., Brom. 174 B7
Holmbury Vw. E5 95 E1
Holmbush Rd. SW15 148 B6
Holmcote Gdns. N5 93 J5
Holmcroft Way, Brom. 192 C5
Holmdale Gdns. NW4 72 A5
Holmdale Rd. NW6 90 D5
Holmdale Rd., Chis. 175 F5
Holmdale Ter. N15 76 B7
Holmdene Av. NW7 55 G6
Holmdene Av. SE24 151 J5
Holmdene Av., Har. 67 H3
Holmdene Cl., Beck. 190 C2
Holme Lacey Rd. SE12 155 F6
Holme Rd. E6 116 B1
Holme Way, Stan. 52 C6
Holmead Rd. SW6 129 E7
Holmebury Cl., Bushey 52 B2
Holmefield Ct. NW3 91 H6
Holmes Av. E17 77 J3
Holmes Av. NW7 56 B5
Holmes Pl. SW10 30 D5
Holmes Rd. NW5 92 B5
Holmes Rd. SW19 167 F7
Holmes Rd., Twick. 162 C2
Holmes Ter. SE1 27 E3
Holmes Ter. SE1 131 G2
Holmesdale Av. SW14 146 B3
Holmesdale Cl. SE25 188 C3
Holmesdale Rd. N6 74 B7
Holmesdale Rd. SE25 188 A5
Holmesdale Rd., Bexh. 158 D2
Holmesdale Rd., Croy. 188 A5
Holmesdale Rd., Rich. 145 J1
Holmesdale Rd., Tedd. 163 F6
Holmesley Rd. SE23 153 H6
Holmewood Gdns. SW2 151 F7
Holmewood Rd. SE25 188 B3
Holmewood Rd. SW2 151 E7
Holmfield Av. NW4 72 A5
Holmhurst Rd., Belv. 139 H5
Holmleigh Rd. N16 94 B1
Holmleigh Rd. Est. N16 94 C1
Holmleigh Rd.
Holms St. E2 13 H1
Holms St. E2 112 D2
Holmshaw Cl. SE26 171 H4
Holmside Ri., Wat. 50 B3
Holmside Rd. SW12 150 A6
Holmsley Cl., N.Mal. 183 F6
Holmstall Av., Edg. 70 C3
Holmwood Cl., Har. 67 J3
Holmwood Cl., Nthlt. 85 H6
Holmwood Gdns. N3 72 D2
Holmwood Gdns., Wall. 200 B6
Holmwood Gro. NW7 54 D5
Holmwood Rd., Chess. 195 G5
Holmwood Rd., Ilf. 99 H2
Holmwood Vil. SE7 135 G5
Woolwich Rd.
Holne Chase N2 73 F6
Holne Chase, Mord. 184 C6
Holness Rd. E15 97 F6
Holroyd Rd. SW15 147 J4
Holstein Way, Erith 138 E3
Holstock Rd., Ilf. 99 F3
Holsworth Cl., Har. 67 J5
Holsworthy Sq. WC1 10 D6
Holsworthy Way, Chess. 195 F5
Holt, The, Ilf. 65 F6
Holt, The, Wall. 200 C4
Holt Cl. N10 74 A4
Holt Cl. SE28 118 B7
Holt Cl., Chig. 65 J5
Holt Ct. E15 96 C5
Clays La.
Holt Rd. E16 136 B1
Holt Rd., Wem. 87 E3
Holt Way, Chig. 65 J5
Holton St. E1 113 G4
Holtwhite Av., Enf. 43 J2
Holtwhites Hill, Enf. 43 H1
Holwell Pl., Pnr. 66 E4
Holwood Pk. Av., Orp. 206 C4
Holwood Pl. SW4 150 D4
Holybourne Av. SW15 147 G7
Holyhead Cl. E3 114 A3
Holyhead Cl. E6 116 C5
Valiant Way
Holyoak Rd. SE11 35 G1
Holyoake Ct. SE16 133 J2
Bryan Rd.
Holyoake Wk. N2 73 F3
Holyoake Wk. W5 105 F4
Holyport Rd. SW6 127 J7
Holyrood Av., Har. 85 E4
Holyrood Gdns., Edg. 70 B3
Holyrood Ms. E16 135 G1
Wesley Av.
Holyrood Rd., Barn. 41 F6
Holyrood St. SE1 28 D2
Holywell Cl. SE3 135 G6
Holywell Cl. SE16 132/133 E5
Masters Dr.
Holywell La. EC2 12 E5
Holywell La. EC2 112 B4
Holywell Row EC2 12 D6
Holywell Row EC2 112 B4
Home Cl., Cars. 199 J2
Home Cl., Nthlt. 103 F3
Home Ct., Felt. 160 A1
Home Fm. Cl., T.Ditt. 180 C7
Home Gdns., Dag. 101 J3
Home Lea, Orp. 207 J5
Home Mead, Stan. 69 F1
Home Pk. Rd. SW19 166 D3
Home Pk. Wk., Kings.T. 181 G4
Home Rd. SW11 149 H2
Homecroft Gdns., Loug. 48 E4
Homecroft Rd. N22 75 J1
Homecroft Rd. SE26 171 F5
Homefarm Rd. W7 104 B6
Homefield Av., Ilf. 81 H5
Homefield Cl. NW10 88 C6
Homefield Cl., Hayes 102 C4
Homefield Gdns. N2 73 G3
Homefield Gdns., Mitch. 185 F2
Homefield Ms., Beck. 190 A1
Homefield Pk., Sutt. 198 E6
Homefield Rd. SW19 166 A6
Homefield Rd. W4 127 F4
Homefield Rd., Brom. 191 J1
Homefield Rd., Edg. 54 D6
Homefield Rd., Walt. 179 E7
Homefield Rd., Wem. 86 D4
Homefield St. N1 12 D2
Homefield St. N1 112 B2
Homelands Dr. SE19 170 B7
Homeleigh Rd. SE15 153 G5
Homemead SW12 168 C2
Homemead Rd., Brom. 192 C5
Homemead Rd., Croy. 186 C6
Homer Cl., Bexh. 159 J1
Homer Dr. E14 134 A4
Homer Rd. E9 95 H6
Homer Rd., Croy. 189 G6
Homer Row W1 15 H2
Homer Row W1 109 H5
Homer St. W1 15 H2
Homer St. W1 109 H5
Homersham Rd., Kings.T. 182 A2
Homerton Gro. E9 95 G5
Homerton High St. E9 95 F5
Homerton Rd. E9 95 H5
Homerton Row E9 95 F5
Homerton Ter. E9 95 F6
Morning La.
Homesdale Cl. E11 79 G5
Homesdale Rd., Brom. 191 J4
Homesdale Rd., Orp. 193 H7
Homesfield NW11 72 D5
Homestall Rd. SE22 153 F5
Homestead, The N11 58 B4
Homestead Gdns., Esher 194 B5

Homestead Paddock N14 42 B5
Homestead Pk. NW2 89 F3
Homestead Rd. SW6 128 C7
Homestead Rd., Dag. 101 F2
Homewillow Cl. N21 43 H6
Homewood Cl., Hmptn. 161 F6
Fearnley Cres.
Homewood Cres., Chis. 175 H6
Honduras St. EC1 11 J5
Honey Cl., Dag. 101 H6
Honey La. EC2 20 A4
Honeybourne Rd. NW6 90 E5
Honeybourne Way, Orp. 207 G1
Honeybrook Rd. SW12 150 C7
Honeycroft, Loug. 48 D4
Honeyden Rd., Sid. 177 E6
Honeyman Cl. NW6 90 A7
Honeypot Cl. NW9 69 J4
Honeypot La. NW9 69 J3
Honeypot La., Stan. 69 J3
Honeysett Rd. N17 76 C2
Reform Row
Honeysuckle Cl., Sthl. 102 E7
Honeysuckle Gdns., Croy. 203 G1
Primrose La.
Honeywell Rd. SW11 149 J6
Honeywood Rd. NW10 107 F2
Honeywood Rd., Islw. 144 D4
Honeywood Wk., Cars. 199 J4
Honister Cl., Stan. 69 E1
Honister Gdns., Stan. 53 E7
Honister Pl., Stan. 69 E1
Honiton Rd. NW6 108 C2
Honiton Rd., Well. 157 J2
Honley Rd. SE6 154 B7
Honnor Gdns., Islw. 143 J3
London Rd.
Honor Oak Pk. SE23 153 F6
Honor Oak Ri. SE23 153 F6
Honor Oak Rd. SE23 171 F1
Hood Av. N14 42 B6
Hood Av. SW14 146 C5
Hood Cl., Croy. 201 H1
Parson's Mead
Hood Ct. EC4 19 F4
Hood Rd. SW20 165 F7
Hood Wk., Rom. 83 H1
Hoodcote Gdns. N21 43 H7
Hook, The, Barn. 41 G6
Hook Fm. Rd., Brom. 192 A5
Hook La., Well. 157 J5
Hook Ri. N., Surb. 196 A3
Hook Ri. S., Surb. 196 A3
Hook Ri. S. Ind. Pk., Surb. 196 A3
Hook Rd., Chess. 195 G5
Hook Rd., Surb. 195 H3
Hook Wk., Edg. 54 C6
Hookers Rd. E17 77 G3
Hooking Grn., Har. 67 H5
Hooks Cl. SE15 152/153 E1
Woods Rd.
Hooks Hall Dr., Dag. 101 J3
Hooks Way SE22 170 D1
Dulwich Common
Hookstone Way, Wdf.Grn. 64 A7
Hoop La. NW11 72 C7
Hooper Rd. E16 115 G6
Hooper St. E1 21 H5
Hooper St. E1 112 D6
Hooper's Ct. SW3 23 J4
Hop Gdns. WC2 18 A6
Hope Cl. N1 93 J6
Wallace Rd.
Hope Cl. SE12 173 H3
Hope Cl., Sutt. 199 F5
Hope Cl., Wdf.Grn. 63 J6
West Gro.
Hope Pk., Brom. 173 F7
Hope St. SW11 149 G3
Hope Wf. SE16 133 F2
St. Marychurch St.
Hopedale Rd. SE7 135 H6
Hopefield Av. NW6 108 B2
Hopes Cl., Houns. 123 G6
Old Cote Dr.
Hopetown St. E1 21 G2
Hopewell St. SE5 132 A7
Hopewell Yd. SE5 132 A7
Hopewell St.
Hopgood St. W12 127 J1
Macfarlane Rd.
Hopkins Cl. N10 58 A7
Cromwell Rd.
Hopkins Ms. E15 115 F1
West Rd.
Hopkins St. W1 17 G4
Hopkinsons Pl. NW1 110 A1
Fitzroy Rd.
Hoppers Rd. N13 59 G2
Hoppers Rd. N21 59 G2
Hoppett Rd. E4 62 E3
Hopping La. N1 93 H6
St. Mary's Gro.
Hoppingwood Av., N.Mal. 183 E3
Hopton Gdns. SE1 27 H1
Hopton Gdns. SE1 131 H1
Hopton Gdns., N.Mal. 183 G6
Hopton Rd. SW16 168 E5
Hopton St. SE1 27 H1
Hopton St. SE1 131 H1
Hopwood Cl. SW17 167 F3
Hopwood Rd. SE17 36 C5
Hopwood Rd. SE17 132 A6
Hopwood Wk. E8 94 D7
Wilman Gro.
Horace Av., Rom. 101 J1
Horace Rd. E7 97 H4
Horace Rd., Ilf. 81 F3
Horace Rd., Kings.T. 181 J3
Horatio Ct. SE16 133 F1
Rotherhithe St.
Horatio Pl. E14 134 C2
Cold Harbour
Horatio Pl. SW19 166 D7
Kingston Rd.
Horatio St. E2 13 H2
Horatio St. E2 112 C2
Horatius Way, Croy. 201 F5
Horbury Cres. W11 108 D7
Horbury Ms. W11 108 C7
Ladbroke Rd.
Horder Rd. SW6 148 B1
Hordle Prom. E. SE15 37 G7
Hordle Prom. N. SE15 37 E7
Hordle Prom. S. SE15 37 E7
Hordle Prom. W. SE15 37 E7
Horizon Way SE7 135 H4
Horle Wk. SE5 151 H2
Lilford Rd.
Horley Cl., Bexh. 159 G5
Horley Rd. SE9 174 B4
Hormead Rd. W9 108 C4
Horn La. SE10 135 G4
Horn La. W3 106 C7
Horn La., Wdf.Grn. 63 G6
Horn Link Way SE10 135 G4
Horn Pk. Cl. SE12 155 H5
Horn Pk. La. SE12 155 H5
Hornbeam Cl. NW7 55 F3
Marsh La.
Hornbeam Cl. SE11 34 E1
Hornbeam Cl., Borwd. 38 A1
Hornbeam Cl., Buck.H. 64 A3
Hornbeam Rd.
Hornbeam Cl., Ilf. 99 G5
Hornbeam Cl., Nthlt. 85 F5
Hornbeam Cres., Brent. 125 E7
Hornbeam Gro. E4 63 E3
Hornbeam La. E4 47 E5
Hornbeam La., Bexh. 159 J2
Hornbeam Rd., Buck.H. 64 A3
Hornbeam Rd., Hayes 102 C5
Hornbeam Ter., Cars. 199 H1
Hornbeam Twr. E11 96 D3
Hollydown Way
Hornbeam Wk., Rich. 163 J3
Hornbeam Way, Brom. 192 D6
Hornbeams Ri. N11 58 A6
Hornblower Cl. SE16 133 H4
Greenland Quay
Hornbuckle Cl., Har. 86 A2
Hornby Cl. NW3 91 G7
Horncastle Cl. SE12 155 G7
Horncastle Rd. SE12 155 G7
Hornchurch Cl., Kings.T. 163 G4
Horndean Cl. SW15 165 G1
Bessborough Rd.
Horndon Cl., Rom. 83 J1
Horndon Grn., Rom. 83 J1
Horndon Rd., Rom. 83 J2
Horne Way SW15 147 J2
Horner La., Mitch. 185 G2
Hornfair Rd. SE7 135 J6
Horniman Dr. SE23 171 E1
Horning Cl. SE9 174 B4
Horns End Pl., Pnr. 66 C4
Horns Rd., Ilf. 81 F6
Hornsey La. N6 92 B1
Hornsey La. N19 74 C7
Hornsey La. Est. N19 74 D7
Hornsey La.
Hornsey La. Gdns. N6 74 C7
Hornsey Pk. Rd. N8 75 F3
Hornsey Ri. N19 74 D7
Hornsey Ri. Gdns. N19 74 D7
Hornsey Rd. N7 93 E2
Hornsey Rd. N19 93 E2
Hornsey St. N7 93 F5
Hornshay St. SE15 133 F6
Hornton Pl. W8 22 A4
Hornton Pl. W8 128 D2
Hornton St. W8 128 D2
Horsa Cl., Wall. 201 E7
Horsa Rd. SE12 155 J7
Horsa Rd., Erith 139 J7
Horse & Dolphin Yd. W1 17 J5
Horse Fair, Kings.T. 181 G2
Horse Guards Av. SW1 26 A2
Horse Guards Av. SW1 130 E1
Horse Guards Rd. SW1 25 J2
Horse Guards Rd. SW1 130 D1
Horse Leaze E6 116 D6
Horse Ride SW1 25 H2
Horse Ride SW1 130 C1
Horse Rd. E7 97 H3
Centre Rd.
Horse Shoe Cres., Nthlt. 103 G2
Horse Shoe Grn., Sutt. 198/199 E2
Aultone Way
Horse Yd. N1 111 H1
Essex Rd.
Horsebridge Cl., Dag. 119 E1
Horsecroft Rd., Edg. 54 D7
Horseferry Pl. SE10 134 C6
Horseferry Rd. E14 113 H7
Horseferry Rd. SW1 25 H6
Horseferry Rd. SW1 130 D4
Horsell Rd. N5 93 G5
Horselydown La. SE1 29 F3
Horselydown La. SE1 132 C2
Horsenden Av., Grnf. 86 B5
Horsenden Cres., Grnf. 86 C5
Horsenden La. N., Grnf. 86 C6
Horsenden La. S., Grnf. 104 D2
Horseshoe Cl. E14 134 C5
Ferry St.
Horseshoe Cl. NW2 89 H2
Horseshoe La. N20 56 A1
Horseshoe La., Enf. 43 J3
Chase Side
Horsfeld Gdns. SE9 156 B5
Horsfeld Rd. SE9 156 A5
Horsford Rd. SW2 151 F5
Horsham Av. N12 57 H5
Horsham Rd., Bexh. 159 G5
Horsham Rd., Felt. 141 F6
Horsley Dr., Croy. 204 C7
Horsley Dr., Kings.T. 163 G5
Horsley Rd. E4 62 C2
Horsley Rd., Brom. 191 H1
Palace Rd.
Horsley St. SE17 36 B5
Horsley St. SE17 132 A6
Horsmonden Cl., Orp. 193 H7
Horsmonden Rd. SE4 153 J5
Hortensia Rd. SW10 30 C7
Hortensia Rd. SW10 129 F7
Horticultural Pl. W4 126 D5
Heathfield Ter.
Horton Av. NW2 90 B4
Horton Br. Rd., West Dr. 120 C1
Horton Cl., West Dr. 120 C1
Horton Ind. Pk., West Dr. 120 C1
Horton Rd. E8 94 E6
Horton Rd., West Dr. 120 D1
Horton St. SE13 154 B3
Horton Way, Croy. 189 G5
Hortus Rd. E4 62 C2
Hortus Rd., Sthl. 123 F2
Hosack Rd. SW17 167 J2
Hoser Av. SE12 173 G2
Hosier La. EC1 19 G2
Hosier La. EC1 111 H5
Hoskins Cl. E16 115 J6
Hoskins Cl., Hayes 121 J5
Cranford Dr.
Hoskins St. SE10 134 D5
Hospital Br. Rd., Twick. 143 H7
Hospital Rd. E9 95 G5
Homerton Row
Hospital Rd., Houns. 143 G3
Hotham Cl., W.Mol. 179 G3
Garrick Gdns.
Hotham Rd. SW15 147 J3
Hotham Rd. SW19 167 F7
Hotham Rd. Ms. SW19 167 F7
Haydons Rd.
Hotham St. E15 114 E1
Hothfield Pl. SE16 133 F3
Lower Rd.
Hotspur Rd., Nthlt. 103 G2
Hotspur St. SE11 34 E3
Hotspur St. SE11 131 G5
Houblon Rd., Rich. 145 H5
Houghton Cl. E8 94 C6
Buttermere Wk.
Houghton Cl., Hmptn. 161 E6
Houghton Rd. N15 76 C5
West Grn. Rd.
Houghton St. WC2 18 D4
Houlder Cres., Croy. 201 H6
Houndsden Rd. N21 43 F6
Houndsditch EC3 20 E3
Houndsditch EC3 112 B6
Houndsfield Rd. N9 44 E7
Hounslow Av., Houns. 143 H5
Hounslow Gdns., Houns. 143 H5
Hounslow Rd. (Feltham), Felt. 160 B1
Hounslow Rd. (Hanworth), Felt. 160 D4
Hounslow Rd., Twick. 143 J6
Houseman Way SE5 132 A7
Hopewell St.
Houston Pl., Esher 194 B1
Lime Tree Av.
Houston Rd. SE23 171 H2
Houston Rd., Surb. 181 E6
Hove Av. E17 77 J5
Hove Gdns., Sutt. 199 E1
Hoveden Rd. NW2 90 B5
Hoveton Rd. SE28 118 C6
Howard Av., Bex. 176 C1
Howard Cl. N11 58 A2
Howard Cl. NW2 90 B4
Howard Cl. W3 106 B6
Howard Cl., Hmptn. 161 J6
Howard Cl., Loug. 48 B6
Howard Dr., Borwd. 38 D4
Howard Ms. N5 93 H4
Hamilton Pk.
Howard Pl. SW1 25 F6
Howard Rd. E6 116 C2
Howard Rd. E11 97 E3
Howard Rd. E17 78 A3
Howard Rd. N15 76 B6
Howard Rd. N16 94 A4
Howard Rd. NW2 90 A4
Howard Rd. SE20 189 F1
Howard Rd. SE25 188 D5
Howard Rd., Bark. 117 G1
Howard Rd., Brom. 173 G7
Howard Rd., Ilf. 99 E4
Howard Rd., Islw. 144 C3
Howard Rd., N.Mal. 183 E3
Howard Rd., Sthl. 103 H6
Howard Rd., Surb. 181 J6
Howard St., T.Ditt. 181 E7
Howard Wk. N2 73 F4
Howard Way, Barn. 40 A5
Howards Cl., Pnr. 66 B2
Howards Crest Cl., Beck. 190 C2
Howards La. SW15 147 H4
Howards Rd. E13 115 G3
Howarth Ct. E15 96 C5
Clays La.
Howarth Rd. SE2 138 A5
Howberry Cl., Edg. 53 G6
Howberry Rd., Edg. 53 G6
Howberry Rd., Stan. 53 G6
Howberry Rd., Th.Hth. 188 A1
Howbury Rd. SE15 153 F3
Howcroft Cres. N3 56 D7
Howcroft La., Grnf. 104 A3
Cowgate Rd.
Howden Cl. SE28 118 D7
Howden Rd. SE25 188 C2
Howden St. SE15 152 D3
Howe Cl., Rom. 83 G1
Howell Cl., Rom. 82 D5
Howell Wk. SE1 35 H2
Howes Cl. N3 72 D3
Howfield Pl. N17 76 C3
Howgate Rd. SW14 146 D3

Howick Pl. SW1 25 G6
Howick Pl. SW1 130 C3
Howie St. SW11 129 H7
Howitt Cl. NW3 91 H6
Howitt Rd.
Howitt Rd. NW3 91 H6
Howland Est. SE16 133 F3
Howland Ms. E. W1 17 G1
Howland St. W1 17 F1
Howland St. W1 110 C5
Howland Way SE16 133 H2
Howletts Rd. SE24 151 J6
Howley Pl. W2 14 D1
Howley Pl. W2 109 F5
Howley Rd., Croy. 201 H3
Hows St. E2 13 F1
Hows St. E2 112 C2
Howsman Rd. SW13 127 G6
Howson Rd. SE4 153 H4
Howson Ter., Rich. 145 H6
Howton Pl., Bushey 52 A1
Hoxton Mkt. N1 12 D4
Hoxton Sq. N1 12 D4
Hoxton Sq. N1 112 B3
Hoxton St. N1 12 E4
Hoxton St. N1 112 B1
Hoy St. E16 115 F6
Hoylake Gdns., Mitch. 186 C3
Hoylake Gdns., Ruis. 84 B1
Hoylake Gdns., Wat. 50 D4
Hoylake Rd. W3 107 E6
Hoyland Cl. SE15 132/133 E7
Commercial Way
Hoyle Rd. SW17 167 H5
Hubbard Dr., Chess. 195 F6
Hubbard Rd. SE27 169 J4
Hubbard St. E15 114 E1
Hubbinet Ind. Est., Rom. 83 J3
Hubert Gro. SW9 151 E3
Hubert Rd. E6 116 A3
Huddart St. E3 114 A5
Huddleston Cl. E2 113 F2
Huddleston Rd. N7 92 D4
Huddlestone Rd. E7 97 F4
Huddlestone Rd. NW2 89 H6
Hudson Ct. E14 134 A5
Napier Av.
Hudson Ct. SW19 167 E7
Hudson Gdns., Orp. 207 J6
Superior Dr.
Hudson Pl. SE18 137 F5
Hudson Rd., Bexh. 159 F2
Hudson Rd., Hayes 121 G6
Hudson's Pl. SW1 33 E1
Huggin Ct. EC4 20 A5
Huggin Hill EC4 20 A5
Huggins Pl. SW2 169 F1
Roupell Rd.
Hugh Dalton Av. SW6 128 C6
Hugh Gaitskell Cl. SW6 128 C6
Hugh Ms. SW1 33 E2
Hugh Pl. SW1 33 H1
Hugh St. SW1 32 E2
Hugh St. SW1 130 B4
Hughan Rd. E15 96 D5
Hughenden Av., Har. 69 E5
Hughenden Gdns., Nthlt. 102 C3
Hughenden Rd., Wor.Pk. 183 G7
Hughendon Ter. E15 96 C4
Westdown Rd.
Hughes Rd., Hayes 102 B7
Hughes Wk., Croy. 187 J7
St. Saviours Rd.
Hugo Rd. N19 92 C4
Hugon Rd. SW6 148 E3
Huguenot Pl. E1 21 G1
Huguenot Pl. E1 112 C5
Huguenot Pl. SW18 149 F5
Huguenot Sq. SE15 152/153 E3
Scylla Rd.
Hull Cl. SE16 133 G2
Hull Pl. E16 136/137 E2
Barge Ho. Rd.
Hull St. EC1 11 J4
Hullbridge Ms. N1 112 A1
Sherborne St.
Hulse Av., Bark. 99 G6
Hulse Av., Rom. 83 H1
Hulse Ter., Ilf. 99 F5
Buttsbury Rd.
Humber Cl., West Dr. 120 A1
Humber Dr. W10 108 A4
Humber Rd. NW2 89 H2
Humber Rd. SE3 135 F6
Humberstone Rd. E13 115 J3
Humberton Cl. E9 95 H5
Marsh Hill
Humbolt Rd. W6 128 B6
Hume Ter. E16 115 J6
Prince Regent La.
Hume Way, Ruis. 66 A6
Humes Av. W7 124 B3
Humphrey Cl., Ilf. 80 C1
Humphrey St. SE1 37 F3
Humphrey St. SE1 132 C5
Humphries Cl., Dag. 101 F4
Hundred Acre NW9 71 F2
Hungerdown E4 62 C1
Hungerford Br. SE1 26 B1
Hungerford Br. SE1 131 E1
Hungerford Br. WC2 26 B1
Hungerford Br. WC2 131 E1
Hungerford La. WC2 26 A1
Hungerford Rd. N7 92 E5
Hungerford St. E1 112/113 E6
Commercial Rd.
Hunsdon Cl., Dag. 101 E6
Hunsdon Rd. SE14 133 G6
Hunslett St. E2 113 F2
Royston St.
Hunston Rd., Mord. 198 E1
Hunt Rd., Sthl. 123 G3
Hunt St. W11 128 A1
Hunt Way SE22 170 D1
Dulwich Common
Hunter Cl. SE1 28 C6
Hunter Cl. SW12 168 A1
Balham Pk. Rd.
Hunter Cl., Borwd. 38 C5
Hunter Ho., Felt. 160 A1
Hunter Rd. SW20 183 J1
Hunter Rd., Ilf. 99 E5
Hunter Rd., Th.Hth. 188 A3
Hunter St. WC1 10 B5
Hunter St. WC1 111 E4
Hunter Wk. E13 115 G2
Hunter Wk., Borwd. 38 C5
Ashley Dr.
Huntercrombe Gdns., Wat. 50 C4
Hunters, The, Beck. 190 C1
Hunters Ct., Rich. 145 G5
Friars La.
Hunters Gro., Har. 69 F4
Hunters Gro., Hayes 122 A1
Hunters Gro., Orp. 207 E4
Hunters Hall Rd., Dag. 101 G4
Hunters Hill, Ruis. 84 C3
Hunters Meadow SE19 170 B4
Dulwich Wd. Av.
Hunters Rd., Chess. 195 H3
Hunters Sq., Dag. 101 G4
Hunters Way, Croy. 202 B4
Brownlow Rd.
Hunters Way, Enf. 43 G1
Hunting Gate Cl., Enf. 43 G3
Hunting Gate Dr., Chess. 195 H7
Hunting Gate Ms., Sutt. 199 E3
Hunting Gate Ms., Twick. 162 B1
Colne Rd.
Huntingdon Cl., Mitch. 187 E3
Huntingdon Gdns. W4 126 C7
Huntingdon Gdns., Wor.Pk. 197 J3
Huntingdon Rd. N2 73 H3
Huntingdon Rd. N9 61 F1
Huntingdon St. E16 115 F6
Huntingdon St. N1 93 F7
Huntingfield, Croy. 203 J7
Huntingfield Rd. SW15 147 G5
Huntings Rd., Dag. 101 G6
Huntley Dr. N3 56 D6
Huntley St. WC1 9 G6
Huntley St. WC1 110 C4
Huntley Way SW20 183 G2
Huntly Rd. SE25 188 B4
Hunton St. E1 13 H6
Hunton St. E1 112 D4
Hunt's Cl. SE3 155 G2
Hunt's Ct. WC2 17 J6
Hunts La. E15 114 C2
Hunts Mead, Enf. 45 G3
Hunts Mead Cl., Chis. 174 C7
Hunts Slip Rd. SE21 170 B3
Huntsman St. SE17 36 C2
Huntsman St. SE17 132 A4
Huntsmans Cl., Felt. 160 B4
Huntsmoor Rd., Epsom 196 D5
Huntspill St. SW17 167 F3
Huntsworth Ms. NW1 7 J6
Hurley Cres. SE16 133 G2
Marlow Way
Hurley Rd. SE11 35 F2
Hurley Rd. SE11 131 G4
Hurley Rd., Grnf. 103 H6
Hurlingham Ct. SW6 148 C3
Hurlingham Gdns. SW6 148 C3
Hurlingham Rd. SW6 148 C2
Hurlingham Rd., Bexh. 139 F7
Hurlingham Sq. SW6 148/149 E3
Peterborough Rd.
Hurlock St. N5 93 H3
Hurlstone Rd. SE25 188 A5
Hurn Ct. Rd., Houns. 142 D2
Renfrew Rd.
Huron Cl., Orp. 207 J6
Winnipeg Dr.
Huron Rd. SW17 168 A2
Hurren Cl. SE3 154 E3
Hurry Cl. E15 97 E7
Hursley Rd., Chig. 65 J5
Tufter Rd.
Hurst Av. E4 62 A4
Hurst Av. N6 74 C6
Hurst Cl. E4 62 A3
Hurst Cl. NW11 72 E6
Hurst Cl., Brom. 205 F1
Hurst Cl., Chess. 196 A5
Hurst Cl., Nthlt. 85 F5
Hurst Est. SE2 138 D5
Hurst La. SE2 138 D5
Hurst La., E.Mol. 179 J4
Hurst Ri., Barn. 40 D3
Hurst Rd. E17 78 B3
Hurst Rd. N21 59 G1
Hurst Rd., Bex. 176 D1
Hurst Rd., Buck.H. 64 A1
Hurst Rd., Croy. 202 A5
Hurst Rd., E.Mol. 179 H3
Hurst Rd., Erith 139 J7
Hurst Rd., Sid. 176 A2
Hurst Rd., Walt. 178 C5
Hurst Rd., W.Mol. 179 E3
Hurst Springs, Bex. 177 E1
Hurst St. SE24 151 H6
Hurst Vw. Rd., S.Croy. 202 B7
Hurst Way, S.Croy. 202 B6
Hurstbourne, Esher 194 C6
Hurstbourne Gdns., Bark. 99 H6
Hurstbourne Rd. SE23 171 H1
Hurstcourt Rd., Sutt. 198 E2
Hurstdene Av., Brom. 205 F1
Hurstdene Gdns. N15 76 B7
Hurstfield, Brom. 191 G5
Hurstfield Rd., W.Mol. 179 G3
Hurstleigh Gdns., Ilf. 80 C1
Hurstmead Ct., Edg. 54 B4
Hurstway Wk. W11 108 A7
Hurstwood Av. E18 79 H4
Hurstwood Av., Bex. 176 E1
Hurstwood Dr., Brom. 192 C3
Hurstwood Rd. NW11 72 B4
Hurtwood Rd., Walt. 179 F7
Huson Cl. NW3 91 H7
Hussars Cl., Houns. 142 E3
Husseywell Cres., Brom. 205 G1
Hutchings St. E14 134 A2
Hutchings Wk. NW11 73 E4
Hutchins Cl. E15 96 C7
Gibbins Rd.
Hutchins Rd. SE28 118 A7
Hutchinson Ter., Wem. 87 G3
Hutton Cl., Grnf. 86 A5
Mary Peters Dr.
Hutton Cl., Wdf.Grn. 63 H6
Hutton Gdns., Har. 51 J7
Hutton Gro. N12 57 E5
Hutton La., Har. 51 J7
Hutton Row, Edg. 54 C7
Pavilion Way
Hutton St. EC4 19 F4
Hutton Wk., Har. 51 J7
Huxbear St. SE4 153 J5
Huxley Cl., Nthlt. 103 E1
Huxley Dr., Rom. 82 B7
Huxley Gdns. NW10 105 J3
Huxley Par. N18 60 A5
Huxley Pl. N13 59 H4
Huxley Rd. E10 96 C2
Huxley Rd. N18 60 A4
Huxley Rd., Well. 157 J3
Huxley Sayze N18 60 A5
Huxley St. W10 108 B3
Hyacinth Cl., Hmptn. 161 G6
Gresham Rd.
Hyacinth Cl., Ilf. 98 E6
Hyacinth Ct., Pnr. 66 C3
Tulip Ct.
Hyacinth Rd. SW15 165 G1
Hycliffe Gdns., Chig. 65 F4
Hyde, The NW9 71 E5
Hyde Cl. E13 115 G2
Hyde Cl., Barn. 40 C3
Hyde Ct. N20 57 G3
Hyde Cres. NW9 71 E5
Hyde Est. Rd. NW9 71 F5
Hyde Ho. NW9 71 E5
Hyde La. SW11 149 H1
Battersea Br. Rd.
Hyde Pk. SW7 23 G1
Hyde Pk. SW7 129 J1
Hyde Pk. W1 23 G1
Hyde Pk. W1 129 J1
Hyde Pk. W2 23 G1
Hyde Pk. W2 129 J1
Hyde Pk. Av. N21 59 J2
Hyde Pk. Cor. W1 24 C3
Hyde Pk. Cor. W1 130 A2
Hyde Pk. Cres. W2 15 G4
Hyde Pk. Cres. W2 109 H6
Hyde Pk. Gdns. N21 59 J1
Hyde Pk. Gdns. W2 15 F5
Hyde Pk. Gdns. W2 109 G7
Hyde Pk. Gdns. Ms. W2 15 F5
Hyde Pk. Gate SW7 22 D4
Hyde Pk. Gate SW7 129 F2
Hyde Pk. Gate Ms. SW7 22 D4
Hyde Pk. Pl. W2 15 H5
Hyde Pk. Pl. W2 109 H7
Hyde Pk. Sq. W2 15 G4
Hyde Pk. Sq. W2 109 H6
Hyde Pk. Sq. Ms. W2 15 G4
Hyde Pk. St. W2 15 G4
Hyde Pk. St. W2 109 H6
Hyde Rd. N1 112 A1
Hyde Rd., Bexh. 159 F2
Hyde Rd., Rich. 145 J5
Albert Rd.
Hyde St. SE8 134 A6
Deptford High St.
Hyde Vale SE10 134 C7
Hyde Wk., Mord. 184 D7
Hyde Way N9 60 C2
Hyde Way, Hayes 121 J4
Hydefield Cl. N21 60 A1
Hydefield Ct. N9 60 B2
Hyderabad Way E15 96 E7
Hydes Pl. N1 93 H7
Compton Av.
Hydeside Gdns. N9 60 C2
Hydethorpe Av. N9 60 C2
Hydethorpe Rd. SW12 168 C1
Hylands Rd. E17 78 D2
Hylton St. SE18 137 J4
Hyndewood SE23 171 G3
Hyndman St. SE15 132 E6
Hynton Rd., Dag. 100 C2
Hyrstdene, S.Croy. 201 H4
Hyson Rd. SE16 132/133 E4
Galleywall Rd.
Hythe Av., Bexh. 139 F7
Hythe Cl. N18 60 D4
Hythe Path, Th.Hth. 188 A3
Hythe Rd. NW10 107 G4
Hythe Rd., Th.Hth. 188 A2
Hyver Hill NW7 38 D6

I

Ian Sq., Enf. 45 G1
Lansbury Rd.
Ibbetson Path, Loug. 49 E3
Ibbotson Av. E16 115 F6
Ibbott St. E1 113 F4
Mantus Rd.
Iberian Av., Wall. 200 D4
Ibis La. W4 146 C1
Ibis Way, Hayes 102 D6
Cygnet Way
Ibscott Cl., Dag. 101 J6
Ibsley Gdns. SW15 165 G1
Ibsley Way, Barn. 41 H5
Ice Wf. Marina N1 10 B1
Iceland Rd. E3 114 A1
Iceni Ct. E3 113 J1
Roman Rd.
Ickburgh Est. E5 94/95 E3
Ickburgh Rd.
Ickburgh Rd. E5 94 E3
Ickleton Rd. SE9 174 B4
Icknield Dr., Ilf. 81 E5
Ickworth Pk. Rd. E17 77 H4
Ida Rd. N15 76 A5
Ida St. E14 114 C6
Iden Cl., Brom. 191 E3
Idlecombe Rd. SW17 168 A6
Idmiston Rd. E15 97 F5
Idmiston Rd. SE27 169 J3

Idmiston Rd., Wor.Pk. 183 F7
Idmiston Sq., Wor.Pk. 183 F7
Idol La. EC3 20 D6
Idonia St. SE8 133 J7
Iffley Rd. W6 127 H3
Ifield Rd. SW10 30 B5
Ifield Rd. SW10 129 E6
Ifor Evans Pl. E1 113 G4
Mile End Rd.
Ightham Rd., Erith 139 G7
Ikea Twr. NW10 88 D5
Ilbert St. W10 108 A3
Ilchester Gdns. W2 14 A5
Ilchester Gdns. W2 108 E7
Ilchester Pl. W14 128 C3
Ilchester Rd., Dag. 100 B5
Ildersly Gro. SE21 170 A2
Ilderton Rd. SE15 133 F7
Ilderton Rd. SE16 133 E5
Ilex Cl., Sun. 178 C2
Oakington Dr.
Ilex Ho. N4 75 F7
Ilex Rd. NW10 89 F6
Ilex Way SW16 169 G5
Ilford Hill, Ilf. 98 D3
Ilford La., Ilf. 98 E3
Ilfracombe Gdns., Rom. 82 B7
Ilfracombe Rd., Brom. 173 F3
Iliffe St. SE17 35 H3
Iliffe St. SE17 131 H5
Iliffe Yd. SE17 35 H3
Ilkeston Ct. E5 95 G4
Overbury St.
Ilkley Cl. SE19 170 A6
Ilkley Rd. E16 115 J5
Ilkley Rd., Wat. 50 D5
Illingworth Cl., Mitch. 185 G3
Illingworth Way, Enf. 44 B4
Ilmington Rd., Har. 69 G6
Ilminster Gdns. SW11 149 H4
Imber Cl. N14 42 C7
Imber Cl., Esher 194 A1
Ember La.
Imber Ct. Trd. Est., E.Mol. 180 A6
Imber Gro., Esher 180 A7
Imber Pk. Rd., Esher 194 A1
Imber St. N1 112 A1
Imer Pl., T.Ditt. 180 C7
Imperial Av. N16 94 C3
Victorian Rd.
Imperial Cl., Har. 67 G6
Imperial College Rd. SW7 22 E6
Imperial College Rd. SW7 129 G3
Imperial Dr., Har. 67 G7
Imperial Gdns., Mitch. 186 B3
Imperial Ms. E6 115 J2
Central Pk. Rd.
Imperial Rd. N22 74 E1
Imperial Rd. SW6 149 F1
Imperial Rd., Felt. 141 H7
Imperial Sq. SW6 149 E1
Imperial St. E3 114 C3
Imperial Way, Chis. 175 F3
Imperial Way, Croy. 201 F6
Imperial Way, Har. 69 H6
Imre Cl. W12 127 H1
Ellerslie Rd.
Inca Dr. SE9 156 E7
Inchmery Rd. SE6 172 B2
Inchwood, Croy. 204 B4
Independent Pl. E8 94 C5
Downs Pk. Rd.
Independents Rd. SE3 155 F3
Blackheath Village
Inderwick Rd. N8 75 F5
Indescon Ct. E14 134 B2
India Pl. WC2 18 C5
India St. EC3 21 F4
India Way W12 107 H7
Indigo Ms. E14 114 C7
Ashton St.
Indigo Ms. N16 94 A3
Indus Rd. SE7 135 J7
Industry Ter. SW9 151 G3
Canterbury Cres.
Ingal Rd. E13 115 G4
Ingate Pl. SW8 150 B1
Ingatestone Rd. E12 97 J1
Ingatestone Rd. SE25 188 E4
Ingatestone Rd., Wdf.Grn. 63 G7
Ingelow Rd. SW8 150 B2
Ingersoll Rd. W12 127 H1
Ingestre Pl. W1 17 G4
Ingestre Rd. E7 97 G4
Ingestre Rd. NW5 92 B4
Ingham Rd. NW6 90 D4
Ingle Cl., Pnr. 67 E3
Inglebert St. EC1 11 E3
Ingleborough St. SW9 151 G2
Ingleby Dr., Har. 86 A3
Ingleby Rd., Dag. 101 H6
Ingleby Rd., Ilf. 98 E1
Ingleby Way, Chis. 174 D5
Ingledew Rd. SE18 137 G5
Inglehurst Gdns., Ilf. 80 C5
Inglemere Rd. SE23 171 G3
Inglemere Rd., Mitch. 167 J7
Inglesham Wk. E9 95 J6
Ingleside Cl., Beck. 172 A7
Ingleside Gro. SE3 135 F6
Inglethorpe St. SW6 148 A1
Ingleton Av., Well. 158 A5
Ingleton Rd. N18 60 D6
Ingleton St. SW9 151 G2
Ingleway N12 57 G6
Inglewood Cl. E14 134 A4
Inglewood Cl., Ilf. 65 J6
Inglewood Copse, Brom. 192 B2
Inglewood Rd. NW6 90 D5
Inglis Barracks NW7 56 B6
Inglis Rd. W5 105 J7
Inglis Rd., Croy. 202 C1
Inglis St. SE5 151 H1
Ingram Av. NW11 73 F7
Ingram Cl. SE11 34 D1
Ingram Cl., Stan. 53 F5
Ingram Rd. N2 73 H4
Ingram Rd., Th.Hth. 187 J1
Ingram Way, Grnf. 104 A1
Ingrave Ho., Dag. 118 B1
Ingrave St. SW11 149 G3
Ingress St. W4 126/127 E5
Devonshire Rd.
Inigo Jones Rd. SE7 136 B7
Inigo Pl. WC2 18 A5
Inkerman Rd. NW5 92 B6
Inkerman Ter. W8 128 D3
Allen St.
Inks Grn. E4 62 C5
Inman Rd. NW10 106 E1
Inman Rd. SW18 149 F7
Inmans Row, Wdf.Grn. 63 G4
Inner Circle NW1 8 B3
Inner Circle NW1 110 A3
Inner Pk. Rd. SW19 166 A1
Inner Ring E., Houns. 140 E3
Inner Ring W., Houns. 140 D3
Inner Temple La. EC4 19 E4
Innes Cl. SW20 184 B2
Innes Gdns. SW15 147 H6
Innes Yd., Croy. 201 J3
Whitgift St.
Inniskilling Rd. E13 115 J2
Innovation Cl., Wem. 105 H1
Inskip Cl. E10 96 B2
Inskip Rd., Dag. 100 D1
Institute Pl. E8 94/95 E5
Amhurst Rd.
Instone Cl., Wall. 201 E7
Integer Gdns. E11 78 D7
Forest Rd.
Interchange E. Ind. Est. E5 95 F1
Theydon Rd.
International Av., Houns. 122 C5
International Trd. Est., Sthl. 122 B3
Inver Cl. E5 95 F2
Theydon Rd.
Inver Ct. W2 14 B4
Inveraray Pl. SE18 137 G6
Old Mill Rd.
Inverclyde Gdns., Rom. 82 D4
Inveresk Gdns., Wor.Pk. 197 F3
Inverforth Cl. NW3 91 F2
North End Way
Inverforth Rd. N11 58 B5
Inverine Rd. SE7 135 H5
Invermore Pl. SE18 137 F4
Inverness Av., Enf. 44 B1
Inverness Dr., Ilf. 65 H6
Inverness Gdns. W8 22 A2
Inverness Ms. E16 136/137 E2
Barge Ho. Rd.
Inverness Ms. W2 14 B5
Inverness Pl. W2 14 B5
Inverness Pl. W2 109 E7
Inverness Rd. N18 60/61 E5
Aberdeen Rd.
Inverness Rd., Houns. 143 F4
Inverness Rd., Sthl. 123 E4
Inverness Rd., Wor.Pk. 198 A1
Inverness St. NW1 110 B1
Inverness Ter. W2 14 B5
Inverness Ter. W2 109 E7
Inverton Rd. SE15 153 G4
Invicta Cl., Chis. 174 D5
Invicta Gro., Nthlt. 103 F3
Invicta Plaza SE1 27 G1
Invicta Rd. SE3 135 G7
Inville Rd. SE17 36 C4
Inville Rd. SE17 132 A5
Inwen Ct. SE8 133 H5
Inwood Av., Houns. 143 J3
Inwood Cl., Croy. 203 H2
Inwood Rd., Houns. 143 H4
Inworth St. SW11 149 H2
Inworth Wk. N1 111 J1
Popham St.
Ion Sq. E2 13 H2
Iona Cl. SE6 154 A7
Iona Cl., Mord. 184 E7
Ipswich Rd. SW17 168 A6
Ireland Cl. E6 116 C5
Bradley Stone Rd.
Ireland Pl. N22 58/59 E7
Whittington Rd.
Ireland Yd. EC4 19 H4
Ireland Yd. EC4 111 H6
Irene Rd. SW6 148 D1
Irene Rd., Orp. 193 J7
Ireton Cl. N10 58 A7
Cromwell Rd.
Ireton St. E3 114 A4
Tidworth Rd.
Iris Av., Bex. 159 E5
Iris Cl. E6 116 B4
Iris Cl., Croy. 203 G1
Iris Cl., Surb. 181 J7
Iris Ct., Pnr. 66 C3
Iris Cres., Bexh. 139 F6
Iris Rd., Epsom 196 B5
Iris Wk., Edg. 54 C4
Ash Cl.
Iris Way E4 61 J6
Irkdale Av., Enf. 44 C1
Iron Br. Cl. NW10 88 E5
Iron Br. Cl., Sthl. 123 J1
Iron Br. Rd., Uxb. 120 D2
Iron Br. Rd., West Dr. 120 D2
Iron Mill Pl. SW18 148/149 E6
Garratt La.
Iron Mill Rd. SW18 149 E6
Ironmonger La. EC2 20 B4
Ironmonger Pas. EC1 12 A5
Ironmonger Row EC1 12 A5
Ironmonger Row EC1 111 J3
Ironmongers Pl. E14 134 A4
Spindrift Av.
Ironside Cl. SE16 133 G2
Kinburn St.
Irvine Av., Har. 68 D3
Irvine Cl. N20 57 H2
Irvine Way, Orp. 193 J7
Irving Av., Nthlt. 102 D1
Irving Gro. SW9 151 F2
Irving Rd. W14 128 A3
Irving St. WC2 17 J5
Irving St. WC2 110 D7
Irving Way NW9 71 F5
Irwin Av. SE18 137 H7
Irwin Gdns. NW10 107 H1
Isabel Hill Cl., Hmptn. 179 H1
Upper Sunbury Rd.
Isabel St. SW9 151 F1
Isabella Cl. N14 42 C7
Isabella Dr., Orp. 207 F4
Isabella Rd. E9 95 F5
Isabella St. SE1 27 G2
Isabella St. SE1 131 H1
Isambard Ms. E14 134 C3
Isambard Pl. SE16 133 F1
Rotherhithe St.
Isel Way SE22 152 B5
East Dulwich Gro.
Isham Rd. SW16 186 E2
Isis Cl. SW15 147 J4
Isis St. SW18 167 F2
Isla Rd. SE18 137 F6
Island Fm. Av., W.Mol. 179 F5
Island Fm. Rd., W.Mol. 179 F5
Island Rd., Mitch. 167 J7
Island Row E14 113 J6
Commercial Rd.
Islay Gdns., Houns. 142 D5
Islay Wk. N1 93 J7
Douglas Rd.
Isledon Rd. N7 93 G3
Islehurst Cl., Chis. 192 D1
Isleworth Business Complex, Islw. 144 C2
St. John's Rd.
Isleworth Prom., Twick. 144 E4
Islington Grn. N1 111 H1
Islington High St. N1 11 F2
Islington High St. N1 111 H2
Islington Pk. Ms. N1 93 G7
Islington Pk. St.
Islington Pk. St. N1 93 G7
Islip Gdns., Edg. 54 D7
Islip Gdns., Nthlt. 85 E7
Islip Manor Rd., Nthlt. 85 E7
Islip St. NW5 92 C5
Ismailia Rd. E7 97 H7
Isom Cl. E13 115 J4
Belgrave Rd.
Ivanhoe Dr., Har. 68 D3
Ivanhoe Rd. SE5 152 C3
Ivanhoe Rd., Houns. 142 D3
Ivatt Pl. W14 128 C5
Ivatt Way N17 75 H3
Ive Fm. Cl. E10 96 A2
Ive Fm. La. E10 96 A2
Iveagh Av. NW10 106 A2
Iveagh Cl. E9 113 G1
Iveagh Cl. NW10 106 A2
Iveagh Ter. NW10 106 A2
Iveagh Av.
Ivedon Rd., Well. 158 C2
Iveley Rd. SW4 150 C2
Ivere Dr., Barn. 40 E6
Iverhurst Cl., Bexh. 158 D5
Iverna Ct. W8 128 D3
Iverna Gdns. W8 128 D3
Iverna Gdns., Felt. 141 G5
Ivers Way, Croy. 204 B7
Iverson Rd. NW6 90 C6
Ives Rd. E16 114 E5
Ives St. SW3 31 H1
Ives St. SW3 129 H4
Ivestor Ter. SE23 153 F7
Ivimey St. E2 13 J3
Ivimey St. E2 112 D3
Ivinghoe Cl., Enf. 44 B2
Ivinghoe Rd., Dag. 100 B5
Ivor Gro. SE9 175 E1
Ivor Pl. NW1 7 J6
Ivor Pl. NW1 109 J4
Ivor St. NW1 92 C7
Ivory Sq. SW11 149 F3
Gartons Way
Ivorydown, Brom. 173 G4
Ivy Cl., Har. 85 F4
Ivy Cl., Pnr. 66 C7
Ivy Cl., Sun. 178 C2
Ivy Cotts. E14 114 B7
Grove Vil.
Ivy Ct. SE16 37 J4
Ivy Cres. W4 126 C4
Ivy Gdns. N8 74 E6
Ivy Gdns., Mitch. 186 D3
Ivy La., Houns. 143 F4
Ivy Pl., Surb. 181 J6
Alpha Rd.
Ivy Rd. E16 115 G6
Pacific Rd.
Ivy Rd. E17 78 A6
Ivy Rd. N14 42 C7
Ivy Rd. NW2 89 J4
Ivy Rd. SE4 153 J4
Ivy Rd. SW17 167 H5
Tooting High St.
Ivy Rd., Houns. 143 H4
Ivy Rd., Surb. 196 A1
Ivy St. N1 12 D1
Ivy St. N1 112 B2
Ivy Wk., Dag. 100 E6
Ivybridge Cl., Twick. 144 D6
Ivybridge Est., Islw. 144 C5
Ivybridge La. WC2 18 B6
Ivychurch Cl. SE20 171 F7
Ivychurch La. SE17 37 F3
Ivydale Rd. SE15 153 G3
Ivydale Rd., Cars. 199 J2
Ivyday Gro. SW16 169 F3
Ivydene, W.Mol. 179 F5
Ivydene Cl., Sutt. 199 F4
Ivyhouse Rd., Dag. 100 D6
Ivymount Rd. SE27 169 G3
Ixworth Pl. SW3 31 G3
Ixworth Pl. SW3 129 H5
Izane Rd., Bexh. 159 F4

J

Jacaranda Cl., N.Mal. 182 E3
Jacaranda Gro. E8 94 C7
Queensbridge Rd.
Jack Barnett Way N22 75 F2
Jack Clow Rd. E15 115 E2
Jack Cornwell St. E12 98 D4
Jack Dash Way E6 116 B4
Jack Walker Ct. N5 93 H4
Jackass La., Kes. 205 H6
Jacklin Grn., Wdf.Grn. 63 G4
Jackman Ms. NW10 88 E3
Jackman St. E8 112 E1

Joyners Cl., Dag. 101 F4
Jubb Powell Ho. N15 76 B6
Jubilee Av. E4 62 C6
Jubilee Av., Rom. 83 H5
Jubilee Av., Twick. 161 J1
Jubilee Cl. NW9 70 D6
Jubilee Cl., Pnr. 66 C2
Jubilee Cl., Rom. 83 H5
Jubilee Cres. E14 134 C3
Jubilee Cres. N9 60 D1
Jubilee Dr., Ruis. 84 D4
Jubilee Gdns., Sthl. 103 G6
Jubilee Pl. SW3 31 H3
Jubilee Pl. SW3 129 H5
Jubilee Rd., Grnf. 104 E1
Jubilee Rd., Sutt. 198 A7
Jubilee St. E1 113 F6
Jubilee Wk., Wat. 50 B4
Jubilee Way SW19 185 E1
Jubilee Way, Chess. 196 A4
Jubilee Way, Sid. 176 A2
Judd St. WC1 10 A4
Judd St. WC1 110 E3
Jude St. E16 115 F6
Judge Wk., Esher 194 B6
Juer St. SW11 129 H7
Julia Gdns., Bark. 118 D2
Julia Garfield Ms. E16 135 H1
Wesley Av.
Julia St. NW5 92 A4
Oak Village
Julian Av. W3 106 B7
Julian Cl., Barn. 40 E3
Julian Hill, Har. 86 B2
Julian Pl. E14 134 B5
Juliana Cl. N2 72/73 E3
East End Rd.
Julien Rd. W5 125 F3
Juliette Rd. E13 115 F2
Junction App. SE13 154 C3
Junction App. SW11 149 H3
Junction Av. W10 107 J3
Harrow Rd.
Junction Ms. W2 15 G3
Junction Pl. W2 15 G3
Junction Rd. E13 115 H2
Junction Rd. N9 60 D1
Junction Rd. N17 76 D3
Junction Rd. N19 92 C4
Junction Rd. W5 125 G4
Junction Rd., Brent. 125 G4
Junction Rd., Har. 68 B6
Junction Rd., S.Croy. 202 A5
Junction Rd. E., Rom. 82/83 E7
Kenneth Rd.
Junction Rd. W., Rom. 82 E7
Juniper Cl., Barn. 40 A5
Juniper Cl., Chess. 195 J6
Juniper Cl., Wem. 87 J5
Juniper Cres. NW1 92 A7
Juniper Gdns. SW16 186 C1
Leonard Rd.
Juniper La. E6 116 B5
Juniper Rd., Ilf. 98 D4
Juniper St. E1 113 F7
Juno Way SE14 133 G6
Jupiter Way N7 93 F6
Jupp Rd. E15 96 D7
Jupp Rd. W. E15 114 C1
Justice Wk. SW3 31 G6
Justin Cl., Brent. 125 G7
Justin Rd. E4 61 J6
Jute La., Enf. 45 H2
Jutland Cl. N19 92/93 E1
Sussex Way
Jutland Rd. E13 115 G4
Jutland Rd. SE6 154 C7
Jutsums Av., Rom. 83 H6
Jutsums La., Rom. 83 H6
Juxon Cl., Har. 67 H1
Augustine Rd.
Juxon St. SE11 34 D1
Juxon St. SE11 131 F4

K

Kaduna Cl., Pnr. 66 A5
Kale Rd., Erith 138 E2
Kambala Rd. SW11 149 G3
Kangley Br. Rd. SE26 171 J5
Kaplan Dr. N21 43 F5
Kara Way NW2 90 A4
Karen Ct. SE4 153 J2
Wickham Rd.
Karen Ct., Brom. 191 F1
Blyth Rd.
Karen Ter. E11 97 F2
Montague Rd.
Karenza Ct., Wem. 69 F7
Lulworth Av.
Karina Cl., Chig. 65 H5
Karoline Gdns., Grnf. 104 A2
Oldfield La. N.
Kashgar Rd. SE18 137 J4
Kashmir Rd. SE7 136 A7
Kassala Rd. SW11 149 J1
Katella Trd. Est., Bark. 117 H3
Kates Cl., Barn. 39 G5
Katharine St., Croy. 201 J3
Katherine Cl. SE16 133 G1
Rotherhithe St.
Katherine Gdns. SE9 156 A4
Katherine Gdns., Ilf. 65 F7
Katherine Rd. E6 98 A7
Katherine Rd. E7 97 J5
Katherine Rd., Twick. 162 D1
London Rd.
Katherine Sq. W11 128 B1
Wilsham St.
Kathleen Av. W3 106 C5
Kathleen Av., Wem. 87 H7
Kathleen Rd. SW11 149 J3
Kay Rd. SW9 151 E2
Kay St. E2 13 J1
Kay St. E2 112 D2
Kay St. E15 96 D7
Kay St., Well. 158 B1
Kayemoor Rd., Sutt. 199 H7
Kean St. WC2 18 C4
Kean St. WC2 111 F6
Keatley Grn. E4 61 J6
Keats Av. E16 135 H1
Wesley Av.
Keats Cl. E11 79 H5
Nightingale La.
Keats Cl. NW3 91 H4
Keats Gro.
Keats Cl. SE1 37 F2
Keats Cl. SW19 167 G6
North Rd.
Keats Cl., Chig. 65 F6
Keats Cl., Enf. 45 G5
Keats Cl., Hayes 102 A5
Keats Gro. NW3 91 G4
Keats Ho., Beck. 172 A6
Keats Pl. EC2 20 B2
Keats Rd., Belv. 139 J3
Keats Rd., Well. 157 H1
Keats Way, Croy. 189 F6
Keats Way, Grnf. 103 H5
Keats Way, West Dr. 120 C4
Keble Cl., Nthlt. 85 J5
Keble Cl., Wor.Pk. 197 F1
Keble Pl. SW13 127 H6
Somerville Av.
Keble St. SW17 167 F4
Kechill Gdns., Brom. 191 G7
Kedelston Ct. E5 95 G4
Redwald Rd.
Kedleston Dr., Orp. 193 J6
Kedleston Wk. E2 112/113 E3
Middleton St.
Keedonwood Rd., Brom. 172 E5
Keel Cl. SE16 133 G1
Keel Cl., Bark. 118/119 E3
Choats Rd.
Keeley Rd., Croy. 201 J2
Keeley St. WC2 18 C4
Keeley St. WC2 111 F6
Keeling Rd. SE9 156 A5
Keely Cl., Barn. 41 H5
Keemor Cl. SE18 136 D7
Llanover Rd.
Keens Cl. SW16 168 D5
Keens Rd., Croy. 201 J4
Keens Yd. N1 93 H6
St. Paul's Rd.
Keep, The SE3 155 G2
Keep, The, Kings.T. 163 J6
Keep La. N11 58 A2
Gardeners Cl.
Keepers Ms., Tedd. 163 F6
Keesey St. SE17 36 B5
Keesey St. SE17 132 A6
Keetons Rd. SE16 132 E3
Keevil Dr. SW19 148 A7
Keighley Cl. N7 92/93 E5
Penn Rd.
Keightley Dr. SE9 175 F1
Keildon Rd. SW11 149 J4
Keir, The SW19 165 J5
West Side Common
Keir Hardie Est. E5 94/95 E1
Springfield
Keir Hardie Ho. W6 127 J6
Lochaline St.
Keir Hardie Way, Bark. 100 A7
Keir Hardie Way, Hayes 102 A3
Keith Connor Cl. SW8 150 B3
Daley Thompson Way
Keith Gro. W12 127 G2
Keith Rd. E17 77 J1
Keith Rd., Bark. 117 G2
Keith Rd., Hayes 121 H3
Kelbrook Rd. SE3 156 B3
Kelby Path SE9 175 E3
Kelceda Cl. NW2 89 G2
Kelfield Gdns. W10 107 J6
Kelfield Ms. W10 108 A6
Kelfield Gdns.
Kell St. SE1 27 H5
Kelland Cl. N8 74 D5
Palace Rd.
Kelland Rd. E13 115 G4
Kellaway Rd. SE3 155 J2
Keller Cres. E12 98 A4
Kellerton Rd. SE13 154 E5
Kellett Rd. SW2 151 G4
Kelling Gdns., Croy. 187 H7
Kellino St. SW17 167 J4
Kellner Rd. SE28 137 J3
Kelly Av. SE15 132 C7
Kelly Cl. NW10 88 D3
Kelly Ct., Borwd. 38 C2
Kelly Ms. W9 108 C5
Woodfield Rd.
Kelly Rd. NW7 56 B6
Kelly St. NW1 92 B6
Kelly Way, Rom. 82 E5
Kelman Cl. SW4 150 D2
Kelmore Gro. SE22 152 D4
Kelmscott Cl. E17 77 J2
Kelmscott Gdns. W12 127 G3
Kelmscott Rd. SW11 149 J5
Kelross Pas. N5 93 J4
Kelross Rd.
Kelross Rd. N5 93 J4
Kelsall Cl. SE3 155 H2
Kelsey La., Beck. 190 A2
Kelsey Pk. Av., Beck. 190 B2
Kelsey Pk. Rd., Beck. 190 A2
Kelsey Sq., Beck. 190 A2
Kelsey St. E2 13 J5
Kelsey St. E2 112 E4
Kelsey Way, Beck. 190 A3
Kelshall Ct. N4 93 J2
Brownswood Rd.
Kelsie Way, Ilf. 65 H7
Kelso Pl. W8 22 B6
Kelso Pl. W8 128 E3
Kelso Rd., Cars. 185 F7
Kelson Ho. E14 134 C3
Kelston Rd., Ilf. 81 E2
Kelvedon Cl., Kings.T. 163 J6
Kelvedon Rd. SW6 128 C7
Kelvedon Way, Wdf.Grn. 64 C6
Kelvin Av. N13 59 F6
Kelvin Av., Tedd. 162 B6
Kelvin Cl., Epsom 196 A6
Kelvin Cres., Har. 52 B7
Kelvin Dr., Twick. 145 E6
Kelvin Gdns., Croy. 187 E7
Kelvin Gdns., Sthl. 103 G6
Kelvin Gro. SE26 170 E3
Kelvin Gro., Chess. 195 H3
Kelvin Ind. Est., Grnf. 85 H7
Kelvin Par., Orp. 207 H1
Kelvin Rd. N5 93 J4
Kelvin Rd., Well. 158 A3
Kelvinbrook, W.Mol. 179 H3
Kelvington Cl., Croy. 189 H7
Kelvington Rd. SE15 153 G5
Kember St. N1 93 F7
Carnoustie Dr.
Kemble Dr., Brom. 206 B3
Kemble Rd. N17 76 D1
Kemble Rd. SE23 171 G1
Kemble Rd., Croy. 201 G3
Kemble St. WC2 18 C4
Kemble St. WC2 111 F6
Kemerton Rd. SE5 151 J3
Kemerton Rd., Beck. 190 B2
Kemerton Rd., Croy. 188 C7
Kemeys St. E9 95 H5
Kemnal Rd., Chis. 175 G4
Kemp Gdns., Croy. 187 J6
St. Saviours Rd.
Kemp Rd., Dag. 100 D1
Kempe Rd. NW6 108 A2
Kempis Way SE22 152 B5
East Dulwich Gro.
Kemplay Rd. NW3 91 G4
Kemp's Ct. W1 17 G4
Kemps Dr. E14 114 A7
Morant St.
Kemps Gdns. SE13 154 C5
Thornford Rd.
Kempsford Gdns. SW5 128 D5
Kempsford Rd. SE11 35 G1
Kempsford Rd. SE11 131 G4
Kempshott Rd. SW16 168 D7
Kempson Rd. SW6 148 D1
Kempt St. SE18 136 D6
Kempthorne Rd. SE8 133 H4
Kempton Av., Nthlt. 85 G6
Kempton Av., Sun. 178 B1
Kempton Cl., Erith 139 J6
Kempton Ct., Sun. 178 B1
Kempton Rd. E6 116 C1
Kempton Rd., Hmptn. 179 F2
Kempton Wk., Croy. 189 H6
Kemsing Cl., Bex. 159 E7
Kemsing Cl., Brom. 205 F2
Kemsing Cl., Th.Hth. 187 J4
Kemsing Rd. SE10 135 G5
Ken Way, Wem. 88 C2
Kenbury Gdns. SE5 151 J2
Kenbury St.
Kenbury St. SE5 151 J2
Kenchester Cl. SW8 131 E7
Kencot Cl., Erith 139 F2
Kendal Av. N18 60 A4
Kendal Av. W3 106 A5
Kendal Av., Bark. 99 H7
Kendal Cl. SW9 35 G7
Kendal Cl. SW9 131 H7
Kendal Cl., Wdf.Grn. 63 F2
Kendal Gdns. N18 60 A4
Kendal Gdns., Sutt. 199 F2
Kendal Par. N18 60 A4
Great Cambridge Rd.
Kendal Pl. SW15 148 C5
Upper Richmond Rd.
Kendal Rd. NW10 89 G4
Kendal St. W2 15 H4
Kendal St. W2 109 H6
Kendale Rd., Brom. 172 E5
Kendall Av., Beck. 189 H2
Kendall Ct. SW19 167 G6
Byegrove Rd.
Kendall Pl. W1 16 B2
Kendall Rd., Beck. 189 H2
Kendall Rd., Islw. 144 D2
Kendalmere Cl. N10 74 B1
Kender St. SE14 133 F7
Kendoa Rd. SW4 150 D4
Kendon Cl. E11 79 H5
The Av.
Kendra Hall Rd., S.Croy. 201 H7
Kendrey Gdns., Twick. 144 B6
Kendrick Ms. SW7 31 E1
Kendrick Pl. SW7 31 E2
Kendrick Pl. SW7 129 G4
Kenelm Cl., Har. 86 D3
Kenerne Dr., Barn. 40 B5
Kenilford Rd. SW12 150 B7
Kenilworth Av. E17 78 A2
Kenilworth Av. SW19 166 D5
Kenilworth Av., Har. 85 F4
Kenilworth Cl., Borwd. 38 C3
Kenilworth Ct. SW15 148 A3
Lower Richmond Rd.
Kenilworth Cres., Enf. 44 B1
Kenilworth Dr., Borwd. 38 C3
Kenilworth Gdns. SE18 156 E2
Kenilworth Gdns., Ilf. 99 J2
Kenilworth Gdns., Loug. 48 C6
Kenilworth Gdns., Sthl. 103 F3
Kenilworth Gdns., Wat. 50 C5
Kenilworth Rd. E3 113 H2
Kenilworth Rd. NW6 108 C1
Kenilworth Rd. SE20 189 G1
Kenilworth Rd. W5 125 H1
Kenilworth Rd., Edg. 54 C3
Kenilworth Rd., Epsom 197 G6
Kenilworth Rd., Orp. 193 F6
Kenley Av. NW9 70 E1
Kenley Cl., Barn. 41 H4
Kenley Cl., Bex. 159 G7
Kenley Cl., Chis. 193 H3
Kenley Gdns., Th.Hth. 187 H4
Kenley Rd. SW19 184 C2
Kenley Rd., Kings.T. 182 B2
Kenley Rd., Twick. 144 D6
Kenley Wk. W11 108 B7
Kenley Wk., Sutt. 198 A4
Kenlor Rd. SW17 167 G5
Kenmare Dr., Mitch. 167 J7
Kenmare Gdns. N13 59 H4
Kenmare Rd., Th.Hth. 187 G6
Kenmere Gdns., Wem. 106 A1
Kenmere Rd., Well. 158 C2
Kenmont Gdns. NW10 107 H3
Kenmore Av., Har. 68 D4
Kenmore Cl., Rich. 126 A7
Kent Rd.
Kenmore Gdns., Edg. 70 B2

Kenmore Rd., Har. 69 G3
Kenmure Rd. E8 95 E5
Kenmure Yd. E8 94/95 E5
Kenmure Rd.
Kennacraig Cl. E16 135 G1
Hanameel St.
Kennard Rd. E15 96 D7
Kennard Rd. N11 57 J5
Kennard St. E16 136 C1
Kennard St. SW11 150 A2
Kennedy Av., Enf. 45 F6
Kennedy Cl. E13 115 G2
Kennedy Cl., Mitch. 186 A2
Kennedy Cl., Orp. 207 G1
Kennedy Cl., Pnr. 51 F6
Kennedy Path W7 104 C4
Harp Rd.
Kennedy Rd. W7 104 B5
Kennedy Rd., Bark. 117 H1
Kennedy Wk. SE17 132 A4
Flint St.
Kennet Cl. SW11 149 G4
Maysoule Rd.
Kennet Rd. W9 108 C4
Kennet Rd., Islw. 144 C3
Kennet Sq., Mitch. 185 H1
Kennet St. E1 29 J1
Kennet St. E1 132 D1
Kennet Wf. La. EC4 20 A5
Kenneth Av., Ilf. 98 E4
Kenneth Cres. NW2 89 H5
Kenneth Gdns., Stan. 52 D6
Kenneth More Rd., 98/99 E3
Ilf.
Oakfield Rd.
Kenneth Rd., Rom. 82 D7
Kenneth Robbins Ho. 60 E7
N17
Kennett Dr., Hayes 102 E5
Kenning St. SE16 133 F2
Railway Av.
Kenning Ter. N1 112 B1
Kenninghall Rd. E5 94 D3
Kenninghall Rd. N18 61 F5
Kennings Way SE11 35 G3
Kennings Way SE11 131 G5
Kennington Grn. SE11 35 E4
Kennington Gro. SE11 34 D5
Kennington La. SE11 35 F3
Kennington La. SE11 131 F5
Kennington Oval 34 D5
SE11
Kennington Oval 131 F6
SE11
Kennington Pk. Est. 35 E6
SE11
Kennington Pk. Gdns. 35 E4
SE11
Kennington Pk. Gdns. 131 H6
SE11
Kennington Pk. Pl. 35 F4
SE11
Kennington Pk. Pl. 131 G6
SE11
Kennington Pk. Rd. 35 F5
SE11
Kennington Pk. Rd. 131 G6
SE11
Kennington Rd. SE1 27 E5
Kennington Rd. SE1 131 G3
Kennington Rd. SE11 27 E6
Kennington Rd. SE11 131 G4
Kenny Dr., Cars. 199 J7
Fountain Dr.
Kenny Rd. NW7 56 B5
Kenrick Pl. W1 16 B1
Kensal Rd. W10 108 B4
Kensington Av. E12 98 B6
Kensington Av., 187 G1
Th.Hth.
Kensington Ch. Ct. 22 A4
W8
Kensington Ch. Ct. 128 E2
W8
Kensington Ch. St. 128 D1
W8
Kensington Ch. Wk. 22 A4
W8
Kensington Ch. Wk. 128 E2
W8
Kensington Cl. N11 58 A6
Kensington Ct. W8 22 B4
Kensington Ct. W8 129 E2
Kensington Ct. 128/129 E3
Gdns. W8
Kensington Ct. Pl.
Kensington Ct. Ms. W8 22 B4
Kensington Ct. Pl. W8 22 B5
Kensington Ct. Pl. W8 129 E3
Kensington Dr., 80 A1
Wdf.Grn.
Kensington Gdns. W2 22 D2
Kensington Gdns. W2 129 F1
Kensington Gdns., Ilf. 98 C1

Kensington Gdns., 181 G3
Kings.T.
Portsmouth Rd.
Kensington Gdns. Sq. 14 A4
W2
Kensington Gdns. Sq. 108 E6
W2
Kensington Gate W8 22 C5
Kensington Gate W8 129 F3
Kensington Gore SW7 22 E4
Kensington Gore SW7 129 G2
Kensington Hall 128 C5
Gdns. W14
Beaumont Av.
Kensington High St. 128 D3
W8
Kensington High St. 128 B4
W14
Kensington Mall W8 128 D1
Kensington Palace 22 A1
Gdns. W8
Kensington Palace 128 E1
Gdns. W8
Kensington Pk. Gdns. 108 C7
W11
Kensington Pk. Ms. 108 C6
W11
Kensington Pk. Rd.
Kensington Pk. Rd. 108 C7
W11
Kensington Pl. W8 128 D1
Kensington Rd. SW7 23 F4
Kensington Rd. SW7 129 G2
Kensington Rd. W8 22 B4
Kensington Rd. W8 129 E2
Kensington Rd., Nthlt. 103 G3
Kensington Rd., Rom. 83 J6
Kensington Sq. W8 22 A4
Kensington Sq. W8 128 E2
Kensington Ter., 202 A7
S.Croy.
Sanderstead Rd.
Kent Av. W13 104 E5
Kent Av., Dag. 119 G4
Kent Av., Well. 157 J5
Kent Cl., Mitch. 187 E4
Kent Cl., Orp. 207 H6
Kent Dr., Barn. 42 A4
Kent Dr., Tedd. 162 B5
Kent Gdns. W13 105 E5
Kent Gdns., Ruis. 66 B6
Kent Gate Way, Croy. 204 A5
Kent Ho. La., Beck. 171 H5
Kent Ho. Rd. SE26 189 G1
Kent Ho. Rd., Beck. 171 H5
Kent Pas. NW1 7 J5
Kent Pas. NW1 109 J3
Kent Rd. N21 60 A1
Kent Rd. W4 126 C3
Kent Rd., Dag. 101 H5
Kent Rd., E.Mol. 179 J4
Kent Rd., Kings.T. 181 G3
The Bittoms
Kent Rd., Rich. 126 A7
Kent Rd., W.Wick. 204 B1
Kent St. E2 13 G1
Kent St. E2 112 C2
Kent St. E13 115 J3
Kent Ter. NW1 7 H4
Kent Ter. NW1 109 H3
Kent Twr. SE20 171 E7
Kent Vw. Gdns., Ilf. 99 H2
Kent Wk. SW9 151 H4
Moorland Rd.
Kent Way SE15 152 C1
Sumner Rd.
Kent Way, Surb. 195 H3
Kent Yd. SW7 23 H4
Kentford Way, Nthlt. 102 E1
Kentish Bldgs. SE1 28 B2
Kentish Rd., Belv. 139 G4
Kentish Town Rd. 92 B7
NW1
Kentish Town Rd. 92 B7
NW5
Kentish Way, Brom. 191 G2
Kentmere Rd. SE18 137 H4
Kenton Av., Har. 68 C7
Kenton Av., Sthl. 103 G7
Kenton Av., Sun. 178 E2
Kenton Ct. W14 128 C3
Kensington High St.
Kenton Gdns., Har. 69 F5
Kenton La., Har. 69 F3
Kenton Pk. Av., Har. 69 G4
Kenton Pk. Cl., Har. 69 F4
Kenton Pk. Cres., Har. 69 G4
Kenton Pk. Rd., Har. 69 F4
Kenton Rd. E9 95 G6
Kenton Rd., Har. 69 G5
Kenton St. WC1 10 A5
Kenton St. WC1 110 E4
Kents Pas., Hmptn. 179 F1
Kentwode Grn. SW13 127 G7

Kenver Av. N12 57 G6
Kenward Rd. SE9 155 J5
Kenway, Rom. 83 J2
Kenway Rd. SW5 30 A2
Kenway Rd. SW5 128 E4
Kenwood Av. N14 42 D5
Kenwood Av. SE14 153 G1
Besson St.
Kenwood Cl. NW3 91 G1
Kenwood Cl., West Dr. 120 D6
Kenwood Dr., Beck. 190 C3
Kenwood Gdns. E18 79 H3
Kenwood Gdns., Ilf. 80 D4
Kenwood Rd. N6 73 J6
Kenwood Rd. N9 60 D1
Kenworthy Rd. E9 95 H5
Kenwyn Dr. NW2 89 E3
Kenwyn Rd. SW4 150 D4
Kenwyn Rd. SW20 183 J1
Kenya Rd. SE7 136 A7
Kenyngton Dr., Sun. 160 A5
Kenyngton Pl., Har. 69 F5
Kenyon St. SW6 148 A1
Keogh Rd. E15 97 E6
Kepler Rd. SW4 150 E4
Keppel Rd. E6 98 C7
Keppel Rd., Dag. 100 E4
Keppel Row SE1 27 J2
Keppel St. WC1 17 J1
Keppel St. WC1 110 D5
Kerbela St. E2 13 H5
Kerbey St. E14 114 B6
Kerfield Cres. SE5 152 A1
Kerfield Pl. SE5 152 A1
Kerri Cl., Barn. 39 J4
Kerridge Ct. N1 94 B6
Kerrison Pl. W5 125 G1
Kerrison Rd. E15 114 D1
Kerrison Rd. SW11 149 H3
Kerrison Rd. W5 125 G1
Kerrison Vil. W5 125 G1
Kerrison Pl.
Kerry Av., Stan. 53 G4
Kerry Cl. E16 115 H6
Kerry Cl. N13 59 F2
Kerry Ct., Stan. 53 G4
Kerry Path SE14 133 J6
Kerry Rd.
Kerry Rd. SE14 133 J6
Kersey Gdns. SE9 174 B4
Kersfield Rd. SW15 148 A6
Kershaw Cl. SW18 149 G6
Westover Rd.
Kershaw Rd., Dag. 101 G3
Kersley Ms. SW11 149 J2
Kersley Rd. N16 94 B3
Kersley St. SW11 149 J2
Kerswell Cl. N15 76 B5
Kerwick Cl. N7 93 F7
Sutterton St.
Keslake Rd. NW6 108 A2
Kessock Cl. N17 76 E5
Kesteven Cl., Ilf. 65 J6
Kestlake Rd., Bex. 158 C6
East Rochester Way
Keston Av., Kes. 205 J5
Keston Cl. N18 60 A3
Keston Cl., Well. 138 C7
Keston Gdns., Kes. 205 J4
Keston Pk. Cl., Kes. 206 C3
Keston Rd. N17 76 A3
Keston Rd. SE15 152 D3
Keston Rd., Th.Hth. 187 G6
Kestrel Av. E6 116 B5
Swan App.
Kestrel Av. SE24 151 H5
Kestrel Cl. NW9 71 E2
Kestrel Cl. NW10 88 D5
Kestrel Cl., Kings.T. 163 G4
Kestrel Ho. EC1 11 J3
Kestrel Ho. EC1 111 H3
Kestrel Ho. W13 104 C4
Kestrel Pl. SE14 133 H6
Milton Ct. Rd.
Keswick Av. SW15 164 E5
Keswick Av. SW19 184 D2
Keswick Bdy. SW15 148 B5
Upper Richmond Rd.
Keswick Cl., Sutt. 199 F4
Keswick Gdns., Ilf. 80 B5
Keswick Gdns., Wem. 87 H4
Keswick Ms. W5 125 H1
Keswick Rd. SW15 148 B5
Keswick Rd., Bexh. 159 G2
Keswick Rd., Orp. 207 J1
Keswick Rd., Twick. 143 J6
Keswick Rd., W.Wick. 204 E2
Kett Gdns. SW2 151 F5
Kettering Rd. SW16 168 C6
Kettlebaston Rd. E10 95 J1
Kettlewell Cl. N11 58 A6
Kevan Ho. SE5 131 J7
Kevelioc Rd. N17 75 J1
Kevin Cl., Houns. 142 D2

Kevington Cl., Orp. 193 J4
Kevington Dr., Chis. 193 J4
Kevington Dr., Orp. 193 J4
Kew Br., Brent. 125 J6
Kew Br. Arches, Rich. 125 J6
Kew Br.
Kew Br. Ct. W4 126 A5
Kew Br. Rd., Brent. 125 J6
Kew Cres., Sutt. 198 B3
Kew Foot Rd., Rich. 145 H4
Kew Gdns. Rd., Rich. 125 J7
Kew Grn., Rich. 126 A6
Kew Meadow Path, 146 A1
Rich.
Kew Palace, Rich. 125 H7
Kew Rd., Rich. 145 H3
Key Cl. E1 113 E4
Keybridge Ho. SW8 34 B6
Keybridge Ho. SW8 131 E6
Keyes Rd. NW2 90 A5
Keymer Rd. SW2 169 F2
Keynes Cl. N2 73 J3
Keynsham Av., 63 E4
Wdf.Grn.
Keynsham Gdns. SE9 156 B5
Keynsham Rd. SE9 156 B5
Keynsham Rd., Mord. 198 E1
Keynsham Wk., Mord. 198 E1
Keyse Rd. SE1 29 F6
Keysham Av., Houns. 142 A1
Keystone Cres. N1 10 B2
Keywood Dr., Sun. 160 A6
Keyworth Cl. E5 95 H4
Keyworth St. SE1 27 H5
Keyworth St. SE1 131 H3
Kezia St. SE8 133 H5
Trundleys Rd.
Khama Rd. SW17 167 H4
Khartoum Rd. E13 115 H3
Khartoum Rd. SW17 167 G4
Khartoum Rd., Ilf. 99 E5
Khyber Rd. SW11 149 H2
Kibworth St. SW8 131 F7
Kidbrooke Gdns. SE3 155 G2
Kidbrooke Gro. SE3 155 G1
Kidbrooke La. SE9 156 B4
Kidbrooke Pk. Cl. 155 H1
SE3
Kidbrooke Pk. Rd. SE3 155 H1
Kidbrooke Way SE3 155 H2
Kidd Pl. SE7 136 B5
Kidderminster Pl., 201 H1
Croy.
Kidderminster Rd.
Kidderminster Rd., 201 H1
Croy.
Kidderpore Av. NW3 90 D4
Kidderpore Gdns. 90 D4
NW3
Kidlington Way NW9 70 E2
Kiffen St. EC2 12 C5
Kilberry Cl., Islw. 144 A1
Kilburn Br. NW6 90 C7
Kilburn High Rd.
Kilburn Bldgs. NW6 108/109 E1
Kilburn High Rd.
Kilburn Gate NW6 6 A1
Kilburn High Rd. NW6 90 C7
Kilburn La. W9 108 A3
Kilburn La. W10 108 A3
Kilburn Pk. Rd. NW6 108 D3
Kilburn Pl. NW6 108 D1
Kilburn Priory NW6 108 E1
Kilburn Sq. NW6 108 D1
Kilburn High Rd.
Kilburn Vale NW6 108/109 E1
Belsize Rd.
Kildare Cl., Ruis. 84 C1
Kildare Gdns. W2 108 D6
Kildare Rd. E16 115 G5
Kildare Ter. W2 108 D6
Kildare Wk. E14 114 A6
Farrance St.
Kildoran Rd. SW2 150 E5
Kildowan Rd., Ilf. 100 A1
Kilgour Rd. SE23 153 H6
Kilkie St. SW6 149 F2
Killarney Rd. SW18 149 F6
Killburns Mill Cl., 200 B4
Wall.
London Rd.
Killearn Rd. SE6 172 D1
Killester Gdns., 197 H4
Wor.Pk.
Killick St. N1 10 C1
Killick St. N1 111 F2
Killieser Av. SW2 168 E2
Killip Cl. E16 115 F6
Killowen Av., Nthlt. 85 J5
Killowen Rd. E9 95 G6
Killyon Rd. SW8 150 C2

Killyon Ter. SW8 150 C2
Kilmaine Rd. SW6 128 B7
Kilmarnock Gdns., Dag. 100 C3
Lindsey Rd.
Kilmarnock Rd., Wat. 50 D4
Kilmarsh Rd. W6 127 J4
Kilmartin Av. SW16 187 F3
Kilmartin Rd., Ilf. 100 A2
Kilmeston Way SE15 37 F7
Kilmington Rd. SW13 127 G6
Kilmorey Gdns., Twick. 144 E5
Kilmorey Rd., Twick. 144 E4
Kilmorie Rd. SE23 171 H1
Kiln Cl., Hayes 121 G6
Brickfield La.
Kiln Ms. SW17 167 G5
Kiln Pl. NW5 92 A5
Kilner St. E14 114 A5
Kilnside, Esher 194 D7
Kilpatrick Way, Hayes 103 E5
Kilravock St. W10 108 B3
Kilsby Wk., Dag. 100 B6
Rugby Rd.
Kilsha Rd., Walt. 178 B6
Kimbell Gdns. SW6 148 B1
Kimbell Pl. SE3 155 J4
Tudway Rd.
Kimber Rd. SW18 148 D7
Kimberley Av. E6 116 B2
Kimberley Av. SE15 153 E2
Kimberley Av., Ilf. 81 G7
Kimberley Av., Rom. 83 J6
Kimberley Dr., Sid. 176 D2
Kimberley Gdns. N4 75 H5
Kimberley Gdns., Enf. 44 C3
Kimberley Gate, Brom. 173 F7
Oaklands Rd.
Kimberley Rd. E4 62 E1
Kimberley Rd. E11 96 D2
Kimberley Rd. E16 115 F4
Kimberley Rd. E17 77 J1
Kimberley Rd. N17 76 D2
Kimberley Rd. N18 61 E6
Kimberley Rd. NW6 108 B1
Kimberley Rd. SW9 151 E2
Kimberley Rd., Beck. 189 G2
Kimberley Rd., Croy. 187 H6
Kimberley Way E4 63 E1
Kimble Rd. SW19 167 G6
Kimbolton Cl. SE12 155 F6
Kimbolton Grn., Borwd. 38 C4
Kimbolton Row SW3 31 G2
Kimmeridge Gdns. SE9 174 B4
Kimmeridge Rd. SE9 174 B4
Kimpton Rd. SE5 152 A1
Kimpton Rd., Sutt. 198 C2
Kimpton Trade Business Cen., Sutt. 198 C2
Kinburn St. SE16 133 G2
Kincaid Rd. SE15 132 E7
Kincardine Gdns. W9 108 C4
Harrow Rd.
Kinch Gro., Wem. 69 J7
Kinder Cl. SE28 118 D7
Kinder St. E1 112/113 E6
Cannon St. Rd.
Kinfauns Rd. SW2 169 G2
Kinfauns Rd., Ilf. 100 A1
King Alfred Av. SE6 172 A3
King & Queen Cl. SE9 174 B4
St. Keverne Rd.
King & Queen St. SE17 36 A2
King & Queen St. SE17 131 J5
King Arthur Cl. SE15 133 F7
King Charles Cres., Surb. 181 J7
King Charles Rd., Surb. 181 J5
King Charles St. SW1 25 J3
King Charles St. SW1 130 D2
King Charles Ter. E1 112/113 E7
Sovereign Cl.
King Charles Wk. SW19 166 B1
Princes Way
King David La. E1 113 F7
King Edward Dr., Chess. 195 H3
Kelvin Gro.
King Edward Ms. SW13 147 G1
King Edward Rd. E10 96 C1
King Edward Rd. E17 77 H3
King Edward Rd., Barn. 40 D4
King Edward St. EC1 19 J3
King Edward St. EC1 111 J6
King Edward III Ms. SE16 132/133 E2
Paradise St.
King Edward Wk. SE1 27 F5
King Edward Wk. SE1 131 G3
King Edward's Gdns. W3 126 A1
King Edwards Gro., Tedd. 163 E6
King Edward's Pl. W3 126 A1
King Edward's Gdns.
King Edwards Rd. E9 113 E1
King Edwards Rd. N9 44 E7
King Edwards Rd., Bark. 117 G1
King Edward's Rd., Enf. 45 G4
King Frederik IX Twr. SE16 133 J3
Finland St.
King Gdns., Croy. 201 H5
King George Av. E16 116 A6
King George Av., Ilf. 81 G5
King George Cl., Rom. 83 J3
King George VI Av., Mitch. 185 J4
King George Sq., Rich. 145 J6
King George St. SE10 134 C7
King Georges Dr., Sthl. 103 F5
King George's Trd. Est., Chess. 196 A4
King Harolds Way, Bexh. 138 D7
King Henry Ms., Orp. 207 J5
Osgood Av.
King Henry St. N16 94 B5
King Henry Ter. E1 112/113 E7
Sovereign Cl.
King Henry's Rd. NW3 91 H7
King Henry's Rd., Kings.T. 182 B3
King Henry's Wk. N1 94 B6
King James St. SE1 27 H4
King James St. SE1 131 H2
King John Ct. EC2 12 E5
King John St. E1 113 G5
King Johns Wk. SE9 174 A1
King Sq. EC1 11 J4
King Stairs Cl. SE16 132/133 E2
Elephant La.
King St. E13 115 G4
King St. EC2 20 A4
King St. EC2 111 J6
King St. N2 73 G3
King St. N17 76 C1
King St. SW1 25 G2
King St. SW1 130 C1
King St. W3 126 B1
King St. W6 127 G4
King St. WC2 18 A5
King St. WC2 110 E7
King St., Rich. 145 G5
King St., Sthl. 123 E3
King St., Twick. 162 D1
King William IV Gdns. SE20 171 F6
St. John's Rd.
King William La. SE10 134/135 E5
Orlop St.
King William St. EC4 20 C6
King William St. EC4 112 A7
King William Wk. SE10 134 C6
Kingcup Cl., Croy. 203 G1
Primrose La.
Kingdon Rd. NW6 90 D6
Kingfield Rd. W5 105 G4
Kingfield St. E14 134 C4
Kingfisher Av. E11 79 H6
Eastern Av.
Kingfisher Cl. SE28 118 C7
Kingfisher Cl., Har. 52 C7
Kingfisher Ct. SW19 166 B2
Queensmere Rd.
Kingfisher Ct., Sutt. 198 B2
Gander Grn. La.
Kingfisher Dr., Rich. 163 E4
Kingfisher Sq. SE8 133 J6
Kingfisher St. E6 116 B5
Kingfisher Wk. NW9 70/71 E2
Eagle Dr.
Kingfisher Way NW10 88 D6
Kingfisher Way, Beck. 189 G5
Kingham Cl. SW18 149 F7
Kingham Cl. W11 128 B2
Kinghorn St. EC1 19 J2
Kinglake Est. SE17 37 E3
Kinglake St. SE17 36 D4
Kinglake St. SE17 132 B5
Kingly Ct. W1 17 F5
Kingly St. W1 17 F4
Kingly St. W1 110 C6
Kings Arbour, Sthl. 122 E5
Kings Arms Ct. E1 21 H2
Kings Arms Yd. EC2 20 B3
Kings Av. N10 74 A3
Kings Av. N21 59 H1
King's Av. SW4 150 D7
King's Av. SW12 168 D1
Kings Av. W5 105 G6
Kings Av., Brom. 173 F6
Kings Av., Buck.H. 64 A2
Kings Av., Cars. 199 H7
Kings Av., Grnf. 103 H6
Kings Av., Houns. 143 H1
Kings Av., N.Mal. 183 E4
Kings Av., Rom. 83 F6
Kings Av., Wdf.Grn. 63 H5
Kings Bench St. SE1 27 H3
Kings Bench Wk. EC4 19 F4
Kings Chace Vw., Enf. 43 G2
Crofton Way
Kings Chase, E.Mol. 179 J3
Kings Cl. E10 78 B7
Kings Cl. NW4 72 A4
Kings Cl., T.Ditt. 180 D6
Kings College Rd. NW3 91 H7
Kings Ct. E13 115 H1
Kings Ct. W6 127 G4
King St.
Kings Ct., Wem. 88 B2
Kings Cres. N4 93 J3
Kings Cres. Est. N4 93 J2
King's Cross Br. N1 10 B3
King's Cross Rd. WC1 10 D3
King's Cross Rd. WC1 111 F3
Kings Dr., Edg. 53 J4
Kings Dr., Surb. 182 A7
Kings Dr., Tedd. 162 A5
Kings Dr., T.Ditt. 180 E6
Kings Dr., Wem. 88 B2
Kings Fm. Av., Rich. 146 A4
Kings Gdns. NW6 90 D7
West End La.
Kings Gdns., Ilf. 99 G1
King's Garth Ms. SE23 171 F2
London Rd.
Kings Grn., Loug. 48 B3
Kings Gro. SE15 133 E7
Kings Hall Rd., Beck. 171 H7
Kings Head Hill E4 46 B7
Kings Head Yd. SE1 28 B2
Kings Highway SE18 137 H6
Kings Hill, Loug. 48 B2
Kings Keep, Kings.T. 181 H4
Beaufort Rd.
Kings La., Sutt. 199 G6
Kings Mead Pk., Esher 194 B7
Kings Ms. SW4 150/151 E5
King's Av.
King's Ms. WC1 10 D6
King's Ms. WC1 111 F5
Kings Ms., Chig. 65 F2
Kings Oak, Rom. 83 G3
King's Orchard SE9 156 B6
Kings Paddock, Hmptn. 179 J1
Kings Par., Cars. 199 H3
Wrythe La.
King's Pas. E11 78 E7
Kings Pas., Kings.T. 181 G2
Kings Pl. SE1 27 J4
Kings Pl. W4 126 C5
Kings Pl., Buck.H. 63 J2
Kings Pl., Loug. 47 J7
Fallow Flds.
King's Reach Twr. SE1 27 F1
King's Reach Twr. SE1 131 G1
Kings Ride Gate, Rich. 146 A4
Kings Rd. E4 62 D1
Kings Rd. E6 115 J1
Kings Rd. E11 78 E7
King's Rd. N17 76 C1
Kings Rd. N18 60 D5
Kings Rd. N22 75 F1
Kings Rd. NW10 89 H7
Kings Rd. SE25 188 D3
King's Rd. SW1 31 H3
King's Rd. SW1 129 J5
King's Rd. SW3 31 H3
King's Rd. SW3 129 J5
King's Rd. SW6 148 E1
King's Rd. SW10 148 E1
Kings Rd. SW14 146 D3
Kings Rd. SW19 166 D6
Kings Rd. W5 105 G5
Kings Rd., Bark. 99 F7
North St.
Kings Rd., Barn. 39 J3
Kings Rd., Felt. 160 C1
Kings Rd., Har. 85 F2
Kings Rd., Kings.T. 163 H7
Kings Rd., Mitch. 186 A3
Kings Rd., Orp. 207 J4
Kings Rd., Rich. 145 J5
Kings Rd., Surb. 195 F1
Kings Rd., Tedd. 162 A5
Kings Rd., Twick. 145 E6
Kings Rd., West Dr. 120 C2
Kings Rd. Bungalows, Har. 85 F3
Kings Rd.
King's Scholars' Pas. SW1 33 F1
King's Ter. NW1 110 C1
Plender St.
Kings Ter., Islw. 144 D3
Worple Rd.
King's Wk., Kings.T. 181 G1
Kings Way, Har. 68 B4
Kingsand Rd. SE12 173 G2
Kingsash Dr., Hayes 102 E4
Kingsbridge Av. W3 125 J2
Kingsbridge Cres., Sthl. 103 F5
Kingsbridge Rd. W10 107 J6
Kingsbridge Rd., Bark. 117 G2
Kingsbridge Rd., Mord. 184 A7
Kingsbridge Rd., Sthl. 123 F4
Kingsbridge Rd., Walt. 178 B7
Kingsbury Circle NW9 70 A5
Kingsbury Rd. N1 94 B6
Kingsbury Rd. NW9 70 B5
Kingsbury Ter. N1 94 B6
Kingsbury Trd. Est. NW9 70 D6
Kingsclere Cl. SW15 147 G7
Kingsclere Pl., Enf. 43 J2
Chase Side
Kingscliffe Gdns. SW19 166 C1
Kingscote Rd. W4 126 D3
Kingscote Rd., Croy. 188 E7
Kingscote Rd., N.Mal. 182 D3
Kingscote St. EC4 19 G5
Kingscourt Rd. SW16 168 D3
Kingscroft Rd. NW2 90 C6
Kingsdale Gdns. W11 128 A1
Kingsdale Rd. SE18 137 J7
Kingsdale Rd. SE20 171 G7
Kingsdown Av. W3 107 E7
Kingsdown Av. W13 125 E2
Kingsdown Cl. SE16 132/133 E5
Masters Dr.
Kingsdown Cl. W10 108 A6
Kingsdown Rd. E11 97 E3
Kingsdown Rd. N19 92 E2
Kingsdown Rd., Sutt. 198 B5
Kingsdown Way, Brom. 191 G7
Kingsdowne Rd., Surb. 181 H7
Kingsfield Av., Har. 67 H4
Kingsfield Ho. SE9 174 A3
Kingsfield Rd., Har. 68 A7
Kingsford Av., Wall. 201 E7
Kingsford St. NW5 91 J5
Kingsford Way E6 116 C5
Kingsgate, Wem. 88 C3
Kingsgate Av. N3 72 D3
Kingsgate Cl., Bexh. 158 E1
Kingsgate Pl. NW6 90 D7
Kingsgate Rd. NW6 90 D7
Kingsgate Rd., Kings.T. 181 H1
Kingsground SE9 156 B7
Kingshall Ms. SE13 154 C3
Lewisham Rd.
Kingshill Av., Har. 69 E4
Kingshill Av., Nthlt. 102 A3
Kingshill Av., Wor.Pk. 183 G7
Kingshill Dr., Har. 68 E3
Kingshold Rd. E9 95 F7
Kingsholm Gdns. SE9 156 A4
Kingshurst Rd. SE12 155 G7
Kingsland NW8 109 H1
Broxwood Way
Kingsland Grn. E8 94 B6
Kingsland High St. E8 94 C5
Kingsland Pas. E8 94 B6
Kingsland Grn.
Kingsland Rd. E2 13 E3
Kingsland Rd. E2 112 B2
Kingsland Rd. E8 112 B2
Kingsland Rd. E13 115 J3
Kingslawn Cl. SW15 147 H5
Howards La.

Kohat Rd. SW19	167	E5
Kossuth St. SE10	134	E5
Kotree Way SE1	**37**	**J2**
Kramer Ms. SW5	128	D5
Kempsford Gdns.		
Kreedman Wk. E8	94	D5
Kreisel Wk., Rich.	125	J6
Kuala Gdns. SW16	187	F1
Kuhn Way E7	97	G5
Forest La.		
Kydbrook Cl., Orp.	193	G7
Kylemore Cl. E6	116	A2
Parr Rd.		
Kylemore Rd. NW6	90	D7
Kymberley Rd., Har.	68	B6
Kynance Gdns., Stan.	69	F1
Kynance Ms. SW7	**22**	**C6**
Kynance Ms. SW7	129	E3
Kynance Pl. SW7	**22**	**C6**
Kynance Pl. SW7	129	F3
Kynaston Av. N16	94	C3
Dynevor Rd.		
Kynaston Av., Th.Hth.	187	J5
Kynaston Cl., Har.	52	A7
Kynaston Cres., Th.Hth.	187	J5
Kynaston Rd. N16	94	B3
Kynaston Rd., Brom.	173	G5
Kynaston Rd., Enf.	44	A1
Kynaston Rd., Th.Hth.	187	J5
Kynaston Wd., Har.	52	A7
Kynersley Cl., Cars.	199	J3
William St.		
Kynock Rd. N18	61	F4
Kyrle Rd. SW11	150	A5
Kyverdale Rd. N16	94	C2
L		
La Tourne Gdns., Orp.	207	F3
Laburnum Av. N9	60	B2
Laburnum Av. N17	60	A7
Laburnum Av., Sutt.	199	H3
Laburnum Cl. E4	61	J6
Laburnum Cl. N11	58	A6
Laburnum Cl. SE15	133	F7
Clifton Way		
Laburnum Ct. E2	112	C1
Laburnum St.		
Laburnum Ct., Stan.	53	F4
Laburnum Cres., Sun.	178	B1
Batavia Rd.		
Laburnum Gdns. N21	59	J2
Laburnum Gdns., Croy.	189	G7
Laburnum Gro. N21	59	J2
Laburnum Gro. NW9	70	C7
Laburnum Gro., Houns.	143	F4
Laburnum Gro., N.Mal.	182	D2
Laburnum Gro., Sthl.	103	F4
Laburnum Ho., Dag.	101	G2
Bradwell Av.		
Laburnum Rd. SW19	167	F7
Laburnum Rd., Hayes	121	J4
Laburnum Rd., Mitch.	186	A2
Laburnum St. E2	112	C1
Laburnum Way, Brom.	192	D7
Lacebark Cl., Sid.	157	J7
Lacey Cl. N9	60	D2
Lacey Dr., Dag.	100	B4
Lacey Dr., Edg.	53	H4
Lacey Dr., Hmptn.	179	F1
Lacey Wk. E3	114	A2
Lackington St. EC2	**20**	**C1**
Lackington St. EC2	112	A5
Lacock Cl. SW19	167	F6
Lacon Rd. SE22	152	D4
Lacy Rd. SW15	148	A4
Ladas Rd. SE27	169	J4
Ladbroke Cres. W11	108	B6
Ladbroke Gro.		
Ladbroke Gdns. W11	108	C7
Ladbroke Gro. W10	108	A4
Ladbroke Gro. W11	108	B6
Ladbroke Ms. W11	128	B1
Ladbroke Rd.		
Ladbroke Rd. W11	128	C1
Ladbroke Rd., Enf.	44	C6
Ladbroke Sq. W11	108	C7
Ladbroke Ter. W11	108	C7
Ladbroke Wk. W11	128	C1
Ladbrook Cl., Pnr.	67	F5
Ladbrook Rd. SE25	188	A3
Ladbrooke Cres., Sid.	176	D3
Ladderstile Ride, Kings.T.	164	B5
Ladderswood Way N11	58	C5
Lady Booth Rd., Kings.T.	181	H2
Lady Dock Path SE16	133	H2
Salter Rd.		
Lady Hay, Wor.Pk.	197	F2
Lady Margaret Rd. N19	92	C4
Lady Margaret Rd. NW5	92	C5
Lady Margaret Rd., Sthl.	103	F5
Lady Somerset Rd. NW5	92	B4
Ladybower Ct. E5	95	H4
Gilpin Rd.		
Ladycroft Gdns., Orp.	207	F5
Ladycroft Rd. SE13	154	B3
Ladycroft Wk., Stan.	69	G1
Ladycroft Way, Orp.	207	F5
Ladyfield Cl., Loug.	49	E4
Ladyfields, Loug.	49	E4
Ladysmith Av. E6	116	B2
Ladysmith Av., Ilf.	81	G7
Ladysmith Rd. E16	115	F3
Ladysmith Rd. N17	76	D2
Ladysmith Rd. N18	61	E5
Ladysmith Rd. SE9	156	D6
Ladysmith Rd., Enf.	44	B3
Ladysmith Rd., Har.	68	B2
Ladywell Cl. SE4	153	J4
Adelaide Av.		
Ladywell Hts. SE4	153	J6
Ladywell Rd. SE13	154	A5
Ladywell St. E15	115	F1
Plaistow Gro.		
Ladywood Av., Orp.	193	H5
Ladywood Rd., Surb.	196	A2
Lafone Av., Felt.	160	C1
Alfred Rd.		
Lafone St. SE1	**29**	**F3**
Lafone St. SE1	132	C2
Lagado Ms. SE16	133	G1
Lagonda Av., Ilf.	65	J6
Laidlaw Dr. N21	43	F5
Chadwick Av.		
Laing Cl., Ilf.	65	G6
Laing Dean, Nthlt.	102	C1
Laings Av., Mitch.	185	J2
Lainlock Pl., Houns.	143	H1
Spring Gro. Rd.		
Lainson St. SW18	148	D7
Laird Ho. SE5	131	J7
Lairdale Cl. SE21	169	J1
Lairs Cl. N7	92/93	E6
Manger Rd.		
Laitwood Rd. SW12	168	B1
Lake, The, Bushey	51	J1
Lake Av., Brom.	173	G6
Lake Cl. SW19	166	C5
Lake Rd.		
Lake Dr., Bushey	51	J2
Lake Gdns., Dag.	101	G5
Lake Gdns., Rich.	163	E2
Lake Gdns., Wall.	200	B3
Lake Ho. Rd. E11	97	G3
Lake Rd. SW19	166	C5
Lake Rd., Croy.	203	J2
Lake Rd., Rom.	82	D4
Lake Vw., Edg.	53	J5
Lakedale Rd. SE18	137	H6
Lakefield Rd. N22	75	H2
Lakehall Gdns., Th.Hth.	187	H5
Lakehall Rd., Th.Hth.	187	H5
Lakehurst Rd., Epsom	196	E5
Lakeland Cl., Har.	52	A6
Lakenheath N14	42	D6
Laker Pl. SW15	148	C6
Lakes Rd., Kes.	205	J5
Lakeside N3	73	E2
Lakeside W13	105	F6
Edgehill Rd.		
Lakeside, Beck.	190	B3
Lakeside, Enf.	42	D4
Lakeside, Wall.	200	B3
Derek Av.		
Lakeside Av. SE28	138	A1
Lakeside Av., Ilf.	80	A4
Lakeside Cl. SE25	188	D2
Lakeside Cl., Chig.	65	J4
Lakeside Cl., Sid.	158	C5
Lakeside Ct. N4	93	H2
Lakeside Ct., Borwd.	38	A5
Cavendish Cres.		
Lakeside Cres., Barn.	41	J5
Lakeside Dr., Brom.	206	B3
Lakeside Rd. N13	59	F4
Lakeside Rd. W14	128	A3
Lakeside Way, Wem.	88	A4
Lakeswood Rd., Orp.	193	E6
Lakeview Ct. SW19	166	B2
Victoria Dr.		
Lakeview Rd. SE27	169	G5
Lakeview Rd., Well.	158	B4
Lakis Cl. NW3	91	F4
Flask Wk.		
Laleham Av. NW7	54	D3
Laleham Rd. SE6	154	C6
Lalor St. SW6	148	B2
Lamb La. E8	94	E7
Lamb St. E1	**21**	**F1**
Lamb St. E1	112	C5
Lamb Wk. SE1	**28**	**D4**
Lambarde Av. SE9	174	D4
Lamberhurst Rd. SE27	169	G4
Lamberhurst Rd., Dag.	101	F1
Lambert Av., Rich.	146	B3
Lambert Rd. E16	115	H6
Lambert Rd. N12	57	G5
Lambert Rd. SW2	151	E5
Lambert St. N1	93	G7
Lambert Wk., Wem.	87	G3
Lambert Way N12	57	F5
Woodhouse Rd.		
Lamberts Pl., Croy.	202	A1
Lamberts Rd., Surb.	181	H5
Lambeth Br. SE1	**34**	**B1**
Lambeth Br. SE1	131	E4
Lambeth Br. SW1	**34**	**B1**
Lambeth Br. SW1	131	E4
Lambeth High St. SE1	**34**	**C2**
Lambeth High St. SE1	131	F4
Lambeth Hill EC4	**19**	**J5**
Lambeth Hill EC4	111	J7
Lambeth Palace Rd. SE1	**26**	**C6**
Lambeth Palace Rd. SE1	131	F3
Lambeth Rd. SE1	**26**	**D6**
Lambeth Rd. SE1	131	F4
Lambeth Rd. SE11	**26**	**D6**
Lambeth Rd. SE11	131	F4
Lambeth Rd., Croy.	187	G7
Lambeth Wk. SE11	**34**	**D1**
Lambeth Wk. SE11	131	F4
Lamble St. NW5	92	A5
Lambley Rd., Dag.	100	B6
Lambolle Pl. NW3	91	H6
Lambolle Rd. NW3	91	H6
Lambourn Cl. W7	124	C2
Lambourn Rd. SW4	150	B3
Lambourne Av. SW19	166	C4
Lambourne Gdns. E4	62	A2
Lambourne Gdns., Bark.	99	J7
Lambourne Rd.		
Lambourne Gdns., Enf.	44	C2
Lambourne Gro., Kings.T.	182	B2
Kenley Rd.		
Lambourne Pl. SE3	155	H1
Shooter's Hill Rd.		
Lambourne Rd. E11	78	C7
Lambourne Rd., Bark.	99	H7
Lambourne Rd., Chig.	65	H4
Lambourne Rd., Ilf.	99	H2
Lambrook Ter. SW6	148	B1
Lamb's Bldgs. EC1	**12**	**B6**
Lambs Conduit Pas. WC1	**18**	**C1**
Lamb's Conduit St. WC1	**10**	**C6**
Lamb's Conduit St. WC1	111	F4
Lambs Meadow, Wdf.Grn.	80	A2
Lambs Ms. N1	111	H1
Colebrooke Row		
Lamb's Pas. EC1	**12**	**B6**
Lamb's Pas. EC1	112	A5
Lambs Ter. N9	60	A2
Lambs Wk., Enf.	43	J2
Lambscroft Av. SE9	173	J3
Lambton Pl. W11	108	C6
Westbourne Gro.		
Lambton Rd. N19	92	E1
Lambton Rd. SW20	183	J1
Lamerock Rd., Brom.	173	F4
Lamerton Rd., Ilf.	81	E2
Lamerton St. SE8	134	A6
Lamford Cl. N17	60	A7
Lamington St. W6	127	H4
Lamlash St. SE11	**35**	**G1**
Lammas Av., Mitch.	186	A2
Lammas Grn. SE26	170	E3
Lammas Pk. W5	125	F2
Lammas Pk. Gdns. W5	125	F2
Lammas Pk. Rd. W5	125	F1
Lammas Rd. E9	95	G7
Lammas Rd. E10	95	H2
Lammas Rd., Rich.	163	F4
Lammermoor Rd. SW12	150	B7
Lamont Rd. SW10	**30**	**D6**
Lamont Rd. SW10	129	F6
Lamorbey Cl., Sid.	175	J1
Lamorna Cl. E17	78	C1
Lamorna Gro., Stan.	69	G1
Lamp Office Ct. WC1	**10**	**C6**
Lampard Gro. N16	94	C1
Lampern Sq. E2	**13**	**J3**
Lampeter Sq. W6	128	B6
Humbolt Rd.		
Lamplighter Cl. E1	113	F4
Cleveland Way		
Lampmead Rd. SE12	155	E5
Lamport Cl. SE18	136	C4
Lampton Av., Houns.	143	H1
Lampton Ho. Cl. SW19	166	A4
Lampton Pk. Rd., Houns.	143	H2
Lampton Rd., Houns.	143	H2
Lanacre Av. NW9	71	F1
Lanark Cl. W5	105	F5
Lanark Pl. W9	**6**	**D5**
Lanark Pl. W9	109	F4
Lanark Rd. W9	**6**	**C4**
Lanark Rd. W9	109	E2
Lanark Sq. E14	134	B3
Lanata Wk., Hayes	102	D4
Ramulis Dr.		
Lanbury Rd. SE15	153	G4
Lancashire Ct. W1	**16**	**E5**
Lancaster Av. E18	79	H4
Lancaster Av. SE27	169	H2
Lancaster Av. SW19	166	A5
Lancaster Av., Bark.	99	H7
Lancaster Av., Mitch.	186	E5
Lancaster Cl. N1	94	B7
Hertford Rd.		
Lancaster Cl. N17	60	D7
Park La.		
Lancaster Cl. NW9	55	F7
Lancaster Cl., Brom.	191	F4
Lancaster Cl., Kings.T.	163	G5
Lancaster Cl., Stai.	140	B6
Lancaster Cotts., Rich.	145	H6
Lancaster Pk.		
Lancaster Ct. SE27	169	H2
Lancaster Ct. SW6	128	C7
Lancaster Ct. W2	**14**	**D6**
Lancaster Ct., Walt.	178	A7
Lancaster Dr. E14	134	C1
Prestons Rd.		
Lancaster Dr. NW3	91	H6
Lancaster Dr., Loug.	48	B6
Lancaster Gdns. SW19	166	B5
Lancaster Gdns. W13	125	E2
Lancaster Gdns., Kings.T.	163	G5
Lancaster Gate W2	**14**	**D6**
Lancaster Gate W2	109	F7
Lancaster Gro. NW3	91	G6
Lancaster Ms. SW18	148/149	E5
East Hill		
Lancaster Ms. W2	**14**	**D5**
Lancaster Ms. W2	109	F7
Lancaster Ms., Rich.	145	H6
Richmond Hill		
Lancaster Pk., Rich.	145	H5
Lancaster Pl. SW19	166	A5
Lancaster Rd.		
Lancaster Pl. WC2	**18**	**C5**
Lancaster Pl. WC2	111	F7
Lancaster Pl., Houns.	142	C2
Lancaster Pl., Ilf.	99	F5
Staines Rd.		
Lancaster Pl., Twick.	144	D6
Lancaster Rd. E7	97	G7
Lancaster Rd. E11	97	E2
Lancaster Rd. E17	77	G2
Lancaster Rd. N4	75	G7
Lancaster Rd. N11	58	D6
Lancaster Rd. N18	60	C5
Lancaster Rd. NW10	89	G5
Lancaster Rd. SE25	188	C2
Lancaster Rd. SW19	166	A5
Lancaster Rd. W11	108	B6
Lancaster Rd., Barn.	41	G5
Lancaster Rd., Enf.	44	A1
Lancaster Rd., Har.	67	G5
Lancaster Rd., Nthlt.	85	J6
Lancaster Rd., Sthl.	103	E7
Lancaster St. SE1	**27**	**H4**
Lancaster St. SE1	131	H2
Lancaster Ter. W2	**15**	**E5**
Lancaster Ter. W2	109	G7
Lancaster Wk. W2	**22**	**E3**
Lancaster Wk. W2	129	F1

Lancaster W. W11	108	A7
Grenfell Rd.		
Lance Rd., Har.	67	J7
Lancefield St. W10	108	C3
Lancell St. N16	94	B2
Stoke Newington Ch. St.		
Lancelot Av., Wem.	87	G4
Lancelot Cres., Wem.	87	G4
Lancelot Gdns., Barn.	42	A7
Lancelot Pl. SW7	**23**	**J4**
Lancelot Pl. SW7	129	J2
Lancelot Rd., Ilf.	65	H6
Lancelot Rd., Well.	158	A4
Lancelot Rd., Wem.	87	G5
Lancer Sq. W8	**22**	**A3**
Lancey Cl. SE7	136	A4
Cleveley Cl.		
Lanchester Rd. N6	73	J5
Lancing Gdns. N9	60	C1
Lancing Rd. W13	104/105	E7
Drayton Grn. Rd.		
Lancing Rd., Croy.	187	F6
Lancing Rd., Ilf.	81	G6
Lancing St. NW1	**9**	**H4**
Lancresse Ct. N1	112	B1
Landcroft Rd. SE22	152	C6
Landells Rd. SE22	152	C6
Landford Rd. SW15	147	J3
Landgrove Rd. SW19	166	D5
Landmann Way SE14	133	G5
Landon Pl. SW1	**23**	**J5**
Landon Pl. SW1	129	J3
Landon Wk. E14	114	B7
Cottage St.		
Landons Cl. E14	134	C1
Landor Rd. SW9	150	E3
Landor Wk. W12	127	G2
Landport Way SE15	**37**	**G7**
Landra Gdns. N21	43	H6
Landridge Rd. SW6	148	C2
Landrock Rd. N8	75	E6
Landscape Rd., Wdf.Grn.	63	H7
Landseer Av. E12	98	D5
Landseer Cl. SW19	185	F1
Brangwyn Cres.		
Landseer Cl., Edg.	70	A2
Landseer Rd. N19	92	E3
Landseer Rd., Enf.	44	D5
Landseer Rd., N.Mal.	182	D7
Landseer Rd., Sutt.	198	D6
Landstead Rd. SE18	137	G7
Lane, The NW8	**6**	**C1**
Lane, The SE3	155	G3
Lane App. NW7	56	B5
Lane Cl. NW2	89	H3
Lane End, Bexh.	159	H3
Lane Ms. E12	98	C3
Colchester Av.		
Lanercost Cl. SW2	169	G2
Lanercost Gdns. N14	42	E7
Lanercost Rd. SW2	169	G2
Lanesborough Pl. SW1	**24**	**B3**
Laneside, Chis.	175	E5
Laneside, Edg.	54	C5
Laneside Av., Dag.	83	F7
Laneway SW15	147	H5
Lanfranc Rd. E3	113	H2
Lanfrey Pl. W14	128	C5
North End Rd.		
Lang St. E1	113	F4
Langbourne Av. N6	92	A2
Langbourne Pl. E14	134	A2
Westferry Rd.		
Langbourne Way, Esher	194	D6
Langbrook Rd. SE3	156	A3
Langcroft Cl., Cars.	199	J3
Langdale Av., Mitch.	185	J3
Langdale Cl. SE17	**35**	**J5**
Langdale Cl. SE17	131	J6
Langdale Cl. SW14	146	B4
Clifford Av.		
Langdale Cl., Dag.	100	C1
Langdale Cl., Orp.	206/207	E3
Grasmere Rd.		
Langdale Cres., Bexh.	139	G7
Langdale Gdns., Grnf.	105	E3
Langdale Rd. SE10	134	C7
Langdale Rd., Th.Hth.	187	G4
Langdale St. E1	112/113	E6
Burslem St.		
Langdon Ct. NW10	106	E1
Langdon Cres. E6	116	D2
Langdon Dr. NW9	88	C1
Langdon Pk. Rd. N6	74	C7
Langdon Pl. SW14	146	C3
Rosemary La.		
Langdon Rd. E6	116	D1
Langdon Rd., Brom.	191	H3
Langdon Rd., Mord.	185	F5
Langdon Shaw, Sid.	175	J5
Langdon Wk., Mord.	185	F5
Langdon Way SE1	**37**	**J2**
Langdons Ct., Sthl.	123	G3
Langford Cl. E8	94	D5
Langford Cl. N15	76	B6
Langford Cl. NW8	**6**	**D1**
Langford Ct. NW8	**6**	**C2**
Langford Ct. NW8	109	F2
Langford Cres., Barn.	41	J4
Langford Grn. SE5	152	B3
Langford Pl. NW8	**6**	**D1**
Langford Pl. NW8	109	F2
Langford Pl., Sid.	176	A3
Langford Rd. SW6	149	E2
Langford Rd., Barn.	41	H4
Langford Rd., Wdf.Grn.	63	J6
Langfords, Buck.H.	64	A2
Langham Cl. N15	75	H3
Langham Rd.		
Langham Dr., Rom.	82	B6
Langham Gdns. N21	43	G5
Langham Gdns. W13	105	E7
Langham Gdns., Edg.	54	C7
Langham Gdns., Rich.	163	F4
Langham Gdns., Wem.	87	F2
Langham Ho. Cl., Rich.	163	G4
Langham Pl. N15	75	H3
Langham Pl. W1	**16**	**E2**
Langham Pl. W1	110	B5
Langham Pl. W4	126/127	E6
Hogarth Roundabout		
Langham Rd. N15	75	H3
Langham Rd. SW20	183	J1
Langham Rd., Edg.	54	C6
Langham Rd., Tedd.	162	E5
Langham St. W1	**17**	**E2**
Langham St. W1	110	B5
Langhedge Cl. N18	60	C6
Langhedge La.		
Langhedge La. N18	60	C5
Langhedge La. Ind. Est. N18	60	C6
Langholm Cl. SW12	150	D7
King's Av.		
Langholme, Bushey	51	J1
Langhorne Rd., Dag.	101	G7
Langland Cres., Stan.	69	H3
Langland Dr., Pnr.	50	E7
Langland Gdns. NW3	91	E5
Langland Gdns., Croy.	203	J2
Langler Rd. NW10	107	J2
Langley Av., Ruis.	84	B1
Langley Av., Surb.	195	G1
Langley Av., Wor.Pk.	198	A2
Langley Ct. SE9	156	D6
Langley Ct. WC2	**18**	**A5**
Langley Ct., Beck.	190	B5
Langley Cres. E11	79	J7
Langley Cres., Dag.	100	C7
Langley Cres., Edg.	54	C3
Langley Cres., Hayes	121	J7
Langley Dr. E11	79	H7
Langley Dr. W3	126	B2
Langley Gdns., Brom.	191	J4
Langley Gdns., Dag.	100	D7
Langley Gdns., Orp.	193	E6
Langley Gro., N.Mal.	182	E2
Langley La. SW8	**34**	**B5**
Langley La. SW8	131	F6
Langley Meadow, Loug.	49	G2
Langley Pk. NW7	54	E6
Langley Pk. Rd., Sutt.	199	F5
Langley Rd. SW19	184	C1
Langley Rd., Beck.	189	H4
Langley Rd., Islw.	144	C2
Langley Rd., Surb.	181	H7
Langley Rd., Well.	138	C6
Langley Row, Barn.	40	C1
Langley St. WC2	**18**	**A4**
Langley St. WC2	110	E6
Langley Way, W.Wick.	204	D1
Langmead Dr., Bushey	52	A1
Langmead St. SE27	169	H4
Beadman St.		
Langmore Ct., Bexh.	158	D3
Regency Way		
Langridge Ms., Hmptn.	161	F6
Oak Av.		
Langroyd Rd. SW17	167	J2
Langside Av. SW15	147	G4
Langside Cres. N14	58	D3
Langston Hughes Cl. SE24	151	H4
Shakespeare Rd.		
Langston Rd., Loug.	49	F5
Langthorn Ct. EC2	**20**	**B3**
Langthorne Rd. E11	96	C3
Langthorne St. SW6	128	A7
Langton Av. E6	116	D3
Langton Av. N20	41	F7
Langton Cl. WC1	**10**	**D4**
Langton Pl. SW18	166	D1
Merton Rd.		
Langton Ri. SE23	152	E7
Langton Rd. NW2	89	J3
Langton Rd. SW9	131	H7
Langton Rd., Har.	51	J7
Langton Rd., W.Mol.	179	J4
Langton St. SW10	**30**	**D6**
Langton St. SW10	129	F6
Langton Way SE3	155	F1
Langton Way, Croy.	202	B4
Langtry Rd. NW8	108	E1
Langtry Rd., Nthlt.	102	D2
Langtry Wk. NW8	91	F7
Alexandra Pl.		
Langwood Chase, Tedd.	163	F6
Langworth Dr., Hayes	102	A6
Lanhill Rd. W9	108	D4
Lanier Rd. SE13	154	C6
Lanigan Dr., Houns.	143	H5
Lankaster Gdns. N2	73	G1
Lankers Dr., Har.	67	F6
Lankton Cl., Beck.	190	C1
Lannock Rd., Hayes	121	H1
Lannoy Rd. SE9	175	F1
Lanrick Rd. E14	114	D6
Lanridge Rd. SE2	138	D3
Lansbury Av. N18	60	A5
Lansbury Av., Bark.	100	A7
Lansbury Av., Felt.	142	B6
Lansbury Av., Rom.	83	E5
Lansbury Cl. NW10	88	C5
Lansbury Est. E14	114	B6
Lansbury Gdns. E14	114	D6
Lansbury Rd., Enf.	45	G1
Lansbury Way N18	60	B5
Lanscombe Wk. SW8	150	E1
Lansdell Rd., Mitch.	186	A2
Lansdown Rd. E7	97	J7
Lansdown Rd., Sid.	176	B3
Lansdowne Av., Bexh.	138	D7
Lansdowne Av., Orp.	207	E1
Lansdowne Cl. SW20	166	A7
Lansdowne Cl., Surb.	196	B2
Kingston Rd.		
Lansdowne Cl., Twick.	162	C1
Lion Rd.		
Lansdowne Ct., Wor.Pk.	197	G2
The Av.		
Lansdowne Cres. W11	108	B7
Lansdowne Dr. E8	94	D6
Lansdowne Gdns. SW8	150	E1
Lansdowne Grn. SW8	150/151	E1
Hartington Rd.		
Lansdowne Gro. NW10	89	E4
Lansdowne Hill SE27	169	H3
Lansdowne La. SE7	136	A6
Lansdowne Ms. SE7	136	A5
Lansdowne Ms. W11	128	C1
Lansdowne Rd.		
Lansdowne Pl. SE1	**28**	**C6**
Lansdowne Pl. SE19	170	C7
Lansdowne Ri. W11	108	B7
Lansdowne Rd. E4	62	A2
Lansdowne Rd. E11	97	F2
Lansdowne Rd. E17	78	A5
Lansdowne Rd. E18	79	G3
Lansdowne Rd. N3	56	C7
Lansdowne Rd. N10	74	C2
Lansdowne Rd. N17	76	C1
Lansdowne Rd. SW20	165	J7
Lansdowne Rd. W11	108	B7
Lansdowne Rd., Brom.	173	G7
Lansdowne Rd., Croy.	202	A2
Lansdowne Rd., Epsom	196	C7
Lansdowne Rd., Har.	68	B7
Lansdowne Rd., Houns.	143	H3
Lansdowne Rd., Ilf.	99	J1
Lansdowne Rd., Stan.	53	F6
Lansdowne Row W1	**24**	**E1**
Lansdowne Ter. WC1	**10**	**B6**
Lansdowne Ter. WC1	111	E4
Lansdowne Wk. W11	128	B1
Lansdowne Way SW8	150	E1
Lansdowne Wd. Cl. SE27	169	H3
Lansfield Av. N18	60	D4
Lant St. SE1	**27**	**J3**
Lant St. SE1	131	J2
Lantern Cl. SW15	147	G4
Lantern Cl., Wem.	87	G5
Lantern Way, West Dr.	120	B2
Warwick Rd.		
Lanterns Ct. E14	134	A2
Lanvanor Rd. SE15	153	F2
Lapford Cl. W9	108	C4
Lapponum Wk., Hayes	102	D5
Lochan Cl.		
Lapse Wd. Wk. SE23	170	E1
Lapstone Gdns., Har.	69	F6
Lapwing Ct., Surb.	196	A3
Chaffinch Cl.		
Lapwing Way, Hayes	102	D6
Lara Cl. SE13	154	C6
Lara Cl., Chess.	195	H7
Larbert Rd. SW16	186	C1
Larch Av. W3	126	E1
Larch Cl. E13	115	H4
Larch Cl. N11	58	A7
Larch Cl. N19	92	C2
Bredgar Rd.		
Larch Cl. SE8	133	J6
Clyde St.		
Larch Cl. SW12	168	B2
Larch Cres., Epsom	196	B6
Larch Cres., Hayes	102	C4
Larch Dr. W4	126	A5
Gunnersbury Av.		
Larch Grn. NW9	70/71	E1
Clayton Fld.		
Larch Gro., Sid.	175	J1
Larch Ms. N19	92	C2
Bredgar Rd.		
Larch Rd. E10	96	A2
Walnut Rd.		
Larch Rd. NW2	89	J4
Larch Tree Way, Croy.	204	A3
Larch Way, Brom.	192	D7
Larchdene, Orp.	206	D2
Larches, The N13	59	J3
Larches Av. SW14	146	D4
Larchwood Rd. SE9	175	E2
Larcom St. SE17	**36**	**A2**
Larcom St. SE17	131	J4
Larcombe Cl., Croy.	202	C4
Larden Rd. W3	127	E1
Largewood Av., Surb.	196	A2
Larissa St. SE17	**36**	**C3**
Lark Row E2	113	F1
Lark Way, Cars.	185	H7
Larkbere Rd. SE26	171	H4
Larken Dr., Bushey	51	J1
Larkfield Av., Har.	69	E3
Larkfield Cl., Brom.	205	F2
Larkfield Rd., Rich.	145	H4
Larkfield Rd., Sid.	175	J3
Larkhall La. SW4	150	D2
Larkhall Ri. SW4	150	C3
Larkhill Ter. SE18	136	D7
Larks Gro., Bark.	99	H7
Larksfield Gro., Enf.	45	E1
Larkshall Ct., Rom.	83	J2
Larkshall Cres. E4	62	C4
Larkshall Rd. E4	62	C5
Larkspur Cl. E6	116	B5
Larkspur Cl. N17	60	A7
Fryatt Rd.		
Larkspur Cl. NW9	70	B5
Larkspur Gro., Edg.	54	C4
Larkspur Way, Epsom	196	C5
Larkswood Ct. E4	62	D5
Larkswood Ri., Pnr.	66	C4
Larkswood Rd. E4	62	A4
Larkway Cl. NW9	70	D4
Larnach Rd. W6	128	A6
Larpent Av. SW15	147	J5
Larwood Cl., Grnf.	86	A5
Lascelles Av., Har.	68	A7
Lascelles Cl. E11	96	D2
Lascotts Rd. N22	59	F6
Lassa Rd. SE9	156	B5
Lassell St. SE10	134	D5
Lasseter Pl. SE3	135	F6
Vanbrugh Hill		
Latchett Rd. E18	79	H1
Latchingdon Ct. E17	77	G4
Latchingdon Gdns., Wdf.Grn.	64	B6
Latchmere Cl., Rich.	163	H5
Latchmere La., Kings.T.	163	J6
Latchmere Pas. SW11	149	H2
Cabul Rd.		
Latchmere Rd. SW11	149	J2
Latchmere Rd., Kings.T.	163	H7
Latchmere St. SW11	149	J2
Lateward Rd., Brent.	125	G6
Latham Cl. E6	116	B6
Oliver Gdns.		
Latham Cl., Twick.	144	D7
Latham Ho. E1	113	G6

Latham Rd., Bexh. 159 G5
Latham Rd., Twick. 144 C7
Lathams Way, Croy. 201 F1
Lathkill Cl., Enf. 44 D7
Lathom Rd. E6 98 C7
Latimer SE17 36 D4
Latimer Av. E6 116 C1
Latimer Cl., Pnr. 66 C1
Latimer Cl., Wor.Pk. 197 H4
Latimer Gdns., Pnr. 66 C1
Latimer Pl. W10 107 J6
Latimer Rd. E7 97 H4
Latimer Rd. N15 76 B6
Latimer Rd. SW19 166 E6
Latimer Rd. W10 107 J6
Latimer Rd., Barn. 40 E3
Latimer Rd., Croy. 201 H3
Abbey Rd.
Latimer Rd., Tedd. 162 C5
Latona Rd. SE15 37 H6
Latona Rd. SE15 132 D6
Lattimer Pl. W4 127 E6
Latton Cl., Walt. 179 E7
Latymer Ct. W6 128 A4
Latymer Rd. N9 60 C1
Latymer Way N9 60 A2
Laud St. SE11 34 C3
Laud St., Croy. 201 J3
Lauder Cl., Nthlt. 102 D2
Lauderdale Dr., Rich. 163 G3
Lauderdale Pl. EC2 111 J5
Beech St.
Lauderdale Rd. W9 6 A4
Lauderdale Rd. W9 108 E3
Laughton Ct., Borwd. 38 D2
Banks Rd.
Laughton Rd., Nthlt. 102 D1
Launcelot Rd., Brom. 173 G4
Launcelot St. SE1 26 E4
Launceston Gdns., Grnf. 105 F1
Launceston Pl. W8 22 C5
Launceston Pl. W8 129 F3
Launceston Rd., Grnf. 105 F1
Launch St. E14 134 C3
Laundress La. N16 94 D3
Laundry La. N1 111 J1
Greenman St.
Laundry Rd. W6 128 B6
Laura Cl. E11 79 J5
Laura Cl., Enf. 44 B5
Laura Pl. E5 95 F4
Lauradale Rd. N2 73 J4
Laurel Av., Twick. 162 C1
Laurel Bank Gdns. SW6 148 C2
New Kings Rd.
Laurel Bank Rd., Enf. 43 J1
Laurel Bank Vil. W7 124 B1
Lower Boston Rd.
Laurel Cl. N19 92 C2
Hargrave Pk.
Laurel Cl. SW17 167 H5
Laurel Cl., Ilf. 65 F6
Laurel Cl., Sid. 176 A3
Laurel Cres., Croy. 204 A3
Laurel Dr. N21 43 G7
Laurel Gdns. E4 46 B7
Laurel Gdns. NW7 54 D3
Laurel Gdns. W7 124 B1
Laurel Gdns., Houns. 142 E4
Laurel Gro. SE20 171 E7
Laurel Gro. SE26 171 G4
Laurel La., West Dr. 120 B4
Laurel Pk., Har. 52 C7
Laurel Rd. SW13 147 G2
Laurel Rd. SW20 183 H1
Laurel Rd., Hmptn. 162 A5
Laurel St. E8 94 C6
Laurel Vw. N12 56 E3
Laurel Way E18 79 F4
Laurel Way N20 56 D3
Laurence Ms. W12 127 G2
Askew Rd.
Laurence Pountney Hill EC4 20 B5
Laurence Pountney La. EC4 20 B5
Laurie Gro. SE14 153 H1
Laurie Rd. W7 104 B5
Laurier Rd. NW5 92 B3
Laurier Rd., Croy. 188 C7
Laurimel Cl., Stan. 52/53 E6
September Way
Laurino Pl., Bushey 51 J2
Lauriston Rd. E9 113 G1
Lauriston Rd. SW19 166 A6
Lausanne Rd. N8 75 G4
Lausanne Rd. SE15 153 F1
Lavell St. N16 94 A4
Lavender Av. NW9 88 C1
Lavender Av., Mitch. 185 H1
Lavender Av., Wor.Pk. 197 J3
Lavender Cl. SW3 31 F6
Lavender Cl., Brom. 192 B6
Lavender Cl., Cars. 200 A4
Lavender Ct., W.Mol. 179 H3
Molesham Way
Lavender Gdns. SW11 149 J4
Lavender Gdns., Enf. 43 H1
Lavender Gdns., Har. 52 B6
Uxbridge Rd.
Lavender Gro. E8 94 C7
Lavender Gro., Mitch. 185 H1
Lavender Hill SW11 149 H4
Lavender Hill, Enf. 43 G1
Lavender Ms., Wall. 200 E6
Lavender Pl., Ilf. 98 E5
Lavender Ri., West Dr. 120 D2
Lavender Rd. SE16 133 H1
Lavender Rd. SW11 149 G3
Lavender Rd., Cars. 200 A4
Lavender Rd., Croy. 187 F6
Lavender Rd., Enf. 44 A1
Lavender Rd., Epsom 196 B5
Lavender Rd., Sutt. 199 G4
Lavender Sq. E11 96 D3
Anglian Rd.
Lavender St. E15 96/97 E6
Manbey Gro.
Lavender Sweep SW11 149 J4
Lavender Ter. SW11 149 H3
Falcon Rd.
Lavender Vale, Wall. 200 D6
Lavender Wk. SW11 149 J4
Lavender Wk., Mitch. 186 A3
Lavender Way, Croy. 189 G6
Lavengro Rd. SE27 169 J2
Lavenham Rd. SW18 166 C2
Lavernock Rd., Bexh. 159 G2
Lavers Rd. N16 94 B3
Laverstoke Gdns. SW15 147 G7
Laverton Ms. SW5 30 B2
Laverton Pl. SW5 30 B2
Laverton Pl. SW5 129 E4
Lavidge Rd. SE9 174 B2
Lavina Gro. N1 10 C1
Lavington Rd. W13 125 E1
Lavington Rd., Croy. 201 F3
Lavington St. SE1 27 H2
Lavington St. SE1 131 H1
Law Ho., Bark. 118 A2
Law St. SE1 28 C5
Law St. SE1 132 A3
Lawdons Gdns., Croy. 201 H4
Lawford Rd. N1 94 B7
Lawford Rd. NW5 92 C6
Lawford Rd. W4 126 C7
Lawless St. E14 114 B7
Lawley Rd. N14 42 B7
Lawley St. E5 95 F4
Lawn, The, Sthl. 123 G5
Lawn Cl. N9 44 C7
Lawn Cl., Brom. 173 H6
Lawn Cl., N.Mal. 182 E2
Lawn Cres., Rich. 146 A2
Lawn Fm. Gro., Rom. 82 E4
Lawn Gdns. W7 124 B1
Lawn Ho. Cl. E14 134 C2
Lawn La. SW8 34 B6
Lawn La. SW8 131 E6
Lawn Pl. SE15 152 C1
Sumner Est.
Lawn Rd. NW3 91 J5
Lawn Rd., Beck. 171 J7
Lawn Ter. SE3 155 E3
Lawn Vale, Pnr. 66 D2
Lawnfield NW2 90 A7
Coverdale Rd.
Lawns, The E4 62 A5
Lawns, The SE3 154/155 E3
Lee Ter.
Lawns, The SE19 188 A1
Lawns, The, Pnr. 51 H7
Lawns, The, Sid. 176 B4
Lawns, The, Sutt. 198 B7
Lawns Ct., Wem. 87 J2
The Av.
Lawnside SE3 155 F4
Lawrence Av. E12 98 D4
Lawrence Av. E17 77 G1
Lawrence Av. N13 59 H4
Lawrence Av. NW7 55 E4
Lawrence Av., N.Mal. 182 D6
Lawrence Bldgs. N16 94 C3
Lawrence Campe Cl. N20 57 G3
Friern Barnet La.
Lawrence Cl. E3 114 A2
Lawrence Cl. N15 76 B3
Lawrence Rd.
Lawrence Ct. NW7 55 E5
Lawrence Cres., Dag. 101 H3
Lawrence Cres., Edg. 70 A2
Lawrence Gdns. NW7 55 F3
Lawrence Hill E4 62 A2
Lawrence La. EC2 20 A4
Lawrence Pl. N1 110/111 E1
Outram Pl.
Lawrence Rd. E6 116 A1
Lawrence Rd. E13 115 H1
Lawrence Rd. N15 76 B4
Lawrence Rd. N18 60 E4
Lawrence Rd. SE25 188 C4
Lawrence Rd. W5 125 G4
Lawrence Rd., Erith 139 H7
Lawrence Rd., Hmptn. 161 F7
Lawrence Rd., Houns. 142 C4
Lawrence Rd., Pnr. 66 D5
Lawrence Rd., Rich. 163 F4
Lawrence Rd., W.Wick. 205 G4
Lawrence St. E16 115 F5
Lawrence St. NW7 55 F4
Lawrence St. SW3 31 G6
Lawrence St. SW3 129 H6
Lawrence Way NW10 88 C4
Lawrence Weaver Cl., Mord. 184/185 E6
Green La.
Lawrie Pk. Av. SE26 171 E5
Lawrie Pk. Cres. SE26 171 E5
Lawrie Pk. Gdns. SE26 171 E4
Lawrie Pk. Rd. SE26 171 E6
Lawson Cl. E16 115 J5
Lawson Cl. SW19 166 A3
Lawson Est. SE1 28 B6
Lawson Est. SE1 132 A3
Lawson Gdns., Pnr. 66 B3
Lawson Rd., Enf. 45 F1
Lawson Rd., Sthl. 103 F4
Lawson Wk., Cars. 199 J7
Fountain Dr.
Lawton Rd. E3 113 H3
Lawton Rd. E10 96 C1
Lawton Rd., Barn. 41 G3
Lawton Rd., Loug. 48 E3
Laxcon Cl. NW10 88 C5
Laxey Rd., Orp. 207 J6
Laxley Cl. SE5 35 H7
Laxley Cl. SE5 131 H7
Laxton Pl. NW1 9 E5
Layard Rd. SE16 133 E4
Layard Rd., Enf. 44 C1
Layard Rd., Th.Hth. 188 A2
Layard Sq. SE16 133 E4
Laycock St. N1 93 G6
Layer Gdns. W3 106 A7
Layfield Cl. NW4 71 H7
Layfield Cres. NW4 71 H7
Layfield Rd. NW4 71 H7
Layhams Rd., Kes. 205 F5
Layhams Rd., W.Wick. 204 D3
Laymarsh Cl., Belv. 139 F3
Laymead Cl., Nthlt. 84 E6
Laystall St. EC1 10 E6
Laystall St. EC1 111 G4
Layton Cres., Croy. 201 G5
Layton Rd. N1 11 F1
Layton Rd., Brent. 125 G5
Layton Rd., Houns. 143 H4
Laytons Bldgs. SE1 28 A3
Layzell Wk. SE9 174 A1
Mottingham La.
Lazar Wk. N7 93 F2
Briset Way
Le May Av. SE12 173 H3
Lea Br. Rd. E5 95 F3
Lea Br. Rd. E10 95 H1
Lea Br. Rd. E17 78 D4
Lea Gdns., Wem. 87 H4
Lea Hall Rd. E10 96 A1
Lea Rd., Beck. 190 A2
Fairfield Rd.
Lea Rd., Enf. 44 A1
Lea Rd., Sthl. 122 E4
Lea Valley Rd. E4 45 G5
Lea Valley Rd., Enf. 45 G5
Lea Valley Trd. Est. N18 61 G5
Lea Valley Viaduct E4 61 G5
Lea Valley Viaduct N18 61 G5
Lea Vw. Hos. E5 94/95 E1
Springfield
Leabank Cl., Har. 86 B3
Leabank Sq. E9 96 A6
Leabank Vw. N15 76 D6
Leabourne Rd. N16 76 D6
Leacroft Av. SW12 149 J7
Leadale Av. E4 62 A2
Leadale Rd. N15 76 D6
Leadale Rd. N16 76 D6
Leadbeaters Cl. N11 57 J5
Goldsmith Rd.
Leadenhall Mkt. EC3 20 D4
Leadenhall Pl. EC3 20 D4
Leadenhall St. EC3 20 D4
Leadenhall St. EC3 112 B6
Leader Av. E12 98 D5
Leadings, The, Wem. 88 C3
Leaf Cl., T.Ditt. 180 B5
Leaf Gro. SE27 169 G5
Leafield Cl. SW16 169 H6
Leafield La., Sid. 177 F4
Leafield Rd. SW20 184 C3
Leafield Rd., Sutt. 198 D2
Leafy Gro., Kes. 205 J5
Leafy Oak Rd. SE12 173 J3
Leafy Way, Croy. 202 C2
Leagrave St. E5 95 F3
Leahurst Rd. SE13 154 D5
Leake Ct. SE1 26 D4
Leake St. SE1 26 D3
Leake St. SE1 131 F2
Lealand Rd. N15 76 C6
Leamington Av. E17 78 A5
Leamington Av., Brom. 173 J5
Leamington Av., Mord. 184 C4
Leamington Av., Orp. 207 H4
Leamington Cl. E12 98 B5
Leamington Cl., Brom. 173 J5
Leamington Cl., Houns. 143 J5
Leamington Cres., Har. 85 E3
Leamington Gdns., Ilf. 99 J2
Leamington Pk. W3 106 D5
Leamington Rd., Sthl. 122 D4
Leamington Rd. Vil. W11 108 C5
Leamore St. W6 127 H4
Leamouth Rd. E6 116 B6
Remington Rd.
Leamouth Rd. E14 114 D6
Leander Ct. SE8 154 A1
Leander Rd. SW2 151 F6
Leander Rd., Nthlt. 103 G2
Leander Rd., Th.Hth. 187 F4
Learner Dr., Har. 85 G2
Learoyd Gdns. E6 116 D7
Leas Cl., Chess. 195 J7
Leas Dale SE9 174 D3
Leas Grn., Chis. 175 J6
Leaside Av. N10 74 A3
Leaside Rd. E5 95 F1
Leasowes Rd. E10 96 A1
Leather Bottle La., Belv. 139 E4
Leather Cl., Mitch. 186 A2
Leather Gdns. E15 114/115 E1
Abbey Rd.
Leather La. EC1 19 F2
Leather La. EC1 111 G5
Leatherbottle Grn., Erith 139 F3
Leatherdale St. E1 113 F4
Portelet Rd.
Leatherhead Cl. N16 94 C1
Leathermarket Ct. SE1 28 D4
Leathermarket Ct. SE1 132 B2
Leathermarket St. SE1 28 D4
Leathermarket St. SE1 132 B2
Leathersellers Cl., Barn. 40 B4
The Av.
Leathsail Rd., Har. 85 H3
Leathwaite Rd. SW11 149 J4
Leathwell Rd. SE8 154 B2
Leaveland Cl., Beck. 190 A4
Leaver Gdns., Grnf. 104 A2
Leavesden Rd., Stan. 52 D6
Leaway E10 95 G1
Lebanon Av., Felt. 160 D5
Lebanon Ct., Twick. 144 E7
Lebanon Gdns. SW18 148 D6
Lebanon Pk., Twick. 144 E7
Lebanon Rd. SW18 148 D5
Lebanon Rd., Croy. 202 B1
Lebrun Sq. SE3 155 H3
Lechmere App., Wdf.Grn. 79 J2
Lechmere Av., Chig. 65 F4
Lechmere Av., Wdf.Grn. 80 A2
Lechmere Rd. NW2 89 H6
Leckford Rd. SW18 167 F2
Leckwith Av., Bexh. 138 E6
Lecky St. SW7 31 E3
Lecky St. SW7 129 G5
Leconfield Av. SW13 147 F3
Leconfield Rd. N5 94 A4

Leda Av., Enf. 45 G1
Leda Rd. SE18 136 C3
Ledbury Est. SE15 132 E7
Ledbury Ms. N. W11 108 D7
Ledbury Rd.
Ledbury Ms. W. W11 108 D7
Ledbury Rd.
Ledbury Pl., Croy. 201 J4
Ledbury Rd.
Ledbury Rd. W11 108 C6
Ledbury Rd., Croy. 201 J4
Ledbury St. SE15 132 D7
Ledrington Rd. SE19 170 D6
Anerley Hill
Ledway Dr., Wem. 69 J7
Lee Av., Rom. 82 E6
Lee Br. SE13 154 C3
Lee Ch. St. SE13 155 E4
Lee Cl. E17 77 G1
Lee Cl., Barn. 41 F4
Lee Conservancy Rd. E9 95 J5
Lee Grn. SE12 155 F5
Lee High Rd.
Lee Gro., Chig. 64 D2
Lee High Rd. SE12 154 D3
Lee High Rd. SE13 154 D3
Lee Pk. SE3 155 F4
Lee Pk. Way N9 61 G4
Lee Pk. Way N18 61 G4
Lee Rd. NW7 56 A7
Lee Rd. SE3 155 F3
Lee Rd. SW19 185 E1
Lee Rd., Enf. 44 D6
Lee Rd., Grnf. 105 F1
Lee St. E8 112 C1
Lee Ter. SE3 154 E3
Lee Ter. SE13 154 E3
Lee Valley Technopark N17 76 D3
Lee Vw., Enf. 43 H1
Leechcroft Av., Sid. 157 J5
Leechcroft Rd., Wall. 200 A3
Leecroft Rd., Barn. 40 B5
Leeds Pl. N4 93 F2
Tollington Pk.
Leeds Rd., Ilf. 99 G1
Leeds St. N18 60 D5
Leefern Rd. W12 127 G2
Leegate SE12 155 F5
Leeke St. WC1 10 C3
Leeke St. WC1 111 F3
Leeland Rd. W13 124 D1
Leeland Ter. W13 124 D1
Leeland Way NW10 89 F4
Leerdam Dr. E14 134 C3
Lees, The, Croy. 203 J2
Lees Pl. W1 16 B5
Lees Pl. W1 110 A7
Leeside, Barn. 40 B5
Leeside Cres. NW11 72 C6
Leeside Rd. N17 61 E6
Leeson Rd. SE24 151 G4
Leesons Hill, Chis. 193 J3
Leesons Way, Orp. 193 J2
Leeward Gdns. SW19 166 C6
Leeway SE8 133 J5
Leeway Cl., Pnr. 51 F7
Leewood Cl. SE12 155 F6
Upwood Rd.
Lefevre Wk. E3 114 A1
Lefroy Rd. W12 127 F2
Legard Rd. N5 93 H3
Legatt Rd. SE9 156 A5
Leggatt Rd. E15 114 C2
Legge St. SE13 154 C5
Leghorn Rd. NW10 107 F2
Leghorn Rd. SE18 137 G5
Legion Cl. N1 93 G6
Legion Ct., Mord. 184 D6
Legion Rd., Grnf. 103 J1
Legion Way N12 57 H7
Legon Av., Rom. 101 J1
Legrace Av., Houns. 142 D2
Leicester Av., Mitch. 187 E4
Leicester Cl., Wor.Pk. 197 J4
Leicester Ct. WC2 17 J5
Leicester Gdns., Ilf. 81 H7
Leicester Pl. WC2 17 J5
Leicester Rd. E11 79 H5
Leicester Rd. N2 73 H3
Leicester Rd. NW10 88 D7
Leicester Rd., Barn. 40 E5
Leicester Rd., Croy. 188 B7
Leicester Sq. WC2 17 J6
Leicester Sq. WC2 110 D7
Leicester St. WC2 17 J5
Leigh Av., Ilf. 80 A4
Leigh Cl., N.Mal. 182 D4
Leigh Ct., Borwd. 38 D2
Banks Rd.
Leigh Ct., Har. 86 B1
Leigh Cres., Croy. 204 B7
Leigh Gdns. NW10 107 J2
Leigh Hunt Dr. N14 58 D1
Leigh Hunt St. SE1 27 J3
Leigh Orchard Cl. SW16 169 F3
Leigh Pl. EC1 19 E1
Leigh Pl., Well. 158 A2
Leigh Rd. E6 98 D6
Leigh Rd. E10 78 C7
Leigh Rd. N5 93 H4
Leigh Rd., Houns. 144 A4
Leigh Rodd, Wat. 51 F3
Leigh St. WC1 10 A5
Leigh St. WC1 110 E4
Leigham Av. SW16 169 E3
Leigham Ct., Wall. 200 C6
Stafford Rd.
Leigham Ct. Rd. SW16 169 E2
Leigham Dr., Islw. 124 B7
Leigham Vale SW2 169 F3
Leigham Vale SW16 169 F3
Leighton Av. E12 98 D5
Leighton Av., Pnr. 66 E3
Leighton Cl., Edg. 70 A2
Leighton Cres. NW5 92 C5
Leighton Gro.
Leighton Gdns. NW10 107 H2
Leighton Gro. NW5 92 C5
Leighton Pl. NW5 92 C5
Leighton Rd. NW5 92 D5
Leighton Rd. W13 124 D2
Leighton Rd., Enf. 44 C5
Leighton Rd., Har. 68 A2
Leighton St., Croy. 201 H1
Leila Parnell Pl. SE7 135 J6
Leinster Av. SW14 146 C3
Leinster Gdns. W2 14 C4
Leinster Gdns. W2 109 F6
Leinster Ms. W2 14 C5
Leinster Ms. W2 109 F7
Leinster Pl. W2 14 C4
Leinster Pl. W2 109 F6
Leinster Rd. N10 74 B4
Leinster Rd. NW6 108 D3
Stafford Rd.
Leinster Sq. W2 108 D6
Leinster Ter. W2 14 C5
Leinster Ter. W2 109 F7
Leisure Way N12 57 G7
Leith Cl. NW9 88 D1
Leith Rd. N22 75 H1
Leith Yd. NW6 108 D1
Quex Rd.
Leithcote Gdns. SW16 169 F4
Leithcote Path SW16 169 F3
Lela Av., Houns. 142 C2
Lelitia Cl. E8 112 D1
Pownall Rd.
Leman St. E1 21 G4
Leman St. E1 112 C6
Lemark Cl., Stan. 53 F5
Lemmon Rd. SE10 134 E6
Lemna Rd. E11 79 E7
Lemonwell Ct. SE9 157 F5
Lemonwell Dr.
Lemonwell Dr. SE9 157 F5
Lemsford Cl. N15 76 D5
Lemsford Ct. N4 93 J2
Brownswood Rd.
Lemsford Ct., Borwd. 38 C4
Lemuel St. SW18 149 E6
Len Freeman Pl. SW6 128 C7
John Smith Av.
Lena Gdns. W6 127 J3
Lena Kennedy Cl. E4 62 B6
Lenanton Steps E14 134 A2
Manilla St.
Lendal Ter. SW4 150 D3
Lenelby Rd., Surb. 196 A1
Lenham Rd. SE12 155 F4
Lenham Rd., Bexh. 139 F6
Lenham Rd., Sutt. 199 E4
Lenham Rd., Th.Hth. 188 A2
Lennard Av., W.Wick. 205 E2
Lennard Cl., W.Wick 205 E2
Lennard Rd. SE20 171 F6
Lennard Rd., Beck. 171 G6
Lennard Rd., Brom. 206 C1
Lennard Rd., Croy. 201 J1
Lennon Rd. NW2 89 J5
Lennox Gdns. NW10 89 F4
Lennox Gdns. SW1 23 J6
Lennox Gdns. SW1 129 J3
Lennox Gdns., Croy. 201 H4
Lennox Gdns., Ilf. 98 C1
Lennox Gdns. Ms. SW1 23 J6
Lennox Gdns. Ms. SW1 129 J3
Lennox Rd. E17 77 J6
Lennox Rd. N4 93 F2
Lenor Cl., Bexh. 159 E4
Lens Rd. E7 97 J7
Lensbury Way SE2 138 C3
Lenthall Rd. E8 94 D7
Lenthall Rd., Loug. 49 G4
Lenthorp Rd. SE10 135 F4
Lentmead Rd., Brom. 173 F3
Lenton Path SE18 137 G6
Lenton Ri., Rich. 145 H3
Evelyn Ter.
Lenton St. SE18 137 G4
Leo St. SE15 133 E7
Leo Yd. EC1 11 H6
Leof Cres. SE6 172 B5
Leominster Rd., Mord. 185 F6
Leominster Wk., Mord. 185 F6
Leonard Av., Mord. 185 F5
Leonard Rd. E4 62 A6
Leonard Rd. E7 97 G4
Leonard Rd. N9 60 C3
Leonard Rd. SW16 186 C1
Leonard Rd., Sthl. 122 D3
Leonard Robbins Path SE28 118 B7
Tawney Rd.
Leonard St. E16 136 B1
Leonard St. EC2 12 C5
Leonard St. EC2 112 A4
Leontine Cl. SE15 132 D7
Leopards Ct. EC1 19 E1
Leopold Av. SW19 166 C5
Leopold Ms. E9 113 F1
Fremont St.
Leopold Rd. E17 78 A5
Leopold Rd. N2 73 G3
Leopold Rd. N18 61 E5
Leopold Rd. NW10 89 E7
Leopold Rd. SW19 166 C4
Leopold Rd. W5 125 J1
Leopold St. E3 113 J5
Leopold Ter. SW19 166 D5
Dora Rd.
Leppoc Rd. SW4 150 D5
Leroy St. SE1 36 D1
Leroy St. SE1 132 B4
Lescombe Cl. SE23 171 H3
Lescombe Rd. SE23 171 H3
Lesley Cl., Bex. 159 H7
Leslie Gdns., Sutt. 198 D7
Leslie Gro., Croy. 202 B1
Leslie Gro. Pl., Croy. 202 A1
Leslie Gro.
Leslie Pk. Rd., Croy. 202 B1
Leslie Rd. E11 96 C4
Leslie Rd. E16 115 H6
Leslie Rd. N2 73 G3
Leslie Smith Sq. SE18 136 D6
Nightingale Vale
Lessar Av. SW4 150 C5
Lessing St. SE23 153 H7
Lessingham Av. SW17 167 J4
Lessingham Av., Ilf. 80 D3
Lessington Av., Rom. 83 J6
Lessness Av., Bexh. 138 D7
Lessness Pk., Belv. 139 F5
Lessness Rd., Belv. 139 G5
Stapley Rd.
Lessness Rd., Mord. 185 F6
Lester Av. E15 115 E3
Leswin Pl. N16 94 C3
Leswin Rd.
Leswin Rd. N16 94 C3
Letchford Gdns. NW10 107 G3
Letchford Ms. NW10 107 G3
Letchford Gdns.
Letchford Ter., Har. 67 H1
Letchworth Av., Felt. 141 J7
Letchworth Cl., Brom. 191 G5
Letchworth Cl., Wat. 50 D5
Letchworth Dr., Brom. 191 G5
Letchworth St. SW17 167 J4
Lethbridge Cl. SE13 154 C1
Lett Rd. E15 96 D7
Letterstone Rd. SW6 128 C7
Varna Rd.
Lettice St. SW6 148 C1
Lettsom St. SE5 152 B2
Lettsom Wk. E13 115 G2
Leucha Rd. E17 77 H5
Levana Cl. SW19 166 B1
Levehurst Way SW4 151 E2
Leven Cl., Wat. 50 D5
Leven Rd. E14 114 C5
Levendale Rd. SE23 171 H2
Lever St. EC1 11 H4
Lever St. EC1 111 H3
Leverett St. SW3 31 H1
Leverholme Gdns. SE9 174 D3
Leverson St. SW16 168 C6
Leverton Pl. NW5 92 C5
Leverton St.
Leverton St. NW5 92 C5
Levett Gdns., Ilf. 99 J4
Levett Rd., Bark. 99 H6
Levine Gdns., Bark. 118 D2
Levison Way N19 92 D2
Grovedale Rd.
Lewes Cl., Nthlt. 85 G6
Lewes Rd. N12 57 H5
Lewes Rd., Brom. 192 A2
Lewesdon Cl. SW19 166 A1
Leweston Pl. N16 76 C7
Lewey Ho. E3 113 J4
Lewgars Av. NW9 70 C6
Lewin Rd. SW14 146 D3
Lewin Rd. SW16 168 D6
Lewin Rd., Bexh. 159 E4
Lewis Av. E17 78 A1
Lewis Cl. N14 42 C7
Orchid Rd.
Lewis Cres. NW10 88 C5
Lewis Gdns. N2 73 G2
Lewis Gro. SE13 154 C3
Lewis Rd., Mitch. 185 G2
Lewis Rd., Rich. 145 G5
Red Lion St.
Lewis Rd., Sid. 176 C3
Lewis Rd., Sthl. 123 E2
Lewis Rd., Sutt. 199 E4
Lewis Rd., Well. 158 C3
Lewis St. NW1 92 B7
Lewis Way, Dag. 101 H6
Lewisham High St. SE13 154 C3
Lewisham Hill SE13 154 C2
Lewisham Pk. SE13 154 B6
Lewisham Rd. SE13 154 B1
Lewisham St. SW1 25 J4
Lewisham Way SE4 153 J1
Lewisham Way SE14 153 J1
Lexden Dr., Rom. 82 B6
Lexden Rd. W3 106 B7
Lexden Rd., Mitch. 186 D4
Lexham Ct., Grnf. 104 A1
Lexham Gdns. W8 30 B1
Lexham Gdns. W8 128 E3
Lexham Gdns. Ms. W8 22 B6
Lexham Gdns. Ms. W8 129 E3
Lexham Ho., Bark. 117 G1
St. Margarets
Lexham Ms. W8 128 D4
Lexham Wk. W8 22 B6
Lexington St. W1 17 G4
Lexington St. W1 110 C6
Lexington Way, Barn. 40 A4
Lexton Gdns. SW12 168 D1
Ley St., Ilf. 99 E2
Leyborne Av. W13 125 E2
Leyborne Pk., Rich. 146 A1
Leybourne Cl., Brom. 191 G6
Leybourne Rd. E11 97 F1
Leybourne Rd. NW1 92 B7
Leybourne Rd. NW9 70 A5
Leybourne St. NW1 92 B7
Hawley St.
Leybridge Ct. SE12 155 G5
Leyburn Cl. E17 78 B4
Church La.
Leyburn Gdns., Croy. 202 B2
Leyburn Gro. N18 60 D6
Leyburn Rd. N18 60 D6
Leycroft Cl., Loug. 48 D5
Leyden St. E1 21 F2
Leydon Cl. SE16 133 G1
Lagado Ms.
Leyfield, Wor.Pk. 197 E1
Leyland Av., Enf. 45 H2
Leyland Gdns., Wdf.Grn. 63 J5
Leyland Rd. SE12 155 G5
Leylang Rd. SE14 133 G7
Leys, The N2 73 F4
Leys, The, Har. 69 J6
Leys Av., Dag. 101 J7
Leys Cl., Dag. 101 J7
Leys Cl., Har. 68 A5
Leys Gdns., Barn. 42 A5
Leys Rd. E., Enf. 45 H1
Leys Rd. W., Enf. 45 H1
Leysdown Av., Bexh. 159 J4
Leysdown Rd. SE9 174 B2
Leysfield Rd. W12 127 G2
Leyspring Rd. E11 97 F1
Leyswood Dr., Ilf. 81 H5
Leythe Rd. W3 126 C2

Leyton Business Cen. E10 96 A2
Leyton Gra. E10 96 B1
Goldsmith Rd.
Leyton Gra. Est. E10 96 B1
Leyton Grn. Rd. E10 78 C6
Leyton Ind. Village E10 77 G7
Leyton Pk. Rd. E10 96 C3
Leyton Rd. E15 96 D5
Leyton Rd. SW19 167 F7
Leyton Way E17 79 E7
Leytonstone Rd. E15 96 E5
Leywick St. E15 114 E2
Lezayre Rd., Orp. 207 J6
Liardet St. SE14 133 H6
Liberia Rd. N5 93 H6
Liberty Av. SW19 185 G1
Liberty Ms. SW12 150 B6
Liberty St. SW9 151 F1
Libra Rd. E3 113 J1
Libra Rd. E13 115 G2
Library Pl. E1 112/113 E7
Cable St.
Library St. SE1 27 G4
Library St. SE1 131 H2
Library Way, Twick. 143 J7
Nelson Rd.
Lichfield Cl., Barn. 41 J3
Lichfield Gdns., Rich. 145 H4
Lichfield Gro. N3 72 E2
Lichfield Rd. E3 113 H3
Lichfield Rd. E6 116 A3
Lichfield Rd. N9 60 D2
Winchester Rd.
Lichfield Rd. NW2 90 B4
Lichfield Rd., Dag. 100 B4
Lichfield Rd., Houns. 142 C3
Lichfield Rd., Nthwd. 66 A3
Lichfield Rd., Rich. 145 J1
Lichfield Rd., Wdf.Grn. 63 E4
Lichfield Sq., Rich. 145 H4
Lichfield Gdns.
Lichlade Cl., Orp. 207 J4
Lidbury Rd. NW7 56 B6
Lidcote Gdns. SW9 151 G2
Liddall Way, West Dr. 120 C1
Liddell Cl., Har. 69 G3
Liddell Gdns. NW10 107 J2
Liddell Rd. NW6 90 D6
Lidding Rd., Har. 69 G5
Liddington Rd. E15 115 F1
Liddon Rd. E13 115 H3
Liddon Rd., Brom. 191 J3
Liden Cl. E17 95 J1
Hitcham Rd.
Lidfield Rd. N16 94 A4
Lidgate Rd. SE15 132 C7
Chandler Way
Lidiard Rd. SW18 167 F2
Lidlington Pl. NW1 9 G2
Lidlington Pl. NW1 110 C2
Lido Sq. N17 76 A2
Lidyard Rd. N19 92 C1
Liffler Rd. SE18 137 H5
Lifford St. SW15 148 A4
Liffords Pl. SW13 147 F2
Lightcliffe Rd. N13 59 G4
Lighter Cl. SE16 133 H4
Lighterman Ms. E1 113 G6
Lightermans Rd. E14 134 A2
Lightermans Wk. SW18 148 D4
Lightfoot Rd. N8 74 E5
Lightley Cl., Wem. 87 J7
Stanley Av.
Ligonier St. E2 13 F5
Lilac Cl. E4 61 J6
Lilac Gdns. W5 125 G3
Lilac Gdns., Croy. 204 A3
Lilac Pl. SE11 34 C2
Lilac Pl. SE11 131 F4
Lilac St. W12 107 G7
Lilburne Gdns. SE9 156 B5
Lilburne Rd. SE9 156 B5
Lilburne Wk. NW10 88 C6
Lile Cres. W7 104 B4
Lilestone Est. NW8 7 E6
Lilestone St. NW8 7 G5
Lilestone St. NW8 109 H4
Lilford Rd. SE5 151 H2
Lilian Barker Cl. SE12 155 G5
Lilian Board Way, Grnf. 86 A5
Lilian Cl. N16 94 B3
Barbauld Rd.
Lilian Gdns., Wdf.Grn. 79 H1
Lilian Rd. SW16 186 C1
Lillechurch Rd., Dag. 100 B6
Lilleshall Rd., Mord. 185 G6

Lilley Cl. E1 29 J2
Lilley La. NW7 54 D5
Lillian Av. W3 126 A2
Lillian Rd. SW13 127 G6
Lillie Rd. SW6 128 B7
Lillie Yd. SW6 128 D6
Lillieshall Rd. SW4 150 B3
Lillington Gdns. Est. SW1 33 G2
Lilliput Av., Nthlt. 103 F1
Lily Cl. W14 128 B4
Lily Dr., West Dr. 120 A3
Wise La.
Lily Gdns., Wem. 105 F2
Lily Pl. EC1 19 F1
Lily Pl. EC1 111 G5
Lily Rd. E17 78 A6
Lilyville Rd. SW6 148 C1
Limbourne Av., Dag. 83 F7
Limburg Rd. SW11 149 J4
Lime Cl. E1 29 J1
Lime Cl. E1 132 D1
Lime Cl., Brom. 192 B4
Lime Cl., Buck.H. 64 A3
Lime Cl., Cars. 199 J2
Lime Cl., Har. 68 D2
Lime Cl., Rom. 83 J4
Lime Ct., Mitch. 185 G2
Lewis Rd.
Lime Cres., Sun. 178 C2
Lime Gro. E4 61 J6
Burnside Av.
Lime Gro. N20 56 C1
Lime Gro. W12 127 J2
Lime Gro., Ilf. 65 J6
Lime Gro., N.Mal. 182 D3
Lime Gro., Orp. 207 E2
Lime Gro., Ruis. 66 B7
Lime Gro., Sid. 157 J6
Lime Gro., Twick. 144 C6
Lime Rd., Rich. 145 J4
St. Mary's Gro.
Lime Row, Erith 139 F3
Northwood Pl.
Lime St. E17 77 H4
Lime St. EC3 20 D5
Lime St. EC3 112 B7
Lime St. Pas. EC3 20 D4
Lime Ter. W7 104 B7
Manor Ct. Rd.
Lime Tree Av., Esher 194 A1
Lime Tree Av., T.Ditt. 194 A1
Lime Tree Gro., Croy. 203 J3
Lime Tree Pl., Mitch. 186 B1
Lime Tree Rd., Houns. 143 H1
Lime Tree Ter. SE6 171 J1
Winterstoke Rd.
Lime Tree Wk., Bushey 52 B1
Lime Tree Wk., W.Wick. 205 F4
Lime Wk. E15 114/115 E1
Church St. N.
Limeburner La. EC4 19 G4
Limeburner La. EC4 111 H6
Limecroft Cl., Epsom 196 D7
Limedene Cl., Pnr. 66 D1
Limeharbour E14 134 B3
Limehouse Causeway E14 113 J7
Limehouse Flds. Est. E14 113 H5
Limehouse Link E14 113 H7
Limekiln Dr. SE7 135 H6
Limekiln Pl. SE19 170 C7
Limerick Cl. SW12 150 C7
Limerston St. SW10 30 D5
Limerston St. SW10 129 F6
Limes, The W2 108 D7
Linden Gdns.
Limes, The, Brom. 206 B2
Limes, The, Har. 68 C2
Limes Av. E11 79 H4
Limes Av. N12 57 F4
Limes Av. NW7 54 E6
Limes Av. NW11 72 B7
Limes Av. SE20 171 E7
Limes Av. SW13 147 F2
Limes Av., Cars. 199 J1
Limes Av., Chig. 65 G6
Limes Av., Croy. 201 G3
Limes Av., The N11 58 B5
Limes Fld. Rd. SW14 146/147 E3
White Hart La.
Limes Gdns. SW18 148 D6
Limes Gro. SE13 154 C4
Limes Pl., Croy. 188 A7
Limes Rd., Beck. 190 B2
Limes Rd., Croy. 188 A7
Limes Row, Orp. 206/207 E5
Orchard Rd.
Limes Wk. SE15 153 E4

Limes Wk. W5 125 G2
Chestnut Gro.
Limesdale Gdns., Edg. 70 C2
Limesford Rd. SE15 153 G4
Limestone Wk., Erith 138 D3
Limetree Cl. SW2 169 F1
Limetree Ter., Well. 158 A3
Hook La.
Limetree Wk. SW17 168 A5
Church La.
Limewood Cl. E17 77 J4
Limewood Cl. 104/105 E6
W13
St. Stephens Rd.
Limewood Ct., Ilf. 80 C5
Limewood Rd., Erith 139 J7
Limpsfield Av. SW19 166 A2
Limpsfield Av., Th.Hth. 187 F5
Linacre Ct. W6 128 A5
Linacre Rd. NW2 89 H6
Linberry Wk. SE8 133 J4
Linchmere Rd. SE12 155 F7
Lincoln Av. N14 58 C3
Lincoln Av. SW19 166 A3
Lincoln Av., Twick. 161 J2
Lincoln Cl. SE25 188 D6
Woodside Grn.
Lincoln Cl., Grnf. 103 J1
Lincoln Cl., Har. 67 F5
Lincoln Ct. N16 76 A7
Lincoln Ct., Borwd. 38 D5
Lincoln Cres., Enf. 44 B5
Lincoln Dr., Wat. 50 C3
Lincoln Gdns., Ilf. 80 B7
Lincoln Grn. Rd., Orp. 193 J5
Lincoln Ms. NW6 108 C1
Willesden La.
Lincoln Ms. SE21 170 A1
Lincoln Rd. E7 98 A6
Lincoln Rd. E13 115 H4
Lincoln Rd. E18 79 G1
Grove Rd.
Lincoln Rd. N2 73 H3
Lincoln Rd. SE25 188 E3
Lincoln Rd., Enf. 44 D5
Lincoln Rd., Felt. 161 F3
Lincoln Rd., Har. 67 F5
Lincoln Rd., Mitch. 186 E5
Lincoln Rd., N.Mal. 182 C3
Lincoln Rd., Sid. 176 B5
Lincoln Rd., Wem. 87 G6
Lincoln Rd., Wor.Pk. 197 H1
Lincoln St. E11 96 E2
Lincoln St. SW3 31 J2
Lincoln St. SW3 129 J4
Lincoln Way, Enf. 44 E5
Lincolns, The NW7 55 F3
Lincoln's Inn WC2 18 D3
Lincoln's Inn WC2 111 G6
Lincoln's Inn Flds. WC2 18 C3
Lincoln's Inn Flds. 111 F6
WC2
Lincombe Rd., Brom. 173 F3
Lind Rd., Sutt. 199 F5
Lind St. SE8 154 B2
Lindal Cres., Enf. 43 E4
Lindal Rd. SE4 153 J5
Lindales, The N17 60 C6
Brantwood Rd.
Linden Av. NW10 108 A2
Linden Av., Enf. 44 D1
Linden Av., Houns. 143 H5
Linden Av., Ruis. 84 A1
Linden Av., Th.Hth. 187 H4
Linden Av., Wem. 87 J5
Linden Cl. N14 42 C6
Linden Cl., Ruis. 84 A1
Linden Cl., Stan. 52 E5
Linden Cl., T.Ditt. 180 C7
Linden Ct. W12 127 J1
Linden Cres., Grnf. 86 C6
Linden Cres., Kings.T. 181 J2
Linden Cres., Wdf.Grn. 63 H6
Linden Gdns. W2 108 D7
Linden Gdns. W4 126 D5
Linden Gdns., Enf. 44 D1
Linden Gro. SE15 153 F3
Linden Gro. SE26 171 F6
Linden Gro., N.Mal. 182 E3
Linden Gro., Tedd. 162 C5
Waldegrave Rd.
Linden Lawns, Wem. 87 J4
Linden Lea N2 73 F5
Linden Leas, W.Wick. 204 D2
Linden Ms. N1 94 A5
Mildmay Gro. N.
Linden Ms. W2 108 D7
Linden Gdns.

Linden Pas. W4 126 D5
Linden Gdns.
Linden Pl., Mitch. 185 H4
Linden Rd. E17 77 J5
High St.
Linden Rd. N10 74 B4
Linden Rd. N11 57 J2
Linden Rd. N15 75 J4
Linden Rd., Hmptn. 161 G7
Linden Wk. N19 92 C2
Hargrave Pk.
Linden Way N14 42 C6
Lindenfield, Chis. 192 E2
Lindens, The N12 57 G5
Lindens, The W4 146 C1
Hartington Rd.
Lindens, The, Croy. 204 C6
Lindens, The, Loug. 48 C5
Lindeth Cl., Stan. 53 F6
Old Ch. La.
Lindfield Gdns. NW3 91 E5
Lindfield Rd. W5 105 F4
Lindfield Rd., Croy. 188 C6
Lindfield St. E14 114 A6
Lindhill Cl., Enf. 45 G1
Lindisfarne Rd. 165 G7
SW20
Lindisfarne Rd., Dag. 100 C3
Lindisfarne Way E9 95 H4
Lindley Est. SE15 37 H7
Lindley Rd. E10 96 B2
Lindley St. E1 113 F5
Lindo St. SE15 153 F2
Selden Rd.
Lindore Rd. SW11 149 J4
Lindores Rd., Cars. 185 F7
Lindrop St. SW6 149 F2
Lindsay Cl., Chess. 195 H7
Lindsay Cl., Stai. 140 A5
Lindsay Dr., Har. 69 H6
Lindsay Rd., Hmptn. 161 H4
Lindsay Rd., Wor.Pk. 197 H2
Lindsay Sq. SW1 33 J3
Lindsay Sq. SW1 130 D5
Lindsell St. SE10 154 C1
Lindsey Cl., Brom. 192 A3
Lindsey Cl., Mitch. 187 E4
Lindsey Gdns., Felt. 141 G7
Lindsey Ms. N1 93 J7
Lindsey Rd., Dag. 100 C4
Lindsey St. EC1 19 H1
Lindsey St. EC1 111 H5
Lindum Rd., Tedd. 163 F7
Lindway SE27 169 H5
Lindwood Cl. E6 116 B5
Northumberland Rd.
Linfield Cl. NW4 71 J3
Linford Rd. E17 78 C3
Linford St. SW8 150 C1
Ling Rd. E16 115 G5
Ling Rd., Erith 139 J6
Lingards Rd. SE13 154 C4
Lingey Cl., Sid. 175 J2
Lingfield Av., Kings.T. 181 H4
Lingfield Cl., Enf. 44 B6
Lingfield Cres. SE9 157 G4
Lingfield Gdns. N9 45 E7
Lingfield Rd. SW19 166 A5
Lingfield Rd., Wor.Pk. 197 J3
Lingham St. SW9 151 E2
Lingholm Way, Barn. 40 A5
Lingmere Cl., Chig. 65 F2
Lingrove Gdns., Buck.H. 63 H2
Beech La.
Lings Coppice SE21 170 A2
Lingwell Rd. SW17 167 H3
Lingwood Gdns., Islw. 124 B7
Lingwood Rd. E5 76 D7
Linhope St. NW1 7 J5
Linhope St. NW1 109 J4
Link, The SE9 174 D3
Link, The W3 106 B6
Link, The, Enf. 45 H1
Link, The, Nthlt. 85 F5
Eastcote La.
Link, The, Pnr. 66 C7
Link, The, Wem. 87 F1
Nathans Rd.
Link La., Wall. 200 D6
Link Rd. N11 58 A4
Link Rd., Dag. 119 H2
Link Rd., Felt. 141 J7
Link Rd., Wall. 200 A1
Link St. E9 95 F6
Link Way, Brom. 192 B7
Link Way, Pnr. 66 D1
Linkfield, Brom. 191 G6
Linkfield, W.Mol. 179 G3
Linkfield Rd., Islw. 144 C2
Linklea Cl. NW9 55 E7
Links, The E17 77 H4

Links Av., Mord. 184 D4
Links Dr. N20 56 D1
Links Gdns. SW16 169 G7
Links Rd. NW2 89 F2
Links Rd. SW17 168 A6
Links Rd. W3 106 A6
Links Rd., W.Wick. 204 C1
Links Rd., Wdf.Grn. 63 G5
Links Side, Enf. 43 G3
Links Vw. N3 56 C7
Links Vw. Cl., Stan. 52 D6
Links Vw. Rd., Croy. 204 A3
Links Vw. Rd., Hmptn. 161 J5
Links Way, Beck. 190 A6
Links Yd. E1 21 H1
Linkside N12 56 C6
Linkside, Chig. 65 F5
Linkside, N.Mal. 183 E2
Linkside Cl., Enf. 43 F3
Linkside Gdns., Enf. 43 F3
Linksway NW4 72 A2
Linkway N4 75 J7
Linkway SW20 183 H3
Linkway, Dag. 100 C4
Linkway, Rich. 163 E2
Linkway, The, Barn. 40 E6
Linkwood Wk. NW1 92 D7
Maiden La.
Linley Cres., Rom. 83 H3
Linley Rd. N17 76 B2
Linnell Cl. NW11 72 E6
Linnell Dr. NW11 72 E6
Linnell Rd. N18 60 D5
Fairfield Rd.
Linnell Rd. SE5 152 B2
Linnet Cl. N9 61 G1
Linnet Cl. SE28 118 C7
Linnet Ms. SW12 150 A7
Linnet Ter., Ilf. 80 D3
Tiptree Cres.
Linnett Cl. E4 62 C4
Linom Rd. SW4 150 E4
Linscott Rd. E5 95 F4
Linsdell Rd., Bark. 117 F1
Linsey St. SE16 37 H1
Linsey St. SE16 132 D4
Linslade Cl., Houns. 142/143 E5
Frampton Rd.
Linslade Cl., Pnr. 66 B3
Linstead Ct. SE9 157 H6
Linstead St. NW6 90 D7
Linstead Way SW18 148 B7
Linster Gro., Borwd. 38 C5
Lintaine Cl. W6 128 B6
Moylan Rd.
Linthorpe Av., Wem. 87 F6
Linthorpe Rd. N16 76 B7
Linthorpe Rd., Barn. 41 H3
Linton Cl., Mitch. 185 J7
Linton Cl., Well. 158 B1
Anthony Rd.
Linton Gdns. E6 116 B6
Linton Gro. SE27 169 H5
Linton Rd., Bark. 99 F7
Linton St. N1 111 J1
Lintons, The, Bark. 99 F7
Lintott Ct., Stai. 140 A6
Linver Rd. SW6 148 D2
Linwood Cl. SE5 152 C2
Linwood Cres., Enf. 44 D1
Linwood Way SE15 37 F7
Linzee Rd. N8 74 E4
Lion Av., Twick. 162 C1
Lion Rd.
Lion Cl. SE4 154 A6
Lion Ct., Borwd. 38 C1
Lion Gate Gdns., Rich. 145 J3
Lion Pk. Av., Chess. 196 A4
Lion Rd. E6 116 C5
Lion Rd. N9 60 D2
Lion Rd., Bexh. 159 F4
Lion Rd., Croy. 187 J5
Lion Rd., Twick. 162 C1
Lion Way, Brent. 125 G7
Lion Wf. Rd., Islw. 144 E3
Lion Yd. SW4 150 D4
Tremadoc Rd.
Lionel Gdns. SE9 156 A5
Lionel Ms. W10 108 B5
Telford Rd.
Lionel Rd. SE9 156 A5
Lionel Rd., Brent. 125 J5
Lions Cl. SE9 173 J3
Liphook Cres. SE23 153 F7
Liphook Rd., Wat. 50 D4
Lippitts Hill, Loug. 47 E1
Lipton Cl. SE28 118 C7
Aisher Rd.
Lipton Rd. E1 113 G6
Bower St.
Lisbon Av., Twick. 161 J2
Lisburne Rd. NW3 91 J4
Lisford St. SE15 152 C1
Lisgar Ter. W14 128 C4
Liskeard Cl., Chis. 175 F6
Liskeard Gdns. SE3 155 G1
Lisle Cl. SW17 168 B4
Lisle St. WC2 17 J5
Lisle St. WC2 110 D7
Lismore Circ. NW5 92 A5
Lismore Cl., Islw. 144 D2
Lismore Rd. N17 76 A3
Lismore Rd., S.Croy. 202 B6
Lismore Wk. N1 93 J6
Clephane Rd.
Liss Way SE15 37 G7
Lissenden Gdns. NW5 92 A4
Lisson Grn. Est. NW8 7 G4
Lisson Grn. Est. NW8 109 H3
Lisson Gro. NW1 7 G6
Lisson Gro. NW1 109 H4
Lisson Gro. NW8 7 F4
Lisson Gro. NW8 109 G3
Lisson St. NW1 15 G1
Lisson St. NW1 109 H5
Lister Cl. W3 106 D5
Lister Cl., Mitch. 185 H1
Lister Gdns. N18 59 J5
Lister Ho. SE3 135 E6
Lister Rd. E11 97 E1
Lister St. E13 115 G3
Sewell St.
Lister Wk. SE28 118 D7
Haldane Rd.
Liston Rd. N17 76 D1
Liston Rd. SW4 150 C3
Liston Way, Wdf.Grn. 63 J7
Listowel Cl. SW9 35 F7
Listowel Rd., Dag. 101 G3
Listria Pk. N16 94 B2
Litchfield Av. E15 96 E6
Litchfield Av., Mord. 184 C7
Litchfield Gdns. NW10 89 G6
Litchfield Rd., Sutt. 199 F4
Litchfield St. WC2 17 J5
Litchfield St. WC2 110 D7
Litchfield Way NW11 73 E5
Lithos Rd. NW3 91 E6
Little Acre, Beck. 190 A3
Little Albany St. NW1 8 E5
Little Argyll St. W1 17 F4
Little Benty, West Dr. 120 A5
Little Birches, Sid. 175 H2
Little Boltons, The SW5 30 B3
Little Boltons, The SW5 129 E5
Little Boltons, The SW10 30 B3
Little Boltons, The SW10 129 E5
Little Bornes SE21 170 B4
Little Britain EC1 19 H2
Little Britain EC1 111 H5
Little Brownings SE23 170 E2
Little Bury St. N9 60 A1
Little Cedars N12 57 F4
Woodside Av.
Little Chester St. SW1 24 C5
Little Chester St. SW1 130 B3
Little College La. EC4 112 A7
Garlick Hill
Little College St. SW1 26 A5
Little Common, Stan. 52 D3
Little Ct., W.Wick. 204 E2
Little Dean's Yd. SW1 26 A5
Little Dimocks SW12 168 B2
Little Dorrit Ct. SE1 28 A3
Little Dorrit Ct. SE1 131 J2
Little Dragons, Loug. 48 A4
Little Ealing La. W5 125 F4
Little Edward St. NW1 8 E3
Little Elms, Hayes 121 G7
Little Essex St. WC2 18 E5
Little Ferry Rd., Twick. 162/163 E1
Ferry Rd.
Little Friday Rd. E4 62 E2
Little Gearies, Ilf. 80 E4
Little George St. SW1 26 A4
Little Gra., Grnf. 104 D3
Perivale La.
Little Grn., Rich. 145 G4
Little Grn. St. NW5 92 B4
College La.
Little Halliards, Walt. 178 A6
Felix Rd.
Little Heath SE7 136 B6
Little Heath, Rom. 82 B4
Little Heath Rd., Bexh. 159 F1
Little Ilford La. E12 98 C4
Little Marlborough St. W1 17 F4
Little Moss La., Pnr. 67 E2
Little New St. EC4 19 F3
Little Newport St. WC2 17 J5
Little Newport St. WC2 110 D7
Little Orchard Cl., Pnr. 66/67 E2
Barrow Pt. La.
Little Oxhey La., Wat. 50 D5
Little Pk. Dr., Felt. 160 D2
Little Pk. Gdns., Enf. 43 J3
Little Plucketts Way, Buck.H. 63 J1
Little Portland St. W1 17 F3
Little Portland St. W1 110 B6
Little Queens Rd., Tedd. 162 C6
Little Redlands, Brom. 192 B2
Little Rd., Croy. 202 B1
Lower Addiscombe Rd.
Little Rd., Hayes 121 J2
Little Russell St. WC1 18 A2
Little Russell St. WC1 110 E5
Little St. James's St. SW1 25 F2
Little St. James's St. SW1 130 C1
Little St. Leonards SW14 146 C3
Little Sanctuary SW1 25 J4
Little Smith St. SW1 25 J5
Little Somerset St. E1 21 F4
Little Strand NW9 71 F2
Little Thrift, Orp. 193 F4
Little Titchfield St. W1 17 F2
Little Trinity La. EC4 20 A5
Little Turnstile WC1 18 C2
Littlebrook Cl., Croy. 189 G6
Littlebury Rd. SW4 150 D3
Littlecombe SE7 135 H6
Littlecombe Cl. SW15 148 A6
Littlecote Cl. SW19 148 A7
Littlecote Pl., Pnr. 67 E1
Littlecroft SE9 156 D3
Littledale SE2 138 A6
Littlefield Cl. N19 92 C4
Tufnell Pk. Rd.
Littlefield Cl., Kings.T. 181 H2
Fairfield W.
Littlefield Rd., Edg. 54 C7
Littlegrove, Barn. 41 H6
Littleheath Rd., S.Croy. 202 E7
Littlejohn Rd. W7 104 C6
Littlemead, Esher 194 A4
Littlemede SE9 174 C3
Littlemoor Rd., Ilf. 99 G3
Littlemore Rd. SE2 138 A2
Littlers Cl. SW19 185 G1
Runnymede
Littlestone Cl., Beck. 172 A6
Abbey La.
Littleton Av. E4 63 F1
Littleton Cres., Har. 86 C2
Littleton Rd., Har. 86 C2
Littleton St. SW18 167 F2
Littlewood SE13 154 C5
Littlewood Cl. W13 125 E3
Littleworth Av., Esher 194 A5
Littleworth Common Rd., Esher 194 A3
Littleworth La., Esher 194 A4
Littleworth Pl., Esher 194 A4
Littleworth Rd., Esher 194 B4
Livermere Rd. E8 112 C1
Liverpool Gro. SE17 36 A4
Liverpool Gro. SE17 132 A5
Liverpool Rd. E10 78 C6
Liverpool Rd. E16 115 E5
Liverpool Rd. N1 111 G2
Liverpool Rd. N7 93 G5
Liverpool Rd. W5 125 G2
Liverpool Rd., Kings.T. 164 A7
Liverpool Rd., Th.Hth. 187 J3
Liverpool St. EC2 20 D2
Liverpool St. EC2 112 B5
Livesey Cl., Kings.T. 181 J3
Livesey Pl. SE15 37 J5
Livingston College Twrs. E10 78 C6
Essex Rd.
Livingstone Pl. E14 134 C5
Ferry St.
Livingstone Rd. E15 114 C1
Livingstone Rd. E17 78 B6
Livingstone Rd. N13 59 E6
Livingstone Rd. SW11 149 G3
Winstanley Rd.
Livingstone Rd., Houns. 143 J4
Livingstone Rd., Sthl. 102 D7
Livingstone Rd., Th.Hth. 187 J2
Livingstone Wk. SW11 149 G3
Livonia St. W1 17 G4
Lizard St. EC1 12 A4
Lizard St. EC1 111 J3
Lizban St. SE3 135 H7
Llanelly Rd. NW2 90 C2
Llanover Rd. SE18 136 D6
Llanover Rd., Wem. 87 G3
Llanthony Rd., Mord. 185 G6
Llanvanor Rd. NW2 90 C2
Llewellyn St. SE16 29 J4
Lloyd Av. SW16 187 E1
Lloyd Baker St. WC1 10 D4
Lloyd Baker St. WC1 111 F3
Lloyd Ct., Pnr. 66 D5
Lloyd Pk. Av., Croy. 202 C4
Lloyd Rd. E6 116 C1
Lloyd Rd. E17 77 G4
Lloyd Rd., Dag. 101 F6
Lloyd Rd., Wor.Pk. 197 J3
Lloyd Sq. WC1 10 E3
Lloyd Sq. WC1 111 G3
Lloyd St. WC1 10 E3
Lloyd St. WC1 111 G3
Lloyd's Av. EC3 21 E4
Lloyd's Av. EC3 112 B6
Lloyds Pl. SE3 155 E2
Lloyd's Row EC1 11 F4
Lloyds Way, Beck. 189 H5
Loampit Hill SE13 154 A2
Loampit Vale SE13 154 B3
Loanda Cl. E8 112 C1
Clarissa St.
Loats Rd. SW2 150 E6
Lobelia Cl. E6 116 B5
Sorrel Gdns.
Locarno Rd. W3 126 C1
High St.
Locarno Rd., Grnf. 103 J4
Lochaber Rd. SE13 154 E4
Lochaline St. W6 127 J6
Lochan Cl., Hayes 102 E4
Lochinvar St. SW12 150 B7
Lochmere Cl., Erith 139 H6
Lochnagar St. E14 114 C5
Lock Chase SE3 155 F3
Lock Cl., Sthl. 123 J2
Navigator Dr.
Lock Rd., Rich. 163 F4
Lockesfield Pl. E14 134 B5
Lockesley Dr., Orp. 193 J6
Lockesley Sq., Surb. 181 G6
Locket Rd., Har. 68 B3
Lockfield Av., Enf. 45 H2
Lockgate Cl. E9 95 J5
Lee Conservancy Rd.
Lockhart Cl. N7 93 F6
Lockhart Cl., Enf. 44/45 E5
Derby Rd.
Lockhart St. E3 113 J4
Lockhurst St. E5 95 G4
Lockie Pl. SE25 188 D3
Lockier Wk., Wem. 87 G3
Lockington Rd. SW8 150 B1
Lockmead Rd. N15 76 D6
Lockmead Rd. SE13 154 C3
Locks La., Mitch. 185 J1
Locksley Est. E14 113 J6
Locksley St. E14 113 J5
Locksmeade Rd., Rich. 163 F4
Lockswood Cl., Barn. 41 J4
Lockwood Cl. SE26 171 G4
Lockwood Ind. Pk. N17 76 E3
Lockwood Sq. SE16 132 E3
Lockwood Way E17 77 G2
Lockwood Way, Chess. 196 A5
Lockyer Est. SE1 28 C3
Lockyer St. SE1 28 C4
Loddiges Rd. E9 95 F7
Loder St. SE15 153 F1
Lodge Av. SW14 146 E3
Lodge Av., Croy. 201 G3
Lodge Av., Dag. 118 A1

Lodge Av., Har. 69 H4
Lodge Cl. N18 59 J5
Lodge Cl., Edg. 53 J6
Lodge Cl., Islw. 144 E1
Lodge Cl., Wall. 200 A1
Lodge Ct., Wem. 87 H5
Lodge Dr. N13 59 G4
Lodge Gdns., Beck. 189 J5
Lodge Hill SE2 138 B7
Lodge Hill, Ilf. 80 B4
Lodge Hill, Well. 138 B7
Lodge La. N12 57 F5
Lodge La., Bex. 158 D6
Lodge La., Croy. 204 A6
Lodge Pl., Sutt. 199 E5
Lodge Rd. NW4 71 J4
Lodge Rd. NW8 7 F4
Lodge Rd. NW8 109 G3
Lodge Rd., Brom. 173 H7
Lodge Rd., Croy. 187 H6
Lodge Rd., Sutt. 198/199 E5
Throwley Way
Lodge Rd., Wall. 200 B5
Lodge Vil., Wdf.Grn. 63 F7
Lodgehill Pk. Cl., Har. 85 H2
Lodore Gdns. NW9 70 E5
Lodore St. E14 114 C6
Lofthouse Pl., Chess. 195 F6
Loftie St. SE16 29 J4
Loftie St. SE16 132 D2
Lofting Rd. N1 93 F7
Loftus Rd. W12 127 H1
Logan Cl., Enf. 45 G1
Logan Cl., Houns. 143 F3
Logan Ms. W8 128 D4
Logan Pl. W8 128 D4
Logan Rd. N9 61 E2
Logan Rd., Wem. 87 H2
Loggetts, The SE21 170 B2
Logs Hill, Brom. 174 B7
Logs Hill, Chis. 174 B7
Logs Hill Cl., Chis. 192 B1
Lolesworth Cl. E1 21 G2
Lollard St. SE11 34 D1
Lollard St. SE11 131 F4
Loman St. SE1 27 H3
Loman St. SE1 131 H2
Lomas Cl., Croy. 204 C7
Lomas Ct. E8 94 C7
Lomas St. E1 21 J1
Lomas St. E1 112 D5
Lombard Av., Enf. 45 F1
Lombard Av., Ilf. 99 H1
Lombard Business Pk. SW19 185 F2
Lombard Ct. EC3 20 C5
Lombard Ct. W3 126 B1
Crown St.
Lombard La. EC4 19 F4
Lombard Rd. N11 58 B5
Lombard Rd. SW11 149 G2
Lombard Rd. SW19 185 E2
Lombard St. EC3 20 C4
Lombard St. EC3 112 A6
Lombard Wall SE7 135 H3
Lombardy Pl. W2 14 A6
Lomond Cl. N15 76 B4
Lomond Cl., Wem. 87 J7
Lomond Gdns., S.Croy. 203 H7
Lomond Gro. SE5 36 B7
Lomond Gro. SE5 132 A7
Loncroft Rd. SE5 37 E5
Loncroft Rd. SE5 132 B6
Londesborough Rd. N16 94 B4
London Br. EC4 28 C1
London Br. EC4 132 A1
London Br. SE1 28 C1
London Br. SE1 132 A1
London Br. St. SE1 28 B2
London Br. St. SE1 132 A1
London Br. Wk. SE1 28 C1
London Br. Wk. SE1 132 B1
London City Airport E16 136 C1
London Flds. E8 94 E7
London Flds. E. Side E8 94 E7
London Flds. W. Side E8 94 D7
London La. E8 95 E7
London La., Brom. 173 F7
London Ms. W2 15 F4
London Rd. E13 115 G2
London Rd. SE1 27 G5
London Rd. SE1 131 H3
London Rd. SE23 170 D1
London Rd. SW16 187 F1
London Rd. SW17 185 J2
London Rd., Bark. 98 E7
London Rd., Brent. 125 F7
London Rd., Brom. 173 F7
London Rd., Croy. 187 H7
London Rd., Enf. 44 A3
London Rd., Har. 86 B2
London Rd., Houns. 144 A3
London Rd., Islw. 144 C2
London Rd., Kings.T. 181 J2
London Rd., Mitch. 185 J2
London Rd. (Beddington Cor.), Mitch. 186 A7
London Rd., Mord. 184 D5
London Rd., Rom. 83 G6
London Rd. (Abridge), Rom. 49 J4
London Rd., Stan. 53 F5
London Rd., Sutt. 198 A3
London Rd., Th.Hth. 187 G5
London Rd., Twick. 144 D5
London Rd., Wall. 200 B4
London Rd., Wem. 87 H6
London Stile W4 126 A5
Wellesley Rd.
London St. EC3 20 E5
London St. W2 15 F4
London St. W2 109 G6
London Wall EC2 20 A2
London Wall EC2 111 J5
London Wall Bldgs. EC2 20 C2
Lonesome Way SW16 186 B1
Long Acre WC2 18 A5
Long Acre WC2 110 E7
Long Deacon Rd. E4 62 E1
Long Dr. W3 106 E6
Long Dr., Grnf. 103 H1
Long Dr., Ruis. 84 D4
Long Elmes, Har. 67 H1
Long Fld. NW9 55 E7
Long Grn., Chig. 65 H4
Long Hedges, Houns. 143 G1
Long La. EC1 19 H1
Long La. EC1 111 H5
Long La. N2 73 F2
Long La. N3 73 F2
Long La. SE1 28 B4
Long La. SE1 132 A2
Long La., Bexh. 138 D7
Long La., Croy. 189 F5
Long Leys E4 62 B6
Long Mark Rd. E16 116 A5
Fulmer Rd.
Long Mead NW9 71 F1
Long Meadow NW5 92 D5
Torriano Av.
Long Meadow Cl., W.Wick. 190 C7
Long Pond Rd. SE3 154 E1
Long Reach Ct., Bark. 117 G2
Long Rd. SW4 150 C4
Long St. E2 13 F3
Long St. E2 112 C3
Long Wk. SE1 29 E5
Long Wk. SE18 136 E6
Long Wk. SW13 147 E2
Long Wk., N.Mal. 182 C3
Long Yd. WC1 10 C6
Long Yd. WC1 111 F4
Longacre Pl., Cars. 200 A6
Beddington Gdns.
Longacre Rd. E17 78 D1
Longbeach Rd. SW11 149 J3
Longberrys NW2 90 C3
Longboat Row, Sthl. 103 F6
Longbridge Rd., Bark. 99 F7
Longbridge Rd., Dag. 100 A4
Longbridge Way SE13 154 C5
Longcliffe Path, Wat. 50 A3
Gosforth La.
Longcroft SE9 174 C3
Longcroft Ri., Loug. 48 D5
Longcrofte Rd., Edg. 53 G7
Longdon Wd., Kes. 206 B4
Longdown Rd. SE6 172 A4
Longfellow Rd. E17 77 J6
Longfellow Rd., Wor.Pk. 197 G2
Longfellow Way SE1 37 G2
Longfield, Brom. 191 F1
Longfield, Loug. 47 J5
Longfield Av. E17 77 H4
Longfield Av. NW7 55 G7
Longfield Av. W5 105 F7
Longfield Av., Wall. 200 A1
Longfield Av., Wem. 87 H1
Longfield Cres. SE26 171 F3
Longfield Dr. SW14 146 B5
Longfield Dr., Mitch. 167 H7
Longfield Est. SE1 37 G2
Longfield Est. SE1 132 C4
Longfield Rd. W5 105 F7
Longfield St. SW18 148 D7
Longfield Wk. W5 105 F6
Longford Av., Felt. 141 H6
Longford Av., Sthl. 103 G7
Longford Cl., Hmptn. 161 G4
Longford Cl., Hayes 102 D7
Longford Gdns.
Longford Ct. E5 95 G4
Pedro St.
Longford Ct. NW4 72 A4
Longford Ct., Epsom 196 C4
Longford Gdns., Hayes 102 D7
Longford Gdns., Sutt. 199 F3
Longford Rd., Twick. 161 G1
Longford St. NW1 8 E5
Longford St. NW1 110 B4
Longford Wk. SW2 151 G7
Longhayes Av., Rom. 82 D4
Longhayes Ct., Rom. 82 D4
Longhayes Av.
Longheath Gdns., Croy. 189 F5
Longhedge Ho. SE26 170 C4
Longhedge St. SW11 150 A2
Longhill Rd. SE6 172 D2
Longhook Gdns., Nthlt. 102 A2
Longhope Cl. SE15 37 E6
Longhope Cl. SE15 132 B6
Longhurst Rd. SE13 154 D5
Longhurst Rd., Croy. 189 E6
Longland Ct. SE1 37 H3
Longland Dr. N20 56 E3
Longlands Ct. W11 108 C7
Portobello Rd.
Longlands Ct., Mitch. 186 A1
Summerhill Way
Longlands Pk. Cres., Sid. 175 H3
Longlands Rd., Sid. 175 H3
Longleat Rd., Enf. 44 B5
Longleat Way, Felt. 141 G7
Longleigh La. SE2 138 C6
Longleigh La., Bexh. 138 C6
Longlents Ho. NW10 106 D1
Longley Av., Wem. 105 J1
Longley Rd. SW17 167 H6
Longley Rd., Croy. 187 H7
Longley Rd., Har. 67 J5
Longley St. SE1 37 H2
Longley St. SE1 132 D4
Longley Way NW2 89 J3
Longmead, Chis. 192 D2
Longmead Dr., Sid. 176 D2
Longmead Rd. SW17 167 J5
Longmead Rd., T.Ditt. 180 B7
Longmeadow Rd., Sid. 175 H1
Longmoor Pt. SW15 165 H1
Norley Vale
Longmoore St. SW1 33 F2
Longmoore St. SW1 130 C4
Longmore Av., Barn. 41 F6
Longnor Rd. E1 113 G3
Longreach Rd., Bark. 117 J4
Longridge La., Sthl. 103 H7
Longridge Rd. SW5 128 D4
Long's Ct. WC2 17 H5
Long's Ct. WC2 110 D7
Longs Ct., Rich. 145 J4
Crown Ter.
Longshaw Rd. E4 62 D3
Longshore SE8 133 J4
Longstaff Cres. SW18 148 D6
Longstaff Rd. SW18 148 D6
Longstone Av. NW10 89 F7
Longstone Rd. SW17 168 B5
Longthornton Rd. SW16 186 C2
Longton Av. SE26 170 D4
Longton Gro. SE26 170 E4
Longville Rd. SE11 35 G1
Longwalk Rd., Uxb. 121 E1
Longwood Dr. SW15 147 G6
Longwood Gdns., Ilf. 80 C4
Longworth Cl. SE28 118 D6
Loning, The NW9 71 E4
Lonsdale Av. E6 116 A4
Lonsdale Av., Rom. 83 J6
Lonsdale Av., Wem. 87 H5
Lonsdale Cl. E6 116 B4
Lonsdale Av.
Lonsdale Cl. SE9 174 A3
Lonsdale Cl., Edg. 53 J5
Orchard Dr.
Lonsdale Cl., Pnr. 51 E7
Lonsdale Cres., Ilf. 80 E6
Lonsdale Dr., Enf. 43 E5
Lonsdale Gdns., Th.Hth. 187 F4
Lonsdale Ms., Rich. 146 A1
Elizabeth Cotts.
Lonsdale Pl. N1 93 G7
Barnsbury St.
Lonsdale Rd. E11 79 F7
Lonsdale Rd. NW6 108 C2
Lonsdale Rd. SE25 188 E4
Lonsdale Rd. SW13 127 G6
Lonsdale Rd. W4 127 F4
Lonsdale Rd. W11 108 C6
Lonsdale Rd., Bexh. 159 F2
Lonsdale Rd., Sthl. 122 D3
Lonsdale Sq. N1 93 G7
Loobert Rd. N15 76 B3
Looe Gdns., Ilf. 81 E3
Loom Ct. E1 13 E6
Loop Rd., Chis. 175 F6
Lopen Rd. N18 60 B4
Loraine Cl., Enf. 45 F5
Loraine Rd. N7 93 F4
Loraine Rd. W4 126 B6
Lord Amory Way E14 134 C2
Lord Av., Ilf. 80 C4
Lord Chancellor Wk., Kings.T. 182 C1
Lord Gdns., Ilf. 80 B4
Lord Hills Br. W2 14 B2
Lord Hills Rd. W2 14 B1
Lord Hills Rd. W2 109 E5
Lord Holland La. SW9 151 G1
Myatt's Flds. S.
Lord Knyvett Cl., Stai. 140 A6
Lord Napier Pl. W6 127 G5
Upper Mall
Lord N. St. SW1 26 A6
Lord N. St. SW1 130 E3
Lord Roberts Ms. SW6 128/129 E7
Moore Pk. Rd.
Lord Roberts Ter. SE18 136 D5
Lord St. E16 136 B1
Lord Warwick St. SE18 136 C3
Lordell Pl. SW19 165 J6
Lorden Wk. E2 13 H4
Lorden Wk. E2 112 D3
Lord's Cl. SE21 169 J2
Lords Cl., Felt. 161 E2
Lord's Vw. NW8 7 F4
Lordship Gro. N16 94 A2
Lordship La. N17 75 J1
Lordship La. N22 75 G2
Lordship La. SE22 152 C6
Lordship La. Est. SE22 170 D1
Lordship Pk. N16 93 J2
Lordship Pk. Ms. N16 93 J2
Allerton Rd.
Lordship Pl. SW3 31 G6
Lordship Rd. N16 94 A2
Lordship Rd., Nthlt. 84 E7
Lordship Ter. N16 94 A2
Lordsmead Rd. N17 76 B1
Lorenzo St. WC1 10 C3
Lorenzo St. WC1 111 F3
Loretto Gdns., Har. 69 H4
Lorian Cl. N12 56 E4
Loring Rd. N20 57 H2
Loring Rd., Islw. 144 C2
Loris Rd. W6 127 J3
Lorn Ct. SW9 151 G2
Lorn Rd. SW9 151 F2
Lorne Av., Croy. 189 G7
Lorne Cl. NW8 7 H4
Lorne Gdns. E11 79 J4
Lorne Gdns. W11 128 A2
Lorne Gdns., Croy. 189 H7
Lorne Rd. E7 97 H4
Lorne Rd. E17 78 A5
Lorne Rd. N4 93 F1
Lorne Rd., Har. 68 C2
Lorne Rd., Rich. 145 J5
Albert Rd.
Lorraine Pk., Har. 52 B7
Lorrimore Rd. SE17 35 H5
Lorrimore Rd. SE17 131 H6
Lorrimore Sq. SE17 35 H5
Lorrimore Sq. SE17 131 H6
Loseberry Rd., Esher 194 A5
Lothair Rd. W5 125 G2
Lothair Rd. N. N4 75 H6
Lothair Rd. S. N4 75 G7
Lothbury EC2 20 B3
Lothbury EC2 112 A6
Lothian Av., Hayes 102 B5
Lothian Cl., Wem. 86 D4
Lothian Rd. SW9 151 H1
Lothrop St. W10 108 B3
Lots Rd. SW10 129 F7
Lotus Cl. SE21 169 J3
Loubet St. SW17 167 J6
Loudoun Av., Ilf. 81 E5

Name	Page	Grid
Loudoun Rd. NW8	**6**	**D1**
Loudoun Rd. NW8	91	F7
Loudoun Rd. Ms. NW8	109	F1
Loudoun Rd.		
Loudwater Rd., Sun.	178	A4
Loudwater Rd., Sun.	178	A4
Lough Rd. N7	93	F6
Loughborough Est. SW9	151	H2
Loughborough Rd.		
Loughborough Pk. SW9	151	H4
Loughborough Rd. SW9	151	G2
Loughborough St. SE11	**34**	**D3**
Loughborough St. SE11	131	F5
Loughton Way, Buck.H.	64	A1
Louis Ms. N10	74	B1
Louisa Gdns. E1	113	G4
Louisa St.		
Louisa Ho. SW15	147	E4
Louisa St. E1	113	G4
Louise Aumonier Wk. N19	74/75	E7
Hillrise Rd.		
Louise Bennett Cl. SE24	151	H4
Shakespeare Rd.		
Louise Rd. E15	97	E6
Louisville Rd. SW17	168	A3
Louvaine Rd. SW11	149	G4
Lovage App. E6	116	B5
Lovat Cl. NW2	89	F3
Lovat Rd. EC3	**20**	**D6**
Lovat Wk., Houns.	122/123	E7
Cranford La.		
Lovatt Cl., Edg.	54	B6
Lovatt Dr., Ruis.	66	A5
Love La. EC2	**20**	**A3**
Love La. EC2	111	J6
Love La. N17	60	C7
Love La. SE18	136	E4
Love La. SE25	189	E3
Love La., Bex.	159	F6
Love La., Mitch.	185	H3
Love La., Mord.	184	D7
Love La., Pnr.	66	E3
Love La., Surb.	195	G2
Love La., Sutt.	198	B5
Love La., Wdf.Grn.	64	C6
Love Wk. SE5	152	A2
Loveday Rd. W13	125	E1
Lovegrove St. SE1	**37**	**J4**
Lovegrove St. SE1	132	D5
Lovegrove Wk. E14	134	C1
Lovekyn Cl., Kings.T.	181	J2
Queen Elizabeth Rd.		
Lovel Av., Well.	158	A2
Lovelace Av., Brom.	192	D6
Lovelace Gdns., Bark.	100	A4
Lovelace Gdns., Surb.	181	G7
Lovelace Grn. SE9	156	C3
Lovelace Rd. SE21	169	J2
Lovelace Rd., Barn.	41	H7
Lovelace Rd., Surb.	181	F7
Lovelinch Cl. SE15	133	F6
Lovell Ho. E8	112	D1
Lovell Pl. SE16	133	H3
Ropemaker Rd.		
Lovell Rd., Rich.	163	F3
Lovell Rd., Sthl.	103	H6
Loveridge Ms. NW6	90	C6
Loveridge Rd.		
Loveridge Rd. NW6	90	C6
Lovers Wk. N3	56	D7
Lovers Wk. NW7	56	C6
Lovers Wk. SE10	134	E6
Lover's Wk. W1	**24**	**B1**
Lover's Wk. W1	130	A1
Lovett Dr., Cars.	185	F7
Lovett Way NW10	88	C5
Lovett's Pl. SW18	148/149	E4
Old York Rd.		
Lovibonds Av., Orp.	207	E3
Low Cross Wd. La. SE21	170	C3
Low Hall Cl. E4	46	A7
Low Hall La. E17	77	H6
Lowbrook Rd., Ilf.	99	E5
Lowden Rd. N9	61	E1
Lowden Rd. SE24	151	H4
Lowden Rd., Sthl.	102	E7
Lowe Av. E16	115	G5
Lowell St. E14	113	H6
Lower Aberdeen Wf. E14	133	J1
Lower Addiscombe Rd., Croy.	202	B1
Lower Addison Gdns. W14	128	B2
Lower Alderton Hall La., Loug.	48	D5
Lower Belgrave St. SW1	**24**	**D6**
Lower Belgrave St. SW1	130	B3
Lower Boston Rd. W7	124	B1
Lower Broad St., Dag.	119	G1
Lower Camden, Chis.	174	C7
Lower Ch. St., Croy.	201	H2
Waddon New Rd.		
Lower Clapton Rd. E5	95	E5
Lower Clarendon Wk. W11	108	B6
Lancaster Rd.		
Lower Common S. SW15	147	H3
Lower Coombe St., Croy.	201	J4
Lower Downs Rd. SW20	184	A1
Lower Drayton Pl., Croy.	201	H2
Drayton Rd.		
Lower George St., Rich.	145	G5
George St.		
Lower Gravel Rd., Brom.	206	B1
Lower Grn. W., Mitch.	185	H3
Lower Grosvenor Pl. SW1	**24**	**D5**
Lower Grosvenor Pl. SW1	130	B3
Lower Gro. Rd., Rich.	145	J6
Lower Hall La. E4	61	H5
Lower Ham Rd., Kings.T.	163	G6
Lower Hampton Rd., Sun.	178	C3
Lower James St. W1	**17**	**G5**
Lower John St. W1	**17**	**G5**
Lower Kenwood Av., Enf.	42	D5
Lower Lea Crossing E14	114	E7
Lower Lea Crossing E16	114	E7
Lower Maidstone Rd. N11	58	C6
Telford Rd.		
Lower Mall W6	127	H5
Lower Mardyke Av., Rain.	119	J2
Lower Marsh SE1	**26**	**E4**
Lower Marsh SE1	131	G2
Lower Marsh La., Kings.T.	181	J4
Lower Merton Ri. NW3	91	H7
Lower Morden La., Mord.	183	J6
Lower Mortlake Rd., Rich.	145	H4
Lower Pk. Rd. N11	58	C5
Lower Pk. Rd., Belv.	139	G3
Lower Pk. Rd., Loug.	48	A5
Lower Queens Rd., Buck.H.	64	A2
Lower Richmond Rd. SW14	146	B3
Lower Richmond Rd. SW15	147	J3
Lower Richmond Rd., Rich.	146	A3
Lower Rd. SE8	133	F3
Lower Rd. SE16	133	F3
Lower Rd., Belv.	139	H3
Lower Rd., Har.	86	A1
Lower Rd., Loug.	48	D2
Lower Rd., Sutt.	199	F4
Lower Robert St. WC2	110/111	E7
John Adam St.		
Lower Sand Hills, T.Ditt.	181	G7
Lower Sloane St. SW1	**32**	**B2**
Lower Sloane St. SW1	130	A4
Lower Sq., Islw.	144	E3
Lower Strand NW9	71	F2
Lower Sunbury Rd., Hmptn.	179	F2
Lower Sydenham Ind. Est. SE26	171	J5
Lower Tail, Wat.	51	E3
Lower Talbot Wk. W11	108	B6
Lancaster Rd.		
Lower Teddington Rd., Kings.T.	181	G1
Lower Ter. NW3	91	F3
Lower Thames St. EC3	**20**	**C6**
Lower Thames St. EC3	112	A7
Lower Wd. Rd., Esher	194	D6
Lowestoft Cl. E5	95	F2
Theydon Rd.		
Lowestoft Ms. E16	136/137	E2
Barge Ho. Rd.		
Loweswater Cl., Wem.	87	G2
Lowfield Rd. NW6	90	D7
Lowfield Rd. W3	106	C6
Lowick Rd., Har.	68	B4
Lowlands Dr., Stai.	140	A5
Lowlands Gdns., Rom.	83	H6
Lowlands Rd., Har.	68	B7
Lowlands Rd., Pnr.	66	C7
Lowman Rd. N7	93	F4
Lowndes Cl. SW1	**24**	**C6**
Lowndes Cl. SW1	130	A3
Lowndes Ct. W1	**17**	**F4**
Lowndes Pl. SW1	**24**	**B6**
Lowndes Pl. SW1	130	A3
Lowndes Sq. SW1	**24**	**A4**
Lowndes Sq. SW1	129	J2
Lowndes St. SW1	**24**	**A5**
Lowndes St. SW1	130	A3
Lowood Ct. SE19	170	C5
Lowood St. E1	112/113	E7
Dellow St.		
Lowry Cres., Mitch.	185	H2
Lowry Rd., Dag.	100	B4
Lowshoe La., Rom.	83	H1
Lowth Rd. SE5	151	J2
Lowther Dr., Enf.	42	E4
Lowther Gdns. SW7	**23**	**F4**
Lowther Gdns. SW7	129	G2
Lowther Hill SE23	153	H7
Lowther Rd. E17	77	H2
Lowther Rd. N7	93	G5
Mackenzie Rd.		
Lowther Rd. SW13	147	F1
Lowther Rd., Kings.T.	181	J1
Lowther Rd., Stan.	69	J3
Loxford Av. E6	116	A2
Loxford La., Ilf.	99	F5
Loxford Rd., Bark.	99	E6
Loxford Ter., Bark.	99	F6
Fanshawe Av.		
Loxham Rd. E4	62	A7
Loxham St. WC1	**10**	**B4**
Loxley Cl. SE26	171	G5
Loxley Rd. SW18	167	G1
Loxley Rd., Hmptn.	161	F4
Loxton Rd. SE23	171	G1
Loxwood Rd. N17	76	B3
Lubbock Rd., Chis.	174	C7
Lubbock St. SE14	133	F7
Lucan Pl. SW3	**31**	**G2**
Lucan Pl. SW3	129	H4
Lucan Rd., Barn.	40	B3
Lucas Av. E13	115	H1
Lucas Av., Har.	85	G2
Lucas Cl. NW10	89	G7
Pound La.		
Lucas Ct., Har.	85	G1
Lucas Gdns. N2	73	F2
Tarling Rd.		
Lucas Rd. SE20	171	F6
Lucas Sq. NW11	72	D6
Hampstead Way		
Lucas St. SE8	154	A1
Lucerne Cl. N13	58	E4
Lucerne Cl., Erith	138/139	E3
Middle Way		
Lucerne Gro. E17	78	D4
Lucerne Ms. W8	128	D1
Kensington Mall		
Lucerne Rd. N5	93	H4
Lucerne Rd., Orp.	207	J1
Lucerne Rd., Th.Hth.	187	H5
Lucey Rd. SE16	**29**	**H6**
Lucey Rd. SE16	132	D3
Lucey Way SE16	**29**	**J6**
Lucien Rd. SW17	168	A4
Lucien Rd. SW19	166	E2
Lucknow St. SE18	137	H7
Lucorn Cl. SE12	155	F6
Lucton Ms., Loug.	48	E4
Luctons Av., Buck.H.	63	J1
Lucy Cres. W3	106	C5
Lucy Gdns., Dag.	100/101	E3
Grafton Rd.		
Luddesdon Rd., Erith	139	G7
Ludford Cl. NW9	70	E2
Ludford Cl., Croy.	201	H4
Warrington Rd.		
Ludgate Bdy. EC4	**19**	**G4**
Ludgate Circ. EC4	**19**	**G4**
Ludgate Hill EC4	**19**	**G4**
Ludgate Hill EC4	111	H6
Ludgate Sq. EC4	**19**	**H4**
Ludham Cl. SE28	118	C6
Rollesby Way		
Ludlow Cl., Brom.	191	G3
Ludlow Cl., Har.	85	F4
Ludlow Mead, Wat.	50	B3
Ludlow Rd., Felt.	160	A4
Ludlow St. EC1	**11**	**J5**
Ludlow Way N2	73	F4
Ludovick Wk. SW15	147	E4
Ludwick Ms. SE14	133	H7
Luffield Rd. SE2	138	B3
Luffman Rd. SE12	173	H3
Lugard Rd. SE15	153	E2
Lugg App. E12	98	D3
Luke Ho. E1	113	E6
Luke St. EC2	**12**	**D5**
Luke St. EC2	112	B4
Lukin Cres. E4	62	D3
Lukin St. E1	113	F6
Lukintone Cl., Loug.	48	B4
Lullingstone Cl., Orp.	176	B7
Lullingstone Cres.		
Lullingstone Cres., Orp.	176	A7
Lullingstone La. SE13	154	D7
Lullingstone Rd., Belv.	139	F6
Lullington Garth N12	56	C5
Lullington Garth, Borwd.	38	B5
Lullington Garth, Brom.	173	E7
Lullington Rd. SE20	170	D7
Lullington Rd., Dag.	100	E7
Lulot Gdns. N19	92	B2
Lulworth SE17	**36**	**B3**
Lulworth Av., Houns.	123	H7
Lulworth Av., Wem.	69	F7
Lulworth Cl., Har.	85	F3
Lulworth Cres., Mitch.	185	H2
Lulworth Dr., Pnr.	66	D6
Lulworth Gdns., Har.	85	E2
Lulworth Rd. SE9	174	B2
Lulworth Rd. SE15	153	E2
Lulworth Rd., Well.	157	J2
Lulworth Waye, Hayes	102	C6
Lumen Rd., Wem.	87	G2
Lumley Cl., Belv.	139	G6
Lumley Ct. WC2	**18**	**B6**
Lumley Gdns., Sutt.	198	B5
Lumley Rd., Sutt.	198	B6
Lumley St. W1	**16**	**C4**
Luna Rd., Th.Hth.	187	J3
Lunar Ho., Croy.	201	J1
Lundin Wk., Wat.	50	D4
Woodhall La.		
Lundy Dr., Hayes	121	H4
Lundy Wk. N1	93	J6
Clephane Rd.		
Lunham Rd. SE19	170	B6
Lupin Cl. SW2	169	H2
Lupin Cl., Croy.	203	G1
Primrose La.		
Lupin Cl., West Dr.	120	A5
Magnolia St.		
Lupin Cres., Ilf.	98/99	E5
Bluebell Way		
Lupton Cl. SE12	173	H3
Lupton St. NW5	92	C4
Lupus St. SW1	**33**	**G3**
Lupus St. SW1	130	B6
Luralda Gdns. E14	134	C5
Saunders Ness Rd.		
Lurgan Av. W6	128	A6
Lurline Gdns. SW11	150	A1
Luscombe Ct., Brom.	190	E2
Luscombe Way SW8	**34**	**A7**
Luscombe Way SW8	130	E7
Lushes Ct., Loug.	48/49	E5
Lushes Rd.		
Lushes Rd., Loug.	49	E5
Lushington Rd. NW10	107	H2
Lushington Rd. SE6	172	B5
Lushington Ter. E8	94	D6
Wayland Av.		
Luther Cl., Edg.	54	C2
Luther King Cl. E17	77	H6
Luther Rd., Tedd.	162	C5
Luton Pl. SE10	134	C7
Luton Rd. E17	77	J3
Luton Rd., Sid.	176	C3
Luton St. NW8	**7**	**F6**

Luton St. NW8 109 G4
Lutton Ter. NW3 91 G4
Flask Wk.
Luttrell Av. SW15 147 H5
Lutwyche Rd. SE6 171 J2
Luxborough La., 64 B3
Chig.
Luxborough St. W1 16 B1
Luxborough St. W1 110 A4
Luxemburg Gdns. 128 A4
W6
Luxfield Rd. SE9 174 B1
Luxford St. SE16 133 G4
Luxmore St. SE4 153 J1
Luxor St. SE5 151 J3
Lyal Rd. E3 113 H2
Lyall Av. SE21 170 B3
Lyall Ms. SW1 24 B6
Lyall Ms. SW1 130 A3
Lyall Ms. W. SW1 24 B6
Lyall St. SW1 130 A3
Lyall St. SW1 24 B6
Lycett Pl. W12 127 G2
Becklow Rd.
Lyconby Gdns., Croy. 189 H7
Lydd Cl., Sid. 175 H3
Lydd Rd., Bexh. 139 F7
Lydden Ct. SE9 157 H6
Lydden Gro. SW18 148 E7
Lydden Rd. SW18 148 E7
Lydeard Rd. E6 98 C7
Lydford Cl. N16 94 B5
Pellerin Rd.
Lydford Rd. N15 76 A5
Lydford Rd. NW2 90 A6
Lydford Rd. W9 108 C4
Lydhurst Av. SW2 169 F2
Lydney Cl. SE15 36 E7
Lydney Cl. SE15 132 B7
Lydney Cl. SW19 166 B2
Princes Way
Lydon Rd. SW4 150 C3
Lydstep Rd., Chis. 174 D4
Lyford Rd. SW18 149 G7
Lygon Pl. SW1 24 D6
Lyham Cl. SW2 151 E4
Lyham Rd. SW2 150 E5
Lyle Cl., Mitch. 186 A7
Lyme Fm. Rd. SE12 155 G4
Lyme Gro. E9 95 F7
St. Thomas's Sq.
Lyme Rd., Well. 158 B1
Lyme St. NW1 92 C7
Lyme Ter. NW1 92 C7
Royal College St.
Lymer Av. SE19 170 C5
Lymescote Gdns., 198 D2
Sutt.
Lyminge Cl., Sid. 175 J4
Lyminge Gdns. 167 H1
SW18
Lymington Av. N22 75 G2
Lymington Cl. E6 116 C5
Valiant Way
Lymington Cl. SW16 186 D2
Lymington Gdns., 197 F5
Epsom
Lymington Rd. NW6 90 E6
Lymington Rd., Dag. 100 D1
Lympstone Gdns. 37 J7
SE15
Lympstone Gdns. 132 D7
SE15
Lyn Ms. E3 113 J3
Tredegar Sq.
Lynbridge Gdns. N13 59 H4
Lynbrook Cl. SE15 36 E7
Lynch Wk. SE8 133 J6
Prince St.
Lynchen Cl., Houns. 142 A1
The Av.
Lyncott Cres. SW4 150 B4
Lyncroft Av., Pnr. 66 E5
Lyncroft Gdns. NW6 90 D5
Lyncroft Gdns. W13 125 F2
Lyncroft Gdns., 143 J4
Houns.
Lyndale NW2 90 C4
Lyndale Av. NW2 90 C3
Lyndale Cl. SE3 135 F6
Lyndhurst Av. N12 57 J6
Lyndhurst Av. NW7 54 E6
Lyndhurst Av. SW16 186 D2
Lyndhurst Av., Pnr. 66 B1
Lyndhurst Av., Sthl. 123 H1
Lyndhurst Av., Sun. 178 A3
Lyndhurst Av., Surb. 196 B1
Lyndhurst Av., 161 F1
Twick.
Lyndhurst Cl. NW10 88 D3
Lyndhurst Cl., Bexh. 159 H3
Lyndhurst Cl., Croy. 202 C3
Lyndhurst Cl., Orp. 207 E4
Lyndhurst Dr. E10 78 C7

Lyndhurst Dr., N.Mal. 183 E6
Lyndhurst Gdns. N3 72 B1
Lyndhurst Gdns. 91 G5
NW3
Lyndhurst Gdns., 99 H6
Bark.
Lyndhurst Gdns., Enf. 44 B4
Lyndhurst Gdns., Ilf. 81 G6
Lyndhurst Gdns., 66 B1
Pnr.
Lyndhurst Gro. SE15 152 B2
Lyndhurst Ri., Chig. 64 D4
Lyndhurst Rd. E4 62 C7
Lyndhurst Rd. N18 60 D4
Lyndhurst Rd. N22 59 F6
Lyndhurst Rd. NW3 91 G5
Lyndhurst Rd., Bexh. 159 H3
Lyndhurst Rd., Grnf. 103 H4
Lyndhurst Rd., 187 G4
Th.Hth.
Lyndhurst Sq. SE15 152 C1
Lyndhurst Ter. NW3 91 G5
Lyndhurst Way SE15 152 C1
Lyndhurst Way, Sutt. 198 D7
Lyndon Av., Pnr. 51 E6
Lyndon Av., Sid. 157 J5
Lyndon Av., Wall. 200 A3
Lyndon Rd., Belv. 139 G4
Lyne Cres. E17 77 J1
Lyne Way NW10 88 E6
Lynne Way, Nthlt. 102 D2
Lynsted Cl., Bexh. 159 H5
Lynsted Cl., Brom. 191 J2
Lynsted Ct., Beck. 189 H2
Churchfields Rd.
Lynsted Gdns. SE9 156 A3
Lynton Av. N12 57 G4
Lynton Av. NW9 71 F4
Lynton Av. W13 104 D6
Lynton Av., Rom. 83 G1
Lynton Cl. NW10 88 E5
Lynton Cl., Chess. 195 H4
Lynton Cl., Islw. 144 C4
Lynton Cres., Ilf. 80 E6
Lynton Est. SE1 37 H2
Lynton Gdns. N11 58 D6
Lynton Gdns., Enf. 44 B7
Lynton Mead N20 56 D3
Lynton Rd. E4 62 B5
Lynton Rd. N8 74 D5
Lynton Rd. NW6 108 C1
Lynton Rd. SE1 37 G2
Lynton Rd. SE1 132 C4
Lynton Rd. W3 106 A7
Lynton Rd., Croy. 187 G6
Lynton Rd., Har. 85 E2
Lynton Rd., N.Mal. 182 D5
Lynton Ter. W3 106 C6
Lynton Rd.
Lynwood Cl. E18 79 J1
Lynwood Cl., Har. 85 E3
Lynwood Dr., Wor.Pk. 197 G2
Lynwood Gdns., 201 F4
Croy.
Lynwood Gdns., Sthl. 103 F6
Lynwood Gro. N21 59 G1
Lynwood Gro., Orp. 193 H7
Lynwood Rd. SW17 167 J3
Lynwood Rd. W5 105 H4
Lynwood Rd., T.Ditt. 194 C2
Lyon Business Pk., 117 H2
Bark.
Lyon Meade, Stan. 69 F1
Lyon Pk. Av., Wem. 87 H6
Lyon Rd. SW19 185 F1
Lyon Rd., Har. 68 C6

Lyon St. N1 93 F7
Caledonian Rd.
Lyon Way, Grnf. 104 B1
Lyons Pl. NW8 7 E5
Lyons Pl. NW8 109 G4
Lyons Wk. W14 128 B4
Lyonsdown Av., 41 F6
Barn.
Lyonsdown Rd., 41 F6
Barn.
Lyoth Rd., Orp. 207 F2
Lyric Dr., Grnf. 103 H4
Lyric Rd. SW13 147 F1
Lysander Gdns., 181 J6
Surb.
Ewell Rd.
Lysander Gro. N19 92 D1
Lysander Rd., Croy. 201 F6
Lysander Way, Orp. 207 F3
Lysia St. SW6 128 A7
Lysias Rd. SW12 150 A6
Lysons Wk. SW15 147 G5
Swinburne Rd.
Lytchet Rd., Brom. 173 H7
Lytchet Way, Enf. 45 F1
Lytcott Dr., W.Mol. 179 F3
Freeman Dr.
Lytcott Gro. SE22 152 C5
Lyte St. E2 113 F2
Bishops Way
Lytham Av., Wat. 50 D5
Lytham Gro. W5 105 H3
Lytham St. SE17 36 B4
Lytham St. SE17 132 A5
Lyttelton Cl. NW3 91 H7
Lyttelton Rd. E10 96 B3
Lyttelton Rd. N2 73 F5
Lyttleton Rd. N8 75 G3
Lytton Av. N13 59 G2
Lytton Cl. N2 73 G5
Lytton Cl., Loug. 49 G3
Lytton Cl., Nthlt. 85 F7
Lytton Gdns., Wall. 200 D4
Lytton Gro. SW15 148 A5
Lytton Rd. E11 78 E7
Lytton Rd., Barn. 41 F4
Lytton Rd., Pnr. 50 E7
Lytton Strachey Path 118 B7
SE28
Titmuss Av.
Lyveden Rd. SE3 135 H7
Lyveden Rd. SW17 167 H6

M

Maberley Cres. SE19 170 D7
Maberley Rd. SE19 188 C1
Maberley Rd., Beck. 189 G3
Mabledon Pl. WC1 9 J4
Mabledon Pl. WC1 110 D3
Mablethorpe Rd. 128 B7
SW6
Mabley St. E9 95 H6
Macaret Cl. N20 41 E7
MacArthur Cl. E7 97 G6
MacArthur Ter. SE7 136 B6
Macaulay Av., Esher 194 C2
Macaulay Ct. SW4 150 B3
Macaulay Rd. E6 116 A2
Macaulay Rd. SW4 150 B3
Macaulay Sq. SW4 150 B4
Macaulay Way SE28 118 B7
Booth Cl.
Macauley Ms. SE13 154 C2
Macbean St. SE18 136 D3
Macbeth St. W6 127 H5
Macclesfield Br. NW1 7 H1
Macclesfield Rd. NW1 109 H2
Macclesfield Rd. EC1 11 J3
Macclesfield Rd. EC1 111 J3
Macclesfield Rd. 189 E5
SE25
Macclesfield St. W1 17 J5
Macclesfield St. W1 110 D7
Macdonald Av., Dag. 101 H3
Macdonald Rd. E7 97 G4
Macdonald Rd. E17 78 C2
Macdonald Rd. N11 57 J5
Macdonald Rd. N19 92 C2
Macduff Rd. SW11 150 A1
Mace Cl. E1 132/133 E1
Kennet St.
Mace St. E2 113 G2
MacFarlane La., Islw. 124 C6
Macfarlane Rd. W12 127 J1
Macfarren Pl. NW1 8 C6
Macgregor Rd. E16 115 J5
Machell Rd. SE15 153 F3
Mackay Rd. SW4 150 B3
Mackennal St. NW8 7 H2
Mackennal St. NW8 109 H2
Mackenzie Rd. N7 93 F6
Mackenzie Rd., Beck. 189 F2

Mackenzie Wk. E14 134 A1
Mackeson Rd. NW3 91 J4
Mackie Rd. SW2 151 G7
Mackintosh La. E9 95 G5
Homerton High St.
Macklin St. WC2 18 B3
Macklin St. WC2 111 E6
Mackrow Wk. E14 114 C7
Robin Hood La.
Macks Rd. SE16 37 J1
Macks Rd. SE16 132 D4
Mackworth St. NW1 9 F3
Mackworth St. NW1 110 C3
Maclaren Ms. SW15 147 J4
Clarendon Dr.
Maclean Rd. SE23 153 H6
Macleod St. SE17 36 A4
Macleod St. SE17 131 J5
Maclise Rd. W14 128 B3
Macoma Rd. SE18 137 G6
Macoma Ter. SE18 137 G6
Maconochies Rd. E14 134 B5
Macquarie Way E14 134 B4
Macready Pl. N7 92/93 E4
Warlters Rd.
Macroom Rd. W9 108 C3
Mada Rd., Orp. 206 E3
Maddams St. E3 114 B4
Maddison Cl., Tedd. 162 C6
Maddock Way SE17 35 H6
Maddock Way SE17 131 H6
Maddocks Cl., Sid. 176 E5
Maddox St. W1 17 E5
Maddox St. W1 110 B7
Madeira Av., Brom. 173 E7
Madeira Gro., 63 J6
Wdf.Grn.
Madeira Rd. E11 96 D1
Madeira Rd. N13 59 H4
Madeira Rd. SW16 169 E5
Madeira Rd., Mitch. 185 J4
Madeley Rd. W5 105 H6
Madeline Gro., Ilf. 99 G5
Madeline Rd. SE20 188 D1
Madge Gill Way E6 116 B1
Ron Leighton Way
Madinah Rd. E8 94 D6
Madison Cres., Bexh. 138 C7
Madison Gdns., 138 C7
Bexh.
Madison Gdns., 191 F3
Brom.
Madras Pl. N7 93 G6
Madras Rd., Ilf. 99 E4
Madrid Rd. SW13 147 G1
Madrigal La. SE5 131 H7
Madron St. SE17 37 E3
Madron St. SE17 132 B5
Mafeking Av. E6 116 A2
Mafeking Av., Brent. 125 H6
Mafeking Av., Ilf. 81 G7
Mafeking Rd. E16 115 F4
Mafeking Rd. N17 76 D2
Mafeking Rd., Enf. 44 C3
Magdala Av. N19 92 B2
Magdala Rd., Islw. 144 D3
Magdala Rd., S.Croy. 202 A7
Napier Rd.
Magdalen Pas. E1 21 G5
Magdalen Rd. SW18 167 F1
Magdalen St. SE1 28 D2
Magdalen St. SE1 132 B1
Magdalene Cl. 152/153 E2
SE15
Heaton Rd.
Magdalene Gdns. E6 116 D4
Magee St. SE11 35 E5
Magee St. SE11 131 G6
Magellan Pl. E14 134 A5
Napier Av.
Maggie Blake's 29 F2
Cause SE1
Magnet Rd., Wem. 87 G2
Magnin Cl. E8 112 D1
Wilde Cl.
Magnolia Cl. E10 96 A2
Magnolia Cl., 164 C6
Kings.T.
Magnolia Ct., Har. 69 J7
Magnolia Ct., Rich. 146 B1
West Hall Rd.
Magnolia Gdns., Edg. 54 C4
Ash Cl.
Magnolia Pl. SW4 150 E5
Magnolia Pl. W5 105 H5
Montpelier Rd.
Magnolia Rd. W4 126 B6
Magnolia St., 120 A4
West Dr.
Magnolia Way, 196 C5
Epsom
Magpie All. EC4 19 F4
Magpie Cl. E7 97 F5

Magpie Cl. NW9	70/71	E2	Malden Rd., N.Mal.	183	E5	Malting Way, Islw.	144	C3	**Mandeville Pl. W1**	16	C3

Magpie Cl. NW9 70/71 E2
 Eagle Dr.
Magpie Cl., Enf. 44 D1
Magpie Hall Cl., 192 B6
 Brom.
Magpie Hall La., 192 C5
 Brom.
Magpie Hall Rd., 52 B2
 Bushey
Magpie Pl. SE14 133 H6
 Milton Ct. Rd.
Magri Wk. E1 113 F5
 Ashfield St.
Maguire Dr., Rich. 163 F4
Maguire St. SE1 29 G3
Maguire St. SE1 132 C2
Mahatma Gandhi Ho., 88 A5
 Wem.
Mahlon Av., Ruis. 84 B5
Mahogany Cl. SE16 133 H1
Mahon Cl., Enf. 44 C1
Maida Av. W2 14 D1
Maida Av. W2 109 E2
Maida Rd., Belv. 139 G3
Maida Vale W9 6 C4
Maida Vale W9 109 E2
Maida Way E4 46 B7
Maiden Erlegh Av., 176 E1
 Bex.
Maiden La. NW1 92 D7
Maiden La. SE1 28 A1
Maiden La. WC2 18 B6
Maiden La. WC2 111 E7
Maiden Rd. E15 97 E7
Maidenstone Hill 154 C1
 SE10
Maids of Honour 145 G5
 Row, Rich.
 The Grn.
Maidstone Av., Rom. 83 J2
Maidstone Bldgs. SE1 28 A2
Maidstone Ho. E14 114 B6
 Carmen St.
Maidstone Rd. N11 58 D6
Maidstone Rd., Sid. 176 D6
Maidstone St. E2 13 J1
Main Av., Enf. 44 C5
Main Dr., Wem. 87 G3
Main Rd., Sid. 175 H3
Main St., Felt. 160 D5
Mainridge Rd., Chis. 174 D4
Maisemore St. SE15 37 J7
Maitland Cl. SE10 134 B7
Maitland Cl., Houns. 143 F3
Maitland Pk. Est. 91 J6
 NW3
Maitland Pk. Rd. 91 J6
 NW3
Maitland Pk. Vil. 91 J6
 NW3
Maitland Pl. E5 94/95 E4
 Clarence Rd.
Maitland Rd. E15 97 F6
Maitland Rd. SE26 171 G6
Maize Row E14 113 J7
 Commercial Rd.
Majendie Rd. SE18 137 G5
Majestic Way, Mitch. 185 J2
Major Rd. E15 96 D5
Major Rd. SE16 29 J5
Makepeace Av. N6 92 A2
Makepeace Rd. E11 79 G4
Makepeace Rd., 102 E2
 Nthlt.
Makins St. SW3 31 H2
Makins St. SW3 129 H4
Malabar St. E14 134 A2
Malam Gdns. E14 114 B7
 Wades Pl.
Malbrook Rd. SW15 147 H4
Malcolm Ct., Stan. 53 F5
Malcolm Cres. NW4 71 G6
Malcolm Dr., Surb. 195 H1
Malcolm Pl. E2 113 F4
Malcolm Rd. E1 113 F4
Malcolm Rd. SE20 171 F7
Malcolm Rd. SE25 188 D6
Malcolm Rd. SW19 166 B6
Malcolm Way E11 79 G5
Malcolms Way N14 42 C6
Malden Av. SE25 188 E4
Malden Av., Grnf. 86 B5
Malden Cres. NW1 92 A6
Malden Grn. Av., 197 F1
 Wor.Pk.
Malden Hill, N.Mal. 183 F3
Malden Hill Gdns., 183 F3
 N.Mal.
Malden Pk., N.Mal. 183 F6
Malden Pl. NW5 92 A5
 Grafton Ter.
Malden Rd. NW5 92 A5
Malden Rd., Borwd. 38 A3

Malden Rd., N.Mal. 183 E5
Malden Rd., Sutt. 198 A4
Malden Rd., Wor.Pk. 183 F7
Malden Way, N.Mal. 183 F5
Maldon Cl. E15 96 D5
 David St.
Maldon Cl. N1 111 J1
Maldon Cl. SE5 152 B3
Maldon Ct., Wall. 200 C5
 Maldon Rd.
Maldon Rd. N9 60 C3
Maldon Rd. W3 106 C7
Maldon Rd., Rom. 83 J7
Maldon Rd., Wall. 200 B5
Maldon Wk., 63 J6
 Wdf.Grn.
Malet Pl. WC1 9 H6
Malet Pl. WC1 110 D4
Malet St. WC1 9 H6
Malet St. WC1 110 D4
Maley Av. SE27 169 H2
Malford Ct. E18 79 G2
Malford Gro. E18 79 F4
Malfort Rd. SE5 152 B3
Malham Cl. N11 58 A6
 Catterick Cl.
Malham Rd. SE23 171 G1
Malins Cl., Barn. 39 H5
Mall, The E15 96 D7
Mall, The N14 58 E3
Mall, The SW1 25 G3
Mall, The SW1 130 C2
Mall, The SW14 146 C5
Mall, The W5 105 H7
Mall, The, Brom. 191 G3
 High St.
Mall, The, Croy. 201 J2
Mall, The, Har. 69 J6
Mall, The, Surb. 181 G5
Mall Rd. W6 127 H5
Mallams Ms. SW9 151 H3
 St. James's Cres.
Mallard Cl. E9 95 J6
Mallard Cl. NW6 108 D2
Mallard Cl. W7 124 B2
Mallard Cl., Barn. 41 G6
 The Hook
Mallard Cl., Twick. 143 G7
 Stephenson Rd.
Mallard Path SE28 137 G3
Mallard Pl., Twick. 162 D3
Mallard Wk., Beck. 189 G5
Mallard Wk., Sid. 176 C5
Mallard Way NW9 70 C7
Mallards Rd., Bark. 117 H3
 Thames Rd.
Mallards Rd., 63 H7
 Wdf.Grn.
Mallet Dr., Nthlt. 85 F5
Mallet Rd. SE13 154 D6
Malling Cl., Croy. 189 F6
Malling Gdns., Mord. 185 F6
Malling Way, Brom. 191 F7
Mallinson Rd. SW11 149 H5
Mallinson Rd., Croy. 200 D3
Mallord St. SW3 31 F5
Mallord St. SW3 129 G6
Mallory Cl. SE4 153 H4
Mallory Gdns., Barn. 42 A7
Mallory St. NW8 7 H5
Mallory St. NW8 109 H4
Mallow Cl., Croy. 203 G1
 Marigold Way
Mallow Mead NW7 56 B7
Mallow St. EC1 12 B5
Malmains Cl., Beck. 190 D5
Malmains Way, Beck. 190 C4
Malmesbury Rd. E3 113 J3
Malmesbury Rd. 115 E5
 E16
Malmesbury Rd. E18 79 F1
Malmesbury Rd., 185 F7
 Mord.
Malmesbury Ter. 115 F5
Malpas Dr., Pnr. 66 D5
Malpas Rd. E8 94 E6
Malpas Rd. SE4 153 J2
Malpas Rd., Dag. 100 D6
Malt St. SE1 37 H5
Malt St. SE1 132 D6
Malta St. EC1 11 H5
Maltby St. SE1 29 F4
Maltby St. SE1 132 C2
Malthouse Dr. W4 127 E6
Malthouse Dr., Felt. 160 D5
Malthouse Pas. 146/147 E2
 SW13
 The Ter.
Malthus Path SE28 138 C1
 Owen Cl.
Malting Ho. E14 113 J7

Malting Way, Islw. 144 C3
Maltings, The, Orp. 207 J1
Maltings Cl. 146/147 E2
 SW13
 Cleveland Gdns.
Maltings Ms., Sid. 176 A3
 Station Rd.
Maltings Pl. SW6 149 F1
Malton Ms. SE18 137 H6
 Malton St.
Malton Ms. W10 108 B6
 Cambridge Gdns.
Malton Rd. W10 108 B6
 St. Marks Rd.
Malton St. SE18 137 H6
Maltravers St. WC2 18 D5
Malva Cl. SW18 148/149 E5
 St. Ann's Hill
Malvern Av. E4 62 D7
Malvern Av., Bexh. 138 E7
Malvern Av., Har. 85 E3
Malvern Cl. SE20 188 D2
 Derwent Rd.
Malvern Cl. W10 108 C5
Malvern Cl., Mitch. 186 C3
Malvern Cl., Surb. 195 H1
Malvern Ct. SE14 133 F7
 Avonley Rd.
Malvern Ct. SW7 31 F2
Malvern Ct. SW7 129 G4
Malvern Dr., Felt. 160 D5
Malvern Dr., Ilf. 99 J4
Malvern Dr., Wdf.Grn. 63 J5
Malvern Gdns. NW2 90 B2
Malvern Gdns. NW6 108 C2
 Carlton Vale
Malvern Gdns., Har. 69 H3
Malvern Gdns., Loug. 48 C6
Malvern Ms. NW6 108 D3
 Malvern Rd.
Malvern Pl. NW6 108 C3
Malvern Rd. E6 116 B1
Malvern Rd. E8 94 D7
Malvern Rd. E11 97 E2
Malvern Rd. N8 75 F3
Malvern Rd. N17 76 D3
Malvern Rd. NW6 108 D3
Malvern Rd., Hmptn. 161 G7
Malvern Rd., Hayes 121 H7
Malvern Rd., Surb. 195 H2
Malvern Rd., Th.Hth. 187 G4
Malvern Ter. N1 111 G1
Malvern Ter. N9 60 C1
 Latymer Rd.
Malvern Way 104/105 E5
 W13
 Templewood
Malwood Rd. SW12 150 B6
Malyons Rd. SE13 154 B5
Malyons Ter. SE13 154 B5
Managers St. E14 134 C1
 Prestons Rd.
Manatee Pl., Wall. 200 D3
 Croydon Rd.
Manaton Cl. SE15 152 E3
Manaton Cres., Sthl. 103 G6
Manbey Gro. E15 96 E6
Manbey Pk. Rd. E15 96 E6
Manbey Rd. E15 96 E6
Manbey St. E15 96 E6
Manbre Rd. W6 127 J6
Manbrough Av. E6 116 C3
Manchester Dr. W10 108 B4
Manchester Gro. E14 134 C5
Manchester Ms. W1 16 B2
Manchester Rd. E14 134 C5
Manchester Rd. N15 76 A6
Manchester Rd., 187 J3
 Th.Hth.
Manchester Sq. W1 16 B3
Manchester Sq. W1 110 A6
Manchester St. W1 16 B2
Manchester St. W1 110 A5
Manchester Way, 101 H4
 Dag.
Manchuria Rd. SW11 150 A6
Manciple St. SE1 28 B4
Manciple St. SE1 132 A3
Mandalay Rd. SW4 150 C5
Mandarin St. E14 114 A7
 Salter St.
Mandarin Way, 102 D5
 Hayes
Mandela Cl. NW10 88 C7
Mandela Rd. E16 115 G6
Mandela St. NW1 110 C1
Mandela St. SW9 131 G7
Mandela Way SE1 37 F2
Mandela Way SE1 132 B4
Mandeville Cl. SE3 135 F7
 Vanbrugh Pk.
Mandeville Cl. SW20 184 B1
Mandeville Ct. E4 61 H4
Mandeville Dr., Surb. 195 G1

Mandeville Pl. W1 16 C3
Mandeville Pl. W1 110 A6
Mandeville Rd. N14 58 B2
Mandeville Rd., Islw. 144 D2
Mandeville Rd., 85 G7
 Nthlt.
Mandeville St. E5 95 H3
Mandrake Rd. SW17 167 J3
Mandrake Way E15 96 E7
Mandrell Rd. SW2 150 E5
Manette St. W1 17 J4
Manette St. W1 110 D6
Manford Way, Chig. 65 H5
Manfred Rd. SW15 148 C5
Manger Rd. N7 93 E6
Mangold Way, Erith 138 E3
Manhattan Wf. E16 135 G2
Manilla St. E14 134 A2
Manister Rd. SE2 138 A3
Manitoba Cl. SE16 133 F2
 Renforth St.
Manitoba Gdns., Orp. 207 J6
 Superior Dr.
Manley Ct. N16 94 C3
 Stoke Newington High St.
Manley St. NW1 110 A1
Mann Cl., Croy. 201 J3
 Salem Pl.
Mannin Rd., Rom. 82 B7
Manning Gdns., Har. 69 G7
Manning Pl., Rich. 145 J6
 Grove Rd.
Manning Rd. E17 77 H5
 Southcote Rd.
Manning Rd., Dag. 101 G6
Manningford Cl. EC1 11 G3
Manningtree Cl. 166 B1
 SW19
Manningtree Rd., 84 B4
 Ruis.
Manningtree St. E1 21 H3
Mannock Dr., Loug. 49 F2
Mannock Rd. N22 75 H3
Manns Cl., Islw. 144 C5
Manns Rd., Edg. 54 A6
Manoel Rd., Twick. 161 J2
Manor Av. SE4 153 J2
Manor Av., Houns. 142 D3
Manor Av., Nthlt. 85 F7
Manor Cl. E17 77 H2
 Manor Rd.
Manor Cl. NW7 54 D5
 Manor Dr.
Manor Cl. NW9 70 B5
Manor Cl. SE28 118 C7
Manor Cl., Barn. 40 B4
Manor Cl., Wor.Pk. 197 E1
Manor Cotts. App. N2 73 F2
Manor Cl. E10 96 B1
 Grange Pk. Rd.
Manor Cl. N2 73 J5
Manor Cl. SW6 148/149 E1
 Bagley's La.
Manor Ct., Twick. 161 J2
Manor Ct., Wem. 87 H5
Manor Ct. Rd. W7 104 B7
Manor Cres., Surb. 182 A6
Manor Dr. N14 42 B7
Manor Dr. N20 57 H3
Manor Dr. NW7 54 D5
Manor Dr., Epsom 196 E6
Manor Dr., Esher 194 C2
Manor Dr., Felt. 160 D5
 Lebanon Av.
Manor Dr., Sun. 178 A2
Manor Dr., Surb. 181 J6
Manor Dr., Wem. 87 J4
Manor Dr., The, 197 E1
 Wor.Pk.
Manor Dr. N., N.Mal. 182 D7
Manor Dr. N., Wor.Pk. 196 E1
Manor Est. SE16 132 E4
Manor Fm. Cl., 196 E1
 Wor.Pk.
Manor Fm. Dr. E4 63 E3
Manor Fm. Rd., 187 G2
 Th.Hth.
Manor Fm. Rd., Wem. 105 G2
Manor Flds. SW15 148 A6
Manor Gdns. N7 93 E3
Manor Gdns. SW20 184 D2
Manor Gdns. W3 124 A4
Manor Gdns. W4 126/127 E5
 Devonshire Rd.
Manor Gdns., Hmptn. 161 H7
Manor Gdns., Rich. 145 J4
Manor Gdns., Ruis. 84 C5
Manor Gdns., S.Croy. 202 C6
Manor Gdns., Sun. 178 A3
Manor Gate, Nthlt. 84 E7
Manor Gro. SE15 133 F6
Manor Gro., Beck. 190 B2
Manor Gro., Rich. 146 A4
Manor Hall Av. NW4 71 J2

Manor Hall Dr. NW4 72 A2
Manor Ho. Dr. NW6 90 A7
Manor Ho. Est., Stan. 52/53 E6
Old Ch. La.
Manor Ho. Way, Islw. 144 E3
Manor La. SE12 155 E6
Manor La. SE13 154 E4
Manor La., Felt. 160 A2
Manor La., Hayes 121 G6
Manor La., Sun. 178 A2
Manor La., Sutt. 199 F5
Manor La. Ter. SE13 154 E4
Manor Ms. NW6 108 D2
Cambridge Av.
Manor Ms. SE4 154 A2
Manor Mt. SE23 171 F1
Manor Par. NW10 107 F2
Station Rd.
Manor Pk. SE13 154 D4
Manor Pk., Chis. 193 G2
Manor Pk., Rich. 145 J4
Manor Pk. Cl., W.Wick. 204 B1
Manor Pk. Cres., Edg. 54 A6
Manor Pk. Dr., Har. 67 H3
Manor Pk. Gdns., Edg. 54 A5
Manor Pk. Par. SE13 154 D4
Lee High Rd.
Manor Pk. Rd. E12 98 A4
Manor Pk. Rd. N2 73 G3
Manor Pk. Rd. NW10 107 F1
Manor Pk. Rd., Chis. 193 F1
Manor Pk. Rd., Sutt. 199 F5
Manor Pk. Rd., W.Wick. 204 B1
Manor Pl. SE17 35 H4
Manor Pl. SE17 131 H5
Manor Pl., Chis. 193 G1
Manor Pl., Felt. 160 A1
Manor Pl., Mitch. 186 C3
Manor Pl., Sutt. 199 E4
Manor Rd. E10 78 A7
Manor Rd. E15 114 E2
Manor Rd. E16 114 E3
Manor Rd. E17 77 H2
Manor Rd. N16 94 A1
Manor Rd. N17 76 D1
Manor Rd. N22 59 E6
Manor Rd. SE25 188 D4
Manor Rd. SW20 184 C2
Manor Rd. W13 104 D7
Manor Rd., Bark. 99 J6
Manor Rd., Barn. 40 B5
Manor Rd., Beck. 190 B2
Manor Rd., Bex. 177 H1
Manor Rd., Chig. 64 E5
Manor Rd., Dag. 101 J6
Manor Rd., E.Mol. 180 A4
Manor Rd., Enf. 44 A2
Manor Rd., Har. 68 D6
Manor Rd., Hayes 102 A6
Manor Rd., Loug. 47 H6
Manor Rd., Mitch. 186 C4
Manor Rd., Rich. 145 J3
Manor Rd. (Chadwell Heath), Rom. 82 D6
Manor Rd., Sid. 175 J3
Manor Rd., Sutt. 198 C7
Manor Rd., Tedd. 162 E5
Manor Rd., Twick. 161 J2
Manor Rd., Wall. 200 B4
Manor Rd., W.Wick. 204 B2
Manor Rd., Wdf.Grn. 64 C6
Manor Rd. N., Esher 194 C3
Manor Rd. N., T.Ditt. 194 D2
Manor Rd. N., Wall. 200 B4
Manor Rd. S., Esher 194 B4
Manor Sq., Dag. 100 D2
Manor Vale, Brent. 125 F5
Manor Vw. N3 72 E2
Manor Way E4 62 D4
Manor Way NW9 70 E3
Manor Way SE3 155 F4
Manor Way SE28 138 C1
Manor Way, Beck. 190 A2
Manor Way, Bex. 177 G1
Manor Way, Borwd. 38 C4
Manor Way, Brom. 192 B6
Manor Way, Har. 67 H4
Manor Way, Mitch. 186 C3
Manor Way, Orp. 193 F4
Manor Way, S.Croy. 202 B6
Manor Way, Sthl. 122 D4
Manor Way, Wor.Pk. 197 E1
Manor Way, The, Wall. 200 B4
Manorbrook SE3 155 G4
Manordene Cl., T.Ditt. 194 D1
Manordene Rd. SE28 118 C6
Manorfield Cl. N19 92 C4
Tufnell Pk. Rd.
Manorfields Cl., Chis. 193 J3
Manorgate Rd., Kings.T. 182 A1
Manorhall Gdns. E10 96 A1
Manorside, Barn. 40 B4
Manorside Cl. SE2 138 C4
Manorway, Enf. 44 B7
Manorway, Wdf.Grn. 63 J5
Manpreet Ct. E12 98 C5
Morris Av.
Manresa Rd. SW3 31 G4
Manresa Rd. SW3 129 H5
Mansard Beeches SW17 168 A5
Mansard Cl., Pnr. 66 D3
Manse Cl., Hayes 121 G6
Manse Rd. N16 94 C3
Mansel Gro. E17 78 A1
Mansel Rd. SW19 166 B6
Mansell Rd. W3 126 D2
Mansell Rd., Grnf. 103 H5
Mansell St. E1 21 G6
Mansell St. E1 112 C6
Mansergh Cl. SE18 136 B7
Mansfield Av. N15 76 A4
Mansfield Av., Barn. 41 J6
Mansfield Av., Ruis. 84 B1
Mansfield Cl. N9 44 D6
Mansfield Hill E4 62 B1
Mansfield Ms. W1 16 D2
Mansfield Pl. NW3 91 F4
New End
Mansfield Rd. E11 79 H6
Mansfield Rd. E17 77 J4
Mansfield Rd. NW3 91 J5
Mansfield Rd. W3 106 B4
Mansfield Rd., Chess. 195 F5
Mansfield Rd., Ilf. 98 D2
Mansfield Rd., S.Croy. 202 A6
Mansfield St. W1 16 D2
Mansfield St. W1 110 B5
Mansford St. E2 13 J2
Mansford St. E2 112 D2
Manship Rd., Mitch. 168 A7
Mansion Cl. SW9 151 G1
Cowley Rd.
Mansion Gdns. NW3 91 E3
Mansion Ho. EC4 20 B4
Mansion Ho. EC4 112 A6
Mansion Ho. Pl. EC4 20 B4
Mansion Ho. St. EC4 20 B4
Manson Ms. SW7 30 D2
Manson Ms. SW7 129 F4
Manson Pl. SW7 30 E2
Manson Pl. SW7 129 G4
Mansted Gdns., Rom. 82 C7
Manston Av., Sthl. 123 G4
Manston Cl. SE20 189 F1
Garden Rd.
Manston Gro., Kings.T. 163 G5
Manstone Rd. NW2 90 B5
Manthorp Rd. SE18 137 F5
Mantilla Rd. SW17 168 A4
Mantle Rd. SE4 153 H3
Mantle Way E15 96/97 E7
Romford Rd.
Mantlet Cl. SW16 168 C7
Manton Av. W7 124 C2
Manton Rd. SE2 138 A4
Mantua St. SW11 149 G3
Mantus Cl. E1 113 F4
Mantus Rd.
Mantus Rd. E1 113 F4
Manus Way N20 57 F2
Blakeney Cl.
Manville Gdns. SW17 168 B2
Manville Rd. SW17 168 A2
Manwood Rd. SE4 153 J5
Manwood St. E16 136 C1
Manygates SW12 168 B2
Mape St. E2 112 E4
Mapesbury Rd. NW2 90 B6
Mapeshill Pl. NW2 89 J6
Maple Av. E4 61 J5
Maple Av. W3 127 E1
Maple Av., Har. 85 H2
Maple Cl. N3 56 D6
Maple Cl. N16 76 D6
Maple Cl. SW4 150 D6
Maple Cl., Buck.H. 64 A3
Maple Cl., Hmptn. 161 F6
Maple Cl., Hayes 102 D3
Maple Cl., Ilf. 65 H5
Maple Cl., Mitch. 186 B1
Maple Cl., Orp. 193 G5
Maple Cl., Ruis. 66 B6
Maple Ct., N.Mal. 182 E3
Maple Cres., Sid. 158 A6
Maple Gdns., Edg. 54 E7
Maple Gate, Loug. 48 D2
Maple Gro. NW9 70 C7
Maple Gro. W5 125 G3
Maple Gro., Brent. 124 E7
Maple Gro., Sthl. 103 F5
Maple Ind. Est., Felt. 160 A3
Maple Way
Maple Leaf Dr., Sid. 175 J1
Maple Leaf Sq. SE16 133 G2
St. Elmos Rd.
Maple Ms. NW6 6 A1
Maple Ms. SW16 169 F5
Maple Pl. W1 9 G6
Maple Rd. E11 79 E6
Maple Rd. SE20 189 E1
Maple Rd., Hayes 102 C3
Maple Rd., Surb. 181 H5
Maple St. W1 17 F1
Maple St. W1 110 C5
Maple St., Rom. 83 J4
Maple Wk. W10 108 A4
Droop St.
Maple Way, Felt. 160 B3
Maplecroft Cl. E6 116 B6
Allhallows Rd.
Mapledale Av., Croy. 202 D2
Mapledene, Chis. 175 F5
Kemnal Rd.
Mapledene Rd. E8 94 C7
Maplehurst Cl., Kings.T. 181 H4
Mapleleafe Gdns., Ilf. 80 E3
Maples Pl. E1 112/113 E5
Raven Row
Maplestead Rd. SW2 151 F7
Maplestead Rd., Dag. 118 B1
Maplethorpe Rd., Th.Hth. 187 H4
Mapleton Cl., Brom. 191 G6
Mapleton Cres. SW18 148 E6
Mapleton Rd. E4 62 C3
Mapleton Rd. SW18 148 E6
Mapleton Rd., Enf. 45 E2
Maplin Cl. N21 43 F6
Maplin Ho. SE2 138 D2
Wolvercote Rd.
Maplin Rd. E16 115 G6
Maplin St. E3 113 J3
Mapperley Dr., Wdf.Grn. 62/63 E7
Forest Dr.
Maran Way, Erith 138 D2
Marban Rd. W9 108 C3
Marble Arch W1 16 A5
Marble Arch W1 109 J7
Marble Cl. W3 126 B1
Marble Dr. NW2 72 A7
Marble Hill Cl., Twick. 145 E7
Marble Hill Gdns., Twick. 144 E7
Marble Ho. SE18 137 J5
Felspar Cl.
Marble Quay E1 29 H1
Marble Quay E1 132 D1
Marbrook Ct. SE12 173 J3
Marcellina Way, Orp. 207 H3
March Rd., Twick. 144 D7
Marchant Rd. E11 96 D2
Marchant St. SE14 133 H6
Sanford St.
Marchbank Rd. W14 128 C6
Marchmont Gdns., Rich. 145 J5
Marchmont Rd.
Marchmont Rd., Rich. 145 J5
Marchmont Rd., Wall. 200 C7
Marchmont St. WC1 10 A5
Marchmont St. WC1 110 E4
Marchside Cl., Houns. 142 D1
Springwell Rd.
Marchwood Cl. SE5 132 B7
Marchwood Cres. W5 105 F6
Marcia Rd. SE1 37 E2
Marcia Rd. SE1 132 B4
Marcilly Rd. SW18 149 G5
Marco Rd. W6 127 J3
Marcon Pl. E8 94 E6
Marconi Rd. E10 96 A1
Marconi Way, Sthl. 103 H6
Marcourt Lawns W5 105 H4
Marcus Ct. E15 115 E1
Marcus Garvey Ms. SE22 152/153 E5
St. Aidan's Rd.
Marcus Garvey Way SE24 151 G4
Marcus St. E15 115 F1
Marcus St. SW18 149 E6
Marcus Ter. SW18 149 E6
Mardale Dr. NW9 70 D5
Mardell Rd., Croy. 189 G5
Marden Av., Brom. 191 G6
Marden Cres., Bex. 159 J5
Marden Cres., Croy. 187 F6
Marden Rd. N17 76 B3
Marden Rd., Croy. 187 F6
Marden Sq. SE16 132 E3
Marder Rd. W13 124 D2
Mare St. E8 113 E1
Marechal Niel Av., Sid. 175 G3
Maresfield, Croy. 202 B3
Maresfield Gdns. NW3 91 F5
Marfleet Cl., Cars. 199 H2
Margaret Av. E4 46 B6
Margaret Bondfield Av., Bark. 100 A7
Margaret Bldgs. N16 94 C1
Margaret Rd.
Margaret Ct. W1 17 F3
Margaret Gardner Dr. SE9 174 C2
Margaret Ingram Cl. SW6 128 C6
John Smith Av.
Margaret Lockwood Cl., Kings.T. 181 J4
Margaret Rd. N16 94 C1
Margaret Rd., Barn. 41 G4
Margaret Rd., Bex. 158 D6
Margaret St. W1 17 E3
Margaret St. W1 110 B6
Margaret Way, Ilf. 80 B6
Margaretta Ter. SW3 31 G5
Margaretta Ter. SW3 129 H6
Margaretting Rd. E12 97 J1
Margate Rd. SW2 150 E5
Margeholes, Wat. 50 E2
Margery Pk. Rd. E7 97 G6
Margery Rd., Dag. 100 D3
Margery St. WC1 10 E4
Margery St. WC1 111 G3
Margin Dr. SW19 166 A5
Margravine Gdns. W6 128 A5
Margravine Rd. W6 128 A6
Marham Gdns. SW18 167 H1
Marham Gdns., Mord. 185 F6
Maria Ter. E1 113 G4
Maria Theresa Cl., N.Mal. 182 D5
Marian Cl., Hayes 102 D4
Marian Ct., Sutt. 198 E5
Marian Pl. E2 112 E2
Marian Rd. SW16 186 C1
Marian Sq. E2 13 J1
Marian St. E2 112/113 E2
Hackney Rd.
Marian Way NW10 89 F7
Maricas Av., Har. 68 A1
Marie Lloyd Gdns. N19 74/75 E7
Hornsey Ri. Gdns.
Marie Lloyd Wk. E8 94 D6
Forest Rd.
Marigold All. SE1 19 G6
Marigold Cl., Sthl. 102/103 E7
Lancaster Rd.
Marigold Rd. N17 61 F7
Marigold St. SE16 132 E2
Marigold Way E4 61 J6
Silver Birch Av.
Marigold Way, Croy. 203 G1
Marina App., Hayes 103 E5
Marina Av., N.Mal. 183 H5
Marina Cl., Brom. 191 G3
Marina Dr., Well. 157 H2
Marina Gdns., Rom. 83 J6
Marina Way, Tedd. 163 G7
Fairways
Marine Dr. SE18 136 C4
Marine Dr., Bark. 117 H3
Thames Rd.
Marine St. SE16 29 H5
Marinefield Rd. SW6 149 E2
Mariner Gdns., Rich. 163 F3
Mariner Rd. E12 98 C4
Dersingham Av.
Mariners Ms. E14 134 D4
Marion Cl., Ilf. 65 G7
Marion Gro., Wdf.Grn. 63 E5
Marion Rd. NW7 55 G5
Marion Rd., Th.Hth. 187 J5
Marischal Rd. SE13 154 D3
Maritime Quay E14 134 A5
Maritime St. E3 113 J4

Name	Page	Grid
Marius Pas. SW17	168	A2
Marius Rd.		
Marius Rd. SW17	168	A2
Marjorams Av., Loug.	48	C2
Marjorie Gro. SW11	149	J4
Marjorie Ms. E1	113	G6
Arbour Sq.		
Mark Av. E4	46	B6
Mark Cl., Bexh.	158	E1
Mark Cl., Sthl.	123	H1
Longford Av.		
Mark La. EC3	**20**	**E5**
Mark La. EC3	112	B7
Mark Rd. N22	75	H2
Mark Sq. EC2	**12**	**D5**
Mark St. E15	96	E7
Mark St. EC2	**12**	**D5**
Marke Cl., Kes.	206	B4
Markeston Grn., Wat.	50	D4
Market Ct. W1	**17**	**F3**
Market Est. N7	92	E6
Market Hill SE18	136	D3
Market La., Edg.	70	C1
Market Ms. W1	**24**	**D2**
Market Ms. W1	130	B1
Market Par. SE15	152	D2
Rye La.		
Market Pl. N2	73	H3
Market Pl. NW11	73	F4
Market Pl. SE16	**37**	**J1**
Market Pl. W1	**17**	**F3**
Market Pl. W1	110	C6
Market Pl. W3	126	C1
Market Pl., Bexh.	159	G4
Market Pl., Brent.	125	F7
Market Pl., Enf.	44	A3
The Town		
Market Pl., Kings.T.	181	G2
Market Rd. N7	92	E6
Market Rd., Rich.	146	A3
Market Row SW9	151	G4
Atlantic Rd.		
Market Sq. E2	**13**	**F3**
Market Sq. E14	114	B6
Chrisp St.		
Market Sq. N9	60	D2
New Rd.		
Market Sq., Brom.	191	G2
Market St. E6	116	C2
Market St. SE18	136	D4
Market Way E14	114	B6
Kerbey St.		
Market Way, Wem.	87	H5
Turton Rd.		
Markfield Gdns. E4	46	B7
Markfield Rd. N15	76	D4
Markham Pl. SW3	**31**	**J3**
Markham Sq. SW3	**31**	**J3**
Markham Sq. SW3	129	J5
Markham St. SW3	**31**	**H3**
Markham St. SW3	129	H5
Markhole Cl., Hmptn.	161	F7
Priory Rd.		
Markhouse Av. E17	77	H6
Markhouse Rd. E17	77	J5
Markmanor Av. E17	77	H7
Marks Rd., Rom.	83	J5
Marksbury Av., Rich.	146	A3
Markway, Sun.	178	C2
Markwell Cl. SE26	170/171	E4
Longton Gro.		
Markyate Rd., Dag.	100	B5
Marl Rd. SW18	149	E4
Marl St. SW18	149	F4
Marl Rd.		
Marlands Rd., Ilf.	80	B3
Marlborough Av. E8	112	D1
Marlborough Av. N14	58	C3
Marlborough Av., Edg.	54	B3
Marlborough Bldgs. SW3	**31**	**H1**
Marlborough Bldgs. SW3	129	H4
Marlborough Cl. N20	57	J3
Marlborough Gdns.		
Marlborough Cl. SE17	**35**	**H2**
Marlborough Cl. SW19	167	H6
Marlborough Cl., Orp.	193	J7
Aylesham Rd.		
Marlborough Ct. W1	**17**	**F4**
Marlborough Ct. W8	128	D4
Marlborough Ct., Wall.	200	C7
Cranley Gdns.		
Marlborough Cres. W4	126	D3
Marlborough Dr., Ilf.	80	B3

Name	Page	Grid
Marlborough Gdns. N20	57	J3
Marlborough Gate Ho. W2	**14**	**E5**
Marlborough Gro. SE1	**37**	**H4**
Marlborough Gro. SE1	132	D5
Marlborough Hill NW8	109	F1
Marlborough Hill, Har.	68	C4
Marlborough La. SE7	135	J6
Marlborough Pk. Av., Sid.	158	A7
Marlborough Pl. NW8	**6**	**C2**
Marlborough Pl. NW8	109	F2
Marlborough Rd. E4	62	A6
Marlborough Rd. E7	97	J7
Marlborough Rd. E15	96/97	E4
Borthwick Rd.		
Marlborough Rd. E18	79	G3
Marlborough Rd. N9	60	C1
Marlborough Rd. N19	92	D2
Marlborough Rd. N22	59	E7
Marlborough Rd. SW1	**25**	**G2**
Marlborough Rd. SW1	130	C1
Marlborough Rd. SW19	167	G6
Marlborough Rd. W4	126	C5
Marlborough Rd. W5	125	G2
Marlborough Rd., Bexh.	158	D3
Marlborough Rd., Brom.	191	J4
Marlborough Rd., Dag.	100	B4
Marlborough Rd., Felt.	160	D2
Marlborough Rd., Hmptn.	161	G6
Marlborough Rd., Islw.	144	E1
Marlborough Rd., Rich.	145	H6
Marlborough Rd., Rom.	83	G4
Marlborough Rd., S.Croy.	201	J7
Marlborough Rd., Sthl.	122	C3
Marlborough Rd., Sutt.	198	D3
Marlborough St. SW3	**31**	**G2**
Marlborough St. SW3	129	H4
Marlborough Yd. N19	92	D2
Marlborough Rd.		
Marler Rd. SE23	171	H1
Marlescroft Way, Loug.	48	E5
Marley Av., Bexh.	138	D6
Marley Cl. N15	75	H4
Stanmore Rd.		
Marley Cl., Grnf.	103	G3
Marley Wk. NW2	89	J5
Lennon Rd.		
Marlingdene Cl., Hmptn.	161	G6
Marlings Cl., Chis.	193	H4
Marlings Pk. Av., Chis.	193	H4
Marlins Cl., Sutt.	199	F5
Turnpike La.		
Marloes Cl., Wem.	87	G4
Marloes Rd. W8	**22**	**A6**
Marloes Rd. W8	128	E3
Marlow Cl. SE20	189	E3
Marlow Ct. NW6	90	A7
Marlow Ct. NW9	71	F3
Marlow Cres., Twick.	144	C6
Marlow Dr., Sutt.	198	A2
Marlow Gdns., Hayes	121	G3
Marlow Rd. E6	116	C3
Marlow Rd. SE20	189	E3
Marlow Rd., Sthl.	123	F3
Marlow Way SE16	133	G2
Marlowe Cl., Chis.	175	G6
Marlowe Cl., Ilf.	81	F1
Marlowe Gdns. SE9	156	D6
Marlowe Rd. E17	78	C4
Marlowe Sq., Mitch.	186	C4
Marlowe Way, Croy.	201	E2
Marlowes, The NW8	109	G1

Name	Page	Grid
Marlton St. SE10	135	F5
Woolwich Rd.		
Marlwood Cl., Sid.	175	H2
Marmadon Rd. SE18	137	J4
Marmion App. E4	62	A4
Marmion Av. E4	61	J4
Marmion Cl. E4	61	J4
Marmion Ms. SW11	150	A3
Taybridge Rd.		
Marmion Rd. SW11	150	A4
Marmont Rd. SE15	152	D1
Marmora Rd. SE22	153	F6
Marmot Rd., Houns.	142	D3
Marne Av. N11	58	B4
Marne Av., Well.	158	A3
Marne St. W10	108	B3
Marnell Way, Houns.	142	D3
Marney Rd. SW11	150	A4
Marnfield Cres. SW2	151	F7
Marnham Av. NW2	90	B4
Marnham Cres., Grnf.	103	H3
Marnock Rd. SE4	153	H5
Maroon St. E14	113	H5
Maroons Way SE6	172	A5
Marquess Rd. N1	94	A6
Marquis Cl., Wem.	87	J7
Marquis Rd. N4	93	F1
Marquis Rd. N22	59	F6
Marquis Rd. NW1	92	D6
Marrabon Cl., Sid.	176	A1
Marrick Cl. SW15	147	G4
Marriots Cl. NW9	71	F6
Marriott Cl., Felt.	141	G6
Marriott Rd. E15	114	E1
Marriott Rd. N4	93	F1
Marriott Rd. N10	73	J1
Marriott Rd., Barn.	40	A3
Marryat Pl. SW19	166	B4
Marryat Rd. SW19	166	A5
Marryat Sq. SW6	148	B1
Marsala Rd. SE13	154	B4
Marsden Rd. N9	60	E2
Marsden Rd. SE15	152	C3
Marsden St. NW5	92	A6
Marsden Way, Orp.	207	J4
Marsh Av., Mitch.	186	A2
Marsh Cl. NW7	55	F3
Marsh Ct. SW19	185	F1
Marsh Dr. NW9	71	F6
Marsh Fm. Rd., Twick.	162	C1
Marsh Grn. Rd., Dag.	119	G1
Marsh Hill E9	95	H5
Marsh La. E10	96	A2
Marsh La. N17	61	E7
Marsh La. NW7	54	E4
Marsh La., Stan.	53	F5
Marsh Rd., Pnr.	66	E4
Marsh Rd., Wem.	105	G2
Marsh St. E14	134	B4
Harbinger Rd.		
Marsh Wall E14	134	A1
Marshall Cl. SW18	149	F6
Allfarthing La.		
Marshall Cl., Har.	68	A7
Bowen Rd.		
Marshall Cl., Houns.	143	F5
Marshall Path SE28	118	B7
Attlee Rd.		
Marshall Rd. E10	96	B3
Marshall Rd. N17	76	A1
Marshall St. W1	**17**	**G4**
Marshall St. W1	110	C6
Marshalls Cl. N11	58	B4
Marshall's Gro. SE18	136	B4
Marshalls Pl. SE16	**29**	**G6**
Marshall's Rd., Sutt.	198	E4
Marshalsea Rd. SE1	**28**	**A3**
Marshalsea Rd. SE1	131	J2
Marsham Cl., Chis.	174	E5
Marsham St. SW1	**25**	**J6**
Marsham St. SW1	130	D3
Marshbrook Cl. SE3	156	A3
Marshfield St. E14	134	C3
Marshgate La. E15	114	B1
Marshgate Path SE28	137	F3
Tom Cribb Rd.		
Marshgate Sidings E15	96	B7
Marshgate La.		
Marshside Cl. N9	61	F1
Marsland Cl. SE17	**35**	**H4**
Marsland Cl. SE17	131	H5
Marston Av., Chess.	195	H6
Marston Av., Dag.	101	G2
Marston Cl. NW6	91	F7
Fairfax Rd.		
Marston Cl., Dag.	101	G3
Marston Rd., Ilf.	80	B1
Marston Rd., Tedd.	162	E5
Marston Way SE19	169	H7

Name	Page	Grid
Marsworth Av., Pnr.	66	D1
Marsworth Cl., Hayes	103	E5
Mart St. WC2	**18**	**B4**
Martaban Rd. N16	94	B2
Martel Pl. E8	94	C6
Dalston La.		
Martell Rd. SE21	170	A3
Martello St. E8	94	E7
Martello Ter. E8	94	E7
Marten Rd. E17	78	A2
Martens Av., Bexh.	159	J4
Martens Cl., Bexh.	159	J4
Martha Ct. E2	112/113	E2
Cambridge Heath Rd.		
Martha Rd. E4	61	J6
Martha Rd. E15	97	E6
Martha St. E1	113	E6
Martham Cl. SE28	118	D7
Marthorne Cres., Har.	68	A2
Martin Bowes Rd. SE9	156	C7
Martin Cl. N9	61	G1
Martin Cres., Croy.	201	G1
Martin Dene, Bexh.	159	F5
Martin Dr., Nthlt.	85	F5
Martin Gdns., Dag.	100	C4
Martin Gro., Mord.	184	D3
Martin La. EC4	**20**	**C5**
Martin Ri., Bexh.	159	F5
Martin Rd., Dag.	100	C4
Martin St. SE28	137	H1
Merbury Rd.		
Martin Way SW20	184	B3
Martin Way, Mord.	184	B3
Martinbridge Ind. Est., Enf.	44	D5
Martindale SW14	146	C5
Martindale Av. E16	115	G7
Martindale Rd. SW12	150	B7
Martindale Rd., Houns.	142	E3
Martineau Cl., Esher	194	A4
Martineau Ms. N5	93	H4
Martineau Rd.		
Martineau Rd. N5	93	H4
Martineau St. E1	113	F7
Martingale Cl., Sun.	178	A4
Martingales Cl., Rich.	163	G3
Martins Cl., W.Wick.	204	D1
Martins Mt., Barn.	40	D4
Martins Rd., Brom.	191	E2
Martins Wk. N10	74	A1
Martins Wk., Borwd.	38	A4
Siskin Cl.		
Martinsfield Cl., Chig.	65	H4
Martlet Gro., Nthlt.	102	D3
Javelin Way		
Martlett Ct. WC2	**18**	**B4**
Martley Dr., Ilf.	80	E5
Martock Cl., Har.	68	D4
Marton Cl. SE6	172	A3
Marton Rd. N16	94	B2
Martys Yd. NW3	91	G4
Hampstead High St.		
Marvell Av., Hayes	102	A5
Marvels Cl. SE12	173	H2
Marvels La. SE12	173	H2
Marville Rd. SW6	128	C7
Marvin St. E8	94/95	E6
Sylvester Rd.		
Marwood Cl. N17	76	D1
Marwood Cl., W.Wick.	205	F2
Deer Pk. Way		
Marwood Cl., Well.	158	B3
Mary Adelaide Cl. SW15	164	E4
Mary Ann Gdns. SE8	134	A6
Mary Cl., Stan.	69	J4
Mary Datchelor Cl. SE5	152	A1
Mary Grn. NW8	109	E1
Mary Kingsley Ct. N19	74/75	E7
Hillrise Rd.		
Mary Lawrenson Pl. SE3	135	F7
Mary Macarthur Ho. W6	128	B6
Field Rd.		
Mary Peters Dr., Grnf.	86	A5
Mary Pl. W11	108	B7
Mary Rose Cl., Hmptn.	179	G1
Ashley Rd.		
Mary Rose Mall E6	116	D5
Frobisher Rd.		
Mary Seacole Cl. E8	112	C1
Clarissa St.		
Mary St. E16	115	F5
Barking Rd.		
Mary St. N1	111	J1
Mary Ter. NW1	110	B1
Maryatt Av., Har.	85	H2

Marybank SE18 136 C4
Maryland Ind. Est. E15 96 D5
Maryland Rd.
Maryland Pk. E15 96 E5
Maryland Pt. E15 96/97 E6
Leytonstone Rd.
Maryland Rd. E15 96 D5
Maryland Rd. N22 59 F6
Maryland Rd., Th.Hth. 187 H1
Maryland Sq. E15 97 E5
Maryland St. E15 96 D5
Maryland Wk. N1 111 J1
Popham St.
Maryland Way, Sun. 178 A2
Marylands Rd. W9 108 D4
Marylebone Flyover NW1 15 F2
Marylebone Flyover W2 15 F2
Marylebone High St. W1 16 C1
Marylebone High St. W1 110 A5
Marylebone La. W1 16 D4
Marylebone La. W1 110 A6
Marylebone Ms. W1 16 D2
Marylebone Ms. W1 110 B5
Marylebone Pas. W1 17 G3
Marylebone Rd. NW1 15 H1
Marylebone Rd. NW1 109 H5
Marylebone St. W1 16 C2
Marylebone St. W1 110 A5
Marylee Way SE11 34 D3
Marylee Way SE11 131 F4
Maryon Gro. SE7 136 B4
Maryon Ms. NW3 91 H4
South End Rd.
Maryon Rd. SE7 136 B4
Maryon Rd. SE18 136 B4
Maryrose Way N20 57 G1
Mary's Cl. N17 76 C1
Kemble Rd.
Mary's Ter., Twick. 144 D7
Masbro Rd. W14 128 A3
Mascalls Ct. SE7 135 J6
Victoria Way
Mascalls Rd. SE7 135 J6
Mascotte Rd. SW15 148 A4
Mascotts Cl. NW2 89 H3
Masefield Av., Borwd. 38 B5
Masefield Av., Sthl. 103 G7
Masefield Av., Stan. 52 C5
Masefield Cres. N14 42 C6
Masefield Gdns. E6 116 D4
Masefield La., Hayes 102 B4
Masefield Rd., Hmptn. 161 F4
Wordsworth Rd.
Masefield Vw., Orp. 207 F3
Masham Ho., Erith 138 D2
Kale Rd.
Mashie Rd. W3 106 E6
Maskall Cl. SW2 169 G1
Maskani Wk. SW16 168 C7
Bates Cres.
Maskell Rd. SW17 167 F3
Maskelyne Cl. SW11 149 H1
Mason Bradbear Ct. N1 94 A6
St. Paul's Rd.
Mason Cl. E16 115 G7
Mason Cl. SE16 37 J3
Mason Cl. SW20 184 A1
Mason Cl., Bexh. 159 H3
Mason Cl., Borwd. 38 C2
Mason Cl., Hmptn. 179 F1
Mason Rd., Sutt. 198/199 E5
Manor Pl.
Mason Rd., Wdf.Grn. 63 E4
Mason St. SE17 36 C1
Mason St. SE17 132 A4
Masons Arms Ms. W1 17 E4
Masons Av. EC2 20 B3
Masons Av., Croy. 201 J3
Masons Av., Har. 68 C4
Masons Ct., Wem. 88 A2
Mayfields
Masons Grn. La. W3 106 A5
Masons Hill SE18 137 E4
Masons Hill, Brom. 191 G3
Mason's Pl. EC1 11 H3
Mason's Pl. EC1 111 H3
Masons Pl., Mitch. 185 J1
Mason's Yd. SW1 25 G1
Mason's Yd. SW19 166 A5
High St. Wimbledon
Massey Cl. N11 58 B5
Grove Rd.
Massie Rd. E8 94 D6
Graham Rd.
Massingberd Way SW17 168 B4
Massinger St. SE17 36 D2
Massingham St. E1 113 G4
Masson Av., Ruis. 84 C6
Mast Ho. Ter. E14 134 A4
Mast Leisure Pk. SE16 133 G3
Master Gunner Pl. SE18 136 B7
Masterman Ho. SE5 36 B7
Masterman Ho. SE5 132 A7
Masterman Rd. E6 116 B3
Masters Dr. SE16 132 E5
Masters St. E1 113 G5
Mastmaker Rd. E14 134 A2
Maswell Pk. Cres., Houns. 143 J5
Maswell Pk. Rd., Houns. 143 H5
Matcham Rd. E11 97 E3
Matchless Dr. SE18 136 D7
Matfield Cl., Brom. 191 G5
Matfield Rd., Belv. 139 G6
Matham Gro. SE22 152 C4
Matham Rd., E.Mol. 180 A5
Matheson Rd. W14 128 C4
Mathews Av. E6 116 D2
Mathews Pk. Av. E15 97 F6
Matilda Cl. SE19 170 A7
Elizabeth Way
Matilda St. N1 111 F1
Matlock Cl. SE24 151 J4
Matlock Cl., Barn. 40 A6
Matlock Ct. SE5 152 A4
Denmark Hill Est.
Matlock Cres., Sutt. 198 B4
Matlock Cres., Wat. 50 C3
Matlock Gdns., Sutt. 198 B4
Matlock Pl., Sutt. 198 B4
Matlock Rd. E10 78 C6
Matlock St. E14 113 H6
Matlock Way, N.Mal. 182 D1
Matrimony Pl. SW8 150 C2
Matson Ct., Wdf.Grn. 62/63 E7
The Bridle Path
Matthew Cl. W10 108 A4
Matthew Ct., Mitch. 186 D5
Matthew Parker St. SW1 25 J4
Matthew Parker St. SW1 130 D2
Matthews Rd., Grnf. 86 A5
Matthews St. SW11 149 J2
Matthews Yd. WC2 18 A4
Matthias Rd. N16 94 A5
Mattingley Way SE15 132 C7
Daniel Gdns.
Mattison Rd. N4 75 G6
Mattock La. W5 125 E1
Mattock La. W13 125 E1
Maud Cashmore Way SE18 136 C3
Maud Gdns. E13 115 F1
Maud Gdns., Bark. 117 J2
Maud Rd. E10 96 C3
Maud Rd. E13 115 F2
Maud St. E16 115 F5
Maude Rd. E17 77 H5
Maude Rd. SE5 152 B1
Maude Ter. E17 77 H4
Maudesville Cotts. W7 124 B1
The Bdy.
Maudlin's Grn. E1 29 H1
Maudslay Rd. SE9 156 C3
Maudsley Ho., Brent. 125 H5
Green Dragon La.
Mauleverer Rd. SW2 150 E5
Maundeby Wk. NW10 88/89 E6
Neasden La.
Maunder Rd. W7 124 C1
Maunsel St. SW1 33 H1
Maunsel St. SW1 130 D4
Maurice Av. N22 75 H2
Maurice Brown Cl. NW7 56 A5
Maurice St. W12 107 H6
Maurice Wk. NW11 73 F4
Maurier Cl., Nthlt. 102 C1
Mauritius Rd. SE10 135 E4
Maury Rd. N16 94 D2
Mavelstone Cl., Brom. 192 B1
Mavelstone Rd., Brom. 192 B1
Maverton Rd. E3 114 A1
Mavis Av., Epsom 197 E5
Mavis Cl., Epsom 197 E5
Mavis Wk. E6 116 B5
Mawbey Est. SE1 37 H4
Mawbey Est. SE1 132 D5
Mawbey Pl. SE1 37 G4
Mawbey Pl. SE1 132 C5
Mawbey Rd. SE1 37 G4
Mawbey St. SW8 130 E7
Mawney Cl., Rom. 83 H2
Mawney Rd., Rom. 83 J4
Mawson Cl. SW20 184 B2
Mawson La. W4 127 F6
Great W. Rd.
Maxey Gdns., Dag. 101 E4
Maxey Rd. SE18 137 F4
Maxey Rd., Dag. 100 E4
Maxfield Cl. N20 41 F7
Maxilla Gdns. W10 108 A6
Cambridge Gdns.
Maxilla Wk. W10 108 A6
Kingsdown Cl.
Maxim Rd. N21 43 G6
Maxted Pk., Har. 68 B7
Maxted Rd. SE15 152 C3
Maxwell Cl., Croy. 201 E1
Maxwell Gdns., Orp. 207 J3
Maxwell Rd. SW6 128 E7
Maxwell Rd., Borwd. 38 B3
Maxwell Rd., Well. 158 A3
Maxwell Rd., West Dr. 120 C4
Maxwelton Av. NW7 54 D5
Maxwelton Cl. NW7 54 D5
May Bate Av., Kings.T. 181 G1
May Cl., Chess. 195 J6
May Ct. SW19 185 F1
May Gdns., Wem. 105 F2
May Rd. E4 62 A6
May Rd. E13 115 G2
May Rd., Twick. 162 B1
May St. W14 128 C5
North End Rd.
May Tree La., Stan. 52 C7
May Wk. E13 115 H2
Maya Rd. N2 73 F4
Mayall Rd. SE24 151 H5
Maybank Av. E18 79 H2
Maybank Av., Wem. 86 C5
Maybank Gdns., Pnr. 66 A5
Maybank Rd. E18 79 H1
Maybells Commercial Est., Bark. 118 D2
Mayberry Pl., Surb. 181 J7
Maybourne Cl. SE26 171 E5
Maybrook Meadow Est., Bark. 100 A7
Maybury Cl., Loug. 48 E4
Maybury Cl., Orp. 193 E5
Maybury Gdns. NW10 89 H6
Maybury Ms. N6 74 C7
Maybury Rd. E13 115 J4
Maybury Rd., Bark. 117 J2
Maybury St. SW17 167 H5
Maychurch Cl., Stan. 53 G7
Maycroft, Pnr. 66 B2
Maycross Av., Mord. 184 C3
Mayday Gdns. SE3 156 B2
Mayday Rd., Th.Hth. 187 H6
Mayerne Rd. SE9 156 A5
Mayes Rd. N22 75 G2
Mayesbrook Rd., Bark. 117 J1
Mayesbrook Rd., Dag. 100 A3
Mayesbrook Rd., Ilf. 100 A3
Mayesford Rd., Rom. 82 C7
Mayeswood Rd. SE12 173 J3
Mayfair Av., Bexh. 158 D1
Mayfair Av., Ilf. 98 C2
Mayfair Av., Rom. 82 D6
Mayfair Av., Twick. 143 J7
Mayfair Av., Wor.Pk. 197 G1
Mayfair Cl., Beck. 190 B1
Mayfair Cl., Surb. 195 H1
Mayfair Gdns. N17 60 A6
Mayfair Gdns., Wdf.Grn. 63 G7
Mayfair Ms. NW1 91 J7
Regents Pk. Rd.
Mayfair Pl. W1 25 E1
Mayfair Pl. W1 130 B1
Mayfair Ter. N14 42 D7
Mayfield, Bexh. 159 F3
Mayfield Av. N12 57 F4
Mayfield Av. N14 58 D2
Mayfield Av. W4 127 E4
Mayfield Av. W13 124 E3
Mayfield Av., Har. 68 E5
Mayfield Av., Orp. 207 J1
Mayfield Av., Wdf.Grn. 63 G7
Mayfield Cl. E8 94 C6
Forest Rd.
Mayfield Cl. SW4 150 D5
Mayfield Cl., T.Ditt. 194 E1
Mayfield Cres. N9 44 E6
Mayfield Cres., Th.Hth. 187 F4
Mayfield Dr., Pnr. 67 F4
Mayfield Gdns. NW4 72 A6
Mayfield Gdns. W7 104 A6
Mayfield Mans. SW18 148 A7
West Hill
Mayfield Rd. E4 62 C2
Mayfield Rd. E8 94 C7
Mayfield Rd. E13 115 F4
Mayfield Rd. E17 77 H2
Mayfield Rd. N8 75 F6
Mayfield Rd. SW19 184 C1
Mayfield Rd. W3 106 B7
Mayfield Rd. W12 127 E2
Mayfield Rd., Belv. 139 J4
Mayfield Rd., Brom. 192 B5
Mayfield Rd., Dag. 100 C1
Mayfield Rd., Enf. 45 G2
Mayfield Rd., Sutt. 199 G6
Mayfield Rd., Th.Hth. 187 F4
Mayfields, Wem. 88 A2
Mayfields Cl., Wem. 88 A2
Mayflower Cl. SE16 133 G4
Greenland Quay
Mayflower Ct. SE16 133 F2
St. Marychurch St.
Mayflower Rd. SW9 150 E3
Mayflower St. SE16 133 F2
Mayfly Cl., Pnr. 66 C7
Mayfly Gdns., Nthlt. 102 D3
Ruislip Rd.
Mayford Cl. SW12 149 J7
Mayford Cl., Beck. 189 G3
Mayford Rd. SW12 149 J7
Maygood St. N1 10 D1
Maygood St. N1 111 F2
Maygrove Rd. NW6 90 C6
Mayhew Cl. E4 62 A3
Mayhill Rd. SE7 135 H6
Mayhill Rd., Barn. 40 B6
Maylands Dr., Sid. 176 D3
Maylands Rd., Wat. 50 C4
Maynard Cl. N15 76 B4
Brunswick Rd.
Maynard Cl. SW6 128/129 E7
Cambria St.
Maynard Path E17 78 C5
Maynard Rd.
Maynard Rd. E17 78 C5
Maynards Quay E1 113 F7
Garnet St.
Maynooth Gdns., Cars. 185 J7
Middleton Rd.
Mayo Rd. NW10 88 E6
Mayo Rd., Croy. 188 A5
Mayola Rd. E5 95 F4
Mayow Rd. SE23 171 G3
Mayow Rd. SE26 171 G4
Mayplace Cl., Bexh. 159 H3
Mayplace La. SE18 137 E7
Mayplace Rd. E., Bexh. 159 H3
Mayplace Rd. E., Dart. 159 J3
Mayplace Rd. W., Bexh. 159 G4
Maypole Cres., Ilf. 65 G7
Mayroyd Av., Surb. 196 A2
Mays Ct. WC2 18 A6
Mays Hill Rd., Brom. 191 E2
Mays La. E4 62 D2
Mays La., Barn. 39 H7
Mays Rd., Tedd. 162 A5
Maysoule Rd. SW11 149 G4
Mayston Ms. SE10 135 G5
Westcombe Hill
Mayswood Gdns., Dag. 101 J6
Mayton St. N7 93 F3
Maytree Cl., Edg. 54 C3
Maytree Gdns. W5 125 G2
South Ealing Rd.
Maytree Wk. SW2 169 G2
Mayville Est. N16 94 B5
King Henry St.
Mayville Rd. E11 96 E3
Mayville Rd., Ilf. 98 E5
Maywood Cl., Beck. 172 B7
Maze Hill SE3 134 E6
Maze Hill SE10 134 E6
Maze Rd., Rich. 126 A7
Mazenod Av. NW6 90 D7
McAdam Dr., Enf. 43 H2
Rowantree Rd.
McAuley Cl. SE1 26 E5
McAuley Cl. SE1 131 G3
McAuley Cl. SE9 156 E5
McCall Cl. SW4 150/151 E2
Jeffreys Rd.

McCall Cres. SE7 136 B5
McCarthy Rd., Felt. 160 D5
McCoid Way SE1 27 J4
McCrone Ms. NW3 91 G6
Belsize La.
McCullum Rd. E3 113 J1
McDermott Cl. SW11 149 H3
McDermott Rd. SE15 152 D3
McDonough Cl., Chess. 195 H4
McDowall Cl. E16 115 F5
McDowall Rd. SE5 151 J1
McEntee Av. E17 77 H1
McEwen Way E15 114 D1
McGrath Rd. E15 97 F6
McGregor Rd. W11 108 C6
McIntosh Cl., Wall. 200 E7
McKay Rd. SW20 165 H7
McKellar Cl., Bushey 51 J2
McKerrell Rd. SE15 152 D1
McLeod Rd. SE2 138 B4
McLeod's Ms. SW7 30 B1
McLeod's Ms. SW7 129 E4
McMillan St. SE8 134 A6
McNair Rd., Sthl. 123 H2
McNeil Rd. SE5 152 B2
McNicol Dr. NW10 106 C2
McRae La., Mitch. 185 J7
Mead, The N2 73 F2
Mead, The W13 104 E5
Mead, The, Beck. 190 C1
Mead, The, Wall. 200 D6
Mead, The, Wat. 50 E3
Mead, The, W.Wick. 204 D1
Mead Cl., Har. 68 A1
Mead Cl., Loug. 48 E2
Mead Ct. NW9 70 C5
Mead Cres. E4 62 C4
Mead Cres., Sutt. 199 H4
Mead Fld., Har. 85 F3
Kings Rd.
Mead Gro., Rom. 82 E3
Mead Path SW17 167 F5
Mead Pl. E9 95 F6
Mead Pl., Croy. 201 H1
Mead Plat NW10 88 C6
Mead Rd., Chis. 175 F6
Mead Rd., Edg. 54 A6
Mead Rd., Rich. 163 F3
Mead Row SE1 27 E5
Mead Ter., Wem. 87 G4
Meadow Way
Mead Way, Brom. 191 F6
Mead Way, Croy. 203 H2
Meadcroft Rd. SE11 35 G6
Meadcroft Rd. SE11 131 H6
Meade Cl. W4 126 A6
Meadfield, Edg. 54 B2
Meadfield Grn., Edg. 54 B2
Meadfoot Rd. SW16 168 C7
Meadgate Av., Wdf.Grn. 64 B5
Meadlands Dr., Rich. 163 G2
Meadow, The, Chis. 175 F6
Meadow Av., Croy. 189 G6
Meadow Bank N21 43 F6
Meadow Cl. E4 62 B1
Mount Echo Av.
Meadow Cl. E9 95 J5
Meadow Cl. SE6 172 A5
Meadow Cl. SW20 183 J4
Meadow Cl., Barn. 40 C6
Meadow Cl., Bexh. 159 F5
Meadow Cl., Chis. 174 E5
Meadow Cl., Esher 194 C3
Meadow Cl., Houns. 143 G6
Meadow Cl., Nthlt. 103 G2
Meadow Cl., Rich. 163 H1
Meadow Cl., Sutt. 198/199 E2
Aultone Way
Meadow Dr. N10 74 B3
Meadow Dr. NW4 71 J2
Meadow Gdns., Edg. 54 B6
Meadow Garth NW10 88 C6
Meadow Hill, N.Mal. 182 E6
Meadow Ms. SW8 34 C6
Meadow Ms. SW8 131 F6
Meadow Pl. SW8 34 B7
Meadow Pl. SW8 131 E7
Meadow Pl. W4 126/127 E7
Edensor Rd.
Meadow Rd. SW8 34 C7
Meadow Rd. SW8 131 F6
Meadow Rd. SW19 167 F7
Meadow Rd., Bark. 99 J7
Meadow Rd., Borwd. 38 B2
Meadow Rd., Brom. 191 E1
Meadow Rd., Dag. 101 F6
Meadow Rd., Esher 194 B6
Meadow Rd., Felt. 160 E2
Meadow Rd., Loug. 48 B5
Meadow Rd., Pnr. 66 D4
Meadow Rd., Rom. 101 J1
Meadow Rd., Sthl. 103 F7
Meadow Rd., Sutt. 199 H5
Meadow Row SE1 27 J6
Meadow Row SE1 131 J3
Meadow Stile, Croy. 201 J3
High St.
Meadow Vw., Har. 86 B1
Meadow Vw., Sid. 158 B7
Meadow Vw. Rd., Th.Hth. 187 H5
Meadow Wk. E18 79 G4
Meadow Wk., Dag. 101 F6
Meadow Wk., Epsom 197 E6
Meadow Wk., Wall. 200 B3
Meadow Way NW9 70 D5
Meadow Way, Chess. 195 H5
Meadow Way, Chig. 65 F3
Meadow Way, Orp. 206 D3
Meadow Way, Ruis. 66 B6
Meadow Way, Wem. 87 G4
Meadow Way, The, Har. 68 B1
Meadow Waye, Houns. 123 E6
Meadowbank NW3 91 J7
Meadowbank SE3 155 F3
Meadowbank, Surb. 181 J6
Meadowbank Cl. SW6 127 J7
Meadowbank Cl., Barn. 39 F5
Meadowbank Gdns., Houns. 142 A2
Meadowbank Rd. NW9 70 D7
Meadowbanks, Barn. 39 G5
Barnet Rd.
Meadowcourt Rd. SE3 155 F4
Meadowcroft, Brom. 192 C3
Meadowcroft Rd. N13 59 G2
Meadowlea Cl., West Dr. 120 A6
Meadows Cl. E10 96 A2
Meadows End, Sun. 178 A1
Meadowside SE9 155 J4
Meadowsweet Cl. E16 116 A5
Monarch Dr.
Meadowview Rd. SE6 171 J5
Meadowview Rd., Bex. 159 E6
Meads, The, Edg. 54 D6
Meads, The, Sutt. 198 B3
Meads La., Ilf. 81 H7
Meads Rd. N22 75 H2
Meads Rd., Enf. 45 H1
Meadvale Rd. W5 105 E4
Meadvale Rd., Croy. 188 C7
Meadway N14 58 D2
Meadway NW11 73 E6
Meadway SW20 183 J4
Meadway, Barn. 40 D4
Meadway, Beck. 190 C1
Meadway, Ilf. 99 H4
Meadway, Surb. 196 C1
Meadway, Twick. 162 A1
Meadway, Wdf.Grn. 63 J5
Meadway, The SE3 154 D2
Heath La.
Meadway, The, Buck.H. 64 A1
Meadway, The, Loug. 48 C6
Meadway Cl. NW11 73 E6
Meadway Cl., Barn. 40 D4
Meadway Cl., Pnr. 51 H6
Highbanks Rd.
Meadway Ct. NW11 73 E6
Meadway Gate NW11 72 D6
Meaford Way SE20 171 E7
Meakin Est. SE1 28 D5
Meakin Est. SE1 132 B3
Meanley Rd. E12 98 B4
Meard St. W1 17 H4
Meard St. W1 110 D6
Meath Rd. E15 115 F2
Meath Rd., Ilf. 99 F3
Meath St. SW11 150 B1
Mechanics Path SE8 134 A7
Deptford High St.
Mecklenburgh Pl. WC1 10 C5
Mecklenburgh Pl. WC1 111 F4
Mecklenburgh Sq. WC1 10 C5
Mecklenburgh Sq. WC1 111 F4
Mecklenburgh St. WC1 10 C5
Medburn St. NW1 9 H1
Medburn St. NW1 110 D2
Medcroft Gdns. SW14 146 C4
Medebourne Cl. SE3 155 G3
Medesenge Way N13 59 H6
Medfield St. SW15 147 H7
Medhurst Cl. E3 113 H2
Arbery Rd.
Medhurst Rd. E3 113 H2
Arbery Rd.
Median Rd. E5 95 F5
Medina Av., Esher 194 B3
Medina Gro. N7 93 G3
Medina Rd.
Medina Rd. N7 93 G3
Medland Cl., Wall. 200 A1
Medlar Cl., Nthlt. 102/103 E2
Parkfield Av.
Medlar St. SE5 151 J1
Medley Rd. NW6 90 D6
Medora Rd. SW2 151 F7
Medusa Rd. SE6 154 B6
Medway Bldgs. E3 113 H2
Medway Rd.
Medway Cl., Croy. 189 F6
Medway Cl., Ilf. 99 F5
Medway Dr., Grnf. 104 C2
Medway Gdns., Wem. 86 D4
Medway Ms. E3 113 H2
Medway Rd.
Medway Par., Grnf. 104 C2
Medway Rd. E3 113 H2
Medway St. SW1 25 J6
Medway St. SW1 130 D3
Medwin St. SW4 151 F4
Meerbrook Rd. SE3 155 J3
Meeson Rd. E15 115 F1
Meeson St. E5 95 H4
Meeting Flds. Path E9 95 F6
Morning La.
Meeting Ho. La. SE15 152 E1
Meetinghouse All. E1 132/133 E1
Wapping La.
Mehetabel Rd. E9 95 F6
Meister Cl., Ilf. 99 G1
Melancholy Wk., Rich. 163 F2
Melanda Cl., Chis. 174 C5
Melanie Cl., Bexh. 158 E1
Melba Way SE13 154 B1
Melbourne Av. N13 59 F6
Melbourne Av. W13 124 D1
Melbourne Av., Pnr. 67 H3
Melbourne Cl., Orp. 193 H7
Melbourne Cl., Wall. 200 C5
Melbourne Rd.
Melbourne Ct. E5 95 H4
Daubeney Rd.
Melbourne Ct. N10 58 B7
Sydney Rd.
Melbourne Ct. SE20 170 D7
Melbourne Gdns., Rom. 82 E5
Melbourne Gro. SE22 152 B4
Melbourne Ho., Hayes 102 C4
Melbourne Ms. SE6 154 C7
Melbourne Ms. SW9 151 G1
Melbourne Pl. WC2 18 D5
Melbourne Pl. WC2 111 F6
Melbourne Rd. E6 116 C1
Melbourne Rd. E10 78 B7
Melbourne Rd. E17 77 H4
Melbourne Rd. SW19 184 D1
Melbourne Rd., Ilf. 99 E1
Melbourne Rd., Tedd. 163 F6
Melbourne Rd., Wall. 200 B5
Melbourne Sq. SW9 151 G1
Melbourne Ms.
Melbourne Ter. SW6 128/129 E7
Waterford Rd.
Melbourne Way, Enf. 44 C6
Melbury Av., Sthl. 123 H3
Melbury Cl., Chis. 174 C6
Melbury Cl., Esher 194 E6
Melbury Ct. W8 128 C3
Melbury Dr. SE5 132 B7
Sedgmoor Pl.
Melbury Gdns. SW20 183 H1
Melbury Rd. W14 128 C3
Melbury Rd., Har. 69 J5
Melbury Ter. NW1 7 H6
Melbury Ter. NW1 109 H4
Melcombe Gdns., Har. 69 J6
Melcombe Pl. NW1 15 J1
Melcombe Pl. NW1 109 J5
Melcombe St. NW1 8 A6
Melcombe St. NW1 109 J4
Meldex Cl. NW7 55 J6
Meldon Cl. SW6 148/149 E1
Bagley's La.
Meldone Cl., Surb. 182 B6
Meldrum Rd., Ilf. 100 A2
Melfield Gdns. SE6 172 B4
Melford Av., Bark. 99 H6
Melford Cl., Chess. 195 J5
Melford Rd. E6 116 C4
Melford Rd. E11 96 E2
Melford Rd. E17 77 H4
Melford Rd. SE22 152 D7
Melford Rd., Ilf. 99 G2
Melfort Av., Th.Hth. 187 H3
Melfort Rd., Th.Hth. 187 H3
Melgund Rd. N5 93 G5
Melina Pl. NW8 6 E4
Melina Pl. NW8 109 G3
Melina Rd. W12 127 H2
Melior Pl. SE1 28 D3
Melior St. SE1 28 C3
Melior St. SE1 132 A2
Meliot Rd. SE6 172 D2
Mell St. SE10 134/135 E5
Trafalgar Rd.
Meller Cl., Croy. 200 E3
Melling Dr., Enf. 44 D1
Melling St. SE18 137 H6
Mellish Cl., Bark. 117 J1
Mellish Gdns., Wdf.Grn. 63 G5
Mellish Ind. Est. SE18 136 B3
Harrington Way
Mellish St. E14 134 A3
Mellison Rd. SW17 167 H5
Mellitus St. W12 107 F6
Mellor Cl., Walt. 179 F7
Mellows Rd., Ilf. 80 C3
Mellows Rd., Wall. 200 D5
Mells Cres. SE9 174 C4
Melody La. N5 93 H5
Melody Rd. SW18 149 F5
Melon Pl. W8 22 A3
Melon Rd. E11 96 E3
Melon Rd. SE15 152 D1
Melrose Av. N22 75 H1
Melrose Av. NW2 89 J5
Melrose Av. SW16 187 F3
Melrose Av. SW19 166 D2
Melrose Av., Borwd. 38 B5
Melrose Av., Grnf. 103 H2
Melrose Av., Mitch. 168 B7
Melrose Av., Twick. 143 H7
Melrose Cl. SE12 173 G1
Melrose Cl., Grnf. 103 H2
Melrose Cl., Hayes 102 A5
Melrose Cres., Orp. 207 G4
Melrose Dr., Sthl. 123 G1
Melrose Gdns. W6 127 J3
Melrose Gdns., Edg. 70 B2
Melrose Gdns., N.Mal. 182 D3
Melrose Rd. SW13 147 F2
Melrose Rd. SW18 148 C6
Melrose Rd. SW19 184 D2
Melrose Rd. W3 126 C3
Stanley Rd.
Melrose Rd., Pnr. 67 F4
Melrose Ter. W6 127 J2
Melsa Rd., Mord. 185 F6
Melthorne Dr., Ruis. 84 C3
Melthorpe Gdns. SE3 156 B1
Melton Cl., Ruis. 84 C1
Melton Ct. SW7 31 F2
Melton Ct. SW7 129 G4
Melton St. NW1 9 G4
Melton St. NW1 110 D3
Melville Av. SW20 165 G7
Melville Av., Grnf. 86 C5
Melville Av., S.Croy. 202 C5
Melville Gdns. N13 59 H5
Melville Pl. N1 111 H1
Essex Rd.
Melville Rd. E17 77 J3
Melville Rd. NW10 88 D7
Melville Rd. SW13 147 G1
Melville Rd., Sid. 176 C2
Melville Vil. Rd. W3 126 D1
High St.
Melvin Rd. SE20 189 F1
Melyn Cl. N7 92 C4
Anson Rd.
Memel Ct. EC1 11 J6
Memel St. EC1 11 J6
Memess Path SE18 136 D6
Memorial Av. E15 114 E3
Memorial Cl., Houns. 123 F6
Mendip Cl. SE26 171 F4

Mendip Cl. SW19 166 B2
Queensmere Rd.
Mendip Cl., Hayes 121 G7
Mendip Cl., Wor.Pk. 197 J1
Mendip Dr. NW2 90 A2
Mendip Rd. SW11 149 F3
Mendip Rd., Ilf. 81 H5
Mendora Rd. SW6 128 B7
Menelik Rd. NW2 90 B4
Menlo Gdns. SE19 170 A7
Menotti St. E2 13 J5
Mentmore Cl., Har. 69 F6
Mentmore Ter. E8 95 E7
Meon Ct., Islw. 144 B2
Meon Rd. W3 126 C2
Meopham Rd., Mitch. 186 C1
Mepham Cres., Har. 51 J7
Mepham Gdns., Har. 51 J7
Mepham St. SE1 26 D2
Mepham St. SE1 131 F1
Mera Dr., Bexh. 159 G4
Merantun Way SW19 185 F1
Merbury Cl. SE13 154 C5
Merbury Rd. SE28 137 H2
Mercator Pl. E14 134 A5
Napier Av.
Mercator Rd. SE13 154 D4
Mercer Cl., T.Ditt. 180 C7
Mercer Pl., Pnr. 66 C2
Crossway
Mercer St. WC2 18 A4
Mercer St. WC2 110 E6
Merceron St. E1 112 E4
Mercers Cl. SE10 135 F4
Mercers Pl. W6 127 J4
Mercers Rd. N19 92 D3
Merchant St. E3 113 J3
Merchiston Rd. SE6 172 D2
Merchland Rd. SE9 175 F1
Mercia Gro. SE13 154 C4
Mercier Rd. SW15 148 B5
Mercury Cen., Felt. 142 B5
Mercury Way SE14 133 G6
Mercy Ter. SE13 154 B4
Mere Cl. SW15 148 A7
Mere Cl., Orp. 206 E2
Mere End, Croy. 189 G7
Mere Side, Orp. 206 D2
Merebank La., Croy. 201 F5
Meredith Av. NW2 89 J5
Meredith Cl., Pnr. 50 D7
Meredith St. E13 115 G3
Meredith St. EC1 11 G4
Meredyth Rd. SW13 147 G2
Meretone Cl. SE4 153 H4
Merevale Cres., Mord. 185 F6
Mereway Rd., Twick. 162 A1
Merewood Cl., Brom. 192 D2
Merewood Rd., Bexh. 159 J2
Mereworth Cl., Brom. 191 F5
Mereworth Dr. SE18 137 F7
Merganser Gdns. SE28 137 G3
Avocet Ms.
Meriden Cl., Brom. 174 A7
Meriden Cl., Ilf. 81 F1
Meridian Gate E14 134 C2
Meridian Pl. E14 134 B2
Meridian Rd. SE7 136 A7
Meridian Trd. Est. SE7 135 H4
Meridian Wk. N17 60 B6
Commercial Rd.
Meridian Way N9 61 F5
Meridian Way N18 61 F6
Meridian Way, Enf. 45 G6
Merifield Rd. SE9 155 J4
Merino Cl. E11 79 J4
Merino Pl., Sid. 158 A6
Blackfen Rd.
Merivale Rd. SW15 148 B4
Merivale Rd., Har. 67 J7
Merlewood Dr., Chis. 192 C1
Merley Ct. NW9 88 C1
Merlin Cl., Croy. 202 B4
Minster Dr.
Merlin Cl., Mitch. 185 H3
Merlin Cl., Nthlt. 102 C3
Merlin Cres., Edg. 69 J1
Merlin Gdns., Brom. 173 G3
Merlin Gro., Beck. 189 J4
Merlin Gro., Ilf. 65 E7
Merlin Rd. E12 98 A2
Merlin Rd., Well. 158 A4
Merlin Rd. N., Well. 158 A4
Merlin St. WC1 11 E4
Merling Cl., Chess. 195 G5
Coppard Gdns.
Merlins Av., Har. 85 F3
Mermaid Ct. SE1 28 B3
Mermaid Ct. SE1 132 A2
Mermaid Ct. SE16 133 J1
Merredene St. SW2 151 F6
Merriam Cl. E4 62 C5
Merrick Rd., Sthl. 123 F2
Merrick Sq. SE1 28 A5
Merrick Sq. SE1 131 J3
Merridene N21 43 H6
Merrielands Cres., Dag. 119 F1
Merrilands Rd., Wor.Pk. 197 J1
Merrilees Rd., Sid. 157 H7
Merrilyn Cl., Esher 194 D6
Merriman Rd. SE3 155 J1
Merrington Rd. SW6 128 D6
Merrion Av., Stan. 53 G5
Merrion Wk. SE17 132 A5
Dawes St.
Merritt Gdns., Chess. 195 F6
Merritt Rd. SE4 153 J5
Merrivale N14 42 D6
Merrivale Av., Ilf. 80 A4
Merrow St. SE17 36 C4
Merrow St. SE17 131 J6
Merrow Wk. SE17 36 C3
Merrow Way, Croy. 204 C6
Merry Hill Mt., Bushey 51 H1
Merry Hill Rd., Bushey 51 H1
Merrydown Way, Chis. 192 B1
Merryfield SE3 155 F2
Merryfield Gdns., Stan. 53 F5
Merryfields Way SE6 154 B7
Merryhill Cl. E4 46 B7
Merryhills Ct. N14 42 C5
Merryhills Dr., Enf. 42 D4
Mersea Ho., Bark. 98 E6
Mersey Rd. E17 77 J3
Mersey Wk., Nthlt. 103 G2
Brabazon Rd.
Mersham Dr. NW9 70 A5
Mersham Pl. SE20 189 E1
Mersham Rd., Th.Hth. 188 A3
Merten Rd., Rom. 83 E7
Merthyr Ter. SW13 127 H6
Merton Av. W4 127 F4
Merton Av., Nthlt. 85 J5
Merton Gdns., Orp. 193 E5
Merton Hall Gdns. SW20 184 B1
Merton Hall Rd. SW19 184 B1
Merton High St. SW19 167 E7
Merton Ind. Pk. SW19 185 F1
Merton La. N6 91 J2
Merton Mans. SW20 184 A2
Merton Pk. Par. SW19 184 C1
Kingston Rd.
Merton Ri. NW3 91 H7
Merton Rd. E17 78 C5
Merton Rd. SE25 188 D5
Merton Rd. SW18 148 D6
Merton Rd. SW19 166 E7
Merton Rd., Bark. 99 J7
Merton Rd., Har. 85 J1
Merton Rd., Ilf. 81 J7
Merton Way, W.Mol. 179 H4
Merttins Rd. SE15 153 G5
Meru Cl. NW5 92 A4
Mervan Rd. SW2 151 G4
Mervyn Av. SE9 175 F3
Mervyn Rd. W13 124 D3
Messaline Av. W3 106 C6
Messent Rd. SE9 155 J5
Messeter Pl. SE9 156 D6
Messina Av. NW6 90 D7
Metcalf Wk., Felt. 160/161 E4
Gabriel Cl.
Meteor St. SW11 150 A4
Meteor Way, Wall. 200 E7
Metheringham Way NW9 70 E1
Methley St. SE11 35 F4
Methley St. SE11 131 G5
Methuen Cl., Edg. 54 A7
Methuen Pk. N10 74 B2
Methuen Rd., Belv. 139 H4
Methuen Rd., Bexh. 159 F4
Methuen Rd., Edg. 54 A7
Methwold Rd. W10 108 A5
Metro Cen., The, Islw. 144 B2
Metropolitan Cen., The, Grnf. 103 H1
Metropolitan Cl. E14 114 A5
Broomfield St.
Mews, The N1 111 J1
St. Paul St.
Mews, The, Ilf. 80 A5
Mews, The, Twick. 144/145 E6
Bridge Rd.
Mews Deck E1 113 E7
Mews Pl., Wdf.Grn. 63 G4
Mews St. E1 29 H1
Mews St. E1 132 D1
Mexfield Rd. SW15 148 C5
Meyer Rd., Erith 139 J6
Meymott St. SE1 27 G2
Meymott St. SE1 131 H1
Meynell Cres. E9 95 G7
Meynell Gdns. E9 95 G7
Meynell Rd. E9 95 G7
Meyrick Rd. NW10 89 G6
Meyrick Rd. SW11 149 G3
Miah Ter. E1 132 D1
Wapping High St.
Miall Wk. SE26 171 H4
Micawber St. N1 12 A3
Micawber St. N1 111 J3
Michael Faraday Ho. SE17 36 C4
Michael Gaynor Cl. W7 124 C1
Michael Rd. E11 97 E1
Michael Rd. SE25 188 B3
Michael Rd. SW6 149 E1
Michaelmas Cl. SW20 183 J3
Michaels Cl. SE13 154 E4
Micheldever Rd. SE12 155 E6
Michelham Gdns., Twick. 162 C3
Michels Row, Rich. 145 H4
Kew Foot Rd.
Michigan Av. E12 98 B4
Michleham Down N12 56 C4
Mickleham Cl., Orp. 193 J2
Mickleham Gdns., Sutt. 198 B6
Mickleham Rd., Orp. 193 J1
Mickleham Way, Croy. 204 D7
Micklethwaite Rd. SW6 128 D6
Midas Metropolitan Ind. Est., The, Mord. 198 A1
Garth Rd.
Middle Dene NW7 54 D3
Middle Fld. NW8 109 G1
Middle Grn. Cl., Surb. 181 J6
Alpha Rd.
Middle La. N8 74 E5
Middle La., Tedd. 162 C6
Middle La. Ms. N8 74/75 E5
Middle La.
Middle Pk. Av. SE9 156 A6
Middle Path, Har. 86 A1
Middle Rd.
Middle Rd. E13 115 G2
London Rd.
Middle Rd. SW16 186 D2
Middle Rd., Barn. 41 H6
Middle Rd., Har. 86 A2
Middle Row W10 108 B4
Middle St. EC1 19 J1
Middle St., Croy. 201 J3
Surrey St.
Middle Temple EC4 19 E5
Middle Temple La. EC4 19 E4
Middle Temple La. EC4 111 G6
Middle Way SW16 186 D2
Middle Way, Erith 138 E3
Middle Way, Hayes 102 C4
Middle Way, The, Har. 68 C2
Middle Yd. SE1 28 C1
Middlefield Gdns., Ilf. 81 E6
Middlefielde W13 104 E5
Middleham Gdns. N18 60 D6
Middleham Rd. N18 60 D6
Middlesborough Rd. N18 60 D6
Middlesex Business Cen., Sthl. 123 G2
Middlesex Ct. W4 127 F4
British Gro.
Middlesex Pas. EC1 19 H2
Middlesex Rd., Mitch. 186 E5
Middlesex St. E1 21 E2
Middlesex St. E1 112 B5
Middlesex Wf. E5 95 F2
Middleton Av. E4 61 J4
Middleton Av., Grnf. 104 A2
Middleton Av., Sid. 176 C6
Middleton Bldgs. W1 17 F2
Middleton Cl. E4 61 J3
Middleton Dr. SE16 133 G2
Middleton Dr., Pnr. 66 A3
Middleton Gdns., Ilf. 81 E6
Middleton Gro. N7 92 E5
Middleton Ms. N7 92/93 E5
Middleton Gro.
Middleton Rd. E8 94 C7
Middleton Rd. NW11 72 D7
Middleton Rd., Cars. 185 H7
Middleton Rd., Mord. 185 F6
Middleton St. E2 112 E3
Middleton Way SE13 154 D4
Middleway NW11 73 E5
Midfield Av., Bexh. 159 J3
Midfield Par., Bexh. 159 J3
Midford Pl. W1 9 G6
Midholm NW11 72 E4
Midholm, Wem. 88 A1
Midholm Cl. NW11 72 E4
Midholm Rd., Croy. 203 H2
Midhope St. WC1 10 B4
Midhurst Av. N10 74 A3
Midhurst Av., Croy. 187 G7
Midhurst Hill, Bexh. 159 G6
Midhurst Rd. W13 124 D2
Midland Cres. NW3 91 F6
Finchley Rd.
Midland Pl. E14 134 C5
Ferry St.
Midland Rd. E10 78 C7
Midland Rd. NW1 9 J2
Midland Rd. NW1 110 D2
Midland Ter. NW2 90 A3
Kara Way
Midland Ter. NW10 107 E4
Midleton Rd., N.Mal. 182 C3
Midlothian Rd. E3 113 J5
Midmoor Rd. SW12 168 C1
Midmoor Rd. SW19 184 A1
Midship Cl. SE16 133 G1
Surrey Water Rd.
Midship Pt. E14 134 A2
Midstrath Rd. NW10 89 E4
Midsummer Av., Houns. 143 F4
Midway, Sutt. 184 C7
Midwinter Cl., Well. 158 A3
Hook La.
Midwood Cl. NW2 89 H3
Miers Cl. E6 116 D1
Mighell Av., Ilf. 80 A5
Milan Rd., Sthl. 123 F2
Milborne Gro. SW10 30 D4
Milborne Gro. SW10 129 F5
Milborne St. E9 95 F6
Milborough Cres. SE12 155 E6
Milcote St. SE1 27 G4
Milcote St. SE1 131 H2
Mildenhall Rd. E5 95 F4
Mildmay Av. N1 94 A6
Mildmay Gro. N. N1 94 A5
Mildmay Gro. S. N1 94 A5
Mildmay Pk. N1 94 A5
Mildmay Pl. N16 94 B5
Boleyn Rd.
Mildmay Rd. N1 94 B5
Mildmay Rd., Ilf. 98/99 E3
Winston Way
Mildmay Rd., Rom. 83 J5
Mildmay St. N1 94 A6
Mildred Av., Borwd. 38 A4
Mildred Av., Hayes 121 G4
Mildred Av., Nthlt. 85 H5
Mile End, The E17 77 G1
Mile End Pl. E1 113 G4
Mile End Rd. E1 113 F5
Mile End Rd. E3 113 F5
Mile Rd., Wall. 200 C1
Miles Dr. SE28 137 H1
Merbury Rd.
Miles Pl. NW1 15 F1
Miles Pl., Surb. 181 J4
Villiers Av.
Miles Rd. N8 75 E3
Miles Rd., Mitch. 185 H3
Miles St. SW8 34 B6
Miles St. SW8 131 E6
Miles Way N20 57 H2
Milespit Hill NW7 55 H5
Milestone Cl. N9 60 D2
Chichester Rd.
Milestone Cl., Sutt. 199 G6
Milestone Rd. SE19 170 C6
Milfoil St. W12 107 G7
Milford Cl. SE2 139 E6

Moat Cft., Well. 158 C3
Moat Dr. E13 115 J2
Boundary Rd.
Moat Dr., Har. 67 J4
Moat Fm. Rd., Nthlt. 85 F6
Moat Pl. SW9 151 F3
Moat Pl. W3 106 B6
Moatside, Enf. 45 G4
Moatside, Felt. 160 C4
Moberley Rd. SW4 150 D7
Modbury Gdns. NW5 92 A6
Queens Cres.
Modder Pl. SW15 148 A4
Model Cotts. SW14 146 C4
Upper Richmond Rd. W.
Model Fm. Cl. SE9 174 B3
Modling Ho. E2 113 G2
Moelwyn Hughes Ct. N7 92 D5
Hilldrop Cres.
Moelyn Ms., Har. 68 D5
Moffat Rd. N13 59 E6
Moffat Rd. SW17 167 H4
Moffat Rd., Th.Hth. 187 J2
Mogden La., Islw. 144 B5
Mohmmad Khan Rd. E11 97 F1
Harvey Rd.
Moira Cl. N17 76 B2
Moira Rd. SE9 156 C4
Moland Mead SE16 133 G5
Crane Mead
Molasses Row SW11 149 F3
Cinnamon Row
Mole Abbey Gdns., W.Mol. 179 G3
New Rd.
Mole Ct., Epsom 196 C4
Molember Ct., E.Mol. 180 B5
Molember Rd., E.Mol. 180 B5
Molescroft SE9 175 F3
Molesey Av., W.Mol. 179 F4
Molesey Dr., Sutt. 198 B2
Molesey Pk. Av., W.Mol. 179 H5
Molesey Pk. Cl., E.Mol. 179 J5
Molesey Pk. Rd., E.Mol. 180 A5
Molesey Pk. Rd., W.Mol. 179 H5
Molesey Rd., W.Mol. 179 E5
Molesford Rd. SW6 148 D1
Molesham Cl., W.Mol. 179 H3
Molesham Way, W.Mol. 179 H3
Molesworth St. SE13 154 C3
Molineaux Pl., Tedd. 162 D5
Mollison Av., Enf. 45 H2
Mollison Dr., Wall. 201 E6
Mollison Way, Edg. 70 A2
Molly Huggins Cl. SW12 150 C7
Molyneux Dr. SW17 168 B4
Molyneux St. W1 15 H2
Molyneux St. W1 109 H5
Mona Rd. SE15 153 F2
Mona St. E16 115 F5
Monarch Cl., Felt. 141 H7
Monarch Cl., W.Wick. 205 F4
Monarch Dr. E16 116 A5
Monarch Ms. E17 78 B5
Monarch Ms. SW16 169 G5
Monarch Pl., Buck.H. 63 J2
Monarch Rd., Belv. 139 G3
Monastery Gdns., Enf. 44 A2
Monaveen Gdns., W.Mol. 179 G3
Monck St. SW1 25 J6
Monck St. SW1 130 D3
Monclar Rd. SE5 152 A4
Moncorvo Cl. SW7 23 G4
Moncrieff Cl. E6 116 B6
Linton Gdns.
Moncrieff Pl. SE15 152 D2
Rye La.
Moncrieff St. SE15 152 D2
Mondial Way, Hayes 121 F7
Monega Rd. E7 97 J6
Monega Rd. E12 98 A6
Money La., West Dr. 120 A3
Monier Rd. E3 96 A7
Monivea Rd., Beck. 171 J7
Monk Dr. E16 115 G6
Monk Pas. E16 115 G7
Monk Dr.
Monk St. SE18 136 D4
Monkchester Cl., Loug. 48 D1
Monkfrith Av. N14 42 B6
Monkfrith Cl. N14 42 B7
Monkfrith Way N14 42 A7
Monkhams Av., Wdf.Grn. 63 G5
Monkhams Dr., Wdf.Grn. 63 H4
Monkhams La., Buck.H. 63 H3
Monkhams La., Wdf.Grn. 63 G5
Monkleigh Rd., Mord. 184 B3
Monks Av., Barn. 41 F6
Monks Av., W.Mol. 179 F5
Monks Cl. SE2 138 D4
Monks Cl., Enf. 43 J2
Monks Cl., Har. 85 H2
Monks Cl., Ruis. 84 D4
Monks Dr. W3 106 A5
Monks Orchard Rd., Beck. 204 A1
Monks Pk., Wem. 88 C6
Monks Pk. Gdns., Wem. 88 B6
Monks Rd., Enf. 43 J2
Monks Way NW11 72 C4
Hurstwood Rd.
Monks Way, Beck. 190 A5
Monks Way, Orp. 207 F1
Monks Way, West Dr. 120 B6
Harmondsworth La.
Monksdene Gdns., Sutt. 199 E3
Monksgrove, Loug. 48 D5
Monksmead, Borwd. 38 C4
Monkswell Ct. N10 74 A1
Pembroke Rd.
Monkswood Gdns., Borwd. 38 D4
Monkswood Gdns., Ilf. 80 D3
Monkton Rd., Well. 157 J2
Monkton St. SE11 35 F1
Monkton St. SE11 131 G4
Monkville Av. NW11 72 C4
Monkwell Sq. EC2 20 A2
Monmouth Av. E18 79 H3
Monmouth Av., Kings.T. 163 F7
Monmouth Cl. W4 126 D3
Beaumont Rd.
Monmouth Cl., Mitch. 186/187 E4
Recreation Way
Monmouth Cl., Well. 158 A4
Monmouth Gro., Brent. 125 H4
Sterling Pl.
Monmouth Pl. W2 108 D6
Monmouth Rd.
Monmouth Rd. E6 116 C3
Monmouth Rd. N9 60 E2
Monmouth Rd. W2 108 E6
Monmouth Rd., Dag. 101 F5
Monmouth Rd., Hayes 121 H4
Monmouth St. WC2 18 A4
Monmouth St. WC2 110 E7
Monnery Rd. N19 92 C3
Monnow Rd. SE1 37 H2
Monnow Rd. SE1 132 D4
Mono La., Felt. 160 B2
Monoux Gro. E17 78 A1
Monro Gdns., Har. 52 B7
Monroe Cres., Enf. 44 E1
Monroe Dr. SW14 146 B5
Mons Way, Brom. 192 B6
Monsal Ct. E5 95 G4
Redwald Rd.
Monsell Rd. N4 93 H3
Monson Rd. NW10 107 G2
Monson Rd. SE14 133 G7
Montacute Rd. SE6 153 J7
Montacute Rd., Mord. 185 G6
Montagu Cres. N18 61 E4
Montagu Gdns. N18 61 E4
Montagu Gdns., Wall. 200 C4
Montagu Mans. W1 16 A1
Montagu Ms. N. W1 16 A2
Montagu Ms. N. W1 109 J5
Montagu Ms. S. W1 16 A3
Montagu Ms. W. W1 16 A3
Montagu Pl. W1 15 J2
Montagu Pl. W1 109 J5
Montagu Rd. N9 61 F3
Montagu Rd. N18 61 E5
Montagu Rd. NW4 71 G6
Montagu Rd. Ind. Est. N18 61 F4
Montagu Row W1 16 A2
Montagu Sq. W1 16 A2
Montagu Sq. W1 109 J5
Montagu St. W1 16 A3
Montagu St. W1 109 J6
Montague Av. SE4 153 J4
Montague Av. W7 124 C1
Montague Cl. SE1 28 B1
Montague Cl. SE1 132 A1
Montague Cl., Walt. 178 A7
Montague Gdns. W3 106 A7
Montague Pl. WC1 17 J1
Montague Pl. WC1 110 D5
Montague Rd. E8 94 D5
Montague Rd. E11 97 F2
Montague Rd. N8 75 F5
Montague Rd. N15 76 D4
Montague Rd. SW19 166 E7
Montague Rd. W7 124 C1
Montague Rd. W13 105 E6
Montague Rd., Croy. 201 H1
Montague Rd., Houns. 143 H3
Montague Rd., Rich. 145 H6
Montague Rd., Sthl. 122 E4
Montague Sq. SE15 133 F7
Clifton Way
Montague St. EC1 19 J2
Montague St. EC1 111 J5
Montague St. WC1 18 A1
Montague St. WC1 110 E5
Montague Waye, Sthl. 122 E3
Montalt Rd., Wdf.Grn. 63 F5
Montana Gdns. SE26 171 J4
Worsley Br. Rd.
Montana Gdns., Sutt. 199 F5
Lind Rd.
Montana Rd. SW17 168 A4
Montana Rd. SW20 183 J1
Montbelle Rd. SE9 174 E3
Montcalm Cl., Brom. 191 G6
Montcalm Cl., Hayes 102 B3
Ayles Rd.
Montcalm Rd. SE7 136 A7
Montclare St. E2 13 F4
Monteagle Av., Bark. 99 F6
Monteagle Way E5 94 D3
Rendlesham Rd.
Monteagle Way SE15 153 E3
Montefiore St. SW8 150 B2
Montego Cl. SE24 151 G4
Railton Rd.
Monteith Rd. E3 113 J1
Montem Rd. SE23 153 J7
Montem Rd., N.Mal. 182 E4
Montem St. N4 93 F1
Thorpedale Rd.
Montenotte Rd. N8 74 C5
Monterey Cl., Bex. 177 J2
Montesole Ct., Pnr. 66 C2
Montford Pl. SE11 34 E4
Montford Pl. SE11 131 G5
Montford Rd., Sun. 178 A4
Montfort Gdns., Ilf. 65 F6
Montfort Pl. SW19 166 A1
Montgolfier Wk., Nthlt. 102/103 E3
Jetstar Way
Montgomery Av., Esher 194 B3
Montgomery Cl., Mitch. 187 E4
Montgomery Cl., Sid. 157 J6
Montgomery Rd. W4 126 C4
Montgomery Rd., Edg. 53 J6
Montholme Rd. SW11 149 J6
Monthope Rd. E1 21 H2
Montolieu Gdns. SW15 147 H5
Montpelier Av. W5 105 F5
Montpelier Av., Bex. 158 D7
Montpelier Gdns. E6 116 A3
Montpelier Gdns., Rom. 82 C7
Montpelier Gro. NW5 92 C5
Montpelier Ms. SW7 23 H5
Montpelier Pl. E1 113 F6
Montpelier Pl. SW7 23 H5
Montpelier Pl. SW7 129 H3
Montpelier Ri. NW11 72 B7
Montpelier Ri., Wem. 87 G1
Montpelier Rd. N3 73 F1
Montpelier Rd. SE15 153 E1
Montpelier Rd. W5 105 G5
Montpelier Rd., Sutt. 199 F4
Montpelier Row SE3 155 F2
Montpelier Row, Twick. 145 F7
Montpelier Sq. SW7 23 H4
Montpelier Sq. SW7 129 H2
Montpelier St. SW7 23 H4
Montpelier St. SW7 129 H2
Montpelier Ter. SW7 23 H4
Montpelier Vale SE3 155 F2
Montpelier Wk. SW7 23 H5
Montpelier Wk. SW7 129 H3
Montpelier Way NW11 72 B7
Montrave Rd. SE20 171 F6
Montreal Pl. WC2 18 C5
Montreal Rd., Ilf. 81 F7
Montrell Rd. SW2 169 E1
Montrose Av. NW6 108 B2
Montrose Av., Edg. 70 C2
Montrose Av., Sid. 158 A7
Montrose Av., Twick. 143 H7
Montrose Av., Well. 157 H3
Montrose Cl., Well. 157 J3
Montrose Cl., Wdf.Grn. 63 G4
Montrose Ct. SW7 23 F4
Montrose Ct. SW7 129 G2
Montrose Cres. N12 57 F6
Montrose Cres., Wem. 87 H6
Montrose Gdns., Mitch. 185 J3
Montrose Gdns., Sutt. 199 E2
Montrose Pl. SW1 24 C4
Montrose Pl. SW1 130 A2
Montrose Rd., Felt. 141 G6
Montrose Rd., Har. 68 B2
Montrose Way SE23 171 G1
Montserrat Av., Wdf.Grn. 62 D7
Montserrat Cl. SE19 170 A5
Montserrat Rd. SW15 148 B4
Monument Gdns. SE13 154 C5
Monument St. EC3 20 C5
Monument St. EC3 112 A7
Monument Way N17 76 C3
Monza St. E1 113 F7
Moodkee St. SE16 133 F3
Moody Rd. SE15 152 C1
Moody St. E1 113 G3
Moon La., Barn. 40 C3
Moon St. N1 111 H1
Moor La. EC2 20 B2
Moor La. EC2 112 A5
Moor La., Chess. 195 H4
Moor Mead Rd., Twick. 144 D6
Moor Pk. Gdns., Kings.T. 165 E7
Moor Pl. EC2 20 B2
Moor St. W1 17 J4
Moorcroft Gdns., Brom. 192 B5
Southborough Rd.
Moorcroft Rd. SW16 168 E3
Moorcroft Way, Pnr. 66 E5
Moordown SE18 156 D1
Moore Cl. SW14 146 C3
Little St. Leonards
Moore Cl., Mitch. 186 B2
Moore Cres., Dag. 118 B1
Moore Pk. Rd. SW6 128 E7
Moore Rd. SE19 169 J6
Moore St. SW3 31 J1
Moore St. SW3 129 J4
Moore Wk. E7 97 G4
Stracey Rd.
Moore Way SE22 170 D1
Lordship La.
Moorefield Rd. N17 76 C2
Moorehead Way SE3 155 H3
Mooreland Rd., Brom. 173 F7
Moorey Cl. E15 115 F1
Stephen's Rd.
Moorfield Av. W5 105 G4
Moorfield Rd., Chess. 195 H5
Moorfield Rd., Enf. 45 F1
Moorfields EC2 20 B2
Moorfields EC2 112 A5
Moorfields Highwalk EC2 112 A5
Fore St.
Moorgate EC2 20 B3
Moorgate EC2 112 A6
Moorgate Pl. EC2 20 B3
Moorhouse Rd. W2 108 D6
Moorhouse Rd., Har. 69 G3
Moorings SE28 118 B7
Moorland Cl., Twick. 143 G7
Telford Rd.
Moorland Rd. SW9 151 H4
Moorlands Av. NW7 55 H6
Moorlands Est. SW9 151 G4
Moormead Dr., Epsom 197 E5
Moorside Rd., Brom. 173 E3

Name	Page	Grid
Moortown Rd., Wat.	50	C4
Moot Ct. NW9	70	A5
Mora Rd. NW2	89	J4
Mora St. EC1	**12**	**A4**
Mora St. EC1	111	J3
Morant Pl. N22	75	F1
Commerce Rd.		
Morant St. E14	114	A7
Morat St. SW9	151	F1
Moravian Pl. SW10	**31**	**F6**
Moravian St. E2	113	F3
Moray Av., Hayes	121	J1
Moray Cl., Edg.	54	B2
Pentland Av.		
Moray Ms. N7	93	F2
Durham Rd.		
Moray Rd. N4	93	F2
Mordaunt Gdns., Dag.	100	E7
Mordaunt Ho. NW10	106	D1
Mordaunt Rd. NW10	106	D1
Mordaunt St. SW9	151	F3
Morden Cl. SE13	154	C2
Morden Ct., Mord.	184	E4
Morden Gdns., Grnf.	86	C5
Morden Gdns., Mitch.	185	G4
Morden Hall Rd., Mord.	185	E3
Morden Hill SE13	154	C2
Morden La. SE13	154	C1
Morden Rd. SE3	155	G2
Morden Rd. SW19	185	E1
Morden Rd., Mitch.	185	F4
Morden Rd., Rom.	83	E7
Morden Ms. SE3	155	G2
Morden St. SE13	154	B1
Morden Way, Sutt.	184	D7
Morden Wf. Rd. SE10	134	E3
Mordon Rd., Ilf.	81	J7
Mordred Rd. SE6	172	E2
More Cl. E16	115	F6
More Cl. W14	128	B4
Morecambe Cl. E1	113	G5
Morecambe Gdns., Stan.	53	G4
Morecambe St. SE17	**36**	**A2**
Morecambe St. SE17	131	J4
Morecambe Ter. N18	60	A4
Morecoombe Cl., Kings.T.	164	B7
Moree Way N18	60	D4
Moreland St. EC1	**11**	**H3**
Moreland St. EC1	111	H3
Moreland Way E4	62	B3
Morell Cl., Barn.	41	F3
Galdana Av.		
Morella Rd. SW12	149	J7
Moremead Rd. SE6	171	J4
Morena St. SE6	154	B7
Moresby Av., Surb.	182	B7
Moresby Rd. E5	94	E1
Moresby Wk. SW8	150	C2
Moreton Av., Islw.	144	B1
Moreton Cl. E5	95	F2
Moreton Cl. N15	76	A6
Moreton Cl. NW7	55	J6
Moreton Gdns., Wdf.Grn.	64	B5
Moreton Pl. SW1	**33**	**G3**
Moreton Pl. SW1	130	C5
Moreton Rd. N15	76	A6
Moreton Rd., S.Croy.	202	A5
Moreton Rd., Wor.Pk.	197	G2
Moreton St. SW1	**33**	**G3**
Moreton St. SW1	130	D5
Moreton Ter. SW1	**33**	**G3**
Moreton Ter. SW1	130	C5
Moreton Ter. Ms. N. SW1	**33**	**G3**
Moreton Ter. Ms. S. SW1	**33**	**G3**
Moreton Twr. W3	126	B1
Morford Cl., Ruis.	66	B7
Morford Way, Ruis.	66	B7
Morgan Av. E17	78	D4
Morgan Cl., Dag.	101	G7
Morgan Rd. N7	93	G5
Morgan Rd. W10	108	C5
Morgan Rd., Brom.	173	G7
Morgan St. E3	113	H3
Morgan St. E16	115	F5
Morgan Way, Wdf.Grn.	64	B6
Morgans La. SE1	**28**	**D2**
Morgans La. SE1	132	B1
Moriatry Cl. N7	92	E4
Morie St. SW18	149	E5
Morieux Rd. E10	95	J1
Moring Rd. SW17	168	A4
Morkyns Wk. SE21	170	B3
Morland Av., Croy.	202	B1
Morland Cl. NW11	91	E1
Morland Cl., Hmptn.	161	F5
Morland Cl., Mitch.	185	H3
Morland Gdns. NW10	88	D7
Morland Gdns., Sthl.	123	H1
Morland Ms. N1	93	G7
Lofting Rd.		
Morland Rd. E17	77	G5
Morland Rd. SE20	171	G6
Morland Rd., Croy.	202	B1
Morland Rd., Dag.	101	G7
Morland Rd., Har.	69	H5
Morland Rd., Ilf.	98	E2
Morland Rd., Sutt.	199	F5
Morley Av. E4	62	D7
Morley Av. N18	60	D4
Morley Av. N22	75	G2
Morley Cl., Orp.	207	E2
Morley Cres., Edg.	54	C2
Morley Cres., Ruis.	84	C2
Morley Cres. E., Stan.	69	F2
Morley Cres. W., Stan.	69	F2
Morley Rd. E10	96	C1
Morley Rd. E15	115	F2
Morley Rd. SE13	154	C4
Morley Rd., Bark.	117	G1
Morley Rd., Chis.	193	F1
Morley Rd., Rom.	82	E5
Morley Rd., Sutt.	198	C1
Morley Rd., Twick.	145	G6
Morley St. SE1	**27**	**F5**
Morley St. SE1	131	G2
Morna Rd. SE5	151	J2
Morning La. E9	95	F6
Morningside Rd., Wor.Pk.	197	H2
Mornington Av. W14	128	C4
Mornington Av., Ilf.	80	D7
Mornington Av., Brom.	191	J3
Mornington Cl., Wdf.Grn.	63	G4
Mornington Ct., Bex.	177	J1
Mornington Cres. NW1	**9**	**F1**
Mornington Cres. NW1	110	C2
Mornington Cres., Houns.	142	B1
Mornington Gro. E3	114	A3
Mornington Ms. SE5	151	J1
Mornington Pl. NW1	**9**	**E1**
Mornington Rd. E4	46	D7
Mornington Rd. E11	97	F1
Mornington Rd. SE8	133	J7
Mornington Rd., Grnf.	103	H5
Mornington Rd., Loug.	49	F3
Mornington Rd., Wdf.Grn.	63	F4
Mornington St. NW1	**8**	**E1**
Mornington St. NW1	110	B2
Mornington Ter. NW1	110	B1
Mornington Wk., Rich.	163	G4
Morocco St. SE1	**28**	**D4**
Morocco St. SE1	132	B2
Morpeth Gro. E9	113	G1
Morpeth Rd. E9	113	F1
Morpeth St. E2	113	G3
Morpeth Ter. SW1	**25**	**F6**
Morpeth Ter. SW1	130	C3
Morpeth Wk. N17	60/61	E7
West Rd.		
Morrab Gdns., Ilf.	99	J3
Morris Av. E12	98	C5
Morris Cl., Croy.	189	H6
Morris Cl., Orp.	207	H3
Morris Ct. E4	62	B3
Flaxen Rd.		
Morris Gdns. SW18	148	D7
Morris Pl. N4	93	G2
Morris Rd. E14	114	B5
Morris Rd. E15	96	E4
Morris Rd., Dag.	101	F2
Morris Rd., Islw.	144	C3
Morris St. E1	113	E6
Morrish Rd. SW2	151	E7
Morrison Av. N17	76	B3
Morrison Rd., Bark.	118	E2
Morrison Rd., Hayes	102	B3
Morrison St. SW11	150	A3
Morriston Cl., Wat.	50	C5
Morse Cl. E13	115	G3
Morshead Rd. W9	108	D3
Morson Rd., Enf.	45	H6
Morston Gdns. SE9	174	C4
Morten Cl. SW4	150	D6
Morteyne Rd. N17	76	A1
Mortgramit Sq. SE18	136	D3
Powis St.		
Mortham St. E15	114	E1
Mortimer Cl. NW2	90	C3
Mortimer Cl. SW16	168	D2
Mortimer Cres. NW6	108	E1
Mortimer Cres., Wor.Pk.	196	D3
Mortimer Dr., Enf.	44	B5
Mortimer Est. NW6	108	E1
Mortimer Mkt. WC1	**9**	**G6**
Mortimer Pl. NW6	108	E1
Mortimer Rd. E6	116	C3
Mortimer Rd. N1	94	B7
Mortimer Rd. NW10	107	J3
Mortimer Rd. W13	105	F6
Mortimer Rd., Mitch.	185	J1
Mortimer Sq. W11	108	A7
St. Anns Rd.		
Mortimer St. W1	**17**	**F2**
Mortimer St. W1	110	C6
Mortimer Ter. NW5	92	B4
Gordon Ho. Rd.		
Mortlake Cl., Croy.	200/201	E3
Richmond Rd.		
Mortlake Dr., Mitch.	185	H1
Mortlake High St. SW14	146	D3
Mortlake Rd. E16	115	H6
Mortlake Rd., Ilf.	99	F4
Mortlake Rd., Rich.	126	A7
Mortlake Ter., Rich.	126	A7
Kew Rd.		
Mortlock Cl. SE15	152/153	E1
Cossall Wk.		
Morton Cres. N14	58	D4
Morton Gdns., Wall.	200	C5
Morton Ms. SW5	**30**	**A2**
Morton Pl. SE1	**26**	**E6**
Morton Rd. E15	97	F7
Morton Rd. N1	93	J7
Morton Rd., Mord.	185	G5
Morton Way N14	58	C3
Morval Rd. SW2	151	G5
Morvale Cl., Belv.	139	F4
Morven Rd. SW17	167	J3
Morville St. E3	114	A2
Morwell St. WC1	**17**	**J2**
Moscow Pl. W2	**14**	**A5**
Moscow Rd. W2	**14**	**A5**
Moscow Rd. W2	108	D7
Moselle Av. N22	75	G2
Moselle Cl. N8	75	F3
Miles Rd.		
Moselle Ho. N17	60	C7
William St.		
Moselle Pl. N17	60	C7
High Rd.		
Moselle St. N17	60	C7
Moss Cl. E1	**21**	**J1**
Moss Cl., Pnr.	67	F2
Moss Gdns., Felt.	160	A2
Moss Gdns., S.Croy.	203	G7
Warren Av.		
Moss Hall Cres. N12	57	E6
Moss Hall Gro. N12	56	E6
Moss La., Pnr.	67	F3
Moss Rd., Dag.	101	G7
Mossborough Cl. N12	57	E6
Mossbury Rd. SW11	149	H3
Mossdown Cl., Belv.	139	G4
Mossford Ct., Ilf.	81	E3
Mossford Grn., Ilf.	81	E3
Mossford La., Ilf.	81	E2
Mossford St. E3	113	J4
Mossington Gdns. SE16	133	F4
Abbeyfield Rd.		
Mosslea Rd. SE20	171	F6
Mosslea Rd., Brom.	192	A5
Mosslea Rd., Orp.	207	F3
Mossop St. SW3	**31**	**H1**
Mossop St. SW3	129	H4
Mossville Gdns., Mord.	184	C3
Moston Cl., Hayes	121	J5
Fuller Way		
Mostyn Av., Wem.	87	J5
Mostyn Gdns. NW10	108	A2
Mostyn Gro. E3	113	J2
Mostyn Rd. SW9	151	G1
Mostyn Rd. SW19	184	C1
Mostyn Rd., Edg.	54	D7
Mosul Way, Brom.	192	B6
Motcomb St. SW1	**24**	**A5**
Motcomb St. SW1	130	A3
Mothers' Sq. E5	95	E4
Motley Av. EC2	112	B4
Scrutton St.		
Motley St. SW8	150	C2
St. Rule St.		
Motspur Pk., N.Mal.	183	F6
Mott St., Loug.	47	F1
Mottingham Gdns. SE9	174	A1
Mottingham La. SE9	173	J1
Mottingham La. SE12	173	J1
Mottingham Rd. N9	45	G6
Mottingham Rd. SE9	174	B2
Mottisfont Rd. SE2	138	A3
Moulins Rd. E9	113	F1
Moulton Av., Houns.	143	E2
Mound, The SE9	174	D3
Moundfield Rd. N16	76	D6
Mount, The N20	57	F2
Mount, The NW3	91	F4
Heath St.		
Mount, The W3	126	C1
High St.		
Mount, The, N.Mal.	183	F3
Mount, The, Wem.	88	B2
Mount, The, Wor.Pk.	197	H4
Mount Adon Pk. SE22	152	D7
Mount Angelus Rd. SW15	147	F7
Mount Ararat Rd., Rich.	145	H5
Mount Ash Rd. SE26	170	E3
Mount Av. E4	62	A3
Mount Av. W5	105	G5
Mount Av., Sthl.	103	G6
Mount Cl. W5	105	F5
Mount Cl., Barn.	42	A4
Mount Cl., Brom.	192	B1
Mount Cor., Felt.	160	D2
Mount Ct. SW15	148	B3
Weimar St.		
Mount Ct., W.Wick.	204	E2
Mount Culver Av., Sid.	176	D6
Mount Dr., Bexh.	158	E5
Mount Dr., Har.	67	F5
Mount Dr., Wem.	88	C2
Mount Echo Av. E4	62	B2
Mount Echo Dr. E4	62	B1
Mount Ephraim La. SW16	168	D3
Mount Ephraim Rd. SW16	168	D3
Mount Est., The E5	94/95	E2
Mount Pleasant La.		
Mount Gdns. SE26	170	E3
Mount Gro., Edg.	54	C3
Mount Ms., Hmptn.	179	H1
Mount Mills EC1	**11**	**H4**
Mount Nod Rd. SW16	169	F3
Mount Pk. Av., Har.	86	A2
Mount Pk. Cres. W5	105	G6
Mount Pk. Rd. W5	105	G5
Mount Pk. Rd., Har.	86	A3
Mount Pk. Rd., Pnr.	66	A5
Mount Pl. W3	126	B1
High St.		
Mount Pleasant SE27	169	J4
Mount Pleasant WC1	**10**	**D6**
Mount Pleasant WC1	111	G4
Mount Pleasant, Barn.	41	H4
Mount Pleasant, Ruis.	84	C2
Mount Pleasant, Wem.	105	H1
Mount Pleasant Cres. N4	75	F7
Mount Pleasant Hill E5	95	F2
Mount Pleasant La. E5	94	E2
Mount Pleasant Pl. SE18	137	G4
Orchard Rd.		
Mount Pleasant Rd. E17	77	H2
Mount Pleasant Rd. N17	76	B2
Mount Pleasant Rd. NW10	89	J7
Mount Pleasant Rd. SE13	154	B6
Mount Pleasant Rd. W5	105	F4
Mount Pleasant Rd., Chig.	65	G4
Mount Pleasant Rd., N.Mal.	182	C3
Mount Pleasant Vil. N4	75	F7
Mount Pleasant Wk., Bex.	159	J5
Mount Rd. NW2	89	H3
Mount Rd. NW4	71	G6
Mount Rd. SE19	170	A6
Mount Rd. SW19	166	D2
Mount Rd., Barn.	41	H5

316 Mou-Nas

Mount Rd., Bexh. 158 D5
Mount Rd., Chess. 195 J5
Mount Rd., Dag. 101 F1
Mount Rd., Felt. 160 E3
Mount Rd., Hayes 122 A2
Mount Rd., Ilf. 98 E5
Mount Rd., Mitch. 185 H2
Mount Rd., N.Mal. 182 D3
Mount Row W1 16 D6
Mount Row W1 110 B7
Mount Sq., The NW3 91 F3
Heath St.
Mount Stewart Av., Har. 69 G6
Mount St. W1 16 C6
Mount St. W1 110 A7
Mount Ter. E1 112/113 E5
New Rd.
Mount Vernon NW3 91 F4
Mount Vw. NW7 54 D3
Mount Vw. W5 105 G4
Mount Vw. Rd. E4 46 C7
Mount Vw. Rd. N4 75 E7
Mount Vw. Rd. NW9 70 D4
Mount Vil. SE27 169 H3
Mountacre Cl. SE26 170 C4
Mountague Pl. E14 114 C7
Mountbatten Cl. SE18 137 H6
Mountbatten Cl. SE19 170 B5
Mountbatten Ct. SE16 133 F1
Rotherhithe St.
Mountbatten Ct., Buck.H. 64 A2
Mountbatten Gdns., Beck. 189 H4
Balmoral Av.
Mountbatten Ms. SW18 167 F1
Inman Rd.
Mountbel Rd., Stan. 68 D1
Mountcombe Cl., Surb. 181 H7
Mountearl Gdns. SW16 169 F3
Mountfield Cl. SE6 154 D7
Mountfield Rd. E6 116 D2
Mountfield Rd. N3 72 D3
Mountfield Rd. W5 105 G6
Mountford St. E1 21 H3
Mountfort Cres. N1 93 G7
Barnsbury Sq.
Mountfort Ter. N1 93 G7
Barnsbury Sq.
Mountgrove Rd. N5 93 H3
Mounthurst Rd., Brom. 191 F7
Mountington Pk. Cl., Har. 69 G6
Mountjoy Cl. SE2 138 B2
Mounts Pond Rd. SE3 154 D2
Mountsfield Ct. SE13 154 D6
Mountside, Felt. 160/161 E3
Hampton Rd. W.
Mountside, Stan. 68 C1
Mountview Ct. N8 75 H4
Green Las.
Mountview Rd., Esher 194 E7
Mountwood, W.Mol. 179 G3
Movers La., Bark. 117 H2
Mowatt Cl. N19 92 D1
Mowbray Rd. NW6 90 B7
Mowbray Rd. SE19 188 C1
Mowbray Rd., Barn. 41 F4
Mowbray Rd., Edg. 54 A4
Mowbray Rd., Rich. 163 F3
Mowbrays Cl., Rom. 83 J1
Mowbrays Rd., Rom. 83 J2
Mowbrey Gdns., Loug. 49 F2
Mowlem St. E2 113 E2
Mowlem Trd. Est. N17 61 F7
Mowll St. SW9 131 G7
Moxon Cl. E13 115 F2
Whitelegg Rd.
Moxon St. W1 16 B2
Moxon St. W1 110 A5
Moxon St., Barn. 40 C3
Moye Cl. E2 13 J1
Moyers Rd. E10 78 C7
Moylan Rd. W6 128 B6
Moyne Pl. NW10 106 A2
Moynihan Dr. N21 43 E5
Moys Cl., Croy. 186 E6
Moyser Rd. SW16 168 B5
Mozart St. W10 108 C3
Mozart Ter. SW1 32 C2
Mozart Ter. SW1 130 A4
Muchelney Rd., Mord. 185 F6
Mud La. W5 105 G5
Mudlarks Way SE7 135 G3
Mudlarks Way SE10 135 G3
Muggeridge Cl., S.Croy. 202 A5
Muggeridge Rd., Dag. 101 H4
Muir Dr. SW18 149 G6
Muir Rd. E5 94 D4
Muir St. E16 136 C1
Newland St.
Muirdown Av. SW14 146 D4
Muirfield W3 107 E6
Muirfield Cl. SE16 132/133 E5
Ryder Dr.
Muirfield Cl., Wat. 50 C4
Muirfield Cres. E14 134 B3
Millharbour
Muirfield Grn., Wat. 50 C4
Muirfield Rd., Wat. 50 D4
Muirkirk Rd. SE6 172 C1
Mulberry Cl. E4 62 A2
Mulberry Cl. N8 74 E5
Mulberry Cl. NW3 91 G4
Hampstead High St.
Mulberry Cl. NW4 71 J3
Mulberry Cl. SE7 136 A6
Mulberry Cl. SE22 152 D5
Mulberry Cl. SW3 129 G6
Beaufort St.
Mulberry Cl. SW16 168 C4
Mulberry Cl., Barn. 41 G4
Mulberry Cl., Nthlt. 102/103 E2
Parkfield Av.
Mulberry Ct., Bark. 99 J7
Westrow Dr.
Mulberry Cres., Brent. 125 E7
Mulberry Cres., West Dr. 120 D2
Mulberry La., Croy. 202 C1
Mulberry Ms., Wall. 200 C6
Ross Rd.
Mulberry Par., West Dr. 120 D3
Mulberry Pl. W6 127 G5
Chiswick Mall
Mulberry Rd. E8 94 C7
Mulberry St. E1 21 H3
Mulberry Wk. SW3 31 F5
Mulberry Wk. SW3 129 G6
Mulberry Way E18 79 H2
Mulberry Way, Belv. 139 J2
Mulberry Way, Ilf. 81 F4
Mulgrave Rd. NW10 89 F4
Mulgrave Rd. SW6 128 C6
Mulgrave Rd. W5 105 G3
Mulgrave Rd., Croy. 202 A3
Mulgrave Rd., Har. 86 D2
Mulgrave Rd., Sutt. 198 D6
Mulholland Cl., Mitch. 186 B2
Mulkern Rd. N19 92 D1
Mull Wk. N1 93 J6
Clephane Rd.
Mullards Cl., Mitch. 199 J1
Muller Rd. SW4 150 D6
Mullet Gdns. E2 13 J2
Mullins Path SW14 146 D3
Mullion Cl., Har. 67 H1
Mullion Wk., Wat. 50 D4
Ormskirk Rd.
Mulready St. NW8 7 G6
Multi Way W3 126/127 E2
Valetta Rd.
Multon Rd. SW18 149 G7
Mulvaney Way SE1 28 C4
Mulvaney Way SE1 132 A2
Mumford Ct. EC2 20 A3
Mumford Rd. SE24 151 H5
Railton Rd.
Muncaster Rd. SW11 149 J5
Muncies Ms. SE6 172 C2
Mund St. W14 128 C5
Mundania Rd. SE22 153 E6
Munday Rd. E16 115 G6
Munden St. W14 128 B4
Mundesley Cl., Wat. 50 C4
Mundford Rd. E5 95 F2
Mundon Gdns., Ilf. 99 G1
Mundy St. N1 12 D3
Mundy St. N1 112 B3
Mungo Pk. Cl., Bushey 51 J2
Munnery Way, Orp. 206 D3
Munnings Gdns., Islw. 144 A5
Munro Dr. N11 58 C6
Munro Ms. W10 108 B5
Munro Ter. SW10 31 E7
Munro Ter. SW10 129 G7
Munslow Gdns., Sutt. 199 G4
Munster Av., Houns. 143 F4
Munster Ct., Tedd. 163 F6
Munster Gdns. N13 59 H4
Munster Ms. SW6 128 B7
Munster Rd.
Munster Rd. SW6 148 C1
Munster Rd., Tedd. 163 F6
Munster Sq. NW1 9 E5
Munster Sq. NW1 110 B3
Munton Rd. SE17 36 A1
Munton Rd. SE17 131 J4
Murchison Av., Bex. 176 D1
Murchison Rd. E10 96 C2
Murdock Cl. E16 115 F6
Rogers Rd.
Murdock St. SE15 132 E6
Murfett Cl. SW19 166 B2
Muriel St. N1 10 D1
Muriel St. N1 111 F2
Murillo Rd. SE13 154 D4
Murphy St. SE1 27 E4
Murphy St. SE1 131 G2
Murray Av., Brom. 191 H2
Murray Av., Houns. 143 H5
Murray Cres., Pnr. 66 D1
Murray Gro. N1 12 B2
Murray Gro. N1 111 J2
Murray Ms. NW1 92 D7
Murray Rd. SW19 166 A6
Murray Rd. W5 125 F4
Murray Rd., Rich. 163 E2
Murray Sq. E16 115 G6
Murray St. NW1 92 D7
Murray Ter. NW3 91 G4
Flask Wk.
Murray Ter. W5 125 G4
Murray Rd.
Mursell Est. SW8 151 F1
Murtwell Dr., Chig. 65 F6
Musard Rd. W6 128 B6
Musard Rd. W14 128 B6
Musbury St. E1 113 F6
Muscal W6 128 B6
Muscatel Pl. SE5 152 B1
Dalwood St.
Muschamp Rd. SE15 152 C3
Muschamp Rd., Cars. 199 H2
Muscovy Ho., Erith 138/139 E2
Kale Rd.
Muscovy St. EC3 21 E6
Museum La. SW7 23 E6
Museum Pas. E2 112/113 E3
Victoria Pk. Sq.
Museum St. WC1 18 A2
Museum St. WC1 110 E6
Musgrave Cl., Barn. 41 F1
Musgrave Cres. SW6 148 D1
Musgrave Rd., Islw. 144 C1
Musgrove Rd. SE14 153 G1
Musjid Rd. SW11 149 G2
Kambala Rd.
Musket Cl., Barn. 41 G5
East Barnet Rd.
Musquash Way, Houns. 142 C2
Muston Rd. E5 94 E2
Mustow Pl. SW6 148 C2
Munster Rd.
Muswell Av. N10 74 B2
Muswell Hill N10 74 B3
Muswell Hill Bdy. N10 74 B3
Muswell Hill Pl. N10 74 B4
Muswell Hill Rd. N6 74 A6
Muswell Hill Rd. N10 74 A4
Muswell Ms. N10 74 B3
Muswell Rd.
Muswell Rd. N10 74 B3
Mutrix Rd. NW6 108 D1
Mutton Pl. NW1 92 B6
Harmood St.
Muybridge Rd., N.Mal. 182 C2
Myatt Rd. SW9 151 H1
Myatt's Flds. N. SW9 151 G1
Eythorne Rd.
Myatt's Flds. S. SW9 151 G2
Mycenae Rd. SE3 135 G7
Myddelton Cl., Enf. 44 C1
Myddelton Gdns. N21 43 H7
Myddelton Pk. N20 57 G3
Myddelton Pas. EC1 11 F3
Myddelton Rd. N8 75 E4
Myddelton Sq. EC1 11 F3
Myddelton Sq. EC1 111 G3
Myddelton St. EC1 11 F4
Myddelton St. EC1 111 G3
Myddleton Av. N4 93 J2
Myddleton Ms. N22 59 E7
Myddleton Rd. N22 59 E7
Myers La. SE14 133 G6
Mylis Cl. SE26 171 E4
Mylius Cl. SE14 153 F1
Kender St.
Mylne St. EC1 11 E2
Mylne St. EC1 111 G3
Myra St. SE2 138 A4
Myrdle St. E1 21 J2
Myrdle St. E1 112 D5
Myrna Cl. SW19 167 H7
Myron Pl. SE13 154 C3
Myrtle Av., Felt. 141 H4
Myrtle Av., Ruis. 66 A7
Myrtle Cl., Barn. 57 J1
Myrtle Cl., West Dr. 120 C3
Myrtle Gdns. W7 124 B1
Myrtle Gro., N.Mal. 182 C2
Myrtle Rd. E6 116 B1
Myrtle Rd. E17 77 H6
Myrtle Rd. N13 59 J3
Myrtle Rd. W3 126 C1
Myrtle Rd., Croy. 204 A3
Myrtle Rd., Hmptn. 161 J6
Myrtle Rd., Houns. 143 J2
Myrtle Rd., Ilf. 99 E2
Myrtle Rd., Sutt. 199 F5
Myrtle Wk. N1 12 D2
Myrtle Wk. N1 112 B2
Myrtleberry Cl. E8 94 C6
Beechwood Rd.
Myrtledene Rd. SE2 138 A5
Mysore Rd. SW11 149 J3
Myton Rd. SE21 170 A3

N

Nadine St. SE7 135 J5
Nafferton Ri., Loug. 48 A5
Nagle Cl. E17 78 D2
Nag's Head Ct. EC1 11 J6
Nags Head La., Well. 158 B3
Nags Head Rd., Enf. 45 F4
Nairn Grn., Wat. 50 A3
Nairn Rd., Ruis. 84 C6
Nairn St. E14 114 C5
Nairne Gro. SE24 152 A5
Naish Ct. N1 111 E1
Nallhead Rd., Felt. 160 C5
Namba Roy Cl. SW16 169 F4
Valley Rd.
Namton Dr., Th.Hth. 187 F4
Nan Clark's La. NW7 55 F2
Nankin St. E14 114 A6
Nansen Rd. SW11 150 A4
Nant Rd. NW2 90 C2
Nant St. E2 112/113 E3
Cambridge Heath Rd.
Nantes Cl. SW18 149 F4
Nantes Pas. E1 21 F1
Naoroji St. WC1 11 E4
Napier Av. E14 134 A5
Napier Av. SW6 148 C3
Napier Cl. SE8 133 J7
Amersham Vale
Napier Cl. W14 128 C3
Napier Rd.
Napier Cl., West Dr. 120 C3
Napier Ct. SW6 148 C3
Ranelagh Gdns.
Napier Gro. N1 12 A2
Napier Gro. N1 111 J2
Napier Pl. W14 128 C3
Napier Rd. E6 116 D1
Napier Rd. E11 96 E4
Napier Rd. E15 115 E2
Napier Rd. N17 76 B3
Napier Rd. NW10 107 H3
Napier Rd. SE25 188 E4
Napier Rd. W14 128 C3
Napier Rd., Belv. 139 F4
Napier Rd., Brom. 191 H4
Napier Rd., Enf. 45 G5
Napier Rd., Houns. 140 A1
Napier Rd., Islw. 144 D4
Napier Rd., S.Croy. 202 A7
Napier Rd., Wem. 87 G5
Napier Ter. N1 93 H7
Napoleon Rd. E5 94 E3
Napoleon Rd., Twick. 145 E7
Napton Cl., Hayes 102/103 E4
Kingsash Dr.
Narbonne Av. SW4 150 C5
Narborough St. SW6 148 E2
Narcissus Rd. NW6 90 D5
Naresby Fold, Stan. 53 F6
Bernays Cl.
Narford Rd. E5 94 D3
Narrow St. E14 113 H7
Narrow Way, Brom. 192 B6
Nascot St. W12 107 J6
Naseby Cl. NW6 91 F7
Fairfax Rd.
Naseby Cl., Islw. 144 B1
Naseby Rd. SE19 170 A6
Naseby Rd., Dag. 101 G3

Naseby Rd., Ilf. 80 C1
Nash Cl., Sutt. 199 G3
Nash Grn., Brom. 173 G6
Nash La., Kes. 205 G5
Nash Pl. E14 134 B1
South Colonnade
Nash Rd. N9 61 F2
Nash Rd. SE4 153 H4
Nash Rd., Rom. 82 D4
Nash St. NW1 8 E4
Nash Way, Har. 69 E6
Nasmyth St. W6 127 H3
Nassau Path SE28 138 C1
Disraeli Cl.
Nassau Rd. SW13 147 F1
Nassau St. W1 17 F2
Nassau St. W1 110 C5
Nassington Rd. NW3 91 H4
Natal Rd. N11 58 E6
Natal Rd. SW16 168 D6
Natal Rd., Ilf. 98 E4
Natal Rd., Th.Hth. 188 A3
Natalie Cl., Felt. 141 G7
Natalie Ms., Twick. 162 A3
Sixth Cross Rd.
Nathan Way SE28 137 H4
Nathaniel Cl. E1 21 G2
Nathans Rd., Wem. 87 F1
Nation Way E4 62 C1
Naval Row E14 114 C7
Naval Wk., Brom. 191 G3
High St.
Navarino Gro. E8 94 D6
Navarino Rd. E8 94 D6
Navarre Rd. E6 116 B2
Navarre St. E2 13 F5
Navarre St. E2 112 C4
Navenby Wk. E3 114 A4
Rounton Rd.
Navestock Cl. E4 62 C3
Mapleton Rd.
Navestock Cres., Wdf.Grn. 79 J1
Navestock Ho., Bark. 118 B2
Navigator Dr., Sthl. 123 J2
Navy St. SW4 150 D3
Naylor Gro., Enf. 45 G5
South St.
Naylor Rd. N20 57 F2
Naylor Rd. SE15 132 E7
Nazareth Gdns. SE15 152 E2
Nazrul St. E2 13 F3
Nazrul St. E2 112 C3
Neagle Cl., Borwd. 38 C1
Balcon Way
Neal Av., Sthl. 103 F4
Neal Cl., Nthwd. 66 A1
Neal St. WC2 18 A4
Neal St. WC2 110 E6
Nealden St. SW9 151 F3
Neale Cl. N2 73 F3
Neal's Yd. WC2 18 A4
Near Acre NW9 71 F1
Neasden Cl. NW10 89 E5
Neasden La. NW10 89 E4
Neasden La. N. NW10 88 D3
Neasham Rd., Dag. 100 B5
Neate St. SE5 37 F5
Neate St. SE5 132 C6
Neath Gdns., Mord. 185 F6
Neathouse Pl. SW1 33 F1
Neatscourt Rd. E6 116 A5
Nebraska St. SE1 28 B4
Nebraska St. SE1 132 A2
Neckinger SE16 29 G5
Neckinger SE16 132 C3
Neckinger Est. SE16 29 G5
Neckinger Est. SE16 132 C3
Neckinger St. SE1 29 G4
Neckinger St. SE1 132 C2
Nectarine Way SE13 154 B2
Needham Rd. W11 108 D6
Westbourne Gro.
Needham Ter. NW2 90 A3
Needleman St. SE16 133 G2
Neeld Cres. NW4 71 H5
Neeld Cres., Wem. 88 A5
Neeld Par., Wem. 88 A5
Harrow Rd.
Neil Wates Cres. SW2 169 G1
Nelgarde Rd. SE6 154 A7
Nella Rd. W6 128 A6
Nelldale Rd. SE16 133 F4
Nello James Gdns. SE27 170 A4
Nelson Cl., Croy. 201 H1
Nelson Cl., Rom. 83 H1
Nelson Ct. SE16 133 F1
Brunel Rd.
Nelson Gdns. E2 13 J3
Nelson Gdns. E2 112 D3
Nelson Gdns., Houns. 143 G6
Nelson Gro. Rd. SW19 185 E1
Nelson Mandela Cl. N10 74 A2
Nelson Mandela Rd. SE3 155 J3
Nelson Pas. EC1 12 A4
Nelson Pl. N1 11 H2
Nelson Pl. N1 111 H2
Nelson Pl., Sid. 176 A4
Nelson Rd. E4 62 B6
Nelson Rd. E11 79 G4
Nelson Rd. N8 75 F5
Nelson Rd. N9 61 E2
Nelson Rd. N15 76 B4
Nelson Rd. SE10 134 C6
Nelson Rd. SW19 167 E7
Nelson Rd., Belv. 139 F5
Nelson Rd., Brom. 191 J4
Nelson Rd., Enf. 45 G6
Nelson Rd., Har. 86 A1
Nelson Rd., Houns. 143 J7
Nelson Rd. (Heathrow Airport), Houns. 140 C1
Nelson Rd., N.Mal. 182 D5
Nelson Rd., Sid. 176 A4
Nelson Rd., Stan. 53 F6
Nelson Rd., Twick. 143 J6
Nelson Sq. SE1 27 G3
Nelson Sq. SE1 131 H2
Nelson St. E1 112 E6
Nelson St. E6 116 C2
Nelson St. E16 115 F7
Huntingdon St.
Nelson Ter. N1 11 H2
Nelson Ter. N1 111 H2
Nelson Trd. Est. SW19 184 E1
Nelson Wk. SE16 133 H1
Rotherhithe St.
Nelson's Row SW4 150 D4
Nelsons Yd. NW1 9 F1
Nemoure Rd. W3 106 C7
Nene Gdns., Felt. 161 F2
Nene Rd., Houns. 141 E1
Nepaul Rd. SW11 149 H2
Nepean St. SW15 147 G6
Neptune Rd., Har. 68 A6
Neptune Rd. (Heathrow Airport), Houns. 141 G1
Neptune St. SE16 133 F3
Nesbit Rd. SE9 156 A4
Nesbitt Cl. SE3 154/155 E3
Hurren Cl.
Nesbitt Sq. SE19 170 B7
Coxwell Rd.
Nesbitts All., Barn. 40 C3
Bath Pl.
Nesham St. E1 29 H1
Nesham St. E1 132 D1
Ness St. SE16 29 H5
Nesta Rd., Wdf.Grn. 63 E6
Nestles Av., Hayes 121 J3
Nestor Av. N21 43 H6
Nether Cl. N3 56 D7
Nether St. N3 72 D1
Nether St. N12 56 D7
Netheravon Rd. W4 127 F4
Netheravon Rd. W7 124 C1
Netheravon Rd. S. W4 127 F5
Netherbury Rd. W5 125 G3
Netherby Gdns., Enf. 42 E4
Netherby Rd. SE23 153 F7
Nethercourt Av. N3 56 D6
Netherfield Gdns., Bark. 99 G6
Netherfield Rd. N12 57 E5
Netherfield Rd. SW17 168 A3
Netherford Rd. SW4 150 C2
Netherhall Gdns. NW3 91 F6
Netherhall Way NW3 91 F5
Netherhall Gdns.
Netherlands Rd., Barn. 41 G6
Netherleigh Cl. N6 92 B1
Netherton Gro. SW10 30 D6
Netherton Gro. SW10 129 F6
Netherton Rd. N15 76 A6
Netherton Rd., Twick. 144 E5
Netherwood N2 73 G2
Netherwood Pl. W14 128 A3
Netherwood Rd.
Netherwood Rd. W14 128 A3
Netherwood St. NW6 90 C7
Netley Cl., Croy. 204 C7
Netley Cl., Sutt. 198 A5
Netley Dr., Walt. 179 F7
Netley Gdns., Mord. 185 F7
Netley Rd. E17 77 J5
Netley Rd., Brent. 125 H6
Netley Rd. (Heathrow Airport), Houns. 141 G1
Netley Rd., Ilf. 81 G5
Netley Rd., Mord. 185 F7
Netley St. NW1 9 F4
Nettleden Av., Wem. 88 A6
Nettlefold Pl. SE27 169 H3
Nettlestead Cl., Beck. 171 J7
Copers Cope Rd.
Nettleton Rd. SE14 153 G1
Nettleton Rd., Houns. 141 E1
Nettlewood Rd. SW16 168 D7
Neuchatel Rd. SE6 171 J2
Nevada Cl., N.Mal. 182 C4
Georgia Rd.
Nevada St. SE10 134 C6
Nevern Pl. SW5 128 D4
Nevern Rd. SW5 128 D4
Nevern Sq. SW5 128 D5
Nevill Rd. N16 94 B4
Nevill Way, Loug. 48 B7
Valley Hill
Neville Av., N.Mal. 182 D1
Neville Cl. E11 97 F3
Neville Cl. NW1 9 J2
Neville Cl. NW6 108 C2
Neville Cl. SE15 132 D7
Neville Cl. W3 126 C2
Acton La.
Neville Cl., Houns. 143 H2
Neville Cl., Sid. 175 J4
Neville Dr. N2 73 F6
Neville Gdns., Dag. 100 D3
Neville Gill Cl. SW18 148 D6
Neville Pl. N22 75 F1
Neville Rd. E7 97 G7
Neville Rd. NW6 108 C2
Neville Rd. W5 105 G4
Neville Rd., Croy. 188 A7
Neville Rd., Dag. 100 D2
Neville Rd., Ilf. 81 F1
Neville Rd., Kings.T. 182 A2
Neville Rd., Rich. 163 F3
Neville St. SW7 31 E3
Neville St. SW7 129 G5
Neville Ter. SW7 31 E3
Neville Ter. SW7 129 G5
Neville Wk., Cars. 185 H7
Green Wrythe La.
Nevilles Ct. NW2 89 G3
Nevin Dr. E4 62 B1
Nevinson Cl. SW18 149 G6
Nevis Rd. SW17 168 A2
New Ash Cl. N2 73 G3
Oakridge Dr.
New Barn St. E13 115 G4
New Barns Av., Mitch. 186 D4
New Barns Way, Chig. 64 E3
New Bond St. W1 17 E5
New Bond St. W1 110 B7
New Brent St. NW4 71 J5
New Br. St. EC4 19 G4
New Br. St. EC4 111 H6
New Broad St. EC2 20 D2
New Broad St. EC2 112 B5
New Bdy. W5 105 G7
New Bdy., Hmptn. 162 A5
Hampton Rd.
New Burlington Ms. W1 17 F5
New Burlington Pl. W1 17 F5
New Burlington St. W1 17 F5
New Burlington St. W1 110 C7
New Butt La. SE8 134 A7
New Butt La. N. SE8 134 A7
Reginald Rd.
New Cavendish St. W1 17 E1
New Cavendish St. W1 110 A5
New Change EC4 19 J4
New Change EC4 111 J6
New Chapel Sq., Felt. 160 B1
New Charles St. EC1 11 H3
New Ch. Rd. SE5 36 A7
New Ch. Rd. SE5 131 J7
New City Rd. E13 115 J3
New Cl. SW19 185 F3
New Cl., Felt. 160 E5
New College Ct. NW3 91 F7
College Cres.
New College Ms. N1 93 G7
Islington Pk. St.
New College Par. NW3 91 G6
College Cres.
New Compton St. WC2 17 J4
New Compton St. WC2 110 D6
New Ct. EC4 18 E5
New Covent Gdn. Mkt. SW8 130 D7
New Coventry St. W1 17 J6
New Crane Pl. E1 133 F1
Garnet St.
New Cross Rd. SE14 133 F7
New End NW3 91 F4
New End Sq. NW3 91 G4
New Era Est. N1 112 B1
Phillipp St.
New Fm. Av., Brom. 191 G4
New Ferry App. SE18 136 D3
New Fetter La. EC4 19 F3
New Fetter La. EC4 111 G6
New Forest La., Chig. 64 D6
New Gdn. Dr., West Dr. 120 B2
Drayton Gdns.
New Globe Wk. SE1 27 J1
New Globe Wk. SE1 131 J1
New Goulston St. E1 21 F3
New Grn. Pl. SE19 170 B6
Hawke Rd.
New Heston Rd., Houns. 123 F7
New Horizons Ct., Brent. 124 D6
Shield Dr.
New Inn Bdy. EC2 12 E5
New Inn Pas. WC2 18 D4
New Inn St. EC2 12 E5
New Inn Yd. EC2 12 E5
New Inn Yd. EC2 112 B4
New James Ct. SE15 152/153 E3
Nunhead La.
New Kent Rd. SE1 27 J6
New Kent Rd. SE1 131 J3
New King St. SE8 134 A6
New Kings Rd. SW6 148 C2
New London St. EC3 21 E5
New Lydenburg St. SE7 135 J3
New Mt. St. E15 96 D7
Bridge Rd.
New N. Pl. EC2 12 D6
New N. Rd. N1 12 C2
New N. Rd. N1 112 A2
New N. Rd., Ilf. 65 G7
New N. St. WC1 18 C1
New N. St. WC1 111 F5
New Oak Rd. N2 73 F2
New Orleans Wk. N19 74 D7
New Oxford St. WC1 17 J3
New Oxford St. WC1 110 D6
New Pk. Av. N13 59 J3
New Pk. Cl., Nthlt. 84 E6
New Pk. Ct. SW2 151 E7
New Pk. Par. SW2 150/151 E6
Doverfield Rd.
New Pk. Rd. SW2 168 D1
New Pl. Sq. SE16 132 E3
New Plaistow Rd. E15 115 E1
New Printing Ho. Sq. WC1 111 F4
Gray's Inn Rd.
New Priory Ct. NW6 90 D7
Mazenod Av.
New Quebec St. W1 16 A4
New Quebec St. W1 109 J6
New Ride SW7 23 J3
New Ride SW7 129 H2
New River Cres. N13 59 H4
New River Wk. N1 93 J6
New River Way N4 76 A7
New Rd. E1 112 E5
New Rd. E4 62 B4
New Rd. N8 74 E5
New Rd. N9 60 D3
New Rd. N17 76 C1
New Rd. N22 75 J1
New Rd. NW7 56 B7
New Rd. (Barnet Gate) NW7 39 F7
New Rd. SE2 138 D4
New Rd., Brent. 125 G6
New Rd., Dag. 119 G1
New Rd., Felt. 141 G6
New Rd. (East Bedfont), Felt. 160 B1
New Rd. (Hanworth), Felt. 160 E5
New Rd., Har. 86 C4
New Rd., Hayes 121 F7
New Rd., Houns. 143 H4
Station Rd.
New Rd., Ilf. 99 H2
New Rd., Kings.T. 164 A7

Norbury Ct. Rd. SW16	186	E2
Norbury Cres. SW16	187	F1
Norbury Cross SW16	186	E3
Norbury Gdns., Rom.	82	D5
Norbury Gro. NW7	54	E3
Norbury Hill SW16	169	G7
Norbury Ri. SW16	186	E3
Norbury Rd. E4	62	A5
Norbury Rd., Th.Hth.	187	J2
Norcombe Gdns., Har.	69	F6
Norcott Cl., Hayes	102	C4
Willow Tree La.		
Norcott Rd. N16	94	D2
Norcroft Gdns. SE22	152	D7
Norcutt Rd., Twick.	162	B1
Norfield Rd., Dart.	177	J4
Norfolk Av. N13	59	H6
Norfolk Av. N15	76	C6
Norfolk Cl. N2	73	H3
Park Rd.		
Norfolk Cl. N13	59	H6
Norfolk Cl., Barn.	42	A4
Norfolk Cl., Twick.	144/145	E6
Cassilis Rd.		
Norfolk Cres. W2	**15**	**H3**
Norfolk Cres. W2	109	H6
Norfolk Cres., Sid.	157	H7
Norfolk Gdns., Bexh.	159	F1
Norfolk Gdns., Borwd.	38	D4
Norfolk Ho. SE3	135	E6
Norfolk Ho. Rd. SW16	168	D3
Norfolk Ms. W10	108	C5
Blagrove Rd.		
Norfolk Pl. W2	**15**	**F3**
Norfolk Pl. W2	109	G6
Norfolk Pl., Well.	158	A2
Norfolk Rd. E6	116	C1
Norfolk Rd. E17	77	G2
Norfolk Rd. NW8	109	G1
Norfolk Rd. NW10	88	E7
Norfolk Rd. SW19	167	H7
Norfolk Rd., Bark.	99	H7
Norfolk Rd., Barn.	40	D3
Norfolk Rd., Dag.	101	H5
Norfolk Rd., Enf.	45	E6
Norfolk Rd., Esher	194	B5
Norfolk Rd., Felt.	160	C1
Norfolk Rd., Har.	67	H5
Norfolk Rd., Ilf.	99	H1
Norfolk Rd., Rom.	83	J6
Norfolk Rd., Th.Hth.	187	J3
Norfolk Row SE1	**34**	**C1**
Norfolk Sq. W2	**15**	**F4**
Norfolk Sq. W2	109	G6
Norfolk Sq. Ms. W2	**15**	**F4**
Norfolk St. E7	97	G4
Norfolk Ter. W6	128	B5
Field Rd.		
Norgrove St. SW12	150	A7
Norhyrst Av. SE25	188	C3
Norland Pl. W11	128	B1
Norland Rd. W11	128	A1
Norland Sq. W11	128	B1
Norlands Cres., Chis.	192	E1
Norlands Gate, Chis.	193	E1
Norley Vale SW15	165	G1
Norlington Rd. E10	96	C1
Norlington Rd. E11	96	C1
Norman Av. N22	75	H1
Norman Av., Felt.	161	E2
Norman Av., Sthl.	103	E7
Norman Av., Twick.	145	E7
Norman Cl., Orp.	207	F3
Norman Cl., Rom.	83	H2
Norman Ct., Ilf.	81	G7
Norman Cres., Houns.	142	D1
Norman Cres., Pnr.	66	C1
Norman Gro. E3	113	H2
Norman Rd. E6	116	C4
Norman Rd. E11	96	D2
Norman Rd. N15	76	C5
Norman Rd. SE10	134	B7
Norman Rd. SW19	167	F7
Norman Rd., Belv.	139	H3
Norman Rd., Ilf.	99	E5
Norman Rd., Sutt.	198	D5
Norman Rd., Th.Hth.	187	H5
Norman St. EC1	**11**	**J4**
Norman Way N14	58	E2
Norman Way W3	106	B5
Normanby Cl. SW15	148	C5
Manfred Rd.		
Normanby Rd. NW10	89	F4
Normand Gdns. W14	128	B6
Greyhound Rd.		
Normand Ms. W14	128	B6
Normand Rd.		
Normand Rd. W14	128	C6
Normandy Av., Barn.	40	C5
Normandy Rd. SW9	151	G1
Normandy Ter. E16	115	H6
Normanhurst Av., Bexh.	158	D1
Normanhurst Dr., Twick.	144/145	E5
St. Margarets Rd.		
Normanhurst Rd. SW2	169	F2
Norman's Bldgs. EC1	111	J3
Ironmonger Row		
Normans Cl. NW10	88	D6
Normans Mead NW10	88	D6
Normansfield Av., Tedd.	163	F7
Normanshire Av. E4	62	C4
Normanshire Dr. E4	62	A4
Normanton Av. SW19	166	D2
Normanton Pk. E4	62	E3
Normanton Rd., S.Croy.	202	B6
Normanton St. SE23	171	G2
Normington Cl. SW16	169	G5
Norrice Lea N2	73	G5
Norris St. SW1	**17**	**H6**
Norroy Rd. SW15	148	A4
Norrys Cl., Barn.	41	J5
Norrys Rd., Barn.	41	J4
Norseman Cl., Ilf.	100	B1
Norseman Way, Grnf.	103	H1
Olympic Way		
Norstead Pl. SW15	165	G2
North Access Rd. E17	77	G6
North Acre NW9	71	E1
North Acton Rd. NW10	106	D2
North Audley St. W1	**16**	**B4**
North Audley St. W1	110	A6
North Av. N18	60	D4
North Av. W13	104	E6
North Av., Cars.	199	J7
North Av., Har.	67	H6
North Av., Hayes	102	A7
North Av., Rich.	146	A1
Sandycombe Rd.		
North Av., Sthl.	103	F7
North Bank NW8	**7**	**G4**
North Bank NW8	109	H3
North Birkbeck Rd. E11	96	D3
North Branch Av. W10	107	J3
Harrow Rd.		
North Carriage Dr. W2	**15**	**G5**
North Carriage Dr. W2	109	G7
North Circular Rd. E4	61	J7
North Circular Rd. E18	79	J2
North Circular Rd. N3	72	E3
North Circular Rd. N12	73	G1
North Circular Rd. N13	59	G5
North Circular Rd. NW2	88	E3
North Circular Rd. NW10	88	C7
North Circular Rd. NW11	72	B4
North Cl., Barn.	39	J5
North Cl., Bexh.	158	D4
North Cl., Dag.	119	G1
North Cl., Felt.	141	G6
North Rd.		
North Colonnade E14	134	A1
North Common Rd. W5	105	H7
North Countess Rd. E17	77	J1
North Ct. W1	**17**	**G1**
North Cray Rd., Bex.	177	F3
North Cray Rd., Sid.	176	E6
North Cres. E16	114	D4
North Cres. N3	72	C2
North Cres. WC1	**17**	**H1**
North Cres. WC1	110	D5
North Cross Rd. SE22	152	C5
North Cross Rd., Ilf.	81	F4
North Dene NW7	54	D3
North Dene, Houns.	143	H1
North Dr. SW16	168	C4
North Dr., Houns.	143	J2
North Dr., Orp.	207	H4
North End NW3	91	F2
North End, Buck.H.	47	J7
North End, Croy.	201	J2
North End Av. NW3	91	F2
North End Cres. W14	128	C4
North End Ho. W14	128	B4
North End Par. W14	128	B4
North End Rd.		
North End Rd. NW11	90	D1
North End Rd. NW8	128	C6
North End Rd. W14	128	B4
North End Rd., Wem.	88	A3
North End Way NW3	91	F2
North Eyot Gdns. W6	127	F5
St. Peter's Sq.		
North Flockton St. SE16	**29**	**H3**
North Gdn. E14	133	J1
Westferry Circ.		
North Gdns. SW19	167	G7
North Glade, The, Bex.	159	F7
North Gower St. NW1	**9**	**G4**
North Gower St. NW1	110	C3
North Grn. NW9	54/55	E7
Clayton Fld.		
North Gro. N6	74	A7
North Gro. N15	76	A5
North Hatton Rd.	141	G1
(Heathrow Airport), Houns.		
North Hill N6	73	J6
North Hill Av. N6	74	A6
North Hyde Gdns.	122	A4
Hayes		
North Hyde La., Houns.	123	E5
North Hyde La., Sthl.	123	E5
North Hyde Rd., Hayes	121	J3
North La., Tedd.	162	C6
North Lo. Cl. SW15	148	A5
Westleigh Av.		
North Mall N9	60/61	E2
St. Martins Rd.		
North Ms. WC1	**10**	**D6**
North Ms. WC1	111	F4
North Par., Chess.	195	H5
North Pk. SE9	156	C6
North Pas. SW18	148	D4
North Peckham Est. SE15	**37**	**E7**
North Peckham Est. SE15	132	C7
North Pl., Mitch.	167	J7
North Pl., Tedd.	162	C6
North Pole La., Kes.	205	F6
North Pole Rd. W10	107	J5
North Ride W2	**15**	**G6**
North Ride W2	109	H7
North Rd. N6	74	A7
North Rd. N7	92	E6
North Rd. N9	60	E1
North Rd. SE18	137	H4
North Rd. SW19	167	F6
North Rd. W5	125	G3
North Rd., Belv.	139	H3
North Rd., Brent.	125	H6
North Rd., Brom.	191	H1
North Rd., Edg.	70	B1
North Rd., Felt.	141	G6
North Rd., Ilf.	99	H2
North Rd., Rich.	146	A3
North Rd., Rom.	82	E5
North Rd., Sthl.	103	G7
North Rd., Surb.	181	G6
North Rd., West Dr.	120	C3
North Rd., W.Wick.	204	B1
North Row W1	**16**	**A5**
North Row W1	109	J7
North Several SE3	154	D2
Orchard Dr.		
North Side	149	G5
Wandsworth Common SW18		
North Sq. N9	60/61	E2
St. Martins Rd.		
North Sq. NW11	72	D5
North St. E13	115	H2
North St. NW4	71	J5
North St. SW4	150	C3
North St., Bark.	99	E6
North St., Bexh.	159	G4
North St., Brom.	191	G1
North St., Cars.	199	J3
North St., Islw.	144	D3
North St. Pas. E13	115	H2
North Tenter St. E1	**21**	**G4**
North Tenter St. E1	112	C6
North Ter. SW3	**23**	**G6**
North Ter. SW3	129	H3
North Verbena Gdns. W6	127	G5
St. Peter's Sq.		
North Vw. SW19	165	H5
North Vw. W5	105	F4
North Vw., Pnr.	66	C7
North Vw. Dr., Wdf.Grn.	80	A2
North Vw. Rd. N8	74	D3
North Vil. NW1	92	D6
North Wk. W2	**14**	**C6**
North Wk., Croy.	204	B5
North Way N9	61	F2
North Way N11	58	C6
North Way NW9	70	B3
North Way, Pnr.	66	C3
North Wf. Rd. W2	**14**	**E2**
North Wf. Rd. W2	109	G5
North Woolwich Rd. E16	135	G1
North Woolwich Roundabout E16	136	A1
North Woolwich Rd.		
North Worple Way SW14	146	D3
Northall Rd., Bexh.	159	J2
Northampton Gro. N1	94	A5
Northampton Pk. N1	93	J6
Northampton Rd. EC1	**11**	**F5**
Northampton Rd. EC1	111	G4
Northampton Rd., Croy.	202	D2
Northampton Rd., Enf.	45	H4
Northampton Sq. EC1	**11**	**G4**
Northampton Sq. EC1	111	H3
Northampton St. N1	93	J7
Northanger Rd. SW16	168	E6
Northbank Rd. E17	78	C2
Northborough Rd. SW16	186	D3
Northbourne, Brom.	191	G7
Northbourne Rd. SW4	150	D4
Northbrook Rd. N22	59	E7
Northbrook Rd. SE13	154	D5
Northbrook Rd., Barn.	40	B5
Northbrook Rd., Croy.	188	A5
Northburgh St. EC1	**11**	**H5**
Northburgh St. EC1	111	H4
Northchurch SE17	**36**	**C3**
Northchurch Rd. N1	94	A7
Northchurch Rd., Wem.	87	J6
Northchurch Ter. N1	94	B7
Northcliffe Cl., Wor.Pk.	197	E3
Northcliffe Dr. N20	56	C1
Northcote, Pnr.	66	C2
Northcote Av. W5	105	H7
Northcote Av., Islw.	144	D5
Northcote Av., Sthl.	103	E7
Northcote Av., Surb.	182	A7
Northcote Rd. E17	77	H4
Northcote Rd. NW10	89	E7
Northcote Rd. SW11	149	H4
Northcote Rd., Croy.	188	A6
Northcote Rd., N.Mal.	182	C4
Northcote Rd., Sid.	175	H4
Northcote Rd., Twick.	144	D5
Northcott Av. N22	75	E1
Northcroft Rd. W13	124	E2
Northcroft Rd., Epsom	196	D7
Northcroft Ter. W13	124/125	E2
Northcroft Rd.		
Northdene, Chig.	65	G5
Northdene Gdns. N15	76	C6
Northdown Gdns., Ilf.	81	H5
Northdown Rd., Well.	158	B2
Northdown St. N1	**10**	**B1**
Northdown St. N1	111	F2
Northern Av. N9	60	C2
Northern Perimeter Rd., Houns.	141	F1
Northern Perimeter Rd. W., Houns.	140	A1
Northern Relief Rd., Bark.	99	E7
Northern Rd. E13	115	H1
Northern Service Rd., Barn.	40	B3
Northernhay Wk., Mord.	184	B4
Northey St. E14	113	H7
Northfield, Loug.	48	A4
Northfield Av. W5	125	E2
Northfield Av. W13	125	E2
Northfield Av., Pnr.	66	D4
Northfield Cl., Brom.	192	B1
Northfield Cl., Hayes	121	J3
Northfield Cres., Sutt.	198	B4

Name	Page	Grid
Northfield Gdns., Dag.	101	F4
Northfield Rd.		
Northfield Pk., Hayes	121	J3
Northfield Path, Dag.	101	F4
Northfield Rd. E6	98	C7
Northfield Rd. N16	76	B7
Northfield Rd. W13	124	E2
Northfield Rd., Barn.	41	H3
Northfield Rd., Borwd.	38	B1
Northfield Rd., Dag.	101	F4
Northfield Rd., Enf.	45	E5
Northfield Rd., Houns.	122	D6
Northfields SW18	148	D4
Northfields Ind. Est., Wem.	106	A1
Northfields Rd. W3	106	B5
Northgate Dr. NW9	70	E6
Northiam N12	56	D3
Northiam St. E9	113	E1
Northington St. WC1	**10**	**D6**
Northington St. WC1	111	F4
Northlands Av., Orp.	207	H4
Northlands St. SE5	151	J2
Northolm, Edg.	54	D4
Northolme Gdns., Edg.	70	A1
Northolme Ri., Orp.	207	H2
Northolme Rd. N5	93	J4
Northolt Av., Ruis.	84	B5
Northolt Gdns., Grnf.	86	C5
Northolt Rd., Har.	85	H4
Northolt Rd., Houns.	140	A1
Northover, Brom.	173	F3
Northport St. N1	112	A1
Northrop Rd., Houns.	141	H1
Northside Rd., Brom.	191	G1
Mitchell Way		
Northspur Rd., Sutt.	198	D3
Northstead Rd. SW2	169	G2
Northumberland All. EC3	**21**	**E4**
Northumberland All. EC3	112	B6
Northumberland Av. E12	97	J1
Northumberland Av. WC2	**26**	**A1**
Northumberland Av. WC2	130	E1
Northumberland Av., Enf.	45	E1
Northumberland Av., Islw.	144	C1
Northumberland Av., Well.	157	H4
Northumberland Cl., Erith	139	J7
Northumberland Cl., Stai.	140	B6
Northumberland Cres., Felt.	141	H6
Northumberland Gdns. N9	60	C3
Northumberland Gdns., Brom.	192	D4
Northumberland Gdns., Islw.	124	D7
Northumberland Gdns., Mitch.	186	D5
Northumberland Gro. N17	60	E7
Northumberland Pk. N17	60	C7
Northumberland Pk., Erith	139	J7
Northumberland Pl. W2	108	D6
Northumberland Pl., Rich.	145	G5
Northumberland Rd. E6	116	B6
Northumberland Rd. E17	78	A7
Northumberland Rd., Barn.	41	F6
Northumberland Rd., Har.	67	F5
Northumberland Row, Twick.	162	B1
Colne Rd.		
Northumberland St. WC2	**26**	**A1**
Northumberland St. WC2	130	E1
Northumberland Way, Erith	159	J1
Northumbria St. E14	114	A6
Northview Cres. NW10	89	F4
Northway NW11	72	E5
Northway, Mord.	184	B3
Northway, Wall.	200	C4
Northway Circ. NW7	54	D4
Northway Cres. NW7	54	D4
Northway Rd. SE5	151	J3
Northway Rd., Croy.	188	C6
Northways Par. NW3	91	G7
College Cres.		
Northweald La., Kings.T.	163	G5
Northwest Pl. N1	**11**	**F1**
Northwick Av., Har.	68	D6
Northwick Circle, Har.	69	F6
Northwick Cl. NW8	**7**	**E5**
Northwick Pk. Rd., Har.	68	C6
Northwick Rd., Wat.	50	C4
Northwick Rd., Wem.	105	G1
Northwick Ter. NW8	**6**	**E5**
Northwick Ter. NW8	109	G4
Northwick Wk., Har.	68	C7
Northwold Dr., Pnr.	66	C3
Cuckoo Hill		
Northwold Est. E5	94	D2
Northwold Rd. E5	94	C2
Northwold Rd. N16	94	C2
Northwood Gdns. N12	57	G5
Northwood Gdns., Grnf.	86	C5
Northwood Gdns., Ilf.	80	D4
Northwood Hall N6	74	C7
Northwood Ho. SE27	170	A4
Northwood Pl., Erith	139	F3
Northwood Rd. N6	74	B7
Northwood Rd. SE23	171	J1
Northwood Rd., Cars.	200	A6
Northwood Rd., Houns.	140	A1
Northwood Rd., Th.Hth.	187	H2
Northwood Way SE19	170	A6
Roman Ri.		
Northwood Way, Nthwd.	50	A7
Norton Av., Surb.	182	B7
Norton Cl. E4	62	A5
Norton Cl., Borwd.	38	A1
Norton Cl., Enf.	44/45	E2
Brick La.		
Norton Folgate E1	**21**	**E1**
Norton Folgate E1	112	B5
Norton Gdns. SW16	186	E2
Norton Rd. E10	95	J1
Norton Rd., Wem.	87	G6
Norval Rd., Wem.	86	E2
Norway Gate SE16	133	H3
East India Dock Rd.		
Norway Pl. E14	113	J6
Norway St. SE10	134	B6
Norwich Ho. E14	114	B6
Cordelia St.		
Norwich Ms., Ilf.	100	A1
Ashgrove Rd.		
Norwich Pl., Bexh.	159	G4
Norwich Rd. E7	97	G5
Norwich Rd., Dag.	119	G2
Norwich Rd., Grnf.	103	H1
Norwich Rd., Th.Hth.	187	J3
Norwich St. EC4	**19**	**E3**
Norwich St. EC4	111	G6
Norwich Wk., Edg.	54	C7
Norwood Av., Wem.	105	J1
Norwood Cl., Sthl.	123	G4
Norwood Cl., Twick.	162	A2
Fourth Cross Rd.		
Norwood Cres., Houns.	141	F1
Norwood Dr., Har.	67	F6
Norwood Gdns., Hayes	102	C4
Norwood Gdns., Sthl.	123	F4
Norwood Grn. Rd., Sthl.	123	G4
Norwood High St. SE27	169	H3
Norwood Pk. Rd. SE27	169	J5
Norwood Rd. SE24	169	H1
Norwood Rd. SE27	169	H2
Norwood Rd., Sthl.	123	F4
Norwood Ter., Sthl.	123	H4
Tentelow La.		
Nota Ms. N3	72	D1
Station Rd.		
Notley St. SE5	**36**	**B7**
Notley St. SE5	132	A7
Notre Dame Est. SW4	150	C4
Notson Rd. SE25	188	E4
Notting Barn Rd. W10	108	A4
Notting Hill Gate W11	128	D1
Nottingdale Sq. W11	128	B1
Wilsham St.		
Nottingham Av. E16	115	J5
Nottingham Ct. WC2	**18**	**A4**
Nottingham Pl. W1	**8**	**B6**
Nottingham Pl. W1	110	A4
Nottingham Rd. E10	78	C6
Nottingham Rd. SW17	167	J1
Nottingham Rd., Islw.	144	C2
Nottingham Rd., S.Croy.	201	J4
Nottingham St. W1	**16**	**B1**
Nottingham St. W1	110	A5
Nottingham Ter. NW1	**8**	**B6**
Nova Ms., Sutt.	198	B1
Nova Rd., Croy.	187	H7
Novar Cl., Orp.	193	J7
Novar Rd. SE9	175	F1
Novello St. SW6	148	D1
Novello Way, Borwd.	38	D1
Nowell Rd. SW13	127	G6
Nower Hill, Pnr.	67	F4
Noyna Rd. SW17	167	J3
Nuding Cl. SE13	154	A3
Nugent Rd. N19	93	E1
Nugent Rd. SE25	188	C3
Nugent Ter. NW8	**6**	**D2**
Nugent Ter. NW8	109	F2
Nugents Ct., Pnr.	66/67	E1
St. Thomas' Dr.		
Nugents Pk., Pnr.	67	E1
Nun Ct. EC2	**20**	**B3**
Nuneaton Rd., Dag.	100	D7
Nunhead Cres. SE15	152	E3
Nunhead Est. SE15	152	E3
Nunhead Grn. SE15	153	E3
Nunhead Gro. SE15	153	E3
Nunhead La. SE15	152	E3
Nunhead Pas. SE15	152	D3
Peckham Rye		
Nunnington Cl. SE9	174	B3
Nunns Rd., Enf.	43	J2
Nupton Dr., Barn.	39	J6
Nursery Av. N3	73	F2
Nursery Av., Bexh.	159	F3
Nursery Av., Croy.	203	G2
Nursery Cl. SE4	153	J2
Nursery Cl. SW15	148	A4
Nursery Cl., Croy.	203	G2
Nursery Cl., Enf.	45	G1
Nursery Cl., Felt.	142	B7
Nursery Cl., Rom.	82	D6
Nursery Cl., Wdf.Grn.	63	H5
Nursery Cl. N17	60	C7
Nursery St.		
Nursery Gdns., Chis.	174	E6
Nursery Gdns., Enf.	45	G1
Nursery Gdns., Houns.	143	F5
Nursery La. E2	112	C1
Nursery La. E7	97	G6
Nursery La. W10	107	J5
Nursery Rd. E9	95	F6
Morning La.		
Nursery Rd. N2	73	G1
Nursery Rd. N14	42	C7
Nursery Rd. SW9	151	F4
Nursery Rd., Loug.	47	J5
Nursery Rd. (High Beach), Loug.	47	H1
Nursery Rd., Pnr.	66	C3
Nursery Rd., Sutt.	199	F4
Nursery Rd., Th.Hth.	188	A4
Nursery Rd. Merton SW19	185	E2
Nursery Rd., Mitch.	185	H3
Nursery Rd. Wimbledon SW19	166	B7
Worple Rd.		
Nursery Row SE17	**36**	**B2**
Nursery Row SE17	132	A4
Nursery Row, Barn.	40	B3
St. Albans Rd.		
Nursery St. N17	60	C7
Nursery Wk. NW4	71	H3
Nurserymans Rd. N11	58	A2
Nurstead Rd., Erith	139	G7
Nutbourne St. W10	108	B3
Nutbrook St. SE15	152	D3
Nutbrowne Rd., Dag.	119	F1
Nutcroft Rd. SE15	132	E7
Nutfield Cl. N18	60	D6
Nutfield Cl., Cars.	199	H3
Nutfield Gdns., Ilf.	99	J2
Nutfield Gdns., Nthlt.	102	C2
Nutfield Rd. E15	96	C4
Nutfield Rd. NW2	89	G2
Nutfield Rd. SE22	152	C5
Nutfield Rd., Th.Hth.	187	H4
Nutfield Way, Orp.	206	D2
Nutford Pl. W1	**15**	**H3**
Nutford Pl. W1	109	H6
Nuthatch Gdns. SE28	137	G2
Nuthurst Av. SW2	169	F2
Nutley Ter. NW3	91	F6
Nutmead Cl., Bex.	177	J1
Nutmeg Cl. E16	114/115	E4
Cranberry La.		
Nutmeg La. E14	114	D6
Nutt Gro., Edg.	53	G2
Nutt St. SE15	**37**	**G7**
Nutt St. SE15	132	C7
Nuttall St. N1	**12**	**E1**
Nuttall St. N1	112	B2
Nutter La. E11	79	J6
Nutwell St. SW17	167	H5
Nuxley Rd., Belv.	139	F6
Nyanza St. SE18	137	G6
Nye Bevan Est. E5	95	G3
Nylands Av., Rich.	146	A1
Nymans Gdns. SW20	183	H3
Hidcote Gdns.		
Nynehead St. SE14	133	H7
Nyon Gro. SE6	171	J2
Nyssa Cl., Wdf.Grn.	64	C6
Gwynne Pk. Av.		
Nyton Cl. N19	92/93	E1
Courtauld Rd.		

O

Name	Page	Grid
Oak Apple Ct. SE12	173	G2
Oak Av. N8	74	E4
Oak Av. N10	58	B7
Oak Av. N17	60	A7
Oak Av., Croy.	204	A2
Oak Av., Hmptn.	161	E5
Oak Av., Houns.	122	D7
Oak Av., West Dr.	120	D3
Oak Bank, Croy.	204	C6
Oak Cl. N14	42	B7
Oak Cl., Sutt.	199	F2
Oak Cottage Cl. SE6	173	F1
Oak Cres. E16	115	E5
Oak Dene W13	104/105	E5
The Dene		
Oak Fm., Borwd.	38	C5
Oak Gdns., Croy.	204	A2
Oak Gdns., Edg.	70	C2
Oak Gro. NW2	90	B4
Oak Gro., Ruis.	84	B1
Oak Gro., Sun.	160	B7
Oak Gro., W.Wick.	204	C2
Oak Gro. Rd. SE20	189	F1
Oak Hall Rd. E11	79	H6
Oak Hill, Surb.	181	H7
Oak Hill, Wdf.Grn.	62	D7
Oak Hill Cl., Wdf.Grn.	62	D7
Oak Hill Cres., Surb.	181	H7
Oak Hill Cres., Wdf.Grn.	62	D7
Oak Hill Gdns., Wdf.Grn.	79	E1
Oak Hill Pk. NW3	91	E4
Oak Hill Pk. Ms. NW3	91	F4
Oak Hill Rd., Surb.	181	H6
Oak Hill Way NW3	91	F4
Oak La. E14	113	J7
Oak La. N2	73	G2
Oak La. N11	58	D6
Oak La., Islw.	144	B4
Oak La., Twick.	144	D7
Oak La., Wdf.Grn.	63	G5
Oak Lo. Av., Chig.	65	G5
Oak Lo. Cl., Stan.	53	F5
Dennis La.		
Oak Lo. Dr., W.Wick.	190	B7
Oak Manor Dr., Wem.	87	J5
Oakington Manor Dr.		
Oak Pk. Gdns. SW19	148	A7
Oak Pl. SW18	148/149	E5
East Hill		
Oak Ri., Buck.H.	64	A3
Oak Rd. W5	105	G7
The Bdy.		
Oak Rd. (Northumberland Heath), Erith	139	J7
Oak Rd., N.Mal.	182	D2
Oak Row SW16	186	C2
Oak St., Rom.	83	J5
Oak Tree Cl. W5	105	F6
Pinewood Gro.		
Oak Tree Cl., Loug.	49	F1
Oak Tree Cl., Stan.	53	F7
Oak Tree Dell NW9	70	C5
Oak Tree Dr. N20	57	E1
Oak Tree Gdns., Brom.	173	H5
Oak Tree Rd. NW8	**7**	**F4**
Oak Tree Rd. NW8	109	H3
Oak Village NW5	92	A4
Oak Way N14	42	B7
Oak Way W3	126	E1
Oak Way, Croy.	189	G6
Oakbank Av., Walt.	179	F7
Oakbank Gro. SE24	151	J4

Oakbrook Cl., Brom. 173 H4
Oakbury Rd. SW6 149 E2
Oakcombe Cl., N.Mal. 182/183 E1
Traps La.
Oakcroft Cl., Pnr. 66 B2
Oakcroft Rd. SE13 154 D2
Oakcroft Rd., Chess. 195 J4
Oakcroft Vil., Chess. 195 J4
Oakdale N14 58 B1
Oakdale Av., Har. 69 H5
Oakdale Av., Nthwd. 66 A2
Oakdale Cl., Wat. 50 C4
Oakdale Gdns. E4 62 C5
Oakdale Rd. E7 97 H7
Oakdale Rd. E11 96 D2
Oakdale Rd. E18 79 H2
Oakdale Rd. N4 75 J6
Oakdale Rd. SE15 153 F3
Oakdale Rd. SW16 169 E5
Oakdale Rd., Wat. 50 C3
Oakdale Way, Mitch. 186 A7
Wolseley Rd.
Oakden St. SE11 35 F1
Oakden St. SE11 131 G4
Oakdene SE15 152/153 E1
Carlton Gro.
Oakdene Av., Chis. 174 D5
Oakdene Av., Erith 139 J6
Oakdene Av., T.Ditt. 194 D1
Oakdene Cl., Pnr. 51 F7
Oakdene Dr., Surb. 182 C7
Oakdene Ms., Sutt. 198 C1
Oakdene Pk. N3 56 C7
Oakdene Rd., Orp. 193 J5
Oake Ct. SW15 148 B5
Oaken Dr., Esher 194 C6
Oaken La., Esher 194 B5
Oakenholt Ho. SE2 138 D2
Hartslock Dr.
Oakenshaw Cl., Surb. 181 H7
Oakes Cl. E6 116 C6
Savage Gdns.
Oakeshott Av. N6 92 A2
Oakey La. SE1 27 E5
Oakey La. SE1 131 G3
Oakfield E4 62 B5
Oakfield Av., Har. 69 E3
Oakfield Cl., N.Mal. 183 F5
Blakes La.
Oakfield Ct. N8 74 E7
Oakfield Ct. NW2 72 A7
Hendon Way
Oakfield Ct., Borwd. 38 B3
Oakfield Gdns. N18 60 B4
Oakfield Gdns. SE19 170 B5
Oakfield Gdns., Beck. 190 A5
Oakfield Gdns., Cars. 199 H1
Oakfield Gdns., Grnf. 104 A4
Oakfield La., Kes. 205 J4
Oakfield Rd. E6 116 B1
Oakfield Rd. E17 77 H2
Oakfield Rd. N3 72 E1
Oakfield Rd. N4 75 G6
Oakfield Rd. N14 58 E3
Oakfield Rd. SE20 171 E7
Oakfield Rd. SW19 166 A3
Oakfield Rd., Croy. 201 J1
Oakfield Rd., Ilf. 99 E2
Oakfield St. SW10 30 C5
Oakfield St. SW10 129 F6
Oakfields Rd. NW11 72 B6
Oakford Rd. NW5 92 C4
Oakhall Ct. E11 79 H6
Oakham Cl. SE6 171 J2
Rutland Wk.
Oakham Cl., Barn. 41 J3
Oakham Dr., Brom. 191 F4
Oakhampton Rd. NW7 56 A7
Oakhill, Esher 194 D6
Oakhill Av. NW3 90 E4
Oakhill Av., Pnr. 66 E2
Oakhill Ct. SW19 166 A7
Oakhill Dr., Surb. 181 H7
Oakhill Path, Surb. 181 H6
Oakhill Pl. SW15 148 D5
Oakhill Rd.
Oakhill Rd. SW15 148 C5
Oakhill Rd. SW16 187 E1
Oakhill Rd., Beck. 190 C2
Oakhill Rd., Orp. 207 J1
Oakhill Rd., Sutt. 199 E3
Oakhouse Rd., Bexh. 159 G5
Oakhurst Av., Barn. 41 H7
Oakhurst Av., Bexh. 138 E7
Oakhurst Cl. E17 78 E4
Oakhurst Cl., Ilf. 81 F1
Oakhurst Cl., Tedd. 162 B5
Oakhurst Gdns. E4 63 F1
Oakhurst Gdns. E17 78 E4
Oakhurst Gdns., Bexh. 139 E7
Oakhurst Gro. SE22 152 D4
Oakhurst Rd., Epsom 196 C6
Oakington Av., Har. 67 G7
Oakington Av., Hayes 121 G4
Oakington Av., Wem. 87 J3
Oakington Dr., Sun. 178 C2
Oakington Manor Dr., Wem. 88 A5
Oakington Rd. W9 108 D4
Oakington Way N8 75 E6
Oakland Pl., Buck.H. 63 G2
Oakland Rd. E15 96 D4
Oakland Way, Epsom 196 D6
Oaklands N21 59 F2
Oaklands, Twick. 143 J7
Oaklands Av. N9 44 E6
Oaklands Av., Esher 194 A1
Oaklands Av., Islw. 124 C6
Oaklands Av., Sid. 157 J7
Oaklands Av., Th.Hth. 187 G4
Oaklands Av., Wat. 50 B1
Oaklands Av., W.Wick. 204 B3
Oaklands Cl., Bexh. 159 F5
Oaklands Cl., Chess. 195 F4
Oaklands Cl., Orp. 193 H6
Oaklands Ct., Wem. 87 G5
Oaklands Est. SW4 150 C6
Oaklands Gro. W12 127 G1
Oaklands La., Barn. 39 H4
Oaklands Pk. Av., Ilf. 99 G2
High Rd.
Oaklands Pl. SW4 150 C4
St. Alphonsus Rd.
Oaklands Rd. N20 40 C7
Oaklands Rd. NW2 90 A4
Oaklands Rd. SW14 146 D3
Oaklands Rd. W7 124 C2
Oaklands Rd., Bexh. 159 F4
Oaklands Rd., Brom. 173 E7
Oaklands Way, Wall. 200 D7
Oaklea Pas., Kings.T. 181 G3
Oakleafe Gdns., Ilf. 80 E3
Oakleigh Av. N20 57 G2
Oakleigh Av., Edg. 70 B2
Oakleigh Av., Surb. 196 A1
Oakleigh Cl. N20 57 J3
Oakleigh Ct., Barn. 41 H6
Church Hill Rd.
Oakleigh Ct., Edg. 70 C2
Oakleigh Cres. N20 57 H3
Oakleigh Gdns. N20 57 F1
Oakleigh Gdns., Edg. 53 J5
Oakleigh Gdns., Orp. 207 H4
Oakleigh Ms. N20 57 F2
Oakleigh Rd. N.
Oakleigh Pk. Av., Chis. 192 D1
Oakleigh Pk. N. N20 57 G1
Oakleigh Pk. S. N20 57 H2
Oakleigh Rd., Pnr. 51 F6
Oakleigh Rd. N. N20 57 G2
Oakleigh Rd. S. N11 58 A3
Oakleigh Way, Mitch. 186 B1
Oakleigh Way, Surb. 196 A1
Oakley Av. W5 106 A7
Oakley Av., Bark. 99 J7
Oakley Av., Croy. 201 E4
Oakley Cl. E4 62 C3
Mapleton Rd.
Oakley Cl. E6 116 B6
Northumberland Rd.
Oakley Cl. W7 104 B7
Oakley Cl., Islw. 144 A1
Oakley Ct., Loug. 48 D2
Hillyfields
Oakley Ct., Mitch. 200 A1
London Rd.
Oakley Cres. EC1 11 H2
Oakley Dr. SE9 175 G1
Oakley Dr. SE13 154 C5
Hither Grn. La.
Oakley Dr., Brom. 206 B3
Oakley Gdns. N8 75 F5
Oakley Gdns. SW3 31 H5
Oakley Gdns. SW3 129 H6
Oakley Pk., Bex. 158 C7
Oakley Pl. SE1 37 F4
Oakley Pl. SE1 132 C5
Oakley Rd. N1 94 A7
Oakley Rd. SE25 188 E5
Oakley Rd., Brom. 206 B3
Oakley Rd., Har. 68 B6
Oakley Sq. NW1 9 G1
Oakley Sq. NW1 110 C2
Oakley St. SW3 31 G5
Oakley St. SW3 129 H6
Oakley Wk. W6 128 A6
Oakley Yd. E2 13 G5
Oaklodge Way NW7 55 F6
Oakmead Av., Brom. 191 G6
Oakmead Gdns., Edg. 54 D4
Oakmead Pl., Mitch. 185 H1
Oakmead Rd. SW12 168 A1
Oakmead Rd., Croy. 186 D6
Oakmeade, Pnr. 51 G6
Oakmere Rd. SE2 138 A6
Oakmoor Way, Chig. 65 H5
Oakmount Pl., Orp. 207 G1
Oakridge Dr. N2 73 G3
Oakridge La., Brom. 172 D5
Downham Way
Oakridge Rd., Brom. 172 D4
Oaks, The N12 57 E4
Oaks, The SE18 137 F5
Oaks, The, Wat. 50 C1
Oaks, The, Wdf.Grn. 63 E6
Oaks Av. SE19 170 B5
Oaks Av., Felt. 160 E2
Oaks Av., Rom. 83 J2
Oaks Av., Wor.Pk. 197 H3
Oaks Gro. E4 62 E2
Oaks La., Croy. 203 F3
Oaks La., Ilf. 81 H5
Oaks Rd., Croy. 202 E5
Oaks Rd., Stai. 140 A6
Oaks Way, Cars. 199 J7
Oaks Way, Surb. 195 G2
Oaksford Av. SE26 170 E3
Oakshade Rd., Brom. 172 D4
Oakshaw Rd. SW18 149 E7
Oakthorpe Rd. N13 59 G5
Oaktree Av. N13 59 H3
Oaktree Gro., Ilf. 99 G5
Oakview Gdns. N2 73 G4
Oakview Gro., Croy. 203 H1
Oakview Rd. SE6 172 B5
Oakway SW20 183 J4
Oakway, Brom. 190 D2
Oakway Cl., Bex. 159 E6
Oakways SE9 156 E6
Oakwood Av. N14 42 D7
Oakwood Av., Beck. 190 C2
Oakwood Av., Borwd. 38 B4
Oakwood Av., Brom. 191 H3
Oakwood Av., Mitch. 185 G2
Oakwood Av., Sthl. 103 G7
Oakwood Cl. N14 42 C6
Oakwood Cl., Chis. 174 C6
Oakwood Cl., Wdf.Grn. 64 B6
Green Wk.
Oakwood Ct. W14 128 C3
Oakwood Cres. N21 43 E6
Oakwood Cres., Grnf. 86 D6
Oakwood Dr. SE19 170 A6
Oakwood Dr., Edg. 54 C6
Oakwood Gdns., Ilf. 99 J2
Oakwood Gdns., Orp. 207 F2
Oakwood Gdns., Sutt. 198 D2
Oakwood Hill, Loug. 48 C6
Oakwood Hill Ind. Est., Loug. 49 F5
Oakwood La. W14 128 C3
Oakwood Pk. Rd. N14 42 D7
Oakwood Pl., Croy. 187 G6
Oakwood Rd. NW11 72 E5
Oakwood Rd. SW20 183 G1
Oakwood Rd., Croy. 187 G6
Oakwood Rd., Orp. 207 F2
Oakwood Rd., Pnr. 66 B2
Oakwood Vw. N14 42 D6
Oakworth Rd. W10 107 J5
Oarsman Pl., E.Mol. 180 B4
Oat La. EC2 19 J3
Oat La. EC2 111 J6
Oates Cl., Brom. 190 D3
Oatfield Rd., Orp. 207 J1
Oatland Ri. E17 77 H2
Oatlands Rd., Enf. 45 F1
Oban Cl. E13 115 J4
Oban Ho., Bark. 117 G2
Wheelers Cross
Oban Rd. E13 115 J3
Oban Rd. SE25 188 A4
Oban St. E14 114 D6
Oberon Cl., Borwd. 38 C1
Oberstein Rd. SW11 149 G4
Oborne Cl. SE24 151 H5
Observatory Gdns. W8 128 D2
Observatory Ms. E14 134 D4
Storers Quay
Observatory Rd. SW14 146 C4
Occupation La. SE18 156 E1
Occupation La. W5 125 G4
Occupation Rd. SE17 35 J3
Occupation Rd. SE17 131 J5
Occupation Rd. W13 125 E2
Ocean Est. E1 113 G4
Ocean St. E1 113 G5
Ocean Wf. E14 134 A2
Ockendon Rd. N1 94 A6
Ockham Dr., Orp. 176 A7
Ockley Rd. SW16 168 E3
Ockley Rd., Croy. 187 F7
Octagon Arc. EC2 20 D2
Octavia Cl., Mitch. 185 H5
Octavia Rd., Islw. 144 C2
Octavia St. SW11 149 H1
Octavia Way SE28 118 B7
Booth Cl.
Octavius St. SE8 134 A7
Odard Rd., W.Mol. 179 G4
Down St.
Oddesey Rd., Borwd. 38 B1
Odessa Rd. E7 97 F4
Odessa Rd. NW10 107 G2
Odessa St. SE16 133 J2
Odger St. SW11 149 J2
Odhams Wk. WC2 18 A4
Odyssey Business Pk., Ruis. 84 B5
Offa's Mead E9 95 H4
Lindisfarne Way
Offenbach Ho. E2 113 G2
Offenham Rd. SE9 174 C4
Offerton Rd. SW4 150 C3
Offham Slope N12 56 C5
Offley Pl., Islw. 124 A7
Thornbury Rd.
Offley Rd. SW9 35 E7
Offley Rd. SW9 131 G7
Offord Cl. N17 60 D7
Offord Rd. N1 93 F7
Offord St. N1 93 F7
Ogilby St. SE18 136 C4
Oglander Rd. SE15 152 C4
Ogle St. W1 17 F1
Ogle St. W1 110 C5
Oglethorpe Rd., Dag. 101 F3
Ohio Rd. E13 115 F4
Oil Mill La. W6 127 G5
Okeburn Rd. SW17 168 A5
Okehampton Cl. N12 57 G5
Okehampton Cres., Well. 158 B1
Okehampton Rd. NW10 107 J1
Olaf St. W11 108 A7
Old Bailey EC4 19 H4
Old Bailey EC4 111 H6
Old Barge Ho. All. SE1 27 E1
Old Barn Cl., Sutt. 198 B7
Old Barrack Yd. SW1 24 B4
Old Barrowfield E15 114/115 E1
New Plaistow Rd.
Old Bellgate Wf. E14 134 A3
Old Bethnal Grn. Rd. E2 13 J3
Old Bethnal Grn. Rd. E2 112 D3
Old Bond St. W1 17 F6
Old Bond St. W1 110 C7
Old Brewers Yd. WC2 18 A4
Old Brewery Ms. NW3 91 G4
Hampstead High St.
Old Br. Cl., Nthlt. 103 G2
Old Br. St., Kings.T. 181 G2
Old Broad St. EC2 20 C4
Old Broad St. EC2 112 A6
Old Bromley Rd., Brom. 172 D5
Old Brompton Rd. SW5 128 D5
Old Brompton Rd. SW7 30 C3
Old Brompton Rd. SW7 128 D5
Old Bldgs. WC2 18 E3
Old Burlington St. W1 17 F5
Old Burlington St. W1 110 C7
Old Castle St. E1 21 F3
Old Castle St. E1 112 C6
Old Cavendish St. W1 16 D3
Old Cavendish St. W1 110 B6
Old Change Ct. EC4 111 J6
Carter La.
Old Chelsea Ms. SW3 31 F6
Old Ch. La. NW9 88 C2
Old Ch. La., Grnf. 104 D3
Perivale La.
Old Ch. La., Stan. 53 F7
Old Ch. Rd. E1 113 G6
Old Ch. Rd. E4 62 A4
Old Ch. St. SW3 31 F4
Old Ch. St. SW3 129 G5
Old Claygate La., Esher 194 D6
Old Clem Sq. SE18 136 D6
Kempt St.

322 Old-Orc

Old Compton St. W1 17 H5
Old Compton St. W1 110 D7
Old Cote Dr., Houns. 123 G6
Old Ct. Pl. W8 22 A3
Old Ct. Pl. W8 128 E2
Old Deer Pk. Gdns., Rich. 145 H3
Old Devonshire Rd. SW12 150 B7
Old Dock Cl., Rich. 126 A6
Watcombe Cotts.
Old Dover Rd. SE3 135 H7
Old Fm. Av. N14 42 C7
Old Fm. Av., Sid. 175 G1
Old Fm. Cl., Houns. 143 F4
Old Fm. Pas., Hmptn. 179 J1
Old Fm. Rd. N2 73 G1
Old Fm. Rd., Hmptn. 161 F6
Old Fm. Rd., West Dr. 120 A2
Old Fm. Rd. E., Sid. 176 A2
Old Fm. Rd. W., Sid. 175 J2
Old Fish St. Hill EC4 19 J5
Old Fleet La. EC4 19 G3
Old Fold Cl., Barn. 40 C1
Old Fold La.
Old Fold La., Barn. 40 C1
Old Fold Vw., Barn. 39 J3
Old Ford Rd. E2 113 F2
Old Ford Rd. E3 113 H2
Old Forge Cl., Stan. 52 D4
Old Forge Ms. W12 127 H2
Goodwin Rd.
Old Forge Way, Sid. 176 B4
Old Fox Footpath, S.Croy. 202 B7
Essenden Rd.
Old Gloucester St. WC1 18 B1
Old Gloucester St. WC1 111 E5
Old Hall Cl., Pnr. 67 E1
Old Hall Dr., Pnr. 66 E1
Old Hill, Chis. 192 D1
Old Hill, Orp. 207 G6
Old Homesdale Rd., Brom. 191 J4
Old Hospital Cl. SW12 167 J1
Old Ho. Cl. SW19 166 B5
Old Ho. Gdns., Twick. 145 F5
Old Jamaica Rd. SE16 29 H5
Old Jamaica Rd. SE16 132 D3
Old James St. SE15 152 E3
Old Jewry EC2 20 B4
Old Jewry EC2 112 A6
Old Kent Rd. SE1 36 D1
Old Kent Rd. SE1 132 B4
Old Kent Rd. SE15 132 B4
Old Kenton La. NW9 70 B5
Old Kingston Rd., Wor.Pk. 196 C3
Old Lo. Pl., Twick. 144/145 E6
St. Margarets Rd.
Old Lo. Way, Stan. 52 D5
Old Maidstone Rd., Sid. 177 F7
Old Malden La., Wor.Pk. 196 D2
Old Manor Dr., Islw. 143 J6
Old Manor Way, Chis. 174 C5
Old Marylebone Rd. NW1 15 H2
Old Marylebone Rd. NW1 109 H5
Old Ms., Har. 68 B5
Hindes Rd.
Old Mill Ct. E18 79 J3
Old Mill Rd. SE18 137 G6
Old Mitre Ct. EC4 111 G6
Fleet St.
Old Montague St. E1 21 H2
Old Montague St. E1 112 D5
Old Nichol St. E2 13 F5
Old Nichol St. E2 112 C4
Old N. St. WC1 18 C1
Old Oak Cl., Chess. 195 J4
Old Oak Common La. NW10 107 E4
Old Oak Common La. W3 107 E5
Old Oak La. NW10 107 E3
Old Oak Rd. W3 107 F7
Old Orchard, Sun. 178 C2
Old Orchard, The NW3 91 J4
Nassington Rd.
Old Palace La., Rich. 145 F5
Old Palace Rd., Croy. 201 H3
Old Palace Ter., Rich. 145 G5
King St.
Old Palace Yd. SW1 26 A5
Old Palace Yd. SW1 130 E3

Old Palace Yd., Rich. 145 F5
Old Paradise St. SE11 34 C1
Old Paradise St. SE11 131 F4
Old Pk. Av. SW12 150 A6
Old Pk. Av., Enf. 43 J4
Old Pk. Gro., Enf. 43 J4
Old Pk. La. W1 24 C2
Old Pk. La. W1 130 A1
Old Pk. Ms., Houns. 123 F7
Old Pk. Ridings N21 43 H6
Old Pk. Rd. N13 59 F4
Old Pk. Rd. SE2 138 A5
Old Pk. Rd., Enf. 43 H3
Old Pk. Rd. S., Enf. 43 H4
Old Pk. Vw., Enf. 43 G3
Old Perry St., Chis. 175 H7
Old Pound Cl., Islw. 144 D1
Old Pye St. SW1 25 H5
Old Pye St. SW1 130 D3
Old Quebec St. W1 16 A4
Old Quebec St. W1 109 J6
Old Queen St. SW1 25 J4
Old Queen St. SW1 130 D2
Old Rectory Gdns., Edg. 54 A6
Old Redding, Har. 51 J4
Old Rd. SE13 155 E4
Old Rd., Enf. 45 F1
Old Rope Wk., Sun. 178 B3
The Av.
Old Royal Free Pl. N1 111 G1
Liverpool Rd.
Old Royal Free Sq. N1 111 G1
Old Ruislip Rd., Nthlt. 102 D2
Old Savill's Cotts., Chig. 65 F4
The Chase
Old Sch. Cl. SW19 184 D2
Old Sch. Cl., Beck. 189 G2
Old Sch. Cres. E7 97 F6
Old Sch. Sq., T.Ditt. 180 C6
Old Seacoal La. EC4 19 G3
Old S. Cl., Pnr. 66 D1
Old S. Lambeth Rd. SW8 34 B7
Old S. Lambeth Rd. SW8 131 E7
Old Spitalfields Mkt. E1 21 F1
Old Spitalfields Mkt. E1 112 C5
Old Sq. WC2 18 D3
Old Sq. WC2 111 F6
Old Sta. Rd., Hayes 121 J3
Old Sta. Rd., Loug. 48 B5
Old Stockley Rd., West Dr. 120 E2
Old St. E13 115 H2
Old St. EC1 11 J5
Old St. EC1 111 J4
Old Swan Yd., Cars. 199 J4
Old Town SW4 150 C3
Old Town, Croy. 201 H3
Old Tram Yd. SE18 137 H4
Lakedale Rd.
Old Woolwich Rd. SE10 134 D6
Old York Rd. SW18 149 E5
Oldacre Ms. SW12 150 B7
Balham Gro.
Oldberry Rd., Edg. 54 D6
Oldborough Rd., Wem. 87 F2
Oldbury Pl. W1 16 C1
Oldbury Pl. W1 110 A4
Oldbury Rd., Enf. 44 D2
Oldfield Cl., Brom. 192 C4
Oldfield Cl., Grnf. 86 B5
Oldfield Cl., Stan. 52 D5
Oldfield Fm. Gdns., Grnf. 104 A1
Oldfield Gro. SE16 133 G4
Oldfield La. N., Grnf. 86 B6
Oldfield La. S., Grnf. 103 J4
Oldfield Ms. N6 74 C7
Oldfield Rd. N16 94 B3
Oldfield Rd. NW10 89 F7
Oldfield Rd. SW19 166 B6
Oldfield Rd. W3 127 F2
Valetta Rd.
Oldfield Rd., Bexh. 159 E2
Oldfield Rd., Brom. 192 C4
Oldfield Rd., Hmptn. 179 F1
Oldfields Circ., Nthlt. 85 J6
Oldfields Rd., Sutt. 198 C3
Oldfields Trd. Est., Sutt. 198 D3
Oldfields Rd.
Oldham Ter. W3 126 C1
Oldhill St. N16 94 D1
Oldridge Rd. SW12 150 A7
Oldstead Rd., Brom. 172 D4
Oleander Cl., Orp. 207 G5

O'Leary Sq. E1 113 F5
Olinda Rd. N16 76 C6
Oliphant St. W10 108 A3
Olive Rd. E13 115 J3
Olive Rd. NW2 89 J4
Olive Rd. SW19 167 F7
Norman Rd.
Olive Rd. W5 125 G3
Oliver Av. SE25 188 C3
Oliver Cl. E10 96 B2
Oliver Rd.
Oliver Cl. W4 126 B6
Oliver Gdns. E6 116 B6
Oliver Gro. SE25 188 C4
Oliver Rd. E10 96 B2
Oliver Rd. E17 78 C5
Oliver Rd., N.Mal. 182 C2
Oliver Rd., Sutt. 199 G4
Oliver-Goldsmith Est. SE15 152 D1
Olivers Yd. EC1 12 C5
Olivette St. SW15 148 A4
Ollards Gro., Loug. 48 A4
Ollerton Grn. E3 113 J1
Ollerton Rd. N11 58 D5
Olley Cl., Wall. 200 E7
Ollgar Cl. W12 127 F1
Olliffe St. E14 134 C3
Olmar St. SE1 37 H5
Olmar St. SE1 132 D6
Olney Rd. SE17 35 J5
Olney Rd. SE17 131 H6
Olron Cres., Bexh. 158 D5
Olven Rd. SE18 137 F7
Olveston Wk., Cars. 185 G6
Olwen Ms., Pnr. 66 D2
Olyffe Av., Well. 158 A2
Olyffe Dr., Beck. 190 C1
Olympia Ms. W2 14 B6
Olympia Way W14 128 B3
Olympic Retail Pk., Wem. 88 B4
Olympic Way, Grnf. 103 H1
Olympic Way, Wem. 88 A4
Olympus Sq. E5 94 D4
Nolan Way
Oman Av. NW2 89 J4
O'Meara St. SE1 28 A2
O'Meara St. SE1 131 J1
Omega Cl. E14 134 B3
Tiller Rd.
Omega Pl. N1 10 B2
Omega St. SE14 154 A1
Ommaney Rd. SE14 153 G1
Omnibus Way E17 78 A2
On The Hill, Wat. 50 E2
Ondine Rd. SE15 152 C4
One Tree Cl. SE23 153 F6
Onega Gate SE16 133 H3
O'Neill Path SE18 136 D6
Kempt St.
Ongar Cl., Rom. 82 C5
Ongar Rd. SW6 128 D6
Onra Rd. E17 78 A7
Onslow Av., Rich. 145 H5
Onslow Cl. E4 62 C2
Onslow Cl., T.Ditt. 194 B1
Onslow Cres., Chis. 192 E1
Onslow Dr., Sid. 176 D2
Onslow Gdns. E18 79 H3
Onslow Gdns. N10 74 B5
Onslow Gdns. N21 43 G5
Onslow Gdns. SW7 31 E3
Onslow Gdns. SW7 129 G5
Onslow Gdns., T.Ditt. 194 B1
Onslow Gdns., Wall. 200 C6
Onslow Ms. E. SW7 31 E2
Onslow Ms. W. SW7 30 E2
Onslow Rd., Croy. 187 F7
Onslow Rd., N.Mal. 183 G4
Onslow Rd., Rich. 145 H5
Onslow Sq. SW7 31 F1
Onslow Sq. SW7 129 G4
Onslow St. EC1 11 F6
Onslow Way, T.Ditt. 194 B1
Ontario St. SE1 27 H6
Ontario St. SE1 131 H3
Ontario Way E14 114 A7
Opal Cl. E16 116 A6
Opal Ms. NW6 108 C1
Priory Pk. Rd.
Opal Ms., Ilf. 98/99 E2
Ley St.
Opal St. SE11 35 G2
Opal St. SE11 131 H4
Openshaw Rd. SE2 138 B4
Openview SW18 167 F1
Ophelia Gdns. NW2 90 B3
The Vale
Ophir Ter. SE15 152 D1
Opossum Way, Houns. 142 C2
Oppenheim Rd. SE13 154 C2

Oppidans Ms. NW3 91 J7
Meadowbank
Oppidans Rd. NW3 91 J7
Orange Ct. E1 29 J2
Orange Gro. E11 96 E3
Orange Gro., Chig. 65 F6
Orange Hill Rd., Edg. 54 C7
Orange Pl. SE16 133 F3
Lower Rd.
Orange St. WC2 17 H6
Orange St. WC2 110 D7
Orange Yd. W1 17 J4
Orangery, The, Rich. 163 F2
Orangery La. SE9 156 C5
Oratory La. SW3 31 F3
Orb St. SE17 36 B2
Orb St. SE17 132 A4
Orbain Rd. SW6 128 B7
Orbel St. SW11 149 H1
Orchard, The N14 42 B5
Orchard, The N21 44 A6
Orchard, The NW11 72 D5
Orchard, The SE3 154 D2
Orchard, The W4 126 D4
Orchard, The W5 105 G5
Orchard, The, Epsom 197 F7
Orchard, The, Houns. 143 J2
Orchard Av. N3 72 D3
Orchard Av. N14 42 C6
Orchard Av. N20 57 G2
Orchard Av., Belv. 139 E6
Orchard Av., Croy. 189 H7
Orchard Av., Felt. 141 G5
Orchard Av., Houns. 123 E7
Orchard Av., Mitch. 200 A1
Orchard Av., N.Mal. 183 E2
Orchard Av., Sthl. 123 E1
Orchard Av., T.Ditt. 194 D1
Orchard Cl. E4 62 A4
Chingford Mt. Rd.
Orchard Cl. E11 79 H4
Orchard Cl. N1 93 J7
Morton Rd.
Orchard Cl. NW2 89 G3
Orchard Cl. SE23 153 F6
Brenchley Gdns.
Orchard Cl. SW20 183 J4
Grand Dr.
Orchard Cl. W10 108 B5
Orchard Cl., Bexh. 158 E1
Orchard Cl., Bushey 52 A1
Orchard Cl., Edg. 53 H6
Orchard Cl., Epsom 196 B6
Orchard Cl., Nthlt. 85 J5
Orchard Cl., Surb. 181 E7
Orchard Cl., Walt. 178 B7
Garden Rd.
Orchard Cl., Wem. 105 H1
Orchard Ct., Islw. 144 A1
Thornbury Av.
Orchard Ct., Twick. 162 A2
Orchard Ct., Wor.Pk. 197 G1
The Av.
Orchard Cres., Edg. 54 C5
Orchard Cres., Enf. 44 C1
Orchard Dr. SE3 154 E2
Orchard Dr., Edg. 53 J5
Orchard Gdns., Chess. 195 H4
Orchard Gdns., Sutt. 198 D5
Orchard Gate NW9 70 E4
Orchard Gate, Esher 194 A1
Orchard Gate, Grnf. 86 E6
Orchard Grn., Orp. 207 H2
Orchard Gro. SE20 170 D7
Orchard Gro., Croy. 189 H7
Orchard Gro., Edg. 70 A1
Orchard Gro., Har. 69 J5
Orchard Gro., Orp. 207 J2
Orchard Hill SE13 154 B2
Coldbath St.
Orchard Hill, Cars. 199 J5
Orchard La. SW20 183 H1
Orchard La., E.Mol. 180 A6
Orchard La., Wdf.Grn. 63 J4
Orchard Ms. N1 94 A7
Southgate Gro.
Orchard Pl. E14 115 E7
Orchard Pl. N17 60 C7
Orchard Ri., Croy. 203 H1
Orchard Ri., Kings.T. 182 C1
Orchard Ri., Rich. 146 B4
Orchard Ri. E., Sid. 157 J5
Orchard Ri. W., Sid. 157 H5
Orchard Rd. N6 74 B7
Orchard Rd. SE3 154/155 E2
Eliot Pl.
Orchard Rd. SE18 137 G4
Orchard Rd., Barn. 40 C4
Orchard Rd., Belv. 139 G4
Orchard Rd., Brent. 125 F6
Orchard Rd., Brom. 191 J1
Orchard Rd., Chess. 195 H4
Orchard Rd., Dag. 119 G1

Orchard Rd., Enf. 45 F5
Orchard Rd., Hmptn. 161 F7
Orchard Rd., Hayes 102 A7
Orchard Rd., Houns. 143 F5
Orchard Rd., Kings.T. 181 H2
Orchard Rd., Mitch. 200 A1
Orchard Rd., 207 E5
(Farnborough), Orp.
Orchard Rd., Rich. 146 A3
Orchard Rd., Rom. 83 H1
Orchard Rd., Sid. 175 H4
Orchard Rd., Sun. 160 B7
Hanworth Rd.
Orchard Rd., Sutt. 198 D5
Orchard Rd., Twick. 144 D5
Orchard Rd., Well. 158 B3
Orchard Sq. W14 128 C5
Sun Rd.
Orchard St. E17 77 H4
Orchard St. W1 16 B4
Orchard St. W1 110 A6
Orchard Ter., Enf. 44 D6
Great Cambridge Rd.
Orchard Way, Beck. 189 H5
Orchard Way, Croy. 189 H7
Orchard Way, Enf. 44 B3
Orchard Way, Sutt. 199 G4
Orchardleigh Av., Enf. 45 F2
Orchardmede N21 44 A6
Orchardson St. NW8 7 E6
Orchardson St. NW8 109 G4
Orchid Cl. E6 116 B5
Orchid Cl., Sthl. 103 E6
Orchid Rd. N14 42 C7
Orchid St. W12 107 G7
Orde Hall St. WC1 10 C6
Orde Hall St. WC1 111 F4
Ordell Rd. E3 113 J2
Ordnance Cl., Felt. 160 A3
Ordnance Cres. SE10 134 D2
Ordnance Hill NW8 109 G1
Ordnance Ms. NW8 7 F1
Ordnance Rd. E16 115 F5
Ordnance Rd. SE18 136 D6
Oregano Dr. E14 114 D6
Oregon Av. E12 98 C4
Oregon Cl., N.Mal. 182 C4
Georgia Rd.
Oregon Sq., Orp. 207 G1
Orestes Ms. NW6 90 D5
Aldred Rd.
Orford Ct. SE27 169 H2
Orford Gdns., Twick. 162 C2
Orford Rd. E17 78 A5
Orford Rd. E18 79 H3
Orford Rd. SE6 172 B3
Organ La. E4 62 C2
Oriel Cl., Mitch. 186 D4
Oriel Ct. NW3 91 F4
Heath St.
Oriel Dr. SW13 127 H6
Oriel Gdns., Ilf. 80 C3
Oriel Pl. NW3 91 F4
Heath St.
Oriel Rd. E9 95 G6
Oriel Way, Nthlt. 85 H7
Orient Ind. Pk. E10 96 A2
Orient St. SE11 35 G1
Orient Way E5 95 G3
Orient Way E10 95 H2
Oriental Rd. E16 136 A1
Oriental St. E14 114 A7
Morant St.
Oriole Way SE28 118 B7
Orion Rd. N11 58 B6
Orissa Rd. SE18 137 H5
Orkney St. SW11 150 A2
Orlando Rd. SW4 150 C3
Orleans Cl., Esher 194 A2
Orleans Rd. SE19 170 A6
Orleans Rd., Twick. 145 E7
Orleston Ms. N7 93 G6
Orleston Rd. N7 93 G6
Orley Fm. Rd., Har. 86 B3
Orlop St. SE10 134 E5
Ormanton Rd. SE26 170 D4
Orme Ct. W2 14 A6
Orme Ct. W2 108 E7
Orme Ct. Ms. W2 14 B6
Orme La. W2 14 A6
Orme La. W2 108 E7
Orme Rd., Kings.T. 182 B2
Orme Sq. W2 14 A6
Ormeley Rd. SW12 168 B1
Ormerod Gdns., 186 A2
Mitch.
Ormesby Cl. SE28 118 D7
Wroxham Rd.
Ormesby Way, Har. 69 J6
Ormiston Gro. W12 127 H1
Ormiston Rd. SE10 135 G5
Ormond Av., Hmptn. 179 H1
Ormond Av., Rich. 145 G5
Ormond Rd.

Ormond Cl. WC1 18 B1
Ormond Cres., 179 H1
Hmptn.
Ormond Dr., Hmptn. 161 H7
Ormond Ms. WC1 10 B6
Ormond Rd. N19 93 E1
Ormond Rd., Rich. 145 G5
Ormond Yd. SW1 25 G1
Ormonde Av., Orp. 207 F2
Ormonde Gate SW3 32 A4
Ormonde Gate SW3 129 J5
Ormonde Pl. SW1 32 B2
Ormonde Ri., 63 J1
Buck.H.
Ormonde Rd. SW14 146 B3
Ormonde Ter. NW8 109 J1
Ormsby Gdns., 103 J2
Grnf.
Ormsby Pl. N16 94 C3
Victorian Gro.
Ormsby Pt. SE18 136/137 E4
Troy Ct.
Ormsby St. E2 13 F1
Ormsby St. E2 112 C2
Ormside St. SE15 133 F6
Ormskirk Rd., Wat. 50 D4
Ornan Rd. NW3 91 H5
Oronsay Wk. N1 93 J6
Clephane Rd.
Orpen Wk. N16 94 B3
Orpheus St. SE5 152 A1
Orpington Gdns. 60 B3
N18
Orpington Rd. N21 59 H1
Orpington Rd., Chis. 193 H3
Orpwood Cl., 161 F5
Hmptn.
Orsett St. SE11 34 D3
Orsett St. SE11 131 F5
Orsett Ter. W2 14 B3
Orsett Ter. W2 109 F6
Orsett Ter., Wdf.Grn. 79 J1
Orston Rd. N1 112 B1
Orton St. E1 29 H2
Orville Rd. SW11 149 G2
Orwell Ct. N5 93 J4
Orwell Rd. E13 115 J2
Osbaldeston Rd. N16 94 D2
Osbert St. SW1 33 H2
Osberton Rd. SE12 155 G5
Osborn Cl. E8 112 D1
Osborn Gdns. NW7 56 A7
Osborn La. SE23 153 H7
Osborn St. E1 21 G2
Osborn St. E1 112 C5
Osborn Ter. SE3 155 F4
Lee Rd.
Osborne Cl., Barn. 41 J3
Osborne Cl., Beck. 189 H4
Osborne Cl., Felt. 160 D5
Osborne Gdns., 187 J2
Th.Hth.
Osborne Gro. E17 77 J4
Osborne Gro. N4 93 G1
Osborne Ms. E17 77 J4
Osborne Gro.
Osborne Pl., Sutt. 199 G5
Osborne Rd. E7 97 H5
Osborne Rd. E9 95 J6
Osborne Rd. E10 96 B3
Osborne Rd. N4 93 G1
Osborne Rd. N13 59 G3
Osborne Rd. NW2 89 H6
Osborne Rd. W3 126 B3
Osborne Rd., Belv. 139 F5
Osborne Rd., 63 H1
Buck.H.
Osborne Rd., Dag. 101 F5
Osborne Rd., Enf. 45 H2
Osborne Rd., Houns. 143 F3
Osborne Rd., 163 H7
Kings.T.
Osborne Rd., Sthl. 103 J6
Osborne Rd., Th.Hth. 187 J2
Osborne Sq., Dag. 101 F4
Osborne Ter. SW17 168 A5
Church La.
Oscar St. SE8 154 A1
Oseney Cres. NW5 92 C6
Osgood Av., Orp. 207 J5
Osgood Gdns., Orp. 207 J5
O'Shea Gro. E3 113 J1
Osidge La. N14 58 A1
Osier Ms. W4 127 F6
Osier St. E1 113 F4
Osier Way E10 96 B3
Osier Way, Mitch. 185 H5
Osiers Rd. SW18 148 D4
Oslac Rd. SE6 172 B5
Oslo Ct. NW8 7 G2
Oslo Sq. SE16 133 H3
Norway Gate
Osman Cl. N15 76 A6
Tewkesbury Rd.

Osman Rd. N9 60 D3
Osman Rd. W6 127 J3
Batoum Gdns.
Osmond Cl., Har. 85 J2
Osmond Gdns., 200 C5
Wall.
Osmund St. W12 107 F6
Braybrook St.
Osnaburgh St. NW1 9 E6
Osnaburgh St. NW1 110 B4
Osnaburgh Ter. NW1 8 E5
Osney Ho. SE2 138 D2
Hartslock Dr.
Osney Wk., Cars. 185 G6
Osprey Cl. E6 116 B5
Dove App.
Osprey Cl. E11 79 G4
Osprey Cl. E17 61 H7
Osprey Cl., Sutt. 198 B2
Gander Grn. La.
Osprey Cl., West Dr. 120 B2
Osprey Ms., Enf. 45 E5
Ospringe Cl. SE20 171 F7
Ospringe Ct. SE9 157 G6
Alderwood Rd.
Ospringe Rd. NW5 92 C4
Osram Rd., Wem. 87 G3
Osric Path N1 12 D2
Osric Path N1 112 B2
Ossian Ms. N4 75 F7
Ossian Rd. N4 75 F7
Ossington Bldgs. W1 16 B1
Ossington St. W2 14 A6
Ossington St. W2 108 E7
Ossory Rd. SE1 37 H4
Ossory Rd. SE1 132 D5
Ossulston St. NW1 9 H2
Ossulston St. NW1 110 D3
Ossulton Pl. N2 73 F3
East End Rd.
Ossulton Way N2 73 F4
Ostade Rd. SW2 151 F7
Osten Ms. SW7 22 B6
Oster Ter. E17 77 G5
Southcote Rd.
Osterley Av., Islw. 124 A7
Osterley Ct., Islw. 144 A1
Osterley Cres., Islw. 144 B1
Osterley Gdns., 187 J2
Th.Hth.
Osterley Ho. E14 114 B6
Giraud St.
Osterley La., Islw. 124 B5
Osterley La., Sthl. 123 G5
Osterley Pk., Islw. 124 A5
Osterley Pk. Rd., Sthl. 123 F3
Osterley Pk. Vw. Rd. 124 B2
W7
Osterley Rd. N16 94 B4
Osterley Rd., Islw. 124 B7
Osterley Views, Sthl. 123 J1
West Pk. Rd.
Ostliffe Rd. N13 59 H5
Oswald Rd., Sthl. 123 E1
Oswald St. E5 95 G3
Oswald Ter. NW2 89 J3
Temple Rd.
Oswald's Mead E9 95 H4
Lindisfarne Way
Osward Pl. N9 60 E2
Osward Rd. SW17 167 J2
Oswell Ho. E1 133 E1
Oswin St. SE11 35 H1
Oswin St. SE11 131 H4
Oswyth Rd. SE5 152 B2
Otford Cl. SE20 189 F1
Otford Cl., Bex. 159 H6
Southwold Rd.
Otford Cl., Brom. 192 D3
Otford Cres. SE4 153 J6
Othello Cl. SE11 35 G3
Otis St. E3 114 C3
Otley App., Ilf. 81 E6
Otley Dr., Ilf. 80 E5
Otley Rd. E16 115 J6
Otley Ter. E5 95 G2
Otley Way, Wat. 50 C3
Ottaway St. E5 94 D3
Stellman Cl.
Ottenden Cl., Orp. 207 H4
Southfleet Rd.
Otter Rd., Grnf. 103 J4
Otterbourne Rd. E4 62 D3
Otterbourne Rd., 201 J2
Croy.
Otterburn Gdns., 124 D7
Islw.
Otterburn Ho. SE5 35 J7
Otterburn Ho. SE5 131 J7
Otterburn St. SW17 167 J6
Otterden St. SE6 172 A4
Otto Cl. SE26 170 E3
Otto St. SE17 35 G6
Otto St. SE17 131 H6

Oulton Cl. E5 95 F2
Mundford Rd.
Oulton Cl. SE28 118 C6
Rollesby Way
Oulton Cres., Bark. 99 J6
Oulton Rd. N15 76 A5
Oulton Way, Wat. 51 E4
Ouseley Rd. SW12 167 J1
Outer Circle NW1 8 B6
Outer Circle NW1 110 B2
Outgate Rd. NW10 89 F7
Outram Pl. N1 111 E1
Outram Rd. E6 116 B1
Outram Rd. N22 74 D1
Outram Rd., Croy. 202 C1
Outwich St. EC3 20 E3
Oval, The E2 112 E2
Oval, The, Sid. 158 A7
Oval Pl. SW8 34 C7
Oval Pl. SW8 131 F7
Oval Rd. NW1 110 B1
Oval Rd., Croy. 202 B1
Oval Rd. N., Dag. 119 H1
Oval Rd. S., Dag. 119 H2
Oval Way SE11 34 D4
Oval Way SE11 131 F5
Overbrae, Beck. 172 A6
Overbrook Wk., Edg. 54 A7
Overbury Av., Beck. 190 B3
Overbury Rd. N15 76 A6
Overbury St. E5 95 G4
Overcliff Rd. SE13 154 A3
Overcourt Cl., Sid. 158 B6
Overdale Av., N.Mal. 182 C2
Overdale Rd. W5 125 F3
Overdown Rd. SE6 172 A4
Overhill Rd. SE22 152 D7
Overhill Way, Beck. 190 D5
Overlea Rd. E5 76 D7
Overmead, Sid. 157 G7
Oversley Ho. W2 108 D5
Overstand Cl., Beck. 190 A5
Overstone Gdns., 189 J7
Croy.
Overstone Rd. W6 127 J3
Overton Cl. NW10 88 C6
Overton Cl., Islw. 144 C1
Avenue Rd.
Overton Ct. E11 79 G7
Overton Dr. E11 79 H7
Overton Dr., Rom. 82 C7
Overton Rd. E10 95 H1
Overton Rd. N14 42 E5
Overton Rd. SE2 138 C3
Overton Rd. SW9 151 G2
Overton Rd., Sutt. 198 D6
Overton Rd. E. SE2 138 D3
Overtons Yd., Croy. 201 J3
Ovesdon Av., Har. 85 F1
Ovett Cl. SE19 170 B6
Ovex Cl. E14 134 C2
Ovington Gdns. SW3 23 H6
Ovington Gdns. SW3 129 H6
Ovington Ms. SW3 23 H6
Ovington Ms. SW3 129 H3
Ovington Sq. SW3 23 H6
Ovington Sq. SW3 129 H3
Ovington St. SW3 23 H6
Ovington St. SW3 129 H3
Owen Cl. SE28 138 C1
Owen Cl., Croy. 188 A6
Owen Cl., Hayes 102 B3
Owen Gdns., 64 B6
Wdf.Grn.
Owen Rd. N13 59 J5
Owen Rd., Hayes 102 B3
Owen St. EC1 11 G2
Owen Wk. SE20 170 D7
Sycamore Gro.
Owen Waters Ho., Ilf. 80 C1
Owen Way NW10 88 C6
Owenite St. SE2 138 B4
Owen's Ct. EC1 11 G3
Owen's Row EC1 11 G3
Owens Way SE23 153 H7
Owgan Cl. SE5 132 A7
Benhill Rd.
Owl Pk., Loug. 47 F2
Oxberry Av. SW6 148 B2
Oxendon St. SW1 17 H6
Oxendon St. SW1 110 D7
Oxenford St. SE15 152 C3
Oxenholme NW1 9 G2
Oxenholme NW1 110 C1
Oxenpark Av., Wem. 69 H7
Oxestalls Rd. SE8 133 H5
Oxford Av. SW20 184 B2
Oxford Av., Hayes 121 J7
Oxford Av., Houns. 123 G5
Oxford Circ. Av. W1 17 F4
Oxford Cl. N9 60 E2
Oxford Cl., Mitch. 186 D3
Oxford Ct. EC4 20 B5
Oxford Ct. W3 106 A6

Oxford Ct., Felt. 160 D4
Oxford Way
Oxford Cres., N.Mal. 182 D6
Oxford Dr., Ruis. 84 C2
Oxford Gdns. N20 57 G1
Oxford Gdns. N21 43 J7
Oxford Gdns. W4 126 A5
Oxford Gdns. W10 108 B6
Oxford Gate W6 128 A4
Oxford Ms., Bex. 159 G7
Bexley High St.
Oxford Pl. NW10 88 D3
Neasden La. N.
Oxford Rd. E15 96 D6
Oxford Rd. N4 93 G1
Oxford Rd. N9 61 E2
Oxford Rd. NW6 108 D2
Oxford Rd. SE19 170 A6
Oxford Rd. SW15 148 B4
Oxford Rd. W5 105 G7
Oxford Rd., Cars. 199 H6
Oxford Rd., Enf. 45 E5
Oxford Rd., Har. 67 J6
Oxford Rd. (Wealdstone), Har. 68 C3
Oxford Rd., Ilf. 99 F4
Oxford Rd., Sid. 176 B5
Oxford Rd., Tedd. 162 A5
Oxford Rd., Wall. 200 C5
Oxford Rd., Wdf.Grn. 63 J5
Oxford Rd. N. W4 126 B5
Oxford Rd. S. W4 126 A5
Oxford Sq. W2 15 H4
Oxford Sq. W2 109 H6
Oxford St. W1 16 B4
Oxford St. W1 110 B6
Oxford Wk., Sthl. 123 F1
Oxford Way, Felt. 160 D4
Oxgate Gdns. NW2 89 H3
Oxgate La. NW2 89 H2
Oxhawth Cres., Brom. 192 D5
Oxhey Dr., Nthwd. 50 B5
Oxhey Dr., Wat. 50 C3
Oxhey La., Har. 51 H5
Oxhey La., Pnr. 51 H5
Oxhey La., Wat. 51 F3
Oxhey Ridge Cl., Nthwd. 50 A5
Oxleas E6 116 E6
Oxleas Cl., Well. 157 G2
Oxleay Ct., Har. 85 G1
Oxleay Rd., Har. 85 G1
Oxleigh Cl., N.Mal. 183 E5
Oxley Cl. SE1 37 G3
Oxley Cl. SE1 132 C5
Oxleys Rd. NW2 89 H3
Oxlip Cl., Croy. 203 G1
Marigold Way
Oxlow La., Dag. 101 G4
Oxonian St. SE22 152 C4
Oxted Cl., Mitch. 185 G3
Oxtoby Way SW16 186 D2
Oyster Catchers Cl. E16 115 H6
Freemasons Rd.
Oyster Row E1 113 F6
Lukin St.
Ozolins Way E16 115 G6

P

Pablo Neruda Cl. SE24 151 H4
Shakespeare Rd.
Pace Pl. E1 112/113 E6
Bigland St.
Pacific Rd. E16 115 G6
Packington Rd. W3 126 C3
Packington Sq. N1 111 J1
Packington St. N1 111 H1
Packmores Rd. SE9 157 G5
Padbury SE17 36 D4
Padbury SE17 132 B5
Padbury Ct. E2 13 G4
Padbury Ct. E2 112 C3
Padcroft Rd., West Dr. 120 A1
Paddenswick Rd. W6 127 G3
Paddington Cl., Hayes 102 D4
Paddington Grn. W2 15 F1
Paddington Grn. W2 109 G5
Paddington St. W1 16 B1
Paddington St. W1 110 A5
Paddock Cl. SE3 155 G2
Paddock Cl. SE26 171 G4
Paddock Cl., Nthlt. 103 G2
Paddock Cl., Orp. 206/207 E4
State Fm. Av.
Paddock Cl., Wor.Pk. 196 E1
Paddock Gdns. SE19 170 B6
Westow St.
Paddock Rd. NW2 89 G3
Paddock Rd., Bexh. 159 E4
Paddock Rd., Ruis. 84 D3
Paddock Way, Chis. 175 G7
Paddocks, The, Barn. 41 J3
Paddocks, The, Wem. 88 B2
Paddocks Cl., Har. 85 H4
Padfield Rd. SE5 151 J3
Padnall Ct., Rom. 82 D3
Padnall Rd.
Padnall Rd., Rom. 82 D4
Padstow Rd., Enf. 43 H2
Padua Rd. SE20 189 F1
Pagden St. SW8 150 B1
Page Cl., Dag. 101 E5
Page Cl., Hmptn. 161 E6
Page Cl., Har. 69 J6
Page Cres., Croy. 201 G5
Page Grn. Rd. N15 76 D5
Page Grn. Ter. N15 76 C5
Page Heath La., Brom. 192 A3
Page Heath Vil., Brom. 192 A3
Page Meadow NW7 55 G7
Page Rd., Felt. 141 G6
Page St. NW7 71 G1
Page St. SW1 33 J1
Page St. SW1 130 E4
Pageant Av. NW9 70 D1
Pageant Cres. SE16 133 H1
Rotherhithe St.
Pageant Wk., Croy. 202 B3
Pageantmaster Ct. EC4 19 G4
Pagehurst Rd., Croy. 188 E7
Pages Hill N10 74 A2
Pages La. N10 74 A2
Pages Wk. SE1 36 D1
Pages Wk. SE1 132 B4
Pages Yd. W4 126/127 E6
Church St.
Paget Av., Sutt. 199 G3
Paget Cl., Hmptn. 162 A4
Paget Gdns., Chis. 193 E1
Paget La., Islw. 144 A3
Paget Pl., Kings.T. 164 C6
Paget Pl., T.Ditt. 194 D1
Brooklands Rd.
Paget Ri. SE18 136 D7
Paget Rd. N16 94 A1
Paget Rd., Ilf. 98 E4
Paget St. EC1 11 G3
Paget Ter. SE18 136 D6
Pagitts Gro., Barn. 40 E1
Pagnell St. SE14 133 J7
Pagoda Av., Rich. 145 J3
Pagoda Gdns. SE3 154 D2
Pagoda Vista, Rich. 145 J2
Paignton Rd. N15 76 B6
Paignton Rd., Ruis. 84 A3
Paines Cl., Pnr. 67 E3
Paines La., Pnr. 66 E1
Pains Cl., Mitch. 186 B2
Painsthorpe Rd. N16 94 B3
Oldfield Rd.
Painters Rd., Ilf. 81 J3
Paisley Rd. N22 75 H1
Paisley Rd., Cars. 199 G1
Pakeman St. N7 93 F3
Pakenham Cl. SW12 168 A1
Balham Pk. Rd.
Pakenham St. WC1 10 D5
Pakenham St. WC1 111 F3
Palace Av. W8 22 B2
Palace Av. W8 129 E1
Palace Ct. NW3 91 E5
Palace Ct. W2 14 A5
Palace Ct. W2 108 E7
Palace Ct., Brom. 191 H1
Palace Gro.
Palace Ct., Har. 69 H6
Palace Ct. Gdns. N10 74 C3
Palace Gdns., Buck.H. 64 A1
Palace Gdns., Enf. 44 A3
Palace Gdns. Ms. W8 128 D1
Palace Gdns. Ter. W8 128 D1
Palace Gate W8 22 C4
Palace Gate W8 129 F2
Palace Gates Rd. N22 74 D1
Palace Grn. W8 22 B3
Palace Grn. W8 129 E2
Palace Grn., Croy. 203 J7
Palace Gro. SE19 170 C7
Palace Gro., Brom. 191 H1
Palace Ms. E17 77 J4
Palace Ms. SW1 32 C2
Palace Ms. SW6 128 C7
Hartismere Rd.
Palace of Industry, Wem. 88 A4
Palace Pl. SW1 25 F5
Palace Rd. N8 74 D5
Palace Rd. N11 58 E7
Palace Rd. SE19 170 C7
Palace Rd. SW2 169 F1
Palace Rd., Brom. 191 H1
Palace Rd., E.Mol. 180 A3
Palace Rd., Kings.T. 181 G4
Palace Rd., Ruis. 84 E4
Palace Rd. Est. SW2 169 F1
Palace Sq. SE19 170 C7
Palace St. SW1 25 F5
Palace St. SW1 130 C3
Palace Vw. SE12 173 G2
Palace Vw., Brom. 191 G3
Palace Vw., Croy. 203 J4
Palace Vw. Rd. E4 62 B5
Palamos Rd. E10 96 A1
Palatine Av. N16 94 C4
Stoke Newington Rd.
Palatine Rd. N16 94 B4
Palermo Rd. NW10 107 G2
Palestine Gro. SW19 185 G1
Palewell Common Dr. SW14 146 D5
Palewell Pk. SW14 146 D5
Paley Gdns., Loug. 49 F3
Palfrey Pl. SW8 34 D7
Palfrey Pl. SW8 131 F7
Palgrave Av., Sthl. 103 G7
Palgrave Rd. W12 127 F3
Palissy St. E2 13 F4
Pall Mall SW1 25 G2
Pall Mall SW1 130 C1
Pall Mall E. SW1 25 J1
Pall Mall E. SW1 130 D1
Pall Mall Pl. SW1 25 G2
Pall Mall Pl. SW1 130 C1
Pallant Way, Orp. 206 D3
Pallet Way SE18 156 B1
Palliser Rd. W14 128 B5
Palm Av., Sid. 176 D6
Palm Cl. E10 96 B3
Palm Gro. W5 125 H3
Palm Rd., Rom. 83 J5
Palmar Cres., Bexh. 159 G3
Palmar Rd., Bexh. 159 G2
Palmeira Rd., Bexh. 158 D3
Palmer Av., Sutt. 197 J4
Palmer Cl., Houns. 143 G1
Palmer Cl., W.Wick. 204 D3
Palmer Cres., Kings.T. 181 H3
Palmer Gdns., Barn. 40 A5
Palmer Pl. N7 93 G5
Palmer Rd. E13 115 H4
Palmer Rd., Dag. 100 D1
Palmer St. SW1 25 H4
Palmer St. SW1 130 D3
Palmers Gro., W.Mol. 179 G4
Palmers La., Enf. 45 E1
Palmers Pas. SW14 146 C3
Palmers Rd.
Palmers Rd. E2 113 G2
Palmers Rd. N11 58 C5
Palmers Rd. SW14 146 C3
Palmers Rd. SW16 187 F2
Palmers Rd., Borwd. 38 B1
Palmerston Cres. N13 59 F5
Palmerston Cres. SE18 137 F6
Palmerston Gro. SW19 166 D7
Palmerston Rd. E7 97 H5
Palmerston Rd. E17 77 J4
Palmerston Rd. N22 59 F7
Palmerston Rd. NW6 90 D7
Palmerston Rd. SW14 146 C4
Palmerston Rd. SW19 166 D7
Palmerston Rd. W3 126 C3
Palmerston Rd., Buck.H. 63 H2
Palmerston Rd., Cars. 199 J4
Palmerston Rd., Croy. 188 A5
Palmerston Rd., Har. 68 C3
Palmerston Rd., Houns. 143 J1
Gresham Rd.
Palmerston Rd., Orp. 207 F4
Palmerston Rd., Sutt. 199 F5
Vernon Rd.
Palmerston Rd., Twick. 144 C6
Palmerston Way SW8 130 B7
Bradmead
Pamela Gdns., Pnr. 66 B5
Pamela Wk. E8 112 D1
Marlborough Av.
Pampisford Rd., S.Croy. 201 H7
Pams Way, Epsom 196 D5
Pancras La. EC4 20 A4
Pancras Rd. NW1 9 H1
Pancras Rd. NW1 110 D2
Pandora Rd. NW6 90 D6
Panfield Ms., Ilf. 80 D6
Cranbrook Rd.
Panfield Rd. SE2 138 A3
Pangbourne Av. W10 107 J5
Pangbourne Dr., Stan. 53 G5
Panhard Pl., Sthl. 103 H7
Pank Av., Barn. 41 F5
Pankhurst Cl. SE14 133 G7
Briant St.
Pankhurst Cl., Islw. 144 C3
Pankhurst Rd., Walt. 178 C7
Panmuir Rd. SW20 183 H1
Panmure Cl. N5 93 H4
Panmure Rd. SE26 170 E3
Pansy Gdns. W12 107 G7
Panther Dr. NW10 88 D5
Pantiles, The NW11 72 C5
Willifield Way
Pantiles, The, Bexh. 139 F7
Pantiles, The, Brom. 192 B3
Pantiles Cl. N13 59 H5
Panton St. SW1 17 H6
Panyer All. EC4 19 J3
Papermill Cl., Cars. 200 A4
Papillons Wk. SE3 155 G2
Papworth Gdns. N7 93 F5
Liverpool Rd.
Papworth Way SW2 151 G7
Parade, The SW11 32 A7
Parade, The SW11 129 J7
Parade, The, Esher 194 B6
Parade, The, Hmptn. 162 A5
Hampton Rd.
Parade, The (Carpenders Pk.), Wat. 50 E3
Parade Ms. SE27 169 H2
Norwood Rd.
Paradise Pas. N7 93 G5
Paradise Pl. SE18 136 B4
Woodhill
Paradise Rd. SW4 150 E2
Paradise Rd., Rich. 145 G5
Paradise Row E2 112/113 E3
Bethnal Grn. Rd.
Paradise St. SE16 132 E2
Paradise Wk. SW3 31 J5
Paradise Wk. SW3 129 J6
Paragon, The SE3 155 F2
Paragon Cl. E16 115 G6
Paragon Gro., Surb. 181 J6
Paragon Ms. SE1 36 C1
Paragon Pl. SE3 155 F2
Paragon Pl., Surb. 181 J6
Berrylands Rd.
Paragon Rd. E9 95 E6
Parbury Ri., Chess. 195 H6
Parbury Rd. SE23 153 H6
Parchmore Rd., Th.Hth. 187 H2
Parchmore Way, Th.Hth. 187 H2
Pardon St. EC1 11 H5
Pardoner St. SE1 28 C5
Pardoner St. SE1 132 A3
Parfett St. E1 21 J2
Parfett St. E1 112 D5
Parfitt Cl. NW3 91 F2
North End
Parfrey St. W6 127 J6
Parham Dr., Ilf. 80 E6
Parham Way N10 74 C2
Paris Gdn. SE1 27 G1
Paris Gdn. SE1 131 H1
Parish Gate Dr., Sid. 157 H6
Parish La. SE20 171 G6
Parish Ms. SE20 171 G7
Parish Wf. Pl. SE18 136 B4
Woodhill
Park, The N6 74 A6
Park, The NW11 90 E1
Park, The SE19 170 B7
Park, The SE23 170/171 E1
Park Hill
Park, The W5 125 G1
Park, The, Cars. 199 J5
Park, The, Sid. 175 J5
Park App., Well. 158 B4
Park Av. E6 116 D1
Park Av. E15 96 E6
Park Av. N3 73 E1
Park Av. N13 59 G3
Park Av. N18 60 D4
Park Av. N22 75 E2
Park Av. NW2 89 H6
Park Av. NW10 105 J3
Park Av. NW11 90 E1
Park Av. SW14 146 D4
Park Av., Bark. 99 F6
Park Av., Brom. 173 F6
Park Av., Cars. 200 A6
Park Av., Enf. 44 B6
Park Av., Houns. 143 H6
Park Av., Ilf. 98 D1
Park Av., Mitch. 168 B7
Park Av. (Farnborough), Orp. 206 C3
Park Av., Sthl. 123 G1

Parr Cl. N9 60 E4
Parr Cl. N18 60 E4
Parr Ct., Felt. 160 C4
Parr Rd. E6 116 A1
Parr Rd., Stan. 69 G1
Parr St. N1 12 B1
Parr St. N1 112 A2
Parrs Pl., Hmptn. 161 G7
Parry Av. E6 116 C6
Parry Cl., Epsom 197 G7
Parry Pl. SE18 137 E4
Parry Rd. SE25 188 B3
Parry Rd. W10 108 B3
Parry St. SW8 34 A5
Parry St. SW8 130 E6
Parsifal Rd. NW6 90 D5
Parsley Gdns., Croy. 203 G1
Primrose La.
Parsloes Av., Dag. 100 D4
Parson St. NW4 71 J4
Parsonage Gdns., Enf. 43 J2
Parsonage La., Enf. 44 A2
Parsonage La., Sid. 177 F4
Parsonage Manorway, Belv. 139 G6
Parsonage St. E14 134 C4
Parsons Cres., Edg. 54 A3
Parsons Grn. SW6 148 D1
Parsons Grn. La. SW6 148 D1
Parsons Gro., Edg. 54 A3
Parsons Hill SE18 136 D3
Powis St.
Parson's Ho. W2 7 E6
Parson's Ho. W2 109 G4
Parson's Mead, Croy. 201 H1
Parsons Mead, E.Mol. 179 J3
Parsons Rd. E13 115 J2
Old St.
Parthenia Rd. SW6 148 D1
Partingdale La. NW7 56 A5
Partington Cl. N19 92 D1
Partridge Cl. E16 116 A5
Fulmer Rd.
Partridge Cl., Barn. 39 J6
Partridge Cl., Bushey 51 H1
Partridge Cl., Stan. 53 H4
Partridge Ct. EC1 111 H4
Percival St.
Partridge Dr., Orp. 207 F3
Partridge Grn. SE9 174 D3
Partridge Rd., Hmptn. 161 F6
Partridge Rd., Sid. 175 H3
Partridge Sq. E6 116 B5
Nightingale Way
Partridge Way N22 75 E1
Parvin St. SW8 150 D1
Pasadena Cl., Hayes 122 B2
Pasadena Cl. Trd. Est., Hayes 122 B2
Pasadena Cl.
Pascal St. SW8 33 J7
Pascal St. SW8 130 D7
Pascoe Rd. SE13 154 D5
Pasley Cl. SE17 35 J4
Pasquier Rd. E17 77 H3
Passey Pl. SE9 156 C6
Passfield Dr. E14 114 B5
Uamvar St.
Passfield Path SE28 118 B7
Booth Cl.
Passing All. EC1 11 H6
Passmore Gdns. N11 58 D6
Passmore St. SW1 32 B2
Passmore St. SW1 130 A4
Pasteur Cl. NW9 71 E2
Pasteur Gdns. N18 59 H5
Paston Cl. E5 95 G3
Caldecott Way
Paston Cl., Wall. 200 C3
Paston Cres. SE12 155 H7
Pastor St. SE11 35 H1
Pastor St. SE11 131 H4
Pasture Cl., Wem. 86 E3
Pasture Rd. SE6 173 F1
Pasture Rd., Dag. 101 F4
asture Rd., Wem. 86 E2
astures, The N20 56 C1
tcham Ter. SW8 150 B1
er St. W8 128 D3
rnoster Row 19 J4
4
oster Sq. EC4 19 H3
Manor Dr., Felt. 141 G7
e SW19 184 E1
Rd. SW16 168 D6
The, Wat. 50 D1
y Cl.
d. SW11 149 H2
/4 150 D6
SW8 150 C1
W8 150 C1
W9 131 H7
114 A3
11 J4

Patricia Ct., Chis. 193 G1
Manor Pk. Rd.
Patricia Ct., Well. 138 B7
Patrick Connolly Gdns. E3 114 B3
Talwin St.
Patrick Pas. SW11 149 H2
Patrick Rd. E13 115 J3
Patriot Sq. E2 113 E2
Patrol Pl. SE6 154 B6
Patshull Pl. NW5 92 C6
Patshull Rd.
Patshull Rd. NW5 92 C6
Patten All., Rich. 145 G5
The Hermitage
Patten Rd. SW18 149 H7
Pattenden Rd. SE6 171 J1
Patterdale Cl., Brom. 173 F6
Patterdale Rd. SE15 133 F7
Patterson Ct. SE19 170 C7
Patterson Rd. SE19 170 C6
Pattina Wk. SE16 133 J1
Pattison Pt. E16 115 G5
Fife Rd.
Pattison Rd. NW2 90 D3
Pattison Wk. SE18 137 F5
Paul Cl. E15 96/97 E7
Paul St.
Paul Gdns., Croy. 202 C2
Paul Julius Cl. E14 114 D7
Paul Robeson Cl. E6 116 D3
Eastbourne Rd.
Paul St. E15 114 D1
Paul St. EC2 12 C6
Paul St. EC2 112 A4
Paulet Rd. SE5 151 H2
Paulhan Rd., Har. 69 G4
Paulin Dr. N21 43 G7
Pauline Cres., Twick. 161 J1
Paul's Wk. EC4 19 H5
Paul's Wk. EC4 111 J7
Paultons Sq. SW3 31 F5
Paultons Sq. SW3 129 G6
Paultons St. SW3 31 F6
Paultons St. SW3 129 G6
Pauntley St. N19 92 C1
Paved Ct., Rich. 145 G5
Paveley Dr. SW11 129 H7
Paveley St. NW8 7 H5
Paveley St. NW8 109 H4
Pavement, The SW4 150 C4
Pavement, The W5 125 H3
Popes La.
Pavement Ms., Rom. 82 D7
Clarissa Rd.
Pavement Sq., Croy. 202 D1
Pavet Cl., Dag. 101 H6
Pavilion Ms. N3 72 D2
Windermere Av.
Pavilion Rd. SW1 24 A6
Pavilion Rd. SW1 129 J2
Pavilion Rd., Ilf. 80 C7
Pavilion St. SW1 24 A6
Pavilion Ter., E.Mol. 180 C4
Pavilion Ter., Ilf. 81 H5
Southdown Cres.
Pavilion Way, Edg. 54 B7
Pavilion Way, Ruis. 84 C2
Pawleyne Cl. SE20 171 F7
Pawsey Cl. E13 115 G1
Plashet Rd.
Pawson's Rd., Croy. 187 J6
Paxford Rd., Wem. 86 E2
Paxton Cl., Rich. 145 J2
Paxton Cl., Walt. 178 C7
Shaw Dr.
Paxton Pl. SE27 170 B4
Paxton Rd. N17 60 C7
Paxton Rd. SE23 171 H3
Paxton Rd. W4 126 E6
Paxton Rd., Brom. 173 G7
Paxton Ter. SW1 33 E5
Paxton Ter. SW1 130 B6
Payne Rd. E3 114 B2
Payne St. SE8 133 J6
Paynell Ct. SE3 154/155 E3
Lawn Ter.
Paynes Wk. W6 128 B6
Paynesfield Av. SW14 146 D3
Peabody Av. SW1 32 D3
Peabody Cl. SE10 154 B1
Devonshire Dr.
Peabody Cl., Croy. 203 F1
Shirley Rd.
Peabody Dws. WC1 10 A5
Peabody Est. EC1 12 A6
Peabody Est. N17 76 B1
Peabody Est. SE1 27 F2
Peabody Est. SE24 151 J7
Peabody Est. SW3 31 H5
Peabody Est. W6 127 J5
The Sq.
Peabody Est. W10 107 J5

Peabody Hill SE21 169 H1
Peabody Hill Est. SE21 151 H7
Peabody Sq. N1 111 H1
Essex Rd.
Peabody Sq. SE1 27 G4
Peabody Sq. SE1 131 H2
Peabody Trust SE1 27 J2
Peabody Trust SE1 131 J1
Peabody Yd. N1 111 J1
Greenman St.
Peace Cl. N14 42 B5
Peace Cl. SE25 188 B4
Peace Gro., Wem. 88 B3
Peace St. SE18 136/137 E6
Nightingale Vale
Peach Rd. W10 108 A3
Peaches Cl., Sutt. 198 B7
Peachum Rd. SE3 135 F6
Peacock St. SE17 35 H2
Peacock Wk. E16 115 H6
Peacock Yd. SE17 35 H2
Peak, The SE26 171 F3
Peak Hill SE26 171 F4
Peak Hill Av. SE26 171 F4
Peak Hill Gdns. SE26 171 F4
Peaketon Av., Ilf. 80 A4
Peal Gdns. W13 104 D4
Ruislip Rd. E.
Peall Rd., Croy. 187 F6
Pear Cl. NW9 70 D4
Pear Cl. SE14 133 H7
Southerngate Way
Pear Pl. SE1 27 E3
Pear Rd. E11 96 D3
Pear Tree Cl. E2 112 C1
Pear Tree Cl., Chess. 196 A5
Pear Tree Cl., Mitch. 185 H2
Pear Tree Ct. EC1 11 F5
Pear Tree Ct. EC1 111 G4
Pear Tree St. EC1 11 H5
Pear Tree St. EC1 111 H4
Pearce Cl., Mitch. 186 A2
Pearce Rd., W.Mol. 179 H3
Pearcefield Av. SE23 171 F1
Pearcroft Rd. E11 96 D2
Peardon St. SW8 150 B2
Peareswood Gdns., Stan. 69 G1
Pearfield Rd. SE23 171 H3
Pearl Cl. E6 116 D6
Pearl Cl. NW2 72 A7
Marble Dr.
Pearl Rd. E17 78 A3
Pearl St. E1 132/133 E1
Penang St.
Pearman St. SE1 27 F5
Pearman St. SE1 131 G2
Pears Rd., Houns. 143 J3
Pearscroft Ct. SW6 149 E1
Pearscroft Rd. SW6 149 E1
Pearse St. SE15 36 E6
Pearson Ms. SW4 150 D3
Edgeley Rd.
Pearson St. E2 13 E1
Pearson St. E2 112 C2
Pearsons Av. SE14 154 A1
Tanners Hill
Peartree Av. SW17 167 F3
Peartree Gdns., Dag. 100 B4
Peartree Gdns., Rom. 83 H2
Peartree La. E1 113 F7
Glamis Rd.
Peartree Rd., Enf. 44 B3
Peartree Way SE10 135 G4
Peary Pl. E2 113 F3
Kirkwall Pl.
Peatfield Cl., Sid. 175 H3
Woodside Rd.
Pebble Way W3 126 B1
Pebworth Rd., Har. 86 D2
Peckarmans Wd. SE26 170 D3
Peckett Sq. N5 93 J4
Highbury Gra.
Peckford Pl. SW9 151 G2
Peckham Gro. SE15 36 E7
Peckham Gro. SE15 132 B7
Peckham High St. SE15 152 D1
Peckham Hill St. SE15 37 H7
Peckham Hill St. SE15 132 D7
Peckham Pk. Rd. SE15 37 J7
Peckham Pk. Rd. SE15 132 D7
Peckham Rd. SE5 152 B1
Peckham Rd. SE15 152 B1
Peckham Rye SE15 152 D3
Peckham Rye SE22 152 D4
Pecks Yd. E1 21 F1
Peckwater St. NW5 92 C5

Pedlars Wk. N7 93 E6
Pedley Rd., Dag. 100 C1
Pedley St. E1 13 G6
Pedley St. E1 112 C4
Pedro St. E5 95 G3
Pedworth Gdns. SE16 133 F4
Rotherhithe New Rd.
Peek Cres. SW19 166 A5
Peel Cl. E4 62 B2
Peel Cl. N9 60 D3
Plevna Rd.
Peel Dr. NW9 71 F3
Peel Dr., Ilf. 80 B3
Peel Gro. E2 113 F2
Peel Pas. W8 128 D1
Peel St.
Peel Pl., Ilf. 80 B2
Peel Prec. NW6 108 D2
Peel Rd. E18 79 F1
Peel Rd. NW6 108 C3
Peel Rd., Har. 68 C3
Peel Rd., Orp. 207 F5
Peel Rd., Wem. 87 G3
Peel St. W8 128 D1
Peerless St. EC1 12 B4
Peerless St. EC1 112 A3
Pegamoid Rd. N18 61 F3
Pegasus Cl. N16 94 A4
Green Las.
Pegasus Pl. SE11 35 E5
Pegasus Way N11 58 B6
Pegg Rd., Houns. 122 D7
Pegley Gdns. SE12 173 G2
Pegwell St. SE18 137 H7
Pekin Cl. E14 114 A6
Pekin St.
Pekin St. E14 114 A6
Peldon Ct., Rich. 145 J4
Peldon Pas., Rich. 145 J4
Worple Way
Peldon Wk. N1 111 H1
Britannia Row
Pelham Av., Bark. 117 J1
Pelham Cl. SE5 152 B2
Pelham Cres. SW7 31 G2
Pelham Cres. SW7 129 H4
Pelham Pl. SW7 31 G2
Pelham Pl. SW7 129 H4
Pelham Rd. E18 79 H3
Pelham Rd. N15 76 C4
Pelham Rd. N22 75 G2
Pelham Rd. SW19 166 D7
Pelham Rd., Beck. 189 F2
Pelham Rd., Bexh. 159 G3
Pelham Rd., Ilf. 99 G2
Pelham St. SW7 31 F1
Pelham St. SW7 129 H4
Pelican Est. SE15 152 C1
Pelican Pas. E1 113 F4
Cambridge Heath Rd.
Pelican Wk. SW9 151 H4
Loughborough Pk.
Pelier St. SE17 36 A5
Pelinore Rd. SE6 172 E2
Pellant Rd. SW6 128 B7
Pellatt Gro. N22 75 G1
Pellatt Rd. SE22 152 C5
Pellatt Rd., Wem. 87 G2
Pellerin Rd. N16 94 B5
Pelling St. E14 114 A6
Pellipar Cl. N13 59 G3
Pellipar Gdns. SE18 136 C5
Pelly Rd. E13 115 G2
Pelter St. E2 13 F3
Pelter St. E2 112 C3
Pelton Rd. SE10 134 E5
Pembar Av. E17 77 H3
Pember Rd. NW10 108 A3
Pemberley Chase (West Ewell), Epsom 196 B5
Pemberley Cl. (West Ewell), Epsom 196 B5
Ruxley Cl.
Pemberton Gdns. N19 92 C3
Pemberton Gdns., Rom. 82 E5
Pemberton Ho. SE26 170 D4
High Level Dr.
Pemberton Pl. E8 94/95 E7
Mare St.
Pemberton Rd. N4 75 G5
Pemberton Rd., E.Mol. 179 J4
Pemberton Row EC4 19 F3
Pemberton Ter. N19 92 C3
Pembridge Av., Twick. 161 F1
Pembridge Cres. W11 108 D7
Pembridge Gdns. W2 108 D7
Pembridge Ms. W11 108 D7
Pembridge Pl. SW15 148 D5
Oakhill Rd.
Pembridge Pl. W2 108 D7

Pembridge Rd. W11 108 D7
Pembridge Sq. W2 108 D7
Pembridge Vil. W2 108 D7
Pembridge Vil. W11 108 D7
Pembroke Av., Har. 68 D3
Pembroke Av., Pnr. 84 D1
Pembroke Av., Surb. 182 B5
Pembroke Cl. SW1 24 C4
Pembroke Cl. SW1 130 A2
Pembroke Cotts. W8 128 D3
Pembroke Sq.
Pembroke Gdns. W8 128 C4
Pembroke Gdns., Dag. 101 H3
Pembroke Gdns. Cl. W8 128 D3
Pembroke Ms. E3 113 H3
Morgan St.
Pembroke Ms. N10 74 A1
Pembroke Rd.
Pembroke Ms. W8 128 D3
Earls Wk.
Pembroke Pl. W8 128 D3
Pembroke Pl., Edg. 54 A7
Pembroke Pl., Islw. 144 B2
Thornbury Rd.
Pembroke Rd. E6 116 C5
Pembroke Rd. E17 78 B5
Pembroke Rd. N8 74 E4
Pembroke Rd. N10 74 A1
Pembroke Rd. N13 59 J3
Pembroke Rd. N15 76 C5
Pembroke Rd. SE25 188 B4
Pembroke Rd. W8 128 D4
Pembroke Rd., Brom. 191 J2
Pembroke Rd., Erith 139 J5
Pembroke Rd., Grnf. 103 H4
Pembroke Rd., Ilf. 99 J1
Pembroke Rd., Mitch. 186 A2
Pembroke Rd., Wem. 87 G3
Pembroke Sq. W8 128 D3
Pembroke St. N1 93 E7
Pembroke Studios W8 128 C3
Pembroke Vil. W8 128 D4
Pembroke Vil., Rich. 145 G4
Pembroke Wk. W8 128 D4
Pembroke Way, Hayes 121 F3
Pembury Av., Wor.Pk. 183 G7
Pembury Cl., Brom. 191 F7
Pembury Ct., Hayes 121 G6
Pembury Cres., Sid. 176 E2
Pembury Pl. E5 94 E5
Pembury Rd. E5 94 E5
Pembury Rd. N17 76 C2
Pembury Rd. SE25 188 D4
Pembury Rd., Bexh. 139 E7
Pemdevon Rd., Croy. 187 G7
Pemell Cl. E1 113 F4
Colebert Av.
Pemerich Cl., Hayes 121 J5
Pempath Pl., Wem. 87 G2
Penally Pl. N1 112 A1
Shepperton Rd.
Penang St. E1 133 E1
Penard Rd., Sthl. 123 G3
Penarth St. SE15 133 F6
Penates, Esher 194 A4
Penberth Rd. SE6 172 C1
Penbury Rd., Sthl. 123 F4
Pencombe Ms. W11 108 C7
Denbigh Rd.
Pencraig Way SE15 132 E6
Penda Rd., Erith 139 H7
Pendall Cl., Barn. 41 H4
Pendarves Rd. SW20 183 J1
Penda's Mead E9 95 H4
Lindisfarne Way
Pendell Av., Hayes 121 J7
Pendennis Rd. N17 76 A3
Pendennis Rd. SW16 168 E4
Penderel Rd., Houns. 143 G5
Penderry Ri. SE6 172 D2
Penderyn Way N7 92 D4
Pendle Rd. SW16 168 B6
Pendlestone Rd. E17 78 B5
Pendragon Rd., Brom. 173 F3
Pendragon Wk. NW9 70 E6
Pendrell Rd. SE4 153 H2
Pendrell St. SE18 137 G7
Pendula Dr., Hayes 102 D4
Pendulum Ms. E8 94 C5
Birkbeck Rd.
Penerley Rd. SE6 172 B1
Penfold Cl., Croy. 201 G3
Epsom Rd.
Penfold La., Bex. 176 D2
Penfold Pl. NW1 15 G1
Penfold Pl. NW1 109 H5
Penfold Rd. N9 61 G1
Penfold St. NW1 7 F6
Penfold St. NW1 109 G4
Penfold St. NW8 7 F6
Penfold St. NW8 109 G4
Penford Gdns. SE9 156 A3
Penford St. SE5 151 H2
Pengarth Rd., Bex. 158 D5
Penge Ho. SW11 149 G3
Wye St.
Penge La. SE20 171 F7
Penge Rd. E13 97 J7
Penge Rd. SE20 188 D3
Penge Rd. SE25 188 D3
Penhall Rd. SE7 136 A4
Penhill Rd., Bex. 158 C7
Penhurst Rd., Ilf. 65 E7
Penifather La., Grnf. 104 A3
Peninsular Cl., Felt. 141 G6
Peninsular Pk. Rd. SE7 135 G4
Penistone Rd. SW16 168 E7
Penketh Dr., Har. 86 A3
Penmon Rd. SE2 138 A3
Penn Cl., Grnf. 103 H2
Penn Cl., Har. 69 F4
Penn Gdns., Chis. 192 E2
Penn La., Bex. 158 D5
Penn Rd. N7 93 E5
Penn St. N1 112 A1
Pennack Rd. SE15 37 G6
Pennack Rd. SE15 132 C6
Pennant Ms. W8 30 A1
Pennant Ms. W8 128 E4
Pennant Ter. E17 77 J2
Pennard Rd. W12 127 J2
Pennards, The, Sun. 178 C2
Penner Cl. SW19 166 B2
Victoria Dr.
Penners Gdns., Surb. 181 H7
Pennethorne Cl. E9 113 F1
Victoria Pk. Rd.
Pennethorne Rd. SE15 132 E7
Pennine Dr. NW2 90 B2
Pennine La. NW2 90 B2
Pennine Dr.
Pennine Way, Hayes 121 G7
Pennington Cl. SE27 170 A4
Hamilton Rd.
Pennington Dr. N21 43 E5
Pennington St. E1 21 J6
Pennington St. E1 112 D7
Pennington Way SE12 173 H2
Penniston Cl. N17 75 J2
Penny Ms. SW12 150 B7
Caistor Rd.
Penny Rd. NW10 106 B3
Pennyfather La., Enf. 43 J3
Pennyfields E14 114 A7
Pennymoor Wk. W9 108 C3
Ashmore Rd.
Pennyroyal Av. E6 116 D6
Penpoll Rd. E8 94 E6
Penpool La., Well. 158 B3
Penrhyn Av. E17 77 J1
Penrhyn Cres. E17 78 A1
Penrhyn Cres. SW14 146 C4
Penrhyn Gro. E17 78 A1
Penrhyn Rd., Kings.T. 181 H3
Penrith Cl. SW15 148 B5
Penrith Cl., Beck. 190 B1
Albemarle Rd.
Penrith Pl. SE27 169 H2
Harpenden Rd.
Penrith Rd. N15 76 A5
Penrith Rd., Ilf. 65 J6
Penrith Rd., N.Mal. 182 D4
Penrith Rd., Th.Hth. 187 J2
Penrith St. SW16 168 C6
Penrose Av., Wat. 50 D2
Penrose Gro. SE17 35 J4
Penrose Gro. SE17 131 J5
Penrose Ho. SE17 35 J4
Penrose Ho. SE17 131 J5
Penrose St. SE17 35 J4
Penrose St. SE17 131 J5
Penry St. SE1 37 E2
Penryn St. NW1 9 H1
Penryn St. NW1 110 D2
Pensbury Pl. SW8 150 C2
Pensbury St. SW8 150 C2
Penscroft Gdns., Borwd. 38 D4
Pensford Av., Rich. 146 A2
Penshurst Av., Sid. 158 A6
Penshurst Gdns., Edg. 54 B5
Penshurst Grn., Brom. 191 F5
Penshurst Rd. E9 95 G7
Penshurst Rd. N17 60 C7
Penshurst Rd., Bexh. 159 F1
Penshurst Rd., Th.Hth. 187 H5
Penshurst Wk., Brom. 191 F5
Hayesford Pk. Dr.
Penshurst Way, Sutt. 198 D7
Pensilver Cl., Barn. 41 H4
Penstemon Cl. N3 56 D7
Penstock Footpath N22 75 E3
Pentavia Retail Pk. NW7 55 F7
Bunns La.
Pentelow Gdns., Felt. 142 A6
Pentire Rd. E17 78 D1
Pentland Av., Edg. 54 B2
Pentland Cl. NW11 90 B2
Pentland Gdns. SW18 149 F6
St. Ann's Hill
Pentland Pl., Nthlt. 102 E1
Pentland St. SW18 149 F6
Pentlands Cl., Mitch. 186 B3
Pentlow St. SW15 147 J3
Pentlow Way, Buck.H. 48 B7
Pentney Rd. E4 62 D1
Pentney Rd. SW12 168 C1
Pentney Rd. SW19 184 B1
Midmoor Rd.
Penton Gro. N1 11 E2
Penton Ho. SE2 138 D2
Hartslock Dr.
Penton Pl. SE17 35 H3
Penton Pl. SE17 131 H5
Penton Ri. WC1 10 D3
Penton Ri. WC1 111 F3
Penton St. N1 10 E1
Penton St. N1 111 G2
Pentonville Rd. N1 10 C2
Pentonville Rd. N1 111 F2
Pentridge St. SE15 132 C7
Pentyre Av. N18 60 A5
Penwerris Av., Islw. 123 J7
Penwith Rd. SW18 166 E2
Penwortham Rd. SW16 168 B6
Penylan Pl., Edg. 54 A7
Penywern Rd. SW5 128 D5
Penzance Pl. W11 128 B1
Penzance St. W11 128 B1
Peony Ct., Wdf.Grn. 62/63 E7
The Bridle Path
Peony Gdns. W12 107 G7
Peploe Rd. NW6 108 A2
Peplow Cl., West Dr. 120 A1
Tavistock Rd.
Pepper All., Loug. 47 G1
Pepper Cl. E6 116 C5
Pepper St. E14 134 B3
Pepper St. SE1 27 J3
Peppermead Sq. SE13 154 A5
Peppermint Cl., Croy. 186 E7
Peppermint Pl. E11 96/97 E3
Birch Gro.
Peppie Cl. N16 94 B2
Bouverie Rd.
Pepys Cres. E16 135 G1
Britannia Gate
Pepys Cres., Barn. 39 J5
Pepys Ri., Orp. 207 J1
Pepys Rd. SE14 153 G1
Pepys Rd. SW20 183 J1
Pepys St. EC3 21 E5
Pepys St. EC3 112 B7
Perceval Av. NW3 91 H5
Perch St. E8 94 C4
Percheron Cl., Islw. 144 D3
Percheron Rd., Borwd. 38 D6
Percival Ct. N17 60 C7
High Rd.
Percival Ct., Nthlt. 85 G5
Percival Gdns., Rom. 82 C6
Percival Rd. SW14 146 C4
Percival Rd., Enf. 44 C4
Percival Rd., Orp. 207 E2
Percival St. EC1 11 G5
Percival St. EC1 111 H4
Percival Way, Epsom 196 C4
Percy Bush Rd., West Dr. 120 C3
Percy Circ. WC1 10 D3
Percy Circ. WC1 111 F3
Percy Gdns., Enf. 45 G5
Percy Gdns., Islw. 144 D2
Percy Gdns., Wor.Pk. 196 E1
Percy Ms. W1 17 H2
Percy Pas. W1 17 G2
Percy Rd. E11 78 E7
Percy Rd. E16 115 E5
Percy Rd. N12 57 F5
Percy Rd. N21 43 J7
Percy Rd. NW6 108 D3
Stafford Rd.
Percy Rd. SE20 189 G1
Percy Rd. SE25 188 D5
Percy Rd. W12 127 G2
Percy Rd., Bexh. 159 E2
Percy Rd., Hmptn. 161 G7
Percy Rd., Ilf. 82 A7
Percy Rd., Islw. 144 D4
Percy Rd., Mitch. 186 A7
Percy Rd., Rom. 83 H3
Percy Rd., Twick. 161 H1
Percy St. W1 17 H2
Percy St. W1 110 D5
Percy Way, Twick. 161 J1
Percy Yd. WC1 10 D3
Peregrine Cl. NW10 88 D5
Peregrine Ct. SW16 169 F4
Leithcote Gdns.
Peregrine Ct., Well. 157 J1
Peregrine Gdns., Croy. 203 H2
Peregrine Ho. EC1 11 H3
Peregrine Ho. EC1 111 H3
Peregrine Way SW19 165 J7
Perham Rd. W14 128 B5
Peridot St. E6 116 B5
Perifield SE21 169 J1
Perimeade Rd., Grnf. 105 F2
Periton Rd. SE9 156 A4
Perivale Gdns. W13 104/105 E4
Bellevue Rd.
Perivale Gra., Grnf. 104 D3
Perivale Ind. Pk., Grnf. 104 E2
Perivale La., Grnf. 104 D3
Perivale New Business Cen., Grnf. 105 E2
Perkin Cl., Wem. 86 E5
Perkin's Rents SW1 25 H5
Perkin's Rents SW1 130 D3
Perkins Rd., Ilf. 81 G5
Perkins Sq. SE1 28 A1
Perks Cl. SE3 154/155 E3
Hurren Cl.
Perpins Rd. SE9 157 H6
Perran Rd. SW2 169 H2
Christchurch Rd.
Perran Wk., Brent. 125 H5
Perren St. NW5 92 B6
Ryland Rd.
Perrers Rd. W6 127 H4
Perrin Rd., Wem. 86 D4
Perrins Ct. NW3 91 F4
Hampstead High St.
Perrins La. NW3 91 F4
Perrin's Wk. NW3 91 F4
Perrott St. SE18 137 F4
Perry Av. W3 106 D6
Perry Ct. E14 134 A5
Napier Av.
Perry Ct. N15 76 B6
Albert Rd.
Perry Gdns. N9 60 B3
Deansway
Perry Garth, Nthlt. 102 C1
Perry Hall Rd., Orp. 193 J6
Perry Hill SE6 171 J3
Perry How, Wor.Pk. 197 F1
Perry Mead, Enf. 43 H2
Perry Ri. SE23 171 H3
Perry Rd., Dag. 119 F4
Perry St., Chis. 175 G6
Perry St. Gdns., Chis. 175 H6
Old Perry St.
Perry Vale SE23 171 F2
Perryfield Way NW9 71 F6
Perryfield Way, Rich. 163 E2
Perryman Ho., Bark. 117 F1
The Shaftesburys
Perrymans Fm. Rd., Ilf. 81 G6
Perrymead St. SW6 148 D1
Perryn Rd. SE16 132/133 E3
Drummond Rd.
Perryn Rd. W3 106 D7
Perrys Pl. W1 17 H3
Persant Rd. SE6 172 E2
Perseverance Pl. SW9 131 G7
Perseverance Pl., Rich. 145 H3
Shaftesbury Rd.
Pershore Cl., Ilf. 81 E5
Pershore Gro., Cars. 185 G6
Pert Cl. N10 58 B7
Perth Av. NW9 70 D7
Perth Av., Hayes 102 C4
Perth Cl. SW20 183 G2
Huntley Way
Perth Rd. E10 95 H1
Perth Rd. E13 115 H2
Perth Rd. N4 93 G1
Perth Rd. N22 75 H1
Perth Rd., Bark. 117 G2
Perth Rd., Beck. 190 C2
Perth Rd., Ilf. 80 D6
Perth Ter., Ilf. 81 F7
Perwell Av., Har. 85 F1

Perwell Ct., Har. 85 F1
Peter Av. NW10 89 H7
Peter James Business Cen., Hayes 122 A2
Peter St. W1 17 G5
Peter St. W1 110 D7
Peterboat Cl. SE10 134/135 E4
Tunnel Av.
Peterborough Gdns., Ilf. 80 B7
Peterborough Ms. SW6 148 D2
Peterborough Rd. E10 78 C5
Peterborough Rd. SW6 148 D2
Peterborough Rd., Cars. 185 H6
Peterborough Rd., Har. 86 B1
Peterborough Vil. SW6 148 E1
Peterchurch Ho. SE15 132/133 E6
Commercial Way
Petergate SW11 149 F4
Peters Cl., Dag. 100 D1
Peters Cl., Stan. 53 G6
Peters Cl., Well. 157 H2
Peters Hill EC4 19 J5
Peter's La. EC1 19 H1
Peters Path SE26 170 E4
Petersfield Cl. N18 59 J5
Petersfield Ri. SW15 165 H1
Petersfield Rd. W3 126 C2
Petersham Cl., Rich. 163 G2
Petersham Cl., Sutt. 198 D5
Petersham Dr., Orp. 193 J2
Petersham Gdns., Orp. 193 J2
Petersham La. SW7 22 C5
Petersham La. SW7 129 F3
Petersham Ms. SW7 22 C6
Petersham Ms. SW7 129 F3
Petersham Pl. SW7 22 C5
Petersham Pl. SW7 129 F3
Petersham Rd., Rich. 145 H6
Petersham Ter., Croy. 200/201 E3
Richmond Grn.
Peterstone Rd. SE2 138 B3
Peterstow Cl. SW19 166 B2
Peterwood Way, Croy. 201 F2
Petherton Rd. N5 93 J5
Petley Rd. W6 127 J6
Peto Pl. NW1 8 E5
Peto Pl. NW1 110 B4
Peto St. N. E16 115 F7
Victoria Dock Rd.
Petrie Cl. NW2 90 B6
Pett St. SE18 136 B4
Petticoat La. E1 21 E2
Petticoat La. E1 112 B5
Petticoat Sq. E1 21 F3
Petticoat Sq. E1 112 C6
Pettits Pl., Dag. 101 G5
Pettits Rd., Dag. 101 G5
Pettiward Cl. SW15 147 J4
Pettman Cres. SE28 137 G3
Petts Hill, Nthlt. 85 H5
Petts Wd. Rd., Orp. 193 F5
Pettsgrove Av., Wem. 87 F5
Petty France SW1 25 G5
Petty France SW1 130 C3
Petworth Cl., Nthlt. 85 F7
Petworth Gdns. SW20 183 H3
Hidcote Gdns.
Petworth Rd. N12 57 H5
Petworth Rd., Bexh. 159 G5
Petworth St. SW11 149 H1
Petyt Pl. SW3 31 G6
Petyward SW3 31 H2
Petyward SW3 129 H4
Pevel Ho., Dag. 101 G2
Pevensey Av. N11 58 D5
Pevensey Av., Enf. 44 A2
Pevensey Cl., Islw. 123 J7
Pevensey Rd. E7 97 F4
Pevensey Rd. SW17 167 G4
Pevensey Rd., Felt. 160 E1
Peverel E6 116 D6
Downings
Peveret Cl. N11 58 B5
Woodland Rd.
Peveril Dr., Tedd. 162 A5
Pewsey Cl. E4 62 A5
Peyton Pl. SE10 134 C7
Pharaoh Cl., Mitch. 185 J7
Pheasant Cl. E16 115 G6
Maplin Rd.
Phelp St. SE17 36 B5
Phelp St. SE17 132 A6
Phelps Way, Hayes 121 J4
Phene St. SW3 31 H5
Phene St. SW3 129 H6
Phil Brown Pl. SW8 150 B2
Heath Rd.
Philbeach Gdns. SW5 128 D5
Philchurch Pl. E1 21 J4
Philimore Cl. SE18 137 H5
Philip Gdns., Croy. 203 J2
Philip La. N15 76 A4
Philip Rd. SE15 152 D3
Peckham Rye
Philip St. E13 115 G4
Philip Wk. SE15 152 D3
Philipot Path SE9 156 C6
Philippa Gdns. SE9 156 A5
Philips Cl., Cars. 200 A1
Phillimore Gdns. NW10 107 J1
Phillimore Gdns. W8 128 D2
Phillimore Gdns. Cl. W8 128 D3
Phillimore Gdns.
Phillimore Pl. W8 128 D2
Phillimore Wk. W8 128 D3
Phillipp St. N1 112 B1
Philpot La. EC3 20 D5
Philpot Path, Ilf. 99 F3
Sunnyside Rd.
Philpot Sq. SW6 148/149 E3
Peterborough Rd.
Philpot St. E1 113 E6
Phineas Pett Rd. SE9 156 B3
Phipp St. EC2 12 D5
Phipp St. EC2 112 B4
Phipps Br. Rd. SW19 185 F2
Phipps Br. Rd., Mitch. 185 F2
Phipp's Ms. SW1 24 D6
Phoebeth Rd. SE4 154 A5
Phoenix Cl. E8 112 C1
Stean St.
Phoenix Cl., W.Wick. 204 E2
Phoenix Dr., Kes. 206 A3
Phoenix Pk., Brent. 125 G5
Phoenix Pl. WC1 10 D5
Phoenix Pl. WC1 111 F4
Phoenix Rd. NW1 9 H3
Phoenix Rd. NW1 110 D3
Phoenix Rd. SE20 171 F6
Phoenix St. WC2 17 J4
Phoenix Way, Houns. 122 C6
Phoenix Wf. SE10 135 F2
Phoenix Wf. Rd. SE1 29 G4
Phyllis Av., N.Mal. 183 H5
Physic Pl. SW3 31 J5
Piazza, The WC2 110/111 E7
Covent Gdn.
Picardy Manorway, Belv. 139 H3
Picardy Rd., Belv. 139 G4
Picardy St., Belv. 139 G3
Piccadilly W1 24 E2
Piccadilly W1 130 B1
Piccadilly Arc. SW1 25 F1
Piccadilly Circ. W1 17 H6
Piccadilly Circ. W1 110 D7
Piccadilly Pl. W1 17 G6
Pickard St. EC1 11 H3
Pickering Av. E6 116 D2
Pickering Cl. E9 95 G7
Cassland Rd.
Pickering Gdns., Croy. 188 C6
Pickering Ms. W2 14 B3
Pickering Pl. SW1 25 G2
Pickering St. N1 111 H1
Essex Rd.
Pickets Cl., Bushey 52 A1
Pickets St. SW12 150 B7
Pickett Cft., Stan. 69 G1
Picketts Lock La. N9 61 F2
Pickford Cl., Bexh. 158 E2
Pickford La., Bexh. 159 E2
Pickford Rd., Bexh. 158 E3
Pickfords Wf. N1 11 J2
Pickfords Wf. N1 111 J2
Pickhurst Grn., Brom. 191 F7
Pickhurst La., Brom. 205 F1
Pickhurst La., W.Wick. 191 E6
Pickhurst Mead, Brom. 191 F7
Pickhurst Pk., Brom. 191 E5
Pickhurst Ri., W.Wick. 190 C7
Pickle Herring St. SE1 132 B1
Tooley St.
Pickwick Cl., Houns. 142/143 E5
Dorney Way
Pickwick Ct. SE9 174 B1
West Pk.
Pickwick Ms. N18 60 B5
Pickwick Pl., Har. 68 B7
Pickwick Rd. SE21 152 A7
Pickwick St. SE1 27 J4
Pickwick Way, Chis. 175 F6
Pickworth Cl. SW8 130/131 E7
Kenchester Cl.
Picton Pl. W1 16 C4
Picton Pl., Surb. 196 A1
Picton St. SE5 132 A7
Piedmont Rd. SE18 137 G5
Pier Head E1 132/133 E1
Wapping High St.
Pier Par. E16 136 D2
Pier Rd.
Pier Rd. E16 136 C2
Pier Rd., Felt. 142 B5
Pier St. E14 134 C4
Pier Ter. SW18 149 F4
Jew's Row
Pier Way SE28 137 G3
Piermont Grn. SE22 152 E5
Piermont Pl., Brom. 192 B2
Piermont Rd. SE22 152 E5
Pierrepoint Arc. N1 111 H2
Islington High St.
Pierrepoint Rd. W3 106 B7
Pierrepoint Row N1 11 G1
Pigeon La., Hmptn. 161 G4
Pigott St. E14 114 A6
Pike Cl., Brom. 173 H5
Pike Rd. NW7 54 D4
Ellesmere Av.
Pikes End, Pnr. 66 B4
Pikestone Cl., Hayes 102/103 E4
Berrydale Rd.
Pilgrim Cl., Mord. 185 E7
Pilgrim Hill SE27 169 J4
Pilgrim St. EC4 19 G4
Pilgrimage St. SE1 28 B4
Pilgrimage St. SE1 132 A2
Pilgrims Cl. N13 59 F4
Pilgrims Cl., Nthlt. 85 J5
Pilgrims Ct. SE3 155 G1
Pilgrim's La. NW3 91 G4
Pilgrims Ms. E14 114 C7
Blackwall Way
Pilgrims Pl. NW3 91 G4
Hampstead High St.
Pilgrims Ri., Barn. 41 H5
Pilgrims Way E6 116 B1
High St. N.
Pilgrims Way N19 92 D1
Pilgrims Way, S.Croy. 202 C5
Pilgrim's Way, Wem. 88 B1
Pilkington Rd. SE15 152 E2
Pilkington Rd., Orp. 207 F2
Pilsdon Cl. SW19 166 A1
Inner Pk. Rd.
Piltdown Rd., Wat. 50 D4
Pilton Est., The, Croy. 201 H2
Pitlake
Pimento Ct. W5 125 G3
Olive Rd.
Pimlico Rd. SW1 32 B3
Pimlico Rd. SW1 130 A5
Pimlico Wk. N1 12 D3
Pinchbeck Rd., Orp. 207 J6
Pinchin St. E1 21 J5
Pinchin St. E1 112 D7
Pincott Pl. SE4 153 G3
Billingford Cl.
Pincott Rd. SW19 185 F1
Pincott Rd., Bexh. 159 G5
Pindar St. EC2 20 D1
Pindar St. EC2 112 B5
Pindock Ms. W9 6 B6
Pine Av. E15 96 D5
Pine Av., W.Wick. 204 B1
Pine Cl. E10 96 B2
Walnut Rd.
Pine Cl. N14 42 C7
Pine Cl. N19 92 C2
Hargrave Pk.
Pine Cl. SE20 189 F1
Pine Cl., Stan. 52 E4
Pine Coombe, Croy. 203 G4
Pine Gdns., Ruis. 84 B1
Pine Gdns., Surb. 182 A6
Pine Glade, Orp. 206 C4
Pine Gro. N4 93 E2
Pine Gro. N20 56 C1
Pine Gro. SW19 166 C5
Pine Ms. NW10 108 A2
Clifford Gdns.
Pine Rd. N11 58 A2
Pine Rd. NW2 89 J4
Pine St. EC1 11 E5
Pine St. EC1 111 G4
Pine Tree Cl., Houns. 142 B1
Pine Wk., Brom. 191 J1
Pine Wk., Surb. 182 A6
Pine Wd., Sun. 178 A1
Pineapple Ct. SW1 25 F5
Pinecrest Gdns., Orp. 207 E4
Pinecroft Cres., Barn. 40 B4
Hillside Gdns.
Pinedene SE15 152/153 E1
Meeting Ho. La.
Pinefield Cl. E14 114 A7
Pinehurst Wk., Orp. 207 H1
Pinelands Cl. SE3 135 F7
St. John's Pk.
Pinemartin Cl. NW2 89 J3
Pines, The N14 42 C5
Pines, The, Sun. 178 A3
Pines, The, Wdf.Grn. 63 G3
Pines Rd., Brom. 192 B2
Pinewood Av., Pnr. 51 H6
Pinewood Av., Sid. 175 H1
Pinewood Cl., Borwd. 38 D1
Pinewood Cl., Croy. 203 H3
Pinewood Cl., Nthwd. 50 B5
Pinewood Cl., Orp. 207 G1
Pinewood Cl., Pnr. 51 H6
Pinewood Dr., Orp. 207 H5
Pinewood Gro. W5 105 F6
Pinewood Rd. SE2 138 D6
Pinewood Rd., Brom. 191 G4
Pinewood Rd., Felt. 160 B3
Pinfold Rd. SW16 168 E4
Pinglestone Cl., West Dr. 120 B7
Pinkcoat Cl., Felt. 160 B3
Tanglewood Way
Pinkerton Pl. SW16 168 D4
Riggindale Rd.
Pinkham Way N11 58 A7
Pinkwell Av., Hayes 121 G4
Pinkwell La., Hayes 121 F4
Pinley Gdns., Dag. 118 B1
Stamford Rd.
Pinnacle Hill, Bexh. 159 H4
Pinnacle Hill N., Bexh. 159 H3
Pinnell Pl. SE9 156 A4
Pinnell Rd. SE9 156 A4
Pinner Ct., Pnr. 67 G4
Pinner Grn., Pnr. 66 C2
Pinner Gro., Pnr. 67 E4
Pinner Hill, Pnr. 66 C1
Pinner Hill Rd., Pnr. 66 C2
Pinner Pk., Pnr. 67 G1
Pinner Pk. Av., Har. 67 H3
Pinner Pk. Gdns., Har. 67 J2
Pinner Rd., Har. 67 H5
Pinner Rd., Pnr. 67 F4
Pinner Vw., Har. 67 J6
Pintail Cl. E6 116 B5
Swan App.
Pintail Rd., Wdf.Grn. 63 H7
Pintail Way, Hayes 102 D5
Pinto Cl., Borwd. 38 D6
Percheron Rd.
Pinto Way SE3 155 H4
Pioneer St. SE15 152 D1
Pioneer Way W12 107 H6
Du Cane Rd.
Pioneers Ind. Pk., Croy. 200 E1
Piper Cl. N7 93 F5
Piper Rd., Kings.T. 182 A3
Piper's Gdns., Croy. 189 H7
Pipers Grn. NW9 70 C5
Pipers Grn. La., Edg. 53 H3
Pipewell Rd., Cars. 185 H6
Pippin Cl. NW2 89 H3
Pippin Cl., Croy. 203 J1
Pippins Cl., West Dr. 120 A3
Piquet Rd. SE20 189 F2
Pirbright Cres., Croy. 204 C6
Pirbright Rd. SW18 166 C1
Pirie Cl. SE5 152 A3
Denmark Hill
Pirie St. E16 135 H1
Pitcairn Cl., Rom. 83 G4
Pitcairn Rd., Mitch. 167 J7
Pitcairn's Path, Har. 85 J3
Eastcote Rd.
Pitchford St. E15 96 D7
Pitfield Cres. SE28 138 A1
Pitfield Est. N1 12 C3
Pitfield Est. N1 112 A3
Pitfield St. N1 12 D3
Pitfield St. N1 112 B3
Pitfield Way NW10 88 C6
Pitfield Way, Enf. 45 F1
Pitfold Cl. SE12 155 G6
Pitfold Rd. SE12 155 G6
Pitlake, Croy. 201 H2
Pitman St. SE5 35 J7
Pitman St. SE5 131 J7
Pitsea Pl. E1 113 G6
Pitsea St.
Pitsea St. E1 113 G6
Pitshanger La. W5 105 E4
Pitshanger Pk. W13 105 F3

Pitt Cres. SW19 166 E4
Pitt Rd., Croy. 187 J5
Pitt Rd., Orp. 207 F4
Pitt Rd., Th.Hth. 187 J5
Pitt St. W8 128 D2
Pittman Gdns., Ilf. 99 F5
Pitt's Head Ms. W1 24 C2
Pitt's Head Ms. W1 130 A1
Pittsmead Av., Brom. 191 G7
Pittville Gdns. SE25 188 D3
Pixfield Ct., Brom. 191 F2
Beckenham La.
Pixley St. E14 113 J6
Place Fm. Av., Orp. 207 G1
Plaistow Gro. E15 115 F1
Plaistow Gro., Brom. 173 H7
Plaistow La., Brom. 173 H7
Plaistow Pk. Rd. E13 115 H2
Plaistow Rd. E13 115 F1
Plaistow Rd. E15 115 F1
Plane St. SE26 170 E3
Plane Tree Cres., Felt. 160 B3
Plane Tree Wk. SE19 170 B6
Central Hill
Plantagenet Cl., Wor.Pk. 196 D4
Plantagenet Gdns., Rom. 82 D7
Broomfield Rd.
Plantagenet Pl., Rom. 82 D7
Broomfield Rd.
Plantagenet Rd., Barn. 41 F4
Plantain Gdns. E11 96 D3
Hollydown Way
Plantain Pl. SE1 28 B3
Plantation, The SE3 155 G2
Plantation Wf. SW11 149 F3
Plasel Ct. E13 115 G1
Plashet Rd.
Plashet Gro. E6 115 J1
Plashet Rd. E13 115 G1
Plassy Rd. SE6 154 B7
Platina St. EC2 12 C5
Plato Rd. SW2 151 E4
Platt, The SW15 148 A3
Platt St. NW1 9 H1
Platt St. NW1 110 D2
Platt's Eyot, Hmptn. 179 G2
Platt's La. NW3 90 D4
Platts Rd., Enf. 45 F1
Plawsfield Rd., Beck. 189 G1
Plaxtol Cl., Brom. 191 J1
Plaxtol Rd., Erith 139 G7
Playfair St. W6 127 J5
Winslow Rd.
Playfield Av., Rom. 83 J1
Playfield Cres. SE22 152 C5
Playfield Rd., Edg. 70 C2
Playford Rd. N4 93 F2
Playgreen Way SE6 172 A4
Playground Cl., Beck. 189 G2
Churchfields Rd.
Playhouse Yd. EC4 19 G4
Plaza W., Houns. 143 H1
Pleasance, The SW15 147 H4
Pleasance Rd. SW15 147 H5
Pleasant Gro., Croy. 203 J3
Pleasant Pl. N1 93 H7
Pleasant Row NW1 110 B1
Pleasant Vw. Pl., Orp. 206/207 E5
High St.
Pleasant Way, Wem. 105 F2
Plender St. NW1 110 C1
Plender St. Est. NW1 110 C1
Plender St.
Pleshey Rd. N7 92 D4
Plevna Cres. N15 76 B6
Plevna Rd. N9 60 D3
Plevna Rd., Hmptn. 179 H1
Plevna St. E14 134 C3
Pleydell Av. SE19 170 C7
Pleydell Av. W6 127 F4
Pleydell Ct. EC4 19 F4
Pleydell Est. EC1 111 J3
Radnor St.
Pleydell St. EC4 19 F4
Plimsoll Cl. E14 114 B6
Grundy St.
Plimsoll Rd. N4 93 G3
Plough Ct. EC3 20 C5
Plough La. SE22 152 C6
Plough La. SW17 167 E5
Plough La. SW19 167 E5
Plough La., Tedd. 162 D5
Plough La., Wall. 200 E4
Plough La. Cl., Wall. 200 E5
Plough Ms. SW11 149 G4
Plough Ter.
Plough Pl. EC4 19 F3
Plough Rd. SW11 149 G3
Plough St. E1 21 H3
Plough Ter. SW11 149 G4
Plough Way SE16 133 G4
Plough Yd. EC2 12 E6
Plough Yd. EC2 112 B4
Ploughmans Cl. NW1 110 D1
Crofters Way
Ploughmans End, Islw. 144 A5
Plover Way SE16 133 H3
Plover Way, Hayes 102 D6
Plowden Bldgs. EC4 111 G6
Middle Temple La.
Plowman Cl. N18 60 A5
Plowman Way, Dag. 100 C1
Plum Cl., Felt. 160 A1
Highfield Rd.
Plum Garth, Brent. 125 G4
Plum La. SE18 137 E7
Plumbers Row E1 21 H2
Plumbers Row E1 112 D5
Plumbridge St. SE10 154 C1
Blackheath Hill
Plummer La., Mitch. 185 J2
Plummer Rd. SW4 150 D7
Plumpton Cl., Nthlt. 85 G6
Plumpton Way, Cars. 199 H3
Plumstead Common Rd. SE18 136 E6
Plumstead High St. SE18 137 H4
Plumstead Rd. SE18 137 E4
Plumtree Cl., Dag. 101 H6
Plumtree Cl., Wall. 200 D7
Plumtree Ct. EC4 19 F3
Plumtree Mead, Loug. 48 D3
Plymouth Rd. E16 115 G5
Plymouth Rd., Brom. 191 H1
Plymouth Wf. E14 134 D4
Plympton Av. NW6 90 C7
Plympton Cl., Belv. 138/139 E3
Halifield Dr.
Plympton Pl. NW8 7 G6
Plympton Rd. NW6 90 C7
Plympton St. NW8 7 G6
Plympton St. NW8 109 H4
Plymstock Rd., Well. 138 C7
Pocklington Cl. NW9 70 E2
Pocock Av., West Dr. 120 C3
Pocock St. SE1 27 G3
Pocock St. SE1 131 H2
Podmore Rd. SW18 149 F4
Poets Rd. N5 94 A5
Poets Way, Har. 68 B4
Blawith Rd.
Point Cl. SE10 154 C1
Point Hill
Point Hill SE10 134 C7
Point of Thomas Path E1 113 F7
Glamis Rd.
Point Pl., Wem. 88 B7
Point Pleasant SW18 148 D4
Pointalls Cl. N3 73 F2
Pointer Cl. SE28 118 D6
Pointers Cl. E14 134 B5
Poland St. W1 17 G4
Poland St. W1 110 C6
Pole Cat All., Brom. 205 F2
Pole Hill Rd. E4 46 C7
Polebrook Rd. SE3 155 J3
Polecroft La. SE6 171 J2
Polehamptons, The, Hmptn. 161 J7
High St.
Polesden Gdns. SW20 183 H2
Polesworth Ho. W2 108 D5
Polesworth Rd., Dag. 100 D7
Pollard Cl. E16 115 G7
Pollard Cl. N7 93 F4
Pollard Rd. N20 57 H2
Pollard Rd., Mord. 185 G5
Pollard Row E2 13 J3
Pollard Row E2 112 D3
Pollard St. E2 13 J3
Pollard St. E2 112 D3
Pollard Wk., Sid. 176 C6
Pollards Cl., Loug. 47 J5
Pollards Cres. SW16 187 E3
Pollards Hill E. SW16 187 F3
Pollards Hill N. SW16 187 E3
Pollards Hill S. SW16 187 E3
Pollards Hill W. SW16 187 E3
Pollards Wd. Rd. SW16 187 E2
Pollen St. W1 17 E4
Pollitt Dr. NW8 7 E5
Polperro Cl., Orp. 193 J6
Cotswold Ri.
Polsted Rd. SE6 153 J7
Polthorne Est. SE18 137 G4
Polthorne Gro. SE18 137 F4
Polworth Rd. SW16 168 E5
Polygon, The SW4 150 C4
Old Town
Polygon Rd. NW1 9 H2
Polygon Rd. NW1 110 D2
Polytechnic St. SE18 136 D4
Pomell Way E1 21 G3
Pomeroy St. SE14 153 F1
Pomfret Rd. SE5 151 H3
Flaxman Rd.
Pomoja La. N19 92 D2
Pond Cl. N12 57 H6
Summerfields Av.
Pond Cl. SE3 155 F2
Pond Cottage La., W.Wick. 204 A1
Pond Cotts. SE21 170 B1
Pond Fld. End, Loug. 47 J7
Pond Hill Gdns., Sutt. 198 B6
Pond Mead SE21 152 A6
Pond Path, Chis. 174/175 E6
Heathfield La.
Pond Pl. SW3 31 G2
Pond Pl. SW3 129 H4
Pond Rd. E15 114 E2
Pond Rd. SE3 155 F2
Pond Sq. N6 92 A1
South Gro.
Pond St. NW3 91 H5
Pond Way, Tedd. 163 F6
Holmesdale Rd.
Ponder St. N7 93 F7
Ponders End Ind. Est., Enf. 45 J4
Pondfield Rd., Brom. 205 E1
Pondfield Rd., Dag. 101 H5
Pondfield Rd., Orp. 207 E3
Pondside Cl., Hayes 121 G7
Providence La.
Pondwood Ri., Orp. 193 H7
Ponler St. E1 112 E6
Ponsard Rd. NW10 107 H3
Ponsford St. E9 95 F6
Ponsonby Pl. SW1 33 J3
Ponsonby Pl. SW1 130 D5
Ponsonby Rd. SW15 147 H7
Ponsonby Ter. SW1 33 J3
Ponsonby Ter. SW1 130 D5
Pont St. SW1 23 J6
Pont St. SW1 129 J3
Pont St. Ms. SW1 23 J6
Pont St. Ms. SW1 129 J3
Pontefract Rd., Brom. 173 F5
Ponton Rd. SW8 33 J6
Ponton Rd. SW8 130 D6
Pontypool Pl. SE1 27 G3
Pool Cl., Beck. 172 A5
Pool Cl., W.Mol. 179 F5
Pool Ct. SE6 172 A2
Pool Rd., Har. 68 A7
Pool Rd., W.Mol. 179 F5
Poole Ct. Rd., Houns. 142/143 E2
Vicarage Fm. Rd.
Poole Rd. E9 95 G6
Poole Rd., Epsom 196 D6
Poole St. N1 112 A1
Pooles Bldgs. EC1 10 E6
Pooles La. SW10 129 F7
Lots Rd.
Pooles La., Dag. 119 E2
Pooles Pk. N4 93 G2
Seven Sisters Rd.
Poolmans St. SE16 133 G2
Poolsford Rd. NW9 71 E4
Poonah St. E1 113 F6
Hardinge St.
Pope Cl. SW19 167 G6
Shelley Way
Pope Rd., Brom. 192 A5
Pope St. SE1 29 E4
Pope St. SE1 132 B2
Popes Av., Twick. 162 B2
Popes Dr. N3 72 D1
Popes Gro., Croy. 203 J3
Popes Gro., Twick. 162 C2
Pope's Head All. EC3 112 A6
Cornhill
Popes La. W5 125 G3
Popes Rd. SW9 151 G3
Popham Cl., Felt. 161 F3
Popham Gdns., Rich. 146 A3
Lower Richmond Rd.
Popham Rd. N1 111 J1
Popham St. N1 111 H1
Poplar Av., Mitch. 185 J1
Poplar Av., Orp. 207 E2
Poplar Av., Sthl. 123 H3
Poplar Bath St. E14 114 B7
Lawless St.
Poplar Business Pk. E14 114 C7
Poplar Cl. E9 95 J5
Lee Conservancy Rd.
Poplar Cl., Pnr. 66 D1
Poplar Ct. SW19 166 D5
Poplar Cres., Epsom 196 C6
Poplar Fm. Cl., Epsom 196 C6
Poplar Gdns., N.Mal. 182 D2
Poplar Gro. N11 58 A6
Poplar Gro. W6 127 J2
Poplar Gro., N.Mal. 182 D3
Poplar Gro., Wem. 88 C3
Poplar High St. E14 114 A7
Poplar Mt., Belv. 139 H4
Poplar Pl. SE28 118 C7
Poplar Pl. W2 14 A5
Poplar Pl. W2 109 E7
Poplar Pl., Hayes 102 A7
Central Av.
Poplar Rd. SE24 151 J4
Poplar Rd. SW19 184 D2
Poplar Rd., Sutt. 198 C1
Poplar Rd. S. SW19 184 D3
Poplar St., Rom. 83 J4
Poplar Vw., Wem. 87 G2
Magnet Rd.
Poplar Wk. SE24 151 J4
Poplar Wk., Croy. 201 J2
Poplar Way, Felt. 160 A3
Poplar Way, Ilf. 81 F4
Poplars, The N14 42 B5
Poplars Av. NW10 89 J6
Poplars Rd. E17 78 B6
Poppins Ct. EC4 19 G4
Poppleton Rd. E11 79 E6
Poppy Cl., Wall. 200 A1
Poppy La., Croy. 189 F7
Porch Way N20 57 J3
Porchester Cl. SE5 151 J4
Porchester Gdns. W2 14 B5
Porchester Gdns. W2 109 E7
Porchester Gdns. Ms. W2 14 B4
Porchester Mead, Beck. 172 B6
Porchester Ms. W2 14 B3
Porchester Ms. W2 109 E6
Porchester Pl. W2 15 H4
Porchester Pl. W2 109 H6
Porchester Rd. W2 14 A3
Porchester Rd. W2 109 E6
Porchester Rd., Kings.T. 182 B2
Porchester Sq. W2 14 B3
Porchester Sq. W2 109 E6
Porchester Ter. W2 14 C4
Porchester Ter. W2 109 F7
Porchester Ter. N. W2 14 B3
Porchester Ter. N. W2 109 E6
Porcupine Cl. SE9 174 B2
Porden Rd. SW2 151 F4
Porlock Av., Har. 85 J1
Porlock Rd. W10 108 A4
Ladbroke Gro.
Porlock Rd., Enf. 44 C7
Porlock St. SE1 28 B3
Porlock St. SE1 132 A2
Porrington Cl., Chis. 192 C1
Port Cres. E13 115 H4
Jenkins Rd.
Portal Cl. SE27 169 G3
Portal Cl., Ruis. 84 A4
Portbury Cl. SE15 152 D1
Clayton Rd.
Portcullis Lo. Rd., Enf. 44 A3
Portelet Rd. E1 113 G3
Porten Rd. W14 128 B3
Porter Rd. E6 116 C6
Porter Sq. N19 92/93 E1
Hornsey Rd.
Porter St. SE1 28 A1
Porter St. W1 16 A1
Porters Av., Dag. 100 B6
Porters Wk. E1 112/113 E7
Pennington St.
Porters Way, West Dr. 120 C3
Portersfield Rd., Enf. 44 B4
Porteus Rd. W2 14 D1
Porteus Rd. W2 109 F5
Portgate Cl. W9 108 C4
Porthcawe Rd. SE26 171 H4
Porthkerry Av., Well. 158 A4
Portia Way E3 113 J4
Portinscale Rd. SW15 148 B5
Portland Av. N16 76 C7
Portland Av., N.Mal. 183 F7
Portland Av., Sid. 158 A6
Portland Cl., Rom. 82 E5
Portland Cres. SE9 174 B2
Portland Cres., Grnf. 103 H4
Portland Cres., Stan. 69 G2
Portland Gdns. N4 75 H6
Portland Gdns., Rom. 82 D5
Portland Gro. SW8 151 F1

Name	Page	Grid
Portland Ms. W1	17	G4
Portland Pl. W1	16	E2
Portland Pl. W1	110	B5
Portland Ri. N4	93	H1
Portland Ri. Est. N4	93	J1
Portland Rd. N15	76	C4
Portland Rd. SE9	174	B2
Portland Rd. SE25	188	D4
Portland Rd. W11	128	B1
Portland Rd., Brom.	173	J4
Portland Rd., Kings.T.	181	H3
Portland Rd., Mitch.	185	H2
Portland Rd., Sthl.	123	F3
Portland Sq. E1	132/133	E1
Watts St.		
Portland St. SE17	36	B3
Portland St. SE17	132	A5
Portland Ter., Rich.	145	G4
Portland Wk. SE17	36	C5
Portman Av. SW14	146	D3
Portman Cl. W1	16	A3
Portman Cl. W1	109	J6
Portman Cl., Bexh.	158	D3
Queen Anne's Gate		
Portman Dr., Wdf.Grn.	80	A2
Portman Gdns. NW9	70	D2
Portman Gate NW1	7	H6
Portman Ms. S. W1	16	B4
Portman Ms. S. W1	110	A6
Portman Pl. E2	113	F3
Portman Rd., Kings.T.	181	J2
Portman Sq. W1	16	B3
Portman Sq. W1	109	J6
Portman St. W1	16	B4
Portman St. W1	110	A6
Portmeadow Wk. SE2	138	D2
Portmers Cl. E17	77	J6
Lennox Rd.		
Portnall Rd. W9	108	C3
Portobello Ct. W11	108	C7
Westbourne Gro.		
Portobello Ms. W11	108	D7
Portobello Rd.		
Portobello Rd. W10	108	C6
Portobello Rd. W11	108	C6
Porton Ct., Surb.	181	F6
Portpool La. EC1	18	E1
Portpool La. EC1	111	G5
Portree Cl. N22	59	F7
Nightingale Rd.		
Portree St. E14	114	D6
Portsdown, Edg.	54	A5
Rectory La.		
Portsdown Av. NW11	72	C6
Portsdown Ms. NW11	72	C6
Portsea Ms. W2	15	H4
Portsea Pl. W2	15	H4
Portslade Rd. SW8	150	C2
Portsmouth Av., T.Ditt.	180	D7
Wesley Av.		
Portsmouth Ms. E16	135	H1
Portsmouth Rd. SW15	147	H7
Portsmouth Rd., Kings.T.	181	F5
Portsmouth Rd., Surb.	181	F5
Portsmouth Rd., T.Ditt.	194	B2
Portsmouth St. WC2	18	C4
Portsoken St. E1	21	F5
Portsoken St. E1	112	C7
Portugal Gdns., Twick.	161	J2
Fulwell Pk. Av.		
Portugal St. WC2	18	C4
Portugal St. WC2	111	F6
Portway E15	115	F1
Portway Gdns. SE18	136	A7
Shooter's Hill Rd.		
Post La., Twick.	162	A1
Post Office App. E7	97	H5
Post Office Ct. EC3	20	C4
Post Office Way SW8	33	H7
Post Office Way SW8	130	D7
Post Rd., Sthl.	123	H3
Postern Grn., Enf.	43	G2
Postmill Cl., Croy.	203	G3
Postway Ms., Ilf.	98/99	E3
Clements Rd.		
Potier St. SE1	28	C6
Potier St. SE1	132	A3
Pott St. E2	113	E3
Potter Cl., Mitch.	186	B2
Potter St., Nthwd.	66	A1
Potter St., Pnr.	66	B1
Potter St. Hill, Pnr.	50	B6
Potterne Cl. SW19	148	A7
Potters Cl., Croy.	203	H1
Potters Cl., Loug.	48	B2
Potters Flds. SE1	132	B1
Tooley St.		
Potters Gro., N.Mal.	182	C4
Potters Hts. Cl., Pnr.	50	B7
Potters La. SW16	168	D6
Potters La., Barn.	40	D4
Potters La., Borwd.	38	C1
Potters Rd. SW6	149	F2
Potters Rd., Barn.	40	E4
Pottery La. W11	108	B7
Portland Rd.		
Pottery Rd., Bex.	177	J2
Pottery Rd., Brent.	125	H6
Pottery St. SE16	132	E2
Poulett Gdns., Twick.	162	D1
Poulett Rd. E6	116	C2
Poulner Way SE15	132	C7
Daniel Gdns.		
Poulters Wd., Kes.	206	A5
Poulton Av., Sutt.	199	G3
Poulton Cl. E8	94/95	E5
Spurstowe Ter.		
Poultry EC2	20	B4
Poultry EC2	112	A6
Pound Cl., Orp.	207	F3
Pound Cl., Surb.	195	F1
Pound Ct. Dr., Orp.	207	G2
Pound La. NW10	89	G6
Pound Pk. Rd. SE7	136	A4
Pound Pl. SE9	156	D6
Pound St., Cars.	199	J5
Pound Way, Chis.	175	F7
Royal Par.		
Poundfield Rd., Loug.	48	D5
Pountney Rd. SW11	150	A3
Poverest Rd., Orp.	193	J5
Powder Mill La., Twick.	161	F1
Powell Cl., Chess.	195	G5
Coppard Gdns.		
Powell Cl., Edg.	53	J6
Powell Cl., Wall.	200	D7
Powell Gdns., Dag.	101	G4
Powell Rd. E5	95	E3
Powell Rd., Buck.H.	47	J1
Powell's Wk. W4	127	E6
Power Rd. W4	126	A4
Powers Ct., Twick.	145	G7
Powerscroft Rd. E5	95	F4
Powerscroft Rd., Sid.	176	C6
Powis Gdns. NW11	72	C7
Powis Gdns. W11	108	C6
Powis Ms. W11	108	C6
Westbourne Pk. Rd.		
Powis Pl. WC1	10	B6
Powis Pl. WC1	111	E4
Powis Rd. E3	114	B3
Powis Sq. W11	108	C6
Powis St. SE18	136	D3
Powis Ter. W11	108	C6
Powle Ter., Ilf.	99	F5
Oaktree Gro.		
Powlett Pl. NW1	92	B6
Harmood St.		
Pownall Gdns., Houns.	143	H4
Pownall Rd. E8	112	C1
Pownall Rd., Houns.	143	H4
Pownsett Ter., Ilf.	99	F5
Buttsbury Rd.		
Powster Rd., Brom.	173	H5
Powys Cl., Bexh.	138	D6
Powys La. N13	58	E5
Powys La. N14	58	E4
Poynders Ct. SW4	150	C6
Poynders Rd.		
Poynders Gdns. SW4	150	C7
Poynders Rd. SW4	150	C6
Poynings Rd. N19	92	C3
Poynings Way N12	56	D5
Poyntell Cres., Chis.	193	G1
Poynter Rd., Enf.	44	D5
Poynton Rd. N17	76	D2
Poyntz Rd. SW11	149	J2
Poyser St. E2	113	E2
Praed Ms. W2	15	F3
Praed St. W2	15	G2
Praed St. W2	109	G6
Pragel St. E13	115	H2
Pragnell Rd. SE12	173	H2
Prague Pl. SW2	150	E5
Prah Rd. N4	93	G2
Prairie St. SW8	150	A2
Pratt Ms. NW1	110	C1
Pratt St.		
Pratt St. NW1	110	C1
Pratt Wk. SE11	34	D1
Pratt Wk. SE11	131	F4
Pratts Pas., Kings.T.	181	H2
Eden St.		
Prayle Gro. NW2	90	A1
Prebend Gdns. W4	127	F3
Prebend Gdns. W6	127	F3
Prebend St. N1	111	J1
Precinct, The, W.Mol.	179	H3
Victoria Av.		
Precinct Rd., Hayes	102	A7
Precincts, The, Mord.	184/185	E6
Green La.		
Premier Cor. W9	108	C2
Kilburn La.		
Premier Pk. NW10	106	B1
Premier Pl. SW15	148	B4
Putney High St.		
Premiere Pl. E14	114	A7
Garford St.		
Prendergast Rd. SE3	155	E3
Prentis Rd. SW16	168	D4
Prentiss Ct. SE7	136	A4
Presburg Rd., N.Mal.	183	E5
Presburg St. E5	95	G3
Glyn Rd.		
Prescelly Pl., Edg.	69	J1
Prescot St. E1	21	G5
Prescott Av., Orp.	192	E6
Prescott Cl. SW16	168	E7
Prescott Grn., Loug.	49	F3
Prescott Ho. SE17	35	H6
Prescott Pl. SW4	150	D3
Presentation Ms. SW2	169	F1
Palace Rd.		
President Dr. E1	132/133	E1
Waterman Way		
President St. EC1	11	J3
Press Rd. NW10	88	D3
Prestage Way E14	114	C7
Prestbury Rd. E7	97	J7
Prestbury Sq. SE9	174	C4
Prested Rd. SW11	149	H4
St. John's Hill		
Prestige Way NW4	71	J5
Heriot Rd.		
Preston Av. E4	62	D6
Preston Cl. SE1	36	D1
Preston Cl., Twick.	162	B3
Preston Dr. E11	79	J5
Preston Dr., Bexh.	158	D1
Preston Dr., Epsom	197	E6
Preston Gdns. NW10	88/89	E6
Church Rd.		
Preston Gdns., Ilf.	80	B6
Preston Hill, Har.	69	J6
Preston Pl. NW2	89	G6
Preston Pl., Rich.	145	H5
Preston Rd. E11	79	E6
Preston Rd. SE19	169	H6
Preston Rd. SW20	165	F7
Preston Rd., Har.	69	H7
Preston Rd., Wem.	87	H2
Preston Waye, Har.	87	H1
Prestons Rd. E14	134	C2
Prestons Rd., Brom.	205	G3
Prestwick Cl., Sthl.	122/123	E5
Ringway		
Prestwick Rd., Wat.	50	D5
Prestwood Av., Har.	69	E4
Prestwood Cl. SE18	138	A7
Prestwood Cl., Har.	69	F4
Prestwood Gdns., Croy.	187	J7
Prestwood St. N1	12	A2
Pretoria Av. E17	77	H4
Pretoria Cl. N17	60	C7
Pretoria Rd.		
Pretoria Cres. E4	62	C1
Pretoria Rd. E4	62	C1
Pretoria Rd. E11	96	D1
Pretoria Rd. E16	115	F3
Pretoria Rd. N17	60	C7
Pretoria Rd. SW16	168	B6
Pretoria Rd., Ilf.	98	E5
Pretoria Rd., Rom.	83	J4
Pretoria Rd. N. N18	60	C6
Prevost Rd. N11	58	A2
Price Cl. NW7	56	B6
Price Cl. SW17	167	J3
Price Rd., Croy.	201	H5
Price Way, Hmptn.	160/161	E6
Victors Dr.		
Price's Yd. N1	111	F1
Pricklers Hill, Barn.	41	E6
Prickley Wd., Brom.	205	F1
Priddy's Yd., Croy.	201	J2
Church St.		
Prideaux Pl. W3	106	D7
Prideaux Pl. WC1	10	D3
Prideaux Pl. WC1	111	F3
Prideaux Rd. SW9	151	E3
Pridham Rd., Th.Hth.	188	A4
Priest Ct. EC2	19	J3
Priest Pk. Av., Har.	85	G2
Priestfield Rd. SE23	171	H3
Priestlands Pk. Rd., Sid.	175	J3
Priestley Cl. N16	76	C7
Ravensdale Rd.		
Priestley Gdns., Rom.	82	B6
Priestley Rd., Mitch.	186	A2
Priestley Way E17	77	G3
Priestley Way NW2	89	G1
Priests Br. SW14	147	E3
Priests Br. SW15	147	E3
Prima Rd. SW9	35	E7
Prima Rd. SW9	131	G7
Primrose Av., Enf.	44	A1
Primrose Av., Rom.	82	B7
Primrose Cl. SE6	172	C5
Primrose Cl., Har.	85	F4
Primrose Cl., Wall.	200	B1
Primrose Dr., West Dr.	120	A3
Wise La.		
Primrose Gdns. NW3	91	H6
Primrose Gdns., Ruis.	84	C5
Primrose Hill EC4	19	F4
Primrose Hill Ct. NW3	91	J7
Primrose Hill Rd. NW3	91	H7
Primrose Hill Studios NW1	110	A1
Fitzroy Rd.		
Primrose La., Croy.	203	G1
Primrose Ms. NW1	91	J7
Sharpleshall St.		
Primrose Ms. SE3	135	H7
Primrose Ms. W5	125	G2
St. Mary's Rd.		
Primrose Rd. E10	96	B1
Primrose Rd. E18	79	H2
Primrose Sq. E9	95	F7
Primrose St. EC2	20	D1
Primrose St. EC2	112	B5
Primrose Wk., Epsom	197	F7
Primrose Way, Wem.	105	G2
Primula St. W12	107	G6
Prince Albert Rd. NW1	7	H2
Prince Albert Rd. NW1	109	H2
Prince Albert Rd. NW8	7	H2
Prince Albert Rd. NW8	109	H2
Prince Arthur Ms. NW3	91	F4
Perrins La.		
Prince Arthur Rd. NW3	91	F5
Prince Charles Dr. NW4	71	J7
Prince Charles Rd. SE3	155	F1
Prince Charles Way, Wall.	200	B3
Prince Consort Dr., Chis.	193	G1
Prince Consort Rd. SW7	22	E5
Prince Consort Rd. SW7	129	F3
Prince Edward Rd. E9	95	J6
Prince George Av. N14	42	C5
Prince George Duke of Kent Ct., Chis.	175	G7
Holbrook La.		
Prince George Rd. N16	94	B4
Prince George's Av. SW20	183	J2
Prince George's Rd. SW19	185	G1
Prince Henry Rd. SE7	136	A7
Prince Imperial Rd. SE18	156	C1
Prince Imperial Rd., Chis.	175	E7
Prince John Rd. SE9	156	B5
Prince of Orange La. SE10	134	C7
Greenwich High Rd.		
Prince of Wales Cl. NW4	71	H4
Church Ter.		
Prince of Wales Dr. SW8	130	B7
Prince of Wales Dr. SW11	149	J1
Prince of Wales Gate SW7	23	G3
Prince of Wales Gate SW7	129	H2
Prince of Wales Pas. NW1	9	F4
Prince of Wales Rd. NW5	92	A6
Prince of Wales Rd. SE3	155	F1

Prince of Wales Rd., Sutt.	199	G2	Princess May Rd. N16	94	B4	Priory Rd. W4	126	D3	Provost Rd. NW3	91	J7

Prince of Wales Rd., Sutt. 199 G2
Prince of Wales Ter. W4 126 E5
Prince of Wales Ter. W8 22 B4
Prince Regent Ct. SE16 133 H1
Rotherhithe St.
Prince Regent La. E13 115 H3
Prince Regent La. E16 115 J5
Prince Regent Rd., Houns. 143 J3
Prince Rd. SE25 188 B5
Prince Rupert Rd. SE9 156 C4
Prince St. SE8 133 J6
Princedale Rd. W11 128 B1
Princelet St. E1 21 G1
Princelet St. E1 112 C5
Prince's Arc. SW1 25 G1
Princes Av. N3 72 D1
Princes Av. N10 74 A3
Princes Av. N13 59 G5
Princes Av. N22 74 D1
Princes Av. NW9 70 B4
Princes Av. W3 126 A3
Princes Av., Cars. 199 J7
Princes Av., Grnf. 103 H6
Princes Av., Orp. 193 H5
Princes Av., Surb. 196 A1
Princes Av., Wdf.Grn. 63 H4
Princes Cl. N4 93 H1
Princes Cl. NW9 70 A4
Princes Cl. SW4 150 C3
Old Town
Princes Cl., Edg. 54 A5
Princes Cl., Sid. 176 D3
Princes Cl., Tedd. 162 A4
Princes Ct. E1 113 E7
Princes Ct. SE16 133 J3
Princes Ct., Wem. 87 H5
Princes Dr., Har. 68 B3
Princes Gdns. SW7 23 F5
Princes Gdns. SW7 129 G3
Princes Gdns. W3 106 A5
Princes Gdns. W5 105 F4
Princes Gate SW7 23 G4
Princes Gate SW7 129 H2
Princes Gate Ct. SW7 23 F4
Princes Gate Ms. SW7 23 F5
Princes Gate Ms. SW7 129 G3
Princes La. N10 74 B3
Princes Ms. W2 14 A5
Princes Pk. Av. NW11 72 B6
Princes Pl. SW1 25 G1
Princes Pl. W11 128 B1
Princes Plain, Brom. 192 B7
Princes Ri. SE13 154 C2
Princes Riverside Rd. SE16 133 G1
Princes Rd. N18 61 F4
Princes Rd. SE20 171 G6
Princes Rd. SW14 146 D3
Princes Rd. SW19 166 D6
Princes Rd. W13 124/125 E1
Broomfield Rd.
Princes Rd., Buck.H. 63 J2
Princes Rd., Ilf. 81 G4
Princes Rd., Kings.T. 164 A7
Princes Rd., Rich. 145 J5
Princes Rd. (Kew), Rich. 145 J1
Princes Rd., Tedd. 162 A4
Princes Sq. W2 14 A5
Princes Sq. W2 108 E7
Princes St. EC2 20 B4
Princes St. EC2 112 A6
Princes St. N17 60 B6
Queen St.
Princes St. W1 17 E4
Princes St. W1 110 B6
Princes St., Bexh. 159 F4
Princes St., Rich. 145 H5
Sheen Rd.
Princes St., Sutt. 199 G4
Princes Ter. E13 115 H1
Princes Way SW19 148 A7
Princes Way, Buck.H. 63 J2
Princes Way, Croy. 201 F5
Princes Way, Ruis. 84 E4
Princes Way, W.Wick. 205 F4
Princes Yd. W11 128 B1
Princedale Rd.
Princess Alice Way SE28 137 G2
Princess Av., Wem. 87 H2
Princess Cres. N4 93 H2

Princess May Rd. N16 94 B4
Princess Ms. NW3 91 G6
Belsize Cres.
Princess Par., Orp. 206 D3
Crofton Rd.
Princess Pk. Manor N11 58 A5
Princess Rd. NW1 110 A1
Princess Rd. NW6 108 D2
Princess Rd., Croy. 187 J6
Princess St. SE1 27 H6
Princess St. SE1 131 H3
Princesses Wk., Rich. 125 H7
Kew Rd.
Princethorpe Ho. W2 14 A1
Princethorpe Ho. W2 108 E5
Princethorpe Rd. SE26 171 G4
Princeton Ct. SW15 148 A3
Felsham Rd.
Princeton St. WC1 18 C1
Princeton St. WC1 111 F5
Pringle Gdns. SW16 168 C4
Print Village SE15 152 C2
Chadwick Rd.
Printer St. EC4 19 F3
Printers Inn Ct. EC4 19 E3
Printing Ho. La., Hayes 121 H2
Printing Ho. Yd. E2 13 E3
Priolo Rd. SE7 135 J5
Prior Av., Sutt. 199 H7
Prior Bolton St. N1 93 H6
Prior Rd., Ilf. 98 D3
Prior St. SE10 134 C7
Prioress Rd. SE27 169 H3
Prioress St. SE1 28 C6
Prioress St. SE1 132 A3
Priors Cft. E17 77 H2
Priors Fld., Nthlt. 84/85 E6
Arnold Rd.
Priors Gdns., Ruis. 84 C5
Priors Mead, Enf. 44 B1
Priory, The SE3 155 F4
Priory Av. E4 61 J3
Priory Av. E17 78 A5
Priory Av. N8 74 D4
Priory Av. W4 127 E4
Priory Av., Orp. 193 G6
Priory Av., Sutt. 198 A4
Priory Av., Wem. 86 C4
Priory Cl. E4 61 J3
Priory Cl. E18 79 G1
Priory Cl. N3 72 C1
Church Cres.
Priory Cl. N14 42 B5
Priory Cl. N20 40 C7
Priory Cl. SW19 184/185 E1
High Path
Priory Cl., Beck. 189 H3
Priory Cl., Chis. 192 C1
Priory Cl., Hmptn. 179 F1
Priory Gdns.
Priory Cl., Hayes 102 B7
Priory Cl., Stan. 52 C3
Priory Cl., Sun. 160 A7
Staines Rd. E.
Priory Cl. (Sudbury), Wem. 86 C4
Priory Ct. E17 77 J3
Priory Ct. EC4 111 H6
Ludgate Hill
Priory Ct. SW8 150 D1
Priory Ct. Est. E17 77 J2
Priory Cres. SE19 169 J7
Priory Cres., Sutt. 198 A4
Priory Cres., Wem. 86 D3
Priory Dr. SE2 138 D5
Priory Dr., Stan. 52 C3
Priory Fld. Dr., Edg. 54 B4
Priory Gdns. N6 74 B6
Priory Gdns. SE25 188 C4
Priory Gdns. SW13 147 F3
Priory Gdns. W4 127 E4
Priory Gdns. W5 105 H3
Hanger La.
Priory Gdns., Hmptn. 161 F7
Priory Gdns., Wem. 86 D4
Priory Grn. Est. N1 10 D1
Priory Grn. Est. N1 111 F2
Priory Gro. SW8 150 E1
Priory La. SW15 147 E6
Priory La., Rich. 126 A7
Forest Rd.
Priory La., W.Mol. 179 H4
Priory Ms. SW8 150 D1
Priory Pk. SE3 155 F3
Priory Pk. Rd. NW6 108 C1
Priory Pk. Rd., Wem. 86 D4
Priory Rd. E6 116 A1
Priory Rd. N8 74 D4
Priory Rd. NW6 108 E1
Priory Rd. SW19 167 G7

Priory Rd. W4 126 D3
Priory Rd., Bark. 99 G7
Priory Rd., Chess. 195 H3
Priory Rd., Croy. 187 G7
Priory Rd., Hmptn. 161 F7
Priory Rd., Houns. 143 J5
Priory Rd., Loug. 48 B4
Priory Rd., Rich. 126 A6
Priory Rd., Sutt. 198 A4
Priory St. E3 114 B3
St. Leonards St.
Priory Ter. NW6 108 E1
Priory Ter., Sun. 160 A7
Staines Rd. E.
Priory Wk. SW10 30 D4
Priory Wk. SW10 129 F5
Priory Way, Har. 67 H4
Priory Way, Sthl. 122 D3
Priory Way, West Dr. 120 B6
Pritchard's Rd. E2 112 D1
Priter Rd. SE16 29 J6
Priter Rd. SE16 132 D3
Priter Way SE16 132 D3
Dockley Rd.
Private Rd., Enf. 44 B5
Probert Rd. SW2 151 G5
Probyn Rd. SW2 169 H2
Procter St. WC1 18 C2
Procter St. WC1 111 F5
Proctor Cl., Mitch. 186 A1
Proctors Cl., Felt. 160 A1
Progress Business Pk., Croy. 201 F2
Progress Way N22 75 G1
Progress Way, Croy. 201 F2
Progress Way, Enf. 44 D5
Promenade, The W4 147 E1
Promenade App. Rd. W4 126 E7
Promenade Mans., Edg. 54 B5
Hale La.
Prospect Business Pk., Loug. 49 F4
Prospect Cl. SE26 170 E4
Prospect Cl., Belv. 139 G4
Prospect Cl., Houns. 143 F1
Prospect Cl., Ruis. 66 D7
Prospect Cotts. SW18 148 D4
Point Pleasant
Prospect Cres., Twick. 143 J6
Prospect Hill E17 78 B4
Prospect Pl. E1 133 F1
Prospect Pl. N2 73 G4
Prospect Pl. N17 76 B1
Prospect Pl. NW2 90 C3
Ridge Rd.
Prospect Pl. NW3 91 F4
Holly Wk.
Prospect Pl., Brom. 191 H3
Prospect Pl., Rom. 83 J2
Prospect Quay SW18 148 D4
Point Pleasant
Prospect Ring N2 73 G3
Prospect Rd. NW2 90 C3
Prospect Rd., Barn. 40 D5
Prospect Rd., Surb. 181 F6
Prospect Rd. (Wdf.Grn.) 63 J5
Prospect St. SE16 132/133 E2
Jamaica Rd.
Prospect Vale SE18 136 B4
Prospero Rd. N19 92 C1
Protea Cl. E16 115 F4
Hermit Rd.
Prothero Gdns. NW4 71 H5
Prothero Ho. NW10 88 D7
Prothero Rd. SW6 128 B7
Prout Gro. NW10 89 E4
Prout Rd. E5 95 E3
Provence St. N1 111 J2
St. Peters St.
Providence Ct. W1 16 C5
Providence Ct. W1 110 A7
Providence La., Hayes 121 G7
Providence Pl. N1 111 H1
Upper St.
Providence Pl., Rom. 83 F2
Providence Rd., West Dr. 120 B1
Providence Row N1 10 C2
Providence Row Cl. E2 112/113 E3
Ainsley St.
Providence Sq. SE1 132 C2
Mill St.
Providence St. N1 111 J2
St. Peters St.
Providence St. E2 13 H3
Provident Ind. Est., Hayes 122 A2
Provost Est. N1 12 B3
Provost Est. N1 112 A2

Provost Rd. NW3 91 J7
Provost St. N1 12 B4
Provost St. N1 112 A3
Prowse Av., Bushey 51 J2
Prowse Pl. NW1 92 B7
Bonny St.
Pruden Cl. N14 58 C2
Prudent Pas. EC2 20 A3
Prusom St. E1 133 E4
Pryors, The NW3 91 G3
Pudding La. EC3 20 C6
Pudding La. EC3 112 A7
Pudding La., Chig. 65 J1
Pudding Mill La. E15 114 B1
Puddle Dock EC4 19 H5
Puffin Cl., Bark. 117 H3
Thames Rd.
Puffin Cl., Beck. 189 G5
Pulborough Rd. SW18 148 C7
Pulborough Way, Houns. 142 C4
Pulford Rd. N15 76 A6
Pulham Av. N2 73 F4
Puller Rd., Barn. 40 B2
Pulleyns Av. E6 116 B3
Pullman Ct. SW2 169 E1
Pullman Gdns. SW15 147 J6
Pullman Pl. SE9 156 B5
Pulross Rd. SW9 151 F3
Pulteney Cl. E3 113 J1
Pulteney Gdns. E18 79 H3
Pulteney Rd.
Pulteney Rd. E18 79 H3
Pulteney Ter. N1 111 F1
Pulton Pl. SW6 128 D7
Puma Ct. E1 21 F1
Pump All., Brent. 125 G7
Pump Cl., Nthlt. 103 G2
Union Rd.
Pump Ct. EC4 19 E4
Pump Hill, Loug. 48 C2
Pump Ho. Cl., Brom. 191 F2
Pump La. SE14 133 F7
Farrow La.
Pump La., Hayes 122 A2
Pump Pail N., Croy. 201 J3
Old Town
Pump Pail S., Croy. 201 J3
Southbridge Rd.
Pumping Sta. Rd. W4 127 E7
Pundersons Gdns. E2 113 E3
Herbert Rd.
Purbeck Av., N.Mal. 183 F6
Purbeck Dr. NW2 90 B2
Purbrook Est. SE1 29 E4
Purbrook St. SE1 29 E5
Purbrook St. SE1 132 B3
Purcell Cres. SW6 128 B7
Purcell Ms. NW10 88/89 E7
Suffolk Rd.
Purcell Rd., Grnf. 103 H5
Purcell St. N1 12 D1
Purcell St. N1 112 B2
Purcells Av., Edg. 54 A5
Purchese St. NW1 9 J1
Purchese St. NW1 110 D2
Purdy St. E3 114 B4
Purelake Ms. SE13 154 D3
Purland Cl., Dag. 101 F1
Purland Rd. SE28 137 J2
Purleigh Av., Wdf.Grn. 64 B6
Purley Av. NW2 90 B3
Purley Cl., Ilf. 80 D2
Purley Pl. N1 93 H7
Islington Pk. St.
Purley Rd. N9 60 A3
Purley Rd., S.Croy. 202 A7
Purley Way, Croy. 187 F7
Purley Way, Pur. 201 G7
Purley Way Cres., Croy. 187 F7
Purley Way
Purneys Rd. SE9 156 A4
Purrett Rd. SE18 137 J5
Purser's Cross Rd. SW6 148 C1
Pursewardens Cl. W13 125 F1
Pursley Rd. NW7 55 H7
Purves Rd. NW10 107 J2
Puteaux Ho. E2 113 G2
Putney Br. SW6 148 B3
Putney Br. SW15 148 B3
Putney Br. App. SW6 148 B3
Putney Br. Rd. SW15 148 B3
Putney Br. Rd. SW18 148 D5
Putney Common SW15 147 J3
Heathfield Pk. Dr.
Putney Gdns., Rom. 82 B6
Putney Heath SW15 147 J6

Name	Page	Grid
Putney Heath La. SW15	148	A6
Putney High St. SW15	148	A4
Putney Hill SW15	148	A6
Putney Pk. Av. SW15	147	G4
Putney Pk. La. SW15	147	H4
Puttenham La., Wat.	50	C3
Pycroft Way N9	60	C4
Pyecombe Cor. N12	56	C4
Pylbrook Rd., Sutt.	198	D3
Pylon Way, Croy.	201	E1
Pym Cl., Barn.	41	G5
Pymers Mead SE21	169	J1
Pymmes Cl. N13	59	F5
Pymmes Cl. N17	60	E3
Pymmes Gdns. N. N9	60	C3
Pymmes Gdns. S. N9	60	C3
Pymmes Grn. Rd. N11	58	B4
Pymmes Rd. N13	59	E6
Pymms Brook Dr., Barn.	41	H4
Pyne Rd., Surb.	196	A1
Pyne Ter. SW19	166	A1
Windlesham Gro.		
Pynfolds SE16	132/133	E2
Paradise St.		
Pynham Cl. SE2	138	A3
Pynnacles Cl., Stan.	53	E5
Pyrland Rd. N5	94	A5
Pyrland Rd., Rich.	145	J6
Pyrles Grn., Loug.	48	E1
Pyrles La., Loug.	48	E2
Pyrmont Gro. SE27	169	H3
Pyrmont Rd. W4	126	A6
Pyrmont Rd., Ilf.	99	F2
High Rd.		
Pytchley Cres. SE19	169	J6
Pytchley Rd. SE22	152	B3

Q

Name	Page	Grid
Quad Rd., Wem.	87	G3
Courtenay Rd.		
Quadrangle, The W2	**15**	**G3**
Quadrangle Ms., Stan.	53	F7
Quadrant, The SE24	151	J5
Herne Hill		
Quadrant, The SW20	184	B1
Quadrant, The, Bexh.	138	D7
Quadrant, The, Rich.	145	H4
Quadrant, The, Sutt.	199	F6
Quadrant Arc. W1	**17**	**G6**
Quadrant Gro. NW5	91	J5
Quadrant Rd., Rich.	145	G4
Quadrant Rd., Th.Hth.	187	H4
Quaggy Wk. SE3	155	G4
Quainton St. NW10	88	D3
Quaker Ct. E1	13	F6
Quaker La., Sthl.	123	G3
Quaker St. E1	**13**	**F6**
Quaker St. E1	112	C4
Quakers Course NW9	71	F1
Quakers La., Islw.	144	D1
Quaker's Pl. E7	98	A5
Quakers Wk. N21	44	A6
Quality Ct. WC2	**18**	**E3**
Quality Ct. WC2	111	G6
Quantock Cl., Hayes	121	G7
Quantock Dr., Wor.Pk.	197	J2
Quantock Gdns. NW2	90	A2
Quarley Way SE15	**37**	**F7**
Quarr Rd., Cars.	185	G6
Quarrendon St. SW6	148	D2
Quarry Pk. Rd., Sutt.	198	C6
Quarry Ri., Sutt.	198	C6
Quarry Rd. SW18	149	F6
Quarter Mile La. E10	96	B4
Quarterdeck, The E14	134	A2
Quay W., Tedd.	162	E5
Quebec Ms. W1	**16**	**A4**
Quebec Rd., Hayes	102	C7
Quebec Rd., Ilf.	81	E7
Quebec Way SE16	133	G2
Queen Adelaide Rd. SE20	171	F6
Queen Alexandra's Ct. SW19	166	C5
Suffield Rd.		
Queen Anne Av. N15	76	C5
Queen Anne Av., Brom.	191	F3
Queen Anne Dr., Esher	194	B7
Queen Anne Ms. W1	**16**	**E2**
Queen Anne Rd. E9	95	G6
Queen Anne St. W1	**16**	**D3**
Queen Anne St. W1	110	B6
Queen Anne Ter. E1	112/113	E7
Sovereign Cl.		

Name	Page	Grid
Queen Anne's Cl., Twick.	162	A3
Queen Anne's Gdns. W4	127	E3
Queen Annes Gdns. W5	125	H2
Queen Annes Gdns., Enf.	44	B6
Queen Annes Gdns., Mitch.	185	J3
Queen Anne's Gate SW1	**25**	**H4**
Queen Anne's Gate SW1	130	D2
Queen Anne's Gate, Bexh.	158	D3
Queen Anne's Gro. W4	126	E3
Queen Annes Gro. W5	125	H2
Queen Annes Gro., Enf.	44	A7
Queen Annes Pl., Enf.	44	B6
Queen Caroline Est. W6	127	J5
Queen Caroline St. W6	127	J4
Queen Elizabeth Gdns., Mord.	184	D4
Queen Elizabeth Rd. E17	77	H3
Queen Elizabeth Rd., Kings.T.	181	J1
Queen Elizabeth St. SE1	**29**	**E3**
Queen Elizabeth St. SE1	132	C2
Queen Elizabeth Wk. SW13	147	H1
Queen Elizabeths Cl. N16	94	A2
Queen Elizabeths Dr. N14	58	E1
Queen Elizabeths Wk. N16	94	A2
Queen Elizabeth's Wk. Wall.	200	D4
Queen Margaret's Gro. N1	94	B5
Queen Mary Av., Mord.	184	A5
Queen Mary Cl., Surb.	196	A3
Queen Mary Rd. SE19	169	H6
Queen Mary's Av., Cars.	199	J7
Queen of Denmark Ct. SE16	133	J3
Queen Sq. WC1	10	B6
Queen Sq. WC1	111	E4
Queen Sq. Pl. WC1	**10**	**B6**
Queen St. EC4	**20**	**A5**
Queen St. EC4	111	J7
Queen St. N17	60	B6
Queen St. W1	**24**	**D1**
Queen St. W1	130	B1
Queen St., Bexh.	159	F3
Queen St., Croy.	201	J3
Church Rd.		
Queen St. Pl. EC4	**20**	**A6**
Queen Victoria Av., Wem.	87	G7
Queen Victoria St. EC4	**19**	**H5**
Queen Victoria St. EC4	111	H7
Queen Victoria Ter. E1	112/113	E7
Sovereign Cl.		
Queenborough Gdns., Chis.	175	G6
Queenborough Gdns., Ilf.	80	D4
Queenhithe EC4	**20**	**A5**
Queenhithe EC4	111	J7
Queens Acre, Sutt.	198	A7
Queens Av. N3	57	F7
Queens Av. N10	74	A3
Queens Av. N20	57	G2
Queen's Av. N21	59	H1
Queens Av., Felt.	160	C4
Queens Av., Grnf.	103	H6
Queens Av., Stan.	69	F3
Queens Av., Wdf.Grn.	63	H5
Queen's Circ. SW8	130	B7
Queenstown Rd.		
Queen's Circ. SW11	130	B7
Queenstown Rd.		
Queens Cl., Edg.	54	A5
Queens Cl., Wall.	200	B5
Queens Rd.		
Queens Club Gdns. W14	128	B6
Queens Ct. SE23	171	F1
Queens Ct., Rich.	145	J6
Queens Cres. NW5	92	A6

Name	Page	Grid
Queens Cres., Rich.	145	J5
Queens Dr. E10	78	A7
Queens Dr. N4	93	H2
Queens Dr. W3	105	J6
Queens Dr. W5	105	J6
Queens Dr., Surb.	182	A7
Queens Dr., T.Ditt.	180	D7
Queen's Elm Sq. SW3	**31**	**F4**
Queens Gdns. NW4	71	J5
Queens Gdns. W2	**14**	**C5**
Queens Gdns. W2	109	F7
Queens Gdns. W5	105	F4
Queen's Gdns., Houns.	143	E1
Queen's Gate SW7	**30**	**E1**
Queen's Gate SW7	129	F3
Queen's Gate Gdns. SW7	**22**	**D6**
Queen's Gate Gdns. SW7	129	F3
Queens Gate Gdns. SW15	147	H4
Upper Richmond Rd.		
Queen's Gate Ms. SW7	**22**	**D4**
Queen's Gate Ms. SW7	129	F2
Queen's Gate Pl. SW7	**22**	**D6**
Queen's Gate Pl. SW7	129	F3
Queen's Gate Pl. Ms. SW7	**22**	**D6**
Queen's Gate Pl. Ms. SW7	129	F3
Queen's Gate Ter. SW7	**22**	**C5**
Queen's Gate Ter. SW7	129	F3
Queen's Gro. NW8	109	G1
Queen's Gro. Ms. NW8	109	G1
Queens Gro. Rd. E4	62	D1
Queen's Head St. N1	111	H1
Queens Head Yd. SE1	**28**	**B2**
Queens Ho., Tedd.	162	C6
Queens La. N10	74	B3
Queens Mkt. E13	115	J1
Green St.		
Queens Ms. W2	**14**	**B5**
Queens Ms. W2	109	E7
Queens Par. N11	57	J5
Colney Hatch La.		
Queens Par. W5	105	J6
Queens Par. Cl. N11	57	J5
Colney Hatch La.		
Queens Pk. Ct. W10	108	A3
Queens Pas., Chis.	174/175	E6
High St.		
Queens Pl., Mord.	184	D4
Queen's Prom., Kings.T.	181	G3
Portsmouth Rd.		
Queens Reach, E.Mol.	180	B4
Queens Ride SW13	147	G3
Queens Ride SW15	147	G3
Queen's Ride, Rich.	164	B1
Queens Ri., Rich.	145	J6
Queens Rd. E11	78	D7
Queens Rd. E13	115	H1
Queen's Rd. E17	77	J6
Queens Rd. N3	73	F1
Queens Rd. N9	60	E3
Queens Rd. N11	58	E7
Queens Rd. NW4	71	J5
Queens Rd. SE14	152	E1
Queens Rd. SE15	152	E1
Queens Rd. SW14	146	D3
Queens Rd. SW19	166	C6
Queens Rd. W5	105	H6
Queens Rd., Bark.	99	F6
Queens Rd., Barn.	40	A3
Queens Rd., Beck.	189	H2
Queens Rd., Brom.	191	G2
Queens Rd., Buck.H.	63	H2
Queens Rd., Chis.	175	E6
Queens Rd., Croy.	187	H6
Queens Rd., Enf.	44	B4
Queens Rd., Felt.	160	B1
Queens Rd., Hmptn.	161	H4
Queens Rd., Houns.	143	H3
Queens Rd., Kings.T.	164	A7
Queens Rd., Loug.	48	B3
Queens Rd., Mitch.	185	G3
Queens Rd., Mord.	184	D4
Queens Rd., N.Mal.	183	F4
Queens Rd., Rich.	145	H7
Queens Rd., Sthl.	122	D2
Queens Rd., Tedd.	162	C6
Queens Rd., T.Ditt.	180	C5
Queens Rd., Twick.	162	C1
Queens Rd., Wall.	200	B5
Queens Rd., Well.	158	B2
Queens Rd., West Dr.	120	C2
Queens Rd. W. E13	115	G2
Queen's Row SE17	**36**	**B5**

Name	Page	Grid
Queen's Row SE17	132	A6
Queen's Ter. E13	115	H1
Queen's Ter. NW8	**7**	**E1**
Queen's Ter. NW8	109	G2
Queens Ter., Islw.	144	D4
Queens Ter. Cotts. W7	124	B2
Boston Rd.		
Queens Wk. E4	62	D1
The Grn. Wk.		
Queens Wk. NW9	88	C2
Queen's Wk. SW1	**25**	**F2**
Queen's Wk. SW1	130	C1
Queens Wk. W5	105	F4
Queen's Wk., Har.	68	B4
Queen's Wk., Ruis.	84	D3
Queen's Wk., The SE1	**28**	**E1**
Queen's Wk., The SE1	132	B1
Queens Way NW4	71	J5
Queens Way, Croy.	201	F6
Queens Way, Felt.	160	C3
Queen's Well Av. N20	57	H3
Queen's Wd. Rd. N10	74	B6
Queens Yd. WC1	**9**	**G6**
Queensberry Ms. W. SW7	**30**	**E1**
Queensberry Pl. SW7	**30**	**E1**
Queensberry Pl. SW7	129	G4
Queensberry Way SW7	**31**	**E1**
Queensborough Ms. W2	**14**	**C5**
Queensborough Pas. W2	**14**	**C5**
Queensborough S. Bldgs. W2	109	F7
Porchester Ter.		
Queensborough Studios W2	**14**	**C5**
Queensborough Ter. W2	**14**	**B5**
Queensborough Ter. W2	109	E7
Queensbridge Pk., Islw.	144	B5
Queensbridge Rd. E2	112	C1
Queensbridge Rd. E8	94	C7
Queensbury Circle Par., Har.	69	H3
Streatfield Rd.		
Queensbury Circle Par., Stan.	69	H3
Streatfield Rd.		
Queensbury Pl., Rich.	145	G5
Friars La.		
Queensbury Rd. NW9	70	D7
Queensbury Rd., Wem.	105	J2
Queensbury Sta. Par., Edg.	69	J3
Queensbury St. N1	93	J7
Queenscourt, Wem.	87	H4
Queenscroft Rd. SE9	156	A5
Queensdale Cres. W11	128	A1
Queensdale Pl. W11	128	B1
Queensdale Rd. W11	128	A1
Queensdale Wk. W11	128	B1
Queensdown Rd. E5	94	E4
Queensferry Wk. N17	76/77	E4
Jarrow Rd.		
Queensgate Gdns., Chis.	193	G1
Queensgate Pl. NW6	90	D7
Queensland Av. N18	59	J6
Queensland Av. SW19	184	E1
Queensland Pl. N7	93	G4
Queensland Rd.		
Queensland Rd. N7	93	G4
Queensmead NW8	109	G1
Queensmead Rd., Brom.	191	F2
Queensmere Cl. SW19	166	A2
Queensmere Rd. SW19	166	A2
Queensmill Rd. SW6	128	A7
Queensthorpe Rd. SE26	171	G4
Queenstown Ms. SW8	150	B2
Queenstown Rd.		
Queenstown Rd. SW8	**32**	**D6**
Queenstown Rd. SW8	130	B6
Queensville Rd. SW12	150	D7
Queensway W2	**14**	**B4**
Queensway W2	109	E6
Queensway, Enf.	45	E4
Queensway, Orp.	193	F5
Queensway, Sun.	178	B2

Queensway, W.Wick. 205 E3
Queenswood Av. E17 78 C1
Queenswood Av., 161 H6
  Hmptn.
Queenswood Av., 143 F2
  Houns.
Queenswood Av., 187 G5
  Th.Hth.
Queenswood Av., 200 D4
  Wall.
Queenswood Gdns. 97 H1
  E11
Queenswood Pk. N3 72 B2
Queenswood Rd. 171 G3
  SE23
Queenswood Rd., 157 J5
  Sid.
Quemerford Rd. N7 93 F5
Quentin Pl. SE13 155 E3
Quentin Rd. SE13 155 E3
Quernmore Cl., 173 G6
  Brom.
Quernmore Rd. N4 75 G6
Quernmore Rd., 173 G6
  Brom.
Querrin St. SW6 149 F2
Quex Ms. NW6 108 D1
  Quex Rd.
Quex Rd. NW6 108 D1
Quick Pl. N1 111 H1
Quick Rd. W4 126 E5
Quick St. N1 11 H2
Quick St. N1 111 H2
Quick St. Ms. N1 11 G2
Quicks Rd. SW19 167 E7
Quickswood NW3 91 H7
  King Henry's Rd.
Quiet Nook, Brom. 206 A3
  Croydon Rd.
Quill La. SW15 148 A4
Quill St. N4 93 G3
Quill St. W5 105 H3
Quilp St. SE1 27 J3
Quilter St. E2 13 H3
Quilter St. E2 112 D3
Quilter St. SE18 137 J5
Quinta Dr., Barn. 39 H5
Quintin Av. SW20 184 C1
Quintin Cl., Pnr. 66 B5
  High Rd.
Quinton Cl., Beck. 190 C3
Quinton Cl., Houns. 122 B7
Quinton Cl., Wall. 200 B4
Quinton Rd., T.Ditt. 194 D1
Quinton St. SW18 167 F2
Quixley St. E14 114 D7
Quorn Rd. SE22 152 B4

R

Rabbit Row W8 128 D1
  Kensington Mall
Rabbits Rd. E12 98 B4
Rabournmead Dr., 84 E5
  Nthlt.
Raby Rd., N.Mal. 182 D4
Raby St. E14 113 H6
  Salmon La.
Raccoon Way, Houns. 142 C2
Rachel Cl., Ilf. 81 G3
Rachel Pt. E5 94 D4
  Muir Rd.
Rackham Cl., Well. 158 B2
Rackham Ms. SW16 168 C6
  Westcote Rd.
Racton Rd. SW6 128 D6
Radbourne Av. W5 125 F4
Radbourne Cl. E5 95 G4
  Overbury St.
Radbourne Cres. E17 78 D2
Radbourne Rd. SW12 150 C7
Radcliffe Av. NW10 107 G2
Radcliffe Av., Enf. 43 J1
Radcliffe Gdns., Cars. 199 H7
Radcliffe Ms., Hmptn. 161 J5
  Taylor Cl.
Radcliffe Rd. N21 59 H1
Radcliffe Rd. SE1 29 E5
Radcliffe Rd., Croy. 202 C2
Radcliffe Rd., Har. 68 D2
Radcliffe Sq. SW15 148 A6
Radcliffe Way, Nthlt. 102 D3
Radcot Pt. SE23 171 G3
Radcot St. SE11 35 F4
Radcot St. SE11 131 G5
Raddington Rd. W10 108 B5
Radfield Way, Sid. 157 G7
Radford Rd. SE13 154 C6
Radford Way, Bark. 117 J3
Radipole Rd. SW6 148 C1
Radius Pk., Felt. 141 J4
Radland Rd. E16 115 F6

Radlet Av. SE26 171 E3
Radlett Cl. E7 97 F6
Radlett Pl. NW8 109 H1
Radley Av., Ilf. 99 J4
Radley Ct. SE16 133 G2
  Thame Rd.
Radley Gdns., Har. 69 H4
Radley Ho. SE2 138 D2
  Wolvercote Rd.
Radley Ms. W8 128 D3
Radley Rd. N17 76 B2
Radley's La. E18 79 G2
Radleys Mead, Dag. 101 H6
Radlix Rd. E10 96 A1
Radnor Av., Har. 68 B5
Radnor Av., Well. 158 B5
Radnor Cl., Chis. 175 H6
  Homewood Cres.
Radnor Cl., Mitch. 187 E4
Radnor Cres. SE18 138 A7
Radnor Cres., Ilf. 80 C5
Radnor Gdns., Enf. 44 B1
Radnor Gdns., Twick. 162 C2
Radnor Ms. W2 15 F4
Radnor Pl. W2 15 G4
Radnor Pl. W2 109 H6
Radnor Rd. NW6 108 B1
Radnor Rd. SE15 37 H7
Radnor Rd. SE15 132 D7
Radnor Rd., Har. 68 A5
Radnor Rd., Twick. 162 C2
Radnor St. EC1 12 A4
Radnor St. EC1 111 J3
Radnor Ter. W14 128 C4
Radnor Wk. E14 134 A4
  Copeland Dr.
Radnor Wk. SW3 31 H4
Radnor Wk. SW3 129 H5
Radnor Wk., Croy. 189 J6
Radnor Way NW10 106 B4
Radstock Av., Har. 68 D3
Radstock St. SW11 129 H7
Raeburn Av., Surb. 182 B6
Raeburn Cl. NW11 73 F6
Raeburn Cl., Kings.T. 163 G7
Raeburn Rd., Edg. 70 A1
Raeburn Rd., Sid. 157 H6
Raeburn St. SW2 151 E4
Rafford Way, Brom. 191 H2
Raft Rd. SW18 148 D4
  North Pas.
Raggleswood, Chis. 192 D1
Raglan Cl., 142/143 E5
  Houns.
  Vickers Way
Raglan Ct. SE12 155 G5
Raglan Ct., S.Croy. 201 H5
Raglan Ct., Wem. 87 J4
Raglan Gdns., Wat. 50 B1
Raglan Rd. E17 78 C5
Raglan Rd. SE18 137 F5
Raglan Rd., Belv. 139 F4
Raglan Rd., Brom. 191 J4
Raglan Rd., Enf. 44 B7
Raglan St. NW5 92 B6
Raglan Ter., Har. 85 H4
Raglan Way, Nthlt. 85 J6
Ragley Cl. W3 126 C2
  Church Rd.
Raider Cl., Rom. 83 G1
Railey Ms. NW5 92 C5
Railshead Rd., Islw. 144 E4
Railton Rd. SE24 151 G5
Railway App. N4 75 G6
  Wightman Rd.
Railway App. SE1 28 C1
Railway App. SE1 132 A1
Railway App., Har. 68 C4
Railway App., Twick. 144 D7
Railway App., Wall. 200 B6
Railway Av. SE16 133 F2
Railway Ms. E3 114 A3
  Wellington Way
Railway Ms. W10 108 B6
  Ladbroke Gro.
Railway Pas., Tedd. 162 D6
  Victoria Rd.
Railway Pl. SW19 166 C6
  Hartfield Rd.
Railway Pl., Belv. 139 G3
Railway Ri. SE22 152 B4
  Grove Vale
Railway Rd., Tedd. 162 C4
Railway Side SW13 147 E3
Railway St. N1 10 B2
Railway St. N1 111 E2
Railway St., Rom. 100 C1
Railway Ter. SE13 154 B5
  Ladywell Rd.
Railway Ter., Felt. 160 A1
Rainborough Cl. 88 C6
  NW10
Rainbow Av. E14 134 B5

Rainbow Quay SE16 133 H3
  Rope St.
Rainbow St. SE5 132 B7
Raine St. E1 133 E1
Rainham Cl. SE9 157 G6
Rainham Cl. SW11 149 H5
Rainham Rd. NW10 107 J3
Rainham Rd. N., Dag. 101 H2
Rainham Rd. S., Dag. 101 H4
Rainhill Way E3 114 A3
Rainsborough Av. 133 H4
  SE8
Rainsford Cl., Stan. 53 F5
  Coverdale Cl.
Rainsford Rd. NW10 106 B3
Rainsford St. W2 15 G3
Rainton Rd. SE7 135 G5
Rainville Rd. W6 127 J6
Raisins Hill, Pnr. 66 C3
Raith Av. N14 58 D3
Raleana Rd. E14 134 C1
Raleigh Av., Hayes 102 B5
Raleigh Av., Wall. 200 D4
Raleigh Cl. NW4 71 J5
Raleigh Cl., Pnr. 66 D7
Raleigh Ct. SE16 133 G1
  Rotherhithe St.
Raleigh Ct., Wall. 200 B6
Raleigh Dr. N20 57 H3
Raleigh Dr., Esher 194 A5
Raleigh Dr., Surb. 196 C1
Raleigh Gdns. SW2 151 F6
  Brixton Hill
Raleigh Gdns., Mitch. 185 J2
Raleigh Ms. N1 111 H1
  Queen's Head St.
Raleigh Ms., Orp. 207 J5
  Osgood Av.
Raleigh Rd. N8 75 G4
Raleigh Rd. SE20 171 G7
Raleigh Rd., Enf. 44 A4
Raleigh Rd., Rich. 145 J3
Raleigh Rd., Sthl. 122 E5
Raleigh St. N1 111 H1
Raleigh Way N14 58 D1
Raleigh Way, Felt. 160 C5
Ralph Ct. W2 14 B3
Ralph Perring Ct., 190 A4
  Beck.
Ralston St. SW3 31 J4
Ralston Way, Wat. 50 D2
Ram Pas., Kings.T. 181 G2
  High St.
Ram Pl. E9 95 F6
  Chatham Pl.
Ram St. SW18 148 E5
Rama Cl. SW16 168 D7
Rama Ct., Har. 86 B2
Ramac Way SE7 135 H4
Rambler Cl. SW16 168 C4
Rame Cl. SW17 168 A5
Ramillies Cl. SW2 151 E6
Ramillies Pl. W1 17 F4
Ramillies Pl. W1 110 C6
Ramillies Rd. NW7 54 E2
Ramillies Rd. W4 126 D4
Ramillies Rd., Sid. 158 B6
Ramillies St. W1 17 F4
Rampart St. E1 112/113 E6
  Commercial Rd.
Rampayne St. SW1 33 H3
Rampayne St. SW1 130 D5
Rampton Cl. E4 62 A3
Rams Gro., Rom. 83 E4
Ramsay Ms. SW3 31 G5
Ramsay Pl., Har. 86 B1
Ramsay Rd. E7 97 E4
Ramsay Rd. W3 126 C3
Ramscroft Cl. N9 44 B7
Ramsdale Rd. SW17 168 A5
Ramsden Rd. N11 57 J5
Ramsden Rd. SW12 150 A6
Ramsey Cl. NW9 71 F6
  West Hendon Bdy.
Ramsey Cl., Grnf. 85 J5
Ramsey Ho., Wem. 87 H6
Ramsey Ms. N4 93 H3
  Monsell Rd.
Ramsey Rd., Th.Hth. 187 F6
Ramsey St. E2 13 J5
Ramsey St. E2 112 D4
Ramsey Wk. N1 94 A6
  Clephane Rd.
Ramsey Way N14 42 C7
Ramsgate Cl. E16 135 H1
  Hanameel St.
Ramsgate St. E8 94 C6
  Dalston La.
Ramsgill App., Ilf. 81 J4
Ramsgill Dr., Ilf. 81 J5
Ramulis Dr., Hayes 102 D4
Ramus Wd. Av., Orp. 207 H5
Rancliffe Gdns. SE9 156 B4
Rancliffe Rd. E6 116 B2

Randall Av. NW2 89 F3
Randall Cl. SW11 149 H1
Randall Cl., Erith 139 J6
Randall Rd. SE11 34 C3
Randall Rd. SE11 131 F4
Randall Row SE11 34 C2
Randell's Rd. N1 111 E1
Randle Rd., Rich. 163 F4
Randlesdown Rd. SE6 172 A4
Randolph App. E16 116 A6
Randolph Av. W9 6 D6
Randolph Av. W9 109 F4
Randolph Cl., Bexh. 159 J3
Randolph Cl., Kings.T. 164 C5
Randolph Cres. W9 6 C6
Randolph Cres. W9 109 F4
Randolph Gdns. NW6 6 A2
Randolph Gdns. NW6 108 E2
Randolph Gro., Rom. 82 C5
  Donald Dr.
Randolph Ho., Croy. 201 J1
Randolph Ms. W9 6 D6
Randolph Ms. W9 109 F4
Randolph Rd. E17 78 B5
Randolph Rd. W9 6 C6
Randolph Rd. W9 109 F4
Randolph Rd., Sthl. 123 F2
Randolph St. NW1 92 C7
Randon Cl., Har. 67 H2
Ranelagh Av. SW6 148 C3
Ranelagh Av. SW13 147 G2
Ranelagh Br. W2 108/109 E5
  Gloucester Ter.
Ranelagh Cl., Edg. 54 A4
Ranelagh Dr., Edg. 54 A4
Ranelagh Dr., Twick. 145 E5
Ranelagh Gdns. E11 79 J5
Ranelagh Gdns. SW6 148 C3
Ranelagh Gdns. W4 126 C7
  Grove Pk. Gdns.
Ranelagh Gdns. W6 127 F3
Ranelagh Gdns., Ilf. 98 D1
Ranelagh Gro. SW1 32 C3
Ranelagh Gro. SW1 130 A5
Ranelagh Ms. W5 125 G2
  Ranelagh Rd.
Ranelagh Pl., 182/183 E5
  N.Mal.
  Rodney Rd.
Ranelagh Rd. E6 116 D1
Ranelagh Rd. E11 96 E4
Ranelagh Rd. E15 115 E7
Ranelagh Rd. N17 76 B3
Ranelagh Rd. N22 75 F1
Ranelagh Rd. NW10 107 F2
Ranelagh Rd. SW1 33 G4
Ranelagh Rd. W5 125 G2
Ranelagh Rd., Sthl. 122 D1
Ranelagh Rd., Wem. 87 G5
Ranfurly Rd., Sutt. 198 D2
Rangefield Rd., Brom. 172 E5
Rangemoor Rd. N15 76 C5
Rangers Rd. E4 47 E7
Rangers Rd., Loug. 47 E7
Rangers Sq. SE10 154 D1
Rangeworth Pl., Sid. 175 J3
  Priestlands Pk. Rd.
Rangoon St. EC3 112 C6
  Northumberland All.
Rankin Cl. NW9 71 E3
Ranleigh Gdns., Bexh. 139 F7
Ranmere St. SW12 168 B1
  Ormeley Rd.
Ranmoor Cl., Har. 68 A4
Ranmoor Gdns., Har. 68 A4
Ranmore Av., Croy. 202 C3
Rannoch Cl., Edg. 54 B2
Rannoch Rd. W6 127 J6
Rannock Av. NW9 70 E7
Ranskill Rd., Borwd. 38 A1
Ransom Rd. SE7 135 J5
  Harvey Gdns.
Ransom Wk. SE7 135 J5
  Woolwich Rd.
Ranston St. NW1 15 G1
Ranulf Rd. NW2 90 C4
Ranwell Cl. E3 113 J1
  Beale Rd.
Ranwell St. E3 113 J1
Ranworth Rd. N9 61 F2
Ranyard Cl., Chess. 195 J3
Raphael Dr., T.Ditt. 180 C7
Raphael St. SW7 23 J4
Raphael St. SW7 129 J2
Rashleigh St. SW8 150 B7
  Peardon St.
Rasper Rd. N20 57 F2
Rastell Av. SW2 168 D2
Ratcliff Rd. E7 97 J5
Ratcliffe Cl. SE12 155 G7
Ratcliffe Cross St. E1 113 G6
Ratcliffe La. E14 113 H6
Ratcliffe Orchard E1 113 G7

Rathbone Mkt. E16 115 F5
Barking Rd.
Rathbone Pl. W1 17 H3
Rathbone Pl. W1 110 D6
Rathbone Pt. E5 94 D4
Nolan Way
Rathbone St. E16 115 F5
Rathbone St. W1 17 G2
Rathbone St. W1 110 C5
Rathcoole Av. N8 75 F4
Rathcoole Gdns. N8 75 F5
Rathfern Rd. SE6 171 J1
Rathgar Av. W13 125 E1
Rathgar Cl. N3 72 C2
Rathgar Rd. SW9 151 H3
Coldharbour La.
Rathlin Wk. N1 93 J6
Clephane Rd.
Rathmell Dr. SW4 150 D6
Rathmore Rd. SE7 135 H5
Rattray Rd. SW2 151 G4
Raul Rd. SE15 152 D1
Raveley St. NW5 92 C4
Raven Cl. NW9 70/71 E2
Eagle Dr.
Raven Ct. E5 94 D3
Stellman Cl.
Raven Rd. E18 79 J2
Raven Row E1 113 E5
Ravenet St. SW11 150 B1
Strasburg Rd.
Ravenfield Rd. SW17 167 J3
Ravenhill Rd. E13 115 J2
Ravenna Rd. SW15 148 A5
Ravenoak Way, Chig. 65 H5
Ravenor Pk. Rd., Grnf. 103 H3
Ravens Cl., Brom. 191 F2
Ravens Cl., Enf. 44 B2
Ravens Ms. SE12 155 G5
Ravens Way
Ravens Way SE12 155 G5
Ravensbourne Av., Beck. 172 D7
Ravensbourne Av., Brom. 172 D7
Ravensbourne Gdns. W13 104 E5
Ravensbourne Gdns., Ilf. 80 D1
Ravensbourne Pk. SE6 154 A7
Ravensbourne Pk. Cres. SE6 153 J7
Ravensbourne Pl. SE13 154 B2
Ravensbourne Rd. SE6 153 J7
Ravensbourne Rd., Brom. 191 G3
Ravensbourne Rd., Twick. 145 F6
Ravensbury Av., Mord. 185 F5
Ravensbury Ct., Mitch. 185 G4
Ravensbury Gro.
Ravensbury Gro., Mitch. 185 G4
Ravensbury La., Mitch. 185 G4
Ravensbury Path, Mitch. 185 G4
Ravensbury Rd. SW18 166 D2
Ravensbury Rd., Orp. 193 J4
Ravensbury Ter. SW18 167 E1
Ravenscar Rd., Brom. 172 E4
Ravenscar Rd., Surb. 195 J2
Ravenscourt Av. W6 127 G4
Ravenscourt Gdns. W6 127 G4
Ravenscourt Pk. W6 127 G3
Ravenscourt Pl. W6 127 H4
Ravenscourt Rd. W6 127 H4
Ravenscourt Sq. W6 127 G3
Ravenscraig Rd. N11 58 B4
Ravenscroft Av. NW11 72 C7
Ravenscroft Av., Wem. 87 J1
Ravenscroft Cl. E16 115 G5
Ravenscroft Cres. SE9 174 C3
Ravenscroft Pk., Barn. 40 A4
Ravenscroft Rd. E16 115 G5
Ravenscroft Rd. W4 126 C4
Ravenscroft Rd., Beck. 189 F2
Ravenscroft St. E2 13 G2
Ravenscroft St. E2 112 C2
Ravensdale Av. N12 57 F4
Ravensdale Gdns. SE19 170 A7
Ravensdale Gdns., Houns. 142 E3
Ravensdale Rd. N16 76 C7
Ravensdale Rd., Houns. 142 E3
Ravensdon St. SE11 35 F4
Ravensdon St. SE11 131 G5
Ravensfield Cl., Dag. 100 D4
Ravensfield Gdns., Epsom 197 E5
Ravenshaw St. NW6 90 C5
Ravenshill, Chis. 192 E1
Ravenshurst Av. NW4 71 J4
Ravenside Cl. N18 61 G6
Ravenside Retail Pk. N18 61 G5
Ravenslea Rd. SW12 149 J7
Ravensmead Rd., Brom. 172 D7
Ravensmede Way W4 127 F4
Ravenstone SE17 36 E4
Ravenstone SE17 132 B5
Ravenstone Rd. N8 75 G3
Ravenstone Rd. NW9 71 F6
West Hendon Bdy.
Ravenstone St. SW12 168 A1
Ravenswood, Bex. 177 E1
Ravenswood Av., Surb. 195 J2
Ravenswood Av., W.Wick. 204 C1
Ravenswood Ct., Kings.T. 164 B6
Ravenswood Cres., Har. 85 F2
Ravenswood Cres., W.Wick. 204 C1
Ravenswood Gdns., Islw. 144 B1
Ravenswood Pk., Nthwd. 50 A6
Ravenswood Rd. E17 78 B4
Ravenswood Rd. SW12 150 B7
Ravenswood Rd., Croy. 201 H3
Ravensworth Rd. NW10 107 H3
Ravensworth Rd. SE9 174 C4
Ravent Rd. SE11 34 D2
Ravent Rd. SE11 131 F4
Ravey St. EC2 12 D5
Ravine Gro. SE18 137 H6
Rawlings St. SW3 31 J1
Rawlings St. SW3 129 J4
Rawlins Cl. N3 72 B3
Rawlins Cl., S.Croy. 203 H7
Rawnsley Av., Mitch. 185 G5
Rawreth Wk. N1 111 J1
Basire St.
Rawson St. SW11 150 A1
Strasburg Rd.
Rawsthorne Cl. E16 136 C1
Kennard St.
Rawstone Wk. E13 115 G2
Rawstorne Pl. EC1 11 G3
Rawstorne St. EC1 11 G3
Rawstorne St. EC1 111 H3
Ray Cl., Chess. 195 F6
Merritt Gdns.
Ray Gdns., Bark. 118 A2
Ray Gdns., Stan. 53 E5
Ray Lo. Rd., Wdf.Grn. 63 J6
Ray Massey Way E6 116 B1
Ron Leighton Way
Ray Rd., W.Mol. 179 H5
Ray St. EC1 11 F6
Ray St. EC1 111 G4
Ray St. Br. EC1 11 F6
Ray Wk. N7 93 F2
Andover Rd.
Raydean Rd., Barn. 40 E5
Raydon St. N19 92 B2
Raydons Gdns., Dag. 101 E5
Raydons Rd., Dag. 100 E5
Rayfield Cl., Brom. 192 B6
Rayford Av. SE12 155 F7
Rayleas Cl. SE18 156 E1
Rayleigh Av., Tedd. 162 B6
Rayleigh Cl. N13 60 A3
Rayleigh Rd.
Rayleigh Ct., Kings.T. 181 J2
Rayleigh Ri., S.Croy. 202 B6
Rayleigh Rd. E16 135 H1
Wesley Av.
Rayleigh Rd. N13 59 J3
Rayleigh Rd. SW19 184 C1
Rayleigh Rd., Wdf.Grn. 63 J6
Raymead NW4 71 J4
Tenterden Gro.
Raymead Av., Th.Hth. 187 G5
Raymere Gdns. SE18 137 G7
Raymond Av. E18 79 F3
Raymond Av. W13 124 D3
Raymond Bldgs. WC1 18 D1
Raymond Cl. SE26 171 F5
Raymond Ct. N10 58 A7
Pembroke Rd.
Raymond Rd. E13 97 J7
Raymond Rd. SW19 166 B6
Raymond Rd., Beck. 189 H4
Raymond Rd., Ilf. 81 G7
Raymond Way, Esher 194 D6
Raymouth Rd. SE16 133 E4
Rayne Ct. E18 79 F4
Rayner Twr. E10 78 A7
Rayners Cl., Wem. 87 G5
Rayners Ct., Har. 85 G1
Rayners Cres., Nthlt. 102 B3
Rayners Gdns., Nthlt. 102 B2
Rayners La., Har. 85 H2
Rayners La., Pnr. 67 F6
Rayners Rd. SW15 148 B5
Raynes Av. E11 79 J7
Raynham Av. N18 60 D6
Raynham Rd. N18 60 D5
Raynham Rd. W6 127 H4
Raynham Ter. N18 60 D5
Raynor Cl., Sthl. 123 F1
Raynor Pl. N1 111 J1
Elizabeth Av.
Raynton Cl., Har. 85 E1
Rays Av. N18 61 F4
Rays Rd. N18 61 F4
Rays Rd., W.Wick. 190 C7
Raywood Cl., Hayes 121 F7
Raywood St. SW8 150 B1
Gladstone Ter.
Reachview Cl. NW1 92 C7
Baynes St.
Read Cl., T.Ditt. 180 D7
Reade Wk. NW10 88/89 E7
Denbigh Cl.
Reading La. E8 94 E6
Reading Rd., Nthlt. 85 H5
Reading Rd., Sutt. 199 F5
Reading Way NW7 56 A5
Reads Cl., Ilf. 98/99 E3
Chapel Rd.
Reapers Cl. NW1 110 D1
Crofters Way
Reapers Way, Islw. 144 A5
Hall Rd.
Reardon Ct. N21 59 J2
Cosgrove Cl.
Reardon Path E1 133 E1
Reardon St. E1 132 E1
Reaston St. SE14 133 G7
Reckitt Rd. W4 126 E5
Record St. SE15 133 F6
Recovery St. SW17 167 H5
Recreation Av., Rom. 83 J5
Recreation Rd. SE26 171 G4
Recreation Rd., Brom. 191 F2
Recreation Rd., Sid. 175 H3
Woodside Rd.
Recreation Rd., Sthl. 122 E4
Recreation Way, Mitch. 186 D3
Rector St. N1 111 J1
Rectory Cl. E4 62 A3
Rectory Cl. N3 72 C1
Rectory Cl. SW20 183 J3
Rectory Cl., Sid. 176 B4
Rectory Cl., Stan. 53 E6
Rectory Cl., Surb. 195 F1
Rectory Cres. E11 79 J6
Rectory Fld. Cres. SE7 135 J7
Rectory Gdns. N8 74 E4
Rectory Gdns. SW4 150 C3
Rectory Gdns., Nthlt. 103 F1
Rectory Grn., Beck. 189 J1
Rectory Gro. SW4 150 C3
Rectory Gro., Croy. 201 H2
Rectory Gro., Hmptn. 161 F4
Rectory La. SW17 168 A6
Rectory La., Edg. 54 A6
Rectory La., Loug. 48 D2
Rectory La., Sid. 176 B4
Rectory La., Stan. 52 E5
Rectory La., Surb. 195 F1
Rectory La., Wall. 200 C4
Rectory Orchard SW19 166 B4
Rectory Pk. Av., Nthlt. 103 F3
Rectory Pl. SE18 136 D4
Rectory Rd. E12 98 C5
Rectory Rd. E17 78 B3
Rectory Rd. N16 94 C3
Rectory Rd. SW13 147 G2
Rectory Rd. W3 126 B1
Rectory Rd., Beck. 190 A1
Rectory Rd., Dag. 101 G7
Rectory Rd., Hayes 102 A6
Rectory Rd., Houns. 142 B1
Rectory Rd., Kes. 206 A7
Rectory Rd., Sthl. 123 F3
Rectory Rd., Sutt. 198 D3
Rectory Sq. E1 113 G5
Reculver Ms. N18 60 D4
Lyndhurst Rd.
Reculver Rd. SE16 133 G5
Red Anchor Cl. SW3 31 G6
Red Barracks Rd. SE18 136 C4
Red Cedars Rd., Orp. 193 H7
Red Hill, Chis. 174 D5
Red Ho. La., Bexh. 158 D4
Red Ho. Sq. N1 93 J6
Clephane Rd.
Red La., Esher 194 D6
Red Lion Cl. SE17 36 A5
Red Lion Ct. EC4 19 F3
Red Lion Hill N2 73 G2
Red Lion La. SE18 136 D7
Red Lion Pl. SE18 156 D1
Shooter's Hill Rd.
Red Lion Rd., Surb. 195 J2
Red Lion Row SE17 36 A5
Red Lion Row SE17 131 J6
Red Lion Sq. SW18 148 D5
Wandsworth High St.
Red Lion Sq. WC1 18 C2
Red Lion Sq. WC1 111 F5
Red Lion St. WC1 18 C1
Red Lion St. WC1 111 F5
Red Lion St., Rich. 145 G5
Red Lion Yd. W1 24 C1
Red Lo. Rd., W.Wick. 190 D6
Red Oak Cl., Orp. 207 E3
Red Path E9 95 J6
Red Pl. W1 16 B5
Red Post Hill SE21 152 A5
Red Post Hill SE24 152 A4
Redan Pl. W2 14 A4
Redan Pl. W2 108 E6
Redan St. W14 128 A3
Redan Ter. SE5 151 J2
Flaxman Rd.
Redberry Gro. SE26 171 F3
Redbourne Av. N3 72 D1
Redbridge Enterprise Cen., Ilf. 99 F2
Redbridge Gdns. SE5 132 B7
Redbridge La. E., Ilf. 80 A6
Redbridge La. W. E11 79 H6
Redburn St. SW3 31 J5
Redburn St. SW3 129 J6
Redcar Cl., Nthlt. 85 H5
Redcar St. SE5 131 J7
Redcastle Cl. E1 113 F7
Redchurch St. E2 13 F5
Redchurch St. E2 112 C4
Redcliffe Cl. SW5 128/129 E5
Warwick Rd.
Redcliffe Gdns. SW5 30 B4
Redcliffe Gdns. SW5 129 E5
Redcliffe Gdns. SW10 30 B4
Redcliffe Gdns. SW10 129 E5
Redcliffe Gdns., Ilf. 98 D1
Redcliffe Ms. SW10 30 B4
Redcliffe Ms. SW10 129 E5
Redcliffe Pl. SW10 30 C6
Redcliffe Pl. SW10 129 F6
Redcliffe Rd. SW10 30 C4
Redcliffe Rd. SW10 129 F5
Redcliffe Sq. SW10 30 B4
Redcliffe Sq. SW10 129 E5
Redcliffe St. SW10 30 B5
Redcliffe St. SW10 129 E6
Redclose Av., Mord. 184 D5
Chalgrove Av.
Redclyffe Rd. E6 115 J1
Redcroft Rd., Sthl. 103 J7
Redcross Way SE1 28 A3
Redcross Way SE1 131 J2
Reddings, The NW7 55 F3
Reddings Cl. NW7 55 F4
Reddins Rd. SE15 37 H6
Reddins Rd. SE15 132 D6
Reddons Rd., Beck. 171 H7
Rede Pl. W2 108 D6
Chepstow Pl.
Redesdale Gdns., Islw. 124 D7
Redesdale St. SW3 31 H5
Redesdale St. SW3 129 J6
Redfern Av., Houns. 143 G7
Redfern Rd. NW10 89 E7
Redfern Rd. SE6 154 C7
Redfield La. SW5 128 D4
Redfield Ms. SW5 128 D4
Redfield La.
Redford Av., Th.Hth. 187 F4
Redford Av., Wall. 200 E6
Redford Wk. N1 111 H1
Britannia Row
Redgate Dr., Brom. 205 H2
Redgate Ter. SW15 148 A6
Lytton Gro.
Redgrave Cl., Croy. 188 C6
Redgrave Rd. SW15 148 A3

Richmond Pk. Rd., 163 H7
Kings.T.
Richmond Pl. SE18 137 F4
Richmond Rd. E4 62 D1
Richmond Rd. E7 97 H5
Richmond Rd. E8 94 C7
Richmond Rd. E11 96 D2
Richmond Rd. N2 73 F2
Richmond Rd. N11 58 E6
Richmond Rd. N15 76 B6
Richmond Rd. SW20 183 H1
Richmond Rd. W5 125 H2
Richmond Rd., Barn. 41 E6
Richmond Rd., Croy. 200 E3
Richmond Rd., Ilf. 99 F3
Richmond Rd., Islw. 144 D3
Richmond Rd., 163 G5
Kings.T.
Richmond Rd., Th.Hth. 187 H3
Richmond Rd., Twick. 145 F6
Richmond St. E13 115 G2
Richmond Ter. SW1 26 A3
Richmond Ter. SW1 130 E2
Richmond Ter. 130/131 E2
Ms. SW1
Parliament St.
Richmond Way E11 97 G2
Richmond Way W12 128 A2
Richmond Way W14 128 A3
Richmount Gdns. 155 G3
SE3
Rick Roberts Way E15 114 C1
Rickard Cl. NW4 71 H4
Rickard Cl. SW2 169 F1
Rickard Cl., West Dr. 120 A3
Rickards Cl., Surb. 195 H1
Rickett St. SW6 128 D6
Rickman St. E1 113 F3
Mantus Rd.
Rickmansworth Rd., 66 B2
Pnr.
Rickthorne Rd. N19 92/93 E2
Landseer Rd.
Rickyard Path SE9 156 B4
Ridding La., Grnf. 86 C5
Riddons Rd. SE12 173 J3
Ride, The, Brent. 125 E5
Ride, The, Enf. 45 F3
Rideout St. SE18 136 C4
Rider Cl., Sid. 157 H6
Ridgdale St. E3 114 B2
Ridge,The, Bex. 159 F7
Ridge, The, Orp. 207 G2
Ridge, The, Surb. 182 A5
Ridge, The, Twick. 144 A7
Ridge Av. N21 43 J7
Ridge Cl. NW4 72 A2
Ridge Cl. NW9 70 D4
Ridge Cl. SE28 137 G2
Ridge Crest, Enf. 43 F1
Ridge Hill NW11 90 B1
Ridge Rd. N8 75 F6
Ridge Rd. N21 59 J1
Ridge Rd. NW2 90 C3
Ridge Rd., Mitch. 168 B7
Ridge Rd., Sutt. 198 B1
Ridge Way SE19 170 B6
Central Hill
Ridge Way, Felt. 160 E3
Ridgebrook Rd. SE3 155 J3
Ridgecroft Cl., Bex. 177 J1
Ridgemont Gdns., 54 C4
Edg.
Ridgemount Av., Croy. 203 G1
Ridgemount Cl. 170/171 E7
SE20
Anerley Pk.
Ridgemount Gdns., 43 H2
Enf.
Ridgeview Cl., Barn. 40 A6
Ridgeview Rd. N20 57 E3
Ridgeway, Brom. 205 G2
Ridgeway, Wdf.Grn. 63 J4
Ridgeway, The E4 62 B2
Ridgeway, The N3 56 E7
Ridgeway, The N11 57 J4
Ridgeway, The N14 59 E2
Ridgeway, The NW7 55 H4
Ridgeway, The NW9 70 E4
Ridgeway, The NW11 90 C1
Ridgeway, The SE28 137 G4
Pettman Cres.
Ridgeway, The W3 126 A3
Ridgeway, The, Croy. 201 F3
Ridgeway, The, Enf. 43 G1
Ridgeway, The, Har. 67 F5
Ridgeway, The 69 F6
(Kenton), Har.
Ridgeway, The, Ruis. 67 G6
Ridgeway, The, Stan. 53 F6
Ridgeway Av., Barn. 41 J6
Ridgeway Cres., Orp. 207 H3
Ridgeway 207 H2
Gdns., Orp.

Ridgeway Dr., Brom. 173 H4
Ridgeway E., Sid. 157 J5
Ridgeway Gdns. N6 74 C7
Ridgeway Gdns., Ilf. 80 B5
Ridgeway Rd. SW9 151 H3
Ridgeway Rd., Islw. 124 B7
Ridgeway Rd. N., 124 B6
Islw.
Ridgeway Wk., 84/85 E6
Nthlt.
Fortunes Mead
Ridgeway W., Sid. 157 H5
Ridgewell Cl. N1 111 J1
Basire St.
Ridgewell Cl. SE26 171 J4
Ridgewell Cl., Dag. 119 H1
Ridgmount Gdns. 9 H6
WC1
Ridgmount Pl. WC1 17 H1
Ridgmount Rd. SW18 149 E5
Ridgmount St. WC1 17 H1
Ridgway SW19 166 A6
Ridgway, The, Sutt. 199 G7
Ridgway Gdns. SW19 166 A7
Ridgway Pl. SW19 166 B6
Ridgwell Rd. E16 115 J5
Riding, The NW11 72 C7
Golders Grn. Rd.
Riding Ho. St. W1 17 F2
Riding Ho. St. W1 110 B5
Ridings, The W5 105 J4
Ridings, The, Sun. 178 A1
Ridings, The, Surb. 182 A5
Ridings Av. N21 43 H4
Ridings Cl. N6 74 C7
Hornsey La. Gdns.
Ridley Av. W13 124 E3
Ridley Rd. E7 97 J4
Ridley Rd. E8 94 C5
Ridley Rd. NW10 107 G2
Ridley Rd. SW19 166 E7
Ridley Rd., Brom. 191 F3
Ridley Rd., Well. 158 B1
Ridley Several SE3 155 H2
Blackheath Pk.
Ridsdale Rd. SE20 188 E1
Riefield Rd. SE9 157 F4
Riesco Dr., Croy. 203 F6
Riffel Rd. NW2 89 J5
Rifle Pl. SE11 35 F5
Rifle Pl. SE11 131 G6
Rifle Pl. W11 128 A1
Rifle St. E14 114 B5
Rigault Rd. SW6 148 B2
Rigby Cl., Croy. 201 G3
Rigby La., Hayes 121 G2
Rigby Ms., Ilf. 98/99 E2
Cranbrook Rd.
Rigden St. E14 114 B6
Rigeley Rd. NW10 107 G3
Rigg App. E10 95 G1
Rigge Pl. SW4 150 D4
Riggindale Rd. SW16 168 D5
Riley Rd. SE1 29 E5
Riley Rd. SE1 132 C3
Riley St. SW10 31 E7
Riley St. SW10 129 G6
Rinaldo Rd. SW12 150 B7
Ring, The W2 15 G5
Ring, The W2 109 G3
Ring Cl., Brom. 173 H7
Garden Rd.
Ring Rd. W12 107 J7
Ringcroft St. N7 93 G5
Ringers Rd., Brom. 191 G3
Ringford Rd. SW18 148 C5
Ringlet Cl. E16 115 H6
Ringlewell Cl., Enf. 44/45 E2
Central Av.
Ringmer Av. SW6 148 B1
Ringmer Gdns. N19 92/93 E2
Sussex Way
Ringmer Pl. N21 44 A5
Ringmer Way, Brom. 192 C5
Ringmore Ri. SE23 153 E7
Ringslade Rd. N22 75 F2
Ringstead Rd. SE6 154 B7
Ringstead Rd., Sutt. 199 G4
Ringway N11 58 C6
Ringway, Sthl. 123 E5
Ringwold Cl., Beck. 171 H7
Ringwood Av. N2 73 J2
Ringwood Av., Croy. 187 E7
Ringwood Cl., Pnr. 66 C3
Ringwood Gdns. E14 134 A4
Inglewood Cl.
Ringwood Gdns. 165 G2
SW15
Ringwood Rd. E17 77 J6
Ringwood Way N21 59 H1
Ringwood Way, 161 G4
Hmptn.
Ripley Cl., Brom. 192 C5
Ringmer Way

Ripley Cl., Croy. 204 C6
Ripley Gdns. SW14 146 D3
Ripley Gdns., Sutt. 199 F4
Ripley Ms. E11 78/79 E7
Wadley Rd.
Ripley Rd. E16 115 J6
Ripley Rd., Belv. 139 G4
Ripley Rd., Enf. 43 J1
Ripley Rd., Hmptn. 161 G7
Ripley Rd., Ilf. 99 J2
Ripley Vil. W5 105 F6
Castlebar Rd.
Riplington Ct. SW15 147 G7
Longwood Dr.
Ripon Cl., Nthlt. 85 G5
Ripon Gdns., Chess. 195 F5
Ripon Gdns., Ilf. 80 B6
Ripon Rd. N9 44 E7
Ripon Rd. N17 76 A3
Ripon Rd. SE18 136 E6
Ripon Way, Borwd. 38 C5
Rippersley Rd., Well. 158 A1
Ripple Rd., Bark. 99 F7
Ripple Rd., Dag. 118 B1
Rippleside 118 C2
Commercial Est., Bark.
Ripplevale Gro. N1 93 F7
Rippolson Rd. SE18 137 J5
Risborough Dr., 183 G7
Wor.Pk.
Risborough St. SE1 27 H3
Risdon St. SE16 133 F2
Renforth St.
Rise, The E11 79 G5
Rise, The N13 59 G4
Rise, The NW7 55 F6
Rise, The NW10 88 D4
Rise, The, Bex. 158 C7
Rise, The, Buck.H. 48 A7
Rise, The, Edg. 54 B5
Rise, The, Grnf. 86 D5
Risedale Rd., Bexh. 159 H3
Riseldine Rd. SE23 153 H6
Rising Sun Ct. EC1 19 H2
Risinghill St. N1 10 E1
Risinghill St. N1 111 F2
Risingholme Cl., Har. 68 B1
Risingholme Rd., Har. 68 B2
Risings, The E17 78 D4
Risley Av. N17 75 J1
Rita Rd. SW8 34 B6
Rita Rd. SW8 131 E7
Ritches Rd. N15 75 J5
Ritchie Rd., Croy. 189 E6
Ritchie St. N1 11 F1
Ritchie St. N1 111 G2
Ritchings Av. E17 77 H4
Ritherdon Rd. SW17 168 A2
Ritson Rd. E8 94 D6
Ritter St. SE18 136 D6
Ritz Par. W5 105 J4
Connell Cres.
Rivaz Pl. E9 95 F6
Rivenhall Gdns. E18 79 F4
River Av. N13 59 H3
River Av., T.Ditt. 180 D7
River Bank N21 43 J7
River Bank, E.Mol. 180 A3
River Bank, T.Ditt. 180 C5
River Bank, W.Mol. 179 F3
River Barge Cl. E14 134 C2
Stewart St.
River Brent Business 124 B3
Pk. W7
River Cl. E11 79 J6
River Cl., Sthl. 123 J2
River Cl., Surb. 181 G5
Catherine Rd.
River Crane Wk., Felt. 160 D1
River Crane Wk., 160 D1
Houns.
River Crane Way, Felt. 161 F2
Watermill Way
River Front, Enf. 44 A3
River Gdns., Cars. 200 A2
River Gdns., Felt. 142 B4
River Gro. Pk., Beck. 189 J1
River La., Rich. 163 G1
River Pk. Gdns., 172 D7
Brom.
River Pk. Rd. N22 75 F2
River Pl. N1 93 J7
River Reach, Tedd. 163 F5
River Rd., Bark. 117 H2
River Rd., Buck.H. 64 B1
River Rd. Business 117 J3
Pk., Bark.
River St. EC1 11 E3
River St. EC1 111 G3
River Ter. W6 127 J5
Crisp Rd.
River Vw., Enf. 43 J3
Chase Side
River Wk., Walt. 178 A6

River Way, Epsom 196 D5
River Way, Loug. 48 D6
River Way, Twick. 161 H2
Riverbank Way, 125 F6
Brent.
Rivercourt Rd. W6 127 H4
Riverdale SE13 154 C3
Lewisham High St.
Riverdale Cl., Bark. 117 H3
Thames Rd.
Riverdale Dr. 166/167 E1
SW18
Strathville Rd.
Riverdale Gdns., 145 F6
Twick.
Riverdale Rd. SE18 137 J5
Riverdale Rd., Bex. 159 F7
Riverdale Rd., Erith 139 H5
Riverdale Rd., Felt. 161 E4
Riverdale Rd., Twick. 145 F6
Riverdene, Edg. 54 C3
Riverdene Rd., Ilf. 98 D3
Riverhead Cl. E17 77 G2
Rivermead, E.Mol. 179 J3
Rivermead Cl., Tedd. 163 E5
Rivermead Ct. SW6 148 C3
Rivermeads Av., 161 G3
Twick.
Rivernook Cl., Walt. 178 C5
Riversdale Rd. N5 93 H3
Riversdale Rd., T.Ditt. 180 D5
Riversfield Rd., Enf. 44 B3
Riverside NW4 71 H7
Riverside SE7 135 H3
Riverside, Twick. 162 E1
Riverside, The, E.Mol. 180 A3
Riverside Av.,E.Mol. 180 A5
Riverside Business 167 E1
Cen. SW18
Riverside Cl. E5 95 F1
Riverside Cl. W7 104 B4
Riverside Cl., 181 G4
Kings.T.
Riverside Cl., Wall. 200 B3
Riverside Ct. E4 46 B6
Chelwood Cl.
Riverside Ct. SW8 33 J5
Riverside Ct. SW8 130 D6
Riverside Dr. NW11 72 B6
Riverside Dr. W4 126 D7
Riverside Dr., Mitch. 185 H5
Riverside Dr., Rich. 163 E2
Riverside Gdns. N3 72 B3
Riverside Gdns. W6 127 H5
Riverside Gdns., Enf. 43 J2
Riverside Gdns., 105 H2
Wem.
Riverside Ind. Est., 118 A3
Bark.
Riverside Ind. Est., Enf. 45 H6
Riverside Ms., 200/201 E3
Croy.
Wandle Rd.
Riverside Pl., Stai. 140 A6
Riverside Rd. E15 114 C2
Riverside Rd. N15 76 D6
Riverside Rd. SW17 167 E4
Riverside Rd., Sid. 177 E3
Riverside Rd. 140 A5
(Stanwell), Stai.
Riverside Wk. SE1 26 C2
Riverside Wk. SE1 131 F1
Riverside Wk., Bex. 158 C7
Riverside Wk., Islw. 144 B3
Riverside Wk., 181 G2
Kings.T.
High St.
Riverside Wk., Loug. 48 E6
Riverside W. 148/149 E4
SW18
Smugglers Way
Riverton Cl. W9 108 C3
Riverview Gdns. 127 H6
SW13
Riverview Gdns., 162 C2
Twick.
Riverview Gro. W4 126 B6
Riverview Pk. SE6 172 A2
Riverview Rd. W4 126 B6
Riverview Rd., Epsom 196 C4
Riverway N13 59 G5
Riverwood La., Chis. 193 G1
Rivington Av., 80 A2
Wdf.Grn.
Rivington Ct. NW10 107 G1
Rivington Cres. NW7 55 F7
Rivington Pl. EC2 12 E4
Rivington St. EC2 12 D4
Rivington St. EC2 112 B3
Rivington Wk. E8 112 D1
Wilde Cl.
Rivulet Rd. N17 59 J7
Rixon Ho. SE18 136/137 E6
Barnfield Rd.

Rixon St. N7 93 G3
Rixsen Rd. E12 98 B5
Roach Rd. E3 96 A7
Roads Pl. N19 92/93 E2
Hornsey Rd.
Roan St. SE10 134 C6
Robarts Cl., Pnr. 66 B5
Field End Rd.
Robb Rd., Stan. 52 D6
Robert Adam St. W1 16 B3
Robert Adam St. W1 110 A6
Robert Cl. W9 6 D6
Robert Cl., Chig. 65 J5
Robert Dashwood Way SE17 35 J2
Robert Dashwood Way SE17 131 J4
Robert Gentry Ho. W14 128 B5
Comeragh Rd.
Robert Keen Cl. SE15 152 D1
Cicely Rd.
Robert Lowe Cl. SE14 133 G7
Robert Owen Ho. SW6 148 A1
Robert St. E16 136 E1
Robert St. NW1 8 E4
Robert St. NW1 110 B3
Robert St. SE18 137 G4
Robert St. WC2 18 B6
Robert St., Croy. 201 J3
High St.
Roberta St. E2 13 H3
Roberta St. E2 112 D3
Roberton Dr., Brom. 191 J1
Roberts Cl. SE9 175 G1
Roberts Cl., Pnr. 66 B5
Field End Rd.
Roberts Cl., Sutt. 198 A7
Roberts Cl., West Dr. 120 B1
Roberts Ms. SW1 24 B6
Robert's Pl. EC1 11 F5
Roberts Rd. E17 78 B1
Roberts Rd. NW7 56 B6
Roberts Rd., Belv. 139 G5
Robertsbridge Rd., Cars. 199 F1
Robertson Rd. E15 114 C1
Robertson St. SW8 150 B2
Robeson St. E3 113 J5
Ackroyd Dr.
Robeson Way, Borwd. 38 C1
Robin Cl. NW7 54 E3
Robin Cl., Hmptn. 161 E5
Robin Ct. SE16 37 H1
Robin Ct. SE16 132 D4
Robin Cres. E6 116 A5
Robin Gro. N6 92 A2
Robin Gro., Brent. 125 F6
Robin Gro., Har. 69 J6
Robin Hill Dr., Chis. 174 B6
Robin Hood Dr., Har. 52 C7
Robin Hood La. E14 114 C7
Robin Hood La. SW15 164 E4
Robin Hood La., Bexh. 159 E5
Robin Hood La., Sutt. 198 D5
Robin Hood Rd. SW19 165 H5
Robin Hood Way SW15 165 E4
Robin Hood Way SW20 165 E4
Robin Hood Way, Grnf. 86 C6
Robina Cl., Bexh. 158 D4
Robinhood Cl., Mitch. 186 C3
Robinhood La., Mitch. 186 C3
Robinia Cl., Ilf. 65 H6
Robinia Cres. E10 96 B2
Robins Ct. SE12 173 J3
Robins Gro., W.Wick. 205 G3
Robinscroft Ms. SE10 154 B1
Sparta St.
Robinson Cres., Bushey 51 J1
Robinson Rd. E2 113 F2
Robinson Rd. SW17 167 H6
Robinson Rd., Dag. 101 G4
Robinson St. SW3 31 J5
Robinsons Cl. W13 104 D5
Robinwood Pl. SW15 164 D4
Robsart St. SW9 151 F2
Robson Av. NW10 107 G1
Robson Cl. E6 116 B6
Linton Gdns.
Robson Cl., Enf. 43 H2
Robson Rd. SE27 169 H3
Roch Av., Edg. 69 J2
Rochdale Rd. E17 78 A7
Rochdale Rd. SE2 138 B5
Rochdale Way SE8 134 A7
Octavius St.
Roche Rd. SW16 187 F1
Roche Wk., Cars. 185 G6
Rochelle Cl. SW11 149 G4
Rochelle St. E2 13 F4
Rochemont Wk. E8 112 C1
Pownall Rd.
Rochester Av. E13 115 J1
Rochester Av., Brom. 191 H2
Rochester Cl. SW16 169 E7
Rochester Cl., Enf. 44 B1
Rochester Cl., Sid. 158 B6
Rochester Dr., Bex. 159 F6
Rochester Dr., Pnr. 66 D5
Rochester Gdns., Croy. 202 B3
Rochester Gdns., Ilf. 80 C7
Rochester Ms. NW1 92 C7
Rochester Pl. NW1 92 C6
Rochester Rd. NW1 92 C6
Rochester Rd., Cars. 199 J4
Rochester Row SW1 33 G1
Rochester Row SW1 130 C4
Rochester Sq. NW1 92 C7
Rochester St. SW1 25 H6
Rochester St. SW1 130 D3
Rochester Ter. NW1 92 C6
Rochester Wk. SE1 28 B1
Rochester Way SE3 155 H1
Rochester Way SE9 156 C3
Rochester Way Relief Rd. SE3 155 H1
Rochester Way Relief Rd. SE9 156 B4
Rochford Av., Loug. 49 F3
Rochford Av., Rom. 82 C5
Rochford Cl. E6 116 A2
Boleyn Rd.
Rochford Grn., Loug. 49 F3
Rochford St. NW5 91 J5
Rochford Wk. E8 94 D7
Wilman Gro.
Rochford Way, Croy. 186 E6
Rock Av. SW14 146 D3
South Worple Way
Rock Gdns., Dag. 101 H5
Rock Gro. Way SE16 37 J1
Rock Hill SE26 170 C4
Rock St. N4 93 G2
Rockbourne Rd. SE23 171 G1
Rockells Pl. SE22 153 E6
Rockford Av., Grnf. 104 D2
Rockhall Rd. NW2 90 A4
Rockhampton Cl. SE27 169 G4
Rockhampton Rd.
Rockhampton Rd. SE27 169 G4
Rockhampton Rd., S.Croy. 202 B6
Rockingham Cl. SW15 147 F4
Rockingham Est. SE1 27 J6
Rockingham Est. SE1 131 J3
Rockingham St. SE1 27 J6
Rockingham St. SE1 131 J3
Rockland Rd. SW15 148 B4
Rocklands Dr., Stan. 69 E2
Rockley Rd. W14 128 A2
Rockmount Rd. SE18 137 J5
Rockmount Rd. SE19 170 A6
Rocks La. SW13 147 G1
Rockware Av., Grnf. 104 A1
Rockways, Barn. 39 F6
Rockwell Gdns. SE19 170 B5
Rockwell Rd., Dag. 101 H5
Rockwood Pl. W12 127 J2
Rocliffe St. N1 11 H2
Rocombe Cres. SE23 153 F7
Rocque La. SE3 155 F3
Rodborough Rd. NW11 90 D1
Roden Ct. N6 74 D7
Hornsey La.
Roden Gdns., Croy. 188 B6
Roden St. N7 93 F3
Roden St., Ilf. 98 D3
Rodenhurst Rd. SW4 150 C6
Roderick Rd. NW3 91 J4
Roding Av., Wdf.Grn. 64 B6
Roding Gdns., Loug. 48 B6
Roding La., Buck.H. 64 B1
Roding La., Chig. 64 D1
Roding La. N., Wdf.Grn. 80 A2
Roding La. S., Ilf. 80 A4
Roding La. S., Wdf.Grn. 80 A4
Roding Ms. E1 29 J1
Roding Rd. E5 95 G4
Roding Rd. E6 116 E5
Roding Rd., Loug. 48 B5
Roding Trd. Est., Bark. 98 E7
Roding Vw., Buck.H. 64 A1
Rodings, The, Wdf.Grn. 63 J6
Rodings Row, Barn. 40 B5
Leecroft Rd.
Rodmarton St. W1 16 A2
Rodmarton St. W1 109 J5
Rodmell Cl., Hayes 102 E4
Rodmell Slope N12 56 C5
Rodmere St. SE10 134/135 E5
Trafalgar Rd.
Rodmill La. SW2 151 E7
Rodney Cl., Croy. 201 H1
Rodney Cl., N.Mal. 182 E5
Rodney Cl., Pnr. 66 E7
Rodney Ct. W9 6 D5
Rodney Gdns., Pnr. 66 B5
Rodney Gdns., W.Wick. 205 G4
Rodney Pl. E17 77 H2
Rodney Pl. SE17 36 A1
Rodney Pl. SE17 131 J4
Rodney Pl. SW19 185 F1
Rodney Rd. E11 79 H4
Rodney Rd. SE17 36 A1
Rodney Rd. SE17 132 A4
Rodney Rd., Mitch. 185 H2
Rodney Rd., N.Mal. 182 E5
Rodney Rd., Twick. 143 G6
Rodney St. N1 10 D1
Rodney St. N1 111 F2
Rodney Way, Rom. 83 G1
Rodway Rd. SW15 147 G7
Rodway Rd., Brom. 191 H1
Rodwell Cl., Ruis. 66 C7
Rodwell Pl., Edg. 54 A6
Whitchurch La.
Rodwell Rd. SE22 152 C6
Roe End NW9 70 C4
Roe Grn. NW9 70 C5
Roe La. NW9 70 B4
Roe Way, Wall. 201 E7
Roebourne Way E16 136 D2
Roebuck Cl., Felt. 160 B4
Roebuck La. N17 60 C6
High Rd.
Roebuck La., Buck.H. 47 J7
Roebuck Rd., Chess. 196 A5
Roedean Av., Enf. 45 F1
Roedean Cl., Enf. 45 F1
Roedean Cres. SW15 146 E6
Roehampton Cl. SW15 147 G4
Roehampton Dr., Chis. 175 F6
Roehampton Gate SW15 146 E6
Roehampton High St. SW15 147 H7
Roehampton La. SW15 147 G4
Roehampton Vale SW15 165 E3
Roffey St. E14 134 C2
Rogate Ho. E5 94 D3
Muir Rd.
Roger St. WC1 10 D6
Roger St. WC1 111 F4
Rogers Gdns., Dag. 101 G5
Rogers Rd. E16 115 F6
Rogers Rd. SW17 167 G4
Rogers Rd., Dag. 101 G5
Rogers Wk. N12 56/57 E3
Brook Meadow
Rojack Rd. SE23 171 G1
Rokeby Gdns., Wdf.Grn. 79 G1
Rokeby Pl. SW20 165 H7
Rokeby Rd. SE4 153 J2
Rokeby St. E15 114 E1
Rokesby Cl., Well. 157 G2
Rokesby Pl., Wem. 87 G5
Rokesly Av. N8 74 E5
Roland Gdns. SW7 30 D3
Roland Gdns. SW7 129 F5
Roland Gdns., Felt. 161 F3
Hampton Rd. W.
Roland Ms. E1 113 G5
Stepney Grn.
Roland Rd. E17 78 D4
Roland Way SE17 36 C4
Roland Way SE17 132 A5
Roland Way SW7 30 D3
Roland Way, Wor.Pk. 197 F2
Roles Gro., Rom. 82 D4
Rolfe Cl., Barn. 41 H4
Rolinsden Way, Kes. 206 A4
Roll Gdns., Ilf. 80 D5
Rollesby Rd., Chess. 196 A6
Rollesby Way SE28 118 C7
Rolleston Av., Orp. 193 E6
Rolleston Cl., Orp. 193 E7
Rolleston Rd., S.Croy. 202 A7
Rollins St. SE15 133 F6
Rollit Cres., Houns. 143 G5
Rollit St. N7 93 F5
Hornsey Rd.
Rolls Bldgs. EC4 19 E3
Rolls Pk. Av. E4 62 A6
Rolls Pk. Rd. E4 62 B5
Rolls Pas. EC4 18 E3
Rolls Rd. SE1 37 G3
Rolls Rd. SE1 132 C5
Rollscourt Av. SE24 151 J5
Rolt St. SE8 133 H6
Rolvenden Gdns., Brom. 174 A7
Rolvenden Pl. N17 76 D1
Manor Rd.
Roma Read Cl. SW15 147 H7
Bessborough Rd.
Roma Rd. E17 77 H3
Roman Cl. W3 126 B2
Avenue Gdns.
Roman Cl., Felt. 142 C5
Roman Ind. Est., Croy. 188 B7
Roman Ri. SE19 170 A6
Roman Rd. E2 113 F3
Roman Rd. E3 113 H2
Roman Rd. E6 116 B4
Roman Rd. N10 58 B7
Roman Rd. NW2 89 J3
Roman Rd. W4 127 F4
Roman Rd., Ilf. 99 E6
Roman Sq. SE28 138 A1
Roman Way N7 93 F6
Roman Way SE15 133 F7
Clifton Way
Roman Way, Cars. 199 J7
Fountain Dr.
Roman Way, Croy. 201 H2
Roman Way, Enf. 44 C5
Roman Way Ind. Est. N1 93 F7
Offord St.
Romanfield Rd. SW2 151 F7
Romanhurst Av., Brom. 191 E4
Romanhurst Gdns., Brom. 190 E4
Romany Gdns. E17 77 H1
McEntee Av.
Romany Gdns., Sutt. 184 D7
Romany Ri., Orp. 207 F1
Romberg Rd. SW17 168 A3
Romborough Gdns. SE13 154 C5
Romborough Way SE13 154 C5
Romero Cl. SW9 151 F3
Stockwell Rd.
Romero Sq. SE3 155 J4
Romeyn Rd. SW16 169 F3
Romford Rd. E7 97 H5
Romford Rd. E12 98 B4
Romford Rd. E15 96 E7
Romford St. E1 21 J2
Romford St. E1 112 D5
Romilly Dr., Wat. 51 E3
Romilly Rd. N4 93 H2
Romilly St. W1 17 H5
Romilly St. W1 110 D7
Rommany Rd. SE27 170 A4
Romney Cl. N17 76 E1
Romney Cl. NW11 91 F1
Romney Cl. SE14 133 F7
Kender St.
Romney Cl., Chess. 195 H4
Romney Cl., Har. 67 G7
Romney Dr., Brom. 174 A7
Romney Dr., Har. 67 G7
Romney Gdns., Bexh. 159 F1
Romney Ms. W1 16 B1
Romney Rd. SE10 134 C6
Romney Rd., N.Mal. 182 D6
Romney Row NW2 90 A2
Brent Ter.
Romney St. SW1 25 J6
Romney St. SW1 130 E3
Romola Rd. SE24 169 H1
Romsey Cl., Orp. 207 E4
Romsey Gdns., Dag. 118 D1
Romsey Rd. W13 104 D7
Romsey Rd., Dag. 118 D1
Ron Leighton Way E6 116 B1
Rona Rd. NW3 92 A4
Rona Wk. N1 94 A6
Clephane Rd.
Ronald Av. E15 115 E3
Ronald Cl., Beck. 189 J4
Ronald St. E1 113 F6
Devonport St.
Ronalds Rd. N5 93 G5
Ronalds Rd., Brom. 191 G1
Ronaldstone Rd., Sid. 157 H6

Ronart St., Har. 68 C3
Stuart Rd.
Rondu Rd. NW2 90 B5
Ronelean Rd., Surb. 195 J3
Ronver Rd. SE12 155 F7
Rood La. EC3 20 D5
Rood La. EC3 112 B7
Rook Wk. E6 116 B6
Allhallows Rd.
Rookby Ct. N21 59 H2
Carpenter Gdns.
Rooke Way SE10 135 F5
Rookeries Cl., Felt. 160 B3
Rookery Cl. NW9 71 F5
Rookery Cres., Dag. 101 H7
Rookery Dr., Chis. 192 D1
Rookery La., Brom. 192 A6
Rookery Rd. SW4 150 C4
Rookery Way NW9 71 F5
Rookfield Av. N10 74 C4
Rookfield Cl. N10 74 C4
Cranmore Way
Rookstone Rd. SW17 167 J5
Rookwood Av., Loug. 49 F3
Rookwood Av., N.Mal. 183 G4
Rookwood Av., Wall. 200 D4
Rookwood Gdns. E4 63 F1
Whitehall Rd.
Rookwood Gdns., Loug. 49 F3
Rookwood Ho., Bark. 117 G2
St. Marys
Rookwood Rd. N16 76 C7
Rootes Dr. W10 108 A4
Rope St. SE16 133 H4
Rope Wk., Sun. 178 C3
Rope Wk. Gdns. E1 21 J4
Rope Yd. Rails SE18 136 E3
Ropemaker Rd. SE16 133 H3
Ropemaker St. EC2 20 B1
Ropemaker St. EC2 112 A5
Ropemakers Flds. E14 113 J7
Narrow St.
Roper La. SE1 29 E4
Roper St. SE9 156 C6
Roper Way, Mitch. 186 A2
Ropers Av. E4 62 C5
Ropers Wk. SW2 151 G7
Brockwell Pk. Gdns.
Ropery St. E3 113 J4
Ropley St. E2 13 H2
Ropley St. E2 112 D2
Rosa Alba Ms. N5 93 J4
Kelross Rd.
Rosaline Rd. SW6 128 B7
Rosamond St. SE26 170 E3
Rosamun St., Sthl. 123 E4
Rosamund Cl., S.Croy. 202 A4
Rosary Cl., Houns. 142 E2
Rosary Gdns. SW7 30 C2
Rosary Gdns. SW7 129 F4
Rosaville Rd. SW6 128 C7
Roscoe St. EC1 12 A6
Roscoff Cl., Edg. 70 C1
Rose All. SE1 28 A1
Rose All. SE1 131 J1
Rose & Crown Ct. EC2 19 J3
Rose & Crown Yd. SW1 25 G1
Rose Av. E18 79 H2
Rose Av., Mitch. 185 J1
Rose Av., Mord. 185 F5
Rose Bates Dr. NW9 70 A4
Rose Ct. E1 112 B5
Sandy's Row
Rose Ct. SE26 170 E2
Rose Ct., Pnr. 66 C3
Nursery Rd.
Rose Dale, Orp. 207 E2
Rose End, Wor.Pk. 198 A1
Rose Gdn. Cl., Edg. 53 H6
Rose Gdns. W5 125 G3
Rose Gdns., Felt. 160 A2
Rose Gdns., Sthl. 103 G4
Rose Gdns., Stai. 140 A7
Diamedes Av.
Rose Glen NW9 70 D4
Rose Hill, Sutt. 199 E2
Rose La., Rom. 82 D3
Rose Lawn, Bushey 51 J1
Rose Sq. SW3 31 F3
Rose Sq. SW3 129 G5
Rose St. WC2 18 A5
Rose Wk., Surb. 182 B5
Rose Wk., W.Wick. 204 D2
Rose Way SE12 155 G5
Rose Way, Edg. 54 C4
Stoneyfields La.
Roseacre Cl. W13 104/105 E5
Middlefielde
Roseacre Rd., Well. 158 B3
Roseary Cl., West Dr. 120 A4
Rosebank SE20 170 E7
Rosebank Av., Wem. 86 C4
Rosebank Cl. N12 57 H5
Rosebank Cl., Tedd. 162 D6
Rosebank Gdns. E3 113 J2
Rosebank Gro. E17 77 J3
Rosebank Rd. E17 78 B6
Rosebank Rd. W7 124 B2
Rosebank Vil. E17 78 A4
Rosebank Wk. NW1 92 D7
Maiden La.
Rosebank Wk. SE18 136 B4
Woodhill
Rosebank Way W3 106 D6
Roseberry Gdns. N4 75 H6
Roseberry Gdns., Orp. 207 H3
Roseberry Pl. E8 94 C6
Roseberry St. SE16 132 E4
Rosebery Av. E12 98 B6
Rosebery Av. EC1 10 E6
Rosebery Av. EC1 111 G4
Rosebery Av. N17 76 D2
Rosebery Av., Har. 85 F4
Rosebery Av., N.Mal. 183 F2
Rosebery Av., Sid. 157 H7
Rosebery Av., Th.Hth. 187 J2
Rosebery Cl., Mord. 184 A6
Rosebery Ct. EC1 111 G4
Rosebery Av.
Rosebery Gdns. N8 74 E5
Rosebery Gdns. W13 104 D6
Rosebery Gdns., Sutt. 199 E4
Rosebery Ms. N10 74 C2
Rosebery Ms. SW2 150/151 E6
Rosebery Rd.
Rosebery Rd. N9 60 D3
Rosebery Rd. N10 74 C2
Rosebery Rd. SW2 150 E6
Rosebery Rd., Houns. 143 J5
Rosebery Rd., Kings.T. 182 B2
Rosebery Rd., Sutt. 198 C6
Rosebery Sq. EC1 10 E6
Rosebery Sq., Kings.T. 182 A2
Rosebine Av., Twick. 144 A7
Rosebury Rd. SW6 149 E2
Rosecourt Rd., Croy. 187 F6
Rosecroft Av. NW3 90 D3
Rosecroft Gdns. NW2 89 G3
Rosecroft Gdns., Twick. 162 A1
Rosecroft Rd., Sthl. 103 G4
Rosecroft Wk., Pnr. 66 D5
Rosecroft Wk., Wem. 87 G5
Rosedale Cl. SE2 138 B3
Finchale Rd.
Rosedale Cl. W7 124 C2
Boston Rd.
Rosedale Cl., Stan. 53 E6
Rosedale Ct. N5 93 H4
Rosedale Gdns., Dag. 100 B7
Rosedale Rd. E7 97 J5
Rosedale Rd., Dag. 100 B7
Rosedale Rd., Epsom 197 G5
Rosedale Rd., Rich. 145 H4
Rosedale Rd., Rom. 83 J2
Rosedale Ter. W6 127 H3
Dalling Rd.
Rosedene NW6 108 A1
Christchurch Av.
Rosedene Av. SW16 169 F3
Rosedene Av., Croy. 187 F7
Rosedene Av., Grnf. 103 G3
Rosedene Av., Mord. 184 D5
Rosedene Gdns., Ilf. 80 D4
Rosedene Ter. E10 96 B2
Rosedew Rd. W6 128 A6
Rosefield Cl., Cars. 199 H5
Alma Rd.
Rosefield Gdns. E14 114 A7
Roseford Ct. W12 128 A2
Rosehart Ms. W11 108 D6
Westbourne Gro.
Rosehatch Av., Rom. 82 D3
Roseheath Rd., Houns. 143 F5
Rosehill, Esher 194 D6
Rosehill, Hmptn. 179 G1
Rosehill Av., Sutt. 199 F1
Rosehill Gdns., Grnf. 86 C5
Rosehill Gdns., Sutt. 199 E2
Rosehill Pk. W., Sutt. 199 F1
Rosehill Rd. SW18 149 F6
Roseland Cl. N17 60 A7
Cavell Rd.
Roseleigh Av. N5 93 H4
Roseleigh Cl., Twick. 145 G6
Rosemary Av. N3 73 E2
Rosemary Av. N9 60 E1
Rosemary Av., Enf. 44 A1
Rosemary Av., Houns. 142 D2
Rosemary Av., W.Mol. 179 G3
Rosemary Cl., Croy. 186 E6
Rosemary Dr. E14 114 D6
Rosemary Dr., Ilf. 80 A5
Rosemary Gdns. SW14 146 C3
Rosemary La.
Rosemary Gdns., Chess. 195 H4
Rosemary Gdns., Dag. 101 F1
Rosemary La. SW14 146 C3
Rosemary Rd. SE15 37 G7
Rosemary Rd. SE15 132 C7
Rosemary Rd. SW17 167 F3
Rosemary Rd., Well. 157 J1
Rosemary St. N1 112 A1
Shepperton Rd.
Rosemead NW9 71 F7
Rosemead Av., Mitch. 186 C2
Rosemead Av., Wem. 87 H5
Rosemont Av. N12 57 F6
Rosemont Rd. NW3 91 F6
Rosemont Rd. W3 106 B7
Rosemont Rd., N.Mal. 182 C3
Rosemont Rd., Rich. 145 H6
Rosemont Rd., Wem. 105 H1
Rosemoor St. SW3 31 J2
Rosemoor St. SW3 129 J4
Rosemount Cl., Wdf.Grn. 64 C6
Chapelmount Rd.
Rosemount Dr., Brom. 192 C4
Rosemount Rd. W13 104 D6
Rosenau Cres. SW11 149 H1
Rosenau Rd. SW11 149 H1
Rosendale Rd. SE21 151 J7
Rosendale Rd. SE24 151 J7
Roseneath Av. N21 59 H1
Roseneath Rd. SW11 150 A6
Roseneath Wk., Enf. 44 B4
Rosens Wk., Edg. 54 B3
Rosenthal Rd. SE6 154 B6
Rosenthorpe Rd. SE15 153 G5
Roserton St. E14 134 C2
Rosery, The, Croy. 189 G6
Roses, The, Wdf.Grn. 63 F7
Rosethorn Cl. SW12 150 C7
Rosetta Cl. SW8 131 E7
Rosetti Ter., Dag. 100 B4
Marlborough Rd.
Roseveare Rd. SE12 173 J4
Roseville Av., Houns. 143 G5
Roseville Rd., Hayes 122 A5
Rosevine Rd. SW20 183 J1
Roseway SE21 152 A6
Rosewell Cl. SE20 170 E7
Rosewood, Esher 194 D2
Rosewood Av., Grnf. 86 D5
Rosewood Cl., Sid. 176 C3
Rosewood Ct., Brom. 191 J1
Rosewood Ct., Rom. 82 C5
Rosewood Gdns. SE13 154 C2
Lewisham Rd.
Rosewood Gro., Sutt. 199 F2
Rosewood Sq. W12 107 G6
Primula St.
Rosewood Ter. SE20 171 F7
Laurel Gro.
Rosher Cl. E15 96 D7
Rosina St. E9 95 G5
Roskell Rd. SW15 148 A3
Roslin Rd. W3 126 B3
Roslin Way, Brom. 173 G5
Roslyn Cl., Mitch. 185 G2
Roslyn Rd. N15 76 A5
Rosmead Rd. W11 108 B7
Rosoman Pl. EC1 11 F5
Rosoman St. EC1 11 F4
Rosoman St. EC1 111 G3
Ross Av. NW7 56 B5
Ross Av., Dag. 101 F2
Ross Cl., Har. 51 J7
Ross Cl., Hayes 121 G4
Ross Ct. SW15 148 A7
Ross Par., Wall. 200 B6
Ross Rd. SE25 188 A3
Ross Rd., Twick. 161 H1
Ross Rd., Wall. 200 C5
Ross Way SE9 156 B3
Rossall Cres. NW10 105 J3
Rossdale, Sutt. 199 H5
Rossdale Dr. N9 45 F6
Rossdale Dr. NW9 88 C1
Rossdale Rd. SW15 147 J4
Rosse Ms. SE3 155 H1
Rossendale St. E5 94 E2
Rossendale Way NW1 92 C7
Rossetti Rd. SE16 132 E5
Rossignol Gdns., Cars. 200 A2
Rossindel Rd., Houns. 143 G5
Rossington St. E5 94 D2
Rossiter Flds., Barn. 40 B6
Rossiter Rd. SW12 168 B1
Rossland Cl., Bexh. 159 H5
Rosslyn Av. E4 63 F2
Rosslyn Av. SW13 147 E3
Rosslyn Av., Barn. 41 H6
Rosslyn Av., Dag. 83 F7
Rosslyn Av., Felt. 142 A6
Rosslyn Cl., W.Wick. 205 F3
Rosslyn Cres., Har. 68 C5
Rosslyn Cres., Wem. 87 H4
Rosslyn Gdns., Wem. 87 H3
Rosslyn Cres.
Rosslyn Hill NW3 91 G4
Rosslyn Ms. NW3 91 G4
Rosslyn Hill
Rosslyn Pk. Ms. NW3 91 G5
Lyndhurst Rd.
Rosslyn Rd. E17 78 C4
Rosslyn Rd., Bark. 99 G7
Rosslyn Rd., Twick. 145 F6
Rossmore Rd. NW1 7 H6
Rossmore Rd. NW1 109 H4
Rosswood Gdns., Wall. 200 C6
Rostella Rd. SW17 167 G4
Rostrevor Av. N15 76 C6
Rostrevor Gdns., Hayes 121 H1
Rostrevor Gdns., Sthl. 123 E5
Rostrevor Ms. SW6 148 C1
Rostrevor Rd. SW6 148 C1
Rostrevor Rd. SW19 166 D5
Rotary St. SE1 27 G5
Roth Wk. N7 93 F3
Durham Rd.
Rothbury Gdns., Islw. 124 D7
Rothbury Rd. E9 95 J7
Rothbury Wk. N17 60 D7
Rotherfield Rd., Cars. 200 A4
Rotherfield St. N1 93 J7
Rotherham Wk. SE1 27 G2
Rotherhill Av. SW16 168 D6
Rotherhithe New Rd. SE16 37 J4
Rotherhithe New Rd. SE16 132 D5
Rotherhithe Old Rd. SE16 133 G4
Rotherhithe St. SE16 133 F2
Rotherhithe Tunnel E1 133 F1
Rotherhithe Tunnel App. E14 133 F2
Rotherhithe Tunnel App. SE16 133 F2
Rothermere Rd., Croy. 201 F5
Rotherwick Hill W5 105 J4
Rotherwick Rd. NW11 72 D7
Rotherwood Cl. SW20 184 B1
Rotherwood Rd. SW15 148 A3
Rothery St. N1 111 H1
Gaskin St.
Rothery Ter. SW9 131 H7
Rothesay Av. SW20 184 B2
Rothesay Av., Grnf. 86 A6
Rothesay Av., Rich. 146 B4
Rothesay Rd. SE25 188 B4
Rothsay Rd. E7 97 J6
Rothsay St. SE1 28 D5
Rothsay St. SE1 132 B3
Rothsay Wk. E14 134 A4
Charnwood Gdns.
Rothschild Rd. W4 126 C4
Rothschild St. SE27 169 H4
Rothwell Gdns., Dag. 100 C7
Rothwell Rd., Dag. 118 C1
Rothwell St. NW1 109 J1
Rotten Row SW1 24 B3
Rotten Row SW1 129 J2
Rotten Row SW7 23 G3
Rotten Row SW7 129 H2
Rotterdam Dr. E14 134 C3
Rouel Rd. SE16 29 H6
Rouel Rd. SE16 132 D3
Rougemont Av., Mord. 184 D6
Round Gro., Croy. 189 G7
Round Hill SE26 171 F2
Roundacre SW19 166 A2
Inner Pk. Rd.
Roundaway Rd., Ilf. 80 C2
Roundel Cl. SE4 153 J4
Adelaide Av.
Roundhay Cl. SE23 171 G2
Roundhill Dr., Enf. 43 F4

Roundmead Av., Loug. 48 D3
Roundmead Cl., Loug. 48 D3
Roundshaw Cen., Wall. 200/201 E7
Meteor Way
Roundtable Rd., Brom. 173 F3
Roundtree Rd., Wem. 86 E5
Roundway, The N17 75 J1
Roundway, The, Esher 194 C5
Roundwood, Chis. 192 E2
Roundwood Av., Uxb. 121 F1
Roundwood Rd. NW10 89 F6
Rounton Rd. E3 114 A4
Roupell Rd. SW2 169 F1
Roupell St. SE1 27 F2
Roupell St. SE1 131 G1
Rous Rd., Buck.H. 64 B1
Rousden St. NW1 92 C7
Rouse Gdns. SE21 170 B4
Routemaster Cl. E13 115 H3
Routh Rd. SW18 149 H7
Routh St. E6 116 C5
Routledge Cl. N19 92 D1
Rover Av., Ilf. 65 J6
Rowallan Rd. SW6 128 B7
Rowan Av. E4 61 J6
Rowan Cl. SW16 186 C1
Rowan Cl. W5 125 H2
Rowan Cl., Ilf. 99 G5
Rowan Cl., N.Mal. 182 E2
Rowan Cl., Stan. 52 C6
Woodlands Dr.
Rowan Cl., Wem. 86 D3
Rowan Cres. SW16 186 C1
Rowan Dr. NW9 71 G4
Rowan Gdns., Croy. 202 C3
Radcliffe Rd.
Rowan Rd. SW16 186 C2
Rowan Rd. W6 128 A4
Rowan Rd., Bexh. 159 E3
Rowan Rd., Brent. 125 E7
Rowan Rd., West Dr. 120 A4
Rowan Ter. W6 128 A4
Bute Gdns.
Rowan Wk. N2 73 F6
Rowan Wk. N19 92 C2
Bredgar Rd.
Rowan Wk. W10 108 B4
Droop St.
Rowan Wk., Barn. 40/41 E5
Station Rd.
Rowan Wk., Brom. 206 C3
Rowan Way, Rom. 82 C3
Rowans, The N13 59 H3
Rowans Way, Loug. 48 C4
Rowantree Cl. N21 60 A1
Rowantree Rd. N21 60 A1
Rowantree Rd., Enf. 43 H2
Rowanwood Av., Sid. 176 A1
Rowben Cl. N20 56 E1
Rowberry Cl. SW6 127 J7
Rowcross St. SE1 37 F3
Rowcross St. SE1 132 C5
Rowdell Rd., Nthlt. 103 G1
Rowden Pk. Gdns. E4 62 A6
Rowden Rd.
Rowden Rd. E4 62 A6
Rowden Rd., Beck. 189 H1
Rowden Rd., Epsom 196 B4
Rowditch La. SW11 150 A2
Rowdon Av. NW10 89 H7
Rowdowns Rd., Dag. 119 F1
Rowe Gdns., Bark. 117 J2
Rowe La. E9 95 F5
Rowe Wk., Har. 85 G3
Rowena Cres. SW11 149 H2
Rowfant Rd. SW17 168 A1
Rowhill Rd. E5 95 E4
Rowington Cl. W2 14 A1
Rowington Cl. W2 108 E5
Rowland Av., Har. 69 F3
Rowland Ct. E16 115 F4
Rowland Cres., Chig. 65 H4
Rowland Gro. SE26 170/171 E3
Dallas Rd.
Rowland Hill Av. N17 59 J7
Rowland Hill St. NW3 91 H5
Rowland Way SW19 184/185 E1
Hayward Cl.
Rowlands Av., Pnr. 51 G6
Rowlands Cl. N6 74 A6
North Hill
Rowlands Cl. NW7 55 G7
Rowlands Rd., Dag. 101 F2
Rowley Av., Sid. 158 B7
Rowley Cl., Wem. 87 J7
Rowley Gdns. N4 75 J7
Rowley Grn. Rd., Barn. 39 F5
Rowley Ind. Pk. W3 126 B3
Rowley La., Barn. 39 F5
Rowley La., Borwd. 38 D1
Rowley Rd. N15 75 J5
Rowley Way NW8 109 E1
Rowlheys Pl., West Dr. 120 B3
Rowlls Rd., Kings.T. 181 J3
Rowney Gdns., Dag. 100 C6
Rowney Rd., Dag. 100 B6
Rowntree Clifford Cl. E13 115 H3
Liddon Rd.
Rowntree Path SE28 118 B7
Booth Cl.
Rowntree Rd., Twick. 162 B1
Rowse Cl. E15 96 C7
Rowsley Av. NW4 71 J3
Rowstock Gdns. N7 92 D5
Rowton Rd. SE18 137 F7
Roxborough Av., Har. 68 A7
Roxborough Av., Islw. 124 C7
Roxborough Pk., Har. 68 B7
Roxborough Rd., Har. 68 A5
Roxbourne Cl., Nthlt. 84 D6
Roxburgh Rd. SE27 169 H5
Roxby Pl. SW6 128 D6
Roxeth Grn. Av., Har. 85 H3
Roxeth Gro., Har. 85 H4
Roxeth Hill, Har. 86 A2
Roxley Rd. SE13 154 B6
Roxton Gdns., Croy. 204 A5
Roxwell Rd. W12 127 G2
Roxwell Rd., Bark. 118 A2
Roxwell Trd. Pk. E10 77 H7
Roxwell Way, Wdf.Grn. 63 J7
Roxy Av., Rom. 82 C7
Roy Gdns., Ilf. 81 H4
Roy Gro., Hmptn. 161 H6
Roy Sq. E14 113 H7
Narrow St.
Royal Albert Dock E16 116 C7
Royal Albert Roundabout E16 116 B7
Royal Albert Way
Royal Albert Way E16 116 A7
Royal Arc. W1 17 F6
Royal Artillery Barracks SE18 136 D5
Repository Rd.
Royal Av. SW3 31 J3
Royal Av. SW3 129 J5
Royal Av., Wor.Pk. 197 E2
Royal Circ. SE27 169 G3
Royal Cl. N16 94 B1
Manor Rd.
Royal Cl., Ilf. 82 A7
Royal Cl., Wor.Pk. 196 E2
Royal College St. NW1 92 C7
Royal Ct. EC3 112 A6
Cornhill
Royal Ct. SE16 133 J3
Royal Cres. W11 128 A1
Royal Cres., Ruis. 84 E4
Royal Cres. Ms. W11 128 A1
Queensdale Rd.
Royal Docks Rd. E6 117 E6
Royal Dr. N11 58 A5
Royal Ex. EC3 20 C4
Royal Ex. EC3 112 A6
Royal Ex. Av. EC3 20 C4
Royal Ex. Bldgs. EC3 20 C4
Royal Ex. Steps EC3 112 A6
Cornhill
Royal Gdns. W7 124 D3
Royal Hill SE10 134 C7
Royal Hospital Rd. SW3 31 J5
Royal Hospital Rd. SW3 129 J6
Royal London Est., The N17 60 E6
Royal Ms., The SW1 25 E5
Royal Ms., The SW1 130 B3
Royal Mint Ct. EC3 21 G6
Royal Mint Ct. EC3 112 C7
Royal Mint Pl. E1 21 G5
Royal Mint St. E1 21 G5
Royal Mint St. E1 112 C7
Royal Mt. Ct., Twick. 162 B3
Royal Naval Pl. SE14 133 J7
Royal Oak Ct. N1 112 B3
Pitfield St.
Royal Oak Pl. SE22 153 E6
Royal Oak Rd. E8 94 E6
Royal Oak Rd., Bexh. 159 F5
Royal Opera Arc. SW1 25 H1
Royal Opera Arc. SW1 130 D1
Royal Orchard Cl. SW18 148 B7
Royal Par. SE3 155 E2
Royal Par. SW6 128 B7
Dawes Rd.
Royal Par. W5 105 H3
Western Av.
Royal Par., Chis. 175 F7
Royal Par., Rich. 146 A1
Station App.
Royal Par. Ms. SE3 155 F2
Royal Par.
Royal Par. Ms., Chis. 175 F7
Royal Pl. SE10 134 C7
Royal Rd. E16 116 A6
Royal Rd. SE17 35 G5
Royal Rd. SE17 131 H6
Royal Rd., Sid. 176 D3
Royal Rd., Tedd. 162 A5
Royal Route, Wem. 87 J4
Royal St. SE1 26 D5
Royal St. SE1 131 F3
Royal Victor Pl. E3 113 G2
Royal Victoria Dock E16 115 H7
Royal Victoria Pl. E16 135 H1
Wesley Av.
Royal Wk., Wall. 200 B3
Prince Charles Way
Royal Windsor Ct., Surb. 196 A1
Royalty Ms. W1 17 H4
Roycraft Av., Bark. 117 J2
Roycraft Cl., Bark. 117 J2
Roycroft Cl. E18 79 H1
Roycroft Cl. SW2 169 G1
Roydene Rd. SE18 137 H6
Roydon Cl. SW11 150 B1
Reform St.
Roydon Cl., Loug. 48 B7
Roydon St. SW11 150 B1
Southolm St.
Royle Cres. W13 104 D4
Royston Av. E4 62 A5
Royston Av., Sutt. 199 G3
Royston Av., Wall. 200 D4
Royston Cl., Houns. 142 B1
Royston Ct. SE24 151 J6
Burbage Rd.
Royston Ct., Rich. 145 J1
Lichfield Rd.
Royston Ct., Surb. 196 A3
Hook Ri. N.
Royston Gdns., Ilf. 80 A6
Royston Gro., Pnr. 51 F6
Royston Par., Ilf. 80 A6
Royston Pk. Rd., Pnr. 51 F6
Royston Rd. SE20 189 G1
Royston Rd., Rich. 145 H5
Royston St. E2 113 F2
Roystons, The, Surb. 182 B5
Rozel Ct. N1 112 B1
Rozel Rd. SW4 150 C2
Rubastic Rd., Sthl. 122 B3
Rubens Rd., Nthlt. 102 C2
Rubens St. SE6 171 J2
Ruberoid Rd., Enf. 45 J3
Ruby Ms. E17 78 A3
Ruby Rd.
Ruby Rd. E17 78 A3
Ruby St. SE15 132 E6
Ruby Triangle SE15 132/133 E6
Sandgate St.
Ruckholt Cl. E10 96 B3
Ruckholt Rd. E10 96 A4
Rucklidge Av. NW10 107 F2
Rudall Cres. NW3 91 G4
Willoughby Rd.
Ruddington Cl. E5 95 H4
Ruddock Cl., Edg. 54 C7
Orange Hill Rd.
Ruddstreet Cl. SE18 137 E4
Ruddy Way NW7 55 G6
Flower La.
Rudland Rd., Bexh. 159 H3
Rudloe Rd. SW12 150 C7
Rudolf Pl. SW8 34 B6
Rudolph Ct. SE22 152 D7
Rudolph Rd. E13 115 F2
Rudolph Rd. NW6 108 D2
Rudyard Gro. NW7 54 C6
Ruffetts, The, S.Croy. 203 E7
Ruffetts Cl., S.Croy. 202 E7
Rufford Cl., Har. 68 D6
Rufford St. N1 111 E1
Rufford Twr. W3 126 B1
Rufus Cl., Ruis. 84 E3
Rufus St. N1 12 D4
Rugby Av. N9 60 C1
Rugby Av., Grnf. 86 A6
Rugby Av., Wem. 87 E5
Rugby Cl., Har. 68 B5
Rugby Gdns., Dag. 100 C6
Rugby Rd. NW9 70 B4
Rugby Rd. W4 126 E2
Rugby Rd., Dag. 100 B7
Rugby Rd., Twick. 144 B6
Rugby St. WC1 10 C6
Rugby St. WC1 111 F4
Rugg St. E14 114 A7
Ruislip Cl., Grnf. 103 H4
Ruislip Rd., Grnf. 103 G3
Ruislip Rd., Nthlt. 102 D3
Ruislip Rd., Sthl. 103 G3
Ruislip Rd. E. W7 104 B4
Ruislip Rd. E. W13 104 A4
Ruislip Rd. E., Grnf. 103 G3
Ruislip St. SW17 167 J4
Rum Cl. E1 113 F7
Rumbold Rd. SW6 129 E7
Rumsey Cl., Hmptn. 161 F6
Rumsey Ms. N4 93 H3
Monsell Rd.
Rumsey Rd. SW9 151 F3
Runbury Circle NW9 88 D2
Runcorn Cl. N17 76 E4
Runcorn Pl. W11 108 B7
Rundell Cres. NW4 71 H5
Runes Cl., Mitch. 185 G4
Runnel Fld., Har. 86 B3
Running Horse Yd., Brent. 125 H6
Pottery Rd.
Runnymede SW19 185 G1
Runnymede Cl., Twick. 143 H6
Runnymede Ct., Croy. 202 C2
Runnymede Cres. SW16 186 D1
Runnymede Gdns., Grnf. 104 A2
Runnymede Gdns., Twick. 143 H6
Runnymede Rd., Twick. 143 H6
Runway, The, Ruis. 84 B5
Rupack St. SE16 133 F2
St. Marychurch St.
Rupert Av., Wem. 87 H5
Rupert Ct. W1 17 H5
Rupert Ct., W.Mol. 179 G4
St. Peter's Rd.
Rupert Gdns. SW9 151 H2
Rupert Rd. N19 92 D3
Holloway Rd.
Rupert Rd. NW6 108 C2
Rupert Rd. W4 127 E3
Rupert St. W1 17 H5
Rupert St. W1 110 D7
Rural Way SW16 168 B7
Ruscoe Rd. E16 115 F6
Ruscombe Way, Felt. 141 J7
Rush, The SW19 184 C1
Kingston Rd.
Rush Grn. Gdns., Rom. 101 J1
Rush Grn. Rd., Rom. 101 J1
Rush Gro. St. SE18 136 C4
Rush Hill Ms. SW11 150 A3
Rush Hill Rd.
Rush Hill Rd. SW11 150 A3
Rusham Rd. SW12 149 J6
Rushbrook Cres. E17 77 J1
Rushbrook Rd. SE9 175 F2
Rushcroft Rd. E4 62 A7
Rushcroft Rd. SW2 151 G4
Rushden Cl. SE19 170 A7
Rushden Gdns. NW7 55 J6
Rushden Gdns., Ilf. 80 D3
Rushdene SE2 138 D3
Rushdene Av., Barn. 41 H7
Rushdene Cl., Nthlt. 102 C3
Rushdene Cres., Nthlt. 102 C2
Rushdene Rd., Pnr. 66 D6
Rushen Wk., Cars. 199 G1
Paisley Rd.
Rushett Cl., T.Ditt. 194 E1
Rushett Rd., T.Ditt. 180 E7
Rushey Cl., N.Mal. 182 D4
Rushey Grn. SE6 154 B7
Rushey Hill, Enf. 43 F4
Rushey Mead SE4 154 A5
Rushford Rd. SE4 153 J6
Rushgrove Av. NW9 71 F5
Rushley Cl., Kes. 206 A4
Rushmead E2 112/113 E3
Florida St.
Rushmead, Rich. 163 E3
Rushmead Cl., Croy. 202 C4

Rushmere Ct., Wor.Pk. 197 G2
The Av.
Rushmere Pl. SW19 166 A5
Rushmoor Cl., Pnr. 66 B4
Rushmore Cl., Brom. 192 B3
Rushmore Cres. E5 95 G4
Rushmore Rd.
Rushmore Rd. E5 95 F4
Rusholme Av., Dag. 101 G3
Rusholme Gro. SE19 170 B5
Rusholme Rd. SW15 148 B6
Rushout Av., Har. 68 E6
Rushton St. N1 12 C1
Rushton St. N1 112 A2
Rushworth Av. NW4 71 G3
Rushworth Gdns.
Rushworth Gdns. NW4 71 G4
Rushworth St. SE1 27 H3
Rushworth St. SE1 131 H2
Rushy Meadow La., Cars. 199 H2
Ruskin Av. E12 98 B6
Ruskin Av., Felt. 141 J6
Ruskin Av., Rich. 126 A7
Ruskin Av., Well. 158 A2
Ruskin Cl. NW11 72 E6
Ruskin Dr., Orp. 207 H3
Ruskin Dr., Well. 158 A3
Ruskin Dr., Wor.Pk. 197 H2
Ruskin Gdns. W5 105 G4
Ruskin Gdns., Har. 69 J4
Ruskin Gro., Well. 158 A2
Ruskin Pk. Ho. SE5 152 A3
Ruskin Rd. N17 76 C1
Ruskin Rd., Belv. 139 G4
Ruskin Rd., Cars. 199 J5
Ruskin Rd., Croy. 201 H2
Ruskin Rd., Islw. 144 C3
Ruskin Rd., Sthl. 102 E7
Ruskin Wk. N9 60 D2
Durham Rd.
Ruskin Wk. SE24 151 J5
Ruskin Wk., Brom. 192 C6
Ruskin Way SW19 185 G1
Rusland Av., Orp. 207 G3
Rusland Hts., Har. 68 B4
Rusland Pk. Rd.
Rusland Pk. Rd., Har. 68 B4
Rusper Cl. NW2 89 J3
Rusper Cl., Stan. 53 F4
Rusper Rd. N22 75 J2
Rusper Rd., Dag. 100 C6
Russell Av. N22 75 H2
Russell Cl. NW10 88 C7
Russell Cl. SE7 135 J7
Russell Cl. W4 127 F6
Russell Cl., Beck. 190 B3
Russell Cl., Bexh. 159 G4
Russell Cl., Ruis. 84 C2
Russell Ct. SW1 25 G2
Russell Dr., Stai. 140 A6
Russell Gdns. N20 57 H2
Russell Gdns. NW11 72 B6
Russell Gdns. W14 128 B3
Russell Gdns., Rich. 163 F2
Russell Gdns., West Dr. 120 D5
Russell Gdns. Ms. W14 128 B2
Russell Gro. NW7 54 E5
Russell Gro. SW9 131 G7
Russell Kerr Cl. W4 126 C7
Burlington La.
Russell La. N20 57 H2
Russell Mead, Har. 68 C1
Russell Pl. NW3 91 H5
Aspern Gro.
Russell Pl. SE16 133 H3
Onega Gate
Russell Rd. E4 61 J4
Russell Rd. E10 78 B6
Russell Rd. E16 115 G6
Russell Rd. E17 77 J3
Russell Rd. N8 74 D6
Russell Rd. N13 59 F6
Russell Rd. N15 76 B5
Russell Rd. N20 57 H2
Russell Rd. NW9 71 F6
Russell Rd. SW19 166 D7
Russell Rd. W14 128 B3
Russell Rd., Buck.H. 63 H1
Russell Rd., Mitch. 185 H3
Russell Rd., Nthlt. 85 J5
Russell Rd., Twick. 144 C6
Russell Rd., Walt. 178 A6
Russell Sq. WC1 10 A6
Russell Sq. WC1 110 D5
Russell St. WC2 18 B5
Russell St. WC2 111 F6
Russell Wk., Rich. 145 J6
Park Hill
Russell Way, Sutt. 198 D5
Russell's Footpath SW16 169 E5
Russet Cres. N7 93 F5
Stock Orchard Cres.
Russet Dr., Croy. 203 H1
Russets Cl. E4 62 D4
Larkshall Rd.
Russett Way SE13 154 B2
Conington Rd.
Russia Ct. EC2 20 A3
Russia Dock Rd. SE16 133 H1
Russia La. E2 113 F2
Russia Row EC2 20 A4
Russia Wk. SE16 133 H2
Rust Sq. SE5 36 B7
Rust Sq. SE5 132 A7
Rusthall Av. W4 126 D4
Rusthall Cl., Croy. 189 F6
Rustic Av. SW16 168 B7
Rustic Pl., Wem. 87 G4
Rustic Wk. E16 115 H6
Lambert Rd.
Rustington Wk., Mord. 184 C7
Ruston Av., Surb. 182 B7
Ruston Gdns. N14 42 A6
Farm La.
Ruston Ms. W11 108 B6
St. Marks Rd.
Ruston Rd. SE18 136 B3
Ruston St. E3 113 J1
Rutford Rd. SW16 168 E5
Ruth Cl., Stan. 69 J4
Rutherford Cl., Borwd. 38 C2
Rutherford Cl., Sutt. 199 G6
Rutherford St. SW1 33 H1
Rutherford St. SW1 130 D4
Rutherford Twr., Sthl. 103 H6
Rutherford Way, Bushey 52 A1
Rutherford Way, Wem. 88 A4
Rutherglen Rd. SE2 138 A6
Rutherwyke Cl., Epsom 197 G6
Ruthin Cl. NW9 70 E6
Ruthin Rd. SE3 135 G6
Ruthven St. E9 113 G1
Lauriston Rd.
Rutland Av., Sid. 158 A7
Rutland Cl. SW14 146 C3
Rutland Cl. SW19 167 H7
Rutland Rd.
Rutland Cl., Bex. 176 D1
Rutland Cl., Chess. 195 J6
Rutland Ct., Enf. 45 F5
Rutland Dr., Mord. 184 C6
Rutland Dr., Rich. 163 G1
Rutland Gdns. N4 75 H6
Rutland Gdns. SW7 23 H4
Rutland Gdns. SW7 129 H2
Rutland Gdns. W13 104 D5
Rutland Gdns., Croy. 202 B4
Rutland Gdns., Dag. 100 C5
Rutland Gdns. Ms. SW7 23 H4
Rutland Gate SW7 23 H4
Rutland Gate SW7 129 H2
Rutland Gate, Belv. 139 H5
Rutland Gate, Brom. 191 F4
Rutland Gate Ms. SW7 23 G4
Rutland Gro. W6 127 H5
Rutland Ms. NW8 108/109 E1
Boundary Rd.
Rutland Ms. E. SW7 23 G5
Rutland Ms. S. SW7 23 G5
Rutland Pk. NW2 89 J6
Rutland Pk. SE6 171 J2
Rutland Pk. Gdns. NW2 89 J6
Rutland Pk.
Rutland Pk. Mans. NW2 89 J6
Walm La.
Rutland Pl. EC1 11 J6
Rutland Pl., Bushey 52 A1
The Rutts
Rutland Rd. E7 98 A7
Rutland Rd. E9 113 F1
Rutland Rd. E11 79 H5
Rutland Rd. E17 78 A6
Rutland Rd. SW19 167 H7
Rutland Rd., Har. 67 J6
Rutland Rd., Hayes 121 G4
Rutland Rd., Ilf. 99 E4
Rutland Rd., Sthl. 103 G5
Rutland Rd., Twick. 162 A2
Rutland St. SW7 23 H5
Rutland St. SW7 129 H3
Rutland Wk. SE6 171 J2
Rutley Cl. SE17 35 G5
Rutlish Rd. SW19 184 D1
Rutter Gdns., Mitch. 185 F4
Rutters Cl., West Dr. 120 D2
Rutts, The, Bushey 52 A1
Rutts Ter. SE14 153 G1
Ruvigny Gdns. SW15 148 A3
Ruxley Cl., Epsom 196 B5
Ruxley Cl., Sid. 176 D6
Ruxley Cor. Ind. Est., Sid. 176 D6
Ruxley Cres., Esher 194 E6
Ruxley La., Epsom 196 D5
Ruxley Ms., Epsom 196 B5
Ruxley Ridge, Esher 194 D7
Ryalls Ct. N20 57 J3
Ryan Cl. SE3 155 J4
Ryan Cl., Ruis. 84 B1
Ryan Dr., Brent. 124 D6
Ryarsh Cres., Orp. 207 H4
Rycott Path SE22 152 D7
Lordship La.
Rycroft Way N17 76 C3
Ryculff Sq. SE3 155 F2
Rydal Cl. NW4 72 B1
Rydal Cres., Grnf. 105 E3
Rydal Dr., Bexh. 159 G1
Rydal Dr., W.Wick. 205 E2
Rydal Gdns. NW9 71 E5
Rydal Gdns. SW15 164 E5
Rydal Gdns., Houns. 143 H6
Rydal Gdns., Wem. 87 F1
Rydal Rd. SW16 168 D4
Rydal Way, Enf. 45 F6
Rydal Way, Ruis. 84 C4
Ryde Pl., Twick. 145 F6
Ryde Vale Rd. SW12 168 B2
Ryder Cl., Brom. 173 H5
Ryder Ct. SW1 25 G1
Ryder Dr. SE16 132 E5
Ryder Ms. E9 95 F5
Homerton High St.
Ryder St. SW1 25 G1
Ryder St. SW1 130 C1
Ryder Yd. SW1 25 G1
Ryders Ter. NW8 6 C1
Rydon St. N1 111 J1
St. Paul St.
Rydons Cl. SE9 156 B3
Rydston Cl. N7 93 F7
Sutterton St.
Rye, The N14 42 C7
Rye Cl., Bex. 159 H6
Rye Hill Pk. SE15 153 F4
Rye La. SE15 152 D1
Rye Pas. SE15 152 D3
Rye Rd. SE15 153 G4
Rye Wk. SW15 148 A5
Chartfield Av.
Rye Way, Edg. 53 J6
Canons Dr.
Ryecotes Mead SE21 170 B1
Ryecroft Av., Ilf. 80 E2
Ryecroft Av., Twick. 143 H7
Ryecroft Cres., Barn. 39 H5
Ryecroft Rd. SE13 154 C5
Ryecroft Rd. SW16 169 G6
Ryecroft Rd., Orp. 193 G6
Ryecroft St. SW6 148 E1
Ryedale SE22 152 E6
Ryefield Ct., Nthwd. 66 A2
Ryefield Cres.
Ryefield Cres., Nthwd. 66 A2
Ryefield Par., Nthwd. 66 A2
Ryefield Cres.
Ryefield Path SW15 165 G1
Ryefield Rd. SE19 169 J6
Ryelands Cres. SE12 155 J6
Ryfold Rd. SW19 166 D3
Ryhope Rd. N11 58 B4
Ryland Ho., Croy. 201 J3
Ryland Rd. NW5 92 B6
Rylandes Rd. NW2 89 G3
Rylett Cres. W12 127 F3
Rylett Rd. W12 127 F2
Rylston Rd. N13 60 A3
Rylston Rd. SW6 128 C6
Rymer Rd., Croy. 188 B7
Rymer St. SE24 151 H6
Rymill St. E16 136 D1
Rysbrack St. SW3 23 J5
Rysbrack St. SW3 129 J3
Rythe Cl., Chess. 195 G6
Ashlyns Way
Rythe Ct., T.Ditt. 180 D7
Rythe Rd., Esher 194 A5

S

Sabbarton St. E16 115 F6
Victoria Dock Rd.
Sabella Ct. E3 113 J2
Sabine Rd. SW11 149 J3
Sable Cl., Houns. 142 C3
Sable St. N1 93 H7
Canonbury Rd.
Sach Rd. E5 95 E2
Sackville Av., Brom. 205 G1
Sackville Cl., Har. 86 A3
Sackville Est. SW16 169 E3
Sackville Gdns., Ilf. 98 C1
Sackville Rd., Sutt. 198 D7
Sackville St. W1 17 G6
Sackville St. W1 110 C7
Sackville Way SE22 170 D1
Dulwich Common
Saddle Yd. W1 24 D1
Saddlers Cl., Barn. 39 H5
Barnet Rd.
Saddlers Cl., Borwd. 38 D6
Farriers Way
Saddlers Cl., Pnr. 51 G6
Saddlers Ms. SW8 151 F1
Portland Gro.
Saddlers Ms., Wem. 86 C4
The Boltons
Saddlers Path, Borwd. 38 D5
Saddlescombe Way N12 56 D5
Sadler Cl., Mitch. 185 J2
Sadlers Ride, W.Mol. 179 J2
Saffron Av. E14 114 D7
Saffron Cl. NW11 72 C5
Saffron Cl., Croy. 186 E6
Saffron Ct., Felt. 141 F7
Staines Rd.
Saffron Hill EC1 11 F6
Saffron Hill EC1 111 G4
Saffron Rd., Rom. 83 J2
Saffron St. EC1 19 F1
Saffron Way, Surb. 195 G1
Sage Cl. E6 116 C5
Bradley Stone Rd.
Sage St. E1 113 F7
Cable St.
Sage Way WC1 10 C4
Saigasso Cl. E16 116 A6
Royal Rd.
Sail St. SE11 34 D1
Sail St. SE11 131 F4
Sainfoin Rd. SW17 168 A2
Sainsbury Rd. SE19 170 B5
St. Agatha's Dr., Kings.T. 163 J6
St. Agathas Gro., Cars. 199 J1
St. Agnes Cl. E9 113 F1
Gore Rd.
St. Agnes Pl. SE11 35 G6
St. Agnes Pl. SE11 131 G6
St. Agnes Well EC1 112 A4
Old St.
St. Aidans Ct. W13 124/125 E2
St. Aidans Rd.
St. Aidans Ct., Bark. 118 B3
Choats Rd.
St. Aidan's Rd. SE22 152 E6
St. Aidans Rd. W13 125 E2
St. Albans Av. E6 116 C3
St. Alban's Av. W4 126 D4
St. Albans Av., Felt. 160 D5
St. Albans Cl. NW11 90 D1
St. Albans Cres. N22 75 G1
St. Alban's Cres., Wdf.Grn. 63 G7
St. Alban's Gdns., Tedd. 162 D5
St. Albans Gro. W8 22 B5
St. Albans Gro. W8 129 E3
St. Alban's Gro., Cars. 185 H7
St. Albans La. NW11 90 D1
West Heath Dr.
St. Albans Ms. W2 15 F1
St. Albans Ms. W2 109 G5
St. Alban's Pl. N1 111 H1
St. Albans Rd. NW5 92 A3
St. Albans Rd. NW10 106 E1
St. Albans Rd., Barn. 40 B1
St. Albans Rd., Ilf. 99 J1
St. Alban's Rd., Kings.T. 163 H6
St. Alban's Rd., Sutt. 198 C4
St. Alban's Rd., Wdf.Grn. 63 G7
St. Albans St. SW1 17 H6
St. Albans Ter. W6 128 B6
Margravine Rd.
St. Albans Twr. E4 61 J6
St. Alban's Vil. NW5 92 A3
Highgate Rd.
St. Alfege Pas. SE10 134 C6
St. Alfege Rd. SE7 136 A6
St. Alphage Gdns. EC2 20 A2

Name	Page	Grid
St. Alphage Highwalk EC2, *London Wall*	112	A5
St. Alphage Wk., Edg.	70	C2
St. Alphege Rd. N9	45	F7
St. Alphonsus Rd. SW4	150	C4
St. Amunds Cl. SE6	172	A4
St. Andrew St. EC4	**19**	**F2**
St. Andrew St. EC4	111	G5
St. Andrews Av., Wem.	86	D4
St. Andrew's Cl. N12, *Woodside Av.*	57	F4
St. Andrews Cl. NW2	89	H3
St. Andrews Cl. SE16, *Ryder Dr.*	132/133	E5
St. Andrew's Cl., Islw.	144	A1
St. Andrew's Cl., Ruis.	84	D2
St. Andrew's Cl., Stan.	69	F2
St. Andrew's Ct. SW18, *Waynflete St.*	167	F2
St. Andrew's Dr., Stan.	69	F1
St. Andrew's Gro. N16	94	A1
St. Andrew's Hill EC4	**19**	**H5**
St. Andrew's Hill EC4	111	H7
St. Andrew's Ms. N16	94	B1
St. Andrews Ms. SE3, *Mycenae Rd.*	135	G7
St. Andrews Pl. NW1	**8**	**E5**
St. Andrews Pl. NW1	110	B4
St. Andrews Rd. E11	78	E6
St. Andrews Rd. E13	115	H3
St. Andrews Rd. E17	77	G2
St. Andrews Rd. N9	45	F7
St. Andrews Rd. NW9	88	D1
St. Andrews Rd. NW10	89	H6
St. Andrews Rd. NW11	72	C6
St. Andrews Rd. W3	107	E7
St. Andrews Rd. W7, *Church Rd.*	124	B2
St. Andrews Rd. W14	128	B6
St. Andrews Rd., Cars.	199	H3
St. Andrews Rd., Croy., *Lower Coombe St.*	201	J4
St. Andrews Rd., Enf.	44	A3
St. Andrews Rd., Ilf.	80	C7
St. Andrews Rd., Sid.	176	D3
St. Andrew's Rd., Surb.	181	G6
St. Andrews Rd., Wat.	50	D3
St. Andrews Sq. W11, *St. Marks Rd.*	108	B6
St. Andrews Sq., Surb.	181	G6
St. Andrews Twr., Sthl.	103	J7
St. Andrews Way E3	114	B4
St. Anna Rd., Barn., *Sampson Av.*	40	A5
St. Anne St. E14, *Commercial Rd.*	113	J6
St. Annes Av., Stai.	140	A7
St. Anne's Cl. N6, *Highgate W. Hill*	92	A3
St. Anne's Cl., Wat.	50	C4
St. Anne's Ct. W1	**17**	**H4**
St. Annes Gdns. NW10	105	J3
St. Annes Pas. E14, *Newell St.*	113	J6
St. Anne's Rd. E11	96	D2
St. Anne's Rd., Wem.	87	G5
St. Anne's Row E14, *Commercial Rd.*	113	J6
St. Ann's, Bark.	117	F1
St. Ann's Cres. SW18	149	F6
St. Ann's Gdns. NW5, *Queens Cres.*	92	A6
St. Ann's Hill SW18	149	E5
St. Ann's La. SW1	**25**	**J5**
St. Ann's Pk. Rd. SW18	149	F6
St. Ann's Pas. SW13	147	E3
St. Anns Rd. N9	60	C2
St. Ann's Rd. N15	75	H5
St. Ann's Rd. SW13	147	F2
St. Anns Rd. W11	108	A7
St. Ann's Rd., Bark., *Axe St.*	117	F1
St. Ann's Rd., Har.	68	B6
St. Ann's St. SW1	**25**	**J5**
St. Ann's St. SW1	130	D3
St. Ann's Ter. NW8	**7**	**F1**
St. Ann's Ter. NW8	109	G2
St. Anns Vil. W11	128	A1
St. Anns Way, S.Croy.	201	H6
St. Anselm's Pl. W1	**16**	**D4**
St. Anselms Rd., Hayes	121	J2
St. Anthonys Av., Wdf.Grn.	63	J6
St. Anthonys Cl. E1	**29**	**H1**
St. Anthonys Cl. E1	132	D1
St. Anthonys Cl. SW17, *College Gdns.*	167	H2
St. Anthony's Way, Felt.	141	J4
St. Antony's Rd. E7	97	H7
St. Arvans Cl., Croy.	202	B3
St. Asaph Rd. SE4	153	G3
St. Aubyn's Av. SW19	166	C5
St. Aubyns Av., Houns.	143	G5
St. Aubyns Cl., Orp.	207	J3
St. Aubyns Gdns., Orp.	207	J2
St. Aubyn's Rd. SE19	170	C6
St. Audrey Av., Bexh.	159	G2
St. Augustine's Av. W5	105	H2
St. Augustines Av., Brom.	192	B5
St. Augustine's Av., S.Croy.	201	J6
St. Augustine's Av., Wem.	87	H3
St. Augustine's Path N5	93	H5
St. Augustines Rd. NW1	92	D7
St. Augustine's Rd., Belv.	139	F4
St. Austell Cl., Edg.	69	J2
St. Austell Rd. SE13	154	C2
St. Awdry's Rd., Bark.	99	G7
St. Awdry's Wk., Bark., *Station Par.*	99	F7
St. Barnabas Cl. SE22, *East Dulwich Gro.*	152	B5
St. Barnabas Cl., Beck.	190	C2
St. Barnabas Ct., Har.	67	J1
St. Barnabas Gdns., W.Mol.	179	G5
St. Barnabas Rd. E17	78	A6
St. Barnabas Rd., Mitch.	168	A7
St. Barnabas Rd., Sutt.	199	G5
St. Barnabas Rd., Wdf.Grn.	79	H1
St. Barnabas St. SW1	**32**	**C3**
St. Barnabas St. SW1	130	A5
St. Barnabas Ter. E9	95	G5
St. Barnabas Vil. SW8	151	E1
St. Bartholomews Cl. SE26	171	F4
St. Bartholomew's Rd. E6	116	B1
St. Benedict's Cl. SW17, *Church La.*	168	A5
St. Benet's Cl. SW17, *College Gdns.*	167	H2
St. Benet's Gro., Cars.	185	F7
St. Benet's Pl. EC3	**20**	**C5**
St. Bernards, Croy.	202	B3
St. Bernard's Cl. SE27, *St. Gothard Rd.*	170	A4
St. Bernard's Rd. E6	116	A1
St. Blaise Av., Brom.	191	H2
St. Botolph Row EC3	**21**	**F4**
St. Botolph St. EC3	**21**	**F4**
St. Botolph St. EC3	112	C6
St. Bride St. EC4	**19**	**G3**
St. Bride St. EC4	111	H6
St. Bride's Av. EC4, *New Br. St.*	111	H6
St. Brides Av., Edg.	69	J1
St. Brides Cl., Erith, *St. Katherines Rd.*	138	D2
St. Bride's Pas. EC4	**19**	**G4**
St. Catherines Cl. SW17, *College Gdns.*	167	H2
St. Catherines Dr. SE14, *Kitto Rd.*	153	G2
St. Catherine's Ms. SW3	**31**	**J1**
St. Catherines Rd. E4	62	A2
St. Chads Cl., Surb.	181	F7
St. Chad's Gdns., Rom.	82	E7
St. Chad's Pl. WC1	**10**	**B3**
St. Chad's Pl. WC1	111	E3
St. Chad's Rd., Rom.	82	E6
St. Chad's St. WC1	**10**	**B3**
St. Chad's St. WC1	111	E3
St. Charles Pl. W10, *Chesterton Rd.*	108	B5
St. Charles Sq. W10	108	A5
St. Christopher's Cl., Islw.	144	B1
St. Christopher's Dr., Hayes	102	B7
St. Christophers Gdns., Th.Hth.	187	G3
St. Christophers Ms., Wall.	200	C5
St. Christopher's Pl. W1	**16**	**C3**
St. Clair Dr., Wor.Pk.	197	H3
St. Clair Rd. E13	115	H2
St. Clair's Rd., Croy.	202	B2
St. Clare Business Pk., Hmptn.	161	J6
St. Clare Cl., Ilf.	80	C2
St. Clare St. EC3	**21**	**F4**
St. Clements Ct. EC4, *Clements La.*	112	A7
St. Clements Ct. N7, *Arundel Sq.*	93	G6
St. Clements Hts. SE26	170	D3
St. Clement's La. WC2	**18**	**D4**
St. Clements St. N7	93	G6
St. Cloud Rd. SE27	169	J4
St. Crispins Cl. NW3	91	H4
St. Crispins Cl., Sthl.	103	F6
St. Cross St. EC1	**19**	**F1**
St. Cross St. EC1	111	G5
St. Cuthberts Gdns., Pnr., *Westfield Pk.*	51	F7
St. Cuthberts Rd. N13	59	G6
St. Cuthberts Rd. NW2	90	C6
St. Cyprian's St. SW17	167	J4
St. Davids Cl. SE16, *Masters Dr.*	132/133	E5
St. Davids Cl., Wem.	88	C3
St. David's Cl., W.Wick.	190	B7
St. David's Ct. E17	78	C3
St. Davids Dr., Edg.	69	J1
St. Davids Pl. NW4	71	H7
St. Davids Sq. E14	134	B5
St. Denis Rd. SE27	170	A4
St. Dionis Rd. SW6	148	C2
St. Donatts Rd. SE14	153	J1
St. Dunstan's All. EC3	**20**	**D5**
St. Dunstans Av. W3	106	D7
St. Dunstans Cl., Hayes	121	J4
St. Dunstan's Ct. EC4, *Fleet St.*	111	G6
St. Dunstans Gdns. W3, *St. Dunstans Av.*	106	D7
St. Dunstan's Hill EC3	**20**	**D6**
St. Dunstan's Hill EC3	112	B7
St. Dunstan's Hill, Sutt.	198	B5
St. Dunstan's La. EC3	**20**	**D6**
St. Dunstan's La., Beck.	190	C6
St. Dunstan's Rd. E7	97	J6
St. Dunstans Rd. SE25	188	C4
St. Dunstans Rd. W6	128	A5
St. Dunstans Rd. W7	124	B2
St. Dunstans Rd., Houns.	142	C2
St. Edmunds Cl. NW8, *St. Edmunds Ter.*	109	J1
St. Edmunds Cl. SW17, *College Gdns.*	167	H2
St. Edmunds Cl., Erith, *St. Katherines Rd.*	138	D2
St. Edmunds Dr., Stan.	68	D1
St. Edmund's La., Twick.	143	H7
St. Edmunds Rd. N9	44	D7
St. Edmunds Rd., Ilf.	80	C6
St. Edmunds Sq. SW13	127	J6
St. Edmunds Ter. NW8	**7**	**H1**
St. Edmunds Ter. NW8	109	H1
St. Edwards Cl. NW11	72	D6
St. Egberts Way E4	62	C1
St. Elmo Rd. W12	127	F1
St. Elmos Rd. SE16	133	H2
St. Erkenwald Ms., Bark., *St. Erkenwald Rd.*	117	G1
St. Erkenwald Rd., Bark.	117	G1
St. Ermin's Hill SW1	**25**	**H5**
St. Ervans Rd. W10	108	B5
St. Fabian Twr. E4, *Iris Way*	61	J6
St. Faiths Cl., Enf.	43	J1
St. Faith's Rd. SE21	169	H1
St. Fillans Rd. SE6	172	C1
St. Francis Cl., Orp.	193	H6
St. Francis Cl., Wat.	50	B1
St. Francis Rd. SE22	152	B4
St. Francis Twr. E4, *Iris Way*	61	J6
St. Francis Way, Ilf.	99	H4
St. Fridewides Ms. E14, *Lodore St.*	114	C6
St. Gabriel's Cl. E11	97	H1
St. Gabriels Rd. NW2	90	A5
St. George St. W1	**17**	**E4**
St. George St. W1	110	B6
St. Georges Av. E7	97	H7
St. Georges Av. N7	92	D4
St. Georges Av. NW9	70	C4
St. Georges Av. W5	125	G2
St. Georges Av., Sthl.	103	F7
St. Georges Circ. SE1	**27**	**G5**
St. Georges Circ. SE1	131	H3
St. Georges Cl. NW11	72	C6
St. George's Cl. SW8, *Patmore Est.*	150	C1
St. Georges Cl., Wem.	86	D3
St. Georges Ct. E6	116	C4
St. Georges Ct. EC4	**19**	**G3**
St. Georges Ct. SW7	**22**	**C5**
St. George's Dr. SW1	**33**	**F3**
St. George's Dr. SW1	130	B4
St. Georges Dr., Wat.	50	E3
St. Georges Flds. W2	**15**	**H4**
St. Georges Flds. W2	109	H6
St. George's Gdns., Surb., *Hamilton Av.*	196	B2
St. Georges Gro. SW17	167	G3
St. Georges Gro. Est. SW17	167	G3
St. Georges Ind. Est., Kings.T.	163	G5
St. Georges La. EC3	**20**	**D5**
St. Georges Ms. NW1, *Regents Pk. Rd.*	91	J7
St. Georges Pl., Twick., *Church St.*	162	D1
St. Georges Rd. E7	97	H6
St. Georges Rd. E10	96	C3
St. Georges Rd. N9	60	D3
St. Georges Rd. N13	59	F3
St. Georges Rd. NW11	72	C6
St. Georges Rd. SE1	**27**	**F5**
St. Georges Rd. SE1	131	G3
St. George's Rd. SW19	166	C6
St. Georges Rd. W4	126	E2
St. Georges Rd. W7	124	C1
St. George's Rd., Beck.	190	B1
St. Georges Rd., Brom.	192	C2
St. Georges Rd., Dag.	100	E5
St. George's Rd., Felt.	160	D4
St. George's Rd., Ilf.	80	C7
St. George's Rd., Kings.T.	164	A7
St. George's Rd., Mitch.	186	B3
St. Georges Rd., Orp.	193	G6
St. Georges Rd., Rich.	145	J3
St. Georges Rd., Sid.	176	D6
St. Georges Rd., Twick.	145	E1
St. Georges Rd., Wall.	200	B5
St. Georges Rd. W., Brom.	192	B1
St. Georges Sq. E7	97	H7
St. Georges Sq. E14, *Narrow St.*	113	H7
St. George's Sq. SE8	133	J4
St. George's Sq. SW1	**33**	**H3**
St. George's Sq. SW1	130	D5

Name	Map	Grid
St. George's Sq., N.Mal.	182/183	E3
High St.		
St. George's Sq. Ms. SW1	**33**	**H4**
St. George's Sq. Ms. SW1	130	D5
St. Georges Ter. NW1	91	J7
Regents Pk. Rd.		
St. Georges Wk., Croy.	201	J3
St. Georges Way SE15	**36**	**D6**
St. Georges Way SE15	132	B6
St. Gerards Cl. SW4	150	C5
St. German's Pl. SE3	155	G1
St. Germans Rd. SE23	171	H1
St. Giles Av., Dag.	101	H7
St. Giles Cl., Dag.	101	H7
St. Giles Av.		
St. Giles Cl., Orp.	207	G5
St. Giles High St. WC2	**17**	**J3**
St. Giles High St. WC2	110	D6
St. Giles Pas. WC2	**17**	**J4**
St. Giles Rd. SE5	132	B7
St. Gilles Ho. E2	113	G2
St. Gothard Rd. SE27	170	A4
St. Gregory Cl., Ruis.	84	C4
St. Helena Rd. SE16	133	G4
St. Helens St. WC1	**10**	**E4**
St. Helens Cres. SW16	187	F1
St. Helens Rd.		
St. Helens Gdns. W10	108	A6
St. Helens Pl. EC3	**20**	**D3**
St. Helens Rd. SW16	187	F1
St. Helen's Rd. W13	124/125	E1
Dane Rd.		
St. Helens Rd., Erith	138	D2
St. Helens Rd., Ilf.	80	C6
St. Helier Av., Mord.	185	F7
St. Heliers Av., Houns.	143	G5
St. Heliers Rd. E10	78	C6
St. Hildas Cl. NW6	90	A7
St. Hildas Cl. SW17	167	H2
St. Hilda's Rd. SW13	127	H6
St. Hughe's Cl. SW17	167	H2
College Gdns.		
St. Hughs Rd. SE20	188/189	E1
Ridsdale Rd.		
St. James Av. N20	57	H3
St. James Av. W13	124	D1
St. James Av., Sutt.	198	D5
St. James Cl. N20	57	H3
St. James Cl. SE18	137	F5
Congleton Gro.		
St. James Cl., Barn.	41	G4
St. James Cl., N.Mal.	183	F5
St. James Cl., Ruis.	84	C2
St. James Gdns., Wem.	87	G7
St. James Gate NW1	92	D7
St. Paul's Cres.		
St. James Gro. SW11	149	J2
Reform St.		
St. James Ms. E14	134	C3
St. James Ms. E17	77	H5
St. James's St.		
St. James Rd. E15	97	F5
St. James Rd. N9	60/61	E2
Queens Rd.		
St. James Rd., Cars.	199	H3
St. James Rd., Kings.T.	181	H2
St. James Rd., Mitch.	168	A7
St. James Rd., Surb.	181	G6
St. James Rd., Sutt.	198	D5
St. James St. W6	127	J5
St. James Wk. SE15	132	C7
Commercial Way		
St. James Way, Sid.	177	E5
St. James's SE14	153	H1
St. James's Av. E2	113	F2
St. James's Av., Beck.	189	H3
St. James's Av., Hmptn.	161	J5
St. James's Cl. SW17	167	J2
St. James's Dr.		
St. James's Cotts., Rich.	145	G5
Paradise Rd.		
St. James's Ct. SW1	**25**	**G5**
St. James's Ct. SW1	130	C3
St. James's Cres. SW9	151	G3
St. James's Dr. SW12	167	J1
St. James's Dr. SW17	167	J1
St. James's Gdns. W11	128	B1
St. James's La. N10	74	B4
St. James's Mkt. SW1	**17**	**H6**
St. James's Palace SW1	**25**	**G3**
St. James's Palace SW1	130	C1
St. James's Pk. SW1	**25**	**H3**
St. James's Pk. SW1	130	D2
St. James's Pk., Croy.	187	J7
St. James's Pas. EC3	**21**	**E4**
St. James's Pl. SW1	**25**	**F2**
St. James's Pl. SW1	130	C1
St. James's Rd. SE1	**37**	**J3**
St. James's Rd. SE1	132	D5
St. James's Rd. SE16	**29**	**J5**
St. James's Rd. SE16	132	D3
St. James's Rd., Croy.	187	H7
St. James's Rd., Hmptn.	161	H5
St. James's Row EC1	**11**	**F5**
St. James's Sq. SW1	**25**	**G1**
St. James's Sq. SW1	130	C1
St. James's St. E17	77	H5
St. James's St. SW1	**25**	**F1**
St. James's St. SW1	130	C1
St. James's Ter. NW8	**7**	**J1**
St. James's Ter. Ms. NW8	109	J1
St. James's Wk. EC1	**11**	**G5**
St. James's Wk. EC1	111	H4
St. Joans Rd. N9	60	C1
St. John Fisher Rd., Erith	138	D3
St. John St. EC1	**11**	**H6**
St. John St. EC1	111	H4
St. Johns Av. N11	57	J5
St. John's Av. NW10	107	F1
St. Johns Av. SW15	148	A5
St. John's Ch. Rd. E9	95	F5
St. Johns Cl. N14	42	C6
Chase Rd.		
St. John's Cl. SW6	128	D7
Dawes Rd.		
St. John's Cl., Wem.	87	H5
St. John's Cotts. SE20	171	F7
Maple Rd.		
St. Johns Cotts., Rich.	145	H4
Kew Foot Rd.		
St. Johns Ct., Buck.H.	63	H1
St. John's Ct., Islw.	144	C2
St. Johns Cres. SW9	151	G3
St. John's Est. N1	**12**	**C2**
St. John's Est. N1	112	A2
St. John's Est. SE1	**29**	**F3**
St. John's Gdns. W11	108	C7
St. Johns Gro. N19	92	C2
St. Johns Gro. SW13	147	F2
Terrace Gdns.		
St. Johns Gro., Rich.	145	H4
Kew Foot Rd.		
St. John's Hill SW11	149	G4
St. John's Hill Gro. SW11	149	G4
St. John's La. EC1	**11**	**G6**
St. John's La. EC1	111	H4
St. John's Ms. W11	108	D6
Ledbury Rd.		
St. Johns Par., Sid.	176	A4
Church Rd.		
St. John's Pk. SE3	135	F7
St. Johns Pas. SE23	171	F1
Davids Rd.		
St. John's Pas. SW19	166	B6
Ridgway Pl.		
St. John's Path EC1	**11**	**G6**
St. Johns Pathway SE23	171	F1
Devonshire Rd.		
St. John's Pl. EC1	**11**	**G6**
St. John's Rd. E4	62	B3
St. John's Rd. E6	116	B1
Ron Leighton Way		
St. Johns Rd. E16	115	G6
St. John's Rd. E17	78	B2
St. Johns Rd. N15	76	B6
St. Johns Rd. NW11	72	C6
St. Johns Rd. SE20	171	F7
St. John's Rd. SW11	149	H4
St. John's Rd. SW19	166	B7
St. John's Rd., Bark.	117	H1
St. Johns Rd., Cars.	199	H3
St. Johns Rd., Croy.	201	H3
Sylverdale Rd.		
St. Johns Rd., E.Mol.	180	A4
St. John's Rd., Felt.	161	E4
St. John's Rd., Har.	68	C6
St. Johns Rd., Ilf.	81	G7
St. John's Rd., Islw.	144	C2
St. John's Rd., Kings.T.	181	F2
St. Johns Rd., Loug.	48	C2
St. John's Rd., N.Mal.	182	C3
St. John's Rd., Orp.	193	G6
St. John's Rd., Rich.	145	H4
St. John's Rd., Sid.	176	B4
St. Johns Rd., Sthl.	122	E3
St. Johns Rd., Sutt.	198	D2
St. John's Rd., Well.	158	B3
St. John's Rd., Wem.	87	G4
St. John's Sq. EC1	**11**	**G6**
St. Johns Ter. E7	97	H6
St. Johns Ter. SE18	137	F6
St. John's Ter. SW15	164	D4
Kingston Vale		
St. Johns Ter. W10	108	A4
Harrow Rd.		
St. Johns Vale SE8	154	A2
St. Johns Vil. N19	92	D2
St. John's Vil. W8	**22**	**B6**
St. Johns Way N19	92	D1
St. John's Wd. Ct. NW8	**7**	**F4**
St. John's Wd. High St. NW8	**7**	**F2**
St. John's Wd. High St. NW8	109	G2
St. John's Wd. Pk. NW8	109	G1
St. John's Wd. Rd. NW8	**6**	**E5**
St. John's Wd. Rd. NW8	109	G4
St. John's Wd. Ter. NW8	**7**	**G1**
St. John's Wd. Ter. NW8	109	G2
St. Josephs Cl. W10	108	B5
Bevington Rd.		
St. Joseph's Cl., Orp.	207	J4
St. Joseph's Ct. SE7	135	H6
St. Josephs Dr., Sthl.	123	E1
St. Joseph's Gro. NW4	71	H4
St. Josephs Rd. N9	45	E7
St. Joseph's Vale SE3	154	D2
St. Jude St. N16	94	B5
St. Jude's Rd. E2	113	E2
St. Julian's Cl. SW16	169	G4
St. Julian's Fm. Rd. SE27	169	G4
St. Julian's Rd. NW6	90	C7
St. Katharines Prec. NW1	**8**	**D1**
St. Katharine's Way E1	**29**	**G1**
St. Katharine's Way E1	132	C1
St. Katherines Rd., Erith	138	D2
St. Katherine's Row EC3	**21**	**E4**
St. Katherine's Wk. W11	108	A7
Hunt St.		
St. Keverne Rd. SE9	174	B4
St. Kilda Rd. W13	124	D1
St. Kilda Rd., Orp.	207	J1
St. Kilda's Rd. N16	94	A1
St. Kilda's Rd., Har.	68	B6
St. Kitts Ter. SE19	170	B5
St. Laurence Cl. NW6	108	A1
St. Lawrence Cl., Edg.	53	J7
St. Lawrence Dr., Pnr.	66	B6
St. Lawrence St. E14	134	C1
St. Lawrence Ter. W10	108	B5
St. Lawrence Way SW9	151	G2
St. Leonards Av. E4	62	E6
St. Leonards Av., Har.	69	F4
St. Leonard's Cl., Well.	158	A3
Hook La.		
St. Leonards Ct. N1	**12**	**A3**
St. Leonards Ct. N1	112	A3
St. Leonard's Gdns., Hours.	122	E7
St. Leonards Gdns., Ilf.	99	F5
St. Leonards Ri., Orp.	207	H4
St. Leonards Rd. E14	114	B5
St. Leonard's Rd. NW10	106	D4
St. Leonard's Rd. SW14	146	B3
St. Leonards Rd. W13	105	F7
St. Leonards Rd., Croy.	201	H3
St. Leonards Rd., Esher	194	C6
St. Leonard's Rd., Surb.	181	G5
St. Leonards Rd., T.Ditt.	180	D6
St. Leonards Sq. NW5	92	A6
St. Leonard's Sq., Surb.	181	G5
St. Leonard's Rd.		
St. Leonards St. E3	114	B3
St. Leonard's Ter. SW3	**31**	**J4**
St. Leonard's Ter. SW3	129	J5
St. Leonards Wk. SW16	169	F7
St. Loo Av. SW3	**31**	**H5**
St. Loo Av. SW3	129	H6
St. Louis Rd. SE27	169	J4
St. Loy's Rd. N17	76	B2
St. Lucia Dr. E15	115	F1
St. Luke's Av. SW4	150	D4
St. Luke's Av., Ilf.	99	E5
St. Lukes Cl. EC1	111	J4
Old St.		
St. Luke's Cl. SE25	189	E6
St. Luke's Est. EC1	**12**	**B4**
St. Luke's Est. EC1	112	A3
St. Lukes Ms. W11	108	C6
Basing St.		
St. Lukes Pas., Kings.T.	181	J1
St. Lukes Rd. W11	108	C5
St. Lukes Sq. E16	115	F6
St. Luke's St. SW3	**31**	**G3**
St. Luke's St. SW3	129	H5
St. Luke's Yd. W9	108	C2
St. Malo Av. N9	61	F3
St. Margarets, Bark.	117	G1
St. Margarets Av. N15	75	H4
St. Margarets Av. N20	57	F2
St. Margarets Av., Har.	85	J3
St. Margarets Av., Sid.	175	G3
St. Margaret's Av., Sutt.	198	B3
St. Margaret's Ct. SE1	**28**	**A2**
St. Margarets Cres. SW15	147	H5
St. Margaret's Dr., Twick.	144	E5
St. Margaret's Gro. E11	97	F3
St. Margaret's Gro. SE18	137	F6
St. Margarets Gro., Twick.	144	D6
St. Margarets La. W8	**22**	**A6**
St. Margarets La. W8	128	E3
St. Margarets Pas. SE13	154/155	E3
Church Ter.		
St. Margarets Rd. E12	97	J2
St. Margaret's Rd. N17	76	B3
St. Margaret's Rd. NW10	107	J3
St. Margarets Rd. SE4	153	J4
St. Margarets Rd. W7	124	B2
St. Margarets Rd., Edg.	54	B5
St. Margarets Rd., Islw.	144	E4
St. Margarets Rd., Twick.	144	E4
St. Margarets Sq. SE4	153	J4
Adelaide Av.		
St. Margaret's St. SW1	**26**	**A4**
St. Margaret's St. SW1	130	D4
St. Margaret's Ter. SE18	137	F5
St. Mark St. E1	**21**	**G4**
St. Mark St. E1	112	C6
St. Marks Cl. SE10	134	C7
Ashburnham Pl.		
St. Marks Cl. W11	108	B6
Lancaster Rd.		
St. Mark's Cl., Barn.	40	E3
St. Marks Cres. NW1	110	A1
St. Marks Gate E9	95	J7
Cadogan Ter.		
St. Mark's Gro. SW10	**30**	**B7**
St. Mark's Gro. SW10	129	E6
St. Mark's Hill, Surb.	181	H6
St. Mark's Pl. SW19	166	C6
Wimbledon Hill Rd.		

Street	Page	Grid
St. Marks Pl. W11	108	B6
St. Marks Ri. E8	94	C5
St. Marks Rd. SE25	188	D4
St. Mark's Rd. W5	125	H1
The Common		
St. Marks Rd. W7	124	B2
St. Marks Rd. W10	108	A6
St. Marks Rd. W11	108	B6
St. Marks Rd., Brom.	191	H3
St. Marks Rd., Enf.	44	C6
St. Marks Rd., Mitch.	185	J2
St. Mark's Rd., Tedd.	163	E7
St. Marks Sq. NW1	110	A1
St. Martins Av. E6	116	A2
St. Martins Cl. NW1	110	C1
St. Martins Cl., Enf.	44	E1
St. Martins Cl., Erith	138	D2
St. Helens Rd.		
St. Martin's Cl., Wat.	50	C4
Muirfield Rd.		
St. Martin's Cl., West Dr.	120	A3
St. Martin's Rd.		
St. Martin's Ct. WC2	110	D7
St. Martin's La.		
St. Martins Est. SW2	169	G1
St. Martin's La. WC2	18	A5
St. Martin's La. WC2	110	E7
St. Martin's Ms. WC2	18	A6
St. Martin's Pl. WC2	18	A6
St. Martins Pl. WC2	110	E7
St. Martins Rd. N9	60	E7
St. Martins Rd. SW9	151	F2
St. Martin's Rd., West Dr.	120	A3
St. Martin's St. WC2	17	J6
St. Martins Way SW17	167	F3
St. Martin's-le-Grand EC1	19	J3
St. Martin's-le-Grand EC1	111	J6
St. Mary Abbots Pl. W8	128	C3
St. Mary Abbots Ter. W14	128	C3
St. Mary at Hill EC3	20	D6
St. Mary at Hill EC3	112	B7
St. Mary Av., Wall.	200	A3
St. Mary Axe EC3	20	D4
St. Mary Axe EC3	112	B6
St. Mary Rd. E17	78	A4
St. Mary St. SE18	136	C4
St. Marychurch St. SE16	133	F2
St. Marys, Bark.	117	G1
St. Marys App. E12	98	C5
St. Marys Av. E11	79	H6
St. Mary's Av. N3	72	B2
St. Mary's Av., Brom.	191	E3
St. Mary's Av., Stai.	140	A7
St. Mary's Av., Tedd.	162	C6
St. Mary's Av. Cen., Sthl.	123	H4
St. Mary's Av. N., Sthl.	123	H4
St. Mary's Av. S., Sthl.	123	H4
St. Marys Cl. N17	76	D1
Kemble Rd.		
St. Marys Cl., Chess.	195	J7
St. Marys Cl., Epsom	197	G7
St. Mary's Cl., Stai.	140	A7
St. Mary's Cl., Sun.	178	A4
Green Way		
St. Marys Ct. E6	116	C4
St. Mary's Ct. SE7	136	A7
St. Mary's Ct. W5	125	G2
St. Mary's Rd.		
St. Mary's Cres. NW4	71	H3
St. Marys Cres., Islw.	124	A7
St. Mary's Cres., Stai.	140	A7
St. Marys Dr., Felt.	141	F7
St. Mary's Gdns. SE11	35	F1
St. Mary's Gdns. SE11	131	G4
St. Mary's Gate W8	22	A6
St. Mary's Gate W8	128	E3
St. Marys Grn. N2	73	F3
Thomas More Way		
St. Mary's Gro. N1	93	H6
St. Mary's Gro. SW13	147	H3
St. Mary's Gro. W4	126	B6
St. Mary's Gro., Rich.	145	J4
St. Marys Mans. W2	14	E1
St. Marys Mans. W2	109	F5
St. Mary's Ms. NW6	90/91	E7
Priory Rd.		
St. Mary's Ms., Rich.	163	F3
Back La.		
St. Marys Path N1	111	H1
St. Mary's Pl. SE9	156	D6
Eltham High St.		
St. Mary's Pl. W5	125	G2
St. Mary's Rd.		
St. Mary's Pl. W8	22	B6
St. Mary's Pl. W8	128	E3
St. Marys Rd. E10	96	C3
St. Marys Rd. E13	115	H2
St. Marys Rd. N8	74/75	E4
High St.		
St. Marys Rd. N9	61	F1
St. Mary's Rd. NW10	107	E1
St. Mary's Rd. NW11	72	B7
St. Mary's Rd. SE15	153	F1
St. Mary's Rd. SE25	188	B3
St. Mary's Rd. (Wimbledon) SW19	166	B5
St. Mary's Rd. W5	125	G2
St. Mary's Rd., Barn.	41	J7
St. Mary's Rd., Bex.	177	J1
St. Marys Rd., E.Mol.	180	A5
St. Mary's Rd., Ilf.	99	F2
St. Marys Rd., Surb.	181	G6
St. Marys Rd. (Long Ditton), Surb.	181	F7
St. Mary's Rd., Wor.Pk.	197	E2
St. Marys Sq. W2	14	E1
St. Mary's Sq. W5	125	G2
St. Mary's Rd.		
St. Marys Ter. W2	14	E1
St. Mary's Ter. W2	109	G5
St. Marys Vw., Har.	69	F5
St. Mary's Wk. SE11	35	F1
St. Mary's Wk. SE11	131	G4
St. Mary's Way, Chig.	64	D5
St. Matthew St. SW1	25	H6
St. Matthew's Av., Surb.	195	H1
St. Matthew's Dr., Brom.	192	C3
St. Matthew's Rd. SW2	151	F4
St. Matthews Rd. W5	125	H1
The Common		
St. Matthew's Row E2	13	H4
St. Matthew's Row E2	112	D3
St. Matthias Cl. NW9	71	F5
St. Maur Rd. SW6	148	C1
St. Merryn Cl. SE18	137	G7
St. Michael's All. EC3	20	C4
St. Michaels Av. N9	45	F7
St. Michael's Av., Wem.	88	A6
St. Michaels Cl. E16	116	A5
Fulmer Rd.		
St. Michael's Cl. N3	72	C2
St. Michaels Cl. N12	57	H5
St. Michaels Cl., Brom.	192	B3
St. Michaels Cl., Erith	138	D2
St. Helens Rd.		
St. Michaels Cl., Wor.Pk.	197	F2
St. Michaels Cres., Pnr.	67	E6
St. Michaels Gdns. W10	108	B5
St. Lawrence Ter.		
St. Michaels Rd. NW2	89	J4
St. Michael's Rd. SW9	151	F2
St. Michaels Rd., Croy.	201	J1
St. Michaels Rd., Wall.	200	C6
St. Michaels Rd., Well.	158	B3
St. Michaels St. W2	15	F3
St. Michaels St. W2	109	H5
St. Michaels Ter. N22	75	E2
St. Mildred's Ct. EC2	112	A6
Poultry		
St. Mildreds Rd. SE12	155	E7
St. Nicholas Glebe SW17	168	A6
St. Nicholas Rd. SE18	137	J5
St. Nicholas Rd., Sutt.	199	E5
St. Nicholas Rd., T.Ditt.	180	C6
St. Nicholas St. SE8	154	A1
Lucas St.		
St. Nicholas Way, Sutt.	198	E4
St. Nicolas La., Chis.	192	B1
St. Ninian's Ct. N20	57	J3
St. Norbert Grn. SE4	153	H4
St. Norbert Rd. SE4	153	H4
St. Olaf's Rd. SW6	128	B7
St. Olaves Ct. EC2	20	B4
St. Olave's Est. SE1	29	E3
St. Olaves Gdns. SE11	34	E1
St. Olaves Rd. E6	116	D1
St. Olave's Wk. SW16	186	C2
St. Olav's Sq. SE16	133	F3
St. Oswald's Pl. SE11	34	C4
St. Oswald's Pl. SE11	131	F5
St. Oswald's Rd. SW16	187	H1
St. Oswulf St. SW1	33	J2
St. Pancras Way NW1	92	C7
St. Patrick's Ct., Wdf.Grn.	63	E7
St. Paul St. N1	111	J1
St. Paul's All. EC4	111	H6
St. Paul's Chyd.		
St. Paul's Av. NW2	89	H6
St. Paul's Av. SE16	133	G1
St. Pauls Av., Har.	69	J5
St. Paul's Chyd. EC4	19	H4
St. Pauls Chyd. EC4	111	H6
St. Paul's Cl. SE7	136	A5
St. Paul's Cl. W5	125	J1
St. Paul's Cl., Cars.	199	H1
St. Pauls Cl., Chess.	195	G4
St. Pauls Cl., Hayes	121	G5
St. Paul's Cl., Houns.	143	E2
St. Paul's Ct. W14	128	A4
Colet Gdns.		
St. Pauls Ctyd. SE8	134	A7
Deptford High St.		
St. Pauls Cray Rd., Chis.	193	G1
St. Paul's Cres. NW1	92	D7
St. Pauls Dr. E15	96	D5
St. Paul's Ms. NW1	92	D7
St. Paul's Cres.		
St. Pauls Pl. N1	94	A6
St. Pauls Ri. N13	59	H6
St. Paul's Rd. N1	93	H6
St. Paul's Rd. N17	60	D7
St. Paul's Rd., Bark.	117	F1
St. Paul's Rd., Brent.	125	G6
St. Paul's Rd., Erith	139	J7
St. Paul's Rd., Rich.	145	J3
St. Paul's Rd., Th.Hth.	187	J3
St. Paul's Shrubbery N1	94	A6
St. Pauls Sq., Brom.	191	G2
St. Paul's Ter. SE17	35	H5
St. Pauls Twr. E10	78	B7
St. Pauls Wk., Kings.T.	164	A7
Alexandra Rd.		
St. Paul's Way E3	113	J5
St. Paul's Way E14	113	J5
St. Paul's Way N3	56	E7
St. Pauls Wd. Hill, Orp.	193	H2
St. Peter's All. EC3	20	C4
St. Peter's Av. E2	13	J2
St. Peter's Av. E17	78	E4
St. Peters Av. N18	60	D4
St. Peter's Cl. E2	13	J2
St. Peter's Cl. E2	112	D2
St. Peters Cl. SW17	167	H2
College Gdns.		
St. Peter's Cl., Barn.	39	H5
St. Peters Cl., Bushey	52	A1
St. Peter's Cl., Chis.	175	G7
St. Peters Cl., Ilf.	81	H4
St. Peter's Cl., Ruis.	84	D2
St. Peter's Ct. NW4	71	J5
St. Peters Ct. SE3	155	F4
Eltham Rd.		
St. Peters Ct. SE4	153	J2
Wickham Rd.		
St. Peters Ct., W.Mol.	179	G4
St. Peter's Gdns. SE27	169	G3
St. Peter's Gro. W6	127	G4
St. Peter's Pl. W9	6	A6
St. Peters Rd. N9	61	F1
St. Peter's Rd. W6	127	G5
St. Peter's Rd., Croy.	202	A4
St. Peters Rd., Kings.T.	182	A2
St. Peter's Rd., Sthl.	103	G5
St. Peter's Rd., Twick.	145	E5
St. Peter's Rd., W.Mol.	179	G4
St. Peter's Sq. E2	13	J2
St. Peters Sq. W6	127	G5
St. Peters St. N1	111	H1
St. Peter's St. S.Croy.	202	A5
St. Peters Ter. SW6	128	B7
St. Peter's Vil. W6	127	G4
St. Peter's Way N1	94	B7
St. Peters Way W5	105	G5
St. Peters Way, Hayes	121	G5
St. Petersburgh Ms. W2	14	A5
St. Petersburgh Ms. W2	108	E7
St. Petersburgh Pl. W2	14	A5
St. Petersburgh Pl. W2	108	E7
St. Philip Sq. SW8	150	B2
St. Philip St. SW8	150	B2
St. Philip's Av., Wor.Pk.	197	H2
St. Philip's Rd. E8	94	D6
St. Philips Rd., Surb.	181	G6
St. Philip's Way N1	111	J1
Linton St.		
St. Quentin Rd., Well.	157	J3
St. Quintin Av. W10	107	J5
St. Quintin Gdns. W10	107	J5
St. Quintin Rd. E13	115	H2
St. Raphael's Way NW10	88	C5
St. Regis Cl. N10	74	B2
St. Ronans Cres., Wdf.Grn.	63	G7
St. Rule St. SW8	150	C2
St. Saviour's Est. SE1	29	F5
St. Saviour's Est. SE1	132	C3
St. Saviour's Rd. SW2	151	F5
St. Saviours Rd., Croy.	187	J6
St. Silas Pl. NW5	92	A6
St. Silas St. Est. NW5	92	A6
St. Simon's Av. SW15	147	J5
St. Stephens Av. E17	78	C5
St. Stephens Av. W12	127	H2
St. Stephens Av. W13	104	E6
St. Stephens Cl. E17	78	B5
St. Stephens Cl. NW8	109	H1
St. Stephens Cl., Sthl.	103	G5
St. Stephens Cres. W2	108	D6
St. Stephens Cres., Th.Hth.	187	G3
St. Stephens Gdn. Est. W2	108	D6
Shrewsbury Rd.		
St. Stephens Gdns. SW15	148	C5
Manfred Rd.		
St. Stephens Gdns. W2	108	D6
St. Stephens Gdns., Twick.	145	F6
St. Stephens Gro. SE13	154	C3
St. Stephens Ms. W2	108	D5
Chepstow Rd.		
St. Stephen's Par. E7	97	J7
Green St.		
St. Stephen's Pas., Twick.	145	F6
Richmond Rd.		
St. Stephen's Rd. E3	113	J2
St. Stephens Rd. E6	97	J7
St. Stephen's Rd. E17	78	B5
Grove Rd.		
St. Stephens Rd. W13	105	E6
St. Stephen's Rd., Barn.	40	A5
St. Stephens Rd., Houns.	143	G6
St. Stephens Rd., West Dr.	120	A1
St. Stephens Row EC4	20	B4
St. Stephens Ter. SW8	131	F7
St. Stephen's Wk. SW7	30	C1
St. Stephen's Wk. SW7	129	F4
St. Swithin's La. EC4	20	B5
St. Swithin's La. EC4	112	A7
St. Swithun's Rd. SE13	154	D5
St. Theresa's Rd., Felt.	141	J4
St. Thomas' Cl., Surb.	195	J1
St. Thomas Cl., Bex.	159	G7
St. Thomas Dr., Orp.	207	F1
St. Thomas' Dr., Pnr.	67	E1
St. Thomas Gdns., Ilf.	99	F6
St. Thomas Pl. NW1	92	D7
St. Thomas Rd. E16	115	G6
St. Thomas Rd. N14	42	D7
St. Thomas' Rd. W4	126	C6
St. Thomas Rd., Belv.	139	J2

St. Thomas St. SE1 **28 B2**
St. Thomas St. SE1 132 A1
St. Thomas's Gdns. 92 A6
NW5
Queens Cres.
St. Thomas's Pl. E9 95 F7
St. Thomas's Rd. N4 93 G2
St. Thomas's Rd. 107 E1
NW10
St. Thomas's Sq. E9 95 E7
St. Thomas's Way 128 C7
SW6
St. Timothy's Ms., 191 H1
Brom.
Wharton Rd.
St. Ursula Gro., Pnr. 66 D5
St. Ursula Rd., Sthl. 103 G6
St. Vincent Cl. SE27 169 H5
St. Vincent Rd., 143 J6
Twick.
St. Vincent St. W1 16 C2
St. Wilfrids Cl., Barn. 41 H5
St. Wilfrids Rd., Barn. 41 G5
St. Winefride's Av. 98 C5
E12
St. Winifreds Cl., 65 F5
Chig.
St. Winifred's Rd., 163 E6
Tedd.
Saints Cl. SE27 169 H4
Wolfington Rd.
Saints Dr. E7 98 A5
Salamanca Pl. SE1 34 C2
Salamanca St. SE1 34 B2
Salamanca St. SE1 131 F4
Salamander Cl., 163 F5
Kings.T.
Salcombe Dr., Mord. 198 A1
Salcombe Dr., Rom. 83 F6
Salcombe Gdns. NW7 55 J6
Salcombe Pk., Loug. 48 A5
High La.
Salcombe Rd. E17 77 J7
Salcombe Rd. N16 94 B5
Salcombe Way, Ruis. 84 A2
Salcott Rd. SW11 149 H5
Salcott Rd., Croy. 201 E3
Sale Pl. W2 15 G2
Sale Pl. W2 109 H5
Sale St. E2 13 H5
Salehurst Cl., Har. 69 H5
Salehurst Rd. SE4 153 J6
Salem Pl., Croy. 201 J3
Salem Rd. W2 14 B5
Salem Rd. W2 109 E7
Salford Rd. SW2 168 D1
Salhouse Cl. SE28 118 C6
Rollesby Way
Salisbury Av. N3 72 C3
Salisbury Av., Bark. 99 H7
Salisbury Av., Sutt. 198 C6
Salisbury Cl. SE17 36 B1
Salisbury Cl., 197 F3
Wor.Pk.
Salisbury Ct. EC4 19 G4
Salisbury Ct. EC4 111 H6
Salisbury Gdns. 166 B7
SW19
Salisbury Gdns., 64 A2
Buck.H.
Salisbury Hall Gdns. 62 A6
E4
Salisbury Ho. E14 114 B6
Hobday St.
Salisbury Ms. SW6 128 C7
Dawes St.
Salisbury Ms., Brom. 192 B5
Salisbury Rd.
Salisbury Pl. SW9 131 H7
Salisbury Pl. W1 15 J1
Salisbury Pl. W1 109 J5
Salisbury Rd. E4 62 A3
Salisbury Rd. E7 97 G6
Salisbury Rd. E10 96 C2
Salisbury Rd. E12 98 A5
Salisbury Rd. E17 78 C5
Salisbury Rd. N4 75 H5
Salisbury Rd. N9 60 D3
Salisbury Rd. N22 75 H1
Salisbury Rd. SE25 188 D6
Salisbury Rd. SW19 166 B7
Salisbury Rd. W13 124 D2
Salisbury Rd., Barn. 40 B3
Salisbury Rd., Bex. 177 G1
Salisbury Rd., Brom. 192 B5
Salisbury Rd., Cars. 199 J6
Salisbury Rd., Dag. 101 H6
Salisbury Rd., Felt. 160 C1
Salisbury Rd., Har. 68 A5
Salisbury Rd., Houns. 142 C3
Salisbury Rd. 141 F5
(Heathrow Airport), Houns.
Salisbury Rd., Ilf. 99 H2
Salisbury Rd., N.Mal. 182 D3

Salisbury Rd., Pnr. 66 A4
Salisbury Rd., Rich. 145 H4
Salisbury Rd., Sthl. 123 E4
Salisbury Rd., 197 F3
Wor.Pk.
Salisbury Sq. EC4 19 F4
Salisbury St. NW8 7 G6
Salisbury St. NW8 109 H4
Salisbury St. W3 126 C2
Salisbury Ter. SE15 153 F3
Salisbury Wk. N19 92 C2
Salix Cl., Sun. 160 B7
Oak Gro.
Salliesfield, Twick. 144 A6
Sally Murray Cl. E12 98 D4
Grantham Rd.
Salmen Rd. E13 115 F2
Salmon La. E14 113 H6
Salmon Rd., Belv. 139 G5
Salmon St. E14 113 J6
Salmon La.
Salmon St. NW9 88 B1
Salmond Cl., Stan. 52 D6
Robb Rd.
Salmons Rd. N9 60 D1
Salmons Rd., Chess. 195 G6
Chalk Rd.
Salomons Rd. E13 115 J5
Salop Rd. E17 77 G6
Saltash Cl., Sutt. 198 C4
Saltash Rd., Ilf. 65 G7
Saltash Rd., Well. 158 C1
Saltcoats Rd. W4 126 E2
Saltcroft Cl., Wem. 88 B1
Salter Cl., Har. 85 F3
Salter Rd. SE16 133 G1
Salter St. E14 114 A7
Salter St. NW10 107 G3
Salterford Rd. SW17 168 A6
Salters Hill SE19 170 A5
Salters Rd. E17 78 D4
Salters Rd. W10 108 A4
Salterton Rd. N7 93 E3
Saltley Cl. E6 116 B6
Dunnock Rd.
Saltoun Rd. SW2 151 G4
Saltram Cl. N15 76 C4
Saltram Cres. W9 108 C3
Saltwell St. E14 114 A7
Saltwood Gro. SE17 36 B4
Salusbury Rd. NW6 108 B1
Salutation Rd. SE10 135 E4
Salvia Gdns., Grnf. 104 D2
Selborne Gdns.
Salvin Rd. SW15 148 A3
Salway Cl., Wdf.Grn. 63 F7
Salway Pl. E15 96/97 E6
Broadway
Salway Rd. E15 96 D6
Sam Bartram Cl. SE7 135 J5
Samantha Cl. E17 77 J7
Sambruck Ms. SE6 172 B1
Samels Ct. W6 127 G5
South Black Lion La.
Samford St. NW8 7 F6
Samford St. NW8 109 G4
Samos Rd. SE20 189 E2
Sampson Av., Barn. 40 A5
Sampson Cl., Belv. 138 D3
Carrill Way
Sampson St. E1 29 J2
Sampson St. E1 132 D1
Samson St. E13 115 J2
Samuel Cl. E8 112 C1
Pownall Rd.
Samuel Cl. SE14 133 G6
Samuel Cl. SE18 136 B4
Samuel Gray Gdns. 181 G1
Kings.T.
Samuel Johnson Cl. 169 G4
SW16
Curtis Fld. Rd.
Samuel Lewis Trust 94 D4
Dws. E8
Amhurst Rd.
Samuel Lewis Trust 93 G7
Dws. N1
Liverpool Rd.
Samuel Lewis Trust 31 G2
Dws. SW3
Samuel Lewis Trust 128 D7
Dws. SW6
Samuel St. SE15 37 F7
Samuel St. SE15 132 C7
Samuel St. SE18 136 C4
Samuels Cl. W6 127 G5
South Black Lion La.
Sancroft Cl. NW2 89 H3
Sancroft Rd., Har. 68 C2
Sancroft St. SE11 34 D3
Sancroft St. SE11 131 F5
Sanctuary, The SW1 25 J4
Sanctuary, The, Bex. 158 D6

Sanctuary, The, 184 D6
Mord.
Sanctuary Rd., 140 D6
Houns.
Sanctuary St. SE1 28 A4
Sandal Rd. N18 60 D5
Sandal Rd., N.Mal. 182 D5
Sandal St. E15 114 E1
Sandale Cl. N16 94 A3
Stoke Newington Ch. St.
Sandall Cl. W5 105 H4
Sandall Rd. NW5 92 C6
Sandall Rd. W5 105 H4
Sandalwood Cl. E1 113 H4
Solebay St.
Sandalwood Rd., 160 B3
Felt.
Sandbach Pl. SE18 137 F4
Sandbourne Av. 184 E3
SW19
Sandbourne Rd. SE4 153 H2
Sandbrook Cl. NW7 54 D6
Sandbrook Rd. N16 94 B3
Sandby Grn. SE9 156 B3
Sandcroft Cl. N13 59 H6
Sandell St. SE1 27 E3
Sanders Cl., Hmptn. 161 J5
Sanders La. NW7 56 A7
Sanders Way N19 92 D1
Sussex Way
Sanderson Cl. NW5 92 B4
Sanderstead Av. 90 B2
NW2
Sanderstead Cl. 150 C7
SW12
Atkins Rd.
Sanderstead Rd. E10 95 H1
Sanderstead Rd., 202 A7
S.Croy.
Sandfield Gdns., 187 H3
Th.Hth.
Sandfield Pas., 187 J3
Th.Hth.
Sandfield Rd., Th.Hth. 187 H3
Sandford Av. N22 59 J7
Sandford Av., Loug. 49 F3
Sandford Cl. E6 116 C4
Sandford Ct. N16 94 B1
Sandford La. N16 94 C2
Lawrence Bldgs.
Sandford Rd. E6 116 B4
Sandford Rd., Bexh. 159 E4
Sandford Rd., Brom. 191 G4
Sandford St. SW6 128/129 E7
King's Rd.
Sandgate La. SW18 167 H1
Sandgate Rd., Well. 138 C7
Sandgate St. SE15 132 E6
Sandham Pt. 136/137 E4
SE18
Troy Ct.
Sandhills, Wall. 200 D4
Sandhurst Av., Har. 67 H6
Sandhurst Av., Surb. 182 B7
Sandhurst Cl. NW9 70 A3
Sandhurst Dr., Ilf. 99 J4
Sandhurst Rd. N9 45 F6
Sandhurst Rd. NW9 70 A3
Sandhurst Rd. SE6 172 D1
Sandhurst Rd., Bex. 158 D5
Sandhurst Rd., Sid. 175 J3
Sandhurst Way, 202 B7
S.Croy.
Sandiford Rd., Sutt. 198 C2
Sandiland Cres., 205 F2
Brom.
Sandilands, Croy. 202 D2
Sandilands Rd. SW6 148 E1
Sandison St. SE15 152 C3
Sandland St. WC1 18 D2
Sandland St. WC1 111 F5
Sandling Ri. SE9 174 D3
Sandlings, The N22 75 G2
Sandlings, The 152/153 E2
SE15
Pilkington Rd.
Sandmere Rd. SW4 150 E4
Sandon Cl., Esher 180 A7
Sandow Cres., Hayes 121 J3
Sandown Av., Dag. 101 J6
Sandown Cl., Houns. 142 A1
Sandown Rd. SE25 188 E5
Sandown Way, Nthlt. 85 G6
Sandpiper Cl. E17 77 G1
Sandpiper Cl. SE16 133 J2
Sandpiper Rd., Sutt. 198 B2
Gander Grn. La.
Sandpit Pl. SE7 136 B5
Sandpit Rd., Brom. 172 E5
Sandpits Rd., Croy. 203 G4
Sandpits Rd., Rich. 163 G2
Sandra Cl. N22 75 J1
New Rd.
Sandra Cl., Houns. 143 H5

Sandridge Cl., Har. 68 B4
Sandridge St. N4 93 J3
Queens Dr.
Sandridge St. N19 92 C2
Sandringham Av. 184 B2
SW20
Sandringham Cl. 166 A1
SW19
Sandringham Cl., 44 B2
Enf.
Sandringham Cl., Ilf. 81 F3
Sandringham Ct. W9 6 D4
Sandringham Cres., 85 G2
Har.
Sandringham Dr., 157 H2
Well.
Sandringham Gdns. 75 E6
N8
Sandringham Gdns. 57 G6
N12
Sandringham Gdns., 142 A1
Houns.
Sandringham Gdns., 81 F3
Ilf.
Sandringham Ms. W5 105 G7
High St.
Sandringham Rd. E7 97 J5
Sandringham Rd. E8 94 C5
Sandringham Rd. E10 78 D6
Sandringham Rd. 75 J3
N22
Sandringham Rd. 89 H6
NW2
Sandringham Rd. 72 B7
NW11
Sandringham Rd., 99 J6
Bark.
Sandringham Rd., 173 G5
Brom.
Sandringham Rd., 140 B5
Houns.
Sandringham Rd., 85 G7
Nthlt.
Sandringham Rd., 187 J5
Th.Hth.
Sandringham Rd., 197 G3
Wor.Pk.
Sandrock Pl., Croy. 203 G4
Sandrock Rd. SE13 154 A3
Sand's End La. SW6 149 E1
Sands Way, Wdf.Grn. 64 B6
Sandstone Pl. N19 92 B2
Sandstone Rd. SE12 173 H2
Sandtoft Rd. SE7 135 H6
Sandwell Cres. NW6 90 D6
Sandwich St. WC1 10 A4
Sandwich St. WC1 110 E3
Sandwick Cl. NW7 55 G7
Sebergham Gro.
Sandy Bury, Orp. 207 G3
Sandy Hill Av. SE18 136 E5
Sandy Hill Rd. SE18 136 E5
Sandy La., Har. 69 J6
Sandy La., Kings.T. 162 D7
Sandy La., Mitch. 186 A1
Sandy La., Nthwd. 50 A5
Sandy La., Rich. 163 F2
Sandy La., Sid. 176 D7
Sandy La., Sutt. 198 B7
Sandy La., Tedd. 162 D7
Sandy La., Walt. 178 B6
Sandy La. Est., Rich. 163 G2
Sandy La. N., Wall. 200 D5
Sandy La. S., Wall. 200 D6
Sandy Ridge, Chis. 174 D6
Sandy Rd. NW3 90 E3
Sandy Way, Croy. 203 J3
Sandycombe Rd., 160 A1
Felt.
Sandycombe Rd., 146 A3
Rich.
Sandycoombe Rd., 145 F6
Twick.
Sandycroft SE2 138 A6
Sandyhill Rd., Ilf. 98 E4
Sandymount Av., 53 F5
Stan.
Sandy's Row E1 21 E2
Sandy's Row E1 112 B5
Sanford La. N16 94 C2
Stoke Newington High St.
Sanford St. SE14 133 H6
Sanford Ter. N16 94 C3
Sanford Wk. N16 94 C2
Sanford Ter.
Sanford Wk. SE14 133 H6
Cold Blow La.
Sanger Av., Chess. 195 H5
Sangley Rd. SE6 154 B7
Sangley Rd. SE25 188 B4
Sangora Rd. SW11 149 G4
Sans Wk. EC1 11 F5
Sans Wk. EC1 111 G4
Sansom Rd. E11 97 E2

Sansom St. SE5 132 A7
Santley St. SW4 151 F4
Santos Rd. SW18 148 D5
Santway, The, Stan. 52 B5
Sapcote Trd. Cen. NW10 89 F5
Saperton Wk. SE11 34 D1
Saperton Wk. SE11 131 F4
Saphora Cl., Orp. 207 G5
Oleander Cl.
Sapphire Cl. E6 116 D6
Sapphire Cl., Dag. 100 C1
Sapphire Rd. SE8 133 H4
Sara Ct., Beck. 190 B1
Albemarle Rd.
Saracen Cl., Croy. 188 A6
Saracen St. E14 114 A6
Saracen's Head Yd. EC3 21 F4
Sarah Ho. SW15 147 F4
Sarah St. N1 12 E3
Saratoga Rd. E5 95 F4
Sardinia St. WC2 18 C4
Sarita Cl., Har. 68 A2
Sarjant Path SW19 166 A2
Queensmere Rd.
Sark Cl., Houns. 123 G7
Sark Wk. E16 115 H6
Sarnesfield Ho. SE15 132/133 E6
Pencraig Way
Sarnesfield Rd., Enf. 44 A3
Church St.
Sarre Rd. NW2 90 C5
Sarsen Av., Houns. 143 F2
Sarsfeld Rd. SW12 167 J1
Sarsfield Rd., Grnf. 105 E2
Sartor Rd. SE15 153 G4
Sarum Ter. E3 113 J4
Satanita Cl. E16 116 A6
Fulmer Rd.
Satchell Mead NW9 71 F1
Satchwell Rd. E2 13 H4
Satchwell Rd. E2 112 D3
Sauls Grn. E11 96/97 E3
Napier Rd.
Saunders Cl. E14 113 J7
Limehouse Causeway
Saunders Ness Rd. E14 134 C5
Saunders Rd. SE18 137 J5
Saunders St. SE11 34 E1
Saunders St. SE11 131 G4
Saunders Way SE28 118 B7
Oriole Way
Saunderton Rd., Wem. 86 E5
Saunton Av., Hayes 121 J7
Savage Gdns. E6 116 C6
Savage Gdns. EC3 21 E5
Savernake Rd. N9 44 D6
Savernake Rd. NW3 91 J4
Savery Dr., Surb. 181 F7
Savile Cl., N.Mal. 183 E5
Savile Cl., T.Ditt. 194 C1
Savile Gdns., Croy. 202 C2
Savile Row W1 17 F5
Savile Row W1 110 C7
Savill Gdns. SW20 183 G3
Bodnant Gdns.
Savill Row, Wdf.Grn. 63 F6
Saville Rd. E16 136 B1
Saville Rd. W4 126 D3
Saville Rd., Rom. 83 F6
Saville Rd., Twick. 162 C1
Saville Row, Brom. 205 F1
Saville Row, Enf. 45 G2
Savona Cl. SW19 166 B7
Savona Est. SW8 130 C7
Savona St. SW8 130 C7
Savoy Av., Hayes 121 H5
Savoy Bldgs. WC2 18 C6
Savoy Cl. E15 114/115 E1
Arthingworth St.
Savoy Cl., Edg. 54 A5
Savoy Ct. WC2 18 B6
Savoy Hill WC2 18 C6
Savoy Pl. WC2 18 B6
Savoy Pl. WC2 111 E7
Savoy Row WC2 18 C5
Savoy Steps WC2 111 F7
Savoy St.
Savoy St. WC2 18 C5
Savoy St. WC2 111 F7
Savoy Way WC2 18 C6
Sawbill Cl., Hayes 102 D5
Sawkins Cl. SW19 166 B2
Sawley Rd. W12 127 G1
Sawtry Cl., Cars. 185 H7
Sawyer Cl. N9 60 D2
Lion Rd.
Sawyer St. SE1 27 J3
Sawyer St. SE1 131 J2
Sawyers Cl., Dag. 101 J6
Sawyer's Hill, Rich. 146 B7
Sawyers Lawn W13 104 C6
Saxby Rd. SW2 150 E7
Saxham Rd., Bark. 117 J1
Saxlingham Rd. E4 62 D3
Saxon Av., Felt. 161 F2
Saxon Cl. E17 78 A7
Saxon Cl., Surb. 181 G6
Saxon Dr. W3 106 B6
Saxon Gdns., Sthl. 102/103 E7
Saxon Rd.
Saxon Rd. E3 113 J2
Saxon Rd. E6 116 C4
Saxon Rd. N22 75 H1
Saxon Rd. SE25 188 A5
Saxon Rd., Brom. 173 F7
Saxon Rd., Ilf. 99 E6
Saxon Rd., Sthl. 123 E1
Saxon Rd., Wem. 88 C3
Saxon Wk., Sid. 176 C6
Saxon Way N14 42 D6
Saxonbury Av., Sun. 178 B3
Saxonbury Cl., Mitch. 185 G3
Saxonbury Gdns., Surb. 195 F1
Saxonfield Cl. SW2 151 F7
Saxton Cl. SE13 154 D3
Sayers Wk., Rich. 145 J7
Stafford Pl.
Sayes Ct. SE8 133 J5
Sayes Ct. St.
Sayes Ct. St. SE8 133 J6
Sayesbury La. N18 60 D5
Scadbury Pk., Chis. 175 J6
Scads Hill Cl., Orp. 193 J6
Scala St. W1 17 G1
Scala St. W1 110 C5
Scales Rd. N17 76 C3
Scampston Ms. W10 108 A6
Scampton Rd., Houns. 140 C6
Southampton Rd.
Scandrett St. E1 132 E1
Scarba Wk. N1 94 A6
Marquess Rd.
Scarborough Rd. E11 96 D1
Scarborough Rd. N4 75 G7
Scarborough Rd. N9 45 F7
Scarborough Rd., Houns. 141 F6
Southern Perimeter Rd.
Scarborough St. E1 21 G4
Scarbrook Rd., Croy. 201 J3
Scarle Rd., Wem. 87 G6
Scarlet Rd. SE6 172 E3
Scarlette Manor Way SW2 151 G7
Papworth Way
Scarsbrook Rd. SE3 156 A3
Scarsdale Pl. W8 22 A5
Scarsdale Rd., Har. 85 J3
Scarsdale Vil. W8 128 D3
Scarth Rd. SW13 147 F3
Scawen Cl., Cars. 200 A4
Scawen Rd. SE8 133 H5
Scawfell St. E2 13 G2
Scawfell St. E2 112 C2
Scaynes Link N12 56 D5
Sceaux Est. SE5 152 B1
Sceaux Gdns. SE5 152 C1
Sceptre Rd. E2 113 F3
Schofield Wk. SE3 135 H7
Dornberg Cl.
Scholars Rd. E4 62 C1
Scholars Rd. SW12 168 C1
Scholefield Rd. N19 92 D1
Schonfeld Sq. N16 94 A2
School Ho. La., Tedd. 163 E7
School La. SE23 170 E2
School La., Kings.T. 181 F1
School Rd.
School La., Pnr. 66 E4
School La., Surb. 196 A1
School La., Well. 158 B3
School Pas., Kings.T. 181 J2
School Pas., Sthl. 123 F1
School Rd. E12 98 C4
School Rd. NW10 106 D4
School Rd., Chis. 193 F1
School Rd., Dag. 119 G1
School Rd., E.Mol. 180 A4
School Rd., Hmptn. 161 J6
School Rd., Houns. 143 J3
School Rd., Kings.T. 181 F1
School Rd., West Dr. 120 A6
School Rd. Av., Hmptn. 161 J6
School Way N12 57 F4
High Rd.
School Way, Dag. 100 C3
Schoolbell Ms. E3 113 H2
Arbery Rd.
Schoolhouse Gdns., Loug. 48 E4
Schoolhouse La. E1 113 G7
Schoolway N12 57 G6
Schooner Cl. E14 134 D3
Schooner Cl. SE16 133 G2
Kinburn St.
Schooner Cl., Bark. 117 H3
Thames Rd.
Schubert Rd. SW15 148 C5
Sclater St. E1 13 F5
Sclater St. E1 112 C4
Scoble Pl. N16 94 C4
Amhurst Rd.
Scoles Cres. SW2 169 G1
Scoresby St. SE1 27 G2
Scoresby St. SE1 131 H1
Scorton Av., Grnf. 104 D2
Scot Gro., Pnr. 50 D7
Scotch Common W13 104 D5
Scoter Cl., Wdf.Grn. 63 H7
Mallards Rd.
Scotia Rd. SW2 151 G7
Scotland Grn. N17 76 D2
Scotland Grn. Rd., Enf. 45 G5
Scotland Grn. Rd. N., Enf. 45 G4
Scotland Pl. SW1 26 A1
Scotland Rd., Buck.H. 63 J1
Scotsdale Cl., Orp. 193 H4
Scotsdale Cl., Sutt. 198 B7
Scotsdale Rd. SE12 155 H5
Scotswood St. EC1 11 F5
Scotswood Wk. N17 60 D7
Scott Cl. SW16 187 F1
Scott Cl., Epsom 196 C5
Scott Cl., West Dr. 120 C4
Scott Ct. W3 126 C2
Petersfield Rd.
Scott Cres., Har. 85 H1
Scott Ellis Gdns. NW8 6 E4
Scott Ellis Gdns. NW8 109 G3
Scott Fm. Cl., T.Ditt. 194 E1
Scott Gdns., Houns. 122 D7
Scott Ho. N18 60 D5
Scott Lidgett Cres. SE16 29 H4
Scott Lidgett Cres. SE16 132 D2
Scott Russell Pl. E14 134 B5
Westferry Rd.
Scott St. E1 112 E4
Scott Trimmer Way, Houns. 143 E2
Scottes La., Dag. 100 D1
Valence Av.
Scotts Av., Brom. 190 D2
Scotts Dr., Hmptn. 161 H7
Scotts Fm. Rd., Epsom 196 C6
Scotts La., Brom. 190 D3
Scotts Rd. E10 96 C1
Scotts Rd. W12 127 H2
Scotts Rd., Brom. 173 G7
Scotts Rd., Sthl. 122 C3
Scott's Yd. EC4 20 B5
Scottwell Dr. NW9 71 F5
Crossway
Scoulding Rd. E16 115 F6
Scouler St. E14 114 D7
Quixley St.
Scout App. NW10 88 E4
Scout La. SW4 150 C3
Old Town
Scout Way NW7 54 D4
Scovell Cres. SE1 27 J4
Scovell Rd. SE1 27 J4
Scrattons Ter., Bark. 118 D2
Scriven St. E8 112 C1
Scrooby St. SE6 154 B6
Scrubs La. NW10 107 G3
Scrubs La. W10 107 G3
Scrutton Cl. SW12 150 D7
Scrutton St. EC2 12 D6
Scrutton St. EC2 112 B4
Scudamore La. NW9 70 C3
Scutari Rd. SE22 153 F5
Scylla Cres., Houns. 141 E7
Scylla Rd. SE15 152 E3
Scylla Rd., Houns. 141 E6
Seabright St. E2 112/113 E3
Bethnal Grn. Rd.
Seabrook Dr., W.Wick. 204 E2
Seabrook Gdns., Rom. 83 G7
Seabrook Rd., Dag. 100 D3
Seacole Cl. W3 106 D5
Seacourt Rd. SE2 138 D2
Seacroft Gdns., Wat. 50 D3
Seafield Rd. N11 58 D4
Seaford Rd. E17 78 B3
Seaford Rd. N15 76 A5
Seaford Rd. W13 124 E1
Seaford Rd., Enf. 44 B4
Seaford Rd., Houns. 140 A5
Seaford St. WC1 10 B4
Seaford St. WC1 111 E3
Seaforth Av., N.Mal. 183 H5
Seaforth Cres. N5 93 J5
Seaforth Gdns. N21 43 F7
Seaforth Gdns., Epsom 197 F4
Seaforth Gdns., Wdf.Grn. 63 J5
Seaforth Pl. SW1 130 C3
Buckingham Gate
Seagrave Rd. SW6 128 D6
Seagry Rd. E11 79 G6
Seagull Cl., Bark. 117 H3
Thames Rd.
Seal St. E8 94 C4
Sealand Rd., Houns. 140 D6
Sealand Wk., Nthlt. 102/103 E3
Wayfarer Rd.
Searle Pl. N4 93 F1
Evershot Rd.
Searles Cl. SW11 129 H7
Searles Dr. E6 116 D5
Winsor Ter.
Searles Rd. SE1 36 C1
Searles Rd. SE1 132 A4
Sears St. SE5 36 B7
Sears St. SE5 132 A7
Seasprite Cl., Nthlt. 102 D3
Seaton Av., Ilf. 99 H5
Seaton Cl. E13 115 H4
New Barn St.
Seaton Cl. SE11 35 F3
Seaton Cl. SE11 131 G5
Seaton Cl. SW15 165 H1
Seaton Cl., Twick. 144 A6
Seaton Gdns., Ruis. 84 A3
Seaton Pt. E5 94 D4
Nolan Way
Seaton Rd., Hayes 121 G4
Seaton Rd., Mitch. 185 H2
Seaton Rd., Twick. 143 J6
Seaton Rd., Well. 138 C7
Seaton Rd., Wem. 105 H2
Seaton St. N18 60 D5
Sebastian St. EC1 11 H4
Sebastian St. EC1 111 H3
Sebastopol Rd. N9 60 D4
Sebbon St. N1 93 H7
Sebergham Gro. NW7 55 G7
Sebert Rd. E7 97 H5
Sebright Pas. E2 13 J2
Sebright Rd., Barn. 40 A2
Secker Cres., Har. 67 J1
Secker St. SE1 27 E2
Second Av. E12 98 B4
Second Av. E13 115 G3
Second Av. E17 78 A5
Second Av. N18 61 F4
Second Av. NW4 72 A4
Second Av. SW14 146 E3
Second Av. W3 127 F1
Second Av. W10 108 B4
Second Av., Dag. 119 H1
Second Av., Enf. 44 C5
Second Av., Hayes 121 J1
Second Av., Rom. 82 C5
Second Av., Walt. 178 B6
Second Av., Wem. 87 G2
Second Cl., W.Mol. 179 J4
Second Cross Rd., Twick. 162 B2
Second Way, Wem. 88 B4
Sedan Way SE17 36 D3
Sedcombe Cl., Sid. 176 B4
Knoll Rd.
Sedcote Rd., Enf. 45 F5
Sedding St. SW1 32 B1
Sedding St. SW1 130 A4
Seddon Rd., Mord. 185 G5
Seddon St. WC1 10 D4
Sedge Rd. N17 61 F7
Sedgebrook Rd. SE3 156 A2
Sedgecombe Av., Har. 69 F5
Sedgeford Rd. W12 127 F1
Sedgehill Rd. SE6 172 A4
Sedgemere Av. N2 73 F3
Sedgemere Rd. SE2 138 C3
Sedgemoor Dr., Dag. 101 G4
Sedgeway SE6 173 F1
Sedgewood Cl., Brom. 191 F7
Sedgmoor Pl. SE5 132 B7
Sedgwick Rd. E10 96 C2
Sedgwick St. E9 95 G5
Sedleigh Rd. SW18 148 C6

Skipworth Rd. E9 113 F1
Skomer Wk. N1 93 J6
Clephane Rd.
Sky Peals Rd., Wdf.Grn. 78 D1
Skyport Dr., West Dr. 120 A7
Slade, The SE18 137 H6
Slade Ho., Houns. 143 F6
Slade Twr. E10 96 B2
Slade Wk. SE17 35 H6
Sladebrook Rd. SE3 156 A2
Sladedale Rd. SE18 137 H5
Slades Cl., Enf. 43 G3
Slades Dr., Chis. 175 F3
Slades Gdns., Enf. 43 G2
Slades Hill, Enf. 43 G3
Slades Ri., Enf. 43 G3
Slagrove Pl. SE13 154 B5
Slaidburn St. SW10 30 D6
Slaidburn St. SW10 129 F6
Slaithwaite Rd. SE13 154 C4
Slaney Pl. N7 93 G5
Hornsey Rd.
Slater Cl. SE18 136 D5
Woolwich New Rd.
Slattery Rd., Felt. 160 C1
Sleaford Grn., Wat. 50 D3
Sleaford St. SW8 33 F7
Sleaford St. SW8 130 C7
Slievemore Cl. SW4 150 D3
Voltaire Rd.
Slingsby Pl. WC2 18 A5
Slippers Pl. SE16 133 E3
Sloane Av. SW3 31 G2
Sloane Av. SW3 129 H4
Sloane Ct. E. SW3 32 B3
Sloane Ct. W. SW3 32 B3
Sloane Ct. W. SW3 130 A5
Sloane Gdns. SW1 32 B2
Sloane Gdns. SW1 130 A4
Sloane Gdns., Orp. 207 F3
Sloane Sq. SW1 32 B2
Sloane Sq. SW1 129 J4
Sloane St. SW1 24 A5
Sloane St. SW1 129 J2
Sloane Ter. SW1 32 A1
Sloane Ter. SW1 129 J4
Sloane Wk., Croy. 189 J6
Slocum Cl. SE28 118 C7
Slough La. NW9 70 C6
Sly St. E1 112/113 E6
Cannon St. Rd.
Smaldon Cl., West Dr. 120 D3
Walnut Av.
Smallberry Av., Islw. 144 C2
Smallbrook Ms. W2 14 E4
Smalley Cl. N16 94 C3
Smalley Rd. Est. N16 94 C3
Smalley Cl.
Smallwood Rd. SW17 167 G4
Smardale Rd. SW18 149 F5
Alma Rd.
Smarden Cl., Belv. 139 G5
Essenden Rd.
Smarden Gro. SE9 174 C4
Smart St. E2 113 G3
Smarts La., Loug. 48 A4
Smarts Pl. N18 60 D5
Fore St.
Smart's Pl. WC2 18 B3
Smeaton Cl., Chess. 195 G6
Merritt Gdns.
Smeaton Rd. SW18 148 D7
Smeaton Rd., Wdf.Grn. 64 C5
Smeaton St. E1 132 E1
Smedley St. SW4 150 D2
Smedley St. SW8 150 D2
Smeed Rd. E3 96 A7
Smiles Pl. SE13 154 C2
Smith Cl. SE16 133 G1
Smith Sq. SW1 26 A6
Smith Sq. SW1 130 E3
Smith St. SW3 31 J3
Smith St. SW3 129 J5
Smith St., Surb. 181 J6
Smith Ter. SW3 31 J4
Smith Ter. SW3 129 J5
Smithfield St. EC1 19 G2
Smithies Ct. E15 96 C5
Smithies Rd. SE2 138 B4
Smith's Ct. W1 17 G5
Smiths Fm. Est., Nthlt. 103 G2
Smiths Yd. SW18 167 F2
Summerley St.
Smith's Yd., Croy. 201 J3
St. Georges Wk.
Smithson Rd. N17 76 A1
Smithwood Cl. SW19 166 B1
Smithy St. E1 113 F5
Smock Wk., Croy. 187 J6
Smokehouse Yd. EC1 19 H1
Smokehouse Yd. EC1 111 H5
Smugglers Way SW18 149 E4
Smyrks Rd. SE17 36 E4
Smyrks Rd. SE17 132 B5
Smyrna Rd. NW6 90 D7
Smythe St. E14 114 B7
Snakes La., Barn. 42 B3
Snakes La. E., Wdf.Grn. 63 J6
Snakes La. W., Wdf.Grn. 63 G6
Snaresbrook Dr., Stan. 53 G4
Snaresbrook Rd. E11 78 E4
Snarsgate St. W10 107 J5
Sneath Av. NW11 72 C7
Snells Pk. N18 60 C6
Sneyd Rd. NW2 89 J4
Snow Hill EC1 19 G2
Snow Hill EC1 111 H5
Snow Hill Ct. EC1 19 H3
Snowberry Cl. E15 96 D4
Snowbury Rd. SW6 149 E2
Snowden St. EC2 12 D6
Snowden St. EC2 112 B4
Snowdon Cres., Hayes 121 F3
Snowdon Dr. NW9 70 E6
Snowdon Rd., Houns. 141 F5
Southern Perimeter Rd.
Snowdown Cl. SE20 189 G1
Snowdrop Cl., Hmptn. 161 G6
Gresham Rd.
Snowman Ho. NW6 109 E1
Snowsfields SE1 28 C3
Snowsfields SE1 132 A2
Snowshill Rd. E12 98 B5
Snowy Fielder Waye, Islw. 144 E2
Soames St. SE15 152 C3
Soames Wk., N.Mal. 182 E1
Socket La., Brom. 191 H7
Soho Sq. W1 17 H3
Soho Sq. W1 110 D6
Soho St. W1 17 H3
Sojourner Truth Cl. E8 94/95 E6
Richmond Rd.
Solander Gdns. E1 112/113 E7
Dellow St.
Solebay St. E1 113 H4
Solent Ri. E13 115 G3
Solent Rd. NW6 90 D5
Solent Rd., Houns. 140 C6
Soley Ms. WC1 10 E3
Solna Av. SW15 147 J5
Solna Rd. N21 60 A1
Solomon Av. N9 60 D4
Solomon's Pas. SE15 152 E4
Solon New Rd. SW4 150 E4
Solon New Rd. Est. SW4 150/151 E4
Solon New Rd.
Solon Rd. SW2 151 E4
Solway Cl. E8 94 C6
Buttermere Wk.
Solway Cl., Houns. 143 E3
Solway Rd. N22 75 H1
Solway Rd. SE22 152 D4
Somaford Gro., Barn. 41 G6
Somali Rd. NW2 90 C4
Somerby Rd., Bark. 99 G7
Somercoates Cl., Barn. 41 H3
Somerfield Rd. N4 93 H2
Somerford Cl., Pnr. 66 A4
Somerford Gro. N16 94 C4
Somerford Gro. N17 60 D7
Somerford Gro. Est. N16 94 C4
Somerford Gro.
Somerford St. E1 112 E4
Somerford Way SE16 133 H2
Somerhill Av., Sid. 158 B7
Somerhill Rd., Well. 158 B2
Somerleyton Pas. SW9 151 H4
Somerleyton Rd. SW9 151 G4
Somers Cl. NW1 9 H1
Somers Cres. W2 15 G4
Somers Cres. W2 109 H6
Somers Ms. W2 15 G4
Somers Pl. SW2 151 F7
Somers Rd. E17 77 J4
Somers Rd. SW2 151 F6
Somersby Gdns., Ilf. 80 C5
Somerset Av. SW20 183 H2
Somerset Av., Chess. 195 G4
Somerset Av., Well. 157 J5
Somerset Cl. N17 76 A2
Somerset Cl., N.Mal. 183 E6
Somerset Cl., Wdf.Grn. 79 G1
Somerset Est. SW11 149 G1
Somerset Gdns. N6 74 A7
Somerset Gdns. N17 60 B7
Somerset Gdns. SE13 154 B2
Somerset Gdns. SW16 187 F3
Somerset Gdns., Tedd. 162 B5
Somerset Rd. E17 78 A5
Somerset Rd. N17 76 C3
Somerset Rd. N18 60 C5
Somerset Rd. NW4 71 J4
Somerset Rd. SW19 166 B4
Somerset Rd. W4 126 D3
Somerset Rd. W13 125 E1
Somerset Rd., Barn. 41 E5
Somerset Rd., Brent. 125 F6
Somerset Rd., Har. 67 J5
Somerset Rd., Kings.T. 181 J2
Somerset Rd., Sthl. 103 F5
Somerset Rd., Tedd. 162 B5
Somerset Sq. W14 128 B2
Somerset Waye, Houns. 122 E6
Somersham Rd., Bexh. 159 E2
Somerton Av., Rich. 146 B3
Somerton Rd. NW2 90 B3
Somerton Rd. SE15 153 E4
Somertrees Av. SE12 173 H2
Somervell Rd., Har. 85 F5
Somerville Av. SW13 127 H6
Somerville Rd. SE20 171 G7
Somerville Rd., Rom. 82 C6
Sonderburg Rd. N7 93 F2
Sondes St. SE17 36 B5
Sondes St. SE17 132 A6
Sonia Ct., Har. 68 C6
Sonia Gdns. N12 57 F4
Woodside Av.
Sonia Gdns. NW10 89 F4
Sonia Gdns., Houns. 123 G7
Sonning Gdns., Hmptn. 161 E6
Sonning Rd. SE25 188 D6
Soper Cl. E4 61 J5
Sophia Cl. N7 93 F6
Mackenzie Rd.
Sophia Rd. E10 96 B1
Sophia Rd. E16 115 H6
Sophia Sq. SE16 113 H7
Rotherhithe St.
Sopwith Av., Chess. 195 H5
Sopwith Cl., Kings.T. 163 J5
Sopwith Rd., Houns. 122 C7
Sopwith Way SW8 32 D7
Sopwith Way SW8 130 B7
Sopwith Way, Kings.T. 181 H1
Sorrel Cl. SE28 138 A1
Sorrel Gdns. E6 116 B5
Sorrel La. E14 114 D6
Sorrell Cl. SE14 133 H7
Southerngate Way
Sorrento Rd., Sutt. 198 E3
Sotheby Rd. N5 93 H3
Sotheran Cl. E8 112 D1
Sotheron Rd. SW6 129 E7
Soudan Rd. SW11 149 J1
Souldern Rd. W14 128 A3
South Access Rd. E17 77 H7
South Acre NW9 71 E2
South Africa Rd. W12 127 H1
South Audley St. W1 16 C6
South Audley St. W1 110 A7
South Av. E4 46 B7
South Av., Cars. 199 J7
South Av., Rich. 146 A2
Sandycombe Rd.
South Av., Sthl. 103 F7
South Av. Gdns., Sthl. 103 F7
South Bank, Chis. 175 F4
South Bank, Surb. 181 H6
South Bank Ter., Surb. 181 H6
South Birkbeck Rd. E11 96 D3
South Black Lion La. W6 127 G5
South Bolton Gdns. SW5 30 B3
South Bolton Gdns. SW5 129 E5
South Carriage Dr. SW1 23 J3
South Carriage Dr. SW1 129 H2
South Carriage Dr. SW7 23 F4
South Carriage Dr. SW7 129 H2
South Cl. N6 74 B6
South Cl., Barn. 40 C3
South Cl., Bexh. 158 D4
South Cl., Dag. 119 G1
South Cl., Mord. 184/185 E6
Green La.
South Cl., Pnr. 67 F7
South Cl., Twick. 161 G3
South Cl., West Dr. 120 C3
South Colonnade E14 134 A1
South Countess Rd. E17 77 J3
South Cres. E16 114 D4
South Cres. WC1 17 H2
South Cres. WC1 110 D5
South Cross Rd., Ilf. 81 F5
South Croxted Rd. SE21 170 A3
South Dene NW7 54 D3
South Dr., Orp. 207 H5
South Ealing Rd. W5 125 G2
South Eastern Av. N9 60 C3
South Eaton Pl. SW1 32 C1
South Eaton Pl. SW1 130 A4
South Eden Pk. Rd., Beck. 190 B6
South Edwardes Sq. W8 128 C3
South End W8 22 B5
South End, Croy. 201 J4
South End Cl. NW3 91 H4
South End Grn. NW3 91 H4
South End Rd.
South End Rd. NW3 91 H4
South End Row W8 22 B5
South End Row W8 129 E3
South Esk Rd. E7 97 J6
South Gdns. SW19 167 G7
South Gipsy Rd., Well. 158 D3
South Glade, The, Bex. 177 F1
South Grn. NW9 70/71 E1
Clayton Fld.
South Gro. E17 77 J5
South Gro. N6 92 A1
South Gro. N15 76 A5
South Gro. Ho. N6 92 A1
Highgate W. Hill
South Hill, Chis. 174 C6
South Hill Av., Har. 85 J3
South Hill Gro., Har. 86 B4
South Hill Pk. NW3 91 H4
South Hill Pk. Gdns. NW3 91 H4
South Hill Rd., Brom. 190 E3
South Huxley N18 60 A5
South Island Pl. SW9 131 F7
South Kensington Sta. Arc. SW7 129 G4
Pelham St.
South Lambeth Pl. SW8 34 B5
South Lambeth Pl. SW8 131 E6
South Lambeth Rd. SW8 131 E7
South La., Kings.T. 181 G3
South La., N.Mal. 182 D4
South La. W., N.Mal. 182 D4
South Lo. Av., Mitch. 186 E4
South Lo. Cres., Enf. 42 D4
South Lo. Dr. N14 42 E5
South Mall N9 60 D3
Plevna Rd.
South Mead NW9 71 F1
South Mead, Epsom 197 E7
South Meadows, Wem. 87 J5
South Molton La. W1 16 D4
South Molton La. W1 110 B6
South Molton Rd. E16 115 G6
South Molton St. W1 16 D4
South Molton St. W1 110 B6
South Norwood Hill SE25 188 B2
South Oak Rd. SW16 169 F4
South Par. SW3 31 F3
South Par. SW3 129 G5
South Par. W4 126 D4
South Pk. SW6 148 D2
South Pk. Cres. SE6 173 F1
South Pk. Cres., Ilf. 99 G3
South Pk. Dr., Bark. 99 H4
South Pk. Dr., Ilf. 99 H4
South Pk. Gro., N.Mal. 182 C4
South Pk. Hill Rd., S.Croy. 202 A5

South Pk. Ms. SW6	148	E3
South Pk. Rd. SW19	166	D6
South Pk. Rd., Ilf.	99	G3
South Pk. Ter., Ilf.	99	H3
South Pk. Way, Ruis.	84	C6
South Penge Pk. Est. SE20	188	E2
South Pl. EC2	**20**	**C1**
South Pl. EC2	112	A5
South Pl., Enf.	45	E7
South Pl., Surb.	181	J7
South Pl. Ms. EC2	**20**	**C2**
South Ri. Way SE18	137	G5
South Rd. N9	60	D1
South Rd. SE23	171	G2
South Rd. SW19	167	F6
South Rd. W5	125	G4
South Rd., Edg.	70	B1
South Rd., Felt.	160	D5
South Rd., Hmptn.	161	H6
South Rd. (Chadwell Heath), Rom.	82	C5
South Rd. (Little Heath), Rom.	82	E6
South Rd., Sthl.	123	F2
South Rd., Twick.	162	A3
South Rd., West Dr.	120	D3
South Row SE3	155	F2
South Sea St. SE16	133	J3
South Side W6	127	F3
South Sq. NW11	72	E6
South Sq. WC1	**18**	**E2**
South St. W1	**24**	**C1**
South St. W1	130	A1
South St., Brom.	191	G2
South St., Enf.	45	G5
South St., Islw.	144	D3
South St., Rain.	119	J2
South Tenter St. E1	**21**	**G5**
South Tenter St. E1	112	C7
South Ter. SW7	**31**	**G1**
South Ter. SW7	129	H4
South Ter., Surb.	181	H6
South Vale SE19	170	B6
South Vale, Har.	86	B4
South Vw., Brom.	191	H2
South Vw. Dr. E18	79	H3
South Vw. Rd. N8	74	D3
South Vw. Rd., Loug.	48	C6
South Vw. Rd., Pnr.	50	B6
South Vil. NW1	92	D6
South Wk., W.Wick.	204	E3
South Way N9	61	F2
South Way N11	58	C6
Ringway		
South Way, Brom.	191	G7
South Way, Croy.	203	H3
South Way, Har.	67	G4
South Way, Wem.	88	A5
South W. India Dock Entrance E14	134	C2
Prestons Rd.		
South Western Rd., Twick.	144	D6
South Wf. Rd. W2	**15**	**E3**
South Wf. Rd. W2	109	G6
South Woodford to Barking Relief Rd. E11	79	J4
South Woodford to Barking Relief Rd. E12	98	D3
South Woodford to Barking Relief Rd. E18	79	J4
South Woodford to Barking Relief Rd., Bark.	98	D3
South Woodford to Barking Relief Rd., Ilf.	98	D3
South Worple Av. SW14	146	E3
South Worple Way SW14	146	D3
Southacre Way, Pnr.	66	C1
Southall La., Houns.	122	B6
Southall La., Sthl.	122	C4
Southall Pl. SE1	**28**	**B4**
Southall Pl. SE1	132	A2
Southam St. W10	108	B4
Southampton Bldgs. WC2	**18**	**E3**
Southampton Gdns., Mitch.	186	E5
Southampton Ms. E16	135	H1
Wesley Av.		
Southampton Pl. WC1	**18**	**B2**
Southampton Pl. WC1	111	E5
Southampton Rd. NW5	91	J5
Southampton Rd., Houns.	140	D6
Southampton Row WC1	**18**	**B1**
Southampton Row WC1	111	E5
Southampton St. WC2	**18**	**B5**

Southampton St. WC2	111	E7
Southampton Way SE5	**36**	**C7**
Southampton Way SE5	132	A7
Southbank, T.Ditt.	180	E7
Southborough Cl., Surb.	195	G1
Southborough La., Brom.	192	B5
Southborough Rd. E9	113	F1
Southborough Rd., Brom.	192	B3
Southborough Rd., Surb.	195	H1
Southbourne, Brom.	191	G7
Southbourne Av. NW9	70	C2
Southbourne Cl., Pnr.	67	E7
Southbourne Cres. NW4	72	B4
Southbourne Gdns. SE12	155	H5
Southbourne Gdns., Ilf.	99	F5
Southbourne Gdns., Ruis.	84	B1
Southbridge Pl., Croy.	201	J4
Southbridge Rd., Croy.	201	J4
Southbridge Way, Sthl.	123	E2
Southbrook Ms. SE12	155	F6
Southbrook Rd. SE12	155	F6
Southbrook Rd. SW16	187	E1
Southbury Av., Enf.	44	D5
Southbury Rd., Enf.	44	A3
Southchurch Rd. E6	116	C2
Southcombe St. W14	128	B4
Southcote Av., Surb.	182	B7
Southcote Rd. E17	77	G5
Southcote Rd. N19	92	C4
Southcote Rd. SE25	189	E6
Southcroft Av., Well.	157	H3
Southcroft Av., W.Wick.	204	C2
Southcroft Rd. SW16	168	A6
Southcroft Rd. SW17	168	A6
Southcroft Rd., Orp.	207	H3
Southdale, Chig.	65	G6
Southdean Gdns. SW19	166	C2
Southdown Av. W7	124	D3
Southdown Cres., Har.	85	H1
Southdown Cres., Ilf.	81	H5
Southdown Dr. SW20	166	A7
Crescent Rd.		
Southdown Rd. SW20	184	A1
Southend Cl. SE9	156	E6
Southend Cres. SE9	156	D6
Southend La. SE6	171	J4
Southend La. SE26	171	J4
Southend Rd. E4	61	H5
Southend Rd. E6	98	C7
Southend Rd. E17	78	B1
Southend Rd. E18	79	G1
Southend Rd., Beck.	172	A7
Southend Rd., Wdf.Grn.	79	J2
Southern Av. SE25	188	C3
Southern Av., Felt.	160	A1
Southern Dr., Loug.	48	C6
Southern Gro. E3	113	J3
Southern Perimeter Rd., Houns.	141	G5
Southern Rd. E13	115	H2
Southern Rd. N2	73	J4
Southern Row W10	108	B4
Southern St. N1	**10**	**C1**
Southern St. N1	111	F2
Southern Way, Rom.	83	G6
Southerngate Way SE14	133	H7
Southernhay, Loug.	48	A5
Southerton Rd. W6	127	J3
Southey Ms. E16	135	G1
Wesley Av.		
Southey Rd. N15	76	B5
Southey Rd. SW9	151	G1
Southey Rd. SW19	166	D7
Southey St. SE20	171	G7
Southfield, Barn.	40	A6
Southfield Cotts. W7	124	C3
Oaklands Rd.		
Southfield Gdns., Twick.	162	C4
Southfield Pk., Har.	67	H4
Southfield Rd. N17	76	B2
The Av.		
Southfield Rd. W4	126	E3

Southfield Rd., Chis.	193	J3
Southfield Rd., Enf.	45	E6
Southfields NW4	71	G2
Southfields, E.Mol.	180	B6
Southfields Ct. SW19	166	B1
Southfields Pas. SW18	148	D6
Southfields Rd. SW18	148	D6
Southfleet Rd., Orp.	207	H3
Southgate Circ. N14	58	D1
The Bourne		
Southgate Gro. N1	94	A7
Southgate Rd. N1	94	A7
Southholme Cl. SE19	188	B1
Southill La., Pnr.	66	A4
Southill Rd., Chis.	174	B7
Southill St. E14	114	B6
Chrisp St.		
Southland Rd. SE18	137	J7
Southland Way, Houns.	144	A5
Southlands Av., Orp.	207	G4
Southlands Dr. SW19	166	A2
Southlands Gro., Brom.	192	B3
Southlands Rd., Brom.	191	J4
Southly Cl., Sutt.	198	D3
Southmead Rd. SW19	166	B1
Southmont Rd., Esher	194	B2
Southmoor Way E9	95	J6
Southold Ri. SE9	174	C3
Southolm St. SW11	150	B1
Southover N12	56	D4
Southover, Brom.	173	G5
Southport Rd. SE18	137	G4
Southridge Pl. SW20	166	A7
Southsea Rd., Kings.T.	181	H4
Southside Common SW19	165	J6
Southspring, Sid.	157	G7
Southvale Rd. SE3	155	E2
Southview Av. NW10	89	F5
Southview Cl. SW17	168	A5
Southview Cl., Bex.	159	F6
Southview Cres., Ilf.	80	E6
Southview Gdns., Wall.	200	C7
Southview Rd., Brom.	172	D4
Southville SW8	150	D1
Southville Rd., T.Ditt.	180	E7
Southwark Br. EC4	**28**	**A1**
Southwark Br. SE1	**28**	**A1**
Southwark Br. EC4	131	J1
Southwark Br. SE1	131	J1
Southwark Br. Rd. SE1	**27**	**H5**
Southwark Br. Rd. SE1	131	H3
Southwark Gro. SE1	**27**	**J2**
Southwark Pk. Est. SE16	133	E4
Southwark Pk. Rd. SE16	**37**	**G1**
Southwark Pk. Rd. SE16	132	C4
Southwark Pl., Brom.	192	C3
St. Georges Rd.		
Southwark St. SE1	**27**	**H1**
Southwark St. SE1	131	H1
Southwater Cl. E14	113	J6
Southwater Cl., Beck.	172	B7
Southway N20	56	D2
Southway NW11	73	E6
Southway SW20	183	J4
Southway, Wall.	200	C4
Southwell Av., Nthlt.	85	G6
Southwell Gdns. SW7	**30**	**C1**
Southwell Gdns. SW7	129	F4
Southwell Gro. Rd. E11	96	E2
Southwell Rd. SE5	151	J3
Southwell Rd., Croy.	187	G6
Southwell Rd., Har.	69	G6
Southwest Rd. E11	96	D1
Southwick Ms. W2	**15**	**F3**
Southwick Pl. W2	**15**	**G4**
Southwick Ms. W2	109	H6
Southwick St. W2	**15**	**G3**
Southwick St. W2	109	H6
Southwold Dr., Bark.	100	A5
Southwold Rd. E5	95	E2
Southwold Rd., Bex.	159	H6
Southwood Av. N6	74	B7
Southwood Av., Kings.T.	182	C1
Southwood Cl., Brom.	192	C4
Southwood Cl., Wor.Pk.	198	A1
Southwood Dr., Surb.	182	C7

Southwood Gdns., Esher	194	D3
Southwood Gdns., Ilf.	80	E4
Southwood La. N6	74	A7
Southwood Lawn Rd. N6	74	A7
Southwood Rd. SE9	174	E2
Southwood Rd. SE28	138	B1
Southwood Smith St. N1	111	G1
Barford St.		
Sovereign Cl. E1	113	E7
Sovereign Cl. W5	105	F5
Sovereign Ct., Brom.	192	C5
Sovereign Ct., W.Mol.	179	F4
Sovereign Cres. SE16	133	H1
Rotherhithe St.		
Sovereign Gro., Wem.	87	G3
Sovereign Ms. E2	**13**	**F1**
Sovereign Pk. NW10	106	B4
Sovereign Rd., Bark.	118	C3
Sowerby Cl. SE9	156	B5
Spa Cl. SE25	188	B1
Spa Grn. Est. EC1	**11**	**F3**
Spa Grn. Est. EC1	111	G3
Spa Hill SE19	188	A1
Spa Rd. SE16	**29**	**F6**
Spa Rd. SE16	132	C3
Space Waye, Felt.	142	A5
Spafield St. EC1	**11**	**E5**
Spalding Cl., Edg.	54/55	E7
Blundell Rd.		
Spalding Rd. NW4	71	J6
Spalding Rd. SW17	168	B5
Spanby Rd. E3	114	A4
Spaniards Cl. NW11	91	G1
Spaniards End NW3	91	F1
Spaniards Rd. NW3	91	F2
Spanish Pl. W1	**16**	**C2**
Spanish Pl. W1	110	A6
Spanish Rd. SW18	149	F5
Spareleaze Hill, Loug.	48	C5
Sparkbridge Rd., Har.	68	B4
Sparks Cl. W3	106	D6
Joseph Av.		
Sparks Cl., Dag.	100	D2
Sparks Cl., Hmptn.	160/161	E6
Victors Dr.		
Sparrow Cl., Hmptn.	160	E6
Sparrow Dr., Orp.	207	F1
Sparrow Fm. Dr., Felt.	142	D7
Sparrow Fm. Rd., Epsom	197	G4
Sparrow Grn., Dag.	101	H3
Sparrows La. SE9	157	F7
Sparsholt Rd. N19	93	F1
Sparsholt Rd., Bark.	117	H1
Sparta St. SE10	154	B1
Spear Ms. SW5	128	D4
Spearman St. SE18	136	D6
Spearpoint Gdns., Ilf.	81	J4
Spears Rd. N19	92	E1
Speart La., Houns.	122	E7
Spedan Cl. NW3	91	E3
Speedwell St. SE8	134	A7
Comet St.		
Speedy Pl. WC1	**10**	**A4**
Speer Rd., T.Ditt.	180	C5
Speirs Cl., N.Mal.	183	F6
Speke Ho. SE5	131	J7
Speke Rd., Th.Hth.	188	A2
Spekehill SE9	174	C3
Speldhurst Cl., Brom.	191	F5
Speldhurst Rd. E9	95	G7
Speldhurst Rd. W4	126	D3
Spellbrook Wk. N1	111	J1
Basire St.		
Spelman St. E1	**21**	**H1**
Spelman St. E1	112	D5
Spence Cl. SE16	133	J2
Vaughan St.		
Spencer Av. N13	59	F6
Spencer Av., Hayes	102	A5
Spencer Cl. N3	72	D2
Spencer Cl. NW10	105	J3
Spencer Cl., Orp.	207	H2
Spencer Cl., Wdf.Grn.	63	J5
Spencer Dr. N2	73	F6
Spencer Gdns. SE9	156	C5
Spencer Gdns. SW14	146	C5
Spencer Hill SW19	166	B6
Spencer Hill Rd. SW19	166	B7
Spencer Ms. SW8	151	F1
Lansdowne Way		
Spencer Ms. W6	128	B6
Greyhound Rd.		
Spencer Pk. SW18	149	G5
Spencer Pas. E2	112/113	E2
Pritchard's Rd.		

Spencer Pl. N1 93 H7
Canonbury La.
Spencer Pl., Croy. 188 A7
Gloucester Rd.
Spencer Ri. NW5 92 B4
Spencer Rd. E6 116 A1
Spencer Rd. E17 78 C1
Spencer Rd. N8 75 F5
Spencer Rd. N11 58 B4
Spencer Rd. N17 76 D1
Spencer Rd. SW18 149 G4
Spencer Rd. SW20 183 H1
Spencer Rd. W3 126 C1
Spencer Rd. W4 126 C7
Spencer Rd., Brom. 173 E7
Spencer Rd., E.Mol. 179 J5
Spencer Rd., Har. 68 B2
Spencer Rd., Ilf. 99 J1
Spencer Rd., Islw. 144 A1
Spencer Rd., Mitch. 186 A3
Spencer Rd. (Beddington Cor.), Mitch. 186 A7
Spencer Rd., S.Croy. 202 B5
Spencer Rd., Twick. 162 B3
Spencer Rd., Wem. 87 F2
Spencer St. EC1 11 G4
Spencer St. EC1 111 H3
Spencer St., Sthl. 122 D2
Spencer Wk. NW3 91 F4
Hampstead High St.
Spencer Wk. SW15 148 A4
Spenser Gro. N16 94 B4
Spenser Ms. SE21 170 A1
Croxted Rd.
Spenser Rd. SE24 151 G5
Spenser St. SW1 25 G5
Spenser St. SW1 130 C3
Spensley Wk. N16 94 A3
Clissold Rd.
Speranza St. SE18 137 J5
Sperling Rd. N17 76 B2
Spert St. E14 113 H7
Spey St. E14 114 C5
Speyside N14 42 C6
Spezia Rd. NW10 107 G2
Spicer Cl. SW9 151 H2
Spicer Cl., Walt. 178 C6
Spice's Yd., Croy. 201 J4
Spigurnell Rd. N17 76 A1
Spikes Br. Rd., Sthl. 103 E6
Spilsby Cl. NW9 70/71 E2
Kenley Av.
Spindle Cl. SE18 136 B3
Spindlewood Gdns., Croy. 202 B4
Spindrift Av. E14 134 B4
Spinel Cl. SE18 137 J5
Spinnaker Cl., Bark. 117 H3
Thames Rd.
Spinnells Rd., Har. 85 F1
Spinney, The N21 43 G7
Spinney, The SW16 168 D3
Spinney, The, Barn. 41 E2
Spinney, The, Sid. 176 E5
Spinney, The, Stan. 53 H4
Spinney, The, Sun. 178 A1
Spinney, The, Sutt. 197 J4
Spinney, The, Wem. 86 D3
Spinney Cl., N.Mal. 182 E5
Spinney Cl., Wor.Pk. 197 F2
Spinney Dr., Felt. 141 F7
Spinney Gdns. SE19 170 C5
Spinney Gdns., Dag. 101 E5
Spinney Oak, Brom. 192 B2
Spinneys, The, Brom. 192 C2
Spirit Quay E1 29 J1
Spital Sq. E1 21 E1
Spital Sq. E1 112 B5
Spital St. E1 21 H1
Spital St. E1 112 D4
Spital Yd. E1 21 E1
Spitfire Est., Houns. 122 C5
Spitfire Way, Houns. 122 C5
Splendour Wk. SE16 133 F5
Verney Rd.
Spode Wk. NW6 90/91 E6
Lymington Rd.
Spondon Rd. N15 76 D4
Spoonbill Way, Hayes 102 D5
Spooner Wk., Wall. 200 D5
Spooners Ms. W3 126 D1
Churchfield Rd.
Sportsbank St. SE6 154 C7
Spottons Gro. N17 75 J1
Gospatrick Rd.
Spout Hill, Croy. 204 A5
Spratt Hall Rd. E11 79 G6
Spray La., Twick. 144 B6
Spray St. SE18 137 E4
Spreighton Rd., W.Mol. 179 H4
Sprimont Pl. SW3 31 J3
Sprimont Pl. SW3 129 J5
Spring Br. Ms. W5 105 G7
Spring Br. Rd.
Spring Br. Rd. W5 105 G7
Spring Cl., Barn. 40 A5
Spring Cl., Borwd. 38 A1
Spring Cl., Dag. 100 D1
Spring Cl. La., Sutt. 198 B6
Spring Cotts., Surb. 181 G5
St. Leonard's Rd.
Spring Ct., Sid. 176 A3
Station Rd.
Spring Dr., Pnr. 66 A6
Eastcote Rd.
Spring Gdns. N5 93 J5
Grosvenor Av.
Spring Gdns. SW1 25 J1
Spring Gdns., Rom. 83 J5
Spring Gdns., Wall. 200 C5
Spring Gdns., W.Mol. 179 J5
Spring Gdns., Wdf.Grn. 63 J7
Spring Gdns. Ind. Est., Rom. 83 J5
Spring Gro. SE19 170 C7
Alma Pl.
Spring Gro. W4 126 A5
Spring Gro., Hmptn. 179 H1
Plevna Rd.
Spring Gro., Loug. 48 A6
Spring Gro., Mitch. 186 A1
Spring Gro. Cres., Houns. 143 J1
Spring Gro. Rd., Houns. 143 J1
Spring Gro. Rd., Islw. 143 J1
Spring Gro. Rd., Rich. 145 J5
Spring Hill E5 76 D7
Spring Hill SE26 171 F4
Spring Lake, Stan. 52 E4
Spring La. E5 95 E1
Spring La. N10 74 A3
Spring La. SE25 188 E6
Spring Ms. W1 16 A1
Spring Pk. Av., Croy. 203 G2
Spring Pk. Dr. N4 93 J1
Spring Pk. Rd., Croy. 203 G2
Spring Pas. SW15 148 A3
Embankment
Spring Path NW3 91 G5
Spring Pl. NW5 92 B5
Spring St. W2 15 E4
Spring St. W2 109 G6
Spring Ter., Rich. 145 H5
Spring Vale, Bexh. 159 H4
Spring Vil. Rd., Edg. 54 A7
Spring Wk. E1 21 H1
Springall St. SE15 133 E7
Springbank N21 43 F6
Springbank Rd. SE13 154 D6
Springbank Wk. NW1 92 D7
St. Paul's Cres.
Springbourne Ct., Beck. 190 C1
Springcroft Av. N2 73 J4
Springdale Ms. N16 94 A4
Springdale Rd.
Springdale Rd. N16 94 A4
Springfield E5 94 E1
Springfield, Bushey 52 A1
Springfield Av. N10 74 C3
Springfield Av. SW20 184 C3
Springfield Av., Hmptn. 161 H6
Springfield Cl. N12 56 E5
Springfield Cl., Stan. 52 D3
Springfield Dr., Ilf. 81 F6
Springfield Gdns. E5 95 E1
Springfield Gdns. NW9 70 D5
Springfield Gdns., Brom. 192 C4
Springfield Gdns., Ruis. 84 B1
Springfield Gdns., W.Wick. 204 B2
Springfield Gdns., Wdf.Grn. 63 J7
Springfield Gro. SE7 135 J6
Springfield La. NW6 108 E1
Springfield Mt. NW9 70 E5
Springfield Pl., N.Mal. 182 C4
Springfield Ri. SE26 170 E3
Springfield Rd. E4 62 E1
Springfield Rd. E6 98 C7
Springfield Rd. E15 115 E3
Springfield Rd. E17 77 J6
Springfield Rd. N11 58 B5
Springfield Rd. N15 76 D4
Springfield Rd. NW8 109 F1
Springfield Rd. SE26 171 E5
Springfield Rd. SW19 166 C5
Springfield Rd. W7 124 B1
Springfield Rd., Bexh. 159 H3
Springfield Rd., Brom. 192 C4
Springfield Rd., Har. 68 B6
Springfield Rd., Hayes 122 C1
Springfield Rd., Kings.T. 181 H3
Springfield Rd., Tedd. 162 D5
Springfield Rd., Th.Hth. 187 J1
Springfield Rd., Twick. 161 G1
Springfield Rd., Wall. 200 B5
Springfield Rd., Well. 158 B3
Springfield Wk. NW6 108 E1
Springfield Wk., Orp. 207 G1
Place Fm. Av.
Springhill Cl. SE5 152 A3
Springhurst Cl., Croy. 203 J4
Springpark Dr., Beck. 190 C3
Springpond Rd., Dag. 101 E5
Springrice Rd. SE13 154 D6
Springvale Av., Brent. 125 G5
Springvale Est. W14 128 B3
Blythe Rd.
Springvale Ter. W14 128 A3
Springwater Cl. SE18 156 D1
Springway, Har. 68 A7
Springwell Av. NW10 107 F1
Springwell Cl. SW16 169 G4
Etherstone Rd.
Springwell Ct., Houns. 142 D2
Springwell Rd. SW16 169 G4
Springwell Rd., Houns. 142 D1
Springwood Cres., Edg. 54 B2
Sprowston Ms. E7 97 G6
Sprowston Rd. E7 97 G5
Spruce Ct. W5 125 H3
Elderberry Rd.
Spruce Hills Rd. E17 78 C2
Spruce Pk., Brom. 191 F4
Cumberland Rd.
Sprucedale Gdns., Croy. 203 G4
Sprules Rd. SE4 153 H2
Spur Rd. N15 76 A4
Philip La.
Spur Rd. SE1 27 E3
Spur Rd. SE1 131 G2
Spur Rd. SW1 25 F4
Spur Rd. SW1 130 C2
Spur Rd., Bark. 117 F3
Spur Rd., Edg. 53 H4
Spur Rd., Felt. 142 B5
Spur Rd., Islw. 124 E7
Spur Rd. Est., Edg. 53 J4
Spurfield, W.Mol. 179 H3
Spurgeon Av. SE19 188 A1
Spurgeon Rd. SE19 188 A1
Spurgeon St. SE1 28 B6
Spurgeon St. SE1 132 A3
Spurling Rd. SE22 152 C4
Spurling Rd., Dag. 101 F6
Spurstowe Rd. E8 94/95 E6
Marcon Pl.
Spurstowe Ter. E8 94 E5
Square, The W6 127 J5
Square, The, Cars. 200 A5
Square, The, Hayes 121 G1
Square, The, Ilf. 80 D7
Square, The, Rich. 145 G5
Square, The, Wdf.Grn. 63 G5
Square Rigger Row SW11 149 F3
York Pl.
Squarey St. SW17 167 F3
Squires Ct. SW19 166 D4
Squires La. N3 73 E2
Squires Mt. NW3 91 G3
East Heath Rd.
Squires Wd. Dr., Chis. 174 B7
Squirrel Cl., Houns. 142 C2
Squirrel Ms. W13 104 D7
Squirrels, The SE13 154 D3
Belmont Hill
Squirrels, The, Pnr. 67 F3
Squirrels Cl. N12 57 F4
Woodside Av.
Squirrels Grn., Wor.Pk. 197 F1
Squirrels La., Buck.H. 64 A3
Squirrels Trd. Est., The, Hayes 122 A3
Squirries St. E2 13 J3
Squirries St. E2 112 D3
Stable Cl., Nthlt. 103 G2
Stable Wk. N2 73 G1
Old Fm. Rd.
Stable Way W10 107 J6
Latimer Rd.
Stable Yd. SW1 25 F3
Stable Yd. SW9 151 F2
Broomgrove Rd.
Stable Yd. SW15 147 J3
Danemere St.
Stable Yd. Rd. SW1 25 F2
Stable Yd. Rd. SW1 130 C1
Stables, The, Buck.H. 47 J7
Stables End, Orp. 207 F3
Stables Ms. SE27 169 J5
Stables Way SE11 35 E3
Stables Way SE11 131 G5
Stacey Av. N18 61 F4
Stacey Cl. E10 78 D5
Halford Rd.
Stacey St. N7 93 G3
Stacey St. WC2 17 J4
Stacey St. WC2 110 D6
Stackhouse St. SW3 23 J5
Stacy Path SE5 132 B7
Harris St.
Stadium Rd. NW2 71 J7
Stadium Rd. SE18 136 C7
Stadium St. SW10 129 F7
Stadium Way, Wem. 87 J4
Staff St. EC1 12 C4
Staffa Rd. E10 95 H1
Stafford Cl. E17 77 J6
Stafford Cl. N14 42 C5
Stafford Cl. NW6 108 D3
Stafford Cl., Sutt. 198 B6
Stafford Ct. W8 128 D3
Stafford Cross, Croy. 201 F5
Stafford Gdns., Croy. 201 F5
Stafford Pl. SW1 25 F5
Stafford Pl. SW1 130 C3
Stafford Pl., Rich. 145 J7
Stafford Rd. E3 113 J2
Stafford Rd. E7 97 J7
Stafford Rd. NW6 108 D3
Stafford Rd., Croy. 201 G4
Stafford Rd., Har. 51 J7
Stafford Rd., N.Mal. 182 C3
Stafford Rd., Sid. 175 H4
Stafford Rd., Wall. 200 C6
Stafford St. W1 25 F1
Stafford St. W1 130 C1
Stafford Ter. W8 128 D3
Staffordshire St. SE15 152 D1
Stag Cl., Edg. 70 C2
Stag La. NW9 70 B2
Stag La. SW15 165 F2
Stag La., Buck.H. 63 H2
Stag La., Edg. 70 B2
Stag Pl. SW1 25 F5
Stag Pl. SW1 130 C3
Stag Ride SW19 165 F3
Staggart Grn., Chig. 65 J6
Stags Way, Islw. 124 C6
Stainbank Rd., Mitch. 186 B3
Stainby Cl., West Dr. 120 B3
Stainby Rd. N15 76 C4
Stainer St. SE1 28 C2
Stainer St. SE1 132 A1
Staines Av., Sutt. 198 A2
Staines Rd., Felt. 141 G7
Staines Rd., Houns. 143 H3
Staines Rd., Ilf. 99 G4
Staines Rd., Twick. 161 G3
Staines Rd. E., Sun. 160 A7
Staines Wk., Sid. 176 C6
Evry Rd.
Stainforth Rd. E17 78 A4
Stainforth Rd., Ilf. 81 G7
Staining La. EC2 20 A3
Staining La. EC2 111 J6
Stainmore Cl., Chis. 193 G1
Stainsbury St. E2 113 F2
Royston St.
Stainsby Pl. E14 114 A6
Stainsby Rd.
Stainsby Rd. E14 114 A6
Stainton Rd. SE6 154 D6
Stainton Rd., Enf. 45 F1
Stalbridge St. NW1 15 H1
Stalham St. SE16 133 E3
Stambourne Way SE19 170 B7
Stambourne Way, W.Wick. 204 C3
Stamford Brook Av. W6 127 F3
Stamford Brook Rd. W6 127 F3
Stamford Cl. N15 76 D4
Stamford Cl. NW3 91 F4
Heath St.
Stamford Cl., Har. 52 B7
Stamford Cl., Sthl. 103 G7

Stamford Cotts. SW10 128/129 E7
Billing St.
Stamford Ct. W6 127 F4
Goldhawk Rd.
Stamford Dr., Brom. 191 F4
Stamford Gdns., Dag. 100 C7
Stamford Gro. E. N16 94 D1
Oldhill St.
Stamford Gro. W. N16 94 D1
Oldhill St.
Stamford Hill N16 94 C2
Stamford Hill Est. N16 94 C1
Stamford Rd. E6 116 B1
Stamford Rd. N1 94 B7
Stamford Rd. N15 76 D5
Stamford Rd., Dag. 118 B1
Stamford St. SE1 27 E2
Stamford St. SE1 131 G1
Stamp Pl. E2 13 F3
Stamp Pl. E2 112 C3
Stanard Cl. N16 76 B7
Stanborough Cl., Hmptn. 161 F6
Stanborough Pas. E8 94 C6
Abbot St.
Stanborough Rd., Houns. 144 A3
Stanbridge Pl. N21 59 H2
Stanbridge Rd. SW15 147 J3
Stanbrook Rd. SE2 138 B2
Stanbury Rd. SE15 153 E1
Stancroft NW9 70 E4
Standard Ind. Est. E16 136 C2
Standard Pl. EC2 12 E4
Standard Rd. NW10 106 C4
Standard Rd., Belv. 139 G5
Standard Rd., Bexh. 159 E4
Standard Rd., Houns. 143 E3
Standen Rd. SW18 148 C7
Standfield Gdns., Dag. 101 G6
Standfield Rd.
Standfield Rd., Dag. 101 G5
Standish Rd. W6 127 G4
Standlake Pt. SE23 171 G3
Stane Cl. SW19 184/185 E1
Hayward Cl.
Stane Way SE18 136 A7
Stanfield Rd. E3 113 H2
Stanford Cl., Hmptn. 161 F6
Stanford Cl., Rom. 83 H6
Stanford Cl., Wdf.Grn. 64 B5
Stanford Ho., Bark. 118 B2
Stanford Pl. SE17 36 D2
Stanford Rd. N11 57 J5
Stanford Rd. SW16 186 D2
Stanford Rd. W8 22 B5
Stanford Rd. W8 129 E3
Stanford St. SW1 33 H2
Stanford Way SW16 186 D2
Stangate Cres., Borwd. 38 E5
Stangate Gdns., Stan. 53 E4
Stanger Rd. SE25 188 D4
Stanhope Av. N3 72 C3
Stanhope Av., Brom. 205 F1
Stanhope Av., Har. 68 A1
Stanhope Cl. SE16 133 G2
Middleton Dr.
Stanhope Gdns. N4 75 H6
Stanhope Gdns. N6 74 B6
Stanhope Gdns. NW7 55 F5
Stanhope Gdns. SW7 30 D1
Stanhope Gdns. SW7 129 F4
Stanhope Gdns., Dag. 101 F3
Stanhope Gdns., Ilf. 98 C1
Stanhope Gate W1 24 C1
Stanhope Gate W1 130 A1
Stanhope Gro., Beck. 189 J5
Stanhope Ms. E. SW7 30 D1
Stanhope Ms. E. SW7 129 F4
Stanhope Ms. S. SW7 30 D2
Stanhope Ms. W. SW7 30 D1
Stanhope Ms. W. SW7 129 F4
Stanhope Par. NW1 9 F3
Stanhope Pk. Rd., Grnf. 103 J4
Stanhope Pl. W2 15 J4
Stanhope Pl. W2 109 J6
Stanhope Rd. E17 78 B5
Stanhope Rd. N6 74 C6
Stanhope Rd. N12 57 F5
Stanhope Rd., Barn. 39 J6
Stanhope Rd., Bexh. 159 E2
Stanhope Rd., Cars. 200 A7
Stanhope Rd., Croy. 202 B3
Stanhope Rd., Dag. 101 F2
Stanhope Rd., Grnf. 103 J5
Stanhope Rd., Sid. 176 A4
Stanhope Row W1 24 D2
Stanhope St. NW1 9 F4
Stanhope St. NW1 110 C3
Stanhope Ter. W2 15 F5
Stanhope Ter. W2 109 G7
Stanier Cl. W14 128 C5
Aisgill Av.
Stanlake Ms. W12 127 J1
Stanlake Rd. W12 127 H1
Stanlake Vil. W12 127 H1
Stanley Av., Bark. 117 J2
Stanley Av., Beck. 190 C2
Stanley Av., Dag. 101 F1
Stanley Av., Grnf. 103 J1
Stanley Av., N.Mal. 183 G5
Stanley Av., Wem. 87 H7
Stanley Cl. SW8 34 C6
Stanley Cl. SW8 131 F6
Stanley Cl., Wem. 87 H7
Stanley Cres. W11 108 C7
Stanley Gdns. NW2 89 J5
Stanley Gdns. W3 126 E1
Stanley Gdns. W11 108 C7
Stanley Gdns., Mitch. 168 A6
Ashbourne Rd.
Stanley Gdns., Wall. 200 C6
Stanley Gdns. Ms. W11 108 C7
Stanley Cres.
Stanley Gdns. Rd., Tedd. 162 B5
Stanley Gro. SW8 150 A2
Stanley Gro., Croy. 187 G6
Stanley Pk. Dr., Wem. 87 J7
Stanley Pk. Rd., Cars. 199 J7
Stanley Pk. Rd., Wall. 200 B6
Stanley Pas. NW1 10 A2
Stanley Rd. E4 62 D1
Stanley Rd. E10 78 B6
Stanley Rd. E12 98 B5
Stanley Rd. E15 114 D1
Stanley Rd. E18 79 F1
Stanley Rd. N2 73 G3
Stanley Rd. N9 60 C1
Stanley Rd. N10 58 B7
Stanley Rd. N11 58 D6
Stanley Rd. N15 75 H4
Stanley Rd. NW9 71 G7
West Hendon Bdy.
Stanley Rd. SW14 146 B4
Stanley Rd. SW19 166 D7
Stanley Rd. W3 126 C3
Stanley Rd., Brom. 191 H4
Stanley Rd., Cars. 200 A7
Stanley Rd., Croy. 187 G7
Stanley Rd., Enf. 44 B3
Stanley Rd., Har. 85 J2
Stanley Rd., Houns. 143 J4
Stanley Rd., Ilf. 99 G2
Stanley Rd., Mitch. 168 A7
Stanley Rd., Mord. 184 D4
Stanley Rd., Nthwd. 66 A1
Stanley Rd., Sid. 176 A3
Stanley Rd., Sthl. 102 E7
Stanley Rd., Sutt. 198 E6
Stanley Rd., Tedd. 162 B4
Stanley Rd., Twick. 162 A3
Stanley Rd., Wem. 87 J6
Stanley St. SE8 133 J7
Stanley Ter. N19 92 E2
Stanleycroft Cl., Islw. 144 B1
Stanmer St. SW11 149 H1
Stanmore Gdns., Rich. 145 J3
Stanmore Gdns., Sutt. 199 F3
Stanmore Hall, Stan. 52 E3
Stanmore Hill, Stan. 52 D3
Stanmore Pk., Stan. 52 E5
Stanmore Pl. NW1 110 B1
Arlington Rd.
Stanmore Rd. E11 97 F1
Stanmore Rd. N15 75 H4
Stanmore Rd., Belv. 139 J4
Stanmore Rd., Rich. 145 J3
Stanmore St. N1 111 F1
Caledonian Rd.
Stanmore Ter., Beck. 190 A2
Stanmore Way, Loug. 48 D1
Stannard Ms. E8 94 D6
Stannard Rd. E8 94 D6
Stannary Pl. SE11 35 F4
Stannary Pl. SE11 131 G5
Stannary St. SE11 35 F5
Stannary St. SE11 131 G6
Stannet Way, Wall. 200 C4
Stannington Path, Borwd. 38 A1
Stansfeld Rd. E6 116 A5
Stansfield Rd. SW9 151 F3
Stansfield Rd., Houns. 142 B2
Stansgate Rd., Dag. 101 G2
Stanstead Cl., Brom. 191 F5
Stanstead Gro. SE6 171 J1
Catford Hill
Stanstead Manor, Sutt. 198 D6
Stanstead Rd. E11 79 H5
Stanstead Rd. SE6 171 G1
Stanstead Rd. SE23 171 G1
Stanstead Rd., Houns. 140 C6
Stansted Cres., Bex. 176 D1
Stanswood Gdns. SE5 132 B7
Sedgmoor Pl.
Stanthorpe Cl. SW16 168/169 E5
Stanthorpe Rd.
Stanthorpe Rd. SW16 168 E5
Stanton Av., Tedd. 162 B5
Stanton Cl., Epsom 196 B5
Stanton Cl., Wor.Pk. 198 A1
Stanton Rd. SE26 171 J4
Stanton Way
Stanton Rd. SW13 147 F2
Stanton Rd. SW20 184 A2
Stanton Rd., Croy. 187 J7
Stanton Sq. SE26 171 J4
Stanton Way
Stanton Way SE26 171 J4
Stanway Cl., Chig. 65 H5
Stanway Ct. N1 112 B2
Hoxton St.
Stanway Gdns. W3 126 A1
Stanway Gdns., Edg. 54 C5
Stanway St. N1 12 E1
Stanway St. N1 112 B2
Stanwell Cl., Stai. 140 A6
Stanwell Gdns., Stai. 140 A6
Stanwell Rd., Felt. 141 F7
Stanwick Rd. W14 128 C4
Stanworth St. SE1 29 F4
Stanworth St. SE1 132 C2
Stanwyck Dr., Chig. 65 F5
Stapenhill Rd., Wem. 86 E3
Staple Inn WC1 19 E2
Staple Inn Bldgs. WC1 18 E2
Staple Inn Bldgs. WC1 111 G5
Staple St. SE1 28 C4
Staple St. SE1 132 A2
Staplefield Cl. SW2 169 E1
Staplefield Cl., Pnr. 50 E7
Stapleford Av., Ilf. 81 H5
Stapleford Cl. E4 62 C3
Stapleford Cl. SW19 148 B7
Stapleford Cl., Kings.T. 182 A3
Stapleford Rd., Wem. 87 G7
Stapleford Way, Bark. 118 B3
Staplehurst Rd. SE13 154 E5
Staplehurst Rd., Cars. 199 H7
Staples Cl. SE16 133 H1
Staples Cor. NW2 89 H1
Staples Cor. Business Pk. NW2 89 H1
Staples Rd., Loug. 48 B3
Stapleton Gdns., Croy. 201 G5
Stapleton Hall Rd. N4 75 F7
Stapleton Rd. SW17 168 A3
Stapleton Rd., Bexh. 139 F7
Stapleton Rd., Orp. 207 J3
Stapley Rd., Belv. 139 G5
Stapylton Rd., Barn. 40 B3
Star & Garter Hill, Rich. 163 H1
Star La. E16 115 E4
Star Path, Nthlt. 103 G2
Brabazon Rd.
Star Pl. E1 21 G6
Star Rd. W14 128 C6
Star Rd., Islw. 144 A2
Star St. E16 115 F5
Star St. W2 15 F3
Star St. W2 109 H5
Star Yd. WC2 18 E3
Starboard Way E14 134 A3
Starch Ho. La., Ilf. 81 G2
Starcross St. NW1 9 G4
Starcross St. NW1 110 C3
Starfield Rd. W12 127 G2
Starling Cl., Buck.H. 63 G1
Starling Cl., Pnr. 66 C3
Starling Ms. SE28 137 G2
Whinchat Rd.
Starling Wk., Hmptn. 160/161 E6
Oak Av.
Starmans Cl., Dag. 119 E1
Starts Cl., Orp. 206 D3
Starts Hill Av., Orp. 207 E4
Starts Hill Rd., Orp. 206 D3
Starveall Cl., West Dr. 120 C3
State Fm. Av., Orp. 207 E4
Staten Gdns., Twick. 162 C1
Lion Rd.
Statham Gro. N16 93 J4
Green Las.
Statham Gro. N18 60 B5
Station App. E7 97 H4
Woodford Rd.
Station App. (Snaresbrook) E11 79 G5
High St.
Station App. N11 58 B5
Friern Barnet Rd.
Station App. N12 56/57 E5
Holden Rd.
Station App. (Woodside Pk.) N12 56 E4
Station App. (Stoke Newington) N16 94 C2
Stamford Hill
Station App. NW10 107 F3
Station Rd.
Station App. SE1 26 D4
Station App. SE1 131 G2
Station App. SE3 155 H3
Kidbrooke Pk. Rd.
Station App. (Mottingham) SE9 174 C1
Station App. (Lower Sydenham) SE26 171 J5
Worsley Br. Rd.
Station App. (Sydenham) SE26 171 F4
Sydenham Rd.
Station App. SW6 148 B3
Station App. SW16 168 D5
Station App. W7 124 B1
Station App., Barn. 41 F4
Station App., Bex. 159 G7
Bexley High St.
Station App., Bexh. 158/159 E2
Avenue Rd.
Station App. (Barnehurst), Bexh. 159 J2
Station App., Brom. 205 G1
Station App., Buck.H. 64 A4
Cherry Tree Ri.
Station App., Chis. 192 D1
Station App. (Elmstead Wds.), Chis. 174 B6
Station App. (Stoneleigh), Epsom 197 G5
Station App. (Hinchley Wd.), Esher 194 C3
Station App., Grnf. 86 A7
Station App., Hmptn. 179 G1
Milton Rd.
Station App., Har. 68 B7
Station App., Hayes 121 J2
Station App., Kings.T. 182 A1
Station App., Loug. 48 B5
Station App. (Debden), Loug. 49 F4
Station App., Orp. 207 J2
Station App., Pnr. 66 E3
Station App. (Hatch End), Pnr. 51 G7
Uxbridge Rd.
Station App., Rich. 146 A1
Station App., Ruis. 84 B5
Station App., Sun. 178 A1
Station App. (Cheam), Sutt. 198 B7
Station App. (Carpenders Pk.), Wat. 50 D3
Prestwick Rd.
Station App., Well. 157 J2
Station App., Wem. 87 E6
Station App., West Dr. 120 B1
Station App. N., Sid. 176 A2
Station App. Rd. W4 126 C7
Station Av. SW9 151 H3
Coldharbour La.
Station Av., N.Mal. 183 E3
Station Av., Rich. 146 A1
Station Par.
Station Cl. N3 72 D1
Station Cl. (Woodside Pk.) N12 56 E4
Station Cl., Hmptn. 179 H1
Station Cres. N15 76 A4
Station Cres. SE3 135 G5
Station Cres., Wem. 87 E6
Station Est., Beck. 189 G4
Elmers End Rd.
Station Est. Rd., Felt. 160 B1
Station Garage Ms. SW16 168 D6
Estreham Rd.
Station Gdns. W4 126 C7
Station Gro., Wem. 87 H6
Station Hill, Brom. 205 G2

Station Ho. Ms. N9 60 D4
Fore St.
Station Par. E11 79 G5
Station Par. N14 58 D1
High St.
Station Par. NW2 89 J6
Station Par. SW12 168 A1
Balham High Rd.
Station Par. W3 106 A6
Station Par., Bark. 99 F7
Station Par., Felt. 142 B7
Station Par., Rich. 146 A1
Station Pas. E18 79 H2
Maybank Rd.
Station Pas. SE15 152/153 E1
Asylum Rd.
Station Path E8 94/95 E6
Amhurst Rd.
Station Pl. N4 93 G2
Seven Sisters Rd.
Station Ri. SE27 169 H2
Norwood Rd.
Station Rd. (Chingford) E4 62 D1
Station Rd. E7 97 G4
Station Rd. E12 98 A4
Station Rd. E17 77 H6
Station Rd. N3 72 D1
Station Rd. N11 58 B5
Station Rd. N17 76 D3
Hale Rd.
Station Rd. N19 92 C3
Station Rd. N21 59 H1
Station Rd. N22 75 F2
Station Rd. NW4 71 G6
Station Rd. NW7 55 E5
Station Rd. NW10 107 F2
Station Rd. SE13 154 C3
Station Rd. SE20 171 F6
Station Rd. (Norwood Junct.) SE25 188 C4
Station Rd. SW13 147 G3
Station Rd. SW19 185 F1
Station Rd. W5 105 J6
Station Rd. (Hanwell) W7 124 B1
Station Rd., Barn. 40 E5
Station Rd., Belv. 139 G3
Station Rd., Bexh. 159 E3
Station Rd., Borwd. 38 A4
Station Rd., Brent. 125 F6
Station Rd., Brom. 191 G1
Station Rd. (Shortlands), Brom. 191 E2
Station Rd., Cars. 199 J4
Station Rd., Chess. 195 H5
Station Rd., Chig. 64 E3
Station Rd. (East Croydon), Croy. 202 A2
Station Rd. (West Croydon), Croy. 201 J1
Station Rd., Edg. 54 A6
Station Rd., Esher 194 A2
Station Rd. (Claygate), Esher 194 A5
Station Rd., Hmptn. 179 G1
Station Rd., Har. 68 C7
Station Rd. (North Harrow), Har. 67 H5
Station Rd., Hayes 121 J3
Station Rd., Houns. 143 H4
Station Rd., Ilf. 98 E3
Station Rd. (Barkingside), Ilf. 81 G3
Station Rd., Kings.T. 182 A1
Station Rd. (Hampton Wick), Kings.T. 181 F1
Station Rd., Loug. 48 B4
Station Rd. (Motspur Pk.), N.Mal. 183 H5
Station Rd., Orp. 207 J2
Station Rd. (Chadwell Heath), Rom. 82 D7
Station Rd., Sid. 176 A4
Station Rd., Sun. 160 A7
Station Rd., Tedd. 162 C5
Station Rd., T.Ditt. 180 C7
Station Rd., Twick. 162 C1
Station Rd., West Dr. 120 B1
Station Rd., W.Wick. 204 C1
Station Rd. N., Belv. 139 H3
Station Sq. (Petts Wd.), Orp. 193 F5
Station St. E15 96 D7
Station St. E16 136 E1
Station Ter. NW10 108 A2
Station Ter. SE5 151 J1
Station Vw., Grnf. 104 A1
Station Way SE15 152 D2
Rye La.
Station Way (Roding Valley), Buck.H. 63 J4
Station Way (Claygate), Esher 194 B6
Station Way (Cheam), Sutt. 198 B6
Station Yd., Twick. 144 D7
Stationers Hall Ct. EC4 111 H6
Ludgate Hill
Staunton Rd., Kings.T. 163 H6
Staunton St. SE8 133 J6
Stave Yd. Rd. SE16 133 H1
Staveley Cl. E9 95 F5
Churchill Wk.
Staveley Cl. N7 92/93 E4
Penn Rd.
Staveley Cl. SE15 152/153 E1
Asylum Rd.
Staveley Gdns. W4 146 D1
Staveley Rd. W4 126 D7
Staverton Rd. NW2 89 J7
Stavordale Rd. N5 93 H4
Stavordale Rd., Cars. 185 F7
Stayner's Rd. E1 113 G4
Stayton Rd., Sutt. 198 D3
Stead St. SE17 36 B2
Stead St. SE17 132 A4
Steadfast Rd., Kings.T. 181 G1
Steam Fm. La., Felt. 141 J4
Stean St. E8 112 C1
Stebbing Way, Bark. 118 A2
Stebondale St. E14 134 C5
Stedham Pl. WC1 18 A3
Steedman St. SE17 35 J2
Steeds Rd. N10 73 J1
Steeds Way, Loug. 48 B3
Steele Rd. E11 96 E4
Steele Rd. N17 76 B3
Steele Rd. NW10 106 C2
Steele Rd. W4 126 C3
Steele Rd., Islw. 144 D4
Steele Wk., Erith 139 H6
Steeles Ms. N. NW3 91 J6
Steeles Rd.
Steeles Ms. S. NW3 91 J6
Steeles Rd.
Steeles Rd. NW3 91 J6
Steel's La. E1 113 F6
Devonport St.
Steelyard Pas. EC4 112 A7
Upper Thames St.
Steen Way SE22 152 B5
East Dulwich Gro.
Steep Cl., Orp. 207 J6
Steep Hill SW16 168 D3
Steep Hill, Croy. 202 B4
Steeple Cl. SW6 148 B2
Steeple Cl. SW19 166 B5
Steeple Ct. E1 112/113 E4
Coventry Rd.
Steeple Wk. N1 111 J1
Basire St.
Steeplestone Cl. N18 59 J5
Steerforth St. SW18 167 E2
Steers Mead, Mitch. 185 J1
Steers Way SE16 133 H2
Stella Rd. SW17 167 J6
Stellar Ho. N17 60 C6
Stellman Cl. E5 94 D3
Stembridge Rd. SE20 188 E2
Stephan Cl. E8 112 D1
Stephen Cl., Orp. 207 J3
Stephen Ms. W1 17 H2
Stephen Rd., Bexh. 159 J3
Stephen St. W1 17 H2
Stephen St. W1 110 D5
Stephendale Rd. SW6 149 E2
Stephen's Rd. E15 115 E1
Stephenson Rd. E17 77 H5
Stephenson Rd. W7 104 C6
Stephenson Rd., Twick. 143 G7
Stephenson St. E16 114 E4
Stephenson St. NW10 107 E3
Stephenson Way NW1 9 G5
Stephenson Way NW1 110 C4
Stepney Causeway E1 113 G6
Stepney Grn. E1 113 F5
Stepney High St. E1 113 G5
Stepney Way E1 112 E5
Sterling Av., Edg. 53 J4
Sterling Av., Pnr. 66 E7
Sterling Cl., Pnr. 84 D1
Sterling Gdns. SE14 133 H6
Sterling Ind. Est., Dag. 101 H4
Sterling Pl. W5 125 H4
Sterling St. SW7 23 H5
Sterling Way N18 60 A5
Stern Cl., Bark. 118/119 E3
Choats Rd.
Sterndale Rd. W14 128 A3
Sterne St. W12 128 A2
Sternhall La. SE15 152 D3
Sternhold Av. SW2 168 D2
Sterry Cres., Dag. 101 G5
Alibon Rd.
Sterry Dr., Epsom 196 E4
Sterry Dr., T.Ditt. 180 B6
Sterry Gdns., Dag. 101 G6
Sterry Rd., Bark. 117 J1
Sterry Rd., Dag. 101 G4
Sterry St. SE1 28 B4
Sterry St. SE1 132 A2
Steucers La. SE23 153 H7
Steve Biko La. SE6 172 A4
Steve Biko Rd. N7 93 G3
Steve Biko Way, Houns. 143 G3
Stevedale Rd., Well. 158 C2
Stevedore St. E1 132/133 E1
Waterman Way
Stevenage Rd. E6 98 D6
Stevenage Rd. SW6 128 A7
Stevens Av. E9 95 F6
Stevens Cl., Beck. 172 A6
Stevens Cl., Hmptn. 161 F6
Stevens Cl., Pnr. 66 C5
Bridle Rd.
Stevens Grn., Bushey 51 J1
Stevens La., Esher 194 D7
Stevens Rd., Dag. 100 B3
Stevens St. SE1 29 E5
Stevens Way, Chig. 65 H4
Stevenson Cl., Barn. 41 G6
Stevenson Cres. SE16 37 J3
Stevenson Cres. SE16 132 E5
Steventon Rd. W12 107 F7
Stew La. EC4 19 J5
Steward St. E1 21 E2
Steward St. E1 112 B5
Stewards Holte Wk. N11 58 B4
Coppies Gro.
Stewart Cl. NW9 70 C6
Stewart Cl., Chis. 175 E5
Stewart Cl., Hmptn. 161 E5
Stewart Rainbird Ho. E12 98 D5
Stewart Rd. E15 96 D4
Stewart St. E14 134 C2
Stewart's Gro. SW3 31 F3
Stewart's Gro. SW3 129 G4
Stewart's Rd. SW8 130 C7
Stewartsby Cl. N18 59 J5
Steyne Rd. W3 126 C1
Steyning Gro. SE9 174 C4
Steyning Way, Houns. 142 C4
Steynings Way N12 56 D5
Steynton Av., Bex. 176 D2
Stickland Rd., Belv. 139 G4
Picardy Rd.
Stickleton Cl., Grnf. 103 H3
Stile Hall Gdns. W4 126 A5
Stile Hall Par. W4 126 A5
Chiswick High Rd.
Stile Path, Sun. 178 A3
Stilecroft Gdns., Wem. 86 E3
Stiles Cl., Brom. 192 C6
Stiles Cl., Erith 139 H5
Riverdale Rd.
Stillingfleet Rd. SW13 127 G6
Stillington St. SW1 33 G1
Stillington St. SW1 130 C4
Stillness Rd. SE23 153 H6
Stilton Cres. NW10 88 C7
Stipularis Dr., Hayes 102 D4
Stirling Cl. SW16 186 C1
Stirling Cor., Barn. 38 D6
Stirling Cor., Borwd. 38 D6
Stirling Gro., Houns. 143 J2
Stirling Rd. E13 115 H2
Stirling Rd. E17 77 H3
Stirling Rd. N17 76 D1
Stirling Rd. N22 75 H1
Stirling Rd. SW9 150 E2
Stirling Rd. W3 126 B3
Stirling Rd., Har. 68 C3
Stirling Rd., Hayes 102 B7
Stirling Rd., Houns. 140 C6
Stirling Rd., Twick. 143 G7
Stirling Rd. Path E17 77 H3
Stirling Wk., N.Mal. 182 C5
Stirling Wk., Surb. 182 B6
Stirling Way, Borwd. 38 D6
Stirling Way, Croy. 186 E7
Stiven Cres., Har. 85 F3
Stock Orchard Cres. N7 93 F5
Stock Orchard St. N7 93 F5
Stock St. E13 115 G2
Stockbury Rd., Croy. 189 F6
Stockdale Rd., Dag. 101 F2
Stockdove Way, Grnf. 104 C3
Stocker Gdns., Dag. 100 C7
Ellerton Rd.
Stockfield Rd. SW16 169 F3
Stockfield Rd., Esher 194 B5
Stockholm Rd. SE16 133 F5
Stockholm Way E1 29 H1
Stockholm Way E1 132 D1
Stockhurst Cl. SW15 147 J2
Stockingswater La., Enf. 45 H3
Stockley Cl., West Dr. 120 E2
Stockley Fm. Rd., West Dr. 120/121 E3
Stockley Rd.
Stockley Pk., Uxb. 121 E1
Stockley Pk. Roundabout, Uxb. 120 E1
Stockley Rd., West Dr. 120 E4
Stockport Rd. SW16 186 D1
Stocks Pl. E14 113 J7
Grenade St.
Stocksfield Rd. E17 78 C3
Stockton Gdns. N17 59 J7
Stockton Rd.
Stockton Gdns. NW7 54 E3
Stockton Rd. N17 59 J7
Stockton Rd. N18 60 D6
Stockwell Av. SW9 151 F3
Stockwell Cl., Brom. 191 H2
Stockwell Gdns. SW9 151 F2
Stockwell Gdns. Est. SW9 151 E2
Stockwell Grn. SW9 151 F2
Stockwell La. SW9 151 F2
Stockwell Ms. SW9 151 F2
Stockwell Rd.
Stockwell Pk. Cres. SW9 151 F2
Stockwell Pk. Est. SW9 151 G2
Stockwell Pk. Rd. SW9 151 F1
Stockwell Pk. Wk. SW9 151 F3
Stockwell Rd. SW9 151 F2
Stockwell St. SE10 134 C6
Stockwell Ter. SW9 151 F1
Stodart Rd. SE20 189 F1
Stofield Gdns. SE9 174 A3
Aldersgrove Av.
Stoford Cl. SW19 148 B7
Stoke Newington Ch. St. N16 94 A3
Stoke Newington Common N16 94 C3
Stoke Newington High St. N16 94 C3
Stoke Newington Rd. N16 94 C5
Stoke Pl. NW10 107 F3
Stoke Rd., Kings.T. 164 C7
Stokenchurch St. SW6 148 E1
Stokes Rd. E6 116 B4
Stokes Rd., Croy. 189 G6
Stokesby Rd., Chess. 195 J6
Stokesley St. W12 107 F6
Stoll Cl. NW2 89 J3
Stoms Path SE6 172 A5
Stonard Rd. N13 59 G3
Stonard Rd., Dag. 100 B5
Stonards Hill, Loug. 48 C6
Stondon Pk. SE23 153 H7
Stondon Wk. E6 116 A2
Stone Bldgs. WC2 18 D2
Stone Bldgs. WC2 111 F5
Stone Cl. SW4 150 C2
Larkhall Ri.
Stone Cl., Dag. 101 F2
Stone Cl., West Dr. 120 C1
Stone Cres., Felt. 141 J7
Stone Hall Gdns. W8 22 A6
Stone Hall Pl. W8 22 A6
Stone Hall Rd. N21 43 F7
Stone Ho. Ct. EC3 20 D3
Stone Pk. Av., Beck. 190 A4
Stone Pl., Wor.Pk. 197 G2
Stone Rd., Brom. 191 F5
Stone St., Croy. 201 G5
Stonebanks, Walt. 178 A7
Stonebridge Common E8 94 C7
Mayfield Rd.
Stonebridge Pk. NW10 88 D7
Stonebridge Rd. N15 76 B5
Stonebridge Way, Wem. 88 B6
Stonechat Sq. E6 116 B5
Peridot St.
Stonecot Cl., Sutt. 198 B1
Stonecot Hill, Sutt. 198 B1
Stonecroft Cl., Barn. 39 H4
Stonecroft Rd., Erith 139 J7

Sudbury Gdns., Croy. 202 B4
Langton Way
Sudbury Hts. Av., Grnf. 86 C5
Sudbury Hill, Har. 86 B2
Sudbury Hill Cl., Wem. 86 C4
Sudbury Rd., Bark. 99 J5
Sudeley St. N1 11 H2
Sudeley St. N1 111 H2
Sudlow Rd. SW18 148 D4
Sudrey St. SE1 27 J4
Suez Av., Grnf. 104 C2
Suez Rd., Enf. 45 H4
Suffield Rd. E4 62 B3
Suffield Rd. N15 76 C5
Suffield Rd. SE20 189 F2
Suffolk Cl., Borwd. 38 D5
Clydesdale Cl.
Suffolk Ct. E10 78 A7
Suffolk Ct., Ilf. 81 H6
Suffolk Ct., Surb. 181 G6
St. James Rd.
Suffolk La. EC4 20 B5
Suffolk Pk. Rd. E17 77 H4
Suffolk Pl. SW1 25 J1
Suffolk Rd. E13 115 F3
Suffolk Rd. N15 76 A6
Suffolk Rd. NW10 89 E7
Suffolk Rd. SE25 188 C4
Suffolk Rd. SW13 127 F7
Suffolk Rd., Bark. 99 G7
Suffolk Rd., Dag. 101 J5
Suffolk Rd., Enf. 45 E5
Suffolk Rd., Har. 67 F6
Suffolk Rd., Ilf. 81 H6
Suffolk Rd., Sid. 176 C6
Suffolk Rd., Wor.Pk. 197 F2
Suffolk St. E7 97 G5
Suffolk St. SW1 25 J1
Sugar Bakers Ct. EC3 112 B6
Creechurch La.
Sugar Ho. La. E15 114 C2
Sugar Loaf Wk. E2 113 F3
Victoria Pk. Sq.
Sugar Quay Wk. EC3 20 E6
Sugar Quay Wk. EC3 112 B7
Sugden Rd. SW11 150 A3
Sugden Rd., T.Ditt. 194 E1
Sugden Way, Bark. 117 J2
Sulgrave Gdns. W6 127 J2
Sulgrave Rd.
Sulgrave Rd. W6 127 J2
Sulina Rd. SW2 151 E7
Sulivan Ct. SW6 148 D3
Sulivan Rd. SW6 148 D3
Sullivan Av. E16 116 A5
Sullivan Cl. SW11 149 H3
Sullivan Cl., W.Mol. 179 G3
Victoria Av.
Sullivan Rd. SE11 35 F1
Sullivan Rd. SE11 131 H4
Sultan Rd. E11 79 H4
Sultan St. SE5 35 J7
Sultan St. SE5 131 J7
Sultan St., Beck. 189 G2
Sumatra Rd. NW6 90 D5
Sumburgh Rd. SW12 150 A6
Summer Av., E.Mol. 180 B5
Summer Gdns., E.Mol. 180 B5
Summer Hill, Borwd. 38 A5
Summer Hill, Chis. 192 D2
Summer Hill Vil., Chis. 192 D1
Summer Rd., E.Mol. 180 B5
Summer Rd., T.Ditt. 180 C5
Summer St. EC1 11 E6
Summer Trees, Sun. 178 B1
The Av.
Summercourt Rd. E1 113 F6
Summerene Cl. SW16 168 C7
Bates Cres.
Summerfield Av. NW6 108 B2
Summerfield La., Surb. 195 G2
Summerfield Rd. W5 105 E4
Summerfield Rd., Loug. 48 A6
Summerfield St. SE12 155 F7
Summerfields Av. N12 57 H6
Summerhill Cl., Orp. 207 H3
Summerhill Gro., Enf. 44 B6
Summerhill Rd. N15 76 A4
Summerhill Way, Mitch. 186 A1
Summerhouse Av., Houns. 142 E1
Summerhouse La., West Dr. 120 A6
Summerhouse Rd. N16 94 B2
Summerland Gdns. N10 74 B3
Summerlands Av. W3 106 C7
Summerlee Av. N2 73 J4
Summerlee Gdns. N2 73 J4
Summerley St. SW18 167 E2
Summers Cl., Sutt. 198 D7
Overton Rd.
Summers Cl., Wem. 88 B1
Summers La. N12 57 G7
Summers Row N12 57 H6
Summersby Rd. N6 74 B6
Summerstown SW17 167 F3
Summerton Way SE28 118 D6
Summerville Gdns., Sutt. 198 C6
Summerwood Rd., Islw. 144 C5
Summit, The, Loug. 48 C1
Summit Av. NW9 70 D5
Summit Cl. N14 58 C2
Summit Cl. NW9 70 D4
Summit Cl., Edg. 54 A7
Summit Ct. NW2 90 B5
Summit Dr., Wdf.Grn. 80 A2
Summit Est. N16 76 D7
Summit Rd. E17 78 B4
Summit Rd., Nthlt. 85 G7
Summit Way N14 58 B2
Summit Way SE19 170 B7
Sumner Av. SE15 152 C1
Sumner Rd.
Sumner Cl., Orp. 207 F4
Sumner Est. SE15 132 C7
Sumner Gdns., Croy. 201 G1
Sumner Pl. SW7 31 F2
Sumner Pl. SW7 129 G4
Sumner Pl. Ms. SW7 31 F2
Sumner Rd. SE15 37 G6
Sumner Rd. SE15 132 C7
Sumner Rd., Croy. 201 G1
Sumner Rd., Har. 67 J7
Sumner Rd. S., Croy. 201 G1
Sumner St. SE1 27 H1
Sumner St. SE1 131 J1
Sumpter Cl. NW3 91 F6
Sun All., Rich. 145 H4
Kew Rd.
Sun Ct. EC3 20 C4
Sun La. SE3 135 H7
Sun Pas. SE16 29 H5
Sun Rd. W14 128 C5
Sun St. EC2 20 D2
Sun St. EC2 112 A5
Sun St. Pas. EC2 20 D2
Sun Wk. E1 21 H6
Sunbeam Cres. W10 107 J4
Sunbeam Rd. NW10 106 C4
Sunbury Av. NW7 54 D5
Sunbury Av. SW14 146 D4
Sunbury Ct., Sun. 178 D2
Sunbury Ct. Island, Sun. 178 D3
Sunbury Ct. Ms., Sun. 178 D2
Lower Hampton Rd.
Sunbury Ct. Rd., Sun. 178 C2
Sunbury Gdns. NW7 54 D5
Sunbury La. SW11 149 G1
Sunbury La., Walt. 178 A6
Sunbury Lock Ait, Walt. 178 B4
Sunbury Rd., Sutt. 198 A3
Sunbury St. SE18 136 C3
Sunbury Way, Felt. 160 C5
Suncroft Pl. SE26 171 F3
Sunderland Ct. SE22 152 D7
Sunderland Mt. SE23 171 G2
Sunderland Rd.
Sunderland Rd. SE23 171 G1
Sunderland Rd. W5 125 G3
Sunderland Ter. W2 14 A3
Sunderland Ter. W2 108 E6
Sunderland Way E12 98 A2
Sundew Av. W12 107 G7
Sundial Av. SE25 188 C3
Sundorne Rd. SE7 135 J5
Sundra Wk. E1 113 G4
Beaumont Gro.
Sundridge Av., Brom. 174 A7
Sundridge Av., Chis. 174 A7
Sundridge Av., Well. 157 G2
Sundridge Ho., Brom. 173 H5
Burnt Ash La.
Sundridge Pl., Croy. 202 D1
Inglis Rd.
Sundridge Rd., Croy. 188 C7
Sunfields Pl. SE3 135 H7
Sunland Av., Bexh. 159 E4
Sunleigh Rd., Wem. 105 H1
Sunley Gdns., Grnf. 104 D1
Sunlight Cl. SW19 167 F6
Sunlight Sq. E2 113 E3
Sunmead Rd., Sun. 178 A3
Sunna Gdns., Sun. 178 B2
Sunningdale N14 58 D5
Wilmer Way
Sunningdale Av. W3 107 E7
Sunningdale Av., Bark. 117 G1
Sunningdale Av., Felt. 160 E2
Sunningdale Av., Ruis. 84 C1
Sunningdale Cl. E6 116 C3
Ascot Rd.
Sunningdale Cl. SE16 132/133 E5
Ryder Dr.
Sunningdale Cl. SE28 118 E6
Sunningdale Cl., Stan. 52 D7
Sunningdale Cl., Surb. 195 H2
Culsac Rd.
Sunningdale Gdns. NW9 70 C5
Sunningdale Gdns. W8 128 D3
Lexham Ms.
Sunningdale Rd., Brom. 192 B4
Sunningdale Rd., Sutt. 198 C4
Sunningfields Cres. NW4 71 H2
Sunningfields Rd. NW4 71 H2
Sunninghill Rd. SE13 154 B2
Sunny Bank SE25 188 D3
Sunny Cres. NW10 88 C7
Sunny Gdns. Par. NW4 71 J2
Great N. Way
Sunny Gdns. Rd. NW4 71 H2
Sunny Hill NW4 71 H3
Sunny Nook Gdns., S.Croy. 202 A6
Selsdon Rd.
Sunny Rd., The, Enf. 45 G1
Sunny Vw. NW9 70 D5
Sunny Way N12 57 H7
Sunnycroft Rd. SE25 188 D3
Sunnycroft Rd., Houns. 143 H2
Sunnycroft Rd., Sthl. 103 G5
Sunnydale, Orp. 206 D2
Sunnydale Gdns. NW7 54 D6
Sunnydale Rd. SE12 155 H5
Sunnydene Av. E4 62 D5
Sunnydene Av., Ruis. 84 A2
Sunnydene Gdns., Wem. 87 F6
Sunnydene St. SE26 171 H4
Sunnyfield NW7 55 F4
Sunnyhill Cl. E5 95 H4
Sunnyhill Rd. SW16 168 E4
Sunnyhurst Cl., Sutt. 198 D3
Sunnymead Av., Mitch. 186 C3
Sunnymead Rd. NW9 70 D7
Sunnymead Rd. SW15 147 H5
Sunnymede Dr., Ilf. 80 E4
Sunnyside NW2 90 C3
Sunnyside SW19 166 B6
Sunnyside, Walt. 178 C5
Sunnyside Dr. E4 46 C7
Sunnyside Pas. SW19 166 B6
Sunnyside Pl. SW19 166 B6
Sunnyside
Sunnyside Rd. E10 96 A1
Sunnyside Rd. N19 74 D7
Sunnyside Rd. W5 125 G1
Sunnyside Rd., Ilf. 99 F3
Sunnyside Rd., Tedd. 162 A4
Sunnyside Rd. E. N9 60 D3
Sunnyside Rd. N. N9 60 C3
Sunnyside Rd. S. N9 60 C3
Sunnyside Ter. NW9 70 D3
Edgware Rd.
Sunray Av. SE24 152 A4
Sunray Av., Brom. 192 B6
Sunray Av., Surb. 196 B2
Sunray Av., West Dr. 120 A2
Sunrise Cl., Felt. 161 F3
Exeter Rd.
Sunset Av. E4 62 B1
Sunset Av., Wdf.Grn. 63 F4
Sunset Gdns. SE25 188 C2
Sunset Rd. SE5 151 J4
Sunset Rd. SE28 138 A2
Sunset Vw., Barn. 40 B2
Sunshine Way, Mitch. 185 J2
Sunwell Cl. SE15 152/153 E1
Cossall Wk.
Superior Dr., Orp. 207 J6
Surbiton Ct., Surb. 181 F6
Surbiton Cres., Kings.T. 181 H4
Surbiton Hall Cl., Kings.T. 181 H4
Surbiton Hill Pk., Surb. 182 A5
Surbiton Hill Rd., Surb. 181 H4
Surbiton Par., Surb. 181 H6
St. Mark's Hill
Surbiton Rd., Kings.T. 181 H4
Surlingham Cl. SE28 118 D7
Surma Cl. E1 13 J6
Surma Cl. E1 112 E4
Surr St. N7 93 E5
Surrendale Pl. W9 108 D4
Surrey Canal Rd. SE14 133 F6
Surrey Canal Rd. SE15 133 F6
Surrey Cres. W4 126 A5
Surrey Gdns. N4 75 J6
Finsbury Pk. Av.
Surrey Gro. SE17 36 D4
Surrey Gro., Sutt. 199 G3
Surrey La. SW11 149 H1
Surrey La. Est. SW11 149 H1
Surrey Lo. SE1 26 E6
Surrey Ms. SE27 170 B4
Hamilton Rd.
Surrey Mt. SE23 171 E1
Surrey Quays Rd. SE16 133 G2
Surrey Rd. SE15 153 G5
Surrey Rd., Bark. 117 H1
Surrey Rd., Dag. 101 H5
Surrey Rd., Har. 67 J5
Surrey Rd., W.Wick. 204 B1
Surrey Row SE1 27 G3
Surrey Row SE1 131 H2
Surrey Sq. SE17 36 D3
Surrey Sq. SE17 132 B5
Surrey St. E13 115 H3
Surrey St. WC2 18 D5
Surrey St. WC2 111 F7
Surrey St., Croy. 201 J3
Surrey Ter. SE17 36 E3
Surrey Ter. SE17 132 B5
Surrey Twr. SE20 171 F7
Surrey Water Rd. SE16 133 G1
Surridge Gdns. SE19 170 A6
Hancock Rd.
Susan Cl., Rom. 83 J3
Susan Rd. SE3 155 H2
Susan Wd., Chis. 192 D1
Susannah St. E14 114 B6
Sussex Av., Islw. 144 B3
Sussex Cl. N19 92/93 E2
Cornwallis Rd.
Sussex Cl., Ilf. 80 C5
Sussex Cl., N.Mal. 183 E4
Sussex Cl., Twick. 144/145 E6
Westmorland Cl.
Sussex Cres., Nthlt. 85 G6
Sussex Gdns. N4 75 J5
Sussex Gdns. N6 73 J5
Great N. Rd.
Sussex Gdns. W2 15 E4
Sussex Gdns. W2 109 G6
Sussex Gdns., Chess. 195 G6
Sussex Ms. E. W2 15 F4
Sussex Ms. W. W2 15 F5
Sussex Pl. NW1 7 J5
Sussex Pl. NW1 109 J4
Sussex Pl. W2 15 F4
Sussex Pl. W2 109 G6
Sussex Pl. W6 127 J5
Sussex Pl., Erith 139 H7
Sussex Pl., N.Mal. 183 E4
Sussex Ring N12 56 D5
Sussex Rd. E6 116 D1
Sussex Rd., Cars. 199 J6
Sussex Rd., Erith 139 H7
Sussex Rd., Har. 67 J5
Sussex Rd., Mitch. 186/187 E5
Lincoln Rd.
Sussex Rd., N.Mal. 183 E4
Sussex Rd., Sid. 176 B5
Sussex Rd., S.Croy. 202 A6
Sussex Rd., Sthl. 122 D3
Sussex Rd., W.Wick. 204 B1
Sussex Sq. W2 15 F5
Sussex Sq. W2 109 G7
Sussex St. E13 115 H3
Sussex St. SW1 32 E4
Sussex St. SW1 130 B5
Sussex Wk. SW9 151 H4
Sussex Way N7 93 E2
Sussex Way N19 92 E1
Sussex Way, Barn. 42 A5
Sutcliffe Cl. NW11 73 E5
Sutcliffe Ho., Hayes 102 A6
Sutcliffe Rd. SE18 137 H6

356 Sut-Tal

Sutcliffe Rd., Well. 158 C2
Sutherland Av. W9 6 C4
Sutherland Av. W9 109 F3
Sutherland Av. W13 104 E6
Sutherland Av., Hayes 122 A4
Sutherland Av., Orp. 193 J6
Sutherland Av., Well. 157 H4
Sutherland Cl., Barn. 40 B4
Sutherland Ct. NW9 70 B5
Sutherland Dr. SW19 185 G1
Willow Vw.
Sutherland Gdns. SW14 147 E3
Sutherland Gdns., Wor.Pk. 197 H1
Sutherland Gro. SW18 148 B6
Sutherland Gro., Tedd. 162 B5
Sutherland Pl. W2 108 D6
Sutherland Pt. E5 94/95 E4
Tiger Way
Sutherland Rd. E17 77 G2
Sutherland Rd. N9 60 D1
Sutherland Rd. N17 60 D7
Sutherland Rd. W4 126 E6
Sutherland Rd. W13 104 D6
Sutherland Rd., Belv. 139 G3
Sutherland Rd., Croy. 187 G7
Sutherland Rd., Enf. 45 G5
Sutherland Rd., Sthl. 103 F6
Sutherland Rd. Path E17 77 G3
Sutherland Row SW1 32 E3
Sutherland Row SW1 130 B5
Sutherland Sq. SE17 35 J4
Sutherland Sq. SE17 131 J5
Sutherland St. SW1 32 D3
Sutherland St. SW1 130 B5
Sutherland Wk. SE17 36 A4
Sutherland Wk. SE17 131 J5
Sutlej Rd. SE7 135 J7
Sutterton St. N7 93 F6
Sutton Cl., Beck. 190 B1
Albemarle Rd.
Sutton Cl., Loug. 48 B7
Sutton Cl., Pnr. 66 A5
Sutton Common Rd., Sutt. 184 C7
Sutton Ct. W4 126 C6
Sutton Ct. Rd. E13 115 J3
Sutton Ct. Rd. W4 126 C7
Sutton Ct. Rd., Sutt. 199 F6
Sutton Cres., Barn. 40 A5
Sutton Dene, Houns. 143 H1
Sutton Est. SW3 31 H3
Sutton Est. SW3 129 H5
Sutton Est. W10 107 J5
Sutton Est., The N1 93 H7
Sutton Gdns., Bark. 117 H1
Sutton Rd.
Sutton Gdns., Croy. 188 C5
Sutton Grn., Bark. 117 H1
Sutton Rd.
Sutton Gro., Sutt. 199 G4
Sutton Hall Rd., Houns. 123 G7
Sutton La., Houns. 143 F3
Sutton La. N. W4 126 C5
Sutton La. S. W4 126 C6
Sutton Par. NW4 71 J4
Church Rd.
Sutton Pk. Rd., Sutt. 198 E6
Sutton Path, Borwd. 38 A2
Stratfield Rd.
Sutton Pl. E9 95 F5
Sutton Rd. E13 115 F4
Sutton Rd. E17 77 G1
Sutton Rd. N10 74 A2
Sutton Rd., Bark. 117 H2
Sutton Rd., Houns. 143 G1
Sutton Row W1 17 J3
Sutton Row W1 110 D6
Sutton Sq. E9 95 F5
Urswick Rd.
Sutton Sq., Houns. 143 F1
Sutton St. E1 113 F6
Sutton Way W10 107 J5
Sutton Way, Houns. 143 F1
Sutton's Way EC1 12 A6
Swaby Rd. SW18 167 F1
Swaffham Way N22 59 H7
White Hart La.
Swaffield Rd. SW18 149 E7
Swain Cl. SW16 168 B6
Swain Rd., Th.Hth. 187 J5
Swains Cl., West Dr. 120 B2
Swains La. N6 92 A3
Swains Rd. SW17 167 J7
Swainson Rd. W3 127 F2
Swaledale Cl. N11 58 A6
Ribblesdale Av.
Swallands Rd. SE6 172 A3
Swallow Cl. SE14 153 F1
Swallow Cl., Bushey 51 J1
Swallow Dr. NW10 88 D6
Kingfisher Way
Swallow Dr., Nthlt. 103 G2
Swallow Gdns. SW16 168 D5
Swallow Pas. W1 17 E4
Swallow Pl. W1 17 E4
Swallow St. E6 116 B5
Swallow St. W1 17 G6
Swallowfield Rd. SE7 135 H5
Swallowfield Way, Hayes 121 G2
Swan App. E6 116 B5
Swan Cl. E17 77 H1
Swan Cl., Croy. 188 B7
Swan Cl., Felt. 161 E4
Swan Ct. SW3 31 H4
Swan Dr. NW9 70 E2
Swan La. EC4 20 B6
Swan La. N20 57 F3
Swan La., Loug. 47 J7
Swan Mead SE1 28 D6
Swan Mead SE1 132 B3
Swan Pas. E1 112 C7
Cartwright St.
Swan Path E10 96 C1
Jesse Rd.
Swan Pl. SW13 147 F2
Swan Rd. SE16 133 F2
Swan Rd. SE18 136 A3
Swan Rd., Felt. 160 E5
Swan Rd., Sthl. 103 H6
Swan Rd., West Dr. 120 A2
Swan St. SE1 28 A5
Swan St. SE1 131 J3
Swan St., Islw. 144 E3
Swan Wk. SW3 31 J5
Swan Wk. SW3 129 J6
Swan Way, Enf. 45 G2
Swan Yd. N1 93 H6
Highbury Sta. Rd.
Swanage Rd. E4 62 C7
Swanage Rd. SW18 149 F6
Swanage Waye, Hayes 102 C6
Swanbridge Rd., Bexh. 159 G1
Swandon Way SW18 149 E4
Swanfield St. E2 13 F4
Swanfield St. E2 112 C3
Swanley Rd., Well. 158 C1
Swanscombe Rd. W4 127 E5
Swanscombe Rd. W11 128 A1
Swansea Ct. E16 136/137 E2
Barge Ho. Rd.
Swansea Rd., Enf. 45 F4
Swansea Rd., Felt. 141 F6
Southern Perimeter Rd.
Swansea Rd., Houns. 141 F6
Southern Perimeter Rd.
Swanshope, Loug. 49 E2
Swansland Gdns. E17 77 H1
McEntee Av.
Swanston Path, Wat. 50 C3
Swanton Gdns. SW19 166 A1
Swanton Rd., Erith 139 H7
Swanwick Cl. SW15 147 F7
Swaton Rd. E3 114 A4
Swaylands Rd., Belv. 139 G6
Swaythling Cl. N18 61 E4
Sweden Gate SE16 133 H3
Swedenborg Gdns. E1 21 J5
Swedenborg Gdns. E1 112 D7
Sweeney Cres. SE1 29 G4
Sweeney Cres. SE1 132 C2
Sweet Briar Grn. N9 60 C3
Sweet Briar Gro. N9 60 C3
Sweet Briar Wk. N18 60 C4
Sweetmans Av., Pnr. 66 D3
Sweets Way N20 57 G2
Swete St. E13 115 G2
Swetenham Wk. SE18 137 F5
Sandbach Pl.
Sweyn Pl. SE3 155 G2
Swift Cl. E17 61 H7
Swift Cl., Har. 85 H2
Swift Rd., Felt. 161 E3
Swift Rd., Sthl. 123 F3
Swift St. SW6 148 C1
Swiftsden Way, Brom. 173 E6
Swinbrook Rd. W10 108 B5
Swinburne Ct. SE5 152 A4
Basingdon Way
Swinburne Cres., Croy. 189 F6
Swinburne Rd. SW15 147 G4
Swinderby Rd., Wem. 87 H6
Swindon Cl., Ilf. 99 H2
Salisbury Rd.
Swindon Rd., Houns. 141 F5
Swindon St. W12 127 H1
Swinfield Cl., Felt. 160 E4
Swinford Gdns. SW9 151 H3
Swingate La. SE18 137 H6
Swinnerton St. E9 95 H5
Swinton Cl., Wem. 88 B1
Swinton Pl. WC1 10 C3
Swinton Pl. WC1 111 F3
Swinton St. WC1 10 C3
Swinton St. WC1 111 F3
Swires Shaw, Kes. 206 A4
Swiss Ter. NW6 91 G7
Swithland Gdns. SE9 174 D4
Swyncombe Av. W5 125 E4
Swynford Gdns. NW4 71 G4
Handowe Cl.
Sybil Ms. N4 75 H6
Lothair Rd. N.
Sybil Phoenix Cl. SE8 133 G5
Sybil Thorndike Ho. N1 93 J6
Clephane Rd.
Sybourn St. E17 77 J7
Sycamore Av. W5 125 G3
Sycamore Av., Sid. 157 J6
Sycamore Cl. E16 114/115 E4
Clarence Rd.
Sycamore Cl. N9 60 D4
Pycroft Way
Sycamore Cl. SE9 174 B2
Sycamore Cl. W3 126/127 E1
Bromyard Av.
Sycamore Cl., Barn. 41 G6
Sycamore Cl., Cars. 199 J4
Sycamore Cl., Edg. 54 C4
Ash Cl.
Sycamore Cl., Felt. 160 A3
Sycamore Cl., Loug. 48/49 E2
Cedar Dr.
Sycamore Cl., Nthlt. 103 E1
Sycamore Ct., Surb. 181 H7
Penners Gdns.
Sycamore Gdns. W6 127 H2
Sycamore Gdns., Mitch. 185 G2
Sycamore Gro. NW9 70 C7
Sycamore Gro. SE6 154 C6
Sycamore Gro. SE20 170 D7
Sycamore Gro., N.Mal. 182 D3
Sycamore Hill N11 58 A6
Sycamore Ms. SW4 150 C3
Sycamore Rd. SW19 165 J6
Sycamore St. EC1 11 J6
Sycamore Wk. W10 108 B4
Fifth Av.
Sycamore Wk., Ilf. 81 F4
Civic Way
Sycamore Way, Tedd. 163 F6
Sycamore Way, Th.Hth. 187 G5
Sydenham Av. N21 43 F5
Sydenham Av. SE26 171 E5
Sydenham Cotts. SE12 173 J2
Sydenham Hill SE23 170 E1
Sydenham Hill SE26 170 D3
Sydenham Hill Est. SE26 170 D3
Sydenham Pk. SE26 171 F3
Sydenham Pk. Rd. SE26 171 F3
Sydenham Ri. SE23 170 E2
Sydenham Rd. SE26 171 F5
Sydenham Rd., Croy. 188 A7
Sydmons Ct. SE23 153 F7
Sydner Ms. N16 94 C4
Sydner Rd.
Sydner Rd. N16 94 C4
Sydney Cl. SW3 31 F2
Sydney Cl. SW3 129 G4
Sydney Gro. NW4 71 J5
Sydney Ms. SW3 31 F2
Sydney Ms. SW3 129 G4
Sydney Pl. SW7 31 F2
Sydney Pl. SW7 129 G4
Sydney Rd. E11 79 H6
Mansfield Rd.
Sydney Rd. N8 75 G4
Sydney Rd. N10 74 A1
Sydney Rd. SE2 138 C3
Sydney Rd. SW20 184 A2
Sydney Rd. W13 124 D1
Sydney Rd., Bexh. 158 D4
Sydney Rd., Enf. 44 A4
Sydney Rd., Felt. 160 A1
Sydney Rd., Ilf. 81 F2
Sydney Rd., Rich. 145 H4
Sydney Rd., Sid. 175 H4
Sydney Rd., Sutt. 198 D4
Sydney Rd., Tedd. 162 C5
Sydney Rd., Wdf.Grn. 63 G4
Sydney St. SW3 31 G3
Sydney St. SW3 129 H4
Sylvan Av. N3 72 D2
Sylvan Av. N22 59 F7
Sylvan Av. NW7 55 F6
Sylvan Av., Rom. 83 F6
Sylvan Est. SE19 188 C1
Sylvan Gdns., Surb. 181 G7
Sylvan Gro. NW2 90 A4
Sylvan Gro. SE15 133 E6
Sylvan Hill SE19 188 B1
Sylvan Rd. E7 97 G6
Sylvan Rd. E11 79 G5
Sylvan Rd. E17 78 A5
Sylvan Rd. SE19 188 C1
Sylvan Rd., Ilf. 99 F2
Hainault St.
Sylvan Wk., Brom. 192 C3
Sylvan Way, Dag. 100 B3
Sylvan Way, W.Wick. 204 E4
Sylverdale Rd., Croy. 201 H3
Sylvester Av., Chis. 174 C6
Sylvester Path E8 94/95 E6
Sylvester Rd.
Sylvester Rd. E8 95 E6
Sylvester Rd. E17 77 J7
Sylvester Rd. N2 73 F2
Sylvester Rd., Wem. 87 F5
Sylvestrus Cl., Kings.T. 182 A1
Sylvia Av., Pnr. 51 F6
Sylvia Ct., Wem. 88 B7
Harrow Rd.
Sylvia Gdns., Wem. 88 B7
Symes Ms. NW1 9 F1
Symons St. SW3 32 A2
Symons St. SW3 129 J4
Syon Gate Way, Brent. 124 D7
Syon La., Islw. 124 E7
Syon Pk. Gdns., Islw. 124 C7
Syon Vista, Rich. 145 G1

T

Tabard Gdn. Est. SE1 28 C4
Tabard Gdn. Est. SE1 132 A2
Tabard St. SE1 28 B4
Tabard St. SE1 132 A2
Tabernacle Av. E13 115 G4
Barking Rd.
Tabernacle St. EC2 12 C6
Tabernacle St. EC2 112 A4
Tableer Av. SW4 150 D5
Tabley Rd. N7 92 E4
Tabor Gdns., Sutt. 198 C6
Tabor Gro. SW19 166 B7
Tabor Rd. W6 127 H3
Tachbrook Est. SW1 33 J4
Tachbrook Est. SW1 130 D5
Tachbrook Ms. SW1 33 F1
Tachbrook Rd., Felt. 141 J7
Tachbrook Rd., Sthl. 122 D4
Tachbrook St. SW1 33 G2
Tachbrook St. SW1 130 C4
Tack Ms. SE4 154 A3
Tadema Rd. SW10 30 D7
Tadema Rd. SW10 129 F7
Tadmor St. W12 128 A1
Tadworth Av., N.Mal. 183 F5
Tadworth Rd. NW2 89 G2
Taeping St. E14 134 B4
Taffy's How, Mitch. 185 H3
Taft Way E3 114 B3
St. Leonards St.
Tagg's Island, Hmptn. 180 A2
Tailworth St. E1 21 H2
Tait Rd., Croy. 188 B7
Takhar Ms. SW11 149 H2
Cabul Rd.
Talacre Rd. NW5 92 A6
Talbot Av. N2 73 G3
Talbot Cl. N15 76 C4
Talbot Ct. EC3 20 C5
Talbot Cres. NW4 71 G5
Talbot Gdns., Ilf. 100 A2
Talbot Ho. E14 114 B6
Giraud St.
Talbot Pl. SE3 154 E2
Talbot Rd. E6 116 D2
Talbot Rd. E7 97 G4
Talbot Rd. N6 74 A6
Talbot Rd. N15 76 C4
Talbot Rd. N22 74 C2
Talbot Rd. SE22 152 B4
Talbot Rd. W2 108 C6
Talbot Rd. W11 108 C6
Talbot Rd. W13 104 D7
Talbot Rd., Brom. 191 H4
Masons Hill
Talbot Rd., Cars. 200 A5
Talbot Rd., Dag. 101 F6
Talbot Rd., Har. 68 C2
Talbot Rd., Islw. 144 D4

Talbot Rd., Sthl. 123 E4
Talbot Rd., Th.Hth. 188 A4
Talbot Rd., Twick. 162 B1
Talbot Rd., Wem. 87 G5
Talbot Sq. W2 15 F4
Talbot Sq. W2 109 G6
Talbot Wk. NW10 88/89 E6
Garnet Rd.
Talbot Wk. W11 108 B6
Talbot Yd. SE1 28 B2
Talfourd Pl. SE15 152 C1
Talfourd Rd. SE15 152 C1
Talgarth Rd. W6 128 B5
Talgarth Rd. W14 128 B5
Talgarth Wk. NW9 70 E5
Talisman Cl., Ilf. 100 B1
Talisman Sq. SE26 170 D4
Talisman Way, Wem. 87 J3
Tall Elms Cl., Brom. 191 F5
Tall Trees SW16 187 F3
Tallack Cl., Har. 52 B7
College Hill Rd.
Tallack Rd. E10 95 J1
Tallis Cl. E16 115 H6
Tallis Gro. SE7 135 H6
Tallis St. EC4 19 F5
Tallis St. EC4 111 G7
Tallis Vw. NW10 88 D6
Tally Ho Cor. N12 57 F5
Talma Gdns., Twick. 144 B6
Talma Rd. SW2 151 G4
Talmage Cl. SE23 153 F7
Tyson Rd.
Talman Gro., Stan. 53 G6
Talwin St. E3 114 B3
Tamar Cl. E3 113 J1
Lefevre Wk.
Tamar Sq., Wdf.Grn. 63 H6
Tamar St. SE7 136 B3
Woolwich Rd.
Tamar Way N17 76 D3
Tamarind Yd. E1 29 J1
Tamarisk Sq. W12 107 F7
Tamesis Gdns., Wor.Pk. 196 E1
Tamian Way, Houns. 142 C4
Tamworth Av., Wdf.Grn. 63 E6
Tamworth La., Mitch. 186 B2
Tamworth Pk., Mitch. 186 B4
Tamworth Pl., Croy. 201 J2
Tamworth Rd., Croy. 201 H2
Tamworth St. SW6 128 D6
Tancred Rd. N4 75 H6
Tandridge Dr., Orp. 207 G1
Tandridge Pl., Orp. 193 G7
Tandridge Dr.
Tanfield Av. NW2 89 F4
Tanfield Rd., Croy. 201 J4
Tangier Rd., Rich. 146 B3
Tangle Tree Cl. N3 73 E2
Tanglebury Cl., Brom. 192 C4
Tanglewood Cl., Croy. 203 F3
Tanglewood Cl., Stan. 52 B2
Tanglewood Way, Felt. 160 B3
Tangley Gro. SW15 147 F6
Tangley Pk. Rd., Hmptn. 161 F6
Tangmere Gdns., Nthlt. 102 C2
Tangmere Gro., Kings.T. 163 G5
Tangmere Way NW9 71 E2
Tanhurst Wk. SE2 138 D3
Alsike Rd.
Tankerton Rd., Surb. 195 J2
Tankerton St. WC1 10 B4
Tankerville Rd. SW16 168 D6
Tankridge Rd. NW2 89 H2
Tanner St. SE1 28 E4
Tanner St. SE1 132 B2
Tanner St., Bark. 99 F6
Tanners Cl., Walt. 178 B6
Tanners End La. N18 60 B4
Tanners Hill SE8 153 J1
Tanners La., Ilf. 81 F3
Tannery Cl., Beck. 189 G5
Tannery Cl., Dag. 101 H3
Tannington Ter. N5 93 G3
Tannsfeld Rd. SE26 171 G5
Tansley Cl. N7 92 D5
Hilldrop Rd.
Tanswell Est. SE1 27 F4
Tanswell St. SE1 27 E4
Tansy Cl. E6 116 D6
Tant Av. E16 115 F6
Tantallon Rd. SW12 168 A1
Tantony Gro., Rom. 82 D3
Tanworth Gdns., Pnr. 66 B2
Tanyard La., Bex. 159 G7
Bexley High St.
Tanza Rd. NW3 91 J4
Tapestry Cl., Sutt. 198 E7
Taplow NW3 91 G7
Taplow SE17 36 D4
Taplow Rd. N13 59 J4
Taplow St. N1 12 A2
Taplow St. N1 111 J2
Tapp St. E1 113 E4
Tappesfield Rd. SE15 153 F3
Tapster St., Barn. 40 C4
Taransay Wk. N1 94 A6
Marquess Rd.
Tarbert Rd. SE22 152 B5
Tarbert Wk. E1 113 F7
Juniper St.
Target Cl., Felt. 141 H6
Tariff Cres. SE8 133 J4
Tariff Rd. N17 60 D6
Tarleton Gdns. SE23 171 E1
Tarling Cl., Sid. 176 B3
Tarling Rd. E16 115 F6
Tarling Rd. N2 73 F2
Tarling St. E1 113 E6
Tarling St. Est. E1 113 F6
Tarn St. SE1 27 J6
Tarnbank, Enf. 43 E5
Tarnwood Pk. SE9 174 C1
Tarquin Ho. SE26 170 D4
Tarragon Cl. SE14 133 H7
Tarragon Gro. SE26 171 G6
Tarrant Pl. W1 15 J2
Tarrington Cl. SW16 168 D3
Tarry La. SE8 133 H4
Tarver Rd. SE17 35 H4
Tarver Rd. SE17 131 H5
Tarves Way SE10 134 B7
Tash Pl. N11 58 B5
Woodland Rd.
Tasker Cl., Hayes 121 F7
Tasker Ho., Bark. 117 G2
Dovehouse Mead
Tasker Rd. NW3 91 J5
Tasman Rd. SW9 151 E3
Tasman Wk. E16 116 A6
Royal Rd.
Tasmania Ter. N18 59 J6
Tasso Rd. W6 128 B6
Tatam Rd. NW10 88 C7
Tate & Lyle Jetty E16 136 B2
Tate Rd. E16 136 C1
Newland St.
Tate Rd., Sutt. 198 D5
Tatnell Rd. SE23 153 H6
Tattersall Cl. SE9 156 B5
Tatton Cres. N16 76 C7
Clapton Common
Tatum St. SE17 36 C2
Tatum St. SE17 132 A4
Tauheed Cl. N4 93 J2
Taunton Av. SW20 183 H2
Taunton Av., Houns. 143 J2
Taunton Cl., Ilf. 65 J6
Taunton Cl., Sutt. 198 D1
Taunton Dr. N2 73 F2
Taunton Dr., Enf. 43 G3
Taunton Ms. NW1 7 J6
Taunton Pl. NW1 7 J5
Taunton Pl. NW1 109 J4
Taunton Rd. SE12 155 E5
Taunton Rd., Grnf. 103 H1
Taunton Way, Stan. 69 H3
Tavern Cl., Cars. 185 H7
Tavern La. SW9 151 G2
Taverner Sq. N5 93 J4
Highbury Gra.
Taverners Cl. W11 128 B1
Addison Av.
Taverners Way E4 62/63 E1
Douglas Rd.
Tavistock Av. E17 77 H3
Tavistock Av., Grnf. 104 D2
Tavistock Cl. N16 94 B5
Crossway
Tavistock Cres. W11 108 C5
Tavistock Cres., Mitch. 186 E4
Tavistock Gdns., Ilf. 99 H4
Tavistock Gate, Croy. 202 A1
Tavistock Gro., Croy. 188 A7
Tavistock Ms. E18 79 G4
Avon Way
Tavistock Ms. W11 108 C6
Lancaster Rd.
Tavistock Pl. E18 79 G3
Avon Way
Tavistock Pl. N14 42 B7
Chase Side
Tavistock Pl. WC1 9 J5
Tavistock Pl. WC1 110 E4
Tavistock Rd. E7 97 F4
Tavistock Rd. E15 97 F6
Tavistock Rd. E18 79 G3
Tavistock Rd. N4 76 A6
Tavistock Rd. NW10 107 F2
Tavistock Rd. W11 108 C5
Tavistock Rd., Brom. 191 F4
Tavistock Rd., Cars. 199 G1
Tavistock Rd., Croy. 202 A1
Tavistock Rd., Edg. 70 A1
Tavistock Rd., Well. 158 C1
Tavistock Rd., West Dr. 120 A1
Tavistock Sq. WC1 9 J5
Tavistock Sq. WC1 110 D4
Tavistock St. WC2 18 B5
Tavistock St. WC2 111 E7
Tavistock Ter. N19 92 D3
Tavistock Wk., Cars. 199 G1
Tavistock Rd.
Taviton St. WC1 9 H5
Taviton St. WC1 110 D4
Tavy Cl. SE11 35 F3
Tavy Cl. SE11 131 G5
Tawney Rd. SE28 118 B7
Tawny Cl. W13 124 E1
Tawny Cl., Felt. 160 A3
Chervil Cl.
Tawny Way SE16 133 G4
Tayben Av., Twick. 144 B6
Taybridge Rd. SW11 150 A3
Tayburn Cl. E14 114 C6
Taylor Av., Rich. 146 B2
Taylor Cl. N17 60 D7
Taylor Cl., Hmptn. 161 J5
Taylor Cl., Houns. 143 J1
Taylor Cl., Orp. 207 J4
Taylor Ct. E15 96 C5
Clays La.
Taylor Rd., Mitch. 167 H7
Taylor Rd., Wall. 200 B5
Taylors Bldgs. SE18 136/137 E4
Spray St.
Taylors Cl., Sid. 175 J4
Taylors Grn. W3 106/107 E6
Long Dr.
Taylors La. NW10 88 E7
Taylors La. SE26 170 E4
Taylors La., Barn. 40 C1
Taymount Ri. SE23 171 F2
Tayport Cl. N1 93 E7
Tayside Dr., Edg. 54 B3
Taywood Rd., Nthlt. 103 F3
Teak Cl. SE16 133 H1
Teal Cl. E16 116 A5
Fulmer Rd.
Teal Pl., Sutt. 198 B2
Gander Grn. La.
Teale St. E2 13 J1
Teale St. E2 112 D2
Tealing Dr., Epsom 196 D4
Teasel Cl., Croy. 203 G1
Teasel Way E15 114 E3
Tebworth Rd. N17 60 C7
Teck Cl., Islw. 144 D2
Tedder Cl., Chess. 195 F5
Tedder Cl., Ruis. 84 B5
West End Rd.
Tedder Rd., S.Croy. 203 F7
Teddington Lock, Tedd. 162 E4
Teddington Pk., Tedd. 162 C5
Teddington Pk. Rd., Tedd. 162 C4
Tedworth Gdns. SW3 31 J4
Tedworth Sq. SW3 31 J4
Tedworth Sq. SW3 129 J5
Tee, The W3 106 E6
Tees Av., Grnf. 104 B2
Teesdale Av., Islw. 144 D1
Teesdale Cl. E2 13 J2
Teesdale Cl. E2 112 E2
Teesdale Gdns. SE25 188 B2
Teesdale Gdns., Islw. 144 D1
Teesdale Rd. E11 79 F6
Teesdale St. E2 112 E2
Teesdale Yd. E2 13 J1
Teeswater Ct., Erith 138 D3
Middle Way
Teevan Cl., Croy. 188 D7
Teevan Rd., Croy. 188 D7
Teignmouth Cl. SW4 150 D4
Teignmouth Cl., Edg. 69 J2
Teignmouth Gdns., Grnf. 104 D2
Teignmouth Rd. NW2 90 A5
Teignmouth Rd., Well. 158 C2
Telcote Way, Ruis. 66 C7
Woodlands Av.
Telegraph Hill NW3 90 E3
Telegraph La., Esher 194 C6
Telegraph Ms., Ilf. 100 A1
Telegraph Pl. E14 134 B4
Telegraph Rd. SW15 147 H7
Telegraph St. EC2 20 B3
Telemann Sq. SE3 155 H3
Telephone Pl. SW6 128 C6
Lillie Rd.
Telfer Cl. W3 126 C2
Church Rd.
Telferscot Rd. SW12 168 D1
Telford Av. SW2 168 E1
Telford Cl. E17 77 H7
Telford Cl. SE19 170 C6
St. Aubyn's Rd.
Telford Cl. W3 126 C2
Church Rd.
Telford Dr., Walt. 178 C7
Telford Rd. N11 58 C6
Telford Rd. NW9 71 G6
West Hendon Bdy.
Telford Rd. SE9 175 G2
Telford Rd. W10 108 B5
Telford Rd., Sthl. 103 H7
Telford Rd., Twick. 143 G7
Telford Ter. SW1 33 F5
Telford Ter. SW1 130 C6
Telford Way W3 106 E5
Telford Way, Hayes 102 E5
Telfords Yd. E1 21 J6
Telham Rd. E6 116 D2
Tell Gro. SE22 152 C4
Tellson Av. SE18 156 A1
Telscombe Cl., Orp. 207 H2
Temeraire St. SE16 133 F2
Albion St.
Temperley Rd. SW12 150 A7
Templar Dr. SE28 118 D6
Templar Ho. NW2 90 C6
Shoot Up Hill
Templar Pl., Hmptn. 161 G7
Templar St. SE5 151 H2
Templars Av. NW11 72 C6
Templars Cres. N3 72 D2
Templars Dr., Har. 52 A6
Temple EC4 111 G7
Temple Av. EC4 19 F5
Temple Av. EC4 111 G7
Temple Av. N20 41 G7
Temple Av., Croy. 203 J2
Temple Av., Dag. 101 G1
Temple Cl. E11 78/79 E7
Wadley Rd.
Temple Cl. N3 72 C2
Cyprus Rd.
Temple Cl. SE28 137 F3
Temple Ct. E1 113 G5
Rectory Sq.
Temple Fortune Hill NW11 72 D5
Temple Fortune La. NW11 72 D6
Temple Fortune Par. NW11 72 C5
Finchley Rd.
Temple Gdns. N21 59 H2
Barrowell Grn.
Temple Gdns. NW11 72 C6
Temple Gdns., Dag. 100 D3
Temple Gro. NW11 72 D6
Temple Gro., Enf. 43 H3
Temple La. EC4 19 F4
Temple Mead Cl., Stan. 52 E6
Temple Mill La. E15 96 B4
Temple Pl. WC2 18 D5
Temple Pl. WC2 111 F7
Temple Rd. E6 116 B1
Temple Rd. N8 75 F4
Temple Rd. NW2 89 J4
Temple Rd. W4 126 C3
Temple Rd. W5 125 G3
Temple Rd., Croy. 202 A4
Temple Rd., Houns. 143 H4
Temple Rd., Rich. 145 J3
Temple Sheen SW14 146 C5
Temple Sheen Rd. SW14 146 B4
Temple St. E2 112 E2
Temple Way, Sutt. 199 G3
Temple W. Ms. SE11 27 G6
Temple W. Ms. SE11 131 H3
Templecombe Rd. E9 113 F1
Templecombe Way, Mord. 184 B5
Templehof Av. NW2 71 J7
Templeman Rd. W7 104 C5
Templemead Cl. W3 106 E6
Templeton Av. E4 62 A4
Templeton Cl. N16 94 B5
Truman's Rd.
Templeton Cl. SE19 188 A1
Templeton Pl. SW5 128 D4
Templeton Rd. N15 76 A6
Templewood W13 105 E5
Templewood Av. NW3 90 E3
Templewood Gdns. NW3 91 E3
Tempsford Av., Borwd. 38 D4
Tempsford Cl., Enf. 43 J3
Gladbeck Way
Temsford Cl., Har. 67 J2

Tenbury Cl. E7 98 A5
Romford Rd.
Tenbury Ct. SW2 168 D1
Tenby Av., Har. 68 E2
Tenby Cl. N15 76 C4
Hanover Rd.
Tenby Cl., Rom. 82 E6
Tenby Gdns., Nthlt. 85 G6
Tenby Rd. E17 77 H5
Tenby Rd., Edg. 69 J1
Tenby Rd., Enf. 45 F3
Tenby Rd., Rom. 83 E6
Tenby Rd., Well. 158 D1
Tench St. E1 132 E1
Tenda Rd. SE16 132/133 E4
Roseberry St.
Tendring Way, Rom. 82 C5
Tenham Av. SW2 168 D1
Tenison Ct. W1 17 F5
Tenison Way SE1 26 E2
Tenison Way SE1 131 F1
Tenniel Cl. W2 14 C4
Tennis Ct. La., E.Mol. 180 C3
Hampton Ct. Way
Tennis St. SE1 28 B3
Tennis St. SE1 132 A2
Tennison Av., Borwd. 38 B5
Tennison Rd. SE25 188 C4
Tenniswood Rd., Enf. 44 C1
Tennyson Av. E11 79 G7
Tennyson Av. E12 98 B7
Tennyson Av. NW9 70 C3
Tennyson Av., N.Mal. 183 H5
Tennyson Av., Twick. 162 C1
Tennyson Cl., Enf. 45 G5
Tennyson Cl., Felt. 141 J6
Tennyson Cl., Well. 157 J1
Tennyson Rd. E10 96 B2
Tennyson Rd. E15 96 E7
Tennyson Rd. E17 77 J6
Tennyson Rd. NW6 108 C1
Tennyson Rd. NW7 55 G5
Tennyson Rd. SE20 171 G7
Tennyson Rd. SW19 167 F6
Tennyson Rd. W7 104 C7
Tennyson Rd., Houns. 143 J2
Tennyson St. SW8 150 B2
Tensing Rd., Sthl. 123 G3
Tent Peg La., Orp. 193 F5
Tent St. E1 112 E4
Tentelow La., Sthl. 123 G5
Tenter Grd. E1 21 F2
Tenter Pas. E1 21 G4
Tenterden Cl. NW4 72 A3
Tenterden Cl. SE9 174 C4
Tenterden Dr. NW4 72 A3
Tenterden Gdns. NW4 72 A3
Tenterden Gdns., Croy. 188 D7
Tenterden Gro. NW4 72 A4
Tenterden Rd. N17 60 C7
Tenterden Rd., Croy. 188 D7
Tenterden Rd., Dag. 101 F2
Tenterden St. W1 16 E4
Tenterden St. W1 110 B6
Terborch Way SE22 152 B5
East Dulwich Gro.
Teredo St. SE16 133 G3
Terence Ct., Belv. 139 F6
Nuxley Rd.
Teresa Ms. E17 78 A4
Teresa Wk. N10 74 B5
Connaught Gdns.
Terling Cl. E11 97 F3
Terling Rd., Dag. 101 G2
Terling Wk. N1 111 J1
Britannia Row
Terminus Pl. SW1 25 E6
Terminus Pl. SW1 130 B3
Terrace, The E4 62/63 E3
Chingdale Rd.
Terrace, The N3 72 C2
Hendon La.
Terrace, The NW6 108 D1
Terrace, The SW13 147 E2
Terrace, The, Har. 86 E1
Terrace, The, Wdf.Grn. 63 G6
Broadmead Rd.
Terrace Gdns. SW13 147 F2
Terrace La., Rich. 145 H6
Terrace Rd. E9 95 F7
Terrace Rd. E13 115 G1
Terrace Rd., Walt. 178 A7
Terrace Wk., Dag. 101 E5
Terrapin Rd. SW17 168 B3
Terretts Pl. N1 93 H7
Upper St.
Terrick Rd. N22 75 E1
Terrick St. W12 107 H6
Terrilands, Pnr. 67 F3
Terront Rd. N15 75 J5
Tessa Sanderson Pl. SW8 150 B3
Tessa Sanderson Way, Grnf. 86 A5
Lilian Board Way
Testerton Wk. W11 108 A7
Tetbury Pl. N1 111 H1
Upper St.
Tetcott Rd. SW10 30 C7
Tetcott Rd. SW10 129 F7
Tetherdown N10 74 A3
Tetty Way, Brom. 191 G2
Teversham La. SW8 151 E1
Teviot Cl., Well. 158 B1
Teviot St. E14 114 C5
Tewkesbury Av. SE23 171 E1
Tewkesbury Av., Pnr. 67 E5
Tewkesbury Cl. N15 76 A6
Tewkesbury Rd.
Tewkesbury Cl., Loug. 48 B6
Tewkesbury Gdns. NW9 70 B3
Tewkesbury Rd. N15 76 A6
Tewkesbury Rd. W13 104 D7
Tewkesbury Rd., Cars. 199 G1
Tewkesbury Ter. N11 58 C6
Tewson Rd. SE18 137 H5
Teynham Av., Enf. 44 A6
Teynham Grn., Brom. 191 G5
Teynton Ter. N17 75 J1
Thackeray Av. N17 76 D2
Thackeray Cl. SW19 166 A7
Thackeray Cl., Har. 85 G1
Thackeray Cl., Islw. 144 D2
Thackeray Dr., Rom. 82 A7
Thackeray Rd. E6 116 A2
Thackeray Rd. SW8 150 B2
Thackeray St. W8 22 B4
Thackeray St. W8 129 E2
Thackrah Cl. N2 73 F2
Thakeham Cl. SE26 170 E5
Thalia Cl. SE10 134 D6
Thame Rd. SE16 133 G2
Thames Av. SW10 149 F1
Thames Av., Dag. 119 H4
Thames Av., Grnf. 104 C2
Thames Bank SW14 146 C2
Thames Circle E14 134 A4
Westferry Rd.
Thames Cl., Hmptn. 179 H2
Thames Ct., W.Mol. 179 H2
Thames Ditton Island, T.Ditt. 180 D5
Thames Gateway, Dag. 119 F2
Thames Meadow, W.Mol. 179 G2
Thames Path SE1 19 F6
Thames Path SE1 111 G7
Thames Path SE7 135 J3
Thames Pl. SW15 148 A3
Thames Rd. E16 136 A1
Thames Rd. W4 126 A6
Thames Rd., Bark. 117 J3
Thames Side, Kings.T. 181 G1
Thames St. SE10 134 B6
Thames St., Hmptn. 179 H1
Thames St., Kings.T. 181 G2
Thames St., Sun. 178 B4
Thames Village W4 146 C1
Thames Wf. E16 135 F1
Thamesbank Pl. SE28 118 C6
Thamesgate Cl., Rich. 162/163 E4
Locksmeade Rd.
Thameshill Av., Rom. 83 J2
Thameside, Tedd. 163 G7
Thameside Ind. Est. E16 136 B2
Thameside Wk. SE28 117 J6
Thamesmead, Walt. 178 A7
Thamesmead Spine Rd., Belv. 159 H4
Thamesmere Dr. SE28 118 A7
Thamesvale Cl., Houns. 143 G3
Thane Vil. N7 93 F3
Thane Wks. N7 93 F3
Thane Vil.
Thanescroft Gdns., Croy. 202 B3
Thanet Dr., Kes. 206 A3
Phoenix Dr.
Thanet Pl., Croy. 201 J4
Thanet Rd., Bex. 159 G7
Thanet St. WC1 10 A4
Thanet St. WC1 110 E3
Thanington Ct. SE9 157 H6
Thant Cl. E10 96 B3
Tharp Rd., Wall. 200 D5
Thatcham Gdns. N20 41 F7
Thatcher Cl., West Dr. 120 B2
Classon Cl.
Thatchers Cl., Loug. 49 F2
Thatchers Way, Islw. 144 A5
Thatches Gro., Rom. 82 E4
Thavies Inn EC1 19 F3
Thaxted Ho., Dag. 101 H7
Thaxted Pl. SW20 166 A7
Thaxted Rd. SE9 175 F2
Thaxted Rd., Buck.H. 48 B7
Thaxton Rd. W14 128 C6
Thayer St. W1 16 C2
Thayer St. W1 110 A5
Thayers Fm. Rd., Beck. 189 H1
Theatre Sq. E15 96 D6
Salway Rd.
Theatre St. SW11 149 J3
Theberton St. N1 111 G1
Theed St. SE1 27 E2
Theed St. SE1 131 G1
Thelma Gdns. SE3 156 A1
Thelma Gdns., Felt. 160/161 E3
Hampton Rd. W.
Thelma Gro., Tedd. 162 D6
Theobald Cres., Har. 67 H1
Theobald Rd. E17 77 J7
Theobald Rd., Croy. 201 H2
Theobald St. SE1 28 B6
Theobalds Av. N12 57 F4
Theobalds Ct. N4 93 J2
Queens Dr.
Theobald's Rd. WC1 18 C1
Theobald's Rd. WC1 111 F5
Theodore Rd. SE13 154 C6
Therapia La., Croy. 187 E6
Therapia Rd. SE22 153 F6
Theresa Rd. W6 127 G4
Therfield Ct. N4 93 J2
Brownswood Rd.
Thermopylae Gate E14 134 B4
Theseus Wk. N1 11 H2
Thesiger Rd. SE20 171 G7
Thessaly Rd. SW8 130 C7
Thetford Cl. N13 59 H6
Thetford Gdns., Dag. 100 D7
Thetford Rd., Dag. 118 D1
Thetford Rd., N.Mal. 182 D6
Thetis Ter., Rich. 126 A6
Kew Grn.
Theydon Gro., Wdf.Grn. 63 J6
Theydon Pk. Rd., Epp. 49 H1
Theydon Rd. E5 95 F2
Theydon St. E17 77 J7
Thicket Cres., Sutt. 199 F4
Thicket Gro. SE20 170 D7
Anerley Rd.
Thicket Gro., Dag. 100 C6
Thicket Rd. SE20 170 D7
Thicket Rd., Sutt. 199 F4
Third Av. E12 98 B4
Third Av. E13 115 G3
Third Av. E17 78 A5
Third Av. W3 127 F1
Third Av. W10 108 B3
Third Av., Dag. 119 H1
Third Av., Enf. 44 C5
Third Av., Hayes 121 J1
Third Av., Rom. 82 C6
Third Av., Wem. 87 G2
Third Cl., W.Mol. 179 H4
Third Cross Rd., Twick. 162 A2
Third Way, Wem. 88 B4
Thirleby Rd. SW1 25 G6
Thirleby Rd. SW1 130 C3
Thirleby Rd., Edg. 70 D1
Thirlmere Av., Grnf. 105 F3
Thirlmere Gdns., Wem. 87 F1
Thirlmere Ho., Islw. 144 C5
Summerwood Rd.
Thirlmere Ri., Brom. 173 F6
Thirlmere Rd. N10 74 B1
Thirlmere Rd. SW16 168 D4
Thirlmere Rd., Bexh. 159 J2
Thirsk Cl., Nthlt. 85 G6
Thirsk Rd. SE25 188 A4
Thirsk Rd. SW11 150 A3
Thirsk Rd., Mitch. 168 A7
Thirston Path, Borwd. 38 A2
Thistle Gro. SW10 30 D3
Thistle Gro. SW10 129 F5
Thistle Mead, Loug. 48 D3
Thistlebrook SE2 138 C3
Thistlebrook Ind. Est. SE2 138 C2
Thistlecroft Gdns., Stan. 69 G1
Thistledene, T.Ditt. 180 B6
Thistledene Av., Har. 85 E3
Thistlemead, Chis. 192 E2
Thistlewaite Rd. E5 95 E3
Thistlewood Cl. N7 93 F2
Thistleworth Cl., Islw. 124 A7
Thistley Cl. N12 57 H6
Summerfields Av.
Thomas a'Beckett Cl., Wem. 86 C4
Thomas Baines Rd. SW11 149 G3
Thomas Darby Ct. W11 108 B6
Thomas Dean Rd. SE26 171 J4
Kangley Br. Rd.
Thomas Dinwiddy Rd. SE12 173 H2
Thomas Doyle St. SE1 27 G5
Thomas Doyle St. SE1 131 H3
Thomas Hardy Ho. N22 59 F7
Thomas La. SE6 154 A7
Thomas More St. E1 21 H6
Thomas More St. E1 112 D7
Thomas More Way N2 73 F3
Thomas Pl. W8 22 A6
Thomas Rd. E14 113 J6
Thomas St. SE18 136 E4
Thomas Wall Cl., Sutt. 198/199 E5
Clarence Rd.
Thompson Av., Rich. 146 A3
Thompson Cl., Ilf. 99 F2
High Rd.
Thompson Rd. SE22 152 C6
Thompson Rd., Dag. 101 F3
Thompson's Av. SE5 35 J7
Thompson's Av. SE5 131 J7
Thompson's La., Loug. 47 F1
Thomson Cres., Croy. 201 G1
Thomson Rd., Har. 68 B3
Thorburn Sq. SE1 37 H2
Thorburn Sq. SE1 132 D4
Thorburn Way SW19 185 G1
Willow Vw.
Thoresby St. N1 12 A3
Thoresby St. N1 111 J3
Thorkhill Gdns., T.Ditt. 194 D1
Thorkhill Rd., T.Ditt. 180 E7
Thorn Av., Bushey 51 J1
Thorn Cl., Brom. 192 D6
Thorn Cl., Nthlt. 103 F3
Thorn Ho., Beck. 189 H1
Thorn Ter. SE15 153 F3
Nunhead Gro.
Thornaby Gdns. N18 60 D6
Thornbury Av., Islw. 124 A7
Thornbury Cl. N16 94 B5
Truman's Rd.
Thornbury Gdns., Borwd. 38 C4
Thornbury Rd. SW2 150 E6
Thornbury Rd., Islw. 144 A1
Thornbury Sq. N6 92 C1
Thornby Rd. E5 95 F3
Thorncliffe Rd. SW2 150 E6
Thorncliffe Rd., Sthl. 123 F5
Thorncombe Rd. SE22 152 B5
Thorncroft Rd., Sutt. 198 E4
Thorncroft St. SW8 130 E7
Thorndean St. SW18 167 F2
Thorndene Av. N11 58 A1
Thorndike Av., Nthlt. 102 D1
Thorndike Cl. SW10 30 C7
Thorndike Cl. SW10 129 F7
Thorndike St. SW1 33 H3
Thorndike St. SW1 130 C4
Thorndon Cl., Orp. 193 J2
Thorndon Gdns., Epsom 196 E4
Thorndon Rd., Orp. 193 J2
Thorndyke Ct., Pnr. 51 F7
Westfield Pk.
Thorne Cl. E11 96 E4
Thorne Cl. E16 115 G6
Thorne Cl., Erith 139 J6
Thorne Pas. SW13 147 E2
Thorne Rd. SW8 130 E7
Thorne St. E16 115 F6
Thorne St. SW13 147 E3
Thorneloe Gdns., Croy. 201 G5
Thornes Cl., Beck. 190 C3
Thornet Wd. Rd., Brom. 192 D3
Thorney Cres. SW11 129 G7
Thorney Hedge Rd. W4 126 B4
Thorney St. SW1 34 A1
Thorney St. SW1 130 E4
Thorneycroft Cl., Walt. 178 C6

Thornfield Av. NW7 72 B1
Thornfield Rd. W12 127 H2
Thornford Rd. SE13 154 C5
Thorngate Rd. W9 108 D4
Thorngrove Rd. E13 115 H1
Thornham Gro. E15 96 D5
Thornham St. SE10 134 B6
Thornhaugh Ms. WC1 9 J6
Thornhaugh St. WC1 17 J1
Thornhaugh St. WC1 110 D4
Thornhill Av. SE18 137 H7
Thornhill Av., Surb. 195 H2
Thornhill Br. Wf. N1 111 F1
Caledonian Rd.
Thornhill Cres. N1 93 F7
Thornhill Gdns. E10 96 B2
Thornhill Gdns., Bark. 99 H7
Thornhill Gro. N1 93 F7
Lofting Rd.
Thornhill Ho. N1 93 G7
Thornhill Rd.
Thornhill Rd. E10 96 B2
Thornhill Rd. N1 93 G7
Thornhill Rd., Croy. 187 J7
Thornhill Rd., Surb. 195 H2
Thornhill Sq. N1 93 F7
Thornlaw Rd. SE27 169 G4
Thornley Cl. N17 60 D7
Thornley Dr., Har. 85 H2
Thornley Pl. SE10 134/135 E5
Caradoc St.
Thornsbeach Rd. SE6 172 C1
Thornsett Pl. SE20 188 E2
Thornsett Rd. SE20 188 E2
Thornsett Rd. SW18 167 E2
Thornside, Edg. 54 A6
High St.
Thornton Av. SW2 168 D1
Thornton Av. W4 127 E4
Thornton Av., Croy. 187 F6
Thornton Av., 120 C3
West Dr.
Thornton Cl., 120 C3
West Dr.
Thornton Ct. SW20 184 A5
Thornton Dene, Beck. 190 A2
Thornton Gdns. 168 D1
SW12
Thornton Gro., Pnr. 51 G6
Thornton Hill SW19 166 B7
Thornton Pl. W1 16 A1
Thornton Pl. W1 109 J5
Thornton Rd. E11 96 D2
Thornton Rd. N18 61 F3
Thornton Rd. SW12 150 D7
Thornton Rd. SW14 146 D3
Thornton Rd. SW19 166 A6
Thornton Rd., Barn. 40 B3
Thornton Rd., Belv. 139 H4
Thornton Rd., Brom. 173 G5
Thornton Rd., Cars. 199 G1
Thornton Rd., Croy. 187 F7
Thornton Rd., Ilf. 98 E4
Thornton Rd., Th.Hth. 187 F7
Thornton Rd. E. 166 A6
SW19
Thornton Rd.
Thornton Rd. Retail 187 F6
Pk., Croy.
Thornton Row, 187 G5
Th.Hth.
London Rd.
Thornton St. SW9 151 G2
Thornton Way NW11 73 E5
Thorntree Rd. SE7 136 A5
Thornville Gro., 185 F2
Mitch.
Thornville St. SE8 154 A1
Thornwood Cl. E18 79 H2
Thornwood Rd. SE13 154 E5
Thorogood Gdns. E15 97 E5
Thorold Rd. N22 59 E7
Thorold Rd., Ilf. 98 E2
Thorparch Rd. SW8 150 D1
Thorpe Cl. W10 108 B6
Cambridge Gdns.
Thorpe Cl., Orp. 207 H2
Thorpe Cres. E17 77 J2
Thorpe Hall Rd. E17 78 C1
Thorpe Rd. E6 116 C1
Thorpe Rd. E7 97 F4
Thorpe Rd. E17 78 C2
Thorpe Rd. N15 76 B6
Thorpe Rd., Bark. 99 G7
Thorpe Rd., Kings.T. 163 H7
Thorpebank Rd. W12 127 G1
Thorpedale Gdns., Ilf. 80 D4
Thorpedale Rd. N4 93 E1
Thorpewood Av. 171 E2
SE26
Thorsden Way SE19 170 B4
Oaks Av.
Thorverton Rd. NW2 90 B3
Thoydon Rd. E3 113 H2

Thrale Rd. SW16 168 C5
Thrale St. SE1 28 A2
Thrale St. SE1 131 J1
Thrasher Cl. E8 112 C1
Stean St.
Thrawl St. E1 21 G2
Thrawl St. E1 112 C5
Threadneedle St. 20 C4
EC2
Threadneedle St. 112 A6
EC2
Three Barrels Wk. 20 A5
EC4
Three Colt St. E14 113 J7
Three Colts Cor. E2 13 H5
Three Colts La. E2 113 E4
Three Cors., Bexh. 159 H2
Three Cups Yd. WC1 18 D2
Three Kings Rd., 186 A3
Mitch.
Three Kings Yd. W1 110 B7
Three Mill La. E3 114 C3
Three Oak La. SE1 29 F3
Threshers Pl. W11 108 B7
Thriffwood SE26 171 F3
Thrift Fm. La., Borwd. 38 B2
Thrigby Rd., Chess. 195 J6
Throckmorten Rd. 115 H6
E16
Throgmorton Av. 20 C3
EC2
Throgmorton Av. 112 A6
EC2
Throgmorton St. 20 C3
EC2
Throgmorton St. EC2 112 A6
Throwley Cl. SE2 138 C3
Throwley Rd., Sutt. 199 E5
Throwley Way, Sutt. 199 E4
Thrupp Cl., Mitch. 186 B2
Thrush Grn., Har. 67 G4
Thrush St. SE17 35 J3
Thruxton Way SE15 37 G7
Thunderer Rd., Dag. 118 E4
Thurbarn Rd. SE6 172 B5
Thurland Rd. SE16 29 H5
Thurland Rd. SE16 132 D3
Thurlby Cl., Har. 68 D6
Gayton Rd.
Thurlby Cl., Wdf.Grn. 64 C5
Thurlby Rd. SE27 169 G4
Thurlby Rd., Wem. 87 G6
Thurleigh Av. SW12 150 A6
Thurleigh Rd. SW12 150 A6
Thurleston Av., Mord. 184 B5
Thurlestone Av. N12 57 J6
Thurlestone Av., Ilf. 99 J4
Thurlestone Rd. SE27 169 G3
Thurloe Cl. SW7 31 G1
Thurloe Cl. SW7 129 H3
Thurloe Pl. SW7 31 F1
Thurloe Pl. SW7 129 G4
Thurloe Pl. Ms. SW7 31 F1
Thurloe Sq. SW7 31 G1
Thurloe Sq. SW7 129 H4
Thurloe St. SW7 31 F1
Thurloe St. SW7 129 G4
Thurlow Cl. E4 62 B6
Higham Sta. Av.
Thurlow Gdns., Ilf. 65 G6
Thurlow Gdns., Wem. 87 G5
Thurlow Hill SE21 169 J1
Thurlow Pk. Rd. SE21 169 H1
Thurlow Rd. NW3 91 G5
Thurlow Rd. W7 124 D2
Thurlow St. SE17 36 C3
Thurlow St. SE17 132 A5
Thurlow Ter. NW5 92 A5
Thurlstone Rd., Ruis. 84 A3
Thurnby Ct., Twick. 162 B3
Thursland Rd., Sid. 176 E5
Thursley Cres., Croy. 204 D7
Thursley Gdns. SW19 166 A2
Thursley Rd. SE9 174 C3
Thurso St. SW17 167 G4
Thurstan Rd. SW20 165 H7
Thurston Rd. SE13 154 B2
Thurston Rd., Sthl. 103 F6
Thurtle Rd. E2 112 C1
Thwaite Cl., Erith 139 J6
Thyer Cl., Orp. 207 F4
Isabella Dr.
Thyra Gro. N12 57 E6
Tibbatts Rd. E3 114 B4
Tibbenham Wk. E13 115 F2
Tibberton Sq. N1 93 J7
Popham Rd.
Tibbets Cl. SW19 166 A1
Tibbet's Cor. SW15 148 A7
Tibbet's Cor. 148 A7
Underpass SW15
West Hill
Tibbet's Ride SW15 148 A7

Tiber Gdns. N1 111 F1
Treaty St.
Ticehurst Cl., Orp. 176 A7
Grovelands Rd.
Ticehurst Rd. SE23 171 H2
Tickford Cl. SE2 138 C2
Ampleforth Rd.
Tidal Basin Rd. E16 115 F7
Tidenham Gdns., 202 B3
Croy.
Tidenham Rd. SW15 147 J5
Tideswell Rd., Croy. 204 A3
Tideway Cl., Rich. 162/163 E4
Locksmeade Rd.
Tidey St. E3 114 A5
Tidford Rd., Well. 157 J2
Tidworth Rd. E3 114 A4
Tiepigs La., Brom. 205 E2
Tiepigs La., W.Wick. 205 E2
Tierney Rd. SW2 168 E1
Tiger La., Brom. 191 H4
Tiger Way E5 94 E4
Tilbrook Rd. SE3 155 J3
Tilbury Cl. SE15 37 G7
Tilbury Rd. E6 116 C2
Tilbury Rd. E10 78 C7
Tildesley Rd. SW15 147 J6
Tile Fm. Rd., Orp. 207 G3
Tile Kiln La. N6 92 B1
Winchester Rd.
Tile Kiln La. N13 59 J5
Tile Kiln La., Bex. 177 J2
Tile Yd. E14 113 J6
Commercial Rd.
Tilehurst Pt. SE2 138 C2
Yarnton Way
Tilehurst Rd. SW18 167 G1
Tilehurst Rd., Sutt. 198 B5
Tileyard Rd. N7 92 E7
Tilford Gdns. SW19 166 A2
Tilia Cl., Sutt. 198 C5
Tilia Rd. E5 94/95 E4
Clarence Rd.
Tilia Wk. SW9 151 H4
Moorland Rd.
Tiller Rd. E14 134 A3
Tillett Cl. NW10 88 C6
Tillett Sq. SE16 133 H2
Tillett Way E2 13 H3
Tilling Rd. NW2 89 J1
Tilling Way, Wem. 87 G2
Tillingbourne Gdns. 72 C3
N3
Tillingbourne Way N3 72 C3
Tillingbourne Gdns.
Tillingham Way N12 56 D4
Tillman St. E1 112/113 E6
Bigland St.
Tilloch St. N1 93 F7
Carnoustie Dr.
Tillotson Rd. N9 60 C2
Tillotson Rd., Har. 51 H7
Tillotson Rd., Ilf. 80 D7
Tilney Ct. EC1 12 A5
Tilney Dr., Buck.H. 63 G2
Tilney Gdns. N1 94 A6
Tilney Rd., Dag. 101 F6
Tilney Rd., Sthl. 122 C4
Tilney St. W1 24 C1
Tilney St. W1 130 A1
Tilson Gdns. SW2 150 E7
Tilson Ho. SW2 150/151 E7
Tilson Gdns.
Tilson Rd. N17 76 D1
Tilt Yd. App. SE9 156 C6
Tilton St. SW6 128 B6
Tiltwood, The W3 106 C7
Acacia Rd.
Timber Cl., Chis. 192 D2
Timber Mill Way SW4 150 D3
Timber Pond Rd. 133 G2
SE16
Timber St. EC1 11 J5
Timbercroft, Epsom 196 E4
Timbercroft La. SE18 137 H6
Timberdene NW4 72 A2
Timberdene Av., Ilf. 81 E1
Timberland Rd. E1 113 E6
Timberwharf Rd. N16 76 D6
Timbrell Pl. SE16 133 J1
Silver Wk.
Time Sq. E8 94 C5
Times Sq., Sutt. 199 E5
Timothy Cl. SW4 150 C5
Elms Rd.
Timothy Rd. E3 113 J5
Timsbury Wk. SW15 165 G1
Tindal St. SW9 151 H1
Tinderbox All. SW14 146 D3
Tine Rd., Chig. 65 H5

Tinniswood Cl. N5 93 G5
Drayton Pk.
Tinsley Rd. E1 113 F5
Tintagel Cres. SE22 152 C4
Tintagel Dr., Stan. 53 G4
Tintagel Gdns. SE22 152 C4
Oxonian St.
Tintern Av. NW9 70 B3
Tintern Cl. SW15 148 B5
Tintern Cl. SW19 167 F7
Tintern Gdns. N14 43 E7
Tintern Path NW9 70/71 E6
Ruthin Cl.
Tintern Rd. N22 75 J1
Tintern Rd., Cars. 199 G1
Tintern St. SW4 151 E4
Tintern Way, Har. 85 H1
Tinto Rd. E16 115 G4
Tinwell Ms., Borwd. 38 C5
Cranes Way
Tinworth St. SE11 34 B3
Tinworth St. SE11 131 F5
Tippetts Cl., Enf. 43 J1
Tipthorpe Rd. SW11 150 A3
Tipton Dr., Croy. 202 B4
Tiptree Cl. E4 62 C3
Mapleton Rd.
Tiptree Cres., Ilf. 80 D3
Tiptree Dr., Enf. 44 A4
Tiptree Est., Ilf. 80 D3
Tiptree Rd., Ruis. 84 B4
Tirlemont Rd., S.Croy. 201 J7
Tirrell Rd., Croy. 187 J6
Tisbury Ct. W1 110 D7
Rupert St.
Tisbury Rd. SW16 186 E2
Tisdall Pl. SE17 36 C2
Tisdall Pl. SE17 132 A4
Titchborne Row W2 15 H4
Titchfield Rd. NW8 109 J1
Titchfield Rd., Cars. 199 G1
Titchfield Wk., Cars. 185 G7
Titchfield Rd.
Titchwell Rd. SW18 149 G7
Tite St. SW3 31 J4
Tite St. SW3 129 J5
Tithe Barn Cl., 181 J1
Kings.T.
Tithe Barn Way, 102 B3
Nthlt.
Tithe Cl. NW7 71 G1
Tithe Cl., Walt. 178 B6
Tithe Fm. Av., Har. 85 G3
Tithe Fm. Cl., Har. 85 G3
Tithe Wk. NW7 71 G1
Titley Cl. E4 62 A5
Titmuss Av. SE28 118 B7
Titmuss St. W12 127 H2
Tiverton Av., Ilf. 80 D3
Tiverton Dr. SE9 175 F1
Tiverton Rd. N15 76 A6
Tiverton Rd. N18 60 B5
Tiverton Rd. NW10 108 A1
Tiverton Rd., Edg. 69 J2
Tiverton Rd., Houns. 143 J2
Tiverton Rd., Ruis. 84 A3
Tiverton Rd., Th.Hth. 187 G5
Willett Rd.
Tiverton Rd., Wem. 105 H2
Tiverton St. SE1 27 J6
Tiverton St. SE1 131 J3
Tiverton Way, Chess. 195 F5
Tivoli Ct. SE16 133 J2
Tivoli Gdns. SE18 136 B4
Tivoli Rd. N8 74 D5
Tivoli Rd. SE27 169 J5
Tivoli Rd., Houns. 142 E4
Toad La., Houns. 143 F4
Tobacco Quay E1 112/113 E7
Wapping La.
Tobago St. E14 134 A2
Manilla St.
Tobin Cl. NW3 91 H7
Toby La. E1 113 H4
Toby Way, Surb. 196 B2
Todds Wk. N7 93 F2
Andover Rd.
Token Yd. SW15 148 B4
Montserrat Rd.
Tokenhouse Yd. EC2 20 B3
Tokyngton Av., Wem. 88 A6
Toland Sq. SW15 147 G5
Tolcarne Dr., Pnr. 66 B3
Toley Av., Wem. 69 H7
Tollbridge Cl. W10 108 B4
Kensal Rd.
Tollesbury Gdns., Ilf. 81 G3
Tollet St. E1 113 G4
Tollgate Dr. SE21 170 B2
Tollgate Dr., Hayes 102 D7
Delamere Rd.
Tollgate Gdns. NW6 6 A1
Tollgate Gdns. NW6 108 E2
Tollgate Rd. E6 116 A5

Tollgate Rd. E16 115 J5
Tollhouse Way N19 92 C2
Tollington Pk. N4 93 F2
Tollington Pl. N4 93 F2
Tollington Rd. N7 93 F4
Tollington Way N7 92 E3
Tolmers Sq. NW1 9 G5
Tolpuddle Av. E13 115 J1
Rochester Av.
Tolpuddle St. N1 10 E1
Tolpuddle St. N1 111 G2
Tolsford Rd. E5 95 E5
Tolson Rd., Islw. 144 D3
Tolverne Rd. SW20 183 J1
Tolworth Cl., Surb. 196 B1
Tolworth Gdns., Rom. 82 D5
Tolworth Pk. Rd., Surb. 195 J2
Tolworth Ri. N., Surb. 182 C7
Elmbridge Av.
Tolworth Ri. S., Surb. 196 C1
Warren Dr. S.
Tolworth Rd., Surb. 195 H2
Tolworth Twr., Surb. 196 B2
Tom Coombs Cl. SE9 156 B4
Well Hall Rd.
Tom Cribb Rd. SE28 137 F3
Tom Gros. Cl. E15 96 D5
Maryland St.
Tom Hood Cl. E15 96 D5
Maryland St.
Tom Jenkinson Rd. E16 135 G1
Tom Mann Cl., Bark. 117 H1
Tom Nolan Cl. E15 114 E2
Tom Smith Cl. SE10 134/135 E6
Maze Hill
Tom Thumbs Arch E3 114 A2
Malmesbury Rd.
Tomahawk Gdns., Nthlt. 102 D3
Javelin Way
Tomlins Gro. E3 114 A3
Tomlins Orchard, Bark. 117 F1
Tomlins Ter. E14 113 J5
Rhodeswell Rd.
Tomlins Wk. N7 93 F2
Briset Way
Tomlinson Cl. E2 13 G4
Tomlinson Cl. E2 112 C3
Tomlinson Cl. W4 126 B5
Oxford Rd. N.
Tompion St. EC1 11 G4
Tomswood Ct., Ilf. 81 F1
Tomswood Hill, Ilf. 65 E7
Tomswood Rd., Chig. 64 D6
Tonbridge Cres., Har. 69 H4
Tonbridge Ho. SE25 188 D3
Tonbridge Rd., W.Mol. 179 E4
Tonbridge St. WC1 10 A3
Tonbridge St. WC1 110 E3
Tonbridge Wk. WC1 110/111 E3
Tonbridge St.
Tonfield Rd., Sutt. 198 C1
Tonge Cl., Beck. 190 A5
Tonsley Hill SW18 149 E5
Tonsley Pl. SW18 149 E5
Tonsley Rd. SW18 149 E5
Tonsley St. SW18 149 E5
Tonstall Rd., Mitch. 186 A2
Tony Cannell Ms. E3 113 J3
Maplin St.
Tooke Cl., Pnr. 66 E1
Took's Ct. EC4 19 E3
Tooley St. SE1 28 C1
Tooley St. SE1 132 A1
Toorack Rd., Har. 68 A2
Tooting Bec Gdns. SW16 168 D4
Tooting Bec Rd. SW16 168 A3
Tooting Bec Rd. SW17 168 A3
Tooting Gro. SW17 167 H5
Tooting High St. SW17 167 H6
Tootswood Rd., Brom. 190 E5
Top Ho. Ri. E4 46 C7
Parkhill Rd.
Top Pk., Beck. 190 E5
Topaz Wk. NW2 72 A7
Marble Dr.
Topcliffe Dr., Orp. 207 G4
Topham Sq. N17 75 J1
Topham St. EC1 11 E5
Topiary Sq., Rich. 145 J3
Topley St. SE9 156 A4
Topmast Pt. E14 134 A2
Topp Wk. NW2 89 J2
Topsfield Cl. N8 74 D5
Wolseley Rd.
Topsfield Par. N8 74/75 E5
Tottenham La.
Topsfield Rd. N8 74 E5
Topsham Rd. SW17 167 J3
Tor Gdns. W8 128 D2
Tor Rd., Well. 158 C1
Torbay Rd. NW6 90 C7
Torbay Rd., Har. 84 E2
Torbay St. NW1 92 B7
Hawley Rd.
Torbitt Way, Ilf. 81 J5
Torbridge Cl., Edg. 53 H7
Torbrook Cl., Bex. 159 E6
Torcross Dr. SE23 171 F2
Torcross Rd., Ruis. 84 B3
Tormead Cl., Sutt. 198 D6
Tormount Rd. SE18 137 H6
Toronto Av. E12 98 C4
Toronto Rd. E11 96 D4
Toronto Rd., Ilf. 99 E1
Torquay Gdns., Ilf. 80 A4
Torquay St. W2 14 A2
Torr Rd. SE20 171 G7
Torre Wk., Cars. 199 H1
Torrens Rd. E15 97 F6
Torrens Rd. SW2 151 F5
Torrens Sq. E15 97 E6
Torrens St. EC1 11 F2
Torrens St. EC1 111 G2
Torres Sq. E14 134 A5
Napier Av.
Torriano Av. NW5 92 D5
Torriano Cotts. NW5 92 C5
Torriano Av.
Torriano Ms. NW5 92 D5
Torriano Av.
Torridge Gdns. SE15 153 F4
Torridge Rd., Th.Hth. 187 H5
Torridon Rd. SE6 172 D1
Torridon Rd. SE13 154 D7
Torrington Av. N12 57 G5
Torrington Cl. N12 57 G4
Torrington Cl., Esher 194 B6
Torrington Dr., Har. 85 H4
Torrington Dr., Loug. 49 F4
Torrington Gdns. N11 58 C6
Torrington Gdns., Grnf. 87 F7
Torrington Gdns., Loug. 49 F4
Torrington Gro. N12 57 H5
Torrington Pk. N12 57 G5
Torrington Pl. E1 29 J2
Torrington Pl. E1 132 D1
Torrington Pl. WC1 17 H1
Torrington Pl. WC1 110 D5
Torrington Rd. E18 79 G3
Torrington Rd., Dag. 101 F1
Torrington Rd., Esher 194 B6
Torrington Rd., Grnf. 105 F1
Torrington Sq. WC1 9 J6
Torrington Sq. WC1 110 D4
Torrington Sq., Croy. 188 A7
Tavistock Gro.
Torrington Way, Mord. 184 D6
Torver Rd., Har. 68 B4
Torver Way, Orp. 207 G3
Torwood Rd. SW15 147 G5
Tothill St. SW1 25 H4
Tothill St. SW1 130 D2
Totnes Rd., Well. 138 B7
Totnes Wk. N2 73 G4
Tottan Ter. E1 113 G6
Tottenhall Rd. N13 59 G6
Tottenham Ct. Rd. W1 9 G6
Tottenham Ct. Rd. W1 110 C4
Tottenham Grn. E. N15 76 C4
Tottenham La. N8 74 E5
Tottenham Ms. W1 17 G1
Tottenham Rd. N1 94 B6
Tottenham St. W1 17 G2
Tottenham St. W1 110 C5
Totterdown St. SW17 167 J4
Totteridge Common N20 55 G2
Totteridge Grn. N20 56 D2
Totteridge La. N20 56 D2
Totteridge Village N20 56 B1
Totternhoe Cl., Har. 69 F5
Totton Rd., Th.Hth. 187 G3
Toulmin St. SE1 27 J4
Toulmin St. SE1 131 J2
Toulon St. SE5 35 J7
Toulon St. SE5 131 J7
Tournay Rd. SW6 128 C7
Toussaint Wk. SE16 29 J5
Tovil Cl. SE20 188 D2
Towcester Rd. E3 114 B4
Tower Br. E1 29 F2
Tower Br. E1 132 C1
Tower Br. SE1 29 F2
Tower Br. SE1 132 C1
Tower Br. App. E1 29 F1
Tower Br. App. E1 132 C1
Tower Br. Piazza SE1 132 C1
Horselydown La.
Tower Br. Rd. SE1 28 D6
Tower Br. Rd. SE1 132 B3
Tower Cl. NW3 91 G5
Lyndhurst Rd.
Tower Cl. SE20 170 E7
Tower Cl., Ilf. 65 E6
Tower Cl., Orp. 207 J2
Tower Ct. WC2 18 A4
Tower Gdns., Esher 194 D7
Tower Gdns. Rd. N17 75 J1
Tower Hamlets Rd. E7 97 F4
Tower Hamlets Rd. E17 78 A3
Tower Hill EC3 21 E6
Tower Hill EC3 112 B7
Tower Hill Ter. EC3 112 B7
Byward St.
Tower La., Wem. 87 G3
Main Dr.
Tower Ms. E17 78 A4
Tower Mill Rd. SE15 36 D6
Tower Pier EC3 29 E1
Tower Pier EC3 132 C1
Tower Pl. EC3 20 E6
Tower Pt., Enf. 44 A4
Tower Ri., Rich. 145 H3
Jocelyn Rd.
Tower Rd. NW10 89 G7
Tower Rd., Belv. 139 J4
Tower Rd., Bexh. 159 H4
Tower Rd., Orp. 207 J2
Tower Rd., Twick. 162 C3
Tower Royal EC4 20 A5
Tower St. WC2 17 J4
Tower St. WC2 110 D6
Tower Ter. N22 75 F2
Mayes Rd.
Tower Vw., Croy. 189 G7
Towers Pl., Rich. 145 H5
Eton St.
Towers Rd., Pnr. 66 E1
Towers Rd., Sthl. 103 G4
Towfield Rd., Felt. 161 F2
Towing Path Wk. N1 10 A1
Town, The, Enf. 44 A3
Town Ct. Path N4 93 J1
Town Fm. Way, Stai. 140 A7
Town La.
Town Fld. Way, Islw. 144 D2
Town Hall App. N16 94 B4
Milton Gro.
Town Hall App. Rd. N15 76 C4
Town Hall Av. W4 126 D5
Town Hall Rd. SW11 149 J3
Town La., Stai. 140 A6
Town Meadow, Brent. 125 G7
Town Quay, Bark. 117 E1
Town Rd. N9 61 E2
Towncourt Cres., Orp. 193 F5
Towncourt La., Orp. 193 G6
Towney Mead, Nthlt. 103 F2
Towney Mead Ct., Nthlt. 103 F2
Towney Mead
Townfield Rd., Hayes 121 J1
Townholm Cres. W7 124 C3
Townley Ct. E15 97 F6
Townley Rd. SE22 152 B5
Townley Rd., Bexh. 159 F5
Townley St. SE17 36 B3
Townmead Rd. SW6 149 F2
Townmead Rd., Rich. 146 B2
Townsend Av. N14 58 D4
Townsend Ind. Est. NW10 106 D2
Townsend La. NW9 70 D7
Townsend Rd. N15 76 C5
Townsend Rd., Sthl. 122 E1
Townsend St. SE17 36 C2
Townsend St. SE17 132 A4
Townsend Yd. N6 92 B1
Townshend Cl., Sid. 176 B6
Townshend Est. NW8 7 G1
Townshend Est. NW8 109 H2
Townshend Rd. NW8 109 H1
Townshend Rd., Chis. 174 E5
Townshend Rd., Rich. 145 J4
Townshend Ter., Rich. 145 J4
Townson Av., Nthlt. 102 A3
Townson Way, Nthlt. 102 A2
Townson Av.
Towpath Wk. E9 95 J5
Towpath Way, Croy. 188 C6
Towton Rd. SE27 169 J2
Toynbec Cl., Chis. 174/175 E4
Beechwood Ri.
Toynbee Rd. SW20 184 B1
Toynbee St. E1 21 F2
Toynbee St. E1 112 C5
Toyne Way N6 73 J6
Gaskell Rd.
Tracey Av. NW2 89 J5
Tracy Ct., Stan. 53 F7
Trade Cl. N13 59 G4
Trader Rd. E6 116 E6
Tradescant Rd. SW8 131 E7
Trading Est. Rd. NW10 106 C4
Trafalgar Av. N17 60 B6
Trafalgar Av. SE15 37 G4
Trafalgar Av. SE15 132 C5
Trafalgar Av., Wor.Pk. 198 A1
Trafalgar Business Cen., Bark. 117 J4
Trafalgar Cl. SE16 133 H4
Greenland Quay
Trafalgar Gdns. E1 113 G5
Trafalgar Gdns. W8 22 B5
Trafalgar Gro. SE10 134 D6
Trafalgar Pl. E11 79 G4
Trafalgar Pl. N18 60 D5
Trafalgar Rd. SE10 134 D6
Trafalgar Rd. SW19 167 E7
Trafalgar Rd., Twick. 162 A2
Trafalgar Sq. SW1 25 J1
Trafalgar Sq. SW1 130 D1
Trafalgar Sq. WC2 25 J1
Trafalgar Sq. WC2 130 D1
Trafalgar St. SE17 36 B3
Trafalgar St. SE17 132 A5
Trafalgar Ter., Har. 86 B1
Nelson Rd.
Trafalgar Way E14 134 C1
Trafalgar Way, Croy. 201 F2
Trafford Cl. E15 96 B5
Trafford Cl., Ilf. 65 J6
Trafford Rd., Th.Hth. 187 F5
Tralee Ct. SE16 132/133 E5
Masters Dr.
Tramway Av. E15 96 E7
Tramway Av. N9 45 E7
Tramway Path, Mitch. 185 J5
Tranby Pl. E9 95 G5
Homerton High St.
Tranley Ms. NW3 91 H4
Fleet Rd.
Tranmere Rd. N9 44 C7
Tranmere Rd. SW18 167 F2
Tranmere Rd., Twick. 143 H7
Tranquil Pas. SE3 155 F2
Tranquil Vale
Tranquil Vale SE3 155 E2
Transay Wk. N1 94 A6
Marquess Rd.
Transept St. NW1 15 G2
Transept St. NW1 109 H5
Transmere Cl., Orp. 193 F6
Transmere Rd., Orp. 193 F6
Transom Cl. SE16 133 H4
Plough Way
Transom Sq. E14 134 B5
Transport Av., Brent. 124 E5
Tranton Rd. SE16 29 J5
Tranton Rd. SE16 132 D3
Traps Hill, Loug. 48 C3
Traps La., N.Mal. 182 E1
Travellers Way, Houns. 142 C2
Travers Cl. E17 77 G1
Travers Rd. N7 93 G3
Treacy Cl., Bushey 51 J2
Treadgold St. W11 108 A7
Treadway St. E2 112 E2
Treaty Rd., Houns. 143 H3
Hanworth Rd.
Treaty St. N1 111 F1
Trebeck St. W1 24 D1
Trebovir Rd. SW5 128 D5
Treby St. E3 113 J4
Trecastle Way N7 92 D4
Carleton Rd.
Tredegar Ms. E3 113 J3
Tredegar Ter.
Tredegar Rd. E3 113 J2
Tredegar Rd. N11 58 D7
Tredegar Sq. E3 113 J3
Tredegar Ter. E3 113 J3
Trederwen Rd. E8 112 D1
Tredown Rd. SE26 171 F5
Tredwell Cl. SW2 169 F2
Hillside Rd.
Tredwell Cl., Brom. 192 B4
Tredwell Rd. SE27 169 H4
Tree Cl., Rich. 163 G1
Tree Rd. E16 115 J6
Treen Av. SW13 147 F3

Treeside Cl., West Dr. 120 A4
Treetops Cl. SE2 139 E5
Treetops Vw., Loug. 47 J6
High Rd.
Treeview Cl. SE19 188 B1
Treewall Gdns., Brom. 173 H4
Trefgarne Rd., Dag. 101 G2
Trefil Wk. N7 93 E4
Trefoil Ho., Erith 138/139 E2
Kale Rd.
Trefoil Rd. SW18 149 F5
Tregaron Av. N8 75 E6
Tregaron Gdns., N.Mal. 182/183 E4
Avenue Rd.
Tregarvon Rd. SW11 150 A4
Tregenna Av., Har. 85 F4
Tregenna Cl. N14 42 C5
Tregenna Ct., Har. 85 G4
Trego Rd. E9 96 A7
Tregothnan Rd. SW9 151 E3
Tregunter Rd. SW10 30 C5
Tregunter Rd. SW10 129 F6
Trehearn Rd., Ilf. 65 G7
Trehern Rd. SW14 146 D3
Treherne Ct. SW9 151 G1
Eythorne Rd.
Treherne Ct. SW17 168 A4
Trehurst St. E5 95 H5
Trelawn Rd. E10 96 C3
Trelawn Rd. SW2 151 G5
Trelawney Cl. E17 78 B4
Orford Rd.
Trelawney Est. E9 95 F6
Trelawney Rd., Ilf. 65 G7
Trellick Twr. W10 108 C4
Trellis Sq. E3 113 J3
Malmesbury Rd.
Treloar Gdns. SE19 170 A6
Hancock Rd.
Tremadoc Rd. SW4 150 D4
Tremaine Cl. SE4 154 A2
Tremaine Rd. SE20 189 E2
Trematon Pl., Tedd. 163 F7
Tremlett Gro. N19 92 C3
Tremlett Ms. N19 92 C3
Trenance Gdns., Ilf. 100 A3
Trench Yd. Ct., Mord. 184/185 E6
Green La.
Trenchard Av., Ruis. 84 B4
Trenchard Cl. NW9 70/71 E1
Fulbeck Dr.
Trenchard Cl., Stan. 52 D6
Trenchard Ct., Mord. 184/185 E6
Green La.
Trenchard St. SE10 134 D5
Trenchold St. SW8 34 A6
Trenchold St. SW8 130 E6
Trenholme Cl. SE20 171 E7
Trenholme Rd. SE20 170 E7
Trenholme Ter. SE20 170 E7
Trenmar Gdns. NW10 107 H3
Trent Av. W5 125 F3
Trent Gdns. N14 42 B6
Trent Rd. SW2 151 F5
Trent Rd., Buck.H. 63 H1
Trent Way, Wor.Pk. 197 J3
Trentbridge Cl., Ilf. 65 J6
Trentham St. SW18 166 D1
Trentwood Side, Enf. 43 F3
Treport St. SW18 149 E7
Tresco Cl., Brom. 172 E6
Tresco Gdns., Ilf. 100 A2
Tresco Rd. SE15 153 E4
Trescoe Gdns., Har. 67 E7
Tresham Cres. NW8 7 G5
Tresham Cres. NW8 109 H4
Tresham Rd., Bark. 99 J7
Tresham Wk. E9 95 F5
Churchill Wk.
Tresilian Av. N21 43 F5
Tressell Cl. N1 93 H7
Sebbon St.
Tressillian Cres. SE4 154 A3
Tressillian Rd. SE4 153 J4
Trestis Cl., Hayes 102/103 E5
Jollys La.
Treswell Rd., Dag. 119 E1
Tretawn Gdns. NW7 55 E4
Tretawn Pk. NW7 55 E4
Trevanion Rd. W14 128 B5
Treve Av., Har. 67 J7
Trevelyan Av. E12 98 C4
Trevelyan Cres., Har. 69 G7
Trevelyan Gdns. NW10 107 J1
Trevelyan Rd. E15 97 F4
Trevelyan Rd. SW17 167 H5
Treveris St. SE1 27 G2
Treverton St. W10 108 A4
Treves Cl. N21 43 F5
Treville St. SW15 147 H7
Treviso Rd. SE23 171 G2
Farren Rd.
Trevithick St. SE8 134 A5
Trevone Gdns., Pnr. 67 E6
Trevor Cl., Barn. 41 G5
Trevor Cl., Brom. 191 F7
Trevor Cl., Har. 52 C7
Kenton La.
Trevor Cl., Islw. 144 C5
Trevor Cl., Nthlt. 102 C2
Trevor Gdns., Edg. 70 D1
Trevor Gdns., Nthlt. 102 C2
Trevor Pl. SW7 23 H4
Trevor Pl. SW7 129 H2
Trevor Rd. SW19 166 B7
Trevor Rd., Edg. 70 D1
Trevor Rd., Hayes 121 H2
Trevor Rd., Wdf.Grn. 63 G7
Trevor Sq. SW7 23 J4
Trevor Sq. SW7 129 J2
Trevor St. SW7 23 H4
Trevor St. SW7 129 H2
Trevose Rd. E17 78 D1
Trevose Way, Wat. 50 C3
Trewenna Dr., Chess. 195 G5
Trewince Rd. SW20 183 J1
Trewint St. SW18 167 F2
Trewsbury Ho. SE2 138 D2
Hartslock Dr.
Trewsbury Rd. SE26 171 G5
Triandra Way, Hayes 102 D5
Triangle, The EC1 111 H4
Goswell Rd.
Triangle, The N13 59 G4
Lodge Dr.
Triangle, The, Bark. 99 F6
Tanner St.
Triangle, The, Hmptn. 179 J1
High St.
Triangle, The, Kings.T. 182 C2
Kenley Rd.
Triangle Ct. E16 116 A5
Tollgate Rd.
Triangle Pas., Barn. 41 F4
Triangle Pl. SW4 150 D4
Triangle Rd. E8 112 E1
Trident Gdns., Nthlt. 102 D3
Jetstar Way
Trident St. SE16 133 G4
Trident Way, Sthl. 122 B3
Trig La. EC4 19 J5
Trigon Rd. SW8 34 D7
Trigon Rd. SW8 131 F7
Trilby Rd. SE23 171 G2
Trim St. SE14 133 J6
Trimmer Wk., Brent. 125 H6
Trinder Gdns. N19 92/93 E1
Trinder Rd.
Trinder Rd. N19 93 E1
Trinder Rd., Barn. 39 J5
Tring Av. W5 125 J1
Tring Av., Sthl. 103 F6
Tring Av., Wem. 88 A6
Tring Cl., Ilf. 81 F5
Trinidad St. E14 113 J7
Trinity Av. N2 73 G3
Trinity Av., Enf. 44 C6
Trinity Buoy Wf. E14 115 F7
Trinity Ch. Pas. SW13 127 H6
Trinity Ch. Rd. SW13 127 H6
Trinity Ch. Sq. SE1 28 A5
Trinity Ch. Sq. SE1 131 J3
Trinity Cl. E8 94 C6
Trinity Cl. E11 97 E2
Trinity Cl. NW3 91 G4
Hampstead High St.
Trinity Cl. SE13 154 D4
Wisteria Rd.
Trinity Cl., Brom. 206 B1
Trinity Cl., Houns. 143 E4
Trinity Cotts., Rich. 145 J3
Trinity Rd.
Trinity Ct. N1 94 B7
Downham Rd.
Trinity Ct. SE7 136 A4
Charlton La.
Trinity Cres. SW17 167 J2
Trinity Gdns. E16 115 F4
Cliff Wk.
Trinity Gdns. SW9 151 F4
Trinity Gro. SE10 154 C1
Trinity Ms. SE20 189 E1
Trinity Ms. W10 108 A6
Cambridge Gdns.
Trinity Path SE26 171 F3
Trinity Pl., Bexh. 159 F4
Trinity Ri. SW2 169 G1
Trinity Rd. N2 73 G3
Trinity Rd. N22 75 E1
Trinity Rd. SW17 167 J2
Trinity Rd. SW18 149 G5
Trinity Rd. SW19 166 D6
Trinity Rd., Ilf. 81 F3
Trinity Rd., Rich. 145 J3
Trinity Rd., Sthl. 122 E1
Trinity Sq. EC3 21 E6
Trinity Sq. EC3 112 B7
Trinity St. E16 115 G5
Vincent St.
Trinity St. SE1 28 A4
Trinity St. SE1 131 J2
Trinity St., Enf. 43 J2
Trinity Wk. NW3 91 F6
Trinity Way E4 61 J6
Trinity Way W3 107 E7
Trio Pl. SE1 28 A4
Tristan Sq. SE3 155 E3
Tristram Cl. E17 78 D3
Tristram Rd., Brom. 173 F4
Triton Sq. NW1 9 F5
Triton Sq. NW1 110 C4
Tritton Av., Croy. 201 E4
Tritton Rd. SE21 170 A3
Triumph Cl., Hayes 121 F7
Triumph Ho., Bark. 118 B3
Triumph Rd. E6 116 C6
Trojan Ct. NW6 90 B7
Willesden La.
Trojan Way, Croy. 201 F3
Troon Cl. SE16 132/133 E5
Masters Dr.
Troon St. E1 113 H6
Trosley Rd., Belv. 139 G6
Trossachs Rd. SE22 152 B5
Trothy Rd. SE1 37 J1
Trott Rd. N10 57 J7
Trott St. SW11 149 H1
Trotwood, Chig. 65 G6
Troughton Rd. SE7 135 H5
Trout Rd., West Dr. 120 A1
Troutbeck Rd. SE14 153 H1
Trouville Rd. SW4 150 C6
Trowbridge Est. E9 95 J6
Osborne Rd.
Trowbridge Rd. E9 95 J6
Trowlock Av., Tedd. 163 F6
Trowlock Island, Tedd. 163 G5
Trowlock Way, Tedd. 163 G6
Troy Ct. SE18 137 E4
Troy Rd. SE19 170 A6
Troy Town SE15 152 D3
Trubshaw Rd., Sthl. 123 H3
Havelock Rd.
Truesdale Rd. E6 116 C6
Trulock Ct. N17 60 D7
Trulock Rd. N17 60 D7
Truman Cl., Edg. 54 B7
Pavilion Way
Truman's Rd. N16 94 B5
Trump St. EC2 20 A4
Trumpers Way W7 124 B3
Trumpington Rd. E7 97 F4
Trundle St. SE1 27 J3
Trundlers Way, Bushey 52 B1
Trundleys Rd. SE8 133 G5
Trundleys Ter. SE8 133 G4
Truro Gdns., Ilf. 80 B7
Truro Rd. E17 77 J4
Truro Rd. N22 59 E7
Truro St. NW5 92 A6
Truslove Rd. SE27 169 G5
Trussley Rd. W6 127 J3
Trust Wk. SE21 169 H1
Peabody Hill
Tryfan Cl., Ilf. 80 A5
Tryon St. SW3 31 J3
Tryon St. SW3 129 J5
Trystings Cl., Esher 194 D6
Tuam Rd. SE18 137 G6
Tubbenden Cl., Orp. 207 H2
Tubbenden Dr., Orp. 207 G4
Tubbenden La., Orp. 207 H3
Tubbenden La. S., Orp. 207 G5
Tubbs Rd. NW10 107 F2
Tudor Av., Hmptn. 161 G6
Tudor Av., Wor.Pk. 197 H3
Tudor Cl. N6 74 C7
Tudor Cl. NW3 91 H5
Tudor Cl. NW7 55 G6
Tudor Cl. NW9 88 C2
Tudor Cl. SW2 151 F6
Elm Pk.
Tudor Cl., Chess. 195 H5
Tudor Cl., Chig. 64 D4
Tudor Cl., Chis. 192 C1
Tudor Cl., Pnr. 66 A5
Tudor Cl., Sutt. 198 A5
Tudor Cl., Wall. 200 C7
Tudor Cl., Wdf.Grn. 63 H5
Tudor Ct. E17 77 H7
Tudor Ct., Felt. 160 C4
Tudor Ct. N., Wem. 88 A5
Tudor Ct. S., Wem. 88 A5
Tudor Cres., Enf. 43 H1
Tudor Cres., Ilf. 65 E6
Tudor Dr., Kings.T. 163 H5
Tudor Dr., Mord. 184 A6
Tudor Est. NW10 106 B2
Tudor Gdns. NW9 88 C2
Tudor Gdns. SW13 146/147 E3
Treen Av.
Tudor Gdns. W3 106 A6
Tudor Gdns., Har. 68 A2
Tudor Rd.
Tudor Gdns., Twick. 162 C1
Tudor Gdns., W.Wick. 204 C3
Tudor Gro. E9 95 F7
Tudor Gro. N20 57 H3
Church Cres.
Tudor Pl. W1 17 H3
Tudor Pl., Mitch. 167 H7
Tudor Rd. E4 62 B6
Tudor Rd. E6 115 J1
Tudor Rd. E9 113 E1
Tudor Rd. N9 45 E7
Tudor Rd. SE19 170 C7
Tudor Rd. SE25 189 E5
Tudor Rd., Bark. 117 J1
Tudor Rd., Barn. 40 D3
Tudor Rd., Beck. 190 B3
Tudor Rd., Hmptn. 161 G7
Tudor Rd., Har. 68 A2
Tudor Rd., Houns. 144 A4
Tudor Rd., Kings.T. 164 A7
Tudor Rd., Pnr. 66 C2
Tudor Rd., Sthl. 102 E7
Tudor St. EC4 19 F5
Tudor St. EC4 111 G7
Tudor Wk., Bex. 159 E6
Tudor Way N14 58 D1
Tudor Way W3 126 A2
Tudor Way, Orp. 193 G6
Tudor Well Cl., Stan. 53 E5
Tudway Rd. SE3 155 H3
Tufnell Pk. Rd. N7 92 C4
Tufnell Pk. Rd. N19 92 C4
Tufter Rd., Chig. 65 J5
Tufton Gdns., W.Mol. 179 H2
Tufton Rd. E4 62 A4
Tufton St. SW1 25 J5
Tufton St. SW1 130 D3
Tugboat St. SE28 137 H2
Tugela Rd., Croy. 188 A6
Tugela St. SE6 171 J2
Tugmutton Cl., Orp. 206/207 E4
Acorn Way
Tuilerie St. E2 13 H1
Tuilerie St. E2 112 D2
Tulip Cl. E6 116 C5
Bradley Stone Rd.
Tulip Cl., Croy. 203 G1
Tulip Cl., Hmptn. 161 F6
Partridge Rd.
Tulip Cl., Sthl. 123 J2
Chevy Rd.
Tulip Ct., Pnr. 66 C3
Tulip Gdns., Ilf. 98 E6
Tulip Way, West Dr. 120 A3
Wise La.
Tull St., Mitch. 185 J7
Tulse Cl., Beck. 190 C3
Tulse Hill SW2 151 G6
Tulse Hill Est. SW2 151 G6
Tulsemere Rd. SE27 169 J2
Tumbling Bay, Walt. 178 A6
Tummons Gdns. SE25 188 B2
Tun Yd. SW8 150 B2
Peardon St.
Tuncombe Rd. N18 60 B4
Tunis Rd. W12 127 H1
Tunley Grn. E14 113 J5
Burdett Rd.
Tunley Rd. NW10 106 E1
Tunley Rd. SW17 168 A1
Tunmarsh La. E13 115 J3
Tunnan Leys E6 116 D6
Tunnel Av. SE10 134 D2
Tunnel Gdns. N11 58 C7
Tunnel Rd. SE16 133 F2
St. Marychurch St.
Tunstall Cl., Orp. 207 H4
Tunstall Rd. SW9 151 F4
Tunstall Rd., Croy. 202 B1
Tunstall Wk., Brent. 125 H6
Tunstock Way, Belv. 139 E3
Tunworth Cl. NW9 70 C6
Tunworth Cres. SW15 147 F6
Tupelo Rd. E10 96 B2
Turenne Cl. SW18 149 F4
Turin Rd. N9 45 F7
Turin St. E2 13 H4
Turin St. E2 112 D3
Turkey Oak Cl. SE19 188 B1
Turk's Head Yd. EC1 19 G1
Turks Row SW3 32 A3
Turks Row SW3 129 J5

Name	Page	Grid
Turle Rd. N4	93	F1
Turle Rd. SW16	186	E2
Turlewray Cl. N4	93	F1
Turley Cl. E15	115	E1
Turnagain La. EC4	**19**	**G3**
Turnage Rd., Dag.	100	E1
Turnberry Cl. NW4	72	A2
Turnberry Cl. SE16	132/133	E5
Ryder Dr.		
Turnberry Cl., Wat.	50	C3
Turnberry Quay E14	134	B3
Pepper St.		
Turnberry Way, Orp.	207	G1
Turnbury Cl. SE28	118	D6
Turnchapel Ms. SW4	150	B3
Cedars Rd.		
Turner Av. N15	76	B4
Turner Av., Mitch.	185	J1
Turner Av., Twick.	161	J3
Turner Cl. NW11	72	E6
Turner Cl. SW9	151	H1
Langton Rd.		
Turner Cl., Wem.	87	G5
Turner Dr. NW11	72	E6
Turner Rd. E17	78	C3
Turner Rd., Edg.	69	J3
Turner Rd., N.Mal.	182	D7
Turner St. E1	112	E5
Turner St. E16	115	F6
Turners Meadow Way, Beck.	189	J1
Turners Rd. E3	113	J5
Turners Way, Croy.	201	G2
Turners Wd. NW11	73	F7
Turneville Rd. W14	128	C6
Turney Rd. SE21	152	A7
Turnham Grn. Ter. W4	126	E4
Turnham Grn. Ter. Ms. W4	126/127	E4
Turnham Grn. Ter.		
Turnham Rd. SE4	153	H5
Turnmill St. EC1	**11**	**F6**
Turnmill St. EC1	111	G4
Turnpike Cl. SE8	133	J7
Amersham Vale		
Turnpike Ho. EC1	**11**	**H4**
Turnpike Ho. EC1	111	H3
Turnpike La. N8	75	F4
Turnpike La., Sutt.	199	F5
Turnpike Link, Croy.	202	B2
Turnpike Way, Islw.	144	D1
Turnpin La. SE10	134	C6
Turnstone Cl. E13	115	G3
Turnstone Cl. NW9	70/71	E2
Kestrel Cl.		
Turpentine La. SW1	**32**	**E3**
Turpin Rd., Felt.	141	J6
Staines Rd.		
Turpin Way N19	92	D2
Elthorne Rd.		
Turpin Way, Wall.	200	B7
Turpington Cl., Brom.	192	B6
Turpington La., Brom.	192	B7
Turpins La., Buck.H.	64	C5
Turquand St. SE17	**36**	**A2**
Turret Gro. SW4	150	C3
Turton Rd., Wem.	87	H5
Turville St. E2	**13**	**F5**
Tuscan Rd. SE18	137	G5
Tuskar St. SE10	134	E5
Tustin Est. SE15	133	F6
Tuttlebee La., Buck.H.	63	G2
Tweedale Rd. E15	96	C5
Tweeddale Rd., Cars.	199	G1
Tweedmouth Rd. E13	115	H2
Tweedy Cl., Enf.	44	C5
Tweedy Rd., Brom.	191	G1
Tweezer's All. WC2	**18**	**E5**
Twelvetrees Cres. E3	114	C4
Twentyman Cl., Wdf.Grn.	63	G5
Twickenham Br., Rich.	145	F5
Twickenham Br., Twick.	145	F5
Twickenham Cl., Croy.	201	F3
Twickenham Gdns., Grnf.	86	D5
Twickenham Gdns., Har.	52	B7
Twickenham Rd. E11	96	D2
Twickenham Rd., Felt.	161	F3
Twickenham Rd., Islw.	144	D3
Twickenham Rd., Rich.	145	F4
Twickenham Rd., Tedd.	162	D5
Twickenham Trd. Est., Twick.	144	C6

Name	Page	Grid
Twig Folly Cl. E2	113	G2
Roman Rd.		
Twilley St. SW18	148	E7
Twin Tumps Way SE28	118	A7
Twine Cl., Bark.	118	B3
Thames Rd.		
Twine Ct. E1	113	F7
Twine Ter. E3	113	J4
Ropery St.		
Twineham Grn. N12	56	D4
Tillingham Way		
Twining Av., Twick.	161	J3
Twinn Rd. NW7	56	B6
Twisden Rd. NW5	92	B4
Twybridge Way NW10	88	C7
Twycross Ms. SE10	134/135	E4
Blackwall La.		
Twyford Abbey Rd. NW10	105	J3
Twyford Av. N2	73	J3
Twyford Av. W3	106	A7
Twyford Cres. W3	126	A1
Twyford Pl. WC2	**18**	**C3**
Twyford Rd., Cars.	199	G1
Twyford Rd., Har.	85	H1
Twyford Rd., Ilf.	99	F5
Twyford St. N1	111	F1
Tyas Rd. E16	115	F4
Tybenham Rd. SW19	184	D3
Tyberry Rd., Enf.	45	E3
Tyburn La., Har.	68	B7
Tyburn Way W1	**16**	**A5**
Tyburn Way W1	109	J7
Tycehurst Hill, Loug.	48	C4
Tye La., Orp.	207	F5
Tyers Est. SE1	**28**	**D3**
Tyers Est. SE1	132	B2
Tyers Gate SE1	**28**	**D3**
Tyers St. SE11	**34**	**C3**
Tyers St. SE11	131	F5
Tyers Ter. SE11	**34**	**C4**
Tyers Ter. SE11	131	F5
Tyeshurst Cl. SE2	139	E5
Tylecroft Rd. SW16	186	E2
Tylehurst Gdns., Ilf.	99	F5
Tyler Cl. E2	**13**	**F1**
Tyler Cl. E2	112	C2
Tyler St. SE10	135	E5
Tylers Cl., Loug.	48	B7
Tyler's Ct. W1	**17**	**H4**
Tylers Gate, Har.	69	H6
Tylers Path, Cars.	199	J4
Rochester Rd.		
Tylney Av. SE19	170	C5
Tylney Rd. E7	97	J4
Tylney Rd., Brom.	192	A2
Tynan Cl., Felt.	160	A1
Sandycombe Rd.		
Tyndale Ct. E14	134	B4
Tyndale La. N1	93	H7
Upper St.		
Tyndale Ter. N1	93	H7
Canonbury La.		
Tyndall Rd. E10	96	C2
Tyndall Rd., Well.	157	J3
Tyne St. E1	**21**	**G3**
Tyneham Rd. SW11	150	A2
Tynemouth Cl. E6	116/117	E6
Covelees Wall		
Tynemouth Rd. N15	76	C4
Tynemouth Rd. SE18	137	J5
Tynemouth Rd., Mitch.	168	A7
Tynemouth St. SW6	149	F2
Type St. E2	113	G2
Tyrawley Rd. SW6	148	E1
Tyrell Cl., Har.	86	B4
Tyrell Ct., Cars.	199	J4
Tyrols Rd. SE23	171	G1
Wastdale Rd.		
Tysoe St. EC1	**11**	**E4**
Tyson Rd. SE23	153	F7
Tyssen Pas. E8	94	C6
Tyssen Rd. N16	94	C3
Tyssen Rd. E8	94	C6
Tyssen St. N1	**12**	**E2**
Tytherton Rd. N19	92	D3

U

Name	Page	Grid
Uamvar St. E14	114	B5
Uckfield Gro., Mitch.	186	A1
Udall St. SW1	**33**	**G2**
Udney Pk. Rd., Tedd.	162	D5
Uffington Rd. NW10	107	G1

Name	Page	Grid
Uffington Rd. SE27	169	G4
Ufford Cl., Har.	51	H7
Ufford Rd.		
Ufford Rd., Har.	51	H7
Ufford St. SE1	**27**	**F3**
Ufford St. SE1	131	G2
Ufton Gro. N1	94	A7
Ufton Rd. N1	94	B7
Uhura Sq. N16	94	B3
Ujima Ct. SW16	168/169	E4
Sunnyhill Rd.		
Ullathorne Rd. SW16	168	C4
Ulleswater Rd. N14	59	E4
Ullin St. E14	114	C5
St. Leonards Rd.		
Ullswater Cl. SW15	164	D4
Ullswater Cl., Brom.	173	E6
Ullswater Ct., Har.	67	G7
Oakington Av.		
Ullswater Cres. SW15	164	D4
Ullswater Rd. SE27	169	H2
Ullswater Rd. SW13	127	G7
Ulster Gdns. N13	59	J4
Ulster Pl. NW1	**8**	**D6**
Ulster Ter. NW1	**8**	**D5**
Ulundi Rd. SE3	135	E6
Ulva Rd. SW15	148	A5
Ravenna Rd.		
Ulverscroft Rd. SE22	152	C5
Ulverston Rd. E17	78	D2
Ulverstone Rd. SE27	169	H2
Ulysses Rd. NW6	90	C5
Umberston St. E1	112/113	E6
Hessel St.		
Umbria St. SW15	147	G6
Umfreville Rd. N4	75	H6
Undercliff Rd. SE13	154	A3
Underhill, Barn.	40	D5
Underhill Pas. NW1	110	B1
Camden High St.		
Underhill Rd. SE22	152	E6
Underhill St. NW1	110	B1
Camden High St.		
Underne Av. N14	58	B2
Undershaft EC3	**20**	**D4**
Undershaft EC3	112	B6
Undershaw Rd., Brom.	173	E3
Underwood, Croy.	204	C5
Underwood, The SE9	174	C2
Underwood Rd. E1	**13**	**H6**
Underwood Rd. E1	112	D4
Underwood Rd. E4	62	B5
Underwood Rd., Wdf.Grn.	64	A7
Underwood Row N1	**12**	**A3**
Underwood Row N1	111	J3
Underwood St. N1	**12**	**A3**
Underwood St. N1	111	J3
Undine Rd. E14	134	B4
Undine St. SW17	167	J5
Uneeda Dr., Grnf.	104	A1
Union Cl. E11	96	D4
Union Cotts. E15	96/97	E7
Welfare Rd.		
Union Ct. EC2	**20**	**D3**
Union Ct., Rich.	145	H5
Eton St.		
Union Dr. E1	113	H4
Canal Cl.		
Union Gro. SW8	150	D2
Union Pk. NW10	106	C3
Acton La.		
Union Rd. N11	58	D6
Union Rd. SW4	150	D2
Union Rd. SW8	150	D2
Union Rd., Brom.	192	A5
Union Rd., Croy.	187	J7
Union Rd., Nthlt.	103	G2
Union Rd., Wem.	87	H6
Union Sq. N1	111	J1
Union St. E15	114	C1
Union St. SE1	**27**	**H2**
Union St. SE1	131	H1
Union St., Barn.	40	B4
Union St., Kings.T.	181	G2
Union Wk. E2	**13**	**E3**
Unity Cl. NW10	89	G6
Unity Cl. SE19	169	J5
Crown Dale		
Unity Way SE18	136	A3
University Cl. NW7	55	F7
University Gdns., Bex.	159	F7
University Pl., Erith	139	H7
Belmont Rd.		
University Rd. SW19	167	G6
University St. WC1	**9**	**G6**
University St. WC1	110	C4
University Way E16	116	D7
Unwin Av., Felt.	141	H5
Unwin Cl. SE15	**37**	**H6**
Unwin Cl. SE15	132	D6

Name	Page	Grid
Unwin Rd. SW7	**23**	**F5**
Unwin Rd., Islw.	144	B3
Upbrook Ms. W2	**14**	**D4**
Upcerne Rd. SW10	129	F7
Upchurch Cl. SE20	171	E7
Upcroft Av., Edg.	54	C5
Updale Rd., Sid.	175	J4
Upfield, Croy.	203	E2
Upfield Rd. W7	104	C4
Upgrove Manor Way SW2	151	G7
Trinity Ri.		
Uphall Rd., Ilf.	99	E5
Upham Pk. Rd. W4	127	E4
Uphill Dr. NW7	55	E5
Uphill Dr. NW9	70	C5
Uphill Gro. NW7	55	E4
Uphill Rd. NW7	54	E4
Upland Ms. SE22	152	D5
Upland Rd.		
Upland Rd. E13	115	F4
Sutton Rd.		
Upland Rd. SE22	152	D5
Upland Rd., Bexh.	159	F3
Upland Rd., S.Croy.	202	A5
Upland Rd., Sutt.	199	G7
Uplands, Beck.	190	A2
Uplands, The, Loug.	48	C3
Uplands, The, Ruis.	84	A1
Uplands Av. E17	77	G2
Blackhorse La.		
Uplands Business Pk. E17	77	G2
Uplands Cl. SW14	146	B5
Monroe Dr.		
Uplands End, Wdf.Grn.	64	B7
Uplands Pk. Rd., Enf.	43	G3
Uplands Rd. N8	75	F5
Uplands Rd., Barn.	58	A1
Uplands Rd., Rom.	82	D3
Uplands Rd., Wdf.Grn.	64	B7
Uplands Way N21	43	G5
Upney La., Bark.	99	H6
Upnor Way SE17	**37**	**E3**
Uppark Dr., Ilf.	81	F6
Upper Abbey Rd., Belv.	139	F4
Upper Addison Gdns. W14	128	B2
Upper Bardsey Wk. N1	93	J6
Clephane Rd.		
Upper Belgrave St. SW1	**24**	**C5**
Upper Belgrave St. SW1	130	A3
Upper Berkeley St. W1	**15**	**J4**
Upper Berkeley St. W1	109	J6
Upper Beulah Hill SE19	188	B1
Upper Brighton Rd., Surb.	181	G6
Upper Brockley Rd. SE4	153	J2
Upper Brook St. W1	**16**	**B6**
Upper Brook St. W1	110	A7
Upper Butts, Brent.	125	F6
Upper Caldy Wk. N1	93	J6
Clephane Rd.		
Upper Camelford Wk. W11	108	B6
Lancaster Rd.		
Upper Cavendish Av. N3	72	D3
Upper Cheyne Row SW3	**31**	**G6**
Upper Cheyne Row SW3	129	H6
Upper Clapton Rd. E5	94	E1
Upper Clarendon Wk. W11	108	B6
Lancaster Rd.		
Upper Dengie Wk. N1	111	J1
Popham Rd.		
Upper Elmers End Rd., Beck.	189	H4
Upper Fm. Rd., W.Mol.	179	F4
Upper Fosters NW4	71	J5
New Brent St.		
Upper Grn. E., Mitch.	185	J3
Upper Grn. W., Mitch.	185	J3
London Rd.		
Upper Grenfell Wk. W11	108	A7
Whitchurch Rd.		
Upper Grosvenor St. W1	**16**	**B6**
Upper Grosvenor St. W1	110	A7
Upper Grotto Rd., Twick.	162	C2
Upper Grd. SE1	**26**	**E1**

Upper Grd. SE1 131 H1
Upper Gro. SE25 188 B4
Upper Gro. Rd., Belv. 139 F6
Upper Gulland Wk. N1 93 J6
Clephane Rd.
Upper Ham Rd., Kings.T. 163 G4
Upper Ham Rd., Rich. 163 G4
Upper Handa Wk. N1 94 A6
Clephane Rd.
Upper Harley St. NW1 8 C5
Upper Harley St. NW1 110 A4
Upper Hawkwell Wk. N1 111 J1
Popham Rd.
Upper Hitch, Wat. 51 E1
Upper Holly Hill Rd., Belv. 139 H5
Upper James St. W1 17 G5
Upper John St. W1 17 G5
Upper Lismore Wk. N1 93 J6
Clephane Rd.
Upper Mall W6 127 G5
Upper Marsh SE1 26 D5
Upper Marsh SE1 131 F3
Upper Montagu St. W1 15 J1
Upper Montagu St. W1 109 J5
Upper Mulgrave Rd., Sutt. 198 C7
Upper N. St. E14 114 A5
Upper Palace Rd., E.Mol. 180 A3
Upper Pk., Loug. 48 A4
Upper Pk. Rd. N11 58 B5
Upper Pk. Rd. NW3 91 J5
Upper Pk. Rd., Belv. 139 H4
Upper Pk. Rd., Brom. 191 H1
Upper Pk. Rd., Kings.T. 164 A6
Upper Phillimore Gdns. W8 128 D2
Upper Ramsey Wk. N1 94 A6
Clephane Rd.
Upper Rawreth Wk. N1 111 J1
Popham Rd.
Upper Richmond Rd. SW15 148 B4
Upper Richmond Rd. W. SW14 146 B4
Upper Richmond Rd. W., Rich. 146 A4
Upper Rd. E13 115 G3
Upper Rd., Wall. 200 D5
Upper St. Martin's La. WC2 18 A5
Upper Selsdon Rd., S.Croy. 202 C7
Upper Sheppey Wk. N1 93 J7
Clephane Rd.
Upper Sheridan Rd., Belv. 139 G4
Coleman Rd.
Upper Shirley Rd., Croy. 203 F2
Upper Sq., Islw. 144 D3
North St.
Upper St. N1 11 F1
Upper St. N1 111 G2
Upper Sunbury Rd., Hmptn. 179 E1
Upper Sutton La., Houns. 123 G7
Upper Tachbrook St. SW1 33 F1
Upper Tachbrook St. SW1 130 C4
Upper Tail, Wat. 51 E3
Upper Talbot Wk. W11 108 B6
Lancaster Rd.
Upper Teddington Rd., Kings.T. 181 F1
Upper Ter. NW3 91 F3
Upper Thames St. EC4 19 H5
Upper Thames St. EC4 111 J7
Upper Tollington Pk. N4 93 G1
Upper Tooting Pk. SW17 167 J2
Upper Tooting Rd. SW17 167 J4
Upper Town Rd., Grnf. 103 H4
Upper Tulse Hill SW2 151 F7
Upper Vernon Rd., Sutt. 199 G5
Upper Walthamstow Rd. E17 78 D4
Upper Wickham La., Well. 138 B7
Upper Wimpole St. W1 16 D1
Upper Wimpole St. W1 110 A5
Upper Woburn Pl. WC1 9 J4
Upper Woburn Pl. WC1 110 D3
Upperton Rd., Sid. 175 J5
Upperton Rd. E. E13 115 J3
Inniskilling Rd.
Upperton Rd. W. E13 115 J3
Uppingham Av., Stan. 69 E1
Upsdell Av. N13 59 G6
Upstall St. SE5 151 H1
Upton Av. E7 97 G7
Upton Cl., Bex. 159 F6
Upton Ct. SE20 171 F7
Blean Gro.
Upton Dene, Sutt. 198 E7
Upton Gdns., Har. 69 E5
Upton La. E7 97 G7
Upton Pk. Rd. E7 97 H7
Upton Rd. N18 60 D5
Upton Rd. SE18 137 F6
Upton Rd., Bex. 159 F6
Upton Rd., Bexh. 158 E4
Upton Rd., Houns. 143 G3
Upton Rd., Th.Hth. 188 A2
Upton Rd. S., Bex. 159 F6
Upway N12 57 H7
Upwood Rd. SE12 155 G6
Upwood Rd. SW16 187 E1
Urlwin St. SE5 35 J6
Urlwin St. SE5 131 J6
Urlwin Wk. SW9 151 G2
Urmston Dr. SW19 166 B1
Ursula Ms. N4 93 J1
Portland Ri.
Ursula St. SW11 149 H1
Urswick Gdns., Dag. 100/101 E7
Urswick Rd.
Urswick Rd. E9 95 F5
Urswick Rd., Dag. 100 D7
Usborne Ms. SW8 34 C7
Usborne Ms. SW8 131 F7
Usher Rd. E3 113 J2
Usk Rd. SW11 149 F4
Usk St. E2 113 G3
Utopia Village NW1 110 A1
Chalcot Rd.
Uvedale Rd., Dag. 101 G3
Uvedale Rd., Enf. 44 A5
Uverdale Rd. SW10 129 F7
Uxbridge Gdns., Felt. 160 D2
Marlborough Rd.
Uxbridge Rd. W3 105 H7
Uxbridge Rd. W5 105 H7
Uxbridge Rd. W7 124 C1
Uxbridge Rd. W12 127 G1
Uxbridge Rd. W13 124 C1
Uxbridge Rd., Felt. 160 C2
Uxbridge Rd., Hmptn. 161 G4
Uxbridge Rd., Har. 51 J7
Uxbridge Rd., Hayes 102 C7
Uxbridge Rd., Kings.T. 181 G4
Uxbridge Rd., Pnr. 51 H7
Uxbridge Rd., Sthl. 123 G1
Uxbridge Rd., Stan. 52 C6
Uxbridge Rd., Uxb. 102 B6
Uxbridge St. W8 128 D1
Uxendon Cres., Wem. 87 H1
Uxendon Hill, Wem. 87 J1

V

Valan Leas, Brom. 191 E3
Valance Av. E4 63 F1
Vale, The N10 74 A1
Vale, The N14 42 D7
Vale, The NW11 90 A3
Vale, The SW3 31 E5
Vale, The SW3 129 G6
Vale, The W3 126 D1
Vale, The, Croy. 203 G2
Vale, The, Felt. 142 B6
Vale, The, Houns. 122 E6
Vale, The, Ruis. 84 C4
Vale, The, Sun. 160 A6
Ashridge Way
Vale, The, Wdf.Grn. 63 G7
Vale Av., Borwd. 38 B5
Vale Cl. N2 73 J3
Church Vale
Vale Cl. W9 6 C4
Vale Cl., Orp. 206 D4
Vale Cotts. SW15 164 D4
Kingston Vale
Vale Ct. W9 6 C4
Vale Cres. SW15 165 E3
Vale Cft., Esher 194 B7
Vale Cft., Pnr. 66 E5
Vale Dr., Barn. 40 C4
Vale End SE22 152 B4
Grove Vale
Vale Gro. N4 75 J7
Vale Gro. W3 126 D1
The Vale
Vale La. W3 106 A5
Vale of Health NW3 91 G3
East Heath Rd.
Vale Par. SW15 164 D4
Kingston Vale
Vale Ri. NW11 90 C1
Vale Rd. E7 97 H6
Vale Rd. N4 75 J7
Vale Rd., Brom. 192 D2
Vale Rd., Epsom 197 F4
Vale Rd., Mitch. 186 D3
Vale Rd., Sutt. 198 E4
Vale Rd., Wor.Pk. 197 F4
Vale Rd. N., Surb. 195 H2
Vale Rd. S., Surb. 195 H2
Vale Row N5 93 H3
Gillespie Rd.
Vale Royal N7 92 E7
Vale St. SE27 170 A3
Vale Ter. N4 75 J6
Valence Av., Dag. 100 D3
Valence Circ., Dag. 100 D3
Valence Wd. Rd., Dag. 100 D3
Valencia Rd., Stan. 53 F4
Valentia Pl. SW9 151 G4
Brixton Sta. Rd.
Valentine Av., Bex. 176 E2
Valentine Ct. SE23 171 G2
Valentine Pl. SE1 27 G3
Valentine Pl. SE1 131 H2
Valentine Rd. E9 95 G6
Valentine Rd., Har. 85 J3
Valentine Row SE1 27 G4
Valentine Row SE1 131 H2
Valentines Rd., Ilf. 98 E1
Valerian Way E15 115 E3
Valeswood Rd., Brom. 173 F5
Valetta Gro. E13 115 G2
Valetta Rd. W3 127 E2
Valette St. E9 95 E6
Valiant Cl., Nthlt. 102 D3
Ruislip Rd.
Valiant Cl., Rom. 83 G2
Valiant Ho. SE7 135 J5
Valiant Path NW9 54/55 E7
Blundell Rd.
Valiant Way E6 116 C5
Vallance Rd. E1 13 J4
Vallance Rd. E1 112 D4
Vallance Rd. E2 13 J4
Vallance Rd. E2 112 D3
Vallance Rd. N22 74 C2
Vallentin Rd. E17 78 C4
Valley Av. N12 57 G4
Valley Cl., Loug. 48 C6
Valley Cl., Pnr. 66 B2
Alandale Dr.
Valley Dr. NW9 70 A6
Valley Flds. Cres., Enf. 43 G2
Valley Gdns. SW19 167 G7
Valley Gdns., Wem. 87 J7
Valley Gro. SE7 135 J5
Valley Hill, Loug. 48 B7
Valley Link Ind. Est., Enf. 45 H6
Valley Ms., Twick. 162 D2
Cross Deep
Valley Rd. SW16 169 F4
Valley Rd., Belv. 139 H4
Valley Rd., Brom. 191 E2
Valley Side E4 62 A2
Valley Side Par. E4 62 A2
Valley Side
Valley Vw., Barn. 40 B6
Valley Wk., Croy. 203 F2
Valleyfield Rd. SW16 169 F5
Valliere Rd. NW10 107 H3
Valliers Wd. Rd., Sid. 175 G1
Vallis Way W13 104 D5
Vallis Way, Chess. 195 G4
Valmar Rd. SE5 151 J1
Valnay St. SW17 167 J5
Valognes Av. E17 77 H1
Valonia Gdns. SW18 148 C6
Vambery Rd. SE18 137 F6
Van Dyck Av., N.Mal. 182 D7
Vanbrough Cres., Nthlt. 102 C1
Vanbrugh Cl. E16 116 A5
Fulmer Rd.
Vanbrugh Dr., Walt. 178 C7
Vanbrugh Flds. SE3 135 F7
Vanbrugh Hill SE3 135 F5
Vanbrugh Hill SE10 135 F5
Vanbrugh Pk. SE3 135 F7
Vanbrugh Pk. Rd. SE3 135 F7
Vanbrugh Pk. Rd. W. SE3 135 F7
Vanbrugh Rd. W4 126 D3
Vanbrugh Ter. SE3 155 F1
Vanburgh Cl., Orp. 207 H1
Vancouver Rd. SE23 171 H2
Vancouver Rd., Edg. 70 B1
Vancouver Rd., Hayes 102 B4
Vancouver Rd., Rich. 163 F4
Vanderbilt Rd. SW18 167 F1
Vanderville Gdns. N2 73 F2
Tarling Rd.
Vandome Cl. E16 115 H6
Vandon Pas. SW1 25 G5
Vandon St. SW1 25 G5
Vandon St. SW1 130 C3
Vandy St. EC2 12 D6
Vandyke Cl. SW15 148 A7
Vandyke Cross SE9 156 B5
Vane Cl. NW3 91 G4
Vane Cl., Har. 69 J6
Vane St. SW1 33 G1
Vanessa Cl., Belv. 139 G5
Vanguard Cl. E16 115 G5
Vanguard Cl., Croy. 201 H1
Vanguard Cl., Rom. 83 H2
Vanguard St. SE8 154 A1
Vanguard Way, Wall. 200 E7
Vanneck Sq. SW15 147 G5
Vanoc Gdns., Brom. 173 G3
Vansittart Rd. E7 97 F4
Vansittart St. SE14 133 H7
Vanston Pl. SW6 128 D7
Vant Rd. SW17 167 J5
Vantage Ms. E14 134 C1
Prestons Rd.
Varcoe Rd. SE16 133 E5
Varden St. E1 112 E6
Vardens Rd. SW11 149 G4
Vardon Cl. N3 72 B1
Claremont Pk.
Vardon Cl. W3 106 D6
Varley Par. NW9 71 E4
Varley Rd. E16 115 H6
Varley Way, Mitch. 185 G2
Varna Rd. SW6 128 B7
Varna Rd., Hmptn. 179 H1
Varndell St. NW1 9 F3
Varndell St. NW1 110 C3
Varsity Dr., Twick. 144 B5
Varsity Row SW14 146 C2
William's La.
Vartry Rd. N15 76 A6
Vassall Rd. SW9 131 G7
Vauban Est. SE16 29 G6
Vauban Est. SE16 132 D3
Vauban St. SE16 29 G6
Vauban St. SE16 132 C3
Vaughan Av. NW4 71 G5
Vaughan Av. W6 127 F4
Vaughan Cl., Hmptn. 160/161 E6
Oak Av.
Vaughan Gdns., Ilf. 80 C7
Vaughan Rd. E15 97 F6
Vaughan Rd. SE5 151 J3
Vaughan Rd., Har. 67 J7
Vaughan Rd., T.Ditt. 180 E7
Vaughan Rd., Well. 157 J2
Vaughan St. SE16 133 J2
Vaughan Way E1 21 H6
Vaughan Way E1 112 D7
Vaughan Williams Cl. SE8 134 A7
Watson's St.
Vauxhall Br. SE1 34 A4
Vauxhall Br. SE1 130 E5
Vauxhall Br. SW1 34 A4
Vauxhall Br. SW1 130 E5
Vauxhall Br. Rd. SW1 33 G1
Vauxhall Br. Rd. SW1 130 C4
Vauxhall Gdns., S.Croy. 201 J6
Vauxhall Gdns. Est. SE11 34 D4
Vauxhall Gro. SW8 34 C5
Vauxhall Gro. SW8 131 F6
Vauxhall St. SE11 34 D4
Vauxhall St. SE11 131 F5
Vauxhall Wk. SE11 34 C3
Vauxhall Wk. SE11 131 F5
Vawdrey Cl. E1 113 F4
Veals Mead, Mitch. 185 H1
Vectis Gdns. SW17 168 B6
Vectis Rd.
Vectis Rd. SW17 168 B6
Veda Rd. SE13 154 A4

Velde Way SE22 152 B5
East Dulwich Gro.
Veldene Way, Har. 85 F3
Velletri Ho. E2 113 G2
Vellum Dr., Cars. 200 A3
Venables Cl., Dag. 101 H4
Venables St. NW8 15 F1
Venables St. NW8 109 G4
Vencourt Pl. W6 127 G5
Venetia Rd. N4 75 H6
Venetia Rd. W5 125 G2
Venetian Rd. SE5 151 J2
Venn St. SW4 150 C4
Venner Rd. SE26 171 F6
Ventnor Av., Stan. 69 E1
Ventnor Dr. N20 56 E3
Ventnor Gdns., Bark. 99 H6
Ventnor Rd. SE14 133 G7
Ventnor Rd., Sutt. 199 E7
Venture Cl., Bex. 158 E7
Venue St. E14 114 C5
Venus Rd. SE18 136 C3
Vera Av. N21 43 G5
Vera Lynn Cl. E7 97 G4
Dames Rd.
Vera Rd. SW6 148 B1
Verbena Cl. E16 115 F4
Cranberry La.
Verbena Cl., West Dr. 120 A5
Magnolia St.
Verbena Gdns. W6 127 G5
Verdant La. SE6 173 E1
Verdayne Av., Croy. 203 G1
Verdun Rd. SE18 138 A6
Verdun Rd. SW13 127 G6
Vere Rd., Loug. 49 F4
Vere St. W1 16 D4
Vere St. W1 110 B6
Vereker Dr., Sun. 178 A3
Vereker Rd. W14 128 B5
Verity Cl. W11 108 B6
Vermeer Gdns. SE15 153 F4
Elland Rd.
Vermont Cl., Enf. 43 H4
Vermont Rd. SE19 170 A6
Vermont Rd. SW18 149 E6
Vermont Rd., Sutt. 198 E3
Verney Gdns., Dag. 100 E4
Verney Rd. SE16 132 D6
Verney Rd., Dag. 100 E5
Verney St. NW10 88 D3
Verney Way SE16 132 E5
Vernham Rd. SE18 137 F6
Vernon Av. E12 98 C4
Vernon Av. SW20 184 A2
Vernon Av., Wdf.Grn. 63 H7
Vernon Cl., Epsom 196 C6
Vernon Ct., Stan. 68/69 E1
Vernon Dr.
Vernon Cres., Barn. 42 A6
Vernon Dr., Stan. 68 D1
Vernon Ms. E17 77 J4
Vernon Rd.
Vernon Ms. W14 128 B4
Vernon St.
Vernon Pl. WC1 18 B2
Vernon Pl. WC1 111 E5
Vernon Ri. WC1 10 D3
Vernon Ri. WC1 111 F3
Vernon Ri., Grnf. 86 A5
Vernon Rd. E3 113 J2
Vernon Rd. E11 97 E1
Vernon Rd. E15 97 E7
Vernon Rd. E17 77 J5
Vernon Rd. N8 75 G3
Vernon Rd. SW14 146 D3
Vernon Rd., Ilf. 99 J1
Vernon Rd., Sutt. 199 F5
Vernon Sq. WC1 10 D3
Vernon St. W14 128 B4
Vernon Yd. W11 108 C7
Portobello Rd.
Veroan Rd., Bexh. 158 E2
Verona Dr., Surb. 195 H2
Verona Rd. E7 97 G7
Upton La.
Veronica Gdns. SW16 186 C1
Veronica Rd. SW17 168 B3
Veronique Gdns., Ilf. 81 E5
Verran Rd. SW12 150 B7
Balham Gro.
Versailles Rd. SE20 170 D7
Verulam Av. E17 77 J6
Verulam Bldgs. WC1 18 D1
Verulam Rd., Grnf. 103 G4
Verulam St. WC1 18 E1
Verwood Dr., Barn. 41 J3
Verwood Rd., Har. 67 J2
Vesey Path E14 114 B6
East India Dock Rd.
Vespan Rd. W12 127 G2
Vesta Rd. SE4 153 H2
Vestris Rd. SE23 171 G2
Vestry Ms. SE5 152 B1
Vestry Rd. E17 78 B4
Vestry Rd. SE5 152 B1
Vestry St. N1 12 B3
Vestry St. N1 112 A3
Vevey St. SE6 171 J2
Veysey Gdns., Dag. 101 G3
Viaduct Pl. E2 112/113 E3
Viaduct St.
Viaduct St. E2 112 E3
Vian St. SE13 154 B3
Vibart Gdns. SW2 151 F7
Vibart Wk. N1 110/111 E1
Outram Pl.
Vicarage Av. SE3 155 G1
Vicarage Cl., Erith 139 J6
Vicarage Cl., Nthlt. 85 F7
Vicarage Cl., Wor.Pk. 196 E1
Vicarage Ct. W8 22 A3
Vicarage Ct., Felt. 141 F7
Vicarage Cres. SW11 149 G1
Vicarage Dr. SW14 146 D5
Vicarage Dr., Bark. 99 F7
Vicarage Dr., Beck. 190 A1
Vicarage Fm. Rd., Houns. 142 E2
Vicarage Flds., Walt. 178 C6
Vicarage Gdns. SW14 146 C5
Vicarage Rd.
Vicarage Gdns. W8 128 D1
Vicarage Gdns., Mitch. 185 H3
Vicarage Gate W8 22 A3
Vicarage Gate W8 128 E2
Vicarage Gro. SE5 152 A1
Vicarage La. E6 116 C3
Vicarage La. E15 97 E7
Vicarage La., Chig. 65 F2
Vicarage La., Ilf. 99 G1
Vicarage Pk. SE18 137 F5
Vicarage Path N8 74 E7
Vicarage Rd. E10 96 B1
Vicarage Rd. E15 97 F7
Vicarage Rd. N17 60 D7
Vicarage Rd. NW4 71 G6
Vicarage Rd. SE18 137 F5
Vicarage Rd. SW14 146 C5
Vicarage Rd., Bex. 177 H1
Vicarage Rd., Croy. 201 G3
Vicarage Rd., Dag. 101 H6
Vicarage Rd., Kings.T. 181 G2
Vicarage Rd. (Hampton Wick), Kings.T. 181 F1
Vicarage Rd., Sutt. 198 E4
Vicarage Rd., Tedd. 162 D5
Vicarage Rd., Twick. 162 B2
Vicarage Rd. (Whitton), Twick. 143 J6
Vicarage Rd., Wdf.Grn. 64 B7
Vicarage Way NW10 88 D3
Vicarage Way, Har. 67 G7
Vicars Br. Cl., Wem. 105 H2
Vicars Cl. E9 113 F1
Northiam St.
Vicars Cl. E15 115 G1
Vicars Cl., Enf. 44 B2
Vicars Hill SE13 154 B4
Vicars Moor La. N21 43 G7
Vicars Oak Rd. SE19 170 B6
Vicars Rd. NW5 92 A5
Vicars Wk., Dag. 100 B3
Viceroy Cl. N2 73 H4
Market Pl.
Viceroy Ct. NW8 7 H1
Viceroy Par. N2 73 H3
High Rd.
Viceroy Rd. SW8 150 E1
Vickers Way, Houns. 143 E5
Victor Gro., Wem. 87 H7
Victor Rd. NW10 107 H3
Victor Rd. SE20 171 G7
Victor Rd., Har. 67 J3
Victor Rd., Tedd. 162 B4
Victor Vil. N9 60 A3
Victor Wk. NW9 70/71 E2
Booth Rd.
Victoria Av. E6 116 A1
Victoria Av. EC2 20 E2
Victoria Av. N3 72 C1
Victoria Av., Barn. 41 G4
Victoria Av., Houns. 143 F5
Victoria Av., Surb. 181 G7
Victoria Av., Wall. 200 A3
Victoria Av., Wem. 88 B6
Victoria Av., W.Mol. 179 G3
Victoria Cl., Barn. 41 G4
Victoria Cl., W.Mol. 179 G3
Victoria Av.
Victoria Cotts., Rich. 145 J1
Victoria Ct., Wem. 88 A6
Victoria Cres. N15 76 B5
Victoria Cres. SE19 170 B6
Victoria Cres. SW19 166 C7
Victoria Dock Rd. E16 115 G7
Victoria Dr. SW19 148 A7
Victoria Embk. EC4 18 C6
Victoria Embk. EC4 111 F7
Victoria Embk. SW1 26 B3
Victoria Embk. SW1 131 E2
Victoria Embk. WC2 18 C6
Victoria Embk. WC2 131 E2
Victoria Gdns. W11 128 D1
Victoria Gdns., Houns. 142 E1
Victoria Gro. N12 57 F5
Victoria Gro. W8 22 C5
Victoria Gro. W8 129 F3
Victoria Ind. Est. NW10 106 E3
Victoria La., Barn. 40 C4
Victoria La., Hayes 121 F5
Victoria Ms. NW6 108 D1
Victoria Ms. SW4 150 B4
Victoria Ri.
Victoria Ms. SW18 167 F1
Victoria Pk. E9 95 H7
Victoria Pk. Rd. E9 113 F1
Victoria Pk. Sq. E2 113 F3
Victoria Pas. NW8 7 E5
Victoria Pl., Rich. 145 G5
Victoria Pt. E13 115 G2
Victoria Rd.
Victoria Retail Pk., Ruis. 84 E5
Victoria Ri. SW4 150 B3
Victoria Rd. E4 63 E1
Victoria Rd. E11 96 E4
Victoria Rd. E13 115 G2
Victoria Rd. E17 78 C2
Victoria Rd. E18 79 H2
Victoria Rd. N4 75 F7
Victoria Rd. N9 60 C4
Victoria Rd. N15 76 D4
Victoria Rd. N18 60 C4
Victoria Rd. N22 74 C1
Victoria Rd. NW4 71 J4
Victoria Rd. NW6 108 C1
Victoria Rd. NW7 55 F5
Victoria Rd. NW10 106 D5
Victoria Rd. SW14 146 D3
Victoria Rd. W3 106 D5
Victoria Rd. W5 105 E5
Victoria Rd. W8 22 C5
Victoria Rd. W8 129 F3
Victoria Rd., Bark. 99 E6
Victoria Rd., Barn. 41 G4
Victoria Rd., Bexh. 159 G4
Victoria Rd., Brom. 192 A5
Victoria Rd., Buck.H. 64 A2
Victoria Rd., Bushey 51 H1
Victoria Rd., Chis. 174 D5
Victoria Rd., Dag. 101 H5
Victoria Rd., Felt. 160 B1
Victoria Rd., Kings.T. 181 J2
Victoria Rd., Mitch. 167 H7
Victoria Rd., Ruis. 84 C5
Victoria Rd., Sid. 175 J3
Victoria Rd., Sthl. 123 F3
Victoria Rd., Surb. 181 G6
Victoria Rd., Sutt. 199 G5
Victoria Rd., Tedd. 162 D6
Victoria Rd., Twick. 144 D7
Victoria Sq. SW1 24 E5
Victoria Sta. SW1 33 E1
Victoria Sta. SW1 130 B4
Victoria Steps, Brent. 125 J6
Kew Br. Rd.
Victoria St. E15 96 E7
Victoria St. SW1 25 F6
Victoria St. SW1 130 C3
Victoria St., Belv. 139 F5
Victoria Ter. N4 93 G1
Victoria Ter. NW10 106/107 E3
Old Oak La.
Victoria Ter., Har. 86 B1
Victoria Vil., Rich. 145 J3
Victoria Way SE7 135 H5
Victoria Wf. E14 113 H7
Victorian Gro. N16 94 B3
Victorian Rd. N16 94 B3
Victors Dr., Hmptn. 161 E6
Victors Way, Barn. 40 C3
Victory Av., Mord. 185 F5
Victory Business Cen., Islw. 144 C3
Victory Pl. E14 113 H7
Northey St.
Victory Pl. SE17 36 A1
Victory Pl. SE17 131 J4
Victory Pl. SE19 170 B6
Westow St.
Victory Rd. E11 79 H4
Victory Rd. SW19 167 F7
Victory Rd. Ms. SW19 167 F7
Victory Rd.
Victory Wk. SE8 154 A1
Ship St.
Victory Way SE16 133 H2
Victory Way, Houns. 122 C5
Victory Way, Rom. 83 H2
Vidler Cl., Chess. 195 F6
Merritt Gdns.
Vienna Cl., Ilf. 80 B2
Coburg Gdns.
View, The SE2 139 E5
View Cl. N6 73 J7
View Cl., Chig. 65 G5
View Cl., Har. 68 A4
View Rd. N6 73 J7
Viewfield Cl., Har. 69 H7
Viewfield Rd. SW18 148 C6
Viewfield Rd., Bex. 176 C1
Viewland Rd. SE18 137 J5
Viga Rd. N21 43 G6
Vigilant Cl. SE26 170 D4
Vignoles Rd., Rom. 83 G7
Vigo St. W1 17 F6
Vigo St. W1 110 C7
Viking Cl. E3 113 H2
Selwyn Rd.
Viking Ct. SW6 128 D6
Viking Gdns. E6 116 B4
Jack Dash Way
Viking Pl. E10 95 J1
Viking Rd., Sthl. 103 E7
Viking Way, Erith 139 J3
Villa Rd. SW9 151 G3
Villa St. SE17 36 C4
Villa St. SE17 132 A5
Villacourt Rd. SE18 138 A7
Village, The SE7 135 J6
Village Arc. E4 62 D1
Station Rd.
Village Cl. E4 62 C5
Village Cl. NW3 91 H5
Ornan Rd.
Village Hts., Wdf.Grn. 63 F5
Village Ms. NW9 88 D2
Village Pk. Cl., Enf. 44 B6
Village Rd. N3 72 B1
Village Rd., Enf. 44 B6
Village Row, Sutt. 198 D7
Village Way NW10 88 D4
Village Way SE21 152 A6
Village Way, Beck. 190 A2
Village Way, Pnr. 67 E7
Village Way E., Har. 67 F7
Villas Rd. SE18 137 F4
Villiers Av., Surb. 181 J5
Villiers Av., Twick. 161 F1
Villiers Cl. E10 96 A2
Villiers Cl., Surb. 181 J4
Villiers Ct. N20 41 F7
Buckingham Av.
Villiers Path, Surb. 181 H5
Villiers Rd. NW2 89 G6
Villiers Rd., Beck. 189 G2
Villiers Rd., Islw. 144 B2
Villiers Rd., Kings.T. 181 J3
Villiers Rd., Sthl. 123 F1
Villiers St. WC2 18 A6
Villiers St. WC2 110 E7
Vincam Cl., Twick. 143 G7
Vince St. EC1 12 C4
Vince St. EC1 112 A3
Vincent Av., Surb. 196 B1
Vincent Cl. SE16 133 H2
Vincent Cl., Barn. 40 D3
Vincent Cl., Brom. 191 H4
Vincent Cl., Ilf. 65 F6
Vincent Cl., Sid. 175 H1
Vincent Cl., West Dr. 120 D6
Vincent Gdns. NW2 89 F3
Vincent Ms. E3 114 A2
Vincent Rd. E4 62 D6
Vincent Rd. N15 75 J4
Vincent Rd. N22 75 G2
Vincent Rd. SE18 137 E4
Vincent Rd. W3 126 C3
Vincent Rd., Croy. 188 B7
Vincent Rd., Dag. 100 E7
Vincent Rd., Houns. 142 D2
Vincent Rd., Islw. 144 A1
Vincent Rd., Kings.T. 182 A3
Vincent Rd., Wem. 87 J7
Vincent Row, Hmptn. 161 J6
Vincent Sq. SW1 33 G1
Vincent Sq. SW1 130 C4
Vincent St. E16 115 F5
Vincent St. SW1 33 H1
Vincent St. SW1 130 D4
Vincent Ter. N1 11 G1
Vincent Ter. N1 111 H2
Vincents Path, Nthlt. 84/85 E6
Arnold Rd.
Vine Cl., Surb. 181 J6
Vine Cl., Sutt. 199 F3
Vine Cl., West Dr. 120 D4
Vine Ct. E1 21 J2
Vine Ct., Har. 69 H6

Vine Gdns., Ilf. 99 F5
Vine Hill EC1 10 E6
Vine La. SE1 28 E2
Vine Pl. W5 125 H1
The Common
Vine Pl., Houns. 143 H4
Vine Rd. E15 97 F7
Vine Rd. SW13 147 F3
Vine Rd., E.Mol. 179 J4
Vine Rd., Orp. 207 J6
Vine Sq. W14 128 C5
Vine St. EC3 21 F5
Vine St. W1 17 G6
Vine St., Rom. 83 J5
Vine St. Br. EC1 11 F6
Vine St. Br. EC1 111 G4
Vine Yd. SE1 28 A3
Vinegar All. E17 78 B4
Vinegar St. E1 132/133 E1
Reardon St.
Vinegar Yd. SE1 28 D3
Viner Cl., Walt. 178 C6
Vineries, The N14 42 C6
Vineries, The, Enf. 44 B3
Vineries Bank NW7 55 H5
Vineries Cl., Dag. 101 G6
Heathway
Vineries Cl., West Dr. 120 D6
Vines Av. N3 72 E1
Viney Rd. SE13 154 B3
Vineyard, The, Rich. 145 H5
Vineyard Av. NW7 56 B7
Vineyard Cl. SE6 172 A1
Vineyard Cl., Kings.T. 181 J3
Vineyard Gro. N3 73 E1
Vineyard Hill Rd. SW19 166 D4
Vineyard Pas., Rich. 145 H5
Paradise Rd.
Vineyard Path SW14 146 D3
Vineyard Rd., Felt. 160 A3
Vineyard Row, Kings.T. 181 F1
Vineyard Wk. EC1 11 E5
Vineyard Wk. EC1 111 G4
Vining St. SW9 151 G4
Vintry Ms. E17 78 A4
Cleveland Pk. Cres.
Viola Av. SE2 138 B4
Viola Av., Felt. 142 C6
Viola Sq. W12 107 F7
Violet Cl. E16 115 E4
Violet Cl., Wall. 200 B1
Violet Gdns., Croy. 201 H5
Violet Hill NW8 6 C2
Violet Hill NW8 109 F2
Violet La., Croy. 201 H5
Violet Rd. E3 114 B4
Violet Rd. E17 78 A6
Violet Rd. E18 79 H2
Violet St. E2 112/113 E4
Three Colts La.
Virgil Pl. W1 15 J2
Virgil St. SE1 26 D5
Virgil St. SE1 131 F3
Virginia Cl., N.Mal. 182 C4
Willow Rd.
Virginia Gdns., Ilf. 81 F2
Virginia Rd. E2 13 F4
Virginia Rd. E2 112 C3
Virginia Rd., Th.Hth. 187 H1
Virginia St. E1 21 J6
Virginia St. E1 112 D7
Virginia Wk. SW2 151 F6
Viscount Cl. N11 58 B5
Viscount Dr. E6 116 C5
Viscount Gro., Nthlt. 102 D3
Wayfarer Rd.
Viscount St. EC1 11 J6
Viscount Way, Houns. 141 H4
Vista, The SE9 156 A6
Vista, The, Sid. 175 J5
Langdon Shaw
Vista Av., Enf. 45 G2
Vista Dr., Ilf. 80 A5
Vista Way, Har. 69 H6
Viveash Cl., Hayes 121 J3
Vivian Av. NW4 71 H5
Vivian Av., Wem. 88 A5
Vivian Cl., Wat. 50 A1
Vivian Gdns., Wat. 50 A1
Vivian Gdns., Wem. 88 A5
Vivian Rd. E3 113 H2
Vivian Sq. SE15 152/153 E3
Scylla Rd.
Vivian Way N2 73 G5
Vivien Cl., Chess. 195 H7
Vivienne Cl., Twick. 145 F6
Voce Rd. SE18 137 G7
Voewood Cl., N.Mal. 183 F6
Volta Way, Croy. 201 F1
Voltaire Rd. SW4 150 D3
Voluntary Pl. E11 79 G6
Vorley Rd. N19 92 C2
Voss Ct. SW16 169 E6
Voss St. E2 13 J4
Voss St. E2 112 D3
Voyagers Cl. SE28 118 C6
Vulcan Cl., Wall. 201 F7
Vulcan Gate, Enf. 43 G2
Vulcan Rd. SE4 153 J2
Vulcan Sq. E14 134 A4
Britannia Rd.
Vulcan Ter. SE4 153 J2
Vulcan Way N7 93 F6
Vyne, The, Bexh. 159 H3
Vyner Rd. W3 106 D7
Vyner St. E2 113 E1
Vyse Cl., Barn. 39 J4

W

Wadbrook St., Kings.T. 53 G7
High St.
Wadding St. SE17 36 B2
Wadding St. SE17 132 A4
Waddington Cl., Enf. 44 B4
Waddington Rd. E15 96 D5
Waddington St. E15 96 D6
Waddington Way SE19 169 J7
Waddon Cl., Croy. 201 G3
Waddon Ct. Rd., Croy. 201 G4
Waddon Marsh Way, Croy. 201 F1
Waddon New Rd., Croy. 201 H3
Waddon Pk. Av., Croy. 201 G3
Waddon Rd., Croy. 201 G3
Waddon Way, Croy. 201 G6
Wades Gro. N21 43 G7
Wades Hill N21 43 G6
Wades La., Tedd. 162 D5
High St.
Wades Ms. N21 43 G7
Wades Hill
Wades Pl. E14 114 B7
Wadeson St. E2 113 E2
Wadeville Av., Rom. 83 F7
Wadeville Cl., Belv. 139 G6
Wadham Av. E17 62 B7
Wadham Gdns. NW3 109 H1
Wadham Gdns., Grnf. 86 A6
Wadham Rd. E17 78 B1
Wadham Rd. SW15 148 B4
Wadhurst Cl. SE20 188 E2
Wadhurst Rd. SW8 150 C1
Wadhurst Rd. W4 126 D3
Wadley Rd. E11 78 E7
Wadsworth Business Cen., Grnf. 105 F2
Wadsworth Cl., Enf. 45 G5
Wadsworth Cl., Grnf. 105 F2
Wadsworth Rd., Grnf. 105 E2
Wager St. E3 113 J4
Waggon Ms. N14 58 C1
Chase Side
Waghorn Rd. E13 115 J1
Waghorn Rd., Har. 69 G3
Waghorn St. SE15 152 D3
Wagner St. SE15 133 F7
Wagstaff Gdns., Dag. 100 C7
Ellerton Rd.
Wagtail Cl. NW9 70/71 E2
Swan Dr.
Waights Ct., Kings.T. 181 H1
Wainfleet Av., Rom. 83 J2
Wainford Cl. SW19 166 A1
Windlesham Gro.
Wainwright Gro., Islw. 144 A4
Waite Davies Rd. SE12 155 F7
Waite St. SE15 37 F5
Waite St. SE15 132 C6
Waithman St. EC4 19 G4
Wakefield Gdns. SE19 170 B7
Wakefield Gdns., Ilf. 80 B6
Wakefield Ms. WC1 10 B4
Wakefield Rd. N11 58 D5
Wakefield Rd. N15 76 C5
Wakefield Rd., Rich. 145 G5
Wakefield St. E6 116 A1
Wakefield St. N18 60 D5
Wakefield St. WC1 10 B5
Wakefield St. WC1 111 E3
Wakeham St. N1 94 A6
Wakehams Hill, Pnr. 67 F3
Wakehurst Rd. SW11 149 H5
Wakelin Rd. E15 114 E2
Wakeling Rd. W7 104 C5
Wakeling St. E14 113 H6
Wakeman Rd. NW10 107 J3
Wakemans Hill Av. NW9 70 D5
Wakering Rd., Bark. 99 F6
Wakerley Cl. E6 116 C6
Truesdale Rd.
Wakley St. EC1 11 G3
Wakley St. EC1 111 H2
Walberswick St. SW8 131 E7
Walbrook EC4 20 B5
Walbrook EC4 112 A7
Walbrook Ho. N9 61 F1
Walbrook Wf. EC4 111 J7
Upper Thames St.
Walburgh St. E1 112/113 E6
Bigland St.
Walcorde Av. SE17 36 A2
Walcot Rd., Enf. 45 J2
Walcot Sq. SE11 35 F1
Walcot Sq. SE11 131 G4
Walcott St. SW1 33 G1
Waldair Ct. E16 136/137 E2
Barge Ho. Rd.
Waldair Wf. E16 136 E2
Waldeck Gro. SE27 169 H3
Waldeck Rd. N15 75 H4
Waldeck Rd. SW14 146 C3
Lower Richmond Rd.
Waldeck Rd. W4 126 A6
Waldeck Rd. W13 105 E6
Waldeck Ter. SW14 146 C3
Lower Richmond Rd.
Waldegrave Av., Tedd. 162 C5
Waldegrave Rd.
Waldegrave Gdns., Twick. 162 C2
Waldegrave Pk., Twick. 162 C4
Waldegrave Rd. N8 75 G3
Waldegrave Rd. SE19 170 C7
Waldegrave Rd. W5 105 J6
Waldegrave Rd., Brom. 192 B4
Waldegrave Rd., Dag. 100 C2
Waldegrave Rd., Tedd. 162 C4
Waldegrave Rd., Twick. 162 C4
Waldegrove, Croy. 202 C3
Waldemar Av. SW6 148 B1
Waldemar Av. W13 125 F1
Waldemar Rd. SW19 166 D5
Walden Av. N13 59 J4
Walden Av., Chis. 174 C4
Walden Cl., Belv. 139 F5
Walden Gdns., Th.Hth. 187 F3
Walden Rd. N17 76 A1
Walden Rd., Chis. 174 C6
Walden St. E1 112 E6
Walden Way NW7 56 A6
Walden Way, Ilf. 65 H7
Waldenshaw Rd. SE23 171 F1
Waldo Cl. SW4 150 C5
Waldo Pl., Mitch. 167 H7
Waldo Rd. NW10 107 G3
Waldo Rd., Brom. 192 A3
Waldram Cres. SE23 171 F1
Waldram Pk. Rd. SE23 171 G1
Waldram Pl. SE23 171 F1
Waldram Cres.
Waldrist Way, Erith 139 F2
Waldron Gdns., Brom. 190 D3
Waldron Ms. SW3 31 F5
Waldron Rd. SW18 167 F3
Waldron Rd., Har. 86 B1
Waldronhyrst, S.Croy. 201 H4
Waldrons, The, Croy. 201 H4
Waldrons Path, S.Croy. 201 J4
Waldstock Rd. SE28 118 A7
Waleran Cl., Stan. 52 C6
Chenduit Way
Waleran Flats SE1 132 B4
Old Kent Rd.
Walerand Rd. SE13 154 C2
Wales Av., Cars. 199 J5
Wales Cl. SE15 132 E7
Wales Fm. Rd. W3 106 D5
Waley St. E1 113 G5
Walfield Av. N20 41 E7
Walford Rd. N16 94 B4
Walfrey Gdns., Dag. 101 E7
Walham Grn. Ct. SW6 128/129 E7
Waterford Rd.
Walham Gro. SW6 128 D7
Walham Ri. SW19 166 B6
Walham Yd. SW6 128 D7
Walham Gro.
Walkden Rd., Chis. 174 D5
Walker Cl. N11 58 C4
Walker Cl. SE18 137 F4
Walker Cl. W7 124 B1
Walker Cl., Hmptn. 161 F6
Fearnley Cres.
Walkers Ct. E8 94 D6
Wilton Way
Walkers Ct. W1 17 H5
Walkers Pl. SW15 148 B3
Felsham Rd.
Walkerscroft Mead SE21 169 J1
Walkford Way SE15 37 F7
Walks, The N2 73 G3
Wall End Rd. E6 98 D7
Wall St. N1 94 A6
Wallace Cl. SE28 118 D7
Haldane Rd.
Wallace Cres., Cars. 199 J5
Wallace Rd. N1 93 J6
Wallace Way N19 92 D2
Giesbach Rd.
Wallbutton Rd. SE4 153 H2
Wallcote Av. NW2 90 A1
Waller Dr., Nthwd. 66 A2
Waller Rd. SE14 153 G1
Wallers Cl., Dag. 119 E1
Wallers Cl., Wdf.Grn. 64 C6
Wallers Hoppit, Loug. 48 B2
Wallflower St. W12 107 F7
Wallgrave Rd. SW5 30 A1
Wallgrave Rd. SW5 128 E4
Wallingford Av. W10 108 A5
Wallington Cor., Wall. 200 B4
Manor Rd. N.
Wallington Rd., Ilf. 81 J7
Wallington Sq., Wall. 200 B6
Woodcote Rd.
Wallis All. SE1 28 A4
Wallis Cl. SW11 149 G3
Wallis Ms. N22 75 G3
Brampton Pk. Rd.
Wallis Rd. E9 95 J6
Wallis Rd., Sthl. 103 H6
Wallis's Cotts. SW2 150 E7
Wallman Pl. N22 75 F1
Bounds Grn. Rd.
Wallorton Gdns. SW14 146 D4
Wallwood Rd. E11 78 D7
Wallwood St. E14 113 J5
Walm La. NW2 90 A5
Walmar Cl., Barn. 41 G1
Walmer Cl. E4 62 B2
Walmer Cl., Orp. 207 G4
Tubbenden La. S.
Walmer Cl., Rom. 83 H2
Walmer Gdns. W13 124 D2
Walmer Ho. N9 44 C7
Walmer Pl. W1 15 J1
Walmer Rd. W10 107 J6
Latimer Rd.
Walmer Rd. W11 108 B7
Walmer St. W1 15 J1
Walmer Ter. SE18 137 F4
Walmgate Rd., Grnf. 104 E1
Walmington Fold N12 56 D6
Walney Wk. N1 93 J6
St. Paul's Rd.
Walnut Av., West Dr. 120 D3
Walnut Cl. SE8 133 J6
Clyde St.
Walnut Cl., Cars. 199 J5
Walnut Cl., Ilf. 81 F4
Civic Way
Walnut Ct. W5 125 H2
Rowan Cl.
Walnut Gdns. E15 96/97 E4
Burgess Rd.
Walnut Gro., Enf. 44 A5
Walnut Ms., Sutt. 199 F7
Walnut Rd. E10 96 A2
Walnut Tree Av., Mitch. 185 H3
De'Arn Gdns.
Walnut Tree Cl. SW13 147 F1
Walnut Tree Cl., Chis. 193 F1
Walnut Tree Cotts. SW19 166 B4
Church Rd.
Walnut Tree Rd. SE10 135 E5
Walnut Tree Rd., Brent. 125 H6
Walnut Tree Rd., Dag. 100 D2
Walnut Tree Rd., Houns. 123 F6
Walnut Tree Wk. SE11 34 E1
Walnut Tree Wk. SE11 131 G4
Walnut Way, Buck.H. 64 A3
Walnut Way, Ruis. 84 C6
Walpole Av., Rich. 145 J2
Walpole Cl. W13 125 F2
Walpole Cl., Pnr. 51 G6
Walpole Cres., Tedd. 162 C5
Walpole Gdns. W4 126 C5
Walpole Gdns., Twick. 162 B2

Walpole Ms. NW8 109 G1
Queen's Gro.
Walpole Ms. SW19 167 G6
Walpole Rd.
Walpole Pk. W5 125 F1
Walpole Pl. SE18 136/137 E4
Anglesea Rd.
Walpole Pl., Tedd. 162 C5
Walpole Rd. E6 97 J7
Walpole Rd. E17 77 H4
Walpole Rd. E18 79 F1
Walpole Rd. (Downhills Way) N17 75 J3
Walpole Rd. (Lordship La.) N17 75 J2
Walpole Rd. SW19 167 G6
Walpole Rd., Brom. 192 A5
Walpole Rd., Croy. 202 A2
Walpole Rd., Surb. 181 H6
Walpole Rd., Tedd. 162 C5
Walpole Rd., Twick. 162 B2
Walpole St. SW3 31 J3
Walpole St. SW3 129 J5
Walrond Av., Wem. 87 H5
Walsham Cl. N16 76 D7
Braydon Rd.
Walsham Cl. SE28 118 D7
Walsham Rd. SE14 153 G2
Walsham Rd., Felt. 142 B7
Walsingham Gdns., Epsom 197 E4
Walsingham Pk., Chis. 193 G2
Walsingham Pl. SW4 149 J4
Clapham Common W. Side
Walsingham Pl. SW11 150 A6
Walsingham Rd. E5 94 D3
Walsingham Rd. W13 124 D1
Walsingham Rd., Enf. 44 A4
Walsingham Rd., Mitch. 185 J5
Walsingham Wk., Belv. 139 G6
Walt Whitman Cl. SE24 151 H4
Shakespeare Rd.
Walter Rodney Cl. E6 98 C6
Stevenage Rd.
Walter St. E2 113 G3
Walter St., Kings.T. 181 H1
Sopwith Way
Walter Ter. E1 113 G6
Walter Wk., Edg. 54 C6
Walters Ho. SE17 35 G6
Walters Rd. SE25 188 B4
Walters Rd., Enf. 45 F5
Walters Way SE23 153 G6
Walters Yd., Brom. 191 G2
Walterton Rd. W9 108 C4
Waltham Av. NW9 70 A6
Waltham Av., Hayes 121 F3
Waltham Dr., Edg. 70 A2
Waltham Pk. Way E17 78 A1
Waltham Rd., Cars. 185 G7
Waltham Rd., Sthl. 122 E3
Waltham Rd., Wdf.Grn. 64 B6
Waltham Way E4 61 J3
Walthamstow Av. E4 62 A7
Walthamstow Business Cen. E17 78 C2
Waltheof Av. N17 76 A1
Waltheof Gdns. N17 76 A1
Walton Av., Har. 85 F5
Walton Av., N.Mal. 183 F4
Walton Av., Sutt. 198 C3
Walton Cl. E5 95 G3
Orient Way
Walton Cl. NW2 89 H2
Walton Cl. SW8 34 B7
Walton Cl. SW8 131 E7
Walton Cl., Har. 68 A4
Walton Cres., Har. 85 F4
Walton Dr. NW10 88 D6
Mitchellbrook Way
Walton Dr., Har. 68 A4
Walton Gdns. W3 106 B5
Walton Gdns., Wem. 87 H2
Walton Grn., Croy. 204 C7
Walton Pl. SW3 23 J5
Walton Pl. SW3 129 J3
Walton Rd. E12 98 D4
Walton Rd. E13 115 J2
Walton Rd. N15 76 C5
Walton Rd., E.Mol. 179 G4
Walton Rd., Har. 68 A4
Walton Rd., Sid. 176 C2
Walton Rd., Walt. 178 C5
Walton Rd., W.Mol. 179 E4
Walton St. SW3 31 H1
Walton St. SW3 129 H4
Walton St., Enf. 44 A1
Walton Way W3 106 B5
Walton Way, Mitch. 186 C4
Walworth Pl. SE17 36 A4
Walworth Pl. SE17 131 J5
Walworth Rd. SE1 35 J1
Walworth Rd. SE1 131 J4
Walworth Rd. SE17 35 J1
Walworth Rd. SE17 131 J4
Walwyn Av., Brom. 192 A3
Wanborough Dr. SW15 165 H1
Wanderer Dr., Bark. 118 B3
Wandle Bank SW19 167 G6
Wandle Bank, Croy. 200 E3
Wandle Ct., Epsom 196 C4
Wandle Ct. Gdns., Croy. 200 E4
Wandle Rd. SW17 167 H2
Wandle Rd., Croy. 201 J3
Wandle Rd. (Waddon), Croy. 201 E3
Wandle Rd., Mord. 185 F4
Wandle Rd., Wall. 200 B2
Wandle Side, Croy. 201 F3
Wandle Side, Wall. 200 B3
Wandle Way SW18 166 E1
Wandle Way, Mitch. 185 J5
Wandon Rd. SW6 129 E7
Wandsworth Br. SW6 149 E3
Wandsworth Br. SW18 149 E3
Wandsworth Br. Rd. SW6 148 E1
Wandsworth Common SW12 149 H6
Wandsworth Common W. Side SW18 149 F5
Wandsworth High St. SW18 148 D5
Wandsworth Plain SW18 148 E5
Wandsworth Rd. SW8 34 A5
Wandsworth Rd. SW8 130 D7
Wangey Rd., Rom. 82 D7
Wanless Rd. SE24 151 J3
Wanley Rd. SE5 152 A4
Wanlip Rd. E13 115 H4
Wannock Gdns., Ilf. 65 E7
Wansbeck Rd. E9 95 J7
Wansdown Pl. SW6 30 A7
Wansey St. SE17 35 J2
Wansey St. SE17 131 J4
Wansford Pk., Borwd. 38 E4
Wansford Rd., Wdf.Grn. 79 J1
Wanstead Cl., Brom. 191 J2
Wanstead La., Ilf. 80 A6
Wanstead Pk. E11 80 A7
Wanstead Pk. Av. E12 98 A2
Wanstead Pk. Rd., Ilf. 98 C1
Wanstead Pl. E11 79 G6
Wanstead Rd., Brom. 191 J2
Wansunt Rd., Bex. 177 J1
Wantage Rd. SE12 155 F5
Wantz Rd., Dag. 101 H4
Wapping Dock St. E1 132/133 E1
Cinnamon St.
Wapping High St. E1 29 H2
Wapping High St. E1 132 D1
Wapping La. E1 113 E7
Wapping Wall E1 133 F1
Warbank La., Kings.T. 165 F7
Warbeck Rd. W12 127 H1
Warberry Rd. N22 75 F2
Warboys App., Kings.T. 164 B6
Warboys Cres. E4 62 C5
Warboys Rd., Kings.T. 164 B6
Warburton Cl. N1 94 B6
Culford Rd.
Warburton Cl., Har. 52 A6
Warburton Rd. E8 95 E7
Warburton Rd., Twick. 161 H1
Warburton St. E8 112/113 E1
Warburton Rd.
Warburton Ter. E17 78 B2
Ward Cl., S.Croy. 202 B5
Ward Rd. E15 114 D1
Ward Rd. N19 92 C3
Wardalls Gro. SE14 133 F7
Wardell Cl. NW7 55 E7
Wardell Fld. NW9 71 E1
Warden Av., Har. 85 F1
Warden Rd. NW5 92 A6
Wardens Fld. Cl., Orp. 207 H6
Wardens Gro. SE1 27 J2
Wardle St. E9 95 G5
Wardley St. SW18 148/149 E7
Garratt La.
Wardo Av. SW6 148 B1
Wardour Ms. W1 17 G4
Wardour St. W1 17 H5
Wardour St. W1 110 D7
Wardrobe Pl. EC4 19 H5
Wardrobe Ter. EC4 19 H5
Wards Rd., Ilf. 81 G7
Ware Pt. Dr. SE28 137 G2
Wareham Cl., Houns. 143 H4
Waremead Rd., Ilf. 80 E5
Warenford Way, Borwd. 38 A1
Warfield Rd. NW10 108 A3
Warfield Rd., Felt. 141 H7
Warfield Rd., Hmptn. 179 H1
Warfield Yd. NW10 108 A3
Warfield Rd.
Wargrave Av. N15 76 C6
Wargrave Rd., Har. 85 J3
Warham Rd. N4 75 G5
Warham Rd., Har. 68 C2
Warham Rd., S.Croy. 201 J5
Warham St. SE5 35 H7
Warham St. SE5 131 H7
Waring Cl., Orp. 207 J6
Waring Dr., Orp. 207 J6
Waring Rd., Sid. 176 C6
Waring St. SE27 169 J4
Warkworth Gdns., Islw. 124 D7
Warkworth Rd. N17 60 A7
Warland Rd. SE18 137 G7
Warley Av., Dag. 83 F7
Warley Av., Hayes 102 A5
Warley Cl. E10 95 J1
Millicent Rd.
Warley Rd. N9 61 F2
Warley Rd., Hayes 102 A6
Warley Rd., Ilf. 80 D1
Warley Rd., Wdf.Grn. 63 H7
Warley St. E2 113 G3
Warlingham Rd., Th.Hth. 187 H4
Warlock Rd. W9 108 D4
Warlters Cl. N7 92/93 E4
Warlters Rd.
Warlters Rd. N7 93 E4
Warltersville Rd. N19 74 E7
Warmington Cl. E5 95 G3
Orient Way
Warmington Rd. SE24 151 J6
Warmington St. E13 115 G4
Barking Rd.
Warminster Gdns. SE25 188 D2
Warminster Rd. SE25 188 C2
Warminster Sq. SE25 188 D2
Warminster Rd.
Warminster Way, Mitch. 186 B1
Warndon St. SE16 133 G4
Warne Pl., Sid. 158 B6
Westerham Dr.
Warneford Rd., Har. 69 G3
Warneford St. E9 113 E1
Warner Av., Sutt. 198 B2
Warner Cl. E15 97 E5
Warner Cl. NW9 71 F7
Warner Cl., Hmptn. 161 F5
Tangley Pk. Rd.
Warner Cl., Hayes 121 G7
Warner Par., Hayes 121 G7
Warner Pl. E2 13 J2
Warner Pl. E2 112 D2
Warner Rd. E17 77 H4
Warner Rd. N8 74 D4
Warner Rd. SE5 151 J1
Warner Rd., Brom. 173 F7
Warner St. EC1 11 E6
Warner St. EC1 111 G4
Warner Ter. E14 114 A5
Broomfield St.
Warner Yd. EC1 10 E6
Warners Cl., Wdf.Grn. 63 G5
Warners La., Kings.T. 163 G4
Warners Path, Wdf.Grn. 63 G5
Warnford Ind. Est., Hayes 121 H2
Warnford Rd., Orp. 207 J5
Warnham Ct. Rd., Cars. 199 J7
Warnham Rd. N12 57 H5
Warple Ms. W3 126/127 E2
Warple Way
Warple Way W3 126 E2
Warren, The E12 98 B4
Warren, The, Hayes 102 A6
Warren, The, Houns. 123 F7
Warren, The, Wor.Pk. 196 D4
Warren Av. E10 96 C3
Warren Av., Brom. 172 E7
Warren Av., Orp. 207 J5
Warren Av., Rich. 146 B4
Warren Av., S.Croy. 203 G7
Warren Cl. N9 45 G7
Warren Cl. SE21 151 J7
Lairdale Cl.
Warren Cl., Bexh. 159 G5
Warren Cl., Hayes 102 C5
Warren Cl., Wem. 87 G2
Warren Ct., Chig. 65 G4
Warren Cres. N9 44 C7
Warren Cutting, Kings.T. 164 D7
Warren Dr., Grnf. 103 H4
Warren Dr., Ruis. 66 D7
Warren Dr., The E11 79 J7
Warren Dr. N., Surb. 196 B1
Warren Dr. S., Surb. 196 C1
Warren Flds., Stan. 53 F4
Valencia Rd.
Warren Footpath, Twick. 145 G6
Warren Gdns. E15 96 D5
Ashton Rd.
Warren Gro., Borwd. 38 D4
Warren Hill, Loug. 47 J6
Warren Ho. E3 114 B3
Bromley High St.
Warren La. SE18 136 E3
Warren La., Stan. 52 D2
Warren Ms. W1 9 F6
Warren Pk., Kings.T. 164 C6
Warren Pk. Rd., Sutt. 199 G6
Warren Pl. E1 113 G6
Pitsea St.
Warren Pond Rd. E4 63 F1
Warren Ri., N.Mal. 182 D1
Warren Rd. E4 62 C2
Warren Rd. E10 96 C3
Warren Rd. E11 97 J1
Warren Rd. NW2 89 F2
Warren Rd. SW19 167 H6
Warren Rd., Bexh. 159 G5
Warren Rd., Brom. 205 G2
Warren Rd., Bushey 51 J1
Warren Rd., Croy. 202 B1
Warren Rd., Ilf. 81 G5
Warren Rd., Kings.T. 164 C6
Warren Rd., Orp. 207 J5
Warren Rd., Sid. 176 C3
Warren Rd., Twick. 143 J6
Warren St. W1 9 F6
Warren St. W1 110 C4
Warren Ter., Rom. 82 D4
Warren Wk. SE7 135 J6
Warren Way NW7 56 B6
Warren Wd. Cl., Brom. 205 F2
Warrender Rd. N19 92 C3
Warrender Way, Ruis. 66 A7
Warrens Shawe La., Edg. 54 B1
Warriner Dr. N9 60 D3
Warriner Gdns. SW11 149 J1
Warrington Cres. W9 6 C6
Warrington Cres. W9 109 F4
Warrington Gdns. W9 6 C6
Warrington Pl. E14 134 C1
Yabsley St.
Warrington Rd., Croy. 201 H3
Warrington Rd., Dag. 100 D2
Warrington Rd., Har. 68 B5
Warrington Rd., Rich. 145 G5
Warrington Sq., Dag. 100 D2
Warrior Sq. E12 98 D4
Warsaw Cl., Ruis. 84 B6
Glebe Av.
Warsdale Dr. NW9 70 D5
Mardale Dr.
Warspite Rd. SE18 136 B3
Warton Rd. E15 96 C7
Warwall E6 116 E6
Warwick Av. W2 6 C6
Warwick Av. W2 109 F4
Warwick Av. W9 6 C6
Warwick Av. W9 109 E4
Warwick Av., Edg. 54 B3
Warwick Av., Har. 85 F4
Warwick Cl., Barn. 41 G5
Warwick Cl., Bex. 159 F7
Warwick Cl., Hmptn. 161 J7
Warwick Ct. SE15 152 D2
Warwick Ct. WC1 18 D2
Warwick Ct., Surb. 195 H2
Hook Rd.
Warwick Cres. W2 14 C1
Warwick Cres. W2 109 F5
Warwick Dene W5 125 H1
Warwick Dr. SW15 147 H3
Warwick Est. W2 14 B2
Warwick Est. W2 108 E5
Warwick Gdns. N4 75 J5
Warwick Gdns. W14 128 C3
Warwick Gdns., Ilf. 99 E1
Warwick Gdns., T.Ditt. 180 C5
Warwick Gro. E5 94 E1

Warwick Gro., Surb. 181 J7
Warwick Ho. St. SW1 25 J1
Warwick Ho. St. SW1 130 D1
Warwick La. EC4 19 H4
Warwick La. EC4 111 H6
Warwick Pas. EC4 19 H3
Warwick Pl. W5 125 G2
Warwick Rd.
Warwick Pl. W9 14 C1
Warwick Pl. W9 109 F5
Warwick Pl. N. SW1 33 F2
Warwick Pl. N. SW1 130 C4
Warwick Rd. E4 62 A5
Warwick Rd. E11 79 H5
Warwick Rd. E12 98 B5
Warwick Rd. E15 97 F6
Warwick Rd. E17 77 J1
Warwick Rd. N11 58 D6
Warwick Rd. N18 60 B4
Warwick Rd. SE20 189 E3
Warwick Rd. SW5 128 C4
Warwick Rd. W5 125 G2
Warwick Rd. W14 128 C4
Warwick Rd., Barn. 40 E4
Warwick Rd., Borwd. 38 D3
Warwick Rd., Houns. 142 B3
Warwick Rd., Kings.T. 181 F1
Warwick Rd., N.Mal. 182 C3
Warwick Rd., Sid. 176 B5
Warwick Rd., Sthl. 123 F3
Warwick Rd., Sutt. 199 F4
Warwick Rd., T.Ditt. 180 C5
Warwick Rd., Th.Hth. 187 G3
Warwick Rd., Twick. 162 B1
Warwick Rd., Well. 158 C3
Warwick Rd., West Dr. 120 B1
Warwick Row SW1 25 E5
Warwick Row SW1 130 B3
Warwick Sq. EC4 19 H3
Warwick Sq. SW1 33 F3
Warwick Sq. SW1 130 C5
Warwick Sq. Ms. SW1 33 F2
Warwick Sq. Ms. SW1 130 C4
Warwick St. W1 17 G5
Warwick St. W1 110 C7
Warwick Ter. SE18 137 G6
Warwick Way SW1 33 F2
Warwick Way SW1 130 C4
Warwick Yd. EC1 12 A6
Warwickshire Path SE8 133 J7
Washington Av. E12 98 B4
Washington Cl. E3 114 C6
Washington Rd. E6 97 J7
St. Stephens Rd.
Washington Rd. E18 79 F2
Washington Rd. SW13 127 G7
Washington Rd., Kings.T. 182 A2
Washington Rd., Wor.Pk. 197 H2
Wastdale Rd. SE23 171 G1
Wat Tyler Rd. SE3 154 C2
Wat Tyler Rd. SE10 154 C2
Watchfield Ct. W4 126 C5
Watcombe Cotts., Rich. 126 A6
Watcombe Pl. SE25 188/189 E5
Albert Rd.
Watcombe Rd. SE25 188 E5
Water Gdns., Stan. 53 E6
Water La. E15 97 E6
Water La. N9 60 E1
Water La. NW1 92 B7
Kentish Town Rd.
Water La. SE14 133 F7
Water La., Ilf. 99 H3
Water La., Kings.T. 181 G1
Water La., Rich. 145 G5
Water La., Sid. 177 F2
Water La., Twick. 162 D1
The Embk.
Water Lily Cl., Sthl. 123 J2
Navigator Dr.
Water Ms. SE15 153 F4
Water Rd., Wem. 105 J1
Water St. WC2 18 D5
Water Twr. Hill, Croy. 202 A4
Water Twr. Pl. N1 111 G1
Liverpool Rd.
Waterbank Rd. SE6 172 B3
Waterbeach Rd., Dag. 100 C6
Waterbrook La. NW4 71 J5
Watercress Pl. N1 94 B7
Hertford Rd.
Waterdale Rd. SE2 138 A6
Waterden Rd. E15 96 A5
Waterer Ri., Wall. 200 D6
Waterfall Cl. N14 58 C3
Waterfall Cotts. SW19 167 G6
Waterfall Rd. N11 58 B4
Waterfall Rd. N14 58 C3
Waterfall Rd. SW19 167 G6
Waterfall Ter. SW17 167 H6
Waterfield Cl. SE28 138 B1
Waterfield Cl., Belv. 139 G3
Waterfield Gdns. SE25 188 B5
Waterford Rd. SW6 149 E1
Watergardens, The, Kings.T. 164 C6
Watergate EC4 19 G5
Watergate, The, Wat. 50 D2
Watergate St. SE8 134 A6
Watergate Wk. WC2 26 B1
Waterhall Av. E4 62 E4
Waterhall Cl. E17 77 G1
Waterhouse Cl. E16 116 A5
Waterhouse Cl. NW3 91 G5
Lyndhurst Rd.
Waterhouse Cl. W6 128 A4
Great Ch. La.
Waterhouse Sq. EC1 19 E2
Waterhouse Sq. EC1 111 G5
Wateridge Cl. E14 134 A3
Westferry Rd.
Waterloo Br. SE1 18 C6
Waterloo Br. SE1 111 F7
Waterloo Br. WC2 18 C6
Waterloo Br. WC2 111 F7
Waterloo Cl. E9 95 F5
Churchill Wk.
Waterloo Est. E2 113 F2
Waterloo Gdns. E2 113 F2
Waterloo Gdns. N1 93 H7
Barnsbury St.
Waterloo Pas. NW6 90 D7
Waterloo Pl. SW1 25 H1
Waterloo Pl. SW1 130 D1
Waterloo Pl., Rich. 145 H5
Sheen Rd.
Waterloo Pl. (Kew), Rich. 126 A6
Waterloo Rd. E6 97 J7
Waterloo Rd. E7 97 F5
Wellington Rd.
Waterloo Rd. E10 78 A7
Waterloo Rd. NW2 89 G1
Waterloo Rd. SE1 27 E3
Waterloo Rd. SE1 131 G2
Waterloo Rd., Ilf. 81 F2
Waterloo Rd., Sutt. 199 G5
Waterloo Ter. N1 93 H7
Waterlow Ct. NW11 72/73 E7
Heath Cl.
Waterlow Rd. N19 92 C1
Waterman St. SW15 148 A3
Waterman Way E1 132 E1
Waterman's Cl., Kings.T. 163 H7
Woodside Rd.
Watermans Wk. SE16 133 H3
Watermead La., Cars. 185 J7
Watermead Rd. SE6 172 C4
Watermead Way N17 76 E3
Watermeadow La. SW6 149 F2
Watermen's Sq. SE20 171 F7
Watermill Cl., Rich. 163 F3
Watermill La. N18 60 B5
Watermill Way SW19 185 F1
Watermill Way, Felt. 161 F2
Watermint Quay N16 76 D7
Waters Gdns., Dag. 101 G5
Waters Pl. SW15 147 J2
Danemere St.
Waters Rd. SE6 172 E3
Waters Rd., Kings.T. 182 B2
Waters Sq., Kings.T. 182 B3
Watersedge, Epsom 196 C4
Watersfield Way, Edg. 53 G7
Waterside, Beck. 190 A1
Rectory Rd.
Waterside Cl. E3 113 J1
Waterside Cl. SE16 29 J4
Waterside Cl., Bark. 100 A4
Waterside Cl., Nthlt. 103 F3
Waterside Cl., Surb. 195 H2
Culsac Rd.
Waterside Dr., Walt. 178 A5
Waterside Pl. NW1 110 A1
Princess Rd.
Waterside Pt. SW11 31 H7
Waterside Pt. SW11 129 H7
Waterside Rd., Sthl. 123 G3
Waterside Trd. Cen. W7 124 B3
Waterside Way SW17 167 F4
Watersmeet Way SE28 118 C6
Waterson St. E2 13 E3
Waterson St. E2 112 B3
Watersplash Cl., Kings.T. 181 H3
Watersplash La., Hayes 122 A4
Watersplash La., Houns. 122 B5
Waterview Ho. E14 113 H5
Waterworks La. E5 95 G2
Waterworks Rd. SW2 151 F6
Waterworks Yd., Croy. 201 J3
Surrey St.
Watery La. SW20 184 C2
Watery La., Nthlt. 102 C2
Watery La., Sid. 176 B6
Wates Way, Mitch. 185 J6
Wateville Rd. N17 75 J1
Watford Cl. SW11 149 H1
Petworth St.
Watford Rd. E16 115 G5
Watford Rd., Har. 86 D2
Watford Rd., Wem. 86 D2
Watford Way NW4 71 G4
Watford Way NW7 71 G4
Watkin Rd., Wem. 88 B3
Watkinson Rd. N7 93 F6
Watling Av., Edg. 54 D7
Watling Ct. EC4 20 A4
Watling Fm. Cl., Stan. 53 F1
Watling Gdns. NW2 90 B6
Watling St. EC4 19 J4
Watling St. EC4 111 J6
Watling St. SE15 36 E6
Watling St., Bexh. 159 H4
Watlings Cl., Croy. 189 H6
Watlington Gro. SE26 171 H5
Watney Mkt. E1 112/113 E6
Commercial Rd.
Watney Rd. SW14 146 C3
Watney St. E1 113 E6
Watneys Rd., Mitch. 186 D5
Watson Av. E6 98 D7
Watson Av., Sutt. 198 B2
Watson Cl. N16 94 A5
Matthias Rd.
Watson Cl. SW19 167 H6
Watson St. E13 115 H2
Watson's Ms. W1 15 H2
Watsons Rd. N22 75 F1
Watson's St. SE8 134 A7
Watsons Yd. NW2 89 F2
North Circular Rd.
Wattisfield Rd. E5 95 F3
Watts Cl. N15 76 B5
Seaford Rd.
Watts Gro. E3 114 B5
Watts La., Chis. 193 E1
Watts La., Tedd. 162 D5
Watts Rd., T.Ditt. 180 D7
Watts St. E1 133 E1
Watts St. SE15 152 C1
Watts Way SW7 23 F5
Wauthier Cl. N13 59 H5
Wavel Ms. N8 74 D4
Wavel Ms. NW6 90/91 E7
Acol Rd.
Wavel Pl. SE26 170 C4
Sydenham Hill
Wavell Dr., Sid. 157 H6
Wavendon Av. W4 126 D5
Waveney Av. SE15 153 E4
Waveney Cl. E1 29 J1
Waverley Av. E4 61 J4
Waverley Av. E17 78 D3
Waverley Av., Surb. 182 B6
Waverley Av., Sutt. 199 E2
Waverley Av., Twick. 161 F1
Waverley Av., Wem. 87 J5
Waverley Cl. E18 79 J1
Waverley Cl., Brom. 192 A5
Waverley Cl., Hayes 121 G4
Waverley Cl., W.Mol. 179 G5
Waverley Cres. SE18 137 G5
Waverley Gdns. E6 116 B5
Oliver Gdns.
Waverley Gdns. NW10 105 J3
Waverley Gdns., Bark. 117 H2
Waverley Gdns., Ilf. 81 F2
Waverley Gdns., Nthwd. 66 A1
Waverley Gro. N3 72 B3
Waverley Ind. Est., Har. 68 A3
Waverley Pl. N4 93 H2
Adolphus Rd.
Waverley Pl. NW8 6 E1
Waverley Pl. NW8 109 G2
Waverley Rd. E17 78 C3
Waverley Rd. E18 79 J1
Waverley Rd. N8 74 D6
Waverley Rd. N17 60 E7
Waverley Rd. SE18 137 G5
Waverley Rd. SE25 188 E4
Waverley Rd., Enf. 43 H4
Waverley Rd., Epsom 197 H5
Waverley Rd., Har. 85 F1
Waverley Rd., Sthl. 103 G7
Waverley Vil. N17 76 C2
Waverley Wk. W2 108 D5
Waverley Way, Cars. 199 H6
Waverton Ho. E3 113 J1
Waverton Rd. SW18 149 F7
Waverton St. W1 24 C1
Waverton St. W1 130 A1
Wavertree Ct. SW2 169 F1
Streatham Hill
Wavertree Rd. E18 79 G2
Wavertree Rd. SW2 169 E1
Waxlow Cres., Sthl. 103 G6
Waxlow Rd. NW10 106 C2
Waxwell Cl., Pnr. 66 D2
Waxwell La., Pnr. 66 D2
Waxwell Ter. SE1 26 D4
Waye Av., Houns. 142 A1
Wayfarer Rd., Nthlt. 102 D4
Wayfield Link SE9 157 G6
Wayford St. SW11 149 H2
Wayland Av. E8 94 D5
Waylands Mead, Beck. 190 B1
Wayleave, The SE28 118 B7
Waylett Pl. SE27 169 H3
Waylett Pl., Wem. 87 G4
Wayman Ct. E8 94 E6
Wayne Cl., Orp. 207 J3
Waynflete Av., Croy. 201 H3
Waynflete Sq. W10 108 A7
Waynflete St. SW18 167 F2
Wayside NW11 90 B1
Wayside SW14 146 C5
Wayside, Croy. 204 B6
Field Way
Wayside Cl. N14 42 C6
Wayside Commercial Est., Bark. 118 A1
Wayside Ct., Twick. 145 F6
Wayside Ct., Wem. 88 A3
Oakington Av.
Wayside Gdns. SE9 174 C4
Wayside Gro.
Wayside Gdns., Dag. 101 G5
Wayside Gro. SE9 174 C4
Wayside Ms., Ilf. 80 D5
Gaysham Av.
Weald, The, Chis. 174 C6
Weald Cl. SE16 132/133 E5
Stevenson Cres.
Weald Cl., Brom. 206 B2
Weald La., Har. 68 A2
Weald Ri., Har. 52 C7
Weald Sq. E5 94/95 E2
Rossington St.
Weald Way, Rom. 83 H6
Wealdstone Rd., Sutt. 198 C2
Wealdwood Gdns., Pnr. 51 H6
Highbanks Rd.
Weale Rd. E4 62 D3
Wear Pl. E2 112 E3
Weardale Gdns., Enf. 44 A1
Weardale Rd. SE13 154 D4
Wearside Rd. SE13 154 B4
Weatherley Cl. E3 113 J5
Weaver Cl. E6 116/117 E7
Trader Rd.
Weaver St. E1 13 H6
Weaver St. E1 112 D4
Weaver Wk. SE27 169 H4
Weavers Cl., Islw. 144 B4
Weavers Ter. SW6 128 D6
Weavers Way NW1 110 D1
Webb Cl. W10 107 J4
Webb Est. E5 76 D7
Webb Gdns. E13 115 G4
Kelland Rd.
Webb Pl. NW10 107 F3
Old Oak La.
Webb Rd. SE3 135 F6
Webb St. SE1 28 D6
Webb St. SE1 132 B3
Webber Row SE1 27 F5
Webber Row SE1 131 H2
Webber St. SE1 27 F3
Webber St. SE1 131 H2
Webbs Rd. SW11 149 J5
Webbs Rd., Hayes 102 B3
Webbscroft Rd., Dag. 101 H4
Webster Gdns. W5 125 G1
Webster Rd. E11 96 C3
Webster Rd. SE16 29 J6
Webster Rd. SE16 132 D3
Wedderburn Rd. NW3 91 G5
Wedderburn Rd., Bark. 117 H1
Wedgewood Wk. NW6 90/91 E5
Lymington Rd.

West Cl., Wem.	87	J1
West Common Rd., Brom.	205	G2
West Common Rd., Kes.	205	H4
West Cotts. NW6	90	D5
West Ct. SE18	156	C1
Prince Imperial Rd.		
West Ct., Wem.	87	F2
West Cromwell Rd. SW5	128	C4
West Cromwell Rd. W14	128	C4
West Cross Cen., Brent.	124	D6
West Cross Route W10	108	A7
West Cross Route W11	108	A7
West Cross Way, Brent.	124	E6
West Dene, Sutt.	198	B6
Park La.		
West Drayton Pk. Av., West Dr.	120	B3
West Dr. SW16	168	C4
West Dr., Har.	52	A6
West Dr. Gdns., Har.	52	A6
West Eaton Pl. SW1	**32**	**B1**
West Eaton Pl. SW1	130	A4
West Eaton Pl. Ms. SW1	**32**	**B1**
West Ella Rd. NW10	88	E7
West End Av. E10	78	C5
West End Av., Pnr.	66	D4
West End Ct., Pnr.	66	D4
West End Gdns., Nthlt.	102	C2
Edward Cl.		
West End La. NW6	108	D1
West End La., Barn.	40	A4
West End La., Hayes	121	F7
West End La., Pnr.	66	D3
West End Rd., Nthlt.	84	C7
West End Rd., Ruis.	84	B5
West End Rd., Sthl.	122	E1
West Gdn. Pl. W2	**15**	**H4**
West Gdns. E1	113	E7
West Gdns. SW17	167	H6
West Gate W5	105	H3
West Grn. Pl., Grnf.	104	A1
Uneeda Dr.		
West Grn. Rd. N15	76	A4
West Gro. SE10	154	C1
West Gro., Wdf.Grn.	63	J6
West Halkin St. SW1	**24**	**B5**
West Halkin St. SW1	130	A3
West Hall Rd., Rich.	146	B1
West Hallowes SE9	174	A1
West Ham La. E15	96	E7
West Ham Pk. E7	97	G7
West Hampstead Ms. NW6	90	E6
West Harding St. EC4	**19**	**F3**
West Heath Av. NW11	90	D1
West Heath Cl. NW3	90	D3
West Heath Dr. NW11	90	D1
West Heath Gdns. NW3	90	D3
West Heath Rd. NW3	90	D2
West Heath Rd. SE2	138	D6
West Hendon Bdy. NW9	71	F6
West Hill SW15	148	A7
West Hill SW18	148	D5
West Hill, Har.	86	B2
West Hill, Wem.	87	J1
West Hill Ct. N6	92	A3
West Hill Pk. N6	91	J2
Merton La.		
West Hill Rd. SW18	148	D6
West Hill Way N20	56	E1
West Holme, Erith	159	J1
West Ho. Cl. SW19	166	B1
West India Av. E14	134	A1
West India Dock Rd. E14	113	J6
West Kentish Town Est. NW5	92	A5
West La. SE16	132	E2
West Lo. Av. W3	126	A1
West Mall W8	128	D1
Palace Gdns. Ter.		
West Mead, Epsom	197	E6
West Mead, Ruis.	84	C4
West Mersea Cl. E16	135	H1
Hanameel St.		
West Ms. N17	60	E6
West Ms. SW1	**33**	**F2**
West Oak, Beck.	190	D1
West Pk. SE9	174	B2
West Pk. Av., Rich.	146	A1
West Pk. Cl., Houns.	123	F6
Heston Gra. La.		
West Pk. Cl., Rom.	82	D5
West Pk. Rd., Rich.	146	A1
West Pk. Rd., Sthl.	123	J1
West Parkside SE10	135	E2
West Pier E1	132/133	E1
Wapping High St.		
West Pl. SW19	165	J5
West Poultry Av. EC1	**19**	**G2**
West Quarters W12	107	G6
West Quay Dr., Hayes	102	E5
West Ramp, Houns.	140	D1
West Ridge Gdns., Grnf.	103	J2
West Rd. E15	115	F1
West Rd. N17	60	E6
West Rd. SW3	**32**	**A4**
West Rd. SW3	129	J6
West Rd. SW4	150	D5
West Rd. W5	105	H5
West Rd., Barn.	58	A1
West Rd., Felt.	141	G6
West Rd., Kings.T.	182	C1
West Rd. (Chadwell Heath), Rom.	82	D6
West Rd., West Dr.	120	C3
West Row W10	108	B4
West Sheen Vale, Rich.	145	J4
West Side Common SW19	165	J5
West Smithfield EC1	**19**	**G2**
West Smithfield EC1	111	H5
West Sq. SE11	**27**	**G6**
West Sq. SE11	131	H3
West St. E2	113	E2
West St. E11	96	E3
West St. E17	78	B5
Grove Rd.		
West St. WC2	**17**	**J4**
West St., Bexh.	159	F4
West St., Brent.	125	F6
West St., Brom.	191	G1
West St., Cars.	199	J3
West St., Croy.	201	J4
West St., Har.	86	A1
West St., Sutt.	198	E5
West St. La., Cars.	199	J4
West Temple Sheen SW14	146	B4
West Tenter St. E1	**21**	**G4**
West Tenter St. E1	112	C6
West Thamesmead Business Pk. SE28	137	H3
Nathan Way		
West Twrs., Pnr.	66	D6
West Vw. NW4	71	J4
West Vw., Felt.	141	F7
West Vw., Loug.	48	C3
West Vw. W5	105	H5
West Wk., Barn.	42	A7
West Wk., Hayes	122	A1
West Warwick Pl. SW1	**33**	**E2**
West Warwick Pl. SW1	130	B4
West Way N18	60	A4
West Way N18	88	D3
West Way, Croy.	203	H2
West Way, Edg.	54	B6
West Way, Houns.	143	F1
West Way, Pnr.	66	D4
West Way, W.Wick.	190	D6
West Way Gdns., Croy.	203	G2
West Woodside, Bex.	159	E7
West World W5	105	H3
Westacott Cl. N19	92	D1
Westall Rd., Loug.	49	E3
Westbank Rd., Hmptn.	161	J6
Westbeech Rd. N22	75	G3
Westbere Dr., Stan.	53	G4
Westbere Rd. NW2	90	B5
Westbourne Av. W3	106	D6
Westbourne Av., Sutt.	198	B2
Westbourne Br. W2	**14**	**C2**
Westbourne Br. W2	109	F5
Westbourne Cl., Hayes	102	B4
Westbourne Cres. W2	**14**	**E5**
Westbourne Cres. W2	109	G7
Westbourne Cres. Ms. W2	**14**	**E5**
Westbourne Dr. SE23	171	G2
Westbourne Gdns. W2	**14**	**A3**
Westbourne Gdns. W2	108	E6
Westbourne Gro. W2	108	D6
Westbourne Gro. W11	108	C7
Westbourne Gro. Ms. W11	108	D6
Westbourne Gro.		
Westbourne Gro. Ter. W2	**14**	**A3**
Westbourne Gro. Ter. W2	108	E6
Westbourne Pk. Ms. W2	**14**	**A3**
Westbourne Pk. Pas. W2	108	D5
Westbourne Pk. Vil.		
Westbourne Pk. Rd. W2	108	D5
Westbourne Pk. Rd. W11	108	B6
Westbourne Pk. Vil. W2	108	D5
Westbourne Pl. N9	60/61	E3
Eastbournia Av.		
Westbourne Rd. N7	93	G6
Westbourne Rd. SE26	171	G6
Westbourne Rd., Bexh.	138	E7
Westbourne Rd., Croy.	188	C6
Westbourne St. W2	**15**	**E5**
Westbourne St. W2	109	G7
Westbourne Ter. SE23	171	G2
Westbourne Dr.		
Westbourne Ter. W2	**14**	**D3**
Westbourne Ter. W2	109	G6
Westbourne Ter. Ms. W2	**14**	**C3**
Westbourne Ter. Ms. W2	109	F6
Westbourne Ter. Rd. W2	**14**	**C2**
Westbourne Ter. Rd. W2	109	F6
Westbridge Rd. SW11	149	G1
Westbrook Av., Hmptn.	161	F7
Westbrook Cl., Barn.	41	G3
Westbrook Cres., Barn.	41	G3
Westbrook Rd. SE3	155	H1
Westbrook Rd., Houns.	123	F7
Westbrook Rd., Th.Hth.	188	A1
Westbrook Sq., Barn.	41	G3
Westbrook Cres.		
Westbrooke Cres., Well.	158	C3
Westbrooke Rd., Sid.	175	G2
Westbrooke Rd., Well.	158	B3
Westbury Av. N22	75	H3
Westbury Av., Esher	194	C6
Westbury Av., Sthl.	103	G4
Westbury Av., Wem.	87	H7
Westbury Cl., Ruis.	66	A7
Westbury Gro. N12	56	D6
Westbury La., Buck.H.	63	J2
Westbury Lo. Cl., Pnr.	66	D3
Westbury Par. SW12	150	B6
Balham Hill		
Westbury Pl., Brent.	125	G6
Westbury Rd. E7	97	H5
Westbury Rd. E17	78	A4
Westbury Rd. N11	58	E6
Westbury Rd. N12	56	D6
Westbury Rd. SE20	189	G1
Westbury Rd. W5	105	H6
Westbury Rd., Bark.	117	G1
Westbury Rd., Beck.	189	H3
Westbury Rd., Brom.	192	A1
Westbury Rd., Buck.H.	63	J2
Westbury Rd., Croy.	188	A6
Westbury Rd., Felt.	160	D1
Westbury Rd., Ilf.	98	D2
Westbury Rd., N.Mal.	182	D4
Westbury Rd., Wem.	87	H7
Westbury St. SW8	150	C2
Westbury Ter. E7	97	H6
Westchester Dr. NW4	72	A3
Westcombe Av., Croy.	187	E6
Westcombe Ct. SE3	135	F7
Westcombe Pk. Rd.		
Westcombe Dr., Barn.	40	D5
Westcombe Hill SE3	135	G6
Westcombe Hill SE10	135	G5
Westcombe Pk. Rd. SE3	135	E6
Westcoombe Av. SW20	183	F1
Westcote Rd. SW16	168	C5
Westcott Cl. N15	76	C6
Ermine Rd.		
Westcott Cl., Brom.	192	B5
Ringmer Way		
Westcott Cres. W7	104	B6
Westcott Rd. SE17	**35**	**H5**
Westcott Rd. SE17	131	H6
Westcourt, Sun.	178	B2
Westcroft Cl. NW2	90	B4
Westcroft Gdns., Mord.	184	C3
Westcroft Rd., Cars.	200	A4
Westcroft Rd., Wall.	200	A4
Westcroft Sq. W6	127	G4
Westcroft Way NW2	90	B4
Westdale Pas. SE18	136	E6
Westdale Rd. SE18	137	E6
Westdean Av. SE12	173	H1
Westdean Cl. SW18	149	E6
Westdown Rd. E15	96	C4
Westdown Rd. SE6	154	A7
Westerdale Rd. SE10	135	G5
Westerfield Rd. N15	76	C5
Westergate Rd. SE2	138	E5
Westerham Av. N9	60	A3
Westerham Dr., Sid.	158	B6
Westerham Rd. E10	78	B7
Westerham Rd., Kes.	206	A6
Westerley Cres. SE26	171	J5
Westerley Ware, Rich.	126	A6
Kew Grn.		
Western Av. NW11	72	A6
Western Av. W3	106	D5
Western Av. W5	105	J4
Western Av., Dag.	101	J6
Western Av., Grnf.	105	G3
Western Av., Nthlt.	103	F1
Western Av. Underpass W5	105	J3
Western Av.		
Western Ct. N3	56	D6
Huntley Dr.		
Western Gdns. W5	106	A7
Western Gateway E16	115	G7
Western La. SW12	150	A7
Western Ms. W9	108	C4
Great Western Rd.		
Western Pl. SE16	133	F2
Canon Beck Rd.		
Western Rd. E13	115	J1
Western Rd. E17	78	C5
Western Rd. N2	73	J4
Western Rd. N22	75	F2
Western Rd. NW10	106	C4
Western Rd. SW9	151	G3
Western Rd. SW19	185	G1
Western Rd. W5	105	G7
Western Rd., Mitch.	185	G1
Western Rd., Sthl.	122	D3
Western Rd., Sutt.	198	D5
Western Ter. W6	127	G5
Chiswick Mall		
Western Trd. Est. NW10	106	C4
Western Vw., Hayes	121	J2
Station Rd.		
Western Way SE28	137	G3
Western Way, Barn.	40	D6
Westernville Gdns., Ilf.	81	F7
Westferry Circ. E14	133	J1
Westferry Rd. E14	134	A1
Westfield, Loug.	47	J5
Westfield Cl. NW9	70	C3
Westfield Cl. SW10	129	F7
Westfield Cl., Enf.	45	H3
Westfield Cl., Sutt.	198	C4
Westfield Dr., Har.	69	G4
Westfield Gdns., Har.	69	G4
Westfield La., Har.	69	G4
Westfield Pk., Pnr.	51	F7
Westfield Pk. Dr., Wdf.Grn.	64	B6
Westfield Rd. NW7	54	D3
Westfield Rd. W13	124	D1
Westfield Rd., Beck.	189	J2
Westfield Rd., Bexh.	159	J2
Westfield Rd., Croy.	201	H2
Westfield Rd., Dag.	101	E4
Westfield Rd., Mitch.	185	J2
Westfield Rd., Surb.	181	G5
Westfield Rd., Sutt.	198	C4
Westfield Rd., Walt.	179	E7
Westfield St. SE18	136	A3
Westfield Way E1	113	H4
Westfields SW13	147	F3
Westfields Av. SW13	147	E3
Westfields Rd. W3	106	B5
Westgate Rd. SE25	188	E4
Westgate Rd., Beck.	190	B1
Westgate St. E8	112	E1
Westgate Ter. SW10	**30**	**B4**
Westgate Ter. SW10	129	E5
Westglade Ct., Har.	69	G5
Westgrove La. SE10	154	C1

Westhay Gdns. SW14 146 B5
Westholm NW11 72 E4
Westholme, Orp. 193 H7
Westholme Gdns., Ruis. 84 A1
Westhorne Av. SE9 155 J6
Westhorne Av. SE12 155 G7
Westhorpe Gdns. NW4 71 J3
Westhorpe Rd. SW15 147 J3
Westhurst Dr., Chis. 175 E5
Westlake Cl. N13 59 G3
Westlake Cl., Hayes 102/103 E4
Lochan Cl.
Westlake Rd., Wem. 87 G2
Westland Cl., Stai. 140 B6
Westland Dr., Brom. 205 F2
Westland Pl. N1 12 B3
Westlands Cl., Hayes 122 A4
Granville Rd.
Westlands Ter. SW12 150 C6
Gaskarth Rd.
Westlea Rd. W7 124 D3
Westleigh Av. SW15 147 H5
Westleigh Dr., Brom. 192 B1
Westleigh Gdns., Edg. 70 A1
Westlinks, Wem. 105 G3
Alperton La.
Westlinton Cl. NW7 56 B6
Frith La.
Westmead SW15 147 H6
Westmead Cor., Cars. 199 H4
Colston Av.
Westmead Rd., Sutt. 199 G4
Westmede, Chig. 65 F6
Westmere Dr. NW7 54 D3
Westmill Ct. N4 93 J2
Brownswood Rd.
Westminster Av., Th.Hth. 187 H2
Westminster Br. SE1 26 B4
Westminster Br. SE1 131 E2
Westminster Br. SW1 26 B4
Westminster Br. SW1 131 E2
Westminster Br. Rd. SE1 26 D4
Westminster Br. Rd. SE1 131 G3
Westminster Cl., Felt. 160 A1
Westminster Cl., Ilf. 81 G2
Westminster Cl., Tedd. 162 D5
Westminster Dr. N13 58 E5
Westminster Gdns. E4 63 E1
Westminster Gdns., Bark. 117 H2
Westminster Gdns., Ilf. 81 F2
Westminster Rd. N9 61 E1
Westminster Rd. W7 124 B1
Westminster Rd., Sutt. 199 G2
Westmoat Cl., Beck. 172 C7
Westmont Rd., Esher 194 B2
Westmoor Gdns., Enf. 45 G2
Westmoor Rd., Enf. 45 G2
Westmoor St. SE7 136 A3
Westmoreland Av., Well. 157 H3
Westmoreland Bldgs. EC1 111 J5
Bartholomew Cl.
Westmoreland Pl. SW1 33 E4
Westmoreland Pl. SW1 130 B5
Westmoreland Pl. W5 105 G5
Mount Av.
Westmoreland Pl., Brom. 191 G3
Westmoreland Rd. NW9 70 A4
Westmoreland Rd. SE17 36 A5
Westmoreland Rd. SE17 132 A6
Westmoreland Rd. SW13 147 F1
Westmoreland Rd., Brom. 191 E5
Westmoreland St. W1 16 C2
Westmoreland St. W1 110 A5
Westmoreland Ter. SW1 32 E4
Westmoreland Ter. SW1 130 B5
Westmoreland Wk. SE17 36 B5
Westmorland Cl. E12 98 A2
Westmorland Cl., Twick. 145 E6
Westmorland Rd. E17 78 A6
Westmorland Rd., Har. 67 H5
Westmorland Sq., Mitch. 186/187 E5
Westmorland Way
Westmorland Ter. SE20 171 E7
Westmorland Way, Mitch. 186 E5
Westmount Rd. SE9 156 C2
Westoe Rd. N9 61 E2
Weston Av., T.Ditt. 180 B7
Weston Av., W.Mol. 179 E3
Weston Ct. N4 93 J3
Queens Dr.
Weston Dr., Stan. 68 E1
Weston Gdns., Islw. 144 B1
Weston Grn., Dag. 101 F4
Weston Grn., T.Ditt. 194 B1
Weston Grn. Rd., Esher 194 A1
Weston Grn. Rd., T.Ditt. 194 B1
Weston Gro., Brom. 191 F1
Weston Pk. N8 75 E6
Weston Pk., Kings.T. 181 H2
Fairfield W.
Weston Pk., T.Ditt. 194 B1
Weston Pk. Cl., T.Ditt. 194 B1
Weston Pk.
Weston Ri. WC1 10 D2
Weston Ri. WC1 111 F2
Weston Rd. W4 126 C3
Weston Rd., Brom. 173 F7
Weston Rd., Dag. 101 E4
Weston Rd., Enf. 44 A1
Weston Rd., T.Ditt. 194 B1
Weston St. SE1 28 C5
Weston St. SE1 132 A3
Weston Wk. E8 94/95 E7
Mare St.
Westover Hill NW3 90 D2
Westover Rd. SW18 149 F6
Westow Hill SE19 170 B6
Westow St. SE19 170 B6
Westpoint Trd. Est. W3 106 B4
Westpole Av., Barn. 42 A4
Westport Rd. E13 115 H4
Westport St. E1 113 G6
Westrow SW15 147 J5
Westrow Dr., Bark. 99 J6
Westrow Gdns., Ilf. 99 J2
Westside NW4 71 H2
Westvale Ms. W3 127 E1
Westview Cl. NW10 89 F5
Westview Cl. W7 104 B6
Westview Cl. W10 107 J6
Westview Cres. N9 44 B7
Westview Dr., Wdf.Grn. 80 A2
Westville Rd. W12 127 G2
Westville Rd., T.Ditt. 194 D1
Westward Rd. E4 61 J5
Westward Way, Har. 69 H6
Westway SW20 183 H3
Westway W2 108 D5
Westway W9 108 D5
Westway W10 108 B6
Westway W12 107 G7
Westway, Orp. 193 G5
Westway Cl. SW20 183 H3
Westways, Epsom 197 F4
Westwell Rd. SW16 168 E6
Westwell Rd. App. SW16 168/169 E6
Westwell Rd.
Westwick Gdns. W14 128 A2
Westwick Gdns., Houns. 142 B2
Westwood Av. SE19 187 J1
Westwood Av., Har. 85 H4
Westwood Cl., Brom. 192 A3
Westwood Gdns. SW13 147 F3
Westwood Hill SE26 170 D5
Westwood La., Sid. 158 A5
Westwood La., Well. 157 J3
Westwood Pk. SE23 153 E7
Westwood Rd. E16 135 H1
Westwood Rd. SW13 147 F3
Westwood Rd., Ilf. 99 J1
Wetheral Dr., Stan. 69 E1
Wetherby Cl., Nthlt. 85 H6
Wetherby Gdns. SW5 30 C2
Wetherby Gdns. SW5 129 F4
Wetherby Ms. SW5 30 A3
Wetherby Pl. SW7 30 C2
Wetherby Pl. SW7 129 F4
Wetherby Rd., Enf. 43 J1
Wetherby Way, Chess. 195 H7
Wetherden St. E17 77 J7
Wetherell Rd. E9 113 G1
Wetherill Rd. N10 74 A1
Wexford Rd. SW12 149 J7
Wey Ct., Epsom 196 C4
Weybourne St. SW18 167 F2
Weybridge Ct. SE16 37 J4
Weybridge Pt. SW11 150 A2
Weybridge Rd., Th.Hth. 187 G4
Weydown Cl. SW19 166 B1
Weyhill Rd. E1 21 J3
Weylond Rd., Dag. 101 F3
Weyman Rd. SE3 155 J1
Weymouth Av. NW7 54 E5
Weymouth Av. W5 125 F3
Weymouth Cl. E6 116/117 E6
Covelees Wall
Weymouth Ct., Sutt. 198 D7
Weymouth Ms. W1 16 D1
Weymouth Ms. W1 110 B5
Weymouth St. W1 16 C2
Weymouth St. W1 110 B5
Weymouth Ter. E2 13 G1
Weymouth Ter. E2 112 C2
Weymouth Wk., Stan. 52 D6
Whadcote St. N4 93 G2
Seven Sisters Rd.
Whalebone Av., Rom. 83 F6
Whalebone Ct. EC2 20 C3
Whalebone Gro., Rom. 83 F6
Whalebone La. E15 96/97 E7
West Ham La.
Whalebone La. N., Rom. 83 E5
Whalebone La. S., Dag. 83 F7
Whalebone La. S., Rom. 83 F7
Wharf La., Twick. 162 D1
Wharf Pl. E2 112 D1
Wharf Rd. E15 114 D1
Wharf Rd. N1 11 J2
Wharf Rd. N1 111 J2
Wharf Rd., Enf. 45 H6
Wharf St. E16 114 E5
Wharfdale Ct. E5 95 G4
Rushmore Rd.
Wharfdale Rd. N1 10 B1
Wharfdale Rd. N1 111 E2
Wharfedale Gdns., Th.Hth. 187 F4
Wharfedale St. SW10 30 A4
Wharfedale St. SW10 128 E5
Wharfside Rd. E16 115 E5
Wharncliffe Dr., Sthl. 124 A1
Wharncliffe Gdns. SE25 188 B2
Wharncliffe Rd. SE25 188 B2
Wharton Cl. NW10 89 E6
Wharton Rd., Brom. 191 H1
Wharton St. WC1 10 D4
Wharton St. WC1 111 F3
Whateley Rd. SE20 171 G7
Whateley Rd. SE22 152 C5
Whatley Av. SW20 184 B3
Whatman Rd. SE23 153 G7
Wheat Sheaf Cl. E14 134 B4
Wheatfield Way, Kings.T. 181 H2
Wheatfields E6 116/117 E6
Oxleas
Wheatfields, Enf. 45 H2
Wheathill Rd. SE20 188 E3
Wheatlands, Houns. 123 G6
Wheatlands Rd. SW17 168 A3
Stapleton Rd.
Wheatley Cl. NW4 71 G2
Wheatley Cres., Hayes 102 A7
Wheatley Gdns. N9 60 B2
Wheatley Rd., Islw. 144 C3
Wheatley St. W1 16 C2
Wheatley's Ait, Sun. 178 A5
Wheatsheaf Cl., Nthlt. 84 E5
Wheatsheaf La. SW6 127 J7
Wheatsheaf La. SW8 34 B7
Wheatsheaf La. SW8 130 E7
Wheatsheaf Ter. SW6 128 C7
Wheatstone Cl., Mitch. 185 H1
Wheatstone Rd. W10 108 B5
Wheel Fm. Dr., Dag. 101 J3
Wheeler Cl., Wdf.Grn. 64 C5
Chigwell Rd.
Wheeler Gdns. N1 110/111 E1
Outram Pl.
Wheelers Cross, Bark. 117 G2
Wheelock Cl., Erith 139 H7
Wheelwright St. N7 93 F7
Whelan Way, Wall. 200 D3
Wheler St. E1 13 F6
Wheler St. E1 112 C4
Whellock Rd. W4 126 E3
Whenman Av., Bex. 177 J2
Whernside Cl. SE28 118 C7
Whetstone Cl. N20 57 G2
Oakleigh Rd. N.
Whetstone Pk. WC2 18 C3
Whetstone Rd. SE3 155 J2
Whewell Rd. N19 93 E2
Whichcote St. SE1 26 E2
Whidborne Cl. SE8 154 A2
Cliff Ter.
Whidborne St. WC1 10 B4
Whidborne St. WC1 111 E3
Whimbrel Cl. SE28 118 C7
Whimbrel Way, Hayes 102 D6
Whinchat Rd. SE28 137 G3
Whinfell Cl. SW16 168 D5
Whinyates Rd. SE9 156 B3
Whipps Cross Rd. E11 78 D5
Whiskin St. EC1 11 G4
Whiskin St. EC1 111 H3
Whisperwood Cl., Har. 52 B7
Whistler Gdns., Edg. 69 J2
Whistler Ms. SE15 132 C7
Commercial Way
Whistler Ms., Dag. 100 B5
Fitzstephen Rd.
Whistler St. N5 93 H4
Whistler Wk. SW10 30 D7
Whistlers Av. SW11 129 G7
Whiston Rd. E2 13 F1
Whiston Rd. E2 112 C2
Whitakers Way, Loug. 48 C1
Whitbread Cl. N17 76 D1
Whitbread Rd. SE4 153 H4
Whitburn Rd. SE13 154 B4
Whitby Av. NW10 106 B3
Whitby Gdns. NW9 70 A3
Whitby Gdns., Sutt. 199 G2
Whitby Rd. SE18 136 C4
Whitby Rd., Har. 85 J3
Whitby Rd., Ruis. 84 B3
Whitby Rd., Sutt. 199 G2
Whitby St. E1 13 F5
Whitcher Cl. SE14 133 H6
Whitcher Pl. NW1 92 C7
Rochester Rd.
Whitchurch Av., Edg. 53 J7
Whitchurch Cl., Edg. 53 J6
Whitchurch Gdns., Edg. 53 J6
Whitchurch La., Edg. 53 G7
Whitchurch Rd. W11 108 A7
Whitcomb Ct. WC2 110 D7
Whitcomb St.
Whitcomb St. WC2 17 J6
Whitcomb St. WC2 110 D7
White Acre NW9 71 E2
White Bear Pl. NW3 91 G4
New End Sq.
White Br. Av., Mitch. 185 G4
Belgrave Wk.
White Butts Rd., Ruis. 84 D3
White Ch. La. E1 21 H3
White Ch. La. E1 112 D6
White Ch. Pas. E1 21 H3
White City Cl. W12 107 J7
White City Est. W12 107 H7
White City Rd. W12 107 H7
White Conduit St. N1 11 F1
White Craig Cl., Pnr. 51 G5
White Gdns., Dag. 101 G6
White Hart Ct. EC2 112 B6
Bishopsgate
White Hart La. N17 60 A7
White Hart La. N22 75 G1
White Hart La. NW10 89 F6
Church Rd.
White Hart La. SW13 147 E3
White Hart La., Rom. 83 G1
White Hart Rd. SE18 137 H4
White Hart Slip, Brom. 191 G2
Market Sq.
White Hart St. SE11 35 F3
White Hart St. SE11 131 G5
White Hart Yd. SE1 28 B2
White Heron Ms., Tedd. 162 C6
White Horse Hill, Chis. 174 D4
White Horse La. E1 113 G4
White Horse Ms. SE1 27 F5
White Horse Rd. E1 113 H6
White Horse Rd. E6 116 C3
White Horse St. W1 24 D2
White Horse St. W1 130 B1
White Horse Yd. EC2 20 B3
White Ho. Dr., Stan. 53 F4
White Kennett St. E1 21 E3
White Lion Ct. EC3 20 D4

White Lion Hill EC4 19 H5
White Lion Hill EC4 111 H7
White Lion St. N1 11 E2
White Lion St. N1 111 G2
White Lo. SE19 169 H7
White Lo. Cl. N2 73 H6
White Lo. Cl., Sutt. 199 F7
White Lyon Ct. EC2 111 J4
Fann St.
White Oak Dr., Beck. 190 C2
White Oak Gdns., Sid. 157 J7
White Orchards N20 40 C7
White Orchards, Stan. 52 D5
White Post La. E9 95 J7
White Post La. SE13 154 A3
White Post St. SE15 133 F7
White Rd. E15 97 E7
White St., Sthl. 122 D2
White Swan Ms. W4 126/127 E6
Bennett St.
Whiteadder Way E14 134 B4
Whitear Wk. E15 96 D6
Whitebarn La., Dag. 119 G1
Whitebeam Av., Brom. 192 D6
Whitebeam Cl. SW9 131 F7
Clapham Rd.
Whitebeam Twr. E17 77 H3
Hillyfield
Whitebridge Cl., Felt. 141 J6
Whitechapel High St. E1 21 G3
Whitechapel High St. E1 112 C6
Whitechapel Rd. E1 21 H2
Whitechapel Rd. E1 112 D5
Whitecote Rd., Sthl. 103 H6
Whitecroft Cl., Beck. 190 D4
Whitecroft Way, Beck. 190 C5
Whitecross Pl. EC2 20 C1
Whitecross St. EC1 12 A5
Whitecross St. EC1 111 J4
Whitefield Av. NW2 71 J7
Whitefield Cl. SW15 148 B6
Whitefoot La., Brom. 172 C4
Whitefoot Ter., Brom. 173 E3
Whitefriars Av., Har. 68 B2
Whitefriars Dr., Har. 68 A2
Whitefriars St. EC4 19 F4
Whitefriars St. EC4 111 G6
Whitegate Gdns., Har. 52 C7
Whitehall SW1 26 A1
Whitehall SW1 130 E1
Whitehall Ct. SW1 26 A2
Whitehall Ct. SW1 130 E1
Whitehall Cres., Chess. 195 G5
Whitehall Gdns. E4 62 D1
Whitehall Gdns. SW1 26 A2
Whitehall Gdns. W3 126 A1
Whitehall Gdns. W4 126 B6
Whitehall La., Buck.H. 63 G2
Whitehall Pk. N19 92 C1
Whitehall Pk. Rd. W4 126 B6
Whitehall Pl. E7 97 G5
Station Rd.
Whitehall Pl. SW1 26 A2
Whitehall Pl. SW1 130 E1
Whitehall Pl., Wall. 200 B4
Bernard Rd.
Whitehall Rd. E4 62 E2
Whitehall Rd. W7 124 D2
Whitehall Rd., Brom. 192 A5
Whitehall Rd., Har. 68 B7
Whitehall Rd., Th.Hth. 187 G5
Whitehall Rd., Wdf.Grn. 62 E2
Whitehall St. N17 60 C7
Whitehaven Cl., Brom. 191 G4
Whitehaven St. NW8 7 G6
Whitehead Cl. N18 60 A5
Whitehead Cl. SW18 149 F7
Whitehead's Gro. SW3 31 H3
Whitehead's Gro. SW3 129 H5
Whitehills Rd., Loug. 48 D3
Whitehorse La. SE25 188 A4
Whitehorse Rd., Croy. 187 J7
Whitehorse Rd., Th.Hth. 188 A6
Whitehouse Av., Borwd. 38 B3
Whitehouse Way N14 58 B2
Whiteledges W13 105 F6
Whitelegg Rd. E13 115 F2
Whiteley Rd. SE19 170 A5
Whiteleys Cotts. W14 128 C4
Whiteleys Way, Felt. 161 G3
Whiteoaks La., Grnf. 104 A2
Whites Av., Ilf. 81 H6
Whites Grds. SE1 28 E4
Whites Grds. SE1 132 B2
Whites Grds. Est. SE1 28 E3
White's Row E1 21 F2
White's Row E1 112 C5
White's Sq. SW4 150 D4
Nelson's Row
Whitestile Rd., Brent. 125 F5
Whitestone La. NW3 91 F3
Heath St.
Whitestone Wk. NW3 91 F3
North End Way
Whitethorn Gdns., Croy. 203 E2
Whitethorn Gdns., Enf. 44 A5
Whitethorn St. E3 114 A4
Whitewebbs Way, Orp. 193 J1
Whitfield Pl. W1 9 F6
Whitfield Rd. E6 97 J7
Whitfield Rd. SE3 154 D1
Whitfield Rd., Bexh. 139 F7
Whitfield St. W1 17 H2
Whitfield St. W1 110 D5
Whitford Gdns., Mitch. 185 J3
Whitgift Av., S.Croy. 201 J5
Whitgift Cen., Croy. 201 J2
Whitgift St. SE11 34 C1
Whitgift St. SE11 131 F4
Whitgift St., Croy. 201 J3
Whiting Av., Bark. 99 E7
Whitings, Ilf. 81 G5
Whitings Rd., Barn. 39 J5
Whitings Way E6 116 D5
Whitland Rd., Cars. 199 G1
Whitley Cl., Stai. 140 B6
Whitley Rd. N17 76 B2
Whitlock Dr. SW19 148 B7
Whitman Rd. E3 113 H4
Whitmead Cl., S.Croy. 202 B6
Whitmore Cl. N11 58 B5
Whitmore Est. N1 112 B1
Whitmore Gdns. NW10 107 J2
Whitmore Rd. N1 112 B1
Whitmore Rd., Beck. 189 J3
Whitmore Rd., Har. 67 J7
Whitnell Way SW15 148 A5
Whitney Av., Ilf. 80 A4
Whitney Rd. E10 78 B7
Whitney Wk., Sid. 176 E6
Whitstable Cl., Beck. 189 J1
Whitstable Ho. W10 108 A6
Whitstable Pl., Croy. 201 J4
Whitta Rd. E12 98 A4
Whittaker Av., Rich. 145 G5
Hill St.
Whittaker Rd. E6 97 J7
Whittaker Rd., Sutt. 198 C3
Whittaker St. SW1 32 B2
Whittaker St. SW1 130 A4
Whittaker Way SE1 37 J2
Whittell Gdns. SE26 171 F3
Whittingstall Rd. SW6 148 C1
Whittington Av. EC3 20 D4
Whittington Ct. N2 73 J5
Whittington Ms. N12 57 F4
Fredericks Pl.
Whittington Rd. N22 58 E7
Whittington Way, Pnr. 67 E5
Whittle Cl. E17 77 H6
Whittle Cl., Sthl. 103 H6
Whittle Rd., Houns. 122 C7
Whittle Rd., Sthl. 123 H2
Post Rd.
Whittlebury Cl., Cars. 199 J7
Whittlesea Cl., Har. 51 J7
Whittlesea Path, Har. 67 J1
Whittlesea Rd., Har. 67 J1
Whittlesey St. SE1 27 E2
Whitton Av. E., Grnf. 86 B5
Whitton Av. W., Grnf. 85 J5
Whitton Av. W., Nthlt. 85 J5
Whitton Cl., Grnf. 87 E6
Whitton Dene, Houns. 143 J5
Whitton Dene, Islw. 144 A5
Whitton Dr., Grnf. 86 D6
Whitton Manor Rd., Islw. 143 J5
Whitton Rd., Houns. 143 H4
Whitton Rd., Twick. 144 C6
Whitton Wk. E3 114 A2
Whitton Waye, Houns. 143 G6
Whitwell Rd. E13 115 G3
Whitworth Pl. SE18 137 E4
Whitworth Rd. SE18 136 D7
Whitworth Rd. SE25 188 B3
Whitworth St. SE10 135 E5
Whorlton Rd. SE15 152 E3
Whymark Av. N22 75 G3
Whytecroft, Houns. 122 D7
Whyteville Rd. E7 97 H6
Wick La. E3 114 A2
Wick Rd. E9 95 G6
Wick Rd., Tedd. 163 E7
Wick Sq. E9 95 J6
Eastway
Wicker St. E1 112/113 E6
Burslem St.
Wickers Oake SE19 170 C4
Wickersley Rd. SW11 150 A2
Wicket, The, Croy. 204 A5
Wicket Rd., Grnf. 104 D3
Wickets Way, Ilf. 65 J6
Wickford St. E1 113 F4
Wickford Way E17 77 G4
Wickham Av., Croy. 203 H2
Wickham Av., Sutt. 197 J5
Wickham Chase, W.Wick. 190 D7
Wickham Cl., Enf. 45 E3
Wickham Cl., N.Mal. 183 F5
Wickham Ct. Rd., W.Wick. 204 C2
Wickham Cres., W.Wick. 204 C2
Wickham Gdns. SE4 153 J3
Wickham Ho. E1 113 G5
Wickham La. SE2 138 A5
Wickham La., Well. 138 A5
Wickham Ms. SE4 153 J2
Wickham Rd. E4 62 C7
Wickham Rd. SE4 153 J3
Wickham Rd., Beck. 190 B2
Wickham Rd., Croy. 203 G2
Wickham Rd., Har. 68 A2
Wickham St. SE11 34 C3
Wickham St. SE11 131 F5
Wickham St., Well. 157 H2
Wickham Way, Beck. 190 C4
Wickliffe Av. N3 72 B2
Wickliffe Gdns., Wem. 88 B2
Wicklow St. WC1 10 C3
Wicklow St. WC1 111 F3
Wicks Cl. SE9 174 A4
Wicksteed Ho., Brent. 125 J5
Green Dragon La.
Wickwood St. SE5 151 H2
Widdecombe Av., Har. 84 E2
Widdenham Rd. N7 93 F4
Widdin St. E15 96 D7
Wide Way, Mitch. 186 D3
Widecombe Gdns., Ilf. 80 B4
Widecombe Rd. SE9 174 B3
Widecombe Way N2 73 G5
Widegate St. E1 21 E2
Widenham Cl., Pnr. 66 C5
Bridle Rd.
Widgeon Cl. E16 115 H6
Maplin Rd.
Widley Rd. W9 108 D3
Widmore Lo. Rd., Brom. 192 A2
Widmore Rd., Brom. 191 G2
Wieland Rd., Nthwd. 50 A7
Wigan Ho. E5 94/95 E1
Warwick Gro.
Wigeon Path SE28 137 G3
Wigeon Way, Hayes 102 D6
Wiggins Mead NW9 55 F7
Wigginton Av., Wem. 88 B6
Wigham Ho., Bark. 99 F7
Wightman Rd. N4 75 G5
Wightman Rd. N8 75 G4
Wigley Rd., Felt. 160 D2
Wigmore Pl. W1 16 D3
Wigmore Pl. W1 110 B6
Wigmore Rd., Cars. 199 G2
Wigmore St. W1 16 B4
Wigmore St. W1 110 A6
Wigmore Wk., Cars. 199 G2
Wigram Rd. E11 79 J6
Wigram Sq. E17 78 C3
Wigston Cl. N18 60 B5
Wigston Rd. E13 115 H4
Wigton Gdns., Stan. 69 H1
Wigton Pl. SE11 35 F4
Wigton Rd. E17 77 J1
Wilberforce Rd. N4 93 H3
Wilberforce Rd. NW9 71 G6
Wilberforce Way SW19 166 A6
Wilbraham Pl. SW1 32 A1
Wilbraham Pl. SW1 129 J4
Wilbury Way N18 60 A5
Wilby Ms. W11 128 C1
Wilcox Cl. SW8 34 B7
Wilcox Cl. SW8 131 E7
Wilcox Cl., Borwd. 38 C1
Wilcox Pl. SW1 25 G6
Wilcox Rd. SW8 34 A7
Wilcox Rd. SW8 130 E7
Wilcox Rd., Sutt. 198 E4
Wilcox Rd., Tedd. 162 A4
Wild Ct. WC2 18 C3
Wild Ct. WC2 111 F6
Wild Goose Dr. SE14 153 F1
Wild Hatch NW11 72 D6
Wild St. WC2 18 B4
Wild St. WC2 111 E6
Wildcroft Gdns., Edg. 53 G6
Wildcroft Rd. SW15 147 J7
Wilde Cl. E8 112 D1
Wilde Pl. N13 59 H6
Medesenge Way
Wilde Pl. SW18 149 G7
Heathfield Rd.
Wilde Rd., Erith 139 H7
Wilder Cl., Ruis. 84 B1
Wilderness, The, E.Mol. 179 J5
Wilderness, The, Hmptn. 161 H4
Park Rd.
Wilderness Rd., Chis. 175 E7
Wilderton Rd. N16 76 B7
Wildfell Rd. SE6 154 B7
Wild's Rents SE1 28 D5
Wild's Rents SE1 132 B3
Wildwood Cl. SE12 155 F7
Wildwood Gro. NW3 91 F1
North End Way
Wildwood Ri. NW11 91 F1
Wildwood Rd. NW11 73 F7
Wildwood Ter. NW3 91 F1
Wilford Cl., Enf. 44 A3
Wilfred Owen Cl. SW19 167 F6
Tennyson Rd.
Wilfred St. SW1 25 F5
Wilfred St. SW1 130 C3
Wilfrid Gdns. W3 106 C5
Wilkes Rd., Brent. 125 H6
Wilkes St. E1 21 G1
Wilkes St. E1 112 C5
Wilkie Way SE22 170 D1
Lordship La.
Wilkin St. NW5 92 B6
Wilkin St. Ms. NW5 92 B6
Wilkin St.
Wilkins Cl., Hayes 121 J5
Wilkins Cl., Mitch. 185 H1
Wilkinson Rd. E16 115 J6
Wilkinson St. SW8 131 F7
Wilkinson Way W4 126 D2
Wilks Gdns., Croy. 203 H1
Wilks Pl. N1 12 E2
Will Crooks Gdns. SE9 155 J4
Willan Rd. N17 76 A2
Willan Wall E16 115 F7
Victoria Dock Rd.
Willard St. SW8 150 B3
Willcocks Cl., Chess. 195 H3
Willcott Rd. W3 126 B1
Willen Fld. Rd. NW10 106 C2
Willenhall Av., Barn. 41 F6
Willenhall Rd. SE18 136 E5
Willersley Av., Orp. 207 G3
Willersley Av., Sid. 175 J1
Willersley Cl., Sid. 175 J1
Willes Rd. NW5 92 B6
Willesden La. NW2 90 A6
Willesden La. NW6 90 A6
Willett Cl., Nthlt. 102 C3
Broomcroft Av.
Willett Cl., Orp. 193 H6
Willett Pl., Th.Hth. 187 G5
Willett Rd.
Willett Rd., Th.Hth. 187 G5
Willett Way, Orp. 193 G5
William Barefoot Dr. SE9 174 D4
William Bonney Est. SW4 150 D4
William Booth Rd. SE20 188 D1
William Carey Way, Har. 68 B7
William Cl. N2 73 G3
King St.
William Cl., Rom. 83 J1
William Cl., Sthl. 123 J2
Windmill Av.
William Dunbar Ho. NW6 108 C2
William Dyce Ms. SW16 168 D4
Babington Rd.
William Ellis Way SE16 29 J6
William IV St. WC2 18 A6

Name	Page	Grid
William IV St. WC2	110	E7
William Gdns. SW15	147	H5
William Guy Gdns. E3	114	B3
Talwin St.		
William Margrie Cl. SE15	152	D2
Moncrieff St.		
William Ms. SW1	**24**	**A4**
William Morley Cl. E6	116	A1
William Morris Cl. E17	77	J3
William Morris Way SW6	149	F3
William Pl. E3	113	J2
Roman Rd.		
William Rd. NW1	**9**	**E4**
William Rd. NW1	110	B3
William Rd. SW19	166	B7
William Rd., Sutt.	199	F5
William Saville Ho. NW6	108	C2
William Sq. SE16	113	H7
Rotherhithe St.		
William St. E10	78	B6
William St. N17	60	C7
William St. SW1	**24**	**A4**
William St. SW1	129	J2
William St., Bark.	99	F7
William St., Cars.	199	H3
Williams Av. E17	77	J1
Williams Bldgs. E2	113	F4
Williams Cl. N8	74	D6
Coolhurst Rd.		
Williams Gro. N22	75	G1
Williams Gro., Surb.	181	F6
William's La. SW14	146	C2
Williams La., Mord.	185	F5
Williams Rd. W13	104	D7
Williams Rd., Sthl.	122	E4
Williams Ter., Croy.	201	G6
Williamson Cl. SE10	135	F4
Lenthorp Rd.		
Williamson Rd. N4	75	H6
Williamson St. N7	93	E4
Williamson Way NW7	56	B6
Willifield Way NW11	72	C5
Willingale Cl., Loug.	49	F2
Willingale Rd.		
Willingale Cl., Wdf.Grn.	64	A6
Willingale Rd., Loug.	49	F3
Willingdon Rd. N22	75	H2
Willingham Cl. NW5	92	C5
Leighton Rd.		
Willingham Ter. NW5	92	C5
Leighton Rd.		
Willingham Way, Kings.T.	182	A3
Willington Ct. E5	95	H3
Mandeville St.		
Willington Rd. SW9	150	E3
Willis Av., Sutt.	199	H6
Willis Rd. E15	115	F1
Willis Rd., Croy.	187	J7
Willis Rd., Erith	139	J4
Willis St. E14	114	B6
Willmore End SW19	184	E1
Willoughby Av., Croy.	201	F4
Willoughby Gro. N17	60	E7
Willoughby La. N17	61	E7
Willoughby Ms. SW4	150	B4
Wixs La.		
Willoughby Pk. Rd. N17	60	E7
Willoughby Pas. E14	134	A1
Willoughby Rd. N8	75	G3
Willoughby Rd. NW3	91	G4
Willoughby Rd., Kings.T.	181	J1
Willoughby Rd., Twick.	145	G6
Willoughby St. WC1	**18**	**A2**
Willoughby Way SE7	135	H4
Willoughbys, The SW14	146/147	E4
Upper Richmond Rd. W.		
Willow Av. SW13	147	F2
Willow Av., Sid.	158	A6
Willow Bank SW6	148	B3
Willow Bank, Rich.	163	E3
Willow Br. Rd. N1	93	J6
Willow Business Cen., Mitch.	185	J5
Willow Cl., Bex.	159	F6
Willow Cl., Brent.	125	F6
Willow Cl., Brom.	192	C5
Willow Cl., Buck.H.	64	A3
Willow Cl., Th.Hth.	187	H6
Willow Cotts., Mitch.	186	C3
Willow Cotts., Rich.	126	A6
Kew Grn.		
Willow Ct. EC2	**12**	**D5**
Willow Ct., Edg.	53	H4
Willow Dene, Pnr.	66	D2
Willow Dr., Barn.	40	B4
Willow End N20	56	D2
Willow End, Nthwd.	50	A6
Willow End, Surb.	195	H1
Willow Fm. La. SW15	147	H3
Queens Ride		
Willow Gdns., Houns.	143	G1
Willow Grn. NW9	70/71	E1
Clayton Fld.		
Willow Grn., Borwd.	38	D5
Libra Rd.		
Willow Gro. E13	115	G2
Willow Gro., Chis.	174	D6
Willow La., Mitch.	185	J5
Willow Mt., Croy.	202	B3
Langton Way		
Willow Pl. SW1	**33**	**G1**
Willow Pl. SW1	130	C4
Willow Rd. NW3	91	G4
Willow Rd. W5	125	H2
Willow Rd., Enf.	44	B3
Willow Rd., N.Mal.	182	C4
Willow Rd., Rom.	83	E6
Willow Rd., Wall.	200	B7
Willow St. E4	46	D7
Willow St. EC2	**12**	**D5**
Willow St. EC2	112	B4
Willow St., Rom.	83	J4
Willow Tree Cl. E3	113	J1
Birdsfield La.		
Willow Tree Cl. SW18	166/167	E1
Cargill Rd.		
Willow Tree Cl., Hayes	102	C4
Willow Tree La., Hayes	102	C4
Willow Tree Wk., Brom.	191	H1
Willow Vale W12	127	G1
Willow Vale, Chis.	174	E6
Willow Vw. SW19	185	G1
Willow Wk. E17	77	J5
Willow Wk. N2	73	G2
Willow Wk. N15	75	H4
Willow Wk. N21	43	F6
Willow Wk. SE1	**37**	**E1**
Willow Wk. SE1	132	B4
Willow Wk., Orp.	206	E3
Willow Wk., Sutt.	198	C3
Willow Way N3	56	E7
Willow Way SE26	171	E3
Willow Way W11	128	A1
Freston Rd.		
Willow Way, Epsom	196	D6
Willow Way, Sun.	178	A4
Willow Way, Twick.	161	H2
Willow Way, Wem.	86	D3
Willow Wd. Cres. SE25	188	B6
Willowbrook Est. SE15	132	C7
Sumner Rd.		
Willowbrook Rd. SE15	**37**	**G6**
Willowbrook Rd. SE15	132	C6
Willowbrook Rd., Sthl.	123	G3
Willowcourt Av., Har.	69	E5
Willowdene N6	73	J7
Denewood Rd.		
Willowdene Cl., Twick.	143	J7
Willowfield Cl. SE18	58/59	E3
Conway Rd.		
Willowhayne Dr., Walt.	178	B7
Willowhayne Gdns., Wor.Pk.	197	J3
Willowmead Cl. W5	105	G5
Willows, The, Buck.H.	64	A3
Willows, The, Esher	194	B6
Albany Cres.		
Willows Av., Mord.	185	E5
Willows Cl., Pnr.	66	C2
Willowtree Way, Th.Hth.	187	G1
Kensington Av.		
Willrose Cres. SE2	138	C5
Wills Cres., Houns.	143	H6
Wills Gro. NW7	55	G5
Wilman Gro. E8	94	D7
Wilmar Gdns., W.Wick.	204	B1
Wilmcote Ho. W2	**14**	**A1**
Wilmcote Ho. W2	108	E5
Wilmer Cl., Kings.T.	163	J5
Wilmer Cres., Kings.T.	163	J5
Wilmer Gdns. N1	112	B1
Wilmer Lea Cl. E15	96	D7
Wilmer Pl. N16	94	C2
Stoke Newington Ch. St.		
Wilmer Way N14	58	D5
Wilmington Av. W4	126	D7
Wilmington Gdns., Bark.	99	G6
Wilmington Sq. WC1	**11**	**E4**
Wilmington Sq. WC1	111	G3
Wilmington St. WC1	**11**	**E4**
Wilmington St. WC1	111	G3
Wilmot Cl. N2	73	F2
Wilmot Cl. SE15	132	D7
Wilmot Pl. NW1	92	C7
Wilmot Pl. W7	124	B1
Boston Rd.		
Wilmot Rd. E10	96	B2
Wilmot Rd. N17	76	A3
Wilmot Rd., Cars.	199	J5
Wilmot St. E2	112	E4
Wilmount St. SE18	136	E4
Wilna Rd. SW18	149	F7
Wilsham St. W11	128	A1
Wilshaw St. SE14	154	A1
Wilsmere Dr., Har.	52	C7
Wilsmere Dr., Nthlt.	85	E6
Wilson Av., Mitch.	167	H7
Wilson Cl., S.Croy.	202	A5
Bartlett St.		
Wilson Cl., Wem.	69	J7
Wilson Cl., West Dr.	120	A6
Hatch La.		
Wilson Dr., Wem.	69	J7
Wilson Gdns., Har.	67	J7
Wilson Gro. SE16	132	E2
Wilson Rd. E6	116	A3
Wilson Rd. SE5	152	B1
Wilson Rd., Chess.	195	J6
Wilson Rd., Ilf.	80	C7
Wilson St. E17	78	C5
Wilson St. EC2	**20**	**C1**
Wilson St. EC2	112	A5
Wilson St. N21	43	G7
Wilsons Pl. E14	113	J6
Salmon La.		
Wilsons Rd. W6	128	A5
Wilstone Cl., Hayes	102/103	E4
Kingsash Dr.		
Wilthorne Gdns., Dag.	101	H7
Acre Rd.		
Wilton Av. W4	127	E5
Wilton Cl., West Dr.	120	A6
Hatch La.		
Wilton Cres. SW1	**24**	**B4**
Wilton Cres. SW1	130	A2
Wilton Cres. SW19	184	C1
Wilton Gdns., W.Mol.	179	G3
Wilton Gro. SW19	184	C1
Wilton Gro., N.Mal.	183	F6
Wilton Ms. SW1	**24**	**C5**
Wilton Ms. SW1	130	A3
Wilton Par., Felt.	160	A2
Highfield Rd.		
Wilton Pk. Ct. SE18	156	D1
Prince Imperial Rd.		
Wilton Pl. SW1	**24**	**B4**
Wilton Pl. SW1	130	A2
Wilton Rd. N10	74	A2
Wilton Rd. SE2	138	C3
Wilton Rd. SW1	**25**	**E6**
Wilton Rd. SW1	130	C3
Wilton Rd. SW19	167	H7
Wilton Rd., Barn.	41	J4
Wilton Rd., Houns.	142	D3
Wilton Rd., Ilf.	98/99	E3
Ilford La.		
Wilton Row SW1	**24**	**B4**
Wilton Row SW1	130	A2
Wilton Sq. N1	112	A1
Wilton St. SW1	**24**	**D5**
Wilton St. SW1	130	B3
Wilton Ter. SW1	**24**	**B5**
Wilton Ter. SW1	130	A3
Wilton Vil. N1	112	A1
Wilton Way E8	94	D6
Wiltshire Cl. NW7	55	F5
Wiltshire Cl. SW3	**31**	**J1**
Wiltshire Gdns. N4	75	J6
Wiltshire Gdns., Twick.	161	J1
Wiltshire Rd. SW9	151	G3
Wiltshire Rd., Th.Hth.	187	G3
Wiltshire Row N1	112	A1
Wilverley Cres., N.Mal.	183	E6
Wimbart Rd. SW2	151	F7
Wimbledon Br. SW19	166	C6
Wimbledon Common SW19	165	G4
Wimbledon Hill Rd. SW19	166	B6
Wimbledon Pk. SW19	166	C2
Wimbledon Pk. Est. SW19	166	B1
Wimbledon Pk. Rd. SW18	148	C7
Wimbledon Pk. Rd. SW19	166	C1
Wimbledon Pk. Side SW19	166	A2
Wimbledon Rd. SW17	167	F4
Wimbledon Sta. SW19	166	C6
The Bdy.		
Wimbolt St. E2	**13**	**H3**
Wimbolt St. E2	112	D3
Wimborne Av., Hayes	102	B6
Wimborne Av., Sthl.	123	G4
Wimborne Cl. SE12	155	F5
Wimborne Cl., Buck.H.	63	H2
Wimborne Cl., Wor.Pk.	197	J1
Wimborne Dr. NW9	70	A3
Wimborne Dr., Pnr.	66	D7
Wimborne Gdns. W13	105	E6
Wimborne Rd. N9	60	D2
Wimborne Rd. N17	76	B2
Wimborne Way, Beck.	189	G3
Wimbourne Av., Orp.	193	J4
Wimbourne Ct. N1	112	A2
Wimbourne St.		
Wimbourne St. N1	**12**	**B1**
Wimbourne St. N1	112	A2
Wimpole Cl., Brom.	191	J4
Stanley Rd.		
Wimpole Cl., Kings.T.	181	J2
Wimpole Ms. W1	**16**	**D1**
Wimpole Ms. W1	110	B5
Wimpole Rd., West Dr.	120	A1
Wimpole St. W1	**16**	**D3**
Wimpole St. W1	110	B6
Wimshurst Cl., Croy.	201	E1
Winans Wk. SW9	151	G2
Wincanton Cres., Nthlt.	85	G5
Wincanton Gdns., Ilf.	80	E2
Wincanton Rd. SW18	148	C7
Winchcomb Gdns. SE9	156	A3
Winchcombe Rd., Cars.	185	G7
Winchelsea Av., Bexh.	139	F7
Winchelsea Cl. SW15	148	A5
Winchelsea Rd. E7	97	G4
Winchelsea Rd. N17	76	B3
Winchelsea Rd. NW10	106	D1
Winchelsey Ri., S.Croy.	202	C6
Winchendon Rd. SW6	128	C7
Winchendon Rd., Tedd.	162	A4
Winchester Av. NW6	108	B1
Winchester Av. NW9	70	A3
Winchester Av., Houns.	123	F6
Winchester Cl. E6	116	B6
Boultwood Rd.		
Winchester Cl. SE17	**35**	**H2**
Winchester Cl. SE17	131	H4
Winchester Cl., Brom.	191	F3
Winchester Cl., Enf.	44	B5
Winchester Cl., Kings.T.	164	B7
Winchester Ct. E17	77	G1
Billet Rd.		
Winchester Dr., Pnr.	66	D5
Winchester Ho. SE18	136	A7
Shooter's Hill Rd.		
Winchester Ms. NW3	91	G7
Winchester Rd.		
Winchester Pk., Brom.	191	F3
Winchester Pl. E8	94	C5
Kingsland High St.		
Winchester Pl. N6	92	B1
Winchester Pl. W3	126	C2
Avenue Rd.		
Winchester Rd. E4	62	C7
Winchester Rd. N6	74	B7
Winchester Rd. N9	60	D1
Winchester Rd. NW3	91	G7
Winchester Rd. Bexh.	158	D2
Winchester Rd., Brom.	191	F3
Winchester Rd., Felt.	161	F3
Winchester Rd., Har.	69	H4

Name	Page	Grid
Wolseley Rd. E7	97	H7
Wolseley Rd. N8	74	D6
Wolseley Rd. N22	75	F1
Wolseley Rd. W4	126	C4
Wolseley Rd., Har.	68	B3
Wolseley Rd., Mitch.	186	A7
Wolseley St. SE1	**29**	**G4**
Wolseley St. SE1	132	C2
Wolsey Av. E6	116	D3
Wolsey Av. E17	77	J3
Wolsey Av., T.Ditt.	180	C5
Wolsey Cl. SW20	165	H7
Wolsey Cl., Houns.	143	J4
Wolsey Cl., Kings.T.	182	B3
Wolsey Cl., Sthl.	123	J3
Wolsey Cl., Wor.Pk.	197	G4
Wolsey Cres., Mord.	184	B7
Wolsey Dr., Kings.T.	163	H5
Wolsey Gdns., Ilf.	65	F6
Wolsey Ms. NW5	92	C6
Wolsey Ms., Orp.	207	J5
Osgood Av.		
Wolsey Rd. N1	94	A5
Wolsey Rd., E.Mol.	180	A4
Wolsey Rd., Enf.	45	E2
Wolsey Rd., Hmptn.	161	H6
Wolsey St. E1	113	F5
Sidney St.		
Wolsey Way, Chess.	196	A5
Wolstonbury N12	56	D5
Wolvercote Rd. SE2	138	D2
Wolverley St. E2	112/113	E3
Bethnal Grn. Rd.		
Wolverton SE17	**36**	**D3**
Wolverton Av.,	182	A1
Kings.T.		
Wolverton Gdns. W5	105	J7
Wolverton Gdns. W6	128	A4
Wolverton Rd., Stan.	53	E6
Wolverton Way N14	42	C5
Wolves La. N13	59	G7
Wolves La. N22	59	G7
Womersley Rd. N8	75	F6
Wonford Cl.,	183	E1
Kings.T.		
Wontner Cl. N1	93	J7
Greenman St.		
Wontner Rd. SW17	167	J2
Wood Cl. E2	**13**	**H5**
Wood Cl. E2	112	D4
Wood Cl. NW9	70	D7
Wood Cl., Har.	68	A7
Wood Dr., Chis.	174	B6
Wood End Av., Har.	85	H4
Wood End Cl., Nthlt.	86	A5
Wood End Gdns.,	85	J5
Nthlt.		
Wood End La., Nthlt.	85	H6
Wood End Rd., Har.	86	A4
Wood End Way,	85	J5
Nthlt.		
Wood La. N6	74	B6
Wood La. NW9	70	E7
Wood La. W12	107	J6
Wood La., Dag.	100	C4
Wood La., Islw.	124	C7
Wood La., Stan.	52	D3
Wood La., Wdf.Grn.	63	F5
Wood Lo. Gdns.,	174	B7
Brom.		
Wood Lo. La.,	204	C3
W.Wick.		
Wood Pt. E16	115	G5
Fife Rd.		
Wood Retreat SE18	137	G7
Wood Ride, Barn.	41	G1
Wood Ride, Orp.	193	G4
Wood Ri., Pnr.	66	A5
Wood St. E16	115	H7
Ethel Rd.		
Wood St. E17	78	C3
Wood St. EC2	**20**	**A4**
Wood St. EC2	111	J6
Wood St. W4	126	E5
Wood St., Barn.	40	A4
Wood St., Kings.T.	181	G1
Wood St., Mitch.	186	A7
Wood Vale N10	74	C5
Wood Vale SE23	170	E1
Wood Vale Est. SE23	153	F6
Wood Way, Orp.	206	D2
Wood Wf. SE10	134	B6
Woodall Cl. E14	114	B7
Lawless St.		
Woodall Cl., Chess.	195	G6
Ashlyns Way		
Woodall Rd., Enf.	45	G6
Woodbank Rd.,	173	F3
Brom.		
Woodbastwick Rd.	171	G5
SE26		
Woodberry Av. N21	59	G2
Woodberry Av., Har.	67	H4
Woodberry Cl., Sun.	160	A6
Ashridge Way		
Woodberry Cres. N10	74	B3
Woodberry Down N4	75	J7
Woodberry Down Est.	75	J7
N4		
Woodberry Gdns. N12	57	F6
Woodberry Gro. N4	75	J7
Woodberry Gro. N12	57	F6
Woodberry Way E4	62	C1
Woodberry Way N12	57	F6
Woodbine Cl.,	162	A2
Twick.		
Woodbine Gro. SE20	171	E7
Woodbine La.,	197	J3
Wor.Pk.		
Woodbine Pl. E11	79	G6
Woodbine Rd., Sid.	175	H1
Woodbine Ter. E9	95	F6
Morning La.		
Woodbines Av.,	181	G3
Kings.T.		
Woodborough Rd.	147	H4
SW15		
Woodbourne Av.	168	D3
SW16		
Woodbourne Cl.	168/169	E3
SW16		
Woodbourne Av.		
Woodbourne Dr.,	194	C6
Esher		
Woodbourne Gdns.,	200	B7
Wall.		
Woodbridge Cl. N7	93	F2
Woodbridge Cl. NW2	89	G3
Woodbridge Ct.,	64	B7
Wdf.Grn.		
Woodbridge Rd.,	99	J5
Bark.		
Woodbridge St. EC1	**11**	**G5**
Woodbridge St. EC1	111	H4
Woodbrook Rd. SE2	138	A6
Woodburn Cl. NW4	72	A5
Woodbury Cl. E11	79	H4
Woodbury Cl., Croy.	202	C2
Woodbury Hill, Loug.	48	B3
Woodbury Hollow,	48	B2
Loug.		
Woodbury Pk. Rd.	104	E4
W13		
Woodbury Rd. E17	78	B4
Woodbury St. SW17	167	H5
Woodchester Sq. W2	**14**	**A1**
Woodchester Sq. W2	108	E5
Woodchurch Cl., Sid.	175	G3
Woodchurch Dr.,	174	A7
Brom.		
Woodchurch Rd. NW6	90	D7
Woodclyffe Dr., Chis.	192	D2
Woodcock Ct., Har.	69	H7
Woodcock Dell Av.,	69	G7
Har.		
Woodcock Hill, Har.	69	G7
Woodcocks E16	115	J5
Woodcombe Cres.	171	F1
SE23		
Woodcote Av. NW7	55	J6
Woodcote Av.,	187	H4
Th.Hth.		
Woodcote Av., Wall.	200	B7
Woodcote Cl., Enf.	45	F6
Woodcote Cl.,	163	J5
Kings.T.		
Woodcote Dr., Orp.	207	G1
Woodcote Ms., Loug.	47	J7
Fallow Flds.		
Woodcote Ms., Wall.	200	B6
Woodcote Pl. SE27	169	H5
Woodcote Rd., Wall.	200	B6
Woodcroft N21	59	F1
Woodcroft SE9	174	C3
Woodcroft, Grnf.	86	D6
Woodcroft Av. NW7	55	E7
Woodcroft Av., Stan.	68	C1
Woodcroft Ms. SE8	133	H4
Croft St.		
Woodcroft Rd.,	187	H5
Th.Hth.		
Woodedge Cl. E4	63	F1
Woodend SE19	169	J6
Woodend, Sutt.	199	F2
Woodend Gdns., Enf.	42	E4
Woodend Rd. E17	78	C2
Wooder Gdns. E7	97	G4
Wooderson Cl. SE25	188	B4
Woodfall Av., Barn.	40	C5
Woodfall Rd. N4	93	G1
Woodfall St. SW3	**31**	**J4**
Woodfall St. SW3	129	J5
Woodfarrs SE5	152	A4
Woodfield Av. NW9	71	E4
Woodfield Av. SW16	168	D3
Woodfield Av. W5	105	F4
Woodfield Av., Cars.	200	A6
Woodfield Av., Wem.	87	F3
Woodfield Cl. SE19	169	J7
Woodfield Cl., Enf.	44	B4
Woodfield Cres. W5	105	F4
Woodfield Dr., Barn.	58	A1
Woodfield Gdns. W9	108	C5
Woodfield Gdns.,	183	F5
N.Mal.		
Woodfield Gro. SW16	168	D3
Woodfield La. SW16	168	D3
Woodfield Pl. W9	108	C4
Woodfield Rd. W5	105	F4
Woodfield Rd. W9	108	C5
Woodfield Rd.,	142	B2
Houns.		
Woodfield Rd., T.Ditt.	194	C2
Lynwood Rd.		
Woodfield Way N11	58	D7
Woodford Av., Ilf.	80	C5
Woodford Av.,	80	B3
Wdf.Grn.		
Woodford Br. Rd., Ilf.	80	A3
Woodford Ct. W12	128	A2
Shepherds Bush Grn.		
Woodford Cres., Pnr.	66	B2
Woodford New Rd.	78	E4
E17		
Woodford New Rd.	79	E1
E18		
Woodford New Rd.,	79	E1
Wdf.Grn.		
Woodford Pl., Wem.	87	H1
Woodford Rd. E7	97	H4
Woodford Rd. E18	79	G4
Woodford Trd. Est.,	80	A3
Wdf.Grn.		
Woodgate Av., Chess.	195	G5
Woodgate Cres.,	50	A6
Nthwd.		
Woodgate Dr. SW16	168	D7
Woodger Rd. W12	127	J2
Goldhawk Rd.		
Woodget Cl. E6	116	B6
Remington Rd.		
Woodgrange Av. N12	57	G6
Woodgrange Av. W5	126	A1
Woodgrange Av.,	44	D6
Enf.		
Woodgrange Av.,	69	F5
Har.		
Woodgrange Cl.,	69	G5
Har.		
Woodgrange Gdns.,	44	D6
Enf.		
Woodgrange Rd. E7	97	H4
Woodgrange Ter.,	44	D6
Enf.		
Great Cambridge Rd.		
Woodhall Av. SE21	170	C3
Woodhall Av., Pnr.	66	E2
Woodhall Dr. SE21	170	C3
Woodhall Dr., Pnr.	66	D1
Woodhall Gate, Pnr.	50	D7
Woodhall La., Wat.	50	D4
Woodhall Rd., Pnr.	50	D7
Woodham Ct. E18	79	F4
Woodham Rd. SE6	172	C3
Woodhatch Cl. E6	116	B6
Remington Rd.		
Woodhaven Gdns.,	81	F3
Ilf.		
Brandville Gdns.		
Woodhayes Rd.	165	J7
SW19		
Woodhead Dr., Orp.	207	H2
Sherlies Av.		
Woodheyes Rd. NW10	88	D5
Woodhill SE18	136	B4
Woodhill Cres., Har.	69	G6
Woodhouse Av.,	104	C2
Grnf.		
Woodhouse Cl., Grnf.	104	C2
Woodhouse Cl.,	121	H3
Hayes		
Woodhouse Eaves,	50	A5
Nthwd.		
Woodhouse Gro. E12	98	B6
Woodhouse Rd. E11	97	F3
Woodhouse Rd. N12	57	G6
Woodhurst Av., Orp.	193	F6
Woodhurst Rd. SE2	138	A5
Woodhurst Rd. W3	106	C7
Woodington Cl. SE9	156	D6
Woodison St. E3	113	H4
Woodknoll Dr., Chis.	192	C1
Woodland App., Grnf.	86	D6
Woodland Cl. NW9	70	C6
Woodland Cl. SE19	170	B6
Woodland Hill		
Woodland Cl., Epsom	197	E6
Woodland Cl.,	63	H3
Wdf.Grn.		
Woodland Cres. SE10	134	E6
Woodland Cres. SE16	133	G2
Woodland Gdns. N10	74	B5
Woodland Gdns.,	144	B2
Islw.		
Woodland Gro. SE10	134	E5
Woodland Hill SE19	170	B6
Woodland Ri. N10	74	B4
Woodland Ri., Grnf.	86	D6
Woodland Rd. E4	62	C1
Woodland Rd. N11	58	B5
Woodland Rd. SE19	170	B5
Woodland Rd., Loug.	48	B3
Woodland Rd.,	187	G4
Th.Hth.		
Woodland St. E8	94	C6
Dalston La.		
Woodland Ter. SE7	136	B4
Woodland Wk. NW3	91	H5
Woodland Wk.	134/135	E5
SE10		
Woodland Gro.		
Woodland Wk., Brom.	172	E4
Woodland Way N21	59	G2
Woodland Way NW7	55	E6
Woodland Way SE2	138	D4
Woodland Way, Croy.	203	H1
Woodland Way,	168	A7
Mitch.		
Woodland Way,	184	C4
Mord.		
Woodland Way, Orp.	193	F4
Woodland Way, Surb.	196	B2
Woodland Way,	204	B4
W.Wick.		
Woodland Way,	63	H3
Wdf.Grn.		
Woodlands NW11	72	B6
Woodlands SW20	183	J4
Woodlands, Har.	67	G4
Woodlands, The N14	58	B1
Woodlands, The SE13	154	D7
Woodlands, The SE19	169	J7
Woodlands, The,	144	C2
Islw.		
Woodlands Av. E11	97	H1
Woodlands Av. N3	57	F7
Woodlands Av. W3	126	B1
Woodlands Av.,	182	C1
N.Mal.		
Woodlands Av., Rom.	82	E6
Woodlands Av.,	84	D1
Ruis.		
Woodlands Av., Sid.	175	H1
Woodlands Av.,	197	F2
Wor.Pk.		
Woodlands Cl. NW11	72	B5
Woodlands Cl.,	38	B4
Borwd.		
Woodlands Cl., Brom.	192	C2
Woodlands Cl.,	194	C7
Esher		
Woodlands Dr., Stan.	52	C6
Woodlands Dr., Sun.	178	C2
Woodlands Gro.	144	B2
Islw.		
Woodlands Pk., Bex.	177	J4
Woodlands Pk. Rd.	75	H5
N15		
Woodlands Pk. Rd.	134	E6
SE10		
Woodlands Rd. E11	96	E2
Woodlands Rd. E17	78	C3
Woodlands Rd. N9	61	F1
Woodlands Rd. SW13	147	F3
Woodlands Rd.,	159	E3
Bexh.		
Woodlands Rd.,	192	B2
Brom.		
Woodlands Rd., Enf.	44	A1
Woodlands Rd., Har.	68	C5
Woodlands Rd., Ilf.	99	F3
Woodlands Rd., Islw.	144	B2
Woodlands Rd., Sthl.	122	D1
Woodlands Rd., Surb.	181	G7
Woodlands St. SE13	154	D7
Woodlands Way	148	C5
SW15		
Oakhill Rd.		
Woodlawn Cl. SW15	148	C5
Woodlawn Cres.,	161	H2
Twick.		
Woodlawn Dr., Felt.	160	D2
Woodlawn Rd. SW6	128	A7
Woodlea Dr., Brom.	191	E5
Woodlea Rd. N16	94	B3
Woodleigh Av. N12	57	H6
Woodleigh Gdns.	169	E3
SW16		
Woodley Cl. SW17	167	J7
Arnold Rd.		
Woodley La., Cars.	199	G3
Woodman La. E4	46	E5
Woodman Path, Ilf.	65	H6

Name	Page	Grid
Woodman St. E16	136	D1
Woodmans Gro. NW10	89	F5
Woodmans Ms. W12	107	H5
Woodmansterne Rd. SW16	168	D7
Woodmere SE9	174	C1
Woodmere Av., Croy.	189	G7
Woodmere Cl. SW11	150	A3
Lavender Hill		
Woodmere Cl., Croy.	189	G7
Woodmere Gdns., Croy.	189	G7
Woodmere Way, Beck.	190	D5
Woodnook Rd. SW16	168	B5
Woodpecker Cl. N9	44	E6
Woodpecker Cl., Bushey	51	J1
Woodpecker Cl., Har.	68	C1
Woodpecker Rd. SE14	133	H6
Woodpecker Rd. SE28	118	C7
Woodquest Av. SE24	151	J5
Woodridge Cl., Enf.	43	G1
Woodridings Av., Pnr.	67	F1
Woodridings Cl., Pnr.	51	E7
Woodriffe Rd. E11	78	D7
Woodrow SE18	136	C4
Woodrow Cl., Grnf.	87	E7
Woodrow Ct. N17	60/61	E7
Heybourne Rd.		
Woodrush Cl. SE14	133	H7
Southerngate Way		
Woodrush Way, Rom.	82	D4
Woods, The, Nthwd.	50	A5
Woods Cl. SE19	170	B6
Woodland Hill		
Woods Ms. W1	**16**	**A5**
Woods Ms. W1	110	A7
Woods Pl. SE1	**28**	**E6**
Woods Rd. SE15	152	E1
Woodseer St. E1	**21**	**G1**
Woodseer St. E1	112	C5
Woodsford SE17	**36**	**B4**
Woodsford Sq. W14	128	B2
Woodshire Rd., Dag.	101	H3
Woodside NW11	72	D5
Woodside SW19	166	C6
Woodside, Buck.H.	63	J2
Woodside Av. N6	73	J5
Woodside Av. N10	73	J5
Woodside Av. N12	57	F4
Woodside Av. SE25	188	E6
Woodside Av., Chis.	175	F5
Woodside Av., Esher	180	B7
Woodside Av., Wem.	105	H1
Woodside Cl., Stan.	52	E5
Woodside Cl., Surb.	182	C7
Woodside Cl., Wem.	105	H1
Woodside Ct. N12	57	F4
Woodside Av.		
Woodside Ct. Rd., Croy.	188	D7
Woodside Cres., Sid.	175	H3
Woodside End, Wem.	105	H1
Woodside Gdns. E4	62	B5
Woodside Gdns. N17	76	B2
Woodside Gra. Rd. N12	57	E4
Woodside Grn. SE25	188	E6
Woodside Gro. N12	57	F3
Woodside La. N12	57	E3
Woodside La., Bex.	158	D6
Woodside Ms. SE22	152	C6
Heber Rd.		
Woodside Pk. SE25	188	D5
Woodside Pk. Av. E17	78	D4
Woodside Pk. Rd. N12	57	E4
Woodside Pl., Wem.	105	H1
Woodside Rd. E13	115	J4
Woodside Rd. N22	59	F7
Woodside Rd. SE25	188	E6
Woodside Rd., Brom.	192	B5
Woodside Rd., Kings.T.	163	H7
Woodside Rd., N.Mal.	182	D2
Woodside Rd., Sid.	175	H3
Woodside Rd., Sutt.	199	F3
Woodside Rd., Wdf.Grn.	63	G4
Woodside Way, Croy.	189	E6
Woodside Way, Mitch.	186	B1
Woodsome Rd. NW5	92	A3
Woodspring Rd. SW19	166	B2
Woodstead Gro., Edg.	53	H6
Woodstock Av. NW11	72	B7
Woodstock Av. W13	124	D3
Woodstock Av., Islw.	144	D5
Woodstock Av., Sthl.	103	F3
Woodstock Av., Sutt.	184	C7
Woodstock Cl., Bex.	177	F1
Woodstock Cl., Stan.	69	H2
Woodstock Ct. SE12	155	G6
Woodstock Cres. N9	44	E6
Woodstock Gdns., Beck.	190	B1
Woodstock Gdns., Ilf.	100	A2
Woodstock Gro. W12	128	A2
Woodstock La. N., Surb.	195	F2
Woodstock La. S., Chess.	195	F4
Woodstock La. S., Esher	194	E5
Woodstock Ms. W1	**16**	**C2**
Woodstock Ri., Sutt.	184	C7
Woodstock Rd. E7	97	J7
Woodstock Rd. E17	78	D2
Woodstock Rd. N4	93	G1
Woodstock Rd. NW11	72	C7
Woodstock Rd. W4	127	E3
Woodstock Rd., Cars.	200	A5
Woodstock Rd., Croy.	202	A3
Woodstock Rd., Wem.	87	J7
Woodstock St. E16	114/115	E6
Victoria Dock Rd.		
Woodstock St. W1	**16**	**D4**
Woodstock Ter. E14	114	B7
Woodstock Way, Mitch.	186	B2
Woodstone Av., Epsom	197	G5
Woodsyre SE26	170	C4
Woodthorpe Rd. SW15	147	H4
Woodtree Cl. NW4	71	J2
Ashley La.		
Woodvale Av. SE25	188	C3
Woodvale Wk. SE27	169	J5
Elder Rd.		
Woodvale Way NW11	90	A3
The Vale		
Woodview Av. E4	62	C4
Woodview Cl. N4	75	H7
Woodview Cl. SW15	164	D4
Woodview Cl., Orp.	207	F2
Crofton Rd.		
Woodville SE3	155	H1
Woodville Cl. SE12	155	G5
Woodville Cl., Tedd.	162	D4
Woodville Gdns. NW11	72	A7
Woodville Gdns. W5	105	H6
Woodville Gdns., Ilf.	80	E3
Woodville Gro., Well.	158	A3
Woodville Rd. E11	97	F1
Woodville Rd. E17	77	H4
Woodville Rd. E18	79	H2
Woodville Rd. N16	94	B5
Woodville Rd. NW6	108	C2
Woodville Rd. NW11	72	A7
Woodville Rd. W5	105	G6
Woodville Rd., Barn.	40	E3
Woodville Rd., Mord.	184	D4
Woodville Rd., Rich.	163	E3
Woodville Rd., Th.Hth.	187	J4
Woodville St. SE18	136	B4
Woodhill		
Woodward Av. NW4	71	G5
Woodward Cl., Esher	194	C6
Woodward Gdns., Dag.	100	C7
Woodward Rd.		
Woodward Gdns., Stan.	52	C7
Woodward Rd., Dag.	100	B7
Woodward Rd. SE22	152	B6
Woodway Cres., Har.	68	D6
Woodwell St. SW18	149	F5
Huguenot Pl.		
Woodyard Cl. NW5	92	A5
Gillies St.		
Woodyard La. SE21	152	B7
Woodyates Rd. SE12	155	G6
Wool Rd. SW20	165	H6
Woolacombe Rd. SE3	155	J1
Woolacombe Way, Hayes	121	H4
Wooler St. SE17	**36**	**B4**
Wooler St. SE17	132	A5
Woolf Cl. SE28	138	B1
Woollaston Rd. N4	75	H6
Woolmead Av. NW9	71	G7
Woolmer Gdns. N18	60	D5
Woolmer Rd. N18	60	D5
Woolmore St. E14	114	C7
Woolneigh St. SW6	148	E3
Woolstaplers Way SE16	**29**	**H6**
Woolstaplers Way SE16	132	D4
Woolston Cl. E17	77	G2
Riverhead Cl.		
Woolstone Rd. SE23	171	H2
Woolwich Ch. St. SE18	136	B3
Woolwich Common SE18	136	D6
Woolwich Ferry Pier E16	136	D2
Woolwich Foot Tunnel E16	136	D2
Woolwich Foot Tunnel SE18	136	D2
Woolwich Garrison SE18	136	C6
Woolwich High St. SE18	136	D3
Woolwich Ind. Est. SE28	137	H3
Hadden Rd.		
Woolwich Manor Way E6	116	E6
Woolwich Manor Way E16	136	E2
Woolwich New Rd. SE18	136	D5
Woolwich Rd. SE2	138	D6
Woolwich Rd. SE7	135	G5
Woolwich Rd. SE10	135	F5
Woolwich Rd., Belv.	138	D6
Woolwich Rd., Bexh.	159	G4
Wooster Gdns. E14	114	D6
Wooster Ms., Har.	67	J3
Fairfield Dr.		
Wooster Pl. SE1	**36**	**C1**
Wootton St. SE1	**27**	**F3**
Wootton St. SE1	131	G1
Worbeck Rd. SE20	189	E2
Worcester Av. N17	60	D7
Worcester Cl. NW2	89	H3
Newfield Ri.		
Worcester Cl., Croy.	203	J2
Worcester Cl., Mitch.	186	B3
Worcester Cres. NW7	54	E3
Worcester Cres., Wdf.Grn.	63	H5
Worcester Dr. W4	127	E2
Worcester Gdns. SW11	149	J5
Grandison Rd.		
Worcester Gdns., Grnf.	85	J6
Worcester Gdns., Ilf.	80	B7
Worcester Gdns., Wor.Pk.	197	E3
Worcester Ms. NW6	90/91	E6
Lymington Rd.		
Worcester Pk. Rd., Wor.Pk.	196	C3
Worcester Rd. E12	98	C4
Worcester Rd. E17	77	G2
Worcester Rd. SW19	166	C5
Worcester Rd., Sutt.	199	E6
Wordsworth Av. E12	98	B6
Wordsworth Av. E18	79	F3
Wordsworth Av., Grnf.	104	A2
Wordsworth Dr., Sutt.	197	J4
Wordsworth Rd. N16	94	B4
Wordsworth Rd. SE1	**37**	**F2**
Wordsworth Rd. SE20	171	G7
Wordsworth Rd., Hmptn.	161	F4
Wordsworth Rd., Wall.	200	C6
Wordsworth Rd., Well.	157	H1
Wordsworth Wk. NW11	72	D4
Wordsworth Way, West Dr.	120	B4
Worfield St. SW11	129	H7
Worgan St. SE11	**34**	**C3**
Worgan St. SE11	131	F5
Worgan St. SE16	133	G3
Worland Rd. E15	97	E7
World's End Est. SW10	**30**	**E7**
World's End Est. SW10	129	G7
Worlds End La. N21	43	F5
Worlds End La., Enf.	43	F5
Worlds End La., Orp.	207	J6
World's End Pas. SW10	**30**	**E7**
Worlidge St. W6	127	J5
Worlingham Rd. SE22	152	C4
Wormholt Rd. W12	107	G7
Wormwood St. EC2	**20**	**D3**
Wormwood St. EC2	112	B6
Wornington Rd. W10	108	B5
Woronzow Rd. NW8	109	G1
Worple Av. SW19	166	A7
Worple Av., Islw.	144	D5
Worple Cl., Har.	85	F1
Worple Rd. SW19	166	B7
Worple Rd. SW20	183	J2
Worple Rd., Islw.	144	D4
Worple Rd. Ms. SW19	166	C6
Worple St. SW14	146	D3
Worple Way, Har.	85	F1
Worple Way, Rich.	145	H5
Worship St. EC2	**12**	**C6**
Worship St. EC2	112	A4
Worslade Rd. SW17	167	G4
Worsley Br. Rd. SE26	171	J4
Worsley Br. Rd., Beck.	171	J5
Worsley Rd. E11	96	E4
Worsopp Dr. SW4	150	C5
Worth Cl., Orp.	207	H4
Worth Gro. SE17	**36**	**B4**
Worthfield Cl., Epsom	196	D7
Worthing Cl. E15	114/115	E2
Mitre Rd.		
Worthing Rd., Houns.	123	F6
Worthington Cl., Mitch.	186	B3
Worthington Rd., Surb.	195	J1
Worthy Down Ct. SE18	156	D1
Prince Imperial Rd.		
Wortley Rd. E6	98	A7
Wortley Rd., Croy.	187	G7
Worton Gdns., Islw.	144	A2
Worton Hall Ind. Est., Islw.	144	B4
Worton Rd., Islw.	144	B3
Worton Way, Houns.	144	A2
Worton Way, Islw.	143	J1
Wotton Rd. NW2	89	J4
Wotton Rd. SE8	133	J6
Wouldham Rd. E16	115	F6
Wragby Rd. E11	97	E3
Wrampling Pl. N9	60	D1
Wrangthorn Wk., Croy.	201	G4
Epsom Rd.		
Wray Av., Ilf.	80	D3
Wray Cres. N4	93	E2
Wrayfield Rd., Sutt.	198	A3
Wraysbury Cl., Houns.	142/143	E5
Dorney Way		
Wrekin Rd. SE18	137	F7
Wren Av. NW2	89	J5
Wren Av., Sthl.	123	F4
Wren Cl. E16	115	F6
Ibbotson Av.		
Wren Cl. N9	61	G1
Chaffinch Cl.		
Wren Cres., Bushey	51	J1
Wren Dr., West Dr.	120	A3
Wren Gdns., Dag.	100	D5
Wren Landing E14	134	A1
Cabot Sq.		
Wren Path SE28	137	G3
Wren Rd. SE5	152	A1
Wren Rd., Dag.	100	D5
Wren Rd., Sid.	176	C4
Wren St. WC1	**10**	**D5**
Wren St. WC1	111	F4
Wrentham Av. NW10	108	A2
Wrenthorpe Rd., Brom.	172	E4
Wrenwood Way, Pnr.	66	B4
Wrestlers Ct. EC3	112	B6
Camomile St.		
Wrexham Rd. E3	114	A2
Wricklemarsh Rd. SE3	155	H1
Wrigglesworth St. SE14	133	G7
Wright Rd. N1	94	B6
Burder Cl.		
Wright Rd., Houns.	122	C7
Wrights All. SW19	165	J6
Wrights Cl. SE13	154	D4
Wisteria Rd.		
Wrights Cl., Dag.	101	H3
Wrights Grn. SW4	150	D4
Nelson's Row		
Wrights La. W8	**22**	**A5**
Wrights La. W8	128	E3

Name	Page	Grid
Wrights Pl. NW10	88	C6
Mitchell Way		
Wrights Rd. E3	113	J2
Wrights Rd. SE25	188	B3
Wrights Row, Wall.	200	B4
Wrights Wk. SW14	146	D3
Wrigley Cl. E4	62	D5
Wrotham Rd. NW1	92	C7
Agar Pl.		
Wrotham Rd. W13	124/125	E1
Mattock La.		
Wrotham Rd., Barn.	40	B2
Wrotham Rd., Well.	158	C1
Wroths Path, Loug.	48	C1
Wrottesley Rd. NW10	107	G2
Wrottesley Rd. SE18	137	F6
Wroughton Rd. SW11	149	J6
Wroughton Ter. NW4	71	J4
Wroxall Rd., Dag.	100	C6
Wroxham Gdns. N11	58	C7
Wroxham Rd. SE28	118	D7
Wroxton Rd. SE15	153	E2
Wrythe Grn., Cars.	199	J3
Wrythe Grn. Rd.		
Wrythe Grn. Rd., Cars.	199	J3
Wrythe La., Cars.	199	F1
Wulfstan St. W12	107	F6
Wyatt Cl. SE16	133	J2
Wyatt Cl., Felt.	160	C1
Wyatt Cl., Hayes	102	A5
Wyatt Dr. SW13	127	J7
Wyatt Pk. Rd. SW2	169	E2
Wyatt Rd. E7	97	G6
Wyatt Rd. N5	93	J3
Wyatts La. E17	78	C3
Wybert St. NW1	**9**	**E5**
Wyborne Way NW10	88	C7
Wyburn Av., Barn.	40	C3
Wych Elm Dr., Brom.	173	F7
London La.		
Wych Elm Pas., Kings.T.	163	J7
Wyche Gro., S.Croy.	201	J7
Wycherley Cl. SE3	135	F7
Wycherley Cres., Barn.	40	E6
Wychwood Av., Edg.	53	G6
Wychwood Av., Th.Hth.	187	J3
Wychwood Cl., Edg.	53	G6
Wychwood Cl., Sun.	160	A6
Wychwood End N6	74	C7
Wychwood Gdns., Ilf.	80	C4
Wychwood Way SE19	170	A6
Roman Ri.		
Wyclif St. EC1	**11**	**G4**
Wycliffe Cl., Well.	157	J1
Wycliffe Rd. SW11	150	A2
Wycliffe Rd. SW19	167	E6
Wycombe Gdns. NW11	90	D2
Wycombe Pl. SW18	149	F6
Wycombe Rd. N17	76	D3
Wycombe Rd., Ilf.	80	C5
Wycombe Rd., Wem.	106	A1
Wydehurst Rd., Croy.	188	D7
Wydell Cl., Mord.	183	J6
Wydeville Manor Rd. SE12	173	H4
Wye Cl., Orp.	193	J7
Wye St. SW11	149	G2
Wyemead Cres. E4	62	E2
Wyevale Cl., Pnr.	66	A3
Wyfields, Ilf.	80/81	E1
Ravensbourne Gdns.		
Wyfold Ho. SE2	138	D2
Wolvercote Rd.		
Wyfold Rd. SW6	128	B7
Wyhill Wk., Dag.	101	J6
Wyke Cl., Islw.	124	C6
Wyke Gdns. W7	124	D3
Wyke Rd. E3	96	A7
Wyke Rd. SW20	183	J2
Wykeham Av., Dag.	100	C6
Wykeham Cl., West Dr.	120	D5
Wykeham Grn., Dag.	100	C6
Wykeham Hill, Wem.	87	J1
Wykeham Ri. N20	56	B1
Wykeham Rd. NW4	71	J5
Wykeham Rd., Har.	68	E4
Wyld Way, Wem.	88	B6
Wyldes Cl. NW11	91	F1
Wildwood Rd.		
Wyldfield Gdns. N9	60	C2
Wyleu St. SE23	153	H7
Wylie Rd., Sthl.	123	G3
Wyllen Cl. E1	113	F4
Wylo Dr., Barn.	39	G6
Wymering Rd. W9	108	D3
Wymond St. SW15	147	J3
Wynan Rd. E14	134	B5
Wynash Gdns., Cars.	199	H5
Wynaud Ct. N22	59	F6
Palmerston Rd.		
Wyncham Av., Sid.	175	H1
Wynchgate N14	58	D1
Wynchgate N21	58	E1
Wynchgate, Har.	52	B7
Wyncroft Cl., Brom.	192	C3
Wyndale Av. NW9	70	A6
Wyndcliff Rd. SE7	135	H6
Wyndcroft Cl., Enf.	43	H3
Wyndham Cl., Orp.	207	F1
Wyndham Cl., Sutt.	198	D7
Wyndham Cres. N19	92	C3
Wyndham Cres., Houns.	143	G6
Wyndham Est. SE5	**36**	**A7**
Wyndham Est. SE5	131	J7
Wyndham Ms. W1	**15**	**J2**
Wyndham Pl. W1	**15**	**J2**
Wyndham Pl. W1	109	J5
Wyndham Rd. E6	98	A7
Wyndham Rd. SE5	131	H7
Wyndham Rd. W13	124	E3
Wyndham Rd., Barn.	57	J1
Wyndham Rd., Kings.T.	163	J7
Wyndham St. W1	**15**	**J1**
Wyndham St. W1	109	J5
Wyndham Yd. W1	**15**	**J2**
Wyneham Rd. SE24	152	A5
Wynell Rd. SE23	171	G3
Wynford Pl., Belv.	139	G6
Wynford Rd. N1	**10**	**C1**
Wynford Rd. N1	111	F2
Wynford Way SE9	174	C3
Wynlie Gdns., Pnr.	66	B2
Wynn Br. Cl., Wdf.Grn.	79	J1
Chigwell Rd.		
Wynndale Rd. E18	79	H1
Wynne Rd. SW9	151	G2
Wynns Av., Sid.	158	A5
Wynnstay Gdns. W8	128	D3
Wynter St. SW11	149	F4
Wynton Gdns. SE25	188	C5
Wynton Pl. W3	106	B6
Wynyard Ter. SE11	**34**	**D3**
Wynyard Ter. SE11	131	F5
Wynyatt St. EC1	**11**	**G4**
Wyre Gro., Edg.	54	B3
Wyre Gro., Hayes	122	A4
Wyresdale Cres., Grnf.	104	C3
Wythburn Pl. W1	**15**	**J4**
Wythens Wk. SE9	156	E6
Wythenshawe Rd., Dag.	101	G3
Wythes Cl., Brom.	192	C2
Wythes Rd. E16	136	B1
Wythfield Rd. SE9	156	C6
Wyvenhoe Rd., Har.	85	J3
Wyvern Gro., Hayes	121	E7
Wyvil Est. SW8	**34**	**A7**
Wyvil Rd. SW8	**34**	**A6**
Wyvil Rd. SW8	130	E6
Wyvis St. E14	114	B5

Y

Name	Page	Grid
Yabsley St. E14	134	C1
Yalding Rd. SE16	**29**	**H6**
Yalding Rd. SE16	132	D3
Yale Cl., Houns.	143	F5
Bramley Way		
Yarborough Rd. SW19	185	G1
Runnymede		
Yardley Cl. E4	46	B5
Yardley La. E4	46	B5
Yardley St. WC1	**10**	**E4**
Yardley St. WC1	111	G3
Yarmouth Cres. N17	76	E5
Yarmouth Pl. W1	**24**	**D2**
Yarnfield Sq. SE15	152	D1
Clayton Rd.		
Yarnton Way SE2	138	D2
Yarnton Way, Erith	139	F3
Yarrow Cres. E6	116	B5
Yateley St. SE18	136	A3
Yates Ct. NW2	90	A6
Yeading Av., Har.	84	E2
Yeading Fork, Hayes	102	C5
Yeading Gdns., Hayes	102	B5
Yeading La., Hayes	102	B6
Yeading La., Nthlt.	102	C3
Yeames Cl. W13	104	D6
Yeate St. N1	94	A7
Yeatman Rd. N6	73	J6
Yeats Cl. NW10	88	E6
Yeats Cl. SE13	154	D2
Eliot Pk.		
Yeend Cl., W.Mol.	179	G4
Yeldham Rd. W6	128	A5
Yellow Hammer Ct. NW9	70/71	E2
Eagle Dr.		
Yelverton Rd. SW11	149	G2
Yenston Cl., Mord.	184	D6
Yeo St. E3	114	B5
Yeoman Cl. E6	116/117	E7
Ferndale St.		
Yeoman Cl. SE27	169	H3
Yeoman Rd., Nthlt.	85	E7
Yeoman St. SE8	133	H4
Yeomans Acre, Ruis.	66	A6
Yeoman's Ms., Islw.	144	B5
Queensbridge Pk.		
Yeoman's Row SW3	**23**	**H6**
Yeoman's Row SW3	129	H3
Yeomans Way, Enf.	45	F2
Yeomans Yd. E1	**21**	**G5**
Yeomen Way, Ilf.	65	F6
Yeovil Cl., Orp.	207	H2
Yeovilton Pl., Kings.T.	163	G5
Yerbury Rd. N19	92	D3
Yester Dr., Chis.	174	B7
Yester Pk., Chis.	174	C7
Yester Rd., Chis.	174	C7
Yew Cl., Buck.H.	64	A2
Yew Gro. NW2	90	A4
Yew Tree Cl. N21	43	G7
Yew Tree Cl., Well.	158	A1
Yew Tree Cl., Wor.Pk.	197	E1
Yew Tree Gdns. (Chadwell Heath), Rom.	83	E5
Yew Tree Rd. W12	107	F7
Yew Tree Wk., Houns.	143	F5
Yew Wk., Har.	86	B1
Yewdale Cl., Brom.	173	E6
Yewfield Rd. NW10	89	F7
Yewtree Cl. N22	74	C1
Yewtree Cl., Har.	67	H4
Yewtree Rd., Beck.	189	J2
Yoakley Rd. N16	94	B2
Yoke Cl. N7	92/93	E6
Ewe Cl.		
Yolande Gdns. SE9	156	B5
Yonge Pk. N4	93	G3
York Av. SW14	146	C5
York Av. W7	124	B1
York Av., Sid.	175	H2
York Av., Stan.	68	E1
York Br. NW1	**8**	**B5**
York Br. NW1	110	A4
York Bldgs. WC2	**18**	**B6**
York Cl. E6	116	C6
Boultwood Rd.		
York Cl. W7	124	B1
York Av.		
York Cl., Mord.	184	E4
York Cres., Borwd.	38	D2
York Cres., Loug.	48	B3
York Gate N14	42	E7
York Gate NW1	**8**	**B6**
York Gate NW1	110	A4
York Gro. SE15	153	F1
York Hill SE27	169	H3
York Hill, Loug.	48	B3
York Hill Est. SE27	169	H3
York Ho., Wem.	87	J4
York Ho. Pl. W8	**22**	**A3**
York Ho. Pl. W8	128	E2
York Ms. NW5	92	B5
Kentish Town Rd.		
York Ms., Ilf.	98	D3
York Rd.		
York Par., Brent.	125	G5
York Pl. SW11	149	G3
York Pl. WC2	**18**	**B6**
York Pl., Dag.	101	J6
York Pl., Ilf.	98	D2
York Rd.		
York Ri. NW5	92	B3
York Ri., Orp.	207	H1
York Rd. E4	62	A5
York Rd. E7	97	G6
York Rd. E10	96	C3
York Rd. E17	77	G5
York Rd. N11	58	D6
York Rd. N18	60	E6
York Rd. N21	44	A7
York Rd. SE1	**26**	**D4**
York Rd. SE1	131	F2
York Rd. SW11	149	F3
York Rd. SW18	149	F3
York Rd. SW19	167	F6
York Rd. W3	106	C6
York Rd. W5	125	F3
York Rd., Barn.	41	F5
York Rd., Brent.	125	G5
York Rd., Croy.	187	G7
York Rd., Houns.	143	H3
York Rd., Ilf.	98	D3
York Rd., Kings.T.	163	J7
York Rd., Nthwd.	66	A2
York Rd., Rich.	145	J5
Albert Rd.		
York Rd., Sutt.	198	D6
York Rd., Tedd.	162	B4
York Sq. E14	113	H6
York St. W1	**16**	**A1**
York St. W1	109	J5
York St., Bark.	117	F1
Abbey Rd.		
York St., Mitch.	186	A7
York St., Twick.	162	D1
York Ter., Erith	159	J1
York Ter. E. NW1	**8**	**C6**
York Ter. E. NW1	110	A4
York Ter. W. NW1	**8**	**B6**
York Ter. W. NW1	110	A4
York Way N1	111	E1
York Way N7	92	D6
York Way N20	57	J3
York Way, Borwd.	38	D2
York Way, Chess.	195	H7
York Way, Felt.	161	F3
York Way Ct. N1	111	E1
York Way Est. N7	92/93	E6
York Way		
Yorkland Av., Well.	157	J3
Yorkshire Cl. N16	94	B3
Yorkshire Gdns. N18	60	E5
Yorkshire Grey Pl. NW3	91	F4
Heath St.		
Yorkshire Grey Yd. WC1	**18**	**C2**
Yorkshire Rd. E14	113	H6
Yorkshire Rd., Mitch.	186	E5
Yorkton St. E2	**13**	**H2**
Yorkton St. E2	112	D2
Young Rd. E16	115	J6
Young St. W8	**22**	**A4**
Young St. W8	128	E2
Youngmans Cl., Enf.	43	J1
Young's Bldgs. EC1	**12**	**A5**
Youngs Rd., Ilf.	81	G5
Yoxley App., Ilf.	81	F6
Yoxley Dr., Ilf.	81	F6
Yukon Rd. SW12	150	B7
Yuletide Cl. NW10	88	E7
Yunus Khan Cl. E17	78	A5

Z

Name	Page	Grid
Zampa Rd. SE16	133	F5
Zander Ct. E2	**13**	**J2**
Zangwill Rd. SE3	156	A1
Zealand Av., West Dr.	120	A7
Zealand Rd. E3	113	H2
Zennor Rd. SW12	168	C1
Zenoria St. SE22	152	C4
Zermatt Rd., Th.Hth.	187	J4
Zetland St. E14	114	B5
Zion Pl., Th.Hth.	188	A4
Zion Rd., Th.Hth.	188	A4
Zoar St. SE1	**27**	**J1**
Zoffany St. N19	92	D2